ASSESSING STUDENTS WITH SPECIAL NEEDS

Eighth Edition

Effie P. Kritikos
Northeastern Illinois University

James A. McLoughlin
Cleveland State University

Rena B. Lewis
San Diego State University

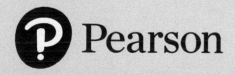

330 Hudson Street, NY NY 10013

In honor of our parents
Kathleen and Peter McLoughlin
Margaret and Willard Bishopp
Aglaia and Tom Papoutsis

And with love to our spouses
Jo Ann McLoughlin
Jim Lewis
Harry Kritikos

Director and Portfolio Manager: Kevin M. Davis
Content Producer: Janelle Rogers
Senior Development Editor: Jill Ross
Media Project Manager: Lauren Carlson
Portfolio Management Assistant: Anne McAlpine
Executive Field Marketing Manager: Krista Clark
Executive Product Marketing Manager: Christopher Barry
Procurement Specialist: Carol Melville

Full Service Project Management: Cenveo® Publisher Services
Cover Designer: Carie Keller, Cenveo® Publisher Services
Cover Image: Qweek/E+/Getty Images
Composition: Cenveo® Publisher Services
Printer/Binder: LSC Communications
Cover Printer: Phoenix Color/Hagerstown
Text Font: Garamond Pro

Credits and acknowledgments borrowed from other sources and reproduced, with permission, in this textbook appear on page.

We would like to thank all of the students who allowed us to use their photos in our book.

Cataloging-in-Publication Data is on file at the Library of Congress

10 2021

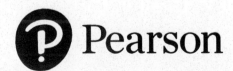 **Pearson**

ISBN 10: 0-13-457570-9
ISBN 13: 978-0-13-457570-4

PREFACE

Assessment is at the center of all good teaching, and this book is designed to provide a clear, comprehensive guide to the assessment of students with mild disabilities. This book will give you an understanding of the assessment process as well as the practical skills needed to assess students with special needs successfully so that you can teach them well. To structure the process, we offer an assessment question model, and we have developed the idea of the Individualized Assessment Plan (IAP). Our basis for the assessment questions and suggested procedures is a combination of best professional practices and legal mandates. This approach allows you sufficient flexibility to explore the areas and types of assessment in which you are particularly interested. In accordance with our belief that educators need useful information, we maintain a strong educational orientation toward assessment.

THE EIGHTH EDITION

This is the eighth edition of *Assessing Students with Special Needs*, and it reflects many changes in professional thought and practice in both special education and general education. Among the topics new to or enhanced in this edition are updated research and assessment tools in each chapter. This already successful book in previous editions builds on a quality book from the last edition and takes it to a new level.

NEW TO THIS EDITION

- Learning objectives are introduced at the beginning of each chapter and summarized at the end of every chapter.
- Breakpoint practices allow students to check their understanding.
- Diversity is addressed in each chapter as related to chapter context.
- Digital videos also are new and include examples of concepts discussed in each chapter.
- Adaptive behavior skills and intellectual performance have been separated into different chapters.
- In addition, oral language and English-language learners have been separated into chapters in order to take a deeper dive into content areas. These in-depth areas of content allow for more detail than competing books.
- Assessments and research articles have been updated. In addition, examples have been added and figures renewed. Legal information has also been updated.

The strengths of this book include the comprehensive nature of the chapter content. This edition presents reviews of dozens of tests, research articles, figures, tables, and legislation in each chapter. This feature allows students to be up to date with current practices and responsibilities. Breakpoint practices allow for formative assessment of future teachers' learning at several points within the chapter. An in-depth authentic case study allows for application of the chapter material. These assessment-to-instruction learning materials allow students to practice learned concepts before entering the classroom. In addition, several short videos are provided to reinforce material throughout the chapters. Multimodal methodology allows for tapping into student learning styles for optimum learning. These features enrich the textbook and provide superior, robust chapters as compared to textbooks by the competition.

Part I, Introduction to Special Education Assessment, includes information on the purposes of assessment, laws and regulations governing assessment, the team approach to assessment, the organization of the assessment process using the Assessment Question Model, and the steps in assessment. Embracing parents and families as a focal point in the assessment process is new to Part I and provides a framework for this text.

Part II, Skills for Special Educators, contains chapters on selecting the tools for assessment, administration, and scoring of standardized tests, and design and use of informal assessment techniques and procedures. All chapters have been updated and revised to increase coverage of techniques for evaluating student progress in classroom instruction.

Part III, Assessment for Special Education Eligibility, centers on the areas most relevant to eligibility assessment: intellectual performance, adaptive behavior, learning disabilities, and classroom behavior and behavioral disorders. In this update, adaptive behavior assessment has its own chapter dedicated to this assessment area.

Part IV, Assessment of Academic Skills, focuses on the assessment of academic, English-language learners, reading, mathematics, writing, and oral language. In this edition, diversity is highlighted in the entire text, with a separate chapter concentrating on English-language learners.

Part V, Important Considerations, provides information on the topics of assessment during the early childhood years and assessment for transition education planning.

This edition also features new tests and assessment procedures, many of which are revised versions of measures described in earlier editions. Approximately 50 new published measures are included. Among the new instruments discussed are:

- *Woodcock-Johnson IV Tests of Achievement*
- *Kaufman Test of Educational Achievement—Third Edition*
- *TerraNova SUPERA*
- *Wechsler Intelligence Scale for Children—Fifth Edition*
- *Wechsler Intelligence Scale for Children—Fifth Edition (Spanish)*
- *Woodcock-Johnson IV Tests of Cognitive Abilities*
- *Diagnostic Adaptive Behavior Scale*
- *Gray Oral Reading Tests—Fifth Edition*
- *Woodcock Reading Mastery Tests—Third Edition*
- *Analytical Reading Inventory—Tenth Edition*
- *Test of Word Reading Efficiency*
- *Informal Reading Inventory—Eighth Edition*
- *Oral and Written Language Scales-II*
- *Test of Early Written Language—3*
- *Test of Written Spelling—5*

- *Woodcock-Muñoz Language Survey—Revised Normative Update*
- *BRIGANCE® Diagnostic Inventory of Early Development—III*
- *BRIGANCE® Comprehensive Inventory of Basic Skills—II*
- *BRIGANCE® Transition Skills Inventory*

FEATURES

Our goal in this book is to provide you with a foundation for understanding the assessment process and with the skills necessary for carrying out meaningful assessments. The chief strength of this text remains its balanced coverage of formal eligibility assessment and the assessment practices that teachers carry out in classrooms. Critiques of the strengths and weaknesses of formal tests and informal procedures help you to select the tools that will supply the information you need.

We have chosen to speak about popular assessment procedures as well as less well-known, but distinctive, measures. On the one hand, popular instruments are discussed in some depth, not necessarily because they are always the best techniques, but because they reflect current practice. On the other hand, information about less well-known tests and techniques is provided to acquaint you with promising procedures. With this comprehensive coverage, you will find out not only what is currently being done (and how well) but also what needs to be changed and how to do that.

In addition, we provide the connection between gathering assessment information and using it to make decisions. There are regular reminders to consider assessment data in relation to the classroom setting and suggestions for making sense out of all the information gathered. This process is described in the context of a team approach to educational assessment but with particular emphasis on the role of the special education teacher.

To make our book a more practical classroom resource, we have included several useful *Assessment in Action* student profiles, sample test profiles, checklists, and illustrations. Also, information boxes throughout the chapters summarize the important characteristics of tests discussed in depth. We have tried to give you a feel for the procedures you will use in assessment and to critique and relate them to one another so that you can better understand how to use them. Each chapter begins with a brief topical outline of its contents and ends with a summary of the important points in the chapter.

SUPPLEMENTAL MATERIALS FOR STUDENTS AND INSTRUCTORS

Online Instructor's Manual with Test Questions
0134254600/9780134254609

Each chapter of the Online Instructor's Manual with Test Questions contains the following: chapter overview, chapter outline, glossary terms, class discussion questions, resources, and suggested activities. In addition, the manual contains test questions (multiple choice, true/false, short answer, and essay) as well as a set of instructional aids that can be used in teaching an assessment course to prospective special educators.

Online PowerPoint Presentations
0134254708/9780134254708

The lecture presentations (in PowerPoint) prepared for the eighth edition highlight the key concepts and content of each chapter.

Instructor Resource Center

To access both the online Instructor's Manual with Test Questions and the Online PowerPoint Presentations, go to *www.pearsonhighered.com*, click on the Instructor's Support button, and then go to the Download Supplements section. Here you will be able to log in or complete a one-time registration for a user name and password. The Instructor Resource Center opens the door to a variety of print and media resources in downloadable, digital format. As a registered faculty member, you can log in directly to premium online products and download resource files directly to your computer.

AUTHORS AND CONTRIBUTORS FOR THE EIGHTH EDITION

Revisions for the eighth edition were completed primarily by Rena B. Lewis, one of the co-authors of the first four editions and primary author of the fifth and sixth. The contributions of James A. McLoughlin to previous editions continue to add to the strength of this book.

Three contributors also participated in the development of the seventh edition, and we thank them for their willingness to share their perspectives and expertise. They are Eleanor W. Lynch, author of Chapter 3, Including Parents and Families in the Assessment Process; Laura J. Hall, author of Chapter 16, Early Childhood Assessment; and Bonnie R. Kraemer, author of Chapter 17, Assessment for Transition Education and Planning.

OUR THANKS

We would like to express our appreciation to the people who assisted in the preparation of this edition. First of all, thanks go to the field reviewers for their feedback and suggestions: April D. Miller, Morehead State University; Anisa N. Goforth, University of Montana-Missoula; Melissa A. Heath, Brigham Young University; Alicia Brophy, University of North Carolina-Wilmington; and Andy V. Pham, Florida International University.

Second, we would like to thank the many publishers and agencies who answered our questions and gave us permission to reproduce their materials. Third, special thanks to our colleagues at Pearson, who helped to birth yet another edition of this book.

BRIEF CONTENTS

CONTENTS

Note: Every effort has been made to provide accurate and current Internet information in this book. However, the Internet and information posted on it are constantly changing, so it is inevitable that some of the Internet addresses listed in this textbook will change.

1

Special Education Assessment

LEARNING OUTCOMES

After reading this chapter, you will be able to:

- Define assessment
- Provide examples of how assessments in the present differ from assessments in the past.
- List the three major purposes of assessment.
- Discuss proper assessment procedures (outlined by IDEA or another organization).
- Compare and contrast the difference between IEPs and 504 plans for general and special education assessment.
- Name members of the collaboration team involved in special education assessment.
- Explain the major components and framework of special education assessment.

KEY TERMS

assessment

individualized education program (IEP)

individual transition plan (ITP)

individual family service plan (IFSP)

prereferral strategies

formal assessment

standardized tests

norm-referenced tests

informal assessment

mild disabilities

Assessment* is the process of gathering information for the purpose of making a decision. Everyone engages in assessment. As human beings, we all gather information, sift and weigh that information, and make decisions based on our judgments and conclusions. When we wake up in the morning, we look outdoors to assess the weather. When we meet friends, loved ones, or acquaintances, we study their demeanor to assess their moods. Before we make a purchase, we weigh the merits of various products. Before we enter the voting booth, we investigate the worthiness of political candidates. And, as teachers, we assess our students.

Educational assessment is an integral part of the instructional process. Teachers observe their students as they enter the classroom, take their seats, and begin (or do not promptly begin) to work. Teachers ask questions and evaluate students' answers. They monitor students' behavior in the classroom and in the other environments of the school.

Sometimes assessment is more structured and systematic. Teachers give quizzes and exams. They assign a written paper or project, and they evaluate the results. Teachers also take part in the school-, district-, and/or statewide administration of standardized tests to evaluate students' progress in mastering the curriculum.

Although assessment is an important skill for all teachers, it is particularly important for special educators—teachers who serve students with disabilities. General education is designed to serve typical learners; special education, in contrast, is designed to meet the individual needs of students with school performance difficulties. The instructional plans for students with disabilities must be highly individualized, which means that special education teachers require precise information about their students' educational strengths and needs. Special education assessment is at the core of this process.

WHAT IS ASSESSMENT?

Special education assessment is the assessment of students to determine strengths and needs. In addition, it is used to determine student eligibility for services, strategies to support students and families, and progress with respect to goals. It can be defined as the systematic process of gathering educationally relevant information to make legal

---

*Words appearing in boldface in the text are defined in the Glossary.

and instructional decisions about the provision of special services. There are many important aspects to this definition. First, assessment is an ongoing process, not a one-time event. Assessments take place when students experience difficulty meeting the demands of the general education curriculum and are referred for consideration for special education services. Once students are found eligible for special education services, assessment continues in the special education classroom and other school environments where the special education teacher and others gather information related to the everyday concerns of instruction.

Second, special education assessment is systematic. In the early stages of the assessment process, an interdisciplinary team meets to plan strategies for the collection of useful information. Professionals—such as special educators, psychologists, and speech-language clinicians—work together to ensure that sufficient information is gathered to answer important questions. Classroom assessment of students with disabilities is also systematic. Teachers regularly monitor students' progress toward important instructional goals and, when necessary, modify instructional strategies.

Third, special education assessment focuses on the collection of educationally relevant information. School performance is a major concern, and teachers and other professionals evaluate students' progress in all pertinent areas of the school curriculum. In addition to academic achievement, professionals are interested in students' language, social, and behavioral skills. Students' learning abilities and strategies for learning are concerns, as are the characteristics of the learning environments in which students are asked to participate. All of these factors contribute to a better understanding of students' strengths and weaknesses and the types of support they may require to succeed in school.

Fourth, special education assessment is purposeful. Information is collected in order to make important decisions about schooling for students with special needs. Those decisions concern issues such as determining whether students meet legal criteria for special education services, selecting the most appropriate program and placement for students, setting instructional goals, choosing instructional methods and materials, and monitoring student progress and the effectiveness of instructional approaches.

Special education assessment extends beyond the school years because infants, preschoolers, and young adults with disabilities are served by special education. In the preschool years, assessment focuses on development in important skill areas such as language, cognition, social-emotional behavior, and sensory and motor skills. In young adulthood, the concern is successful transition from the world of school into the world of work, higher education, careers, and other areas of adult life.

The term *assessment* is sometimes confused with two other terms: *testing* and *diagnosis.* Tests are one type of assessment technique, and, as such, they are one of the many strategies used to gather information about students with special needs. Assessment is much broader; it is the entire data collection process and the decisions that result from that process. Testing is only one of the activities that takes place in assessment, just as the use of textbooks or any other instructional tool is only one small part of the teaching process.

Diagnosis is a term borrowed from the medical profession. In a medical context, the cause of a condition is identified or diagnosed so that appropriate treatment can be offered. The diagnosis typically results in a label such as "autism," and that label is linked to treatment. In contrast, educational assessment is not designed to establish causes, assign labels to students, or determine educational treatments based on labels. When students are identified as having disabilities, that designation is given only to document eligibility for special services. Furthermore, special instructional programs are developed for individual students based on their strengths and weaknesses in school learning, not on labels for global syndromes or conditions. In other words, special educators would conclude from an assessment that a student has needs in the area of reading, rather than labeling the student with dyslexia.

ASSESSMENT PAST AND PRESENT

Educational assessment practices for students with disabilities have been shaped by a variety of disciplines, forces, and trends. Changes in education, psychology, and medicine, and in the beliefs that society holds regarding the educational process continue to influence how schools gather assessment information to make decisions about the students they serve.

While the measurement of personality and other psychological factors was a topic of study in the late 1800s, the work of Alfred Binet (1857–1911) and others led to the major development of assessment techniques in the early 1900s. Assessments were created to meet a variety of needs, including the screening of students in public schools and the evaluation of military personnel and potential employees. These early efforts became the prototypes for many current group and individual tests in psychology and education.

Controversy over the nature of intelligence has affected the assessment practices used with students with disabilities. One debate centers on whether intelligence is one entity or whether it is made up of a set of factors. Some tests attempt to address a variety of factors that comprise intelligence; these factors are then analyzed to identify individual strengths and weaknesses within the global set of abilities that make up intellectual performance.

Another cause for discussion is the question of whether intelligence is modifiable. Most professionals consider intelligence a product of the interaction between people and their environment and, therefore, subject to change. Educational assessment of students with disabilities now incorporates procedures that analyze the environment as well as the person's abilities.

The field of medicine has had a profound effect on the development of educational assessment procedures. Many of the pioneers in special education were physicians who identified and described children with various types of disabilities and began the search for the causes and treatments of those disabilities. Some of these searches were successful, such as the development of vaccines to prevent diseases like polio. Others continue today in areas such as gene therapy and the use of sophisticated medical technologies to study the brain functioning of persons with dyslexia and attention-deficit/hyperactivity disorders.

For many years, educators were hampered by the use of a medical model in the assessment of students with disabilities. Students were diagnosed with a condition (e.g., intellectual disabilities or learning disabilities) and an educational treatment was prescribed based upon knowledge about that condition rather than the characteristics of the individual student. In some cases, the condition was assumed to be permanent; in others (most notably, learning disabilities), educators sought to cure the disability through educational remediation. Considerable progress has been made toward developing an assessment model that is more relevant to educational concerns. While identification of a specific disability is still part of current practice, the focus in assessment is the study of the individual student, his or her strengths and weaknesses, and the ways in which the instructional environment can be adapted to address the student's educational needs.

Other fields have also contributed to the assessment practices in special education. Tests of perception allow the study of how information is processed through vision, hearing, and other senses. Psychoeducational test batteries combine the analysis of psychological and educational factors. Applications of behavioral psychology have resulted in the use of several systems for behavioral observations of students in their school environments, including a special interest in the curriculum and the instructional tasks with which students interact. Other forms of informal assessment, like interviewing, have been borrowed and adapted from fields such as anthropology and sociology.

With the end of World War II and the baby boom in the 1950s, services for students with disabilities grew tremendously, with a subsequent growth in assessment procedures, particularly tests. Tests designed for administration to individual students were developed in all academic areas—and in language, social skills, and vocational skills—with the help of commercial publishers. In addition, special educators and other professionals created informal procedures directly related to classroom needs. Criterion-referenced testing played a major role in linking assessment and instructional programming.

Unfortunately, many misuses and abuses of assessment procedures accompanied this growth. Invalid and unreliable measures were used, sometimes administered by untrained individuals. Some assessments were too narrow; some discriminated on the basis of the student's language, cultural background, or gender. Results were used inappropriately, with students erroneously labeled with a disability. The rights of students with disabilities and of their parents to due process under law were violated (Birnbaum, 2006).

In 1975, the passage of PL 94-142, the Education for All Handicapped Children Act, exerted a strong, positive influence on the content and procedures used in the assessment of students with disabilities. The **individualized education program** (IEP) required a statement of (1) the child's current level of educational performance; (2) annual goals, including short-term objectives; (3) specific special education and related services to be provided; (4) the degree to which a child was able to participate in the general curriculum; (5) the dates for the beginning of services and the anticipated length the services would be in effect; and (6) appropriate objective criteria and evaluation procedures and schedules for determining how well the short-term objectives were being attained (Murdick, Gartin, & Crabtree, 2002).

In 1990, through the Individuals with Disabilities Education Act (IDEA), also known as PL 101-476, transition services were more clearly defined so that services to children between the ages of 18 and 21 could be further described and applied. An **individual transition plan** (ITP) was also required, with discussion involving school-to-adult transition beginning by age 14 and no later than age 16. In addition, the student's IEP was to contain a statement of the transition services needed before the student left school.

In 1991, IDEA or PL 102-119 was reauthorized in order to reauthorize Part H, the section that deals with young children and funding for their services. Federal funds were allocated to help states educate infants, toddlers, preschoolers, children, and youth with disabilities (Murdick et al., 2002). Rather than require an IEP for children between birth and 3 years of age, an **individual family service plan** (IFSP) was required. Professionals were to support the family and the child in determining its needs and deciding how those needs could best be met. The IFSP included information about the child's status, family

information, outcomes, early intervention services, dates, duration of services, service coordinator(s), and transition information (Murdick et al., 2002).

 Breakpoint Practice 1.1
Click here to check your understanding of IEP, ITP and IFSP.

The changes introduced in PL 94-142 are maintained and extended throughout the years by new versions such as PL 108-446, the Individuals with Disabilities Education Improvement Act of 2004 (IDEA 2004). First and foremost, this law guarantees that students with disabilities shall receive a free, appropriate, public education in the least restrictive educational environment. In the area of assessment, the law mandates a set of due process procedures to protect students and their parents and detailed guidelines to correct past problems. A team must adequately assess students with disabilities, and an IEP must be developed. In addition, state departments of education must comply with federal requirements to receive funding for special education programming.

IDEA 2004 places special emphasis on assessment of students' involvement with and progress in the general education curriculum. These areas must be addressed in the development of IEPs as well as how students will participate in state and district assessments of school achievement. The IEP team must also consider a range of special factors, including positive behavioral interventions and supports for students with behavioral problems, the language needs of students who are not proficient in English, and any requirements students might have for assistive technology devices and services.

Trends within the fields of education and special education have also influenced the development of assessment techniques and procedures. In the early years of special education, assessment focused solely on students and their deficits. That approach gave way to increased emphasis on the school curriculum and the specific instructional tasks with which students were experiencing difficulty. At present, the approach is more balanced. Both the student and the educational environment are of interest, particularly the ways in which interactions occur between individuals and school demands. In addition, influences from educational theories such as constructivism have contributed to special educators' perspectives on assessment. In the constructivist view, students construct their own knowledge by building on the prior knowledge they bring with them to the learning situation (Bell, 2010; Bransford, Brown, & Cocking, 2000; Cegelka, 1995a).

One challenge that special education continues to face is the development of appropriate procedures to assess culturally and linguistically diverse students who are suspected of having a disability (Benson, 2003; Waitoller & Artiles, 2013). Unsolved problems in this area have contributed to overrepresentation of some groups in special education programs and underrepresentation of others (Artiles & Trent, 1994; Losen & Orfield, 2002; Patton, 1998; Sullivan, 2011). This issue is likely to persist as the population of the United States becomes more diverse in the next decades.

The movement to educate students with disabilities in more inclusive settings has created a greater need for both general and special education teachers to have tools to assess these students in multiple environments, including the general education classroom. Educators of students with disabilities are held accountable for ongoing evaluation of learning. They need to monitor student progress frequently, without the necessity of administering standardized tests. Such tests are too costly in terms of both time and money, and their results do not translate directly to classroom interventions. Instead, educators have turned to **curriculum-based assessments**, that is, procedures and techniques that evaluate student growth in relation to the current classroom curriculum. Curriculum-based approaches such as criterion-referenced assessment, curriculum-based measurement, and portfolio assessment produce results that assist in the development of instructional goals, objectives, and procedures.

Major educational reforms in the United States are making profound changes in the assessment and evaluation of all students, including those with disabilities. By the mid-1990s, most states had adopted sets of academic standards and begun to link assessment of educational outcomes to these standards (American Federation of Teachers, 1996; Olson, 2006). In this evaluation model, results of standards-based assessments are used as the basis for judging student performance, deciding whether schools and teachers are functioning appropriately, and even forcing fundamental changes in teaching methods and the structure of schools.

The standards movement became even more prominent with passage of President George W. Bush's education initiative, "No Child Left Behind." According to Bush (2001), this initiative has four major goals:

- *Increase Accountability for Student Performance:* States, districts, and schools that improve achievement will be rewarded. Failure will be sanctioned. Parents will know how well their child is learning, and that schools will be held accountable for their effectiveness with annual state reading and math assessments in grades 3–8.
- *Focus on What Works:* Federal dollars will be spent on effective, research-based programs and practices. Funds will be targeted to improve schools and enhance teacher quality.
- *Reduce Bureaucracy and Increase Flexibility:* Additional flexibility will be provided to states and school districts, and flexible funding will be increased at the local level.
- *Empower Parents:* Parents will have more information about the quality of their child's school. Students in persistently low-performing schools will be given choice.

As states, districts, and schools face increasing pressure to provide comparative data about the scholastic abilities of American students, the issues surrounding inclusion of students with disabilities in high-stakes testing become a major concern. Federal special education laws require that students with disabilities participate in state and local assessments of academic achievement alongside their general education peers. Although it is important to ensure that students with disabilities are not excluded, at the same time, appropriate test accommodation and modifications as well as alternative measures must be provided to guarantee valid and reliable evaluation.

In summary, special educational assessment today can be described in the following ways:

- Special education assessment, like special education instruction, is individualized. It is tailored to the needs of each student with disabilities.
- Assessment data are used to make decisions about the eligibility of students for special education services and about the types of services that are provided. Thus, decisions are both legal and instructional.
- Assessment focuses on educationally relevant information so that an appropriate IEP can be developed, implemented, and monitored.
- Assessment also focuses on the student's involvement with and progress in the general education curriculum.
- The student is not the only subject of assessment. The learning environment is also evaluated as well as the student's interactions with classroom tasks.
- A variety of procedures are used in assessment. Assessment is not limited to the administration of standardized tests.
- Assessment is characterized by a team approach. Parents and both special and general educators are important members of that team.
- Professionals strive for nonbiased assessment of all students, particularly those from culturally and linguistically diverse groups.
- Assessment does not stop when instruction starts. Instructional programs are continuously monitored and evaluated.

PURPOSES OF ASSESSMENT

Special education assessment has several purposes because it plays a role in each phase of programming for students with disabilities. From the first indication of a learning problem, special education teachers and others gather information to aid in decision making. In general, this information is used to document eligibility for special education services and/or adaptations of the general education curriculum and to plan and monitor the effectiveness of an IEP. The main purposes of

assessment are directly related to the steps in the special education assessment process: identification and referral, determination of eligibility, program planning, and program implementation and evaluation. These steps are described briefly in the paragraphs that follow. A more detailed discussion can be found in Chapter 2.

Identification and Referral

Identification of students who may have disabilities is the first purpose of assessment. Two identification procedures are used: screening and prereferral strategies. Screening is a large-scale data collection activity used to quickly identify those students out of the entire school population who may be in need of further study. For example, most schools administer vision and hearing screening tests at regular intervals throughout the grades. When potential problems are detected, students are referred for a more in-depth evaluation.

Prereferral strategies, in contrast, are aimed at solving the school performance problems of individual students. Prereferral interventions begin when a general education teacher consults with others at the school site about a student experiencing difficulty in school. Information is gathered about the student's performance in areas of concern and about the instructional environment. In most cases, the prereferral team will develop a set of adaptations and modifications in an attempt to meet the student's academic and behavioral needs. These interventions are implemented, and data are collected to determine their effectiveness. If the results suggest a persistent learning problem, the student may be referred for consideration for special education services.

Determination of Eligibility

Second, special education assessment is performed to determine whether a student meets eligibility criteria for special education services. Eligibility is based on two interrelated criteria: the student must have a school performance problem, and that problem must be related to a disability. Each state develops its own eligibility requirements based upon federal laws, and individual districts may set additional guidelines for assessment. Eligibility assessment is much more thorough than assessment for screening or prereferral. Also, it is individualized; the assessment team determines what types of information it needs to gather for each individual student. Then, students are assessed to determine their present levels of performance in areas related to the suspected disability. Typically, this involves investigation of the student's school skills, intellectual performance, hearing and vision, social and behavioral status, and language abilities. Information is also collected about the student's school history, current classroom performance, and the characteristics of the learning environment. Special attention is paid to the student's progress in the general education curriculum and the types of support needed to maximize the student's probability of success in the general education classroom.

Program Planning

Third, educational assessment data are used to plan the IEP. After the student's educational needs are identified and prioritized, annual goals are developed. The IEP team decides what types of special education and related services the student will receive and what kinds of supplementary aids and services will be needed to maintain the student within the general education classroom, if at all possible. The IEP indicates who will accomplish the goals and objectives, the settings in which services will take place, and the amount of time services will require. The plan also outlines how the student's progress will be monitored and how parents will be informed about their child's progress.

Program Implementation and Evaluation

The fourth reason for assessment is to monitor the student's progress in the educational program. Information is gathered by teachers (and others, as appropriate) about the effects of instruction and other types of interventions. This type of assessment is usually performed at frequent intervals, perhaps weekly or even daily. A variety of procedures are used, although the most common are informal techniques such as observation of student behavior, review of student work, and direct

measurement of performance in skill areas of interest. At this stage in the process, assessment and instruction blend together, with assessment data providing the information needed to guide instructional modifications.

ENHANCEDetext
Video Example 1.1
Classroom lessons are guided by the student's progress in the educational program. Watch this video to see how sorting, counting and graphing are taught and monitored in the classroom.

The final purpose of special education assessment is program evaluation. Federal special education laws require that the IEP of all students with disabilities be reviewed periodically. School staff and parents examine the progress of the student and the results of the program and decide if special education services should be continued as is, modified, or discontinued. In addition, the student's eligibility for special education services is typically reviewed every 3 years. These types of program evaluation are designed to ensure that students with disabilities receive appropriate interventions and that those interventions continue only as long as they are required.

TYPES OF ASSESSMENT PROCEDURES

Many types of assessment procedures are available, and they vary along several dimensions, including the amount of professional expertise required for their use. In general, special education assessment techniques can be divided into two major types: formal and informal strategies. Both are employed in all phases of assessment, although formal strategies are often considered more useful for gathering information for eligibility decisions and informal strategies are more useful for classroom instructional decisions.

Formal assessment strategies are structured assessment procedures with specific guidelines for administration, scoring, and interpretation of results. The most common example, **standardized tests**, sometimes referred to as **norm-referenced tests**, are designed to compare the performance of one individual to that of a normative group. Thus, their use is limited to students who are very similar to the group used in developing the test.

Norm-referenced tests may be designed for group or individual administration and are available for most academic subjects, intellectual performance, and other areas of learning. Directions for administration, scoring, and interpretation of these measures are usually very explicit. As a result, professionals require training before they can be considered skilled in the use of a specific test. Test results are expressed in quantitative scores such as standard scores and percentile ranks, and as Chapter 5 explains, the test manual provides information about factors such as the development of the test, the standardization sample, and quality of the test as a measurement tool. Results of norm-referenced tests are used in a number of ways, including documentation of eligibility for special education and identification of general strengths and weaknesses in school learning.

Tests can be designed for administration to a group of individuals or to one person. Group procedures often penalize students with disabilities because they may require students to read, follow directions independently, and work under timed conditions. Because students with disabilities often lack these skills, results of group tests tend to underestimate their abilities. However, group tests are the norm in general education because they are more efficient and require much less time to administer. When students with disabilities participate in such assessments, accommodations are often necessary.

Tests that are individually administered are preferred in special education. The professional administering the test (usually called the examiner or tester) establishes rapport with the student and makes sure he or she understands the directions for the test tasks. Skills are measured separately, so that it is possible to separate out a student's performance in reading from his or her skills or knowledge in other areas such as mathematics, science, or social studies. In many cases, students respond orally, so that poor writing skills are not penalized when writing is not the object of assessment. In addition, professionals can carefully observe students as they interact with test tasks to gain further insight into their strengths, weaknesses, and general work behaviors.

The Assessment Tool Table of Contents at the start of this book lists each of the individual and group tests (and other published measures) discussed in depth in this text. Informal assessment strategies are also included in the Index. Inclusion of a test or strategy should not be considered an endorsement; some of the measures that we have described, though popular, do not meet recommended standards for technical adequacy. Test descriptions throughout this book include information about technical adequacy as well as the training required by examiners. In some cases, administration is limited to members of certain professional groups. For example, most states restrict the use of individual aptitude measures to licensed school psychologists.

Informal assessment procedures are used in educational assessments to determine current levels of performance, document student progress, and direct changes in the instructional program. A distinction is often made between the formal measures just described and these less formal techniques.

Informal procedures are usually less structured or are structured differently from standardized tests. Rather than administering a formal test, a teacher might observe a student with behavior problems, give the class a test on the spelling words studied that week, or assign mathematics homework. Like most informal measures, these are designed by the teacher rather than by a commercial publisher. Also, their purpose is to gather information directly related to instruction. There is an element of subjectivity in the design of informal measures as well as in their administration, scoring (if they are scored), and interpretation. In fact, interpretation is often quite difficult because of a lack of guidelines.

Although informal procedures lack the kinds of scores yielded by standardized tests, their results are relevant to instruction because they can be expressed in instructional terms. Informal assessment tools vary in how directly they measure student performance and instructional conditions. Some involve the student directly, whereas others rely on informants such as teachers and parents. Observation, curriculum-based assessments, and other informal procedures are discussed in detail in Chapter 6, the chapter on classroom assessment.

Because informal assessment strategies have a clear connection to the curriculum, the potential usefulness of the results they produce is high. However, it is important to point out that just because an assessment technique is informal does not mean that it is appropriate for all students with disabilities. Informal measures may contain barriers like those in group, formal tests. For example, a classroom quiz might be timed or a math assignment might require reading and writing skills. As is the case with formal measures, accommodations are often necessary.

ENHANCEDetext
Video Example 1.2

? Breakpoint Practice 1.2
Click here to check your understanding of formal and informal assessment.

504 PLANS, IEPS, AND STUDENTS WITH SPECIAL NEEDS

Special educational assessment involves students with disabilities. As defined by federal law, these disabilities include:

> intellectual disability, a hearing impairment (including deafness), a speech or language impairment, a visual impairment (including blindness), a serious emotional disturbance (hereinafter referred to in this part as "emotional disturbance"), an orthopedic impairment, autism, traumatic brain injury, other health impairment; a specific learning disability, deaf-blindness, or multiple disabilities who, by reason thereof, needs special education and related services. (IDEA 2004 Final Regulations, §300.8(a)(l))

Students qualifying for services are entitled to receive a free and appropriate education from special educators and other professionals.

IDEA 2004, like its 1997 predecessor, expands the definition of "child with a disability" to include young children ages 3 through 9 who are "experiencing developmental delays . . . and who, by reason thereof, need special education and related services" (IDEA 2004, Part A, Section 602(3)(B)). This allows young children to receive special services without the need to label them as having a specific disability. The law requires that delays be documented in one or more of these areas: physical, cognitive, communication, social or emotional, or adaptive development.

Another group of students benefiting from federal protections are those identified as having attention-deficit/hyperactivity disorders (ADHD). This disorder involves issues with attention and behaviors of impulsivity and overactivity. A student with ADHD could be distractible, often moving around. A student with attention-deficit disorder (ADD) has issues of attention without impulsivity and overactivity. The student with ADD appears inattentive. The U.S. Department of Education ruled in 1991 that students with ADHD are eligible for services under Section 504 of the Rehabilitation Act of 1973. The regulations for IDEA 2004 include both ADHD and ADD in the list of conditions covered under the "other health impairment" disability category. According to the federal definition, other health impairment "means having limited strength, vitality or alertness, *including a heightened alertness to environmental stimuli,* that results in limited alertness with respect to the educational environment" (IDEA 2004 Final Regulations, §300.8(c)(9), emphasis added). This limitation may be due to a variety of health problems, including both attention-deficit disorder and attention-deficit/hyperactivity disorder. It is important that students with ADHD or ADD who need a 504 plan are provided this plan. This is different from an IEP because a 504 plan is not special education, whereas an IEP is. When a student qualifies for a 504 plan, accommodations are made in the classroom. This plan is required under civil rights law. The student does not meet a special education classification but requires accommodations.

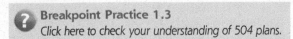

Breakpoint Practice 1.3
Click here to check your understanding of 504 plans.

This book focuses on educational assessment of students with mild disabilities. **Mild disabilities** include intellectual disabilities, emotional disturbance, speech-language impairments, and learning disabilities. Because their disabilities are mild, these students are often members of general education classrooms and receive special education services on a part-time basis. As Table 1–1 indicates, federal laws recognize the need for special education services for students with disabilities in the aforementioned areas. Students with specific learning disabilities comprise the largest group of all students with disabilities, followed

TABLE 1–1
Mild Disabilities

Intellectual Disability	Significantly subaverage general intellectual functioning, existing concurrently with deficits in adaptive behavior and manifested during the developmental period, that adversely affects a child's educational performance. (IDEA 2004 Final Regulations, §300.8(c)(6))
Emotional Disturbance	A condition exhibiting one or more of the following characteristics over a long period of time, to a marked degree, that adversely affect a child's educational performance: (A) An inability to learn that cannot be explained by intellectual, sensory, or health factors. (B) An inability to build or maintain satisfactory interpersonal relationships with peers and teachers. (C) Inappropriate types of behavior or feelings under normal circumstances. (D) A general pervasive mood of unhappiness or depression. (E) A tendency to develop physical symptoms or fears associated with personal or school problems. Emotional disturbance includes schizophrenia. The term does not apply to children who are socially maladjusted, unless it is determined that they have an emotional disturbance (IDEA 2004 Final Regulations, §300.8(c)(4))
Specific Learning Disabilities	A disorder in one or more of the basic psychological processes involved in understanding or in using language, spoken or written, that may manifest itself in the imperfect ability to listen, think, speak, read, write, spell, or to do mathematical calculations, including conditions such as perceptual disabilities, brain injury, minimal brain dysfunction, dyslexia, and developmental aphasia. . . . Specific learning disability does not include learning problems that are primarily the result of visual, hearing, or motor disabilities, of mental retardation, of emotional disturbance, or of environmental, cultural, or economic disadvantage. (IDEA 2004 Final Regulations, §300.8(c)(10))

Source: Building the Legacy US Department of Education.

by students with speech-language impairments, students with autism, and students with intellectual disabilities (National Center for Educational Statistics, 2015).

From an educational perspective, students with mild disabilities share many common psychological, academic, and social-behavioral problems that require assessment. Students with attention-deficit/hyperactivity disorder also share these characteristics. The educational assessment strategies described in this book apply to these types of students. Many of the procedures are also useful for students with other types of disabilities; however, educational assessment for students with severe disabilities and those with sensory and physical disabilities requires special considerations beyond the scope of this text.

This book is primarily concerned with school-aged students with classroom-related learning problems. However, procedures for the assessment of preschool children and their families are described in Chapter 16 and those for the assessment of adolescents and young adults in transition programs in Chapter 17.

COLLABORATION AND THE TEAM APPROACH IN SPECIAL EDUCATION ASSESSMENT

Important educational decisions about students with disabilities are made by teams rather than by a single individual. The team approach brings together individuals from different perspectives who contribute their expertise to the decision-making process. The team may be composed of the student's parents and professionals representing general education, special education, psychology, speech and language disorders, medicine, and other areas as needed. Each team member gathers data about the student and interprets them from his or her perspective, sharing the data with others on the team. The team then analyzes all contributions, including those of the student's parents, in an attempt to make the most appropriate decision.

The team approach is not new to special education, although it has gained impetus in recent years. Federal laws such as the Individuals with Disabilities Education Act and its amendments explicitly require that teams rather than individuals make the following decisions:

1. Evaluation of the eligibility of students for special education and related services;
2. Formulation of IEPs;
3. Evaluation and modification of IEPs; and
4. Periodic review of the need for special education and related services.

The membership of educational decision-making teams varies. Different purposes require different numbers of team members and the representation of different disciplines. For example, the team that assesses a student for eligibility for special services is likely to have more members than the team responsible for formulating the IEP for the same student. The needs of the student also influence team membership. A student with several severe disabilities is likely to require a larger team representing more disciplines than a student with a mild disability.

Federal laws require that team decisions take into consideration several areas of student functioning, if those areas are pertinent to the educational needs of a specific student. Table 1–2 lists several possible areas of concern and the team members who are the primary sources of information for each area. Although certain team members take major responsibility for assessment in certain areas, any team member may provide additional information.

This book is written from the perspective of one member of the team, the special educator. Although many of the assessment procedures described here can be used by other professionals, the special educator is the team member who focuses on the needs of students with disabilities. Having the dual responsibilities of assessment and instruction, the special educator is in a unique position to maintain an educational focus in the special education assessment process.

School Personnel

General and special education teachers who are involved directly with the student on a day-to-day basis are necessary team members. Teachers

TABLE 1–2
Primary Sources of Information about Student Functioning

TEAM MEMBER		TYPE OF INFORMATION					
	Health	Social and Emotional Status	General Ability	School Performance	Communicative Status	Motor Skills	Transition Factors
Educators		*		*	*		*
Parents	*	*			*	*	*
Students		*		*			*
Psychologists		*	*	*			
Speech-Language Pathologists					*		
Medical Personnel	*					*	
Counselors and Social Workers		*					
Transition Specialists							*
Motor Skills Specialists						*	*

are able to provide information on all aspects of student development, especially academic performance and social and emotional status.

General education teachers contribute valuable information about students' social skills in dealing with their peers. They are also the major source of information about the instructional programs and procedures used in their classroom and have firsthand knowledge about the student's response to those programs and procedures. Their assessment procedures often consist of group-administered achievement tests, informal tests and inventories, classroom observations, and portfolios. Consequently, they can describe how well the student with a disability is progressing in the general education curriculum compared to others in the classroom. These types of information are particularly useful in determining the kinds of adaptations and accommodations the student will need to succeed in the regular classroom environment.

Special educators offer a somewhat different perspective. Their assessment procedures are generally more individualized; they gather formal and informal data not only about academic skills but also about performance in areas such as language and behavior. This information, when added to that of general educators, helps the team to make decisions about the types of services needed by students with disabilities.

Special education teachers are often members of school-based teams that collaborate with and provide consultation to classroom teachers. In this role, special educators may perform classroom observations and work with the team to develop possible strategies to address learning and behavioral problems in the general education environment. When students are referred for consideration for special education services, special educators play a major role in the assessment process, serving as important members of the team, with responsibility for gathering information about the student's current levels of performance in a number of areas.

School administrators on educational decision-making teams may include building principals, directors of special education, or other supervisory personnel. Building principals or vice principals are often included to enlist their cooperation in the education of students with disabilities at the school site and to encourage their support of special education and inclusion programs. Special education administrators and other supervisory personnel are able to share their knowledge of the special education programming options available in the school district or division.

Families and Students

The intent of federal special education laws is to encourage the meaningful participation of parents of students with disabilities and the students themselves, when appropriate, in the educational decision-making process. Parents and other family members have much to contribute to the team. They are knowledgeable about their child's behavior and have acted as the child's teacher as part of their caregiving role.

Like educators, parents provide information on many aspects of the student's current performance. However, parents and other family members have a somewhat different perspective because their observations take place in the home, neighborhood, and community. Another important contribution of parents is information about their student's past educational experiences, health history, and progress through the stages of development. Parents can complete questionnaires about their children or be interviewed by school personnel. They can be observed at home while interacting with their child, or they can be asked to gather informal observational data about their child in the home environment. When parents become full participants in the team process, they contribute to better educational decisions and are more likely to support their child's instructional program.

Students themselves are also members of some educational teams, particularly in the higher grades. Students can contribute information about all aspects of school performance as well as their feelings, attitudes, goals, and aspirations for the future. Students assist in the data collection process in many ways. In addition to participating in assessment procedures such as formal tests and informal inventories, they may answer interview questions, complete rating scales, or answer questions on a questionnaire.

School Support Personnel

Psychologists, speech-language pathologists, and assistive technology specialists often support general and special educators, and they are frequently members of educational decision-making teams. During assessment, school psychologists gather data to help determine whether students are eligible for special education programs. In this role, the school psychologist is usually the professional responsible for administering and interpreting results of formal tests to determine the general intelligence level.

Assessment reports prepared by the psychologist address concerns about the student's level of general ability, the status of specific skills involved in learning, and emotional and behavioral status. When combined with results of academic reports from teachers, psychological reports allow the team to compare a student's actual classroom performance with expected levels of achievement. In planning the educational program, psychologists can assist in establishing reasonable goals and provide information about the student's specific learning abilities.

Speech-language pathologists are involved in the assessment and instruction of students with speech and language disorders. They are responsible for evaluating the communication skills of students, referring students to other specialists as needed, providing direct instructional services, and consulting with other professionals working with those students.

The assessment procedures used by speech-language professionals are both formal and informal; they frequently solicit input from educators about a student's classroom speech and language performance. Special educators may screen students for speech and language problems, and then refer students with suspected problems to speech-language pathologists for more in-depth evaluation. Speech-language pathologists provide speech-language diagnoses. Furthermore, knowledge of the communicative status of a student helps the team understand academic and behavioral problems with speech or language components. In planning the IEP, speech-language pathologists specify goals for the student and indicate how others can support those goals. For some students with disabilities, speech-language instruction is the only special service received; for others, it is one of several services.

Assistive technology (AT) specialists are relatively new members of educational teams.

Their role involves the use of assistive technology to increase the student's ability to participate in the educational program. IDEA 2004 specifically requires that the IEP team "consider whether the child needs assistive technology devices and services" (IDEA 2004 Final Regulations, §300.324(a)(2)(v)). The AT specialist assists by evaluating the current functioning levels of the student and the ways in which devices such as adapted computers, communication devices, and aids for students with visual and hearing impairments might improve current performance.

ENHANCEDetext

Video Example 1.3

Watch this video to see assistive technology in action in the classroom.

Medical Personnel

Medical information about the student is obtained from the student's physician, the school nurse, and other medical specialists. This information may include results of vision and hearing screenings, the student's health history, as well as his or her current physical status.

All students should be screened for possible visual and hearing impairments. This screening is generally carried out by the school nurse (or the school health aide), who then refers students with possible problems to the appropriate specialists. The results of screening and any subsequent evaluations are reported to the team by the school nurse. Of particular interest to the team is how vision and hearing problems affect assessment performance and subsequent programming.

The school nurse or physician may also report information about any relevant health problems, conditions, or diseases. Pediatricians, neurologists, psychiatrists, and other physicians may be involved. Also of interest is whether the student is currently receiving any medical treatment, such as drug therapy. All medical information should be reported so that the educational implications are clear. The team must consider data from the assessment of classroom performance and other areas of functioning in light of any medical problems.

Social Workers and Counselors

Social workers and school counselors provide information about the social and emotional status of the student. In the schools, social workers assist by preparing a social or developmental history of the student conducting group and individual counseling with the child and his or her family, working with problems in a student's living situation that affect adjustment in school, and mobilizing school and community resources.

The assessment procedures used by social workers include interviews and home visits. Data gathered regarding a student's background and home environment could help the team interpret other assessment data. Social workers may also assist team members, particularly parents, in identifying goals and strategies for action at home and in the community.

Counselors also help in the area of emotional development. Counseling services, according to federal special education laws, may be provided by a variety of professionals such as social workers, psychologists, school counselors, and vocational rehabilitation counselors. Counselors use both formal and informal procedures to gather information about the emotional and social development of the student and sometimes that of other family members. Counselors can add important information to the student profile. For instance, data from counseling may indicate the need for specific goals or may shape decisions about placement or instructional strategies.

Transition Specialists

Current federal laws require that the IEPs for older students contain a description of the transition services needed by the students to meet post-secondary goals "related to training, education, employment, and, where appropriate, independent living skills" (IDEA 2004 Final Regulations, §300.320(b)(l)). Professionals who contribute to assessment and instruction in this area include vocational rehabilitation counselors; special education teachers at the secondary level who provide instruction in areas related to transition; and persons with special training in the assessment, instruction, and coordination skills needed for the provision of transition services. While transition specialists focus on this area in assessment, other team members—such as teachers, parents, and students themselves—can also contribute valuable information.

Motor Skills Specialists

Information about the motor development of the student may be obtained from adaptive physical education teachers, physical therapists, and occupational therapists. In addition, the school nurse or a physician, such as an orthopedic surgeon, may also provide information about motor skills.

The adaptive physical education teacher is involved with the instruction of students who require special physical education programs, and he or she can provide information about the student's current motor abilities. Teachers, psychologists, and others may also have input about the student's gross and fine motor skills. In some cases, motor skill problems may be related to other kinds of difficulties, such as poor handwriting. Adaptive physical education teachers specify goals for the student and assist team members in programming for motor needs.

Physical and occupational therapists also contribute information. Some authors distinguish between physical therapists, who are concerned with gross motor development, and occupational therapists, who work with fine motor development. According to the American Physical Therapy Association (2013), physical therapists assist individuals with limited movement and performance of activities due to medical or health problems. In contrast, occupational therapists provide assistance to help students in body functions and body structures involved in everyday life activities (American Occupational Therapy Association, 2011). Both kinds of therapists use specialized assessment procedures; their data may be supplemented by results of interviews or experiences of other team members.

Teachers can report on classroom demands for motor skills and their observations of the student's strengths and weaknesses. Parents may also have useful data. The IEP contains goals related to motor development, if necessary, and allows the therapists to suggest strategies that are useful in the development of better motor coordination or realistic transition goals.

Other Personnel

Occasionally, team members other than those just described are needed to present important information about the student. Tutors or para-professional aides who work closely with the student may provide insight based on their experiences. Members of the community, such as employers or work supervisors, may be able to give the team a better understanding of realistic vocational goals and needed transition services. Other family members, such as grandparents, can sometimes supplement input from the parents and student.

In summary, the purpose of the team approach is to assemble all the information necessary for educational decision making through members' combined skills, knowledge, experience, and expertise. Teams are viewed as being more objective than individuals because they represent multiple viewpoints. Teams differ in size depending on the types of decisions under consideration. However, as a general rule, teams should be kept as small as possible so that parents feel comfortable making contributions. In some cases, such as some IEP teams, only the parents and educators may participate. In others, there is a need for wider representation because several different types of information are required.

ENHANCEDetext
Video Example 1.4
Watch this video to learn more about IEP teams.

A FRAMEWORK FOR SPECIAL EDUCATION ASSESSMENT

One of the best ways to ensure effective practice in special education assessment is to use a systematic structure or framework to guide the process of collecting data, analyzing results, and making important educational decisions. In this book, the framework is based on the steps in the assessment process and the important assessment questions that must be addressed in each step. As Figure 1–1 illustrates, the four steps in the assessment process are related to five major assessment questions.

Is There a School Performance Problem?

This major question is asked in the first step of the assessment process—identification of potential problems and possible referral for in-depth special education assessment. Students with possible school problems are identified through routine screening procedures or through teacher referral. The student's general education teacher may bring the student to the attention of a school-based team in an attempt to find solutions for the student's learning problems. Several types of assessment data can be collected, including school history data (e.g., past grades and results of tests of achievement); information from parents about family background and the student's medical, developmental, and educational history; current grades and classroom work samples; and reports of current teachers about the types of instructional approaches used and their success.

Classroom assessment procedures can also be used to determine whether a learning problem exists. Systematic behavioral observations may identify a pattern of events affecting the student's achievement. Teachers may see a pattern of difficulty when they systematically analyze classroom activities and subsequent student responses. The general education curriculum itself serves as the framework for assessment as the student's proficiency in component skills and performance at different levels are examined.

Based on this information, teachers may make instructional and environmental modifications and note an immediate change in the student's school performance. In this way, any student with temporary or situational learning problems will be identified, and further concern and assessment can be avoided. Students who do not respond to these efforts and whose learning difficulties are clearly documented are then referred for in-depth assessment. The outcome of the questioning is the identification of general problem areas, an assessment of their approximate severity, and a clear indication of the need for further assessment.

Is the School Performance Problem Related to a Disability?

After a student has been formally referred for consideration for special education services, an assessment team forms to determine the student's eligibility. Students with learning problems qualify for special education only if they meet the criteria for a disability as set forth in federal, state, and local guidelines. Although these criteria differ somewhat from one location to another, two major requirements must be met: the student has a school performance problem and that problem is related to a disability. According to federal special education laws, the disability must have an adverse effect on school performance. The presence of a disability alone, without an accompanying school problem, is not sufficient. Likewise, students with school performance problems that are not related to disabilities are not eligible for special education.

Steps in Assessment   *Assessment Questions*

Identification and Referral   Is there a school performance problem?

Determination of Eligibility   Is the school performance problem related to a disability?

What are the student's levels of academic achievement and strengths and weaknesses in school learning?

What are the student's levels of intellectual performance and adaptive behavior?

What are the student's levels of development of specific learning abilities and learning strategies?

What is the status of classroom behavior and social-emotional development?

Program Planning   What are the student's educational needs?

What is the level of achievement and strengths and weaknesses in
- Reading?
- Mathematics?
- Written and oral language?

What is relationship of learning problems to classroom demands?

What educational program is required to meet those needs?

What are the annual goals?

What special factors must be considered?

What types of special education and related services are needed?

What types of supplementary aids, services, modifications, and supports are needed? What types of testing accommodations?

What transition services are needed?

Program Implementation and Monitoring   How effective is the educational program?

Is the student making adequate progress in the educational program?

How does the educational program need to be modified?

Does the student continue to require special education services?

FIGURE 1–1
Framework for Special Education Assessment

19

Students with all types of disabilities show school performance problems. These problems are documented with referral information, results of academic achievement tests, and data concerning the student's ability to conform to classroom behavioral requirements. All students are also assessed to determine general aptitude for learning. In the case of most mild disabilities, students show average or above-average intellectual performance. However, in the case of intellectual disabilities, intellectual performance as well as adaptive behavior skills are below average. A learning disability is documented by poor performance in one or more specific learning abilities or learning strategies. Students identified as being emotionally disturbed must meet criteria related to classroom behavior, interpersonal relationships, and social-emotional development. To gather the information necessary to make these types of decisions, four assessment questions are asked.

What Are the Student's Levels of Academic Achievement and Strengths and Weaknesses in School Learning?

The information needed here is an individualized assessment of the student's current school achievement. Although there is already strong indication of possible learning problems, additional data are gathered to describe the student's strengths and weaknesses. Norm-referenced achievement tests, administered individually, indicate the student's overall achievement level in relationship to other students of the same age or in the same grade. These results help to determine whether a serious problem exists. Other procedures, such as interviews, classroom observations, and analysis of student work samples, help to describe the student's current skill levels. An academic assessment should identify global areas of need for further assessment and indicate the more severe problem areas.

What Are the Student's Levels of Intellectual Performance and Adaptive Behavior?

These two areas are assessed to determine general aptitude for learning. Intellectual functioning involves a composite of skills related to thinking, problem solving, and general academic aptitude. Adaptive behavior involves the ability to cope with environments other than the school classroom. Included are self-help, communication, and social and interpersonal skills. Normative data are needed in each area. The team must determine how students perform in comparison with their peers and whether that performance falls within average ranges. This information must be related to academic and other performance data before final judgments are made.

Norm-referenced tests, administered individually, provide information about intellectual performance. Both formal and informal procedures are appropriate for assessing adaptive behavior skills. Parents, teachers, and others familiar with the student may be interviewed or asked to complete adaptive behavior rating scales. School and home observations and examination of cultural practices contribute to a clearer understanding of the student's mastery of functional skills. Results of these assessments indicate whether students are markedly different from peers in global cognitive skills and adaptive behavior. This information is useful in making decisions about the presence of mild disabilities and in designing the IEP.

What Are the Student's Levels of Development of Specific Learning Abilities and Learning Strategies?

Specific learning abilities are generally considered to underlie academic skills and other areas of development. Examples are specific abilities such as attention, perception, and memory. Learning strategies, in contrast, relate to the ways in which students use their learning abilities in the completion of school tasks. Students with learning disabilities often experience difficulty not only in one or more specific abilities but also in strategies for learning.

There are several formal procedures for the evaluation of specific learning abilities. These include both norm-referenced tests and standardized rating forms for teachers. Learning strategies, in contrast, are typically studied with less formal measures and procedures. Examples are observations, checklists and rating scales, and interviews of teachers and students themselves. Results of these assessments are used to determine whether students have significant problems in specific learning abilities or strategies. This information may shed light on problems the student is encountering in academic and behavioral areas; it is also necessary for documentation of the disability of learning disabilities.

What Is the Status of Classroom Behavior and Social-Emotional Development?

To answer this question, the team assesses the student's classroom behavior, including conduct problems, interactions with teachers and peers, and the influences of the physical and instructional environments on the student's ability to meet expectations. Of interest is whether the student currently has the necessary social and behavioral skills to engage in learning activities in a general education classroom setting.

Many types of procedures are used in the assessment of behavioral status. For example, results of norm-referenced rating scales completed by parents, teachers, and others are used to identify which behaviors at school and in other environments are considered inappropriate for the student's age, grade, and gender. Systematic behavioral observations are used to study specific behaviors; particular attention is paid to the conditions under which the problem behavior occurs and the consequences of the behavior. Other procedures include sociograms, analyzing interactions between the student and the teacher, and examining any relationships between behavior and medical and psychological considerations. Results of these assessments identify problems in the area of behavior and contribute to decisions about whether the student meets criteria for disabilities such as emotional disturbance. In addition, information about specific behavioral problems is useful for planning intervention programs.

What Are the Student's Educational Needs?

Once it has been established that the student is likely to meet the criteria for special education services, questions about educational needs should be considered. Two major assessment questions are asked. The first relates to the basic school skills: reading, mathematics, written language,

and oral language. Students with disabilities frequently have difficulties in one or more of these areas, and their problems with skill acquisition impede the learning of other school subjects, such as science and history. The second major question related to the student's educational needs asks about the relationship between school performance problems and the demands of the student's classroom or classrooms.

What Are the Student's Educational Needs in Reading? Mathematics? Written and Oral Language?

The needed information in each skill area is the same: (a) an indication of the current level of performance and whether achievement is below average compared to other students; (b) specific strengths and weaknesses; and (c) the relationship of skills in one area to skills in other areas, such as the influence of reading upon mathematics. Both formal and informal devices and procedures are needed to gather this information.

Three main areas of concern in assessment of reading achievement are the student's ability to recognize or decode words, to comprehend what is read, and to use reading as a tool to learn new material. Formal tests provide information about the student's overall level of reading performance in relation to peers; these tests also help pinpoint skill areas that are possible strengths or potential weaknesses for the student. These skill areas are then studied in more detail using informal procedures such as criterion-referenced tests, informal reading inventories, teacher-made checklists, and analyses of reading errors and reading materials.

In mathematics, the areas of concern in the assessment of educational needs are computation, problem solving, and application skills. Like reading, both formal and informal techniques are used. For example, assessment may begin with a diagnostic mathematics test. Informal procedures such as classroom observations and analyses of student work samples are then used to gather additional information about areas of need.

Spelling, handwriting, and composition skills are the major concerns in the study of written language. Assessment often begins with a broad-based test of writing skills that includes collection of a student-writing sample. Rating scales may be used to evaluate handwriting, formal tests to evaluate spelling skills, and informal procedures to gain more information about the student's ability to write connected text. As with other academic skills, both formal and informal procedures contribute to the team's understanding of the student's educational needs.

In oral language, the major areas to be assessed relate to the student's ability to understand and express the four dimensions of oral language: phonology, syntax, semantics, and pragmatics. These dimensions are concerned with the sound system of language, language rules, the meaningful aspects of language, and the use of language for communication. Also of interest with regard to students who speak languages other than English is their proficiency in English and in the other language spoken. Again, both formal and informal measures are used in the assessment of educational needs. In many cases, assessment duties in oral language are shared with speech-language pathologists and bilingual educators.

The outcome of the assessment of educational needs is a clear statement about the student's levels of performance, strengths, and weaknesses in each important area. When reviewing results, it is important to examine how task demands influence performance. For example, a student might do well in written computation but have difficulty with mental computation. The learning strategies of the student become more apparent when performance varies based on the characteristics of the task.

It is also important to ask how problems in one area might influence performance in another area. For example, poor oral reading skills might be related to poor spelling skills. Relationships such as this may suggest a common underlying factor and lead to a plan for an instructional intervention.

The results of academic assessments should be considered in relation to the results of assessment for specific disabilities. Information about the student's general aptitude for learning, specific learning abilities and strategies, and classroom behavior and social-emotional development may aid the analysis of his or her educational needs, thereby facilitating the program planning process. For example, classroom conduct problems interfere with all types of learning, and interventions for students with these needs may focus on different skills than interventions for students whose difficulties are primarily academic. The educational plan for a student who does not complete assignments despite having the necessary skills, for instance, might address work completion first, rather than acquisition of new skills.

Medical, social, and cultural factors may also affect student performance. Among the medical considerations are the student's general health status, vision, hearing, and motor development. Important social factors may include characteristics of the family constellation (e.g., primary caregivers in the home, the number and age of siblings), emphasis on literacy at home, and provisions for doing homework. Cultural factors include linguistic differences, forms of communication, and cultural perceptions of the value of school learning.

What Is the Relationship of Learning Problems to Classroom Demands?

To obtain a clear picture of educational needs, the student's current school performance must be considered within the context of classroom demands: the physical environment of the classroom and the tasks, methods, and materials used in instruction. Task analysis is a useful technique to determine what aspects of a learning task are creating difficulty for the student. If the student lacks prerequisite skills, these can become part of instruction. Sometimes it is also necessary to modify the task itself; for example, allowing students to answer questions orally rather than in writing may dramatically improve their performance on a science test.

The classroom learning environment can be studied through observations, interviews, and analysis of instructional materials. Possible questions the assessment team might ask are:

1. What are the features of instructional materials? What prerequisite skills are required? What objectives do the materials address? Is the pace of instruction appropriate? Is the format clear? Do these materials match the learning needs of the student?

2. What instructional procedures are used by the teacher? Does the teacher use modeling, prompting, and reinforcement? Are the methods of instruction appropriate for the needs of the student?

3. Are the physical surroundings (lighting, heating, work space, noise level) conducive to learning? Will the physical environment facilitate the student's learning rather than impede it?

Poor student performance in one or more skill areas may be directly related to inappropriate classroom conditions. If this is the case, then the problem lies with the environment, not with the student. Environmental modifications become a priority, and these data can guide the changes.

The assessment team can make better decisions when planning the instructional program by noting interrelationships between the different types of information gathered and integrating the findings of the various members of the assessment team. This helps to put the results of the assessment in context. For example, although poor vision may partially explain a reading disability, both corrective lenses and an instructional program in reading may be necessary. Or a problem in academic achievement may be considered less extreme if the student's general ability to learn is low, if he or she is inattentive in class, if the tasks in the classroom have an inappropriate response requirement, or if the student has a hearing loss. Noting interrelationships produces a clearer understanding of the student's educational needs.

What Educational Program Is Required to Meet Those Needs?

The team of concerned professionals and the student's parents (as well as the student in some cases) is now ready to develop an educational plan. For students with disabilities, there are several areas to consider. Requirements for the IEP, spelled out in federal laws such as IDEA 2004, form the basis for this group of assessment questions.

What Are the Annual Goals?

The first step in development of the plan is a description of the student's most pressing educational needs and identification of priority goals. First, the student's current levels of performance in important areas are described. Second, the team determines which problems identified in the assessment process constitute the most important educational needs. To do this, it is necessary to consider the student's age and grade in school, the concerns and priorities of the parents and those of the student, and the family's culture and value system. For example, if a junior in high school is concerned about preparing for a career, instruction in basic phonics skills may not be considered as important as learning to read job-related vocabulary words.

Next, the team sets annual goals for the student. These goals shape the direction of the student's program and become the guidelines for evaluation of its effectiveness. In the language of IDEA 2004, the IEP must contain "a statement of measurable annual goals, including academic and functional goals" (IDEA 2004, §614(d)(i)(II)). Benchmarks or short-term objectives may then be identified for each goal. Although no longer required by federal law, these objectives represent the intermediate steps the student must complete to reach the annual goals; as such, they guide teachers and others responsible for implementing the program.

What Special Factors Must Be Considered?

In developing the educational plan, the team must consider several special factors when identifying goals and making decisions about services. These factors are:

- The needs of students with behavioral problems, including the need for positive behavioral interventions and supports;
- The language needs of students with limited proficiency in English;
- The need for instruction in Braille for students who are blind or visually impaired;
- The communication needs of all students, including those who are deaf or hard of hearing; and
- The need for assistive technology devices and services for all students.

These factors focus on important dimensions, although it is unlikely that all will apply to any one individual.

What Types of Special Education and Related Services Are Needed?

The next step involves making decisions about the special education and related services needed to implement the educational program. A range of special education services is available, depending on the severity of the student's needs. These services include full-time placement in a special classroom, part-time services outside the general education classroom from a resource or itinerant teacher, and instruction provided in the general education classrooms by special education personnel. The last two options are the most common because the majority of students with disabilities spend at least part of the school day in the general education environment.

Related services are other types of services required by the student in order to benefit from special education. Included in this category are speech-language pathology and audiology services, physical and occupational therapy, social work services, and counseling.

What Types of Supplementary Aids, Services, Modifications, and Supports Are Needed?

Federal special education law requires that the IEP specify the ways in which the educational environment is to be modified to support the participation of the student with disabilities. The intent is to make the educational environment, including the general education classroom, more accessible to students with disabilities. Supplementary aids and services are defined as "aids, services, and other supports that are provided in regular education classes, other education-related settings, and in extracurricular and nonacademic settings to enable children with disabilities to be educated with nondisabled children to the maximum extent appropriate" (IDEA 2004 Final Regulations, §300.42).

Thus, the team must consider how best to include the student in the general education program and develop strategies to make that inclusion successful. Examples of some of the types of supports that might be provided are consultation to the general education teacher, special learning materials, in-class instruction delivered by special education personnel, and modification of assignments or tests by the classroom teacher.

What Types of Accommodations Are Needed for Testing?

IDEA 2004 requires that students with disabilities participate in state and district assessments of academic achievement administered to general education students. In developing the IEP, the team decides what types of modifications are needed, if any, in the administration of these tests. The team can also determine that these assessments are not appropriate for a particular student; in that case, an alternative assessment procedure must be described.

What Transition Services Are Needed?

According to IDEA 2004, transition services are "a coordinated set of activities for a child with a disability that is designed to be within a results-oriented process, . . . to facilitate movement from school to post-school activities" (§602(34)(A)). When the student reaches the age of 16, the IEP must contain appropriate postsecondary goals and a description of the transition services needed to attain those goals. The types of services to be provided may include "(i) Instruction; (ii) Related services; (iii) Community experiences; (iv) The development of employment and other post-school adult living objectives; and (v) If appropriate, acquisition of daily living skills and provision of a functional vocational evaluation" (IDEA 2004 Final Regulations, §300.43(a)(2)).

How Effective Is the Educational Program?

Once the IEP is implemented, its evaluation begins. The question here concerns the effectiveness of the educational program. Teachers and others responsible for implementation collect data as they provide services. At periodic intervals, parents receive progress reports, and the IEP is reviewed most typically on an annual basis. Every few years, the student's need for special education services is reconsidered. All of these actions require assessment information, and all are directed toward one goal—modification of the program, if necessary. Three assessment questions relate to the evaluation process.

Is the Student Making Adequate Progress in the Educational Program?

Assessment of the student's progress begins when instruction begins. Teachers observe the student during instruction, analyze the responses the student makes, and evaluate performance on classroom learning tasks, assignments, and tests. These data are collected to gauge the effectiveness of instructional strategies. If the student is not progressing at the expected rate, the instructional approach must be modified.

The IEP for each student contains not only annual goals but also a plan for measuring progress toward those goals. The assessment procedures outlined in that plan may be limited to the curriculum-based measures most often used by teachers or may include other more formal measures. In any event, teachers must inform parents of their child's progress on a regular basis. IDEA 2004 requires that parents receive progress reports at least as often as report cards are issued for general education students.

How Does the Educational Program Need to Be Modified?

Under current law, the IEP team must evaluate the educational plan at least once each year and modify it as needed. Prior to the IEP meeting, assessment information is collected in order to describe the student's current level of performance in each annual goal area. The team reviews the student's progress and discusses the effectiveness of the instructional program. Then a decision is made about whether the program should continue and, if so, how it should be modified. Typical modifications are a revised set of annual goals and changes in the types of services and supports provided.

Does the Student Continue to Require Special Education Services?

Every 3 years, or more often if necessary, the student's eligibility for special education services must be reevaluated. This process may require the collection of assessment data about the student's disability if the team believes such information is necessary. The purpose of this evaluation is to ensure that special education services are not provided when they are no longer needed—and that students who continue to require assistance from special education will receive that assistance.

In this textbook, students with mild disabilities are the focus, although both formal and informal assessment procedures and strategies can be used with all students. The assessment process is implemented by a team of professionals, with the special educator playing a central role. Educational assessment questions are used to structure this process (as well as this textbook). That is, they guide the choice of assessment procedures and the ultimate use of the information that is gathered.

Assessment in Action
Meet Sandy

Sandy is 10 years old and in the fifth grade. She was referred for special education because of poor academic performance throughout her school years. Sandy is in your classroom, and you have identified that she has problems processing information and paying attention to directions. You have attempted prereferral strategies in the classroom, and she still exhibits difficulties. Sandy's mother has left you a message with questions regarding the evaluation process, including the paperwork and her legal rights. Sandy is also bilingual. Her mother has requested involvement of an interpreter or a bilingual professional in Spanish.

What information do you provide Sandy's mother?

What other individuals should be involved in the discussion?

What are Sandy's rights?

Sandy's family should be informed of their rights in writing and in their native language. Sandy's mother should be informed about safeguards that will be used during the evaluation process. Furthermore, all participants in the evaluation of Sandy should be actively involved in the process. Participants include the psychologist, the social worker, occupational and speech therapists, as well as special education and inclusion teachers. Teachers should list pre-referral strategies used in the classroom. More input should also be obtained from Sandy.

Sandy has the right to a free, appropriate public education in the least restrictive environment based on a nondiscriminatory assessment. The informal and formal assessment tools should be written in her native language. They should be administered by properly trained administrators, and the instruments should be standardized for the purpose for which they are being used. Any variation in the standardization procedures should be noted and described in the evaluation report. Her family members should have a voice in the decision-making process. Sandy is entitled to due process and to protections under the law that will provide her an individualized education based on her needs.

Multicultural Considerations

Multicultural considerations and discriminatory practices have shaped and continue to shape the field of special education in relation to changes in the law. Cases have changed the rules regarding special education services, and specific aspects of assessment are addressed within these laws. Students should be tested in their native and primary language. The parents should also be informed of their rights and are provided interpretation of test results in their native language. Cultural rules are provided in the laws so that students are given every opportunity to succeed. These considerations include bias-free testing and placement.

Researchers have supported the use of prereferral of students in need of special education services to reduce overidentification and underidentification of students who are culturally or linguistically diverse (Nelson, Smith, Taylor, Dodd, & Reavis, 1991; Sullivan, 2011). Important considerations during the prereferral process include carefully choosing the individuals on the prereferral team and addressing proactively differences in language that can affect communication and collaboration. Also, learning styles must be considered, as well as concepts of time (importance of being exactly on time) and cooperation (working in groups versus competition) during the process (Dodd, Nelson, & Spint, 1995).

Standardized tests are also flawed when evaluating students who are culturally and linguistically diverse. Many of these tests do not provide fair opportunities for the students who speak a language other than English. Using performance-based, curriculum-based, and dynamic assessment could increase the validity of the assessment process (Salend, Garrick-Duhaney, & Montgomery, 2002; National Joint Committee on Learning Disabilities, 2010).

SUMMARY

As you reflect on this chapter and the impact that practice and application has on learning, consider the following main points:

- Assessment is a systematic process for gathering information about the educational needs of children and adolescents with disabilities. Special education assessment is the assessment of students to determine strengths and needs. In addition, it is used to determine student eligibility for services, strategies to support students and families, and progress with respect to goals.

- In the past, assessments were created to meet a variety of needs, including the screening of students in public schools and the evaluation of military personnel and potential employees. Today, assessment focuses on educationally relevant information so that an appropriate individualized education program can be developed, implemented, and monitored.

- The main purposes of assessment are directly related to the steps in the special education assessment process: identification and referral, determination of eligibility, program planning, and program implementation and evaluation.

- Special education assessment techniques may utilize formal and informal strategies. Both strategies are employed in all phases of assessment, although formal strategies are often considered more useful for gathering information for eligibility decisions and informal strategies more useful for classroom instructional decisions.

- A 504 plan is different from an IEP because a 504 plan is not special education, whereas an IEP is special education. When a student qualifies for a 504 plan, accommodations are made in the classroom. This plan is required under civil rights law. The student does not meet a special education classification but requires accommodations.

- The collaboration team involved in special education assessment may be composed of the student's parents and professionals representing general education, special education, psychology, speech and language disorders, medicine, and other areas as needed. Each team member gathers data about the student and interprets it from his or her perspective, sharing it with others on the team.

- A framework for special education involves the use of a systematic structure to guide the process of collecting data, analyzing results, and making important educational decisions. This framework could include the identification and referral, determination of eligibility, program planning, and program implementation and monitoring.

Studio 8/Pearson Education, Inc.

2

The Assessment Process

LEARNING OUTCOMES

After reading this chapter, you will be able to:

- Name and describe two main types of decisions made by special educators in the assessment process.

- Name and describe the four main steps in the assessment process.

- Provide examples of three identification and referral stages special educators use in special education assessment.

- Define the individualized assessment plan professionals use in discussion regarding determination of eligibility.

- Discuss elements of the IEP professionals use in program planning.

- Provide definitions of two monitoring techniques in program implementation and monitoring.

KEY TERMS

individualized education program (IEP)
due process
individualized assessment plan (IAP)
least restrictive environment (LRE)

curriculum-based assessments
curriculum-based measurement (CBM)
response to intervention (RTI)

Special education assessment is a systematic process designed to gather the information needed to make important decisions about students' educational programs. The types and number of assessment procedures vary at different stages in that process because the reasons for gathering data are different. This chapter text describes the entire assessment sequence, beginning with identification of possible learning problems and ending with the monitoring and evaluation of special education services. First, however, it is useful to describe the types of decisions that educational teams must make and the ways in which these decisions influence the collection of assessment data.

Assessment in Action
William and the Challenges of Second Grade

William is a 7-year-old student in the second grade. His teacher, Ms. Trapp, is concerned about his behavior in school and his achievement. On the group tests administered to all students, William scored in the average range in reading but experienced difficulty with mathematics. He has trouble remembering number facts from one day to the next and often becomes confused when trying to solve a computational problem. William's classroom behavior is also a concern. He doesn't seem to attend to directions and is often disruptive when he is supposed to be working independently. His assignments, both in-class and homework, are rarely completed.

Ms. Trapp is an experienced teacher who is familiar with the signs of learning problems in young children. She is worried about William and seeks help from the student study team at her school. She collects response to intervention data and tries various instructional interventions. She uses manipulatives, peer tutors, and additional resources for home use prior to lessons (i.e., outlines, notes, and additional manipulatives). While examining the academic and environmental demands in the classroom, she decides to slow the pace of William's lessons and add more visual cues and prompts. She also tells William that he'll be able to visit the classroom computer center only if he completes all of his work and is less disruptive. Ms. Trapp carefully observes William to see if changes occur but sees only minimal improvements in his behavior.

William's mother is also concerned about his school problems and his behavior at home. It upsets her that he doesn't listen and won't do what he's told to do. She's tried to help him with his schoolwork at home, but he refuses to work on assignments and study his math facts. William's mother wonders if there is something wrong with him. When Ms. Trapp talks with William's mother, they agree that further study of William's school problems is needed. Ms. Trapp refers William for assessment.

TYPES OF DECISIONS

Special education assessment provides the information needed to make two types of decisions: legal decisions and instructional decisions. These decisions differ in several important ways.

Legal Decisions

The determination of eligibility for special services and the reevaluation of eligibility are essentially legal decisions. These decisions concern the person who will receive special education services. Their purpose is to determine whether individual students meet the legal requirements for one or more disabilities to allow allocation of special education funds, resources, and personnel.

Federal special education laws such as IDEA 2004 specify two major eligibility criteria: The student must be determined to have a disability, and that disability must have an adverse effect on the student's educational performance. These criteria guide the assessment process by indicating the essential information needed. Federal laws and state regulations also define each disability. However, federal definitions tend to be general descriptions of conditions, as can be seen in Table 1–1 in Chapter 1. State guidelines may provide more specificity, although they usually do not mandate particular assessment procedures. In most cases, these decisions are left to the professional judgment of team members. Considerable expertise is needed to put legal definitions into operation.

Legal decisions about mild disabilities require the contributions of several team members, including parents, general and special educators, school psychologists, speech-language pathologists, and school nurses. Other professionals—such as physicians, adaptive physical education teachers, school social workers, and assistive technology specialists—participate when necessary.

In making decisions about the existence of mild disabilities, most states require assessment information about three areas of functioning: (1) general intellectual performance, (2) educational performance, and (3) performance related to specific disabilities. Table 2–1 compares the general criteria for the various mild disabilities in these three areas. Note that the terms *behavioral disorder* is used instead of emotional disturbance and *intellectual disability* instead of mental retardation; the latter terms are legal terms not favored by educators.

General intellectual performance is assessed in all mild disabilities. It is assessed by individual tests of intelligence and, in cases where intellectual disability is suspected, measures of adaptive behavior. Intellectual disability is indicated when performance falls within the below-average range. In other mild disabilities, the opposite is true. Intellectual performance must be at least average.

Educational performance is also a concern for all mild disabilities (Zentall & Beike, 2012). In intellectual disability, the pattern is typically poor performance in most or all areas. In contrast, other mild disabilities require low or

TABLE 2–1
Comparison of Eligibility Criteria

DISABILITY	GENERAL INTELLECTUAL FUNCTIONING	EDUCATIONAL PERFORMANCE	INDEX OF DISABILITY
Intellectual Disability	Below average	Below average in most areas	Low or below average in adaptive behavior and most other areas
Learning Disability	Average or above	Low or below average in at least one area	Low or below average in at least one specific learning ability or learning strategy
Behavioral Disorder	Average or above	Low or below average in at least one area	Low or below average in at least one area of behavior
Attention-Deficit/ Hyperactivity Disorder (OHI)	Average or above	Low or below average in at least one area	Low or below average in attention, activity level, or both

below-average performance in only one area. However, it is not uncommon for older students with learning disabilities, behavioral disorders, and other health impaired (OHI) disorders to show poor performance in several school skills.

The third major area of concern, the index of disability, differs across the four mild disabilities. Intellectual disability is a comprehensive disability affecting school skills, adaptive behavior, and most other areas of functioning. Learning disabilities are indicated when students have deficits in one or more specific learning abilities or learning strategies, despite adequate general intellectual performance. Both behavioral disorders and attention-deficit/hyperactivity disorders require evidence of specific types of behavioral problems. Like learning disabilities, these disabilities occur despite adequate intellectual performance.

Eligibility decisions rely heavily on results of norm-referenced measures such as standardized tests. These instruments provide information that allows the team to compare a student's performance with that of other students. For example, results of academic achievement measures may indicate that the student's school performance is sufficiently different from that of age or grade peers to warrant considering it to be a problem. Salvia, Ysseldyke, and Bolt (2006) maintain that norm-referenced tools could provide data that could protect students from inappropriate labeling, if used correctly. Guidelines for interpreting standardized test results for eligibility decisions are presented in Chapter 4.

Informal assessment procedures also play a role in legal decisions. Checklists, interviews, rating scales, observations, portfolios, criterion-referenced tests, and other informal measures are used to confirm the results of norm-referenced tests and to provide information not available from standardized measures. The team approach to making legal decisions helps to ensure that all important areas of functioning are considered and that the assessment procedures selected are the most appropriate for the task at hand.

 Breakpoint Practice 2.1
Click here to check your understanding of the different types of special education assessment decisions.

Instructional Decisions

Planning, monitoring, and evaluating the student's special education program require instructional decisions. In fact, once a student has been found eligible for special education services, the majority of decisions to be made are instructional rather than legal. The major concerns are the content of the student's curriculum (i.e., what to teach), the instructional methods used to implement the curriculum (i.e., how to teach), and the overall effectiveness of the instructional program.

The first step is preparation of an **individualized education program,** or **IEP,** for the student. Results of the eligibility assessment are reviewed, and additional information is gathered as needed. The student's current levels of performance in important skill areas then serve as a basis for identifying annual goals and short-term objectives, selecting appropriate services and curricular modifications for the student, and planning strategies for evaluation of the individualized program.

Once the IEP is implemented, the teacher and other professionals responsible for delivering educational services continue to make instructional decisions. These decisions are an integral part of the teaching process; data collection is ongoing, and instructional decisions are made on a regular and frequent basis. Instruction takes place, the teacher gathers data on the student's response to instruction, and modifications are made based on the student's progress. This cycle is repeated continuously as the teacher monitors the effects of the intervention.

More formal evaluations of the instructional effort also take place. Several times during the school year, the teacher communicates with the student's parents about progress toward the annual goals specified in the IEP. This typically occurs when report cards are prepared for all students in the school. In present practice, the entire IEP is reviewed at least once each year by the student's parents and teachers. Progress toward the student's goals is reported, the effectiveness of the educational program is discussed, and a new plan is developed for the coming year. Instructional decisions require specific information about the student's performance in relation to the classroom program. Because of this requirement, informal assessment strategies are more useful than formal measures. Although standardized test results may help the assessment team identify areas of strength and weakness for the IEP, these measures are not designed for frequent assessment of progress toward specific instructional goals. Informal techniques such as observation, informal inventories, portfolios, and criterion-referenced tests are more appropriate.

ENHANCEDetext
Video Example 2.1
Watch this video to see the implementation of a student's IEP.

STEPS IN THE ASSESSMENT PROCESS

Table 2–2 presents the steps in the assessment process. There are four main phases in assessment: identification and referral; determination of eligibility; program planning; and program implementation and evaluation. Each phase is made up of several steps, and the overall sequence parallels the purposes of assessment, the types of educational decisions to be made, and the assessment questions introduced in Chapter 1.

Two major factors influence the steps in assessment: (1) special education laws and regulations at the national, state, and local levels and (2) professional beliefs about preferred assessment practices. IDEA 2004 and its predecessors guarantee free, appropriate, public education to all students with disabilities. This guarantee requires that all students with possible disabilities be identified and, if appropriate, assessed. Accompanying this guarantee are strict guidelines for the ways in

TABLE 2–2
Steps in Educational Assessment

Identification and Referral
- Screening and teacher identification of students with school problems
- Prereferral intervention strategies
- Referral and notification of parents

Determination of Eligibility
- Design of the individualized assessment plan (IAP)
- Parental permission for assessment
- Administration, scoring, and interpretation of assessment procedures
- Reporting results
- Decisions about eligibility

Program Planning
- Design of the individualized education program (IEP)
- Parental agreement to the IEP

Program Implementation and Evaluation
- Implementation of the IEP
- Ongoing monitoring of student progress
- Annual review of the IEP
- Periodic reevaluation of eligibility

which assessments must be carried out. Students and their parents are protected by legal requirements for due process, procedural safeguards, nondiscriminatory assessment, placement in the least restrictive educational environment, confidentiality of information, and development and regular monitoring of the IEP. States must conform to these regulations to receive federal aid for special education services.

Due process procedures are designed to safeguard the rights of students with disabilities and their parents (O'Halloran, 2008). This legal requirement has been described as a practice that balances fairness for both families and educational professionals in the outcome of special education assessment (Turnbull, Strickland, & Brantley, 1982). Due process provides protection to the consumers of the assessment process—for example, by requiring that parents give their consent before their child is assessed.

Although laws and regulations provide the general structure for assessment, specific procedures must be developed at the state and local levels. For example, there is considerable variation among states in the terminology used to identify the different disabilities; within states, there are differences in the forms that local districts develop to document referrals, parental consent for assessment, and IEPs. This flexibility allows professionals to consider local needs and act upon their beliefs about preferred practices in assessment.

IDENTIFICATION AND REFERRAL

The first phase in the assessment process is the identification of students with possible disabilities. This phase involves the largest number of students. However, identification does not necessarily result in referral for special education assessment. In some cases, students are referred for consideration for other types of services, such as bilingual education. In others, school problems are resolved through classroom interventions during the prereferral stage. When problems persist despite such efforts, students may be referred for assessment to determine their eligibility for special education.

Screening and Teacher Identification

According to federal special education laws, state education agencies are responsible for "child find," that is, the identification, location, and evaluation of all students with disabilities. States use several types of child find strategies, including mass media information campaigns, in an attempt to make the general public more aware of the needs of individuals with disabilities. These campaigns stress the signs and symptoms of disabilities as well as the availability of services within the state or a particular region.

School districts and other educational agencies also participate in child find activities. Screening procedures are used to gather information about large groups of students to identify those in need of more in-depth assessment. Teachers and other staff members are alerted to signs of various disabilities as well as the prereferral and

referral processes. Teachers may be asked to complete checklists or rating forms for each of their students to help identify those with potential problems. School records may be examined to locate students with poor report card grades or low performance on group achievement tests.

Anyone within the community may identify a child with a possible disability. In the preschool years, parents often bring their child to the attention of education professionals. Once the child has entered the elementary grades, it is typically the general education teacher who first notices a potential problem. This is particularly true for mild disabilities because these disabilities often first become apparent when students are unable to meet classroom academic and behavioral expectations. When teachers identify students with problems in school, the first step is not referral. Instead, prereferral strategies are used in an attempt to ameliorate the problem.

Prereferral Strategies

General education teachers are expected to make modifications in a student's instructional program before beginning formal procedures for referring that student for special education assessment. The purpose of this prereferral intervention stage is twofold. First, many students who experience minor or transitory learning and behavior problems can be helped to succeed by relatively simple adaptations of the standard curriculum, of instructional procedures, or of the behavior management program within the general education classroom. Also, there may be resources within the school, in addition to special education, that can assist the student; examples are peer tutoring programs and bilingual education. Second, when prereferral strategies are not effective in improving the student's performance, the information gathered during this stage provides direction for the special education team in its decisions about eligibility, intervention strategies, and placement options.

In many schools, the prereferral intervention stage is coordinated by a team of professionals (e.g., a child study or student assistance team) that includes general educators as well as special educators. A teacher with a student who is experiencing difficulty in school may ask the team for assistance in identifying strategies for modifying the classroom learning environment to improve the student's chances for success. Prereferral strategies can take many forms: conferences with students and parents, review of school records and results of medical screenings, changes in instruction, introduction of learning aids, and modifications of the classroom behavior management system. Checklists such as this are used to document the adaptations made in general education so that their effectiveness can be evaluated.

When prereferral interventions do not bring about desired changes, one option open to the team is referral for special education assessment. The team or the student's classroom teacher may institute the referral. Others interested in the student's welfare can also make referrals: parents, tutors, physicians, or even the student himself or herself. However, general education teachers remain the most common source of special education referrals.

Referral and Parental Notification

Referrals are initiated when the parent, teacher, or another professional completes a referral form. Although forms differ from district to district, most require the person making the referral to describe the student's problem, tell how long the problem has been occurring, and discuss the types of classroom modifications that have been introduced in an attempt to solve the problem.

Once a student is formally referred for special education assessment, a chain of events is set in motion. School districts usually have an individual or team that receives referrals from schools in the district or, in the case of new students, from other agencies or individuals. A team forms and processes the referral by alerting the student's parents and by gathering all available data.

Federal special education law requires that parents be informed of any referral in writing. They must also be informed whenever any testing for possible special education program changes will take place. Parents have the right to participate in the assessment and in subsequent decisions about their child's program. They must give their permission for assessment and should receive an explanation of the results and any proposed action. They can ask for an independent evaluation, inspect all school records, and request a mediation due process hearing whenever they disagree with a proposed action, such as placement in special education.

Students with disabilities have the right to be represented in assessment and other matters. When no parent or guardian can be identified, when his or her whereabouts are unknown, or when the student is a ward of the state, the state or local education agency can assign a surrogate parent. The person chosen must be qualified to serve the best interests of the child. He or she represents the student in all the matters mentioned here and cannot be employed by the school district.

DETERMINATION OF ELIGIBILITY

The eligibility determination stage of assessment begins with careful planning. Parents are informed of the assessment plan, and their participation in team deliberations is encouraged. When the assessment has been carried out, results are reported, and team members, including the student's parents, make legal decisions about eligibility for special education services.

Design of the Individualized Assessment Plan

Assessment of students with suspected disabilities must be systematic. To ensure this, a plan of action should be developed by the professionals responsible for the assessment. In this text, we call that plan an **individualized assessment plan,** or **IAP.** Although it is not a legal requirement, the IAP serves to individualize the assessment process so that each student's unique needs are addressed. Standard sets of assessment procedures, administered by some districts to all students referred for special education assessment, are neither appropriate nor useful.

An IAP describes the steps in assessment and the procedures used in each step. It should address the reason the student was referred for assessment, focus on areas relevant to education, and provide information needed for decisions concerning instructional design, placement, and other aspects of the educational program. The three main concerns are (1) the student's skills and abilities (including performance in the areas related to the suspected disability), (2) the general education curriculum and the tasks with which the student is having difficulty, and (3) the classroom learning environment. The IAP may also consider physical, social, and behavioral characteristics as they relate to the student's educational needs. For example, a student may have a severe reading disability due in part to a vision disorder.

Chapter 1 presented a framework for special education assessment that suggested important assessment questions for each stage of the process. Those questions can be used to develop the IAP. Questions are arranged in sequential order, and each major question is followed by a set of more detailed questions. For example, depending on the answers to broad questions such as "What are the student's levels of achievement and strengths and weaknesses in school learning?" the team might also ask, "What are the student's strengths and weaknesses in mathematics?"

IAPs include formal and/or informal assessment procedures, depending on the questions under consideration. The questions may address any area relevant to education; examples are academic skills (e.g., reading), social-emotional concerns (self-concept), and the physical environment of the classroom (seating arrangement). The types of information needed to answer the assessment question often influence the choice of assessment procedures. For example, norm-referenced tests provide information to answer questions about level of proficiency, but they do not describe specific skill deficits. A parent interview, rather than a formal test, would be used to gather data about a student's family history and medical background. Other criteria for the selection of appropriate assessment procedures are described in Chapter 4.

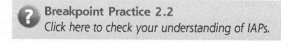

Breakpoint Practice 2.2
Click here to check your understanding of IAPs.

Federal special education laws make several specific provisions for evaluation. Before a student receives special education services, a team of qualified professionals must assess the student to determine eligibility. This team is made up of individuals similar to those who serve on the IEP team. According to IDEA 2004, such teams should include:

- The student's parents;
- A general education teacher if the student is or may be participating in general education;
- A special education teacher;
- A representative of the educational agency who can provide or supervise special education services and who is knowledgeable about the general curriculum and resources available within the agency;
- An individual able to interpret assessment results and their educational implications (this individual may be one of the professionals just listed);
- Others, as needed, with special expertise or knowledge about the student; and
- If appropriate, the student.

The law makes clear that one of the major purposes of the evaluation is to gather information for program planning. IDEA 2004 also places great emphasis on the general education curriculum. In development of the educational program, the team must describe how the disability affects the student's involvement with and progress in the general curriculum.

In designing the IAP, the evaluation team should follow these principles:

1. Focus assessment on the education of the student; consider noneducational factors only as they contribute to understanding the educational problem.
2. Plan the assessment by asking important assessment questions, and then select procedures that will gather the information needed to answer those questions.
3. Choose assessment procedures of the highest quality.
4. Coordinate the efforts of team members. Avoid duplication and take advantage of the expertise of persons with different perspectives.
5. Begin assessment in each area of interest by surveying general performance; continue assessment with more in-depth procedures only if a problem is identified.

6. Consider not only the student but also the learning tasks and the instructional environment.
7. Compare findings from different procedures to confirm the accuracy of assessment results. Be sure to include information about the student's current classroom performance in this comparison.

Decisions about eligibility for special education and program planning are important. These principles help to ensure that students are assessed accurately, fully, and fairly so that useful information is available for decision making.

Parental Permission for Assessment

Once an assessment plan has been developed, the student's parents must give their permission before the assessment can take place. Federal special education laws require that parents be notified in writing. The notice must be given a reasonable time before the school proposes to do the assessment, and it must include information about procedural safeguards, a clear explanation of the reasons for the assessment, and a description of each assessment procedure to be used.

There are additional legal requirements. The request for permission for assessment and all related communications must be clearly written in understandable language. When necessary, the notice must be translated into the parents' native language or other mode of communication (e.g., Braille), unless this is not feasible. If the parents do not use a written language for communication, the notice must be translated orally. The educational agency must document that these procedures have been followed. The goal is to ensure that, when parents agree to the assessment, the consent they give is an informed consent.

Administration, Scoring, and Interpretation of Assessment Procedures

Guidelines for administration, scoring, and interpretation of formal assessment procedures such as norm-referenced tests are discussed in detail in Chapter 5. These guidelines are supplemented by the specific directions that appear in the manuals that accompany published tests.

Chapter 6 describes similar procedures for informal assessment procedures such as observations, interviews, and inventories. Although manuals are not available for most informal measures, principles of good practice guide professionals in their use of these assessment tools.

Like other aspects of the assessment process, special education laws govern the selection and use of assessment procedures. For example, assessment devices must be technically sound, and standardized tests must be administered by trained professionals who follow the directions provided by the test producer. A more complete discussion of these legal requirements appears in Chapter 4.

Reporting Results

When students are assessed for possible special education services, results must be reported to parents, whether or not the student is ultimately found to be eligible for services. The results are presented at a meeting of the evaluation team, and parents are to serve as members of this team. Parents must be clearly told if the student has a disability and is eligible for special education services. If so, the components of an IEP are developed.

Federal special education laws also specify that parents must be informed of their right to have access to all school records concerning their child's identification, assessment, and placement in special education. In some cases, parents may wish to examine the records to better understand the school's basis for concern. In addition, the school system must provide information about where parents can obtain an independent educational evaluation, if requested.

Decisions About Eligibility

Decisions about eligibility are usually made at the team meeting when results are reported. These legal decisions are based on the eligibility criteria in federal laws and regulations as well as state and district policies. According to federal guidelines, the team must decide whether the student has a disability and, if so, if that disability adversely affects school performance. The disability must be one covered by federal law. Also, students with school performance problems due to limited proficiency in English or lack of appropriate instruction in reading or math are not considered disabled.

ENHANCEDetext
Video Example 2.2
Watch this video to see how families are involved as children's advocates in the assessment process.

PROGRAM PLANNING

The team now turns its attention to instructional matters and meets to develop the educational plan for the student. Once the student's parents have agreed to the proposed plan, the student's special education program can begin.

Design of the Individualized Education Program

The IEP meeting must take place within 30 days of the determination that the student has a disability and is in need of special education services. The IEP must be developed before the student begins to receive special services and must be implemented without any undue delay after the meeting. Furthermore, a similar meeting must be held regularly (most typically annually) to reexamine the appropriateness of the IEP and revise it, if necessary.

The IEP team is composed of the same members as the assessment team. Thus, the team includes the student's parents and the professionals who will provide services to the student, such as special education teachers, general education teachers, and others as needed. Other required team members include a representative of the educational agency who has knowledge about special education, the general curriculum, and school resources (often the school principal or vice principal) and a person who is knowledgeable about the interpretation of assessment results (often the special education teacher or school psychologist). Students themselves may serve as members of the IEP team, when appropriate.

Schools must take steps to encourage parents to attend IEP meetings and participate in the development of their child's IEP.

1. Parents must be notified early enough in advance of the meeting that they have an opportunity to attend.
2. Parents must be informed of the purpose of the meeting, its time and location, and the persons who will attend.
3. Meetings must be scheduled at a mutually agreed-upon time and place.
4. When parents cannot attend, the school must use other means of communication to ensure parental participation (e.g., individual and conference telephone calls).
5. An IEP meeting may be held without the student's parents if the parents choose not to attend. In this case, the school must keep detailed records of all attempts to communicate with the parents and any responses.
6. At the meeting, every effort must be made to ensure that parents understand the proceedings. This may involve the use of interpreters for parents who are deaf or those who speak languages other than English.
7. Parents must receive a copy of their child's IEP at no cost.

Professionals and parents make decisions about the student's educational program based on the data gathered in the assessment. Many types of assessment data are needed to develop the components of the IEP. In fact, the full array of educational assessment procedures described in Chapter 1 may be used to make these instructional decisions.

TABLE 2–3
IEP Requirements

Content of the IEP (§300.320(a))

(a)   *General.* As used in this part, the term *individualized education program* or IEP means a written statement for each child with a disability that is developed, reviewed, and revised in a meeting in accordance with §§300.320 through 300.324, and that must include—

(1)   A statement of the child's present levels of educational achievement and functional performance, including—

(i)   How the child's disability affects the child's involvement and progress in the general curriculum (i.e., the same curriculum as for nondisabled children); or

(ii)   For preschool children, as appropriate, how the disability affects the child's participation in appropriate activities;

(2)   (i)   A statement of measurable annual goals, including academic and functional goals designed to—

(A)   Meet the child's needs that result from the child's disability to enable the child to be involved in and make progress in the general education curriculum; and

(B)   Meet each of the child's other educational needs that result from the child's disability;

(ii)   For children with disabilities who take alternate assessments aligned to alternate achievement standards, a description of benchmarks or short-term objectives;

(3)   A description of—

(i)   How the child's progress toward meeting the annual goals described in paragraph (2) of this section will be measured; and

(ii)   When periodic reports on the progress the child is making toward meeting the annual goals (such as through the use of quarterly or other periodic reports, concurrent with the issuance of report cards) will be provided;

(4)   A statement of the special education and related services and supplementary aids and services, based on peer-reviewed research to the extent practicable, to be provided to the child, or on behalf of the child, and a statement of the program modifications or supports for school personnel that will be provided to enable the child—

(i)   To advance appropriately toward attaining the annual goals;

(ii)   To be involved in and make progress in the general curriculum . . . and to participate in extracurricular and other nonacademic activities; and

(iii) To be educated and participate with other children with disabilities and nondisabled children in the activities described in this section;

(5)   An explanation of the extent, if any, to which the child will not participate with nondisabled children in the regular class and in the activities described paragraph (a)(4) of this section;

(6)   (i)   A statement of any individual appropriate accommodations that are necessary to measure the academic achievement and functional performance of the child on State and districtwide assessments. . . .

(ii)   If the IEP Team determines that the child shall take an alternate assessment on a particular State or districtwide assessment of student achievement, a statement of why—

(A)   The child cannot participate in the regular assessment; and

(B)   The particular alternate assessment selected is appropriate for the child; and

(7)   The projected date for the beginning of the services and modifications described in paragraph (a)(4) of this section, and the anticipated frequency, location, and duration of those services and modifications.

TABLE 2–3   *continued*

Transition (§300.320(b))

(b) Transition services. Beginning not later than the first IEP to be in effect when the child is 16, or younger if determined appropriate by the IEP Team, and updated annually, thereafter, the IEP must include—

   (1) Appropriate measurable postsecondary goals based upon age-appropriate transition assessments related to training, education, employment, and, where appropriate, independent living skills; and

   (2) the transition services (including courses of study) needed to assist the child in reaching those goals.

Consideration of Special Factors (§300.324(2))

   (i) In the case of a child whose behavior impedes the child's learning or that of others, consider the use of positive behavioral interventions and supports, and other strategies, to address that behavior;

   (ii) In the case of a child with limited English proficiency, consider the language needs of the child as such needs relate to the child's IEP;

   (iii) In the case of a child who is blind or visually impaired, provide for instruction in Braille and the use of Braille unless the IEP Team determines, after an evaluation of the child's reading and writing skills, needs, and appropriate reading and writing media (including an evaluation of the child's future needs for instruction in Braille or the use of Braille), that instruction in Braille or the use of Braille is not appropriate for the child;

   (iv) Consider the communication needs of the child, and in the case of a child who is deaf or hard of hearing, consider the child's language and communication needs, opportunities for direct communications with peers and professional personnel in the child's language and communication mode, academic level, and full range of needs, including opportunities for direct instruction in the child's language and communication mode; and

   (v) Consider whether the child needs assistive technology devices and services.

Source: Building the Legacy US Department of Education.

Specific guidelines govern the content of the IEP. According to current federal laws, the IEP must contain information about:

1. The student's present levels of educational achievement and functional performance;
2. Measurable annual goals;
3. Needed special education and related services, supplementary aids and services, and program modifications and supports;
4. The extent to which the student will not participate with nondisabled students in the general education classroom and other school activities;
5. Procedures for the student's participation in state- or districtwide assessments of student achievement;
6. Strategies for measuring progress toward annual goals and informing parents of that progress;
7. Transition services for older students; and
8. When appropriate, special factors such as behavioral needs, language needs, instruction in Braille, communication needs, and assistive technology devices and services.

Table 2–3 presents excerpts from the Final Regulations for IDEA 2004 that address the content of the IEP.

Although federal laws mandate the components of the IEP, the IEP form itself is not. The form is developed by individual school districts or other educational agencies, causing some variation from one locale to another.

Several components of the IEP focus on the general education curriculum and the student's access to and participation in that curriculum. In describing the student's present levels of educational performance, the team must address the effects of the disability on the student's ability to participate in the general curriculum. The team must develop annual goals related to involvement and progress in the general curriculum. The team can specify several types of services for the student, if these are needed. These services include not only special education and related services, but also services and supports in the general education classroom. In addition, the team must describe how the student will participate in the state- or districtwide assessments of achievement (or, if participation is not considered appropriate, the alternative assessment procedures). The IEP must identify strategies for measuring the student's progress toward annual goals and specify a schedule for notifying parents of that progress; that schedule must be at least as frequent as the report card schedule for students without disabilities. Finally, the IEP team must explain any placement that constitutes a removal from the general education classroom. Although current federal laws do not require that students with disabilities remain in the general education classroom at all times, the IEP team must justify any removal to another educational setting or any action that curtails students' ability to participate in extracurricular activities or other nonacademic school activities.

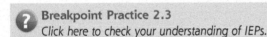

Breakpoint Practice 2.3
Click here to check your understanding of IEPs.

Placement of students with disabilities is governed by the principle of **least restrictive environment (LRE)**. The IDEA 2004 Final Regulations define LRE in this way:

> To the maximum extent appropriate, children with disabilities . . . are educated with children who are nondisabled, and special classes, separate schooling or other removal of children with disabilities from the regular educational environment occurs only when the nature or severity of the disability is such that education in regular classes with the use of supplementary aids and services cannot be achieved satisfactorily. (§300.114(a)(2))

These regulations also require that local educational agencies maintain a continuum of alternative placements for students with disabilities. This continuum must include services provided in conjunction with regular class placement (e.g., resource rooms and itinerant instruction) as well as separate placements, such as special classes, special schools, home instruction, and instruction in hospitals and institutions. Although these requirements appear somewhat contradictory, they are not. In fact, they underscore one of the most important assumptions underlying the provision of special education services: All decisions about students with disabilities, including decisions about placement, must be made on an individual basis. Thus, the IEP team considers the needs of an individual student in order to design an educational program tailored to that student's unique needs.

Parental Agreement to the IEP

After parents and professionals work together to design the student's educational program, the parents must give their consent before the IEP can be implemented. Parents must approve the provisions of the IEP, including the educational services to be provided to the student. As with other important decisions, parents must give informed consent. This means that the IEP must be explained to parents in clear, understandable language with written or oral translations, as needed. The school must document that this and all other due process procedures have been followed.

Sometimes the parents and the school do not agree on one or more aspects of the IEP, such as the amount of support to be provided or the placement recommended for the student. In such cases, several options are available to both parties in the dispute. The first is voluntary mediation. In mediation, the parents and the educational agency meet with an impartial mediator in an attempt to resolve the dispute. If the conflict is resolved, a written mediation agreement must result.

If mediation does not end in an agreement, or if either party does not choose to participate, the next option is an impartial due process hearing. At such hearings, parents have the right to be advised by legal counsel and by persons knowledgeable about students with disabilities. The educational agency must inform the parents of free or low-cost legal services and other relevant services, if available in the area. An impartial hearing officer presides over the deliberations; that officer may not be an employee of the state or local educational agency. At the hearing, both parties have the right to present evidence, confront and cross-examine witnesses, and call their own witnesses. Both parties must disclose evaluations and recommendations they plan to present at least 5 days prior to the hearing. A record of the hearing, the finding of facts, and the decision must be provided to parents at no cost.

Decisions made in impartial due process hearings are final, unless the parents and/or school wish to appeal to the state educational agency. The decision made by the state is final, unless either party wishes to take civil action. Civil actions can be brought in a state or U.S. district court.

Federal special education laws set up timelines for conducting both the impartial due process hearing and the state-level review so that decisions are made in an expeditious manner. In most cases, the student remains in the current educational placement during this period, unless the parents and the school system agree to an alternative placement. However, there are special procedures for placement in alternative educational settings for students charged with serious offenses such as use of illegal drugs or carrying a weapon to school.

Several modifications to IDEA took place in regards to eligibility and IEPs. Students with disabilities must have accessible materials. In addition, several language changes to parental consent are included in the updated law. For example, the phrase "reasonable efforts to obtain consent from the parent for an initial evaluation" was added. Language regarding "special education environment" was changed to "special class." In addition, stronger language was added to encourage districts to purposefully involve family members in the IEP meetings. Clarification language was added in regards to transfer students. Also, a requirement was added to inform the IEP team, if changes were made to the IEP (Wright, 2006).

PROGRAM IMPLEMENTATION AND MONITORING

Once the student's parents have given their consent, the IEP can be implemented. The student's progress in the program is monitored, and the IEP is reviewed and revised on a regular basis, typically annually. Also, at least every 3 years, the student's eligibility for special education is reconsidered. The purpose of these evaluation strategies is to determine whether the student's educational program is effective and, if it is not, to modify the program so that it more adequately meets the student's needs.

IEP Implementation and Ongoing Monitoring of Progress

The IEP must be implemented as soon as possible after it has been designed by the team and approved by the student's parents. All persons with responsibility for delivering services must have access to the IEP and be informed of their specific responsibilities in its implementation. This includes general education teachers involved in the student's education as well as special education teachers and others such as counselors and speech-language pathologists. In particular, professionals must be made aware of the supports, accommodations, and modifications to be provided to the student.

The IEP sets forth the annual goals for the educational program, and these goals become the framework for evaluation of the student's progress. The IEP must specify how the team will assess progress toward annual goals and how that progress will be reported to parents. Several types of assessment procedures are used to gather the data needed to monitor progress, but in most cases, informal assessment strategies are preferred. For example, observations, analysis of work samples, criterion-referenced tests, and informal inventories provide information about student performance and help professionals determine whether changes should be made in the instructional program.

In addition, the IEP describes the student's participation in state- or districtwide assessments of student achievement. There are three possible options. First, the student can participate in the assessments under conditions identical to those for typical students. Second, modifications may be made in administration procedures. For example, the student may be given extra time to complete a test or be allowed to type, rather than handwrite, essays. Third, if the IEP team determines that participation in such assessments is not appropriate for the student, the team must explain why and describe how the student will be assessed to monitor his or her progress in the general curriculum. Strategies for making decisions about test accommodations and modifications are discussed later in this book in Chapter 4.

ENHANCEDetext
Video Example 2.3
What are the components of an IEP? Watch this video to see how IEP goals are shared.

Annual Review of the IEP

At minimum, the IEP must be reviewed on an annual basis. In this review, the team evaluates the student's progress toward the annual goals. Both formal and informal assessment procedures may be used to gather data for this review. Norm-referenced tests may be administered to determine whether the student's performance has improved in relation to the performance of age or grade peers. Teachers and other team members may report results of classroom observations, portfolio assessments, criterion-referenced testing, and interviews with students and parents. These data are used to decide whether the educational program described in the IEP should be continued, modified, or discontinued. If the annual goals have been achieved and no further special education needs are apparent, the student may be dismissed from special education. However, if all goals have not been fully accomplished or if additional goals are necessary, the IEP is revised and the student continues to receive special education services.

Schools must provide the special education and other services listed on the IEP and make a good-faith effort to assist students to meet their annual goals and objectives. However, schools and teachers may not be held accountable if students fail to meet those goals. When students do not achieve as expected, parents have the right to ask that the IEP be revised. For example, parents might request a change in the types of services provided to their child or an increase in the amount of services.

Although the law now requires annual review of the IEP, IDEA 2004 authorizes a feasibility study of multiyear IEPs in a limited number of states. Multiyear IEPs would address no more than 3 years and would focus on natural transition points for students (e.g., the transition from middle school to high school). Gartin and Murdick (2005) explain that this change is in response to criticisms of the amount of paperwork required in special education.

Curriculum-Based Measurements

Over the past few years, **curriculum-based measurements (CBMs)** have been used often in the classroom for purposes of continuous assessment tied to instruction. Although CBMs are utilized in the classroom, they are not necessarily informal assessment (Hosp, Hosp, & Howell, 2012). CBMs are criterion-based measurements and generally have reliability and validity established. In addition, standardized procedures are used.

Curriculum-based measurement (CBM) is a measurement tool used for assessing students' academic growth repeatedly over time, providing additional strategies to support students' needs, and ascertaining the need for additional diagnostic testing (Howell & Nolet, 1999). Curriculum-based measurement was developed to utilize formative measurement information in evaluating and improving instructional efficacy (Deno, 1985). This avenue of repeated measures provides teachers with the data as tools to monitor and adjust their instruction (Deno & Mirkin, 1977).

Deno (2003) studied the literature and offered the general characteristics and uses of CBM. General characteristics include reliability and validity,

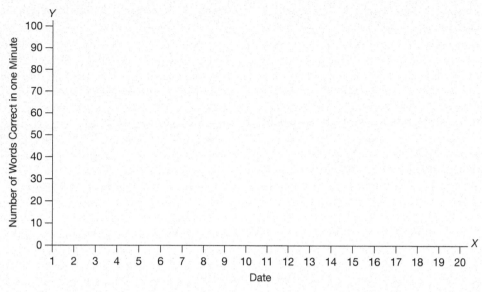

FIGURE 2–1
Aim Line

standard tasks, specific instructional materials, specifics in terms of administration and scoring, sampling through direct observation, repeated sampling, time efficiency, and ease of teaching. General uses include improving instructional programs, predicting performance, developing normative samples, increasing collaboration, identifying high-risk students, appraising prereferral interventions, decreasing bias, finding different identification systems, investigating inclusion placements, predicting performance on high-stakes tests, looking at content area growth, evaluating English language learners (ELLs) (Esparza, Brown & Sanford, 2011), and predicting performance in the early grade levels.

Fuchs and Fuchs (1999) offered criteria for successful measurement structures, which include meeting standards for reliability and validity; modeling growth over time; being affected by instructional adaptations quickly; not involving just one specific instructional program; and being quick, inexpensive, and efficient.

CBM is progress monitoring rather than mastery measurement (Fuchs, 2006b). Safer and Fleischman (2005) also tap into the concept of monitoring instruction through continuous assessment. They discuss a rate of progress through the

use of probes and their connection to improved instruction. That is, the teacher looks at samples of skills the student is expected to learn by the end of the year. The teacher examines the probes on a weekly, biweekly, or monthly basis. Teachers can then graph the students' progress to see if instruction must be altered. Altered instruction would then yield better student outcomes. Students could also be involved in graphing and self-monitoring. Students can take responsibility for meeting with the teacher if the aim line is not reached three days in a row (see Figure 2–1). Data would be shared with family members.

Swain (2005) tapped into the students' self-monitoring, that is, the self-determination aspect of CBM. She studied goal-setting awareness, knowledge, and setting daily reading goals in students with learning disabilities. Students in the goal-setting treatment group increased knowledge but had difficulty setting realistic goals.

Progress monitoring has been tied into standards-based assessment and connected positively to accountability, expectations, and outcomes (Quenemoen, Thurlow, Moen, Thompson, & Morse, 2003). Monitoring of the student's progress provides a continuous feedback loop to the teacher and student, which improves assessment and instruction outcomes (Fuchs & Fuchs, 1986a, 1986b). Furthermore, this method provides graphic displays of each individual's data and qualitative accounts of student demonstrations of skills (Fuchs & Fuchs, 2002). More specifically, this method can be used for designing effective individualized programs, including setting goals and monitoring progress toward goals (Fuchs, 2006a).

In concentrating on the instructional or intervention aspect of this **CBM** process, **response to intervention*** (RTI) (Gresham, 1991) is a concept that is critical to the discussion of students with and without disabilities (Fuchs, 2006b). Gresham (1991) referred to RTI as a change in performance due to intervention. He also described resistance to intervention as academic performance that does not change in response to research-based intervention.

RTI has also been discussed as a possible alternative to using a questioned discrepancy model (VanDerHeyden & Jimerson, 2005; Vellutino, Scanlon, & Lyon, 2000) when identifying learning disabilities (Massanari, 2004; Fuchs, Fuchs, & Compton, 2012). Researchers included issues such as variability in the number of standard deviations used in this model, differentiation and difficulties with reliability, and waiting until student failure occurs (Vaughn & Fuchs, 2003). Mellard (2004) notes the following as strengths of RTI: high-quality instruction, instruction grounded in research, students' assessment in the classroom curriculum, universal screening, progress monitoring, interventions grounded in research, progress monitoring during interventions, and technical adequacy.

RTI looks at student performance after educational interventions (Hoover, 2010). Instruction is changed based on what the data reveal regarding the effectiveness of those interventions. Different methods work for different students. Several tiers of this method reveal useful information regarding the student. As we progress in the three-tier continuum of interventions, intensity increases (Barnett, Daly, Jones, & Lentz, 2004), and identification of difficulties becomes more evident (Fuchs, 2006b). Those tiers include tier one, where the student fails to show improvement (even with research-based interventions) in the general education classroom. In tier two, a multidisciplinary team attempts to problem-solve different and more intense interventions regarding the student in question. In tier three, an eligibility evaluation for special education services takes place (CASP Board of Directors, 2003).

Therefore, CBMs provide us not only with tools for monitoring and enhancing student growth and reflecting and changing our instructional practices, but also with information in the area of diagnostic evaluation. Fuchs and Fuchs (2002) described identifying students with disabilities and the notion of nonresponders. In their dual discrepancy approach, they refer to this notion as students who are nonresponsive to otherwise effective instruction. Traditionally, special educators have looked at a discrepancy between achievement and intelligence measures. However, we can look at learning disabilities from a different perspective. We are providing specialized instruction to students who perform below expectations and show a significantly lower learning rate. Utilizing CBM, we can identify and enhance learning in nonresponders.

In terms of showing a need for special education services, a CBM must show that discrepancies exist in performance and growth rate between the student and his or her peers, the student's learning rate with adaptations is below level, and special education services result in enhanced progress (Fuchs & Fuchs, 1997; Tindal, 2013).

Periodic Reevaluation of Eligibility

A review of each student's eligibility for special education must be held every 3 years, or more often if requested by the student's parent or teacher. The purpose of this review is to determine whether the student continues to require special education services. As with the initial eligibility decision, a team meets to plan the data collection process. Existing information about the student is reviewed, an assessment plan is prepared, and parents are asked for their consent before the assessment is conducted. In some cases, the team may decide that no additional information is needed to make the eligibility decision. If so, the team notifies the parents of its determination that further assessment is not necessary. If the parents agree with this decision, the student's eligibility is reviewed using existing information. If the parents disagree, they have the right to request that an assessment take place.

MULTICULTURAL CONSIDERATIONS

Students who speak a language other than English are at risk of an incorrect and inappropriate diagnosis (Kritikos, 2004; Ortiz, Robertson, Wilkinson, Liu, McGhee, & Kushner, 2011; Sullivan, 2011). DeMatthews, Edwards, and Nelson (2014) investigated the identification of special education disability as related to a group of nonnative English-speaking students. Results revealed a lack of guidance and support for educational professionals serving nonnative English speaking students.

McCloskey and Schicke Athanasiou (2000) investigated the assessment practices of school psychologists related to individuals who were linguistically diverse. They found that some school psychologists used curriculum-based, dynamic, and portfolio assessment. However, most used traditional norm-referenced tests.

Researchers have investigated whether biases related to individuals who are culturally and/or linguistically diverse exist within informal tools used by professionals. VanDerHeyden and Witt (2005) investigated the relationship among the components of teacher referral, race, gender, high and low student achievement, and assessment. More specifically, they examined the efficacy of teacher referral and assessment problem solving. They used the Problem Validation Screening (PVS), a universal screening tool, to examine these aspects. Results revealed that PVS was a more accurate instrument than teacher referral in identifying students at risk for learning difficulties. Teachers were 61 percent accurate compared to a PVS accuracy of 86 percent in referring Caucasian students. Teachers were 78 percent accurate compared to a PVS accuracy

of 90 percent in referring minority students for evaluations. Furthermore, teachers were 63 percent accurate compared to a PVS accuracy of 87 percent in referring males, and they were 69 percent accurate compared to a PVS accuracy of 85 percent in identifying females. These results reveal important information regarding teacher referral efficacy and curriculum-based assessment related to race and gender. This tool can benefit teachers in increasing appropriate assessment and instruction to students.

In addition, Kranzler, Miller, and Jordan (1999) researched racial/ethnic and gender bias involving reading CBM in African American and Caucasian students. Results revealed no significant differences in grades 2 and 3. However, racial/ethnicity bias was revealed in grades 4 and 5, and gender bias was found in grade 5. Results revealed overestimates for African American students and the opposite effect for Caucasian students. Furthermore, overestimates for girls and underestimates for boys were noted.

MacMillan (2000) also explored the area of reading and CBM related to gender. The researcher found growth in reading for all students. However, small gender differences were found. Girls outperformed boys.

Evans-Hampton, Skinner, Henington, Sims, and McDaniel (2002) investigated cultural bias and CBM. They focused on math performance and timing in African American and Caucasian students. Specifically, they evaluated data involving digits correct per minute and percentage of digits correct. No difference was found between the two groups in terms of timing groups. Therefore, CBM shows positive results in the area of culture.

Seaman, Guggisberg, Malyn, Payne, and Scheibe (2001) investigated the validity of a copying curriculum-based fluency measure. They found that females performed significantly better than boys at the fifth- and sixth-grade levels. Malecki and Jewell (2003) also investigated writing CBM as it relates to gender. They found that girls performed significantly better than boys did at all grade levels. Teachers should increase their awareness regarding these outcomes and consider this information while assessing students.

Assessment in Action
William

Once his teacher, Ms. Trapp, refers William, an assessment plan is developed and approved by William's mom. The professionals making up the assessment team begin collecting information by reviewing William's school records, interviewing his mother and teacher, observing William's behavior in the second grade classroom, analyzing samples of William's schoolwork, and administering tests and other measures of reading, mathematics, language arts, intellectual performance, and other areas of interest.

At the completion of assessment, William's mother meets with the team to learn about the results and help make decisions about William's educational program. Team members report that William scores within the average range in intellectual performance and is doing acceptable work in reading and language arts. However, his mathematics skills fall far below grade level, and his behavior problems are quite severe. His teacher considers him disruptive and hard to motivate, and classroom observations reveal a pattern of verbal outbursts, negative remarks, physical threats to peers, and out-of-seat behavior. The team and William's mother conclude that William meets the eligibility criteria for special education services for students with behavioral disorders. The next step in the process is development of an individualized education program for William to address his needs in the areas of behavior and mathematics.

SUMMARY

- Special education assessment provides the information needed to make two types of decisions: legal decisions and instructional decisions. The determination of eligibility for special services and the reevaluation of eligibility are legal decisions. Their purpose is to determine whether individual students meet legal requirements for one or more disabilities in order to allow allocation of special education funds, resources, and personnel.

  Planning, monitoring, and evaluating the student's special education program require instructional decisions. The major areas are the content of the student's curriculum (i.e., what to teach), the instructional methods used to implement the curriculum (i.e., how to teach), and the overall effectiveness of the instructional program.

- Four main steps in the assessment process include identification and referral, determination of eligibility, program planning, and program implementation and evaluation. An example of identification and referral includes prereferral intervention strategies. In addition, administration, scoring, and interpretation of assessment procedures are art of the determination of eligibility. Program planning includes the design of the IEP. Furthermore, program implementation and evaluation would involve implementation of the IEP.

- Identification does not necessarily result in referral for special education assessment. In some cases, students are referred for consideration for other types of services, such as bilingual education. In others, school problems are resolved through classroom interventions during the prereferral stage. When problems persist despite such efforts, students may be referred for assessment to determine their eligibility for special education. Screening and teacher identification, prereferral strategies, and referral and identification are examples of identification and referral stages special educators use in special education assessment.

- Assessment of students with suspected disabilities must be systematic. To ensure this, a plan of action should be developed by the professionals responsible for the assessment. In this text, we call that plan an individualized assessment plan, or IAP. Although it is not a legal requirement, the IAP serves to individualize the assessment process so that each student's unique needs are addressed.

- The IEP must be implemented as soon as possible after the team has designed it and it has been approved by the student's parents. All persons with responsibility for delivering services must have access to the IEP and be informed of their specific responsibilities in its implementation.

The IEP sets forth the annual goals for the educational program, and these goals become the framework for evaluation of the student's progress. The IEP must specify how the team will assess progress toward annual goals and how that progress will be reported to parents. Several types of assessment procedures are used to gather the data needed to monitor progress, but in most cases, informal assessment strategies are preferred. In addition, the IEP describes the student's participation in state- or districtwide assessments of student achievement.

- Once the student's parents have given their consent, the IEP can be implemented. The student's progress in the program is monitored, and the IEP is reviewed and revised on a regular basis, typically annually. Also, at least every 3 years, the student's eligibility for special education is reconsidered. The purpose of these evaluation strategies is to determine whether the student's educational program is effective and, if it is not, to modify the program so that it more adequately meets the student's needs.

3

Micromonkey/Fotolia

Including Parents and Families in the Assessment Process

By Eleanor W. Lynch

LEARNING OUTCOMES

After reading this chapter, you will be able to:

- Describe three examples of benefits in parent–professional partnerships in assessment.
- Provide three examples of strategies educational professionals could use to develop parent–professional partnerships in the assessment process.
- Discuss three elements that are important in the assessment of children from diverse cultural and linguistic backgrounds and partnering with their families.
- Summarize three elements that are important in communicating effectively with parents and families.
- Choose and explain three strategies educational professionals use to effectively interview and conference with parents and families.

Teachers and other educational specialists know students through their performance and behavior at school. They seldom, however, have the opportunity to get to know students within the larger context of students' family and community. Yet a great deal can be learned about each child or teen through his or her parents, others in the family, friends, and mentors within the community. Parents or primary caregivers are typically the experts on their own son, daughter, grandchild, niece, or nephew (Dardig, 2008). The wealth of knowledge that they possess makes them important partners in both assessment and program development. Parents may go through a number of different emotions as they first realize that their child has a disability or learning difference. It is essential that educational professionals are sensitive to this aspect of working with families.

Parental perspective and input is important for all teachers, but for those who work with children with special needs, it is imperative. Parents and family members can play vital roles in accurately assessing learning needs, planning effective programs, and monitoring the success of those programs for students with disabilities. For example, Nokali, Bachman, and Votruba-Drzal (2010) reported that parent involvement suggested improvement in students' appropriate behaviors and social skills.

The importance of parents has been recognized in special education law since passage of PL 94-142 in 1975, and the commitment to parental involvement continues to be a strong component of the 2004 amendments of the Individuals with Disabilities Education Act (IDEA) and its regulations.

For most students, parents are the primary adults in their lives. Increasingly, however, other relatives have responsibility for parenting. U.S. Census Bureau figures reported by the Children's Defense Fund (2014) indicate that in 2012, 5.5 million children under the age of 18 lived in homes headed by grandparents. More than 958,000 of these children had no parent living within the home. As kinship care increases, the importance of extending parent involvement to include other family members is becoming clear. Although IDEA clearly states who may legally serve in the decision-making role, schools can encourage parents and parent surrogates to include others in the family or community who can contribute to a better understanding of the student in the assessment process.

Greater cultural diversity in the United States also suggests a need to be more inclusive when defining families and seeking their participation. Strategies for socializing children, expectations for behavior and performance, and child-rearing practices differ across cultures and ethnic groups (Hanson & Lynch, 2004; Lynch & Hanson, 2004a;

Kritikos, LeDosquet, & Melton, 2012). In addition, services offered to families do not always meet parents' belief of need regarding services for their family member (Wade, Mildon, & Matthews, 2006).

It is not unusual for differences in expectations to exist between the culture of the home and the culture of the school. For example, some families may emphasize the importance of being a contributing member of a group (cooperation) as opposed to individual achievement (competition) (Chan & Lee, 2004; Jacob, 2004; Joe & Malach, 2004; Santos & Chan, 2004; Willis, 2004; Zuñiga, 2004). Students may work more effectively with instruction and assessment, which emphasizes collaborative activities (Creighton & Szymkowiak, 2014). Children whose families emphasize cooperation over competition may not raise their hands to respond to teachers' questions. They may share answers with classmates; and they may not respond even when they know the answer. These behaviors may cause teachers to erroneously conclude that such students are unprepared, cheating, or don't understand—all because students have been taught at home to respond in ways that are not rewarded in schools. Understanding how each family's culture shapes its children can be very important to accurate and appropriate assessment. Therefore, this chapter focuses on parent *and* family involvement in assessment and planning for students with learning difficulties. Legal regulations determine who is invited to participate in assessments, attend individualized education program (IEP) meetings, make and formalize decisions related to a student's assessment, program, and placement; but teachers and administrators can create a climate in which both parents and other members of the family and community important to them and to their son or daughter feel comfortable.

This chapter also emphasizes a model of parent/family–professional collaboration and partnership that is based on respect, differentiated roles, and mutual problem solving. In this model, the ultimate goal is parent and family empowerment—empowerment that will result in optimal educational support and advocacy for students with learning difficulties (Dunst, Trivette, & Deal, 1988; Epstein, 1990; Kroth & Edge, 1997; Hooper & Umansky, 2009).

PARENT–PROFESSIONAL PARTNERSHIPS IN ASSESSMENT

Benefits of Parent–Professional Partnerships

The value of **partnerships** between parents and professionals is well established (Summers, Hoffman, Marquis, Turnbull, & Poston, 2005; Mueller, Singer, & Draper, 2008). When parents and professionals work in partnership, beginning with identification and referral and extending to assessment, eligibility determination, intervention, and progress monitoring, students receive better services.

In assessing students with disabilities, working in partnership with parents or other family members can be invaluable (Garfinkel, 2010), and it is the express intent of the 2004 amendments to IDEA that the role of parents be strengthened. Parents know more about their own sons and daughters than anyone else, and they are typically the constant in their child's life (Cutler, 1995). When professionals trust parent input, mutual trust is more likely to develop in collaborative educational assessment relationships (LeDosquet, 2010). Parents and primary caregivers of young children can provide professionals with information about the child's development, current and emerging skills, activity level, language and communication, and strategies that they use for redirection. In the elementary and middle school years, they can provide teachers with information about their son's or daughter's performance in applied academic skills such as reading signs, books, newspapers, or magazines; managing their allowance or using money to make purchases; understanding the rules of games; and gaining general knowledge of the world around them. They can also provide information about their child's social interactions, motivation, memory, and activity level. Parents often provide valuable insights into their son's or daughter's self-concept—information that can be used to help teachers understand the motivation of students with learning difficulties to use instructional strategies or participate in school activities and events. As students enter high school and transition into young adulthood, parents contribute additional information about functional skills, applied academic skills, work experience and work habits, motivation, interpersonal relationships, and post-school goals and aspirations.

In addition to providing information, parents and family members can become part of the data-gathering process. Parents can "take data" in a variety of situations to help teachers determine whether students are generalizing school skills into other settings. They can also gauge the validity of test scores by watching their son's or daughter's performance or seeing the profile of results. They may, for example, be able to tell the teacher that their child knows the answer to items that she or he failed in a test situation, or they may be surprised at seeing a higher level of performance than they see at home.

Finally, families have the *right* to be involved in the assessment process. They also have the responsibility of serving as their child's advocates. Parents and families may take a variety of roles while advocating for their child with disabilities. Trainor (2010) gives examples, which involve expert, strategy, change, and intuitive roles. McCloskey (2010) describes parental positioning in the context of navigating special education services. Rights that mandate parental inclusion in assessment have existed since the inception of IDEA in 1975 (at that time PL. 94-142). Schools and agencies providing special education programs and services must: (1) notify parents of a referral for assessment, (2) obtain parental permission for assessment, (3) provide information to parents concerning assessment results, (4) request and actively seek parental participation in IEP development, (5) obtain parental permission for a child to be placed in special education programs or receive special education services, (6) review the IEP at least annually with opportunity for parental input, and (7) give parents the right to an appeal process regarding the decisions made. In addition, the right to a nonbiased assessment—one that does not discriminate on the basis of language, race, culture, gender, socioeconomic status, religion, or other child and family characteristics—is also guaranteed in special education legislation.

Parental rights related to assessment were strengthened in the 1997 Amendments to IDEA, and they include: (1) *informed* parental consent prior to assessment or *reevaluation;* (2) right to seek an independent educational evaluation; and (3) inclusion of parent input in determining eligibility for special education. Parental rights continue to be an important part of this law and its implementation. Parents' legal rights are clearly stipulated; and these rights represent recommended practice.

Parent and Professional Roles in Assessment

In any partnership or collaboration, it is important to understand each participant's role and expectations. Understanding the different ways in which parents and teachers contribute to the assessment process and the expectations that each may have is a first step in the collaboration. Correa (1991) describes the roles that parents and professionals play in special education. For parents, these roles include giving developmental and contextual information, applying strategies in the home context, and serving as their child's advocate. Professionals also have roles that have expanded in recent years. It is important that preservice teachers' receive information to support their work with families of students with disabilities (Mulholland & Blecker, 2008). According to Correa, this information includes supplying student progress data, sharing assessment results, providing school event information, showing cultural sensitivity, and being a good collaborator. In assessment, parent and professional roles are parallel, with each partner's role supporting and enriching the other. Both parents and professionals can (1) participate in identification and referral for assessment; (2) gather assessment information about the student; (3) ensure that cultural, linguistic, and sociocultural diversity are taken into account in assessment, interpretation of findings, and program development; (4) discuss and interpret findings and results; (5) develop and implement interventions; and (6) monitor student progress. Table 3–1 illustrates ways in which parent and professional roles overlap and are complementary and the contributions that each can make to the assessment process.

Parental involvement cannot be judged normatively, however. The extent of parents' involvement varies depending on their comfort with schools and professionals; life situation; cultural, linguistic, and economic background; beliefs about and expectations of professionals; and the extent to which professionals create a collaborative climate that facilitates partnership. Although most parents are involved daily in their children's lives and informal education, they may not be comfortable assuming all of the roles that are suggested in Table 3–1.

TABLE 3–1
Roles of Parents and Professionals in the Assessment Process

1. Identify learning and behavior issues and problems and design preferral strategies to prevent referral for special education assessment.	**Parents:** Bring concerns to professionals; describe concerns; keep records that support concerns; suggest or work with professionals to develop strategies to manage the behavior or address learning difficulties. **Professionals:** Bring concerns to parents; describe concerns in clear language; share documentation supporting concerns; seek parents' observations about the issue; suggest and work with them to develop strategies to manage the behavior or address learning difficulties.
2. Participate in identification and referral for assessment.	**Parents:** Bring concerns to professionals; describe concerns; keep records that support concerns and areas of strength; make formal referral; agree to assessment; talk with son or daughter about the assessment process. **Professionals:** Bring concerns to parents; describe concerns; keep records that support concerns and areas of strength; talk with family about referral; explain referral, identification, and assessment process and procedures to parents in clear, jargon-free language; assist parents with procedures required for informed consent; talk with student about concerns, the assessment process, and procedures; solicit student's suggestions regarding the issues of concern.
3. Gather assessment information about the student.	**Parents:** Provide relevant developmental, health, and behavioral history; identify current concerns; describe son's or daughter's performance at home and in other nonschool environments; discuss relevant family information such as cultural identity, home language, expectations for son or daughter; provide data from daily perspective about the concerns being assessed. **Professionals:** Discuss assessment procedures, processes, and concerns with parents; solicit parents' ideas and information on the concerns being assessed; select culturally, linguistically, and concern-appropriate assessment strategies, instruments, and criteria; conduct assessment.
4. Ensure that cultural, linguistic, and sociocultural diversity are taken into account in assessment, interpretation of findings, and program development.	**Parents:** Share cultural, linguistic, and sociocultural information that may influence assessment outcomes and interpretation of assessment results. **Professionals:** Talk with parents and family members about the importance of cultural, linguistic, and sociocultural issues in understanding their son's or daughter's needs; select assessment instruments and strategies that are nonbiased; provide support and information consistent with cultural and personal preferences throughout the assessment process; ensure that interpreters are available to families who are more comfortable communicating in a language in which professionals are not fluent; maintain confidentiality.
5. Discuss and interpret findings and results.	**Parents:** Talk with professionals about the findings; provide interpretations based on daily life with your son or daughter; ask questions; seek clarifications. **Professionals:** Explain assessment findings clearly without jargon; seek parental and family input on interpretations; determine validity of findings from parents' point of view.
6. Develop and implement interventions.	**Parents:** Reinforce learning informally at home; participate with professionals when possible on carryover of specific interventions such as behavior management; talk with son or daughter openly and positively about interventions; stay informed about son's or daughter's program and services; advocate for quality in all aspects of the program. **Professionals:** Design instructional and behavioral plans; solicit parents' input on plans and strategies; implement plans.
7. Monitor student progress.	**Parents:** Observe son or daughter at home and in other nonschool settings; describe changes (or lack of change) to professionals; talk with son or daughter about his or her progress. **Professionals:** Collect data on effectiveness of the interventions; share data with parents; seek parental suggestions for modifying interventions.

ENHANCEDetext
Video Example 3.1
Watch this video to see an example of parental involvement.

DEVELOPING PARENT–PROFESSIONAL PARTNERSHIPS IN THE ASSESSMENT PROCESS

Parent–Professional Partnerships: Dimensions and Strategies

The range and variations among family constellations, circumstances, resources, and preferences are staggering. Just as student differences require individualization, so, too, do strategies for encouraging parents and family members to become partners in the assessment process. While there is no recipe for successful partnerships, a number of studies focus on the dimensions of successful partnerships and the behaviors that parents and professionals view as supporting these dimensions (e.g., Blue-Banning, Summers, Frankland, Nelson, & Beegle, 2004). In their focus groups and individual interviews with parents and professionals, Blue-Banning et al. identified six themes or dimensions of collaborative partnerships: communication, commitment, equality, skills, trust, and respect. These themes are not surprising when one considers what most people want in any relationship.

However, to be effective, these overarching dimensions must be built on specific behaviors— ways of being and interacting that parents and professionals in the study viewed as collaborative. Each of the dimensions viewed as foundational to successful partnerships in Blue-Banning et al.'s study is described next, as are strategies for encouraging those behaviors.

Communication

Communications that were clear, frequent, open, honest, tactful, and positive were viewed as supporting collaboration. Listening was also a behavior that supported successful partnership. The following strategies may be used to support improved communication:

- Demystify "special educationese" in all communications.
- Call, e-mail, send a note, or write something in the student's communication book to parents when their son or daughter does something well or has a good day.
- Increase the frequency of communication with parents, particularly positive communication.
- Communicate negatives factually; avoid assigning blame; and enlist parents in problem solving.
- Invite communication through class newsletters, websites, and an open-door policy.

Commitment

Caring, flexibility, consistency, and accessibility were seen as characteristics of commitment. Showing sensitivity to emotions, providing encouragement, and seeing children and families as individuals rather than as cases further supported a sense of commitment. School personnel may want to consider the following strategies:

- Clearly mark entrances and signage so that families know how to approach the school building and don't feel lost when they enter the campus.
- Immediately acknowledge parents' presence in the office, classroom, or meeting room and indicate that someone will be with them soon.
- Use signage, personnel who speak, and materials written in the languages that predominate

among the families whose children attend the school.

- Provide privacy and ensure confidentiality in all interactions that involve personal information.
- Maintain an open-door policy and welcome parents when they come to school.
- Conduct events and use approaches that incorporate community needs or ways of doing things: for example, a room where family members can drop in and have tea, a web page about the school that includes information on referral and assessment or after-school programs.
- Convene a diverse group of parents and school personnel to "audit" the school grounds, policies, and practices to determine how family friendly they are.

Equality

Advocacy for children's and families' needs, reciprocity, empowering parents, and validation were viewed as supporting collaboration, as were fostering harmony and avoiding power plays. The following strategies may contribute to equality among team members:

- Become active in advocacy efforts for children and families, and share information (print materials, websites, DVDs, etc.) with parents.
- Listen to parents and maintain communication that is conversational rather than a professional monologue.
- Provide information about assessment (and all topics) in approachable formats such as frequently asked questions (FAQs), web-based fact sheets, and videotaped demonstrations.
- With parental permission, enlist veteran parents to share their experiences and serve as mentors or guides during the assessment process.
- Provide families with specific ways to give input such as sharing their child's strengths and needs with you over a cup of coffee, making a list of their child's strengths, completing behavioral checklists, or charting the number of words that the child requests help with when reading a story.
- Use the input that families provide, and make it clear that it is useful and valued.

- Coach parents prior to assessments on what will take place, what tests and strategies are being used, why they have been selected, and what can be learned from each.
- In settings with other team members, avoid "inside" jokes, personal comments to colleagues, and any other behavior that makes parents feel like outsiders.
- Sit beside parents during meetings and check to make sure that their questions and concerns are being heard.

Skills

Nothing substitutes for professional expertise: knowing what action to take, taking the action, monitoring progress, and being willing to learn. The following can help teachers and other school personnel increase their skills:

- Become fully qualified for the job through the state's credentialing or certification standards.
- Seek continuing education that is relevant to the specific job as well as broader issues in special education and service delivery.
- Read professional journals and apply knowledge that supports recommended practice.
- Be a contributor as a guest lecturer at a local college or university, action researcher, professional development organizer, or presenter.
- Participate in reflective practice and ongoing evaluation of programs and practices within the school and district.

Trust

Reliability, dependability, truthfulness, discretion, and keeping children safe were behaviors that enabled parents and professionals to trust one another. Although each of the characteristics is self-explanatory, several strategies for encouraging trust follow:

- Do what you promise or agree to do.
- Become known as "someone you can always count on."
- Follow through in a timely manner.
- Put students' safety at the top of the list.
- Speak honestly and factually.

ENHANCEDetext
Video Example 3.2
Watch this video to see an example of parental involvement.
https://www.youtube.com/watch?v=vbyhao0FtaQ

- Don't gossip about children or families.
- When you make a mistake or misjudgment, admit it.

Respect

Being courteous and nonjudgmental were viewed as elements of respect in relationships between parents and professionals. A nonbiased, nondiscriminatory approach, as well as nonintrusive interactions, were also seen as supportive of successful partnerships. Several strategies for expressing respect follow:

- Learn and observe behaviors that respect cultural preferences when interacting with families whose culture, ethnicity, race, and/or language may be different from your own.
- Use formal forms of address (Mr., Ms., Mrs., Dr.) until you are given permission to be less formal.
- If cultural practices are unfamiliar and surprising, learn more about their importance to the family. Do not express shock or disgust.
- Incorporate family values and preferences into every aspect of their child's education.

These general strategies provide the threshold that allows parents and other family members to enter into collaborative partnerships. Each can be tailored to the particular family, situation, and professional involved, and each can contribute to more effective partnerships between parents and professionals. Professionals need to engage families (Ferrel, 2012) in collaborative decision making beyond the extent mandated by IDEA (Olivos, Gallagher, & Aguilar, 2010). In addition, increasing family involvement in daily classroom activities could further increase student support in school and home contexts (Staples & Diliberto, 2010). Using these strategies could help decrease tensions, which sometimes exist between families and educational professionals.

ASSESSMENT OF CHILDREN FROM DIVERSE CULTURAL AND LINGUISTIC BACKGROUNDS AND PARTNERING WITH THEIR FAMILIES

Nonbiased Assessment

Nonbiased assessment is one of the cornerstones of IDEA and best practices. Therefore, assessment strategies, instruments, practices, and procedures must be examined for their appropriateness and validity across cultures, languages, and life experiences. For example, a low score on a test of English reading comprehension for a monolingual, Spanish-speaking, 10-year-old whose family recently moved to the United States from another country cannot be considered valid. Although the previous example seems obvious in the extreme, bias is often more subtle. The results of an assessment conducted in English with a high school student who seems to have fluent English may also be biased and inaccurate. Although the student may comfortably engage in everyday conversation in English, he or she may not have the language proficiency to respond to academic material. The difference in language mastery that supports basic interpersonal communication skills (BICS) versus the mastery that is described as cognitive academic language proficiency (CALP) dramatically influences assessment outcomes (Cummins, 1981). Similarly, a child who has been

ENHANCEDetext
Video Example 3.3
Watch this video to see a teacher discuss community building in the classroom.

taught to be cooperative, not competitive, may not raise her hand to respond even when she knows the correct answer, or she may try not to excel and call attention to herself in class.

Encouraging Family Participation

Parents who do not speak the language of the school, who are unfamiliar with schooling in the United States or schooling in general, or who come from groups that have not been welcomed in America's schools may be reluctant to be active participants in assessment (Brandon & Brown, 2009). Rather than interpreting their reluctance as lack of involvement, professionals have an obligation to reach out to find ways to make participation a possibility (Lynch & Hanson, 2004a; Lynch & Stein, 1987). An initial step in reaching out is the examination of one's own attitudes, beliefs, and behaviors—developing an awareness of one's own habits, customs, and stereotypes that are culturally based (Harry, 1992b). The majority of education professionals place a high value on education, and their background, socioeconomic status, and years of university study suggest that their life experiences may have been different from those of their students and students' families. In today's schools, poverty, racial discrimination, and recent immigration are typically more common for students and their families than for teachers and other professionals. Thus, professionals may need to develop new strategies for interacting with and learning from parents who differ from themselves on many dimensions.

Although examples of diversity that relate to cultural and linguistic differences between parents and professionals are most often selected, other differences may bias assessment results and/or make it difficult for parents to participate. For example, the results of a test of general information may be accurate, but they may be completely unrelated to the *ability* of a middle school student whose family does not have a stable place to live. Tests in basic skill areas may be equally accurate but nonpredictive for such a student. Without experience in reading or using money, test performance will not be optimal. Likewise, parents facing crises in the most basic areas of survival such as adequate housing, food, health care, and ability to earn a living cannot be expected to participate actively in assessment without considerable support.

Culture, language, and life circumstances influence family–professional partnerships in the assessment process. In discussing these issues in relation to the assessment of young children, Lynch and Hanson (2004b) describe several issues that are equally applicable to collaborating with families of students with learning difficulties from a wide range of diverse backgrounds.

Partnering with families who view professionals as "experts" presents challenges when establishing a collaborative relationship. When parents consider disagreement, questioning, and speaking out to be rude or disrespectful or feel that their own life experience gives them little to say to a professional, it can be difficult to engage them as active participants. To mediate this barrier, professionals may want to use a bilingual/bicultural/sociocultural mediator who can talk with parents about family concerns and, with parental permission, share this information with professionals on the assessment team. Written checklists or questionnaires in the family's preferred language may provide another alternative to overcoming the barrier of professional as expert. However, written materials may create other difficulties such as inappropriate reading levels, nonexistent or inadequate translations, or formats that are unfamiliar to some families. Sometimes a conversation, free of jargon, that encourages parents to talk about their child's strengths and needs as well as their own concerns can be the most effective way to approach families who view professionals as experts.

Concept of self can be defined by individualism or by reliance on self. It can also be defined by collectivism or by membership in a group. The concept of time differs for many families. One family may value efficiency over time, which is typical in the United States. However, other families may focus on the value of a task at hand and less on time deadlines. Locus of control is another area where family beliefs may differ. Some may use an external locus of control where fate or luck controls behavior, whereas others may use an internal locus of control. In this latter example, personal efforts affect outcomes (Kritikos, LeDosquet, & Melton, 2012). Please see Figure 3–1.

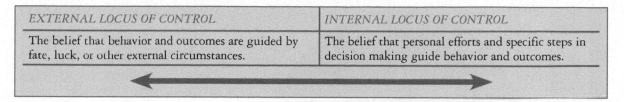

EXTERNAL LOCUS OF CONTROL	INTERNAL LOCUS OF CONTROL
The belief that behavior and outcomes are guided by fate, luck, or other external circumstances.	The belief that personal efforts and specific steps in decision making guide behavior and outcomes.

FIGURE 3–1
External versus Internal Locus of Control.

Assessment Instruments and Strategies

A primary consideration in selecting instruments and strategies is the availability of the instrument in the student's primary language. This issue is critical not only to achieving a nonbiased assessment, but also to gathering accurate information. Assuming that parents share their child's primary language, it also enables them to understand what is being asked if they are observing the assessment or talking with professionals about the results. If an appropriate instrument is available in the child's primary language, finding an assessor who is fluent in the language or an interpreter who can assist is the next step. Use of a nonfluent assessor or someone who is fluent but not trained in assessment or the instrument being used leads to inaccurate findings and loss of parental confidence in the assessment process.

Another important issue related to selecting appropriate instruments and strategies is their face validity or the assessor's ability to explain why various items are included. For example, the ability to remember a sequence of numbers forward and backward measures concentration and short-term memory, skills that are extremely important to learning letter–sound relationships, solving mathematical problems, and completing a task in sequential order. However, to a family member without training in assessment or much knowledge of the underlying skills needed for school success, remembering a series of numbers may seem meaningless. Explaining what is being measured and why it is important provides a bridge that enables parents to participate.

Sharing Information

Sharing information clearly and caringly about assessment processes, procedures, and results is part of the larger issue of communication discussed later in this chapter. However, its importance cannot be overemphasized. For most of us, any sort of assessment—a physical exam, a test in a university class, or a weigh-in after a month of dieting—produces anxiety. For families of children with learning difficulties, the anxiety may be increased. Therefore, giving information clearly and sensitively is critical. The meaning of disability varies from person to person and family to family (Hanson & Lynch, 1992; Kroth & Edge, 1997). Learning for the first time that one's son or daughter has a disability may have different meanings across cultures as well (Harry, 1992a). For example, if the culture prizes boys over girls, learning that a son has a learning difficulty may be more difficult for the family to accept. Or if academic achievement is a lower priority for a family than getting along well with others, learning that a child has learning problems may be somewhat easier to accept than learning that the child has a behavior disorder. Regardless of what professionals expect the family's reaction to be, communicating caringly is essential.

Clarity of communication is also critical. In an ethnographic study that involved low-income Puerto Rican families in the United States, Harry (1992a) described the difficulties that arise when differences in family and professional language interfere with shared meaning. Some Puerto Rican families interpreted cognitive disability to mean "crazy" (loco), and this interpretation of their child's problem had no validity for them. Others could not understand how an assessment could determine that their son or daughter had cognitive disability when the child was learning to speak English—a skill that they did not possess. Being clear about the meaning of words that are used in assessment and helping families

FIGURE 3–2
Family Systems Model

incorporate the meaning into their own context are two of the most important ways in which professionals can support families to become partners. Please see Figure 3–2 above.

COMMUNICATING EFFECTIVELY WITH PARENTS AND FAMILIES

In addition to the characteristics described in an earlier section that support the development of successful parent–professional partnerships, other qualities, characteristics, and communication strategies have been linked to effective interactions with parents and other family members. Communicating effectively with families has become a central part of service delivery for

professionals who work with young children (see Chapter 16). Its importance should also be stressed at other age levels. This section reviews communication strategies that can enhance interactions as teachers and other school personnel talk with, interview, and conference with parents of students with learning difficulties.

Qualities of Effective Communicators

The professional literature contains many discussions of the qualities of effective communicators and specific communication skills that can be used to build and improve interactions and relationships. Beckman, Frank, and Newcomb (1996) discuss three qualities that professionals can bring to their interactions with parents that can lay the groundwork for effective communication: respect, nonjudgmental attitude, and empathy. This is not surprising: consider how good friends and confidants are likely to possess these three qualities.

Respect for families of students with disabilities is critical—respect for their knowledge, opinions, points of view, concerns, advocacy, and sometimes their withdrawal from professional contacts and requests. Differences between parental and professional views of the student's behavior, performance, and potential often occur. This, too, is not surprising. The differences inherent in school and home environments and value systems often produce differences in perspectives (Kroth & Edge, 1997). However, respect, even in disagreement, is as foundational to effective communication as it is to developing successful partnerships.

Maintaining a *nonjudgmental attitude* is another quality of an effective communicator (Beckman et al., 1996). When parents trust professionals to listen without criticizing, they are more likely to share information, ask questions, or seek help with problems they are experiencing. Parenting is a complex job filled with moment-to-moment decision making, and some parenting decisions are better than others. Parents can't always help with their son or daughter's homework or implement the carefully designed behavioral support plan that has been developed at school. Freedom to discuss what they can and cannot do without being made to feel inadequate or incompetent is important to most people. Recognizing that parents are responsible for the entire family, *not* just their son or daughter with a disability, can help professionals recognize that the family's values and priorities may be different from the professional's.

Empathy, the characteristic that Beckman et al. (1996) consider foundational to communicating effectively with parents, is the ability to identify with another's feelings and to see the world from his or her perspective. This does not mean that the professional's response is "I know just how you feel" when a family shares its concerns. No one can know how another individual feels, but it is possible to acknowledge parents' feelings and provide emotional and cognitive support when they express their joys, fears, and frustrations.

Specific Communication Skills

In addition to the qualities that effective communicators possess, there are specific skills that aid in interpersonal communication. Communication does not always involve talking. Skills are both verbal and nonverbal, and often the nonverbal skills are the most valuable and most difficult to learn. *Listening* is one of the most important components of communicating. According to Kroth and Edge (1997), individuals with strength in this area work at understanding messages and ask questions to confirm understanding. When a professional is building and maintaining partnerships with parents and other family members, listening is an essential skill. Listening is not a passive role in which the words of another sweep over the listener with little impact. Instead, listening is active and requires the listener's full attention and engagement in the speaker's content and feeling. Listening is one way to show respect, to learn, and to help parents engage in problem solving as they present information. Good listeners are comfortable with and allow silences to occur. They use their face and posture to demonstrate their attentiveness, and they focus on what is being said rather than on what they are going to say next. Finally, good listeners respond to content and feeling by acknowledging that they have understood both.

Verbal communication skills are also important in parent–professional interactions. Turnbull and Turnbull (2001) discuss several types of verbal response, including furthering responses, paraphrasing, responding to affect, questioning, and summarizing. *Furthering responses* is a technique used to encourage others to continue to speak or elaborate. Saying "uh-huh" and reiterating what has been said in the language of the family are "furthering" strategies (Turnbull & Turnbull). *Paraphrasing* is a restatement of what has been said using one's own words. It can be used to clarify, to ensure that the message has been clearly understood, and to demonstrate interest and attention to parents' comments.

Responding to affect requires that professionals understand parents' feelings when they provide information. Whether the feeling is one of joy, triumph, sadness, or anger, the professional responds by verbalizing the feelings accurately and with the same degree of intensity as the feeling was expressed (Turnbull & Turnbull, 2001). For example, a parent's comment such as the following, "It's *really* difficult for Nathan now that his little sister is reading better than he is" might elicit the following response: "You're feeling sad and concerned about Nathan as he falls behind his sister in reading." Or the following joyful comment from a parent, "Polly couldn't quit smiling! It was the first time she had ever been invited to a classmate's birthday party" might produce this response, "It sounds as if you are overjoyed about her happiness and thrilled about her acceptance."

Questioning and summarizing are also cited as valuable communication techniques (Turnbull & Turnbull, 2001). Types of questioning have been discussed. For example, open-ended questions elicit more information than close-ended questions and enable parents to respond in ways that are comfortable for them. Close-ended questions typically produce limited responses, do not encourage elaboration, and may sound more like interrogation than collaboration. For example, stating "Tell me the kinds of things Jason does when he works with you at your store" is likely to provide much richer information than asking "Does Jason use the cash register at your store?"

Summarizing provides a way to ensure that parents' primary points have been heard accurately. Summarizing may aid in problem solving, bring closure to one part of the interview, or conclude the meeting. All of these techniques support positive parent–professional communication and encourage family–professional collaboration and partnerships.

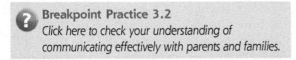

? Breakpoint Practice 3.2
Click here to check your understanding of communicating effectively with parents and families.

INTERVIEWING AND CONFERENCING WITH PARENTS AND FAMILIES

Every interaction with parents—whether written or spoken; on the phone, through e-mail or in person; or one to one or through an interpreter—is an opportunity to support family–professional collaboration. However, interviewing families

and conferencing with them provide extended opportunities to develop or maintain a positive partnership. Interviews are typically conducted to gather information. **Conferences** are usually held to share information, discuss the assessment and develop the IEP, or talk about progress. Using the communication skills described in the preceding section, in the following paragraphs we discuss principles that support effective collaboration in interviews and conferences. Because these principles are similar for both interviewing and conferencing, they are discussed together.

Although family interviews are used extensively in gathering information about very young children to develop individual family service plans for students with severe disabilities, they are used less frequently in relation to mild disabilities. Keogh (1999) advocates including information about family structure, climate, and *especially* daily routines as a way of extending assessment to capture information that may improve professionals' ability to design optimal interventions. The following section suggests strategies for conducting family interviews or conferencing with families. Family interviews are also discussed in Chapter 16.)

ENHANCEDetext
Video Example 3.4
Watch this video to see a parent discuss the driving force in the inclusion movement: parental involvement.

Preparing for the Interview or Conference

Inviting families to participate in an interview or a conference is the first step. Contact can be made by note, telephone, or e-mail—whatever approach is preferred by the family or is likely to be the most effective. The way the request for an interview is presented is important, especially if families have not been invited to participate in the assessment process in recent years. Professionals should communicate the idea that parental input is an important and valued part of assessment. An informal conversation with parents about their son or daughter's strengths and needs—as well as the parents' goals, expectations, and preferences—would be helpful. If the team wants to address specific issues or types of information, it may be helpful to let parents know in the initial contact so that they can formulate their thoughts prior to the meeting.

Communicating the purpose of a conference is equally important. Some families may perceive an invitation to a conference or IEP meeting as intimidating. If they are unfamiliar with professionals, schooling, or special education processes and procedures, they may view the conference with anxiety. Parents whose previous contacts with teachers and schools have been negative may assume that this meeting, too, will be filled with bad news. Being clear about the goals of the conference—whether it is to discuss assessment results, to work together to develop the best educational program, or to consider the types of support services—can relieve anxiety. Parents who have already participated in an interview, contributed information to the assessment, and become acquainted with school professionals, procedures, and processes are likely to feel more positive and confident about meeting with the team to develop the IEP.

Determining whether *any special accommodations,* such as an interpreter for the deaf or an interpreter/translator in another language, are needed for parents' participation is another part of planning. Finding a mutually convenient time and place for the interview or conference is the next step. Conferences are usually conducted at school to make it easier to share work samples or involve other team members. However, interviews can also be conducted in the home or someplace in the neighborhood that is comfortable and provides adequate privacy for parents to share information confidentially.

Interviews conducted in the home often provide school personnel with a much deeper understanding of a child's experiences and opportunities. Seeing the student's surroundings, meeting other family members, and having the student see the teacher at his or her home can support the home–school alliance. Interviews in the home are more time consuming, but the time is usually well spent. When considering an interview in the home, several factors are important: (1) the family's comfort and willingness, (2) appropriateness based on the student's age, and (3) the safety of visiting professionals. Families vary in their willingness to invite "outsiders" into their home. Many will be pleased or even honored to have their son or daughter's teacher visit; others will find it intrusive. Only families can make that decision, so providing choices for the interview location is important. Although it is not uncommon for teachers of young children to conduct home visits, it becomes less common as students get older. For a teacher of a middle or high school student to come to the student's home may cause the student to be embarrassed or teased by peers. Whenever a visit to a student's home is likely to cause discomfort for the family or student, it is not appropriate. Finally, there is the factor of the professional's safety. Some neighborhoods are not safe for the families who live there; they may be particularly unwelcoming to strangers.

If *arranging for an interpreter* is necessary, ensure that someone who is trained in interpreting and is fluent in the family's language and dialect is available. Working through interpreters requires preparation. The nature and content of the interview or conference should be shared with interpreters prior to the meeting. A glossary of specific terms or words that will be used should be provided so that the interpreter can determine the best way to present the underlying concept when direct translation would be inaccurate or inappropriate. Giving the interpreter and family an opportunity to talk prior to the interview can also be an important strategy. It provides family members with a contact in their own language and allows them to ask questions about the process. It enables each to become comfortable with the other's way of speaking, pacing, and vocabulary so that the time available for the interview can be optimized. For more information on working through interpreters, see Langdon, Siegel, Halog, and Sánchez-Boyce (1994) and Lynch (2004).

Formulating questions or strategies for presenting information is an important part of the planning process. In an interview, open-ended approaches are often preferable (e.g., Keogh, 1999; Kroth & Edge, 1997; Wayman, Lynch, & Hanson, 1990). However, an outline of what is to be covered is an important aid as professionals become comfortable with interviewing families. In some instances, having families tell their story may be an appropriate way to initiate the interview (Keogh); in others, general questions about the family's observations of the child's behavior, interests, or skills may provide the best approach. In both of these examples, the interviewer can follow up on parents' responses and focus on areas of particular concern or importance. Sometimes the interviewer may want specific information that can be elicited by questions such as the following: "When you take Anthony to a restaurant, how does he behave?" "You mentioned that Teresa enjoys going to the mall with her friends. Does she make purchases independently or does she need help?" "What does Jamal do from the time he gets home from school to the time he goes to bed?" General suggestions for planning and conducting interviews follow; for more specific guidelines, refer to Kroth and Edge (1997).

Planning for a conference is also important. Conferences are often structured only to allow professionals to present information. Often, conference structure and the time allocated do not include opportunities to seek information from parents or to engage in discussion or joint problem solving. Recommended practice suggests that conferences should be structured thoughtfully to provide information in clear, jargon-free, family-friendly language *and* to engage parents in discussion and dialogue about the information presented.

Conducting Interviews and Conferences

The *opening* of an interview or conference provides an opportunity to establish rapport and reduce each participant's anxiety. It is also the time to introduce those present and to clarify the purpose and goals of the meeting. The amount of time allotted for this portion can only be judged by the family's preferences and the amount of time available. Some families expect and need an extended warm-up time; others want to minimize the "small talk" and "get down to business." Family preferences may be a matter of comfort, the amount of time available, or cultural style and expectations. As professionals become more experienced in working with families, judging when to go slowly or when to move on becomes easier.

Conferences, especially those that involve several team members, are often time limited. When this is the case, it is helpful for the teacher to talk or meet with parents prior to an official meeting so that parents can talk with others, process information, and formulate questions. When a meeting must be concluded at a specific time, it is important that all parties be made aware of the time limitation at the outset. That allows the most important issues to be addressed. Decision making should occur *only* after families have had an opportunity to review the information, ask questions, and seek clarification.

Because most interviewers need to take notes, the opening of an interview is also the time to explain why notes are necessary and to request the family's permission. This author has found it helpful to keep the notepad in full view and to go over the notes at the end of the interview so that families know what has been written. Another strategy to ensure that families do not feel threatened by note taking is to use carbonless copy paper and leave a set of the notes with the family at the end of the interview. Novice interviewers often express a desire to audiotape interviews. Although an audiotape can be helpful in reconstructing what was said, it requires additional time to replay and/or transcribe. Therefore, audiotaping is recommended only when an exact transcription is needed.

Notes in conferences may be more or less formal. In a parent–teacher conference, teachers may want to jot down notes. In that case, the strategies mentioned in the previous paragraph are equally applicable. In a more formal conference or IEP meeting with several participants, a designated recorder is typically responsible for completing district forms. These, too, should be discussed and shared with the family and not finalized until they have had the opportunity to review them.

The *interview or conference* with families should be nonthreatening in content and approach. In interviews, families can be encouraged to tell their story and describe their son's or daughter's strengths and needs, or asked to respond to specific questions related to providing an appropriate educational program. Questions about motivation, interest, and self-concept as well as learning, performance, goals, and aspirations may be included in this portion of the interview. The interviewer can follow up on parents' responses as needed or use parents' comments as prompts to pursue more specific information.

In conferences, parents may be asked their opinions, experiences, and observations related to the material being presented. They should also be asked what questions and concerns they would like to discuss. Setting an informal agenda at the beginning of the conference enables each participant to be heard.

All people respond to reinforcement, and many of us respond to social approval. Although the interviewer should show interest in parents' comments, it is important not to inadvertently provide reinforcement for certain types of content. For example, if the interviewer nods, smiles, and says "that's interesting" every time parents mention something related to their child's social skills, parents are likely to try to provide more information in that area and omit other areas of importance. If parents stray from the topic or avoid certain areas, it is appropriate to gently redirect them to the issue. The same strategies can be used to ensure that conferences are focused.

Interviews should not be one way with only professionals posing questions. Families should also have opportunities to ask questions, request information, and seek the interviewer's opinion. One of the goals of family–professional collaboration is the give and take between parents and professionals. An interview that models this is consistent with the collaborative model being promoted. The same is true for conferences.

If the interview or conference is being conducted through an interpreter, several additional issues need to be considered. A relaxed style that allows for comfortable pacing is an important element. Pausing to allow time for translation and recognizing that not as much can be covered in translated interactions are also important. Instead of speaking to the translator, the professional should speak to the parents and respond to them as their words are being translated.

In *closing* the interview or conference, the professional may want to summarize what has been addressed and share notes that were taken. It is also the time to ask if parents or other family members have "anything else" they want to ask or share. In addition to expressing appreciation for their time and willingness to participate, professionals should give parents a clear statement of the next steps in the assessment or implementation process as well as the accompanying timelines. In an assessment, a schematic diagram that includes steps in the process and projected timelines for each step may be helpful.

Interpreting, Reporting, and Using Information from Interviews and Conferences

Interpreting information shared by families can be simple or complex. In educational situations, interpretation is typically straightforward, relying on the facts and perceptions voiced by parents. The goal of interpretation is to extrapolate the information that provides insight and knowledge about the student's behavior, skills, motivation, and so forth so that it can be used to optimize the educational program. A search for underlying meaning, family dynamics, or pathology is *not* a goal of this sort of interviewing. Rather, it is important to learn about things such as the parents' objection to a job training experience that would place their daughter in a business downtown or their son's sudden interest in writing now that he is communicating with friends by e-mail or text messaging.

Reporting interview information is typically done in a summary of the interview. Although background information that parents feel is important to understanding their son or daughter is included, the focus is on information that is relevant to educational planning. For family–professional collaboration to become a reality, parents must feel safe that the information they share will be used appropriately and that confidentiality will be maintained.

Information that parents discuss in conferences is usually not reported formally. Instead, the teacher or other relevant professional incorporates it into the program planning and implementation.

Incorporating information in planning and placement is the ultimate goal of the interview process. Learning that Jillian is a baseball fan and that her math activities centered on batting averages, box scores, and lifetime scoring records are motivating to her can be used to design instruction that is both engaging and relevant. Realizing that Felix likes to read along with taped versions of adventure stories may provide an adaptation that will support his literacy skills. Knowing that Caleb is a computer whiz may provide avenues for improving his self-concept and increasing opportunities for him to engage in higher-order thinking skills.

There are many common strategies in interviewing and conferencing with parents and families. Although strategies and approaches will be tailored to fit each parent and professional, the underlying qualities of effective communicators—respect, nonjudgmental attitude, and empathy—are foundational to effective interviewing and conferencing as well as to developing and maintaining parent–professional partnerships.

In conclusion, working with parents and other family members in the assessment process brings critical information to educational planning and decision making, and the collaborative process strengthens the home–school alliance. Family perspectives help teachers set priorities, target educational objectives, and monitor the effectiveness of instructional strategies and behavioral interventions. Professional knowledge and expertise helps parents understand their son's or daughter's learning difficulties, find ways to support instruction in daily routines, and partner with professionals in evaluating outcomes.

Assessment in Action
A Family's Point of View

Latanya will soon be 4½ years old and has intellectual, language, and motor delays. She has been in an integrated preschool program near her home and is included in all of her family's activities. Her parents strongly believe that it is important for Latanya to be part of the community and to adapt regular activities and expectations to enable her to participate. Now that Latanya is approaching age 5, transition planning has begun; and school personnel are planning an assessment. Because of the partnership that they have developed with Latanya's parents, the first step was for Latanya's teacher, Ms. Beech, to meet with them to learn about their current concerns, preferences regarding Latanya's kindergarten placement, and what additional information they would like to have about the transition process.

Latanya's parents and Ms. Beech have just completed a very productive meeting. Ms. Beech shared her concerns and discussed the types of assessments that are typically part of transition planning. Latanya's parents expressed their desire to learn more about Latanya's communication abilities. They want to find a strategy that will help her communicate more effectively when she is in a new and unfamiliar setting. They also expressed their desire to have her attend the neighborhood school where she can be in a kindergarten class with support from other specialists. Finally, they want to know more about how to prepare Latanya and her new teacher for the transition. Based on their input, Latanya's teacher, Ms. Beech, will ask for assessments from the speech and language specialist as well as the assistive technology and augmentative communication specialist. She will also observe the classroom that Latanya's parents had mentioned and several others so that she will be better informed about the types of adaptations that might be needed within a variety of environments and what Latanya's parents can do to help a new teacher get acquainted with Latanya and respond to her special needs. In their meeting, Ms. Beech shared her concerns about Latanya's motor skills. She suggested that a more thorough work-up by a pediatric orthopedist prior to the transition assessment might provide important information to the physical therapist, and they will schedule that assessment. Because of the collaborative partnership that Ms. Beech and Latanya's parents had established, planning for the assessment went smoothly. This will enable school personnel and the family to gather the information needed to make placement decisions supporting Latanya's needs.

SUMMARY

- When parents and professionals work in partnership extending from identification and referral to assessment, eligibility determination, intervention, and progress monitoring, students receive better services. In addition, when professionals trust parent input, mutual trust is more likely to develop in collaborative educational assessment relationships (LeDosquet, 2010). The parents and primary caregivers of young children can provide professionals with information about the child's development, current and emerging skills, activity level, language and communication, and redirection strategies. Also, parents and family members can become part of the data-gathering process.

- Blue-Banning et al. identified six themes or dimensions of collaborative partnerships: communication, commitment, equality, skills, trust, and respect. One strategy to improve family and educational professionals' collaboration is to demystify "special educationese" in all communications. Another strategy involves calling, e-mailing, sending a note, or writing something in the student's communication book to parents when their son or daughter does something well or has a good day.

  Increasing the frequency of communication with parents, especially positive communication, is yet another strategy.

- Parents who do not speak the language of the school, who are unfamiliar with schooling in the United States or schooling in general, or who come from groups that have not been welcomed in America's schools may be reluctant to be active participants in assessment (Brandon & Brown, 2009). Rather than interpreting their reluctance as lack of involvement, professionals have an obligation to find ways to make participation a possibility (Lynch & Hanson, 2004a; Lynch & Stein, 1987). When parents consider disagreement, questioning, and speaking out to be rude or disrespectful or feel that their own life experience gives them little to say to a professional, it can be difficult to engage them as active participants.

  To mediate this barrier, professionals may want to use a bilingual/bicultural/sociocultural mediator who can talk with parents about family concerns and, with parental permission, share this information with professionals on the assessment team. Written checklists or questionnaires in the family's preferred language may provide another alternative to the barrier of professional as expert. However, written materials may create other difficulties such as inappropriate reading levels, nonexistent or inadequate translations, or formats that are unfamiliar to some families. Sometimes a conversation that is free of jargon and that encourages parents to talk about their son's or daughter's strengths and needs as well as their own concerns can be the most effective way to approach families who view professionals as experts.

- *Respect* for families of students with disabilities is critical—respect for their knowledge, opinions, points of view, concerns, advocacy, and sometimes their withdrawal from professional contacts and requests. Maintaining a *nonjudgmental attitude* is another quality of an effective communicator (Beckman et al., 1996). When parents trust professionals to listen without criticizing, they are more likely to share information, ask questions, or seek help with problems that they are experiencing. *Listening* is one of the most important components of communicating. According to Kroth and Edge (1997), individuals with strength in this area work at understanding messages and ask questions to confirm understanding. When a professional is building and maintaining partnerships with parents and other family members, listening is an essential skill.

- The way the request for an interview is presented is important, especially if families have not been invited to participate in the assessment process in recent years. Professionals should communicate the idea that parental input is an important and valued part of assessment. An informal conversation with parents about their son or daughter's strengths and needs—as well as the parents' goals, expectations, and preferences—would be helpful. *Communicating the purpose of a conference* is equally important. Some families may feel intimidated by an invitation to a conference or IEP meeting. If they are unfamiliar with professionals, schooling, or the special education processes and procedures, they may view the conference with anxiety. *Formulating questions or strategies for presenting information* is an important part of the planning process. In an interview, open-ended approaches are often preferable (e.g., Keogh, 1999; Kroth & Edge, 1997; Wayman, Lynch, & Hanson, 1990).

4

Syda Productions/Fotolia

Selection of Assessment Tools to Promote Fair Assessment

LEARNING OUTCOMES

After reading this chapter, you will be able to:

- Provide examples of core criteria for the selection of assessment tools.
- Discuss major concepts when evaluating different types of measurement.
- Distinguish between and evaluate reliability and validity when selecting tools for assessment.
- Discuss types of test scores and other assessment results.
- Describe issues, problems, and opportunities that educators might encounter while promoting nonbiased assessment.

KEY TERMS

nominal	ratio
ordinal	mode
interval	median

mean

range

standard deviation

correlation

norm-referenced test

criterion-referenced test

reliability

validity

standard error of measurement

raw score

age scores

grade scores

percentile rank

standard scores

normal curve equivalent (NCE)

stanines

Assessment is an information-gathering activity. Its purpose is to provide answers to important educational questions, whether these concern identification and placement, instructional planning (Foegan & Morrison, 2010), or monitoring of student progress and program effectiveness (Fuchs, Fuchs, & Zumeta, 2008). The assessment process begins with careful planning, and one of the most critical preparatory steps is selection of appropriate tools.

The tools selected for assessment influence the success of the data-gathering process. Inaccurate measures produce useless and potentially harmful information; tools that are inappropriate, even if their results are accurate, fail to provide the type of information necessary to assist educational decision making. Inappropriate tools may therefore lead to invalid results and interpretations.

The appropriateness of an assessment tool depends on the context in which the evaluator will use that instrument. Although poor quality measures that yield inaccurate results are never appropriate, most tools provide information useful for some purposes, some students, and some situations. In judging the worth of a measure or strategy, the professional first assures its technical adequacy and then determines its value for the particular assessment task.

In the early days of special education services, criticism of assessment practices centered on the inappropriate use of assessment tools, specifically the misuse of standardized intelligence tests with culturally and linguistically diverse students. Leaders such as Lloyd Dunn (1968) charged that special classes for students with intellectual disabilities contained disproportionate numbers of children from minority groups. Researchers such as Jane Mercer (1973) attributed this overrepresentation to reliance on a single test score, the IQ for placement decisions. The appropriateness of standard intelligence measures for diverse students was challenged in the courts. *Diana v. State Board of Education* (1970) questioned the use of English-language IQ tests with children whose home language was Spanish. *Larry P. v. Riles* (1972, 1979, 1984) sought to establish the discriminatory nature of dominant culture intelligence measures for African American students.

Although some controversies surrounding testing continue, assessment practices today are much improved. One major impetus for this change was the enactment of federal and state laws setting forth specific guidelines for special education assessment and placement. Another important factor has been the development of professional standards of practice by groups such as the Council for Exceptional Children (CEC), the major professional organization in the field of special education. Table 4–1 presents the CEC's professional standards related to assessment.

TABLE 4–1
Professional Standards in Assessment from the Council for Exceptional Children

INITIAL PREPARATION STANDARDS

Initial Preparation Standard 1: Learner Development and Individual Learning Differences
1.0	Beginning special education professionals understand how exceptionalities may interact with development and learning and use this knowledge to provide meaningful and challenging learning experiences for individuals with exceptionalities.

Key Elements
1.1	Beginning special education professionals understand how language, culture, and family background influence the learning of individuals with exceptionalities.
1.2	Beginning special education professionals use understanding of development and individual differences to respond to the needs of individuals with exceptionalities.

Initial Preparation Standard 2: Learning Environments
2.0	Beginning special education professionals create safe, inclusive, culturally responsive learning environments so that individuals with exceptionalities become active and effective learners and develop emotional well being, positive social interactions, and self-determination.

Key Elements
2.1	Beginning special education professionals, through collaboration with general educators and other colleagues, create safe, inclusive, culturally responsive learning environments to engage individuals with exceptionalities in meaningful learning activities and social interactions.
2.2	Beginning special education professionals use motivational and instructional interventions to teach individuals with exceptionalities how to adapt to different environments.
2.3	Beginning special education professionals know how to intervene safely and appropriately with individuals with exceptionalities in crisis.

Council for Exceptional Children. (2015). What Every Special Educator Must Know: Professional Ethics and Standards. Arlington, VA: CEC 1

Initial Preparation Standard 3: Curricular Content Knowledge
3.0	Beginning special education professionals use knowledge of general and specialized curricula to individualize learning for individuals with exceptionalities.

Key Elements
3.1	Beginning special education professionals understand the central concepts, structures of the discipline, and tools of inquiry of the content areas they teach, and can organize this knowledge, integrate cross-disciplinary skills, and develop meaningful learning progressions for individuals with exceptionalities.
3.2	Beginning special education professionals understand and use general and specialized content knowledge for teaching across curricular content areas to individualize learning for individuals with exceptionalities.
3.3	Beginning special education professionals modify general and specialized curricula to make them accessible to individuals with exceptionalities.

Initial Preparation Standard 4: Assessment
4.0	Beginning special education professionals use multiple methods of assessment and data sources in making educational decisions.

TABLE 4–1 *continued*

Key Elements	
4.1	Beginning special education professionals select and use technically sound formal and informal assessments that minimize bias.
4.2	Beginning special education professionals use knowledge of measurement principles and practices to interpret assessment results and guide educational decisions for individuals with exceptionalities.
4.3	Beginning special education professionals, in collaboration with colleagues and families, use multiple types of assessment information in making decisions about individuals with exceptionalities.
4.4	Beginning special education professionals engage individuals with exceptionalities to work toward quality learning and performance and provide feedback to guide them.

Council for Exceptional Children. (2015). What Every Special Educator Must Know: Professional Ethics and Standards. Arlington, VA: CEC 2

Initial Preparation Standard 5: Instructional Planning and Strategies

5.0	Beginning special education professionals select, adapt, and use a repertoire of evidence-based instructional strategies to advance learning of individuals with exceptionalities.

Key Elements	
5.1	Beginning special education professionals consider individual abilities, interests, learning environments, and cultural and linguistic factors in the selection, development, and adaptation of learning experiences for individuals with exceptionalities.
5.2	Beginning special education professionals use technologies to support instructional assessment, planning, and delivery for individuals with exceptionalities.
5.3	Beginning special education professionals are familiar with augmentative and alternative communication systems and a variety of assistive technologies to support the communication and learning of individuals with exceptionalities.
5.4	Beginning special education professionals use strategies to enhance language development and communication skills of individuals with exceptionalities.
5.5	Beginning special education professionals develop and implement a variety of education and transition plans for individuals with exceptionalities across a wide range of settings and different learning experiences in collaboration with individuals, families, and teams.
5.6	Beginning special education professionals teach to mastery and promote generalization of learning.
5.7	Beginning special education professionals teach cross-disciplinary knowledge and skills such as critical thinking and problem solving to individuals with exceptionalities.

Council for Exceptional Children. (2015). What Every Special Educator Must Know: Professional Ethics and Standards. Arlington, VA: CEC 3

Initial Preparation Standard 6: Professional Learning and Ethical Practice

6.0	Beginning special education professionals use foundational knowledge of the field and their professional ethical principles and practice standards to inform special education practice, to engage in lifelong learning, and to advance the profession.

continued

TABLE 4–1 *continued*

Key Elements	
6.1	Beginning special education professionals use professional ethical principles and professional practice standards to guide their practice.
6.2	Beginning special education professionals understand how foundational knowledge and current issues influence professional practice.
6.3	Beginning special education professionals understand that diversity is a part of families, cultures, and schools, and that complex human issues can interact with the delivery of special education services.
6.4	Beginning special education professionals understand the significance of lifelong learning and participate in professional activities and learning communities.
6.5	Beginning special education professionals advance the profession by engaging in activities such as advocacy and mentoring.
6.6	Beginning special education professionals provide guidance and direction to paraeducators, tutors, and volunteers.
Initial Preparation Standard 7: Collaboration	
7.0	Beginning special education professionals collaborate with families, other educators, related service providers, individuals with exceptionalities, and personnel from community agencies in culturally responsive ways to address the needs of individuals with exceptionalities across a range of learning experiences.
Key Elements	
7.1	Beginning special education professionals use the theory and elements of effective collaboration.
7.2	Beginning special education professionals serve as a collaborative resource to colleagues.
7.3	Beginning special education professionals use collaboration to promote the well being of individuals with exceptionalities across a wide range of settings and collaborators.

Sources: Council for Exceptional Children. (2015). What Every Special Educator Must Know: Professional Ethics and Standards. Arlington, VA: CEC 4. From *CEC Initial Level Special Educator Preparation Standards, 2012, Council for Exceptional Children.* Retrieved March 25, 2015, from *https://www.cec.sped.org/~/media/Files/Standards/Professional%20Preparation%20Standards/Initial%20Preparation%20Standards%20with%20Elaborations.pdf.* Reprinted with permission.

CRITERIA FOR THE SELECTION OF ASSESSMENT TOOLS

One purpose of the landmark special education law, the Education for All Handicapped Children Act of 1975, was the establishment of a set of procedures to guard against inappropriate assessment and placement practices. This law provided safeguards to prevent recurrence of past abuses. These safeguards are preserved and strengthened in the current federal statute, IDEA 2004, as Table 4–2 illustrates. Federal laws and regulations and the state laws resulting from them mandate appropriate assessment procedures. In some cases, actual practice may fall short of intended goals.

Legal Guidelines for Assessment

The regulations for IDEA 2004 provide specific guidelines for the evaluation and placement of students with disabilities in special education programs. This law focuses on the use of assessment information for legal decisions, that is, decisions about identification and determination of eligibility for special education services. This type of information has implications for long-range

TABLE 4–2
Legal Safeguards Against Assessment Abuses

PAST ABUSES	IDEA SAFEGUARDS
Students evaluated for special education without notice to parents or parental consent	Parents must be given notice prior to evaluation; parents must give informed consent before evaluation. [§300.503(a), 300.300(a)]
Culturally biased tests used in evaluation	Assessment procedures must be selected and administered so that they are not discriminatory on a racial or cultural basis. [§300.304(c)(1)(i)]
Non-English-speaking students assessed in English	Measures must be provided and administered in the language and form most likely to yield accurate information, unless clearly not feasible. [§300.304(c)(1)(ii)]
Tests administered by untrained or poorly trained personnel	Trained and knowledgeable personnel must administer assessment instruments according to the instructions provided by the makers of the instruments. [§300.304(c)(1)(iv) and (v)]
Poor quality assessment instruments used for evaluation	Assessment instruments must be technically sound; they must be used for the purpose for which they are valid and reliable. [§300.304(b)(3); §300.304(c)(1)(iii)]
Tests used that penalized students with disabilities	Measures for individuals with disabilities must accurately reflect the aptitudes, skills, or knowledge areas being assessed, not skill limitations due to the disability, unless those limitations are the subject of assessment. [§300.304(c)(3)]
Placement in services for students with intellectual disabilities based solely on IQ scores	No one measure or procedure may be used as the sole criterion for determination of a disability or of the educational program. [§300.304(b)(2); §300.304(c)(2)]
Placement decisions made without a complete evaluation of the student	Individuals must be assessed in all areas of the suspected disability. A variety of measures must be used to gather information about functional, developmental, and academic performance. [§300.304(c)(4)]
Assessment focused only on the disability, not the educational program	Assessment must provide information directly relevant to the child's educational needs. [§300.304(c)(6)]

The numbers in brackets refer to sections of the *Final Regulations* for IDEA 2004 (*Federal Register*, 2006).

instructional decisions, such as those associated with design of the individualized education program (IEP). However, no attempt is made to regulate classroom assessment and the day-to-day instructional decisions practitioners face.

IDEA 2004 includes several guidelines for the selection of assessment tools and the conduct of the assessment process.

Assessment Is Nondiscriminatory

Federal special education law expressly forbids three types of discrimination. First, assessment tools must be free of racial and cultural bias. Tests and other procedures must be selected on this basis, and care must be taken to prevent the intrusion of bias into test administration. Second, if a student's native language is not English, every effort must be made to provide assessment tools in the student's language. This mandate extends not only to individuals who speak languages other than English, but also to those whose mode of communication is not spoken language. For example, students with hearing impairments who communicate through sign language should be assessed in sign language. However, because appropriate assessment tools are not available in all languages, assessment may proceed if testing in the native language is clearly not feasible.

Third, assessment tools must not discriminate on the basis of disability. Unless the purpose of assessment is to study the disability, tests and other procedures should bypass the student's problem. Specifically, the law states that tests must be chosen so that sensory, motor, and speaking disabilities do not interfere with the assessment of other skills and abilities. For instance, if the purpose of assessment is to study spelling achievement, the student with impaired motor skills should not be required to write his or her answers.

Assessment Focuses on Educational Needs

The major purpose of assessment is to determine educational needs. Although the presence of a disability must be established to support eligibility for special education services, simply identifying a student as having a learning disability or intellectual disability is insufficient. Attention must also be directed to the specific educational needs resulting from the disability. In addition, assessment must focus on the student's ability to participate in the general curriculum and the progress he or she has made in that curriculum.

Assessment Is Comprehensive

All important areas of student performance must be studied. Although tests of intellectual performance may be used, they must be accompanied by other measures that assess educational needs. The results of a single measure must never be the sole basis for placement in special education. The assessment must be comprehensive so that no important area of performance is neglected. Health, vision, hearing, social and emotional status, general intelligence, academic performance, communicative status, and motor abilities may be considered, if these are areas of potential need for the student under assessment. Several sources must be consulted for information about the student. These include results of formal and informal assessments carried out by special educators and other professionals, input from parents, and classroom teachers' observations and recommendations.

Assessment Tools Are Technically Adequate and Administered by Trained Professionals

Assessment devices must be reliable measurement tools that have been validated for the specific purpose for which they will be used. They must display adequate technical quality to ensure accurate results. If the goal is study of reading achievement, the instrument chosen must be a valid measure of reading achievement. Assessment must also be conducted by trained professionals. The administration, scoring, and interpretation rules specified in the measure's manual must be scrupulously followed.

Rights of Students with Disabilities and Their Parents Are Protected During Assessment

Throughout the assessment process, safeguards protect the rights of individuals with disabilities and their parents or guardians. As Chapters 2 and 3 discussed, parents must be notified when a student is referred for assessment; they must receive information about their rights; and they must give informed consent before assessment begins. No student may be placed in special education without a comprehensive assessment that includes evaluation of his or her educational needs. The student's progress in special education must be evaluated on a regular basis (typically annually), and a complete reevaluation must be conducted at least every 3 years. Parents may review school records that concern their child's identification, assessment, and placement in special education; they also have the right to an explanation of the assessment results. In addition, parents participate as members of the IEP team and assist in developing their child's educational program.

Professional Guidelines

There are several sources of guidance in the selection of assessment tools in addition to legal requirements. An important resource is *Standards for Educational and Psychological Testing* (1999), prepared by a joint committee of the American Educational Research Association, the American Psychological Association, and the National Council on Measurement in Education. This guide for test users and producers contains standards for tests, manuals, and reports; it also includes standards for reports of research on reliability and validity and standards for the use of tests. The *Code of Fair Testing Practices in Education* (2004) from the Joint Committee on Testing Practices provides guidelines to test users in selecting, administering, scoring, interpreting, and reporting the results of educational tests.

Test catalogues, websites of test publishers, test manuals, and other information provided by producers of assessment tools may also aid in the selection process. Test catalogues and publishers' websites provide an overview of available instruments, particularly newer ones, and often include brief descriptions of each measure. However, the more detailed information needed for selection decisions can be found in test manuals. Manuals should discuss important characteristics of the instrument, including purpose, the procedures used for development, and data on psychometric quality. Not all manuals are complete, and few seek to emphasize the weak points of the measure, so the buyer must beware.

The Mental Measurements Yearbook series offers assistance in the evaluation of specific measures. Issued every few years by the Buros Institute of Mental Measurements, these references contain reviews of commercially available psychological, educational, and vocational tests. The most recent edition, the *Nineteenth Mental Measurements Yearbook* (Carlson, Geisinger, & Jonson, 2014), includes information on more than 250 tests. The companion series, *Tests in Print*, serves as an index to the yearbooks. A newer resource is the web-based *Test Reviews Online,* which contains reviews of more than 3,500 tests from the *Yearbook* series. This service is available at no cost to students through some college and university libraries; reviews may also be purchased online for $15 per test.

Another online service is *TestLink* from the Educational Testing Service (*www.ets.org*). This searchable database contains more than 25,000 tests, and brief test descriptions are available at no charge. *Tests* (Maddox, 2003) is a print collection of test reviews. The fifth edition of this guide contains descriptions of approximately 2,000 tests used commonly in psychology, education, and business.

Professional journals are the best source for research relating to assessment and for critical reviews of newly developed assessment tools. *Assessment for Effective Intervention*, published by the Council for Educational Diagnostic Services of the Council for Exceptional Children (CEC), focuses on special education assessment. Other journals that often contain articles about assessment tools and their use in special education are *Exceptional Children, Journal of Special Education*, and *Remedial and Special Education*, as well as those journals that address specific disabilities (e.g., *Journal of Learning Disabilities, Learning Disabilities Research and Practice, Behavioral Disorders*, and *American Journal on Intellectual and Developmental Disabilities*).

Evaluation Criteria

Whether an assessment team is faced with choosing the tools to gather information for an eligibility decision or a classroom teacher is searching for a measure to evaluate academic progress, the task is the same: selection of the most accurate, effective, and efficient means of data collection. The questions that follow provide a structure for evaluation of assessment tools.

Does the Tool Fit the Purpose of Assessment?

A technically excellent assessment device is useless if it does not provide the particular information needed to answer an assessment question. Because the type of tool needed is related to the purpose of the assessment, the ways in which assessment information will be used must be clear. If the goal is to answer questions about a student's standing in relation to his or her peers, then norm-referenced measures are appropriate. If questions concern classroom behaviors, observational strategies are indicated. For questions about the mastery of specific academic skills, the most valuable information sources may be criterion-referenced tests, informal inventories, classroom quizzes, and teacher checklists.

The form in which assessment results appear is also important. Sometimes comparative scores such as percentile ranks or standard scores are necessary; for other purposes, a simple frequency count of the number of times a student performs a particular behavior will suffice.

Other considerations are the content and scope of the measure—the specific achievement, aptitude, or attitude areas that are assessed. If the goal is study of a student's reading abilities, a test of mathematics skills is obviously inappropriate. Less apparent is the choice between a global achievement test designed to screen for problems in reading and other academic subjects and a diagnostic reading test that assesses decoding, structural analysis, comprehension, and vocabulary skills. Before it is possible to select the most appropriate tool, the purpose of the assessment must be clearly understood.

Is the Tool Appropriate for the Student?

The assessment instrument or strategy must fit the student's needs and abilities. If norm-referenced measures are used, the student's characteristics must be consistent with those of the norm group with which the test was standardized. The age or grade of the student is also important because test norms are generally arranged by chronological age or grade in school. For instance, if a 5-year-old is administered a test normed with 6- to 12-year-olds, it is impossible to convert his or her responses to norm-referenced test scores.

With any type of measure, the assessment tasks must be compatible with the skills of the student. No student should be asked to attempt tasks that are clearly beyond his or her current functioning level. In addition to the content and difficulty level of the assessment task, other important skill considerations are:

- *Presentation Mode*, or the method by which the test task is presented to the student. Is the student required to listen, read, look at figures or pictures, or attend to a demonstration?
- *Response mode*, or the method by which the student must answer the question or perform the specified task. Must the student speak, make a check or darken a square, write words or sentences, or point to the correct response?
- *Group versus individual administration*, or whether the student takes part in assessment as one of a group or as the only participant.
- *Time factors* such as the length of the assessment, particularly as it relates to the student's attention span, and whether the student is required to respond under timed conditions.

Tools should capitalize on the student's strengths rather than penalize weaknesses. Individual measures are more appropriate for students with difficulty maintaining attention during group testing. Students who write poorly should be assessed with measures that allow oral responses, unless the purpose of assessment is the study of writing skills. The assessment device should not discriminate against the student on the basis of race, culture, language, gender, or disability.

Is the Tool Appropriate for the Tester?

The assessment device must match the skills and qualifications of the professional using it. No tool should be selected unless adequately trained personnel are available to take responsibility for administration of the measure, scoring of student responses, and interpretation of results. In untrained hands, even the best instruments can produce erroneous information.

Is the Tool Technically Adequate?

Before confidence can be placed in the results of an assessment tool, its quality must be demonstrated. The techniques used to construct the measure must be sound, it must produce reliable data, and it must show validity. Information on the measurement characteristics of norm-referenced standardized measures is generally presented in the test manual or technical supplement. The same types of information may be available for less formal measures such as rating scales, criterion-referenced tests, checklists, and inventories. However, in many cases, the technical quality of informal instruments remains unknown. Although some technical considerations may not be relevant for certain types of informal measures (e.g., standardization procedures in the case of unstandardized instruments), an assessment tool's reliability and validity and the methods used in its construction are always important.

Is the Tool an Efficient Data Collection Mechanism?

An efficient measure produces the needed information with minimum expenditure of time and effort. Administration, preparation by the tester, scoring of assessment results, and interpretation of data are all factors to consider. Ease of use also influences efficiency; more difficult procedures typically take longer and introduce greater possibility of error. Measures are considered effective and efficient when their results are worth the time and effort of both student and professional.

If no available measure is appropriate for a particular assessment task, several options remain open. Two or more existing measures can be combined to produce a tool sufficiently comprehensive to collect the needed information, or an instrument or data collection strategy can be modified to fit the purposes of assessment and the characteristics of the student. However, when adaptations are made in procedures for standardized tests, test norms can no longer be used. Such measures should be considered informal, and their results should be interpreted cautiously. Another alternative is to construct a new assessment tool that satisfies the demands of the situation. This solution is not simple and should be reserved for cases in which modification of available measures is clearly unacceptable. Devising a new assessment tool is time consuming, and unless technical adequacy of the new device can be demonstrated, its quality remains unknown.

In many assessment situations, a professional or team puts together an assessment battery—a collection of tools designed to answer several assessment questions. For instance, in determining whether a student is eligible for special education, the team may pose a series of questions that necessitate the use of many types of assessment strategies. In selecting the measures for an assessment battery, these principles should be followed:

1. The assessment battery must be comprehensive and complete, but unnecessary duplication should be avoided.
2. An attempt should be made to select measures that include a variety of different activities.
3. In selecting the tools for an initial assessment, measures to substantiate the reasons for referral should be included.
4. In general, results of group measures should be used only as screening information.
5. If two procedures appear equally appropriate, the more efficient one should be selected.
6. If possible, only measures with known technical adequacy should be included in the battery.

EVALUATING MEASUREMENT TYPES

We will introduce some terminology used in the study of measurement. Everyone is familiar with common units of measurement—inches, centimeters, miles, pounds, pints, liters, and degrees. Each represents a scale for quantifying some physical property such as distance, weight, or temperature. Educational assessment is less precise because it deals with human, rather than physical, properties; the goal is the quantification of psychological dimensions such as aptitude, attitude, and achievement.

Measurement Scales

There are four types of measurement scales: nominal, ordinal, interval, and ratio scales.

A **nominal** scale is the least powerful or meaningful scale. This scale can be thought of as a naming or identification tool. Categories are used for identification purposes. For example, the students in a classroom could be categorized on the basis of hair color and sorted into brunettes, redheads, and blondes. In nominal measurement, no values are assigned to categories; categories are simply different from one another. As a result, it is impossible to add, subtract, multiply, or divide this type of information. This restricts the ways in which nominal scales can be statistically analyzed.

Students in Ms. Harris's Classroom

Brunettes	Redheads	Blondes
Eddie	Joseph	Lucy
Julie	Vicki	Carrie
Suzie	Stephen	Eleni

The next level of the scales of measurement is the **ordinal** scale. This scale serves as a ranking tool. So, persons or other subjects of study are placed in sequence. In the classroom, the teacher might rank students according to their artistic performance. Maria, the class artist, is ranked first; then Henry, a skilled cartoonist; then Susette, a fair painter; and so forth. Ordinal scales only place individuals in position relative to one another; no assumption can be made about the distance between individuals. From the teacher's ranking of the points, we know Maria performed more artistically than either Henry or Susette, but we do not know how much more. Maria may be just a little more proficient than Henry, or she may be six times more talented. Like nominal data, ordinal data cannot be arithmetically manipulated.

Student	Rank
Maria	1
Henry	2
Susette	3

With **interval** scales, there are equal intervals (numbers are equidistant) between the units of measurement, and the scale begins at an arbitrary starting point. A quiz, for example, would yield interval data; John might earn a score of 10, Sally 8, Rose 6, and Harvey 5. Individuals can be ordered according to their scores; in addition, the distance between scores can be discussed. The distance between John's score of 10 and Sally's score of 8 is the same as the distance between Sally's score of 8 and Rose's score of 6. However, interval scales do not begin with a true zero; if a student earns a score of zero on a classroom quiz, it does not mean that he or she has zero information about the subject assessed. Thus, it is impossible to multiply or divide interval data; one cannot say that John's score of 10 represents two times as much knowledge as Harvey's score of 5. Despite this, most common statistical techniques are appropriate for interval data. Many psychological variables measured in educational assessment are arranged on interval scales.

Student	Quiz Score
John	10
Sally	8
Rose	6
Harvey	5

The **ratio** scale is considered the most sophisticated scale. This fourth level of measurement possesses all of the qualities indicated in the previous three scales in addition to a true zero.

Ratio scales allow all arithmetic operations, including multiplication and division, and any type of statistical procedure can be used. Unfortunately, few variables of interest in educational assessment are arranged on ratio scales; those that are include physical properties such as height and weight as well as some physiological measures.

Day	Length of Temper Tantrum in Seconds
Monday	120
Tuesday	123
Wednesday	96
Thursday	34
Friday	0

Monday's tantrum lasted 24 seconds longer than Wednesday's tantrum and 3 seconds less than Thursday's tantrum.

 Breakpoint Practice 4.1
Click here to check your understanding of measurement scales.

Descriptive Statistics

Descriptive statistics assist in summarizing information from all types of scales. Measures of central tendency describe a set or distribution of data with one index that represents the entire set. For example, instead of listing the exam scores of all 35 members of a class, the class mode, median, or mean can be computed. The **mode** is the most common value among a set of values, the score that occurs most frequently. If a distribution includes the following scores:

Score (x)
100
92
92
90

the most commonly occurring score is 92. If no number occurs more than once, there is no mode.

Note that in this case the mode is not 0. In the following distribution of scores:

Score (x)
100
100
92
92
90
90
90

the most commonly occurring number or score is 90. If the distribution were as follows:

Score (x)
100
100
92
92
90

then there would be two modes, or a bimodal distribution.

The **median** is the middle score in a set of scores; one-half of the scores are higher than the median score and one-half are lower. If a set of scores were even, then the two numbers in the middle would be averaged. For example, if a distribution included the following scores:

Score (x)
99
92
90
86

90 and 92 would be averaged. So $92 + 90/2 = 91$. Therefore, 91 is the median. Remember that to determine the median correctly, it is helpful to rank the numbers from largest to smallest and thus minimize error.

The **mean** is the arithmetic average of the scores and is computed by adding all scores together and dividing by the number of scores. This method is often used in informal assessment. For example, when teachers calculate grades for scores on teacher-made tests, they use a mean. For example, if distribution included the following scores

Score (x)
99
93
92
90
86

the total or sum would be 460. Dividing by the number of scores, or 5, produces a result of 92. Therefore, the mean or average of this distribution is 92.

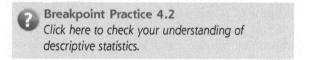

Breakpoint Practice 4.2
Click here to check your understanding of descriptive statistics.

If data are nominal, the only measure of central tendency that can be used is the mode. With ordinal data, the median is appropriate, as is the mode. Interval data allow the calculation of all three measures. For most interval data, the mean is the most accurate descriptor of central tendency. However, the median is a better choice if the distribution contains extreme scores.

Measures of variability are another type of descriptive statistic. Their purpose is description of the spread or dispersion of a distribution. Sets of scores, even those with identical means and medians, can differ in variability. One set might have scores clustering around the mean (e.g., 59, 60, 61), whereas another might have scattered scores (e.g., 40, 60, 80). The **range** can be used to describe scatter; it is the distance between the highest and lowest scores in the distribution. With interval data, a better estimate of variability is **standard deviation**. The standard deviation takes each score's relationship to the mean into account; the higher the standard deviation, the more variability within a set of scores. The computational formula for standard deviation (σ) is

$$\sigma = \sqrt{\dfrac{\Sigma X^2 - \dfrac{(\Sigma X^2)}{N}}{N}}$$

where Σ signifies the addition operation, X the test scores, and N the number of cases. To determine ΣX^2, each score is squared; then the squares are added. To determine $(\Sigma X)^2$, the scores are first added; then the total sum is squared.

 ENHANCEDetext
Video Example 4.1
Watch this video to learn more about calculating mean and standard deviation using Excel.
https://www.youtube.com/watch?v=62i1fqKhNhg

A third type of descriptive statistic is measures of **correlation**. These measures express the degree of relationship between two sets of scores. If two measures are highly correlated, the scores from one measure can be used to predict performance on the other. Several measures of correlation are available, but the most common one is the Pearson product-moment correlation coefficient. The Pearson *r*, as it is often called, is appropriate for interval data. Correlation coefficients range in value from −1.00 to +1.00. A coefficient of 0 indicates no relationship between two sets of scores. A coefficient of +1.00 indicates a perfect positive correlation; individuals with the highest scores in the first set of scores also achieved the highest scores in the second set. A perfect negative correlation is represented by a coefficient of −1.00; in this case, the persons with the highest scores in the first data set obtained the lowest scores in the second. Educators utilize coefficients when choosing and interpreting the value of specific tests.

Correlational techniques are frequently used to analyze the technical adequacy of assessment tools, particularly in the study of reliability and validity. It is essential that professionals be able to interpret correlational data (Best & Kahn, 2005) in order to appropriately use assessment tools. Correlations measure the relationship between two or more sets of scores (Cohen, Cohen, West, & Aiken, 2003).

The direction of a correlation coefficient refers to whether it is positive or negative; magnitude is the size of the coefficient. However, a correlation coefficient of .73 does not mean 73 percent of a perfect relationship between sets of scores. On the one hand, an example of a positive relationship could be the number of classes a college student participates in and class activity scores. In this case, both sets of scores increase. If both sets of scores decrease, a positive relationship is also found. On the other hand, an example of a negative relationship could be the number of parties a college student attends and their test scores. In this case, one set of scores increases while the other set decreases.

To determine the usefulness of the correlation coefficient, the coefficient of determination is computed; this is simply the square of the correlation coefficient. Thus, if the Pearson *r* is either −.70 or +.70, the coefficient of determination is 49 percent (.70 × .70 = .49 or 49%). This percentage indicates the degree to which one set of scores can be used to predict the other. As Ary, Jacobs, Sorensen, and Walker (2013) explain, when finding a correlation between two factors of .80 or more, 64 percent of the variance in one factor (e.g., achievement) is connected with variance in the related factor (i.e., intelligence test results).

 Breakpoint Practice 4.3
Click here to check your understanding of correlation coefficients.

Test Norms and Other Standards of Comparison

Some types of assessment tools compare an individual's performance with an outside reference or standard. With norm-referenced tests, the standard is the performance of a norm group, and with criterion-referenced tests, the standard is a curricular goal. For a tool to be appropriate for assessment, its standard of comparison must fit the purpose of assessment and the needs and characteristics of the student.

A norm group serves as the outside reference for **norm-referenced tests**. The test is administered to a large number of individuals selected to represent the types of persons with whom the test will be used. For instance, for a measure of beginning reading skills, the norm group might be a representative sample of kindergartners and first and second graders. Test norms are then derived from the performance of persons in the norm group. If results are to have meaning for a particular student, the norm group must be an appropriate standard against which to evaluate the student's performance. Factors to consider in determining the appropriateness of test norms are:

1. *Age, grade, and gender of norm group members.* These characteristics must match the characteristics of the student. Many of the psychological variables of interest in educational assessment differ by gender and across age groups and grade levels. Thus, it is incorrect to administer a test to a student beyond the age or grade of the norms and then use the closest age or grade group to estimate results.

2. *Method of selection.* Norm groups are samples intended to represent some population of interest. Because randomly selected samples are most likely to approximate the characteristics of a population, norm groups obtained through this method are preferable. Samples selected only because of their accessibility to the test producer are unsatisfactory.

3. *Representativeness of the norm group.* A representative sample includes members from all important segments of the population. If the goal were to construct a national norm group representative of American schoolchildren, it would be unsuitable to select only 6-year-olds or only females. Important population characteristics in test construction are age, gender, geographic region (e.g., the Eastern Seaboard, the South, the Midwest), location of residence (rural, urban, suburban), ethnicity, and some index of socioeconomic status. Variables pertinent to school populations are grade, school placement (general versus special education), type of disability, and language or languages spoken.

4. *Size of the norm group.* Generally, larger samples produce more accurate results. If the norm group is divided into age or grade levels for which separate norms are provided, the size of these subgroups should also be considered.

5. *Recency of test norms.* Test norms should reflect current standards of student performance. Norms established with first graders in 1998 may be a poor index for evaluating the first graders of 2015. Both test norms and test content should be periodically updated for subject areas that change over time.

It has been suggested that the norm groups of all tests used for special education purposes should include individuals with disabilities (Fuchs, Fuchs, Benowitz, & Barringer, 1987). This makes sense if the purpose of assessment is to compare a student's performance to that of the total school population, including both students with and without disabilities. However, because in eligibility decisions it is necessary to determine whether achievement problems exist, the appropriate standard of comparison is the performance of students placed in general education classrooms. Norm groups drawn from general education classrooms will likely include students with mild disabilities, and test manuals should describe the characteristics of these students as fully as possible.

Criterion-referenced tests and other informal devices also provide a standard against which student performance can be compared. These measures determine whether students have mastered specific skills; they compare a student's performance to the desired curricular goal rather than to the performance of other students. Again, the appropriateness of the standard must be evaluated. Just as norm groups may not approximate the characteristics of a student, the content of a published criterion-referenced measure may not represent the student's current skill repertoire or the curriculum taught in the student's classroom. Even if a measure has been developed for curriculum-based assessment in a specific district, it may not reflect current instruction in all schools and classrooms within that district.

The manual accompanying the measure is the best source of information about test norms and other standards of comparison. Test producers are expected to provide a complete manual that describes the purpose of the measure, the method of its construction, characteristics of the norm group or other standard, and results of reliability and validity studies. However, not all manuals include these components.

Technical quality refers to the adequacy of an assessment tool as a measurement device. Four major characteristics of an instrument are considered in the evaluation of technical quality: reliability, validity, measurement error, and, for norm-referenced and criterion-referenced measures, the reference group or standard against which a student's performance is compared.

RELIABILITY AND VALIDITY

Reliability

Reliability refers to consistency. In everyday language, a reliable person is one who can be counted on. A reliable assessment tool produces consistent results. For example, if a reliable test were to be administered several times to the same individual, the person's scores would remain stable and would not randomly fluctuate. Anastasi and Urbina (1997) define reliability in terms of consistency of scores achieved by the same test takers over different times, sets of items, or other testing conditions.

Correlational techniques are the most usual methods for studying reliability. Although there are no set rules for determining if a correlation coefficient is of adequate magnitude, it appears logical to set .80 as a minimum. If two sets of scores are related at this level, the coefficient of determination is 64 percent, meaning that approximately two-thirds of the variance in the first set of scores is associated with the variance in the second. Explanation of this proportion of the variance should be regarded as a minimum standard. Salvia, Ysseldyke, and Bolt (2010) recommend a minimum level of .60 for group data used for administrative purposes, .80 for individual data that influence screening decisions, and .90 for individual data considered for important decisions such as placement in special education. Gay (1990) maintains that test selection for tests of achievement and aptitude should include a minimum cut-off of .90.

There are several types of reliability. *Test-retest reliability* refers to the consistency of a measure from one administration to another. This is typically studied with some segment of the norm group; the measure is administered once during norming and then again to the same group of individuals after a brief period, perhaps a few weeks. *Equivalent-forms reliability* is of interest when there is more than one form of the same measure and these forms are used interchangeably. To determine if different forms of the same measure produce consistent results, all forms are administered to the same group and results are correlated.

Split-half reliability concerns a measure's internal consistency and is studied with one form of a measure and one group. After administration, the measure is divided in half (e.g., into odd-numbered and even-numbered items), and the scores from each half are correlated. The Kuder–Richardson procedures provide another approach to the study of internal consistency. Instead of splitting an instrument in half and comparing one half to the other, these methods consider the equivalence of all items and produce an estimate of interitem consistency.

The last major type of reliability is *interscorer reliability*, also called *interrater* or *interobserver reliability*. This type is concerned with the consistency among persons who evaluate the performance of the individual being assessed; it is most important when scoring standards are subject to interpretation. If two different professionals rate a student's responses to test items, their ratings should be consistent.

Perhaps the most typical assessment situation in which scorer reliability is a factor is in the use of observational techniques. When two observers collect data on the same student, they must ensure consistency. To calculate interobserver reliability, observation records are compared to determine the number of times observers agreed and disagreed on their ratings of behavior. The percentage of agreement is then computed with the following formula:

$$\text{\% of agreements} = \frac{\text{Number of agreements}}{\text{Number of agreements} + \text{Number of disagreements}} \times 100$$

The minimum acceptable rate of agreement between observers is 80 percent (Cooper, Heron, & Heward, 1987; Sulzer-Azaroff & Mayer, 1977).

> **? Breakpoint Practice 4.4**
> *Click here to check your understanding of reliability.*

Validity

Validity refers to whether an assessment tool actually measures what it purports to measure. If a test claims to assess skill in driving a car but includes only multiple-choice questions on the parts of an engine, it is clearly invalid. Also, measurement tools can be valid for one purpose but not for another. For example, a test may be a valid method of screening for academic difficulties but not for differentiating among types of reading problems. According to the legal guidelines for assessment in federal law, assessment tools used with students with disabilities must be validated for the specific purpose for which they are used. Thus, studies of a measure's validity should include individuals with disabilities as subjects if that measure is to be used for special education purposes (Cohen & Spenciner, 2010; Fuchs et al., 1987).

Validity is related to reliability. No measure can be considered valid if it produces inconsistent results. Valid instruments are reliable instruments, although a measure can lack validity and still be reliable. Validity is concerned with the content of the measure and whether that content enables the measure to perform its intended function.

Content validity is defined as the degree to which test sample items represent defined content domain or universe of knowledge (Ary et al., 2013). Content validity, an important consideration in the evaluation of any measure, is particularly critical with criterion-referenced tests, inventories, and other informal instruments that compare student performance to curricular standards. Determination of a measure's content validity is a matter of judgment rather than statistical analysis. Factors to consider are:

- What content area does the measure claim to assess? What are the boundaries of that area?
- Does the measure attempt to assess the entire universe of content, or does it include only a sampling from that universe?
- If the measure assesses only a portion of the content universe, is the sample a representative one?

- Is it complete? Are all important elements included?
- What types of tasks are used to assess content? Are these appropriate for the skill or knowledge being assessed?

The content validity of an assessment tool must be evaluated in relation to the assessment task. Even if an instrument does an adequate job of measuring the content area, it may be inappropriate for a particular student or the specific question guiding the assessment.

Another type of validity is *criterion-related validity*. The instrument is validated in terms of some outside criterion. For example, a new test of academic achievement might be validated against an existing achievement test, school grades, or teacher ratings of academic performance. This assumes, of course, that the criterion chosen is itself a valid measure of the content area.

There are two types of criterion-related validity: predictive and concurrent. *Predictive validity* refers to a measure's ability to predict future performance. It is studied by administering the measure in question to a group of individuals and then, sometime in the future, administering the criterion measure to the same group. For example, the predictive validity of a school readiness test could be established by administering it at the start of kindergarten, then correlating its results with teacher ratings of academic performance at the end of first grade. *Concurrent validity* is concerned with a measure's relationship to some current criterion. It is studied by administering both the measure in question and the criterion measure to the same group at the same time. For example, the concurrent validity of a new algebra test could be established by correlating its results with student grades in algebra.

The correlation coefficients resulting from the study of criterion-related validity are examined to determine their direction and magnitude. As a general rule, the greater the magnitude of a positive correlation between a measure and its criterion, the more support for that measure's validity. Unlike the study of reliability, there are no set rules for judging whether a validity coefficient is of adequate magnitude. At minimum, however, the correlation should be statistically significant

(Anastasi, 1988). That is, there should be reason to believe that the relationship between the two measures is not simply due to chance. Information about statistical significance should be provided in the test's manual or technical report; statistical significance cannot be determined by inspecting the correlation coefficient's magnitude.

In evaluating criterion-related validity, the appropriateness of the criterion measure must be considered. If a test of reading skills is under study, another reading test should be selected as the criterion, not a test of general aptitude. The criterion should address and be a valid measure of the content of interest. Examples of measures include another test, observations, or grades (Kritikos, 2010). According to Ary et al. (2013), appropriate criterion measures are relevant to the content area, and they are reliable and free from bias.

A third type of validity is *construct validity,* or the degree to which an instrument measures the theoretical construct it intends to measure (Hallgren, 2012). Some assessment devices claim to measure constructs such as intelligence, social competence, visual perception, and auditory processing. Theoretical constructs are not directly observable; they must be inferred from observed behaviors. The construct validity of a measure can be studied with correlational techniques. For example, if a new test of construct X is found to relate to an established measure of construct X, the validity of the new test is supported. Other methods of determining construct validity include factor analysis, investigation of age differentiation for measures of developmental constructs, and validation by experimental intervention (Anastasi & Urbina, 1997).

> **Breakpoint Practice 4.5**
> *Click here to check your understanding of validity.*

> ▶ **ENHANCEDetext**
> **Video Example 4.2**
> *Watch this video to learn more about practical application of reliability and validity.*
> https://www.youtube.com/watch?v=fnF2hrLZHoA

Factors That Influence Validity

Reliability. If the reliability is low, then validity is low because if a test is not consistent, then it is not an effective test.

Examinee factors. Life experiences of the examinee, such as death, divorce, a fight, lack of sleep, and hunger. Furthermore, physical problems such as respiratory, endocrine, vision, auditory, social/emotional, attention-deficit/hyperactivity, substance abuse, and home/personal issues can negatively affect testing (AAIDD, 2010; Spinelli, 2011).

Test factors: Unclear test instructions, unfamiliarity with test items, inappropriate test procedures, unfair test items, and language fluency.

Examinee factors. Scoring errors, biased testing.

Norms. Individuals in the norm group should be representative of the test taker.

Measurement Error

Error intrudes into any measurement system, and assessment is no exception. If a test, even the most reliable and valid one, were to be administered twice to the same student by the same examiner, the scores obtained would likely differ—even if testing conditions were identical, the test was administered and scored correctly each time, and the student had not acquired new skills from one administration to the next. Test scores and other assessment results are observed scores made up of two parts—a hypothetical true score and an error component. The less error reported in an observed score, the more precise the measurement tool.

Although measurement error is inevitable, it can be quantified by a statistic called the **standard error of measurement.** This statistic can be determined if the standard deviation and reliability of the measure are known. Most manuals for norm-referenced tests provide information on standard error, or it can be calculated with the formula

$$SE_m = \sigma\sqrt{1 - r}$$

in which SE_m represents standard error of measurement, σ the standard deviation, and r reliability.

Measurement error is related to both the variability of scores and reliability. As variability increases, so does error. However, as reliability increases, error decreases. Thus, to reduce measurement error, professionals should select instruments with low variability and high reliability.

The standard error of measurement is an indicator of the technical quality of an assessment tool and assists with interpretation of results. As explained in the next chapter, standard error is used to construct confidence intervals around observed scores. This allows a student's performance to be reported as a range of scores where it is highly probable the true score lies, rather than as a single score known to include both the true score and error.

TEST SCORES AND OTHER ASSESSMENT RESULTS

Another consideration in the selection of assessment tools is the type of results needed to answer the assessment questions. Assessment data must be in a form that allows their use in various educational decisions. With informal measures, comparing a student's performance to curricular goals or classroom behavioral expectations can produce simple data such as the number of skills mastered or the number of inappropriate behaviors observed. Sometimes, that is the type of information needed. At other times, the more sophisticated results of norm-referenced tests are necessary to answer the assessment questions.

Results of Informal Measures

Most informal assessment results are straightforward, easy to understand, and descriptive. Frequency counts are a typical example; they simply report the number of occurrences of a behavior. For example, findings from informal inventories are often expressed as the number of questions, problems, or items answered correctly. Frequency data are easily converted to percentages. If a student answers 8 out of 10 items correctly on a classroom quiz, the percentage correct is 80. Informal assessments also yield duration data. Duration refers to time elapsed; if a student begins work on an assignment at 9:00 A.M. and completes it at 9:25 A.M., the duration of this activity is 25 minutes.

Frequency counts and percentages are interval data that can be manipulated by addition or subtraction. A student's performance can be compared by examining the difference between the number or percentage correct on each occasion. For example, a student may answer 20 out of 45 questions correctly at the beginning of September but improve to 35 out of 45 correct by the end of October; this represents an increase of 15 questions. Duration data are ratio data; time scales have true zeros and may be added, subtracted, multiplied, or divided. Thus, it is correct to say duration has doubled if a student increases the time spent on homework each evening from 30 minutes to 1 hour.

Some informal measures produce nominal data. Criterion-referenced tests, for example, may yield categorical findings. The student's performance on many criterion-referenced measures is classified as either demonstrating or failing to demonstrate skill mastery; no other descriptive information is provided. Checklists also produce a form of categorical data. If a teacher checks all items that describe a student's typical classroom behavior, in effect each item is classified as either representative or not representative of the student's typical behavior.

Other informal assessments provide ordinal data. Rating scales list a set of descriptions in some logical order: "The spelling performance of this student is (a) below grade level, (b) at grade level, (c) above grade level." The task is to select the most appropriate description. Rating instruments are considered ordinal scales unless they are Likert-type. Likert-type scales appear to be divided into equal intervals. For instance, a student may be asked to express degree of agreement with the statement "My favorite school subject is science" by selecting one of the following options:

1	2	3	4	5
Strongly Disagree	Disagree	Neutral	Agree	Strongly Agree

Likert-type scales are generally assumed to produce interval data.

Some informal measures are described as age-referenced or grade-referenced. For example, an informal inventory may be referenced to the

TABLE 4–3
Results Available from Selected Informal Measures

TYPE OF MEASURE	TYPICAL RESULTS	TYPE OF DATA
Criterion-referenced test	Pass/fail; the skill is mastered or not mastered	Nominal
Classroom quiz or inventory	Number or percentage correct	Interval
Observation	Number of occurrences of a behavior	Interval
	Duration of a behavior	Ratio
Rating scale	Verbal description (e.g., "usually punctual")	Ordinal
	A numerical rating with Likert-type scales	Interval

subject matter of specific grade levels; it may include first-grade spelling words, second-grade spelling words, and so forth. Such measures usually are not norm-referenced. If age or grade standards are derived from some source other than the performance of a norm group, the way in which these standards were determined must be carefully evaluated.

Age and grade ratings are ordinal data. Such scales place skills, traits, or other characteristics into some order; however, distances between points on these scales do not represent equal intervals. As with nominal scales, data from ordinal scales cannot be treated arithmetically.

Table 4–3 presents several informal assessment tools, their typical result, and the type of data they produce. This information can assist in selecting the most appropriate informal measure for an assessment purpose. If the assessment question demands numerical information, a measure yielding interval or ratio data is needed. Examples of numerical questions are "How many sight words can Sue Ellen read?" and "How much time does John take to complete his biology assignment?" Nominal scales are indicated if the assessment question is concerned with classification. An example of a categorical question is "Can Erin type 40 words per minute with no errors?" Ordinal scales fill the gap between numerical and categorical data; they provide descriptive information and answer questions about relative standing. One example is "How would Joan's handwriting be characterized: neat and legible, messy but still legible, or illegible?"

Norm-Referenced Test Scores

The results of norm-referenced tests take many forms: age and grade equivalents, percentile ranks, stanines, standard scores, and so forth. The **raw score** is common to all norm-referenced measures. Raw scores are similar to scores on classroom quizzes. They are not related to the performance of a norm group, and they are used only to obtain other scores. In most cases, raw scores are an index of the number of test items answered correctly. They must be converted to derived scores before a student's test performance can be compared to a norm group.

Age and Grade Equivalents

Many norm-referenced measures provide **age scores** and/or **grade scores** (also called age and/or grade equivalents). These derived scores express test performance in terms of the familiar units of chronological age or grade in school. For example, a student may receive an age score of 7 years, 6 months on a test of spoken language or a grade score of 4.5 on a reading achievement test. Of all norm-referenced scores, age and grade equivalents appear to be the easiest to understand and interpret, but they are quite complicated and thus subject to misinterpretation.

Age and grade scores are derived from the performance of the norm group. For example, if the third graders in the norm group earn an average raw score of 20, a grade equivalent of 3 is assigned to a raw score of 20. Anyone who achieves a raw score of 20 on this test will earn a grade equivalent of 3. Decimal grade equivalents (e.g., 3.1, 3.2, 3.3, and so forth) are usually derived by interpolating data already available, rather than by testing separate groups of students or the same group at successive intervals. Also, the range of grade equivalents in test norms may exceed the range of grades of individuals within the norm group. For example, if a test was normed with only fourth, fifth, and sixth graders, its grade equivalent scores may extend below fourth grade and above sixth grade. If the average performance of grade 6 students is a raw score of 40, a grade equivalent of 9.5 may be assigned to a raw score of 48. Such scores are obtained by extrapolation; the known scores of sixth graders within the norm group are extended to produce estimates of how students in higher grades would have performed, had they taken the test.

Age and grade equivalents are ordinal data. Although an equal-interval time scale underlies chronological age and grade in school, there is not a one-to-one correspondence between time and skill mastery. The gain in achievement in reading from grade 1.0 to grade 1.5 is much greater than the gain from grade 10.0 to grade 10.5; the intervals do not represent equal units of measurement (Maloney & Larrivee, 2007).

The deceptive simplicity of age and grade equivalents leads to their misinterpretation. Thus, professionals should select norm-referenced measures that offer other types of derived scores, either in addition to or instead of age and grade equivalents. Miller, Linn, and Gronlund (2009) report misconceptions in using grade equivalents. Misconceptions include age equivalents used as grade placements, units treated as equal across a score range, comparison of grade equivalents across tests and use of score extrapolations. Maloney and Larrivee (2007) add that age equivalents are imprecise for individuals who score high or low raw scores.

Percentile Ranks

Another type of derived score is the **percentile rank**. The percentile rank for a particular raw score indicates the percentage of individuals within the norm group who achieved this raw score or a lower one. If a raw score of 40 corresponds to a percentile rank of 62, this means that 62 percent of the norm group earned raw scores of 40 or less. A student whose raw score converts to the 62nd percentile can be said to perform at a level equal to or greater than that of 62 percent of the norm group and at a level lower than that of the remaining 38 percent of the norm group. It is important to note that the difference in the middle of the curve could be less than the difference at the ends of the normal curve (Venn, 2014).

Usually, tests provide separate tables of percentile rank norms for different age or grade levels. One table may list norms for students age 6–0 to 6–11, another for students age 7–0 to 7–11, and so forth. This allows more precise descriptions of student performance. For example, it may be possible to say that a 12-year-old performed at the 75th percentile when compared with age 12 students in the norm group.

Percentile ranks are relatively easy to understand as long as they are not confused with percentages. A percentile rank refers to a percentage of persons; percentage correct refers to a percentage of test items. A student may answer only 50 percent of the items on a test correctly but perform at the 99th percentile for his or her age. Percentile rank data indicate relative position within the norm group (Salvia & Ysseldyke, 2007).

Standard Scores

Standard scores are available on many norm-referenced measures. These derived scores transform raw scores to a new scale with a set mean and standard deviation. Standard scores are useful for comparing the performance of the same individual on two different measures, as long as the raw score distributions of the measures are similar. They also provide a standard scale for reporting norms for various age or grade groups within the total standardization sample.

Standard score distributions can be constructed using any mean or standard deviation; the values are arbitrary. The z score is one type of standard score, and its distribution has a mean of 0 and a standard deviation of 1. Many norm-referenced tests set the mean of the standard score distribution at 100 and the standard deviation at 15. On these tests, if a student's raw score converts to a standard score of 100, the student

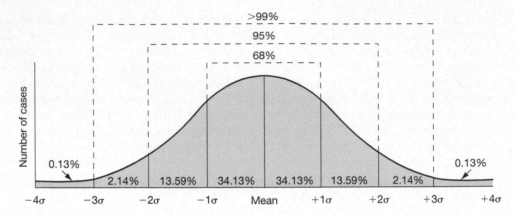

FIGURE 4–1
Normal Distribution
Source: Building the Legacy US Department of Education.

performed at the mean. A standard score of 115 indicates performance one standard deviation above the mean, and a standard score of 85 indicates performance one standard deviation below the mean.

The values selected for the mean and standard deviation of standard score distributions vary from measure to measure and sometimes among different parts of the same measure. For example, measures that provide two sets of standard scores—one for overall test performance and the other for performance on individual subtests—may use two separate score distributions to differentiate the scores. An example is the *Stanford-Binet Intelligence Scales, Fifth Edition* (Roid, 2003). Its total test scores, called IQ scores, have a mean of 100 and a standard deviation of 15. In contrast, the standard scores for the individual subtests have a mean of 10 and a standard deviation of 3. The term *scaled score* is frequently used to refer to subtest standard scores.

Separate standard score norms may be provided by age or grade. However, whatever the distribution for a particular standard score, the same scale is used for all students taking the test. A standard score mean of 100 is used to indicate average performance, whatever the student's age or grade. Thus, a 6-year-old would earn a standard score of 100 if his or her raw score equaled the mean of the 6-year-old segment of the norm group, and a 12-year-old would earn a standard score of 100 if his or her raw score equaled the mean of the 12-year-old segment of the norm group.

Comparison of standard scores from one test to another makes sense only if the raw score distributions of the two measures are similar. One way to ensure similarity is to select measures with raw score distributions that are normal or have been normalized by the test producer. As Figure 4–1 shows, most scores in a normal distribution are found in the middle and fewer at the extremes. When a distribution is normal, it is possible to determine the exact percentage of cases that fall within any portion of the curve. The majority of cases fall in the center portion; 68 percent of the scores of a normally distributed measure occur in the range from one standard deviation below the mean to one standard deviation above—that is, from −1 to +1 standard deviations. Approximately 14 percent of the scores fall between −1 and −2 standard deviations, with the same percentage found between +1 and +2 standard deviations; thus, the range from −2 to +2 standard deviations includes approximately 95 percent of the cases. When the range is extended to include from −3 to +3 standard deviations, it accounts for more than 99 percent of the cases.

Standard scores based on normal distributions have special characteristics. They allow a student's performance to be related to the mean and standard deviation of the norm group, and they can be directly converted into percentile ranks. Figure 4–2 presents this relationship. If a student scores one standard deviation above the mean on a measure that is normally distributed, the

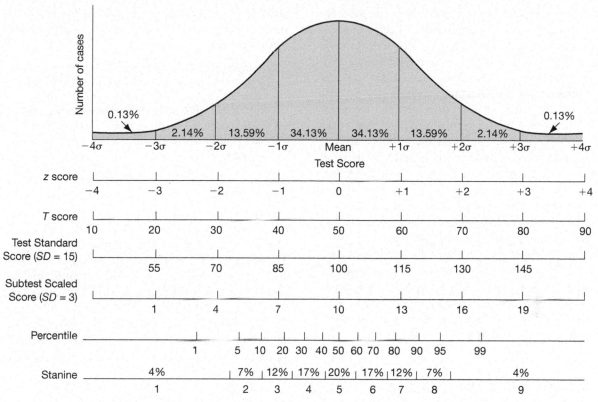

FIGURE 4–2
Relationships Among Different Types of Scores in a Normal Distribution

percentile rank of that score is 84. A score equal to the mean earns a percentile rank of 50, and if a score lies one standard deviation below the mean, its percentile rank is 16. Thus, test performance can be described in relation to the mean and to a percentage of the norm group. With a measure in which the mean is 100, the standard deviation is 15, and scores are normally distributed, a standard score of 70 indicates performance that is (1) two standard deviations below the mean of the norm group and (2) equal to or greater than the performance of 2 percent of the norm group. Because they provide these two types of information, normalized standard scores are particularly useful in the interpretation of norm-referenced test results.

Another type of standard score that is often available is the **normal curve equivalent (NCE)**. NCE scores are normalized standard scores that were developed to assist in the analysis of student progress in federally sponsored educational

programs. The NCE distribution is divided into 99 equal units, with a mean of 50 and a standard deviation of 21.06. Rudner and Schater (2002) recommend that NCE scores be used to report results for groups of students. Among the advantages of NCE scores that these authors identify are that they allow you to:

- compare the performance of students who take different levels or forms of the same test within a test battery.
- evaluate gains over time.
- combine data from different tests.
- compute meaningful summary statistics. (p. 42)

Stanines

Stanines are another type of derived score. The stanine distribution is divided into nine segments, or standard nines, each of which is .5 standard deviation in width. Figure 4–2 illustrates the relationship among stanines, percentile ranks, and other standard scores. It also lists the percentage of cases expected to fall within each stanine if raw scores are normally distributed. Because stanines represent a range of performance rather than a specific score, the data they provide are less precise than those from standard scores.

It is apparent that norm-referenced measures offer a variety of different scores, and the types available from a particular measure should be considered as part of the selection process. In general, if the purpose of assessment is to compare a student's performance to that of a norm group, the most informative type of score is the normalized standard score. However, the same information can be obtained from a measure that is not normally distributed if it provides both standard scores and percentile ranks. Whenever possible, tests that offer only age or grade equivalents should be avoided. If age or grade scores are used, either percentile ranks or standard scores, or both, should accompany them.

PROMOTING NONBIASED ASSESSMENT

The potential for bias is not limited to the selection, administration, and interpretation of assessment devices (Gravois & Rosenfield, 2006; Oakland, 1980; Winzer & Mazurek, 1998). Bias can enter at any point in the special education process: prior to assessment in referral, screening, and the selection of assessment tools; during assessment in the utilization of data collection strategies and in relation to student and examiner characteristics; and after assessment in placement, program planning, and reevaluation. Nevertheless, a major concern in preventing bias is the selection of appropriate assessment tools.

Issues in Assessment of Culturally and Linguistically Diverse Students

Major challenge facing the field of special education is the appropriate use of standardized tests with students from diverse ethnic, cultural, and linguistic groups. Research indicates that students who are culturally and/or linguistically diverse are most acutely affected by these large-scale assessments (Horn, 2003). Laosa (1977) summarizes one major objection to standardized testing for these students:

> Standardized tests are biased and unfair to persons from cultural and sociocultural minorities since most tests reflect largely white, middle-class values and attitudes and they do not reflect the experiences and the linguistic, cognitive, and other cultural styles and values of minority group persons. (p. 10)

This is a validity concern. With students who do not speak English, it is obvious that an achievement test written in English is an invalid measure of academic performance. Sotelo-Dynega et al. (2013) report that when higher levels of cultural knowledge and the English language are necessary, it may be discriminatory because of the required values or beliefs related to answering test questions appropriately.

The problems associated with assessment of diverse students have stimulated a number of proposed solutions, although no solution has escaped criticism.

Translation of Measures into Languages Other Than English

For assessment of students whose primary language is not English, it is recommended that tests and test directions be translated into the student's home language. Many of the standardized tests commonly used in special education assessment have been translated into Spanish. Several approaches have been used, including backward translation (i.e., translating from English into Spanish and then back again into English to discover significant discrepancies).

However, translating a measure from one language to another does not eliminate the possibility of bias. The translation must preserve not only the literal and cultural meanings of the original, but also the difficulty level of each test item. For example, translation of the gender of a language, word order, developmental levels of vocabulary, and words often not having direct translations can influence students' performance on tests. Translations often deal with surface issues and fail to look at these deeper variables (Abedi, Hofstetter, & Lord, 2004). The measure must also be renormed with an appropriate standardization sample. If a Spanish-language version of a test is intended for use in the United States, norming it with a sample of students from Mexico City is likely inappropriate. A related concern is regional differences. The Spanish spoken by students in Los Angeles may vary from that spoken by students in New York or Miami.

Use of Interpreters

Another strategy for assessing students who speak languages other than English is the use of interpreters. The professional conducting the assessment can act as an interpreter, or another professional or member of the community could be asked to assist. This practice is not recommended. Every effort should be made to contract a bilingual evaluator (Artiles, Ortiz, & Alba, 2002). Spontaneous translations of test instructions and items are likely to include inaccuracies, and, like any departure from the test's standardization conditions, they make the use of test norms impossible. Friends or family members may give away answers to help students. In addition, when family members are used to interpret, their task may upset family dynamics. Furthermore, when members from the community are utilized, confidentiality issues may be present (Cheng & Hammer, 1992). Nonetheless, tests and other assessment tools are not available in all languages, and it is sometimes necessary to rely on interpreters.

Culture-Fair Tests

One method proposed to combat cultural bias is the development of culture-free and culture-fair measures. These measures attempt to minimize factors that may depress the performance of diverse students such as high verbal demands, timed tasks, and emphasis on school learning. One of the first efforts to produce such measures was Cattell's *Culture Fair Intelligence Tests* (Cattell, 1950; Cattell & Cattell, 1960, 1963, 1977). The *Leiter International Performance Scale-3* (Roid & Miller, 2013) and other nonverbal measures of intelligence may also be culture-fair tests.

Results of attempts to produce culture-fair tests have been disappointing (Winzer & Mazurek,

1998). For example, the Culture Fair Intelligence Tests are not often used because they are generally not free from bias (Tucker, 2009). In fact, culture-fair measures may be just as discriminatory as the culturally biased verbal tests they were designed to replace. Even nonverbal measures require some degree of verbal mediation as the student thinks about the test questions and how to respond. According to Gonzales (1982), a culturally fair measure must meet the following criteria:

1. The same predictions can be made from the results across cultures or given populations.
2. Language and reading are kept to a minimum.
3. Adequate representation of the target population is in the norming.
4. Subjects should not be penalized by time factors.
5. Target populations must have the opportunity to learn the material.
6. Item content must be familiar to all groups. (p. 385)

Culture-Specific Measures

Another strategy is the development of measures that relate directly to specific cultures. An early example is the *Black Intelligence Test of Cultural Homogeneity* (Williams, 1972). This 100-item, multiple-choice test was designed to assess knowledge of the black experience and culture (Samuda, 1975). Although culture-specific measures can promote understanding of diverse cultures, they may not solve bias problems. Culture-specific measures are often not transportable from one region of the country to another. In addition, their predictive validity may be less than adequate (Duffey, Salvia, Tucker, & Ysseldyke, 1982).

Separate Norms

An alternative to culture-specific measures is the construction of separate norms for diverse students and dominant culture students. Students would be compared to members of their own community to indicate whether a disability is present (Manly, 2005). However, this practice would further encourage separation of these two groups (Alley & Foster, 1978). Gonzales (1982) recommends that separate local norms be established for diverse students only when their cultural and linguistic characteristics are significantly different from those of the dominant culture, as with some groups of Native American students. Valenzuela and Cervantes (1998) do not agree with using local norms when labeling and placement result in that process.

Modification/Accommodations of Test Administration Procedures

Accommodations are noted within No Child Left Behind. Furthermore, although IDEA and Section 504 of the Americans with Disabilities Act also allow for assessment accommodations, sometimes they are not used (Gagnon & McLaughlin, 2004). Test administration procedures can be altered in an attempt to improve student performance. For example, students could be allowed unlimited time or more frequent breaks to perform tasks that usually have strict time limits (Abedi et al., 2004).

When administration procedures are altered, however, norm-referenced tests become informal procedures. Such modifications prevent the use of the test's norms and invalidate the comparative power of standardized tests. It may be useful to administer a test under standard conditions and then repeat administration with modified procedures.

A related strategy is to train students in test-taking skills (Duffey et al., 1982). If students are unfamiliar with testing procedures or certain assessment tasks, lack of preparation may hinder their performance. For example, many group tests require students to write responses on separate answer sheets. Preparing students by providing practice activities may help make them less anxious about testing and increase their ability to cope with test tasks.

Dynamic Assessment

In this approach, originally described by Feuerstein and his colleagues (1979), tests are administered using a test–teach–retest format. The examiner presents a test task, observes the student interacting with the task, and then coaches the student in an attempt to improve performance. The purpose is study of the student's learning ability or "latent capacity" in the words of Sternberg and Grigorenko (2002), not his or her current intellectual performance. Feuerstein's measure, the *Learning Potential Assessment Device,* is described in Chapter 7. Like other approaches in which standard administration procedures are modified, results must be considered informal because test norms cannot be used. However, as Winzer and Mazurek (1998) point out, because the methods used have yielded positive instructional results, those suggestions may be useful. Pena (2001) notes that dynamic assessment takes into consideration not only the individual's skills, but also his or her learning potential. Fuchs et al. (2011) used dynamic assessment to forecast student response to teaching methods in screening third-grade mathematics performance.

Replacement of Standardized Tests with Informal Procedures

A more controversial proposal is to replace standardized measures with informal procedures such as criterion-referenced tests. Criterion-referenced tests evaluate a student's performance without reference to the performance of other students. Furthermore, criterion-referenced tests provide direction for instruction based on the individual student's needs. Rhodes, Ochoa, and Ortiz (2005) suggested using informal measures to support results from formal measures.

The fact that an assessment tool is informal, however, does not mean that it is nondiscriminatory. Criterion-referenced tests and other informal tools can be subjective (Laosa, 1977), and their results can be interpreted in a biased manner. In addition, replacement of standardized testing with informal assessment would be expensive in terms of time, personnel, and resources (Duffey et al., 1982).

Guidelines for the Selection of Nondiscriminatory Assessment Tools

By law, assessment devices and procedures must be nondiscriminatory. One difficulty in implementing this requirement is the lack of agreement about what constitutes nondiscriminatory assessment. Alley and Foster (1978) describe nondiscriminatory measures as revealing comparable assessment performance among cultural groups. Under this definition, all groups would need to perform equally well on a measure, with similar means and similar variability. However, the relative performance of groups is only one criterion (Lambert, 1981). Other concerns are the instrument's predictive validity, factor-analytic structure, and variance in item scores.

Another major impediment to nondiscriminatory assessment is the scarcity of appropriate assessment tools for diverse populations. There is little agreement about which norm-referenced tests are nondiscriminatory; few measures are available in languages other than English, and most of these are in Spanish.

The potential for bias can be minimized, however, if assessment tools are carefully evaluated and selected. With norm-referenced measures, it is important to determine if the norm group is representative of the race, culture, and gender of the student. It is also necessary to consider how many of the individuals in the norm group have characteristics similar to those of the student (Luckner, Sebald, Cooney, Young, & Muir, 2006). Although a norm group may accurately represent the general population by including the proper proportion of individuals from diverse groups, the total number of such individuals may be very small. Some tests avoid this difficulty by using several norm groups of approximately equal size; separate norms are offered by gender, ethnic group, or some other population variable.

Another step in evaluation is the review of test items for cultural bias. If items demand an experiential background inconsistent with that of the student, the student will probably perform poorly. There are many examples of test items that illustrate cultural bias (Popham, 2012). Williams (1974), as cited by Alley and Foster (1978), suggests that culture influences how a person responds to the test question "When is Washington's birthday?" If the person thinks of George Washington, the answer is February 22; if he or she thinks of Booker T., the answer is April 5.

Because norm-referenced tests have been the most criticized, they are associated with the issue of nonbiased assessment. Professionals today are aware of the ways these tests can be misused, so they attempt to select nondiscriminatory measures (Rudner & Shafer, 2002). However, other types of assessment tools can also be biased. The informal nature of an instrument or strategy is no guarantee that it is nondiscriminatory. For example, Bailey and Harbin (1980) report that wording or content bias could be found in criterion-referenced measures.

Identifying appropriate assessment tools for students whose communication mode is not English poses special problems. Difficulties do not arise if the student speaks only one language, if technically adequate tools are available in that language, and if a professional who is fluent in the language has the assessment expertise necessary for the use of these tools. Unfortunately, this is seldom the case.

A final consideration is the disability of the student. Unless the purpose of assessment is exploration of that disability, the tools for assessment should minimize its effects. If a student's academic disability is in the skill area of reading, measures in which the tester presents questions orally or through demonstration are most appropriate. Other characteristics sometimes associated with disabilities are short attention span, impulsivity, poor self-concept, and expectation for failure. These factors should be considered in selecting assessment procedures.

The evaluation guide in Figure 4–3 can be used to review and critique norm-referenced tests and other assessment tools. It summarizes the important factors in selecting measures that produce nonbiased, accurate, and useful results.

ENHANCEDetext
Video Example 4.3
Watch this video to learn more about nonbiased assessment practices.
https://www.youtube.com/watch?v=F7ZVlltjM8s

Guide for the Evaluation of Assessment Tools

Name of measure _____

Author(s) _____ Date _____

Publisher _____ Cost _____

DESCRIPTION OF THE MEASURE
1. Purpose(s) of the measure, as stated in the manual
2. Type of measure (e.g., norm-referenced test, inventory, checklist)
3. Content area(s) assessed (description of each area and, if applicable, a list of subtests)
4. Student requirements
    a. Language
    b. Presentation mode
    c. Response mode
    d. Group or individual administration
    e. Time factors
5. Tester requirements
    a. Necessary training
    b. Administration time and other time requirements
    c. Ease of use
6. Test norms or other standards
    a. Type of reference (e.g., norm group or curricular goals)
    b. If applicable, characteristics of norm group
        (1) Age, grade, gender
        (2) Method of selection
        (3) Representativeness
        (4) Size
        (5) Recency of norms
    c. If applicable, description of curricular standards
        (1) Content domain
        (2) Representativeness of item pool
        (3) Completeness of item pool
        (4) Appropriateness of tasks
7. Reliability
    a. Test-retest reliability
    b. Equivalent-form reliability
    c. Internal consistency
    d. Scorer reliability
8. Validity
    a. Content validity
    b. Criterion-related validity (predictive and/or concurrent)
    c. Construct validity
9. Results
    a. Types of scores or other results
    b. Standard error of measurement
10. Other comments

CONSIDERATION IN NONBIASED ASSESSMENT
1. Is the norm group or other standard of comparison appropriate for the student in terms of race, ethnicity, culture, and gender?
2. Are test items free from cultural bias?
3. Is the language of the measure appropriate for the student?
4. Does the measure bypass the limitations imposed by the disability?

CONCLUSIONS
1. Does the tool fit the purpose of assessment?
2. Is the tool appropriate for the student?
3. Is the tool appropriate for the tester?
4. Is the tool technically adequate?
5. Is the tool an efficient data-collection mechanism?

FIGURE 4–3
Guide for the Evaluation of Assessment Tools

Assessment in Action
Akis

Akis is a student currently enrolled in a public school kindergarten class. His teacher, Mr. Chang, has concerns regarding his performance in class. Akis is barely keeping up with the other students. His difficulties include using phonics skills, following directions, and being unkind to fellow students. Furthermore, he performed marginally on his state assessment test in the areas of language and cognition. His school district is known for doing very well on standardized tests (it is rewarded financially for good results).

Akis was born in the United States. He is of Greek descent, and he and his parents appear to speak English fluently. Akis attended preschool for a couple of years before starting kindergarten. His mother reports developmental milestones well within normal limits. She also reports that he learned to speak English a year and a half prior to entering kindergarten. He is simultaneously learning literacy skills in Greek and English at home and at Greek school. He speaks and hears English 50 percent of the time and Greek 50 percent of the time. The family notes that his strengths are in language and gross motor skills and that his areas of need are social and emotional. He has had several ear infections each year. Overall, they report that he appears to be within normal limits.

SUMMARY

As you reflect on the impact that practice and application have on learning, consider the following main points:

- In order to best select assessment tools, it is important to provide examples of core criteria. For example, you should find answers to important educational questions, indicate identification and placement, instructional planning, or monitoring of student progress and program effectiveness, and consider legal and professional guidelines influence selection criteria.

- You should specify major concepts in evaluating measurement types, including tools that fit the purpose of assessment and are appropriate for the student to be studied. The tools used should be both technically adequate and efficient methods of data collection. Technical quality includes consideration of the suitability of the reference group with which the student is to be compared and the psychometric characteristics of the instrument, such as reliability, validity, and measurement error.

- When you evaluate reliability, you should indicate the reliability types considered. Some examples include, test–retest reliability, equivalent-forms reliability, split-half reliability, and interscorer reliability. Ways to evaluate validity include criterion-related validity, predictive validity, concurrent validity, and construct validity.

- Because different types of test scores and other assessment results will be used in the evaluation of students, you must be able to provide examples, such as raw score, age score, grade score, percentile rank, standard score, normal curve equivalent, and stanine.

- When you assess students, it is critical to indicate issues that are essential to avoiding bias in all stages of assessment. Issues include translation of measures, use of interpreters, culture-fair tests, culture-specific measures, separate norms, modifications/accommodations of procedures, dynamic assessment, and replacement of formal measures with informal measures.

5

Shutterstock

Standardized Tests

LEARNING OUTCOMES

After reading this chapter, you will be able to:

- Specify three major concepts that professional testers plan for in the preparation for testing.
- Indicate key aspects professionals consider while recording student answers during test administration.
- Specify examples of behavior that seasoned professionals look for while observing of test takers.
- Discuss raw and derived scores in relation to a professional scoring a test.
- Explain four considerations professionals take into account in interpreting test results.
- Specify major technology concepts professionals use in assessment.
- Provide examples of modifications used by professionals related to testing procedures.
- Provide examples of avoiding bias in testing.

KEY TERMS

tests	ceiling
rapport	chronological age
protocol	raw scores
demonstration	confidence intervals
basal	computer-assisted testing

Tests are the best-known type of assessment measures. They are part of the school experience from the early grades to the college classroom. No one passes through the educational system without taking a weekly quiz, a test at the end of a unit, or a final exam. Tests range from informal measures devised by teachers for classroom use to structured instruments known as norm-referenced standardized tests. These formal tests are also a regular feature of education, whether they are achievement tests administered at intervals throughout the grades, aptitude measures used for college admission, or individual tests used in special education.

In standardized testing, test tasks are presented under standard conditions so that the student's performance can be contrasted to the performance of a norm group. The resulting data are comparative; the student's level of functioning is described in relation to typical or average performance. This type of information is necessary in screening and in determining eligibility; the goal is selection of students whose performance is so divergent from that of others that special attention is warranted. Results also help professionals to plan instruction by identifying curriculum areas in which students fail to perform as well as their peers and, in evaluation, to document changes in performance relative to age and grade-level expectations.

Norm-referenced tests must be administered and scored in strict accordance with the standard conditions described in the test manual. If the conditions under which the test was normed are not duplicated, then the student's performance cannot be compared to the performance of the norm group. At the same time, the tester must ensure the full and active participation of the student. Because tests elicit only a sample of behavior, test performance must be an accurate representation of the student's capabilities. These concerns are as old as the history of standardized testing. As Terman and Merrill reported in 1937:

> Three requirements must be satisfied: (1) the standard procedures must be followed; (2) the child's best efforts must be enlisted by the establishment and maintenance of adequate rapport; and (3) the responses must be correctly scored. It can hardly be said that any one of the three is more important than the others, for all are absolutely essential. (p. 52)

ENHANCEDetext
Video Example 5.1
Tests are the most common form of assessment.
Watch this video to find out more about IDEA and
accommodations for students with special needs.

PREPARATION FOR TESTING

Testing does not begin immediately after an appropriate measure has been selected. The tester (i.e., the professional responsible for test administration) must first ensure that he or she is adequately prepared to administer and score the test. Then, the testing environment is readied, and the student is carefully introduced to the testing experience.

Preparation of the Tester

Most standardized tests are designed for use by trained testers—professionals who have mastered the skills of test administration and scoring. Preparation programs for professionals—such as special educators—typically include training in assessment, with supervised practice in the use of standardized measures. Anastasi and Urbina (1997) note that supervised training for administration of individual testing is critical. Furthermore, scaffold practice could take over one year, with multiple demonstrations and practice experiences.

Tests differ in the amount of training needed to guarantee valid administration. Some measures, such as individual intelligence tests, require extensive preparation; in many states, school psychologists are the only school personnel licensed to administer them. Other tests, such as the achievement tests used by special educators, presume that the tester is knowledgeable about and trained in standardized testing procedures but holds no special license or certification. For example, some manuals say that persons properly prepared by training and/or self-study can administer tests.

It is the professional responsibility of the tester to administer only those tests he or she is trained for or, after extensive study, similar tests. Measures administered by untrained testers produce highly questionable results that must be considered invalid. Incorrect administration may also render a test invalid for future use with a student if, for example, an inexperienced tester reveals the correct answers. Practice is necessary but not sufficient in learning new tests; the tester must receive feedback on the accuracy of his or her performance. No new test should be considered learned until a qualified professional has checked the tester's administration and scoring skills; it is too easy to make mistakes and allow them to become habits.

In addition, the evaluator must select the most appropriate assessment for the purposes desired. Matching the decisions to be made, the student characteristics, and the content of the assessment are all important parts of this decision.

Preparation of the Testing Environment

The testing environment consists of the room where the test is administered, the seating arrangements, the testing equipment, and the participants. This environment can influence test performance. Think, for example, of trying to concentrate on an important examination in a stifling hot or noisy room. The tester should make every effort to create a comfortable testing environment.

The testing room should be just large enough to accommodate the testing procedures. Unless gross motor tasks such as running are part of the test, an office-sized room provides sufficient space. Large rooms such as classrooms are not recommended because they often contain distractions. The room's lighting, temperature, and ventilation should be adequate. Light from windows should not shine in the eyes of either tester or student. Nonglare lighting is best, particularly when test materials are printed on shiny pages. Test administration should not be attempted in rooms with inadequate lighting, extremes of temperature, or poor ventilation.

The testing room should be in a quiet location, away from the playground, gymnasium, cafeteria, and music room. A constant noise source, such as an air conditioner, is permissible as long as it does not interfere with communication between the tester and student. The room should be free of visual distractions such as colorful bulletin boards, posters, and other attention-drawing stimuli; windows with interesting views should be curtained or masked. The goal is to make the test the most interesting aspect of the room.

The room should be secured so that people cannot walk in and interrupt. The tester can post a notice on the door stating that testing is in progress; persons who use the room can be informed that it will be occupied. Despite these precautions, interruptions such as a fire drill or other emergency may occur.

It is often impossible to find an ideal testing room, particularly with the time and space constraints in most public schools. Fortunately, valid tests can be given in less than ideal conditions as long as the tester is sensitive to the student's behavior. The student is observed carefully, and if noises or other environmental factors appear to interfere with concentration, testing is immediately discontinued. The testing environment checklist in Figure 5–1 can assist the tester in evaluating the adequacy of the room and other important factors.

Testing should not be attempted if seating arrangements are inadequate: if the student or tester must stand, if chairs are so low or high as to affect vision, if no work surface is available, or if the work surface is very small or not level. Ideal seats are comfortable, straight-backed chairs. Chairs should be of correct size, so that the student's feet comfortably touch the floor; chairs should not swivel. Chairs with attached desks or work surfaces are unsuitable. They offer too little space for test materials, do not allow the tester to sit close to the student, and, if slanted, permit test materials to slide onto the floor.

A table is the most appropriate work surface. The tester and student should be able to sit and write comfortably at the table. Rectangular or square tables are preferred; the surface should be large enough to hold necessary materials, yet narrow enough for the tester to reach across to the student's side. Many standardized tests are designed so that the tester can sit across the table from the student; this arrangement facilitates the observation of student behavior and discourages the student from attempting to view the test manual and score sheet. Other tests require that students sit across the corner of the table from the tester.

The tester should gather all materials needed for administration (the examiner's manual, pencils and paper, and so forth) and place these in the testing room before the start of the test. If the tester discovers a vital piece of equipment missing once administration has begun, testing should be discontinued at a logical breaking point (such as between subtests) and the missing item obtained.

Most tests include stimulus material to be shown to the student, an examiner's manual for the tester, and score sheets or student record booklets. Other equipment may be furnished as part of the test kit, or the tester may need to obtain materials from the classroom. Generally, testers provide writing implements for themselves and the student. Several sharpened pencils of the size and type used by the student in the classroom should be available; these may have erasers if not prohibited by the test manual. The tester will also need several pencils with erasers. Some tests require precise timing of student responses. If timing must be accurate to the second, appropriate devices include a stopwatch, digital with output in seconds, or a clock or watch with a second hand; if minutes must be timed, a wristwatch or clock will suffice. Timing devices should be silent so they do not distract the student.

When the materials are arranged, the test kit is placed near the tester on either the floor or a separate chair. Materials are then transferred to the table as needed. All distracting materials

Testing Environment Checklist

The Room	Optimal	Adequate	Poor
Size	☐	☐	☐
Lighting	☐	☐	☐
Temperature/ventilation	☐	☐	☐
Noise level	☐	☐	☐
Freedom from distractions	☐	☐	☐
Freedom from interruptions	☐	☐	☐

Seating	Optimal	Adequate	Poor
Chairs	☐	☐	☐
Table	☐	☐	☐
Arrangement	☐	☐	☐

Equipment	Available	Not Applicable	Not Available
Test materials	☐	☐	☐
Writing implements	☐	☐	☐
Timing device	☐	☐	☐

	Optimal	Adequate	Poor
Arrangement	☐	☐	☐

Participants	Present
Student	☐
Tester	☐
Other(s)	☐

Explain: _____

Summary
☐ The testing environment was adequate for administration of a valid test.
☐ The testing environment was not adequate for administration of a valid test because
_____
_____

FIGURE 5–1
Testing Environment Checklist

should be removed from the student's view and reach. No extraneous items—such as books or toys—should clutter the table.

There should be no one in the testing room but the tester and the student. However, a parent may need to accompany a young child into the room to help acclimate the child to the new environment. Parents or others should leave the room before test administration begins; observation is best done through a one-way glass, if available. If, for some reason, parents must remain, they should be observers out of the child's view, not participants. Unless specifically allowed by the test manual, parents or others should not administer test items.

Preparation of the Student

Scheduling the test at an optimal time, seeing to the student's physical needs, and preparing the student psychologically are critical components in testing. If these factors are neglected by an insensitive tester, the student's attitude may be affected, and it may become impossible to elicit optimal performance.

Schools are busy places. Schedules for classes, lunch, buses, and special events such as assemblies must be considered when setting up a time and place for testing. Usually, the tester coordinates scheduling with the classroom teacher. Most teachers, concerned about schoolwork missed during testing, prefer that the student leave the classroom during his or her best subject or during the subjects with which he or she experiences difficulty.

Students' preferences must also be considered. Test performance will likely be affected if students are removed from the classroom during a favorite activity; their attention may be on recess, art, or whatever they are missing rather than on the testing situation. Many students work more efficiently at certain times of the day, such as the early morning or midafternoon. The classroom teacher should be consulted to determine when the student is most alert, and, if possible, the test should be scheduled for that time.

Because tests are usually scheduled well in advance, the tester must check the student's physical and emotional status on the day of the test. If the student is ill, the test should be postponed. A toothache, cold, or other physical ailment can depress performance; pain may distract the student, a cold could impair hearing, and even an over-the-counter medication can interfere with normal functioning. Emotional well-being also affects test performance. If the student is upset (e.g., by the illness of a family member or the death of a pet), testing should be delayed. If the tester learns after testing that the student was under physical or mental stress, test results should be considered invalid or, at a minimum, they should be interpreted with great caution.

Before beginning the test, the tester should attend to the students' physical needs. Students are best able to focus attention on test tasks if they are not distracted by pressing physiological needs, such as hunger and thirst. Students should visit the drinking fountain and restroom before the test and during breaks. Some students, particularly younger children, will not ask to go to the restroom, even when they are in dire need of a toilet break. In addition, the tester must make sure that students are wearing eyeglasses, hearing aids, or other required prosthetic devices. If the student is receiving medication, the tester should find out if it has been administered that day and, if so, the medication's possible effects on test performance.

Preparing a student psychologically for testing is called *establishing* **rapport**. This procedure involves a good working relationship between the examiner and the test taker. The test taker should feel comfortable with and interested in responding to the tasks of the test. To establish good rapport, the tester should follow these steps:

1. *Introduction of the tester to the student.* The introduction should be friendly and unhurried and should convey the tester's pleasure at meeting the student. The tester gives his or her name and some indication of profession. For example, the tester might say, "My name is Ms. Geller, and I'm a teacher who visits this school twice a week."

2. *Elicitation of general information from the student.* The tester engages the student in conversation by asking for his or her full name, age, grade, and favorite school subjects. This allows the student a chance to relax and provides the tester with some indication of the student's manner of expression and knowledge of personal information.

3. *Explanation of the purpose of testing.* The meeting should be presented as an occasion for work ("We're going to do some work together") rather than play ("Today, we're going to play some games"). If students believe the test is merely a game, they may not put forth their best effort. However, the word "test" should be avoided because students may associate testing with past failures.

4. *Description of test activities.* The tester should explain exactly what will happen during the test situation. This will prepare the student and may relieve some anxiety. Some tests provide instructions describing test activities for the tester to read to the student. Table 5–1 explains important points to cover during pretest preparation.

5. *Encouragement of student questions.* Students should be provided the opportunity to ask questions about the test. The tester determines if the student understands what will occur and also gauges the student's readiness to begin. Discussion continues until the student becomes comfortable, or, if the student is obviously upset and ill at ease, testing is postponed.

TABLE 5–1
Pretest Information for Students

Before test administration begins, each of the following factors should be explained by the tester in language appropriate to the student's age and ability level.

Length of the Test
Tell the student approximately how long the test will take either in terms of hours and minutes or classroom activities ("You'll be back in Ms. Lloyd's room before lunchtime").

Test Activities
Briefly describe the types of activities involved: listening, looking at pictures, talking, reading, writing, doing math, and so forth. If several different activities are required, let the student know that test tasks will change.

Test Difficulty
If appropriate, inform the student that there will be both easy and difficult items. Let the student know that he or she is not expected to answer every question correctly because some were designed for older age groups.

Confirmation of Responses
Advise the student that he or she will not be told if answers are right or wrong. The tester cannot give information about response accuracy.

Timed Tests
If parts of the test are timed, tell the student so he or she will know that speed is important. If a stopwatch will be used for timing, show it to the student and demonstrate its use.

TEST ADMINISTRATION

The goal in administration of standardized tests is to obtain the best possible sample of student behavior under standard conditions. Strict adherence to the test manual's guidelines for administration and scoring is an absolute necessity. The manual usually provides instructions and test items to be read to the student. These words often appear in color or bold print and must be read verbatim. The tester may tell the student that he or she must "read some directions." The tester should not attempt to recite information from memory, and test items and directions may not be paraphrased, unless specifically allowed by the manual. However, they should be read in a natural tone of voice. The test manual also specifies the order of administration if there are several parts or subtests within the test. Often, the subtests must be given in a set order that the tester may not vary. The manual informs the tester if it is permissible to delete some subtests and, if so, which ones.

Testing requires strict conformance to administration rules, together with the establishment of a dynamic working relationship between student and tester. Achieving this balance is particularly difficult for educators because of the differences between testing and teaching. The teacher automatically praises, prompts, and provides information; the tester can do none of these and yet must maintain an atmosphere of encouragement to promote the student's best efforts. As early as 1905, Binet and Simon observed that inexperienced examiners could affect the validity of test reports. Examples of examiner behaviors that could negatively impact test results include assisting the test taker and talking too much (Kessen, 1965).

Because each test is different, it is always necessary to refer to the manual for specific administration rules. However, standardized measures have many commonalities, making it possible to provide a set of general guidelines, as shown in Table 5–2.

Recording Student Responses

The tester is often responsible for keeping a record of student responses. As the student replies to each question, the tester writes down the answer on the score sheet or record booklet. Once the test record form has been filled in, it is known as the test **protocol**. The protocol serves as the minutes

TABLE 5–2
General Guidelines for Test Administration

Test administration is a skill, and testers must learn how to react to typical student comments and questions. The following general guidelines apply to the majority of standardized tests.

Student Requests for Repetition of Test Items
Students often ask the tester to repeat a question. This is usually permissible as long as the item is repeated verbatim and in its entirety. However, repetition of memory items that measure the student's ability to recall information is not allowed.

Asking Students to Repeat Responses
Sometimes the tester must ask the student to repeat a response. Perhaps the tester did not hear what the student said, or the student's speech is difficult to understand. However, the tester should make every effort to see or hear the student's first answer. The student may refuse to repeat a response or, thinking that the request for repetition means the first response was unsatisfactory, answer differently.

Student Modification of Responses
When students give one response, then change their minds and give a different one, the tester should accept the last response, even if the modification comes after the tester has moved to another item. However, some tests specify that only the first response may be accepted for scoring.

Confirming and Correcting Student Responses
The tester may not in any way—verbal or nonverbal—inform a student whether a response is correct. Correct responses may not be confirmed; wrong responses may not be corrected. This rule is critical for professionals who both teach and test, because their first inclination is to reinforce correct answers.

Reinforcing Student Work Behavior
Although testers cannot praise students for their performance on specific test items, good work behavior can and should be rewarded. Appropriate comments are, "You're working hard" and "I like the way you're trying to answer every question." Students should be praised between test items or subtests to ensure that reinforcement is not linked to specific responses.

Encouraging Students to Respond
When students fail to respond to a test item, the tester can encourage them to give an answer. Students sometimes say nothing when presented with a difficult item, or they may comment, "I don't know" or "I can't do that one." The tester should repeat the item and say, "Give it a try" or "You can take a guess." The aim is to encourage the student to attempt all test items.

Questioning Students
Questioning is permitted on many tests. If, in the judgment of the tester, the response given by the student is neither correct nor incorrect, the tester repeats the student's answer in a questioning tone and says, "Tell me more about that." This prompts the student to explain so that the response can be scored. However, clearly wrong answers should not be questioned.

Coaching
Coaching differs from encouragement and questioning in that it helps a student arrive at an answer. The tester must *never* coach the student. Coaching invalidates the student's response; test norms are based on the assumption that students will respond without examiner assistance. Testers must be very careful to avoid coaching.

Administration of Timed Items
Some tests include timed items; the student must reply within a certain period to receive credit. In general, the time period begins when the tester finishes presentation of the item. A watch or clock should be used to time student performance.

of the testing situation. Because this record is used to evaluate and score the student's responses, it must be both accurate and complete. Recording student responses takes skill, and several rules should be followed.

Concealment of the Test Protocol

The test protocol is hidden from student view. Students should not be allowed to look at it unless, of course, it is necessary for test administration. A protocol may contain correct answers to the questions, and should students see them, test results would be invalidated. The protocol also contains the tester's record and evaluation of the student's responses. Seeing how answers were scored would provide students information about response accuracy; knowing they made several errors might upset some students and affect test performance.

Hiding the protocol may take some manipulation of test materials because the tester must manage several objects at the same time (manual, protocol, stimulus materials for the student, writing implements, and perhaps a stopwatch). The method used to conceal the protocol depends on the specific materials involved and the tester's preference. Some testers place the protocol behind a propped-up test manual; others keep it on a clipboard that rests on the edge of the table. Each tester should find his or her most comfortable method.

Verbatim Recording of Student Responses

The tester keeps an exact record of student responses for scoring purposes and for help in interpreting results. It is often of interest to examine not only which test items the student missed but also what responses he or she gave to these items. For example, knowing what types of errors a student made on a reading test may be just as valuable as knowing the score, particularly when planning instructional strategies. The specific information noted by the tester in verbatim recording depends on the nature of the test task. The tester may make a prose record of student comments or simply write the number of the picture selected by the student from four options. The conventional notation for recording

an "I don't know" response is *DK*, and that for indicating the student did not answer, *NR* (no response).

Accurate Scoring During Administration

Some tests require that the tester make an on-the-spot decision as to whether the student's response is correct. Each response must be carefully but quickly evaluated; otherwise, the student will lose interest. The response is scored and then recorded. Recording systems vary across measures. On some tests, correct responses are denoted by a 1 and incorrect responses by a 0; on others, + indicates a correct answer and − an incorrect answer. Testers must observe the recording conventions of the particular test so that other professionals can interpret the protocol. If a different system is used for some reason, the tester should write a key for that system on the protocol.

Use of Recording Devices

Unless allowed by the manual, no recording equipment, such as tape recorders or video cameras, should be introduced into the testing environment. Many novice testers tape-record a session and then later review the tape to check their scoring of student responses or even to enter student responses on the protocol. This is a bad practice for several reasons. Mechanical devices are typically not part of the standard conditions for test administration, and recording equipment may distract the student. Even if recording is unobtrusive, tapes should not be trusted as the sole source of results. Breakdowns do occur; and if a tape were to fail, the only recourse would be readministration of the test. Although taping practice sessions can assist in learning a new test, testers should acquire the skills of recording student responses during test administration. Few practicing professionals have the leisure to review tapes of each testing session.

Administering Test Items

Before beginning the test, the tester and student should complete the identification section of the test form. Most forms provide space for the name of the student, the tester's name, the date of testing, and pertinent student data, such as age, gender, grade, and teacher. If appropriate, the student can fill in a portion of the form. Recording this information is a necessary step in testing; a form with only the student's first name is virtually useless. At minimum, a protocol should contain the student's full name, the date of testing, and the tester's name.

Some tests are designed so that each item is administered to each student; students begin with the first item and continue until the last is completed. More typically, standardized tests cover a wide range of difficulty, and students attempt only that portion of the test appropriate to their skill level. For example, no student could complete all items in measures for use with grades 1 through 12. Some items would likely be too easy and others too hard, and the time required for test administration would be prohibitive. Test items are arranged in order of difficulty, and whereas one student might receive items 10 to 30, another might attempt items 50 to 95.

Demonstration items may be provided for administration at the start of the test or subtest. Demonstration items are activities similar to, but usually easier than, test tasks. They acquaint students with the type of items to follow and, if necessary, allow the tester to teach the student how to perform test tasks. The rules of teaching, not testing, apply to the presentation of demonstration items. The tester can and should coach the student, reinforce correct answers, and correct wrong ones. If the tester cannot elicit correct responses to these items, testing should be discontinued. Demonstration items are never included in the student's score.

Most test manuals tell how to locate the appropriate point within the test to begin presentation of items. For some students, the very first item is the suggested starting place; for others, it would be unrealistic to begin at the easiest item. Because guidelines differ across measures, the test manual must always be consulted. For example, a test manual might recommend beginning at item 1 for children aged 5 and at item 30 for children aged 6.

After selecting a starting point, the tester presents items to the student in an attempt to locate items of appropriate difficulty. The basal,

or range of successful performance, is determined. Testing then continues to establish the ceiling, or the level at which the student is no longer successful.

The **basal** is the point in the test at which it can be assumed that the student would receive full credit for all easier items. To establish a basal, the tester administers items until the student has correctly completed some specified number of items. The student is then given credit for passing earlier, easier items, even though these were not administered. The basal allows the tester to skip items that would be too easy for the student, thereby saving time. The student, having answered several questions correctly, begins the test with a feeling of success.

Tests vary as to the number of items required to establish a basal. On some, the student must correctly answer three consecutively numbered items; for example, a basal would be established by correct responses for items 9, 10, and 11. On other measures, the student must correctly answer five or even eight consecutively numbered items for the tester to assume success on all easier items.

Determining the basal is not always easy. The tester begins administration at the suggested starting point and proceeds through the test items. If a 10-year-old is to be tested and the manual recommends beginning with item 20 for students ages 10 to 12, the tester begins with item 20. As shown in the following example, the student answers the question correctly, and the tester writes a + in the space next to the item number. The student also answers items 21 and 22 correctly. Because the basal requirement is three consecutive correct responses, a basal is established. The tester will continue administration with item 23.

BASAL: 3 consecutive correct responses

    18. _____

    19. _____

(10)20. _____+_____ *First item administered*

    21. _____+_____ *Second item administered*

    22. _____+_____ *Third item administered*

In this example, the starting point designated by the manual was appropriate for the student.

Items were not too difficult, and the student quickly achieved three consecutive correct responses. This is not always the case. Sometimes the first or second item administered to the student is answered incorrectly. When this happens, the tester has to present items out of order to establish the basal. Generally, when a student makes an error during the search for the basal, the tester immediately begins to proceed backward through the test. Table 5–3 explains this procedure.

Suggested starting points can also be too low. For example, the student may begin with item 5 and answer the next 15 questions correctly. At the start of a test, if there is an indication that items are too easy for the student, the tester may move forward to more difficult items. Testers should take care, however, not to present very difficult items before students have achieved some success. It is far worse to discourage students than to use extra administration time presenting easy items.

TABLE 5–3
Establishing the Basal

Sometimes the tester begins a test at exactly the right starting point, and the basal is easily achieved as the student correctly answers the first several questions. It is just as usual, however, for the student to miss one of the first items presented. When this occurs, the tester must present earlier, easier items.

Presume that a sixth grader was given a test in which the basal is four consecutive correct responses. The recommended starting point for sixth grade students is item 11, and the tester began there. The student answered the first item correctly but missed item 12. Here is what the protocol looked like at this point.

BASAL: 4 consecutive correct responses

8. _____

9. _____

10. _____

(6)11. _____+_____ *First item administered*

1̶2̶. _____−_____ *Second item administered*

13. _____

14. _____

The basal cannot be established without four consecutive correct responses. The tester proceeds backward until a basal of four consecutively numbered correct items is established. As shown in the following example, after the student missed item 12, the tester administered item 10, then item 9, then item 8. When the student answered these correctly, there was a basal. Testing will continue with item 13.

BASAL: 4 consecutive correct responses

8. _____+_____ *Fifth item administered*

9. _____+_____ *Fourth item administered*

10. _____+_____ *Third item administered*

(6)11. _____+_____ *First item administered*

1̶2̶. _____−_____ *Second item administered; when missed, tester moved to item 10*

13. _____

14. _____

In this example, the tester moved backward item by item until a basal was achieved. However, some tests require that the tester skip back several items or move back to a previous page. The tester should check each manual for specific instructions.

Once the basal is determined, testing continues until a ceiling is reached. The **ceiling** is defined as the point at which it can be assumed that the student would receive no credit for all more difficult test items. The ceiling is established by a specified number of incorrect responses; the test ends when the ceiling is determined. Like basals, tests differ in the number of items required for the ceiling. Some measures specify three incorrect responses on consecutively numbered items; others require 5, 8, or even 10 consecutive errors. A ceiling can also be defined in terms of a range of items; for example, the ceiling might be five errors within seven consecutive responses.

Ceilings are established the same way as basals, except the tester seeks a series of incorrect responses. In the following example, the ceiling is three consecutive incorrect responses. The suggested starting item for third graders is item 3. The tester, therefore, began at item 3; a basal was achieved when the third grader answered items 3, 4, and 5 correctly. The student then missed items 6, 7, and 8, establishing a ceiling.

BASAL: 3 consecutive correct responses
CEILING: 3 consecutive incorrect responses

1.	
2.	
(3) 3.	+
4.	+
5.	+
6.	−
7.	−
8.	−

Students often achieve a basal and then answer several questions correctly before missing any. When they encounter items that are difficult for them, they may answer some correctly and others incorrectly before reaching the ceiling. The following example depicts this type of response pattern. The tenth-grade student began the test at the recommended starting point, item 15. The student answered several items correctly and did not make an error until item 19. Item 20 was correct, 21 incorrect, and 22 correct; a ceiling was established with errors on items 23, 24, and 25.

BASAL: 3 consecutive correct responses
CEILING: 3 consecutive incorrect responses

(10) 15.	+	21.	−
16.	+	22.	+
17.	+	23.	−
18.	+	24.	−
19.	−	25.	−
20.	+	26.	

The test manual is the best source for information about suggested starting points and basal and ceiling rules. Some test forms also provide this information. Although they are no substitute for studying the manual, these brief notations on the test record serve as reminders during test administration.

Ending the Test and Retesting

The testing session should include periodic breaks to ward off fatigue. The length of the session and the endurance of the participants determine how often these breaks should occur. With elementary students, a short rest period should be given at least every half hour; more frequent breaks may be necessary with preschool children. Secondary grade students and adults can usually work from 45 minutes to an hour before needing a rest period. Breaks should occur at a logical stopping point in administration, such as at the end of a test or subtest. During the break, students should be encouraged to stand up, move about, and visit the restroom and drinking fountain.

Testing ends when all scheduled activities are completed, the time allotted is exhausted, or the student is no longer able to work efficiently owing to fatigue or loss of concentration. At the end of the session, the tester should thank the student for his or her cooperation and explain what will happen next. This might include further testing on another day, a meeting of the student and tester to go over results, or testing with another professional. The tester answers any questions the student may have and then accompanies the student back to the classroom. The tester should review the session as soon as possible and attempt to evaluate the quality of his or her relationship with the student and the adequacy of the administration process.

It may be necessary to readminister a test at some later date. Readministration of achievement measures to assess progress is routine; students may be given a reading test at the beginning of the school year and then again at the end to measure their growth. Sometimes, however, retesting must occur after only a brief interval. For example, the tester may need to readminister the test within a period of days or weeks, if the original administration was invalidated due to tester error or a student health problem.

Retesting can take place immediately if the test has multiple forms. For instance, if the results of form A were invalid for some reason, form B could be administered the next day. To determine the equivalency of alternate forms of a test, the tester should check the manual's description of equivalent-form reliability.

For measures with only one form, readministration should be delayed as long as possible, preferably for 2 to 4 weeks. If this is impossible, the results of the second administration should be interpreted cautiously because a practice effect is likely. The test manual may provide information on how scores are affected by practice in a test-retest situation.

OBSERVATION OF TEST BEHAVIOR

Skilled testers handle the mechanics of test administration automatically so that they can concentrate on observing the student's behavior during testing. How students act in the testing situation—what they do and say, how they approach a task, and what their general work methods are—is important in interpreting results. The student who is eager, attentive, and anxious to perform well during testing is quite different from the student who is withdrawn and uncooperative. Such behavioral descriptions assist in interpretation of results and provide a beginning for planning instructional strategies.

Observation is a process of collecting data on student behavior. In the observation of test behavior, the tester records information about the student's words and actions. Observational data are objective, precise descriptions of how students behave, and they easily communicate what occurred during testing. Statements such as "Jacob left his seat 13 times during the first 10 minutes of testing" provide useful assessment information. Judgments or opinions such as "Janice was shy and retiring" or "Darren was easily distracted" do not provide useful assessment information unless substantiated by observational data. The specific techniques used in observation of student behavior are explained in Chapter 10. One of the first things the tester should observe is the student's approach to the testing situation. How does the student act when presented with directions and the first few tasks? Is he or she able to adjust quickly to the demands of this new working environment? The tester should be alert for both verbal and nonverbal clues. Students may comment, "I don't wanna stay here," "I like writing with pencils," or " I'm ready to work." They may also express themselves by actions, such as failure to establish eye contact. Also of interest is how students begin the first test task. Some start working immediately, whereas others appear to have difficulty focusing their attention on a new activity.

The tester should also observe the student's style of responding: the response mode selected, the latency between question and answer, the length of the response, and so forth. Table 5–4 describes several important dimensions of response style.

Another major concern is the general work style of the student. The following factors should be considered in observation:

1. *Activity level.* The tester should note obvious signs of activity (standing up, walking around the testing room), as well as more subtle behaviors. Students can be very active without ever leaving their seats. They can squirm around, tap their fingers, and jiggle their legs up and down. High activity levels can distract the student from the test tasks, thereby lowering test performance.
2. *Attention to task.* Some students are able to sustain attention to test tasks for several minutes or for the entire administration period; others appear to become distracted after a very short time. The tester can quantify inattention by counting the number of student remarks unrelated to test activities or the

TABLE 5–4
Observation of Response Style

Response Mode

Which response mode—verbal or nonverbal—does the student favor? If a question can be answered either by pointing to a response or by saying it, which mode does the student select? With questions requiring a yes or no response does the student speak or gesture? Some students accompany even written responses with talk; others speak only when absolutely necessary.

Latency

Latency is the delay between presentation of the test task and the beginning of a response. Students may begin to answer as soon as or even before the tester finishes introducing the tasks; others may delay a few seconds. Some students wait for as long as a minute but then respond correctly. Very short or very long response latencies are noteworthy, particularly in relation to classroom performance.

Length

The length of an answer is not necessarily an indication of its accuracy; depending upon the content of the response and the scoring standards of the test, a brief response may earn as many points as a lengthy one. Verbal responses of students may be characterized by brevity or length. Such patterns should be noted by the tester.

Organization

Although the organization of a response may not be germane to scoring, it is important. A response may be logical and well organized; an equally correct one may be rambling and poorly ordered. How students organize answers provides information about their ability to structure, order, and clearly present their thoughts.

Method of Expressing Inability to Respond

The tester should watch for the student's method of responding when he or she does not know the answer to a question. Some will simply say, "I don't know." Others will say they don't know but will then attempt to explain their inability to answer ("That's fifth grade stuff and I haven't had it yet") or will substitute something they do know ("I can't spell *dog* but I can do *cat:* c-a-t"). Students who express ignorance before the tester has finished the question or who routinely respond to certain types of questions with "I can't do that" should be encouraged to attempt the item. With students who say nothing when they do not know an answer, the tester should wait a reasonable length of time and then encourage the student to at least take a guess. It is important to consider the student's typical response latency so as not to confuse a long delay before answering with an inability to respond.

Idiosyncratic Responses

Occasionally students will give responses that appear to have no relationship to the question. The tester should repeat the question to make sure the student understood what was asked, then ask the student to explain the answer. This is done by repeating the student's answer in a questioning tone and saying, "Tell me what you mean."

number of times the student looks away from test materials. When the student's attention is away from the task 25 percent or more of the time, the tester should consider taking a break or ending the session.

3. *Perseverance.* When presented with an activity, is the student able to persevere until the task is finished? Or does the student give up after a brief attempt? The tester can collect data by timing how long the student works on a particular task.

4. *Need for reassurance.* Many students, anxious about their performance, query the tester about the accuracy of their responses. Even though it has been explained at the beginning of the test that the tester cannot tell them if their answers are right or wrong, students often end a response with the question, "Is that right?" The tester should reiterate that it is against the rules to let them know. An attempt should be made to reassure such students with positive comments such as, "You're working hard." The tester should begin to collect observational data if students persist with this concern.

Comments made during testing may provide information about student attitudes and feelings.

Students may talk about how they perceive their abilities ("I'm dumb in school" or "I can do puzzles real good") or their performance on various test tasks ("I can read pretty well now" or "I'm lousy at spelling"). They may also comment about the test by asking, "Can I do more of these?" or "Are we almost done?" Testers should listen when students talk, answer when appropriate, and record any statements that may be useful in interpreting results.

Testers should also be alert to any warning signs of disabilities. The student's speech should be considered in terms of its intelligibility, articulation, pitch, and volume. Loud or unclear speech may be an indication of hearing problems, as are frequent requests for repetition of test items. Symptoms of vision problems include bringing reading materials close to the face, having red and watery eyes, and rubbing the eyes. If any aspect of the student's test behavior suggests possible speech, hearing, vision, physical, or emotional problems, the tester should refer the student to the appropriate professional for further assessment. If some severe difficulty is confirmed, test results will probably be invalid.

As observational data are collected during testing, they should be recorded. Testers should not trust their memories, particularly their recall of student comments. Some test forms provide space for notations about behaviors; others include checklists for use in rating the student's behavior. However, because space is limited on most forms, experienced testers often bring along extra paper to record observational data and student comments.

SCORING THE TEST

The standard conditions that form the basis of norm-referenced tests also apply to conversion of student responses into test scores. Scoring is a critical step that transforms the student's test responses into comparative data. Accuracy is imperative; every count and calculation must be correct. The amount of time and number of computations required for scoring differ with each test. Some are scored quickly with few calculations, whereas others may take as long or longer to score than to administer.

Tests should be scored as soon as possible after administration. At this time, the tester should also review the observational data because these may aid in the interpretation of numerical scores. Many experienced testers score the test right after it is given and again later to recheck their accuracy.

Sometimes in scoring, it is necessary to know the student's exact **chronological age**—the number of years and months since birth. Calculation of the student's actual age at the time of testing requires both the student's birth date and the date of testing. Table 5–5 explains the computational procedure. Chronological age (CA) is generally written as two numbers separated by a hyphen. For instance, CA 6-3 refers to 6 years, 3 months. The hyphen cannot be replaced with a decimal point. CA 10.6 is not the same as CA 10-6. CA 10.6 is 10 years and 6/10 of a year, an older age than 10 1/2; CA 10–6 is 10 years, 6 months, equal to 10 1/2 years.

Computing Raw Scores

Raw scores, the first to be computed by the tester, describe the number of points earned by a student on a test or subtest. The first step is to determine which test items were answered correctly. This is often done during administration. The tester then assigns point values to each correct response. On many tests, each item is simply worth 1 point; on others, a student can earn 0, 1, 2, or 3 points, depending on response accuracy. Items within a test can vary in point value. For example, easier items may be worth 1 point; more difficult items, 2 points; and the most difficult, 3 points. The test manual provides scoring guidelines with information on item point values.

The raw score is computed by adding the total number of points earned by the student to the total number of points assumed to be earned. Credit is given for the items below the basal that, although not administered, were assumed to be answered correctly. If items below the basal take on a range of possible points, the student is credited with the highest number; for instance, if correct responses receive either 1, 2, or 3 points, it is assumed that the student would have earned a score of 3, had the item actually been administered.

TABLE 5–5
Calculating Chronological Age

To determine the student's exact age at the time of testing, subtract the birth date from the test date. The year, month, and day of testing are written first, then the same information for the student's date of birth.

To subtract, the tester begins with the right-hand column and first subtracts days, then months, and finally years.

Year	Month	Day	
2007	11	29	Date of testing
−1995	8	11	Date of birth
12	3	18	Chronological age

If borrowing is required, convert 1 year into 12 months and 1 month into 30 days. In the following example, it was necessary to borrow 1 month (from 6 months) to convert 4 days to 34 days.

Year	Month	Day	
	5	34	
2007	6̸	4̸	Date of testing
−1993	3	31	Date of birth
14	2	3	Chronological age

In the next example, both years and months were converted before subtracting. First, 2 months were reduced to 1, and 8 days were increased to 38; then 2008 years were reduced to 2007 and 1 month increased to 13.

Year	Month	Day	
	13		
2008	1̸	38	
2̸0̸0̸7̸	2̸	8̸	Date of testing
−1998	10	28	Date of birth
9	3	10	Chronological age

Chronological age is generally reported in terms of years and months but not days. However, the number of days is considered. The convention is to add 1 month if the number of days is greater than 15; if days equal 15 or less, the number of months is not changed. Thus,

8 years, 4 months, 9 days = 8–4

10 years, 6 months, 20 days = 10–7

Table 5–6 presents an example of raw score computation. The test began at item 3, and a basal was achieved when the student correctly answered items 3, 4, and 5. Incorrect responses on items 8, 9, and 10 established the ceiling. Because each item is worth 1 point, the student earned a total of 4 points by correctly answering questions 3, 4, 5, and 7. Credit must also be given for items 1 and 2, the items below the basal assumed to be correct. When the number of points earned (4) is added to the number of points assumed to be earned (2), a total raw score of 6 is obtained.

Converting Raw Scores to Derived Scores

Raw scores must be converted to other scores for a student's performance to be contrasted with that of the norm group. Depending on the test, several types of derived scores may be available: age equivalents, grade equivalents, percentile ranks, standard scores, and others.

Test manuals provide tables for converting raw scores into other scores. The student's raw score is computed, the correct norms table is located, and the derived score is read from the table. Table 5–7 presents sample test norms for students age 9–0 to 9–6.

TABLE 5–6
Computing Raw Scores

Steps in Computing the Raw Score

Step 1: Rate each response correct or incorrect.
Step 2: Assign point values to each response.
Step 3: Calculate number of points earned (in the example below, 4).
Step 4: Calculate number of points assumed earned (2).
Step 5: Add the number of points earned and the number of points assumed earned (4 + 2 = 6).

Example of Raw Score Computation

BASAL: 3 consecutive correct responses
CEILING: 3 consecutive incorrect responses
Each item is worth 1 point.

1. _____
2. _____
3. ____+____
4. ____+____
5. ____+____
6. ____−____
7. ____+____
8. ____−____
9. ____−____
10. ____−____

RAW SCORE ___6___

TABLE 5–7
Sample Norms Table

AGE 9–0 TO 9–6				
Raw Score	Age Equivalent	Grade Equivalent	Percentile Rank	Standard Score
1	—	—	—	—
2	6–0	1.0	5	75
3	6–9	1.7	15	84
4	7–5	2.4	20	87
5	8–2	2.9	35	94
6	9–0	3.5	50	100
7	9–5	3.8	55	102
8	9–11	4.4	60	104
9	10–5	4.8	75	110
10	11–0	5.5	85	116
11	12–1	6.2	90	119
12	—	—	—	—

The tester finds the student's raw score in the first column and then reads across to determine age equivalent, grade equivalent, percentile rank, and standard score. For example, a raw score of 5 for someone age 9–3 would be equivalent to a percentile rank of 35 and a standard score of 94. When no scores are listed for a particular raw score, the student's performance is considered either above or below norms. On the sample norms table, a raw score of 1 would be below norms, and a raw score of 12 above norms.

Sometimes the tester must consult more than one table to obtain all needed scores. For instance, one table may be used to convert raw scores to percentile ranks and a second to convert percentile ranks to standard scores. Tests also differ in how tables are arranged; raw scores can be listed across the top of the table, down the left-hand side, or even down the middle. Testers should be careful to select appropriate tables for the age or grade of the student and to read each table accurately. Some testers find it helpful to use a ruler or index card to help keep their place.

Many test protocols include graphs or profiles for plotting the student's derived scores. This visual representation may assist in interpreting and explaining test results to students and parents. Test manuals provide instructions for plotting the profile; as with all aspects of scoring, accuracy should be a prime concern.

INTERPRETING TEST RESULTS

Results of standardized tests are used to make educational decisions. Tests are administered and scored, and their results interpreted to determine how students perform in relation to age or grade peers. Interpretation of results involves a number of considerations. These include determining the relationship of test behavior to test scores, weighing which test scores provide the most valuable information, allowing for measurement error when reporting results, and evaluating test performance in relation to norm-referenced criteria.

Test Behavior

During test administration, the tester observes the student's behavior. Observational data are then evaluated in relation to the student's scores. Some important questions the tester should consider in interpreting test behavior are:

1. Did the student show *consistent* test behavior? Or did behavior change from task to task or from early in the testing session to later?
2. What types of behaviors were exhibited during tests or subtests that assessed the student's *strengths*—that is, the areas in which the student earned the highest scores?
3. What types of behaviors were exhibited during tests or subtests that assessed the student's *weaknesses?*
4. Was the student's test behavior *representative* of usual classroom behavior? Of behavior in the home?

These factors influence test performance. For example, a student may attend well to the tasks presented at the start of assessment, whether those tasks represent strengths or weaknesses. However, he or she may soon lose interest in testing and respond quickly and carelessly. Or a student may refuse to attempt all tasks relating to a certain skill, such as reading or mathematics. Test behaviors should be described in detail when reporting results.

Choice of Test Scores

A standardized test may offer several types of scores—age and grade equivalents, percentile ranks, standard scores, and so forth. In interpreting test results, it is necessary to choose the scores that will be most useful for quantifying the student's performance and for reporting results to parents and professionals.

As Chapter 4 explained, age and grade equivalents appear to be the simplest scores to interpret but are, in fact, quite complicated. Their use is not recommended for this and other reasons. One major limitation is that they do not provide information about whether a student's performance is within average limits. If a 7-year-old earns a score of age 6 on a measure, this does not indicate the student's standing in relation to others of the same age. The performance of the student could be quite average for 7-year-olds or could fall below the average range of functioning for this age group. If a student in grade 4.3 earns an achievement score of grade 3.9, is the difference significant enough to suggest an achievement problem? Age and grade scores are not useful for answering such questions.

Age and grade scores only appear to provide precise information about a student's instructional or developmental level. If a student earns a grade score of 7.3, this means only that he or she earned a raw score roughly equivalent to that of the seventh-grade students in the norm group, if there were seventh-grade students in the norm group and the score is not the result of extrapolation. Grade scores do not describe the student's current instructional level. They are not even indicative of which test questions were answered correctly. Two students can earn the same age or grade score but not answer any of the same questions correctly. So, if a fourth-grade child obtains a grade equivalent of 6.8 in arithmetic, it does *not* mean that she is proficient in the arithmetic processes taught in the sixth grade. She performed well on fourth-grade arithmetic. However, she did not display mastery of sixth-grade arithmetic material.

Unfortunately, sometimes age and grade equivalents are the only available scores from a particular test. In this situation, they should be reported, but findings should be worded carefully to prevent misinterpretation.

Breakpoint Practice 5.1
Click here to check your understanding of grade equivalents.

Age-equivalent scores are reported in a similar fashion.

Percentile rank scores are preferable to age and grade equivalents because they are comparative scores. They are straightforward indicators of an individual's standing within a group and are easily interpreted. Percentile rank scores are reported by referring to that portion of the norm group against which the student is being compared.

ENHANCEDetext
Video Example 5.2
Watch this video to learn more about percentile rank.
https://www.youtube.com/watch?v=Eq1R9JsZP8w

Standard scores have many advantages. They are comparative, and when based on a normal or normalized distribution of raw scores, they can be directly translated into percentile ranks. Also, because standard scores have a uniform mean and standard deviation, they can be compared from one subtest to the next and from one test administration to another.

In addition, standard scores provide information about whether a student's performance is within average limits. They describe the relationship of a student's score to the average score of the comparison group within the norming sample. For example, if standard scores on a particular test are distributed with a mean of 100 and a standard deviation of 15, a standard score of 70 indicates performance two standard deviations below the mean performance of the comparison group for students of any grade or age. That comparison group would be the grade 8 students within the norm group if an eighth grader's performance is being evaluated; if a first grader is under study, the comparison group would be the first graders within the norm group. Percentile ranks can be reported along with the student's standard scores.

Measurement Error

Test scores, like any other measurement, always contain some element of error. Even if a test is administered and scored in strict adherence to standardization conditions, the scores will be observed scores, consisting of the student's hypothetical true score plus an error component. Fortunately, with standardized tests, the standard error of measurement can be used to estimate the amount of error likely to occur within scores. As Chapter 4 explained, the standard error of measurement is based on the test's reliability and standard deviation. Tests with poor reliability and large standard deviations produce large standard errors. The smaller the standard error of measurement, the more accurate the results. In most cases, standard errors are reported in the test manual. If not, they can be calculated by means of the formula provided in Chapter 4.

The standard error of measurement is used to construct **confidence intervals** around observed scores. With confidence intervals, a student's performance is reported as a range of scores in which it is highly likely that the true score will fall, rather than as a single score known to include both the true score and error. For example, if a student received a score of 95 +/− 3, the chances that his true score falls between 92 and 98 are about 68 percent.

The procedure for constructing confidence intervals is quite straightforward. After an observed score has been obtained and the standard error of measurement for that score is known, a decision is made about the degree of confidence desired. The tester may be satisfied with 68 percent confidence that the student's true score will fall within the range of scores to be constructed. Or a higher degree of confidence may be called for, such as 90, 95, or even 99 percent. The standard error of measurement is then multiplied by a factor related to the level of confidence. The factors, the z scores associated with the confidence levels, are:

CONFIDENCE LEVEL DESIRED	FACTOR BY WHICH STANDARD ERROR IS MULTIPLIED
68%	1.00
85%	1.44
90%	1.64
95%	1.96
99%	2.58

The product of the standard error times the factor is added to the student's observed score to determine the upper limit of the range. The product is then subtracted from the student's observed score to determine the lower limit.

For example, a student's observed score is 100, and the standard error of measurement for that score is 5. If the desired confidence level is 68 percent, the standard error (5) will be multiplied by the factor (1) to equal 5. The upper limit of the confidence interval becomes 105 (100 + 5), and the lower limit 95 (100 − 5). The student's score is reported as 100 ± 5, with a probability of 68 percent that the student's true score lies within that range.

If a more conservative estimate is needed, the confidence level could be set at 95 percent. In this

case, the standard error (5) would be multiplied by 1.96 to equal 10. The confidence interval would then extend from 90 to 110, increasing the chances that this range would include the student's true score to 95 out of 100. When the level of confidence is increased, the width of the confidence interval also increases. In the previous example, increasing the confidence level from 68 to 95 percent changed the range of scores within the confidence interval from 95–105 to 90–110. The magnitude of the standard error of measurement also affects the width of the confidence interval. Consider these examples:

EXAMPLE 1	
Observed score	100
Standard error of measurement	5
Confidence level	68%
Confidence interval	95 to 105
EXAMPLE 2	
Observed score	100
Standard error of measurement	20
Confidence level	68%
Confidence interval	80 to 120

In these examples, the student's observed score and the level of confidence remain the same. When the standard error is 5, the confidence interval is 95 to 105. However, when the standard error increases to 20, the confidence interval becomes much larger. Tests with small standard errors of measurement allow more precision in the estimation of true scores.

Criteria for Evaluating Test Performance

Norm-referenced tests compare one student's performance against the performance of counterparts in the norm group. Standard score ranges should be used for this purpose.

Many standardized measures provide guidelines for test interpretation. These systems often are based on a set of standard score ranges, each of which is given a descriptive label. For example, the manual for one of the older measures of intellectual performance (Wechsler, 2003b) uses these labels to describe its standard score (IQ) ranges: "very superior" (IQ 130 and above), "superior" (the range from IQ 120 to129), "high average" (the range from 110 to 119), "average" (the range from IQ 90 to 109), "low average" (the range from IQ 80 to 89), "borderline" (the range from IQ 70 to 79), "intellectually deficient" (IQ 69 and below). However, this system is not used consistently from test to test. Some measures use different labels to describe student performance, and on others, the ranges into which standard scores are divided are defined in a different way.

Although there is no universally accepted system for describing ranges of performance, judicious use of standard score ranges can facilitate the interpretation of test results. In this book, we describe ranges of standard scores in terms of their distance from the test mean. Score ranges are defined in standard deviation units—within one standard deviation of the mean, between one and two standard deviations below the mean, and so forth. Ranges of performance are also defined in relation to the percentage of population each includes.

Thus, the *average range of performance* is the standard score range within one standard deviation from the mean. On a test with standard scores distributed with a mean of 100 and a standard deviation of 15, this range extends from standard score 85 to standard score 115. If the test is normally distributed, that range encompasses 68 percent of the norm group.

The *low-average range of performance* is the standard score range between one and two standard deviations below the mean. It extends from standard score 70 to standard score 84 and includes approximately 14 percent of the population. Similarly, the *high-average range of performance* is defined as the standard score range between one and two standard deviations above the mean. It includes standard scores 116 to 130 and represents approximately 14 percent of the population.

At the extreme ends of the distribution are the *below-average range of performance* and the *above-average range of performance*. Each represents approximately 2 percent of the population. The below-average range encompasses standard scores 69 and below, and the above-average range encompasses standard scores 131 and above. Figure 5–2 shows the ranges of performance in relation to the normal distribution.

Labels such as "average" and "low average" are arbitrary, although in this system they are tied to percentages of the population. Deciding that a score indicates below-average performance

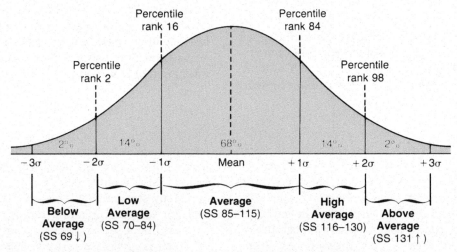

SS = standard score with a mean of 100 and a standard deviation of 15

FIGURE 5–2
Test Interpretation Using Standard Score Ranges

by a standard such as "2 years below grade level" is even more arbitrary and is fraught with measurement difficulties. When linked with percentile ranks, standard score ranges fulfill the purpose of norm-referenced testing and compare the student's performance with that of his or her peers.

In reporting the results of standardized tests, keep in mind several factors. First, note that standard scores are preferred over other types of scores. Second, report scores as confidence intervals rather than as single scores, noting the level of confidence associated with the interval. Third, describe scores in relation to their range of performance, such as average, low average, and so on. Following these recommendations, a standard score of 79 on a test with a standard score mean of 100, a standard deviation of 15, and a standard error of measurement of 3 would be reported in the following way:

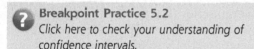

Breakpoint Practice 5.2
Click here to check your understanding of confidence intervals.

TECHNOLOGY IN ASSESSMENT

In the past decades, computer and technology use in American schools has increased dramatically, and today almost every teacher and student has access to a computer, laptop, or other portable hand-held device. Computer devices store, sort, and retrieve large amounts of information quickly, and this capability can expedite many aspects of the assessment process. As the following paragraphs discuss, technology can aid in the administration of tests, test scoring, interpretation of results, and report writing.

Test Administration

Just as technology can help deliver instruction to students, it can also aid in administering some types of tests. In this application of computer technology to assessment, the student sits down at a desk computer, laptop, or iPad, reads the on-screen instructions, and types in answers to

questions or taps on images. The computer program then evaluates the student's responses, calculates test scores, and prepares a written report for the teacher.

Computer-assisted testing is sometimes used with children and adolescents with disabilities. Some professionals have issues with this type of testing primarily because test administration by computer may depress student performance. Students with mild disabilities, as a group, have difficulty reading, writing, controlling their behavior, and focusing their attention on task. Using computers for test administration could exacerbate these difficulties. Although reading and keyboarding demands are concerns, the major drawback is the inability of the computer to monitor the student's behavior, provide motivation and encouragement, observe the student's interaction with the task, and direct the student's attention back to the task as necessary. For some professionals, individual administration of standardized tests by a trained examiner remains the preferred practice for students with disabilities.

Few standardized measures have been designed for (or converted to) computer administration, and most of those available are adult measures (e.g., career counseling tools and adult personality tests). However, development efforts continue, and computer-based measures of academic skills are becoming more common. Some are informal measures designed to help teachers track students' progress through the curriculum. Reading programs assisting in the monitoring of reading progress can be timesaving for teachers. Storing data and reducing paperwork for teachers are positive aspects of technology for progress monitoring. Others are more formal tests of academic achievement. In some cases, these new devices use "computerized-adaptive testing." That is, not all test items are presented to all students; items are selected based on the student's performance.

As more technologies become available for use in special education, professionals will need to learn how to evaluate, select, and interpret the results of these instruments, taking into account the ways in which the introduction of a computer alters the testing situation. The American

Psychological Association (2004), based on the *Code of Fair Testing Practices in Education*, made several recommendations for professionals who provide testing in education regardless of mode used in presentation.

Test Scoring

At present, the most common—and most useful—application of technology to assessment is computation of test scores. Test scoring using technology is not a new application. Publishers of group-administered measures such as the achievement tests used in general education have long provided computer scoring services to schools. Another development is the use of computers by teachers at the school site for test scoring. Within the past decade, several programs have been developed for scoring the individual tests commonly used in special education. These programs represent an excellent use of computer technology; they decrease the probability of computation errors in scoring and speed up the scoring process, freeing the professional for other, more meaningful duties.

Most test-scoring programs for individual tests require that the professional administer the test and compute the raw scores for each subtest. Identifying information such as the student's name is entered into the program along with raw scores, and there may be choices to make about the types of scores to be calculated. It usually takes only a minute or two to enter the necessary data, and then only a few seconds for the computations. This is a substantial timesaving—for some tests it takes 15 or even 30 minutes to compute derived scores by hand.

Test-scoring programs are available for many of the individual measures used in special education. In fact, some of the newer individual tests can only be scored by technology. The publisher of the test typically develops software, although in some cases, publishers may certify as accurate a program developed by another agency. Publishers tend to develop scoring programs for selected tests—those that are most popular and difficult and/or time consuming to score. Price options of scoring programs vary, but some start at 35 dollars per year. Other options include a charge per form (e.g., 2 dollars per form), three-year subscription and five-year subscription.

Test Interpretation and Reporting

Most scoring programs allow teachers to store student data for later use and to view score reports on the screen before printing them. The type of information included in the report varies from program to program, although all provide the basic information found on hand-scored protocols: identification information about the student and derived scores. Other common options are profiles of test results, score comparisons, and narrative explanations of results.

Scoring programs often go beyond simple reporting of scores and begin to contribute to the interpretation of test results. For example, the report may contain descriptions of each subtest on the test, a report of the student's scores, and comparison of the student's performance to that of the norm group. The report might also include analysis of any discrepancies in the student's performance on various subtests (e.g., reading versus math), analysis of any discrepancies between results on this measure and those on other measures (e.g., aptitude versus achievement), and profiles or graphs of the student's scores. In some cases, reports may even offer instructional recommendations based on test performance.

 ENHANCEDetext
Video Example 5.3
Watch this video to learn more about test interpretation.
https://www.youtube.com/watch?v=npZCcDUB7eg

When evaluating a computer program for test interpretation, it is extremely important to understand the decision-making rules the program uses to arrive at its conclusions. For example, one program might identify skill areas as weaknesses when standard scores fall below 85, whereas another program uses standard score 70 as the cut-off. Clearly, the interpretations resulting from these two programs are not comparable. Computer-generated test interpretations are best used as an aid to decision making, not as a substitute for the deliberations of the assessment team. Fortunately, most scoring programs allow testers to select the type of results they wish to print, so that interpretative reports can be omitted in favor of score reports.

MODIFICATION OF TESTING PROCEDURES

In many cases, test manuals dictate the exact words the tester is to use in presenting tasks to students, how the student may respond, and the ways the tester may respond to the student. If specified procedures are not followed, norm-referenced scores become meaningless because the norms assume administration under standard conditions. However, professionals sometimes believe that test results do not adequately reflect the student's capabilities. Certain administration requirements may, in fact, depress a student's performance. For example, a student may be able to complete a test task successfully but not within the required time limits. On most timed tests, students receive no credit for a late, albeit correct, response.

It *is* possible to modify administration procedures for standardized tests, although tests should be given under standard conditions before attempting any modification. In this way, the student's performance under both standard and altered conditions can be studied.

Results of tests administered under altered conditions must be interpreted with great caution. An example is allowing a fourth-grade student to use a calculator for a computation test normed with students who were provided only paper and pencil. With the aid of the calculator, the student's test score may improve; he or she may achieve a score indicating average performance for a fourth grader. However, it is no longer possible to compare the student's performance to that of students in the norm group. If the norm group had been supplied with calculators, perhaps the performance of the student in question would fall within the low-average or below-average range. There is simply no way to determine this. However, despite the necessity for caution in interpretation, results from tests given under altered conditions can provide

useful information about the student's capabilities to perform test tasks. Results may also suggest ways to alter instructional strategies and requirements to increase chances for classroom success.

Before modifying administration procedures, the professional should consider the possible problems that may arise if the test is to be used again in the future with the same student. If the student somehow learns the questions and responses and is able to recall those responses, the test can no longer be used to compare the student's performance with the performance of others.

Sattler (1988) discusses the modification of administration procedures and calls this practice "testing of limits." He notes that one may gain additional information regarding the individual by going beyond the standard test procedures.

Administration conditions can be modified in several ways to determine if students are able to improve their performance. Test directions specifically indicate what type of changes are allowed within a test for validity and reliability purposes. Furthermore, states have allowable changes for standardized tests. In addition, students' IEPs typically indicate which changes were suggested in the past for that particular student. Methods include the following:

1. *Instructions* to the student may be paraphrased in simpler language.
2. The tester can provide a *demonstration* of how test tasks are to be performed.
3. *Time limits* for the completion of tasks can be extended or removed.
4. The *presentation mode* for tasks may be changed. For example, the tester could read items aloud to the student rather than requiring the student to read them.
5. The *response mode* required of the student may be changed. For example, instead of writing the answers, the student could respond orally.
6. The student may be allowed to use *aids* such as paper and pencil or a calculator.
7. The tester may provide the student with *prompts*. For example, the tester could perform

the first step in the test task. Or the tester could question the student about his or her problem-solving method and then suggest an alternate approach.

8. The tester may give *feedback* to the student. This could include confirmation of correct responses or even correction of incorrect responses.

9. *Positive reinforcement* could be offered for correct responses and other appropriate work behaviors.

10. The *physical location* of the test may be changed. The test could be administered on the floor rather than at a table, or in a playroom rather than a testing room.

11. The *tester* may be changed. Someone with whom the student is comfortable, such as a parent or classroom teacher, could administer the test.

12. The tester may *break up testing into smaller segments* for some students. For example, students who tire easily owing to health impairments or attention issues may warrant this change in test administration.

When administration procedures are altered, the modification should be described in the report of test results. Results obtained under nonstandard conditions are reported as **alternate scores.** Although interpretation of these scores is difficult, successful performance with modified tasks may provide clues to ways for improving student functioning. For example, praising a student for each completed test item may increase the number of questions he or she is willing to attempt. Or spelling may improve when the student is allowed to spell orally rather than write the words. Although these results are not determined in accordance with the rules of standardized testing, they may help identify specific problems in learning and suggest remedies for these problems.

 Breakpoint Practice 5.3
Click here to check your understanding of assessment modification.

AVOIDING BIAS IN TESTING

The potential for bias in assessment does not end with careful selection of assessment instruments. Even if standardized tests are deemed the most appropriate tools, discrimination remains a possibility during test administration and scoring and in the critical step of test interpretation.

Bias can be introduced into test administration in a number of ways. One important consideration is the professional preparation of the tester. Testing skill is absolutely essential for nonbiased assessment. Placing a standardized test in the hands of an untrained examiner is as poor a practice as selecting a technically inadequate measure.

Professionals should also have knowledge about the types of students they assess, particularly individuals from cultures different from their own. Information about variations in age, gender, cultural group, and disability and the potential impact of these factors on test performance is essential.

Tester attitudes are another important factor. If the tester holds strong beliefs about certain groups, he or she may fail to see students as individuals. For example, the belief that girls do not excel in mathematics may influence how diligently the tester attempts to elicit a female student's optimal performance on a math test. Tester attitudes affect expectations, which in turn affect test administration and scoring practices.

The working relationship between the student and tester is critical. Testers may need to take special care in building rapport with students of races, cultures, or experiential backgrounds different from their own. The tester may represent an unfamiliar culture to such students, requiring extra effort to help them feel at ease in the testing situation (Winzer & Mazurek, 1998). These authors note that testers familiar to the student and those perceived as warm, friendly, and trustworthy are most likely to elicit optimal performance. However, most studies have not supported a difference in test results based on the race of the evaluator (Kaplan & Saccuzzo, 2012).

It has been suggested that culturally and linguistically diverse students be tested only by examiners from the same group. For example, Alley and Foster (1978) consider the matching of tester and student on race a simplistic approach to nonbiased assessment. They explain that it overlooks the impact of socioeconomic differences within cultures, the need for empathy on the examiner's part, and the issue of tester competence. However, researchers find that this is not necessarily the case. Klein, Le, and Hamilton (2001) investigate math test scores based on race matching. They report that race matching did not affect test scores in their fourth-grade participants.

Selection of the tester becomes an important issue when the student's primary mode of communication is not English. Testers must be chosen carefully for students who speak a language other than English and for students who are deaf and communicate using sign language. In best practice, the tester will be able to communicate directly with the student using the student's communication mode. However, this is not always possible, particularly for students who speak one of the less common languages. When an interpreter must be used to translate the tester's questions to the student and the student's answers to the tester, standardized tests cannot be used for comparative purposes. At best, they provide informal information that must be evaluated with great care.

The potential for bias is also present during the interpretation of test results. Professionals can have a positive influence on this portion of the assessment process by using appropriate procedures for interpretation of test scores, by understanding the limitations of standardized testing, by examining the attitudes they hold toward students from diverse cultures, and by becoming more familiar with the languages and cultures of the students they assess.

 Breakpoint Practice 5.4
Click here to check your understanding of testing procedures.

Assessment in Action: Mrs. Duffy
Mrs. Duffy Reports Test Results

Mrs. Duffy is one of the special education teachers at Rosa Parks High School. She's a seasoned educator with years of experience serving on assessment teams, administering all sorts of measures to students with special needs, and reporting assessment results to parents and other professionals. Mrs. Duffy is convinced that test results should be reported as ranges of scores rather than single numbers. The use of ranges emphasizes that test scores, like other types of measurement, are subject to error. When she meets with parents to discuss results, Mrs. Duffy explains percentile rank scores and how these scores describe the student's performance in relation to others of the same grade or age. She also talks about standard scores and how they can assist in interpretation. For example, take the case of Shawna, a tenth grader having difficulty keeping up with her reading assignments.

Test Results for Shawna:

Subtest	Standard Score Range	Percentile Rank Range	Description
Reading	75–81	5–10	Low Average
Mathematics	94–100	34–50	Average

When Mrs. Duffy presents test results to Shawna's mother and stepfather, she points out that Shawna is doing quite well in math in comparison with others in grade 10. In that subject, Shawna's performance is better than 34 to 50 percent of her grade peers. Mrs. Duffy tells Shawna's family that the standard score range 94 to 100 indicates average performance in mathematics. In contrast, Shawna's reading skills appear less advanced. She scores better than only 5 to 10 percent of grade peers in reading, and her standard score range of 75 to 81 indicates low-average performance. Mrs. Duffy suggests to Shawna's mother and stepfather that assessment continue to learn more about Shawna's reading skills, strengths, and needs and how best to help her become a better performing student.

SUMMARY

- A professional responsible for test administration takes part in significant preparation before testing a student. Three major concepts or areas must be taken into consideration. First, preparation of the tester includes training in assessment with supervised, scaffolded practice in the use of standardized measures. Second, preparation of the testing environment needs to be taken into consideration. The tester should make every effort to create a comfortable testing environment. Third, student preparation is very important to this process. Scheduling the test at an optimal time, seeing to the student's physical needs, and preparing the student psychologically is a critical component in testing.

- Some key terms in test administration are essential in achieving a valid result. Recording student responses takes skill, and several rules should be followed. The test protocol is hidden from student view. In addition, the tester keeps an exact record of student responses for scoring purposes and for assistance in interpreting results. Accurate scoring needs to take place during administration. Standardized tests cover a wide range of difficulty, and students attempt only that portion of the test appropriate to their skill level. After selecting a starting point, the tester presents items to the student in an attempt to locate items of appropriate difficulty. The basal, or range of successful performance, is determined. Testing then continues to establish the ceiling, or the level at which the student is no longer successful. Testing ends when all scheduled activities are completed, the time allotted is exhausted, or the student is no longer able to work efficiently due to fatigue or loss of concentration.

- Seasoned professionals look for certain behaviors while observing of test takers. Observation is a process of collecting data on student behavior. In the observation of test behavior, the tester records information about the student's words and actions. Observational data are objective, precise descriptions of how students behave, and they easily communicate what occurred during testing. Testers pay special attention to how students act in the testing situation, what they do and say, how they approach a task, what their work methods are, activity level, attention to task perseverance, and need for reassurance.

- Professional scoring of a test requires knowledge of computing chronological age, raw scores, and score conversion. Sometimes in scoring, it is necessary to know the student's exact chronological age—the student's number of years and months since birth. The raw score is then computed by adding the total number of points earned by the student to the total number of points assumed to be earned. After the student's raw score is computed, the correct norms table is located, and the derived score is read from the table.

- Tests are administered and scored by professionals, and their results are interpreted to determine how students perform in relation to age or grade peers. Interpretation of results involves a number of key considerations. These include determining the relationship of test behavior to test scores, weighing which test scores provide the most valuable information, allowing for measurement error when reporting results, and evaluating test performance in relation to norm-referenced criteria.

- Technology can support educational professionals in the administration of tests, test scoring, interpretation of results, and report writing. As more technologies become available for use in special education, professionals will need to learn how to evaluate, select, and interpret the results of these instruments, taking into account the ways in which the introduction of a computer alters the testing situation. At present, the most common—and most useful— application of technology to assessment is computation of test scores. Scoring programs often go beyond simple reporting of scores and begin to contribute to the interpretation of test results.

- It *is* possible to modify administration procedures for standardized tests, although tests should be given under standard conditions before attempting any modification. Examples of modification of testing procedures include changes in instructions, demonstrations, time limits presentation, and response mode.

- Bias can be introduced into test administration in a number of ways. Examples of avoiding bias in testing include selection of the tester, communication mode, and interpretation of test results. One important consideration is the professional preparation of the tester. In addition, the tester should be able to communicate directly with the student using the student's communication mode. Professionals should also use appropriate procedures for the interpretation of test scores, understand the limitations of standardized testing, examine the attitudes they hold toward students from diverse cultures, and become more familiar with the languages and cultures of the students they assess.

6

Hero Images Inc./Alamy Stock Photo

Classroom Assessment

LEARNING OUTCOMES

After reading this chapter, you will be able to:

- Define and explain the three major types of classroom assessments: obtrusive and nonobtrusive, curriculum based, and informant.

- Name and explain error analysis and rubrics techniques used when analyzing student work.

- Discuss the three steps in task analysis.

- Name the six steps in designing informal inventories.

- Define and discuss true–false, multiple choice, and matching in classroom tests and quizzes.

- Define criterion-referenced tests.

- Describe the three steps in designing diagnostic probes and diagnostic teaching.

- Give an example of spelling and computational scores derived in curriculum-based measurement.

- Compare and contrast checklists and rating scales.

- Compare and contrast questionnaires and interviews.

- Describe the three types of portfolio assessment according to Salend.

- Discuss the frequency of collecting data concern in managing classroom data.
- Name the four purposes of grading and report cards according to Airasian.
- Discuss the limitations of reliability and validity in interpreting classroom assessment results.
- Name the four questions to use in avoiding bias in classroom assessment noted in this chapter.

KEY TERMS

informal assessment

classroom assessment

curriculum-based assessment

observation

work sample analysis

response analysis

error analysis

rubric

task analysis

structural task analysis

inventories

classroom quizzes

criterion-referenced tests

diagnostic probes

diagnostic teaching

curriculum-based measurement

checklists

rating scales

questionnaires

interviews

clinical interviews

portfolio assessment

Teachers use informal classroom assessment techniques every day—when they observe the behavior of a student, when they examine a student's paper and attempt to find a pattern of errors, or when they interview a student about the procedures he or she has used to solve a problem or answer a question. The major advantage of these authentic assessment techniques is their relevance to instruction. In fact, many of the informal assessment strategies used in special education can be viewed as curriculum-based measures. Informal techniques provide information about the student's current levels of performance, aid in the selection of instructional goals and objectives, point to the need for instructional modifications, document student progress, and suggest directions for further assessment. Whereas norm-referenced measures focus on the student's ability to function in a structured testing situation, informal measures more closely approximate typical classroom conditions. In addition, these measures are useful not only for the evaluation of student performance but also for the study of instructional settings and curricular tasks. This chapter describes the many different types of informal assessment tools available to teachers.

Informal assessment tools—often called classroom assessments—help the professional gather information about the current status of the student, the task, or the setting. Tools are designed to describe current conditions, not to predict future performance. There are several important areas of difference between informal classroom measures and formal measures such as norm-referenced tests.

1. *Standard of reference.* With norm-referenced tests, the student's performance is compared to that of a norm group. With informal measures, the student's performance is compared to specific instructional concerns such as the sequence of learning tasks within the curriculum of the school or the conduct standards of a particular classroom.

2. *Technical adequacy.* Most informal tools are not standardized, and few provide information about reliability and validity. If teachers design informal measures for use in their own classrooms, no information about psychometric quality is available unless it is gathered by the teachers themselves. It is not that the quality of informal assessment is poor; rather, it is generally unknown.

3. *Efficiency.* Norm-referenced tests are usually efficient measures. When evaluating the efficiency of an informal assessment tool, the time and personnel requirements for its design, administration, scoring, and interpretation must all be taken into account. Designing, administering, and scoring an informal tool is a time-consuming process. However, administration procedures are often quite straightforward in comparison to those for norm-referenced tests. Paraprofessionals such as instructional aides can be trained to administer some of the easier informal measures. Despite this assistance, the teacher must be involved in the critical steps of designing the measure and interpreting its results. Even in administration, some measures require the expertise of a professional familiar with the school curriculum and the expectations for performance within the classroom-learning environment.

4. *Specificity.* Formal measures generally assess larger segments of the curriculum, and their coverage of these segments is selective rather than comprehensive. A norm-referenced test may include a broad range of items chosen to represent a general curriculum area, but only a few test items or none measure each specific skill within that curriculum area. In contrast, informal measures tend to focus on one or more subskills within the curriculum in an attempt to assess them thoroughly. Their purpose is to gather sufficient information that will allow teachers to monitor student progress or make instructional planning decisions.

TYPES OF CLASSROOM ASSESSMENTS

There are many types of informal assessment techniques, and it is useful to have some way of conceptualizing them. One important dimension is whether informal strategies introduce a test task into the assessment situation—that is, to determine how obtrusive they are. With procedures such as observation, no test task is presented to the student; he or she is simply observed within the natural environment of the classroom or whatever setting is of interest. Informal inventories, classroom quizzes, and criterion-referenced tests, in contrast, exemplify assessment procedures in which something is added to the environment; the tester introduces test tasks to the student in order to observe how these specific tasks are carried out.

A second dimension of interest is whether measures are direct or indirect. Direct measures attempt to answer an assessment question about a particular student or classroom condition by assessing that characteristic or condition. If the question concerns a student's ability to read a fourth-grade science text, the student is asked to read the science text. Indirect measures rely on a less direct source, such as an informant (usually, someone other than the student). An indirect means of determining a student's ability to read a science text would be to interview the student's teacher.

As Table 6–1 illustrates, the dimensions of directness and obtrusiveness can be used to sort informal assessment techniques into three types: (1) observation, task analysis, and other direct and unobtrusive procedures; (2) curriculum-based assessment techniques such as inventories and criterion-referenced tests that are direct but obtrusive; and (3) procedures using informants such as checklists and interviews that are indirect and obtrusive.

TABLE 6–1
Classroom Assessments

	UNOBTRUSIVE	OBTRUSIVE
Direct	Observation	Informal inventories
	Analysis of student work	Classroom quizzes
	Task analysis	Criterion-referenced tests
		Diagnostic probes and diagnostic teaching
		Curriculum-based measurement
Indirect		Checklists and rating scales
		Questionnaires and interviews

Observation, Task Analysis, and Analysis of Student Work

These are fundamental assessment strategies that are basic to all types of assessment; skill in their use is critical for any assessment professional. These techniques allow the direct examination of student behaviors, tasks, and settings without introducing test tasks. They are important tools for gathering assessment information in the classroom, where they also serve as instructional tools. In addition, they are often used in conjunction with other data collection strategies. For example, observation of the student's test behavior is a critical part of norm-referenced testing. Observation and other direct, unobtrusive procedures can be adapted for use with individuals of any age, in any curriculum area, and in any instructional setting or assessment situation.

Teachers are continually watching and listening to their students. They may not call this procedure **observation**, but by taking note of what their students say and do, teachers are conducting simple observations. When a potential problem is discovered during casual observation, more systematic observational procedures can begin. Although observational techniques are often associated with the study of classroom conduct problems, they are just as appropriate for the study of academic, social, self-help, and vocational skills. Informal behavior techniques, such as functional behavioral assessment and observation recordings are discussed in Chapter 10.

Curriculum-Based Assessment

Many types of informal assessments are curriculum-based. These measures and strategies assess school skills directly. Their content is determined by the standard, school curriculum or the special course of study designed to meet the needs of a particular student with a disability. They are obtrusive because they require that a test task or a series of tasks be added to the instructional environment. However, curriculum-based techniques are used often in classrooms, and their results relate directly to instructional decision making.

Curriculum-based assessment can use any type of informal assessment strategy, even observation. However, the most common techniques are informal inventories, classroom tests and quizzes, and criterion-referenced tests. Other useful approaches are diagnostic probes, diagnostic teaching, curriculum-based measurement (CBM).

Measures Using Informants

Checklists, rating scales, questionnaires, and interviews are informal assessment procedures that make use of the expertise of an informant—a teacher, a parent, an employer, the student, or a peer. These measures are obtrusive and indirect; they access information about nonobservables such as values, beliefs, and opinions or past events. Informants are used in assessment for three purposes. First, they can provide a historical perspective. For example, the student's parents are likely the best source of information about acquisition of developmental milestones in the preschool years. Second, informants who have had extensive experience with the student can summarize their observations and offer opinions, judgments, and interpretations. A teacher, for instance, can provide information about the student's current levels of performance in each of the subject areas taught in the classroom. Third, informants can comment on less observable concerns such as attitudes, values, and perceptions. Students can describe their attitudes toward school, for example.

There is always, however, the danger of inaccuracy when information is gathered indirectly. Informants may not recall past events with clarity; their opinions may be based on incomplete information. They may even report less than the truth. Information gathered from informants is subjective and should be interpreted as such. If this word of caution is kept in mind, informants can be a valuable addition to the assessment process. In fact, for some assessment questions, informants may be the only source of information available to the teacher.

The measures used to gather data from informants are flexible. They can be designed to assess almost any domain: health and developmental history, educational background, current educational status, social and interpersonal skills, and attitudes toward school subjects. Such measures can be tightly structured, prompting the informant for every specific response. Or they can be quite open-ended, providing the informant with general questions that he or she can choose how to answer.

The sections that follow discuss in detail each of the major types of classroom assessment techniques used by teachers to gather information about the instructional status and progress of students with disabilities. The first of these techniques is observation, followed by analysis of tasks and student work samples, several curriculum-based assessment strategies such as informal inventories and classroom quizzes, and measures using informants, including interviews and questionnaires. Later sections of this chapter describe portfolio assessment, an approach combining several different assessment techniques, techniques

for managing classroom assessment data, and considerations in grading and preparing student report cards. The chapter ends with suggestions for interpreting classroom assessment results and avoiding bias in classroom assessment.

 Breakpoint Practice 6.1
Click here to check your understanding of classroom assessment.

ANALYZING STUDENT WORK

Teachers also employ observation to study students' products. The teacher obtains a sample of student work—a written assignment, a test, an essay, an art project, or even a tape recording of oral reading responses or a classroom discussion—and analyzes it to determine areas of successful performance and areas requiring assistance. **Work sample analysis** is most often used to assess academic skills, but it can be applied to any area in which a product results. This technique is a special type of observation, and it is sometimes referred to as permanent product analysis or outcome recording (Alberto & Troutman, 1990; Cooper, 1981; Groth, 2014).

Response Analysis

This technique considers both the correct and incorrect responses of the student. Like other types of observation, it involves the steps of describing the behavior, selecting a measurement system, and deciding on a data-reporting system. In **response analysis**, the teacher is usually interested in these dimensions of human behavior: frequency, duration, rate, and percentage.

Figure 6–1 presents a work sample and several examples of the ways in which responses can be analyzed. Most typically, the teacher will select only one or two aspects of the student's behavior for study. In this response analysis, the teacher is focusing on Louie's spelling. Although Louie's essay contains several errors, the response analysis shows that 78 percent of the words were spelled correctly.

Task: Students are asked to write a short description of a favorite animal.
Transcription of Louie's essay:
   My favorit animl is giraf. They got a long nek and spots. They eat lets and trees and are very tall. They run fast in the jugle.

Time begun: <u>9:20 a.m.</u>   Time finished: <u>9:35 a.m.</u>

Response Analysis

Dimension	Analysis Results

Frequency
Number of words written = 27
Number of words spelled correctly = 21
Number of words spelled incorrectly = 6

Duration
Number of minutes required to write essay = 15

Rate
Rate of writing words

$$\frac{\text{Number of words written}}{\text{Number of minutes writing}} = 1.8 \text{ words per minute}$$

Rate of spelling words correctly

$$\frac{\text{Number of words spelled correctly}}{\text{Number of minutes of writing}} = 1.4 \text{ words per minute}$$

Percentage
Percentage of words spelled correctly

$$\frac{\text{Number of words spelled correctly}}{\text{Number of words written}} \times 100 = 78\%$$

Percentage of words spelled incorrectly

$$\frac{\text{Number of words spelled incorrectly}}{\text{Number of words written}} \times 100 = 22\%$$

FIGURE 6–1
Response Analysis of a Student Work Sample

Like other types of observation, response analysis should not be limited to a single sample of student behavior. Several work samples should be gathered over a period of time to determine the student's typical manner of responding. Results of response analyses can be graphed to facilitate interpretation.

Error Analysis

A second, more common approach to the study of student work samples is **error analysis**, which has a long history in special and remedial education. In the 1930s, Monroe (1932) suggested a procedure for the study of oral reading in which errors were categorized as additions, omissions, substitutions, repetitions, and so forth. Today, error analysis techniques are available for most subject areas.

The goal of error analysis is to identify error patterns. The work sample is scored, all errors are noted, and then an attempt is made to sort the errors into meaningful categories. For example, on a math worksheet of 15 single-digit multiplication problems, Casey made six errors that fell into the following categories:

ERROR	ERROR CATEGORY
$8 \times 6 = 54$	8 fact/6 fact
$9 \times 7 = 64$	9 fact/7 fact
$9 \times 8 = 81$	9 fact/8 fact
$8 \times 7 = 48$	8 fact/7 fact
$8 \times 8 = 62$	8 fact
$9 \times 9 = 72$	9 fact

Results are then summarized to locate patterns of errors:

ERROR CATEGORY	FREQUENCY OF OCCURRENCE
9 fact	3
8 fact	4
7 fact	2
6 fact	1

Casey has difficulty with some, but not all, multiplication facts. The problems that Casey missed required knowledge of the 6, 7, 8, and 9 facts. All errors took place in problems with some number multiplied by either 8 or 9. Because of this error pattern, the teacher's next move would be to assess Casey's knowledge of 8 and 9 multiplication facts with a criterion-referenced test or informal inventory.

The key to a successful error analysis is identification of one or more patterns of errors. However, not all error patterns are as easily detected as the one in the previous example. Sometimes a pattern does not emerge; the student may make several different types of errors, or mistakes may seem random. In many ways, error analysis is a subjective technique, relying on judgments made by the teacher. He or she must decide which responses should be marked as errors, select the category system for classifying errors, and then determine if the student's mistakes fall into some sort of pattern. Also, there are no set criteria for judging the number or proportion of errors that constitute a possible problem. Thus, the results of error analyses are best viewed as a guide for further assessment.

Rubrics

Another method of analyzing student work is through the use of a **rubric**. Rubrics are often associated with portfolio assessment, a technique that combines several assessment strategies (discussed later in this chapter). Rubrics require the use of observational techniques as well as professional judgment. They can be either analytic or holistic. An analytic rubric is a set of separate, short explanations regarding levels of student performance (Airasian, 1996). With an analytic rubric, each skill is assessed separately; that is, there is a separate score for each criterion (Cohen & Spencine, 2007). The performance levels may be indicated by a numerical scale (e.g., 1 through 4) or by verbal labels. Examples of labels are *independent, expanding, emergent,* and *missing* (Kritikos, LeDosquet, & Melton, 2011). To assist the professional using the rubric, each performance level is linked to a description of student performance exemplary of that level.

Figure 6–2 provides an example of an analytic rubric. This measure, the Analytic Reading Rubric, has four separate numerical rating categories with short explanations for each category. Three separate skills are evaluated. For example, in the first section (Reads target words), in order to perform at the highest level, the student must demonstrate reading target words independently. The teacher rates the student on each of the areas presented and then computes an average rating.

In the holistic rubric, an overall evaluation of the product is given in terms of quality. A holistic rubric generally takes less time to develop than an analytic rubric. The skills are evaluated as a whole; criteria are not assessed separately. Performance levels and descriptors are also used in a holistic rubric. See Figure 6–3.

ENHANCEDetext
Video Example 6.1
Watch this video to find out more about rubrics.

Math Problem-Solving Portfolio Rating Form

Student's name:_____

Check one:
_____ Sample One
_____ Sample Two
_____ Final Sample

To Be Completed by Student:

1. Date submitted:

2. What does this problem say about you as a problem solver?

3. What do you like best about how you solved this problem?

4. How will you improve your problem solving skill on the next problem?

To Be Completed by Teacher *(circle the appropriate rating):*

1. Quality of Reflection

Rating	Description
5	Has excellent insight into his/her problem-solving abilities and clear ideas of how to get better.
4	Has good insight into his/her problem-solving abilities and some ideas of how to get better.
3	Reflects somewhat on problem-solving strengths and needs. Has some idea of how to improve as a problem-solver.
2	Seldom reflects on problem-solving strengths and needs. Has little idea of how to improve as a problem-solver.
1	Has no concept of him/herself as a problem-solver.

2. Mathematical Knowledge

5	Shows deep understanding of the problems, math concepts, and principles. Uses appropriate math terms, and all calculations are correct.
4	Shows good understanding of math problems, concepts, and principles. Uses appropriate math terms most of the time. Few computational errors.
3	Shows understanding of some of the problems, math concepts, and principles. Uses some terms incorrectly. Contains some computation errors.
2	Errors in the use of many problems. Many terms used incorrectly.
1	Major errors in problems. Shows no understanding of math problems, concepts, and principles.

3. Strategic Knowledge

Rating	Description
5	Identifies all the important elements of the problem. Reflects an appropriate and systematic strategy for solving the problem; gives clear evidence of a solution process.
4	Identifies most of the important elements of the problem. Reflects an appropriate and systematic strategy for solving the problem and gives clear evidence of a solution process most of the time.
3	Identifies some important elements of the problem. Gives some evidence of a strategy to solve the problems, but process is incomplete.
2	Identifies few important elements of the problem. Gives little evidence of a strategy to solve the problems, and the process is unknown.
1	Uses irrelevant outside information. Copies parts of the problem; no attempt at solution.

continued

FIGURE 6–2
Sample Rubric for Portfolio Evaluation

Source: Tombari, Martin L.; Borich, Gary D., Authentic Assessment in the Classroom: Applications and Practice, 1st Ed., © 1999. Reprinted and Electronically reproduced by permission of Pearson Education, Inc., Upper Saddle River, New Jersey.

FIGURE 6–2 *continued*

4. Communication

5	Gives a complete response with a clear, unambiguous explanation; includes diagrams and charts when they help clarify explanation; presents strong arguments that are logically developed.
4	Gives good response with fairly clear explanation, which includes some use of diagrams and charts; presents good arguments that are mostly but not always logically developed.
3	Explanations and descriptions of problem solution are somewhat clear but incomplete; makes some use of diagrams and examples to clarify points, but arguments are incomplete.
2	Explanations and descriptions of problem solution are weak; makes little, if any, use of diagrams and examples to clarify points; arguments are seriously flawed.
1	Ineffective communication; diagrams misrepresent the problem; arguments have no sound premise.

SUM OF RATINGS: _____
AVERAGE OF RATINGS: _____
Comments:

FIGURE 6–3
Holistic Rubric—Reading

	EXCEPTIONAL (4)	COMPETENT (3)	DEVELOPING (2)	MINIMAL (1)
Reads target words	Reads target words independently	Reads target words with assistance	Reads some of the target words	Looks at pictures but does not read words
Fluency	Uses cues to achieve fluency	Uses some strategies to achieve fluency	Knows some letters and struggles to achieve some fluency	Does not attempt to read pictures or has incorrect attempt
Meaning	Derives meaning	Uses some strategies to derive meaning	Uses memorized language	Has limited knowledge of print

EXCEPTIONAL	COMPETENT	DEVELOPING	MINIMAL
Student reads target single words independently without assistance. Student uses various cues to achieve fluency and derive meaning.	Student reads target single words with assistance. Student knows most letters. Student uses some strategies to achieve fluency and derive meaning.	Student enjoys being read to. Student knows some letters. Student reads some of the target words. Student uses memorized language.	Student enjoys being read to. Student looks at pictures. Limited knowledge of print.

TASK ANALYSIS

Task analysis is an unobtrusive informal technique that focuses on curricular tasks rather than student performance. It is as much an instructional technique as an assessment strategy, and its purpose is to break down complex tasks into teachable subcomponents. Task analysis can be defined as focusing on, dividing, and describing task elements (Howell, Kaplan, & O'Connell, 1979; Cegelka, 1995b; Browder, Trela, & Jimenez, 2007).

The major role of task analysis in the instructional process is to assist in curricular design and specification of the instructional sequence. An instructional goal is selected and analyzed to determine the specific subskills that will support its accomplishment. Then, the subskills or task subcomponents are arranged for instruction in an order that facilitates their acquisition. This arrangement is completed in three steps:

1. Identify a specific instructional goal or objective.
2. Analyze the instructional objective into its essential component parts (i.e., the movements, actions, or responses that, when taken cumulatively, constitute the instructional objective).
3. Determine the entry level of the skill and specify the prerequisite skills (in other words, state at what point the particular skill sequence begins) (Berdine & Cegelka, 1980, p. 160).

The problem of analyzing a task into its subcomponents can be done by temporal order, by developmental sequence, by difficulty level, and by structural task analysis. The method selected is determined to some extent by the nature of the task under consideration.

Methods of Identifying Task Subcomponents

Analysis by Temporal Order

Some tasks follow a temporal order. For example, in washing one's hands, the tap water must be turned on before the hands can be rinsed. The teacher may choose to teach such tasks in the order they are performed or, in some cases, may proceed in a backward order by beginning with the last subtask in the sequence. This is called backward chaining; it is most useful when the task is difficult for the learner. By beginning at the end, backward chaining assures successful task completion in the early stages of learning.

Analysis by Developmental Sequence

Task subcomponents can also be ordered by developmental sequence. Affleck, Lowenbraun, and Archer (1980) explain a developmental sequence consisting of skill stages constructed from earlier learned information. One of the best examples is the traditional curriculum for the arithmetic operations of addition, subtraction, multiplication, and division. There is a definite hierarchy of subskills, and difficulty with a later skill may be due to failure to master an earlier, prerequisite skill.

Analysis by Difficulty Level

Some tasks have neither a definite temporal order nor a natural developmental sequence; however, they can be analyzed according to the ease with which their subcomponents can be acquired. A good example is the skill of writing letters in manuscript. This skill can be task analyzed by dividing lowercase letters into several clusters, beginning with the least difficult (Affleck et al., 1980, p. 90):

Straight line letters	lti
Straight line and slant letters	vxwyz
Circle and curve letters	ocs
Circle and line letters	abepgdq
Curve and line letters	jhmknfru

In assessment, task analysis serves a somewhat different purpose than it serves in instruction. It is used with tasks in which a student experiences difficulty. Troublesome tasks are analyzed, and the student's ability to perform each subtask or task subcomponent is assessed to locate the source of the difficulty. For example, if writing sentences with correct capitalization and punctuation appears to be a problem for Jorge, the teacher can task-analyze this skill and then assess Jorge's ability to perform each step in the developmental sequence. A sample skill hierarchy for capitalization and punctuation appears in Table 6–2. To utilize this sequence for assessment, informal measures such as criterion-referenced tests are designed for each step of interest. With Jorge, the teacher could begin by assessing the skills listed for third graders and then work backward through the sequence to identify prerequisite skills that have not yet been mastered. Instruction would then focus on mastery of these skills.

There are several strategies for conducting a task analysis in assessment. If the task in question is part of the standard curriculum, the teacher may have access to curriculum guides, scope and sequence charts, or published materials that describe the task's subcomponents. Otherwise, it

is up to the teacher to determine the important task components. This is usually easiest for tasks with a definite temporal sequence. The teacher can perform the task and note each step that is taken. An educator can then perform the task multiple times using those steps in order to check the validity of the sequence. In this process, steps can be altered, as needed (Berdine & Cegelka, 1980).

It is also important to determine if the task can be performed in more than one acceptable sequence. For example, the task of tying one's shoe involves several successful sequences. Thus, the teacher should observe other adults and, if possible, students as they complete the task.

With tasks that do not follow a temporal order, subcomponents and their sequence must be determined by logic. One method is to list all the subtasks or subcomponents that appear to be involved in the task. These are then arranged in

TABLE 6–2
Hierarchy for Capitalization and Punctuation Skills

Grade 1

Copies sentences correctly.

Capitalizes first word of a sentence.

Capitalizes first letter of a proper name.

Uses period at the end of a sentence.

Uses question mark after a written question.

Uses period after numbers in a list.

Grade 2

Capitalizes titles of compositions.

Capitalizes proper names used in written compositions.

Uses comma after salutation and after closing of a friendly letter.

Uses comma between day of the month and the year.

Uses comma between names of city and state.

Grade 3

Capitalizes the names of months, days, holidays; first word in a line of verse; titles of books, stories, poems; salutation and closing of letters and notes; and names of special places.

Begins to apply correct punctuation for abbreviations, initials, contractions, items in a list, quotations, questions, and exclamations.

Uses proper indentation for paragraphs.

Note: From *Teaching Students with Learning Problems* (5th ed.) by C. Mercer and A. Mercer. 1998, Upper Saddle River, NJ: Merrill/Prentice Hall. Copyright 1998 by Prentice Hall, Inc. Reprinted by permission.

order, ranging from the least difficult to the most difficult, or by utility, ranging from the most necessary for task completion to the least necessary. Obviously, such a task analysis is somewhat subjective, and two teachers generating a subtask sequence for the same skill might disagree. However, flaws in the task analysis usually become apparent in the assessment phase. If the student can perform each subtask but not the task itself, an important subtask has likely been omitted. If the student can perform what are considered to be difficult subcomponents but cannot perform easier ones, then the specified sequence is incorrect, at least for that student.

Structural Task Analysis

Another approach that may provide instructional information is an analysis of task demands (McLoughlin & Kershman, 1978; Courtrade, Browder, Spooner, & DiBiase, 2010). Rather than specifying task subcomponents and sequence, the goal is to describe the task in terms of the demands placed upon the learner. This is sometimes called a **structural task analysis**, and it includes consideration of the following task characteristics:

- *Task directions.* The directions for completing the task may be presented verbally or in writing. They vary in number and can be either clear and concise or complex and confusing.
- *Presentation mode.* This refers to the way in which information necessary for task completion is provided to the learner; for example, the student may be required to listen to, read, or look at one or more sources of information.
- *Response mode.* This is the method used by the student in performing the task. The student may need to respond orally or make some sort of written response such as writing numbers, letters, words, sentences, or paragraphs.
- *Quantity requirements.* This task dimension is concerned with the number of responses the student must produce: the number of questions to answer, problems to solve, sentences to write, and so on.
- *Time requirements.* Some tasks are timed, and their successful completion depends on the speed of the learner.

- *Accuracy requirements.* These criteria specify the accuracy standards for successful task performance. For example, a teacher might require a minimum of 80 percent accuracy on in-class assignments.

Structural analysis of a classroom task helps identify specific instructional expectations. When these expectations are known, one can consider ways to modify the task demands to facilitate successful performance. In assessment, diagnostic probes are used to evaluate the effects of changing task demands systematically. This strategy is described in the next section.

ENHANCEDetext
Video Example 6.2
Watch this video to find out more about classroom assessment in action.

INFORMAL INVENTORIES

Informal **inventories** assess a student's performance in a school skill area, and their standard of comparison is the curriculum. For example, the teacher may wonder about a new student's knowledge of geography, American history, or punctuation and capitalization rules. Inventories provide data to answer these types of questions about present levels of functioning.

Inventories are screening devices that assess selected portions of curricular areas; they are not intended to measure mastery of every fact, concept, and subskill in a particular domain. Because they assess only representative skills, they can sample a greater number of skill areas. For example, an arithmetic inventory might present some, but not all, addition fact problems, some subtraction facts, and some multiplication and division facts. The intent is to identify the general level of student functioning within the curricular area. However, more precise measures such as criterion-referenced tests are needed to find out about student performance in relation to all skills within this domain.

Inventories are similar in many ways to classroom quizzes, although they are typically used for different purposes. Inventories are more of a preteaching assessment tool rather than a measure of progress. They are usually administered before instruction to determine where a need for instruction exists. Also, inventories generally cover a larger segment of the curriculum than is covered by quizzes. A spelling inventory might contain selected words from several levels of difficulty (grade 1, grade 2, and so forth), whereas a classroom spelling test would include only those words for which instruction had been provided.

Inventories are commercially available for many subject areas, but the most common one is the informal reading inventory. Teachers should understand the steps involved in designing an inventory so that they can create such a measure if an appropriate one is not readily available. To design an informal inventory, the teacher should:

1. Determine the curriculum area in which the student is to be assessed.
2. Isolate a portion of the curriculum appropriate for the student's age, grade, and skill level.
3. Analyze the curriculum into testable and teachable segments. As in task analysis, the curriculum may be broken down into sequential steps, developmental steps, or difficulty levels.
4. Prepare test items for each segment of the curriculum, emphasizing the most important aspects of each segment.
5. If necessary, reduce the number of test items so that the inventory is of manageable length.
6. Sequence the test items from easiest to most difficult or in random order if the student is expected to answer all items.

An example of an informal handwriting inventory could include test items that are representative of the content domain but include only selected subskills. The teacher could analyze the skill of handwriting into developmental steps: Students learn to print their name, then print the lowercase and capital letters, and so forth (Lewis & Doorlag, 2006). Because students usually acquire these skills in this order, the test items are arranged in the developmental sequence to assure successful performance for students who have not yet mastered more advanced skills. However, test items are sometimes arranged in random order. If students are expected to answer all test items, random order reduces the possibility that clues from one item will help them answer others.

Because informal inventories do not typically include performance standards, students do not pass or fail these measures. Instead, the goal is to estimate the students' current levels of performance and identify areas in the curriculum requiring further assessment. Educators determine strengths and needs based on these instruments (Nilsson, 2008). Teachers should be cautious about basing instruction solely on the results of informal inventories. First, the quality of an inventory, like that of most informal measures, is usually unknown. With no information about reliability and validity, it is difficult to judge a measure's accuracy. However, Strickland and Turnbull (1990) maintain that informal inventories could include content and criterion validity types. Second, because inventories do not usually contain standards for acceptable performance, the professional must decide how many errors constitute a potential skill weakness. If a student misses one or two items out of several of a particular type, is this a cause for concern? With informal inventories, the teacher is responsible for making that judgment.

If the teacher determines that inventory results indicate a potential problem area, the next step is to assess the skill area more closely. For example, if a student completes an addition skills inventory and performs successfully until encountering regrouping problems, the teacher should find out more about the student's skills in regrouping. The teacher could construct a criterion-referenced test to assess these skills and, if results indicated they were not yet mastered, begin instruction at this point in the curriculum.

CLASSROOM TESTS AND QUIZZES

Like informal inventories, **classroom quizzes** and tests assess a student's performance in a school skill area using the curriculum as the standard of comparison. Quizzes are screening devices and therefore assess only a subset of skills selected to be representative of the curricular area under study.

A major difference between informal inventories and classroom quizzes is the purpose for which they are used. On the one hand, quizzes—or, as they are sometimes called, tests or examinations—assess whether students have acquired some body of knowledge or skills taught by the teacher. They are measures of progress, and their results are used to evaluate the effects of teaching and learning. Inventories, on the other hand, are typically used to plan instruction. Another difference is the comprehensiveness of the measure; quizzes tend to cover smaller segments of the curriculum than do inventories.

Teachers usually design classroom quizzes, although sample test items may be available in teachers' manuals for textbooks or instructional materials. The first step in the development of a quiz is to identify the content of the instructional unit to be assessed. Because instruction has already taken place, instructional objectives should be available, and these objectives are used to generate quiz items. If time constraints permit, each important objective should be represented by at least one quiz item.

The next step is to determine the types of items to be included in the quiz. Objective items are those for which the correct answer is readily identifiable (e.g., true–false and multiple-choice questions). Objective items are easily scored but time consuming to construct. In contrast, more subjective items such as essay questions require less time to construct but are more difficult to score because the teacher must exercise judgment in evaluating student responses. In selecting the type of items to prepare, the teacher must also consider the nature of the subject matter to be assessed. Some curriculum areas, particularly those with a body of factual information, lend themselves well to measurement by objective questions. Other areas are better assessed with essays and other types of more subjective questions. The most common types of quiz items used by classroom teachers are:

- *True–false.* In this type of question, the student determines whether a statement is true or false.
- *Multiple choice.* The student selects a word, phrase, or sentence that best completes a partial statement or answers a question.
- *Matching.* The student selects from one set of words, phrases, or sentences the one that best fits each of the words, phrases, or sentences in another set.
- *Completion.* The student finishes an incomplete sentence by furnishing a word or phrase.
- *Short answer.* The student provides a brief response such as a definition, a list of steps or examples, or a short description.
- *Problem.* The student solves some sort of mathematical problem.
- *Essay.* The student provides a prose response, usually of some length.

Airasian (2005) presents several rules for writing items for classroom quizzes:

1. Avoid ambiguous and confusing wording and sentences.
2. Use appropriate vocabulary.
3. Keep questions short and to the point.
4. Write items that have one correct answer.
5. Give information about the nature of the desired answer.
6. Do not provide clues to the correct answer. (pp. 185–191)

Although teachers should avoid embedding clues within questions, it is important that items are clear enough to give students direction for responding. This is particularly true for essay questions. Vague questions often result in vague, disorganized responses.

In designing tests and quizzes for students with special needs, it is also important to consider academic skill demands. Students must be able to read quiz questions; a test is not an adequate measure of a curriculum area if a student fails because he or she could not decode the questions. For students with writing skill problems, objective items requiring a response of only one letter or number would be less difficult than, for example, an essay exam. Another concern is the physical appearance of the quiz. The print should be clear and readable, and pages should be uncluttered.

Classroom quizzes can be power tests or speed tests. With power tests, there are no time limits because the aim is to determine the extent of the student's knowledge in the curriculum area under assessment. In general, classroom quizzes should be power measures unless the instructional goal requires that students perform both accurately and quickly. However, with skill subjects, particularly basic academic skills, speed is often important.

The reliability of classroom quizzes can be determined by means of the Kuder–Richardson 21 formula, an estimate of interitem consistency. The teacher needs to know three things to use this formula: K, the number of items in the test; $\overline{X}$, the mean of the scores; and σ^2, the variance of the scores (computed by squaring the standard deviation). These values are used in the following formula to yield r, the total test reliability:

$$r = \frac{K\sigma^2 - \overline{X}(K - \overline{X})}{\sigma^2(K - 1)}$$

It is also possible to gather information about the characteristics of specific quiz items. One concern, the difficulty of the item, is determined by calculating the proportion of students who respond to the item correctly. To do so, simply divide the number of students with correct responses by the total number of students attempting the item. Brown (1981) recommends separating the class into two groups of students—those who score in the upper half on the quiz and those who score in the lower half—in order to use the following formula:

$$\text{Item difficulty} = \frac{\substack{\text{Proportion} \\ \text{correct} \\ \text{(upper half)}} + \substack{\text{Proportion} \\ \text{correct} \\ \text{(lower half)}}}{2}$$

The proportion correct for the upper half of the class is determined by dividing the number of upper-half students who answered the item correctly by the total number of students in the upper half; the proportion for the lower half is determined in the same way. This allows the teacher to compare the difficulty levels for these two segments of the class. Brown (1981) suggests that a difficulty level of .60 to .75 (60 to 75 percent of students responding correctly) is appropriate for most classroom exam items. However, Gallagher (1998) maintains that the acceptable item difficulty level (or item-achievement rank) should be set by the teacher based on the nature of the assessment task and the expectations for student performance.

The discrimination index of a quiz item is a measure of how well the item differentiates between students who score well and those who do not. To determine the discrimination index, use this formula (Brown, 1981):

$$\substack{\text{Item} \\ \text{discrimination}} = \substack{\text{Proportion} \\ \text{correct} \\ \text{(upper half)}} - \substack{\text{Proportion} \\ \text{correct} \\ \text{(lower half)}}$$

According to Gay (1990), when an item's discrimination index is greater than .30, that item is doing an adequate job of distinguishing between upper- and lower-half students. If the discrimination index is less than .30, the item should be reexamined and possibly rewritten. The index can be a negative number. For example, if 50 percent of the upper-half students and 80 percent of the lower-half students answer a quiz question correctly, the item's discrimination index would be −30, a sign that the question is a misleading one. There are some situations in which a teacher would not want an item to discriminate. For example, the instructional goal might be that all students will tell time to the nearest minute with 100 percent accuracy.

Some objective items offer students a choice of responses. For instance, with multiple-choice questions, the student must select one response from several possible answers presented. With this type of item, it is important to look at the wrong answers, sometimes called distractors. To conduct this type of analysis, the teacher records the number of students who select each of the possible responses. If a particular distractor is chosen by a large proportion of students, this may signal a poorly written item or an area of misunderstanding that merits further explanation or instruction.

CRITERION-REFERENCED TESTS

Like informal inventories and classroom quizzes, **criterion-referenced tests (CRTs)** compare a student's performance to the goals of the curriculum rather than to the performance of a norm group. However, CRTs typically sample more restricted curricular domains than those sampled by inventories. An inventory might reveal a possible problem in decoding short vowels; a criterion-referenced test would identify the short vowels the student could read and those he or she could not. Another important feature of CRTs is their emphasis on mastery. These measures are scored as pass or fail: either the student has mastered the skill under study or the student has not. This has direct implications for instruction; unmastered skills or their prerequisites may become the next curricular goal.

Placement tests are quite similar to criterion-referenced tests. Often furnished as part of an instructional material or textbook series, placement tests identify the point within the material where instruction should begin. Placement tests assess mastery of the content presented by the text or material. When the student achieves a specified level of accuracy, it is assumed that the content has been mastered. When he or she drops below this specified mastery level, the starting point for instruction is identified. Competency tests, too, are much like CRTs. A common school use of competency tests is to determine whether students have met state or district standards for high school graduation. Again, specific skills are assessed, and performance is compared to a pre-specified level of mastery.

Criterion-referenced tests, placement tests, and competency tests are all commercially available. CRTs are easy to construct, and teachers may wish to design their own to match their instructional goals. Usually, however, teachers use the placement tests that accompany commercial materials, although it is certainly possible to adapt or even construct such measures. Because competency tests are used with large groups of students, perhaps even an entire school

population, they are typically developed at the school or district level or purchased from a test publisher.

CRTs can be used to assess any behavior for which an instructional objective can be specified. They are easy to design, but their construction does require an investment of time and energy. The major steps are:

1. Decide what specific questions you want answered about a student's behavior. What ability (i.e., skill and knowledge) do you want to test?
2. Write a performance objective, which describes how you are going to test the student. It should include (1) what the student must do (i.e., what behavior must be engaged in); (2) under what conditions the student will engage in this behavior; and (3) how well the student must perform in order to pass the test.
3. Use the performance objective to help you construct (i.e., write) your CRT. All of the necessary components of a CRT may be found in your performance objective. These components are (1) the directions for administration and scoring, (2) the criterion for passing the test, and (3) the materials and/or test items necessary. (Howell, Kaplan, & O'Connell, 1979, pp. 96–97)

Questions about student performance can be generated from many sources. After observing a student in the classroom for a few days, the teacher can easily come up with several! Standardized test results may also suggest areas for further assessment. Other valuable sources are the results of informal measures such as inventories and work sample analyses.

Once an assessment question is specified, an instructional objective is selected. If the question concerns a standard area of the curriculum, it is likely that the appropriate instructional objective will be available in a curriculum guide or a similar source. If necessary, the teacher can construct the objective by specifying three things: the desired student behavior, stated in observable terms; the conditions under which the behavior should occur; and the criterion for acceptable performance of the behavior (Mager, 1975). Just as a target behavior must be pinpointed before it can be observed, the behavior to be assessed with a CRT must be clearly specified. For example, "knowing the alphabet" is too imprecise. It could be interpreted in many ways—reciting the alphabet, writing it in manuscript or cursive, saying the names or sounds of the letters, and so forth. If the teacher is interested in whether the student can recite the alphabet, the objective can begin as:

> *Say the names of the letters of the alphabet in order from memory.*

The teacher then specifies the conditions under which the behavior should occur. What directions will the teacher provide? What materials will be available to the student? What constraints will be imposed upon performance? For the alphabet recitation example, the teacher decided to give one simple direction ("Say the alphabet"). No time constraints were imposed, and no materials were necessary. The objective is:

> *When told by the teacher to "say the alphabet," the student will say the names of the letters of the alphabet in order from memory.*

The last step is to set the criterion for acceptable performance. How well must the student perform to demonstrate mastery of the skill? Are any errors allowed? If so, how many or what percentage? Howell et al. (1979) suggest establishing criteria by means of "expert" populations. They recommend that the teacher identify individuals who possess the skill being assessed by the CRT, then administer the CRT to this group and use their minimum level of performance as the mastery standard. This may not be necessary with some skills if the teacher believes that the skill should be performed without errors. If this is the case in alphabet recitation, the objective becomes:

> When told by the teacher to "say the alphabet," the student will say the names of the letters of the alphabet in order from memory with no errors.

The criterion-referenced test in Figure 6–4 measures this instructional objective. The information at the beginning of the test is derived from the objective. The student behavior becomes

Criterion-Referenced Test

Task: Say the alphabet in order from memory.

Materials: Score sheet

Directions (to student): "Say the alphabet."

Directions (to tester): Record student responses verbatim. Do not allow the student to look at the score sheet.

Scoring: Count correct if the student says each of the 26 letters of the alphabet in the correct order. Count correct if letter names are intelligible even if not articulated perfectly. Count as incorrect if a letter name is omitted, added, or said out of order.

Criterion for Acceptable Performance: 100% accuracy

Score Sheet

Skill: Knowledge of the alphabet

Task: Say names of letters of the alphabet in order from memory

Student ______________________ Date ______________

Age ______________ Grade ______________ Tester ______________

Student responses (record verbatim):

FIGURE 6–4
Criterion-Referenced Test and Score Sheet

the test task; the conditions under which the behavior is to be performed provide information about needed materials and directions, for both the student and the tester; and the objective's criterion for acceptable performance becomes the criterion for passing the CRT. Additional scoring standards may also be necessary. In this case, the teacher decided to allow mispronunciations of letter names if they were intelligible. On the score sheet, the teacher records identifying information about the student and the test and then writes down the student's responses.

If a student passes a CRT, the teacher assumes that the student has mastered the objective, and assessment can progress to the next instructional step. If a student does not pass, the teacher moves backward through the curricular sequence and assesses a prerequisite skill. Instructional planning can begin once the skills the student has mastered are established.

However, the teacher must exercise some caution in interpreting results. First, CRTs tell only what a student can or cannot do; because they are not normed, they do not tell what a particular student is expected to do. If a student fails a CRT on shoe tying, the instructional implication appears to be to teach this skill. Although this skill would likely be appropriate for a young, school-aged child, it would not be for a toddler. Other factors to be considered before translating CRT results into instructional action are the age of the student, the age-appropriateness of the skill, and the priority of the skill in relation to other possible instructional goals.

Another caveat common to all informal measures is the lack of information about reliability and validity. Teachers can improve the CRTs they construct by specifying standard procedures for test administration and scoring and by establishing mastery levels empirically rather than arbitrarily; procedures are also available for determining the reliability and validity of CRTs (Howell et al., 1979).

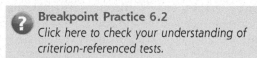

Breakpoint Practice 6.2
Click here to check your understanding of criterion-referenced tests.

DIAGNOSTIC PROBES AND DIAGNOSTIC TEACHING

Diagnostic probes and diagnostic teaching involve the systematic manipulation of instructional conditions to determine the most appropriate strategy for teaching a particular skill to a student. The difference between these two procedures relates to the thoroughness with which they evaluate instructional alternatives. On the one hand, diagnostic probes are typically brief, one-time measures of a single instructional option. Diagnostic teaching, on the other hand, takes place over an extended time period to investigate fully the differential effects of various instructional interventions.

Diagnostic Probes

Diagnostic probes are used to discover whether changing some aspect of a classroom task will have a positive effect on student performance. For example, if the history teacher observes that a student is having difficulty with the daily quizzes on reading assignments, the teacher could design one or several diagnostic probes to investigate the relationship between the demands of the task and the student's ability to perform. The daily quiz could be modified in a number of ways; depending on the type of difficulty the student is experiencing. For instance, if the student answers the first few questions but does not complete the quiz, the amount of time allowed for this task could be increased or the number of questions reduced. Or if the student's writing skills appear to interfere with performance, the student could be permitted to respond orally or to tape-record answers.

The general procedures for the design of a diagnostic probe are:

1. The student's performance is assessed under the standard instructional condition.
2. Some aspect of the task or the instructional conditions that relate to the task is modified.
3. The student's performance is assessed under the modified condition and compared with previous performance.

This sequence of steps usually takes place within one instructional session. The teacher observes a possible performance problem and identifies a possible solution. Data are collected before the modification is made to establish the student's current performance level and again after the modification is in place. If necessary, a series of diagnostic probes are devised until the teacher has sufficient information to design a diagnostic teaching sequence.

The teacher can make several types of changes to improve student performance. Two major types of modifications relate to task characteristics and the instructional strategies used to teach the task. Structural task analysis is a useful way to analyze task characteristics. Among the factors to be considered are the difficulty level of the task; the conditions under which the student is expected to perform; the directions provided for task completion; presentation and response modes; and requirements for quantity, speed, and accuracy.

Table 6–3 summarizes several general methods of adapting instruction. Included are strategies for modifying the task itself and for changing the instructional conditions that relate to task performance. These suggestions are by no means exhaustive, but they do provide some direction for the development of diagnostic probes. Dimensions of instruction to consider are the methods used to present new information to students (lecture, discussion, demonstration, and so forth), the number and type of practice opportunities available, the way feedback is provided, the consequences for successful performance, the instructional materials, and the pace of instruction.

Another type of instructional change involves modifying the strategies that the student uses to approach the classroom task. It is the student's behavior that is altered, not a condition of instruction. The first step is observation of the student's interaction with the task. The methods the student employs in task performance are analyzed, and ineffective strategies are identified. Then the teacher attempts to modify the student's strategy or substitute another, more effective strategy. For example, if a student's handwriting is poor and he or she grips the pencil awkwardly, the teacher may attempt to change the student's hand position. Or if a student studies new biology terms by staring at a page in the text, the teacher may demonstrate an alternative technique that requires active rehearsal.

Diagnostic probes are most useful for gathering preliminary information about the possible effectiveness of an instructional modification. Only in rare instances do probes yield sufficient information to justify making a change in the instructional environment. Probes provide hypotheses about modifications that may make a difference in student performance. These hypotheses can then be tested through diagnostic teaching.

Diagnostic Teaching

Diagnostic teaching systematically evaluates the relative effectiveness of two or more instructional techniques. It assists the teacher in deciding on an instructional strategy for a particular student or group. The teacher carefully monitors student performance while presenting instruction first in one manner and then in another. Assessment data collected under each instructional condition are then compared to determine the more effective teaching technique.

For example, if Yvonne is having difficulty learning multiplication facts, the teacher might want to try some different types of practice activities for this skill. First, the teacher would identify the current instructional condition and assess the student's performance under this condition. In Yvonne's case, worksheets are the current practice activity; over a 1-week period, Yvonne has received scores ranging from 30 percent correct to 55 percent correct. Next, the teacher decides on a new instructional strategy. This decision may be based on the results of a series of diagnostic probes. For multiplication facts, two alternatives to worksheets are flash card drills and computer-based drill and practice programs. These techniques allow practice of the skill while providing the learner with immediate feedback about the accuracy of her responses. The teacher then implements one of the new instructional approaches for a few days and continues to collect student performance data, usually on a daily basis.

TABLE 6–3
Designing Diagnostic Probes

INSTRUCTIONAL DIMENSION	POSSIBLE MODIFICATIONS
Task Characteristics	
The difficulty level of the task	Divide the task into component subtasks for the student to perform separately; or substitute an easier, prerequisite task
The conditions under which the task is performed	Alter the conditions by allowing the use of aids (e.g., calculators for mathematics tasks) or by providing cues and prompts
Task directions	Simplify and reduce the number of directions; provide oral as well as written directions
Presentation mode	Change the presentation mode to one that takes advantage of the student's strengths (e.g., change to oral presentation for students with reading problems); or present information in more than one way
Response mode	Change the response mode to one that takes advantage of the student's strengths (e.g., change to oral responses for students with poor writing skills)
Quantity requirement	Reduce the number of required student responses
Speed requirement	Increase the amount of time allowed for task performance; or remove time limits altogether
Accuracy requirement	Decrease the standards for successful task performance
Instructional Procedures	
Presentation of new information to students	Change the method of instruction to a more direct approach (e.g., use lecture or demonstration rather than discussion or discovery); or explain new information in several different ways; or, increase the number of times new information is presented
Practice opportunities for students	Increase the number of practice opportunities provided to students; improve the quantity and quality of feedback students receive during practice; alter the types of practice activities to relate more directly to target behaviors
Feedback to students on task performance	Give feedback more often; relate feedback not only to the accuracy of the response but also to the specific aspect of the task that the student performed correctly or incorrectly
Consequences to students for successful performance	Make the consequences for success more attractive
Learning materials	Revise or modify learning materials (e.g., textbooks, workbooks, worksheets) to a simpler level; or, substitute alternate materials
Pace of instruction	Slow the pace of instruction so less information is presented and practiced at one time
Providing students with alternate strategies for task performance	Change the way in which students approach the task by modifying current strategies; or introduce new, more effective strategies

Note: From *Teaching Special Students in General Education Classrooms* (7th ed.) by R. B. Lewis and D. H. Doorlag, © 2006, Upper Saddle River, NJ: Merrill/Prentice Hall. Copyright 2006 by Prentice Hall, Inc. Reprinted by permission.

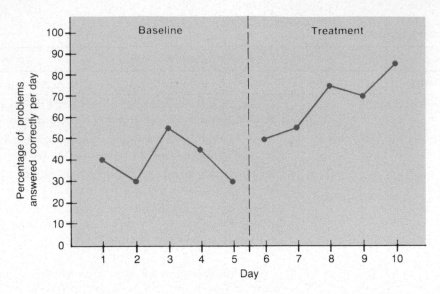

FIGURE 6–5
Diagnostic Teaching Results

The steps in diagnostic teaching are:

1. Identify the current instructional condition, the baseline condition.
2. Select or design an informal assessment tool to monitor student performance.
3. Assess the student's performance under the current instructional condition. Daily data collection for a 1-week period usually provides an adequate picture of current performance.
4. Select one or more new instructional strategies to evaluate.
5. Implement the first new instructional strategy for a brief period (e.g., 1 week). This is the first intervention phase.
6. Continue to regularly assess the student's performance.
7. Implement a second new instructional strategy, if desired.
8. Continue to regularly assess the student's performance.
9. Plot performance data for the baseline condition and the intervention phases on a graph. Compare performance across the conditions.

Only one thing at a time should be changed in diagnostic teaching. The baseline condition and the treatment phase should differ in only one important instructional variable. The instructional factor that produced the change in student behavior can then be identified. For instance, if the teacher changes the practice activity and sees an increase in student accuracy, the change in performance can be linked to the change in the practice activity. However, if several changes occur (e.g., a new practice activity is introduced, a peer tutor replaces the teacher, and the amount of instructional time is doubled), the teacher cannot attribute improved student performance to any single modification.

Figure 6–5 presents the results of the intervention with Yvonne, the girl having difficulty learning multiplication facts. Yvonne's teacher collected daily data on the percentage of questions Yvonne answered correctly. As can be seen from the graph, the new treatment—the flash card drill—appears to be a more effective instructional strategy than worksheet activities for Yvonne.

CURRICULUM-BASED MEASUREMENT

Curriculum-based measurement (CBM), as its name implies, is a curriculum-based assessment strategy. Like informal inventories and classroom quizzes, CBM is a direct approach to the assessment of students' current skill levels in important

TABLE 6–4
CBMs for Basic Skills

AREA	TESTING DURATION	DESCRIPTION AND TYPES OF SCORES DERIVED
Reading	1 minute	Students read passages orally, and the number of words read correctly and errors are counted.
Spelling	2 minutes	Students write words that are dictated orally, and the number of words spelled correctly and correct letter sequences are counted.
Mathematics Computation	2–5 minutes	Students write answers to computation problems, and the number of correct digits are counted.
Written Expression	3 minutes	After being given a story starter or topic sentence, students write a story. Number of words written, spelled correctly, and correct word sequences may be counted.

Note: From "Curriculum-Based Measurement and Problem-Solving Assessment: Basic Procedures and Outcomes" (p. 225) by M. R. Shinn and D. D. Hubbard, 1993, in E. L. Meyen, G. A. Vergason, and R. J. Whelan (Eds.), *Educating Students with Mild Disabilities*, Denver: Love. Copyright 1993 by Love Publishing Company. Adapted by permission.

school subjects. However, CBM differs from other informal techniques because of the types of skills selected for assessment and the frequency with which assessment takes place.

In CBM, brief probes are used to collect samples of critical target behaviors such as reading words aloud and writing numbers and words. For example, to assess oral reading proficiency, students read a passage aloud for 1 minute while the teacher tabulates the number of words read correctly. As Table 6–4 illustrates, the behavior samples are very brief (1 to 5 minutes) and assessment focuses on basic skills. Correct performance is the major concern; the processes underlying performance are not.

Probes are administered frequently (e.g., twice weekly), data are graphed, and the results are analyzed to determine whether the student's progress is adequate. For CBM to be effective, the behaviors of interest should be assessed directly, and measurement should be frequent so that needed instructional changes can be made quickly. A large body of research in special education supports the usefulness of CBM for monitoring student progress and modifying instruction based on student performance (Deno, 1985; Deno & Fuchs, 1988; Deno, Marston, & Mirkin, 1982; Deno, Mirkin, & Chiang, 1982; Deno, Mirkin, Lowry, & Kuehnle, 1980; Fuchs, 1986; Fuchs, Deno, & Mirkin, 1984; Shinn & Hubbard, 1993; Barnett, Daly, Jones, & Lentz, 2004; Esparza Brown & Sanford, 2011).

One of the most important aspects of CBM is the graphing of student performance data. A visual depiction of the student's progress helps teachers identify when changes need to be made to improve the rate of skill acquisition.

CBM can assist in making decisions about instructional modifications (Hasbrouck, Woldbeck, Ihnot, & Parker, 1999). In each, the *y*-axis is labeled *WCPM* for "words correct per minute." The numbers along the *x*-axis are the weeks of the school year. Each dot is a data point the student's score on one CBM probe. The dots are connected to show the student's progress throughout the year. The oblique line beginning at the first data point is the aim line. It represents the expected progress for the student. CBM graphs also show the relationship between student performance and the interventions selected by the teacher. The letters at the top of the graphs (e.g., A, B) indicate an intervention change. The interventions on the graphs can show the results of a change in the interest level of the reading material, attendance issues resolved, and adjustments to the student's reading group.

Hasbrouck et al. (1999) recommend that teachers adopt CBM as a strategy for evaluating student progress and making decisions about the need for changes in instruction. According to these authors, CBM gives quick feedback to constituents, teachers are able to respond to students immediately, and visual results reveal the effectiveness of the program.

Scott and Weishaar (2003) provide step-by-step procedures for development of a CBM system to assess student progress in reading. Among their recommendations are decision rules for determining when instructional changes should be made. According to these authors, changes are indicated when data points fall consistently above (or below) the aim line. No changes are indicated if data points cluster around the aim line. Scott and Weishaar suggest that teachers consider three consecutive data points when applying these rules.

CHECKLISTS AND RATING SCALES

Checklists and rating scales are still other types of classroom assessment strategies. They are structured assessments in which specific questions are posed and an informant selects a response rather than generating one. These measures are usually administered in written form to adult informants, although they can be presented orally to young children.

Checklists, provide the informant with a list of descriptions, and the task is simply to check each description that applies to the student under assessment. The teacher, parent, or other informant reads each description, making a check beside each that is accurate. Checklists can be used for a variety of purposes, and Figure 6–6 presents an example of a social studies curriculum list. In this curriculum list for teachers, the teacher considers each educational objective and then marks those attained by the student.

Cooper and TenBrink (2003) provide suggestions to teachers who decide to develop their own checklists. According to these authors, a well-designed checklist:

1. is relatively short.
2. uses clear statements for each item.
3. focuses on observable characteristics or behaviors.
4. includes only important characteristics or behaviors.
5. is arranged sequentially or logically (p. 15).

Rating scales require more from informants than a yes–no response. A description or statement is presented, and informants express their agreement with the description by selecting one

---

Curriculum Checklist: Social Studies

Understanding Maps

_____1. States definition of latitude

_____2. States definition of longitude

_____3. Demonstrates understanding of grid coordinating system

_____4. States definition of contour lines

_____5. Demonstrates understanding of N, S, E and W

_____6. Demonstrates understanding of measurement units (metric system)

_____7. Demonstrates understanding of scale

_____8. Appropriately uses a compass

_____9. Appropriately uses a protractor

FIGURE 6–6
Curriculum Checklist: Social Studies

of a series of ratings. Among the most common rating instruments are Likert-type scales (Likert, 1932), as noted in Chapter 3. The informant considers each statement and then chooses one of the specified responses: Strongly Agree, Agree, Neutral, Disagree, or Strongly Disagree. The responses to Likert-type scale items are often tied to numerical values (e.g., Strongly Disagree = 1). This allows the informant's responses to be statistically summarized. For example, if a teacher responds to several items about a student's school achievement the teacher's ratings can be summarized by calculating the mean. Rating scales are used for many purposes in education. A very common one is grading. The traditional letter grades of A, B, C, D, and F make up a rating scale. Another example includes a student opinion survey, as included in Figure 6–7.

ENHANCEDetext
Video Example 6.4
Watch this video to find out more about checklists.

QUESTIONNAIRES AND INTERVIEWS

Questionnaires are written measures designed to elicit information from informants. They can be very structured and contain questions similar to those found on checklists and rating scales. They may also contain other types of structured questions such as multiple-choice and true–false items. Less structured, open-ended questions can also be included.

Interviews are the oral equivalent of questionnaires. An interview might be more appropriate than a questionnaire in several situations: if there is a literacy barrier, if the informant needs help in feeling at ease before questioning begins, and if the task directions are complex and need explanation. In addition, an interviewer can guide the informant through the questioning, keep him or her on track, and probe for additional information when necessary.

Interviews are often used to gather information from parents, professionals, and students. With students who have academic difficulties, interviews are usually preferable to questionnaires. Questions indicating which school subjects are strongest, weakest and reasons why appear to be effective during these types of interviews. In addition, questions regarding changes that could be made also have been suggested (Strickland & Turnbull, 1990).

Interviews, questionnaires, and other assessments that rely on informants are indirect measures. The value of their results depends on the informant's accuracy. Poor memory of past events, inadequate interpretation of current observations, faulty judgment, and lack of veracity can result in poor

ENHANCEDetext
Video Example 6.3
Watch this video to find out more about rating scales.

Ranking is another strategy that can be used to question informants. In a ranking task, several alternatives are presented, and the person must place them in order. For example, a student might be asked to rank several school activities by writing a number 1 by his or her favorite, a number 2 by the next favorite, and so forth. Ranking measures are sometimes valuable for obtaining information about preferences. However, they are less common than either checklists or rating scales, possibly because their results are somewhat more difficult to interpret.

Curriculum Checklist: Social Studies—Primary[a]

Understanding One's Community

_____ 1. States that people live together in families.
_____ 2. Tells that families live together in homes.
_____ 3. Gives the name of his community.
_____ 4. Tells his address.
_____ 5. States that all communities are not the same.
_____ 6. Tells the occupation of his parents.
_____ 7. Names some essential elements of a community such as homes, stores, and churches.
_____ 8. Tells the name of some community helpers such as the doctor, grocer, etc.

Parent Problem Behavior Checklist[b]

Directions: Read through the following list carefully and circle the number in front of each statement that describes a problem related to your child.

1. Lacks self confidence
2. Is hypersensitive—feelings easily hurt
3. Is frequently depressed—sad
4. Is easily flustered and confused
5. Is unsure
6. Is very distracted
7. Has short attention span and poor powers of concentration
8. Behavior not predictable—is sometimes good, sometimes bad
9. Exhibits poor muscular coordination—clumsy and awkward
10. Often has physical complaints: headaches, stomachaches, etc.
11. Is nervous and jittery—easily startled
12. Usually feels tired—drowsy
13. Is shy, bashful
14. Is attention-seeking, engages in "show-off" behavior
15. Quarrels and fights with other children

Student Opinion Survey

Directions: Please read each statement and report how strongly you agree or disagree by circling the corresponding number category to the right.

Strongly Agree- 5
Agree- 4
Neutral- 3
Disagree- 2
Strongly Disagree- 1

1. Math class is difficult.	5	4	3	2	1
2. Math class is fun.	5	4	3	2	1
3. Math class has many hands-on activities.	5	4	3	2	1
4. Math homework takes too much time.	5	4	3	2	1
5. Directions to math assignments are clear.	5	4	3	2	1
6. Math concepts are applicable to real life.	5	4	3	2	1
7. I like group activities in math.	5	4	3	2	1
8. I like math worksheets.	5	4	3	2	1
9. Doing well in math class is important.	5	4	3	2	1

FIGURE 6–7

Examples of Checklists

Note: From *Developing and Implementing Individualized Education Programs* (3rd ed.) (p. 480) by B. B. Strickland and A. P. Turnbull, 1990, Upper Saddle River, NJ: Merrill/Prentice Hall. Copyright 1990 by Prentice Hall Publishing Company. Reprinted by permission. From "Parent Problem Behavior Checklist" by S. C. Larsen. Reprinted in *Educational Assessment of Learning Problems: Testing for Teaching* (p. 115) by G. Wallace and S. C. Larsen, 1978, Boston: Allyn & Bacon. Copyright 1978 by Allyn & Bacon. Reprinted by permission of Stephen C. Larsen.

information. The teacher must be aware of these possibilities when interpreting reports of informants.

Clinical Interviews

Clinical interviews are a special type of assessment procedure. They are interviews in which the student acts as informant and the interview questions are designed to identify the strategies the student uses when attempting to perform a task. For example, the teacher may be interested in learning more about how students go about solving mathematics problems, planning essays, or studying textbook chapters. Clinical interviews focus on the process the student follows in completing a task. The product is of secondary interest.

Some strategies are observable. Thus, when conducting a clinical interview, the professional carefully notes the student's behaviors. However, cognitive strategies cannot be observed, and the student's report becomes the basis of information about this aspect of task performance. The teacher takes note of what the student does and then asks the student to describe the thinking process that accompanies those actions.

Clinical interviews usually take place while the student is performing a task. For example, if the task is solving mathematics word problems, the student is supplied with several problems at an appropriate level of difficulty. Then, to find out about nonobservable strategies, the professional directs the student to "think out loud as you solve these problems." Then he or she watches, listens to the student's report, and asks questions to clarify meaning or to probe areas that were not discussed.

In some cases, interviews are conducted immediately after the student has finished the task. In the assessment of writing skills, for instance, it is not wise to interrupt the student in the act of composition. Instead, the interview takes place as soon as the student has finished writing. There should be no delay between completion of the task and start of the interview. Otherwise, the student may not be able to recall the exact series of steps taken in responding to the task.

Clinical interviewing is a sophisticated assessment technique. It requires expertise in the use of observation and interviewing techniques, knowledge of the curriculum area under assessment, and

knowledge of the types of cognitive strategies that students are likely to employ in various types of tasks. The resulting data are subjective in that they are an informant's report of nonobservable behaviors. However, clinical interviews are the most direct means of gathering information about students' cognitive strategies and may provide important directions for structuring the teaching process.

Breakpoint Practice 6.3
Click here to check your understanding of interview and questionnaires.

PORTFOLIO ASSESSMENT

Portfolio assessment is one of the informal assessment strategies most often in use in classrooms today. What makes portfolio assessment different from other popular classroom approaches is that although it is based on analysis of student work samples, it may also include results of other types of data collection techniques such as observation, informal inventories and tests, and questionnaires and interviews.

Portfolios consist of student work assembled in chronological order to demonstrate achievement skills (Feuer & Fulton, 1993; Airasian, 2005). Portfolios can be developed at any grade level for any subject area. Examples are writing, reading/language arts, mathematics, science, the arts, and career preparation programs, including teacher education (Martin, 1999; Wolf, 1991; Cawley, Hayden, Cade, & Baker-Kroczynski, 2002).

ENHANCEDetext
Video Example 6.5
Watch this video to find out more about portfolios.

Portfolios are most valuable when they are systematically planned. Salend (1998) presents these guidelines:

1. Identify the goals of the portfolio.
2. Determine the type of portfolio to be used.
3. Establish procedures for organizing the portfolio.
4. Choose a range of authentic classroom products that relate to the objectives of the portfolio.
5. Record the significance of items included in students' portfolios.
6. Review and evaluate portfolios periodically (pp. 37–40).

The goals for the portfolio should be consistent with the instructional goals for the student (Oosterhof, 2003; Barrett, 2005). For example, the portfolio for a student with individualized education program (IEP) goals in reading, spelling, and written expression might emphasize accomplishments in the language arts. According to Salend (1998), the types of portfolios are (1) the showcase portfolio, containing examples of the student's best work; (2) the cumulative portfolio, documenting changes over time; (3) the goal-based portfolio, demonstrating progress toward specific goals such as those on the IEP; (4) the process portfolio, showing the steps the student follows in the development of products; and (5) the reflective portfolio, emphasizing the reflections of students, teachers, and parents on the learning process.

Once a framework is established, the teacher can plan the organization of the portfolio. There are a number of possibilities, including arranging the portfolio by instructional goal, by subject matter area (e.g., reading, mathematics), by themes, or in chronological order (Gelfer & Perkins, 1998). The next step is the selection of student work samples. Portfolios can contain almost anything that documents the student's progress such as drafts, papers, chapter summaries, art projects, science project reports, quizzes. and other work (Grady, 1992). Photos, audiotapes, videotapes, and other media can supplement print documents. Gelfer and Perkins also suggest including assessments such as teacher-made tests, curriculum-based assessments, and criterion-referenced tests. For example, in classrooms where CBM is used, the graphs showing the student's progress might become part of the portfolio.

The Vermont Portfolio Project has developed guidelines for writing and mathematics portfolios (Abruscato, 1993). The writing portfolio contains six samples of writing completed during the school year as well as the student's response to a "uniform writing assessment," a formal assignment given to all students within a grade level. The work samples are:

1. a table of contents;
2. a "best piece";
3. a letter;
4. a poem, short story, play, or personal narrative;
5. a personal response to a cultural, media, or sports exhibit or event or to a book, current issue, math problem, or scientific phenomenon;
6. one prose piece from any curriculum area other than English or language arts (for fourth graders) and three prose pieces from any curriculum area other than English or language arts (for eighth graders); and
7. the piece produced in response to the uniform writing assessment, as well as related outlines, drafts, and so on (Abruscato, 1993, p. 475).

The mathematics portfolio contains five to seven best pieces, other work samples, and a letter to the portfolio evaluator.

In addition to student products, portfolios should contain information about the significance of the works included. When work samples are those selected by the student, that fact should be indicated in some way. For example, the student might write or tape-record a short explanation of why a particular piece was chosen. Grady (1992), Stiggins (2001), and Davies and Le Mahieu (2003) suggest that student self-evaluations be incorporated into the portfolio. Student self-evaluations may take the form of an ongoing journal in which students reflect on their progress or written responses to specific questions from the teacher. Questionnaires completed by students and by parents can also be placed in the portfolio to provide information on topics such as students' preferred classroom activities and parents' reports of home study habits. Teachers, too, can make contributions to the portfolio. Among the possibilities are observations, progress notes, teacher comments about specific work samples, and records of student teacher and parent–teacher conferences (Gelfer & Perkins, 1998; Grady, 1992; Pierce & O'Malley, 1992; Salend, 1998; Goe & Holdheide, 2011).

The final step is evaluation of the contents of the portfolio. Unlike other types of work sample analysis procedures, the goal is not the identification of error patterns or the number and types of correct and incorrect responses. Instead, the task is to determine whether students are able to demonstrate proficiency in the performance of significant relevant tasks. To do this, standards or criteria must be established; the most common type is a rubric. (Rubrics were discussed earlier in this chapter and an example appeared in Figure 6–2.)

Portfolio assessment, like many other types of informal assessment, carries with it an element of subjectivity. In a sense, it is similar to gathering information from informants with tools such as rating scales and checklists. The teacher (or another judge) considers standards for performance and then rates student work samples in reference to those standards. However, the standards are not objective. They are holistic, qualitative descriptions that require the evaluator to exercise judgment. With an assessment strategy such as this, interrater reliability is a major concern (Oosterhof, 1994). Validity is another concern, particularly the predictive validity of portfolio assessment in relation to future success in school and adult pursuits. As is the case with other informal tools, however, information about the psychometric quality of portfolio assessment is seldom available.

Another potential disadvantage of portfolio assessment is the amount of time that is required, particularly for periodic evaluations (Oosterhof, 1994; Trice, 2000). Pierce and O'Malley (1992) present these suggestions for reducing time demands:

- Make the data collection part of daily instructional routines;
- Make students responsible for collecting information on a regular basis;
- Identify specific items that go into the portfolio and list them on a portfolio analysis form;
- Initially, use portfolios with only two or three students who need intensive monitoring;
- Use staggered data collection cycles where assessment data are collected from only a few students daily or weekly;

- Share responsibilities of data collection and interpretation with other school staff so that individual teachers do not become overwhelmed by the process; and
- Create common planning times for teachers and other staff involved in portfolio development. (p. 14)

MANAGING CLASSROOM DATA

No matter what techniques are used in classroom assessment, it is necessary to develop a system for managing student data. Not every piece of information can be saved, so decisions must be made about what types of information are most important. Then, that information must be organized in some way so that it can be retrieved when it is needed for making instructional decisions or reporting student progress.

Lewis and Doorlag (2006) noted that educators should choose data methods and types of systematic recordkeeping procedures. The first step is determining what areas are to be assessed as part of the instructional process, and the IEP provides guidance here. Assessment should focus on the student's progress toward his or her annual goals as well as any new areas of educational need that become apparent during the school year. The teacher then selects the methods to be used in classroom assessment. Again, the IEP provides guidance because it describes the strategies to be used by the educational team in monitoring the student's progress. However, in many cases, the assessment techniques listed on the IEP are quite general, and the teacher must decide on specific strategies for data collection.

Any of the assessment procedures discussed in this chapter can be used to collect information in the classroom. The choice of a specific technique must be made based on the types of assessment questions the teacher is attempting to answer. For example, curriculum-based measurement provides precise information if the question concerns the rate of accurate performance in basic school skills such as reading words or solving computational problems. If the question concerns higher-level skills and the student's ability to complete authentic tasks, portfolio assessment allows teachers to make judgments about changes in skill development over time.

The next concern is the frequency of assessment. At minimum, some evaluation of progress in important goal areas should take place at least once each week. In areas of particular concern (e.g., new problem behaviors), it may be necessary to gather data more frequently. Weekly assessment is usually not a time-consuming process. For example, depending on the assessment question to be answered, teachers might evaluate student work samples, conduct a brief classroom observation, or administer a 1-minute probe as part of a CBM program. Of course, a more extensive evaluation of student performance is necessary when report cards are to be prepared or when the IEP is reviewed and revised.

After data have been collected, the teacher decides what types of records to maintain. In some cases such as portfolio assessment, the student's actual work samples will be preserved. In others, results of the assessment will be recorded on a graph, in a gradebook, or in some other form such as teacher notes. Whatever is saved must then be stored. There is no perfect storage system; teachers need to experiment to discover the one that works best for them. Some teachers use gradebooks; others use index cards, notebooks, or file folders to store assessment data; still others keep their records on a computer. Data may be organized by subject area (reading, math, language arts, etc.) or by student; within these categories, information is usually arranged in chronological order. No matter what system is chosen, it should be one that allows easy retrieval of information. Assessment data are of no use if they cannot be located. The system should also include provisions for the storage of confidential information such as students' EEPs and test protocols and reports of eligibility assessments.

GRADING AND REPORT CARDS

Grades and report cards are part of the school experience for all students. Although grading procedures may be modified for students who receive special education services, the purposes remain the same. Based on a review of the literature, Bradley and Calvin (1998) identify six major purposes of grading:

- To measure progress toward the achievement of identified goals

- To ensure that students have mastered specific content
- To identify certain students for special programs or courses
- To provide information for planning
- To motivate students to continue to perform well or to perform better
- To compare performance to that of other students (p. 25)

Airasian (2005) suggests that grades serve four purposes: informational, administrative, motivational, and guidance. In their administrative role, grades help educators make decisions about issues such as eligibility for graduation and promotion to the next grade.

There are several philosophical approaches to grading (Silva, Munk, & Bursuck, 2005). Before grades can be assigned, teachers must identify the standard (or standards) of comparison they will use to evaluate a student's performance. In norm-referenced grading, a student is evaluated in relation to the performance of others; in criterion-referenced grading, grades are assigned in relation to preestablished performance standards (Airasian, 2005). Another option is what Christiansen and Vogel (1998) call the *self-referenced viewpoint:* Students are graded in relation to their own past performance. In other words, they are graded on the amount of progress they have achieved. Guskey and Jung (2009) discuss team collaboration in viewing a student's IEP and determining grade-level standards or modified standards based on accommodations and modifications.

Federal law requires that parents of students with disabilities receive information about their child's progress toward IEP goals. Progress reports must be issued at least as frequently as the report cards designed for the parents of typical students. In many cases, students with disabilities participate in the general education curriculum and, as part of that experience, receive the same types of report cards as their peers without disabilities. When this occurs, it is necessary for general and special education teachers to collaborate in the grading process. Christiansen and Vogel (1998) present these guidelines for collaborating teachers:

1. Determine district, state, and federal policies and guidelines regarding grading.

2. Identify your own theoretical approaches to grading.
3. Identify your colleagues' theoretical approaches to grading.
4. Cooperatively determine the grading practices for individual students. (pp. 32–33)

Teachers should become aware of the policies that guide the grading process and then learn about each other's philosophical approach to grading. The next step is discussion of the specific procedures to use in assigning grades to individual students with disabilities.

Individualization is the key. Students with disabilities who are included in general education classrooms often require accommodations in instruction as well as assessment, and grading practices should reflect this requirement. However, fairness is also important. Giving a student an *A* for completing half the work expected of others in the classroom seems unfair unless the criterion for successful performance is clearly stated. One approach is to develop differentiated standards for specific assignments. For example, the checklist in Figure 6–8 lists

Name Jonathan Smith   Date 1-2-98

Checklist for the Business Letter

Requirements (Components)	possible points	points earned	Comments
Heading	4	4	
Inside Address	4	4	
Greeting	2	2	
Spacing	3	3	
Body: 2 Support Statements	8 6	6	2 required supports
Complete Sentences	10	/	Not graded. Need to work on punctuation. Capitals look good!
Correct Spelling	3	/	Not graded. Practice editing on computer.
Written in Pen	2	2	
Readable	5	5	
Closing	2	2	
Signature	1	1	
TOTAL	42 29	29	

Grade A 100%

Attachments: rough copy
                final copy

_____   _____
Student Signature   Parent Signature

FIGURE 6–8
Differentiated Grading Standards for an Assignment
Note: From "Grading Modified Assignments: Equity or Compromise?" (p. 27) by D. F. Bradley and M. B. Calvin, 1998. *Teaching Exceptional Children, 31*(2). Copyright 1998 by The Council for Exceptional Children. Reprinted by permission.

the number of points possible to earn for each component of the assignment—writing a business letter. In this case, the standards have been changed: The student was expected to include two support statements (rather than three), and spelling and sentence structure were not evaluated. The student received a grade of *A* because he earned 29 of 29 possible points; however, it is clear that this *A* is based on differentiated standards.

Report cards and/or progress reports for students with disabilities can also reflect differentiated grading procedures. As Figure 6–9 shows, there are several methods for reporting progress to parents. Some are adaptations of the standard report card (examples 1 and 2); others replace or supplement the standard report card with information about the student's progress toward or achievement of IEP goals and objectives (example 3). This last approach is likely to

Report cards are a major way for teachers to inform parents of their children's progress in school. However, with students with special needs, grading performance in general education classes is often difficult. How should the teacher grade Judy, who is included in the fourth grade class but is successfully completing math assignments at the third grade level? Here are some alternatives:

1. State the student's current grade level in the academic subject, and grade the student's performance at that grade level.
   Judy, Grade 4
   Math grade level _3_
   Math performance at Grade 3 level _B_

2. State the student's current grade level in the academic subject, and grade the student's work behaviors rather than skill performance.
   Judy, Grade 4
   Math grade level _3_
   Works independently _B_
   Completes assignments _B+_
   Neatness _B_

3. State the student's IEP goals and objectives in the academic subject, and indicate which have been met and which still require work.
   Judy, Grade 4
   Goal: By the end of the school year, Judy will perform math computation problems at the 3.5 grade level. _in progress_
   Objectives:
   a. Judy will add and subtract two-digit numbers with regrouping with 90% accuracy. _achieved_
   b. Judy will write multiplication facts with 90% accuracy. _achieved_
   c. Judy will multiply two-digit numbers with regrouping with 90% accuracy. _in progress_
   d. Judy will write division facts with 90% accuracy. _in progress_

Other options include replacing traditional letter grades with simplified grading systems such as pass/fail or satisfactory/needs improvement (McLoughlin & Lewis, 2001). Teachers also can assign multiple grades in a subject area; for example, the student might earn one grade for reading achievement and another for effort in reading activities (Banbury, 1987).

FIGURE 6–9
Alternative Approaches to Report Cards
Note: From *Teaching Special Students in General Education Classrooms* (7th ed.) by R. B. Lewis and D. H. Doorlag, © 2006, Upper Saddle River, NJ: Merrill/Prentice Hall. Copyright 2006 by Prentice Hall, Inc. Reprinted by permission.

become more popular as districts implement federal special education requirements for keeping parents informed of their child's progress in school.

Bradley and Calvin (1998) present several suggestions to "level the playing field" in grading practices for students with disabilities. These suggestions include the following.

- Use points and percentages to grade differentiated assignments, rather than letter grades. For instance, if the length of an assignment is shortened, the student can be graded on the amount of work required and can earn 100 percent when points are converted into percentages (Polloway et al., 1994).
- Match grading criteria for certain students with IEP goals and objectives. Criteria for some may vary from the criteria for the majority of the class. For example, if you require students to respond in complete sentences, you may accept partial sentences from a student who is currently working on writing in complete sentences as an IEP goal, without taking off points or lowering the grade. You may want to add a comment to the paper that encourages continued effort on that skill (Polloway et al., 1994).
- Develop scoring rubrics that delineate the standards for grading and share them with students and parents when introducing assignments. It is appropriate to develop more than one scoring rubric for an assignment to differentiate (even for students without disabilities; see Gersten et al., 1996; Wiggins, 1996).
- Use a variety of grading approaches to obtain grades. For example, include a grade for effort in your overall calculation, use portfolios of student work, include student self-assessment, and use student contracting to determine assignments and grading criteria (Bursuck et al., 1996; Friend & Bursuck, 1996).
- Avoid grading students strictly on effort or learning behaviors. All culminating grades should contain some type of academic component (Gersten et al., 1996, pp. 28–29).

ENHANCEDetext
Video Example 6.6
Watch this video to see a teacher explaining grading to students.

INTERPRETING CLASSROOM ASSESSMENT RESULTS

One of the hallmarks of informal classroom assessment is its relevance to instruction. When teachers design informal procedures to answer specific assessment questions about their students, results are immediately applicable to the solution of instructional problems. The data assist in identifying areas for further assessment, in describing the student's current classroom performance, and in planning or modifying instructional strategies.

Despite the advantages of informal measures, there are also limitations that become apparent in the interpretation of assessment results, as follow.

Technical Adequacy

The greatest limitation of informal assessment tools is the lack of information about reliability and validity (Bennett, 1982). In many cases, the professional simply does not know whether a particular informal procedure is technically adequate. If technical data are not available for a measure, interpretation of its results must be approached with great caution.

All measurements contain error. With norm-referenced tests, the amount of error can be estimated using the standard error of measurement, and confidence intervals are constructed around observed scores to quantify the error factor. However, when there is insufficient psychometric information, the professional is left with the knowledge that assessment results are inaccurate, but the degree of inaccuracy is unknown.

The procedures for gathering information about the technical quality of some types of informal tools have been discussed throughout this chapter. For example, interrater reliability can be determined in observation, and there are techniques to study the reliability and other characteristics of criterion-referenced tests. Professionals should take advantage of any such available procedures.

At minimum, content validity should be evaluated. This type of validity relates to how well the tool fulfills the purpose of assessment by addressing the content of interest. Among the most important considerations are whether the assessment device includes a representative sample of the content domain and whether the assessment tasks are appropriate. If the student's problem is fighting on the playground, an observation conducted during shop class does not assess the domain of interest. If oral reading is the concern, the assessment task should be reading out loud, not matching words and pictures.

Selection of the Appropriate Tools for Assessment

The more direct the measure, the more useful the results. For example, if the student's handwriting skills are a concern, direct measures such as observation and work sample analysis provide instructionally relevant information. Reviewing the student's report card grades in handwriting is a less direct measure.

However, it is necessary to consider the purposes of assessment to determine whether a tool is appropriate. If the purpose is to find out if the student's handwriting skills are adequate for success in a general education classroom, interviewing the classroom teacher may be the most direct means of gathering the needed information.

Many informal assessment tools provide professionals with a wealth of information. However, the amount of data can become overwhelming and confuse, rather than facilitate, decision making. Assessment should be a carefully planned, systematic process. Once it has been learned that a student's spelling performance is satisfactory, it is not useful to continue gathering information about spelling. Only areas that represent educational needs should be assessed in depth. The more intensive informal procedures—criterion-referenced testing, diagnostic teaching, and clinical interviews—should be reserved for in-depth assessment.

Quality of the Sample of Behavior

All formal and informal measures rely on behavior samples. It is impractical to observe all behaviors of a student or test skill in solving all the possible mathematics computation problems. Thus, interpretation of assessment results must take into account the quality of the behavior sample. This holds true for all types of informal assessment tools, ranging from observation and work sample analysis to curriculum-based measures to procedures that rely on informants.

If the student's behavior is being assessed, that is the behavioral sample that is evaluated for representativeness. When persons other than the student contribute information, the representativeness of their behaviors must also be considered. The performance of teachers and parents, like that of students, can fluctuate over time.

Criteria for Evaluating Performance

One of the major difficulties in interpreting the results of many types of informal procedures is the lack of guidelines for determining whether a problem exists and, if one does, whether it is serious enough to warrant an intervention. In most cases, it is left up to the professional to set the criteria. If an observation shows that the student talks out in English class once every 10 minutes on the average, the teacher must decide if this is a problem. Likewise, there are no set standards for evaluating the adequacy of a writing sample with 20 percent of the words misspelled.

Criterion-referenced tests do include performance criteria that are often based on professional judgment rather than empirical evidence. If a professional has set 80 percent accuracy as the standard for mastery on a CRT, other professionals may disagree and choose 70, 90, or even 100 percent as the criterion.

For the most part, informal procedures are designed to describe the behaviors that students exhibit, the tasks they can complete, and the skills that are mastered and those that continue to require instruction. However, such procedures make no attempt to match the student's current performance with the performance appropriate for age, grade, and ability. For example, a CRT will reveal whether or not a student is able to multiply 3-digit by 3-digit numbers. Results will not show that this skill is not expected of first and second graders. Again, the professional must make this decision.

ENHANCEDetext
Video Example 6.7
Watch this video to find out more about criterion-referenced assessment.

Translating Results into Instruction

If limitations are kept firmly in mind, professionals can draw upon and then act on conclusions from informal data. Then assessment continues as information is collected to evaluate the effectiveness of instruction. By building ongoing assessment into the program, the teacher can monitor student progress and determine when instruction is working and when modifications are needed.

Bennett (1982) provides several suggestions for increasing the usefulness of informal data in planning the instructional program.

1. Recognize that a variety of reasons may exist for a child's correct or incorrect performance on assessment tasks.
2. Determine reasons for correct and incorrect performance.
3. Determine the conditions under which the child performs the task best.
4. Use informal procedures as complements to formal procedures. (p. 339)

The third suggestion is important. The assessment process tends to focus on the student's problems. The information gathered describes inappropriate behaviors, unlearned skills, and unmastered tasks. But even more crucial is learning how to help the student succeed. A major purpose of assessment must be identification of the classroom conditions and instructional strategies that are likely to improve student performance.

Bennett's last suggestion also deserves comment. Informal assessment is best viewed as a complement to formal assessment. Neither type of procedure is best; both have their uses. Informal assessment is particularly valuable when it augments the results of standardized testing. For example, if a student's score on a formal reading test falls below the average range of performance for age peers, informal assessment can provide critical information about that student's reading performance. Among the possible informal strategies are observing the student during reading instruction, administering an informal reading inventory, analyzing correct and incorrect oral reading responses, interviewing the student to learn about attitudes toward reading and preferences in reading materials, designing a diagnostic teaching sequence, and conducting a clinical reading interview. Informal procedures can be a rich source of information for instruction. When coupled with formal tests, they complete the assessment picture.

AVOIDING BIAS IN CLASSROOM ASSESSMENT

Unlike norm-referenced tests, informal measures have not been criticized as contributors to discriminatory assessment and placement practices. In fact, the opposite has occurred. Informal measures—criterion-referenced tests in particular—have been suggested as one possible solution to the problem of bias in assessment. Because CRTs compare performance to the goals of the local curriculum rather than to the performance of a norm group, it is assumed that the standard of comparison is fair. In addition, informal measures tend to assess skill areas in more depth than do norm-referenced tests, and thus they are more sensitive to small changes in pupil behavior.

Teacher-constructed tests may also contain discriminatory language and content (Bailey & Harbin, 1980). If teachers are insensitive to and have insufficient information about the languages and cultures of their students, they may prepare biased measures. In constructing or selecting informal assessment tools, teachers should consider the same issues in nondiscriminatory assessment that they attend to when evaluating norm-referenced tests:

- Is the standard of comparison appropriate for the student in terms of race, ethnicity, culture, and gender?
- Are test items free from cultural bias?
- Is the language appropriate for the student?
- Does the measure bypass the limitations imposed by the disability?

Other considerations are the time, money, and personnel resources needed to implement a comprehensive criterion-referenced testing system (Duffey, Salvia, Tucker, & Ysseldyke, 1982), the narrow scope of such measures (Oakland, 1980), and the lack of information about their reliability and validity (Harris & Wolf, 1979).

Although informal measures may not replace norm-referenced tests as the instrument of choice for eligibility assessment, they do offer obvious advantages for classroom use. Teachers can design informal tools to answer specific assessment questions about a particular student. Results assist in making decisions about further assessment, current performance, and modification of instruction. Thus, results are instructionally relevant and directly applicable to classroom practice.

McCormack (1976) maintains that the assessment tools that best meet your needs are the ones you construct. Such measures must also be nonbiased to meet the needs of all students. According to Bailey and Harbin (1980), this can be done if:

1. The importance of the skills measured by the instrument and taught in the curriculum are agreed upon by culturally diverse groups within the school system.
2. Criterion-referenced items are constructed so as not to measure the skills of children from a particular cultural group unfairly.
3. Alternative instructional strategies are incorporated to meet the learning needs of individual children (p. 593).

Assessment in Action (Two Applications)

Ms. Swaderski Monitors Her Students' Reading Progress

Ms. Swaderski is worried about the reading skills of her third graders this year. Her students seem less skilled than the youngsters she taught last year, and she thinks that she might need to alter her plans for instruction. Ms. Swaderski attended a workshop at the beginning of the year where she learned about using curriculum-based measurement to monitor the progress of students in reading, math, and other subjects. She decides to try this approach.

Ms. Swaderski's first step is to obtain the materials necessary to assess her students. The reading specialist, Mr. Jersey, is able to help and lends her one of the school's copies of a published measure, the *Reading Fluency*

Progress Monitor (Ihnot, 2006). This measure is part of *Read Naturally* (Ihnot, 2000, 2001, 2003), a program designed to increase reading fluency. Ms. Swaderski begins by asking each of her students to read three grade-3 passages. She times the students and then determines the number of words read correctly per minute. She then calculates each student's average score and plots that score on a graph. Ms. Swaderski can also consult the norms provided in the *Read Naturally* program. For example, in the fall, grade-3 students who fall at the 50th percentile in reading fluency read 71 words per minute correctly. Ms. Swaderski now has baseline data on her students, and she plans to check their progress in reading at least once per month.

Mr. Sikora Gives a Test
Mr. Sikora is one of the new special education teachers at Hilltop High School this year. He's been teaching for two years, but, until now, he's been assigned to the middle school. Mr. Sikora is going to be teaching ninth-grade math, and he expects that he'll know many of his students because he was their math teacher in eighth grade last year. Mr. Sikora decides to start the semester by finding out how many math skills the students recall from last year. In order to do that, he needs to make some decisions about what types of assessment tools he's going to use.

Because of his experience during the past two years, Mr. Sikora is very familiar with the district's math curriculum for eighth grade. After reviewing the textbook and his lesson plans from last year, he's able to identify the five major skill areas that make up that curriculum. One approach he could take is to develop detailed measures for each of these skill areas. He decides against that approach because it would require a great deal of class time. Instead, he plans to construct a type of test called an informal math inventory in order to sample a variety of subskills from each of the major skill areas. Although not all subskills will be included, the coverage will be adequate for Mr. Sikora to reach general conclusions about the math performance of his students. Then, in areas where students experience difficulty, he can continue assessment. Possibilities include error analyses of students' responses on the informal math inventory, the development of criterion-referenced tests to assess mastery of specific skills, and clinical math interviews to find out how students are going about the problem-solving process.

SUMMARY

- Classroom assessment can include (1) observation, task analysis, and other direct and unobtrusive procedures; (2) curriculum-based assessment techniques such as inventories and criterion-referenced tests that are direct but obtrusive; and (3) procedures using informants such as checklists and interviews that are indirect and obtrusive.

- A common approach to analyzing student work is error analysis. Error analysis techniques are available for most subject areas. The goal is identification of error patterns. The work sample is scored, all errors are noted, and then an attempt is made to sort the errors into meaningful categories. Another method of analyzing student work is through the use of a rubric. Rubrics are often associated with portfolio assessment, a technique combining several assessment strategies. Rubrics require the use of observational techniques as well as professional judgment.

- Task analysis is done in three steps: 1. Identify a specific instructional goal or objective. 2. Analyze the instructional objective into its essential component parts (i.e., the movements, actions, or responses that, when taken cumulatively, constitute the instructional objective). 3. Determine the entry level of the skill and specify the prerequisite skills (in other words, state at what point the particular skill sequence begins) (Berdine & Cegelka, 1980, p. 160).

- To design an informal inventory, the teacher should: 1. Determine the curriculum area in which the student is to be assessed. 2. Isolate a portion of the curriculum appropriate for the student's age, grade, and skill level. 3. Analyze the curriculum into testable and teachable segments. As in task analysis, the curriculum may be broken down into sequential steps, developmental steps, or difficulty levels. Prepare test items for each segment of the curriculum, emphasizing the most important aspects of each segment. 5. If necessary, reduce the number of test items so that the inventory is of manageable length. 6. Sequence the test items from easiest to most difficult, or in random order if the student is expected to answer all items.

- The most common types of quiz items used by classroom teachers are: *True–false.* In this type of question, the student determines whether a statement is true or false. *Multiple choice.* The student selects a word, phrase, or sentence that best completes a partial statement or answers a question. *Matching.* The student selects from one set of words, phrases, or sentences the one that best fits each of the words, phrases, or sentences in another set.

- Criterion-referenced tests (CRTs) compare a student's performance to the goals of the curriculum rather than to the performance of a norm group. However, CRTs typically sample more restricted curricular domains than those sampled by inventories. An inventory might reveal a possible problem in decoding short vowels; a criterion-referenced test would identify the short vowels the student could read and those he or she could not. Another important feature of CRTs is their emphasis on mastery.

- The general procedures for the design of a diagnostic probe are: 1. The student's performance is assessed under the standard instructional condition. 2. Some aspect of the task or the instructional conditions that relate to the task is modified. 3. The student's performance is assessed under the modified condition and compared with previous performance.

- Examples of scores derived in curriculum-based measurement include the following: Students write words that are dictated orally, and the number of words spelled correctly and correct letter sequences are counted. Students write answers to computation problems, and the number of digits are counted.

- Checklists and rating scales are structured assessments in which specific questions are posed and an informant selects a response rather than generating one. These measures are usually administered in written form to adult informants, although they can be presented orally to young children. With checklists, the informant is provided with a list of descriptions, and the task is simply to check each description that applies to the student under assessment. Rating scales require more from informants than a yes–no response. A description or statement is presented, and informants express their agreement with the description by selecting one of a series of ratings.

- Questionnaires are written measures designed to elicit information from informants. They can be very structured and contain questions similar to those found on checklists and rating scales. They may also contain other types of structured questions such as multiple-choice and true–false items. Less structured, open-ended questions can also be included. Interviews are the oral equivalent of questionnaires.

- According to Salend (1998), the types of portfolios are (1) the showcase portfolio, containing examples of the student's best work; (2) the cumulative portfolio, documenting changes over time; (3) the goal-based portfolio, demonstrating progress toward specific goals such as those on the IEP; (4) the process portfolio, showing the steps the student follows in the development of products; and (5) the reflective portfolio, emphasizing the reflections of students, teachers, and parents on the learning process.

- When managing classroom data, the frequency of assessment is always a concern. At minimum, some evaluation of progress in important goal areas should take place at least once each week. In areas of particular concern (e.g., new problem behaviors), it may be necessary to gather data more frequently.

- Airasian (2005) suggests that grades serve four purposes: informational, administrative, motivational, and guidance. In their administrative role, grades help educators make decisions about issues such as eligibility for graduation and promotion to the next grade.

- A limitation of informal assessment tools is the lack of information about reliability and validity. In many cases, the professional simply does not know whether a particular informal procedure is technically adequate. If the student's behavior is being assessed, that is the behavioral sample that is evaluated for representativeness. When persons other than the student contribute information, the representativeness of their behaviors must also be considered. The performance of teachers and parents, like that of students, can fluctuate over time.

- In constructing or selecting informal assessment tools, teachers should consider the same issues in nondiscriminatory assessment that they attend to when evaluating norm-referenced tests: Is the standard of comparison appropriate for the student in terms of race, ethnicity, culture, and gender? Are test items free from cultural bias? Is the language appropriate for the student? Does the measure bypass the limitations imposed by the disability?

7

Wavebreakmediamicro/123rf.com

Intellectual Performance

LEARNING OUTCOMES

After reading this chapter, you will be able to:

- Discuss considerations in assessment of learning aptitude regarding purposes, issues and trends, and current practices.

- Define and explain componential, contextual, and experiential elements in Sternberg's triarchic theory of intelligence.

- Give five examples of sources of information about learning aptitude.

- Define and describe the levels and scoring for the *Otis-Lennon School Ability Test—Eighth Edition* group test of intellectual performance.

- Describe three examples of individual tests of intellectual performance and discuss scoring options for these tests.

- Identify the five composites and explain the scoring options for the *Wechsler Intelligence Scale for Children–Fifth Edition*.

- Name the seven composites and explain the scoring options for the *Woodcock-Johnson IV Tests of Cognitive Abilities*.

- Identify subtests in the *Kaufman Assessment Battery for Children—Second Edition*, including mental processing scales.

- Describe the *System of Multicultural Pluralistic Assessment (SOMPA)* as an approach to nonbiased assessment of intellectual performance.

KEY TERMS

learning aptitude
intelligence

The conceptualization of intelligence and academic, social, and emotional effects is complex. In cases where a known syndrome or condition exists, developmental milestone delays and difficulties in certain areas are sometimes expected. For example, walking may not begin until the age of 2 and ½ years instead of 1 year of age. In general, the more severe the disability, the more the delay will be in reaching milestones. The early childhood range will be discussed in Chapter 16; this chapter will focus on the elementary school years.

Often, families find out about their children's intellectual disabilities when the children begin to have difficulty in school. This may be the case for students with mild intellectual disabilities, which account for about 95 percent of all cases of intellectual disabilities. Teachers may have concerns that the student is falling behind in completing assignments, understanding concepts, and keeping up with other students, and they may share these concerns with the parents. When family–school collaboration points to further assessment, the team gathers information about the student's current functioning in several major domains. One of these domains is general aptitude for learning.

General aptitude is important to consider in the assessment of students with poor school performance. Some students with disabilities show below-average general aptitude and, as a consequence, below-average school achievement. Others achieve poorly in school despite average potential for learning.

When students are referred for special education assessment, the team may begin by evaluating current school performance. If an achievement problem is documented, the team moves to a study of the student's cognitive and behavioral characteristics. The assessment question being addressed at such a point is this: *Is the school performance problem related to a disability?*

The team typically starts to investigate the possibility of a disability by evaluating general learning aptitude. The assessment of learning aptitude is traditionally associated with standardized measures of intellectual performance, known also as intelligence (IQ) tests. However, general aptitude for learning can also be estimated by assessing adaptive behavior—the student's ability to adapt to and comply with environmental demands. Thus, the team is able to pose more specific questions: *What is the student's current level of intellectual performance? What is the student's current functioning level in adaptive behavior?* The area of adaptive behavior will be discussed in Chapter 8.

CONSIDERATIONS IN ASSESSMENT OF LEARNING APTITUDE

Learning aptitude refers to an individual's capacity for altering behavior when presented with new information or experiences. Learning aptitude is required in many environments, and the classroom is only one example. Thus, general learning aptitude is assessed to gain a better understanding of the student's ability to cope with the demands of the instructional and other environments that require changes in behavior.

Purposes

General learning aptitude is a concern in the identification of several different disabilities. The disability most directly related to learning aptitude is intellectual disability. It was defined in 1983 by the American Association on Mental Retardation (AAMR, which has now changed its name to the American Association on Intellectual and Developmental Disabilities [AAIDD]). In Rosa's Law of 2010 (P.L. 111-256), the federal government requested that all agencies use the term "intellectual disability" rather than the term "mental retardation." This AAID 11th edition of the definition of intellectual disability—the one also used in federal law—continues to conceptualize intellectual disability as a developmental phenomenon that becomes apparent before the age of 18. It identifies two important indicators of intellectual disability: below-average intellectual performance and impaired adaptive behavior (Schalock et al., 2010).

This definition is not only based on five important assumptions from the 10th edition listed below, but also includes a discussion of supports:

1. Limitations in present functioning must be considered within the context of community environments typical of the individual's age peers and culture.
2. Valid assessment considers cultural and linguistic diversity as well as differences in communication, sensory, motor, and behavioral factors.
3. Within an individual, limitations often coexist with strengths.
4. An important purpose of describing limitations is to develop a profile of needed supports.
5. With appropriate personalized supports over a sustained period, the life functioning of the person with intellectual disability generally will improve. (p. 13)

Supports are resources and strategies that allow an individual with intellectual disabilities to fully participate in their community. Supports may include agencies, individuals, monetary assets, assistive devices, and other resources (American Association on Intellectual Disabilities, 2010).

Intelligence is a complex construct, and many attempts have been made to define it. According to Wechsler (1974), the author of several measures of intellectual functioning, the definition of intelligence includes the conceptualization of one's ability to deal with his or her environment or context. In the current AAIDD definition (AAMR, 2010), intelligence is described as "general mental capacity." Areas of mental capacity include planning, resolving issues, and understanding multifaceted ideas, among other areas.

In assessment, intellectual functioning is operationalized as performance on standardized tests of intelligence. Such measures claim to assess reasoning abilities, learning skills, and problem-solving abilities. However, most intelligence tests are essentially measures of verbal abilities and skills in dealing with numbers and other abstract symbols (Anastasi & Urbina, 1997). Because these skills and abilities are required in school learning, tests of intelligence are best viewed as measures of scholastic, not general, aptitude.

In intellectual disability, intellectual performance must be below average, *and* there must be deficits in adaptive behavior. Poor scores on tests of intelligence are not sufficient evidence to support the identification of intellectual disability. The individual must also be unable to meet age-level expectations in important areas of adaptive behavior.

General learning aptitude is also a concern with other disabilities. In learning disabilities and behavioral disorders, the possibility of intellectual disability must be ruled out. Thus, intelligence tests are used to gather evidence of average potential for learning. In addition, one factor previously considered in identification of learning disabilities is a discrepancy between expected and actual achievement. Tests of intellectual performance provide the basis for predicting expected achievement. Strengths and needs across subcomponents of achievement are investigated. Assessment of adaptive behavior is less usual with learning disabilities and behavioral disorders, even though it can provide important information about the student's ability to cope with nonscholastic environments.

Issues and Trends

Intelligence testing has engendered more controversy than any other area in special education assessment. The issues raised by the intelligence testing debate concern the nature and definition of intelligence, the relative contributions of heredity and environment to intellectual performance, the usefulness and accuracy of IQ tests, and the appropriateness of these measures for members of diverse ethnic, cultural, and linguistic groups (Ebel, 1977; Herrnstein, 1971; Holtzman & Wilkinson, 1991; Jones, 1988; Losen & Orfield, 2002; Patton, 1998; Perrone, 1977; Tyler, 1969; Valenzuela & Cervantes, 1998).

One factor underlying the controversies is a basic misunderstanding of the purpose of intelligence tests. Measurement of current intellectual performance has become confused with measurement of innate potential. Intelligence tests do not assess potential; they sample behaviors already learned in an attempt to predict future learning. They are built upon the premise that current performance is an indicator of future performance. Individuals who have learned from their environment and are able to perform certain tasks are assumed able to continue learning and achieving. Robinson and Robinson (1976) commented that intelligence tests did not completely capture what educators needed to know regarding prediction of school performance.

The use of intelligence tests in special education drew heated criticism in the 1970s, particularly in relation to the labeling of culturally and linguistically diverse students and their placement in special education. The major issue was the finding that special classes for students with intellectual disability contained disproportionate numbers of students from diverse groups (Jones & Wilderson, 1976; Mercer, 1973). This overrepresentation was attributed to many factors, including reliance solely on IQ scores for special education placement and the cultural loadings of intelligence measures.

In addition, the practice of administering English-language tests of intelligence to students whose primary language was not English resulted in lawsuits such as *Diana v. The State Board of Education* (1970, 1973) and *Guadalupe v. Tempe Elementary School District* (1972). Other litigation charged that intelligence tests were culturally biased and therefore discriminated against members of diverse groups (*Larry P. v. Riles,* 1972, 1979, 1984; *Parents in Action on Special Education*

v. Joseph P. Hannon, 1980). The courts clearly supported the use of tests in the child's own language. However, test bias decisions have been contradictory. In the *Larry P.* case, it was ruled that intelligence tests are culturally biased and must not be used to assess African American students for possible placement in classes for students with mild intellectual disability; in the *Parents in Action* case, the court held that intelligence tests are not racially or culturally biased.

In the mid-1970s, legislative action was taken in an attempt to address the concerns about intelligence testing held by professionals, parents of students identified as disabled, and others. The Education for All Handicapped Children Act of 1975 contained two major provisions to safeguard against testing abuses. The first was its adoption of what was then named the American Association on Mental Retardation definition of intellectual disability. In this definition, intellectual disability is identified by concurrent deficits in intellectual performance and adaptive behavior. Social adaptation has long been of interest to professionals in the field of intellectual disability (Cegelka & Prehm, 1982). However, the need to consider nonscholastic performance was underscored by the findings of Mercer (1973) and others that some students who were labeled with an intellectual disability in school performed quite adequately at home and in their community.

The second major provision of federal law is a set of procedures for special education assessment. These procedures, described in detail in Chapter 2, require that testing be conducted in the language of the student, that measures be nondiscriminatory and validated for the purpose for which they are used, and that no single test score be the sole basis for determining special education placement.

Today, school systems and professional educators are aware of clear guidelines for the appropriate use of intelligence tests in special education assessment. That is not to say that procedures mandated by law are followed in all instances or that all questions about intelligence testing have been answered. Debate continues over measures of intellectual performance, their proper use, and social consequences (Benson, 2003; Bersoff, 1981; Carroll & Horn, 1981; Geisinger, 1992; Helms, 1992; Losen & Orfield, 2002; Reschly, 1981; Scarr, 1981; Winzer & Mazurek, 1998).

ENHANCEDetext
Video Example 7.1
Watch this video to find out more about scaffolding while working on cognitive skills.

Current Practices

Assessment of general learning aptitude takes place in both general and special education. In general education, school districts administer group intelligence tests to elementary grade populations, although this practice is far less common than group achievement testing. At the secondary level, measures such as the *Scholastic Aptitude Test (SAT)* (n.d.) of the College Entrance Examination Board are used to predict success in higher education.

Group measures of general learning aptitude share the drawbacks of group achievement tests for lower performing students. In nationwide testing programs such as the *SAT* special administration procedures are available for students with disabilities. In general, however, individual tests are preferred because they provide a more accurate picture of current academic aptitude.

Individual tests of intellectual functioning are part of the assessment battery for most students under serious consideration for special education services. Information about general learning aptitude is needed for initial decisions for many disabilities as well as for the periodic reevaluation of eligibility. As a rule, individual tests of intelligence are administered in educational settings only by school psychologists—specially trained and licensed professionals who perform this kind of assessment. However, some of the newer individual intelligence tests may be administered by professionals such as teachers, without specific formal training. This may bring about a major change in the way school assessment teams operate. If this change occurs, it will be necessary to make sure that the professionals responsible for assessment of intellectual performance are adequately trained in the administration, scoring, and interpretation of these tests.

The first intelligence test was developed in 1905 in France by Alfred Binet and Theodore Simon. This measure, adapted for use in the United States and revised several times, is the *Stanford-Binet Intelligence Scale.* The individual measure most often used in schools today, the *Wechsler Intelligence Scale for Children–Fifth Edition,* is one of a family of intelligence tests developed by David Wechsler. The Wechsler scale, along with the *Tests of Cognitive Abilities* of the *Woodcock-Johnson IV,* are discussed in this chapter. Other measures of intellectual performance, such as the *Stanford-Binet Intelligence Scales—Fifth Edition* and the *Kaufman Assessment Battery for Children—Second Edition,* are also described.

THEORIES OF INTELLIGENCE

The study of intelligence also continues. Many researchers have influenced the depth and possibilities of the theoretical development of the concept of intelligence. Binet and Simon (1905) discussed ability as a total package or product. They did not look at single aspects of intelligence when measuring ability. They also used age as a measuring stick. They looked at how older children had higher capabilities than younger children and used those findings to separate tasks to calculate mental age.

Spearman (1927) further defined general intellectual ability by offering the factorial approach. He contributed the general ("g") factor and the specific ("s") factor. The general ("g") factor dealt with activities that could not be linked with particular situations, and the specific ("s") factor dealt with activities that could be linked with situations. Thorndike (1927) proposed that three factors were involved in intelligence: abstract intelligence, mechanical intelligence, and social intelligence. Abstract intelligence was connected with verbal and mathematical symbols. Mechanical intelligence dealt with the ability to utilize objects in a significant way. Social intelligence involved dealing with people.

Piaget (1952) has been a major contributor in the conceptualization and assessment of intelligence. He used a developmental model; that is, he posited that behavior develops in a certain order over time. He defined developmental stages or periods: the sensorimotor period (1 ½ to 2 years of age), the preoperational period (1 ½ to 7 years of age), concrete operations period (7 to 11 years of age, and formal operations period (11 years and older). The sensorimotor period involves a child using his or her senses to understand his or her environment. The preoperational period has two stages: the preconceptual stage (1 ½ to 4 years of age) and the intuitive stage (3 to 7 years of age). The preconceptual stage deals with the child's awareness of objects and his or her relation to them. The intuitive stage deals with constancy and the recognition of other points of view. The concrete operations stage involves the child's understanding of quantity, length, and number. The formal operations period deals with reasoning/metalinguistic (thinking about language) activities.

Vygotsky's (1978) theory of intellectual development is based on a sociocultural perspective. He viewed the child as an active learner in his or her environment. Social language is the tool that the child uses to learn from adults or more knowledgeable peers. This interactive process points to a critical focus on culture as shaping the intellectual process. Also, the idea of scaffolding, where a more knowledgeable adult or peer gives less and less support in a learning process as a child becomes more independent, is a key component in the instructional process stressed today in classrooms. Furthermore, increasing the opportunity for active learning via interaction in small groups is another strategy widely used today in the classroom. Vygotsky's work has great implication for teaching all students.

Gardner (1993) proposes seven original intelligences: logicomathematical (i.e., numerical and reasoning tasks), linguistic (i.e., language), musical, spatial (i.e., visual spatial), bodily kinesthetic (i.e., bodily movement), interpersonal (i.e., interactions with others), and intrapersonal (i.e., understanding of oneself). The theory involves analyzing strengths and weaknesses in various areas. Because verbal and quantitative skills are traditionally two of the seven typically examined and emphasized (Diaz-Lefebvre, 2004), this is groundbreaking information. Furthermore, it promotes an assessment-to-instruction loop. Knowing student strengths feeds into activities in which the teacher can use strengths to support needs.

In Sternberg's theory, human intelligence is conceptualized in terms of the individual's mental mechanisms for processing information, the tasks or situations that involve the use of intelligence, and the sociocultural context in which the individual lives (Sternberg, Okagaki, & Jackson, 1990). Sternberg (1988) discusses componential, contextual, and experiential elements in his triarchic theory of intelligence. The componential element involves internal intellectual factors, including the process, activities, and encoding involved in problem solving. Metacognitive, performance, and knowledge acquisition components are prominent in this discussion. The experiential element deals with how humans respond to new tasks or problems, as well as responses to highly familiar circumstances. The contextual element involves culture and behaviors. Adaptation, selection of a better environment, and shaping of the existing environment are key components of this element. These can be investigated further as analytic, creative, and practical intelligence (Viadero, 1995).

Furthermore, Sternberg has developed a theory of successful intelligence (Sternberg, 1999) and methods of teaching for this successful intelligence (Sternberg & Grigorenko, 2000). Individuals find ways to be successful; that is, they know their assets and make the most of those strengths, while recognizing their needs and compensating for them. Sternberg and Grigorenko (2004) noted that there is no single correct way of teaching or assessing students. They encouraged teachers to teach analytically (analyze, critique, judge, compare and contract, evaluate, and assess), creatively (create, invent, discover, imagine, suppose, and predict), and practically (apply, use, put into practice, implement, employ, and render practical). This is an example of the assessment-to-instruction loop regarding intelligence offered by these researchers.

Of particular interest is the intertwining of intelligence and adaptive skills in many of these definitions. The social aspect and the application of behavior in context are seen throughout the evolution of notions of cognition. The inherent interdependence of the concepts is remarkable. In fact, attempting to re-create a setting out of context for this particular type of testing is complex and difficult. Many questions regarding the meaning of the outcome of this type of testing arise. Three theories are more prevalent when looking at the connection between test development and theory. According to Esters and Ittenbach (1999), these theories include the fluid-crystallized theory of intelligence (Horn & Cattell, 1966); planning, attention, simultaneous, and successive theory (Das, Naglieri, & Kirby, 1994); and the three-stratum theory of intelligence (Carroll, 1993).

The nine factors involved in the fluid-crystallized theory of intelligence are (1) fluid reasoning, (2) crystallized intelligence, (3) visual processing, (4) auditory processing, (5) processing speech, (6) short-term memory, (7) long-term retrieval, (8) quantitative knowledge, and (9) correct decision speed. Li, Lindenberger, Hommel, Aschersleben, Prinz, and Baltes (2004) examined fluid and crystallized abilities in relation to maturation. They found support for the dynamic development of fluid and crystallized abilities. Fluid abilities appeared to expand in earlier child development and decrease earlier during aging compared to crystallized abilities. Furthermore, they found that crystallized abilities depend on fluid abilities.

Kaufman, Kaufman, Chen, and Kaufman (1996) investigated seven subtests measuring six Horn abilities. Based on Horn and Hofer's (1992) findings, they looked at vulnerable abilities, which decline with brain damage or age (broad visualization, short-term acquisition, and retrieval), and maintained abilities (quantitate ability and long-term retrieval). Kaufman et al. (1996) found that crystallized (application of knowledge and quantitative mathematical)

abilities were maintained. They also found that fluid and broad visualization were vulnerable. Short-term acquisition and retrieval was also maintained. Results from long-term retrieval produced conflicting findings. The Weschler Series, Stanford-Binet Scales, and Woodcock-Johnson Psycho-Educational Battery-Revised, Test of Cognitive Ability appear to be in accord with the fluid-crystallized theory of intelligence (Esters & Ittenbach, 1999).

In the planning, attention, simultaneous, and successive (PASS) theory, individuals process stimuli that they find relevant while tuning out stimuli that they do not find useful. The Kaufman series are tests that corroborate this theory (Esters & Ittenbach, 1999). Furthermore, the cognitive assessment system (Naglieri & Das, 1997) is based on PASS. However, research results (Kranzler & Keith, 1999) revealed that the PASS model did not provide a particularly good fit to the test (CAS).

The three-stratum theory of intelligence includes (1) general intelligence, (2) broad abilities, and (3) more specific abilities. It blends key features of Spearman's theory and Horn and Cattell's theory (Bickley, Keith, & Wolfle, 1995). Also, this theory addresses individual differences. Carroll (1997) classified the three strata into "narrow" abilities (stratum I), "broad" abilities (stratum II), and "general" ability (stratum III). Stratum I included about 70 specific abilities, with each regarding a specific Stratum II factor (i.e., originality, reading comprehension). Stratum II included fluid intelligence, crystallized intelligence, broad auditory perception, broad visual perception, broad retrieval capacity, broad cognitive speed, general memory and learning, and processing speed. Stratum III was analogous to the "g, or general factor mental ability" (Carroll, 1993). This factor is a single measure of intelligence.

Bickley et al. (1995) tested the three-stratum theory of cognitive abilities across the life span via factor analysis. Results revealed support for the theory, but they did not support the changes in organization of cognitive abilities across the lifetime. Facon and Facon-Bollengier (1999 studied the effect of chronological age and fluid intelligence on the crystallized intelligence of individuals with intellectual disabilities, age 6 to 20. They found that chronological age (experience) and fluid intelligence both accounted for a large portion of crystallized intelligence.

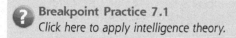

Breakpoint Practice 7.1
Click here to apply intelligence theory.

SOURCES OF INFORMATION ABOUT LEARNING APTITUDE

There are several sources of information about learning aptitude in addition to formal measures. For example, the student's performance in actual learning situations at school or at home may provide clues about ability to acquire new skills and information. However, norm-referenced measures are usually the best source of comparative information about learning aptitude, at least for majority group students whose characteristics match those of the norm group. Informal measures are less useful in this area of assessment and are best used to verify and elaborate the results of formal measures.

School Records

School records contain information about the student's past performance. Unlike achievement, learning aptitude is a relatively stable characteristic, and past performance data may be worth considering.

Group Intelligence Test Results

Results of any current or past group tests of intellectual performance should be reviewed. Keeping in mind the limitations of group administration procedures for students with school performance problems, the team can evaluate test results to determine the student's standing in relation to age or grade peers.

Individual Intelligence Test Data

The student may have been referred for individual assessment in the past, and individual intelligence test data may be available. If the assessment took place within the recent past, results should be compared with current findings. If an individual intelligence test has been administered very recently (e.g., within the last year), the assessment team may decide that another administration is unnecessary.

Developmental and School Histories

School records may contain the student's developmental history, furnished by the student's parents, perhaps at the time of entry to school. Histories typically provide information about the student's early development and, therefore, are most useful in the lower elementary grades. Included may be the ages at which developmental milestones such as talking and walking were achieved, any birth or other medical problems, family history, and data about attendance in early education programs. Developmental histories may suggest delays in early development, a possible indication of depressed learning aptitude. Similarly, school histories may reveal information on retentions, past referrals, chronic problems in school learning, or teachers' comments about the student's general learning aptitude.

The Student

The student assists the study of learning aptitude by participating in test administration and, on occasion, performing nonschool tasks under observation. Students can also talk about how they perceive their own abilities as learners.

Individual Tests of Intellectual Performance

The most usual way of gathering information about general learning aptitude is through the administration of individual intelligence tests. During the hour or more of test administration, the tester observes the speed and accuracy with which the student completes each task. The tester also notes the way the student approaches each problem and plans and implements a strategy for a solution.

Teachers

Teachers observe the student in everyday learning situations and are important sources of information about aptitude.

Observed Learning Aptitude

Teachers can report about how a student learns new skills, information, and classroom routines and procedures. Does the student learn as quickly as class peers? Is more practice needed or are a greater number of explanations indicated? How does the student go about learning, and what instructional strategies have proven successful in facilitating learning?

Developmental History

If school records do not contain the student's developmental history, parents can provide it. This information is most useful for younger elementary children; for older students, school histories are of interest.

Observed Learning Aptitude

Like teachers, parents have numerous opportunities to observe learning aptitude. Within their child's first few years of life, parents watch a great variety of learning experiences: the first step, the first words, the first friends, and the first moves toward independence as children begin to acquire skills in caring for themselves. Parents may be able to compare one child's rate of learning with siblings or age mates. They may also identify

ENHANCEDetext

Video Example 7.2

Watch this video to find out more about cognitive assessment.

tasks the child learns easily and tasks he or she finds difficult.

GROUP TESTS OF INTELLECTUAL PERFORMANCE

Group intelligence tests are sometimes used in general education; their results may be available for students referred for special education assessment. Like all group-administered measures, their scores are likely to be low estimates of actual abilities of students with school performance problems. In particular, most group intelligence tests rely heavily on reading skills. Poor scores on these measures may reflect poor reading ability as opposed to below-average intellectual performance. Because of this and the other limitations, results of group intelligence tests should be used only as an indicator of the need for further assessment with individual tests.

Group tests of intellectual performance are typically designed with several levels; so one test series can be used for grades 1–12. The content of group tests varies somewhat, but most attempt to assess both verbal and quantitative reasoning skills. Some tests provide separate measures of verbal and nonverbal abilities, and others contain several subtests, each of which addresses a different cognitive skill. Most, however, produce total test scores that are similar to IQ scores that indicate overall cognitive functioning. Other summary scores such as percentile ranks and stanines for total test performance are usually also available.

As with group achievement tests, test items are typically in multiple-choice format. The tester presents directions orally, and the student reads each question and responds in writing. Most tests are timed, and older students record their responses on separate answer sheets.

Many of the group tests available today are current editions of long-used measures. The *Otis-Lennon School Ability Test—Eighth Edition* (Otis & Lennon, 2002), for example, is the modern version of the *Otis Group Intelligence Scale,* one of the earliest measures of its type developed in the United States. The *Otis-Lennon* is available in seven levels for students in kindergarten through grade 12. Its subtests assess verbal and nonverbal abilities; results include School Ability Index (SAI) scores, percentile ranks, and stanines for Verbal, Nonverbal, and total test performance. In contrast, the *Cognitive Abilities Tests* (Lohman & Hagen, 2001) provide 13 levels for kindergarten through grade 12, and each level is arranged in three batteries: Verbal, Quantitative, and Nonverbal. Results include standard age scores, percentile ranks, and stanines for each battery and for a total test composite.

Like group achievement measures, group intelligence measures are most useful in screening programs. When group measures are administered to large segments of the school population, results should be reviewed to identify students who need further assessment.

INDIVIDUAL TESTS OF INTELLECTUAL PERFORMANCE

Individual tests may be designed for a special age group, such as preschool children or students between the ages of 6 and 18, or they may be appropriate for the entire age range from early childhood through adulthood. Unlike group tests, individual tests are usually available in only one version that is divided into sections by either subtests or age levels. Subtests contain items that attempt to assess the same skill or ability, and test items are arranged in order of difficulty. When tests are broken into age levels, each age level usually contains a variety of tasks that assess different skills and abilities.

Most individual tests of intellectual performance assess both verbal and nonverbal reasoning. Verbal skills may be emphasized, but nonverbal abilities are evaluated by means of figural or mathematical problem-solving tasks. Measures of memory are often included, as are visual-motor coordination tasks. Academic skill demands are deemphasized on individual intelligence tests. Reading is not required, and written responses are usually limited to drawing

or writing numbers. Information is presented orally or with pictures or objects, and students answer orally or with some type of motoric response.

Several well-known individual tests of intellectual performance are listed in Table 7–1. Each is described in terms of age span and types of results. The next sections of this chapter discuss intelligence measures for school-aged children, beginning with the *Wechsler Intelligence Scale for Children–Fifth Edition.*

 Breakpoint Practice 7.2
Click here to apply your knowledge of individual intelligence assessment.

WECHSLER INTELLIGENCE SCALE FOR CHILDREN–FIFTH EDITION*

The *Wechsler Intelligence Scale for Children–Fifth Edition (WISC–V)* (Wechsler, 2014) is the individual test most often used to assess the general intellectual performance of school-aged individuals. It replaces the previous edition, the *Wechsler Intelligence Scale for Children—Fourth Edition (WISC–IV)* (Wechsler, 2003a). The Wechsler family of tests spans all age levels. The *Wechsler Preschool and Primary Scale of Intelligence–Fourth Edition (WPPSI–IV)* (Wechsler, 2012) is appropriate for children between the ages of 2–6 and 7–7, and the *Wechsler Adult Intelligence Scale–Fourth Edition (WAIS)–IV* (Wechsler, 2008) is used for persons between the ages of 16 and 90–11. The *Wechsler Abbreviated Scale of Intelligence—Second Edition* (2011) provides a quick estimate of intellectual performance for ages 6 to 90–11. A Spanish-language version has also been developed specifically for U.S. students who are Spanish speakers: the *Wechsler Intelligence Scale for Children–Fourth Edition Spanish* (Wechsler, 2005).

The *WISC–V* assesses general intellectual functioning by sampling performance on many

---

Wechsler Intelligence Scale for Children and *WISC–IV* are registered trademarks of Harcourt Assessment.

TABLE 7–1
Individual Tests of Intellectual Performance

NAME (AUTHOR)	AGES	RESULTS
Columbia Mental Maturity Scale— Third Edition (Burgemeister, Blum, & Lorge, 1972)	3 years, 6 months to 9 years, 11 months	Age score, percentile rank, stanine, Maturity Index
Comprehensive Test of Nonverbal Intelligence-2 (Hammill, Pearson, & Wiederholt, 1997)	6–0 to 89–11	Standard scores, percentile ranks, and age equivalents
Das-Naglieri Cognitive Assessment System-2 (Naglieri & Das, 1997)	5–0 to 17–11	Standard scores for Scales (Planning, Attention, Simultaneous, and Successive); subtest scaled scores
Hammill Multiability Intelligence Test (Hammill, Bryant, & Pearson, 1998)	5–0 to 17–11	Standard scores and percentile ranks for Composites (General, Verbal, and Nonverbal Intelligence); subtest standard scores, percentile ranks, and age equivalents
Kaufman Adolescent & Adult Intelligence Test (Kaufman & Kaufman, 1993)	11 to 85+	IQ scores (Fluid, Crystallized, and Composite Intelligence), subtest scaled scores, and percentile ranks
Kaufman Assessment Battery for Children—Second Edition (Kaufman & Kaufman, 2004a)	3 to 18	Global standard scores (Mental Processing Index, Fluid-Crystallized Index, and Nonverbal Index), scores for five scale indexes (Sequential, Simultaneous, Planning, Learning, Knowledge), subtest scaled scores, and percentile ranks
Learning Potential Assessment Device (Feuerstein, Rand, & Hoffman, 1979)	Children and youth	Clinical description of the student's cognitive modifiability
Leiter International Performance Scale– Third Edition (Roid & Miller, 1997)	3–0 to 75+	IQ score; subtest standard scores, percentile ranks, and age equivalents
McCarthy Scales of Children's Abilities (McCarthy, 1972)	2 1/2 to 8 1/2	General Cognitive Index, MA, and scaled scores for five scales: Verbal, Perceptual Performance, Quantitative, Memory, and Motor
Naglieri Nonverbal Ability Test–Second edition (Naglieri, 2003)	4–0 to 18	Standard score, percentile rank, age equivalent
Raven Progressive Matrices (Raven, 1938, 1947, 1962, 1998, 2015)	5 to adult	Percentile rank
Slosson Intelligence Scale–Revised (Nicholson & Hibpshman, 1990)	3–0 to adult	Mean Age Equivalent, Total Test Standard Score, percentile rank, stanine
Stanford-Binet Intelligence Scales, Fifth Edition (Roid, 2003)	2 to 90+	Verbal, Nonverbal, Full Scale, and Abbreviated intelligence scores; factor indexes (Fluid Reasoning, Knowledge, Quantitative Reasoning, Visual-Spatial Processing, Working Memory); subtest scores
Swanson-Cognitive Processing Test (Swanson, 1996)	4–11 to 76	Standard scores for Composites (Semantic, Episodic, Total) and Components (Auditory, Visual, Prospective, Retrospective) for Initial, Gain, and Maintenance testing; subtest scale scores

TABLE 7–1   *continued*

NAME (AUTHOR)	AGES	RESULTS
System of Multicultural Pluralisti Assessment (Mercer & Lewis, 1977b)	5 to 11	School Functioning Level (*WISC–R* IQ scores) and Estimated Learning Potential (*WISC–R* results rescored using alternate norms)
Test of Nonverbal Intelligence (4th ed.) (Brown, Sherbenou, & Johnsen, 1997)	6–0 to 89–11	Age-based standard scores, percentile rank, stanines
Universal Nonverbal Intelligence Test-2 (Bracken & McCallum, 1998)	5–0 to 21–11	Standard scores. percentile ranks, confidence intervals for all quotients, scaled scores, and age equivalents
Wechsler Abbreviated Scale of Intelligence-Second Edition (2011)	6 to 90–11	Verbal IQ, Performance IQ, and Full Scale IQ
Wechsler Adult Intelligence Scale–Fourth Edition (Wechsler, 2008)	16 to 90–11	Verbal IQ, Performance IQ, and Full Scale IQ; factor-based index scores
Wechsler Intelligence Scale for Children–Fifth Edition (Wechsler, 2014a)	6–0 to 16–11	Composite Index scores (Full Scale IQ, Verbal Comprehension, Visual Spatial, Fluid Reasoning, Working Memory, Processing Speed); subtest scaled scores
Wechsler Preschool and Primary Scale of Intelligence–Fourth Edition (Wechsler, 2012)	2–6 to 7–3	Verbal IQ, Performance IQ, Full Scale IQ, and subtest scaled scores
Woodcock-Johnson IV Tests of Cognitive Abilities (Schrank, Mather, & McGrew, 2014)	Age 2 to 90+, Grade K–12 and college	Age and grade equivalents, standard scores, percentile ranks, and Relative Proficiency Index (RPI) scores for individual subtests; General Intellectual Ability; cognitive composites; CHC factors; narrow cognitive abilities and other clinical clusters

different types of activities. According to Wechsler (1974), intelligence is not a single trait, but multidimensional. In special education assessment, the *WISC–V* is often used to gain an overall estimate of the student's current global intellectual performance. This measure may also provide information about strengths and weaknesses in specific areas of aptitude.

The *WISC–V* contains 15 subtests; 7 are primary and 9 are secondary. These primary subtests are used for Full Scale IQ (FSIQ). Subtests are classified according to five different composites: the Verbal Comprehension Index, Visual Spatial Index, Fluid Reasoning Index, Working Memory Index, and Processing Speed Index.

Verbal Comprehension Index subtests require students to listen to questions and answer orally. To preserve the confidentiality of the test items,

the examples cited are similar, but not identical, to *WISC–V* tasks.

- *Similarities* (Primary). The student must describe how two things (pony and cow, or car and airplane) are alike.

- *Vocabulary* (Primary). On early items, the student is asked to name a picture. On later items, the tester says a word and the student must tell its meaning. The tester asks, "What is a _____?" or "What does _____ mean?"

- *Comprehension* (Secondary). The student answers questions that require general knowledge and social reasoning such as "What are some reasons why we need firefighters?"

- *Information* (Secondary). The student responds orally to general information questions such as "How many eyes do you have?" and "From what animal do we get hamburger?"

WECHSLER INTELLIGENCE SCALE FOR CHILDREN–FIFTH EDITION (WISC–V)

D. Wechsler (2014)

Type: Norm-referenced test

Major Content Areas: General verbal aptitude, general performance aptitude

Type of Administration: Individual

Administration Time: about 60 minutes (primary battery)

Age/Grade Levels: Ages 6–0 to 16–11

Types of Scores: Overall IQ score (Full Scale IQ), four composite scores (Verbal Comprehension Index, Visual Spatial Index, Working Memory Index, Fluid Reasoning, and Processing Speed Index), scaled scores for each subtest

Technology Aids: Q-Interactive/Global web-based scoring and reporting

Typical Uses: A wide-range measure of general intellectual performance and specific cognitive abilities

Cautions: This test is not appropriate for students who do not understand and speak English

Publisher: Pearson (http://www.pearsonclinical.com/psychology/products/100000771/wechsler-intelligence-scale-for-childrensupsupfifth-edition—wisc-v.html#tab-details)

Visual Spatial Index subtests are spatial reasoning tasks. The student listens to oral directions, looks at stimulus materials, and responds motorically.

- *Block Design* (Primary). On this timed subtest, the student is given several colored cubes or blocks and a picture of a design. The cubes must be arranged into an identical design.
- *Visual Puzzles* (Secondary). Timed subtest involves the student looking at a completed puzzle and selecting options to redo puzzle.

Fluid Reasoning Index subtests are abstract conceptual reasoning tasks. The task is to use conceptual reasoning from visual information.

- *Matrix Reasoning* (Primary). The student is shown a matrix with one design missing. The task is to identify which of five choices correctly completes the pattern.
  - *Figure Weights* (Primary). The student is shown a scale with missing weight. The task is to identify the quantitative response that will balance the scale.

- *Picture Concepts* (Secondary). The student is shown two rows of drawings and must select one drawing from the top row that goes with one drawing from the bottom row. More difficult items contain three rows of drawings.
- *Arithmetic* (Secondary). The tester reads arithmetic problems to the student, and the student must respond orally within 30 seconds. All computations must be done mentally; paper and pencil are not furnished. Visuals are used with the first few test items.

The subtests that make up the Working Memory Index composite score all require recall. Only one presentation of each item is allowed.

- *Digit Span* (Primary). The tester reads a series of numbers to the student at the rate of one digit per second. On the first portion of the test, the student attempts to repeat the digits in the order read by the tester. On the second portion, digits are repeated backwards.
  - *Picture Span* (Secondary). The tester looks at one or more pictures. The student then puts the pictures in order.

- *Letter-Number Sequencing* (Secondary). The tester reads a series containing both numbers and letters at a rate of one per second. The student must first repeat the numbers in order beginning with the lowest, then the letters in alphabetical order.

The fifth composite, the Processing Speed Index, assesses how well students are able to complete precise tasks under timed conditions.

- *Coding* (Primary). In this paper-and-pencil task, the student is shown a code, such as one geometric design for each of the digits. Then rows of digits are presented, and the student must write in the correct geometric design for each digit. The code remains available to the student during the task. The task is timed.
- *Symbol Search* (Secondary). The student is shown a symbol and must determine if its match appears in a row of three symbols. Older students see two target symbols and must determine if either appears in a row of five symbols. Students respond by marking the "yes" or the "no" box. The task is timed.
- *Cancellation* (Secondary). The student is shown several target pictures (e.g., different types of fruit). The student must locate the target pictures in an array and then cross them out. In the first task, the pictures in the array are scattered throughout the page; in the second, they are arranged in rows. Both tasks are timed.

The *WISC–V* is appropriate for students who can sustain attention for extended periods of time. This test is long and may be administered in more than one session. English-language competence is a necessity. Students must be able to understand test directions and questions and answer questions in English. Both oral and motor responses are required. No skills are needed in reading or written expression, but mental arithmetic is assessed.

Technical Quality

The *WISC–V* was standardized on 2,200 students ages 6 through 16, and equal numbers of males and females were included at each age level. An updated normative sample was selected to resemble the United States 2010 census data. The variables used in the stratified sampling plan were race/ethnicity, geographic region, and parent education. The final sample approximated the total population on these variables.

The normative sample included a small portion of special populations of students (e.g., students with mild or moderate intellectual disability, attention-deficit/hyperactivity disorder, gifted and talented, speech-language impairment, and autism disorder). The manual provides percentages of students included in the normative sample, as well as percentages in the U.S. population. English-language learners were also included in special group studies.

Internal consistency of the *WISC–V* was studied for each index through the split-half method with the Spearman-Brown formula. Average reliability coefficients ranged from .88 to .96, whereas average reliability coefficients for subtests ranged from .88 to .94. Test-retest reliability is adequate across ages for Full Scale IQ, and interscorer reliability coefficients fell at or above .97 across subtests.

The concurrent validity of the *WISC–V* was studied with a number of tests, including the *WISC–IV*. Other test correlations included the WPPSI–IV, WAIS–IV, Wechsler Individual Achievement Test–III, Kaufman Test Educational Assessment-3, Vineland-II, and Behavior Assessment System for Children-2. Correlations were adequate.

Validity was also investigated through factor-analytic studies and studies with special groups (e.g., students with traumatic brain injury). Factor analyses support the four separate composite ability areas of the *WISC–V*. Results of research with special groups support the usefulness of this test for differential diagnosis.

Administration Considerations

According to the manual, *WISC–V* examiners should have a qualification level "c," which is considered a "high level of expertise in test interpretation." Licensed school psychologists are usually the only professionals permitted to administer individual intelligence tests like the *WISC–V* in school settings. Other professionals, however, should be knowledgeable about such tests, even if they are not responsible for their administration and scoring.

Results and Interpretation

The *WISC–V* provides an overall global IQ score, scores for each of the composite indexes, and subtest scaled scores. Derived scores are determined by age norms, not grade norms.

Composite scores include Full Scale IQ, Verbal Comprehension Index, Visual Spatial, Fluid Reasoning Index, Working Memory Index, and Processing Speed Index. These composites are standard scores distributed normally with a mean of 100 and a standard deviation of 15. Tables in the manual allow the tester to report standard score results in ranges using either a 90 percent or 95 percent confidence level. Percentile rank scores are also available for each of the composites. Subtest scaled scores are standard scores distributed normally with a mean of 10 and a standard deviation of 3.

The Record Form for the *WISC–V* provides profiles for plotting both subtest and composite results. Q-Interactive and Q-Global are available to assist in further analyses of test results. In other words, one could hand-score or use Web-based automatic scoring. The other two types of analyses available on the test form—Determining Strengths and Weaknesses and Process Analysis—involve subtest rather than composite results.

IQ and scaled scores can be interpreted using the standard score range system suggested in Chapter 5. However, Wechsler provides a somewhat different system. IQ scores between 90 and 109 are considered Average, and this range incorporates approximately 50 percent of the population. IQs of 80 to 89 are rated as Low Average, 70 to 79 as Very Low, and 69 and below as Extremely Low. Above the mean, IQs 110 to 119 are classified as High Average, 120 to 129 as Very High, and 130 and above as Extremely High.

Results of individual tests such as the *WISC–V* provide information about one criterion for intellectual disability—subaverage intellectual functioning. According to the American Association on Intellectual Disabilities (2010), intellectual disability is indicated when there is a substantial limitation in general intellectual functioning. That significant limitation is operationalized by the use of two standard deviations below the mean. Standard error of measurement is also taken into account.

This guideline takes into account the standard error of measurement (SEM) of IQ scores and the clinical judgment of the assessment team. On the *WISC–V*, .88–1.34 SEM are reported on subtests and 2.9 to 5.24 on scales. Norm tables provide results at two confidence levels: 90 percent and 95 percent. At the 90 percent level, a Full Scale IQ score of 70 would fall in the range 66 to 76, and an IQ of 72 would fall in the range 68 to 78. Determination of whether these scores indicate a substantial limitation is left to the assessment team. Of course, the individual's adaptive behavior must also be evaluated.

In summary, the *WISC–V* appears to be an appropriate individual measure of general intellectual functioning. It is well standardized and reliable, and the available validity data are adequate. The results of this measure provide information about general levels of intellectual performance as well as more specific mental abilities. The Wechsler tests have a long history, and they are well known and widely accepted in education.

ENHANCEDetext
Video Example 7.3
Watch this video to find out more about intelligence tasks.

WOODCOCK-JOHNSON IV TESTS OF COGNITIVE ABILITIES

The *Woodcock-Johnson IV (WJ–IV)* will be discussed in Chapter 11, where one-half of the battery, the *Tests of Achievement,* will be discussed as a measure of school performance. The other portion, the *Tests of Cognitive Abilities,* is presented here.

The *Tests of Cognitive Abilities* serve a variety of purposes. First, they provide an estimate of overall intellectual functioning, similar to a global IQ score. Second, they produce measures of predicted achievement in school subjects such as reading, math, oral and written language, and academic knowledge. Third, subtests are clustered into three broad cognitive composites: General Intellectual Ability (GIA score-first seven subtests), Brief Intellectual Ability (BIA-first three subtests), and Gf-Gc Composite (Two Gf and Two Gc subtests) (new). Fourth, subtests are also clustered into seven cognitive factors to allow description of more specific abilities. The factors, based on the Horn-Cattell theory of intellectual processing (Woodcock & Mather, 1989), are Comprehension-Knowledge, Fluid Reasoning, Short-Term Working Memory, Cognitive Processing Speed, Auditory Processing, Long-Term Retrieval, and Visual Processing. Fifth, results are available for six narrow cognitive abilities and clinical clusters: Quantitative Reasoning, Auditory Memory Span, Number Facility, Perceptual Speed, Vocabulary, and Cognitive Efficiency. It is also possible to contrast expected and actual achievement by comparing a student's performance on the *Tests of Cognitive Abilities* with achievement scores from the other portion of the battery.

There are 18 cognitive ability tests arranged in two levels: the standard battery (subtests 1 through 10) and the extended battery (subtests 11 through 18). An oral language battery also exists. As with the *Woodcock-Johnson IV* achievement tests, the standard battery is administered first; then portions of the extended battery are selected if further information is needed. Alternate forms are not available for the *Tests of Cognitive Abilities.*

The 14 cognitive ability subtests that make up the seven cognitive factors are described next.

Comprehension-Knowledge (Gc)

- *Test 1, Oral Vocabulary.* In Synonyms, the student hears a word and gives its synonym; in Antonyms, the student provides an antonym for the word read by the tester.

WOODCOCK-JOHNSON IV (WJ IV) TESTS OF COGNITIVE ABILITIES

Schrank, Mather, McGrew (2015)

Type: Norm-referenced test

Major Content Areas: Broad intellectual ability, three cognitive categories, seven broad cognitive factors, six narrow cognitive abilities and clinical clusters, and several types of scholastic aptitude

Type of Administration: Individual

Administration Time: Less than one hour for standard battery

Age/Grade Levels: Ages 2 to 90+; Preschool, Grades K–12, college, adult

Types of Scores: Grade and age equivalents, standard scores, percentile ranks, and actual and predicted discrepancies

Technology: *WJ IV* online scoring and reporting system

Typical Uses: A broad-based measure of general cognitive functioning, specific cognitive abilities, and academic aptitudes

Cautions: Administration rules vary from subtest to subtest. Results are available for over 40 standard and extended subtests and clusters, making interpretation complicated. Results should be interpreted with some caution owing to some concerns about the internal consistency and test-retest reliability of a few subtests.

Publisher: Riverside Publishing (*www.riverpub.com*)

- *Test 8, General Information.* This subtest asks students to tell where they would find a specific object or what they would do with that object.

Fluid Reasoning (Gf)

- *Test 2, Number Series* (previously in WJ Diagnostic Supplement). The student is presented with a numerical sequence missing a number. Then the student completes that numerical sequence after applying rules.
- *Test 9, Concept Formation.* The student is shown two sets of drawings, one set of which is inside boxes. The student must tell one or more concepts that differentiate the boxed drawings. Examples are color, size, shape, and number. In this subtest, error responses are corrected.

Short-Term Working Memory (Gwm)

Provides for a less narrow expression of short-term memory than the previous version.

- *Test 10, Numbers Reversed.* The tester or Test Tape reads a series of digits at a rate of one digit per second; the student repeats the digits in backward order.
  - *Test 3, Verbal Attention* (new). The tester provides a response to a question after listening to orally presented material. Both working memory and attention are involved in this activity.

Cognitive Processing Speed (Gs)

- *Test 4, Letter-Pattern Matching* (new). Student identifies (circles) grapheme patterns that match when presented with six options.
- *Test 17, Pair Cancellation.* This paper-and-pencil task requires the student to look at rows of small drawings and draw a circle around each pair that occurs in a specified sequence (e.g., each house that is followed by a tree). Three minutes are allowed.

Auditory Processing (Ga)

- *Test 5, Phonological Processing* (new). The student accesses word retrieval through the use of phonology. Three aspects include word access (i.e., student provides with certain phonemic information), word fluency (i.e., student names as many words as possible that start with a certain sound in a minute), and substitution (i.e., student substitutes a portion of a word to create a new word).

- *Test 12, Nonword Repetition* (new). The student listens to and repeats words like stimuli.

Long-Term Retrieval (Glr)

- *Test 13, Visual-Auditory Learning.* The tester teaches the student a series of visual symbols that stand for words. Then the student is asked to "read" sentences made up of the symbols. The tester corrects student errors or supplies a word if the student hesitates for more than 5 seconds.
  - *Test 6, Story Recall* (previously the second half of Quantitative Concepts). The student listens to a story and through bolded words presents the story.

Visual Processing (Gv)

- *Test 7, Visualization.* (new). The student first indicates visual-spatial recognition and then manipulates multidimensional visual information. For example, the student notes two or three portions of a shape.
- *Test 14, Picture Recognition.* The student is shown a stimulus page with one or more drawings on it; after 5 seconds, a new page is revealed that contains some of the stimulus drawings and others that are similar. The student must identify the stimulus drawings.

Students must be able to attend to test tasks for several minutes at a time to participate in *Woodcock-Johnson IV* administration. English-language skills are a necessity, except perhaps for Processing Speed subtests. However, a Spanish-language version of the *Woodcock-Johnson III* battery, the *Batería III Woodcock-Muñoz* (Woodcock, Muñoz-Sandoval, McGrew, & Mather, 2005), is available.

No reading is required. The most typical response mode is oral, although some subtests require that the student points to the answer and others are paper-and-pencil tasks. Speeded and nonspeeded subtests are included in the *WJ IV*. The student must be able to discriminate colors on the Analysis-Synthesis subtest. A color pretest is included.

Technical Quality

Internal consistency, as measured by the split-half method (as well as an alternate procedure for timed tests), is adequate for most subtests and all cluster scores. However, median reliability coefficients fall below .80 across ages for Picture Recognition ($r = .74$). Furthermore, median reliability for visual processing is .86 for the cluster. This is below the .9 cut-off. Test-retest reliability of all speeded *WJ IV* subtests revealed median reliability coefficients between .85 (Number-Pattern Matching) and .91 (Letter-Pattern Matching) in the cognitive subtests for rate of correct response. Nonspeeded tests were not included in the dataset.

In terms of concurrent validity, the *WJ IV* was compared to the WISC IV, WAIS IV, WPPSI III, Kaufman Assessment Battery for Children, Second Edition, Stanford-Binet Intelligence Scales, Fifth Edition, and the Differential Abilities Scales, Second Edition. Results suggest support for the validity of the *WJ IV*. Results of the GIA revealed correlations between .72 and .86.

Administration Considerations

The *Tests of Cognitive Abilities*, like the achievement portion of the *WJ IV*, are somewhat difficult to administer because of variations from subtest to subtest. For example, in Oral Vocabulary the whole page is tested, and the decision is made using the six lowest incorrect and six highest correct. In Letter-Pattern Matching, time is the deciding factor. In Memory for Words, the four lowest incorrect and four highest correct are used. These variations require an alert test administrator.

The *Tests of Cognitive Abilities* begin with standard introductory remarks that are read to all students. Then the tester selects the subtests to be administered. Suggested starting points are given by the student's estimated ability level, not by actual grade placement.

Results and Interpretation

Like the achievement portion of the *WJ IV*, the *Tests of Cognitive Abilities* produce a great number of results. In general, the same types of scores are available. The overall score, General Intellectual Ability (Standard Scale), summarizes performance on the standard battery. The extended scale version of this score summarizes results from both the standard and extended batteries. Results are also reported by subtest, by cognitive category, by cognitive factor, and by clinical

cluster. More than 40 subtest and cluster results are produced, and each result can be expressed in a number of ways: age and grade equivalent, standard score, percentile rank, and Relative Proficiency Index (RPI) score. Standard scores are distributed with a mean of 100 and a standard deviation of 15.

Results are plotted on a series of profiles to assist in interpretation. These include the Age/Grade Profile and the Standard Score/Percentile Rank profile. In addition, procedures are provided for comparing discrepancies in performance across cognitive ability areas and between predicted achievement and actual achievement; these procedures are discussed in the next chapter.

The *Tests of Cognitive Abilities* are an interesting set of measures that span a wide age range. The *WJ IV* addresses a number of cognitive factors, and several of these factors are of particular interest in the assessment of learning disabilities. The drawbacks of this measure include its length (a total of 18 subtests) and the difficulties associated with interpreting the large number of scores and profiles produced.

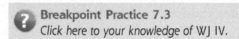

Breakpoint Practice 7.3
Click here to your knowledge of WJ IV.

OTHER INDIVIDUAL MEASURES OF INTELLECTUAL PERFORMANCE

The assessment team can choose from several other individual tests of intellectual performance. The *Kaufman Assessment Battery for Children— Second Edition,* is a revised version of an aptitude measure first published in the 1980s. Also available are age scales such as the *Slosson Intelligence Scale–Revised* and the 1973 *Stanford-Binet Intelligence Scale,* in which test items are arranged by age levels rather than by subtest. The *Stanford-Binet Intelligence Scales—Fifth Edition,* and the previous edition, represents a major revision of this classic test; it is no longer an age scale. Two newer measures are the *Hammill Multiability Intelligence Test,* a companion to the *Hammill Multiability Achievement Test*, described in Chapter 6, and the *Das-Naglieri Cognitive Assessment System.* Nonverbal measures of intellectual performance are discussed in the section on approaches to nonbiased assessment.

Kaufman Assessment Battery for Children—Second Edition

The *KABC–II* (Kaufman & Kaufman, 2004a) is an individual measure designed to be administered by professionals such as school psychologists trained in individual intelligence testing. The battery is appropriate for children ages 3–0 to 18–11. It contains only mental processing subtests; unlike the first edition of this measure, no achievement subtests are included. However, a companion test, the *Kaufman Test of Educational Achievement—Second Edition* (Kaufman & Kaufman, 2004b), was co-normed with the *KABC-II*.

The test authors indicate that the *KABC-II* is based on two different theoretical models. The examiner must decide which model to adopt before administration because overall composites are based on slightly different sets of subtests depending on the model. The first model, Luria's neuropsychological model, is concerned with areas such as sequential and simultaneous processing, learning ability, and planning ability; the composite score derived for this model is the Mental Processing Index. The second model, the Cattell-Horn-Carroll model, describes broad and narrow cognitive abilities; among the areas assessed are short-term memory, visual processing, long-term storage and retrieval, fluid reasoning, and crystallized ability. The composite score for the Cattell-Horn-Carroll model is called the Fluid-Crystallized Index. Also available as an overall score on this test is the Nonverbal Index. All global scores are distributed with a mean of 100 and a standard deviation of 15.

The *KABC-II* contains 20 subtests. Subtests are classified as Core, Supplementary, or Nonverbal, and different ages are assigned depending on those classifications. For example, the Number Recall subtest can be administered to children ages 4–18 as a Core subtest or to those ages 3 as a Supplementary subtest. Also, the Hand Movements subtest can be administered to ages 4–18 as a Supplementary subtest or to ages 3–18 as a Nonverbal subtest.

The 20 subtests are listed below according to the mental processing scales to which each pertains. Ages are provided for Core subtests only.

Sequential
- Number Recall (ages 4–18)
- Word Order (ages 3–18)
- Hand Movements

Simultaneous
- Block Counting (ages 13–18)
- Conceptual Thinking (ages 3–6)
- Face Recognition (ages 3–4)
- Pattern Reasoning (ages 5–6)
- Rover (ages 6–18)
- Story Completion
- Triangles (ages 3–12)
- Gestalt Closure

Planning
- Pattern Reasoning (ages 7–18)
- Story Completion (ages 7–18)

Learning
- Atlantis (ages 3–18)
- Rebus (ages 4–18)
- Atlantis Delayed
- Rebus Delayed

Knowledge
- Expressive Vocabulary (ages 3–6)
- Riddles (ages 3–18)
- Verbal Knowledge (ages 7–18)

Some of the *KABC–II* subtests have unusual names (e.g., Rover, Atlantis, and Rebus), so that it is difficult to get a sense of what test tasks they might contain. The Rover subtest is a maze-like task in which a child must navigate a grid to give the dog a bone. On the Atlantis subtest, the child is required to learn to associate nonsense words with pictures. On the Rebus subtest, the child learns to associate words with drawings called rebuses.

One important feature of the *KABC–II* is the Nonverbal Scale. It is composed of four or five subtests, depending on the age of the student. For example, children ages 3–4 are given Hand Movements, Conceptual Thinking, Face Recognition, and Triangles. Those ages 7–18 are given Hand Movements, Block Counting, Triangles, Pattern Recognition, and Story Completion. All subtests making up the Nonverbal Scale must be able to be administered in pantomime, and students must be able to respond motorically. According to the manual, individuals appropriate for the Nonverbal Scale include students who are deaf or hard of hearing, students with moderate to severe speech or language disabilities, and children who are English-language learners (Kaufman & Kaufman, 2004a).

Stanford-Binet Intelligence Scale—Fifth Edition

The 1986 edition of the *Stanford-Binet* (Thorndike, Hagen, & Sattler) changed the basic nature of this classic test. Instead of being arranged by age levels, it was organized by subtests. The current edition (Roid, 2003) continues this organization, although the number of subtests has been reduced and the factor scores are somewhat different.

Designed for persons age 2 through adult, the *Stanford-Binet 5* contains 10 subtests that assess both verbal and nonverbal abilities:

Verbal

• Verbal Fluid Reasoning
• Verbal Knowledge
• Verbal Quantitative Reasoning
• Verbal Visual-Spatial Processing
• Verbal Working Memory

Nonverbal

• Nonverbal Fluid Reasoning
• Nonverbal Knowledge
• Nonverbal Quantitative Reasoning
• Nonverbal Visual-Spatial Processing
• Nonverbal Working Memory

The verbal and nonverbal subtests, when combined, assess five cognitive factors: Fluid Reasoning, Knowledge, Quantitative Reasoning, Visual-Spatial Processing, and Working Memory.

Results on the *Stanford-Binet 5* include four intelligence scores: Full Scale, Abbreviated, Nonverbal, and Verbal. Standard scores are also available for the five factors; these and the intelligence scores are distributed with a mean of 100 and a standard deviation of 15. Subtest standard scores are distributed with a mean of 10 and a standard deviation of 3.

Several important changes were made in the *Stanford-Binet* in its fourth and fifth editions. These changes may help to overcome some of the criticisms of earlier versions of the *Stanford-Binet*, particularly concerns about overemphasis of verbal aptitude. As research accumulates on this measure, it will become possible to make comparisons between it and other tests such as the *WISC–IV* and the *Woodcock-Johnson III* that attempt to assess a variety of intellectual abilities.

Hammill Multiability Intelligence Test

The *Hammill Multiability Intelligence Test (HAMIT)* by Hammill, Bryant, and Pearson (1998) is a measure of intellectual performance developed in conjunction with the *Hammill Multiability Achievement Test (HAMAT)*. The *HAMIT* is designed for students ages 6–0 to 17–11; only one form is available.

According to its manual, the *HAMIT* is a "special use version" (p. vii) of the *Detroit Tests of Learning Aptitude–4* (Hammill, Bryant, & Pearson, 1998). The *DTLA–4* ts discussed in the next chapter as a measure of specific learning abilities. Eight of the 10 *DTLA–4* subtests have been incorporated intact into the *HAMIT*. These subtests are:

Verbal Subtests

• Word Opposites
• Sentence Imitation
• Basic Information
• Word Sequences

Nonverbal Subtests

• Design Sequences
• Design Reproduction
• Symbolic Relations
• Story Sequences

HAMIT results include three composite quotients: General Intelligence (based on all subtests), Verbal Intelligence, and Nonverbal Intelligence. These scores are distributed with a mean of 100 and a standard deviation of 15. Subtest standard scores are distributed with a mean of 10 and a standard deviation of 3. The manual provides guidelines for determining whether significant discrepancies exist between *HAMIT* quotients and results of measures of academic achievement such as the *HAMAT, PIAT–R, WIAT, Woodcock-Johnson–R,* and *WRAT3*.

Das-Naglieri Cognitive Assessment System

The *Das-Naglieri Cognitive Assessment System (CAS)* by Naglieri and Das (1997) is based on the PASS theory of cognitive processing. PASS, as noted earlier, stands for Planning, Attention, Simultaneous, and Successive (i.e., sequential). The *CAS* is designed to assess these processes in students ages 5–0 to 17–11. The Basic Battery contains eight subtests, two measuring each of the four processes:

Planning

- Matching Numbers
- Planned Codes

Attention

- Expressive Attention
- Number Detection

Simultaneous

- Nonverbal Matrices
- Verbal-Spatial Relations

Successive

- Word Series
- Sentence Repetition

The Standard Battery contains 12 subtests—one additional subtest in each of the four PASS areas.

Results include standard scores for the Full Scale and each of the four PASS Scales. Subtest scaled scores are also available. The manual provides guidelines for determining whether discrepancies exist between results from the *CAS* and the *Woodcock-Johnson–R*.

ENHANCEDetext
Video Example 7.4
Watch this video to find out more about intelligence assessment.

APPROACHES TO NONBIASED ASSESSMENT OF INTELLECTUAL PERFORMANCE

Concern about the potential bias of traditional measures of intellectual performance has led to the development of alternative strategies for the assessment of learning aptitude of culturally and linguistically diverse students. One early effort was the design of the *Culture Fair Intelligence Tests* (Cattell, 1950; Cattell & Cattell, 1960, 1963, 1977). These group-administered measures stress figural reasoning and deemphasize verbal skills and school learning. Another approach has been the nonstandard use of traditional measures such as IQ tests. Examples are the *System of Multicultural Pluralistic Assessment* and the *Learning Potential Assessment Device*. Most common today, however, are nonverbal tests of intellectual performance and measures in languages other than English. The next paragraphs describe some of the nonverbal tests available today as well as other approaches to nonbiased assessment. Measures in languages other than English are discussed in Chapter 13.

Nonverbal Measures of Intellectual Performance

Nonverbal measures of intelligence may be useful for students with hearing, speech, or language disorders, or for those whose language is not English. The nonverbal subtests on the *Stanford-Binet 5*, for example, deemphasize verbal skills and are sometimes considered a nonverbal intelligence measure, even though directions are given verbally. Other well-known nonverbal tests include the *Raven Progressive Matrices,* the *Leiter International Performance Scale–,* and the *Test of Nonverbal Intelligence—Fourth Edition*.

Raven Progressive Matrices

The *Raven Progressive Matrices* are nonverbal tests in which the student is shown a design or matrix with a part missing. The student must then select, from several choices, the piece that best completes the matrix. This task requires figural reasoning and is the only task used on the three versions of the *Matrices.* These are the *Standard Progressive Matrices* (Raven, 1938) for ages 6 to 18+, the *Coloured Progressive Matrices* (Raven, 1947) for ages 5 to 11 and adults with mental and physical impairments, and the *Advanced Progressive Matrices* (Raven, 1962) for age 12 through adults. These tests were originally standardized in England, but recent American norms are available from the tests' U.S. distributor, Harcourt Assessment. Portions of the manual were updated in 1988, 1994, 1998, and 2015 (Raven, 2015).

Leiter International Performance Scale– Third Edition

The *Leiter*–(Roid, Miller, Pomplun, & Koch, 2013) is an update of the revised nonverbal measure of intellectual performance published by Leiter in 1997. Like its predecessor, the *Leiter–3* is completely nonverbal. A typical test task requires the student to place response cards in the correct order based on a stimulus design. The Cognitive Scales of the *Leiter–3* contain five subtests; Classification and Analogies, Sequential Order, Form Completion, Figure-Ground, and Matching/Repeated Patterns (optional). The Attention and Memory Scales include five subtests; Forward Memory, Reverse Memory, Attention Sustained, Attention Divided, and Nonverbal Stroop. The *Leiter–3* is appropriate for ages 3–0 to 75+. Results include an overall IQ score as well as subtest standard scores, percentile ranks, and age equivalents.

Test of Nonverbal Intelligence (4th ed.)

The *Test of Nonverbal Intelligence* (4th ed.) *(TONI–4)* (Brown, Sherbenou, & Johnsen, 2010) is a more modern nonverbal measure. On this test, the examiner gives simple oral instructions, and the subject responds by pointing, nodding, or blinking to one of several possible answers. Test items assess problem solving with abstract, figural designs. The student is shown a set of figures with one or more figures missing. The individual must determine the rule or rules governing the set (e.g., matching, analogies, progressions) and then select the figure that best completes the set from several options.

The *TONI–4* offers two alternate forms with 60 items each. Results are reported as standard scores, with a mean of 100 and a standard deviation of 15. Percentile ranks and stanines are also available. The test was re-normed on 2,272 individuals from 33 states with appropriate representation to demographic changes in race, gender, ethnicity, geographic location, parental education, and socioeconomic status, ages 6–0 to 89–11. Individuals with disabilities were included in the sample. Internal consistency, test-retest, interscorer, and alternate forms reliability are adequate, and results of validity studies indicate that *TONI–4* results are related to results from other nonverbal measures of intelligence such as CTONI 2 and TONI 3. The *TONI–4* is a useful tool for the measurement of nonverbal problem-solving ability. Test directions are also available in Spanish, French, German, Chinese, Vietnamese, Korean, and Tagalog. Testing time is 15 to 20 minutes.

Newer Measures

Other, more modern, nonverbal measures are the *Naglieri Nonverbal Ability Test—Second Edition* (NNAT-2) (Naglieri, 2011) and the *Universal Nonverbal Intelligence Test—Second Edition (UNIT-2)* (Bracken & McCallum, 2015). The Naglieri can be administered in 30 minutes or less. It contains only one type of task, a figural matrix task. Here the student must look at choices and identify the one that completes the pattern. Results include an overall standard score, percentile rank, stanines, normal curve equivalents, and age equivalent. This test includes a home report available in English and in Spanish. The *UNIT-2* can be administered in 30 minutes for the standard battery, 15 minutes for the abbreviated battery, and 45 minutes for the full battery. This test contains six subtests, each of which requires only a motor response. They are: Symbolic Memory, Nonsymbolic Quantity, Analogic Reasoning, Spatial Memory, Numerical Series, and Cube Design,. Among the results are a Full Scale Intelligence Quotient and quotients for Memory, Reasoning, and Quantitative.

Other Approaches to Nonbiased Assessment

Traditional measures of intellectual performance such as the *WISC* and Raven's *Progressive Matrices* have been used in nontraditional ways in an attempt to improve assessment practices for culturally and linguistically diverse students. The first assessment system described here, the *SOMPA,* represents an interesting early approach to nonbiased assessment, although it did not gain widespread acceptance. The second strategy that is described, dynamic assessment, is a general approach that appears more promising. The third and fourth measures included in this section are the *Learning Potential Assessment Device,* one example of a dynamic assessment system, and the *WISC–V,* described earlier.

System of Multicultural Pluralistic Assessment

The *System of Multicultural Pluralistic Assessment (SOMPA)* (Mercer & Lewis, 1977b) is a battery of nine measures designed to provide information about the general learning aptitude of children ages 5 to 11 from diverse sociocultural backgrounds and white, African American, and Hispanic ethnic groups. The *SOMPA* assesses performance from three separate perspectives: Medical, Social System, and Pluralistic.

Medical measures evaluate the student's current health status to determine whether pathological conditions are interfering with physiological functioning. Social System measures determine whether the student is meeting performance expectations for school and social roles. Academic role performance is assessed with the *WISC–R.* Social role performance is assessed with the *Adaptive Behavior Inventory for Children (ABIC)* (Mercer & Lewis, 1977a), a parent interview form that elicits information about the student's ability to cope with nonacademic environments.

The pluralistic perspective of the *SOMPA* is concerned with whether the student is meeting performance expectations for age and sociocultural group. The Sociocultural Scales assess the student's current environment. Then the *WISC–R* is rescored to compare the student with his or her sociocultural group rather than with standard norms. The new *WISC–R* scores are then considered measures of Estimated Learning Potential (ELP).

The *SOMPA* has been heavily criticized for its lack of national norms (standardization took place in California only), its failure to include school performance tasks, its lack of validity data for the ELP score, and its failure to provide guidelines for use of the battery in educational decisions (Clarizio, 1979; Goodman, 1979; Oakland, 1979). Sattler (1988) is particularly critical of the ELP score.

Dynamic Assessment

Kanevsky (2000) observes that "static," established intelligence tests produce lower intelligence scores for students who are culturally and linguistically diverse. Because of this finding, there has been great interest in moving away from static measures of current performance toward dynamic measures of thinking processes with students from diverse backgrounds.

Sternberg and Grigorenko (2002) identify major differences between traditional static tests and the use of dynamic testing. First, static tests focus on skills already observed, while dynamic testing focuses on ongoing, newly learned skills. In addition, the nature of the relationship between the examiner and the student is different in these two approaches. In static testing, the examiner is neutral and does not give the student feedback on the quality of his or her responses. In dynamic testing, the relationship between examiner and student is interactive and the examiner provides feedback.

Several attempts have been made to develop dynamic assessment systems. Among those described by Sternberg and Grigorenko (2002) are the *Learning Potential Assessment Device* (discussed next), the work of Budoff and colleagues on learning potential testing (e.g., Budoff, 1987), the testing-the-limits approach (e.g., Carson & Wiedl, 1992), and the *Swanson-Cognitive Processing Test* (Swanson, 1996).

Learning Potential Assessment Device

The assessment system proposed by Feuerstein and colleagues (1979) is another nontraditional approach to evaluation of learning aptitude. According to Feuerstein, children learn through interactions with adults in mediated learning experiences. In these interactions, the adult "mediates" the world to the child by choosing, concentrating on, and responding to contextual information. In Feuerstein's view, cultural deprivation results from inadequate mediated learning; culturally deprived children have not assimilated their own culture.

In the *Learning Potential Assessment Device (LPAD),* the tester becomes a teacher and attempts to provide the student with mediated learning. To accomplish this, the *LPAD* is administered using a test-teach-test format. This device is actually a collection of measures, some adapted from experimental tasks, others from published instruments such as Raven's *Progressive Matrices.* The student first performs reasoning tasks without assistance from the examiner. The examiner then steps into the instructional role and attempts to provide the student with more sophisticated strategies for task solution. Test tasks are then presented again without coaching. This approach is sometimes called *interactive* or **dynamic assessment.**

The aim is to assess the student's cognitive modifiability rather than current intellectual status. The examiner observes the student's performance and forms a judgment about deficient cognitive functions and the ability to learn. Test tasks are not normed, and scores are not emphasized. Instead, the *LPAD* is intended for clinical use, and its results are primarily descriptive rather than quantitative.

This measure and the accompanying intervention program, Instrumental Enrichment (Feuerstein et al., 1980), are still under study (Feuerstein et al., 1981; Feuerstein, Miller, Rand, & Jensen, 1981; Frisby & Braden, 1992; Harth, 1982). Although the *LPAD* is an interesting system that attempts to address the central question of ability to learn, it is unlikely to be widely used in schools. It is a clinical measure tied to the expertise of the individual examiner and produces results that appear less objective than those of traditional tests.

WISC–V

The *WISC–V,* described earlier in this chapter, is an example of the use of dynamic assessment within a norm-referenced frame of reference. On this test, examiners can choose to continue assessment of specific cognitive skills by administering process subtests when results of standard subtests suggest areas of difficulty. For example, standard verbal comprehension subtests that require students to produce a verbal response can be followed by process tests in which the task is one of selecting the correct answer, not producing it. Other types of adaptations include doing away with bonus points for speed and examining the processes by which students complete test tasks. What is interesting about this approach is that it is possible to determine norm-referenced scaled scores for each of the process subtests administered to the student. Also, discrepancy comparisons can be made to find out if there are significant differences between performance on standard subtests versus performance on process subtests tapping the same cognitive abilities.

 Breakpoint Practice 7.4
Click here to apply nonbiased assessment information.

For example, consider the results of the learning aptitude assessment for Joyce, the fourth grader with school performance problems.

At this level of questioning, the major goal is to obtain a global picture of the student's aptitude. In the process of investigation, however, the team may note indications of specific strengths and weaknesses. Consider the case of Joyce.

Assessment in Action
Joyce

Joyce, a student in Mr. Harvey's fourth-grade class, has been referred for special education assessment. The team began by investigating Joyce's current school performance, and results of individual achievement tests suggested low to below-average achievement in reading, spelling, and handwriting.

Next the team will assess Joyce's general aptitude for learning. Intellectual disability is not suspected because Joyce appears to be able to learn some types of material quite easily. For example, her mathematics performance is average for her age and grade. Other disabilities remain a possibility, so the school psychologist will administer an individual test of intellectual performance—the *Wechsler Intelligence Scale for Children–Fifth Edition.* The results of this measure, along with the data gathered in reviews of school records and interviews with Joyce's classroom teacher, will assist the team in studying the relationship between poor school performance and possible disabilities.

Results of individual achievement tests have confirmed that Joyce is experiencing difficulty in reading, spelling, and handwriting. Continuing the assessment, the team begins an investigation of general learning aptitude. No results of group intelligence tests are found in the school records, and the brief developmental history that Joyce's mother completed at the beginning of the school year does not suggest major developmental delays. Mr. Harvey, Joyce's teacher, reports that Joyce learns some skills quite easily, and Joyce's parents confirm this. Consequently, intellectual disability is not suspected, and the team does not plan to assess adaptive behavior.

The school psychologist, Ms. Kellett, meets with Joyce and administers the *Wechsler Intelligence Scale for Children– Fifth Edition.* Joyce scores within the average range in general intellectual functioning and Perceptual Reasoning. Joyce's performance falls within the average to high-average range on Verbal Comprehension and within the low average to average range on Working Memory and Processing Speed. Joyce shows unusual discrepancies between Index scores. A difference of 34 points between Verbal Comprehension and Working Memory occurred in only 1.1 percent of the standardization sample; a difference of 31 points between Verbal Comprehension and Processing Speed occurred in only 2.6 percent of the standardization sample.

The assessment team concludes that Joyce shows average general intellectual performance with possible weaknesses in specific cognitive abilities. The team will continue assessment and explore the possibility of learning disabilities.

SUMMARY

- General learning aptitude is a concern in the identification of several different disabilities. The disability most directly related to learning aptitude is intellectual disability. Intelligence testing has engendered more controversy than any other area in special education assessment. The issues raised by the intelligence testing debate concern the nature and definition of intelligence, the relative contributions of heredity and environment to intellectual performance, the usefulness and accuracy of IQ tests, and the appropriateness of these measures for members of diverse ethnic, cultural, and linguistic groups (Ebel, 1977; Herrnstein, 1971; Holtzman & Wilkinson, 1991; Jones, 1988; Losen & Orfield, 2002; Patton, 1998; Perrone, 1977; Tyler, 1969; Valenzuela & Cervantes, 1998).

  Assessment of general learning aptitude takes place in both general and special education. In general education, school districts administer group intelligence tests to elementary grade populations, although this practice is far less common than group achievement testing. At the secondary level, measures such as the *Scholastic Aptitude Test (SAT)* (n.d.) of the College Entrance Examination Board are used to predict success in higher education.

- Sternberg (1988) discusses componential, contextual, and experiential elements in his triarchic theory of intelligence. The componential element involves internal intellectual factors, including the process, activities, and encoding involved in problem solving. Metacognitive, performance, and knowledge acquisition components are prominent in this discussion. The experiential element deals with how humans respond to new tasks or problems, as well as responses to highly familiar circumstances. The contextual element involves culture and behaviors. Adaptation, selection of a better environment, and shaping of the existing environment are key components of this element. These can be investigated further as analytic, creative, and practical intelligence (Viadero, 1995).

- School records contain information about the student's past performance. Unlike achievement, learning aptitude is a relatively stable characteristic, and past performance data may be worth considering. Teachers observe the student in everyday learning situations and are important sources of information about aptitude. The student assists the study of learning aptitude by participating in test administration and, on occasion, performing nonschool tasks under observation. Students can also talk about how they perceive their own abilities as a learner.

Results of any current or past group tests of intellectual performance should be reviewed. Keeping in mind the limitations of group administration procedures for students with school performance problems, the team can evaluate test results to determine the student's standing in relation to age or grade peers. If school records do not contain the student's developmental history, parents can provide it. This information is most useful for younger elementary children; for older students, school histories are of interest.

- The *Otis-Lennon School Ability Test—Eighth Edition* (Otis & Lennon, 2002) is the modern version of the *Otis Group Intelligence Scale,* one of the earliest measures of its type developed in the United States. The *Otis-Lennon* is available in seven levels for students in kindergarten through grade 12. Its subtests assess verbal and nonverbal abilities; results include School Ability Index (SAI) scores, percentile ranks, and stanines for Verbal, Nonverbal, and total test performance.

- An example of an individual test is the *Comprehensive Test of Nonverbal Intelligence-2* (Hammill, Pearson, & Wiederholt, 1997). Test scores include standard scores, percentile ranks, and age equivalents. Another example is the *Universal Nonverbal Intelligence Test-2* (Bracken & McCallum, 1998). Standard scores, percentile ranks, confidence intervals for all quotients, scaled scores, and age equivalents are test score options. A third example of an individual test is the *Slosson Intelligence Scale–Revised* (Nicholson & Hibpshman, 1990). Test scores include Mean Age Equivalent, Total Test Standard Score, percentile rank, and stanine.

- The *WISC–V* contains 15 subtests; 7 are primary and 9 are secondary. These primary subtests are used for Full Scale IQ (FSIQ). Subtests are classified according to five different composites: the Verbal Comprehension Index, Visual Spatial Index, Fluid Reasoning Index, Working Memory Index, and Processing Speed Index.

Score types for the WISC-V include Overall IQ score (Full Scale IQ), five composite scores (Verbal Comprehension Index, Visual Spatial Index, Working Memory Index, Fluid Reasoning, and Processing Speed Index), and scaled scores for each subtest.

- Subtests of the *WJ IV* are clustered into seven cognitive factors to allow description of more specific abilities. The factors, based on the Horn-Cattell theory of intellectual processing (Woodcock & Mather, 1989), are Comprehension-Knowledge, Fluid Reasoning, Short-Term Working Memory, Cognitive Processing Speed, Auditory Processing, Long-Term Retrieval, and Visual Processing. More than 40 subtest and cluster results are produced, and each result can be expressed in a number of ways: age and grade equivalent, standard score, percentile rank, and Relative Proficiency Index (RPI) score. Standard scores are distributed with a mean of 100 and a standard deviation of 15.

- Subtests from the *Kaufman Assessment Battery for Children—Second Edition* include **Sequential (Number** Recall, Word Order, Hand Movements), **Simultaneous** (Block Counting, Conceptual Thinking, Face Recognition, Pattern Reasoning, Rover, Story Completion, Triangles, Gestalt Closure), *Planning* (Pattern Reasoning, Story Completion), *Learning* (Atlantis, Rebus, Atlantis Delayed, Rebus Delayed), and *Knowledge* (Expressive Vocabulary, Riddles, Verbal Knowledge).

- The *System of Multicultural Pluralistic Assessment (SOMPA)* (Mercer & Lewis, 1977b) is a battery of nine measures designed to provide information about the general learning aptitude of children ages 5 to 11 from diverse sociocultural backgrounds and white, African American, and Hispanic ethnic groups. The *SOMPA* assesses performance from three separate perspectives: Medical, Social System, and Pluralistic.

Medical measures evaluate the student's current health status to determine whether pathological conditions are interfering with physiological functioning. Social System measures determine whether the student is meeting performance expectations for school and social roles. The pluralistic perspective of the *SOMPA* is concerned with whether the student is meeting performance expectations for age and sociocultural group.

8

Hero Images/Getty Images

Adaptive Behavior

LEARNING OUTCOMES

After reading this chapter, you will be able to:

- Compare and contrast the *Adaptive Behavior Assessment System–Third Edition* and the *Adaptive Behavior Inventory* adaptive behavior measures.

- List and discuss the components of Part One and Part Two in the *AAMR Adaptive Behavior Scale-School—Second Edition*.

- Explain the purpose and identify domains of the *Vineland Adaptive Behavior Scales—Second Edition* as other measures of adaptive behavior.

- Give three examples of the types of procedures used in answering the assessment questions.

- Discuss reliability and validity issues in approaches to nonbiased assessment of adaptive behavior.

KEY TERM

adaptive behavior

Adaptive behavior skills are related to both personal independence and social responsibility (American Association on Mental Retardation [AAMR], 1992). The way individuals deal with demands and changes in their environment are what we think of as adaptive behavior skills. Individuals learn these skills first at home and community and then in school and work settings. The key disposition that aids individuals with disabilities begins with skill building early on, from toddler age into adulthood. These everyday actions, not "maximal" performance (Beirne-Smith, Ittenbach, & Patton, 2006), guide the way individuals perform in the context of their activities.

Adaptive behavior has been defined as competency with "personal independence" and social concern in relation to their age and context (Grossman, 1983). The American Association of Intellectual and Developmental Disabilities (AAIDD) includes conceptual, social, and practical skills (AAIDD, aaidd.org) in its discussion of adaptive behavior. Conceptual skills often involve verbal and quantitative concepts. Some examples of conceptual skills are receptive and expressive language, reading and writing, money concepts, and self-direction (AAIDD, 2015; Sattler & Hoge, 2006). Examples of social skills are interpersonal skills, responsibility, self-esteem, gullibility, naiveté, following of rules, obedience to laws, and victimization. Practical skills include personal skills (i.e., eating, dressing, mobility, toileting), instrumental activities of daily living (i.e., taking medication, preparing meals, using the phone, managing money, using transportation, and doing housekeeping activities), and occupational skills (i.e., maintaining a safe environment) (AAIDD, 2015; Sattler & Hoge, 2006).

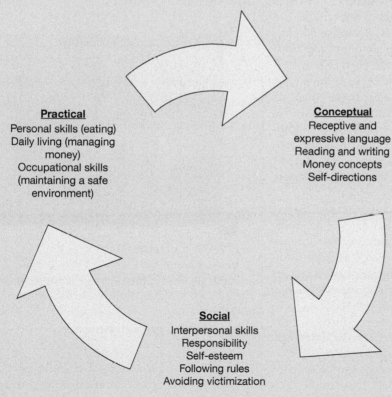

Practical
Personal skills (eating)
Daily living (managing money)
Occupational skills (maintaining a safe environment)

Conceptual
Receptive and expressive language
Reading and writing
Money concepts
Self-directions

Social
Interpersonal skills
Responsibility
Self-esteem
Following rules
Avoiding victimization

FIGURE 8–1
Conceptual, Social, and Practical Skills

The adaptive behavior construct was shaped over the past century. Doll (1927) discussed social competence skills and adaptive behavior, which led to the development of the Vineland Maturity Scale (Doll, 1935). Heber (1961) included the concept of adaptive behavior in the definition of intellectual disabilities in the manual of the American Association of Mental Deficiency in 1961. Maturation, learning, and social adjustments were at the core of the meaning of adaptive behavior. More adaptive behavior tests were developed based on this definitional inclusion (Tasse et al., 2012).

In 1983, Grossman (1983) provided more detail on the skills comprising adaptive behavior in major age groups. For example, sensorimotor and communication skills are two skill areas during infancy and early childhood. Daily life skills are an example of childhood adaptive behavior skills and vocation skills during the adult years. Expected adaptive behavior varies with the age of the individual, as those skill expectations increase with age (Tasse, 2013). For example, preschool children are expected to learn to walk, talk, and interact with family members. School-aged children are expected to widen their circle of acquaintances and add academic skills to their repertoire.

In 1992 (Luckasson et al., 1992) added the concept of 10 adaptive skills areas to the construct of adaptive behavior skills, as these were added to the then AAMR definition of intellectual disabilities. Luckasson et al. (2002) then included conceptual, social, and practical areas in the AAMR definition of intellectual disabilities (Emerson, Hatton, & Thompson, 2004).

The most recent AAID definition (2010) sets specific standards for the determination of significant limitations in adaptive behavior (two standard deviations below the mean), as significant limitations to conceptual, social, or practical are included. The *Diagnostic and Statistical Manual of Mental Disorders—Fifth Edition* (DSM-V) includes impairment in one adaptive domain instead of the previous two adaptive skills criteria as diagnostic criteria for intellectual disabilities (APA, 2013).

A student's adaptive behavior can be assessed by direct observation. Because this would be a time-consuming process, it is more usual to rely on information provided by informants such as parents, teachers, and others who know the student well. Evaluators could increase the reliability of informant data by using multiple informants and achieving good rapport with informants (Tasse et al., 2012). Self-report could be included in the assessment of adaptive skills, but this form of assessment should not be the basis of a diagnosis. For example, individuals may overestimate their adaptive behavior skills (Greenspan & Switzky, 2006).

Current Adaptive Behavior

Adaptive behavior can be assessed by direct observation, especially if available informants are not able to provide important information. Students themselves may be used as informants. Older students may be able to report whether they can tell time, make change, or get along with peers. As with all informants, students' responses may not be accurate, particularly if the questions are unclear to them.

ENHANCEDetext
Video Example 8.1
Watch this video to find out more about social skills.

Current Adaptive Behavior in Nonscholastic School Activities

Teachers also observe their students participating in many activities that are unrelated to academic learning. For instance, they see students at play during recess and observe social interactions throughout the day. They may also see students in community settings on field trips. From this experience base, teachers can provide at least partial information about the student's current adaptive behavior.

Parents

Parents and other family members are the best source concerning the student's performance at home, in the neighborhood, and in the community. Their perspective is valuable because of their lifetime experience with their child in a wide range of activities and environments.

Current Adaptive Behavior at Home and in the Community

Parents are the primary source of information about the student's nonschool adaptive behavior Two methods used to gather these data are interviews and questionnaires. For example, the assessment team can interview the student's parents about the student's current social interaction skills, personal hygiene, responsibility for household chores, handling of money, use of public transportation, and so forth.

Adaptive behavior is also of concern in the assessment of general learning aptitude, particularly when intellectual disability is the disability under consideration. Most states include impaired adaptive behavior as one of the requirements for intellectual disabilities (Bruininks et al., 1982). However, adaptive behavior is not routinely assessed in the identification of learning disabilities and behavioral disorders. This is unfortunate because many students with these mild disabilities experience difficulty in meeting expectations in nonscholastic environments as well as in the classroom. Ditterline, Banner, Oakton, and Becton (2008) discussed adaptive behavior in the realm of profiles and mean scores associated with learning disability, emotional disturbance and autism. Pugliese et al. (2014) related lower adaptive skills scores with lower executive functioning skills in children with autism spectrum disorder. Panerei et al. (2014)

found similar results. They focused on the areas of socialization and weak ability to acclimate to changing contexts. Ventola, Steinberg, Chawarska, and Klin (2014) found that the social skill difficulties associated with autism spectrum disorders could be examined with the focus of differential diagnosis.

Adaptive behavior is typically evaluated by interviewing parents, teachers, or others who are well acquainted with the student or by having them complete questionnaires. In 1935, the first edition of the *Vineland Social Maturity Scale,* a parent interview form, was published by Doll; it has been revised several times, with the latest edition appearing in 2005. This scale and others, including the *AAMR Adaptive Behavior Scale—Second Edition–School* are discussed in a later section of this chapter.

Both intelligence tests and measures of adaptive behavior seek to determine how well the student can adapt to and cope with environmental demands. However, these devices assess different environments. Tests of intellectual performance relate to the academic demands of school, whereas adaptive behavior measures look at performance in nonschool environments that require personal care, communication, social, civic, and vocational skills. By looking at both of these dimensions, it is possible to derive a more global picture of the student's current aptitude for learning.

Utilizing practical social aspects in light of age and cultural appropriateness is a vital part of assessing adaptive skills. Many of the tests used in the measurement of adaptive skills are called adaptive behavior tests. The focus of those tests differs based on the authors' theoretical framework regarding adaptive behavior. This explains the variability in terms of items on some of the major standardized tools (Sattler, 2002). Furthermore, many of the adaptive behavior norm-referenced tests do not have appropriate validity or reliability established. These factors, in combination with cultural bias and the different expectations from people who interact with the individual in a variety of contexts, are complex when considering the assessment of adaptive skills (Pierangelo & Giuliani, 2006).

Breakpoint Practice 8.1
Click here to check your understanding of adaptive behavior skills.

ADAPTIVE BEHAVIOR MEASURES

Adaptive behavior is usually not measured directly. Instead, the student's parents or teachers act as informants about the student's current non-academic functioning. Interviews are typically used with parents, whereas written questionnaires are used with teachers.

Several norm-referenced measures of adaptive behavior are available today, as Table 8–1 illustrates. This table lists the names of the measures, the ages for which each is appropriate, the person or persons who act as informants, and the type of measure (e.g., interview). The next section describes the *AAMR Adaptive Behavior Scale—Second Edition-School* and several other measures.

AAMR ADAPTIVE BEHAVIOR SCALE–SCHOOL (2ND ED.)

The *AAMR Adaptive Behavior Scale–School—Second Edition (ABS–S:2)* by Lambert, Nihira, and Leland (1993) is the most current edition of a series of adaptive behavior measures for preschoolers and K–2 students developed by the AAMR, now the AAIDD. A new measure for adolescents and adults, the *Supports Intensity Scale* (Thompson et al., 2004), is discussed in the next section.

The *ABS–S:2* is an indirect measure of adaptive and maladaptive behaviors. Norms extend from age 3 to age 21 for individuals with intellectual disabilities; those for students without intellectual disabilities begin at age 3 but extend only to age 18. According to its manual, results of the *ABS–S:2* can be used to identify strengths and weaknesses in adaptive behavior, to determine if students show below-average performance in this area, and to document student progress. This tool can be used for evaluation of adaptive behavior in children with autism and behavior difficulties.

The *ABS–S:2* is a print questionnaire. It can be completed by professionals such as teachers if they are sufficiently familiar with the student's skill levels. If they are not, the scale can be used as an interview; the professional asks the questions, and a parent or another person who knows the student well answers.

Part One of the *ABS–S:2* addresses adaptive behavior skills related to personal independence. It includes nine domains: Independent Functioning (e.g., eating, toilet use, dressing), Physical Development, Economic Activity, Language Development, Numbers and Time, Prevocational/Vocational Activity, Self-Direction, Responsibility, and Socialization. Part Two is concerned with social behaviors, including those that can be classified as maladaptive. There are seven Part Two domains: Social Behavior, Conformity, Trustworthiness, Stereotyped and Hyperactive Behavior, Self-Abusive Behavior, Social Engagement, and Disturbing Interpersonal Behavior. The five factors this test taps into are personal self-sufficiency, community self-sufficiency, personal-social responsibility, social adjustment, and personal adjustment.

Technical Quality

The *ABS–S:2* was standardized with two groups: 2,074 students with intellectual disabilities from 40 states and 1,254 individuals without intellectual disabilities from 44 states. Both samples appear to resemble the general school-aged population in race and geographic region; however, rural students are overrepresented. Eighty-seven percent of the students in the sample of students without intellectual disabilities were placed in general education classes. The sample of students with intellectual disabilities includes individuals with IQ scores of less than 20 (12 percent), those with IQ scores from 20 to 49 (48 percent), and those with IQ scores from 50 to 70 (40 percent). Fifty percent of these students were placed in self-contained special education classes; 68 percent lived at home.

The reliability of the *ABS–S:2* appears adequate. Average internal consistency correlation coefficients fall above .80 for all domain and factor scores for both norm groups. Interrater reliability

TABLE 8–1
Measures of Adaptive Behavior

NAME (AUTHOR)	AGES	INFORMANT	TYPE OF MEASURE
AAMR *Adaptive Behavior Scale Residential and Community—Second Edition* (Nihira, Leland, & Lambert, 1993)	18 to 60+	Teacher or other professional Parent	Questionnaire Interview
AAMR *Adaptive Behavior Scale–School—Second Edition* (Lambert, Nihira, & Leland, 1993)	3 to 21	Teacher Parent	Questionnaire Interview
Adaptive Behavior Assessment System–Third Edition (Harrison, 2015)	0 to 89	Parent/Primary Caregiver Teacher/ Daycare Provider Parent Teacher Adult	Rating Scale
Adaptive Behavior Evaluation Scale–Revised Second Edition: 4–12 Years, School Version and *Home Version* (McCarney & Arthaud, 2006a)	4 to 12	Teacher Parent	Questionnaire
Adaptive Behavior Evaluation Scale–Revised Second Edition: 13–18 Years, School Version and *Home Version* (McCarney & Arthaud, 2006b)	13 to 18	Teacher Parent	Questionnaire
Adaptive Behavior Inventory (Brown & Leigh, 1986)	5–0 to 18–11	Teacher	Questionnaire
Adaptive Behavior Inventory for Children (Mercer & Lewis, 1977a)	5 to 11	Parent	Interview
Checklist of Adaptive Living Skills (Morreau & Bruininks, 1991)	Infants to mature adults	Teacher	Questionnaire
Diagnostic Adaptive Behavior Scale (AAIDD, 2013)	4 to 21	Teacher or Parent	Interview
Scales of Independent Behavior–Revised (Bruininks, Woodcock, Weatherman, & Hill, 1996)	Infants to 80+ years	Parent or Teacher	Interview or Questionnaire
Supports Intensity Scale (Thompson et al., 2004)	16 to 72	Adults with disabilities Family members Professionals	Interview
Vineland Adaptive Behavior Scales—Second Edition (Sparrow, Cicchetti, & Bella, 2005b)			
• Survey Interview Form	• Birth to 90	• Parent	• Interview
• Parent/Caregiver Rating Form	• Birth to 90	• Parent	• Questionnaire
• Expanded Interview Form	• Birth to 90	• Parent	• Interview
• Teacher Rating Form	• 3 to 18+	• Teacher	• Questionnaire
Weller-Strawser Scales of Adaptive Behavior for the Learning Disabled (Weller & Strawser, 1981)	Students identified as having a learning disability	Teacher	Questionnaire

AAMR ADAPTIVE BEHAVIOR SCALE–SCHOOL (2ND ED.) (ABS–S:2)

N. Lambert, K. Nihira, & H. Leland (1993)

Type: Norm-referenced questionnaire (or interview)

Major Content Areas: Adaptive and maladaptive behavior

Type of Administration: Print questionnaire or individual interview

Administration Time: Approximately 30 minutes

Age/Grade Levels: Ages 3 to 21 (students with intellectual disabilities); ages 3 to 18 (students without intellectual disabilities)

Types of Scores: Standard scores and percentile ranks for 16 domains and 5 factors; age equivalents for Part One domains and factors

Computer Aids: *ABS–S:2 Scoring Software and Report System*

Typical Uses: An indirect measure of several dimensions of adaptive and maladaptive behavior

Cautions: The classification system recommended in the manual for *ABS–S:2* scores is somewhat unusual

Publisher: PRO-ED (*www.proedinc.com*)

---

also appears satisfactory. Validity was studied in a number of ways. Part One of the *ABS–S:2* shows moderate correlations with results of other measures of adaptive behavior. As would be expected, results of Part Two, the portion of the *ABS–S:2* that assesses maladaptive behavior, are not related to results of other adaptive behavior scales. Similar findings are reported for studies of the relationships between Parts One and Two of the *ABS–S:2* and tests of intellectual performance.

The technical quality of the *ABS–S:2* is much improved over that of the previous edition. The standardization samples have been broadened to include students from more than two states; the samples are described in detail; reliability is adequate; and there is information about the relationship of this scale to other measures of adaptive behavior.

Administration Considerations

Either professionals or paraprofessionals may complete the *ABS–S:2* as a questionnaire, but trained professionals are needed when the scale is used as an interview form with parents. The manual advises the use of an interpreter if the student's parents communicate in a language other than English.

Results and Interpretation

Raw scores for each of the 16 domains can be converted into percentile ranks and standard scores using either the intellectual disabilities or the student without intellectual disabilities norms. Domain standard scores are distributed with a mean of 10 and a standard deviation of 3. The standard score classification system recommended in the manual is somewhat unusual. Standard scores of 6 and 7 are described as "Below Average"; those in the 4–5 range as "Poor"; and those from 1–3 as "Very Poor." Age-equivalent scores can be obtained for Part One domains only.

The *ABS–S:2* Profile/Summary Form is used to convert students' scores on individual items to factor scores. There are five factors—three derived from Part One items and two from Part Two items:

- The *Personal Self-Sufficiency* factor is composed of items from the Independent Functioning and Physical Development domains.

- The *Community Self-Sufficiency* factor is composed of items from the Independent Functioning, Economic Activity, Language development, Numbers and Time, and Prevocational/Vocational Activity domains.
- The *Personal-Social Responsibility* factor is composed of items from the Prevocational/Vocational Activity, Self-Direction, Responsibility, and Socialization domains.
- The *Social Adjustment* factor is composed of items from the Social Behavior, Conformity, and Trustworthiness domains.
- The *Personal Adjustment* factor is composed of items from the Stereotyped and Hyperactive Behavior and Self-Abusive Behavior domains.

Raw factor scores are computed and converted to percentile ranks and quotients. Again, either the intellectual disabilities or the students without intellectual disabilities norms can be used. Quotients are standard scores distributed with a mean of 100 and a standard deviation of 15. The manual classifies quotients from 80 to 89 as "Below Average." Those from 70 to 79 are considered "Poor," and those below 70, "Very Poor." Age-equivalent scores can be obtained for Part One factors only.

The *ABS–S:2* appears to be a useful measure for the study of several dimensions of adaptive and maladaptive behaviors in school-aged students. In addition, this version of the scale shows many improvements over the previous version. However, results are best used to identify areas of need; further assessment will likely be necessary to plan instructional programs for individual students.

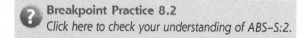

Breakpoint Practice 8.2
Click here to check your understanding of ABS–S:2.

OTHER MEASURES OF ADAPTIVE BEHAVIOR

Several measures of adaptive behavior in addition to the *ABS–S:2* are available to professionals. These include the most recent update of the *Vineland Social Maturity Scale* (Doll, 1935, 1965),

one of the earliest measures of adaptive behavior. This measure is described in the following sections along with the *Scales of Independent Behavior–Revised* (a companion to the *Woodcock-Johnson–R*), the *Supports Intensity Scale* for adolescents and adults, and the *Adaptive Behavior Evaluation Scale—Revised Second Edition*.

Vineland Adaptive Behavior Scales

The *Vineland Adaptive Behavior Scales—Second Edition (Vineland–II)* (Sparrow, Cicchetti, & Balla, 2005b) is the most current version of Doll's classic measure of adaptive behavior. Doll's instrument was a parent interview form, but the *Vineland–II* contains three measures for parents—the Survey Interview Form, Parent/Caregiver Rating Form, and Expanded Interview Form—as well as a Teaching Rating Form.

The three measures for parents and other caregivers are appropriate for ages birth to 90 years. The Survey Interview Form is administered using a semistructured interview format; that is, the interviewer uses his or her own words to probe respondents about the student's current functioning. Interview items are not read. When the interviewer has gathered sufficient information about the student's participation in specific activities, he or she rates the student on the scale's items. A Spanish version of the Survey Interview Form is available.

The Expanded Interview Form also utilizes a semistructured format to question parents about their child's adaptive behavior skills. Although it covers the same domains as the Survey Interview Form, it is more comprehensive, making it a better choice when in-depth information about adaptive behavior is needed for program planning purposes.

The Parent/Caregiver Rating Form, designed for use with parents and others who know the student or adult well, assesses the same adaptive behavior domains as the Survey Interview Form using the same questions and the same organization. Less technical names are used to denote various skill areas (e.g., "receptive" under "Communication Domain" is replaced with "Listening and Understanding" under "Communication") to communicate more clearly with respondents who may be unfamiliar with professional terms. With this measure, the informant reads the items himself or herself and circles a response on the form. Each item presents a skill or behavior (e.g., "Brushes teeth"), and the informant selects one of these responses to indicate how often the student performs the behavior without assistance: 2, usually; 1, sometimes; 0, never; or DK (don't know).

The Teacher Rating Form, like the Parent/Caregiver Rating Form, is a print instrument where the teacher or other professional reads the question and writes a response on the form. This version of the *Vineland II* is designed for school-aged individuals ages 3 to 18+ (norms for age 18 are used for students through age 21). The Teacher

Rating Form addresses many but not all of the domains assessed on the parent measures, and it adds areas of interest with school-aged individuals (e.g., the Academic Subdomain and the School Community Subdomain under the Daily Living Skills Domain). For information about the content of the various versions of the *Vineland II,* see Table 8–2.

The Survey Interview Form and the Parent/Caregiver Rating Form were standardized in 2003–2004 with a national sample of 3,695 persons ages birth through 90 years. Included in the sample as respondents were parents and caregivers of individuals with disabilities such as attention-deficit/hyperactivity disorder, behavioral disorder, learning disabilities, and intellectual disabilities. The Teacher Rating Form was standardized with

TABLE 8–2
Contents of the *Vineland II*

DOMAIN	SUBDOMAIN	SURVEY INTERVIEW FORM	PARENT/ CAREGIVER RATING FORM	TEACHER RATING FORM
Communication	Receptive/Listening and Understanding*	X	X	X
	Expressive/Talking	X	X	X
	Written/Reading and Writing	X	X	X
Daily Living Skills	Personal/Caring for Self	X	X	X
	Domestic/Caring for Home	X	X	
	Community/Living in the Community	X	X	
	Academic			X
	School Community			X
Socialization/Social Skills and Relationships*	Interpersonal Relationships/ Relating to Others	X	X	X
	Play and Leisure Time/Playing and Using Leisure Time	X	X	X
	Coping Skills/Adapting	X	X	X
Motor Skills/Physical Activity	Gross/Using Large Muscles	X	X	X
	Fine/Using Small Muscles	X	X	X
Maladaptive Behavior	Internalizing/Section A	X	X	X
	Externalizing/Section B	X	X	
	Other/Section C	X	X	
	Critical Items/Section D	X	X	

*The domain and subdomain names appearing after the slash (/) are the terms used in the Parent/Caregiver Rating Form. The names appearing before the slash are used in the other two measures.

a national sample of 2,570 persons, ages 3 through 18. This sample includes teachers of students with disabilities, and it appears representative of the U.S. population in terms of race/ethnicity, mother's educational level, and geographic region.

Standard scores are computed for each adaptive behavior domain and for the Composite score, a summary of the four domains. Standard scores are distributed, with a mean of 100 and a standard deviation of 15. Subdomain results are expressed in *v*-scale scores, a standard score with a mean of 15 and a standard deviation of 3. Results for Maladaptive Behavior are also reported in *v*-scale scores. It is possible to determine an Adaptive Level for each domain and subdomain and to compare performance across domains and subdomains. A computer program is available to assist in scoring the *Vineland II*.

ENHANCEDetext
Video Example 8.2
Watch this video to find out more about a functional curriculum.

The *Vineland II* is much improved over the previous version, which offered only a parent interview and teacher questionnaire. The *Vineland II* provides professionals with a choice of four measures, two of which are rating scales that can be completed by informants themselves without the need for an interview process. The unusual semistructured interview format required by the Survey and Expanded Interview

Forms on the *Vineland II* may prevent the use of these measures by teachers and other professionals in some school settings. According to the *Vineland II* manual, graduate-level training in psychology or social work and experience in assessment is required in order to administer this test (Sparrow, Cicchetti, & Balla, 2005a, p. iv). These authors do concede that many types of professionals, including educational diagnosticians, may be qualified to administer the interview portions of the *Vineland II*.

Scales of Independent Behavior–Revised

The *Scales of Independent Behavior–Revised (SIB–R)* (Bruininks, Woodcock, Weatherman, & Hill, 1996) are considered companion measures to the *Woodcock-Johnson Psycho-Educational Battery–Revised*, the version of the *Woodcock-Johnson* preceding the *WJ–III*. The *SIB–R* adds adaptive behavior and problem behavior to the domains of cognitive ability and achievement assessed in this multidimensional battery.

The *SIB–R* is a structured interview that is appropriate for gathering information about persons ranging in age from infancy through 80+ years. The respondent can be anyone who knows the child or adult well. The *SIB–R* can also be used as a checklist; for example, knowledgeable respondents can answer questions directly on the *SIB–R* form, rather than being interviewed.

The *SIB–R* is made up of four Adaptive Behavior clusters, each of which contains several subscales:

Motor Skills
- Gross-Motor Skills
- Fine-Motor Skills

Social Interaction and Communication Skills
- Social Interaction
- Language Comprehension
- Language Expression

Personal Living Skills
- Eating and Meal Preparation
- Toileting

- Dressing
- Personal Self-Care
- Domestic Skills

Community Living Skills

- Time and Punctuality
- Money and Value
- Work Skills
- Home/Community Orientation

These 14 subscales require 45 to 60 minutes to administer, and results are summarized by a Broad Independence (Full Scale) score. A Short Form is also available, as well as an Early Development Form for children from birth to age 6 and students with severe disabilities.

An optional Problem Behavior Scale assesses eight areas of maladaptive behavior organized into three clusters:

Internalized Maladaptive Behavior

- Hurtful to Self
- Unusual or Repetitive Habits
- Withdrawal or Inattentive Behavior

Asocial Maladaptive Behavior

- Socially Offensive Behavior
- Uncooperative Behavior

Externalized Maladaptive Behavior

- Hurtful to Others
- Destructive to Property
- Disruptive Behavior

Norms are based on a national sample of more than 2,100 persons. A variety of scores are available, including age equivalents, percentile ranks, standard scores, Relative Mastery Indexes (RMIs), and Maladaptive Behavior Indexes (MBIs). In addition, an overall Support Score can be calculated. The Support Score, which takes into consideration both adaptive and maladaptive behaviors, indicates the intensity of support that will be required by the student (i.e., Pervasive, Extensive, Frequent, Limited, Intermittent, Infrequent, or No Support). The concept of looking at the amount of support required instead of (or in addition to) specific strengths and weaknesses is consistent with current thinking in the field of intellectual and developmental disabilities.

Supports Intensity Scale

The *Supports Intensity Scale* (Thompson et al., 2004) is the newest measure of adaptive behavior developed under the auspices of the AAIDD. This measure, designed to gather information about the types of supports required by individuals ages 16 to 17, is an interview to be used with informants such as family members, teachers and other professionals, and adolescents and adults themselves. Items list activities, and the informant supplies three ratings for each: the frequency with which support is needed for this activity, the amount of time needed for support each day, and the type of support required (e.g., none, monitoring, prompting, partial or full physical assistance).

Six different areas in which support may be needed are rated:

- Home Living Activities
- Community Living Activities
- Lifelong Learning Activities
- Employment Activities
- Health and Safety Activities
- Social Activities

Also included is a supplemental scale on protection and advocacy as well as a scale covering any needed medical or behavioral supports. Results can be expressed as standard scores and percentile ranks, and then plotted on a profile. Most important, however, is the ease with which results can be translated into an individualized support plan for an adolescent or adult with needs in the area of adaptive behavior.

Adaptive Behavior Evaluation Scale–Revised Second Edition

The *Adaptive Behavior Evaluation Scale–Revised Second Edition (ABES–R2)* (McCarney & Arthaud, 2006a, 2006b) includes versions for two age groups: 4 to 12 and 18 to 18; at each age group are both a School and a Home Version. All are print rating scales designed to be completed by persons who are familiar with the student being assessed.

The most interesting feature of the *ABES–R2* is that the skills it measures are linked to the three major categories of adaptive behavior identified in the 2002 AAMR definition of retardation: conceptual, social, and practical. Thus, the 10 subscales of this measure are organized in this way:

Conceptual

- Communication
- Functional Academics

Social

- Social
- Leisure
- Self-Direction

Practical

- Self-Care
- Home Living
- Community Use
- Health and Safety
- Work

Results include standard scores for the three domains and each of the 10 subscales as well as a total score called the Adaptive Skills Quotient. Accompanying each version of the *ABES–RS* is an intervention manual with instructional goals and objectives and strategies for intervention in the areas assessed by this measure.

 Breakpoint Practice 8.3
Click here to check your understanding of specific adaptive behavior tests.

ANSWERING THE ASSESSMENT QUESTIONS

The assessment team gathers information about intellectual performance and adaptive behavior to arrive at an estimate of the student's current learning aptitude. In evaluating assessment results, the team compares and contrasts the student's academic aptitude, which is measured by tests of intellectual performance, with current levels of functioning in nonacademic activities. The disability of intellectual disability is indicated only when both intellectual performance and adaptive behavior are below average. In learning disabilities and behavioral disorders, intellectual performance must be within the average range, and adaptive behavior may be either adequate or below average.

Types of Procedures

Several types of assessment strategies are used to study learning aptitude: group tests of intellectual performance, individual intelligence tests, school records, parent interviews, questionnaires and checklists for teachers, and direct observation of students' adaptive behavior. Each of these methods is likely to produce somewhat different results.

Results from measures of intellectual performance are not expected to be equivalent to those from measures of adaptive behavior. These two strategies assess different skill domains, and although there is some relationship between academic aptitude and adaptive behavior (Harrison, 1987), students may perform poorly in one of these areas but adequately in the other.

Intellectual performance is assessed with group and individual tests, and parents and teachers may provide supplementary information about the student's aptitude for school learning. Individual tests are preferred over group measures. In special education assessment, there is no substitute for individually administered tests of intellectual performance. The information provided by parents and teachers is useful to corroborate test results; if major discrepancies occur, the team should continue its investigation, perhaps by administering a second individual test. Like group test results, the reports of parents and teachers should be considered preliminary data—less accurate than results of individual measures. As Robinson and Robinson (1976) observe, larger percentages of labels of intellectual disability have been assigned to students when teachers and physicians used subjective measures.

Adaptive behavior may be assessed directly through presentation of test tasks or by observation, but usually informants are asked about the student's typical performance. Direct measurement can be very time consuming; for a comprehensive assessment, the professional would have to observe and evaluate the student's behavior in a wide range of situations. The primary persons who serve as informants regarding adaptive behavior are parents and teachers. Because of their different perspectives, parents and teachers may provide different estimates of the student's current functioning (Harrison, 1987). Parents see their child in settings that impose quite different demands from those of the classroom. Also, parents and children share experiences over a number of years. Teachers, in contrast, see students in academic situations and nonscholastic school activities. They are usually acquainted with students for only one school year, but they are able to evaluate the performance of a particular child in relation to the typical performance of age mates. Neither the parent's nor the teacher's perspective is the "right" one. Each is able to provide only part of the picture of adaptive behavior.

Another factor that influences adaptive behavior assessment is the method used to question informants. The typical strategies are face-to-face interviews and print questionnaires. Interviews allow personal contact, and the interviewer can explain the purpose of the assessment, answer any questions, and probe the informant's unclear responses. In addition, interviews do not require reading and writing skills. However, interviews take more time than do print methods, and respondents may be more willing to answer personal questions on paper. Interviews typically are used with parents, and print methods with teachers, but of course there are exceptions.

Nature of the Assessment Tasks

Assessment instruments differ in the ways they attempt to measure learning aptitude. Among the important differences are the comprehensiveness of measures and tasks that assess the domains of interest. In the evaluation of intellectual performance, most measures attempt to be comprehensive. Individual intelligence tests typically sample several types of reasoning skills, although some of the nonverbal tests restrict assessment to one type (e.g., figural reasoning or problem solving).

However, the comprehensiveness of a measure is influenced by the nature of its assessment tasks. For example, the *WISC–V*, the *Woodcock-Johnson IV*, and the *Stanford-Binet 5* are designed to evaluate several different reasoning skills. In contrast, tests such as the 1973 *Stanford-Binet* and the *Slosson Intelligence Scale—Revised* emphasize verbal tasks. At the opposite extreme, nonverbal tests like the *TONI–4* deemphasize verbal abilities and rely solely on performance tasks to evaluate intellectual performance.

Tests that differ on the nature of the tasks used to assess performance may produce quite different results. For example, if a student were to score notably higher on *Stanford-Binet 5* nonverbal subtests than on verbal subtests, the results of nonverbal tests would probably produce higher estimates of current intellectual performance than the results of tests emphasizing verbal abilities. This would not necessarily mean that either type of measure was inappropriate, only that each provided merely part of the picture.

The content across adaptive behavior measures is quite similar (Kamphaus, 1987). Most scales include items that assess self-help or daily living skills, socialization and interpersonal relations, and independent functioning in the home and community. Questions about communication skills, motor development, and sensory capabilities are also common. Some measures include additional areas. The *Vineland II* Maladaptive Behavior domain and the Problem Behavior Scale on the *SIB–R* are examples. Although measures may be similar in content, they vary in the persons used as informants and the ways that information is collected. These differences may influence the estimated level of current adaptive behavior.

Documentation of Learning Aptitude

The broad assessment question that guides the team in its study of the student's learning aptitude is this: *Is the school performance problem related to a disability?* This question is multifaceted, and the team usually begins its investigation by gathering data about one major concern: general learning aptitude. Two specific assessment questions provide the structure for this part of the process: *What is the student's current level of intellectual performance? What is the student's current functioning level in adaptive behavior?*

Information is gathered from many sources. School records are reviewed for results of group tests of intellectual performance and data on the student's developmental and school history. Intellectual performance is assessed with individual norm-referenced tests, which are usually administered by school psychologists. To obtain information about adaptive behavior, teachers and parents may be interviewed or asked to complete questionnaires.

The team reviews assessment results and attempts to describe the student's current levels of learning aptitude. These descriptions are norm-referenced; they depict the student's standing in relation to peers. If current performance is within the below-average range in both intellectual performance and adaptive behavior, the team may decide that the student meets eligibility criteria for intellectual disability,—provided, of course, that a school performance problem has been documented. If intellectual functioning is not below average, the student may still be eligible for special education services. In such a case, it would be necessary to satisfy eligibility criteria for either learning disabilities or behavioral disorders.

Measurement Issues

Measurement of adaptive behavior skills has been controversial (Arias, Verdugo, Navas, & Gomez, 2013). Researchers have noted measurement issues regarding adaptive behavior skills (Reschly, Myers, & Hartel, 2002). Kampaus (1987) and Greenspan (1999) reported that the construct of adaptive skills was vague. Kramer et al. (2012) added that an unclear definition brings together a variety of

behaviors. Reschly et al. (2002) noted that adaptive behavior measures have been used to confirm intellectual disability. These researchers also reported floor and ceiling effects, as many of the measures have traditionally been normed on individuals ages 3 to 21. Adults within the norm group have had intellectual disabilities. In addition, an item sampling exists owing to wide age bands within many tests. Also, because diagnostic testing is high stakes, informant interviewing may present validity and reliability issues. The researchers also noted that small normative samples have been typically used with adaptive behavior measures as compared to intellectual diagnostic testing.

AVOIDING TEST BIAS

In evaluating adaptive skills, it is important to consider the possible testing effect of language and cultural differences. For example, in the home living category, one comes from a country where dishwashers, washers, and driers were not available within the home. Also, perhaps the individual was not responsible for doing laundry. It would be a validity error to negatively evaluate the individual in the home living category.

ENHANCEDetext
Video Example 8.3
Watch this video to find out more about providing services to students with adaptive skill issues.

Possibly different eye contact and proximity rules exist within one's family or among society members. It may be that individuals in this student's home country use facial expressions quite differently to communicate feelings and emotions. Some cultures expect individuals to use a poker face so that emotions are not revealed. Another example would be appropriateness of taking the bus. In terms of self-direction, perhaps parents were responsible for scheduling. In the area of health and safety, it may be that one's religion prohibits certain or all medications or contact with physicians. In one's home country, academics could have been viewed as purely lecture and question-and-answer instruction. Leisure activities could have been controlled according to religious rules. Work may not have been allowed for certain age groups or genders.

If the assessor is unfamiliar with the person's culture, at least two of the adaptive skill areas could be judged inappropriately. The validity of a formal or informal measure is seriously in question. The fact that in some adaptive behavior measures a second person is involved in judging whether the behavior is present and appropriate adds to the possibility of error. This validity aspect, coupled with cultural- and/or language-biased testing affecting intelligence testing, could have detrimental effects on an appropriate diagnosis of the student. The possible results are alarming.

Many parts of culture, such as ethnic background, gender, age, and socioeconomic status, influence adaptive skills. What may be seen as appropriate in one context may not be viewed as appropriate in another context. The lens of the assessor is also important when considering the assessment of adaptive skills. Information on many adaptive skills tests relies on secondhand information from a reporter. The reporter records information based on his or her memory of events and/or observations. Errors and biases are risk factors that can affect outcomes in this type of assessment. The reporters may not have seen the student's behavior in various settings. The student may behave in a different way in front of the reporter. Furthermore, the individual reporting and/or scoring of the student's adaptive behavior

skills is the filter that guides determination as to what is appropriate.

Our beliefs filter these expectations. The adult administering the test may want a certain outcome, which can influence the results. The test administrator may be a family member, teacher, speech-language pathologist, social worker, counselor, aide, or nurse. As an example, Tasse and Lecavalier (2000) compared parent and teacher ratings on the Nisonger Child Behavior Rating Form, a measure of emotional disabilities. They found that, even though no significant differences were evident on two social competence subscales, differences in three behavioral subscales (i.e., conduct problem, insecure/anxious, and hyperactive) were noted. Because of the different expectations that individuals bring with them as reporters or raters, the reliability and validity of the results of these types of tests are in jeopardy.

The label of intellectual disability cannot be applied unless an adaptive domain is affected. The issue of referral of students should not be overlooked (Hosp, 2003). O'Reilly, Northcraft, and Sabers (1989) introduced the concept of confirmation bias. That is, an evaluator draws conclusions that align with a preferred hypothesis, even though data are missing. Referral rates for individuals who are African American and Latino are higher. Therefore, it is critical that students be assessed in their authentic contexts (Arc, *http://www.thearc.org*). The more sources of credible information and the more context involved when that assessment information is gathered, the more reliable and valid the assessment results will be.

The Individuals with Disabilities Education Act (P.L. 94-142) increased the role of adaptive behavior in identifying students with intellectual disabilities. The home-to-school connection is extremely important in the assessment of adaptive behavior skills. Voelker, Shore, Hakim-Larson, and Bruner (1997) found that teachers rated children more positively in global and specific domains of adaptive behavior than did caregivers. The Vineland Adaptive Behavior Scales were utilized in this study. The study involved 59 children with multiple disabilities. The mean age of the children was 6 years. Communication and collaboration among teachers and caregivers would help bridge this gap and make the assessment more valid.

Different values and rule systems involving social rules can affect pragmatic skills (social language). In fact, when the communication interaction rules at school are different from the rules at home, social language differences can be misperceived as language disorders (Iglesias, 1985). The rules often are different in different contexts within schools (cafeteria, playground, classroom, gym, and hallway).

Damico and Damico (1993) specifically concentrated on social language in individuals who are diverse and reviewed variations that should be addressed early with school-aged children. They included the areas of language code difference and its impact on intelligibility and socialization. Conversation-style shifting and bias were included in the discussion of dialect and style. In addition, conversational discontinuities were discussed. Contextualization cues (verbal and nonverbal) were highlighted in this review. The impact of social language variation included misperceptions, stereotyping, miscommunication, and bias. The authors noted that professionals must be familiar with these issues and attempt to improve the process.

Researchers have indicated that culture-driven social rules within the classroom can be barriers to the learning process (Cheng, 1996). Westby (1997) specifically targeted students who are culturally and linguistically diverse when she looked at social information regarding the context in which students learn. She used data from observations and interviews of teachers of elementary school children. Those data indicated that students who are from cultures that value interdependence, obedience to authority, and passive learning may have problems with learning the academic content in a classroom where the teacher expects students to be independent. Students who do not master social content may not fully acquire academic content. Students who do not fully acquire academic content, as well as social content, may be viewed as having a behavioral or learning disability.

It is also important to look at how caregivers view services provided by the school system.

Shapiro, Monzo, Rueda, Gomez, and Blesher (2004) found that Latina mothers noted five primary concerns relating to developmental disabilities and service systems: poor communication, low effort by the provider, negative attitudes of professionals, negative treatment by professionals, and the central role of the mothers in preserving the well-being of the child. It was also troubling that the mothers appeared to separate themselves from the provider. To improve professional services, it is important to be aware of these areas.

Kritikos and Birnbaum (2004) interviewed 12 caregivers of African American children with mild cognitive disabilities on their views and experiences regarding needs and services provided for their families. These researchers found that the most common concerns included curriculum and instructional needs. Caregivers also noted that if they could provide suggestions for teachers who provide services to students with disabilities, they would urge increasing teacher involvement with students.

 Breakpoint Practice 8.4
Click here to check your understanding of avoiding test bias.

Assessment in Action
Sam

Sam is a student in your eleventh-grade class. He is in a vocational high school where students with mild to moderate intellectual disabilities take courses with a thematic unit focus. One theme involves the restaurant industry. During the math focus, students use calculators to add food charges, tax, and tip. During the reading focus, students learn food (e.g., soup) and restaurant (e.g., restrooms) sight words. During the science focus, students learn about health issues, such as the length of time chicken should be left in the refrigerator, freezer, and/or oven.

Sam does well in these areas of study. He has difficulty when the activities are applied in social settings, and he also has difficulty with social language. He does not easily read social cues and has problems expressing his emotions and language intentions. His employer has serious concerns and wants to terminate him immediately. Sam does not understand why his boss is upset with him and wants to let him go. What do you say to Sam's boss? What do you say to Sam? How could you have prevented this situation? What do you do to salvage the practicum? What do you do in terms of the assessment-to-instruction link?

When considering the information in this chapter, several solutions may come to mind. Discussion of the problem issues with Sam and the employer separately and then together would help clarify matters for both parties. During the work practicum at the restaurant, several issues arose. Defining those issues is critical for a more successful outcome. For example, was Sam sick and did not call to say he would not work his shift?

Does he give food away and/or eat while he is on the job? Does he cough and sneeze in the food? Answers to these types of questions mean that more specific targeted remediation information could then be addressed. Intervention would vary based on the identified issues. Practicing and evaluating the follow-up of these skills on the job would be important.

Discussion with Sam's boss regarding how you will assess the problem, as well as reassurance that you or a representative will be there to provide extensive supports for Sam, should help. Using these strategies before a problem occurs could have prevented this scenario, or it could have reduced the severity of the problem. In addressing the assessment-to-instruction link, assessment of Sam's preferences, skills, particular job skills, needs in particular skills, and practice on the job would be key.

SUMMARY

- The *Adaptive Behavior Assessment System–Third Edition* was published in 2015 and can be used with individuals from birth to 89. A rating scale is used for this test. Forms include Parent/Primary Caregiver, Teacher/Daycare Provider, Parent, and Teacher and Adult. The Adaptive Behavior Inventory was published in 1986 and can be used with individuals aged 5–0 to 18–11. A questionnaire is used for this test, and forms include a Teacher Form.

- Part One of the *ABS–S:2* addresses adaptive behavior skills related to personal independence. It includes nine domains: Independent Functioning (e.g., eating, toilet use, dressing), Physical Development, Economic Activity, Language Development, Numbers and Time, Prevocational/Vocational Activity, Self-Direction, Responsibility, and Socialization. Part Two is concerned with social behaviors, including those that can be classified as maladaptive. There are seven Part Two domains: Social Behavior, Conformity, Trustworthiness, Stereotyped and Hyperactive Behavior, Self-Abusive Behavior, Social Engagement, and Disturbing Interpersonal

Behavior. The five factors this test taps into are personal self-sufficiency, community self-sufficiency, personal-social responsibility, social adjustment, and personal adjustment.

- The *Vineland Adaptive Behavior Scales–Second Edition (Vineland–II)* (Sparrow, Cicchetti, & Balla, 2005b) is the most current version of Doll's classic measure of adaptive behavior. Domains include Communication, Daily Living Skills, Socialization/Social Skills and Relationships, Motor Skills/Physical Activity, and Maladaptive Behavior.

- Adaptive behavior may be assessed directly through the presentation of test tasks or by observation, but usually informants are asked about the student's typical performance. Direct measurement can be very time consuming; for a comprehensive assessment, the professional would have to observe and evaluate the student's behavior in a wide range of situations. The primary persons who serve as informants regarding adaptive behavior are parents and teachers.

- The lens of the assessor is important when considering the assessment of adaptive skills. Information on many adaptive skills tests relies on secondhand information from a reporter. The reporter records information based on his or her memory of events and/or observations. Errors and biases are risk factors that can affect outcomes in this type of assessment. The reporters may not have seen the student's behavior in various settings. The student may behave in a different way in front of the reporter. Furthermore, the individual reporting and/or scoring the student's adaptive skills is the filter that guides determination as to what is appropriate.

Adam Haglund/Apelöga AB/Alamy Stock Photo

9

Learning Disabilities

LEARNING OUTCOMES

After reading this chapter, you will be able to:

- Compare and contrast specific learning abilities and learning strategies in discussing considerations in the assessment of learning disabilities.

- Identify and discuss three examples of sources of information about specific learning abilities.

- Name and describe a tool screening for sensory impairments.

- Name and describe a tool screening for learning disabilities.

- Explain the process of discrepancy analysis for Identification of learning disabilities.

- Explain the response-to-Intervention approach to identification of learning disabilities.

- Define perceptual skills and how those skills are measured in the discussion of measures of perceptual-motor skills and other specific learning abilities.

- Identify a test battery for specific ability assessment and discuss its components.

- Give three examples of questions teachers could ask students in the assessment of learning strategies.

- Discuss why it is important to identify the nature of the assessment tasks of an instrument when answering the assessment questions.

KEY TERMS

specific learning abilities

learning strategies

psychological processes

acuity

discrepancy analysis

response-to-intervention (RTI)

clinical approach

curriculum-based measurement

perception

memory

attention

gross-motor skills

fine-motor skills

Specific learning abilities and strategies are one of the assessment team's major concerns in considering a student's eligibility for special education services. Students may show school performance problems despite average intellectual performance; one reason for this discrepancy may be their difficulties with specific learning abilities. Such students are usually identified as having learning disabilities. Individuals with other disabilities may also experience difficulty in certain learning abilities and strategies. For example, attention problems are often associated with students identified with behavior disorders.

In planning a student's evaluation, the special education team poses several questions about disabilities. The major concern is this: *Is the school performance problem related to a disability?* Assessment usually begins with study of the student's current school performance and general aptitude for learning. Then the team continues by investigating other domains, including specific learning abilities.

Vision and hearing are important considerations for all students, including those with possible difficulties with specific learning abilities. Screening for vision and hearing problems is routinely conducted in schools. The results of screening procedures should be reviewed when students are referred for special education assessment. Although vision and hearing are not considered specific learning abilities, they are closely related. Thus, the assessment team asks, *What is the status of the student's sensory abilities?*

Until quite recently, federal law required that the assessment team document a discrepancy between expected and actual school performance in order to establish the presence of a learning disability. That requirement led to assessment questions such as, *Is there a substantial discrepancy between the student's actual achievement and the achievement level expected for that student?* Those opposed to the use of the discrepancy criterion urge instead that the assessment team determine whether the student has failed to respond to instruction (e.g., Vaughn & Fuchs, 2003; Vellutino, Scanlon, & Lyon, 2000). That recommendation would lead to an assessment question about the student's classroom progress when provided with an effective instructional program: *What type of progress does the student make when high-quality interventions are provided?*

Assessment of specific learning abilities has traditionally emphasized discrete ability areas such as memory, visual perception, and auditory discrimination. Professionals are also becoming interested in how students use their specific abilities in situations requiring learning, that is, in their learning strategies and study skills. These concerns have led the team to pose two assessment questions: *What is the student's current level of development in specific learning abilities? What is the student's current functioning level in strategies for learning and study skills?*

At this stage in assessment, the team attempts to identify specific strengths and weaknesses in the student's repertoire of skills for school learning. Performance and/or achievement relative to age or grade level based on group comparison are considerations in examining this pattern of strengths and weaknesses (PSW model) (Office of Special Education Programs [OSEP], 2006). Observations made in the evaluation of academic and adaptive behavior may prove useful if they indicate potential difficulties in specific learning abilities and strategies.

CONSIDERATIONS IN THE ASSESSMENT OF LEARNING DISABILITIES

The assessment of learning disabilities is a complicated subject, perhaps because the definition of learning disabilities has been a matter of debate ever since this disability was first recognized by the educational community and included in federal and state laws. At present, the assessment process is complicated by the dictates of the Individuals with Disabilities Education Act (IDEA) of 2004, which defines learning disabilities (LDs) as a psychological processing disorder and yet allows schools to use either discrepancy analysis or a response-to-intervention approach (discussed later in this chapter) in the identification of LD. On one hand, discrepancy analysis looks for an important difference between the student's actual achievement in school and that predicted by his or her aptitude for learning. On the other hand, in the response-to-intervention approach, students who fail to thrive academically when high-quality instruction is presented are candidates for LD identification.

This chapter discusses the various components in the assessment of learning disabilities. These procedures are used first to determine if in-depth assessment of the suspected disability is required: screening for visual and hearing impairments, brief screening measures for learning disabilities, discrepancy analysis, and the response-to-instruction process. Second are more in-depth procedures: measures of perceptual-motor skills and other specific learning abilities,

test batteries for specific ability assessment, and measures for assessing learning strategies. The chapter ends by describing how to answer the assessment questions asked about students with possible learning disabilities.

Learning Abilities and Strategies

The term **specific learning abilities** refers to an individual's capacity to participate successfully in certain aspects of the learning task or in certain types of learning. Among the specific abilities that interest educators are attention, perception, memory, and the processes of receiving, associating, and expressing information. Specific abilities are more circumscribed than general learning aptitude; they usually do not affect all areas of learning. In young children, the development of specific abilities is often viewed as a precursor to the acquisition of academic skills. In this context, specific abilities may be regarded as readiness skills; this type of assessment is described in Chapter 16 on evaluation in the preschool years. Specific abilities are also a concern for older students who fail to acquire basic academic skills at the expected rate.

Learning strategies are a newer area of interest. Educators are concerned with the ways that individuals utilize specific learning abilities in situations that require the acquisition of new skills or information. Alley and Deshler (1979) discuss procedures involved with holding and using information in multiple contexts in defining learning strategies. Lenz, Ellis, and Scanlon (1996) add the components of planning, implementation, and evaluation of task performance. Whereas assessment of specific abilities is essentially a static process, learning strategy assessment is dynamic. Its primary focus is the methods employed by the individual to interact with the demands of the learning task.

Purposes

Learning abilities and strategies are assessed to determine the student's strengths and weaknesses in using various types and methods of learning. This information may help those who plan instructional interventions for any student, and it is also important in determining whether school performance problems are related to the condition of learning disabilities.

> The disability of specific learning disabilities is defined by federal law as . . . a disorder in one or more of the basic psychological processes involved in understanding or in using language, spoken or written, that may manifest itself in the imperfect ability to listen, think, speak, read, write, spell, or to do mathematical calculations. (*Federal Register*, 2006, §300.8(c)(10))

In this definition, the term **psychological processes** refers to learning abilities such as attention, perception, and memory. Learning disabilities are viewed as specific ability deficits that contribute to performance problems in basic school skills.

In determining whether students are eligible for special education services for learning disabilities, one of the steps that the assessment team typically takes is the evaluation of current levels of development in specific abilities. Processing issues are characteristic of specific learning disabilities (Johnson, Humphrey, Mellard, Woods, & Swanson, 2010). Historically, however, eligibility criteria specified by federal special education laws did not directly address specific learning abilities. Instead, the major criterion was a severe discrepancy between achievement and intellectual ability. In addition, it was necessary to demonstrate that the discrepancy was not the result of (1) failure to provide appropriate learning experiences or (2) other disabilities or conditions or of environmental, cultural, or economic disadvantage.

This remains true today, even with the movement away from discrepancy analysis and toward the response-to-intervention model. Still, the RTI method has received criticism regarding providing enough evidence to support a learning disability (Fiorello, Hale, & Snyder, 2006; Fiorello, Hale, Snyder, Forrest, & Teodori, 2008; 2009; CASP, 2004). Fiorello notes that low achievement in itself is not enough to support a learning disability. The PSW model ties assessment and instruction in that patterns point to targets of instructional methodology for the individual student (Mascalo, Alfonso, & Flanagan, 2014). An assessment of specific learning abilities and strategies is only one part of the process of establishing eligibility for learning disabilities services.

This type of assessment is not limited to students with suspected learning disabilities. For students with disabilities in other areas, the assessment team may gather information about specific abilities and strategies in an attempt to better understand individual learning problems. Students with intellectual disabilities and those with behavioral disorders may also show strengths in certain areas and weaknesses in others. Knowledge about study skills and learning strategies may provide the team with important data for planning the educational intervention program.

Issues and Trends

The study of specific abilities and strategies in the field of special education has focused on one population—students with learning disabilities. The issues and trends discussed here have resulted from learning disabilities research and practice but clearly have implications for the assessment of students with other types of disabilities.

The learning disabilities literature has long debated the definition of this condition, appropriate procedures for its assessment, and effective strategies for educational intervention (Lerner, with Kline, 2006; Lewis, 1988; Vaughn & Fuchs, 2003). Much controversy has centered on the notion of specific learning abilities. In the early years of the field, special educators hypothesized that school achievement problems were related to deficits in specific learning abilities and that achievement could be improved by either remediating (remedying) the weakness or circumventing it by teaching through the student's strengths. For example, a student with poor reading skills might also score poorly on measures of visual perception. In the remediation of deficits approach, educational treatment focuses on improving the student's visual perception in the hope that he or she would then become able to acquire skills in reading. In the utilization of strengths approach, the educational program in reading emphasizes auditory skills such as phonics and avoids visual skills such as sight word recognition. This second approach is also known as the preferred modality method because students are typically classified according to their strongest learning modality, auditory, or kinesthetic.

Many of the pioneers in the learning disabilities field developed tests and other measures to detect specific deficits. For example, Frostig worked in the area of visual perception (Frostig & Horne, 1964; Frostig, Lefever, & Whittlesey, 1966), Kephart in perceptual-motor skills (Roach & Kephart, 1966), and Kirk in psycholinguistic processing (Kirk & Kirk, 1971; Kirk, McCarthy, & Kirk, 1968). Instructional programs designed to remediate problem areas accompanied several of these measures. The tests identified needs; the companion educational programs provided activities to remediate those needs.

In the 1970s, researchers began to study the effectiveness of these interventions. First to come under scrutiny were perceptual and perceptual-motor treatments (Coles, 1978; Hallahan & Cruickshank, 1973; Hammill & Larsen, 1974b; Larsen, Rogers, & Sowell, 1976), particularly tests and instructional programs that focused on visual perceptual deficits (Hammill, Goodman, & Wiederholt, 1974; Hammill & Wiederholt, 1972; Larsen & Hammill, 1975; Wiederholt & Hammill, 1971). In assessing the usefulness of perceptual-motor training programs, Hammill (1982) concluded that training efficacy was not demonstrated. The effectiveness of remediating weak psycholinguistic abilities was also debated (Hammill & Larsen, 1974a; Kavale, 1981; Larsen, Parker, & Hammill, 1982; Minskoff, 1975; Newcomer & Hammill, 1975, 1976; Sowell, Parker, Poplin, & Larsen, 1979; Sternberg & Taylor, 1982; Torgesen, 1979).

In their critical appraisal of the deficit remediation approach, Arter and Jenkins (1979) concluded that research data revealed academic performance was not typically improved by efforts to teach specific abilities. Similar conclusions have been reached in evaluations of the preferred modality approach (Larrivee, 1981; Myers & Myers, 1980; Ringler & Smith, 1973; Tarver & Dawson, 1978; Waugh, 1973).

In addition to the criticism of the instructional programs derived from specific ability tests, many of the instruments themselves have come under attack. The major charge has been lack of adequate technical quality (Arter & Jenkins, 1979; Coles, 1978; Salvia & Ysseldyke, 1998).

Although newer measures of specific abilities tend to be technically adequate, older tests often fail to meet minimum reliability and validity requirements.

Despite the controversies surrounding evaluation and training of specific learning abilities, many special educators remain interested in their assessment. One indicator of this interest is the popularity of the learning styles approach to instruction (Carbo, 1982, 1984; Carbo, Dunn, & Dunn, 1986; Dunn, 1984, 1988; Dunn, Dunn, & Price, 1979), a strategy that includes assessment of students' perceptual preferences. However, like its predecessor, the preferred modality method, the learning styles approach has been heavily criticized (e.g., Snider, 1992; Stahl, 1988).

Another issue in specific ability assessment is definition of learning disabilities. Most of the traditional definitions emphasize perceptual and/or information-processing deficits, and the characteristics they describe are difficult to operationalize into assessment practices. A newer definition, proposed by the National Joint Committee on Learning Disabilities (NJCLD) (1994), shifts focus away from specific abilities, instead emphasizing performance problems in basic school skills:

> *Learning disabilities* is a general term that refers to a heterogeneous group of disorders manifested by significant difficulties in the acquisition and use of listening, speaking, reading, writing, reasoning, or mathematical abilities. These disorders are intrinsic to the individual and presumed to be due to central nervous system dysfunction.

In contrast, the definition adopted by the Learning Disabilities Association (LDA) in 1986 and currently (LDA, 2015) stresses the long-term nature of the disability and its effects on both school and nonschool performance. Unfortunately, neither of these definitions translates directly into a plan for assessment. The NJCLD published a policy regarding the implications for research and practice for individuals with learning disabilities. In this document, the committee reports that progress has been made in the area of the assessment of learning disabilities, however the committee notes that there is controversy in the

ENHANCEDetext
Video Example 9.1
Watch this video to find out more about specific learning disabilities.

area of eligibility determination based on current assessment tools (NJCLD, 2011).

One important trend is the movement toward consideration of learning strategies, in addition to or in place of specific learning abilities. Researchers have identified characteristic strategies of students with learning disabilities, and evidence suggests that learning strategies are susceptible to training (Hallahan, 1980; Schumaker, Deshler, Alley, Warner, & Denton, 1982; Swanson, 1989, 1993; Wong, 1980). Swanson (1999), in a large-scale study of intervention research, concludes that strategy instruction is the one intervention approach that narrows the achievement gap between students with learning disabilities and their general education peers. Although results are promising, further study is critical. There is a particular need to develop reliable and valid measures of learning strategies and study skills appropriate for classroom use. If practitioners are to assess the learning strategies and study skills of students with school performance problems, they will require a set of technically adequate assessment tools.

Another important trend is the recent interest in phonological awareness and its relationship to the development of beginning reading skills (Lerner, 2006). According to the National Research Council, phonological awareness deals with the relationship between meaning and noticing sounds

(Snow, Burns, & Griffin, 1998, p. 52). There is evidence to suggest that deficits in phonological processing contribute to difficulty in the acquisition of decoding and spelling skills (e.g., Felton & Wood, 1989; Wagner & Torgesen, 1987). Like the early remediation of deficits approach in learning disabilities, interest in phonological awareness has led to the development of assessment devices and intervention programs. However, there appears to be research support for the usefulness of training phonological skills in young children (e.g., O'Connor, Jenkins, Leicester, & Slocum, 1993; Torgesen & Barker, 1995; Wagner, Torgesen, & Rashotte, 1993). Measures of phonological processing are discussed in Chapter 13, the chapter on reading assessment.

A third important direction is the movement away from the use of the discrepancy concept in the identification of learning disabilities. The President's Commission on Excellence in Special Education (2002) recommended that federal laws be amended to eliminate the IQ/achievement discrepancy regarding the identification of a learning disability. This Commission also recommended that assessment focus on the student's response to instruction.

There is widespread support in the field for the movement away from reliance on ability-achievement discrepancies as the major criterion for learning disabilities identification (Marston, Muyskens, Lau, & Canter, 2003; Vaughn & Fuchs, 2003; Vaughn, Linan-Thompson, & Hickman, 2003; Vellutino et al., 2000). However, experts are quick to point out that the alternative model, response to instruction, is not without problems (e.g., Fuchs, 2003; Fuchs, Mock, Morgan, & Young, 2003). L. Fuchs identifies a number of critical decisions that must be made before assessing students' response to instruction. For example, it must be determined when and how often, academic performance will be measured. Is it sufficient to assess only at the end of an intervention; should assessment take place both before and after the intervention; or should it occur regularly throughout the intervention, perhaps on a weekly or more frequent basis? Another critical decision is determining the amount of growth that indicates adequate progress in response to instruction—and the amount that signals a student's lack of responsiveness. Such decisions will directly affect educational services for students with learning disabilities.

Current Practices

Learning abilities and strategies are a concern in both general and special education. In general education, young children in the early elementary grades often take part in group readiness testing. Readiness tests evaluate development in preacademic skills such as listening, memory, matching, letter recognition, and language. Results of such measures may be available for students with disabilities, but, like all group test results, should be interpreted with caution. Sensory abilities are also of interest in general education, and most schools routinely screen students for possible hearing and vision impairments. These results are extremely important for students referred for special education assessment because undetected vision or hearing problems can contribute to difficulties in school performance.

In special education, the assessment team often decides to evaluate specific learning abilities, particularly if learning disabilities are suspected. The team may begin with a screening device such as the *Learning Disabilities Evaluation Scale–Renormed—Second Edition* or the *Learning Disabilities Diagnostic Inventory.* The team may also use one or more of the many currently available individual tests. Some of these measures are designed to assess one ability area. Examples include the *Goldman-Fristoe-Woodcock Test of Auditory Discrimination* and the *Bruininks-Oseretsky Test of Motor Proficiency—Second Edition.* Other measures, such as the *Detroit Tests of Learning Aptitude—Fourth Edition*, attempt to evaluate several different abilities.

Another tactic is administration of those portions of individual tests of intellectual performance that include measures of specific abilities. For instance, the team may be interested in the specific learning abilities assessed by the *Wechsler Intelligence Scale for Children—Fifth Edition* or the *Stanford-Binet Intelligence Scale—Fifth Edition.*

Great caution must be exercised in selecting tests or subtests to ensure that reliable and valid measures are chosen. If no adequate formal measure can be found, the team may decide to use informal techniques. This is often the case in the assessment of learning strategies and study skills because few formal measures are available. Caution is needed here, too. Validity and reliability are just as important in the selection of informal measures as they are in the selection of formal measures. If technical data are not available for an informal test or procedure, the team should make every effort to gather such data, or it should select another measure.

Depending on state and local regulations for the identification of learning disabilities, the special education team may also need to conduct a discrepancy analysis. This does not usually involve gathering new data. Results of current achievement tests are compared with results of current measures of intellectual performance to determine whether important differences exist between actual and expected achievement. Newer measures routinely provide systems for conducting these analyses. For example, the *Woodcock-Johnson IV* (Schrank, Mather, & McGrew, 2014a, 2014b; Shrank, McGrew, & Mather, 2014a, 2014b) provides such a system so that results from the *WJ III Tests of Achievement* can be evaluated in relation to results from its *Tests of Cognitive Abilities* (Schrank, McGrew, & Mather (2015). Similarly, the *Wechsler Intelligence Scale for Children–Fifth Edition* (Wechsler, 2014a) can be used to evaluate results from its companion achievement measure, the *Wechsler Individual Achievement Test–Third Edition* (2009) (Wechsler, 2014b).

It is also possible that state and local regulations may require the assessment team to gather data on the student's response to instruction before making decisions about eligibility for special education services. The section later in this chapter on the RTI approach discusses this process.

Table 9–1 presents information about current federal requirements related to determining if students meet eligibility requirements for learning disabilities. The first section of the table deals with requirements for states. Each state is responsible for developing or adopting criteria for the determination. However, there are two limitations: (1) states must allow schools to use

TABLE 9–1
IDEA 2004 Requirements for the Determination of Learning Disabilities

Requirements for State Departments of Education Regarding Learning Disabilities

- States "must adopt...criteria for determining whether a child has a specific learning disability."
- States "must not require the use of a severe discrepancy between intellectual ability and achievement for determining whether a child has a specific learning disability."
- States "must permit the use of a process based on the child's response to scientific, research-based intervention" (IDEA, 2004 Final Regulations, §300.307(a)).

Requirements for Team Decisions about Learning Disabilities Eligibility

(a) The group...[i.e., the assessment team, including the student's parents] may determine that a children has a specific learning disability...if—

    (1) The child does not achieve adequately for the child's age or to meet State-approved grade-level standards in one or more of the following areas, when provided with learning experiences and instruction appropriate for the child's age or State-approved grade-level standards:

        (i) Oral expression.

        (ii) Listening comprehension.

        (iii) Written expression.

        (iv) Basic reading skill.

        (v) Reading fluency skills.

        (vi) Reading comprehension.

        (vii) Mathematics calculation.

        (viii) Mathematics problem solving.

    (2) (i) The child does not make sufficient progress to meet age or State-approved grade-level standards in one or more of the areas identified...[above] when using a process based on the child's response to scientific, research-based intervention; or

        (ii) The child exhibits a pattern of strengths and weaknesses in performance, achievement, or both, relative to age, State-approved grade-level standards, or intellectual development, that is determined by the group to be relevant to the identification of a specific learning disability....

    (3) The group determines that its findings...are not primarily the result of—

        (i) A visual, hearing, or motor disability;

        (ii) Intellectual disability;

        (iii) Emotional disturbance;

        (iv) Cultural factors;

        (v) Environmental or economic advantage; or

        (vi) Limited English proficiency. (IDEA 2004 Final Regulations, §300.309)

Required Documentation for Learning Disabilities Eligibility Decisions

(a) ...the documentation of the determination of eligibility...must contain a statement of—

    (1) Whether the child has a specific learning disability;

    (2) The basis for making the determination...;

    (3) The relevant behavior, if any, noted during the observation of the child and the relationship of that behavior to the child's academic functioning;

    (4) The educationally relevant medical findings, if any;

continued

TABLE 9–1   *continued*

   (5) Whether—

      (i) The child does not achieve adequately for the child's age or meet State-approved grade-level standards . . . ; and

      (ii) (A) The child does not make sufficient progress to meet age of State-approved grade-level standards . . . ; or

          (B) The child exhibits a pattern of strengths and weaknesses in performance, achievement, or both, relative to age, State-approved grade-level standards or intellectual development. . . . ;

   (6) The determination of the group concerning the effects of a visual, hearing, or motor disability; intellectual disability; emotional disturbance; cultural factors; environmental or economic disadvantage; or limited English proficiency on the child's achievement level; and

   (7) If the child has participated in a process that assesses the child's response to scientific, research-based intervention—

      (i) The instructional strategies used and the student-centered data collected; and

      (ii) The documentation that the child's parents were notified about—

          (A) The State's policies regarding the amount and nature of student performance data that would be collected and the general education services that would be provided;

          (B) Strategies for increasing the child's rate of learning, and

          (C) The parents' right to request an evaluation. (IDEA 2004 Final Regulations, §300.311)

Source: Building the Legacy US Department of Education.

the RTI approach, if they wish, and (2) states may not require schools to document a significant discrepancy between expected and actual school performance.

The second section of the table presents three specific requirements for eligibility. First, the student must show a performance problem in one of the basic school subjects (e.g., reading, mathematics). Second, the child must either show poor progress in school even when provided with high-quality interventions, or there must be a pattern of strengths and weaknesses. That pattern may indicate discrepancies between various areas of performance or between actual achievement and that predicted by measures of intellectual performance. Third, the student's school performance problem must not be due primarily to another disability (e.g., hearing impairment, intellectual disability), cultural or language factors, or environmental or economic disadvantage.

The third section of the table lists the documentation that is required when the assessment team determines that a student meets eligibility criteria for learning disabilities. Note that medical findings are to be included, if relevant, and

that the team must report results of an observation of the student.

 Breakpoint Practice 9.1
Click here to check your understanding of the assessment of learning disabilities.

SOURCES OF INFORMATION ABOUT SPECIFIC LEARNING ABILITIES

There are several sources of information about students' specific learning abilities, learning strategies, and study skills: school records, teachers, parents, and the students themselves.

School Records

School records may provide some clues to a student's past or current levels of functioning. Of particular importance are records of results of periodic vision and hearing screenings.

Readiness Test Results

Results of group tests of school readiness may be available for some students. Readiness measures are usually administered at the end of kindergarten or at the beginning of first grade, so results are most meaningful for first and second graders.

Results of Vision and Hearing Screening

The team should review the student's health record to determine the dates and results of vision and hearing screenings. If possible problems were indicated, the team should check to see if the student was referred for further assessment and what the results were. Were recommended treatments carried out? For example, if corrective lenses were prescribed, were eyeglasses or contact lenses purchased, and does the student wear them as directed? If there is no record of recent vision and hearing checks, the team should arrange for these as soon as possible.

Information about Aptitude and Achievement

There may be some information in the school records that points to discrepancies between the student's aptitude for learning and actual achievement. For example, past teachers may have commented about the student's failure to achieve to capacity. Or the school record may contain results of group achievement and intelligence tests administered earlier in the student's school career. Although these types of data are historical rather than current, they may indicate a continuing pattern of performance.

The Student

The student is an important participant both in the formal assessment of specific abilities and strategies and in informal assessment. Older students in particular can assist the team by describing their strategies for learning.

Individual Measures of Specific Learning Abilities

Students may participate in the administration of individual tests of specific abilities when technically adequate measures are available. Specific ability tests are often designed for elementary grade students. With older students, the team may administer pertinent subtests of individual tests of intellectual performance. During test administration, the student is carefully observed to determine the strategies he or she uses for task completion.

Current Learning Strategies and Study Skills

Informal techniques are typically used to evaluate these. Students can be observed in the classroom to determine what methods they use to learn new material. For example, an observer can record a student's behaviors during lectures, class discussions, or independent work periods. Interviewing is another technique. Students can be asked to describe the study methods they use in school and at home. They can also be interviewed while engaged in a learning task. In addition, samples of the student's work may provide clues about poor work habits or inefficient study strategies.

Teachers

Teachers have many opportunities to observe the specific learning abilities, strategies, and study skills of students in their classroom.

Current Abilities and Strategies for Learning

Teachers can describe how students go about learning new skills and information. In particular, teachers should be asked to discuss any learning problems that the student exhibits. For example, does the student have difficulty paying attention to relevant aspects of the task at hand? Is he or she unable to remember previously learned material? Teachers can also report about students' current study skills. Does the student listen to directions and ask questions when necessary? Is he or she able to follow directions?

Current Aptitude and Achievement

Teachers may be able to comment about the match between the achievement expected of a particular student and that student's current performance. For instance, a teacher may observe that a student appears to understand the course material in class discussions but performs poorly on written examinations.

Progress in the School Curriculum and Response to Instruction

Teachers are probably the best source of information about how students are progressing in the school curriculum. Teachers also can comment on how students respond to different types of instruction and what approaches have been most successful in the past. If a new intervention is being tried to improve a student's academic progress, the teacher can report on the effectiveness of the approach and how well the student is now performing.

Parents

Like teachers, parents have many opportunities to observe their child in learning situations. Parents also have information about their child's current health status and medical history in relation to vision and hearing problems.

History of Treatment for Vision and Hearing Problems

If school records do not contain information about the student's vision and hearing, parents may be able to supply this information. If routine vision or hearing checks at school or by the family physician indicated possible problems, the student's parents can describe what treatments, if any, were recommended and carried out. If necessary, parents can refer school personnel to the appropriate medical professional for more information.

Home Observations of Current Learning Abilities and Strategies

Based on observations of their child in many learning situations, parents can describe typical strategies for learning and recurrent problems. They may comment, for example, on their child's attention span, perseverance in problem solving, or ways of remembering things. Parents can also describe the study strategies used at home to complete class assignments.

SCREENING FOR SENSORY IMPAIRMENTS

A first priority in assessing any student referred for school performance problems is to determine his or her current status in vision and hearing. Undetected and untreated sensory impairments can interfere with school learning. Sensory acuity in

hearing and vision is the concern in screening. **Acuity** refers to the ability of the sense organ to register stimuli. Sensory screening programs identify students in need of in-depth assessment. These persons are then referred to appropriate health professionals for a comprehensive examination.

Vision

Vision can be impaired in many ways. Students may have difficulty seeing objects at a distance. In this condition, known as nearsightedness or myopia, near vision is clearer than far vision. Farsightedness, or hyperopia, is the opposite; vision is clearer for objects at a distance. A third type of disorder, astigmatism, is a condition in which vision is blurred or distorted. Myopia, hyperopia, and astigmatism are considered refractive disorders. They are very common among school-aged children but are usually correctable with eyeglasses or contact lenses (Caton, 1985). When a vision problem can be corrected, it is not considered a disability.

Other types of vision problems are muscle disorders, restricted peripheral vision, and impairments in color vision. Muscle disorders involve the external muscles that control eye movement. An example is strabismus, or "crossed eyes," in which a muscle imbalance prevents the eyes from focusing simultaneously on the same object. Peripheral, or "side," vision refers to the wideness of the visual field. If peripheral vision is severely impaired, the visual field is limited so that the individual sees objects only directly in front of him or her; this condition is known as tunnel vision. Tunnel vision, if uncorrected, is considered a severe enough disability to be included as a type of legal blindness. Disorders can also occur in color vision, reducing the ability to distinguish between colors. Although color blindness is not considered a disability, it can have a deleterious effect on some aspects of school performance. Teachers must know when they have color-blind students so color-cued materials and other educational uses of color can be minimized.

The most usual method of screening for vision problems is the Snellen Chart. This chart, used with older children and adults, contains several different letters of the alphabet. The letters vary in size, with the largest placed at the top. The individual stands 20 feet away from the chart and attempts to read all of the letters, first covering one eye and then the other. A modified version of the chart is available for young children and those unable to read. It contains only the letter *E*, but that letter is rotated into four different positions (Figure 9–1). The person responds by telling or showing which way the letter is pointing.

The Snellen Chart measures far-distance vision, and results are expressed as a fraction. For instance, the fraction 20/20 indicates normal vision. The numerator of the fraction stands for the distance the individual stands from the chart when reading the letters, and the denominator stands for the distance at which persons with normal vision are able to read the same letters. Thus, a person with 20/100 vision is able to read at 20 feet what a person with normal vision can read at 100 feet. Students are considered legally blind when visual acuity is 20/200 or less in the better eye after the best possible correction or have a visual field of 20 degrees or less (Social Security Administration, 2002).

Far-distance vision, though important, is only one of the areas in which visual disorders may occur. To detect possible problems in other aspects of visual acuity, different techniques are available. For instance, the Keystone Telebinocular device allows appraisal of far-distance vision, near-distance vision, depth perception, color discrimination, and other abilities. Other instruments that assess several aspects of visual acuity include the Titmus Vision Tester and the Bausch & Lomb Orthorater. Such devices offer a more comprehensive picture of the student's current vision than the standard chart method provides.

Teachers, other professionals, and parents can assist in the detection of potential vision problems by being aware of warning signs. These include physical manifestations such as red or watery eyes, a pronounced squint, irritation of the eyelids, irregularities of the pupils, or obvious muscle imbalances such as crossed eyes (National Society to Prevent Blindness, 1977; Smolensky, Bonvechio, Whitlock, & Girard, 1968). Among the behavioral symptoms are lack of attention to information presented visually, holding of reading materials very close to or far away from the eyes, and inability to see the chalkboard and other distant objects (Beverstock, 1991; Smolensky et al., 1968).

When potential vision problems are identified, the student is referred to an appropriate vision specialist, usually an ophthalmologist or an optometrist. Ophthalmologists are physicians who specialize in eye disorders. Not only

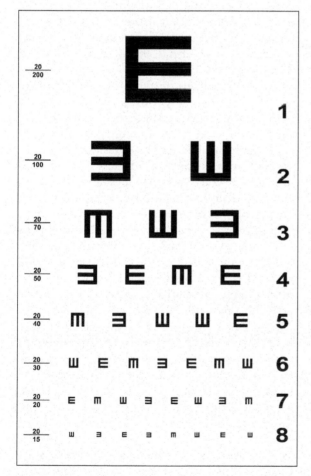

FIGURE 9–1
Snellen Chart
Source: oriontrail/Shutterstock

do they conduct comprehensive vision examinations, they may also prescribe drugs or perform surgery. Optometrists conduct vision examinations and prescribe corrective lenses, but they are not physicians and do not provide medical or surgical treatment. A third professional, the optician, prepares corrective lenses according to the optometrist's or ophthalmologist's prescription.

Many visual impairments can be treated through medical intervention, surgery, and/or the relatively simple prescription of corrective lenses. If vision specialists recommend a treatment regimen, the school should be aware of what is occurring and cooperate as necessary. For example, if eyeglasses are prescribed to correct poor near-distance vision, the classroom teacher can assist by making sure the student wears the glasses during reading and writing activities.

Hearing

The two primary types of hearing loss are conductive and sensorineural. With conductive losses, some obstruction or interference in the outer or middle ear blocks the transmission of sound. The inner ear is intact, but sound does not reach it. Among school-aged children, conductive losses are the most common type of hearing impairments (Frank, 1998). They may be caused by excessive buildup of wax in the auditory canal or collection of fluid in the middle ear (otitis media). Many conductive losses can be corrected by medical or surgical treatment (Moores & Moores, 1988). For example, fluid in the middle ear can be treated with a surgical procedure called a myringotomy, in which a small tube is placed in the eardrum to allow drainage (Frank, 1998). Hearing aids usually benefit individuals with conductive losses.

Sensorineural losses are caused by damage to the inner ear. Sound travels to the inner ear but is not transmitted to the brain. Sensorineural hearing losses are not as responsive to medical and surgical treatment as are conductive hearing losses (Heward, 2006), although hearing aids that amplify sounds may prove beneficial. Individuals

can also show a mixed hearing loss—both a conductive and a sensorineural hearing loss.

Hearing screening, like vision screening, is routine in most schools today. However, teachers and parents should also be aware of symptoms of hearing loss, so that they can initiate hearing checks for students with possible problems. This is particularly important because some hearing losses are intermittent; a student with impaired hearing may be able to pass a routine screening (Frank, 1998). Some of the signs of hearing loss are physical problems associated with the ears, poor articulation of sounds and confusion of similar sounding words, turning of the head toward the source of sound, extreme watchfulness when people are speaking in an attempt to lip read, frequent requests to speakers for repetitions, speaking in a monotone, and speaking very quietly (Smolensky et al., 1968; Stephens, Blackhurst, & Magliocca, 1982).

The dimensions of sound that are important in the assessment of hearing are intensity and frequency. Intensity refers to the loudness of sound and is measured in units called decibels (dB). Zero decibels is the threshold of normal hearing. At a distance of 5 feet, a whisper registers 20 dB, conversational speech 40 to 65 dB, and a loud shout 85 dB (Green, 1981). The frequency of a sound refers to its pitch, whether it is high or low. For example, the keys on a piano are arranged by pitch, from low to high. Frequency is measured in hertz units (Hz), and the range of frequencies considered most important for hearing conversational speech is from 500 to 2000 Hz (Heward, 2006).

In school hearing screening programs, an instrument called a pure tone audiometer is used to produce sounds of different frequencies and intensities. Students are usually tested individually. The student wears earphones, listens for tones generated by the audiometer, and then raises a hand or pushes a button when a tone is heard. In pure tone audiometric screening, or sweep testing, tones are generated at several frequencies, first for one ear, then for the other. If the student fails this screening procedure, it is typically repeated at a later date. The next step is a pure tone threshold test, which is usually

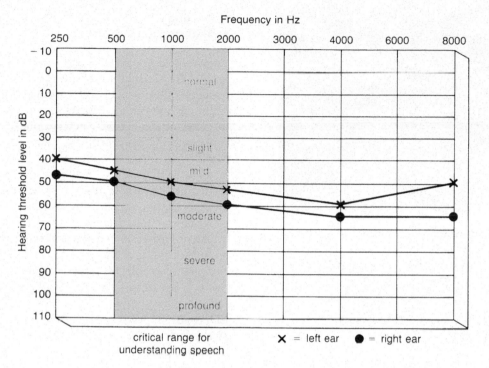

FIGURE 9–2
Sample Audiogram
Note: From *Exceptional Children* (8th ed.) (p. 378) by W. L. Heward, © 2006. Reprinted with permission of Prentice Hall, Inc., Upper Saddle River, NJ.

administered by a trained professional such as an audiologist. In this procedure, sounds are presented at several frequencies, and the intensity is varied to determine the exact decibel level at which the student can detect the sound.

Figure 9–2 shows the record of a pure tone threshold test for a student with a mild hearing impairment. This graph is called an audiogram. The horizontal axis is marked off in frequency units, and the range of frequencies critical for speech is shaded. The vertical axis represents the hearing threshold level, the lowest intensity at which sound can be detected. For example, at 500 Hz, the student was able to hear sounds at 45 dB with the left ear (marked on the audiogram by an *x*) and sounds at 50 dB with the right ear (marked by a •). Persons with normal hearing would be able to detect sounds at intensities somewhere between 0 and 10 dB. If a person's threshold exceeds normal limits, a hearing loss is

indicated. For example, if the threshold is 60 dB, a 60-dB loss is reported.

When possible hearing losses are identified, students are referred to hearing specialists. Otologists are physicians who specialize in disorders of the ear; they conduct comprehensive hearing examinations and provide medical and surgical treatments. Audiologists are not physicians, although they often work closely with otologists. The audiologist evaluates hearing and prescribes hearing aids for losses that cannot be corrected. Otologists and audiologists use several techniques in addition to pure tone audiometry to evaluate hearing. These include tympanometry (to detect problems with the eardrum and middle ear), speech audiometry (to determine the threshold levels for speech), and special assessment procedures for infants, young children, and other persons who are difficult to test (Frank, 1998; Green, 1981; Moores & Moores, 1988).

ENHANCEDetext
Video Example 9.2
Watch this video to find out more about audiometry.

SCREENING FOR LEARNING DISABILITIES

School screening programs often attempt to identify students with possible problems in areas other than vision and hearing impairments. One example is learning disabilities, the most commonly identified disability in U.S. schools (U.S. Department of Education, 2005). Some districts develop their own screening measures to locate students in need of more in-depth assessment. Others use published measures such as the *Learning Disability Evaluation Scale–Renormed—Second Edition* (McCarney & Arthaud, 2007) and the *Learning Disabilities Diagnostic Inventory* (Hammill & Bryant, 1998).

The *Learning Disability Evaluation Scale–Renormed (LDES–R2)* is a questionnaire designed to be completed by teachers, clinical, or other school personnel who are familiar with the student under consideration. Items contain a description of problem behaviors, and the teacher rates the frequency with which these behaviors occur ("not developmentally appropriate for age," "rarely or never," "inconsistently," "consistently"). Items are divided into seven subscales:

- Listening
- Thinking
- Speaking
- Reading
- Writing

- Spelling
- Mathematical Calculations

These possible problem areas correspond directly to the areas listed in the federal definition of learning disabilities. Embedded within the subscales are items that address attention, auditory discrimination, visual perception, fine-motor skills, information processing, and several types of memory.

The *LDES–R2* was standardized with 4,473 students. The sample appears to approximate the U.S. population as a whole, as related to gender, geographical area, residence, race and occupation of parents. Internal consistency, test-retest (.6–.7 on subscales), and interrater (.68–.83) reliabilities are available. Content validity was conducted. Results of the *LDES–R2* appear to be related to results of the *LDDI*. In addition, the *LDES–R2* appears to be able to discriminate students with learning disabilities and general education students.

Results of the *LDES–R2* are reported by subscale and by total test. Separate norms are available for males and females ages 6 to 18. Subscale raw scores are converted to standard scores (mean = 10, SD = 3). The total test score is expressed as a Learning Quotient (mean = 100, SD = 15) and percentile rank. Accompanying the *LDES–R2* are two books—one with suggested interventions for teachers, Learning Disability Intervention Manual-Revised (McCarney, Bauer, & House, 2006) and the other with recommendations for parents, Parent's Guide to Learning Disabilities (McCarney & Bauer, 1991).

The *Learning Disabilities Diagnostic Inventory (LDDI)* is a similar measure. This teacher questionnaire, designed for use with students ages 8–0 to 18–11, contains six scales:

- Listening
- Speaking
- Reading
- Writing
- Mathematics
- Reasoning

On each item, the teacher rates the frequency with which the student displays the problem behavior: "Frequently" (1, 2, or 3), "Sometimes" (4, 5, or 6), or "Rarely" (7, 8, or 9). Like the *LDES–R,* the *LDDI* contains items that are related to specific abilities, such as perception, motor skills, memory, and information processing.

In the standardization of the *LDDI,* 522 teachers rated 2,152 students with identified learning disabilities. Teachers were primarily special educators. Each scale was normed separately, using only those students with identified problems in the area being assessed. Reliability of the *LDDI* appears adequate. Validity was studied in a number of ways, including investigation of the profiles of three groups of students. Of the students with learning disabilities, 86 percent had *LDDI* profiles likely or possibly characteristic of learning disabilities. In contrast, 10 percent of achieving students and 30 percent of students with intellectual disability had such profiles. These findings suggest that the *LDDI* correctly categorizes most, but not all, students.

Raw scores on the six scales are converted to stanines and percentile ranks. No total test score is available. Results are entered in a profile table, which classifies scores by their likelihood of indicating a processing disorder. For example, scales with scores that fall below stanine 6 are identified as "Likely." The examiner then completes the Diagnostic Conclusions section of the form. The final result is a statement about the student's likelihood of having a learning disability.

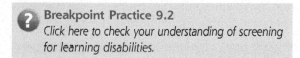

Breakpoint Practice 9.2
Click here to check your understanding of screening for learning disabilities.

DISCREPANCY ANALYSIS FOR IDENTIFICATION OF LEARNING DISABILITIES

Historically, one of the major criteria for the identification of learning disabilities was a discrepancy between expected and actual performance. It was assumed that a learning disability would have a negative effect on school functioning, so students would not achieve as well as would be expected from their general intellectual level. In the past, federal laws required the establishment of a severe discrepancy between ability and achievement in one or more subject matter areas. IDEA 2004 does not continue this requirement; in fact, it mandates that states cannot require schools to establish a discrepancy. However, it also does not prohibit the use of discrepancy analysis techniques in the identification of learning disabilities. Although IDEA 2004 clearly favors the RTI approach over the use of discrepancies, it is likely that many states will continue to allow schools to conduct discrepancy analyses, particularly until the RTI approach is better understood and the implications of its use in practice are clearer.

In **discrepancy analysis** for the identification of learning disabilities, the assessment team compares the student's current performance in one or more areas of achievement with that student's expected performance, as measured by current performance on a test of intellectual performance, to determine if there is an important difference between actual and expected achievement. It is also possible to look for discrepancies between areas of achievement (e.g., reading versus mathematics performance), but this approach is much less common.

The discrepancy notion appears clear and straightforward until it must be operationalized. At that point, numerous questions arise. These include the choice of measures, the setting of standards to determine how large the difference must be to indicate a discrepancy, and how large that discrepancy must be to be considered severe enough to warrant attention in special education. The simplest of these decisions is the choice of measures. In practice, ability is assessed with tests of intellectual performance such as the *WISC–V* and achievement with tests of academic performance such as the *Wechsler Individual Assessment Test–Third Edition (WIAT-3).*

The most typical approach today for determining the magnitude and the importance of discrepancies between ability and achievement is the use of tests with built-in systems for discrepancy analysis. Computer programs are available to assist with scoring and discrepancy analyses for many of these measures.

In some cases, one instrument includes measures of both intellectual performance and academic achievement. One example is the *Woodcock-Johnson IV*. In others, tests of aptitude and achievement are separate but linked through common standardization procedures. Companion tests include the *WISC–V* and the *WIAT–3;* the two Hammill measures, the *Hammill Multiability Intelligence Test* (Hammill, Bryant, & Pearson, 1998) and the *Hammill Multiability Achievement Test* (Hammill, Hresko, Ammer, Cronin, & Quinby, 1998); and the *Kaufman Assessment Battery for Children—Second Edition* (Kaufman & Kaufman, 2004a) and the *Kaufman Test of Educational Achievement—Third Edition* (Kaufman & Kaufman, 2014). Occasionally, tests that are not part of a system will provide sufficient information for discrepancy analyses (e.g., the *Woodcock Reading Mastery Tests—Third Edition,* which allows comparison of reading performance with results from older aptitude measures such as the *WISC–V* and the *Woodcock-Johnson–IV*). However, not all tests offer systems for discrepancy analysis, and those that do often employ different methods.

One of the sets of measures most often used for discrepancy analysis is the *Woodcock-Johnson IV* battery, which includes tests of both cognitive abilities and school achievement. Among the many results that can be obtained are scores for three types of discrepancies: intracognitive, intra-achievement, and aptitude-achievement discrepancies. Intracognitive discrepancies compare results on the various cognitive factors formed as composite scores from results of cognitive subtests. Similarly, intra-achievement discrepancies compare results on composite achievement scores. Although these types of discrepancies provide information about the student's strengths and weaknesses, they are typically not used as part of the process for identification of learning disabilities. However, Mather and Healey (1989) maintain that intracognitive discrepancies should be considered in identification because they provide valuable information about the nature of the learning disability.

On the *Woodcock-Johnson IV,* the system for analyzing aptitude-achievement discrepancies makes use of both aptitude and achievement cluster scores. For aptitude measures, professionals can choose between a global score (General Intellectual Ability), a language score (Oral Language Ability), or predicted achievement cluster scores designed to predict performance in reading, mathematics, and written language. It is important to consider which cognitive subtests are combined to form the predicted achievement scores because they may be the ones in which an individual with learning disabilities does poorly. If this occurs, there may not be a significant discrepancy between the student's lowered aptitude score and a low achievement score.

Another concern is the use of composite scores as measures of students' academic achievement. The Broad Reading cluster, for example, contains these three reading tests from the *Woodcock-Johnson IV* standard battery: Letter-Word Identification, Passage Comprehension, and Sentence Reading Fluency. When considering cluster scores, it is important also to examine the results of the subtests that make up the cluster. In a cluster with three subtests, a student may do well on two and poorly on the other one, ending up with an average score for the cluster.

The Wechsler tests are another family of tests often used for discrepancy analysis. The Wechsler intelligence scales are likely the most popular across the age levels from preschool to adults. In school-aged individuals, the *WISC–V* is often the test of choice, and its results can be used with its companion measure, the *Wechsler Individual Achievement Test–Third Edition,* to conduct discrepancy analyses. The test manuals provide procedures, or the examiner can use the computer-scoring program available from the test publisher.

Student performance on any of the *WIAT–3* subtests or composite scores can be compared to *WISC–V* Full Scale, Verbal Comprehension, Visual Spatial Reasoning and Fluid Reasoning Index scores to determine if discrepancies exist. The approach typically used is called the predicted-achievement method. The student's score on one of the achievement measures is subtracted from his or her score on one of the ability composites to determine a difference score. Each difference score is examined to determine (1) if the difference is significant (i.e., if it is greater than the predicted difference at either the .01 or .05 levels of significance), and (2) the frequency with which differences of this magnitude occurred in the norming sample. Consider the example of Judy.

Judy, a fourth grader referred for school performance problems, has been tested with the *WISC–V* and several measures of academic achievement, including the Spelling subtest from the *WIAT–3*. To determine whether Judy's measured achievement is different from her current intellectual performance, the assessment team decides to conduct a discrepancy analysis.

Using the predicted-achievement method recommended in the *WIAT–3* manual, Judy's Full Scale IQ on the *WISC–V* is used to determine predicted-achievement scores. Judy's Full Scale IQ score was 94 and her Spelling score on the *WIAT–3* was 69. The difference score, then, is 25 (computed by subtracting 69 from 94). The team consults the appropriate tables and finds that this difference is not only significant at the .01 level, but also rare. Less than 1 percent of the norming sample showed a discrepancy of this magnitude between expected and actual spelling achievement. Therefore, the team concludes that it is probable that Judy's current performance in spelling is discrepant from her intellectual performance.

In attempting to determine whether a discrepancy exists between expected and actual achievement, the assessment team should consider the following suggestions:

1. When comparing ability and achievement scores, use scores from valid and reliable tests with comparable norm groups.
2. When using tests with built-in discrepancy analysis systems, be aware of the way in which these systems go about comparing expected and actual achievement. In particular, consider which measure(s) of learning aptitude are used to determine the student's expected level of achievement. When aptitude or achievement scores are composites, also consider the student's performance on the subtests or other components that make up the composite scores.
3. Whatever method of discrepancy analysis is used, confirm that the discrepancy exists within the school environment. Substantiate

that the student's actual classroom performance is below expectation levels.
4. Keep in mind that a discrepancy between ability and achievement is only one of the criteria for identification of learning disabilities.

This last point is an important one. The Council for Learning Disabilities (1986) maintains that the high incidence rates in programs for students with learning disabilities are due to the inclusion of students whose low achievement or underachievement is caused by factors other than learning disabilities. The Learning Disabilities Association (1990) underscores this point with its assertion that educators must not misperceive students' performance as underachievement when it is actually a specific learning disability.

 Breakpoint Practice 9.3
Click here to check your understanding of identifying specific learning disabilities.

THE RESPONSE-TO-INTERVENTION APPROACH TO IDENTIFICATION OF LEARNING DISABILITIES

The **response-to-intervention (RTI)** approach, as it is described in IDEA 2004 and its regulations, is based on an examination of the student's ability to profit from high-quality instruction in order to show progress in the school curriculum. Students who show lack of progress despite what the law calls "scientific, research-based intervention" may meet eligibility requirements for the disability of learning disabilities.

It is important to understand that the RTI approach takes place during the prereferral stage of assessment, before the student is formally referred for special education assessment (Lerner, 2003). It is also important to recognize that students who show lack of progress under RTI may or may not have learning disabilities (Vaughn & Fuchs, 2006). Just as with the discrepancy analysis model, the RTI approach only determines whether there is underachievement.

The RTI approach is in many ways a preventative program. All students, including those who may have learning disabilities, receive early intervention for academic difficulties. Unlike the discrepancy model where academic problems must be severe before they are considered important, there is no need for students to "wait to fail" before receiving assistance (Vaughn & Fuchs, 2003).

There are many different RTI models but all appear to include multiple levels or tiers within a broader continuum of services. The first level or tier is general education where all students should be provided research-based instruction. The final level or tier is special education where students with extraordinary needs are provided research-based instruction designed to respond to those needs.

The National Joint Committee on Learning Disabilities (NJCLD) (2005), in a position paper on RTI, identifies core concepts of RTI. They report that students should receive high quality instruction, their response to that instruction should be monitored, and decisions should be made based on that progress data. In a way, what is being described is a **clinical approach** to teaching. Similar to diagnostic teaching, the goal is to introduce a new intervention when students encounter difficulty, then gather data to determine the effectiveness of that intervention. Note also that one of the assessment techniques discussed earlier in this text, **curriculum-based measurement,** would be ideal for the purpose of monitoring student progress and assisting teachers to make instructional decisions based on data.

In their discussion of the multitiered model for RTI, the National Joint Committee (2005) describes three distinct tiers:

Tier 1: High-quality instructional and behavioral supports are provided for all students in general education.

Tier 2: Students whose performance and rate of progress lag behind those of peers in their classroom, school, or district receive more specialized prevention or remediation within general education.

Tier 3: Comprehensive evaluation is conducted by a multidisciplinary team to determine eligibility for special education and related services. (2005, pp. 3–4)

Thus, Tier 1 represents high-quality education for every student. Tier 2, which also takes place in general education, provides more intensive interventions when students fall behind. According to this system, Tier 3 is assessment for special education services. It could also be conceptualized as the most intensive type of intervention for students with school performance problems: special education designed to meet the unique needs of students with disabilities.

According to the National Research Center on Learning Disabilities (2011), Tier 1 is the responsibility of general education, Tier 2 the joint responsibility of general and special education, and Tier 3 the responsibility of special education. Drawing on the work of the Office of Special Education Programs Technical Assistance Center, the National Center on Learning Disabilities suggests that the most students (80 percent) receive the support they need in general education Tier 1 programs. Tier 2 provides assistance for 15 percent of students, and Tier 3 for the 5 percent of the students with the most intensive needs.

Other conceptualizations of the RTI approach have included different numbers of tiers or different notions about the function of each tier. Reschly (2005), for example, argues for four tiers, with Tier 2 providing small group interventions and Tier 3 individualized interventions. Reschly maintains that all students should participate in Tier 1, with Tier 2 serving 20 percent and Tiers 3 and 4 serving 5 percent.

Several authors have discussed the drawbacks of RTI, despite its obvious advantage of bringing earlier intervention to students in trouble academically. The concerns of these authors generally revolve around the inability of RTI to authoritatively identify learning disabilities. Kavale (2005) reported that the RTI is limited in SLD identification, as nonresponsiveness is not a diagnostic criterion.

Vaughn and Fuchs (2006) identify a number of additional concerns, including questions about the involvement of parents in RTI, the need to maintain due process guarantees, the possible shortage of knowledgeable teaching staff to implement RTI, and the lack of high-quality academic interventions in all subjects for all ages.

It is important to keep in mind that widespread use of the RTI approach is in its infancy in U.S. schools. The final regulations providing structure to IDEA 2004 were not published until August 2006. Thus, as states decide whether to add RTI to their requirements for eligibility for services for students with learning disabilities and as schools and teachers begin to implement this approach, new ideas will likely emerge and some of the concerns perceived as insurmountable problems will be solved. However, research should continue to determine how effective RTI is as an early intervention effort and as a means to locate students who might meet criteria for learning disabilities.

ENHANCEDetext
Video Example 9.3
Watch this video to find out more about Response to Intervention.

MEASURES OF PERCEPTUAL-MOTOR SKILLS AND OTHER SPECIFIC LEARNING DISABILITIES

Once it has been established that the student has an achievement problem despite average or above intellectual performance and/or the provision of high-quality instruction delivered as part of an RTI approach, the assessment team may decide to continue looking for evidence of a learning disability by examining the student's specific learning abilities, including those related to perception, motor skills, memory, and attention. Traditional measures of specific learning abilities are concerned with factors such as attention, perception,

and memory and with the information-processing abilities of reception, association, and expression. Specific abilities are difficult to delimit and define because they are based on inferences about mental processes. For instance, it is impossible to observe or measure directly how a person perceives incoming sensory information. It is possible only to study the person's overt responses or his or her report of the experience and then make inferences about what may have occurred during perception.

Perception can be defined as the psychological ability to process or use the information received through the senses (Lerner, 2000). Perception depends on the physiological ability of the sense organs to receive information. Visual and auditory acuity are of primary concern to educators, but there is also interest in information received through other senses, particularly tactile and kinesthetic input. Tactile information is received through the sense of touch, and kinesthetic information from the feelings of muscles and body movements.

Memory is the ability to recall previously learned information. The memory process can be described in many ways. For example, memory can be differentiated according to the period of time that has elapsed since original learning. Educators are usually most concerned with long-term memory ability, but information must pass through short-term memory before it is stored for long-term recall.

Attention is the process whereby an individual's awareness is directed toward some stimulus or set of stimuli (Kirk & Chalfant, 1984). Attention can be considered a prerequisite not only for other specific abilities such as memory and perception, but also for any type of learning activity. Although the importance of attention cannot be denied, it is very difficult to separate it from other factors.

Information processing refers to the set of abilities that govern the way people receive and respond to incoming information. The three major components of information processing are reception of information, association of incoming information with previously stored information, and expression. Information processes are also referred to as psychological processes. The term *psycholinguistic abilities* describes the psychological processing of linguistic information. Language disorders are often a concern in the assessment of information-processing abilities, as are disorders of thinking and reasoning. In fact, measures of information processing often share many characteristics of language and intellectual performance tests.

Table 9–2 presents a listing of measures of specific learning abilities, although the older ones are no longer widely used in educational assessment, particularly those related to perception. The next sections of this chapter briefly describe several tests of specific learning abilities. Discussion of the older measures is limited because of the technical problems of many of these instruments and because these measures represent a traditional, rather than a contemporary, approach to assessment of learning disabilities.

Tests of Perception

Measures of perceptual abilities usually focus on either auditory or visual perception, rather than on the perceptual process as a whole. Among the assessment concerns in visual perception are visual discrimination, figure–ground discrimination, spatial relationships, and form perception (Wallace & McLoughlin, 1979).

Discrimination is the ability to detect likenesses and differences among stimuli, and figure–ground discrimination is the ability to differentiate relevant stimuli (the figure) from irrelevant stimuli (the background). Spatial relationships refer to perception of the relative positions of objects in space, and form perception is concerned with the size, shape, and position of visual stimuli. In auditory perception, auditory discrimination and auditory blending are of interest (Wallace & McLoughlin, 1979). Auditory blending is the ability to combine separate sounds into a whole.

Visual perception was considered one of the most important specific abilities in early assessment programs because of the hypothesized relationship between visual perception deficits and reading disorders. One of the best-known early measures is the *Developmental Test of Visual Perception* (Frostig et al., 1966). This test is not commonly used in schools today because of its failure to separate motor skills from perceptual skills, the

age and limited representativeness of its standardization sample, the low reliabilities of subtests, and the lack of adequate evidence of validity (Hammill & Wiederholt, 1972).

A new version of the *Developmental Test of Visual Perception* by Hammill, Pearson, and Voress was published in 2013. The *DTVP–3* overcomes the problems of the first edition by separating the assessment of visual perception and visual-motor skills and by meeting the criteria for psychometric quality. It was standardized on 1,035 children from a standardization sample that resembled the U.S. population in race, ethnicity, geographic region, urban-rural residence, and handedness. Internal consistency, test-retest, and interscorer reliability are adequate. The *DTVP-3* total test score (General Visual Perception) shows good agreement with results from other measures of visual perception and visual-motor skills.

Designed for students ages 4–0 to 12–11, the *DTVP–3* contains five subtests:

1. *Eye–Hand Coordination.* The student must draw a line from one drawing to another in straight or curved lines.
2. *Copying.* The student draws a copy of a geometric design; the model is present while the student draws.
3. *Figure–Ground.* The student is shown a set of geometric forms (e.g., circle, square, star) and must tell which of these forms appear in a drawing composed of several forms and perhaps a distracting background.
4. *Visual Closure.* The student sees a complete figure. He or she must then select from a series of incomplete figures the one that, if completed, would match the stimulus.
5. *Form Constancy.* The student must find a stimulus shape in drawings in which it is a different size, a different color, in a different position, and/or shown against a distracting background.

Results of the *DTVP–3* include subtest standard scores (mean = 10, SD = 3) and three composite standard scores (mean = 100, SD = 15). The composites are General Visual Perception, which includes Motor Reduced and Motor Enhanced subtests; Motor-Reduced Visual Perception, and Visual-Motor Integration.

TABLE 9–2

Measures of Specific Learning Abilities

Name (Author)	Ages	SPECIFIC ABILITIES ASSESSED			
		Perception	Motor Skills	Memory and Attention	Information Processing
Auditory Discrimination Test—Second Edition (Reynolds, 1987; Wepman, 1975)	4 to 8–11	*			
Bender-Gestalt Test II (Decker & Brannigan, 2003; Koppitz, 1963, 1975)	4 to 85		*		
Bruininks-Oseretsky Test of Motor Proficiency—Second Edition (Bruininks & Bruininks, 2005; Bruininks, 1978)	4–0 to 21–11		*		
Detroit Tests of Learning Aptitude—Fourth Edition (Hammill, 1998)	6–0 to 17–11		*	*	*
Detroit Tests of Learning Aptitude–Adult (Hammill & Bryant, 1991a)	16–0 to 79–11		*	*	*
Detroit Tests of Learning Aptitude–Primary—Third Edition (Hammill & Bryant, 2005)	3–0 to 9–11	*	*	*	*
Developmental Test of Visual Perception—Third Edition (Hammill, Pearson, & Voress, 2013; 1993)	4–0 to 12–11	*	*		
Developmental Test of Visual Perceptions–Adolescent and Adult (Reynolds, Pearson, & Voress, 2002)	11–0 to 74–11	*	*		
Developmental Test of Visual-Motor Integration–Fifth Edition (Beery VMI) (Beery & Beery, 2004, 2005, 2010)	2–0 and up adults	*	*		
Goldman-Fristoe-Woodcock Auditory Skills Test Battery (Goldman, Fristoe, & Woodcock, 1976)	3 to adult	*		*	
Goldman-Fristoe-Woodcock Test of Auditory Discrimination (Goldman, Fristoe, & Woodcock, 1970)	5–0 to adult	*			
Illinois Test of Psycholinguistic Abilities-3 (Hammill, Mather, & Roberts; 2001; Kirk, McCarthy, & Kirk, 1968)	5–0 to 12–11	*	*	*	*
Learning Disabilities Diagnostic Inventory (Hammill & Bryant, 1998)	8–0 to 18–11	*	*	*	*
Learning Disabilities Evaluation Scale-R2 (McCarney & Arthaud, 2007; McCarney, 1996)	6 to 18	*	*	*	*
Motor-Free Visual Perception Test—Third Edition (Colarusso & Hammill, 2003)	4–0 to 94–0 and above	*			
Purdue Perceptual-Motor Survey (Roach & Kephart, 1966)	6 to 10		*		
Test of Gross Motor Development–2 (Ulrich, 2000)	3–0 to 10–11		*		
Test of Memory and Learning-2 (Reynolds & Voress, 2007; Reynolds & Bigler, 1994)	5–0 to 59–11			*	
Test of Visual-Motor Integration (Hammill, Pearson, & Voress, 1996)	4–0 to 17–11	*	*		
Wechsler Memory Scale–Fourth Edition (Wechsler, 1997b, 2009)	16 to 90–11			*	

Another measure of several visual perception skills is the *Motor-Free Visual Perception Test—Third Edition (MVPT–4)* (Colarusso & Hammill, 2015). Unlike most perceptual measures, it offers norms not only for children but also for adolescents and adults. In fact, norms extend from 4 to 80+ years. Five different tasks are used to assess visual perception:

1. *Figure–Ground.* The student must determine in which of four drawings a stimulus figure is embedded.
2. *Spatial Relationships.* The student is shown a stimulus figure and then must determine which of four drawings contains it; in the drawings, the stimulus may be a different size, a different color, or in a different position.
3. *Visual Memory.* The student views a stimulus figure for 5 seconds. The stimulus is removed, and the student must select a figure identical to it from four choices.
4. *Visual Closure.* The student identifies which of four drawings, if completed, would be identical to a stimulus figure.
5. *Visual Discrimination.* When shown four drawings, the student selects the one that is different from the other three.

Although the *MVPT–4* assesses several skills, only total test scores are available. These include a percentile rank, standard score, and age equivalent. A confidence interval can be constructed around the standard score.

The technical quality of the *MVPT–4* is better than that of many tests of specific abilities published in the 1960s and 1970s. The standardization sample was composed of 2,700 children and adults. Weighting procedures were used to ensure that the standardization sample was equivalent to the general population on characteristics such as region, race/ethnicity, gender, urban–rural residence, and disability status. Test reliabilities appear adequate. The manual provides information about the relationship of the original version of the *MVPT* to other measures of visual perception; correlations are adequate.

Auditory perception has also been a concern in special education assessment, particularly in relationship to speech and language problems. Measures that evaluate several auditory skills are available. For example, the *Goldman-Fristoe-Woodcock Auditory Skills Test Battery* (Goldman, Fristoe, & Woodcock, 1976) contains tests that assess aspects of auditory selective attention, discrimination, and memory, along with sound–symbol relationships. However, auditory discrimination has been the main focus in assessing auditory perceptual skills.

The *Goldman-Fristoe-Woodcock Test of Auditory Discrimination* (Goldman, Fristoe, & Woodcock, 1970) is an individual, norm-referenced test of discrimination under both quiet and noise conditions. It is designed for ages 5–0 through adulthood. The individual looks at four line drawings, listens to a tape, and then selects the drawing that depicts the word read on the tape. The four drawings have names that are similar in sound (e.g., *wake, rake, lake,* and *make*). This test was standardized on a limited sample representing only three states, and small samples were used to study test-retest reliability and concurrent validity. More information is needed to substantiate the technical adequacy of this measure.

One of the best-known measures of perceptual ability is the *Auditory Discrimination Test-2* by J. M. Wepman (1975). In the late 1980s, this test was standardized on a national sample of more than 1,800 children ages 4 through 8 (Wepman & Reynolds, 1987). This test is used for phoneme discrimination. About 5 minutes are required for administration. Two alternate forms are provided, and the test task is the same on each: The tester reads a pair of words, and the student listens and tells whether the words are same or different. Of the 40 word pairs read to the student, 30 differ in only one sound (e.g., *tub* versus *tug*), and 10 pairs contain identical words.

Standard scores are available on the Wepman test for the first time with the second edition. They are normalized T-scores with a mean of 50 and a standard deviation of 10. The student's raw score is converted to a standard score, a percentile rank, and a Qualitative Score, which describes current functioning level (i.e., very good development, above-average ability, average ability, below-average ability, or below the level of adequacy). The test-retest and alternate form reliability of the Wepman test appears satisfactory, and its validity is supported by moderate correlations with other measures of auditory discrimination.

The Wepman test has typically been used as a screening device to identify students with poor auditory discrimination skills. However, before using this measure, the student's ability to comprehend the concepts of *same* and *different* and sustain attention during test administration must be considered, along with the tester's ability to accurately pronounce the word pairs.

Tests of Motor Skills

Motor skills are required in many school endeavors. In the classroom, for example, handwriting is a very important mode of expression. The development of motor skills may be delayed in students with physical impairments such as cerebral palsy. Physicians have the major responsibility for treatment of physical impairments but are often assisted by physical therapists, occupational therapists, and adaptive physical education teachers.

Problems in motor skill development may also occur in students without obvious physical impairments. The two major areas of concern to educators are gross-motor development and fine-motor development. **Gross-motor skills,** such as running, jumping, and throwing, involve the large muscles of the body. In contrast, **fine-motor skills** involve the small muscles. Examples of school-related fine-motor tasks are cutting with scissors, tracing, copying, and writing. Many of these skills involve both fine-motor ability and visual perception; this combination is called eye–hand coordination. Other motor skills of interest are balance, rhythm, laterality, directionality, body image, and body awareness (Wallace & McLoughlin, 1979).

Some measures of motor development are comprehensive in an attempt to assess both gross- and fine-motor skills. An early example is the *Purdue Perceptual-Motor Survey* (Roach & Kephart, 1966). It evaluates five types of motor skills: Balance and Posture, Body Image and Differentiation, Perceptual-Motor Match, Ocular Control, and Form Perception. This measure is no longer widely used.

A more recent measure is the *Bruininks-Oseretsky Test of Motor Proficiency-2* (Bruininks & Bruininks, 2005), which is based on the *Lincoln-Oseretsky Motor Development Scale* (Sloan, 1954). The *Bruininks-Oseretsky* is an individual, norm-referenced test for students ages 4 to 21–11; it contains eight subtests:

Subtest 1: Fine Motor Precision

Subtest 2: Fine Motor Integration

Subtest 3: Manual Dexterity

Subtest 4: Bilateral Coordination

Subtest 5: Balance

Subtest 6: Running Speed and Agility

Subtest 7: Upper Limb Coordination

Subtest 8: Strength

The *Bruininks-Oseretsky 2* produces a standard score and an age equivalent for each subtest. Composite scores are available for Fine Manual Control, Manual Coordination, Body Coordination, Strength and Agility, Total Motor Composite, Gross Motor Composite, and Fine Motor Composite.

The *Bruininks-Oseretsky 2* is a well-constructed test that appears to be useful for the assessment of fine- and gross-motor functioning. It was standardized on a sample of 1,520 students across 38 states, selected to resemble the U.S. population. Test-retest and interrater reliability are adequate, and content validity appears satisfactory.

The *Test of Gross Motor Development–2 (TGMD–2)* (Ulrich, 2000), assesses two areas of gross motor development in children ages 3 to 11: locomotor skills and object control skills. On the Locomotor subtest, students are asked to demonstrate skills such as running, hopping, and leaping. The Object Control subtest includes tasks such as striking a ball with a bat, bouncing a ball, and catching a ball. The test manual clearly describes the procedures for administration and the criteria for evaluating student performance. Results include subtest standard scores and percentiles and a global standard score, the Gross Motor Development Quotient.

The *TGMD–2* was standardized with 1,208 children from eight states. This sample resembled the U.S. population in terms of characteristics such as geographic region, race, urban–rural residence, and educational attainment of parents. The manual provides evidence to support the reliability of the *TGMD–2,* its content validity, and its ability to differentiate between children with and without disabilities. Results from a small-scale study also support the relationship between results from the *TGMD–2* and those from another motor skills measure.

Many of the instruments developed to assess motor skills are concerned with only one ability: the fine-motor skill of eye–hand coordination. This skill is emphasized because it is required in many educational activities, most notably handwriting. Among the measures designed to evaluate eye–hand coordination are the *Bender Visual-Motor Gestalt Test* (Bender, 1938) and its adaptation for young children (Koppitz, 1963, 1975), the Visual-Motor Integration subtests of the *Developmental Test of Visual Perception—Third Edition* (described earlier), the *Developmental Test of Visual-Motor Integration—Fifth Edition* (Beery & Beery, 2004, 2006), and the *Test of Visual-Motor Integration* (Hammill, Pearson, & Voress, 1996). All of these tests require students to copy geometric designs. On the *Bender Gestalt Test for Young Children* (Koppitz, 1963, 1975), for instance, children ages 5 to 11 copy nine geometric designs. Although the *Bender Gestalt* has been recommended as an indicator of intellectual functioning level, minimal brain dysfunction, and emotional disturbance (Koppitz, 1975), it is best viewed simply as a test of eye–hand coordination.

The *Developmental Test of Visual-Motor Integration—Fifth Edition* is a popular measure of eye–hand coordination that was first published in 1967. The fourth edition includes updated norms, including norms for adults, and two new supplemental subtests (in addition to Visual-Motor Integration): Visual Perception and Motor Coordination. The original measure, the Visual-Motor Integration subtest, is available in a full format (for ages 2 through adult) and a short format (for ages 2 through 7). The *VMI* may be administered individually or to groups; administration requires 15 minutes or less. Norms are provided for ages 2–0 through 18–11 and, in the norm supplement, for adults 19–0 through 99–11.

The fifth edition of the *VMI* was standardized with 2,512 children and adolescents. The standardization sample appears representative of the nation as a whole in ethnicity, urban–rural residence, geographic region, and socioeconomic status. Reliability of the *VMI* is adequate, and results appear related to those of other measures of eye–hand coordination.

The Visual-Motor Integration subtest is to be administered first. It contains 24 geometric forms to be copied by the student. Testing continues until the student fails three consecutive forms. Although administration of this subtest is fairly easy, scoring can be quite complicated. Each item is scored pass or fail using the criteria and examples provided in the manual, and a protractor is needed to evaluate some forms. For example, to pass the form called Vertical-Horizontal Cross [+], the student's drawing must contain two lines that are fully intersecting *and* continuous, *and* at least one-half of each line must be within 20 degrees of its correct orientation.

On the Visual Perception subtest, the student looks at a stimulus design and then must find an identical design in an array of possible responses. On the Motor Coordination subtest, the student attempts to draw lines within the boundaries of a design. Global scores are available for each of the three subtests, and each can be expressed as a standard score, percentile rank, and age equivalent.

The *Test of Visual-Motor Integration (TVMI)* is a similar measure. Designed for ages 4–0 to 17–11, it contains 30 forms for students to copy. Younger students complete items 1 to 18 and older students (ages 11 to 18) items 13 to 30. The *TVMI* may be administered to individuals or groups in 15 to 30 minutes. One difference between this measure and the *VMI* is that students may earn 0, 1, 2, or 3 points on each item, depending on the accuracy of their response. Results include a standard score, percentile rank, and age equivalent for total test performance.

Measures of Memory and Attention

Like perception, memory is often separated into two separate abilities on the basis of sensory input channel. Although the auditory-visual distinction may be of interest, memory can be described in several other important ways:

- *Type of information to be recalled.* In some memory tasks, the information to be stored for later retrieval is familiar and meaningful to the learner. This type of information is usually easier to recall than unfamiliar or nonmeaningful material.
- *Time since original learning.* Another variable is the amount of time that intervenes between original learning and recall. Short-term memory tasks require recall immediately after learning. Long-term memory tasks impose an interval of at least several seconds or minutes between learning and recall.
- *Type of memory.* This dimension distinguishes between the recognition of information learned previously and its recall. In recognition memory, the learner simply says whether or not information has been presented earlier. In recall memory, a more difficult task, the learner must reproduce the information.
- *Organization of recall.* In memory tasks, information can be retrieved in more than one way. Free recall is the retrieval of information in any order. In contrast, serial recall requires a fixed order. Serial recall is required in school tasks such as counting from 1 to 100 and reciting the alphabet in order. In paired-associate recall, the learner associates a response with a particular stimulus; when the stimulus is produced, the learner must recall the response. A common classroom task that requires paired-associate recall is saying letter names when written letters are presented.

Despite the many types of memory required in classroom learning, the majority of memory tests assess only short-term recall, usually in the serial mode. The most usual type of memory task on norm-referenced measures is short-term serial recall of nonmeaningful information. Auditory memory is often assessed with digit span tasks, in which students listen to and attempt to repeat series of numbers. Visual memory tasks are more varied; some use non-meaningful shapes or isolated letters, and others employ pictures or photographs.

Most of the commonly used measures of memory are subtests from tests of intellectual performance or comprehensive specific ability batteries; several of these are described in Table 9–3. One notable exception is the *Test of Memory and Learning 2 (TOMAL2)* (Reynolds & Voress, 2007; Reynolds & Bigler, 1994). This comprehensive measure for students ages 5 years, 0 months through 59 years, 11 months contains eight core and six supplementary subtests of memory functioning. Subtests are classified as verbal or nonverbal, and they assess a range of memory abilities including sequential, free recall, and associative memory as well as immediate, delayed, and cued recall. Results include an overall composite (Composite Memory Index) and these supplemental summary scores:

- Verbal Delayed Recall Index
- Learning Index
- Attention and Concentration Index
- Sequential Memory Index
- Free Recall Index
- Associative Recall Index

The *Wechsler Memory Scale–Fourth Edition* (Wechsler, 2009) is another useful instrument. However, it is designed for adolescents and adults with norms extending from ages 16 to 90.

Attention is another specific ability of interest in special education assessment. It is a difficult ability to measure because a learner's attention cannot be separated from the task. When persons attend, they attend *to* something, and that task or situation may influence how well attentional resources are deployed. Because of the inability to isolate attention from other factors, attention is often assessed informally through observation.

Before attending behavior can be observed, it must be operationally defined. For instance, paying attention to a workbook assignment might be defined by behaviors such as looking at the workbook page and writing answers to questions on the page. Of course, such observable behaviors are only indicators of the process of attention. Attention is inferred when the student engages in behaviors related to task completion.

Another source of information is the reports of teachers and parents. Persons who know the student well act as informants by participating in

TABLE 9–3
Measures of Memory on Tests of Intellectual Performance

TYPE OF MEMORY	AUDITORY OR VISUAL	MEANINGFUL OR NONMEANINGFUL	TYPE OF INFORMATION	TEST	SUBTEST
Short-term recognition	Visual	Meaningful	People's faces	KABC–II	Face Recognition
		Nonmeaningful	Objects	WJ IV	Picture Recognition
Short-term serial Recall	Auditory	Meaningful	Sentences	DTLA–4	Sentence Imitation
				S–B	Verbal Working Memory
		Nonmeaningful	Isolated words	DTLA–4	Word Sequences
				K–ABC II	Word Order
				WJ IV	Memory for Words
			Digits	K–ABC II	Number Recall
				WISC–V	Digit Span
				WJ IV	Numbers Reversed
			Digits and letters	WISC–V	Letter-Number Sequencing
				WJ IV	Object Number Sequencing
	Visual	Nonmeaningful	Geometric forms	DTLA–4	Design Reproduction
			Hand movements	K–ABC II	Hand Movements
			Letters	DTLA–4	Reversed Letters
			Unrelated objects	DTLA–4	Design Sequences
Long-term paired associate recall	Visual and Auditory	Meaningful	Words associated with a category	WJ IV	Retrieval Fluency
		Nonmeaningful	Words associated with shapes	WJ IV	Visual-Auditory Learning

Key to test names:
DTLA–4—Detroit Tests of Learning Aptitude–4 (Hammill, 1998)
KABC–II—Kaufman Assessment Battery for Children—Second Edition (Kaufman & Kaufman, 2004a)
S-B—Stanford-Binet Intelligence Scale—Fifth Edition (Roid, 2003)
WISC–V—Wechsler Intelligence Scale for Children—Fifth Edition (Wechsler, 2014)
WJ IV—Woodcock-Johnson IV (Schrank et al. 2014b)

interviews and completing questionnaires and rating scales. This is the strategy most often used in assessment when attention-deficit/hyperactivity disorders (ADHD) are suspected. Chapter 10 discusses procedures for the assessment of attention deficits, hyperactivity, and impulsivity.

 Breakpoint Practice 9.4
Click here to check your understanding of perceptual motor skill testing.

TEST BATTERIES FOR SPECIFIC ABILITY ASSESSMENT

Whereas some measures are designed to assess one particular learning ability, others attempt a more comprehensive evaluation. Such measures are made up of several subtests, each focusing on one or more specific abilities. Historically, the best-known measures of this type are the *Illinois Test of Psycholinguistic Abilities,* an information-processing test battery developed by Kirk, McCarthy, and

Kirk (1968), and the *Detroit Tests of Learning Aptitude* (Baker & Leland, 1967). The newest version of the *Detroit Tests of Learning Aptitude* is described in the next section. The 1968 edition of the *Illinois Test of Psycholinguistic Abilities* has also been revised. However, the third edition of the *ITPA* (Hammill, Mather, & Roberts, 2001) is designed to measure language skills rather than specific learning abilities. Thus, it is discussed in a later chapter of this book that deal with assessment of oral language skills.

Detroit Tests of Learning Aptitude (4th ed.)

The original version of this test was developed in the 1930s by Baker and Leland and then revised in 1967. In 1984, Hammill published a new version. The *Detroit Tests of Learning Aptitude—Second Edition* (DTLA–2), as this edition was called, was a complete revision and restandardization. The current edition is the *Detroit Tests of Learning Aptitude—Fourth Edition*, or *DTLA–4* (Hammill, 1998). Versions for young children (Hammill & Bryant, 2005) and for adults (Hammill & Bryant, 1991a) are also available.

The *DTLA–4* is an individual, norm-referenced test designed to assess a variety of specific cognitive abilities. It is appropriate for students ages 6–0 to 17–11, and it contains 10 subtests:

- *Word Opposites.* The tester says a word and the student must say a word that is opposite in meaning.
- *Design Sequences.* The student is shown a page with a series of designs. The page is removed, and the student must reproduce the series using blocks. If an error is made, the tester shows the page again; no more than three trials are allowed.
- *Sentence Imitation.* The tester says a sentence, and the student must repeat it verbatim.
- *Reversed Letters.* The tester says a series of letters at a rate of one per second; the student must write the letters in reverse order.
- *Story Construction.* The student is shown a picture and must make up a story about it.
- *Design Reproduction.* The student is shown a geometric design. After 5 seconds, the design is removed. After 5 more seconds, the student is asked to draw the design.

- *Basic Information.* The tester asks questions related to daily life, science, geography, and history, and the student responds orally.
- *Symbolic Relations.* The student is shown a page with several designs at the top. One design (or more) is missing. The student must find the design that completes the pattern in the choices at the bottom of the page.
- *Word Sequences.* The tester says a series of unrelated words and the student must repeat them in order.
- *Story Sequences.* The tester presents a set of pictures that tell a story, and the student must put them in order. The student puts a chip with the number 1 on it on the first picture, a chip with a number 2 on the second, and so on.

Administration of the *DTLA–4* requires 50 minutes to 2 hours.

On the *DTLA–4,* standard scores and percentile ranks are computed for each subtest, and subtest results can be combined into several Composite scores. See Figure 9–3 for a sample *DTLA–4* protocol. Subtest standard scores are distributed with a mean of 10 and a standard deviation of 3; Composite scores are distributed with a mean of 100 and a standard deviation of 15. The General Mental Ability Composite is a total test score that reflects performance on all subtests; the Optimal Composite summarizes performance on the four subtests in which the student earned the highest scores. According to the *DTLA–4* manual, this score "represents the best estimate of mental ability when inhibiting factors are suppressed" (p. xii). Subtest results can also be combined into Domain Composites and Theoretical Composites.

The *DTLA–4* assesses three domains: Linguistic, Attentional, and Motoric. Two Composite scores are provided for each domain; one of these scores emphasizes the ability under consideration, and the other deemphasizes it. For example, in the Linguistic Domain, the Verbal Composite includes subtests that stress word knowledge and use, whereas subtests that contribute to the Nonverbal Composite deemphasize verbal abilities. In the Attentional Domain, subtests that require attention, concentration, and short-term memory make up the Attention-Enhanced Composite; subtests that stress long-term memory contribute to the

DTLA–4

Detroit Tests of Learning Aptitude

Profile/Summary Form

Fourth Edition

Section I.   Identifying Information

Name _Luis_   Female ☐   Male ☑   Grade _6_

	Year	Month	Day
Date Tested	97	11	16
Date of Birth	85	7	8
Age	12	4	8

School _Bedichek Middle_

Examiner's Name _Dr. Rivera_

Examiner's Title _Diagnostician_

Section II.   Record of DTLA–4 Subtest Scores

Subtest	Raw Score	%ile	Standard Score	Age Equivalent	Rating
I. Word Opposites (WO)	33	37	9	11-3	Average
II. Design Sequences (DS)	122	37	9	11-3	Average
III. Sentence Imitation (SI)	15	37	9	11-3	Average
IV. Reversed Letters (RL)	38	75	12	16-9	Average
V. Story Construction (SC)	14	50	10	11-9	Average
VI. Design Reproduction (DR)	36	63	11	13-0	Average
VII. Basic Information (BI)	11	5	5	8-3	Poor
VIII. Symbolic Relations (SR)	15	16	7	8-6	Below Average
IX. Word Sequences (WS)	12	37	9	10-0	Average
X. Story Sequences (SS)	27	25	8	9-9	Average

Section III.   Profile of DTLA–4 Subtest Scores

Standard Scores	Word Opposites	Design Sequences	Sentence Imitation	Reversed Letters	Story Construction	Design Reproduction	Basic Information	Symbolic Relations	Word Sequences	Story Sequences	Standard Scores
20	·	·	·	·	·	·	·	·	·	·	20
19	·	·	·	·	·	·	·	·	·	·	19
18	·	·	·	·	·	·	·	·	·	·	18
17	·	·	·	·	·	·	·	·	·	·	17
16	·	·	·	·	·	·	·	·	·	·	16
15	·	·	·	·	·	·	·	·	·	·	15
14	·	·	·	·	·	·	·	·	·	·	14
13	·	·	·	·	·	·	·	·	·	·	13
12	·	·	·	×	·	·	·	·	·	·	12
11	·	·	·	·	·	×	·	·	·	·	11
10	·	·	·	·	×	·	·	·	·	·	10
9	×	×	×	·	·	·	·	·	×	·	9
8	·	·	·	·	·	·	·	·	·	×	8
7	·	·	·	·	·	·	·	×	·	·	7
6	·	·	·	·	·	·	·	·	·	·	6
5	·	·	·	·	·	·	×	·	·	·	5
4	·	·	·	·	·	·	·	·	·	·	4
3	·	·	·	·	·	·	·	·	·	·	3
2	·	·	·	·	·	·	·	·	·	·	2
1	·	·	·	·	·	·	·	·	·	·	1

Additional copies of this form (#8564) may be purchased from PRO-ED, 8700 Shoal Creek Blvd., Austin, TX 78757-6897. 512/451-3246, Fax 512/451-8542

FIGURE 9–3

Sample *Detroit Tests of Learning Aptitude—Fourth Edition* Results

Note: From *Detroit Tests of Learning Aptitude* (4th ed.) (pp. 64–65) by D. D. Hammill, 1998, Austin, TX: PRO-ED. Copyright 1998 by PRO-ED. Reprinted by permission.

Section IV. Workspace for Computing Composites

Global Composites	WO	DS	SI	RL	SC	DR	BI	SR	WS	SS	Sum of Std. Scores	Quotient	%ile
General Mental Ability	9	9	9	12	10	11	5	7	9	8	89	92	30
Optimal (select highest four scores)	9			12	10	11					42	103	58

DOMAIN COMPOSITES:

	WO	DS	SI	RL	SC	DR	BI	SR	WS	SS			

Linguistic

	WO	DS	SI	RL	SC	DR	BI	SR	WS	SS	Sum of Std. Scores	Quotient	%ile
Verbal	9		9		10		5		9		42	89	23
Nonverbal		9		12		11		7		8	47	96	39

Attentional

	WO	DS	SI	RL	SC	DR	BI	SR	WS	SS	Sum of Std. Scores	Quotient	%ile
Attention-Enhanced		9	9	12		11			9	8	58	98	45
Attention-Reduced	9				10		5	7			31	85	16

Motoric

	WO	DS	SI	RL	SC	DR	BI	SR	WS	SS	Sum of Std. Scores	Quotient	%ile
Motor-Enhanced		9		12		11				8	40	100	50
Motor-Reduced	9		9		10		5	7	9		49	87	19

THEORETICAL COMPOSITES:

	WO	DS	SI	RL	SC	DR	BI	SR	WS	SS			

Cattell and Horn

	WO	DS	SI	RL	SC	DR	BI	SR	WS	SS	Sum of Std. Scores	Quotient	%ile
Fluid Intelligence		9		12		11		7			39	98	45
Crystallized Intelligence	9		9		10		5		9	8	50	89	23

Das

	WO	DS	SI	RL	SC	DR	BI	SR	WS	SS	Sum of Std. Scores	Quotient	%ile
Simultaneous Processing	9		9		10	11	5	7			51	90	25
Successive Processing		9		12					9	8	38	97	42

Jensen

	WO	DS	SI	RL	SC	DR	BI	SR	WS	SS	Sum of Std. Scores	Quotient	%ile
Associative Level		9	9	12		11			9		50	100	50
Cognitive Level	9				10		5	7		8	39	85	16

Wechsler

	WO	DS	SI	RL	SC	DR	BI	SR	WS	SS	Sum of Std. Scores	Quotient	%ile
Verbal Scale	9		9		10		5		9		42	89	23
Performance Scale		9		12		11		7		8	47	96	39

FIGURE 9–3   *continued*

Attention-Reduced Composite. Similarly, on the Motoric Domain, subtests with high motor skill demands are combined into the Motor-Enhanced Composite, and those that are relatively motor-free comprise the Motor-Reduced Composite. One of the purposes of the *DTLA–4* is "to determine strengths and weaknesses among developed mental abilities" (p. 24), and the Domain Composites provided by this measure facilitate this task.

Subtest results can also be combined into what the *DTLA–4* calls Theoretical Composites. Each of these sets of scores represents a different theory of intelligence. For example, the Wechsler Composites are called Verbal Scale and Performance Scale, reflecting the two major scales on older Wechsler tests such as the *WISC–III*. In fact, the Wechsler Composites are identical to the *DTLA–4*'s Linguistic Domain Composite scores: Verbal and Nonverbal. Other Theoretical Composites are Cattell and Horn (Fluid and Crystallized Intelligence), Das (Simultaneous and Successive Processing), and Jensen (Associative and Cognitive Levels). According to the *DTLA–4* manual, the Cattell and Horn model separates intelligence into two sets of abilities: fluid intelligence, which emphasizes nonverbal, culture-free processes, and crystallized intelligence, which emphasizes skills acquired through direct instruction or from one's culture. In the Das model, simultaneous processing involves working with stimuli that are presented concurrently, while successive processing involves sequential stimuli. Jensen's model includes associative level thinking, in which there is a high correspondence between the forms of the stimulus and the required response, and cognitive level thinking, in which stimulus input must be transformed to produce a response.

The *DTLA–4* was renormed with 1,350 persons from 37 states. However, some members of the norm group were tested in 1989–1990 as part of the development of the *DTLA–3*, and others were tested in 1996–1997. The sample included ages 6–0 to 17–11, and it appears to approximate the national population in race, ethnicity, urban–rural residence, geographic area, and family income. Students with disabilities made up 11 percent of the sample.

Internal consistency and test-retest reliability are adequate for *DTLA–4* Composite scores and for most subtests. Some subtests show reliability coefficients below .80, although all coefficients equal or exceed .70. For example, the subtest with the lowest average internal consistency (.79) is Story Construction; across ages, its reliability coefficients range from .73 to .85. Across ages, test-retest reliability coefficients fall below .70 for three subtests: Design Sequences (.71), Reversed Letters (.73), and Story Sequences (.76). However, reliability coefficients for all composite scores are .90 or above.

Validity was studied in a number of ways, including investigation of the relationship of the *DTLA–4* to other measures of intellectual performance. Note, however, that the concurrent validity studies reported in the manual refer to the third edition of the *DTLA;* the *DTLA–4* manual explains that the items on these two editions are virtually identical. The General Mental Ability Composite score on the *DTLA–3* shows good agreement with the Broad Cognitive Ability (Standard) score on the *Woodcock-Johnson–R* ($r = .91$) and the Mental Processing score of the *K–ABC* ($r = .82$). Other *DTLA–3* Composite scores show mixed results. An example is the *K–ABC.* Sequential and Simultaneous Processing scores would be expected to be related to the *DTLA–3* Successive and Simultaneous Processing Composites. Although the two measures of sequential processing are related ($r = .84$), the Simultaneous Composite of the *DTLA–3* shows a stronger correlation with the *K–ABC* Sequential score ($r = .80$) than with the *K–ABC* Simultaneous score ($r = .70$).

Factor-analytic studies with the *DTLA–4* provide partial confirmation. The manual states that "[b]ecause the DTLA–4 subtests were constructed to measure cognitive abilities, we expected they would load on a single factor" (p. 152). The first factor analysis identified one dominant factor, general mental ability. In the second analysis, two factors were identified: verbal and nonverbal ability. Confirmatory factor analyses supported the three domains on the *DTLA–4* (Linguistic, Attentional, and Motoric) and the four theoretical composites.

Other Versions of the DTLA

The *Detroit Tests of Learning Aptitude–Primary— Third Edition (DTLA–Primary: 3)* is a downward extension of the *DTLA–4* for children ages 3–0 to 9–11. It employs many of the same kinds of test tasks and produces the same General Ability and Domain Composites as the *DTLA–4.* There are three major differences between the tests. First, the *DTLA–Primary: 3* is not organized by subtests. Second, 100 items of all types are merged into one sequence by difficulty level. Also, the *Primary: 3* contains some tasks that are not found on the version for older students; examples are articulation, draw-a-person, motor directions, oral directions, picture identification, and visual discrimination. Third, the Theoretical Composites of the *DTLA–4* are not available on the *Primary: 3.*

The *Detroit Tests of Learning Aptitude-Adult (DTLA–A)* is designed for ages 16–0 to 79–11. It contains 12 subtests, 9 of which are equivalent to subtests on the *DTLA–4.* The three subtests that are not found on the version for school-aged individuals are Mathematical Problems, Quantitative Relations, and Form Assembly. The *DTLA–A* provides the same types of results as the *DTLA–4:* subtest standard scores, General and Optimal Mental Ability Composites, Domain Composites (Linguistic, Attentional, and Motoric), and Theoretical Composites.

The *Hammill Multiability Intelligence Test (HAMIT)* by Hammill, Bryant, and Pearson (1998), which was described in the previous chapter, is a shorter version of the *DTLA–4.* It contains 8 subtests rather than 10. The two subtests that were omitted are Reversed Letters and Story Construction. The *HAMIT* produces only three composite scores: General, Verbal, and Nonverbal Intelligence.

Intelligence Tests as Measures of Specific Cognitive Abilities

Results of tests of intellectual performance are sometimes used to provide information about students' specific learning abilities. When specific abilities are the focus of assessment, the scores of interest are individual subtest results and composite scores that result from combinations of subtests, not global IQ scores.

This practice began with the criticism leveled at early tests of specific abilities. Faced with a shortage of technically adequate specific ability tests, practitioners turned to well-respected instruments such as the Wechsler family of intelligence tests. Also, the norms of some specific ability measures did not extend into the middle and high school grades, limiting their usefulness to younger age ranges. Another impetus for this practice was the introduction of a new generation of intelligence tests designed to provide not only estimates of overall aptitude for learning, but also information about more specific cognitive abilities.

The individual intelligence test most often used as an information source about specific abilities is the *WISC–V,* the *Wechsler Intelligence Scale for Children–Fifth Edition* (Wechsler, 2014). *WISC–V* results are available for most students who are assessed for possible special education placement, and these results are examined to determine strengths and weaknesses in various cognitive abilities.

Table 9–4 presents several of the newer tests of intellectual performance and the cognitive abilities they measure. The *DTLA–4* is included because it can be classified as either a test of intellectual performance or a measure of specific learning abilities. As can be seen from this table, the *WISC–V* provides five factor-based Index scores in addition to an overall Full Scale IQ; the *Woodcock-Johnson IV* assesses three cognitive performance clusters, seven broad cognitive factors, and six narrow cognitive abilities and clinical factors. The fifth edition of the *Stanford-Binet Intelligence Scale* provides a Verbal and a Nonverbal IQ as well as information about five specific ability areas. The *Kaufman Assessment Battery for Children, Second Edition* (Kaufman & Kaufman, 2004a) yields scores for both sequential and simultaneous processing along with three other specific ability areas.

ENHANCEDetext
Video Example 9.4
Watch this video to find out more about assessment to instruction connection.

TABLE 9–4
Specific Abilities Assessed by Tests of Intellectual Performance

TEST	SCORES REPRESENTING SPECIFIC ABILITIES
Wechsler Intelligence Scale for Children—Fifth Edition	Verbal Comprehension Visual Spatial Fluid Reasoning Working Memory Processing Speed
Woodcock-Johnson IV	Short-Term Working Memory Perceptual Speed Cognitive Processing Speed Auditory Processing Long-Term Retrieval Visual Processing Auditory Memory Span Number Facility Cognitive Efficiency
Stanford-Binet Intelligence Scale—Fifth Edition	Fluid Reasoning Knowledge Quantitative Reasoning Visual-Spatial Processing Working Memory
Kaufman Assessment Battery for Children—Second Edition	Sequential Processing Simultaneous Processing Planning Learning Knowledge
Detroit Tests of Learning Aptitude—Fourth Edition	Verbal Composite Nonverbal Composite Attention-Enhanced Composite Attention-Reduced Composite Motor-Enhanced Composite Motor-Reduced Composite Verbal Scale Performance Scale Fluid Intelligence Crystallized Intelligence Simultaneous Processing Successive Processing Associative Level Cognitive Level

ASSESSMENT OF LEARNING STRATEGIES

In recent years, interest has shifted from the study of isolated specific abilities to consideration of learning strategies. Learning strategies are the methods that students employ when faced with a learning task. This change is due in part to the criticism leveled against traditional specific ability assessments and treatment programs. It is also due to current research findings about the nature of learning disabilities.

Research Findings

Research results indicate that many students with learning disabilities are characterized by inefficient and ineffective strategies for learning (Lewis, 1983). This finding has been reported in relation to the specific learning abilities of both attention and memory. Hallahan and Reeve (1980) in their summary of research on selective attention noted that students with learning disabilities might have weaknesses in the area of limited strategies regarding recognizing cues.

Research on memory supports this theory (Swanson & Cooney, 1996; Torgesen, 1980). Students with learning disabilities tend to recall less information than students without disabilities. They approach the learning task differently and are less likely to engage in active rehearsal during the study period. However, when students with learning disabilities are required to rehearse, their recall improves, sometimes to the level of typical students (Torgesen & Goldman, 1977). These findings led Torgesen (1977) to hypothesize that students with learning disabilities are passive learners. Swanson (1989) disagrees; in his review of research, he uses the term *actively inefficient* to describe students with learning disabilities.

Deshler and other researchers at the University of Kansas have carried out a series of studies on the learning characteristics of adolescents identified as having learning disabilities (e.g., Alley, Deshler, Clark, Schumaker, & Warner, 1983; Deshler, Schumaker, Alley, Warner, & Clark, 1982; Schumaker, Deshler, Alley, & Warner, 1983).

Their results indicate that many adolescents with learning disabilities exhibit immature executive functioning; that is, these students are unable to create and apply an appropriate strategy to a novel problem (Schumaker et al., 1983). In addition, the study skills and strategies of secondary-aged students with learning disabilities are deficient. Among the areas of difficulty are note taking, attention to teachers' statements, listening comprehension, scanning of textbook passages, monitoring of writing errors, and test-taking skills (Deshler et al., 1982).

Although deficient learning strategies and study skills appear to characterize students with learning disabilities, these strategies may be susceptible to training (Lerner, 2000; Lewis, 1983). Torgesen's (1980) work in memory illustrates this point. Research at the University of Kansas on the efficacy of learning strategy interventions also supports the feasibility of training (Deshler et al., 1982). The Strategy Instruction Model (SIM) developed at the University of Kansas begins with assessment of the student's current strategies for learning. New strategies are then taught, first in isolation, then with controlled academic materials, and finally with actual school texts and assignments (Deshler, Alley, Warner, & Schumaker, 1981). Three types of strategies are included in SIM: acquisition strategies, storage strategies, and strategies for the demonstration and expression of knowledge (Lenz et al., 1996).

Approaches to Assessment

Although progress has been made in the development of instructional models, the assessment of learning strategies has received little attention. Pressley, Borkowski, Forrest-Pressley, Gaskins, and Wile (1993) suggested that a formal information-processing tool was unavailable to fully encapsulate the concept. However, these authors suggest that the *Surveys of Problem-Solving and Educational Skills* (Meltzer, 1987) is a promising measure. In practice, professionals tend to rely on informal assessment tools to gather information about learning strategies. Specific ability tests do not provide sufficient information because they measure abilities in isolation rather than in the context of actual learning tasks. More pertinent data are produced by observations, work sample analyses, student questionnaires and interviews, and teacher interviews.

Of note is a measure related to learning strategies, the *School Motivation and Learning Strategies Inventory* (Stroud & Reynolds, 2006). It is a self-report measure available in two forms, one for younger students (ages 8 to 12) and the other for teens (ages 13 to 18). Students rate themselves on items that address eight scales related to Student Strengths and three scales related to Student Liabilities. These scales are:

Student Strengths

> Study Strategies
> Note-Taking/Listening Skills
> Reading/Comprehension Strategies
> Writing/Research Skills
> Test-Taking Strategies
> Organizational Techniques
> Time Management
> Time Management/Organizational
>   Techniques

Student Liabilities

> Low Academic Motivation
> Test Anxiety
> Concentration/Attention Difficulties

T-scores (with a mean of 50 and standard deviation of 10) and percentile ranks are available for each of the scales. It is not possible to compute an overall score.

Suggestions for the design of informal tools for the assessment of learning strategies are available in the study skills literature. However, study skills are not the same as learning strategies. The term *learning strategy* is usually reserved for the general cognitive strategies that students apply to tasks in which learning is expected: strategies for the deployment of attention, for the rehearsal of skills and information to be learned, for generating and evaluating solutions to problems, and so forth. In contrast, study skills are more closely tied to specific school tasks and often require at least rudimentary proficiency in reading and writing. Despite these differences, both learning strategies and study skills are concerned with the student's *use* of specific abilities. Evaluation of study habits can provide some insight into the ways the student interacts with the learning task.

According to Cohen and de Bettencourt (1983), students are responsible for five aspects of independent learning activities: following directions, approaching tasks, obtaining assistance, getting feedback, and gaining reinforcement. These five components could form the basis for designing an observation of student study behavior.

Brown (1978) discusses study behaviors and suggests methods for informal assessment. First, the student's work habits should be observed within the context of the classroom. Among the factors to be considered are the frequency and duration of on-task and off-task behaviors; any classroom conditions or events that appear to distract the student; and variations in performance from one time or one subject matter area, or one teacher to another. A second assessment method is discussion with the student. Students can be asked to describe their usual methods of approaching and completing class assignments.

Students can be interviewed while they are working on a study task or just after they have completed it. This allows the interviewer to ask specific questions about a particular task. Students simply report their actions, rather than attempting to recall or make judgments about their typical behaviors. Some questions that could be asked in situations in which students are learning new information are:

- Think about things you just did in studying _____. What did you do first?
- Did you begin by looking over the information to be learned?
- Did you try to organize the information in any way? If so, how did you organize it?
- Was there anything in the material that you didn't understand? If there was, how did you try to figure it out?

- In your studying, did you do anything to help remember the information? What did you do? Did you look at it? Say it to yourself? Picture it in your mind? Take notes? Outline the information?
- Can you recall the information now? Do you think you'll be able to remember it tomorrow?
- Will you study this information again? If so, will you use the same study methods?

These questions attempt to elicit student comments about the use of strategies such as previewing, organizing, problem solving, and rehearsing. In light of the research findings about students' lack of active task participation, the questions about rehearsal techniques are of special interest. Some students may report using verbal rehearsal—the material to be learned is said aloud or subvocally. Others may talk about visual imagery—the construction of mental visual images—as a strategy for learning. Both verbal rehearsal and visual imagery have been found useful as mnemonic devices or memory aids for students with learning disabilities (Rose, Cundick, & Higbee, 1983). Students who report no rehearsal strategy or say they simply look at the material may be in need of strategy training.

The *Study Skills Counseling Evaluation (SSCE)* (Demos, 1976) is a published assessment device designed to quickly recognize study needs. It is a print questionnaire with norms for high school students, 2-year college students, and 4-year college students.

The *SSCE* contains 50 items that assess five study skill areas:

- Study–Time Distribution
- Study Conditions
- Taking Notes
- Preparing and Taking Examinations
- Other Habits and Attitudes

The student reads each statement (e.g., "I study in several short sessions") and then marks the best description of his or her current study habits: very often, often, sometimes, seldom, or very seldom. The *SSCE* total test raw score is converted to a percentile rank. In addition, the manual provides guidelines for rating performance in each of the study skill areas as Very Strong, Strong, Average, Weak, or Very Weak. These ratings can be plotted on a summary profile to provide a graphic representation of strengths and weaknesses.

The *SSCE* is a normed instrument, but very little information is provided in the manual about the standardization sample. Although this is a concern, the *SSCE* could be used as an informal device, or local norms could be developed. In interpreting results of this or other self-report measures, it must be remembered that not every student is able—or willing—to provide totally accurate information.

Most published study skills questionnaires are designed for high school and college students. The *Study Attitudes and Methods Survey* (Michael, Michael, & Zimmerman, 1985) includes the dimensions of academic interest and drive, study habits, and lack of study anxiety. An older measure, the *Survey of Study Habits and Attitudes* (Brown & Holtzman, 1967a, 1967b), extends down to grade 7 and is available in both English and Spanish. It evaluates study methods, motivation for studying, and attitudes toward scholastic activities.

Levine, Clarke, and Ferb (1981) report the results of a study in which students with learning disabilities, ages 9 and above, rated themselves on several dimensions of learning behavior. The instrument, the *Self-Administered Student Profile,* was made up of quotations gathered from children with learning disabilities. The items represented the categories of Memory, Selective Attention, Visual-Spatial Orientation, Gross Motor Function, Fine Motor Function, Sequential Organization, Language, Academic Performance, Social Interaction, and Overall Working Efficiency.

The most common problems identified by students in this study were in the areas of memory and selective attention. For example, 45 percent of the sample reported: "A lot of times I do things too fast without thinking"; 36 percent said, "It's hard for me to keep my mind on work in school"; and 28 percent said, "I have trouble remembering things the teacher just said a little while ago." In general, there was good agreement between students' reports and those of their teachers, parents, and clinic staff.

Assessment of learning strategies is a relatively new endeavor in special education, and, at present, assessment teams rely primarily on informal techniques if there is interest in evaluating strategies for learning and study skills. The previous paragraphs have provided some suggestions about important factors to consider in designing student observations, interviews, and questionnaires. Upcoming chapters on the assessment of academic skills include additional recommendations for the study of learning strategies as they relate to reading, mathematics, and written language.

 Breakpoint Practice 9.5
Click here to check your understanding of learning strategies.

ANSWERING THE ASSESSMENT QUESTIONS

The assessment team gathers several types of information to describe the student's current specific learning abilities and strategies. Visual and auditory acuity are checked to determine whether a sensory impairment is influencing school performance. In some cases, teachers will complete questionnaires designed to identify students at risk for learning disabilities. The assessment team may compare a student's performance on a broad-range test of achievement with results from a test of intellectual performance to determine if discrepancies exist. In some schools, students with achievement problems will be provided with additional or improved instruction during the prereferral stage, and their progress will be carefully monitored to determine if this level of intervention will result in success. If a discrepancy is identified or students fail to progress when high-quality instruction is provided, specific ability tests may be administered if perceptual-motor skills, memory, or information-processing abilities are of interest. Test batteries assessing several specific abilities may be administered. Results of tests of intellectual performance

may also be considered, if they provide information about specific cognitive abilities. The team may use informal techniques such as observations, questionnaires, and interviews to learn more about learning strategies and study skills.

Types of Procedures

A wide range of assessment techniques is used to study specific learning abilities, learning strategies, and study skills in an attempt to determine if students meet the eligibility criteria for learning disabilities. Because these techniques provide information for several different assessment questions, they are not expected to produce equivalent results. For example, the evaluation of sensory acuity is a separate procedure from the evaluation of specific learning abilities. A student may perform adequately in both of these areas, in neither, or in only one.

Results of specific ability measures are not expected to be equivalent to the findings of informal evaluations of learning strategies and study skills. There are several reasons why. First, students may perform differently in these two areas of functioning. An individual can show adequate specific abilities when these are assessed in isolation but may have difficulty applying them in actual school learning tasks. A student also might compensate for poor specific abilities by developing appropriate learning strategies and study skills.

Second, the types of measures typically used in the evaluation of specific learning abilities are quite different from those used to assess learning strategies and study skills. Most specific ability measures are individual, norm-referenced tests. In contrast, learning strategies and study skills are usually assessed informally. Students are observed while they are engaged in learning activities or are questioned about study strategies through interviews or questionnaires. Such informal techniques do not produce comparative data. For example, if an observation reveals that a student attends to the teacher's lecture in 60 percent of the time intervals sampled, this may or may not indicate typical performance for the student's age and grade.

A third consideration is the directness of the measures. Specific ability tests and student observations are more direct methods of assessment than are interviews and questionnaires used to elicit students' descriptions of their typical learning strategies and study skills. Indirect measures that rely on informants may produce less accurate results than direct assessment of the behaviors under consideration.

Technical quality is a fourth concern. Most specific ability measures are standardized tests, with information available concerning their standardization, reliability, and validity. Most informal learning strategy measures do not have such information. Yet norm-referenced tests are not always preferable to informal strategy assessments. Many of the older norm-referenced measures of specific learning abilities fail to meet minimum criteria for adequate reliability and validity and, thus, should not be used as tools in educational decision making. In many cases, informal measures are the only alternative to technically inadequate tests. Regardless, technical quality is still an important concern. The assessment team should attempt to identify informal techniques that are documented as both reliable and valid.

Nature of the Assessment Tasks

Assessment devices that appear to measure the same skill or ability may, in fact, be measuring quite different factors. This may occur because different test tasks are used for assessment. For example, evaluation of auditory discrimination is the purpose of both the *Goldman-Fristoe-Woodcock Test of Auditory Discrimination* and the *Wepman Auditory Discrimination Test—Second Edition*, but these measures demand different skills. On the Wepman, the student simply listens to the tester read a pair of words. No visual stimuli are presented, and the test is administered in a quiet environment. The student responds by saying whether the words presented were the same or different. In contrast, the *Goldman-Fristoe-Woodcock* uses a taped presentation, and the student hears one word. The student is also shown four pictures and must select the picture that represents the word read on the tape. This test includes two subtests: one in which the listening environment is quiet and the other in which a noisy environment is simulated.

Tests of visual perception may also use dissimilar assessment tasks. For instance, the *Developmental Test of Visual Perception—Third Edition* requires students to draw, whereas the *Motor-Free Visual Perception Test–3* does not. Each of these two tests assesses several areas of visual perception, but only figure–ground perception, spatial relationships, and visual closure are common to both measures.

Several types of assessment tasks evaluate memory. Some emphasize the auditory presentation of information, whereas others stress visual input. The required response mode may be verbal or motor. Most memory tasks assess short-term recall, but the type of information to be recalled varies widely: numbers, words, sentences, shapes, pictures of common objects, photographs of people's faces, and so on. The student may be required to recall in the exact order of presentation, in reverse order, or in no particular order. Because there are important differences between test tasks, it is possible for a student to perform well on one type of memory task and poorly on another.

Documentation of Learning Disabilities

Specific learning abilities and strategies are one major concern of the assessment team as it attempts to answer the question, *Is the school performance problem related to a disability?* The disability condition under consideration in this phase of the assessment process is learning disabilities. Five specific assessment questions are pertinent:

1. What is the status of the student's sensory abilities?
2. Is there a substantial discrepancy between the student's actual achievement and the achievement level expected for that student?
3. What type of progress does the student make when high quality interventions are provided?
4. What is the student's current level of development in specific learning abilities?
5. What is the student's current functioning level in strategies for learning and study skills?

The first question, relating to vision and hearing, is asked for all students referred for special education assessment. The others are most likely to be asked when learning disabilities are suspected. Both question two (discrepancy analysis) and question three (RTI) would be posed during the prereferral stage, before a formal referral was made for special education assessment. Though possible, it is unlikely that both procedures would be used to gather information about the same student. Questions four and five come into play when a referral has been made and the team decides to gather information related to possible learning disabilities.

The assessment team gathers information from many sources to answer these questions. School records are reviewed for results of group measures of school readiness and vision and hearing screenings. Results of ability and achievement tests may be compared, or the team may review results of high-quality interventions provided under an RTI approach in general education. Specific learning abilities are assessed with individual norm-referenced tests, including specific ability measures and tests of intellectual performance. To evaluate learning strategies and study skills, students are observed, or they may complete questionnaires or participate in interviews. Teachers and parents contribute by sharing observations of the student's specific abilities and strategies.

ENHANCEDetext
Video Example 9.5
Watch this video to find out more about answering the assessment questions.

Assessment in Action
Joyce

Joyce, a student in Mr. Harvey's fourth-grade class, has been referred for special education assessment because of concerns about her current classroom functioning. Thus far in the assessment process, it has been established that Joyce has a school performance problem despite having average intellectual performance.

The team will next consider Joyce's specific learning abilities and strategies. The first areas of investigation will be vision and hearing; the team will consult school records to determine the results of the most recent screenings. On the *WISC–V,* Joyce showed low performance on measures of working memory and processing speed. The team will investigate these possible problem areas further by observing Joyce's learning strategies in classroom tasks and by interviewing Joyce and her fourth-grade teacher. For example, Ms. Gale, the special education resource teacher, will observe Joyce's techniques for learning new spelling words and then will interview Joyce about her choice of strategies. In addition, Ms. Gale will administer the *Detroit Tests of Learning Aptitude—Fourth Edition*, a norm-referenced test that assesses several specific learning abilities.

At this point in Joyce's assessment, the team has substantiated the school performance problems noted by Mr. Harvey, Joyce's fourth-grade teacher. It has also been established that Joyce's current intellectual performance is within the average range. The assessment team then moves on to an investigation of specific learning abilities and strategies.

School records are reviewed for the results of Joyce's most recent hearing and vision tests. Both vision and hearing were checked at the beginning of the year when Joyce entered the school district, and no problems were noted. According to Joyce's parents, she has never been treated for a vision or hearing impairment.

The assessment team decides to begin with a discrepancy analysis. The team uses the predicted-achievement method to evaluate the observed difference between Joyce's performance on the *WISC–V* Full Scale, a measure of aptitude, and her performance on the *WIAT–3* Spelling subtest, a measure of achievement. From the analysis results, the team determines that the discrepancy between aptitude and spelling achievement is likely a true difference.

When Joyce was given the *WISC–V,* the assessment team noticed two possible areas of difficulty: the Working Memory and Processing Speed factors. To learn more about Joyce's attention to tasks and memorization strategies, the resource teacher, Ms. Gale, observes Joyce as she studies her new spelling words for the week. No attentional problems are noted. Joyce starts the task immediately and appears to remain on task during the entire study period. However, because she writes slowly, she requires more time to complete the assignment than the other students in the class.

Joyce's assigned task is to study each word and then write it 10 times. Ms. Gale observes that Joyce begins by slowly writing her name on her paper. She then copies five new words from the book to the first line of her paper. Joyce's strategy for writing each word 10 times is this: To write the first word, *home,* she copies the *h* 10 times down her paper, then she copies the *o* 10 times, and so forth, until she has finished that word. She repeats this procedure with each of the new spelling words. After the observation, Ms. Gale talks with Joyce about her study tactics. Joyce says she has always written her spelling words that way because it is quicker. When asked what she did to try to remember how to spell the words, Joyce says she looked at their shapes.

Ms. Gale then interviews Joyce's teacher, Mr. Harvey, who reports that Joyce seems to remember some things, such as math facts, quite well but has difficulty with reading and spelling words. He also mentions that Joyce has problems remembering a series of oral directions. He often has to repeat instructions for her, especially if they contain several steps. Ms. Gale also questions Joyce's teacher about fine-motor skills. According to Mr. Harvey, Joyce prints most of her assignments. Her printing is large, the spacing is poor, and many of the letters are difficult to read.

To gather more information about Joyce's memory and motor skills, Ms. Gale administers the *Detroit Tests of Learning Aptitude—Fourth Edition.* Joyce's overall General Mental Ability Composite on this measure is within the average range of performance. However, her scores fall within the low-average range on the Attention-Enhanced and Motor-Enhanced Composites. She earned her lowest subtest score on Reversed Letters, a measure of short-term memory with a motor component. These test results are in agreement with the results of the informal assessments of specific learning abilities. In addition, because the *DTLA–4* is a norm-referenced measure, these results suggest that Joyce performs memory and motor tasks less well than the majority of her peers.

The assessment team concludes that there is evidence to suggest that Joyce's underachievement is related to poor memory, inefficient memorization strategies, and a possible problem in fine-motor skills. Although learning disabilities seem highly probable, the team will continue its assessment by studying Joyce's classroom behavior and social-emotional status.

SUMMARY

- The term *specific learning abilities* refers to an individual's capacity to participate successfully in certain aspects of the learning task or in certain types of learning. Learning strategies are a newer area of interest. Educators are concerned with the ways that individuals utilize specific learning abilities in situations that require the acquisition of new skills or information. Whereas assessment of specific abilities is essentially a static process, learning strategy assessment is dynamic.

- School records, students, and teachers are three examples of sources of information. School records may provide some clues to a student's past or current levels of functioning. Of particular importance are records of results of periodic vision and hearing screenings. The student is an important participant both in the formal assessment of specific abilities and strategies and in informal assessment. Older students in particular can assist the team by describing their strategies for learning. Teachers have many opportunities to observe the specific learning abilities, strategies, and study skills of students in their classroom.

- The Snellen Chart measures far-distance vision, and results are expressed as a fraction. For instance, the fraction 20/20 indicates normal vision. The numerator of the fraction stands for the distance the individual stands from the chart when reading the letters, and the denominator stands for the distance at which persons with normal vision are able to read the same letters.

- The *Learning Disability Evaluation Scale–Renormed (LDES–R2)* is a questionnaire designed to be completed by teachers, clinical, or other school personnel who are familiar with the student under consideration. Items contain a description of problem behaviors, and the teacher rates the frequency with which these behaviors occur. Items are divided into seven subscales (Listening, Thinking, Speaking, Reading, Writing, Spelling, and Mathematical Calculations).

- In discrepancy analysis for the identification of learning disabilities, the assessment team compares the student's current performance in one or more areas of achievement with that student's expected performance, as measured by current performance on a test of intellectual performance, to determine if there is an important difference between actual and expected achievement. It is also possible to look for discrepancies between areas of achievement (e.g., reading versus mathematics performance), but this approach is much less common.

- The response-to-intervention (RTI) approach, as it is described in IDEA 2004, is based on an examination of the student's ability to profit from high-quality instruction in order to show progress in the school curriculum. Students who show lack of progress despite what the law calls "scientific, research-based intervention" may meet eligibility requirements for the disability of learning disabilities.

- Perception can be defined as the psychological ability to process or use the information received through the senses (Lerner, 2000). Perception depends on the physiological ability of the sense organs to receive information. Visual and auditory acuity are of primary concern to educators, but there is also interest in information received through other senses, particularly tactile and kinesthetic input. Measures of perceptual abilities usually focus on either auditory or visual perception, rather than on the perceptual process as a whole. Among the assessment concerns in visual perception are visual discrimination, figure–ground discrimination, spatial relationships, and form perception (Wallace & McLoughlin, 1979).

- The *DTLA–4* is an individual, norm-referenced test designed to assess a variety of specific cognitive abilities. It is appropriate for students ages 6–0 to 17–11, and it contains 10 subtests. Those are Word Opposites, Design Sequences, Sentence Imitation, Reversed Letters, Story Construction, Design Reproduction, Basic Information, Symbolic Relations, Word Sequences, and Story Sequences.

- In recent years, interest has shifted from the study of isolated specific abilities to consideration of learning strategies. Learning strategies are the methods that students employ when faced with a learning task. Students can be interviewed while they are working on a study task or just after they have completed it. This allows the interviewer to ask specific questions about a particular task. Students simply report their actions rather than attempt to recall or make judgments about their typical behaviors. Some questions that could be asked in situations in which students are learning new information are: Did you begin by looking over the information to be learned? Did you try to organize the information in any way? If so, how did you organize it? Was there anything in the material that you didn't understand? If there was, how did you try to figures it out?

- Assessment devices that appear to measure the same skill or ability may, in fact, be measuring quite different factors. This may occur because different test tasks are used for assessment. For example, evaluation of auditory discrimination is the purpose of both the *Goldman-Fristoe-Woodcock Test of Auditory Discrimination* and the Wepman *Auditory Discrimination Test—Second Edition*, but these measures demand different skills. On the Wepman, the student simply listens to the tester read a pair of words. No visual stimuli are presented, and the test is administered in a quiet environment. The student responds by saying whether the words presented were the same or different. In contrast, the *Goldman-Fristoe-Woodcock* uses a taped presentation, and the student hears one word. The student is also shown four pictures and must select the picture that represents the word read on the tape. This test includes two subtests: one in which the listening environment is quiet and the other in which a noisy environment is simulated.

10

lisafx/123rf/Asset Library

Classroom Behavior and Behavioral Disorders

LEARNING OUTCOMES

After reading this chapter, you will be able to:

- Name and describe the two major approaches to the identification of Behavior disorders in considerations in assessment of classroom behavior.

- List and explain three examples of sources of information about classroom behavior.

- Describe the Behavior Rating Profile—Second Edition in behavior rating scales and checklists.

- Discuss the use of direct observation in the assessment of behavior.

- Explain the purpose of functional behavioral assessment.

- Compare and contrast attention deficit and hyperactivity.

- Describe The *Piers-Harris 2* as a measure of self-concept and peer acceptance.

- Compare and contrast school attitudes and interests.

- Discuss the importance of assessing the learning environment with the ecological approach in the assessment of behavior issues.

- Provide and explain three types of assessment information when answering the assessment questions involved in the assessment of behavior.

KEY TERMS

continuous recording   hyperactivity
sequence analysis   attention-deficit/hyperactivity disorder
functional assessment   sociometric techniques

Some students are referred for special education assessment because their school behavior is judged inappropriate. Such students may be disruptive in class, disturbing instruction. They may be inattentive and/or may show excessive activity. They may be disobedient, unresponsive, or even aggressive. They fail to meet the teacher's expectations for appropriate classroom conduct, and their behavior calls attention to itself. These students may be eligible for special education services if they meet the criteria for the disability of behavioral disorders and if this disability adversely affects school performance. Of course, students with behavioral disorders are not the only ones who exhibit inappropriate classroom behaviors. School conduct problems may also be found in students with mild intellectual disabilities, learning disabilities, or students not identified with any disability.

Problem behaviors are the most obvious concern in assessment of classroom behavior, but there are several other important dimensions. These include the student's self-concept and self-esteem, the student's acceptance by peers, and the student's interests and attitudes toward school. Also important are the characteristics of the classroom learning environment and its effects on the student's ability to behave appropriately. These dimensions of behavior are key considerations for all students referred for special education assessment.

Assessment of classroom behavior starts with a general question: *What is the student's current status in classroom behavior and in social-emotional development?* Answers to this question provide the team with an overall view of the student's current behavioral competence. More specific questions may be asked if preliminary data indicate a need. For example, if the student under study appears to exhibit inappropriate behaviors, the team may ask, *Is there evidence of a severe conduct problem?* and *What are the characteristics of the classroom-learning environment?* The first question helps the team describe the student's current performance, and the second focuses attention on classroom factors that may influence behavior. If self-concept or peer interactions were of concern, the assessment question would be, *What is the student's current status in self-concept and acceptance by peers?* To find out more about the student's perceptions of school and ways to motivate him or her, the team could ask, *What are the student's current interests and attitudes toward school and learning?* For some students, all of these questions are pertinent. With other students, the team may concentrate on one or two areas.

The results of the classroom behavior assessment assist the team in determining eligibility for special education services for individuals with behavioral disorders. Results also provide the basis for designing instructional programs to improve classroom behavior. Specific information is needed for program design, so the assessment tools selected for the study of classroom behavior usually include observation and other informal techniques. Formal, norm-referenced measures may also be used, but informal assessment is stressed. In evaluating Joyce's classroom behavior, for example, the team relied heavily on techniques such as interviews, observations, and inventories.

CONSIDERATIONS IN ASSESSMENT OF CLASSROOM BEHAVIOR

Classroom behavior is a broad term that encompasses a range of nonacademic school behaviors. Included are the student's conduct within the school setting, response to school rules, interpersonal relationships with teachers and other students, and self-concept and attitude toward school. A classroom behavior problem can interfere with academic performance; similarly, poor academic achievement can influence classroom conduct, precipitating inappropriate social behaviors.

Purposes

Classroom behavior and social-emotional development are assessed to gain information about a student's current ability to meet the nonacademic demands of the classroom and other learning environments. The student's classroom behavior is an important consideration when planning instructional programs. It is also of interest in identifying mild disabilities, particularly behavioral disorders.

Students with behavioral disorders are characterized by the seriously inappropriate behaviors they exhibit over time. In federal law, this disability is called emotional disturbance:

(i) *Emotional disturbance* means a condition exhibiting one or more of the following characteristics over a long period of time and to a marked degree that adversely affects a child's educational performance:

(a) An inability to learn, which cannot be explained by intellectual, sensory, or health factors.

(b) An inability to build or maintain satisfactory interpersonal relationships with peers and teachers.

(c) Inappropriate types of behaviors or feelings under normal circumstances.

(d) A general pervasive mood of unhappiness or depression.

(e) A tendency to develop physical symptoms or fears associated with personal or school problems.

(ii) Emotional disturbance includes schizophrenia. The term does not apply to children who are socially maladjusted, unless it is determined that they have an emotional disturbance. (*Federal Register*, 2006, §300.8(c)(4))

To meet eligibility criteria for the disability of serious emotional disturbance, students must show a behavior disorder that is both severe and persistent. In addition, the disorder must act as a negative influence on school performance.

The definition lists several characteristics of behavior disorders; the student must display one or more of these traits. One possible disorder is an inability to learn. Students whose learning problems can be explained by other disabilities are excluded from consideration here. For example, if a student's difficulties in learning can be attributed to an intellectual disability, that student is not considered emotionally disturbed under the "inability to learn" criterion. Other characteristics listed as indicators of emotional disturbance are unsatisfactory interpersonal relationships, inappropriate behavior, depression and other mood disorders, and fears and physical symptoms associated with school and personal problems.

In assessment, two major approaches may be used for identification of behavior disorders. In the first approach, teachers, instructional aides, parents, and others who are well acquainted with the student provide information about the student's current behavioral status. The purpose is to determine whether important persons in the environment perceive the student's behavior as inappropriate. Various assessment strategies are used to gather information from informants: rating scales, checklists, interviews, and questionnaires. Some of these resources provide norms in addition to eliciting informants' judgments. In the second approach, emphasis is on direct observation of the student and the environment in which the student is experiencing difficulty. According to Algozzine, Ruhl, and Ramsey (1991), assessment should consider measureable behavior in the school context.

Direct observation and the questioning of informants are not mutually exclusive. In fact, both are typically used. Teachers and parents point to the existence of a behavior problem, and direct observation allows intensive study of that problem.

Issues and Trends

Many of the issues related to assessment of classroom behavior are tied to issues within the field of behavioral disorders. One basic concern is what to call this disability. *Emotional disturbance* (ED) is the more traditional term and the one used in federal law. However, many educators prefer the term *behavioral disorders* (BD) because it emphasizes behaviors, and behaviors can be changed. The professional organization for educators of students with this disability is the Council for Children with Behavioral Disorders (a division of the Council for Exceptional Children), and the journal it publishes is *Behavioral Disorders.*

Differences in terminology are reflections of theoretical differences. There are several theoretical approaches to the study of behavioral disorders; in each, the disability is viewed in a somewhat different way. As Table 10–1 shows, each theoretical model has its own way of describing disordered behavior, goals for educational intervention, and methods of instruction. Each also approaches assessment differently. For example, the behavioral model holds that behavioral disorders are the result of learning; the student has learned inappropriate behaviors or failed to learn appropriate behaviors. Its focus is on the overt behaviors of the student. In contrast, the ecological approach emphasizes the student's interactions with the environment. Behavioral disorders are seen as problems in interaction, not as a dysfunction within the student. In assessment, both student and environmental characteristics are studied.

Another major issue is definition of the disability. As Shea (1978) observed, the term *behavior disorders* has no shortage of definitions. According to Hallahan and Kauffman (1991), defining this disability is difficult for several reasons. The authors note that differences related to conceptual models and functions of individuals who provide services to children, difficulty in appropriate definitions of mental health and typical behavior, difficulty in measuring behavior and emotion, and coexisting conditions complicate defining behavior disorders.

Deciding if behaviors are inappropriate is a somewhat subjective process. The same behavior may be judged appropriate at one age but not at another. For example, ceaseless activity and exploration are expected of 2-year-olds but not of sixth graders. Culture and gender influence behavioral expectations. What is viewed as normal play among boys may be labeled aggressive in girls. Because it is not possible to set up one standard for normal behavior, it is also difficult to state criteria for disordered behavior, except in severe cases. Obviously, there would be little debate over the inappropriateness of behaviors such as assault or arson.

At present, school practices in the assessment and treatment of behavioral disorders appear to be influenced most by the behavioral model. In this approach, applied behavioral analysis techniques are used to identify behaviors of interest, to observe and measure those behaviors, and then to change them through manipulation of environmental events (Alberto & Troutman, 1990; Cooper, Heron, & Heward, 1987). The ecological perspective has also gained support, at least in assessment (Barnhill, 2005; Swap, 1974; Thurman, 1977). For example, in the functional behavioral assessment approach, there is interest not only in the behavior of the student but also in the influences of the environment in which the student must function (Hanley, 2012).

Current Practices

Classroom behavior is a concern of all teachers, and assessment of student behavior is a regular occurrence in both general and special education. At the classroom level, teachers typically rely on informal techniques such as observation to gather information about student behavior. When assessment is conducted to determine a student's eligibility for special programs, more formal techniques and instruments may be used.

In general, special education assessment begins with the questioning of informants. Most typically, informants are interviewed or asked to complete one of the many available behavioral rating scales or checklists. Many of the commonly used rating scales are formal, normed instruments. This chapter describes several of these rating scales, including the *Behavior Rating*

TABLE 10–1
Theories of Behavioral Disorders

	PSYCHO-ANALYTIC APPROACH	PSYCHO-EDUCATIONAL APPROACH	HUMANISTIC APPROACH	ECOLOGICAL APPROACH	BEHAVIORAL APPROACH
The Problem	A pathological imbalance among the dynamic parts of the mind (id, superego, ego)	Involvement with both underlying psychiatric disorders and readily observable misbehavior and underachievement	Belief that the student is out of touch with his or her own feelings and cannot find fulfillment in traditional educational settings	Belief that the student interacts poorly with the environment; student and environment affect each other reciprocally and negatively	Belief that the student has learned inappropriate responses and failed to learn appropriate ones
Purpose of Educational Practices	Use of psychoanalytic principles to help uncover underlying mental pathology	Concern for unconscious motivation/underlying conflicts and academic achievement/positive surface behavior	Emphasis on enhancing self-direction, self-evaluation, and emotional involvement in learning	Attempt to alter entire social system so that it will support desirable behavior when intervention is withdrawn	Manipulation of student's immediate environment and the consequences of behavior
Characteristics of Teaching Methods	Reliance on individual psychotherapy for student and parents; little emphasis on academic achievement; highly permissive atmosphere	Emphasis on meeting individual needs of the students; reliance on creative projects and creative arts	Use of nontraditional educational settings in which the teacher serves as resource and catalyst rather than as director of activities; nonauthoritarian, open, affective, personal atmosphere	Involvement of all aspects of a student's life, including classroom, family, neighborhood, and community, in teaching useful life and educational skills	Measurement of responses and subsequent analyses of behaviors to change them; emphasis on reward for appropriate behavior

Note: From David P. Hallahan and James M. Kauffman, *Exceptional Children: Introduction to Special Education* (6th ed.), 1994, p. 229. Reprinted with permission of Allyn & Bacon.

Profile—Second Edition, the *Behavior Evaluation Scale–3,* and the *Social Skills Rating System.*

Both formal and informal measures are available to study other aspects of student behavior such as attention disorders and hyperactivity, self-concept, and acceptance by peers. These too are described here. Formal measures are typically selected if the goal of assessment is to determine whether a problem exists. If the goal is to gather information for program planning, informal tools are preferred. Informal techniques are also used to investigate the student's interests and attitudes toward school as well as the classroom learning environment and its effects on student behavior.

As Table 10–2 shows, current practices in the educational assessment of behavior problems incorporate many types of formal measures. However, tests of personality are seldom included. Personality tests are indirect measures, not direct measures of behavior or even attitude or opinion surveys. For example, on projective tests, the student is presented with ambiguous stimuli, and then personality traits are inferred from the student's descriptions of these stimuli. One problem with such measures is their lack of technical adequacy (Taylor, 2000). Another is their lack of educational relevance. Because of these limitations, personality measures are rarely used in schools today.

ENHANCEDetext
Video Example 10.1
Watch this video to find out more about behavior difficulties.

SOURCES OF INFORMATION ABOUT CLASSROOM BEHAVIOR

Several sources can contribute information about the student's current and past classroom behavior: school records, parents, teachers, and the student himself or herself. In addition, the student's peers may be questioned about their perceptions to determine how well the student is accepted by classmates.

School Records

School records may help the team gain a historical perspective of the student's classroom behavior problem. If the problem is long-standing, particular attention should be paid to the results of past interventions.

Discipline and Attendance Records

Educational records usually contain information about school disciplinary actions. For example, if the student has been sent to the principal or vice principal for breaking classroom or school rules, there will likely be a record of the incident and the disciplinary action that resulted. The team should examine these records to determine whether the student has a history of conduct problems. Also, attendance records should be reviewed for information about truancy, chronic tardiness, and excessive school absences. If the student has come into conflict with the law, school records may contain information about the charges and their disposition (probation, referrals for counseling or other services, jail sentences, and so forth). In addition, the team should take special note of any information about reported incidents of child abuse, alcohol or substance abuse, or attempted suicide.

Observations of Former Teachers

The student's former teachers may have left some written records of their observations of the student's classroom behavior. The team should consider report cards from previous years, copies of letters from teachers to parents, and any past referrals for special education assessment.

TABLE 10–2
Formal Measures of Classroom Behavior and Related Concerns

NAME (AUTHORS)	AGES OR GRADES
Classroom Behavior and Social-Emotional Development	
BASC-3 (Behavior Assessment System for Children, Third Edition) (Reynolds & Kamphaus, 2015)	Ages 2–0 to 21–11
Behavior Evaluation Scale–Fourth Edition (McCarney & Arthaud, 2014)	Ages 4 to 18
Behavior Rating Profile—Second Edition (Brown & Hammill, 1990)	Grades 1–12 and ages 6–6 to 18–6
Behavioral and Emotional Rating Scale-2 (Epstein & Sharma, 2004)	Ages 5–0 to 18–11
Burks' Behavior Rating Scales-2 (Burks & Gruber, 2006)	Ages 4 to 18
Child Behavior Checklist (Achenbach, 2001)	Ages 6 to 18
Comprehensive Behavior Rating Scale for Children (Neeper, Lahey, & Frick, 1990)	Ages 6 to 14
Devereux Behavior Rating Scales–School Form (Naglieri, LeBuffe, & Pfeiffer, 1993)	Ages 5 to 18
Emotional and Behavior Problem Scale–Second Edition (McCarney & Arthaud, 2001)	Ages 5 to 18
Mooney Problem Check Lists (Mooney & Gordon, 1950)	Grades 7–12 and college
Revised Behavior Problem Checklist (Quay & Peterson, 1987, 1996)	Grades K–8 regular class; grades K–12 special class
Scale for Assessing Emotional Disturbance-2 (Epstein & Cullinan, 2010)	Ages 5 to 18
School Behavior Checklist (Miller, 1977)	Ages 4 to 13
School Social Skills Rating Scale (Brown, Black, & Downs, 1984)	School ages
Social Skills Rating System (Gresham & Elliott, 1990)	Ages 3–0 to 4–11 and grades K–12
Social-Emotional Dimension Scale-2 (Hutton & Roberts, 2004)	Ages 6–0 to 18–11
Vineland Social-Emotional Early Childhood Scales (Sparrow, Balla, & Cicchetti, 1998)	Ages birth to 6
Walker Problem Behavior Identification Checklist, Revised (Walker, 1983)	Ages 2 to 5 and grades K–6
Attention Disorders and Hyperactivity	
Attention-Deficit Disorders Evaluation Scale–Fourth Edition (McCarney & Arthaud, 2013)	Ages 4 to 18
Attention-Deficit/Hyperactivity Disorder Test-2 (Gilliam, 2015	Ages 5 to 17
BASC Flex Monitor (Reynolds & Kamphaus, 2016)	Ages 2–0 to 18–11
Children's Attention and Adjustment Survey (Lambert, Hartsough, & Sandoval, 1990)	Grades K–5
Self-Concept	
Conners' Rating Scales–3 (Conners, 2008)	Ages 6 to 18
Coopersmith Self-Esteem Inventories (Coopersmith, 1981)	Ages 8 to adult
Culture-Free Self-Esteem Inventories—Third Edition (Battle, 2002)	Grades 2–9 and ages 6–0 to 18–11
Multidimensional Self Concept Scale (Bracken, 1992)	Grades 5–12
Piers-Harris Children's Self Concept Scale—Second Edition (Piers & Herzberg, 2002)	Grades 2–12 and ages 7 to 18

TABLE 10–2 *continued*

NAME (AUTHORS)	AGES OR GRADES
Dimensions of Self-Concept (Michael, Smith, & Michael, 1984)	Grades 4–12 and college
Self-Esteem Index (Brown & Alexander, 1991)	Ages 8–0 to 18–11
Student Self-Concept Scale (Gresham, Elliott, & Evans-Fernandez, 1992)	Grades 3–12
Tennessee Self-Concept Scale—Second Edition (Fitts & Warren, 1996)	Ages 7 through adult
Peer Acceptance	
Behavior Rating Profile—Second Edition (Brown & Hammill, 1990)	Grades 1–12 and ages 6–6 to 18–6
Peer Attitudes toward the Handicapped Scale (Bagley & Greene, 1981)	Grades 4–8

Past Services

Also of interest are any services that the student received in relation to behavioral problems. For example, the student may have received school counseling services, or the school may have suggested counseling services to the student's family. If records are available, the team should attempt to determine the types of services provided and the effects of those services on the student's behavior.

The Student

The student assists in the assessment of classroom behavior by participating in observations and by answering questions about current behavior, attitudes, and perceptions.

Current Classroom Behavior

Direct observation of student behavior is one of the most valuable techniques for gathering data about classroom conduct. The student's role in this assessment technique is simply to behave as usual. This is facilitated if the observer takes care not to call attention to the observation process or to the particular student under study.

Current Attitudes and Perceptions

The student can also participate by acting as an informant about his or her own behavior and attitudes. For instance, some behavior rating scales are designed to be completed by students, allowing them to rate their own behaviors. In the assessment of self-concept, interests, and attitudes toward school, students are the primary source of information. They may complete interest inventories, talk about their attitudes about school and learning, or reply to questions on measures of self-concept.

Teachers

Teachers have the best opportunity of all professionals to observe and evaluate the student's day-to-day behavior in the classroom. Teachers are also an excellent source of information about the characteristics of the classroom-learning environment.

Observations of Current Behavior

Behavioral rating scales and checklists are often used to gather information from teachers about student behavior. These measures allow teachers to share their observations of the student's typical behavior patterns and their judgments about the appropriateness of the student's classroom conduct. Interviews are also useful for eliciting teachers' opinions, particularly about environmental factors that may precipitate behavioral problems.

Characteristics of the Learning Environment

Teachers can provide firsthand information about the characteristics of their classroom. Among the major considerations are the teacher's rules for classroom conduct, strategies for rewarding appropriate behavior, and standard disciplinary techniques. Because there may be wide variations among the behavioral demands of different classrooms, it is important to consider the teacher's standards when interpreting his or her reports of problem behaviors.

Peers

Peers are usually not participants in special education assessment, but in the area of classroom behavior, they can contribute information about the student's social acceptance and interpersonal relationships.

Peer Acceptance and Interactions

Peers can be involved in the assessment process in two major ways. The first area of interest is the general attitudes of typical peers toward students with learning and behavior problems. These attitudes can be surveyed through interviews or with a questionnaire designed for this purpose. Such instruments provide information about peer attitudes toward students with disabilities in general. To find out about acceptance of a particular student, it is necessary to use sociometric techniques, another assessment strategy. These techniques sample students' opinions about the peers with whom they would like to work and play. The results provide a picture of the social interactions within a classroom, identifying students who are and are not accepted by their classmates.

Parents

Parents may be unfamiliar with classroom behavior, but they can discuss their child's behavior in the home and other nonschool settings.

Observations of Current Behavior

A student with classroom behavior problems may or may not act inappropriately at home. The same types of inappropriate behavior could occur both at school and at home; the student could show a different set of problem behaviors at home; or home behavior could be acceptable. Parents can discuss their observations of their child's typical conduct and any concerns they might have. They can describe what approaches they have used in trying to improve problem behaviors and the results of these efforts. If the problem is long-standing, parents may be able to share information about intervention programs in which the child and, perhaps, the family have participated.

Characteristics of the Home Environment

Because the rules for behavior at home may be quite different from school demands, parents should be asked to describe the behavioral expectations they hold for their child. Also of interest are their strategies for encouraging appropriate behavior and discouraging inappropriate behavior. What type of discipline system is used in the home? What consequences does the child face for breaking the rules? The child's parents can also provide information about family makeup. Are both parents present in the home? Does the child have brothers and sisters? Are there other individuals or family members living in the home as part of the family? In addition, the assessment team should be alert to any major changes or stresses within the family such as divorce, unemployment, or the protracted illness or death of a family member. Such changes affect family dynamics and may have an influence on the student's ability to behave appropriately in school.

 Breakpoint Practice 10.1
Click here to check your understanding of sources of information regarding behavior.

BEHAVIOR RATING SCALES AND CHECKLISTS

A wide variety of rating scales and checklists are available for assessing classroom behavior. These measures vary in several ways: the age of the student to be rated, the person or persons used as informants, the types of behaviors included on the scale, and the scores produced. The following sections describe scales that focus on in-school behaviors.

Behavior Rating Profile—Second Edition

The *Behavior Rating Profile—Second Edition (BRP–2)* is an interesting norm-referenced measure because it attempts to provide a comprehensive picture of the student's current behavioral status. Information

> ## BEHAVIOR RATING PROFILE—SECOND EDITION (BRP–2)
>
> ### L. L. Brown & D. D. Hammill (1990)
>
> **Type:** Norm-referenced teacher rating scale, parent rating scale, student checklist, and sociogram
>
> **Major Content Areas:** School behavior, home behavior, and interpersonal relationships
>
> **Type of Administration:** Individual for teachers, parents, and students; group for peers
>
> **Administration Time:** 10–15 minutes for teachers, 20 minutes for parents, 15–30 minutes for students, 15 minutes for peers
>
> **Age/Grade Levels:** Ages 6–6 to 18–6, grades 1–12
>
> **Types of Scores:** Standard scores, percentile ranks
>
> **Computer Aids:** N/A
>
> **Typical Uses:** Identification of students with possible behavioral disorders who may be in need of further assessment
>
> **Cautions:** On the *Student Rating Scales* some students may require assistance in reading the checklist items
>
> **Publisher:** PRO-ED (*www.proedinc.com*)

can be gathered from four types of informants—students themselves, teachers, parents, and peers—to assess the student's performance in the home, at school, and in interpersonal relationships.

The *BRP–2* is made up of four measures that correspond to the different types of informants. The self-rating scale, called the *Student Rating Scales,* is composed of 60 items. One-third of the items are concerned with school behaviors, one-third with home behaviors, and one-third with peer interactions. For instance, "I often break rules set by my parents" is a home item, whereas "I can't seem to concentrate in class" is a school item. The student reads each item and checks whether it is true or false. If necessary, the tester may read the questions aloud to the student and explain the meaning of unknown words.

The *Teacher Rating Scale* is made up of 30 descriptions of school behaviors. The teacher reads each item and determines whether the description is "very much like the student," "like the student," "not much like the student," or "not at all like the student." An example of an item on the teacher scale is "The student doesn't follow class rules." The manual recommends that the student be present in the classroom at least a month before teacher or peer ratings are taken.

The *Parent Rating Scale* is quite similar to the teacher scale, except that it contains descriptions of home behaviors (e.g., "My child is shy; clings to parents"). Each description is rated as "very much like my child," "like my child," "not much like my child," or "not at all like my child." The *Parent Rating Scale* can be completed by the child's mother or father (or other caregivers), or both parents can rate their child independently.

The peer portion of the *BRP–2* is not a rating scale. Instead, a sociometric technique is used, and the student's classmates are asked questions such as "Which of the students in your class would you most (least) like to . . .?" Several sets of questions are available, each tapping a different aspect of interpersonal relationships. For example, students can name the peers they would most like to have as friends. According to the *BRP–2* manual, a minimum of 20 peers must participate for scoring to be accurate.

As Figure 10–1 illustrates, results from the *BRP–2* can be plotted on a profile. Standard scores are produced by each of the rating scales and the sociograms, and percentile ranks are also available. Standard scores are distributed with a mean of 10 and a standard deviation of 3; the range of average performance is standard score 7

BRP-2

Behavior Rating Profile
Second Edition

PROFILE AND RECORD FORM

Section I. Identifying Information

Student's Name MICKEY R.

Parents'/Guardians' Names SARAH ; MICHEAL R.

School GOLDWYN MIDDLE SCHOOL Grade 6

Teacher's Name/Subject Taught D. ROSE - HOMEROOM
E. ARDENE - LANGUAGE ART
M. BLUNDEN - P.E.

Examiner's Name B. HARTLEY

Examiner's Title DIAGNOSTICIAN

	Year	Month
Date of BRP-2 Testing	89	3
Student's Date of Birth	77	8
Student's Age at Testing	11	7

Section II. Results of the BRP-2

	Raw Score	PR	SS	SEm
Student Rating Scales: Home	8	9	6	1
Student Rating Scales: School	7	9	6	1
Student Rating Scales: Peer	10	25	8	1
Teacher Rating Scale/Teacher #1	7	.4	2	1
Teacher Rating Scale/Teacher #2	7	.4	2	1
Teacher Rating Scale/Teacher #3	11	1	3	1
Parent Rating Scale/Mother	14	.1	1	1
Parent Rating Scale/Father	9	.1	1	1
Sociogram/Question #1	8	63	11	1
Sociogram/Question #2	10	63	11	1
Sociogram/Question #3	10	63	11	1

Section III. Results of Other Tests

	Test Name	Date of Testing	Equivalent Quotient
1.	IPC	3/89	89
2.	DTLA-2	2/89	92
3.	DAB TOTAL	2/89	80
4.			
5.			

Section IV. Profile of Scores

Standard Scores: Mean = 10. Standard Deviation = 3

FIGURE 10–1

Sample Behavior Rating Profile–Second Edition Results

Note: From *Behavior Rating Profile* (2nd ed.) (p. 27) by L. L. Brown and D. D. Hammill, 1990, Austin, TX: PRO-ED. Copyright 1990 by PRO-ED. Reprinted by permission.

through 13. Several scores are available from the *BRP–2,* depending on which of the scales were administered. If the student under study completed the *Student Rating Scales,* three separate scores are reported: Home, School, and Peer. There is one score for each teacher who rated the student and one for each parent. Also, each sociometric question answered by the student's peers produces a score. Data can be gathered from all of these sources, or, depending on the purposes of assessment, only one portion of the *BRP–2* can be selected for administration.

The *BRP–2* was standardized on approximately 2,500 general education students, 1,500 teachers, and 2,000 parents from 26 states. The internal consistency of the scales appears adequate, as does the test-retest reliability (with the exception of the *Student Rating Scales* for grades 1 and 2 students). The standard error of measurement is low. On the parent, teacher, and student scales, standard error ranges from .4 to 1.6 standard score points over all grade levels.

Concurrent validity was studied by examining the relationships between *BRP–2* scores and results from other rating scales. In general, *BRP–2* results were found to be consistent with those from other measures. The diagnostic validity of the *BRP–2* was investigated by comparing the ratings of five groups of students, and different group profiles emerged. Normal students and those identified as gifted achieved higher scores than did students with disabilities. Among students with disabilities, the lowest scores were earned by students with intellectual disabilities, followed by students identified as emotionally disturbed. The scores of students with learning disabilities fell between those of normal students and the scores of students with emotional disturbance.

The *BRP–2* appears to be a reliable and valid tool for gathering information from a range of informants about perceptions of a student's behavior in several different ecologies. It is one of the few instruments that allows students to rate themselves and that involves peers in the assessment process.

Other Measures That Use Informants

Two other measures of behavior of interest to educators are the *Behavior Evaluation Scale–4* (McCarney & Arthaud, 2014) and the *Social Skills Rating System* (Gresham & Elliott, 1990).

Behavior Evaluation Scale–4

The *BES–4* is a potentially useful measure because it is linked to the federal definition of emotional disturbance. There are four variations of this measure: Long and Short versions, each of which include both Home and School scales. The Long version of the rating form for parents is also available in Spanish.

The Long version of the *BES–4* is designed for school use. Appropriate for grades pre-K through 12, this instrument contains 76 descriptions of student behaviors, and teachers rate each behavior according to the frequency with which it occurs. There are seven choices ranging from "not personally observed or is developmentally advanced for age group" to "continuously throughout the day."

The *BES–4* is designed to gather information about the five types of behavior disorders described in federal law. Each item on the scale relates to one of these disorders, and results are available for five subscales: Learning Problems, Interpersonal Difficulties, Inappropriate Behavior, Unhappiness/Depression, and Physical Symptoms/Fears. Separate norms for males and females are available for both age and grade. Subscale standard scores are distributed with a mean of 10 and a standard deviation of 3; an overall score called the Behavior Quotient is distributed with a mean of 100 and a standard deviation of 15. The *BES–4* manual recommends that only professionals who are familiar with the student's patterns of behavior be selected as raters. Thus, the informant might be the teacher with primary instructional responsibility for the student; with secondary students, more than one teacher should complete the scale.

The *BES–4* School Version was standardized with 2,446 students from 16 states. This standardization sample appears to represent the national population in race. Test-retest, interrater, and internal consistency reliabilities of the *BES–4* are adequate. Validity is supported by studies of the relationship of *BES–4* results with those from other measures; in addition, the scale appears to differentiate between students with identified behavioral disorders and normally achieving students.

BEHAVIOR EVALUATION SCALE–4 (BES–4), LONG SCHOOL VERSION

S. B. McCarney & T. J. Arthaud (2014)

Type: Norm-referenced teacher rating scale

Major Content Areas: The characteristics of serious emotional disturbance as identified in federal law (e.g., inability to learn, inability to build or maintain satisfactory interpersonal relationships)

Type of Administration: Individual

Administration Time: 15–20 minutes for rating scale

Age/Grade Levels: Grades pre-K–12

Types of Scores: Standard scores and percentiles for each subscale; overall quotient and percentile rank

Computer Aids: *BES–4:L Quick Score*

Typical Uses: Identification of strengths and weaknesses in the behavioral domains described in federal law

Publisher: Hawthorne Educational Services (*www.hes-inc.com*)

Social Skills Rating System

The *SSRS* has three levels to accommodate children from age 3 through students in grade 12. The preschool level (ages 3–0 to 4–11) includes a parent and a teacher rating scale. At the elementary level (grades K–6), there are three scales: one for parents, one for teachers, and a third for students in grades 3–6. The secondary level (grades 7–12) provides rating scales for parents, teachers, and students.

On each of the instruments, the informant reads descriptions of behavior, then rates each according to the frequency with which it occurs ("never," "sometimes," or "very often"). On all scales except the elementary student scale, informants also identify the importance of each behavior ("not important," "important," "critical"). Informants should know the student well and be able to read at the grade 3 level. Instructions and items can be read aloud to students with reading problems.

There is some variation in the behaviors assessed by the various instruments. Parents are asked to consider two behavioral domains: social skills and problem behaviors. Teachers, in contrast, rate three domains: social skills, problem behaviors, and academic competence. Students rate themselves only on social skills. Results for

each scale (Social Skills, Problem Behaviors, and Academic Competence) are expressed in standard scores (mean = 100, SD = 15) and percentile ranks. Separate results are obtained for each rater.

Two of the scales are divided into subscales so that professionals can compare the frequency with which different types of behaviors occur. The Social Skills subscales are Cooperation, Assertion, Responsibility, Empathy, and Self-Control. Subscales for Problem Behaviors are Externalizing, Internalizing, and Hyperactivity. Frequency of behavior is described as "more," "average," or "fewer." The manual defines "average" using one standard deviation as a ruler. With Social Skills, higher frequencies are desirable; with Problem Behaviors, lower frequencies are desirable. Results are entered for all raters on the Graphic Profile Summary so that comparisons can be made across subscales and across parent, teacher, and student informants.

An interesting feature of the *SSRS* is its attempt to link assessment with instruction. In fact, the summary protocol is called the Assessment-Intervention Record. In addition to considering scale and subscale results, the assessment team is directed to analyze responses to individual rating scale items to identify possible instructional targets. Four types of items are of interest: social

SOCIAL SKILLS RATING SYSTEM (SSRS)

F. M. Gresham & S. N. Elliott (1990)

Type: Norm-referenced teacher rating scale, parent rating scale, and student rating scale

Major Content Areas: Social skills, problem behaviors, and academic competence

Type of Administration: Individual

Administration Time: 15–20 minutes for teachers and students, approximately 20 minutes for parents

Age/Grade Levels: Preschool (ages 3 to 5), Elementary (grades K–6), and Secondary (grades 7–12) forms for parents and teachers; Elementary (grades 3–6) and Secondary (grades 7–12) forms for students

Types of Scores: Standard scores, percentile ranks for scales; for each subscale, classification of social skills and problem behaviors by frequency

Computer Aids: *SSRS ASSIST*

Typical Uses: Identification of strengths and weaknesses in social skill development

Cautions: Grade 3 reading level is required; however, items can be read to students. The student standardization sample appears to differ from the national population in several ways, including underrepresentation of Hispanic students. Reliability falls below acceptable levels on some subscales; of particular concern is the test-retest reliability of the elementary grade student instrument.

Publisher: Pearson Assessments (*pearsonassessments.com*)

skills strengths, social skills performance deficits, social skills acquisition deficits, and problem behaviors. In social skills, only those items identified by the rater as "important" or "critical" are considered. Strengths are behaviors that occur "very often." Performance deficits refer to behaviors that occur "sometimes," and acquisition deficits to those that "never" occur. With problem behaviors, those that occur "very often" are of interest.

The *SSRS* was standardized on approximately 4,000 students, 1,000 parents, and 300 teachers from 18 states. Students who spend at least 75 percent of their time in special education classes made up 17 percent of the sample (*n* = 219). Separate norms are available on the *SSRS* by age and by gender; separate norms for students with disabilities are provided on the elementary teacher scale. However, the student sample appears different from the national population in several respects. When compared to the nation as a whole, the student standardization sample contains more students with disabilities, fewer Hispanic students (6.1 percent versus 11.5 percent

for the nation), fewer students from the Northeast and West, and fewer rural students.

Internal consistency and test-retest reliabilities are generally adequate for scale and subscale results on the teacher instruments. The parent and student instruments, however, show reliability coefficients below .80 on several subscales. Of particular concern is test-retest reliability for the elementary grade student instrument; the coefficient for the total scale is .68, and those for the subscales range from .52 to .66. The validity of the *SSRS* is supported by correlations between its results and those from other rating scales.

Comparison of Behavior Rating Scales and Checklists

The *BRP–2*, the *BES–4*, and the *SSRS* are but three of the many behavior rating scales and checklists available, as were shown in Table 10–2. Most of these measures are designed for school-aged populations, particularly elementary grade students. Measures for preschool children are much more rare; among those available are the

Social Skills Rating System and the *Vineland Social-Emotional Early Childhood Scales* (Sparrow et al., 1998).

Most behavior rating scales and checklists use teachers, or teachers and parents, as informants. The student and peers are involved less often. Exceptions are the *Behavior Rating Profile—Second Edition,* which includes teachers, parents, students, and peers, and the *Social Skills Rating System,* which includes teachers, parents, and students. Another exception is *BASC-3 (Behavior Assessment System for Children)* (Reynolds & Kamphaus, 2015), although its self-report is designed to assess personality traits rather than behavior.

Measures also vary on the types of behaviors they ask informants to consider and the theoretical frameworks used to interpret behavioral ratings. For example, the research instrument developed by Quay and Peterson (1987, 1996), the *Revised Behavior Problem Checklist,* classifies student behaviors according to six domains: Conduct Disorder, Socialized Aggression, Attention Problems-Immaturity, Anxiety-Withdrawal, Psychotic Behavior, and Motor Excess. Gresham (1982) reports that the *BPC* is the teacher rating scale with the strongest base of empirical support.

The *Child Behavior Checklist* (Achenbach, 1991) organizes behaviors into internalizing (e.g., anxious/depressed, withdrawn) and externalizing (e.g., attention problems, aggressive behavior). The Achenbach System of Empirically Based Assessment (Achenbach & Reescorla, 2001) is the updated version of the Child Behavior Checklist. It is available in 58 languages and consists of a Preschool form (18 months through 5 years), the Teacher-Completed Form and the Parent-Completed Form (6 through 18 years of age), and the Youth Self-Report (11 through 18 years of age). The system includes a Direct Observation Form and Profile for conducting child and youth interviews. It is a very detailed and well-researched behavioral evaluation system (Beyda Lorie, 2010).

The Teacher-Completed Form, which takes 15 to 20 minutes to complete, includes 113 items (including a section related to adaptive behaviors). Items are scored (0–2) across eight syndrome scales: Withdrawn/Depressed, Anxious/Depressed, Somatic Complaints, Rule-Breaking Behavior, Social Problems, Thought Problems, Aggressive Behavior, and Attention Problems. In addition, all forms have DSM-oriented scales.

Standard scores include T-scores and percentile ranks for each syndrome and DSM-oriented scale. Gender scores are also available. Normative data were based on a large, nationally representative sample. Reliability information includes test-retest, interrater, and internal consistency. Content, construct, concurrent, and discriminative validity data are also available.

The *BASC-3* addresses both externalizing and internalizing problems as well as school problems, other problems, and adaptive skills. This test was designed to measure positive and maladaptive behaviors. The BASC-3 consists of teacher (TRS), parent (PRS) and student (SRP) forms. The teacher and parent forms take approximately 10 to 20 minutes to complete and measure three available age groups, while the student form takes about 30 minutes and has three different age-group options. Three age groups for teacher and parent forms include 2 through 5 (preschool), 6 through 11 (child), and 12 through 21 years (adolescent). The three age groups for self-report include 8 through 11 (child), 12 through 21 (adolescent), and 18 through 25 (college). The parent and student forms are also available in Spanish.

Clinical Scales, Adaptive Scales, Composites, Content Scales, and Clinical Indexes are available with this test. Clinical Scale items include Hyperactivity, Aggression, Conduct Problems, Anxiety, Depression, Somatization, Attention Problems, Learning Problems, Atypicality and Withdrawal. Adaptive Scale items include Activities of Daily Living, Adaptability, Social Skills, Leadership, Study Skills, and Functional Communication. The forms measure IDEA, as well as, DSM 5 classifications. Standardized T scores and percentiles are available for the BASC-3.

Normative sample appears adequate, as age, gender, ethnicity, geographic region, residence, and parent education characteristics were provided. The manual includes adequate internal consistency, test-retest, and interrater reliability. Content, criterion-related, construct, and concurrent validity information is also adequate. BASC-3

Intervention Guide and Materials are available (Vannest, Reynolds, & Kamphaus, 2013).

The purpose of some measures is the assessment of personality rather than behavior disorders. For example, the *Burks' Behavior Rating Scales* (Burks & Gruber, 2006) is intended to measure cluster items into seven scales, such as Disruptive Behavior, Emotional Problems, Social Withdrawal, Ability Deficits, Physical Deficits, Weak Self-Confidence, and Attention and Impulse Control Problems. At the other extreme are measures such as the *Behavior Rating Profile—Second Edition* and the *Behavior Evaluation Scale–4* that focus on observable behaviors.

Many behavior rating scales and checklists are available to screen students with possible behavioral disorders, so it is necessary to select the most appropriate measure for the assessment task at hand. Psychometric quality, theoretical characteristics, the type of informants consulted, and the age and grade of the student must be considered. In addition, there may be considerable overlap among the factors measured by similar teacher scales; one teacher rating scale or checklist is usually sufficient. If adaptive behavior has been assessed, results should be reviewed because adaptive behavior measures often include questions about student behavior, interpersonal relationships, and social-emotional development.

ENHANCEDetext
Video Example 10.2
Watch this video to find out more about behavior disorders.

DIRECT OBSERVATION

Behavior rating scales and checklists provide preliminary information about student conduct problems. Like teacher and parent interviews, they are screening techniques. Further study is needed for two reasons. First, rating scales, checklists, and interviews rely on informants rather than direct evaluation of student behavior. Direct measures are needed to substantiate the existence of a behavioral problem. Second, the results of many screening measures are too general to assist in program planning.

Direct observation of student behavior is the recommended procedure for in-depth study of the possible problem behaviors identified by rating scales, checklists, and interviews. Observation is a versatile assessment technique that can be used to study any type of student behavior—appropriate or inappropriate, academic or social, at home or at school. In the assessment of school behavior problems, data are gathered about the frequency and/or duration of specific student behaviors within the classroom-learning environment. The assessment team may decide to use direct observation to describe the student's behavior problems or as the basis for a functional assessment of those problems.

The first step in planning an observation is to decide which behavior will be studied. It is possible to observe and record all of the behaviors that a student displays within a certain time period, but observations usually focus on one or more specific behaviors. Results of rating scales, checklists, and teacher and parent interviews may suggest possible behaviors of concern. These sources are most useful for identifying possible inappropriate behaviors because they tend to focus on classroom conduct problems. In classroom observations, it is also important to consider the student's academic behaviors. Wallace and Kauffman (1986) have identified four significant classes of academic behavior: (1) accepting tasks provided by the teacher, (2) completing tasks within a reasonable amount of time, (3) working neatly and accurately, and (4) participating in group activities.

Because observation involves the examination of student behaviors within the context of the natural environment, it produces information that often cannot be obtained from any other type of assessment procedure. According to Borich (1999), the least structured type of observation is the narrative report. In narrative reporting, the observer simply describes events in writing. The description may be of one type of event or incident (anecdotal record) or of a sequence of events (ethnographic record). In anecdotal recording, the observer is interested in a specific type of event (Oosterhof, 2003). For example, a teacher might keep written records of a student's outbursts in class. In ethnographic recording, the observer attempts to describe everything that is occurring. For instance, a teacher observing a lesson in a colleague's classroom would attempt to record not only the actions of the teacher but also those of individual students. Both types of narrative reporting are relatively easy to carry out. However, interpretation of results is difficult because descriptions are often subjective.

Systematic observation techniques help the teacher in specifying, recording, and analyzing student behaviors. In the most basic type of systematic observation, the teacher observes and records all the behaviors a student exhibits during some set time period. In contrast to narrative reporting, the teacher is concerned with specific student behaviors rather than more global events. This technique, called **continuous recording** or narrative recording (Cooper, 1981), provides preliminary information to help the teacher determine if there is a problem that requires further study. For example, Figure 10–2 presents the record of a continuous observation of Leticia's behavior. The teacher decided to conduct this observation because Leticia seemed to be out of her seat "constantly" during times when she was expected to work at her desk. However, in analyzing the results of the observation, Leticia left her seat only five times in the half-hour period, and all of her excursions had reasonable purposes.

Sequence analysis is a second observational technique that is useful for gaining an overall picture of a student's performance (Sulzer-Azaroff & Mayer, 1977). As with continuous recording, the teacher observes and records all of the student's behaviors within a specified time period. In addition, an attempt is made to record the events or actions preceding and following each behavior. Identification of the antecedents and consequences of a student's behaviors provides information about how events in the environment may

---

Student: Leticia   Date: January 8, 2008

Observer: Ms. Brown

Classroom Activity: Independent seatwork

Reason for Observation: Leticia seems to be out of her seat constantly when she should be at her seat working on her worksheet.

Time	Event
11:00–11:02	Leticia comes in from the playground, goes directly to her desk, and sits
11:02–11:05	Leticia sits while teacher hands out and explains spelling worksheet
11:05–11:08	Leticia gets pencil from desk, reads worksheet
11:08–11:09	Leticia begins to write, breaks pencil
11:09–11:13	Leticia gets up, walks to pencil sharpener, sharpens pencil, returns to seat
11:13–11:18	Leticia writes on worksheet
11:18–11:20	Leticia drops pencil on floor, gets up, picks up pencil, returns to seat
11:20–11:25	Leticia writes on worksheet
11:25–11:27	Leticia gets up, places worksheet in folder on teacher's desk
11:27–11:28	Leticia returns to seat, puts pencil in desk, looks around room
11:28–11:30	Leticia gets up, walks to teacher's desk, asks teacher if she can get a drink of water, teacher tells Leticia to return to her seat
11:30	Leticia begins to return to seat, lunch bell rings

FIGURE 10–2
Continuous Observation

TABLE 10–3
Sequence Analysis

TIME	ANTECEDENT	BEHAVIOR	CONSEQUENCE
8:45	Teacher asks working group who would like to demonstrate part one of a project.	Andy raises two fingers.	Teacher asks Joe to demonstrate part one of project.
8:48	Teacher asks the working group a question regarding the material.	Andy pounds on desk.	Teacher warns Andy to use appropriate behavior or a privilege will be taken away.
8:50	Teacher asks working group who would like to demonstrate part two of a project and reminds group members to raise hand.	Andy raises hand.	Teacher praises Andy and asks him to demonstrate part two of the project.

influence the student's actions. Consider the sequence analysis of John's classroom behavior in Table 10–3. Few conclusions can be drawn if only the student's actions are considered. However, when antecedents and consequences are taken into account, a more complete picture of the instructional interaction emerges. John's hand-raising behavior appears to be influenced by the actions of the teacher.

Continuous recording and sequence analysis are most often used in the initial stages of assessment to determine if a student's behavior merits further study. They provide a global picture of the student's actions in relationship to situational variables and assist the teacher in selecting specific behaviors that require intervention. However, they are time-consuming procedures and are best considered as screening tools to identify specific student behaviors for further observation.

As soon as a particular behavior or set of behaviors has been selected for study, plans can be made for conducting an observation focusing on these specific behaviors. The teacher follows several steps.

Describe the Behavior to Be Observed

First, the behavior or behaviors of interest are clearly and precisely described. This facilitates communication among persons conducting the observation and allows for discussion of results with the student, parents, and concerned professionals.

To conduct an observation, the behaviors must be both observable and measurable. A behavior is considered observable if its performance can be detected by an outside observer; "understanding the reading assignment" is not an observable behavior but "writing answers to comprehension questions" is. Descriptions of observable behaviors usually contain an action verb. Verbs such as *write, point to, name,* and *throw* describe actions that an observer can see or hear; verbs such as *understand, know, appreciate,* and *perceive* do not.

Behaviors that have clearly definable beginnings and endings are discrete behaviors; examples are writing spelling words and reading a paragraph aloud. Counting their frequency or timing their duration measures discrete behaviors. Some behaviors are not discrete; for example, it is difficult to detect the precise starting and ending points of behaviors such as staying on task and swearing in the classroom. Nondiscrete behaviors are also measurable because during any given time period an observer can determine whether a student is displaying the behavior.

Select a Measurement System

If the behavior of interest is a discrete behavior, it is possible to measure its frequency, its duration, or both. *Frequency* refers to the number of times a behavior occurs; for example, the teacher may be interested in the frequency with which Joe completes math assignments. *Duration* is a measure of

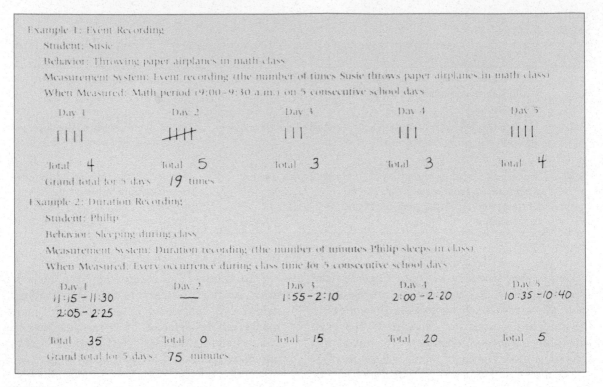

FIGURE 10–3
Observing Discrete Behaviors: Event and Duration Recording

the length of a behavior—that is, how long it lasts in terms of seconds, minutes, or hours. For instance, if punctuality is a concern, information can be collected on the number of minutes late Seng arrives to class each day. Or a parent may have identified a young child's tantruming behavior as a target for observation; for this behavior, it may be important to consider both duration and frequency.

The following measurement systems are used to collect data about discrete behaviors (Alberto & Troutman, 1990):

- *Event recording.* The frequency of the behavior is noted in event recording. The observer simply makes a notation each time the behavior of interest occurs. The first example in Figure 10–3 shows how the teacher tallied Susie's behavior of throwing paper airplanes in class.

- *Duration recording.* Here the observer records the time a behavior begins and the time it ends to determine its length. The second example in

Figure 10–3 is the teacher's daily record of the amount of time Philip spent sleeping in class.

Latency recording is another option. In this system, the observer determines the amount of time it takes a student to begin doing something. For example, the teacher might be interested in how long it takes Jennifer to begin reading her library book after she returns to the classroom from recess.

For nondiscrete behaviors such as working independently or talking with peers, the use of interval recording and time sampling is recommended (Alberto & Troutman, 1990; Cooper, Heron, & Heward, 1987). With these techniques, the observer determines whether a behavior occurs during a specified time period. The class day, period, or activity is broken down into short intervals of a few minutes or even a few seconds, and a record of the presence or absence of the target behavior is kept for each interval. These techniques can also be used with discrete

Momentary Time Sampling

Student: Fred

Behavior: Writing on assigned worksheets

Measurement System: Momentary time sampling (determination if the behavior is occurring at the end of the interval)

Length of Interval: 3 minutes

When Measured: Independent study time (10:30–11:00 a.m.)

Interval Ends		Interval Ends	
10:33	X	10:48	X
10:36	O	10:51	O
10:39	X	10:54	O
10:42	X	10:57	X
10:45	O	11:00	O

X = Fred was writing on a worksheet at the end of the interval.

O = Fred was not writing on a worksheet at the end of the interval.

Results: Fred wrote on assigned worksheets in 5 of the 10 time intervals sampled, or 50%.

FIGURE 10–4

Observing Nondiscrete Behaviors: Interval Recording

behaviors if a complete record of every occurrence is not necessary.

Several variations of interval recording and time sampling are available:

- *Whole-interval recording.* The student is observed for the entire interval, and the observer notes if the target behavior occurs continuously throughout the interval. Observation intervals are very brief, usually lasting only a few seconds.
- *Partial-interval time recording.* The student is observed for the entire interval, but the observer notes only if the behavior occurred at least once during the interval. Again, time intervals are very brief.
- *Momentary time sampling.* The student is observed only at the end of each interval. At that time, the observer checks to see if the behavior is occurring. Intervals are usually longer—3, 5, or even 15 minutes—making this a more convenient method for classroom teachers. However, it is less accurate than interval recording techniques because much of the student's behavior goes unobserved.

Figure 10–4 provides an example of momentary time sampling. Note that the X indicates occurrence of the target behavior and the O indicates nonoccurrence. Results are expressed as the number or percentage of time intervals in which the behavior of interest was displayed.

Set Up the Data Collection System

The next step in planning an observation is to determine logistics. Questions to be answered include the following:

- When and where will the observation take place?
- How many observation periods will there be, and how frequently will these occur?
- Who will act as the observer?
- How will observational data be recorded?

Determining the time and place of the observation must take into account the nature of the behavior. With infrequent behaviors, it may be desirable to collect observational data for each occurrence. However, if the behavior occurs frequently, it is usually impractical to observe every

TABLE 10–4
Classroom Observation Techniques for Teachers

It is not necessary to stop teaching to observe; in fact, it is almost impossible to teach without observing. Try the following suggestions for integrating observations into your classroom procedures:

1. Carry a small card such as an index card; on it list the names of one or two target students and the problem behaviors you wish to observe (e.g., hitting, being out of seat, talking to others). Place a tally mark on the card (and possibly the time of the behavior) each time the behavior occurs. Start this system with one or two students and gradually expand it as your skills improve.

2. Require students to record on their in-class work their starting and finishing time. This approach permits the calculation of rate as well as frequency and accuracy data. Students can also note the times they leave and return to their desks; then the total amount of time in-seat each day or each period can be calculated.

3. Carry a stopwatch to measure the duration of behaviors. For example, start the watch each time Maynard leaves his seat, and stop it when he returns. Continue this (without resetting the watch), and time each occurrence of the behavior. At the end of the observation period, note the total amount of time recorded.

4. To count behaviors without interfering with the operation of the class, use wrist counters (golf counters), supermarket counters, paper clips moved from one pocket to another, navy beans in a cup, and other inexpensive devices.

5. Have a seating chart in front of you as you talk to the class. Place a tally mark by a student's name for each target behavior, such as asking a question, talking out, or answering a question correctly.

6. Recruit volunteers to observe in the classroom. Older students, parents, senior citizens, college students, or other students in the class can be excellent observers. If the teacher has developed a method to record the data and has clearly stated the behavior to be observed, a nonprofessional should be able to conduct the observation.

Note: From *Teaching Special Students in General Education Classrooms* (7th ed.) by R. B. Lewis and D. H. Doorlag, © 2006, Upper Saddle River, NJ: Merrill/Prentice Hall. Copyright 2006 by Prentice Hall, Inc. Reprinted by permission.

instance. Instead, it makes sense to select those times and settings where the behavior is of greatest concern. For example, if Henry's rough play on the playground during recess is a possible problem, he should be observed on the playground at that time.

One observation is not sufficient. More than one observation should be planned, and these should take place over time. A common practice is to observe daily for a minimum of 5 days. Observation should continue until a complete picture of the behavior has emerged. For example, if a behavior occurs only 3 or 4 times daily from Monday through Thursday but 10 times on Friday, it is advisable to observe for at least another week to determine if frequency will level off or continue to increase. There are two exceptions to the rule of multiple observations. Only one observation is needed if the behavior of interest is one that is not present in the student's repertoire (e.g., the student has not learned how to subtract) or if the behavior is one that endangers the student or others.

The professional who designs the observation system usually collects data. If the teacher is the observer, there is less disruption in classroom routine and less danger that the presence of an outsider will cause students to act differently. Although it takes some advance planning, teachers can collect observational data while they are teaching. Several techniques for facilitating teacher observations are presented in Table 10–4. Other professionals, instructional aides, volunteers, or even students may also conduct classroom observations if the behavior is clearly stated, procedures are well specified, and observers are adequately trained.

Results of observations should be recorded on paper during the observational period or immediately thereafter to ensure that data are not forgotten. Although tally sheets such as those shown in Figures 10–5 are the most usual way of recording data, there is no set format. However, record forms should be designed to allow easy entry of

Example 1: Event Recording, Graphing Actual Frequency of Occurrence

Target Behavior: Throwing paper airplanes in math class

When Measured: Math period (9:00–9:30 a.m.) on 5 consecutive school days

[Observational sessions are equal in duration and offer equal opportunity for the behavior to occur.]

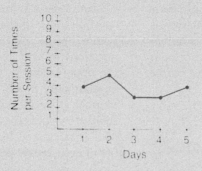

Example 2: Event Recording, Graphing Rate of Occurrence

Target Behavior: Talking out in class

When Measured: Independent work time for 5 consecutive school days

[Observational sessions offer equal opportunity for the behavior to occur but are of unequal duration.]

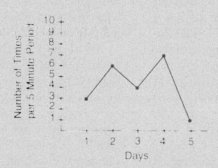

Example 3: Duration Recording, Graphing Percentage of Time

Target Behavior: Tantruming

When Measured: Grocery shopping for 5 consecutive shopping trips

[Observational sessions offer equal opportunity for the behavior to occur but are of unequal duration.]

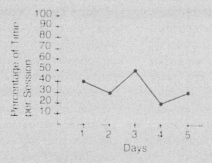

FIGURE 10–5
Reporting Observation Results for Discrete Behaviors

information and encourage accurate reporting. Some teachers carry observational record forms on clipboards, and others enter data on index cards or in small notebooks. There is no set method; teachers should experiment until they find a comfortable strategy. Another option for recording data is audio- or videotaping. Although an observer is still required to listen to or view tapes to summarize results, taping is permanent. If a behavior is missed or is difficult to interpret, the tape can be replayed for clarification.

 Breakpoint Practice 10.2
Click here to check your understanding of recording methods.

Select a Data-Reporting System

Observational data can be reported in statements such as "Susie threw paper airplanes in math class 19 times in a 5-day period." However, the more usual practice is to present results in a visual format such as a graph or chart. Graphs communicate large amounts of information quickly and facilitate the detection of trends and patterns. The most typical procedure is to plot observation results on a line graph where the *x*-axis, or abscissa, represents time and the *y*-axis, or ordinate, represents the behavior.

The simplest way to present frequency data is to plot the observed number of occurrences of the target behavior. The *y*-axis becomes a scale for the number of times the behavior is exhibited, and the *x*-axis depicts the different observational sessions. This procedure makes sense, however, only if all observational sessions are of equal duration and if each offers the student the same opportunity to perform the target behavior. If observations vary in duration, then it is more appropriate to report rate data than frequency data. For example, if the teacher observed the student 10 minutes on Monday, 15 minutes on Tuesday, and 12 minutes on Wednesday, results could be compared across observational sessions by converting the number of occurrences of the behavior into the *number of occurrences per minute* (calculated by dividing the observed number of occurrences by the number of minutes in the observational

session). If, on Monday, the behavior occurred 20 times during the 10-minute observation period, its rate of occurrence would be 2 times per minute. That rate could then be directly compared to the rate of occurrence on Tuesday (e.g., 1.3 times per minute), Wednesday, and so forth.

Likewise, if the behavior of interest is the number of times the student correctly answers questions in science class, the student may have the opportunity to respond to 15 questions one day but only 8 the next. In such situations, the number of occurrences of the target behavior should be converted into *percentage of occurrences*. This is calculated by dividing the observed number of occurrences by the number of opportunities for occurrence during the observational period; this quotient is then multiplied by 100. If, for example, the student answered 10 out of 15 questions correctly, the percentage correct would be 67. That percentage could then be directly compared to percentages achieved at other times when the student was provided with a different number of opportunities.

With duration data, it is possible to plot the actual number of seconds, minutes, or hours that the behavior persisted. However, if observational sessions vary in length, duration data should be converted to percentage data to express the *percentage of time* in which the behavior occurred. Dividing the observed duration of the behavior by the total length of the observation period and then multiplying the quotient by 100 accomplish this. Figure 10–5 presents examples of some of the ways that graphing can depict frequency and duration data for discrete behaviors.

Graphs can also present results of observations of nondiscrete behaviors. Whatever technique is used to record data—whole-interval recording, partial-interval recording, or momentary time sampling—results can be plotted as the number of intervals in which the behavior occurred. If there is variation across observation sessions in the total number of time intervals observed, frequency data should be converted to percentage data. For example, Sara may stare out of the window in 13 of the 24 time intervals sampled on Monday and in 32 of the 55 time intervals sampled on Tuesday. Comparison becomes possible when these results are stated in terms of percentages: Sara's target behavior occurred in 54 percent of the time intervals sampled on Monday and in 58 percent of the time intervals sampled on Tuesday.

Carry Out the Observations

The final step is to actually carry out the planned observations. As this occurs, the observer should be alert to potential problem areas. Is the target behavior stated with sufficient precision? Is the measurement system appropriate for this behavior? Do data collection procedures provide an adequate sampling of the student's typical responses? If two or more observers are involved in the data collection, interobserver reliability becomes an important concern. As Chapter 3 discussed, the percentage of agreement among observers is easily calculated. However, if percentage of agreement falls below 80, interobserver reliability is in question. It may be necessary to describe the target behavior with more precision or to provide observers with additional training.

Describe the Behavior to Be Observed

Before a behavior can be observed, it must be described clearly and precisely. "The student is disruptive" is too general a statement; it must be translated into one or more precise descriptions. For example, a disruptive student might be described as one who talks or yells out during class without permission. Talking and yelling are behaviors that can be observed and counted, and as such they are suitable targets for observation.

Select a Measurement System

Several systems are available for the measurement of behaviors. Discrete behaviors can be measured by counting their frequency and/or by timing their duration. With nondiscrete behaviors such as talking with peers, interval recording or time sampling is used. The observation period is broken into several short time intervals, and the observer notes whether the behavior is or is not occurring at some point in each interval.

Set Up the Data Collection System

There are several considerations in setting up the data collection system: who will collect the data,

when and where the observations will occur, how many observations will take place, and how data will be recorded. In general, observations should be scheduled at the time and location where the target behavior is most likely to occur. The student's teacher may collect observational data, or another member of the assessment team may act as observer. Several observations should be conducted; one observation is not sufficient to provide a picture of the student's typical pattern of behavior. If classroom conduct is the concern, the student should be observed daily for a minimum of five school days.

Select a Data-Reporting System

The results of observations are usually graphed. Graphs communicate large amounts of information quickly and allow identification of trends and patterns in behaviors. Graphs can be used to report any type of observational data: frequency, rate, and percentage of occurrence; duration; percentage of time; and so forth. A graph that reports the results of a series of observations of several behaviors is depicted in Figure 10–6. In this example, Michael was observed during the daily classroom work period to determine how long each day he sat at his seat and worked quietly on his assignment without talking with others. Also of interest were three behaviors incompatible with quiet, independent, and in-seat work: being out-of-seat, talking with peers, and talking with the teacher.

Carry Out the Observations

Observations are carried out, and then the final step—interpretation of results—takes place. Data are evaluated to determine whether or not a behavior problem exists—that is, whether or not intervention is needed. The process of making this decision is complex. Observations are informal techniques without norms or other guidelines to assist in evaluating whether a particular student's behavior is acceptable. There are no criteria that indicate how frequent or of what duration a behavior must be to warrant special attention. Thus, professionals must rely on their own best judgments when interpreting observation results.

Eaves (1982) has proposed a possible alternative. In Eaves's model, information is collected

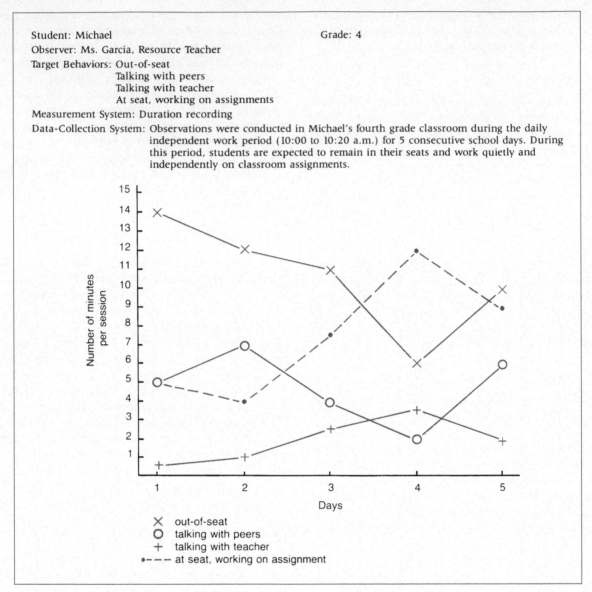

Student: Michael   Grade: 4
Observer: Ms. Garcia, Resource Teacher
Target Behaviors: Out-of-seat
                  Talking with peers
                  Talking with teacher
                  At seat, working on assignments
Measurement System: Duration recording
Data-Collection System: Observations were conducted in Michael's fourth grade classroom during the daily
                  independent work period (10:00 to 10:20 a.m.) for 5 consecutive school days. During
                  this period, students are expected to remain in their seats and work quietly and
                  independently on classroom assignments.

X   out-of-seat
O   talking with peers
+   talking with teacher
•—–— at seat, working on assignment

FIGURE 10–6
Sample Graph of Observation Results

about student behavior in two ways: important persons in the student's environment complete Rating scales, and student behavior is directly observed. A major feature of this model is that local or regional norms are developed for specific student behaviors. Observation becomes a norm-referenced technique, and it is possible to determine how one student's behavior compares to that of age or grade peers. In an example provided by Eaves, a student showing disruptive behavior 24 percent of the time scores at the 98th percentile in disruptiveness. One who is noncompliant 1.8 percent of the time scores at the 99th percentile in noncompliance. Such a system would greatly facilitate the interpretation of observational data. However, as Eaves points out, this proposal is not yet a reality. Before such a system could be used, standardized observation schedules would have to be developed and normative data collected for different regions, age levels, and types of classrooms.

FUNCTIONAL BEHAVIORAL ASSESSMENT

Functional assessment (also called *functional behavioral assessment*) is an informal assessment technique that includes direct observation. However, it goes beyond observation because it is designed to gather the information needed to plan positive behavioral interventions for students with challenging behaviors. According to the regulations for IDEA 2004, when an individualized education program (IEP) team plans a program for a student "whose behavior impedes [his or her] learning or that of others," that team must consider "the use of positive behavioral interventions and supports, and other strategies to address that behavior" (*Federal Register*, 2006, §300.324(a)(2)). Functional assessments are also required when students with IEPs are removed from a placement due to disciplinary reasons.

The primary purpose of functional assessment is to determine the reason(s) for a student's inappropriate behaviors so that a successful behavior change program can be implemented. Put simply, the goal is to understand the function of the inappropriate behavior for the student. To do this, it is necessary to understand the relationship between the student's behavior and environmental, social, cultural, and physiological factors (Fahmie & Iwata, 2011). Quinn, Gable, Rutherford, Nelson, and Howell (1998) maintain that functional behavior assessment centers on the factors that begin, keep, or finish the problem behavior. Sequence analysis, which was described in Chapter 6, is a simple kind of functional assessment because it attempts to determine relationships between behaviors and their antecedents and consequences (O'Neill et al., 1997).

Functional assessment makes use of a variety of informal assessment techniques. Two techniques are always included: direct observation of the student in order to fully describe the behavior

in question, and interviews with persons knowledgeable about the student and the behavior. In some cases, other techniques are also used. Examples are record reviews (e.g., medical and educational histories), task and work sample analyses, and curriculum-based assessments such as informal inventories and skill probes.

According to Artesani (2001), functional assessment is a process designed to result in a more complete consideration of students' problem behaviors. O'Neill et al. (1997) identify five primary outcomes of the functional assessment process:

1. A clear *description of the problem behaviors,* including classes or sequences of behaviors that frequently occur together
2. Identification of the events, times, and situations that *predict* when the problem behaviors *will* and *will not* occur across the full range of typical daily routines
3. Identification of the *consequences that maintain the problem behaviors* (i.e., what functions the behaviors appear to serve for the person)
4. Development of one or more *summary statements* or hypotheses that describe specific behaviors, a specific type of situation, in which they occur, and the outcomes or reinforcers maintaining them in that situation
5. Collection of *direct observation data* that support the summary statements that have been developed (p. 3)

There are several approaches to functional analysis, and each identifies a somewhat different set of procedures (e.g., Chandler & Dahlquist, 2002; Fitzsimmons, 1998; LRE for LIFE Project, 1997; O'Neill et al., 1997; PACER Center, 1994; Quinn et al., 1998; Shippen, Simpson, & Criters, 2003; Witt, Daly, & Noell, 2000). However, all include these basic steps: (1) identification and description of the target behavior, (2) identification of factors that influence the behavior, (3) formulation and testing of a hypothesis to explain the behavior, and (4) development of a positive behavioral support plan.

Describing the Behavior

The first step is identification of the behavior of interest. As with any type of behavioral strategy, the behavior must be both observable and measurable. Its description must be precise. The next step is to gather observational data in order to fully describe the behavior (Iwata & Dozier, 2008). Depending on the type of behavior under consideration, any of the observational strategies discussed in Chapter 6 can be used: narrative reporting, continuous recording, sequence analysis, event recording, duration recording, interval recording, or time sampling. O'Neill et al. (1997) recommend that data be collected for a minimum of 2 to 5 days using time-sampling procedures. The LRE for LIFE Project (1997) suggests at least 3 days of observation. The student should be observed in a variety of settings to determine the conditions under which the behavior occurs or fails to occur.

Identifying Factors That Influence the Behavior

The use of informants to learn about influences on the student's behavior is what sets functional assessment apart from standard behavioral observations. Although results of direct observations help to describe the behavior, rarely do they explain its causes. In order to arrive at hypotheses about possible causes, it is necessary to gather information from other sources. Those sources are the persons who know the student best: the student himself or herself and the student's teachers and others who work with him or her in the educational setting.

Interviews are typically used for data collection, although questionnaires may be appropriate in some situations. According to O'Neill et al. (1997), there are several topics to pursue in the interview. The informant should be asked to describe the behavior or behaviors of interest, including their frequency, duration, and intensity. The behavior should then be considered in relation to three factors: setting events, antecedents, and consequences. Setting events are events removed in time from the behavior that may affect its occurrence. O'Neill et al. identify seven important areas to consider: medications, medical or physical problems, sleep cycles, eating routines and diet, daily schedule, numbers of people, and staffing patterns and interactions. Antecedents are the events that immediately precede the behavior and may predict its occurrence. They include time of day, physical setting, people, and

the activity in which the student is engaged (O'Neill et al.). Consequences or outcomes are what occur after the behavior.

Quinn et al. (1998) add that it is necessary to take into consideration the student's ability to perform the classroom task that appears to precipitate the problem behavior. There are two possibilities: a skill deficit (the student is unable to perform the task because he or she does not possess the necessary skills) or a performance deficit (the student has the needed skills but for some reason fails to perform).

Generating a Hypothesis

The goal of functional assessment is to gather sufficient information to be able to develop a hypothesis to explain the student's behavior. This hypothesis must take into account the behavior itself and the setting events, antecedents, and consequences that affect it. Determining the function or purpose of the behavior is part of this process. Lewis and Sugai (1999) report that typically children use problem behavior to obtain something or prevent something from occurring.

O'Neill et al. (1997) suggest that the team conducting the functional assessment develop a summary statement or hypothesis describing the behavior and the factors influencing it.

Program Planning

The hypothesis about the reasons for the student's behavior can be verified through direct observation and/or by systematic manipulation of setting events, antecedents, and consequences. Once the assessment team is satisfied that it has sufficient data to support the hypothesis, the next step is development of an intervention plan.

Figure 10–7 presents an individual positive behavioral support plan for a third grader named Emily (Lewis & Sugai, 1999). The problem behaviors are described, along with their individual hypothesized functions. For example, the team believes that Emily interrupts academic instruction to gain the attention of the teacher and peers. Next, the team has identified replacement behaviors that will serve the same functions for Emily. For example, instead of blurting out answers during instruction, she will raise her

Student __Emily__ DOB __7/25/88__ Grade __3__
Teacher __Mr. Leigh /Ms. Fernandez__ School __Twin Peeks Elem__
Plan case manager __Mr. Sugal__ Phone __555-5555__
IEP: Y N Plan start date __4/1/99__
Team will reconvene every __10__ days to monitor plan

Briefly describe the problem behavior(s)

Disrupts instruction during reading and math—blurts out answers, makes loud noises, makes jokes. Occurs 10-15 times per half hour class period.

Interrupts peer activities during centers and free time—grabs materials, calls peers names, physically places self at table. Occurs 80% of the time.

Briefly describe the function the problem behavior(s) serve the student (Testable Explanation)

During academic periods, Emily interrupts instruction to access teacher and peer attention.

During peer lead activities, Emily interrupts to access peer attention.

Briefly describe a desired replacement behavior(s) that will serve a similar function as the current problem behavior

Emily will raise her hand before speaking.
Emily will remain on-task 90% of the period.
Emily will talk only about task related topics.
Emily will ask peer permission prior to joining activities.
Emily will make neutral or positive comments toward peers.

Develop a behavioral objective incorporating the replacement behavior(s)

During academic periods, Emily will remain on-task 90% of intervals for 5 consecutive days.

During independent activities, Emily will make neutral or positive comments toward peers in 80% of the opportunities for 5 consecutive days.

List/describe a data collection system to monitor replacement behavior and desired criteria

Academic periods-momentary time sampling, 1 minute intervals. On-task = listening to the teacher, comments relative to task, raise hand before speaking, working on assignments in 90% of the intervals.

Independent activities - event recording, record positive/neutral comments and negative comments. Positive/neutral comments in 80% of opportunities. Opportunities = neutral/positive + negative comments.

Outline the instructional strategies to teach the desired replacement behavior

Emily will receive social skill instruction outlining key "on task" behaviors. Emily will also be taught to "self-manage" her on-task behavior.

Emily will receive social skill instruction focusing on appropriate peer initiations and interactions. Peer tutors will be recruited to assist in instruction.

Briefly describe the antecedent strategies that will accompany the above instructional strategies (e.g., pre-corrects, prompts, academic accommodations, schedule changes)

Pre-corrects will be used to prompt Emily on key social skills prior to academic and independent periods. Emily will be prompted to use her self-management sheet prior to academic periods.

Peers will be prompted to follow class rules including ignoring students who do not comply with the rules.

Emily will receive a pre-correct prior to independent periods. Peer tutors will be prompted to assist Emily.

Outline the consequent strategies for the problem/ replacement behavior (e.g., differential reinforcement, verbal praise, error correction statements)

During academic periods, the teacher will praise Emily approximately every 3-4 minutes if she is on-task. If Emily meets daily criteria on her self-management card, she can earn free-time minutes and select a peer to play with. If Emily is off-task, the teacher will provide specific verbal praise to a nearby compliant peer. If Emily continues to remain off-task, the teacher will use a simple redirective statement.

Peers who participated in the social skills training will provide verbal support to Emily if she successfully demonstrates the use of key social skills. If Emily meets her daily criteria, she can earn computer time and select a peer to work with. If Emily does not comply with the rules of the activity, the teacher will provide brief redirective statements.

Briefly describe what strategies will be used to promote generalized responding

The above strategies will be incorporated during all academic periods, including mainstream classes. "Peer tutors" will be used during other independent times (e.g., recess, cafeteria) once Emily meets criteria in the classroom.

Team Members and their responsibilities for implementation

Member	Responsibilities
Mr. Leigh	Instruction & Data Collection
Ms. Fernandez	Monitor self-management in classroom
Ms. McCathren	Monitor program during lunch and recess
Ms. Garrison	Develop social skill lessons & self-management plan

FIGURE 10–7

Sample Positive Behavior Support Plan

Note: From "Effective Behavior Support: A Systems Approach to Proactive Schoolwide Management" (p. 15) by T.J. Lewis and G. Sugai, 1999, *Focus on Exceptional Children,* 31(6). Copyright 1999 by Love Publishing Company. Reprinted by permission.

hand before speaking. The plan includes objectives related to the replacement behaviors and a data collection system for monitoring Emily's progress. Finally, four types of intervention strategies are specified: the types of instruction Emily will receive, the antecedent strategies to be used during instruction, the consequent strategies for both the problem and replacement behaviors, and strategies for generalizing replacement behaviors to other situations.

ENHANCEDetext
Video Example 10.3
Watch this video to find out more about incentives for appropriate behavior in the classroom.

ATTENTION DEFICITS AND HYPERACTIVITY

In recent years, there has been increased interest in problem behaviors related to attention and activity level (Lerner & Lerner, 1991; Lerner & Lowenthal, 1993; Lerner, Lowenthal, & Lerner, 1995; Shaywitz & Shaywitz, 1992; Silver, 1992). Attention deficits refer to difficulties in focusing and sustaining attention; **hyperactivity** is excessive activity. Both of these problem behaviors are difficult to define because they depend on the age of the student and the situation in which the behavior is displayed. Two-year-olds are expected to be more active and have shorter attention spans than 10-year-olds; a higher level of activity is expected on the ball field than in the classroom.

Despite the inherent definitional problems, students with difficulties in these areas are often identified as having attention-deficit disorder (ADD) or **attention-deficit/hyperactivity disorder (ADHD)**. These disorders are quite common; the Council for Exceptional Children (1992) estimates that 3 to 5 percent of school-aged children have ADD. Although not considered a separate disability under federal laws, ADD and ADHD were added by the 1997 IDEA Amendments to the list of conditions covered under the category "other health impairment." The *Diagnostic and Statistical Manual of Mental Disorders—Fifth Edition* (2013) of the American Psychiatric Association provides diagnostic criteria for attention and hyperactivity disorders. According to the *DSM–V*, children must show at least six criteria (out of nine) from the inattention and/or hyperactivity and impulsivity criteria. These symptoms must be present for at least 6 months before the age of 12 in more than one environment (e.g., home, school, workplace).

Several of the behaviors described in the *DSM–V* definition may be caused by factors other than ADD or ADHD. For example, Ortiz (1991), cited by the Council for Exceptional Children (1992), warns that most behaviors typically associated with ADD are also characteristics of ELL, Silver (1992) cautions that the ADHD label should be applied only when behaviors of hyperactivity, distractibility, and/or impulsivity are both chronic and pervasive.

Several measures are available to assist professionals in the assessment of attention deficits and hyperactivity. Items related to attention and activity levels often appear on rating scales and checklists that survey a range of classroom behaviors. For example, hyperactivity is one of the subscales of Problem Behaviors on the *Social Skills Rating System* (Gresham & Elliott, 1990), and Motor Excess is one of five behavioral domains on the *Revised Behavior Problem Checklist* (Quay & Peterson, 1987). In contrast, measures such as the *Attention Deficit Disorders Evaluation Scale–Fourth Edition* (McCarney & Arthaud, 2013) and the *Conners' Rating Scales-3* (Conners, 2008) are more limited in scope because their major purpose is study of attention deficits and hyperactivity.

Attention Deficit Disorders Evaluation Scale–Fourth Edition

The ADDES–4 is a rating scale designed for use with school-aged children and adolescents. Both a school and a home version are available, and each contains descriptions of behaviors that reflect inattention, impulsivity, and hyperactivity. These descriptions are designed to relate directly to the *DSM–V* diagnostic criteria for ADHD. The informant rates each behavior according to the frequency with which it occurs. The scale includes six ratings: "not developmentally appropriate for age" (0), "not observed" (1), "one to several times per month" (2), "one to several times per week" (3), "one to several times per day" (4), and "one to several times per hour" (5). These quantifiers may help make this scale less subjective than those found in other instruments.

Two types of results are produced by the *ADDES–4:* standard scores for the two subscales (Inattentive and Impulsive-Hyperactive) and a total scale percentile rank. Standard scores are distributed with a mean of 10 and a standard deviation of 3. It should be noted that separate norms are available for male and female students. Also, Spanish Rating Forms can be ordered for both the Home and School versions. Another feature of the *ADDES–4* is a *DSM–V* worksheet that allows professionals to identify which characteristics from the definition were identified as problem areas by the teacher or parent rating the student. Also available are supplementary books with recommended instructional activities for teachers (McCarney, 1994) and parents (McCarney & Bauer, 1995a).

The American Psychiatric Association (1994) identifies several characteristics related to attention-deficit/hyperactivity disorder. The first set of characteristics relates to inattention and the second to hyperactivity-impulsivity. Three classifications are possible: ADHD, Combined Type (if the individual meets criteria for both Inattention and Hyperactivity-Impulsivity); ADHD, Predominantly Inattentive Type (if the individual meets criteria for Inattention but not Hyperactivity-Impulsivity); and ADHD, Predominantly Hyperactive-Impulsive Type (if the individual meets criteria for Hyperactivity-Impulsivity but not Inattention).

Inattention

Six (or more) of the following symptoms of inattention have persisted for at least 6 months to a degree that is maladaptive and inconsistent with developmental level:

Inattention

(a) often fails to give close attention to details or makes careless mistakes in schoolwork, work, or other activities

(b) often has difficulty sustaining attention in tasks or play activities

(c) often does not seem to listen when spoken to directly

(d) often does not follow through on instructions and fails to finish schoolwork, chores, or duties in the workplace (not due to oppositional behavior or failure to understand instructions)

(e) often has difficulties organizing tasks and activities

(f) often avoids, dislikes or is reluctant to engage in tasks that require sustained mental effort (such as schoolwork or homework)

(g) often loses things necessary for tasks or activities (e.g., toys, school assignments, pencils, books, or tools)

(h) is often easily distracted by extraneous stimuli

(i) is often forgetful in daily activities

Hyperactivity-Impulsivity

Six (or more) of the following symptoms of hyperactivity-impulsivity have persisted for at least 6 months to a degree that is maladaptive and inconsistent with developmental level:

Hyperactivity

(a) often fidgets with hands or feet or squirms in seat

(b) often leaves seat in classroom or in other situations in which remaining seated is expected

(c) often runs about or climbs excessively in situations in which it is inappropriate (in adolescents or adults, may be limited to subjective feelings of restlessness)

(d) often has difficulty playing or engaging in leisure activities quietly

(e) is often "on the go" or often acts as if "driven by a motor"

(f) often talks excessively

Impulsivity

(g) often blurts out answers before questions have been completed

(h) often has difficulty waiting in turn

(i) often interrupts or intrudes on others (e.g., butts into conversations or games) (pp. 83–84).

Note: Reprinted with permission from the *Diagnostic and Statistical Manual of Mental Disorders, Fourth Edition.* Copyright 1994, American Psychiatric Association.

The school version of the *ADDES–4* was standardized with 3,356 students in 20 states. The standardization sample is representative of race, urban–rural residence, and geographic region. Test-retest, internal consistency, and interrater reliability are adequate. The validity of the *ADDES–4* is supported by its relationship to other measures of ADHD and by its ability to differentiate between students with and without attention-deficit/hyperactivity disorder.

Conners' Rating Scales–3

Perhaps the best-known measures of ADHD are the *Conners' Rating Scales–3,* a set of several tools for use by parents and teachers of students ages 6 to 18. Both a short and a long form are available for the parent and teacher scales; short and long adolescent self-report scales are available as well. Spanish-language versions of all scales can be purchased from the publisher.

Teachers and parents read descriptions of student behaviors and choose one of four ratings: "not true at all (never, seldom)" (0), "just a little true (occasionally)" (1), "pretty much true (often, quite a bit)" (2), or "very much true (very often, very frequent)" (3). The short form of the teacher scale contains 41 items, and the long form contains 115. The short form for parents contains 45 items, and the long form has 110.

The short-form rating scales produce three subscale scores (Oppositional, Cognitive Problems/Inattention, and Hyperactivity) and the Conners' ADHD Index score. Scores include Content Scores, the Conners' Global Index score, and the *DSM–V* Symptom Subscales. The *DSM–V* Symptom Subscales include rating scale items that assess Oppositional Defiant Disorder. Raw scores are plotted on profiles where their equivalent *T*-scores can be determined. *T*-scores are distributed with a mean of 50 and a standard deviation of 10. On the *CRS–3,* higher scores are indicative of possible problem areas. Norms are available by age and gender; separate norms

---

ATTENTION DEFICIT DISORDERS EVALUATION SCALE— FOURTH EDITION (ADDES–4), HOME VERSION AND SCHOOL VERSION

S. B. McCarney & T. J. Arthaud (2013)

Type: Norm-referenced teacher rating scale and parent rating scale

Major Content Areas: Inattention and impulsivity-hyperactivity

Type of Administration: Individual

Administration Time: 15 to 20 minutes (school version), 15 minutes (home version)

Age/Grade Levels: Ages 4–18

Types of Scores: Standard scores for two subscales; overall percentile rank

Computer Aids: *ADDES-4 Quick Score*

Typical Uses: Identification of possible problems in attention and/or activity level

Cautions: The standardization sample for the school version shows variation from the U.S. population in race, urban–rural residence, and geographic distribution.

Publisher: Hawthorne Educational Services (*www.hes-inc.com*)

RATING SCALES–REVISED (CRS–3)

C. K. Conners (2008)

Type: Norm-referenced teacher rating scales, parent rating scales, and adolescent self-rating scales

Major Content Areas: Problem behaviors including inattention and hyperactivity

Type of Administration: Individual

Administration Time: 5 to 10 minutes (short form), 15 to 20 minutes (long form)

Age/Grade Levels: Ages 6 to 18

Types of Scores: *T*-scores for subscales

Technology Aids: software and online scoring

Typical Uses: Identification of possible problems in attention and/or hyperactivity

Cautions: Results should be interpreted with caution because of concerns about interrater reliability.

Publisher: Multi-Health Systems Inc. (*www.mhs.com*)

are provided for African American/Black students for the adolescent self-rating scales.

According to the manual, the *CRS–3* was standardized with a sample reflective of the population with over 1,400 respondents from 45 states in the U.S. This sample included not only parents and teachers but also adolescents who completed self-ratings. All students were in general education; students in special education classes were excluded from the samples. The sample for each of the *CRS–3* measures is described in terms of the ages of students, their ethnicity, and median annual household income.

The internal consistency reliability of the *CRS–3* is adequate; however, test-retest ranges from .71–.98 and interrater reliability falls below .70 for several subscales of the long forms of the parent and teacher scales. In terms of validity, results from the long and short forms of *CRS–3* measures appear to be related. However, there have been questions regarding agreement between parent and teacher ratings.

In conclusion, it is important to remember that measures that assess specific behaviors such as hyperactivity, impulsivity, and inattention play the same role in assessment as the more general behavior rating scales and checklists. They help identify possible areas of need that may warrant further evaluation. If further assessment is needed, direct observation is the recommended procedure.

 Breakpoint Practice 10.3
Click here to check your understanding of attention deficits and hyperactivity.

SELF-CONCEPT AND PEER ACCEPTANCE

Students with school performance problems may have poor self-concepts, perceiving themselves as failures in academic pursuits. Students may also experience difficulty in their interactions with classmates. Their peers may fail to accept them as friends or as regular members of the classroom social group. The next sections describe several of the measures available for exploring these areas.

Self-Concept

Both formal, norm-referenced measures and informal assessment devices are available for the study of self-concept and self-esteem. The next sections describe four norm-referenced measures: the *Piers-Harris Children's Self-Concept Scale, Coopersmith Self-Esteem Inventories, Multidimensional Self-Concept Scale,* and *Self-Esteem Index.*

Piers-Harris Children's Self-Concept Scale—Second Edition

The *Piers-Harris 2* is a popular norm-referenced measure of self-concept. It is a self-report instrument for students in grades 4–12. Originally designed as a research instrument, the *Piers-Harris 2* is often used in schools as a screening device to identify students who have possible self-concept problems.

The *Piers-Harris* is made up of 60 declarative statements such as "My classmates make fun of me," "I am smart," and "I give up easily." Students are expected to read the statements themselves. If they are unable to do so, the tester can read items aloud. Items are written at a second-grade reading level, and both positive and negative statements are included. Students respond by circling "yes" if they feel the statement describes them or "no" if they feel the statement does not.

Raw scores on the *Piers-Harris* range from 0 to 60, with higher scores indicating more positive self-concepts. Raw scores can be converted to percentile ranks, stanines, and *T*-scores. *T*-scores are standard scores that are distributed with a mean of 50 and a standard deviation of 10.

In addition to a Total score, six cluster scores can also be obtained:

- Behavioral Adjustment
- Intellectual and Social Status
- Physical Appearance and Attributes
- Freedom from Anxiety
- Popularity
- Happiness and Satisfaction

The *Piers-Harris 2* was standardized with a national sample of 1,387 students ages 7 to 18. This norm group is a vast improvement from that used in the previous edition of this measure; it is a national sample rather than a collection of students from only one school district. However, the *Piers-Harris 2* norm group fails to approximate the general U.S. population on some important variables. For example, in terms of race/ethnic background, the norm group appears to contain a lower percentage of Hispanic/Latino students than the United States as a whole (7.4 percent versus 17.1 percent). In terms of geographic region, 13.3 percent of the sample represented the West, whereas U.S. Census figures indicate that 22.5 percent of the population resides in that area. The reliability of the

---

PIERS-HARRIS CHILDREN'S SELF-CONCEPT SCALE— SECOND EDITION (PIERS-HARRIS 2)

E. V. Piers & D. S. Herzberg (2002)

Type: Norm-referenced student checklist

Major Content Areas: Total self-concept and six self-concept clusters

Type of Administration: Group

Administration Time: 10 to 15 minutes

Age/Grade Levels: Grades 2–12, ages 7 to 18

Types of Scores: Percentile ranks, stanines, *T*-scores

Computer Aids: Publisher offers machine scoring services and a PC software program for administration and/or scoring

Typical Uses: Used in the identification of students with possible needs in the area of self-concept development

Cautions: Second-grade reading level required. If students have difficulty reading test items, the tester can read them aloud.

Publisher: Western Psychological Services (*www.wpspublish.com*)

Piers-Harris 2 appears adequate. With respect to validity, correlations between the earlier version of the *Piers-Harris* and other measures of self-concept range from the .30s to the .80s. More positively, the correlation between total scores on the *Piers-Harris 2* and the second edition of the *Tennessee Self-Concept Scale* (Fitts & Warren, 1996) was .66.

Coopersmith Self-Esteem Inventories

The *Coopersmith Self-Esteem Inventories* are another well-known set of measures available for the assessment of self-concept, although they are quite old. Three measures make up the set: the School Form, the Adult Form, and a teacher rating scale entitled *Behavioral Academic Self-Esteem* (Coopersmith & Gilberts, 1981). Of interest here is the School Form, the only one of the three measures that is normed.

The School Form of the *Coopersmith* contains 58 statements such as "I have a low opinion of myself" and "I'm proud of my schoolwork." Both positive and negative statements are included. Students read each statement and then check whether the statement is "like me" or "unlike me." The tester is allowed to read the statements aloud if students have difficulty reading. If a short form of the measure is desired, only the first 25 items are administered. However, norms are not available for the short form.

Items on the *Coopersmith* school inventory are divided into four subscales: General Self, Social Self-Peers, Home-Parents, and School-Academics. Raw scores from each of the subscales are added together; the sum is then multiplied by 2 to produce the Total Self raw score. In addition, a Lie Scale is used to evaluate the veracity of students' responses. Total Self-scores can be converted to percentile ranks, but norms are not available for subscale scores or for the Lie Scale.

Norms for the *Coopersmith* School Form were developed by Kimball (1973) with a sample of approximately 7,600 public school students in grades 4–8. According to Coopersmith (1981), the standardization sample included all socioeconomic levels, African American and "Spanish-surname students" (p. 17). No further description is offered. Coopersmith advises caution in the use of these norms and strongly recommends the development of local norms. The *Coopersmith*'s reliability appears adequate, and there is some support for its validity. The manual states that significant correlations have been found between the *Coopersmith* and other measures of self-esteem.

The *Coopersmith* used as an informal device. If norms are desired, local norms should be

---

MULTIDIMENSIONAL SELF CONCEPT SCALE (MSCS)

B. B. Bracken (1992)

Type: Norm-referenced student rating scale

Major Content Areas: Global self-concept; social, competence, affect, academic, family, and physical self-concept

Type of Administration: Individual (or group)

Administration Time: 20–30 minutes

Age/Grade Levels: Grades 5–12

Types of Scores: Standard scores and percentile ranks for total test and each subscale

Computer Aids: N/A

Typical Uses: Identification of strengths and weaknesses in several dimensions of self-concept

Cautions: Students of color are somewhat underrepresented in the standardization sample; students from southern states are overrepresented

Publisher: PRO-ED (*www.proedinc.com*)

SELF-ESTEEM INDEX (SEI)

L. Brown & J. Alexander (1991)

Type: Norm-referenced student rating scale

Major Content Areas: Overall self-esteem; perceptions of familial acceptance, academic competence, peer popularity, and personal security

Type of Administration: Individual (or group)

Administration Time: Approximately 30 minutes

Age/Grade Levels: Ages 8–0 to 18–11

Types of Scores: Standard scores and percentile ranks for each of the four scales and for total test

Computer Aids: N/A

Typical Uses: Identification of strengths and weaknesses in several areas of self-esteem

Cautions: Some students may have difficulty reading the items on the *SEI*. No information is available on test-retest reliability.

Publisher: PRO-ED (*www.proedinc.com*)

developed. In addition, Coopersmith (1981) recommends supplementing the results of the student checklist with teacher ratings and observations.

Multidimensional Self Concept Scale

Newer instruments include the *Multidimensional Self Concept Scale (MSCS)* (Bracken, 1992) and the *Self-Esteem Index (SEI)* (Brown & Alexander, 1991). The *MSCS* is a self-report scale for students in grades 5–12. Students read 150 statements such as "I often feel dumb" and "I enjoy life," then rate each according to how well it applies to them ("Strongly agree," "Agree," "Disagree," "Strongly disagree"). Six areas of self-concept are addressed: social, competence, affect, academic, family, and physical. Standard scores and percentile ranks are available for each of these areas and for total test. The statements on the scale are written at the third-grade level; the tester may read them aloud to the student, as needed, and explain the meanings of any unknown words.

The *MSCS* was standardized on approximately 2,500 students from nine states. African American and Hispanic students are somewhat underrepresented in the sample; students from the northeastern portion of the country are underrepresented; and those from the South are overrepresented (52.5

versus 35 percent for the nation). Internal consistency reliability coefficients fall at or above .86 for both genders and all grade levels on all scales and total test. Test-retest reliability coefficients range from .73 to .90. *MSCS* total test results show strong correlations with total scores on the *Coopersmith Self-Esteem Inventory* ($r = .73$) and the *Piers-Harris Children's Self-Concept Scale* ($r = .85$).

Self-Esteem Index

The *Self-Esteem Index* is a self-report rating scale for students ages 8–0 to 18–11. It contains 80 statements that students rate as "always true," "usually true" "usually false," or "always false." Each statement contributes to one of four self-esteem scales: perception of familial acceptance, perception of academic competence, perception of peer popularity, and perception of personal security. The *SEI* is designed for either group or individual administration. The examiner may assist students with word meanings, but the manual discourages oral administration.

Results include standard scores and percentile ranks for each of the four scales as well as a total test Self-Esteem Quotient. The *SEI* was standardized with 2,455 students from 19 states; students identified as seriously emotionally disturbed were excluded from the sample. The standardization sample appears to approximate the U.S. population in terms of geographic region, urban–rural residence, ethnicity, and race. Internal consistency reliability coefficients fall at or above .80 for ages 9 through 18; at age 8, four of the five reported coefficients in the .70s. No information is provided on test-retest reliability. *SEI* results show low to moderate correlations with teachers' ratings of student self-esteem (.21 to .43); however, much stronger correlations are reported between the *SEI's* Self-Esteem Quotient and total test results of the *Piers-Harris* (.77) and the *Coopersmith* (.83).

Other Measures

Another newer instrument is the *Culture-Free Self-Esteem Inventories—Third Edition* (Battle, 2002). This set of measures contains self-report inventories for three age levels: primary grades, intermediate grades, and adolescents. This edition of the *Culture-Free* is improved because the standardization sample is described in some detail in the manual. However, that sample does not appear representative of the U.S. population on all-important variables, and there remains concern about the label "culture-free" as applied to this test. However, the manual suggests that the test is unbiased because only a few of its items were found to show differences between African American and non-African American students and between Hispanic American and non-Hispanic American students in the norm group.

Several informal student checklists are also available for the study of self-concept. Students can also be interviewed about their perceptions of self-worth, or some types of observational data can be collected. For example, it is possible to count the number of negative statements a student makes about himself or herself and compare that total with the number of positive statements. Some students make frequent comments such as "I'm dumb" or "I can't do that," whereas others are much more positive in their self-appraisal.

Peer Acceptance

Attitude scales are used to evaluate general education students' perceptions of individuals with school performance problems. These scales provide information about peer attitudes toward students with disabilities in general. They do not assess how well peers accept a particular student.

One example of a general attitude scale is the *Peer Attitudes toward the Handicapped Scale (PATHS)* (Bagley & Greene, 1981). Although the *PATHS* is no longer in print, it provides a model for obtaining information about students' attitudes toward others with disabilities. The *PATHS* consists of a series of paragraphs that describe students with disabilities and the problems they experience. Descriptions of pupils with physical, learning, and behavioral problems are included.

To find out how a particular student is perceived by his or her classmates, **sociometric techniques** are used (Asher & Taylor, 1981). The most common technique is the nomination method. Students nominate the peers they would most or least like to associate with in some activity. Several activities appropriate for the students' age are presented: playing a game, working on a class art project, attending a school assembly, and so forth. For example, students can be asked to respond to questions such as:

1. Name the students in this class you would most (least) like to play with during recess.
2. Name the students you would most (least) like to sit next to in class.
3. Name the students you would most (least) like to work with on a class assignment.

A measure of this kind is included in the *Behavior Rating Profile—Second Edition* (Brown & Hammill, 1990), described earlier in this chapter, and norms are provided for students in grades 1–12. Or sociometric data can be collected informally. Class results are then analyzed to determine how many positive and negative nominations each student received.

Rating scales can also be used to collect sociometric data. For instance, on the *Peer Acceptance Scale* (Bruininks, Rynders, & Gross, 1974), each student in the class rates every other student using the picture rating scale. The possible ratings are "Friend" (illustrated by two persons playing together), "All Right," and "Wouldn't Like." An advantage of this procedure is that results are available for all members of the group, not just for those students nominated by their peers.

Sociometric instruments such as the ones just described can be used to determine how well their peers accept individual students. However, student ratings of other students must remain confidential. Students should be encouraged not to share their responses with others (Lewis & Doorlag, 2006), and teachers should not report results to students. Informing students that their peers poorly accept them is likely to have a negative effect on self-concept.

ENHANCEDetext
Video Example 10.4
Watch this video to find out more about classroom management.

SCHOOL ATTITUDES AND INTERESTS

A student's interests and attitudes may be related to how well that student performs in school. Poor academic achievement, frustration in complying with classroom rules, and difficulty relating to teachers and peers do not lead to positive attitudes toward the school experience. Similarly, disinterest and negative attitudes can contribute to school performance problems. The relationships among interests, attitudes, and school behaviors are complex, usually making it impossible to determine which factors were causes and which were effects.

Attitudes Toward School

Several measures are available for gathering information from students about their perceptions of the school experience. These measures assess students' attitudes toward various school subjects or their attitude toward specific classroom practices. In both of these important areas, the majority of assessment tools are informal and include interviews, questionnaires, and checklists.

A few formal measures have been developed to assess school attitudes. One example is the *Estes Attitude Scales (EAS)* (Estes, Estes, Richards, & Roettger, 1981), which is now out of print. The elementary version of the *EAS* contains three attitude scales: Mathematics, Reading, and Science. The tester reads statements such as "It is easy to get tired of math" and "Reading is fun for me" aloud to the students. Students respond by checking "I agree," "I don't know," or "I disagree."

The secondary version of the *EAS* assesses attitudes toward English and social studies in addition to math, reading, and science. Reading is required, but test items are written at a grade 6 reading level. Examples of secondary level items are "Work in English class helps students do better work in other classes" and "Much of what is taught in social studies is not important." Students respond to each statement by checking "I strongly agree," "I agree," "I cannot decide," "I disagree," or "I strongly disagree."

If comparative information is not needed, informal measures of attitudes toward school may suffice. Interviews or questionnaires could be used to elicit students' views about the school subjects they like most and least and those they perceive as most and least valuable.

Several informal devices are available for assessing students' perceptions of classroom practices. For example, the attitude survey is appropriate for use with secondary students. A questionnaire could contain items that pertain to school attitudes, self-concept, interactions with teachers, and peer relationships. Another technique for gathering information about attitudes involves the use of incomplete sentences. For example, students could be asked to complete sentences such as the following:

- For me, school is _____.
- Learning new things in school makes me feel _____.

- When the teacher asks me to read out loud in class, I _____.
- When I have math problems to solve, I _____.
- In my opinion, writing a story or an essay is _____.

Student Interests

Interests are assessed to learn more about students' likes and dislikes. Information about students' preferences among subjects may prove useful in academic counseling. Knowledge of preferred leisure activities may help teachers select rewards for classroom behavior management programs or choose high-interest instructional materials.

The simplest way to find out about interest is to ask students to describe their favorite activities—the things that they most enjoy doing. Kroth (1975) has developed an informal survey consisting of a series of open-ended questions about student preferences, which include areas, such as friends, games and after school activities.

THE LEARNING ENVIRONMENT

The assessment techniques described so far have focused primarily on student: problem behaviors (including attention deficits and hyperactivity), self-concept, acceptance by peers, interests, and attitudes toward school. Although this is a necessary part of the assessment process, it is also important to consider the characteristics of the classroom and the other environments where the student must function. In the ecological approach to assessment, both student and environmental characteristics are of interest.

Ecological assessment studies the match (or mismatch) between the behaviors of the student and the constraints imposed by the environment. Thurman (1977) has identified three factors to consider: (1) the student's deviant or nondeviant behavior, (2) the student's functional competence, and (3) the tolerance of the microecology (i.e., the classroom) for deviant and/or incompetent student behaviors. Environments with a high tolerance for differences accept greater ranges of student behaviors.

Smith, Neisworth, and Greer (1978) also recommend comprehensive assessment of the learning environment. In addition to evaluation of student performance, they identify four major environments for assessment: instructional (curriculum, methods, and materials), social, services within the school and classroom, and physical.

The next sections describe strategies for assessing school learning environments. Included are techniques for gathering information about the expectations teachers hold for behavior, the instructional demands placed on the student in the classroom learning environment, interactions between students and teachers, and physical characteristics of the environment.

Observations, interviews, and other informal procedures are typically used to assess the classroom-learning environment. One published system for this purpose is *Functional Assessment of Academic Behavior (FAAB)* (Ysseldyke & Christenson, 2002), the current version of *The Instructional Environment Scale-II (TIES-II)* (Ysseldyke & Christenson, 1993). *FAAB* takes into account three different domains: Instructional Support for Learning, Home Support for Learning, and Home-School Support for Learning. The school portion of the system contains a classroom observation, a structured student interview, and a structured teacher interview. When these data have been collected, the classroom segment of the Instructional Environment Checklist is completed. It describes the learning environment in terms of 12 factors identified as critical for student learning. The factors are Instructional Match, Instructional Expectations, Classroom Environment, Instructional Presentation, Cognitive Emphasis, Motivational Strategies, Relevant Practice, Informed Feedback, Academic Engaged Time, Adaptive Instruction, Progress Evaluation, and Student Understanding. *FAAS* is not a normed measure, but each of the factors is described in detail, and examples of appropriate practices are provided.

Behavioral Expectations

Teachers differ in the behavioral expectations they hold for students. The same student behavior may be considered appropriate by one teacher but inappropriate by another. Thus, when investigating student behavior problems, it is necessary to consider the teacher's standards for classroom conduct. The most straightforward way of gathering this information is to interview the teacher. Classroom observations are another useful source of data.

One area of interest is classroom rules. In many classrooms, the rules for behavior are stated explicitly so that students understand which behaviors are acceptable and which are not. Rules may even be posted on a bulletin board as a reminder to students. Affleck, Lowenbraun, and Archer (1980) recommend that classroom rules be scarce and clear, list desired behavior, and be applied.

In some classrooms, the rules for conduct are not clearly spelled out. This, if students are confused about the rules for behavior, they may be unable to comply with those rules. To help students understand class rules, Clarizio and McCoy (1983) suggest simple rules, which are physically posted and explained, with as few distractions as possible.

The classroom behavior management system is closely related to the rules for conduct. This system may be a formal, explicit contingency management program or a less formal approach. Among the questions to consider in studying the classroom behavior management system are the following:

- Do students have a clear understanding of the expectations for classroom conduct? Are they aware of which behaviors are considered acceptable and which are considered unacceptable?
- Are students aware of the consequences of appropriate and inappropriate behavior?
- What happens in the classroom when students behave appropriately? Is appropriate behavior rewarded in some way?
- What types of rewards or reinforcers are provided? Are students rewarded with social reinforcers such as teacher praise? Can they earn activity reinforcers such as free time in the media center or the opportunity to do a special art project? Are tangible rewards like stars, notes home to parents, or school supplies used for reinforcement? Are edible rewards provided?

- Is there a formal system for rewarding appropriate behavior? For example, do students earn points for good behavior and later trade their points for reinforcers? If a formal system is in place, does it include provisions for inappropriate behavior?
- What happens in the classroom when students behave inappropriately? Is inappropriate behavior ignored, or are there consequences?
- What are the consequences of inappropriate behavior? Does the teacher verbally rebuke the student? Does the student lose privileges or previously earned rewards? Is the student sent to the principal or kept in at recess or after school?
- Are consequences delivered consistently to all students at all times?
- How does the classroom behavior management system relate to the rules of the school and the school's behavior management system?

Instructional Demands

The instructional demands in the classroom-learning environment can influence student behavior. If students are faced with academic expectations that they are unable to fulfill, they may react by displaying inappropriate classroom behaviors. In assessing problem classroom behaviors, it is important to consider not only the behavior itself, but also the instructional events and conditions that precede it. Clarizio and McCoy (1983) suggest several questions to ask about the antecedents of problem behaviors regarding the context of difficult behavior. Those include timing, subject area, individuals within context, and academic requirements noted within problem behaviors. These questions relate to instructional antecedents, but the consequences of a problem behavior in terms of instruction are also important. What happens when a student behaves inappropriately? Do the academic demands change in some way?

The school curriculum has a major impact on the instructional conditions of the classroom because curriculum dictates what students are taught. The curriculum specifies not only the particular skills and information students should learn, but also the scope of these skills and the sequence of instruction.

Instructional materials, methods, and activities are used to implement the curriculum. Whereas curriculum is concerned with *what* is taught, instruction is concerned with *how* new skills and information are taught. Included under instructional considerations are learning materials such as texts and workbooks, specific learning activities such as classroom and homework assignments, and the instructional methods used by the teacher to present new information. In evaluating instructional materials, some major characteristics to consider are content, instructional procedures, opportunities for practice, initial and ongoing assessment, review activities, and motivational value.

Many of the factors considered in the evaluation of instructional materials are also pertinent to the evaluation of classroom learning activities. In addition, these questions may prove useful:

1. Do the learning activities match the instructional goals and objectives for the student?
2. Has the student mastered the prerequisite skills necessary for the learning activity?
3. Are the directions for the activity clear and comprehensible?
4. Does the activity present information in a way that is appropriate for the student? For example, if the task requires the student to read, is the level of the reading material appropriate for the student?
5. Are the types of responses required by the activity appropriate for the student?
6. Does the activity provide adequate opportunity for practice of newly learned skills and information?
7. Is there adequate feedback to students about the accuracy of their responses?
8. Is the activity motivating? Is some type of reinforcement provided for successfully completing the activity?
9. Is the classroom environment conducive to participation in and completion of the learning activity?

Popham and Baker (1970) provide additional questions that focus on the student's involvement with the learning task: Does the student know the point of the activity? Precisely what is expected? The value of the activity? Does the student have adequate practice to do the task well?

Also of interest are teachers' instructional strategies and the ways they attempt to modify instruction for students with learning problems. Lewis and Doorlag (2006) discuss four kinds of instructional adaptations teachers can make when students encounter problems with classroom learning tasks. The most drastic modification involves removing the task that students are experiencing difficulty with and substituting an alternative task. This adaptation should be considered a last resort. Lewis and Doorlag (2006) reported several other changes that can be tried first, including modifying the learning materials and activities, changing the procedures used to teach new skills and information, and altering the requirements for successful task completion. The teacher can be observed or interviewed to determine what types of instructional modifications have been tried and the results. In addition, when the student, rather than the learning environment, is under assessment, this hierarchy for altering instructional procedures can form the basis of a series of diagnostic probes or diagnostic teaching sequences.

Putnam, Deshler, and Schumaker (1993) describe a system for analysis of the demands of the instructional setting for students at the secondary level. Among the domains of interest are requirements for student assignments, tests, and class participation. A hierarchical approach is used. Each domain is analyzed to determine required performance areas. Then each performance area is analyzed to identify the elements that comprise it. For example, classroom tests require three performance areas: preparing for the test, answering test questions, and following directions. The demand elements involved in following test directions are readability, length, sentence structure, and clarity. Once instructional demands have been analyzed, it becomes possible to identify the learning strategies that students require to meet those demands.

Student–Teacher Interactions

Interactions between teacher and student are one of the key factors in the classroom-learning environment. Teachers can influence student conduct and academic performance by how they react to students' appropriate and inappropriate behaviors. For example, if a student volunteers to answer questions in class but is repeatedly ignored by the teacher, the student may stop attempting to participate or may resort to inappropriate behavior to gain the teacher's attention.

Assessment of student–teacher interactions is best accomplished by observation. The assessment team can design its own observation system or adopt one of the many available systems and modify it, if necessary. For example, the *Brophy-Good Teacher-Child Dyadic Interaction System* (Brophy & Good, 1969) is designed to assess the verbal interactions between the teacher and each individual student in the classroom. For each interaction, information is gathered about the classroom activity, the initiator of the interaction, the nature of the interaction, the appropriateness of the student's response, and the type of feedback provided by the teacher. Chapman, Larsen, and Parker (1979) describe the five types of student–teacher interactions of interest in the *Brophy-Good* system. Those include replying to questions, reading aloud, explaining, and discussion regarding supplies, homework, or a behavioral issue. In this system, data are recorded on each interaction as it occurs, so that the sequence of events in classroom interactions can be analyzed.

The *Flanders' Interaction Analysis Categories* (Flanders, 1970), another system for observing teacher–student interactions, targets three types of behavior for observation: teacher talk, pupil talk, and silence. These behaviors are further broken down into 10 categories used for coding. The observer uses the codes to record the type of interaction that occurs every 4 seconds for a short period of time each day over several days.

The *EBASS (EcoBehavioral Assessment System Software)* (Greenwood Carta, Kamps, & Delquadri, 1997) is a computer-based classroom observation system developed at the Juniper Gardens Children's Project at the University of Kansas. This well-designed system includes three instruments, one of which is appropriate for both general and special education K–12 classrooms. That instrument, the *MS-CISSAR,* allows the observer to gather data about student, teacher, and ecological events. For example, three types of student events are observed: academic responses, competing responses, and task management (e.g., raising hand, manipulating materials). Teacher events include teacher definition (e.g., regular teacher, special educator, aide), teacher position, teacher behavior, teacher focus, and teacher approval.

Among the events under study in the classroom ecology are setting (e.g., regular classroom, resource room), physical arrangement, activity, task, and instructional grouping. In using the *EBASS,* a trained observer enters data directly on a portable computer. That data can then be analyzed in several ways, including the percentage of occurrence of any specific type of event and analysis of the student's academic engagement over time.

Observation systems such as the *Brophy-Good, Flanders,* and *EBASS* may be modified as needed. Depending on the purpose of the observation, it may become necessary to add or delete behavioral categories. The behaviors of interest in observation depend on the particular situation: the grade level of the classroom, the specific classroom activities, the characteristics of the student and teacher, and the assessment questions under study. However, an unfavorable learning environment is indicated when observations show few interactions between students and teacher and few positive teacher responses to student behaviors.

Students may be able to contribute information about student–teacher interactions or at least their perceptions of those interactions. For example, rating scales are designed to probe students' opinions of the teacher's performance. Scales contain several descriptions of teacher behavior in language tailored to the level of elementary or secondary students. Included on the scales are items relating to the teacher's attention to individual differences and strategies for providing praise and encouragement.

The Physical Environment

Physical conditions can influence the effectiveness of the classroom-learning environment. A noisy room, poorly arranged surroundings, and uncomfortable temperatures can impair both students' and teachers' ability to perform at their best. Reynolds and Birch (1977) have developed a system for evaluating the physical conditions of classrooms, including factors such as space and facility accommodations, teaching-learning settings, and instructional materials. Whatever classroom space is available should be arranged carefully to facilitate instruction.

In arranging the classroom, there are a great many alternatives to the traditional configuration of straight rows of desks. Turnbull and Schulz (1979) recommend that classroom-learning environments include such features as individual and group work areas, manipulative and listening centers, and rest and recreation areas. There are a number of options for arranging seating for classroom instruction: students can be seated at a table, on a rug, or on the floor; in chairs; or in more permanent arrangements such as groupings of desks and chairs.

Comprehensive checklists for evaluating the physical environment of the classroom and the school have been developed by Smith et al. (1978). Among the areas of concern are the safety of the learning environment, its accessibility to students with physical impairments and other disabilities, and physical factors such as lighting, temperature, noise, and color.

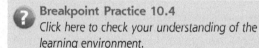

Breakpoint Practice 10.4
Click here to check your understanding of the learning environment.

ANSWERING THE ASSESSMENT QUESTIONS

The assessment team can choose to gather several types of information in its study of the student's current classroom behavior. Behavior rating scales and checklists serve as screening measures to identify possible problem behaviors. If problems are indicated, assessment continues with in-depth study of the behaviors of interest by direct observation or functional assessment. The characteristics of the learning environment are also investigated to determine whether classroom factors are contributing to the student's behavioral difficulties. With some students, other dimensions of behavior may be assessment concerns—the student's self-concept, acceptance by peers, attitudes toward school, and current interests.

Types of Procedures

The assessment techniques used to study classroom behavior supply information for several different assessment questions; thus, they are not expected to produce equivalent results. Dimensions such as classroom behavior and self-concept are viewed as separate concerns, and results in one area are not expected to duplicate results in the other.

Assessment of classroom behavior relies heavily on the information provided by informants. Teachers, parents, peers, and students themselves share their views through rating scales, checklists, interviews, and questionnaires. In interpreting these data, it is important to recognize that measures depending on informants are indirect. Whenever possible, results of indirect measures should be confirmed with more direct techniques.

Another characteristic of the strategies used in the study of classroom behavior is that many are informal techniques. Some dimensions of classroom behavior do not lend themselves to norm-referenced assessment; an example is the study of environmental influences. Available norm-referenced tools tend to be either screening devices like behavior rating scales and checklists or measures of student characteristics such as self-concept. However, some of these normed instruments have been criticized because of poor or unsubstantiated technical quality.

Informal measures have both advantages and disadvantages. In general, informal tools are designed to provide instructional information, and their results are more detailed and specific than those from formal measures. If the purpose in assessment is to learn more about the student and the learning environment so that an instructional program can be devised, informal techniques are preferred. However, a major disadvantage of informal measures is that their technical quality is typically unknown. They may be valid and reliable or technically inadequate. Therefore, results of informal measures must be interpreted with caution, particularly when used for decisions about program eligibility.

Nature of the Assessment Tasks

Assessment devices that appear to measure the same behavioral domains may, in fact, evaluate quite different dimensions. In selecting measures for the study of classroom behavior and interpreting their results, it is important to take into account how each measure goes about assessment.

Behavioral rating scales and checklists provide an excellent example of the range of variations that can occur among measures with similar purposes. For example, rating scales and checklists differ in the person or persons they select to act as informants; the identity of the informant is an important consideration in selecting an assessment tool. Teachers and parents view students from different perspectives, and if classroom behavior is the major concern, teachers are likely the better source of information. The observations of parents may be different from those of teachers, and peers may disagree with both teachers and parents. If students are given the opportunity to rate themselves, their self-perceptions may provide another perspective that is different from the perceptions of others. One way to account for divergent views from various informants is to include them all in the assessment process.

Rating scales and checklists can also vary on several other dimensions. These include types of student behaviors that informants are asked to consider; the underlying theoretical frameworks that influence the selection of behaviors and the methods used to derive results; and the ways in which informants are required to respond. Because of these areas of possible difference, rating scales and checklists that appear similar may, in fact, measure quite different aspects of student behavior.

Other types of procedures also bear scrutiny. Observations of student behaviors are influenced by the way the behavior is defined, the measurement system selected, the times and places that observations occur, the number of times the student is observed, and so forth. Similarly, observations of student–teacher interactions are affected by the coding system used to categorize behaviors. On sociograms, the specific questions that students are asked may determine their willingness to accept or reject a particular peer. Important differences are also likely to be found among measures of self-concept, attitude scales, and informal interest inventories.

Documentation of Classroom Behavior

Classroom behavior is one of the primary concerns of professionals on the assessment team as they attempt to answer the question, *Is the school performance problem related to a disability?* However, classroom behavior is an important consideration

for all students referred for special education assessment, not only for those who qualify for services for behavioral disorders. The general question under study is, *What is the student's current status in classroom behavior and social-emotional development?* This question is pertinent for any student with a school performance problem because of the possible relationship between poor achievement and inappropriate school behavior.

More specific questions about classroom behavior include the following:

- Is there evidence of a severe conduct problem? Of an attention deficit or hyperactivity?
- What are the characteristics of the classroom learning environment?
- What is the student's current status in self-concept and acceptance by peers?
- What are the student's current interests and attitudes toward school and learning?

These specific questions may be germane for some students but not for others.

The assessment team gathers data from many sources to answer the questions about classroom behavior. School records are reviewed for information about disciplinary history and attendance. Current behavior is studied by administering norm-referenced rating scales and checklists to informants such as teachers and parents. If the results of these screening measures point to possible problems, classroom observations are conducted and information is gathered about the environment in which the student is expected to perform. With some students, other dimensions of classroom behavior are of interest, and the assessment team may investigate the student's self-concept, level of acceptance by peers, or current interests and attitudes toward school. In the study of classroom behavior, teachers, parents, the student, and even peers share their observations and perceptions of the student's ability to conform to the behavioral expectations of the classroom-learning environment.

In analyzing the assessment results, the team's task is to describe the student's current behavioral status. This description is based to some extent on the norm-referenced data provided by behavior rating scales and checklists. However, many of the techniques used to study specific aspects of the student's behavior are informal strategies. Informal techniques are an excellent source of instructional information but do not provide comparative data. Thus, the team must proceed cautiously in interpreting the results and in drawing conclusions about performance deficiencies.

Determining program eligibility for students with behavioral disorders rests upon documentation of a severe and persistent behavioral disability. The assessment team must demonstrate that a behavioral disorder exists, that it is neither a mild nor a transitory problem, and that the disorder exerts an adverse effect on school performance. Several types of disorders are possible: an inability to learn that is not explainable by other factors, unsatisfactory relationships with peers and teachers, inappropriate behaviors and feelings, a general mood of unhappiness or depression, and physical symptoms or fears developed in association with school or personal problems.

Classroom behavior is also an important concern for students who do not exhibit behavioral disorders. For instance, professionals may be interested in documenting behaviors related to ADHD such as inattention, distractibility, impulsivity, and hyperactivity. In addition, any student, with or without disabilities, can require educational intervention at some time during his or her school career because of a behavioral difficulty. Consider, for instance, the case of Joyce, the fourth grader with school performance problems.

Assessment in Action
Joyce

The assessment team has almost finished its initial evaluation of Joyce; the fourth grader referred for academic skill problems. The team has established that Joyce has a school performance problem despite average intellectual performance and that her underachievement is likely due to a learning disability. Next, the team will consider Joyce's classroom behavior.

Although Joyce's teacher reported no classroom conduct problems, the team is interested in Joyce's relationships with her peers. To study this further, the team will observe Joyce interacting with her fourth-grade classmates. The observer, Ms. Gale, will look at Joyce's peer interactions in the classroom and in at

least one nonacademic setting such as the lunchroom or the playground. In the classroom observation, Ms. Gale will also take note of the characteristics of the learning environment and Joyce's interactions with her teacher. The team is also interested in Joyce's self-concept and her attitudes toward school and learning. In a previous interview, Joyce's parents described her as a generally happy child who has many friends in her neighborhood. This year, however, they noticed that Joyce doesn't seem to like school as much as she used to. She's not interested in practicing her reading or other academic skills at home, and she sometimes talks about how different she feels from the other students in her class.

To assess Joyce's self-concept, the team will administer one of the self-concept measures designed for elementary grade students. At present, the team plans to evaluate Joyce's attitudes toward school informally. An informal interest inventory will be used to find out about Joyce's current preferences in school and leisure activities. If more information is needed, Ms. Gale will interview Joyce.

The assessment team continues its study of Joyce by investigating several aspects of classroom behavior. Conduct problems are not a concern—Joyce's teacher had reported earlier that Joyce was a well-behaved student. However, to learn more about Joyce's interactions with peers and her teacher, the team has decided to begin assessment by observing Joyce's interactions in the classroom and in nonacademic activities such as recess.

Ms. Gale, the resource teacher, conducts a series of observations over several days. One purpose of these observations is to determine how Joyce relates to her peers in the fourth-grade classroom, and no problems are noted in this area. Joyce appears to have many friends among the boys and girls in her class. She interacts socially with the other students in the classroom, and at recess she is always included in one of the play groups.

The second purpose of observation is study of the classroom-learning environment and Joyce's interactions with her teacher, Mr. Harvey. Although Joyce does not exhibit inappropriate classroom behavior, some areas of difficulty are identified. First Joyce frequently asks the teacher to repeat or further explain the directions for academic tasks. This occurs at an average of three times per hour, a much higher rate than that of other students in the class. In addition, Joyce often requests help from the teacher when attempting to complete her classroom assignments. Again, her request rate is high in comparison to that of other students. Because of Joyce's requests for attention, Mr. Harvey interacts with her more frequently than he does with most other students. Despite this attention, Joyce often fails to complete her work on time. Seventy percent of her assignments are turned in either late or unfinished.

The *Self-Esteem Index* is administered to Joyce to learn more about her self-concept and self-perceptions. Items are read to her because of her difficulties in reading. Test norms are not used, but Joyce's responses are tallied for the four types of questions included on the *SEI*. In only one area, perceptions of academic competence, does the majority of Joyce's responses indicate a negative self-concept.

Ms. Gale then interviews Joyce about her attitudes toward school. Joyce reports that she likes some parts of school, such as art and recess and sometimes math, but that she is "dumb" in reading and spelling. She says she might like to read stories and books if she knew how, but that reading is "very hard to do." Joyce completes an informal interest inventory with Ms. Gale's assistance. Joyce's least favorite school activities are reading, doing workbooks, and writing her spelling words. For leisure activities, she prefers playing with her friends and her new puppy. She says she does not read for pleasure, but she sometimes looks at magazines and books with pictures.

In reviewing these results, the assessment team concludes that Joyce's peer interactions are satisfactory and her classroom behavior is acceptable. However, the team notes that Joyce appears to have difficulty remembering and understanding the directions for classroom assignments. Joyce's difficulties may be due in part to problems in memory and in part to the difficulty level of her classroom work. Thus, the team suggests that Joyce's classroom teacher provide her with less difficult assignments in an attempt to decrease her need for assistance and increase her rate of completion. The team also determines that Joyce shows needs in the areas of self-concept and attitude toward school. These needs probably are related to her poor academic performance.

The team has now gathered sufficient information to make a decision about Joyce's eligibility for special education services. School performance problems in reading, spelling, and handwriting have been documented, and the disability of learning disabilities has been substantiated through the identification of deficits in memory, memorization strategies, and fine motor coordination. Mental retardation, sensory impairments, and behavioral disorders have been ruled out as causes of Joyce's difficulties in academic achievement. Given these data, the team concludes that Joyce meets the eligibility criteria for programs for students with learning disabilities. The next steps in assessment will focus on gathering data about Joyce's specific instructional needs to plan her individualized program.

SUMMARY

- In assessment, there are two major approaches to the identification of behavior disorders. In the first approach, teachers, instructional aides, parents, and others who are well acquainted with the student provide information about the student's current behavioral status. In the second approach, emphasis is on direct observation of the student and the environment in which the student is experiencing difficulty.

- Disciplinary actions, teacher observations, and student reflections provide sources of information regarding classroom behavior. Educational records usually contain information about school disciplinary actions. For example, if the student has been sent to the principal or vice principal for breaking classroom or school rules, there will likely be a record of the incident and the disciplinary action that resulted. The student's former teachers may have left some written records of their observations of the student's classroom behavior. The team should consider report cards from previous years, copies of letters from teachers to parents, and any past referrals for special education assessment. The student also assists in the assessment of classroom behavior by participating in observations and by answering questions about current behavior, attitudes, and perceptions.

- The *Behavior Rating Profile—Second Edition (BRP–2)* is a norm-referenced measure that attempts to provide a comprehensive picture of the student's current behavioral status. Information can be gathered from four types of informants—students themselves, teachers, parents, and peers—to assess the student's performance in the home, at school, and in interpersonal relationships. The *BRP–2* is made up of four measures that correspond to the different types of informants.

- Direct observation of student behavior is the recommended procedure for in-depth study of the possible problem behaviors identified by rating scales, checklists, and interviews. Observation is a versatile assessment technique that can be used to study any type of student behavior—appropriate or inappropriate, academic or social, at home or at school. In the assessment of school behavior problems, data are gathered about the frequency and/or duration of specific student behaviors within the classroom-learning environment. The assessment team may decide to use direct observation to describe the student's behavior problems or as the basis for a functional assessment of those problems.

- The primary purpose of functional assessment is to determine the reason(s) for a student's inappropriate behaviors so that a successful behavior change program can be implemented. Put simply, the goal is to understand what function the inappropriate behavior serves for the student. To do this, it is necessary to understand the relationship between the student's behavior and environmental, social, cultural, and physiological factors.

- Attention deficits refer to difficulties in focusing and sustaining attention; hyperactivity is excessive activity. Both of these problem behaviors are difficult to define because they depend on the age of the student and the situation in which the behavior is displayed. Two-year-olds are expected to be more active and have shorter attention spans than 10-year-olds; a higher level of activity is expected on the ball field than in the classroom.

- The *Piers-Harris 2* is a popular norm-referenced measure of self-concept. It is a self-report instrument for students in grades 4–12. The *Piers-Harris 2* is often used in schools as a screening device to identify students who have possible self-concept problems.

The *Piers-Harris* is made up of 60 declarative statements that students are expected to read themselves. In addition to a Total score, six cluster scores can be obtained: Behavioral Adjustment, Intellectual and Social Status, Physical Appearance and Attributes, Freedom from Anxiety, Popularity, and Happiness and Satisfaction.

- A student's interests and attitudes may be related to how well that student performs in school. Poor academic achievement, frustration in complying with classroom rules, and difficulty relating to teachers and peers do not lead to positive attitudes toward the school experience. Similarly, disinterest and negative attitudes can contribute to school performance problems. The relationships among interests, attitudes, and school behaviors are complex, usually making it impossible to determine which factors were causes and which were effects.

- It is important to consider the characteristics of the classroom and the other environments where the student must function. In the ecological approach to assessment, both student and environmental characteristics are of interest. Ecological assessment studies the match (or mismatch) between the behaviors of the student and the constraints imposed by the environment. Thurman (1977) has identified three factors to consider: (1) the student's deviant or nondeviant behavior, (2) the student's functional competence, and (3) the tolerance of the microecology (i.e., the classroom) for deviant and/or incompetent student behaviors. Environments with a high tolerance for differences accept greater ranges of student behaviors.

- The assessment team can choose to gather several types of information in its study of the student's current classroom behavior. Behavior rating scales and checklists serve as screening measures to identify possible problem behaviors. If problems are indicated, assessment continues with in-depth study of the behaviors of interest by direct observation or functional assessment. The characteristics of the learning environment are also investigated to determine whether classroom factors are contributing to the student's behavioral difficulties. With some students, other dimensions of behavior may be assessment concerns—the student's self-concept, acceptance by peers, attitudes toward school, and current interests.

11

Academic Achievement

LEARNING OUTCOMES

After reading this chapter, you will be able to:

- Compare and contrast No Child Left Behind and Every Student Succeeds Act for considerations in assessment of academic achievement.

- Identify and discuss three examples of sources of information about school performance.

- List and discuss the four reasons noted regarding why group tests of academic achievement are not optimal for lower achieving students.

- Explain the *Dynamic Assessment of Test Accommodations* in the context of test accommodations for students with special needs.

- Compare and contrast the age groups appropriate for *WJ IV* and *WIAT III* in discussing individual tests of academic achievement.

- Describe the six subtests of the *Peabody Individual Achievement Test–Revised/ Normative Update*.

- Identify and describe two examples of subtests in the *Woodcock-Johnson IV Tests of Achievement*.

- Identify and describe two examples of subtests in the *Wechsler Individual Achievement Test–Third Edition*.

- Explain the *Wide Range Achievement Test-4* in other individual measures of academic achievement.

- Identify and describe two ways curriculum-based measurement strategies could be helpful in the assessment process.

- Describe an example of assessment technique differences in answering the assessment questions.

KEY TERMS

school performance

norm-referenced tests

individual tests

accommodations

School performance is usually equated with academic achievement. Parents and educators alike tend to view adequate performance in reading, language arts, mathematics, and other school subjects as the primary index of success in school. Although factors such as classroom behavior, study skills, and interpersonal skills may provide the foundation for successful achievement, school performance is evaluated in terms of classroom functioning, report card grades, and scores on achievement tests.

Students with special needs are characterized by school performance problems. They may have difficulty with one or two of the standard school subjects, or they may be unable to cope with any of the demands of the general education curriculum. Poor school performance is one of the most common reasons why students are referred by teachers, parents, and others for special education assessment.

However, referral for special education assessment should not be the teacher's first response to a student's academic achievement problem. In fact, it should be one of the last steps. Identification of an academic problem should signal investigation of the student's current levels of proficiency *and* the instructional factors within the class-room. The teacher can implement one or a series of instructional modifications and gather data to determine if this change improves the student's performance.

In many school systems, teams of educators (sometimes called "child study com-mittees") meet on a regular basis to help educators solve instructional problems. Teachers can use this resource as a prereferral strategy. The teacher describes the student's academic difficulties so that the team can suggest ways to modify the classroom-learning environment to improve the student's performance or to circum-vent the academic skill problem. Or the team may recommend other resources such as remedial reading services or evaluation for the bilingual education program as alternatives to special education assessment.

Of course, special education is the appropriate option for some students. When this is the case, the teacher can assist by providing the assessment team with specific information about the student's current classroom performance. Among the types of information that the teacher can contribute are samples of the student's work, records of classroom activities and the student's success (or lack of success) in these activities, observational data, test scores, and data on the effects of instructional modifications.

When students are first referred for special education assessment, the team asks, *Is there a school performance problem?* Academic status is also a concern in planning the special education program, evaluating its effectiveness, and determining the continuing eligibility of students with disabilities for specialized services. School performance is generally assessed with measures of academic achievement, and the assessment team asks, *What is the student's current level of academic achievement? Are there apparent strengths and weaknesses in the various areas of school learning?*

At this level of questioning, the special education team is concerned with the student's overall academic performance. Once it has been established that a school skill problem exists, the team will do an in-depth examination of the student's performance in each pertinent area. Here, the focus is on assessment strategies that provide a global picture of the student's current achievement status.

CONSIDERATIONS IN ASSESSMENT OF ACADEMIC ACHIEVEMENT

In the assessment process, school performance is generally operationalized as academic achievement. In the elementary grades, the main concerns are the basic subjects of reading, spelling, writing, and mathematics. In the later elementary, middle, and high school grades, the focus of the curriculum shifts to content area subjects such as science, history, and English and to vocational areas. However, basic school subjects such as reading and mathematics remain an important assessment consideration even during the high school years for lower-performing students who have not yet mastered these skills.

Purposes

School performance is assessed for several reasons. It is a standard area of concern for classroom teachers, and school systems routinely evaluate the achievement status of their entire population.

In special education, poor school performance is a necessary condition for the provision of extraordinary instructional services. Once students begin to receive special education services, their progress in the acquisition of school skills becomes an important evaluation concern.

In seeking information about a student's school performance, the assessment team evaluates current academic achievement in relation to the demands of the general education curriculum. Results from achievement measures help the team discover whether the student has benefited from past instruction and has the necessary skills to learn successfully in the general education environment. If a school performance problem is identified, it may be determined that there is a mismatch between the needs of the student and the learning environment of the general education classroom. The team may then decide that the student requires special education services. Before eligibility for special education is determined, however, the relationship of the school performance problem to a disability must also be documented.

Academic achievement assessment may also contribute information to instructional decisions. Global measures of school learning are useful for identifying the major curriculum areas in which students may require special assistance. Such measures also contribute information about the effectiveness of special education programs by monitoring students' progress toward instructional goals. Of course, general measures of academic achievement can provide only preliminary information for instructional decisions. Their results must be supplemented with results from more specific tests and informal techniques to gain an accurate picture of students' strengths and weaknesses in various school subjects.

Issues and Trends

School performance and its assessment have raised many issues over past decades. Although most of these issues pertain to general education, they influence special education because most students with disabilities spend at least part of the school day in regular classrooms. One theme that has recurred time and time again is public concern over the quality of the American educational system. In the 1970s, this resulted in the back-to-basics movement and minimum competency testing for grade advancement and high school graduation (Copperman, 1979; Gallup, 1978; Munday, 1979; Pipho, 1978). In the 1980s, the focus shifted to excellence in education, and several major commissions issued reports that criticized the state of public education and offered recommendations for improvement. Best known of the more than 25 reports is that of the National Commission on Excellence in Education (1983), in which authors noted that the country was "at risk" in the area of education.

Among the reforms called for in these reports was increased emphasis on content area curricula in the sciences, social studies, mathematics, English, foreign languages, and computer science. Longer school days and years, firmer discipline requirements, higher expectations and grading criteria, and improved preparation and remuneration of teachers were also stressed. States were quick to take action on these recommendations. For example, more than half of the states increased the number of academic units required for high school graduation (Bodner, Clark, & Mellard, 1987).

In 1990, President George H. W. Bush and the nation's governors agreed upon six national education goals for the year 2000. These goals became the foundation for the Goals 2000: Educate America Act of 1994 passed during the following, Clinton administration. With agreement on national goals for public education came a call for national performance standards and a national achievement test to assess students' progress. By the late 1990s, most states had adopted common academic standards for student performance and common measures for the assessment of student achievement of those standards.

The No Child Left Behind Act of 2001, the education initiative of President George W. Bush, strengthened the standards movement even further. No Child Left Behind (NCLB) focused on increased accountability for states at a federal level (U.S. Department of Education, 2002b). Among the law's accountability provisions was the requirement that states test all children in grades 3–8 in math and reading by 2005 and in science by 2007. Results were to be reported by state, district, and school and used to identify schools in need of improvement. Parents of children in schools that failed to improve would have the ability to choose to transfer their children to other district schools (U.S. Department of Education, 2002a).

Unlike most earlier reform efforts, No Child Left Behind made specific references to students with disabilities. It also required that states seeking federal NCLB grants develop plans that coordinated with other federal efforts such as the Individuals with Disabilities Education Act (IDEA) and other special education laws. This is an important proviso because students receiving special education services often receive a major part of their education alongside their general education peers. In the 1980s, some in the field of special education advocated for full-time placement of students with disabilities in general education (e.g., Stainback & Stainback, 1985, 1988, 1992; Stainback, Stainback, & Forest, 1989; Wang & Walberg, 1988; Will, 1986). Others objected, warning that more than one placement option must be available if students' needs are to be addressed on an individualized basis (Fuchs & Fuchs, 1988, 1994; Hallahan, Keller, McKinney, Lloyd, & Bryan, 1988; Schumaker & Deshler, 1988). The result was movement toward greater inclusion of students with disabilities, although other placement options remained available. For example, in the fall of 2002, 96 percent of students with disabilities ages 6 to 11 were educated in regular school buildings; more than 75 percent spent at least 20 percent of the school day in general education classrooms (U.S. Department of Education, 2006).

In December 2015, President Barack Obama signed the Every Student Succeeds Act. This act shifts the accountability to the states rather than the Department of Education. President Obama noted that the idea of accountability was important; however, in practice there were issues with No Child Left Behind. Critics noted that testing was overtaking instruction time, and resources were not supported by federal funds to support needs in schools (Dee & Jacob, 2010). Dee and Jacob (2010) also reported that while mathematics achievement performance increased, the area of reading performance did not show gains. This new law allows educators to break up testing throughout the year. In addition, states decide whether or not to adopt Common Core Standards (Public Law 114-95).

Current Practices

Assessment of academic achievement is a routine practice in general education today. Classroom teachers regularly assess pupil growth, and when students with disabilities are members of general education classrooms, they typically take part in these assessment activities. They may also participate in schoolwide testing programs, including the periodic administration of group achievement tests to monitor academic progress.

One problematic feature of general education assessment for students with learning problems is group test administration. Although group measures can provide some information, students with disabilities typically perform poorly on them. Unfortunately, the standards-based tests of academic achievement now mandated by states or districts use group rather than individual administration procedures. Although students with disabilities seldom participated in such assessments in the past, federal special education laws now require their inclusion. Some students will be able to participate in the assessments designed for their general education peers, whereas others will require accommodations. Study of the effects of test accommodations for students with disabilities has begun, and preliminary results are beginning to become available (Elliott, Kratochwill, & Schulte, 1998; National Research Council, 1997; Rogers, Lazarus, & Thurlow, 2014). Recommendations for test accommodations for students with disabilities are presented later in this chapter.

Because of the problems associated with group measures, individual tests of academic achievement are preferred for students with disabilities, particularly when information is being collected for decisions about eligibility for special education. Individual administration allows the tester to direct the student's attention toward the test task, provide encouragement, and explain requirements. The student can be observed carefully to determine whether environmental factors influence performance. In addition, many individual tests attempt to separate out skills so that assessment of one does not require mastery of another. Thus, reading skills are not required except on measures of reading. The necessity for writing skills is also minimized, except when these are the area of evaluation.

One of the first steps in special education assessment is the administration of an individual **norm-referenced test** of academic achievement. Tests that survey several areas of the curriculum, usually basic skill subjects, are most usual. Because the purpose at this point in the assessment process is to determine whether significant school performance problems exist, norm-referenced measures are appropriate. There has been much debate over the relative merits of norm-referenced versus criterion-referenced measures in achievement testing (Ebel, 1977; Perrone, 1977; Popham, 1978; Rudman, 1977), but norm-referenced tests remain the most common strategy for eligibility assessment. Norm-referenced measures provide the comparative information necessary for determining eligibility, and they are much more time-efficient. Criterion-referenced tests and other informal measures are typically used after eligibility has been established to provide more detailed descriptions of student performance in areas of educational need.

At present, three of the major **individual tests** used to assess academic achievement in special education are the *Peabody Individual Achievement Test—Revised/Normative Update*, the *Woodcock-Johnson IV Tests of Achievement,* and the *Wechsler Individual Achievement Test—Third Edition*. These measures are described in later sections of this chapter, along with others such as the *Wide Range Achievement Test—Fourth Edition,* the *Diagnostic Achievement Battery—Fourth Edition*, and the *Hammill Multiability Achievement Test*. In addition, two types of informal strategies are discussed later: criterion-referenced tests and curriculum-based measures. Although curriculum-based assessment relies on informal tools such as classroom quizzes, it has gained popularity as a method for determining whether students show school performance problems in the general education classroom.

 Breakpoint Practice 11.1
Click here to check your understanding of considerations in assessment of academic achievement.

SOURCES OF INFORMATION ABOUT SCHOOL PERFORMANCE

The assessment team can gather information about the student's school performance in several ways. In addition to individual tests of academic achievement, four major sources of information are school records, students themselves, teachers, and parents.

School Records

School records provide information about the student's past performance and educational history. Although current performance is the main concern, the team needs a picture of how the student has functioned in previous years and the type of services received. Records may also contain some current data, such as this year's report card grades.

School Grades

Both current and past report card grades and teachers' comments should be reviewed. Is the problem new, or does it reflect a continuing pattern of school performance difficulty? Do grades suggest academic achievement deficiencies in all areas or only in selected subjects?

Retentions

School records may show that a student has been retained or considered for retention. If retention was suggested, was poor academic achievement one of the major reasons? If the student was retained, what grade or grades were repeated? What were the effects of the grade repetition?

Special Services

Referral to special services may be part of a student's record. Has the student been recommended for remedial tutoring, bilingual evaluation, special education assessment, or other services? If so, what were the reasons for the referral, and what was its disposition? Did special services result in substantial improvement of school performance?

Attendance Record

Has the student been absent an excessive number of days in this school year or past years? What were the reasons for the attendance problem? Also consider the number of schools the student has attended. Was the student enrolled in several different schools over the past few years? If so, how similar were the academic curricula to the current course of study?

Group Achievement Test Results

With the cautions about group testing in mind, records should be examined to determine the student's scores on current and past group tests of academic achievement, measures of attainment of academic standards, and any other assessments relating to academic achievement. What tests were administered, and what types of accommodations were provided to the student? Are the student's scores indicative of a problem in school performance? Does he or she consistently score within the bottom one-third of age or grade peers in one or more academic areas? Are past and present results approximately the same, or is a problem just beginning to become apparent?

The Student

The assessment team can involve students in the evaluation process in several ways.

Individual Achievement Tests

One of the first steps after referral for special education services is participation in individual achievement tests. These measures provide an overview of the student's current standing in relation to other students in the major school subjects. In evaluating the results of these tests, the team considers both the student's behavior during the testing situation and the final scores.

Current Classroom Performance

School records and teachers provide some information about current classroom performance, but the student is the primary source. The team may want to observe the student in the classroom to see how he or she responds to instruction. Does the student participate by listening and watching, asking questions, and attempting to respond to the teacher's questions? What level of accuracy does the student achieve in classwork? In independent academic activities, is the student able to sustain attention, work without assistance, and achieve an acceptable level of accuracy? Samples of student work can also be analyzed.

Attitudes, Viewpoints, and Academic Goals

Interviews help determine students' perceptions of their own performance. Information can also be gathered with questionnaires, if the measures do not exceed the student's current reading and writing skills. Among the areas the team may wish to explore are the student's attitudes toward school, favorite and most disliked school subjects, and perceptions of the reason for referral. In addition, students can report on their academic goals and perhaps their vocational aspirations. They may perceive a difficult subject as unimportant to their academic or vocational future and therefore expend little energy in attempting to master it.

Teachers

Teachers are an important source of information about current classroom functioning. Often the teacher initiates the referral for special education assessment after careful observation of the student's daily performance. Teachers should be consulted about several different aspects of school performance.

Reason for Referral

If the student's general education teacher was the source of the referral for special education assessment, the team should interview this teacher to find out more about the reasons for referral. Is the student able to meet regular classroom expectations for achievement in any subject areas? In what specific areas is the student experiencing difficulty? How does the student's performance compare with that of the rest of the class?

Past Classroom Performance

The student's former teachers may also be of assistance. They can describe classroom performance in past years, perhaps documenting a history of learning difficulties. Or they may be able to report about instructional strategies that proved successful.

Current Classroom Performance

Current teachers can provide up-to-date report card grades, results of classroom quizzes, and samples of assignments and other completed work. They can also report their daily observations of the student in the instructional environment. In addition, teachers can describe the academic level and quality of work the student is able to perform. Is the student using grade-level materials? If so, is he or she able to master these? If the student is placed in more elementary materials, what is their level? Are they appropriate for current skills? Is the student attentive during instruction? Does he or she participate by asking and answering questions? Is the student able to work independently?

Instructional Modifications

Past and present teachers can provide information about the modification of instruction. If the student is unable to meet the classroom demands, what changes were made to increase the probability of success? What were the results of these changes? Does the student require more complete explanations of new concepts than are required by most learners? Is it necessary to repeat and explain task instructions? Does the student need more opportunities for practice? Does allowing the student additional time increase accuracy? Or is it necessary to assign less or easier work?

Parents and Other Family Members

Whereas teachers have the best opportunity for observing academic performance in the classroom, parents and other family members are best able to report about the use of academic skills at home and in the community.

Reason for Referral

If the student's parents initiated the referral for special education assessment, the team will want to find out why. Are the student's parents concerned about academic achievement? What led to this concern—poor grades, lack of skills or difficulty with academic tasks, or discrepancies between siblings' performance?

Past Educational Performance

Parents can usually provide information about when their child first began showing signs of academic difficulties. Parents often become concerned about their child's school achievement long before the school takes official notice. Sometimes this is due to unrealistic expectations and aspirations for their child. Many times, however, parents make an accurate assessment because they know their child well and have ample opportunity to observe his or her performance.

Current Performance at Home and in the Community

Parents and others in the family are the best source of information about how the student uses academic skills in the home and community. For example, parents can talk about how their child handles money, if and what he or she reads for pleasure, and how the child copes with composition tasks such as writing notes to family members. Parents can also report whether their child can tell time and make change, and whether he or she is able to read road signs, television schedules, and restaurant menus. Parents make a valuable contribution to the assessment team's study of school performance.

ENHANCEDetext
Video Example 11.1
Watch this video to find out more about academic achievement.

GROUP TESTS OF ACADEMIC ACHIEVEMENT

Group academic achievement tests are typically administered in general, not special, education. Their results help evaluate the performance of individuals and classes and determine the effectiveness of school programs. Many students with special needs take group tests along with their peers in the general education classroom.

Group tests of academic achievement usually contain several levels, so that one test series can be used from the earliest elementary grades through high school. The subject areas assessed are the basic skills of reading, mathematics, and language arts. Many tests also evaluate reference or study skills and content area subjects such as science and social studies. Because group administration procedures do not allow oral responses, assessment of reading is limited to silent reading skills. Handwriting, written expression, and written spelling are rarely included because test items tend to be multiple choice to facilitate scoring.

Students are usually furnished with test booklets that contain the items and directions. Directions are also orally presented to the group. Younger students may be allowed to record their answers directly in the test booklets, but older students use separate answer sheets. Some group measures provide practice tests that introduce students to the types of questions used and procedures for marking the answer sheet. Group tests can be scored by hand, and publishers may offer machine-scoring services. With sophisticated computer-generated reports, results can be presented by class, grade, school, district, pupil, and test item.

Many types of scores are available for group measures. The most typical are grade equivalents, percentile ranks, and stanines. Many tests also link items to instructional objectives, so individual or class reports include a listing of mastered and unmastered skills.

Popular group tests of academic achievement include the *TerraNova, Third Edition* (2015) (Terra Nova online), the *Iowa Assessments* (Hoover, Dunbar, & Frisbie, 2001, 2003, 2011), the *Metropolitan Achievement Tests—Eighth Edition* (2001), and the *Stanford Achievement Tests—Tenth Edition* (2002).

These are traditional group tests in multiple-choice format, although some tests are beginning to include items that tap higher-order thinking skills.

The administration procedures used in group testing are not optimal for lower-performing students for several reasons:

- Group tests require reading ability, even when assessing skills other than reading.
- Group tests are often timed.
- Students must write their answers, usually on a separate answer sheet.
- Group administration procedures assume that students can work independently, monitor their own behavior, and sustain attention to test tasks.

When interpreting results of group testing, it should be remembered that these measures tend to produce a low estimate of the performance of students with disabilities. In addition, very low test scores tend to be less reliable than scores within the average range.

However, group tests do have some uses in special education, particularly in the screening process. Results of the achievement tests administered at regular grade intervals should be reviewed carefully to identify students needing further assessment. Such tests can also provide information about the academic progress of students with disabilities in relation to their peers in the general education classroom.

TEST ACCOMMODATIONS FOR STUDENTS WITH SPECIAL NEEDS

Federal law requires IEP teams to determine what accommodations, if any, are needed by students with disabilities to allow their participation in the state-, district-, or schoolwide testing programs designed to assess the academic progress of all students. Most students with mild disabilities should be able to take part in these general education assessments, although many will require accommodations. For students with more severe disabilities who are unable to participate even with accommodations, the individualized education program (IEP) team must develop alternate

assessments (Heumann & Warlick, 2000; Towles-Reeves, Kleinert, Muhomba, 2009). Salend (1998) suggests portfolio assessment be used as an alternate assessment; Ysseldyke and Olsen (1999) recommend a combination of approaches such as observations, interviews or surveys, record reviews, and performance-based tests.

Testing **accommodations** have been defined as an alteration in how a student performs an assessment (Elliott, Kratochwill, & Schulte, 1998). The testing modifications, discussed in Chapter 5, are examples of possible accommodations. It is important to recognize that accommodations can be used with assessment procedures other than norm-referenced tests. Students with disabilities who are members of general education classrooms often benefit when classroom assessment techniques are modified to accommodate their learning problems.

Like other aspects of the IEP, testing accommodations must be determined on an individual basis. There is no predetermined set of accommodations that fits with any particular disability label. The accommodations selected by the team must be listed on the IEP, and it makes sense that these modifications be consistent with those used during instruction. It is important to preserve the validity of the test; a listening task is not a valid measure of reading skills.

Several authors have developed organizational frameworks that describe the range of possible test accommodations. One approach, the Assessment Accommodation Checklist (Elliott, Kratochwill, & Gilbertson, 1998), lists more than 70 accommodations within these eight domains:

- Motivation
- Assistance prior to administration of test
- Scheduling
- Setting
- Assessment directions
- Assistance during assessment
- Use of equipment or adaptive technology
- Changes in format (Elliott, Kratochwill, & Schulte, 1998, p. 11)

For example, scheduling modifications might include extending the time limits for a test or breaking administration into several short segments, rather than one long time period.

Assistance during assessment could involve changing standard presentation and response modes. Instead of having to read test questions, the student might listen as they are read aloud by the teacher; instead of having to write a response, the student might dictate it.

Erickson, Ysseldyke, Thurlow, and Elliott (1998) present a simpler system. They divide testing accommodations into four types: timing, setting, presentation, and response. Timing accommodations are similar to the scheduling modifications described previously. Setting changes include administering the test in a different location or to a small rather than large group. Presentation accommodations involve changes such as reading the test aloud, providing test materials in an alternate format (e.g., large print, Braille, or audiotape), and repeating directions. In response accommodations, the student is permitted to answer test questions in an alternate manner such as by dictating or using a word processor.

States differ in the types of accommodations they allow for students with disabilities participating in mandated testing programs. According to a recent report (State-Wide Assessment Programs, 1998), half or more of the 50 states permitted these modifications:

- *Timing:* flexible scheduling, extra time, multiple/extra testing sessions
- *Setting:* small-group administration, separate test session
- *Presentation:* large-print, Braille or sign language, audiotaped instructions/questions

Modifications in response mode were less frequent. Twenty-one states allowed students to use word processors and 12 permitted audiotaped responses.

This situation is likely to change as state departments of education and local school districts begin to make serious attempts to implement the mandate for testing accommodations for students with disabilities. According to federal law, the IEP team makes decisions about accommodations, and those decisions become part of the educational plan for each student with disabilities.

Even in states where there are several testing accommodation options, however, not all options

are used with equal frequency. Roszmann-Millican and Walker (1998), in a study of the accommodations used in Kentucky, found that the most common were readers for oral administration (30 percent of students) and paraphrasing or repeating directions (26 percent). Modifications of response mode were less common: scribes for dictation of responses (16 percent) and technology (11 percent).

Chiu and Pearson (1999), in a review of the research on the effects of test accommodations, found evidence that appropriate accommodations resulted in improved performance on achievement measures for students with disabilities and for those who were English-language learners. These authors report that the type of accommodation most often studied was increased time.

Research continues in the area of testing accommodations and the broader issue of high-stakes testing and students with disabilities (e.g., Bolt & Thurlow, 2004; Cox, Herner, Demczyk, & Nieberding, 2006; Ysseldyke, Nelson, et al., 2004; Zhang, Wang, Ding, & Liu, 2014). Bolt and Thurlow (2004) found mixed support for the positive benefit of five common types of accommodations: dictated responses, extended time, large-print Braille, and use of sign language interpreters for test instructions. In another investigation, Cox et al. analyzed the number of different types of accommodations allowed by states and the percentage of students with disabilities participating in high-stakes assessment. Higher participation rates were found in states with higher numbers of accommodations available to students.

Dynamic Assessment of Test Accommodations (DATA) (Fuchs, Fuchs, Eaton, & Hamlett, 2003) is a tool that IEP teams might consider using when making decisions about the types of test accommodations to provide individual students. Designed for students in grades 2–7, the *DATA* evaluates students' performance in math computation, math application, and reading comprehension under varying conditions. In math computation, students attempt problems under two conditions: no accommodation and extended time. Performance in math application skills is evaluated under four conditions: no accommodation, extended time, calculator, and reader (the tester reads questions aloud). There are also four conditions for reading comprehension: no accommodations, large print, extended time, and read aloud (i.e., the student reads aloud). In each skill area, the tester determines the number of correct responses under each of the conditions and then calculates the difference between the student's score with no accommodations versus his or her scores under each of the accommodations studied. The *DATA* provides criteria to use when making the decisions about the effectiveness of the different accommodation types.

When the IEP team is discussing possible test modifications, it is helpful to begin with an organizational framework such as one of those discussed here. Such frameworks describe the range of options available to the student so that potentially valuable accommodations are not overlooked. Also important to consider are the language and culture of the student. Culturally and linguistically diverse students with disabilities may require other types of accommodations such as translation of the test and modification of items that are culturally inappropriate (Valenzuela & Cervantes, 1998).

INDIVIDUAL TESTS OF ACADEMIC ACHIEVEMENT

Individual achievement tests are preferred for assessment of school performance in special education. Like group measures, they are designed for a wide span of grades, usually kindergarten through grade 12. Instead of having separate versions for different grade levels, individual tests are usually limited to one version that includes a wide range of items arranged in order of difficulty.

As Table 11–1 shows, most individual achievement tests assess the basic skills of reading, mathematics, and spelling. Content subjects such as science and social studies are not included as often. Because these tests are individually administered, student responses can be written, oral, or even gestural. This allows the assessment of oral as well as silent reading and permits students with poor writing skills to bypass this difficulty when answering questions in other subject matter areas.

The following sections describe and critique three of the individual academic achievement tests used most often in special education. The *Peabody Individual Achievement Test—Revised/ Normative Update* is discussed first. Next are the achievement portion of the *Woodcock-Johnson IV,* and the *Wechsler Individual Achievement Test— Third Edition.*

PEABODY INDIVIDUAL ACHIEVEMENT TEST– REVISED/NORMATIVE UPDATE

The *Peabody Individual Achievement Test—Revised/ Normative Update (PIAT–R/NU)* is a norm-referenced measure commonly used in special education for identifying academic deficiencies. This test was originally published in 1970 (Dunn & Markwardt) and revised in 1989 (Markwardt). A new version with updated norms appeared in 1998 (Markwardt). According to its manual, the *PIAT–R/NU* provides screening across six content areas (Markwardt, 1989).

The *PIAT–R/NU* is made up of six subtests: General Information, Reading Recognition, Reading Comprehension, Mathematics, Spelling, and Written Expression. The most typical response format on the *PIAT–R/NU* is multiple choice. The student is shown a test plate with four possible answers and is asked to select the correct response.

- *General Information.* On this subtest, questions are read aloud by the tester. There are no visuals, and no choices are presented. The student listens to the question and responds orally. Test items sample several areas of knowledge, including science, social studies, fine arts, humanities, and recreation.
- *Reading Recognition.* The first 16 test items, in multiple-choice format, begin with simple matching questions. Students must select the letter or word identical to the stimulus, then progress to items that require students to locate words that begin with the same sound as that of a pictured object. Beginning with item 17, students are presented with words to read orally. Words are presented in isolation without context cues.

TABLE 11–1
Individual Tests of Academic Achievement

Name (Author)	Ages or Grades	SUBJECT AREAS ASSESSED				
		Reading	Math	Spelling	Written Language	Content Subjects
BRIGANCE® Diagnostic Comprehensive Inventory of Basic Skills—Revised (Brigance, 1999)	Grade pre-K–9, Age 5–0 to 13–0	*	*	*	*	
Basic School Skills Inventory—Third Edition (Hammill, Leigh, Pearson, & Maddox, 1998)	Age 4–0 to 8–11	*	*	*		
Diagnostic Achievement Battery—Third Edition (Newcomer, 2001)	Age 6–0 to 14–11	*	*	*	*	
Diagnostic Achievement Test for Adolescents—Second Edition (Newcomer & Bryant, 1993)	Age 12–0 to 18–11	*	*	*	*	*
Hammill Multiability Achievement Test (Hammill, Hresko, Ammer, Cronin, & Quinby, 1998)	Age 7–0 to 17–11	*	*	*		*
Kaufman Test of Educational Achievement, Third Edition (Kaufman & Kaufman, 2014)	Age 4–6 to 25–11	*	*	*	*	*
Peabody Individual Achievement Test–Revised/ Normative Update (Markwardt, 1998)	Age 5–0 to 22–11, grade K–12	*	*	*	*	*
Wechsler Individual Achievement Test—Third Edition (2009)	Age 4–0 to 50–11, grade pre-K–16	*	*	*	*	
Wide Range Achievement Test— Fourth Edition (Wilkinson & Robertson, 2006)	Age 5–0 to 94–11	*	*	*		
Woodcock-Johnson IV Tests of Achievement (Schrank, Mather, & McGrew, 2014)	Age 2 to 90+, grade K–12 and college	*	*	*	*	*

- *Reading Comprehension.* Students read a sentence silently and then select the picture that best depicts that sentence from a set of four pictures. The sentence may not be read more than once, and the student is not allowed to look at the sentence after the pictures have been exposed.

- *Mathematics.* On most items, the tester reads a question as the student views four possible responses. Test items begin with exercises

PEABODY INDIVIDUAL ACHIEVEMENT TEST–REVISED/ NORMATIVE UPDATE (PIAT–R/NU)

F. C. Markwardt (1998)

Type: Norm-referenced test

Major Content Areas: General information, reading, mathematics, spelling, and written expression

Type of Administration: Individual

Administration Time: Approximately 1 hour

Age/Grade Levels: Grades K through 12, ages 5–0 to 22–11

Types of Scores: Grade and age equivalents, standard scores, percentile ranks, stanines; for the Written Expression subtest, grade-based stanines, and developmental scaled scores

Computer Aids: *PIAT–R/NU ASSIST*

Typical Uses: A broad-based screening measure for the identification of strengths and weaknesses in academic achievement

Cautions: In administration, special rules apply concerning "false" basals and ceilings. Scoring is complicated by the need to use two sets of standard errors of measurement, one for raw scores and age/grade equivalents, and another for standard scores. Results of the optional Written Expression subtest should be interpreted cautiously due to concerns about reliability. Information is needed about the *PIAT–R/NU's* concurrent validity.

Publisher: Pearson Assessments (*www.pearsonassessments.com*)

that require matching of numerals and progress to areas such as numeration, basic operations, measurement, geometry, graphs and statistics, estimation, algebra, and advanced mathematics.

- *Spelling.* This subtest begins with multiple-choice items in which the student must discriminate the one response of four that is different; more difficult items require students to select a letter that makes a particular sound. Beginning with item 16, the format of this subtest changes; the student is shown four ways of spelling a word and is asked to identify the correct spelling after hearing the word pronounced and read in a sentence.

- *Written Expression.* This optional subtest contains two levels. Level I is designed for students in kindergarten and grade 1, and Level II for grades 2 through 12. In Level I, students are asked to write their name, copy letters and

words, and write letters, words, and sentences from dictation. In Level II, students are shown a stimulus picture and directed to write a story about that picture within a 20-minute time period. The tester can choose from two stimulus pictures, Prompt A and Prompt B.

Students must be able to attend to test tasks for several minutes at a time to participate in *PIAT–R/NU* administration. English-language skills are a necessity for comprehension of directions and questions. However, the multiple-choice format used in several subtests reduces response requirements; students can answer either by pointing to the correct response, saying the answer, or saying the number of the answer. The student is required to speak only in General Information and later items of the Reading Recognition subtest. Writing is required only in the Written Expression subtest. Reading skills are not needed for the Mathematics and General Information subtests because the tester reads the questions to the student. Only the Written Expression subtest (Level II) is timed.

 Breakpoint Practice 11.2
Click here to check your understanding of individual academic achievement testing.

Technical Quality

The *PIAT–R/NU* was renormed in 1995–1996 with 3,184 students in kindergarten through grade 12 and 245 young adults (ages 18–22). Approximately half of the students were males and half were females. Students were excluded if they were not proficient in English, but students in gifted and special education programs were included. The sample was selected to resemble the U.S. population as reflected in 1994 U.S. Census data. The final sample appears to resemble the nation as a whole in terms of geographic region, parental education level (an indicator of socioeconomic status), and race or ethnic group. Also, the sample appears to be representative of K–12 students who receive services in special and gifted education. For example, 5.9 percent of the sample was identified as learning disabled, similar to the 5.5 percent figure reported by the U.S. Department of Education (1995).

The *PIAT–R/NU* appears most appropriate for students in kindergarten through grade 12, although norms are also available for individuals ages 18 to 22. It is not appropriate for students who do not speak English. It is interesting to note that the 1995–1996 renorming study revealed changes in academic performance since the 1986 norming of the *PIAT–R*. Markwardt (1998) reports:

> The average level of performance tends to have fallen at the earliest grades (grades 1 through 3) but has stayed the same or, in some cases, increased at the secondary level. . . . For below-average students, performance in the NU norm sample tends to be lower than in the original PIAT–R standardization sample. (p. 121)

Reliability and validity are also of concern in evaluating the technical quality of a norm-referenced test. However, the 1998 manual for the *PIAT–R/NU* does not provide new information;

instead, it reports on the reliability and validity of the *PIAT–R* and its predecessor, the *PIAT.* On the *PIAT–R,* reliability was studied by several methods. For the five required *PIAT–R* subtests and the Total Test score, split-half and Kuder–Richardson reliability coefficients were above the suggested .80 minimum at all grade and age levels. Test-retest reliability was generally adequate for these subtests, although coefficients fell in the .70s for some subtests for grade 6/age 12 students.

Reliability was studied somewhat differently for the optional subtest, Written Expression. Level I of that subtest shows high interrater reliability (.90 for kindergarten and .95 for grade 1); however, internal consistency coefficients ranged from .60 to .69, and test-retest reliability was .56. On Level II of Written Expression, most internal consistency coefficients fell at .80 or above. In contrast, the median correlation coefficient for interrater reliability was .58 for Prompt A and .67 for Prompt B. In addition, the average degree of relationship between student performance on Prompt A and on Prompt B was .63, indicating less than satisfactory alternate-form reliability.

Concurrent validity of the *PIAT–R* was studied by assessing its relationship to the *Peabody Picture Vocabulary Test–Revised (PPVT–R)* (Dunn & Dunn, 1981). The median correlation coefficient between *PPVT–R* results and results of individual *PIAT–R* subtests ranged from .50 to .72. Factor analysis was also used to investigate the *PIAT–R*'s validity. Three factors emerged, all of which appear to represent verbal skills. The first, described in the manual as "a general verbal-educational ability factor" (p. 72), includes the General Information, Mathematics, and Reading Comprehension subtests. The second factor includes Spelling and Reading Recognition and appears to relate more to verbal skills associated with symbol systems. The third factor is associated with the Reading Comprehension and Written Expression (Level II) subtests.

There is a need for more information about the relationship of the *PIAT–R/NU* to other tests of academic achievement. Although the 1995–1996 renorming study included not only the *PIAT–R* but also three other achievement measures, the *PIAT–R/NU* manual does not discuss the relationships between results of these tests. The manual does provide summaries of more than 50 validity studies of the original *PIAT*. In general, the 1970 *PIAT* showed moderate correlations with individual measures such as the *Wide Range Achievement Test* (Jastak & Jastak, 1978), the *Woodcock-Johnson Psycho-Educational Battery* (Woodcock & Johnson, 1977), the *Woodcock Reading Mastery Tests* (Woodcock, 1973), and the *KeyMath Diagnostic Arithmetic Test* (Connolly, Nachtman, & Pritchett, 1971, 1976). However, all of these tests have undergone revisions.

Administration Considerations

According to the *PIAT–R/NU* manual, only "minimal" (p. 3) qualifications are required for test administration. Before results are used for educational decisions, however, the manual advises that testers study the administration and scoring procedures and practice test administration. Interpretation of test results requires additional expertise, particularly in the areas of measurement and curriculum.

The *PIAT–R/NU* is relatively easy to administer and score, and Parts II and III of the manual provide guidelines for these procedures. The testing materials include the manual, four administration booklets, and the Test Record in which the examiner records the student's responses and the student writes responses for the Written Expression subtest. The administration booklets are in easel format. The tester sits across the corner of the table from the student so that the tester can view both sides of the easel, as needed.

Subtests must be administered in a standard order, beginning with General Information, and the Test Record and test easels are arranged in that order. It is possible to omit a subtest, but the standard order must be maintained for the remaining subtests. The Reading Comprehension subtest is not administered to students who receive raw scores of less than 19 on the Reading Recognition subtest; when this occurs, the Reading Recognition raw score is also entered as the raw score for Reading Comprehension.

The *PIAT–R/NU* begins with standard introductory remarks that the tester reads to all

students. Training exercises are available for all required subtests and for Level I of Written Expression. For the first subtest, General Information, the Test Record lists suggested starting places by grade level. According to the manual, the tester should adjust this starting place if there is reason to suspect that the student's achievement is either below or above that of typical grade peers. For the remaining required subtests, the suggested starting place is the raw score earned by the student on the previous subtest. Procedures for the Written Expression subtest are somewhat different. Level I is administered to students showing less than grade 2 achievement in written expression skills, and Level II to those with grade 2 achievement or better; it is also possible to administer both levels.

There is no basal or ceiling on the Written Expression subtest; all items are administered on Level I, and Level II consists of only one task. On all other subtests, the basal is five consecutively numbered correct items, and the ceiling is five errors out of seven consecutively numbered items. The manual suggests that if the student misses the first item administered, the tester moves backward five items in an attempt to locate the student's optimal performance range. It is possible on the *PIAT–R/NU* to encounter situations in which students appear to attain more than one basal or ceiling. For example, a student might answer items 5 to 9 correctly, miss item 10, then answer items 11 to 15 correctly. In this case, the lower-numbered items (5 to 9) are considered a "false basal"; the *higher-numbered* range of items (11 to 15) is considered the true basal, and failures below that basal are disregarded. Likewise, if two ceilings are established, that composed of *lower-numbered* items is considered the true ceiling; successes above that ceiling are disregarded.

Only Level II of the Written Expression subtest is timed. Students are allowed 20 minutes to write a story. However, the manual advises that students be encouraged to respond within 30 seconds to Mathematics items and within 15 seconds on other subtests.

The *PIAT–R/NU* Test Record is well designed. It states clearly the basal and ceiling rules and suggested starting points at the beginning of each subtest. The tester should circle the number of the first item administered and draw a bracket around the basal items and the ceiling items. As each item is administered, the student's response is recorded on the protocol and scored. On multiple-choice items, the number of the student's response is entered; on open-ended items, the tester records the student's actual response. Incorrect answers are indicated by a diagonal slash through the item number. Criteria for evaluating performance on the Written Expression subtest are presented in the manual and Test Record. For example, in Level II, the tester uses a 24-item rating scale to evaluate the story the student has written. The scoring guidelines should be carefully followed, and as a check for accuracy, the manual suggests that a second professional be asked to score students' stories.

Results and Interpretation

The *PIAT–R/NU* offers several types of total test and subtest scores. Both age and grade norms are available, and the tester must decide whether to compare the student's performance with that of age or grade peers. Grade norms are generally the most appropriate, and the *PIAT–R/NU* provides grade norms for fall, winter, and spring test administrations. However, if the student is placed in an ungraded or special class, the tester may choose to use age peers for comparison.

A variety of scores are available for the five required subtests, including grade or age equivalents, standard scores, and percentile ranks. Standard scores are distributed with a mean of 100 and a standard deviation of 15. Using the interpretation system suggested in Chapter 4, the range of average performance on the *PIAT–R/NU* is standard score 85 to 115. The manual provides guidelines for determining if differences between required subtests are statistically significant.

Confidence intervals can be constructed around each score. The Test Record provides standard error of measurement values for raw scores by grade and age levels and by confidence level (68, 90, and 95 percent). Somewhat different procedures are used for standard scores; the tester must refer to an appendix in the manual for the standard errors of measurement. Values are usually decimals, which are rounded to the nearest whole number. For numbers ending in .5, the number is rounded up if it is odd (e.g., 3.5) and down if it is even (e.g., 4.5). Standard scores are converted to percentile ranks by means of a table.

These types of results are not available for the Written Expression subtest. Raw scores on both Level I and Level II are converted to grade-based stanines. Stanines are a nine-point scale distributed with a mean of 5 and a standard deviation of approximately 2. On Level II, it is also possible to determine developmental scaled scores that allow comparison of a student's performance to that of all individuals within the standardization sample. These scores range from 1 to 15; the mean is 8 and the standard deviation is approximately 3. In addition to subtest scores, the tester can obtain a Total Reading Composite, Written Language Composite, and Total Test score. Total Reading includes both reading subtests, and the Total Test score is a composite of the five required subtests. The Written Language score combines the Spelling and Written Expression subtests. All global scores can be expressed as standard scores and percentile ranks.

PIAT–R/NU results can be plotted on two profiles: the Developmental Score Profile for age or grade equivalents, and the Standard Score Profile. General guidelines are provided on the Test Record for evaluating whether differences between scores indicate true differences in achievement; however, the manual should be consulted for specific criteria in determining whether differences are statistically significant.

Figure 11–1 presents sample *PIAT–R/NU* results for Joyce, the fourth grader with possible school performance problems. Note that grade norms were used to evaluate her performance and a 68 percent confidence level was selected. The confidence interval for Joyce's Total Test performance is standard score 80 to 84. The chances that this range of scores includes Joyce's true score are about 68 out of 100. It can be concluded that, in overall academic achievement, Joyce is currently functioning within the low-average range of performance when compared to grade peers. Inspection of the Standard Score Profile shows no overlap between some sets of scores (e.g., Mathematics and

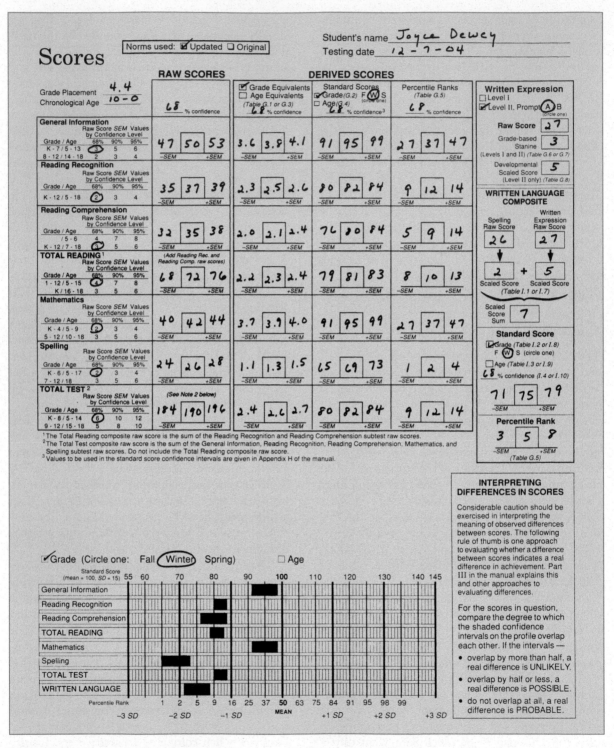

FIGURE 11–1

Sample Results from the *Peabody Individual Achievement Test–Revised/Normative Update*

Note: From Test Record, *Peabody Individual Achievement Test–Revised/Normative Update* by F. C. Markwardt Jr., 1998, Circle Pines, MN: American Guidance Service. Copyright 1998 by American Guidance Service, Inc. Reprinted by permission.

WOODCOCK-JOHNSON IV (WJ IV) TESTS OF ACHIEVEMENT

F. A. Schrank, N. Mather, & K. S. McGrew (2014)

Type: Norm-referenced test

Major Content Areas: Reading, oral language, mathematics, written language, and academic knowledge

Type of Administration: Individual

Administration Time: Approximately 60 minutes for standard battery

Age/Grade Levels: Ages 2 to 95+; Grades K–12, college

Types of Scores: Grade and age equivalents, standard scores, percentile ranks, Relative Proficiency Index (RPI) scores, CALP Level

Technology: web-based scoring

Typical Uses: A broad-based screening measure for the identification of strengths and weaknesses in academic achievement

Cautions: Results are available for more than 40 subtests and skill areas, making interpretation complicated. Caution is needed in interpreting the results of the Handwriting subtest due to low test-retest and interrater reliability. Little information is available regarding alternate form reliability.

Publisher: Houghton Mifflin Harcourt (*http://www.hmhco.com*)

Spelling). By consulting the manual, it is possible to determine that a standard score difference of 26 between these two subtests (Mathematics standard score 95 − Spelling standard score 69) is statistically significant at the .01 level for students in grade 4. Similarly, according to the table in the manual, there is a significant difference at the .05 level between Joyce's performance in Mathematics and Reading Recognition but no significant difference between Mathematics and Reading Comprehension.

In evaluating *PIAT–R/NU* results, it is sometimes useful to analyze the student's responses to individual test items. For subtests with multiple-choice formats, this may not prove very informative. However, some young or immature children will select their answers by position, perhaps choosing responses in the upper right quadrant of the page. The tester should check the student's response pattern for this. On the General Information, Reading Recognition, and Written Expression subtests, items are open-ended rather than multiple choice. Response analysis of these subtests may provide clues to the student's storehouse of general knowledge, word attack strategies, and a variety of writing skills.

ENHANCEDetext
Video Example 11.2
Watch this video to find out more about adapting lessons in instruction.

The *PIAT–R/NU* appears to be a useful tool for the assessment of school performance across a range of academic subjects. It includes measures of general knowledge and skills such as reading, mathematics, spelling, and composition. Caution is necessary, however, in interpreting results of the Written Expression subtest because its reliability is not well established. If information about writing skills is desired, the tester may choose to use this subtest as an informal measure. Like most other broad-based achievement measures that survey several academic subjects, the *PIAT–R/NU* does not produce results specific enough to provide direction for instructional planning; its main function is the identification of school subjects in which the student shows poor performance in relation to age or grade peers. It is also important to note that the *PIAT–R/NU* assesses some skills with test tasks that are not similar to typical classroom activities. For instance, classroom spelling tasks usually require students to write spelling words, not select the correct spelling from several choices.

WOODCOCK-JOHNSON IV TESTS OF ACHIEVEMENT

The *Woodcock-Johnson IV (WJ IV)* is a norm-referenced measure made up of 38 subtests in the *Tests of Cognitive Abilities* and the *Tests of Achievement.* Of concern here is the portion of the *Woodcock-Johnson IV* that focuses on academic achievement. However, one feature of the *WJ IV* is its capacity to assess both learning aptitude and academic performance within one assessment system. This feature was discussed in Chapter 7 in relation to the assessment of intellectual performance.

The *Woodcock-Johnson* was originally published in 1977. The revised 1989 version featured several new subtests, two alternate forms for the achievement measure, and a new organization of subtests into two levels: standard batteries and supplemental batteries. The third version, the *Woodcock-Johnson III,* featured several revised subtests, introduced new subtests and clusters (e.g., those assessing oral language skills), and replaced handscoring with computerized scoring. The 2007 *Woodcock-Johnson III Normative Update*

included new norms and new scoring software, but no alterations in the test tasks themselves or in administration procedures. However, a new brief form of the *Woodcock-Johnson III* was available on the *Normative Update.* Called Form C/Brief Battery, it was composed of nine of the original *Woodcock-Johnson III* subtests.

The *WJ IV Tests of Achievement* are designed to provide information about reading, mathematics, written language, and academic knowledge. Oral Language is now a third component of the overall *WJ IV.* Three forms, Form A, Form B, and Form C are available for the *WJ IV.* Form C is for follow-up testing with another evaluator. The standard achievement battery contains 11 subtests (called "tests" on the *WJ IV*), and the extended battery contains 9 subtests. The paragraphs that follow describe the subtests by curriculum area. In each area, standard battery subtests are discussed first and then extended battery subtests.

Reading

- *ACH-1, Letter-Word Identification*—On early items, the student hears a letter name and finds the letter on a page. Or, when shown a letter, the student says its name. On more difficult items, the student is asked to pronounce real words.
- *ACH-4, Passage Comprehension*—Early items present a colored picture and a choice of small line drawings called "rebuses." The student points to the rebus that represents the picture. Next, the student finds the picture that best represents a written phrase. Finally, the student is asked to silently read a series of passages. In each passage is a blank space where one word has been omitted, and the student's task is to say a word that correctly completes the sentence.
- *ACH-7, Word Attack*—On early items, the student must find the letter on a page that produces a sound read aloud by the examiner. On later items, the student reads nonsense words aloud. A pronunciation key is provided for the tester.
  - *ACH-8, Oral Reading* (new)—Students read sentences to examiner. Examiner then judges accuracy of the sentence.

- *ACH-9, Sentence Reading Fluency*—Students are given 3 minutes to read sentences, then mark "yes" if the sentence is true and "no" if it is false.
- *ACH-12, Reading Recall* (new) (Extended Battery). Student is read story and retells story.
- *ACH-15, Word Reading Fluency* (new) (Extended Battery)—Student circles words that are related.
- *ACH-17, Reading Vocabulary* (Extended Battery)—The subtest is divided into three parts: Synonyms, Antonyms, and Analogies. On the first two parts, the student reads a word aloud and then must supply either a word that means the same or one that has an opposite meaning. On the third part, the student reads three words and then supplies the word that completes the analogy.

Mathematics

- *ACH-2, Applied Problems*—The student solves word problems. In the beginning items, the tester reads a question while the student looks at a drawing. On later items, the student is shown the word problem that the tester reads aloud. Answers are given orally on this subtest, but the student may use pencil and paper for computation.
  - *ACH-5, Calculation*—The student is provided with pages that contain computation problems and writes the answer to each. Beginning items include simply writing dictated numerals and problems involving simple number facts and basic operations. Also included are problems requiring manipulation of fractions and more advanced calculations using algebra, geometry, trigonometry, and calculus.
- *ACH-10, Math Facts Fluency*—Students are given 3 minutes to write the answers to number fact problems.
- *ACH-13, Number Matrices* (new) (Extended Battery)—The student solves number grids both vertically and horizontally.

Written Language

- *ACH-3, Spelling*—Early items include making marks, drawing lines, and writing individual letters. On later items, the test takes on a dictation format where the tester dictates a word and the student attempts to write its correct spelling.
- *ACH-6, Writing Samples*—This subtest is made up of a series of brief writing prompts to which the student responds. Early items only require one-word answers. On later items, students must write a complete sentence. Prompts vary in specificity and complexity. For example, in some items, the student must write a sentence describing a drawing; in others, a phrase must be expanded into a sentence or the student must write a sentence to complete a paragraph.
- *ACH-11, Sentence Writing Fluency*—Students are given 7 minutes to write sentences. Students write to a series of prompts, each of which contains a drawing and three words. Sentences must describe the picture using the words provided.
- *ACH-14, Editing* (Extended Battery)—The student is shown a sentence or sentences with one error. After reading the passage silently, the student must locate the error and tell how to correct it. The tester may tell the student an occasional word but not an entire sentence. This subtest contains items that assess punctuation and capitalization, spelling, and usage.

Cross Domain Cluster

- *ACH-16, Spelling of Sounds* (Extended Battery)—Through audio recording the student writes the nonsense word heard.
- *ACH-18, Science* (Extended Battery)—
- *ACH-19, Social Studies* (Extended Battery)—
- *ACH-20, Humanities* (Extended Battery)—

For ACH 18-20 the tester reads questions aloud, and the student replies orally (or, on early items, by pointing). Drawings accompany some of the questions. Items sample areas such as general scientific knowledge, geography, economics, art, music, and literature.

Within most academic areas are two or more subskills that make up the general skill. For example, reading is broken into Broad Reading, Basic Reading Skills, Reading Comprehension, Reading Fluency, and Reading Rate. In selective testing, the standard reading measures (Letter–Word Identification, Passage Comprehension, Word Attack, Oral Reading and Sentence Reading Fluency) would be administered; then, if Basic Reading Skills appeared to be a problem, the tester could choose to give the supplementary subtests Reading Recall and Word Reading Fluency. Reading Vocabulary also is added to create a Reading Comprehension cluster.

Students must be able to attend to test tasks for several minutes at a time to participate in *WJ IV* administration. English-language skills are a necessity (except for the Calculation subtest). However, a Spanish-language version of the *WJ III* battery, the *Batería III Woodcock-Muñoz* (Woodcock, Muñoz-Sandoval, McGrew, & Mather, 2005) is available.

Reading skills are required on the reading and written expression subtests. Students respond orally on many subtests. However, writing is required on Word Reading Fluency, Calculation, Math Facts Fluency, all written expression subtests (except Editing), Spelling of Sounds, Writing Samples, and Sentence Writing Fluency. The three fluency subtests are timed. An audiotape recording is used in the administration of Spelling of Sounds.

Technical Quality

The *Woodcock-Johnson IV* was standardized with a total of 7,416 individuals from preschool ($n = 664$), K–12 ($n = 3,891$), college ($n = 775$) and adult ($n = 2,086$) age groups across 46 states and the District of Columbia. The sample was selected to resemble the national population on a range of variables such as geographic region, community type, sex, country of birth, race/ethnicity, parent education, and school type; weighting procedures were used to assure that the sample distribution conformed to the population distribution on these variables according to 2010 U.S. Census projection information (Laforte, McGrew, & Schrank, 2014).

The psychometric characteristics of the *WJ IV* are reported in the technical manual (Schrank et al., 2014). Several types of reliability were studied, including split-half, alternate forms, and test-retest. Internal consistency, as measured by the split-half method (as well as an alternate procedure for timed tests), appears adequate for all subtest and cluster scores. Alternate-forms reliability for Form A and B, A and C, and B and C reveal coefficients within an appropriate range (most above .9), except Sentence Writing Fluency for Form B and C at .79. Test-retest reliability median coefficients for the Achievement portion of the *WJ IV* were above .80 (except Science at .76).

The validity of the *WJ IV* is described in the technical manual (Schrank et al., 2014) in terms of the relationship between test content and the cognitive abilities theory upon which the measure was based; the developmental patterns of performance that emerge when test takers of various age groups are compared; and comparison of *WJ IV* to other measures of cognitive, oral language and achievement. The performance of "clinical samples" (individuals with disabilities and those identified as gifted) in comparison with typical children and adults were also described. Results suggest support for the validity of the *WJ IV* Achievement Tests.

In general, the psychometric quality of the *WJ IV* is quite high.

Administration Considerations

The *WJ IV* is designed for use by professionals trained in the administration and interpretation of individual tests. In learning this measure, testers should study the procedures for administration and scoring and practice test administration under the supervision of an experienced examiner. Interpretation of test results requires additional expertise; professionals should be well grounded in measurement and curriculum and be thoroughly familiar with the range of scores available on the *WJ IV.*

The achievement portion of the *WJ IV* is quite easy to administer. One complication is that administration rules vary from subtest to subtest. For example, some tests require oral responses and some motoric responses (writing).

Instructions in the easel-style test notebooks are clear and complete. The first page of each subtest contains information on basal and ceiling rules and suggested starting points. Then each test page provides complete instructions for administration. What the tester should tell the student is provided. As needed, the tester is provided with a list of student responses that require questioning and the exact wording for queries. Test pages also provide pronunciation guides for difficult words. The *WJ IV Tests of Achievement* begin with standard introductory remarks that are read to all students. Then the tester selects the subtests to be administered. Choices can be made from both the standard and the extended batteries based on the assessment questions under consideration.

On most subtests, starting points are recommended based on the student's estimated achievement level. The three fluency subtests are timed. Administration continues for 3 minutes for both Reading Fluency and Math Facts Fluency and for 5 minutes for Sentence Writing Fluency. Each subtest has different basal and ceiling rules. Basal and ceiling rules are different for each test. Testing on the *WJ IV* proceeds in complete page units. Thus, when the basal is met, the tester finishes giving the items on that test page before moving backward to the beginning of an earlier page. A similar procedure is used in establishing the ceiling.

During administration of most subtests, the tester records the student's responses by writing a 1 for a correct answer and a 0 for an incorrect answer or no response (Mather & Wendling, 2014). On tests where the student writes responses in the separate Subject Response Booklet, the tester attempts to observe and score the student's responses as they are written. The test record form provides some space to record verbatim responses and notes about the student's test behavior.

Raw scores are calculated in the usual manner for *WJ IV* achievement subtests. Proceeding from raw scores to final test results on the *WJ IV* requires the software program provided by the publisher. The 2014 version of this program is titled *WJ IV Interpretation and Instructional Interventions Program Online Scoring and Reporting Package* (Wendling & Schrank, 2015). *WJ IV* Online Scoring and Reporting App are also available. Estimated scores are on the right hand of the recording form.

Results and Interpretation

Results of the *WJ IV* academic tests can be reported by subtest, by academic area clusters (e.g., Broad Mathematics), and by subskill clusters (e.g., Math Calculation Skills). More than 40 subtest and cluster results are produced, and each result can be expressed in a variety of scores based on either age or grade norms.

The *WJ IV* manual differentiates among four types of information yielded by the test: informal information (e.g., test observations), level of development (e.g., age and grade equivalents), proficiency (e.g., Relative Proficiency Index), and relative standing in a group. The last type, relative group standing, includes standard scores and percentile rank scores. Confidence intervals can be constructed around standard scores and percentile ranks, and standard scores are distributed with a mean of 100 and a standard deviation of 15. The first part of the computerized score report, the Table of Scores, presents these results as well as information about any discrepancies among the academic skill areas. In addition, it is possible to print a standard score/percentile rank profile as part of the test report. The parent report can also contain a summary in which the student's scores are categorized using the classifications Very Advanced, Advanced, Average to Advanced, Average, Limited to Average, Limited, Very Limited, or Extremely Limited. On the *WJ IV,* the Average category ranges from standard score 90 to 110 (percentile ranks 25 to 75). Low Average corresponds to standard score 80 to 89, Low to 70 to 79, and Very Low to 69 and below.

According to the *WJ IV* manual, age and grade equivalents provide information about level of development. Standard scores and percentile rank are provided in chart form. Proficiency information, in contrast, is conveyed by the Relative Proficiency Index (RPI). The RPI score is used to provide predictions about the level of performance the student will attain on tasks similar to the ones tested. The RPI is stated as a fraction, the denominator of which is 90. The denominator indicates the percentage of mastery (90 percent) of average students. The numerator denotes the particular student's percentage of mastery. Thus, an RPI of 25/90 indicates that when average students at the

---

WECHSLER INDIVIDUAL ACHIEVEMENT TEST–SECOND EDITION (WIAT–III) (2009)

Type: Norm-referenced test

Major Content Areas: Reading, mathematics, spelling, written expression, listening comprehension, and oral expression

Type of Administration: Individual

Administration Time: 35 minutes to 1 hour 45 minutes, depending on student's age

Age/Grade Levels: Grades Pre-K through 16, ages 4–0 to 50–11

Types of Scores: Grade and age equivalents, standard scores, percentile ranks, normal curve equivalents, stanines

Technology Aids: Q-Interactive web-based administration and Q-Global web-based scoring

Typical Uses: A broad-based measure for identification of strengths and weaknesses in listening, speaking, and academic skills

Cautions: Care is required when scoring the Reading Comprehension, Written Express, and Oral Expression subtests. Reliability falls below .80 for some subtests at some age/grade levels.

Publisher: Pearson (*pearsonclinical.com*)

---

subject's age or grade level achieve 90 percent mastery, the subject would be expected to perform with 25 percent mastery. CALP Levels are used to describe a student's proficiency in the English language, particularly those aspects of language related to cognition and academic performance. The term *CALP,* which was defined by Cummins (1984), stands for *cognitive-academic language proficiency.*

In summary, the *Woodcock-Johnson IV* appears to be a useful measure for the assessment of school performance across a wide range of academic areas and ages. The current version links evaluators to evidence-based and formative interventions. Its purpose is the identification of skill areas in which students show poor performance in relation to age or grade peers. An issue is administration time, if the tester chooses to assess several academic skill areas in depth. The vast number of scores and profiles produced complicates the interpretation process.

 Breakpoint Practice 11.3
Click here to check your understanding of WJ IV-Achievement.

WECHSLER INDIVIDUAL ACHIEVEMENT TEST– SECOND EDITION

The *Wechsler Individual Achievement Test—Third Edition (WIAT–III),* first published in 1992 and revised in 2002 and then 2009, is an achievement measure designed to accompany the Wechsler tests of intellectual performance: the *Wechsler Preschool and Primary Scale of Intelligence–IV* (Wechsler, 2012), the *Wechsler Intelligence Scale for Children–V* (Wechsler, 2014), and the *Wechsler Adult Intelligence Scale–IV* (Wechsler, 2008). Its manual describes the *WIAT–III* as an inclusive, individual test used for the assessment of individuals from pre-kindergarten to adult.

The *WIAT–III* contains 16 subtests. Five assess reading (Early Reading Skills, Word Reading, Pseudoword Decoding, Reading Comprehension, Oral Reading Fluency); five math (Numerical Operations, Math Problem Solving, Math Fluency-Addition, Math Fluency-Subtraction, Math Fluency-Multiplication); four written language (Alphabet Writing Fluency, Spelling, Sentence Composition, Essay Composition); and two oral language (Listening Comprehension,

Oral Expression) (Maccow, 2011). According to its manual, the *WIAT-III* assesses all achievement areas included in the federal definition of learning disabilities: oral expression, listening comprehension, basic reading skills, reading comprehension, mathematics calculation, mathematics reasoning, written expression, and total achievement. In addition, achievement results can be compared with results of one of its companion tests of intellectual performance; this feature was discussed in Chapter 7. The subtests of the *WIAT–III* are described in the following paragraphs:

Reading

- *Early Reading Skills.* On early items, student names alphabet letters. Then student makes rhyming words, notes words with same beginning and ending sounds, matches sounds with letters, words with pictures.
- *Word Reading.* On early items, the student finds the letter is the same, names letters, identifies rhyming words, and points to pictures of words that begin or end with the same sound. Later items require the student to read rows of words aloud.
- *Pseudoword Decoding.* The student is asked to read nonsense words aloud.
- *Reading Comprehension.* The student reads a sentence or short passage aloud or silently and answers one or more questions read aloud by the tester.
  - *Oral Reading Fluency.* Student reads passages and orally answers questions.

Mathematics

- *Math Problem Solving.* The student uses oral responses and gestures after hearing the examiner's mathematics applications questions orally and with visual cues.
- *Numerical Operations.* The student writes answers to mathematics computation problems in a separate Response Booklet. The first few items require the student to differentiate numbers from other symbols, find matching numbers, fill in the missing number, write numbers from dictation, and count aloud. Later problems range from one-digit addition and subtraction to operations with fractions, decimals, algebraic equations, and geometry.

- *Math Fluency (Addition, Subtraction, Multiplication).* The student solves written addition, subtraction, and multiplication problems (60-second time limit).

Written Language

- *Alphabet Writing Fluency.* Student writes letters in lower- and uppercase (print or cursive).
- *Spelling.* Here, the student writes letters and words to dictation. The student writes letters when given the letter name or the sound represented by a letter. On later items, the teacher reads a word aloud, then within the context of a sentence.
- *Sentence Composition.* Student forms and combines sentences.
- *Essay Composition.* Student writes an essay based on a stimulus.

Oral Language

- *Listening Comprehension.* This subtest begins with receptive vocabulary items; the tester reads a word, and the student must point to one of four drawings that best depicts the word. On sentence comprehension items, the student identifies the drawing that best depicts the sentence read aloud by the tester. On expressive vocabulary items, the student looks at a picture and listens to a sentence describing it, and then must label the picture.
- *Oral Expression.* The student says a word that matches with a picture provided. Then the student is given a category (e.g., fruit) and asked to name as many fruits as he or she can tell in a story and give oral directions. Student also repeats sentences.

Technical Quality

The *WIAT–III* was standardized with a total sample of 3,000 individuals, 2,775 of whom were students in grades pre-K through 12 (ages 4 to 19). Approximately half of the students were male and half female. The sample was selected based on 2005 U.S. Census data, and the final sample appears to resemble the nation's population in terms of race/ethnicity, geographic region, and parents' educational levels (an index of socioeconomic status). According to the *WIAT–III* manual, students who did not understand or speak English were excluded. Individuals with diagnosed disabilities were included in the sample.

The *WIAT-III* appears appropriate for pre-kindergarten through grade 12 students who speak and understand English. Norms for school-aged individuals are based on a large national sample that represents the general U.S. population on several variables. Norms for older persons appear adequate, though based on smaller samples.

Three types of reliability were studied for the *WIAT–III* internal consistency, test-retest, and interrater. Internal consistency, evaluated using the split-half method, is adequate across all grades and ages for composite scores, although correlation coefficients dropped below the recommended minimum of .80 for the Listening Comprehension subtest for grade 9 (.79) and Alphabet Writing Fluency was at .69 for the fall. For spring, Listening Comprehension was .76 for fourth grade, .78 for eighth grade, and .77 for eleventh grade. In Early Reading Skills a .72 coefficient was reported for grade 3. In Reading Comprehension a .79 coefficient was reported for grade 4. A coefficient of .69 was reported for Alphabet Writing Fluency. Reliability coefficients such as these cause the standard error of measurement to increase, thereby reducing the precision of test results.

Test-retest reliability is adequate for *WIAT–III* composite scores. However, coefficients for subtests ranged from .73 to .93. Coefficients for the average of all grades falling below .8 included Listening Comprehension (.75), Sentence Composition (.79), and Alphabet Writing Fluency (.69). Interrater reliability was above .9 for all subtests.

The concurrent validity of the *WIAT–III* was studied by evaluating its relationship to other individual tests of achievement, group tests of achievement, school grades, and other measures. Those include the WPPSI-III, WISC-IV, WAIS-IV, WNV, and DAS-II. In general, results are adequate.

Administration Considerations

The *WIAT–III* manual says that professionals should be appropriately trained to administer and interpret this type of instrument. Before using this test to gather data for educational decision making, however, the tester should practice both administration and scoring. Testers should pay special attention to the scoring guidelines provided for subtests in which judgment is required.

Although the scoring procedures require careful study and take time to administer (Burns, 2010), the *WIAT–III* is quite easy to administer. The testing materials include the manual, a double-sided stimulus book (in easel format), word cards for Word Recall and Pseudoword Decoding, the Record Form, a new separate Response Booklet for Oral Fluency, and the Scoring Assistant and Technical Manual on CD. Other materials needed include a pencil without eraser, scratch paper, an audio recorder, and a timing mechanism. As with other tests using easels, the student and tester sit across the corner of a table from each other.

Subtests must be administered in the order they appear in the test easels and Record Form. It is possible to omit a subtest if the order is preserved. The tester begins each subtest by reading directions aloud to the student. Starting points are based on grade level. The *WIAT-III* uses the term *reverse rule* for basal and *discontinue rule* for ceiling. On most subtests, the basal is 3 and the ceiling 4. The Reading Comprehension and Oral Reading Fluency subtests use item sets for starting points. Timing is required for portions of each achievement area.

The *WIAT-III* Record Form is well designed, with ample room for recording students' responses. For each subtest, there are reminders of the time guidelines, basal, ceiling, and suggested starting points. To score items, the tester simply circles the appropriate number. Examples of score choices include (Sentence Building) incorrect with multiple errors (0), one or two errors (1), correct—no errors (2). The manual (and stimulus books) provide guidelines for evaluating students' responses on these subtests.

Results and Interpretation

The *WIAT–III* offers both age and grade norms. Grade norms are provided for fall, winter, and spring test administrations, but the manual cautions that age-based standard scores are required if the tester is interested in calculating aptitude-achievement discrepancies.

Subtest raw scores can be converted to a variety of derived scores, including standard scores, percentile ranks, age and grade equivalents, normal curve equivalents, stanines, and growth scale values. Standard scores are distributed with a mean of 100, and a standard deviation of 15 and confidence intervals can be constructed around standard scores.

The same types of scores are available for the *WIAT–III* composites. There are five composites: reading, mathematics, written language, oral language, and total. The Reading composite raw score is computed by adding the raw scores of the five reading subtests. Similarly, the Mathematics composite is based on the five math subtests, the Written Language composite on the two writing subtests, and so on. The Total composite reflects all subtests. The standard scores for *WIAT–III* composites are distributed with a mean of 100 and a standard deviation of 15. The first page of the *WIAT–III* record form, called the Summary Report, contains space for identification information about the student and a table for recording the student's derived scores. The back page contains a table used in analyzing ability-achievement discrepancies and a profile for plotting standard scores.

The Test Record is also designed to help professionals analyze the errors that students make. For example, on math tests, there is a list of the skills assessed by each item. Qualitative observation checklists are provided on several subtests to record the strategies used by the student when difficult items are encountered.

In summary, the *WIAT–III* appears to be a useful tool for assessing current school performance across a number of subject areas. These include reading (both decoding and comprehension), mathematics (both computation and problem solving), and written language (both spelling and composition). Unlike some measures, the *WIAT–III* does not assess science, social studies, or other content subjects. However, it does provide information about oral language, an area that is rarely assessed by individual achievement tests. Results of the *WIAT–III* are best used to identify

school subjects in which the student shows poor performance in relation to age or grade peers.

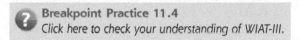

Breakpoint Practice 11.4
Click here to check your understanding of WIAT-III.

OTHER INDIVIDUAL MEASURES OF ACADEMIC ACHIEVEMENT

Several other individual measures of academic achievement are available to the assessment team. One is the *Wide Range Achievement Test—Fourth Edition,* the most recent version of a classic test that dates from the 1930s. Another, the *Diagnostic Achievement Battery—Fourth Edition*, assesses spoken language as well as the basic school skills. The *Hammill Multiability Achievement Test,* a newer measure, assesses basic skills and general information. Also of interest are criterion-referenced tests of achievement, such as the *BRIGANCE® Diagnostic Comprehensive Inventory of Basic Skills–Revised,* although these are typically used in later stages of assessment to gather information for instructional planning.

Wide Range Achievement Test— Fourth Edition

The *Wide Range Achievement Test—Fourth Edition* or *WRAT4* (Wilkinson & Robertson, 2006) is a norm-referenced measure of basic skills for grades K–12 and ages 5–0 to 74–11. According to the manual, the *WRAT4* provides an efficient measurement tool. Although some portions of the *WRAT4* can be administered to small groups, individual administration is preferred. Administration requires 30 to 45 minutes for ages 8 up and between 15 and 25 minutes for younger children.

Two forms are available for the *WRAT4*—the Blue form and the Green form. Each form contains four subtests, which should be administered in the order in which they are described below.

- *Word Reading.* On this subtest, students read lists of words aloud. Words are presented in isolation; each must be pronounced correctly within a specified time limit. A letter reading section is administered to children age 7 and younger and to older students who fail to meet the specified criterion on the oral reading section. In this section, students name letters.

- *Sentence Comprehension.* This subtest was added to the *WRAT* with the fourth edition. Students are shown one or two sentences with one word missing. They must read the sentence(s) silently, then say the missing word. The Sentence Completion subtest is not administered to individuals who score poorly on the Word Reading subtest.
- *Spelling.* Students write spelling words from dictation. The tester reads the word, then a sentence containing the word, and the student must write the word on the test form within a specified time period. A letter writing section is administered to young children and to older students who do not meet the specified criterion level on the dictation section of the subtest. Here, students write their name and letters from dictation.
- *Math Computation.* Students write answers to arithmetic problems. They are given a page of computation problems and asked to solve as many as possible within 15 minutes. Items range from simple addition and other basic operations to computations involving fractions, decimals, and percentages. An oral math section is administered to young children and to older students who fail to meet the specified criterion on the written section. Here, students are timed but respond orally. Activities include counting objects, reading numbers, and answering oral addition and subtraction problems.

Students require several skills in order to participate in *WRAT4* administration. They must be able to sustain attention to test tasks, respond with test time limits, and understand English directions and questions. Response requirements are demanding. Students must write their answers on two of the subtests and respond orally on the other two. In addition, both oral and silent reading skills are needed for the reading subtests. On Math Computation, reading tasks include reading numbers aloud in the oral math section and reading written directions for some of the computation problems.

The fourth edition of the *WRAT4* was standardized with a stratified national sample of 3,021 persons ranging in age from 5 to 94+ years. The sample was selected to represent the national population in terms of gender, race/ethnicity, educational attainment, and geographic region. A portion of the age-based sample ($n = 1,800$) was used to develop grade-based norms. Included were students with "educational disabilities"; the most common disability identified ($n = 49$) was specific learning disabilities. Reliability of the *WRAT4* appears adequate, including alternate form reliability. In concurrent validity studies, results of the *WRAT4* showed moderate correlations with other tests of academic performance, including the *WIAT–II,* the *Woodcock-Johnson III,* and *Kaufman Test of Educational Achievement, Second Edition* (Kaufman & Kaufman, 2004b).

The fourth edition of the *WRAT* provides an expanded repertoire of scores. Scores are available for each of the four subtests, and a Reading Composite score can be computed from the results of the two reading subtests. For the first time, both age and grade norms are available, and with grade norms, the tester can choose to use either fall or spring norms. Results are reported as standard scores (distributed with a mean of 100 and a standard deviation of 15) and percentile ranks. Confidence intervals are used to report standard score results. The tester selects a confidence interval of 85, 90, or 95 percent and then determines from a table in the manual the standard scores representing that interval. Results can be plotted on a profile on the front of the test form. It is also possible to compare standard score results from one subtest to another to determine if there are significant differences between scores.

The *WRAT4* is a much-improved version of this vintage measure. One good addition is the new reading comprehension subtest (i.e., Sentence Comprehension). Although this subtest only requires students to read a sentence or two, it does move the reading process beyond the simple word identification skills required in the Word Reading subtest. Even more important are the changes relative to scoring. Grade norms have been added to age norms, and results are reported as standard score confidence intervals. These improvements make the *WRAT4* one of the measures that should be considered when professionals are looking for a quick, reliable measure of basic school skills.

Diagnostic Achievement Battery— Fourth Edition

The *Diagnostic Achievement Battery—Fourth Edition (DAB—4)* by Newcomer (2014) is an individual achievement test for students ages 6–0 to 14–11. It is designed to assess skills in spoken language (listening and speaking), written language (reading and writing), and mathematics. The test includes eight subtests, although it is permissible to administer only a portion of these. Those subtests are Listening Comprehension, Synonyms, Alphabet/ Phonics/Word Identification, Reading Comprehension, Punctuation/Capitalization, Spelling, Mathematics Reasoning, and Mathematics Calculation. Composites include Spoken Language, Reading, Writing, Mathematics and Total Basic Academic Skills. Punctuation/Capitalization, Spelling, and Mathematics Calculation subtests could be administered in small groups in order to increase the evaluator's time efficiency.

Materials include the manual, student booklet, protocols, assessment probes, and audio CD.

The *DAB–4* offers assessment probes for each of its subtests. According to the manual, these probes allow the tester to go further than typical standardized testing by probing students' comprehension of test instructions, the thinking processes used in answering test questions, and their potential to learn to perform test tasks. The assessment probes provide qualitative information and are not scored.

Standard scores and percentile ranks are available for each *DAB–4* subtest. In addition, several composite scores can be determined. These include the Total Basic Academic Skills, Spoken Language, Reading, Writing, and Mathematics. Standard scores for subtests include means of 10 with standard deviations of 3, while composites include means of 100 with standard deviations of 15.

Hammill Multiability Achievement Test

The *Hammill Multiability Achievement Test (HAMAT)* by Hammill et al. (1998) is an easy-to-use measure of basic academic skills. Designed for students ages 7–0 to 17–11, the *HAMAT* provides two alternate forms: Form A and Form B. The *HAMAT* was developed in conjunction with a measure of intellectual performance, the *Hammill Multiability Intelligence Test (HAMIT)* (Hammill, Bryant, & Pearson, 1998).

Four subtests are included on the *HAMAT*:

- Reading
- Writing
- Arithmetic
- Facts

A novel task is used to assess reading skills. Students read brief passages, and, in each passage, three sentences are incomplete. In place of one of the words in the original sentence is a bracket enclosing four words in bold type. The student must select the word that correctly completes the sentence. In the Writing subtest, the student writes sentences from dictation; spelling, capitalization, and punctuation must be correct for the student to receive credit. In Arithmetic, the student writes answers to computation problems, and in Facts, he or she answers questions related to school subjects such as science, social studies, and language arts.

Reading is required only on the Reading subtest. In Facts, the tester reads the questions to the student. The student writes sentences in Spelling, writes answers to computation problems in Arithmetic, and circles words in Reading. Subtests are not timed. The *HAMAT* can be administered in 30 minutes to 1 hour, depending on the individual student.

Only age norms are available. Quotients (i.e., standard scores) are available for each subtest along with age equivalents, grade equivalents, and percentile ranks. A total test score, the General Achievement Quotient, is based on performance on all subtests. Quotients are distributed with a mean of 100 and a standard deviation of 15. The *HAMAT* manual also provides tables for comparing differences between subtest scores (e.g., Reading versus Writing) and for comparing the total test score with results of measures of intellectual performance.

Criterion-Referenced Tests

The purpose of criterion-referenced tests is evaluation of student performance in relation to specific instructional objectives. Test items are tied to objectives, so results are immediately applicable to instructional planning. However, because criterion-referenced tests are designed to thoroughly assess mastery of specific skills and subskills, they typically take a long time to administer. The detailed information they provide, though very appropriate for instructional decisions, is not the type of information needed for eligibility decisions. Therefore, criterion-referenced measures are most often used in the later stages of assessment to pinpoint specific skills for instruction. But if criterion-referenced test results are available for a student referred for special education assessment, the team should consider these data in its study of the student's current levels of school performance.

Perhaps the most popular set of criterion-referenced tests (CRTs) is the Brigance series. Although they are called inventories, these measures are CRTs based on instructional objectives. The series includes tests for early childhood, the elementary grades, and the secondary grades as well as a Spanish-language version for grades K through 8 and versions designed for students in secondary or postsecondary vocational programs.

The elementary version of this measure is called the *BRIGANCE*® Diagnostic *Comprehensive Inventory of Basic Skills–Revised (CIB–R)* (Brigance, 1999), and its tests are clustered into five major areas:

- Readiness
- Oral Language
- Reading
- Writing
- Mathematics

Overall, the *CIB–R* contains more than 150 separate criterion-referenced tests. However, it is very long.

A feature of the *CIB–R* is that some tests have been standardized. The technical manual (Glascoe, 1999) or scoring software can be used to determine standard scores, percentile ranks, grade equivalents, and age equivalents for all Readiness tests (ages 5–0 to 6–6+) and 10 tests of reading and math. Norms are available for ages 5–0 to 6–6+ (readiness) and 6–0 to 13–0 (reading and math).

ENHANCEDetext
Video Example 11.3
Watch this video to find out more about learning options in academic achievement.

CURRICULUM-BASED MEASUREMENT STRATEGIES

As Chapter 6 explained, curriculum-based measurement is a method of evaluating student performance using the school curriculum as the standard of comparison. It differs from formal tests because authentic curricular context is used (Deno & Fuchs, 1988, p. 483). According to Tucker (1985), student performance on this genuine curricular measurement is a true test of school performance.

Curriculum-based measurement is most useful for gathering information for instructional decisions. According to Blankenship (1985), curriculum-based measures provide important data at three stages in the teaching process: (1) at the planning stage before instruction begins, (2) immediately after instruction to determine whether mastery has occurred, and (3) periodically throughout the year to evaluate long-term retention. Curriculum-based measures have been shown to be valid, sensitive to pupil growth, and cost effective (Marston & Magnusson, 1985).

It has also been suggested that curriculum-based measurement is a useful strategy in gathering information for decisions about pupil eligibility for services such as special education

(Deno, 1985; Marston & Magnusson, 1985; Peterson, Heistad, Peterson, & Reynolds, 1985). Deno describes a simple procedure for peer referencing of curriculum-based measures. To obtain classroom or grade-level "norms," the measure is administered to general education students; their average performance on the curricular task is then used as the standard for evaluating the performance of an individual student. In one example provided by Deno, an individual sixth grader was reading from 30 to 55 words per minute, whereas the average rate for grade 6 students was 120 words per minute.

Curriculum-based measures do discriminate between successful members of general education classes and those with achievement problems. Marston and Magnusson (1985) compared general education, Title I, and special education students on the number of words read correctly; general education students were superior to the other two groups. Peterson and colleagues (1985) used a cut-off score on reading and math curriculum-based measures to discriminate between achievers and nonachievers; 100 percent of the special education students studied fell below the 20th percentile cut-off on one or both measures, whereas 89 percent of general education students fell above the 20th percentile on both reading and math.

Results of curriculum-based measures can add to the database that the assessment team assembles to determine whether a student shows poor school performance. Measures can be peer referenced with norms based on one classroom, a grade level within a school, or an entire district; or the assessment tool can stand by itself, with the curriculum as the standard of comparison. The resulting information is best used in eligibility decisions as an indicator of the magnitude of the school performance problem. In the prereferral stage, for example, curriculum-based measures can help teachers not only identify students who are not responding to instruction, but also evaluate the effects of instructional modifications introduced in the regular classroom.

However, curriculum-based measurement is most valuable as one source of information for planning and monitoring instruction. As Blankenship (1985) suggests, data from curriculum-based measures can be used in the IEP process not only to review the student's progress, but also to recommend goals and objectives.

ANSWERING THE ASSESSMENT QUESTIONS

The assessment team gathers information about the student's academic achievement to determine current levels of school performance. One major concern in the assessment of any skill or ability is the technical adequacy of the measurement tool. Measures of academic achievement should be selected for use only after careful consideration of the evidence supporting their reliability and validity. Results should be interpreted with caution, with the measure's limitations kept firmly in mind.

Two other factors that are important in evaluating assessment results are the types of procedures used in data collection and the nature of the assessment tasks.

Types of Procedures

Many types of procedures are used to gather information about school performance: group and individual measures, norm-referenced and criterion-referenced tests, curriculum-based measures, school record reviews, observations, work sample analyses, questionnaires, and interviews of informants. Each of these methods is likely to produce somewhat different results because each approaches the question of current school performance from a different perspective.

Group tests of academic achievement generally underestimate the school performance abilities of students with academic difficulties. Group tests depend heavily on reading skills and independent work skills—two areas in which lower-performing students tend not to excel. Individual measures tend to produce more accurate estimates of current performance and permit the sampling of a broader range of student skills. Therefore, they are preferred in special education.

Norm-referenced measures provide the most appropriate type of results for determining the existence and severity of a school performance problem. Although criterion-referenced measures are superior in describing specific instructional needs, norm-referenced test results tell where the student's performance falls in relation to other students. Such data are necessary for legal decisions such as eligibility for special education services.

Test results must be confirmed with information about how the student is coping with the demands of the current instructional environment. School records provide historical data and may contain current report card grades. School grades are one index of school performance, although they may be based on subjective criteria and provide little information about a student's standing in relation to peers. Classroom observations and analyses of student work samples add descriptive data about specific student actions and responses. If considered in relationship to the teacher's expectations and the standards for classroom performance, such data may corroborate school grades and test results. Curriculum-based measures also serve to document academic difficulties, particularly if their results reflect peer performance standards as well as curricular goals. Judgmental information is available from informants who are knowledgeable about the student's current school performance. Parents, teachers, and others have observed the student over long periods of time, forming opinions about the student's academic competence. The student can also provide information.

Nature of the Assessment Tasks

Assessment techniques differ in the ways they attempt to measure academic skills. There are obvious differences between group and individual administration, criterion-referenced standards and norm-referenced standards, and direct measures and techniques using informants.

Less obvious perhaps are the variations among the individual norm-referenced tests commonly used to assess achievement.

Comprehensiveness

This concern relates to the number of academic skills assessed and the breadth of coverage within each skill area. For example, a test may say that it measures mathematics skills, but it may limit coverage to simple computation. Of the individual achievement tests described in this chapter, the *WRAT4* is clearly the least comprehensive.

Of the three measures discussed in depth in this chapter, all assess reading recognition skills, math computation, and spelling. Reading comprehension, mathematical problem solving, and written expression are added by the *PIAT–R/NU,* the *WJ IV,* and the *WIAT–III.* Only the *WIAT–III* and *WJ IV* include measures of listening and speaking; only the *PIAT–R/NU* and the *WJ IV* assess content area knowledge. All of these tests require written responses, allowing analysis of the student's handwriting. Areas covered only by the *WJ IV* are knowledge of word meanings, editing, and fluency in reading, writing, and math.

Test Tasks

The ways that skill areas are assessed differ from measure to measure. Task characteristics such as timing factors, type of question, presentation mode, and response mode may influence student performance. Also, some test tasks approximate typical classroom activities, whereas others do not.

The methods used by the *PIAT–R/NU,* the *WRAT4,* the *WJ IV,* and the *WIAT–III* to assess reading recognition are very similar. The test task is oral reading of isolated words. However, test tasks for reading comprehension are quite different. The *WJ IV* uses a cloze procedure whereby the student reads a passage with a word omitted and then attempts to supply the missing word. On the *PIAT–R/NU,* the student reads a passage and then selects the drawing that best illustrates the meaning of the sentence. Neither of these tasks resembles typical classroom reading comprehension activities. The task on the *WIAT–III* is much closer: the student reads a passage and then answers questions about it.

In Spelling, the *WRAT4, WIAT–III,* and the *WJ IV* subtest use a written test format. This task should be familiar to most students because it is routinely used in classroom assessment. On the *PIAT–R/NU,* spelling items are multiple choice and do not require writing. The student must differentiate between the correctly spelled word and three misspelled versions. This is a recognition task, whereas written spelling is a recall task. The Editing subtest of the *WJ IV* assesses the proofreading skills of error detection and correction, and is much more realistic than the *PIAT–R/NU* task.

Math computation is evaluated by written tests on the *WRAT4,* the *WIAT–III,* and the *WJ IV* Calculation subtest. This format is often used in classroom practice activities and quizzes; most adults also solve computation problems with paper and pencil (or with calculators). The *PIAT–R/NU* again presents multiple-choice questions.

The *PIAT–R/NU,* the *WIAT–III,* and the *WJ IV* assess composition skills. The writing task for older students on the *PIAT–R/NU* is quite open-ended. Students must write a story that describes a stimulus picture. The more difficult items on the *WIAT–III* use a similar format: the student writes a paragraph and/or an essay. *The WJ IV,* in contrast, provides a variety of prompts designed to elicit brief, one-sentence writing samples. On the Writing Samples subtest, students write sentences to describe a drawing, expand a phrase, or complete a paragraph. On the Sentence Writing Fluency subtest, students write sentences in response to prompts containing a drawing and three words.

Content area knowledge is assessed by the General Information subtest on the *PIAT–R/NU* and the Academic Knowledge subtest on the *WJ IV.* The test format is the same: The tester asks a question and the student answers orally.

An important difference between the *PIAT–R/NU* and the other tests is the *PIAT–R/NU*'s use of multiple-choice questions. This is both a strength and a limitation. Because the *PIAT–R/ NU* bypasses writing skills on its Spelling and Mathematics subtests, it is a more appropriate measure of these subjects for students with severe writing disabilities or those with physical disabilities that impede writing. However, writing is integral to classroom spelling and mathematics tasks and to the use of these skills in adult life. Also, with multiple-choice questions, students are not asked to recall information, only to recognize

it. If one of the concerns in assessment is classroom performance in either spelling or mathematics, measures requiring recall of information and written responses should be administered in place of or in addition to the *PIAT–R/NU.*

One of the major differences between the *WRAT4* and the other measures is its imposition of time limits. Speed requirements may penalize students who work accurately but slowly. However, classroom success usually depends on both speed and accuracy, particularly in the upper elementary grades and beyond.

Motivational Factors

In addition to comprehensiveness of content and the methods used to assess skills, tests may vary in their appeal to the student. For students with a history of school failure, tests that look like school tasks may seem demanding, difficult, or even forbidding. The *PIAT–R/NU,* the *WIAT– III,* and the *WJ IV* appear less threatening than many, because they are in easel format and the test pages include drawings in addition to words and numbers. In contrast, the *WRAT4* test form gives every appearance of schoolwork. The Spelling Subtest page contains three columns of blank lines to write spelling words, and the middle pages of the test form are covered with math computation. In addition, the *WRAT4* imposes stringent ceiling rules. For example, the student must misspell 10 words in a row before the Spelling subtest is discontinued. Prolonging a failure experience to this extent may affect the student's willingness to attempt other test tasks.

Documentation of School Performance

The assessment question that guides the team in its study of the student's academic functioning is this: *Is there a school performance problem?* The team determines the student's current levels of achievement in important school subjects and decides whether there are apparent strengths and weaknesses in the various areas of learning. To do this, the team gathers information from many different sources.

Usually, the team will examine past records including group test data, interview the student's parents and teachers, observe and possibly interview the student, and administer an individual test of academic achievement. In some cases, a second individual test will be used to add to or help corroborate the results of the first. The team must also gather evidence that the student's academic difficulty is evident in the classroom, not just on standardized tests. Usually, this is not an issue because poor classroom performance is often the reason for the original referral. However, the team must try to explain any discrepancies between teacher reports and test results.

In its review of assessment results, the team attempts to describe the student's current levels of academic performance. At this point in the assessment process, these descriptions focus on the student's standing in relation to others.

Assessment in Action
Nathaniel

Nathaniel is one of your ninth-grade students whose performance indicates evidence of a learning disability. Nathaniel also receives speech and language services three times a week for 20-minute sessions. Nathaniel transferred from a middle school in your district. Other students in class consider Nathaniel to be amusing because he entertains them by acting silly.

Nathaniel has a couple of good friends. During informal conversation, he often answers questions inappropriately. Nathaniel changes topics often and stumbles on his pronunciation of multisyllabic words (i.e., *refrigerator, meaningful*). In addition, he does not seem to follow conversations. Nathaniel sometimes mispronounces words. He speaks to peers and teachers in the same manner. The goals and activities of the speech-language pathologist involve work in semantics, pragmatics, and phonology.

Nathaniel reads and writes several levels below grade level. He attempts to avoid completing tasks during the school day and rarely turns in homework. You collaborate with his general education teachers and provide in-class support for Nathaniel. You also collaborate with his speech-language pathologist. Your primary focus is on his reading and

writing skills. You are to collect informal assessment information to satisfy his IEP requirements. You have attempted to collaborate with his parents, but they have many work and family demands and are often unavailable to meet on a school day.

The assessment battery includes formal and informal measures in the areas of intelligence, adaptive skills, achievement, and speech and language assessment. When looking at Nathaniel's scores, you see that his intelligence and adaptive skills are in the low-average category. You see achievement skills 1 and ½ standard deviations below the mean, and speech and language skills 2 standard deviations below the mean. Achievement skills show strengths in performance-based measures and needs in verbal measures. Math subtest scores are significantly higher than verbal scores.

Nathaniel often tells you that he wants to drop out of school. He notes that he has a lot better things to do than show up in class each day. Nathaniel also states that he does not understand how this information has anything to do with him or how it could help him in the future. How do you respond to Nathaniel? What do you tell his parents? What do you say to his other teachers?

Nathaniel needed to understand how services could help him. You also needed to understand which activities and goals would motivate him. More involvement from Nathaniel in the planning and self-monitoring process would benefit him. Discussion with parents to increase awareness and improve authentically meaningful instruction and assessment could be a positive motivator for all involved. Working around the parents' schedule to increase participation would be beneficial. Discussion with the team of professionals about infusing strategies would also be helpful. Increasing Nathaniel's self-assessment would also improve his involvement in the process. You could formulate a rubric collaboratively, and both you and Nathaniel could score the rubric. Meaningful discussion could arise from comparing these results. Working in the area of need as a basis for the development of rubrics could serve as stimulating activities. Nathaniel could choose one of three activities to increase self-determination, motivation, and self-esteem.

SUMMARY

- The Every Student Succeeds Act shifts accountability from the Department of Education to the state. President Obama noted that the idea of accountability is important; however, in practice there were issues with No Child Left Behind. Critics noted that testing was overtaking instruction time and resources were not supported by federal funds to support needs in schools (Dee & Jacob, 2010). This new law allows educators to break up testing throughout the year. In addition, states decide whether or not to adopt Common Core Standards (Public Law 114-95).

- School records, teachers, and family members are important sources of information. School records provide information about the student's past performance and educational history. Teachers are an important source of information about current classroom functioning. Whereas teachers have the best opportunity for observing academic performance in the classroom, parents and other family members are best able to report about the use of academic skills at home and in the community.

- The administration procedures used in group testing are not optimal for lower-performing students for several reasons. Group tests require reading ability, even when assessing skills other than reading. Group tests are often timed. Students must write their answers, usually on a separate answer sheet. Group administration procedures assume that students can work independently, monitor their own behavior, and sustain attention to test tasks.

- *Dynamic Assessment of Test Accommodations (DATA)* (Fuchs, Fuchs, Eaton, & Hamlett, 2003) is a tool that IEP teams might consider using when making decisions about the types of test accommodations to provide individual students. Designed for students in grades 2–7, the *DATA* evaluates students' performance in math computation, math application, and reading comprehension under varying conditions.

- The WIAT-III is appropriate for administration to individuals 4–0 to 50–11, while the *WJ-IV* could be used with individuals who are 2–0 to 90+ years of age.

- The *PIAT–R/NU* is made up of six subtests: General Information, Reading Recognition, Reading Comprehension, Mathematics, Spelling, and Written Expression. The most typical response format on the *PIAT–R/NU* is multiple choice. The student is shown a test plate with four possible answers and is asked to select the correct response.

- Two examples of subtests from the *WJ IV*—Tests of Achievement include the Oral Reading and Sentence Reading Fluency subtests. In the *Oral Reading* subtest, students read sentences to the examiner. The examiner then judges the accuracy of the sentence. In *Sentence Reading Fluency* students are given 3 minutes to read sentences, then mark "yes" if the sentence is true and "no" if it is false.

- Two examples of subtests from the WIAT-3 are Pseudoword Decoding and Reading Comprehension. In *Pseudoword Decoding*, the student is asked to read nonsense words aloud. In *Reading Comprehension* the student reads a sentence or short passage aloud or silently, and answers one or more questions read aloud by the tester.

- The *Wide Range Achievement Test—Fourth Edition* or *WRAT4* (Wilkinson & Robertson, 2006) is a norm-referenced measure of basic skills for grades K–12 and ages 5–0 to 74–11. According to the manual, the *WRAT4* provides an efficient measurement tool. Although some portions of the *WRAT4* can be administered to small groups, individual administration is preferred.

- Curriculum-based measurement strategies could be helpful in the assessment process. Curriculum-based measures do discriminate between successful members of general education classes and those with achievement problems. In addition, results of curriculum-based measures can add to the database that the assessment team assembles to determine whether a student shows poor school performance.

- The ways that skill areas are assessed differ from measure to measure. Task characteristics such as timing factors, type of question, presentation mode, and response mode may influence student performance. Also, some test tasks approximate typical classroom activities, whereas others do not.

12

WavebreakMediaMicro/Fotolia

Assessment of English Language Learners

LEARNING OUTCOMES

After reading this chapter, you will be able to:

- Identify and explain four common phonological variations in Black English in assessing students who speak dialects of U.S. English.

- Describe two purposes of assessing students who are English-language learners.

- Identify and describe two examples of dimensions of teacher behavior that may influence students' ability to listen effectively within the context of the classroom.

- Describe the concept of language loss while addressing the assessment questions.

KEY TERMS

English-language learner (ELL)
first language
dialects
mainstream American English (MAE)
code switching

bilingual education
basic interpersonal communication
   skills (BICS)
cognitive-academic language
   proficiency (CALP)

For students who speak nonstandard versions of English, assessment centers on identification and description of the dialect in order to ensure that this language difference is not considered a language disorder. For students from homes where languages other than English are spoken, the first step is determining the student's proficiency in English, the home language, and any other languages spoken. Students who are English-language learners may require bilingual education services or other types of language interventions. When **English-language learners (ELLs)** are under consideration for special education services, care must be taken to conduct assessments in all languages in which students possess some skill. For this to occur, it may be necessary to employ informal assessment strategies rather than standardized tests and to enlist the aid of interpreters in the data collection process.

Language is a common assessment area for students who are English-language learners.

Also interested in development of oral language is another group of professionals: teachers of ELLs, sheltered English, and English immersion, among other terms. These teachers are charged with helping their students to develop English-language skills. These educators are only required to speak English. For example, in sheltered English the teacher provides modifications to the curricular material. Unlike bilingual educators who are required to also speak the student's native language, their role does not include continued development of students' home languages.

When students have difficulty with communication in the general education classroom, they may be referred for special education assessment and/or bilingual assessment. The purpose of bilingual assessment, like that of special education assessment, is to determine whether the student is eligible for special services and, if so, what services are needed. If the student is identified as an ELL, special services may be offered. Among the services available in some school districts are bilingual education programs in which instruction takes place both in English and in the students' language, and ELL programs in which English is taught as a second language.

Similar techniques are used to assess students' proficiency in languages other than English, and the same language dimensions are of interest. In bilingual assessment, the language that the child speaks upon entry to school is called the **first language** (L1), or the home, native, or heritage language. The second language that the child learns is usually English and is called L2. The purpose of language assessment for English learners is to determine the extent of their language proficiency in both languages so that learning needs can be identified. The language in which the student is most proficient is called the dominant, or primary, language. Also of interest, particularly with older students, is language preference. The language in which a speaker is most proficient may not be the language in which he or she prefers to converse.

Whatever languages the student speaks, the ability to use oral language in everyday communication situations should not be neglected in assessment. Pragmatics is one facet of the application of language skills and is a necessary assessment concern. It is also important to evaluate the student's ability to deal with the form and meaning of language in everyday interactions. Tests measure language competence, but language performance is another matter. Although a student may define a word correctly on a test, he or she does not necessarily use the word correctly in discourse or, indeed, ever use the word in communication situations.

ASSESSING STUDENTS WHO SPEAK DIALECTS OF U.S. ENGLISH

Not all persons who speak English pronounce the speech sounds in the same way; nor do they use the same syntax, morphology, and vocabulary. The variations that occur within languages are called **dialects**, and there are many dialects of English. For example, the English spoken in Great Britain is not the same as that spoken in America, in Canada, or in Australia. Within the United States, there are regional variations. Words are pronounced differently in Maine, New York, Louisiana, Texas, and California, and variations occur in grammatical structure and word meaning. In addition, some American English dialects are related to population characteristics rather than to geographic region. Examples are Black English and the English spoken by some persons whose first language is Spanish.

Many variations of English are spoken in the United States, and standard American English is only one of them. Standard American English is also referred to as **mainstream American English (MAE)** (Willis, 2004). Other dialects should be considered different from, but not inferior to, Standard English. This is the issue of language difference versus language deficit (Polloway & Smith, 1982; Winzer & Mazurek, 1998). The deficit position holds that any dialect other than Standard English is a restricted code and therefore represents a deficit; it is substandard, rather than non-Standard, English. The difference position, based primarily on studies of the dialect of English spoken by African Americans, maintains that non-Standard English is a complete linguistic system, different from, but not inferior to, the standard dialect. Most educators today support the difference position. As Taylor (1990) comments, there is not a better or best dialect.

The language a child or adult uses for communication is influenced by several factors. Wiig and Semel (1984) suggest considering aspects such as first language culture, socioeconomic status, race/ethnicity, gender, age, and context, among other factors.

> The context factor, which Wiig and Semel name "situation-context," refers to the setting in which a particular communication takes place. Speakers alter their language to fit the communicative context. This is called style or **code switching**, and bidialectical speakers are able to change from one dialect to another depending on the situation, setting, and audience of the communication. For example, a person who speaks non-Standard English in one context (e.g., a conversation with a close friend) may speak Standard English in another (e.g., a job interview) (Cohen & Plaskon, 1980). Al-Hourani and Afizah (2013) report that four factors affect code switching; context, discussion topics, age, and relationship among conversation participants.

In discussing the possible goals of language instruction for non-Standard English speakers, Cohen and Plaskon (1980) review three alternatives: eradication of the nonstandard dialect, complete acceptance of the nonstandard dialect, and bidialectalism. Of these options, the last is most commonly accepted. Teaching students to speak Standard English while maintaining their competence in the original dialect allows them to meet linguistic demands in a variety of communication settings.

Dialectical Differences

Dialects differ along the major dimensions of language: phonology, morphology, syntax, semantics, and pragmatics. However, the areas of dialectical difference that have been studied most extensively are phonological differences and variations in morphology and syntax.

Perhaps the most common dialect in the United States is Black English, also called Ebonics and African American Vernacular English (AAVE) (Polloway & Smith, 1982; Sealey-Ruiz, 2005; Willis, 2004). Although there are systematic differences between Black English and Mainstream American English, Wiig and Semel (1984) point out that most Black English utterances follow Standard English-language rules.

Pronunciation of speech sounds is one area of difference. Engquist (1974) describes the most common phonological variations in Black English:

1. Softening of the *r* sound (e.g., sister/sistah, poor/po', Carter/Cahtuh).
2. Lessening of the *l* sound (e.g., help/hep, all/awe, tool/too).

3. Weakening of final consonants in clusters (e.g., past/pass, hold/hol, bent/ben).
4. Specific sound substitutions (e.g., *f* for *th,* as in mouth/mouf; *d* for *th,* as in this/dis; *i* for *e,* as in pen/pin; *ah* for *i,* as in I/ah). (as cited in Polloway & Smith, 1982, pp. 72–73)

Some phonological characteristics of Black English have morphological consequences. According to Bartel, Grill, and Bryen (1973), the most common morphological variations involve omissions of the final sounds of words. Final sounds are omitted in verbs (present, past, and future tenses), possessives, and plurals. For instance, when final /t/ and /d/ sounds are omitted, past tense verbs sound like present tense verbs ("pass" for "passed") (Cohen & Plaskon, 1980). When the final /l/ sound is omitted, future tense sounds like present ("she" for "she'll"). When the final /s/ or /z/ sound is omitted, singular verbs sound like plural verbs ("hit" for "hits"), and plural nouns sound like singular nouns ("cent" for "cents").

In Black English, variations occur in all parts of speech, but most often in verbs. Use of the verb *to be* in Black English is quite different from Standard English. For example, the copula may be omitted (e.g., "He tired") or *be* used in place of other verb forms (e.g., "They always *be* messing around") (Ruddell, 1974).

Dialectical differences also occur in English speakers whose first language is Spanish. English is influenced by the first language, and several phonological, morphological, and syntactical variations result. The speech sounds in Spanish are not the same as those in English. Spanish has 18 consonant and 5 vowel sounds; English has 24 consonant and 12 to 14 vowel sounds (Merino, 1992). For example, Spanish does not have the vowel sounds in *pig, fat,* or *sun* (Wiig, 1982a). Thus, when Spanish-speakers learn English, they substitute phonemes they can pronounce for those not in their speech sound repertoire. For example, "chip" is pronounced "cheap," and "vat" is pronounced "bat" (Taylor, 1990).

Similarly, the morphology, syntax, and semantics of the Spanish language may interfere with English expression. A word or phrase in one language may convey an entirely different meaning when translated into another. Condon, Peters, and Sueiro-Ross (1979) cite these examples from Lado (1968):

- The Spanish compliment "Qué grueso estás," which is translated literally as "how fat you are," becomes an insult in English.
- The use of the name "Jesús" for a boy is quite common in Hispanic society but not in the Anglo-Saxon community, where it is regarded as inappropriate, if not sacrilegious.
- To be "informal" in Spanish is "to be neglectful," but to be so in English simply conveys the notion of "casual" behavior. (Condon et al., 1979, p. 82)

Word order and vocabulary differences between the two languages may also have an influence. For example, a student whose first language is Spanish might say, "The car red is mine" (rather than "The red car is mine") or "I have thirst" (rather than "I am thirsty") (Wiig, 1982a). Descriptions of some of the syntactical variations of Spanish-influenced English are provided in Table 12–1. Information is available about the characteristics of other, less common dialectical variations of English. Interested readers should refer to Wiig and Semel (1984) for descriptions of Appalachian English and the Southern White dialect, to Adler and Birdsong (1983) for the phonological characteristics of Mountain English, and to Cheng (1987) for a discussion of the influences of the Asian languages on English.

Assessment Strategies

Dialect must be considered in the assessment of oral language. A dialect is not a language disorder, but it can be mistaken for one if the professional conducting the assessment does not recognize its influence on receptive and expressive language. Terrell and Terrell (1983) discuss three types of errors that can occur if the role of dialect is not well understood. First, professionals can assume that all students from diverse groups are normal dialect speakers and thus fail to assess their language competence. Second, if students are assessed, professionals can overcompensate for dialect and assume that true disorders are dialectical characteristics. Third, professionals can undercompensate for dialect and mistake dialectical differences for language disorders.

TABLE 12–1
Syntactical Characteristics of Spanish-Influenced English

FEATURES	ENVIRONMENTS	EXAMPLES
Forms of *to be*	Absent in present progressive	He getting hungry (He is getting hungry)
Pronouns	Absent as subjects of sentences when subject obvious from preceding sentence	Carol left yesterday. I think is coming back tomorrow (Carol left yesterday. I think she is coming back tomorrow)
Third person (-*s*)	Absent in third-person verb agreements	He talk fast (He talks fast)
Past (-*ed*)	Absent in past tense inflections	He walk fast yesterday (He walked fast yesterday)
Go with *to*	Future markings	He go to see the game tomorrow (He is going to see the game tomorrow)
No or *don't*	Imperatives	No do that (Don't do that)
The for possessive pronoun	With body parts	I hurt the finger (I hurt my finger)
Present tense markings	Progressive environments	I think he come soon (I think he is coming soon)
Locative adverbs	Placed near verb	I think he putting down the rifle (I think he is putting the rifle down)

Note: From Anderson, Noma B.; Shames, George H., *Human Communication Disorders: An Introduction*, 8Th Ed., © 2011. Reprinted and Electronically Reproduced by Permission of Pearson Education, Inc., New York, NY.

Dialect is a concern in the assessment of skills other than oral language. Adler and Birdsong (1983), in their discussion of bias in standardized testing, point out the effects of dialect on students' performance on measures of auditory discrimination. For example, on the *Auditory Discrimination Test* by Wepman (1975), Adler and Birdsong identify six pairs of words that may sound alike to children who speak dialects (e.g., "tub/tug" and "pen/pin"). This is a serious problem. In the second edition of the *Auditory Discrimination Test* (Reynolds, 1987), a 7-year-old making six errors scores at the 16th percentile.

Dialectical differences also affect performance of academic skills. Variations in the pronunciation of phonemes may result in what appear to be decoding errors in reading. Written language may be affected, too. If students spell words as they pronounce them, their spelling will not conform to Standard English expectations. Similarly, dialectical variations in morphology, syntax, and semantics can result in compositions that contain non-Standard English sentences and paragraphs.

Unfortunately, there are no widely accepted standardized techniques for the assessment of language competence in students who speak dialects. Terrell and Terrell (1983) observe that "culture-fair" linguistic tests are not developed as quickly and readily as linguistic tests for Standard English speakers. This presents a major obstacle to the responsible professional. Whether a student speaks a dialect must be established in assessment. It cannot be assumed because of some ethnic, cultural, or social characteristic.

One strategy for the assessment of speakers of dialects is to rely on informal procedures. Leonard and Weiss (1983) recommend the collection of spontaneous speech samples in naturalistic settings; these samples are analyzed for instances of dialectical usage. However, in some cases, dialectical variations are similar to the speech produced by young, normally developing children and older children with language disorders. For example, both these children and persons who speak Black English may omit -*s* endings on possessives and plurals. Thus, it is most productive to concentrate on dialectical variations that are different from the variations that occur in normal development.

Sentence repetition is another useful informal technique (Adler & Birdsong, 1983). Sentence repetition tasks are based on the assumption that when children are asked to repeat a sentence, they will reconstruct the sentence and say it in their own dialect. Adler and Birdsong also suggest strategies for determining whether a particular utterance is nonstandard (dialectical) or substandard (an error). One approach is to interview other children who speak the dialect. If a significant number of children (e.g., 50 percent) use the linguistic pattern, it can be assumed to be part of the dialect.

Once the characteristics of the student's dialectical language have been established, it is possible to begin selecting tools for assessment. This process must take into account the possibility of bias. Taylor and Payne (1983) suggest that the language characteristics of individual test items be analyzed. Such an analysis would take into account the language characteristics of each test item, in relation to Mainstream American English and the dialect of the student. In many cases, items will be answered in one way if the rules of Standard English are followed and in another way (that would be scored as incorrect) if the rules of the nonstandard dialect are followed.

When tests contain such items, professionals face a limited number of options. The best solution is to eliminate the test from the battery and substitute another, more appropriate test. If a better measure is not available, the test can still be eliminated and informal procedures used in its place. Sometimes, however, comparative data are needed, and informal procedures will not suffice. In such cases, there are two legitimate courses of action. First, the test can be renormed with members of the student's language group (Adler & Birdsong, 1983; Taylor & Payne, 1983). This is an expensive and impractical option unless a large number of students need revised norms. The second approach is to administer the test in the standard fashion and report two types of results: the student's score in relation to test norms and the expectations for standard English, and an alternate score in which dialectical responses (if correct according to the rules of the dialect) are scored as correct. Like all

alternate scores, these must be interpreted with caution. However, by using this technique, the characteristics of the student's language are considered rather than ignored, and the student is not penalized for language differences. In addition, some information is produced about the student's relative proficiency in Standard English and the dialect.

ENHANCEDetext
Video Example 12.1
Watch this video of teachers discussing a student's progress.

ASSESSING STUDENTS WHO ARE ENGLISH-LANGUAGE LEARNERS

The number of persons in the United States who speak languages other than the language at home exceeds 61 million (Camarota & Zeigler, 2014). The number of school-aged children who are English learners is also increasing (U.S. Census Bureau, 2013). In fact, the growth rate for this group is more rapid than that of the general school population (Baca & Almanza, 1991), and the great majority of these students speak Spanish as their first language. In the year 2013, more than one in five individuals in the U.S. population between the ages 5 and 17 spoke languages other than English at home (U.S. Census Bureau, 2013). Spanish was the most common alternative to English. Other common languages were Russian, Hmong, Arabic, Korean, Japanese, Chinese, Portuguese, Farsi (Hopstock & Stephenson, 2003), Tagalog, and Vietnamese (Camarota & Zeigler, 2014).

Assessment of students who speak languages other than English has two purposes. The first is to determine the student's language proficiency, both in the first or home language (L1) and in English, the language of the school. With most students, English is the second language (L2), although English can be the third or even fourth language of the child. Assessment of language proficiency provides professionals with information about the student's relative competence in each language, so that the language or languages of assessment can be determined. Once this decision is made, assessment continues to explore the need for educational intervention.

With this population, intervention can take several forms, and one recommended by many experts is **bilingual education**. Bilingual education programs are designed primarily for students who are English-language learners—that is, for those who are not yet proficient in English. Bergin (1980) describes the major components of bilingual instructional programs, which include L1 and content area instruction, cultural context, and English-language learning.

Several different models are used in the United States to deliver bilingual education (Baca, 1998; Gollnick & Chinn, 1990). In transitional models, first-language instruction is provided only as a transition to English; when English skills have been developed, English becomes the language of instruction. In contrast, full bilingual models attempt to develop competency in both languages. Instruction takes place in the first language and in English for all school subjects throughout the program.

The development and maintenance of both languages has several advantages. Bilingualism itself is an advantage. The ability to communicate in more than one language is a strength that the regular curriculum of secondary schools attempts to impart to monolingual students via foreign language instruction. In addition, Cummins (1981, 1983) suggests that first- and second-language academic skills are interdependent. This is the theory of common underlying proficiency. Although the surface features of the first and second languages may differ, the cognitive and academic skills learned in one language will transfer to another language. Cummins (1983) explains

this concept in relation to a Spanish-English bilingual program. He reports that by developing language-reading skills in L1, language literacy and academic skills in L2 are facilitated.

In the past decade, bilingual programs have fallen into disfavor in schools, and their number has dwindled. One reason is the English-only political movement that promotes English as the sole language in U.S. society and schools (García, 2006). Another is the federal No Child Left Behind law with its requirements for improvements in academic achievement and increased accountability of schools. A third factor is the number of different languages represented in some schools. It is usually not practical to offer bilingual programs in the 5, 10, or even 20 languages spoken in the homes of students in many elementary schools. Qualified teachers may not be available, and the numbers of students making up some language groups may be small.

Bilingual programs have given way in many districts to programs designed to teach English-language learners. Other terms used to describe such programs are ESOL (English for speakers of other languages), sheltered English, and English immersion. These programs aim to help English learners develop English-language skills as quickly as possible so that they can be successful in general education classrooms.

When students are identified as both ELLs *and* as people with a disability, decisions about appropriate services become more complex. In some cases, the student will receive both bilingual (or ELL) and special education services. In other cases, a bilingual special education program may be available. Special and bilingual/ELL services can be combined in a number of ways: bilingual education with support from special education; special education with bilingual support services; special education with a bilingual teacher; and special education with a bilingual aide, volunteer, or peer tutor (Plata, 1982; Yates & Ortiz, 1998).

Language Proficiency

Payan (1989) defines language proficiency as

> the degree to which the student exhibits control over the use of language, including the measurement of *expressive* and *receptive* language skills in

the areas of phonology, syntax, vocabulary, and semantics and including the area of pragmatics or language use within various domains or social circumstances. (p. 127)

Proficiency in one language is judged independently from proficiency in other languages. It is possible for students to show proficiency in both the first language (L1) and English (L2), in L1 but not in L2, or in L2 but not in L1. Language proficiency is not a simple, unitary skill. According to Cummins (1981), language proficiency has two dimensions: **basic interpersonal communication skills (BICS)** are the spoken skills of the language community and are acquired by almost all community members; and **cognitive-academic language proficiency (CALP)** contrast is the set of language skills needed to function in the academic environment of schools.

In second-language learning, proficiency in basic interpersonal communication is acquired much more quickly than is cognitive-academic proficiency (Cummins, 1982). In face-to-face interpersonal communications, a variety of extralingual supports are available to assist communication: intonation, facial expression, loudness of voice, gestures, body language, and so forth. The communication is context-embedded. In the classroom, there are fewer extralingual cues, making the communication situation more context-reduced.

These differences have important implications for assessment. Evidence of competence in basic communication skills does not guarantee that the student will also speak and understand the language necessary for classroom communications. While a student is learning a second language, a "silent period" could take place, as the student is listening before attempting to speak the new language (Diaz-Rico, 2008). In addition, a mixture of the two languages, called "interlanguage," often takes place (Telléz & Waxman, 2005). Mercer (1983) contends that in order to properly assess a bilingual student, the evaluator must evaluate that student's skills in sociolinguistic communication performance. It is essential that both languages be assessed in the areas of language, achievement, and intelligence skills.

Current practices in the assessment of language proficiency include two major steps. The home language is determined through a language background questionnaire or interview, and the student's skills are assessed with one of the available language proficiency measures (Gonzalez, Brusca-Vega, & Yawkey, 1997). The language background questionnaire or interview is used to gather information from the child's parents about which language or languages are spoken in the home. If a language other than English is spoken, this alerts the school that the student *may* also speak this language. As Payan (1989) comments, linguistic background questionnaires typically provide contextual information in terms of language, as well as general remarks regarding the student's communication skills.

To determine the child's language proficiency, it is necessary to assess the child. Several formal measures are available for this purpose, as Table 12–2 illustrates. However, with few exceptions, these measures are designed for students whose first language is Spanish. Although Spanish-speakers are the largest language minority group in the United States, many professionals are also interested in assessing the language proficiency of students who speak languages other than Spanish. As Lynch and Lewis (1987) observed, a major problem in assessment is a lack of assessment tools in languages other than English. The authors note that there is a dearth of measures for Asian languages.

Cheng (1987) presents several informal tools for assessing the oral language skills of Asian students. In addition, she lists a number of language proficiency tests appropriate for this population that are available from school districts and other noncommercial sources. Roussel (1991) also provides information on language assessment tools for speakers of languages other than English; Langdon (1992) describes measures of language proficiency for speakers of Spanish.

Most of the formal instruments that assess language proficiency in Spanish and English are designed to determine the student's dominant language. The dominant language (also called the primary language) is the language in which the student is most proficient. A more complex method of categorizing language proficiency was recommended in the *Lau Remedies* (Office for Civil Rights, 1975). The *Lau Remedies* were proposed by a federal task force established in response to

TABLE 12–2
Measures of Language Proficiency

NAME (AUTHOR)	AGES OR GRADES	LANGUAGE(S)	ORAL LANGUAGE SKILLS ASSESSED
Basic Inventory of Natural Language (Herbert, 1996)	Grades pre-K to adult	Spanish, English, and 30 other languages	A language sample is scored for fluency, complexity, and average sentence length
Ber-Sil Elementary and Secondary Spanish Tests (Beringer, 1984, 1987)	Ages 5 to 12 and 13 to 17	Spanish, Tagalog, Ilokano; Elementary also available in Cantonese, Mandarin, Korean, Persian	Receptive vocabulary
Bilingual Syntax Measure I and II (Burt, Dulay, & Hernández-Chávez, 1978)	Grades pre-K to 12	Spanish, English	Expressive syntax
Bilingual Verbal Ability Tests Normative Update (Muñoz-Sandoval, Alvarado, & Ruef, 2005)	Ages 5–0 to adult	Spanish, English, and 15 other languages	Receptive and expressive vocabulary
Dos Amigos Verbal Language Scales, 1996 Edition (Critchlow, 1996)	Ages 5 to 13	Spanish, English	Expressive vocabulary
IPT (Idea Proficiency Tests) 2004 Oral Language Proficiency Tests (2004)	Grades pre-K–12	Spanish, English	Vocabulary, comprehension, syntax, and verbal expression (including articulation)
Language Assessment Scales-Oral (Duncan & DeAvila, 1990)	Grades 1 to 12	Spanish, English	Phonemic, lexical, syntactical, and pragmatic aspects of language
Woodcock-Muñoz Language Survey–Revised Normative Update (Schrank, Wendling, Alvarado, & Woodcock, 2010)	Ages 2–0 to 90+	Spanish, English	Receptive and expressive semantics

the landmark *Lau v. Nichols* case (1974). The issue in this class-action suit was denial of equal educational opportunity to non-English-speaking students by providing instruction only in English. The *Lau Remedies* recognize five categories of language proficiency, which Cegelka (1988) describes as follows:

1. Monolingual speaker of a language other than English; speaks this language exclusively.
2. Predominantly speaks the language other than English, although some English is spoken.
3. Bilingual, speaks both English and primary language with equal ease.

4. Predominantly speaks English, though not exclusively.
5. Monolingual speaker of English; speaks this language exclusively. (p. 555)

One issue in the use of tests that assess languages other than English is who will administer them. According to Juárez (1983), native-English-speakers should administer English versions of tests, and native-minority-language speakers should administer minority-language versions. Bilingual professionals are able to fill both roles, provided, of course, they have adequate training in test administration. Some measures attempt to minimize the need for proficiency by the tester in languages other than English by using audiotapes to present test items. This practice may help standardize administration procedures, but it does not eliminate the need for a tester who can speak the student's own language, understand the student's communications, and record responses to test items.

Another issue relates to the equivalency of language proficiency measures. Wald (1982) reports the results of a study that compared these three measures: the *Basic Inventory of Natural Language (BINL),* the *Bilingual Syntax Measure (BSM),* and the *Language Assessment Scales (LAS).* Minimal correlations were found among the measures, and each identified a different portion of the population as English language learners. With the *BINL,* 73 percent of the students participating in the study were identified as English-language learners. Fewer were identified by the *LAS* (30 percent), and the smallest percentage by the *BSM* (19 percent).

Juárez (1983) contends that informal measures tend to be more precise than formal measures when it comes to language performance in ELLs. Generally, informal techniques are the only alternative if pragmatics is the concern. In addition, for many languages, informal assessment may be the only approach available if there is interest in evaluating both basic interpersonal communication skills and cognitive-academic language proficiency. Among the available informal strategies are observation of the student in communication situations, collection and analysis of samples of the student's natural language, and administration of informal inventories and criterion-referenced tests to evaluate specific receptive and expressive language skills.

One example of a well-designed informal measure is the teacher observation form described by Echevarria and Graves (2007) and shown in Figure 12–1. Called the *Student Oral Language Observation Matrix or SOLOM,* it prompts the teacher to observe five aspects of oral language: comprehension, fluency, vocabulary, pronunciation, and grammar. For each of these oral language components, the SOLOM provides five descriptions of student performance ranging from lowest to highest in terms of language proficiency. For example, in the area of Comprehension, the

descriptions range from (1) "cannot understand even simple conversation" to (5) "understands everyday conversation and normal classroom discussions without difficulty."

Special Education Assessment for English-Language Learners

When students who speak languages other than English are referred for special education assessment, a first step is the study of language proficiency. If one language is clearly dominant, then special education assessment will take place in that language. For example, if the student speaks only Spanish, Spanish-language assessment tools should be selected.

When students show some proficiency in both English and their first language, then the decision about the language of assessment is not as straightforward. In general, the best course of action in this situation is to assess in both languages. Baca and Cervantes (1989) explain that collecting information from both L1 and L2 provides educators with more complete data. This evidence allows for a better determination of interventions and supports.

The language of assessment is not the only consideration. The history of special education has been marked by controversy over the assessment of students from diverse groups and the disproportionate placement of such students in special education classes for individuals with intellectual disabilities. Although concerns about testing abuses and inappropriate placement abated somewhat with the passage of federal special education laws, with guarantees of due process and requirements for nondiscriminatory assessment, the issues continue to command attention today. For example, Wilkinson, Ortiz, Robertson, and Kushner (2006) reported that English-language learners received special education services in reading because of inadequate comprehensive assessments. As Gonzalez et al. (1997) report, in today's schools culturally and linguistically diverse students are not appropriately identified with disabilities. Yzquierdo, Blalock, and Torres-Velásquez (2004) caution that students who are speakers of languages other than English often are not assessed in their home language during evaluation for special education services.

Teacher Observation
Student Oral Language Observation Matrix (SOLOM)

Student's Name: _____   Grade: _____   Examiner: _____
Language Observed: _____   Date: _____

LEVEL	1	2	3	4	5
(A) Comprehension	Cannot understand even simple conversation.	Has great difficulty following what is said. Can comprehend only "social conversation" spoken slowly and with frequent repetitions.	Understands most of what is said at slower than normal speed with repetitions.	Understands nearly everything at normal speed, although, occasional repetition may be necessary.	Understands everyday conversation and normal classroom discussions without difficulty.
(B) Fluency	Speech is so halting and fragmentary as to make conversation virtually impossible.	Usually hesitant; often forced into silence by language limitations.	Speech in everyday conversation and classroom discussions is frequently disrupted by the student's search for the correct manner of expression.	Speech in everyday conversation and classroom discussion is generally fluent, with occasional lapses while searching for the correct manner of expression.	Speech in everyday conversation and classroom discussion is fluent and effortless, approximating that of a native speaker.
(C) Vocabulary	Vocabulary limitations so extreme as to make conversation virtually impossible.	Misuse of words and very limited vocabulary make comprehension quite difficult.	Frequently uses the wrong words; conversation somewhat limited because of inadequate vocabulary.	Occasionally uses inappropriate terms and/or must rephrase ideas because of lexical inadequacies.	Use of vocabulary and idioms approximates that of a native speaker.
(D) Pronunciation	Pronunciation problems so severe as to make speech virtually unintelligible.	Very hard to understand because of pronunciation problems. Must frequently repeat in order to make him/herself understood.	Pronunciation problems necessitate concentration on the part of the listener and occasionally lead to misunderstanding.	Always intelligible though one is conscious of a definite accent and occasional inappropriate intonation patterns.	Pronunciation and intonation approximates that of a native speaker.
(E) Grammar	Errors in grammar and word order so severe as to make speech virtually unintelligible.	Grammar and word order errors make comprehension difficult. Must often rephrase and/or restrict him/herself to basic patterns.	Makes frequent errors of grammar and word order which occasionally obscure meaning.	Occasionally makes grammatical and/or word order errors which do not obscure meaning.	Grammatical usage and word order approximates that of a native speaker.

The student oral language observation matrix (SOLOM) has five (5) categories on the left: A. Comprehension, B. Fluency, C. Vocabulary, D. Pronunciation, and E. Grammar. It also has five numbers along the top, one (1) being the lowest mark to five (5) being the highest mark. According to your observation, indicate with an (X) across the square in each category which best describes the child's abilities. Those students whose checkmarks (Xs) are to the right of the darkened line will be considered for reclassification, if test scores and achievement data also indicate English proficiency.

FIGURE 12–1
Teacher Observation Form for Oral Language
Note: From *Sheltered Content Instruction* by J. Echevarria and A. Graves, 2007, p. 15. Copyright 2007 by Pearson Education, Inc. Reprinted with permission.

In response to problems related to discrimination and the use of inappropriate assessment techniques, the National Academy of Sciences Panel on Selection and Placement of Students in Programs for the Students with Intellectual Disabilities was formed. The report of that panel, *Placing Children in Special Education: A Strategy for Equity* (Heller, Holtzman, & Messick, 1982), addresses both assessment and instruction, and a two-phase comprehensive assessment process is recommended for eligibility decisions.

The first phase in assessment should be study of the student's learning environment and investigation of the nature and quality of general education classroom instruction. Messick (1984) notes that educators must rule out contextual learning deficits and apply additional supportive instruction before referral for evaluation.

Four types of information are gathered during the first phase of the comprehensive assessment process:

1. Evidence that the school is using programs and curricula shown to be effective not just for students in general but for the various ethnic, linguistic, and socioeconomic groups actually served by the school in question.

2. Evidence that the students in question have been adequately exposed to the curriculum by virtue of not having missed many lessons due to absence or disciplinary exclusions from class, and that the teacher has implemented the curriculum effectively (e.g., evidence that the teacher makes effective use of the flexibility afforded by the curriculum in choosing instructional strategies and materials, that the child receives appropriate direction, feedback, and reinforcement, that other children in the class are performing acceptably, etc.).

3. Evidence that the child has not learned what was taught.

4. Evidence that systematic efforts were, or are being, made to identify the learning difficulty and to take corrective instructional action, such as introducing remedial approaches, changing the curriculum materials, or trying a new teacher. (Messick, 1984, p. 5)

The second phase of assessment is undertaken only if it is established that an achievement problem exists despite the provision of appropriate instruction in the regular classroom. Current thinking in the field of bilingual special education endorses and extends this approach. As Baca and Almanza (1991) explain, the first concern is prevention of disabilities. In their view, prevention is a protection from weak instruction.

A second concern is that prereferral services should be part of the school's response to academic learning problems. Only when appropriate instructional interventions have not proved successful should a student be referred for special education assessment. Ortiz and Garcia (1988) agree. In their eight-step model, when students experience academic difficulties, systematic efforts are made to not only recognize difficulties, but also to remediate based on that information. Among the areas to consider are the characteristics of the teacher, the student's exposure to the curriculum, student characteristics, instructional approaches, and the methods used to monitor student progress.

With students who speak languages other than English, special education assessment is conducted in the language or languages in which students are most proficient. Several measures are available in a variety of skill areas for Spanish-speaking students, as Table 12–3 shows. As with language proficiency tests, Spanish is the language most often represented on non-English-language versions of special education assessment devices. Most of the measures listed in Table 12–3 have English-language counterparts that have been discussed earlier.

Obviously, the methods used to develop Spanish-language tests affect both technical adequacy and educational usefulness. Payan (1989) warns that non-English-language tests should not be direct translations of English-language tests. Literal translation may not take into account the subtle differences between languages and cultures, so items on the non-English version of the test become either more difficult or easier than their English-language counterparts.

The characteristics of the standardization sample are a critical concern in selection of tests for speakers of languages other than English. Tests based on English-language measures may not have been renormed with speakers of the language in question. If that is the case, professionals are

TABLE 12–3
Assessment Devices for Spanish-Speaking Students

ASSESSMENT AREA	NAME (AUTHOR)	ENGLISH-LANGUAGE COUNTERPART
Academic Achievement	*Aprenda: La prueba de logros en español, Tercera edición* (2006)	Coordinated with *Stanford Achievement Test Series*
	Batería III Woodcock-Muñoz (Woodcock, Muñoz-Sandoval, McGrew, & Mather, 2005)	*Woodcock-Johnson III* (Woodcock, McGrew, & Mather, 2001b)
	BRIGANCE® Assessment of Basic Skills-Revised, Spanish Edition (Brigance, 2007)	*BRIGANCE® Diagnostic Comprehensive Inventory of Basic Skills–Revised* (Brigance, 1999)
	Logramos—Third Edition (2014)	*Iowa Tests of Basic Skills* (Hoover, Dunbar, & Frisbie, 2001, 2003, 2012)
	Prueba de Lectura & Lenguaje Escrito (Test of Reading and Writing) (Hammill, Larsen, Wiederholt, & Fountain-Chambers, 1982)	None
	TerraNova SUPERA (2011)	Linked to *TerraNova* assessment series
	Woodcock-Muñoz Language Survey-Revised Normative Update (Schrank et al., 2010)	Test includes both Spanish and English subtests
Intellectual Performance	*Batería III Woodcock-Muñoz* (Woodcock et al., 2005)	*Woodcock-Johnson III* (Woodcock, McGrew, & Mather, 2001a)
	Wechsler Intelligence Scale for Children—Fifth Edition Spanish (Wechsler, 2014)	*Wechsler Intelligence Scale for Children–Fifth Edition* (Wechsler, 2014)
Adaptive Behavior	*Scales of Independent Behavior-Revised* (Bruininks, Woodcock, Weatherman, & Hill, 1996)	A Spanish version offers a Spanish-language test book and an English-language manual and response booklets.
	Vineland Adaptive Behavior Scales—Second Edition (Sparrow, Cicchetti, & Balla, 2005b)	A Spanish-language version of the Survey Interview Form is available.
Specific Learning Abilities	*Batería III Woodcock-Muñoz* (Woodcock et al., 2005)	*Woodcock-Johnson III* (Woodcock et al., 2001a)
	Prueba Illinois de Habilidades Psicolingüísticas (Hammill, Mather, Roberts, & Frias, 2009)	*Illinois Test of Psycholinguistic Abilities—Third Edition* (Hammill, Mather, & Roberts, 2001)
	Survey of Study Habits and Attitudes, Spanish Edition (Brown & Holtzman, 1967b)	*Survey of Study Habits and Attitudes* (Brown & Holtzman, 1967a)
Classroom Behavior	*Achenbach System of Empirically Based Assessment* (Achenbach, 2010)	Latino Spanish version available
	Perfil de Evaluación de Comportamiento (Brown & Hammill, 1982)	*Behavior Rating Profile* (Brown & Hammill, 1983)
Language*	*Boehm Test of Basic Concepts—Third Edition* (Boehm, 2000)	Directions for administration in both English and Spanish are provided
	Prueba de Desarrollo Inicial de Lenguaje (Hresko, Reid, & Hammill, 1982)	*Test of Early Language Development—Third Edition* (Hresko, Reid, & Hammill, 1999)
	Screening Test of Spanish Grammar (Toronto, 1973)	*Northwestern Syntax Screening Test* (Lee, 1971)
	Test de Vocabulario en Imágenes Peabody (Dunn, Lugo, Padilla, & Dunn, 1986)	*Peabody Picture Vocabulary Test–Fourth Edition* (Dunn & Dunn, 2007)
	Woodcock-Muñoz Language Survey-Revised Normative Update (Schrank et al., 2010)	Test includes both Spanish and English subtests

*See also the measures of language proficiency described in Table 12–2.

forced to develop local norms or use the test as an informal measure; norms developed with English speakers are inappropriate for non-English-speaking students. If norms are available, the characteristics of the standardization sample must be carefully evaluated. As with English, there are many dialects of Spanish and of other languages. Lynch and Lewis (1987) caution that it may not be appropriate to generalize language tests across countries, even when the populations in these countries speak the same language.

The selection of appropriate tools for assessment becomes even more difficult when students speak languages other than Spanish. Often, no technically adequate measures are available in the student's language. When this occurs, professionals could choose not to assess the student or assess with English-language measures. However, neither of these tactics is acceptable. Failure to assess may result in inappropriate placement of the student in special education or retention in general education. Testing non-English speakers with English-language tests is clearly discriminatory.

More acceptable options include the use of interpreters to assist in the administration of English-language measures and the development of informal measures in the student's language. Interpreters are not a perfect solution, although in many cases they may be the only alternative if the language of the student is not a common one. Plata (1982) describes several pitfalls in the use of interpreters for test administration:

(a) On-the-spot translation is very difficult, especially when the interpreter does not know the technical language found in test items.

(b) Many words lose their meaning in the translation process.

(c) The interpreter may not know all the possible terms or dialects applied to a word or concept, especially if the child being tested is from a different geographic region than that of the interpreter.

(d) There may be hostile feelings toward the examiner if an interpreter feels that he or she is "being used" to "cover up" the examiner's inadequacies or if the interpreter perceives the remuneration to be minimal for doing the work of a highly paid professional (p. 4).

ENHANCEDetext
Video Example 12.2
Watch this video to find out more about lesson plans and English-language learners.

Plata (1982), however, concedes that the use of interpreters adds useful information that would not be available. When English-language tests are administered via an interpreter, test norms no longer apply. Results should be viewed as alternate scores, or more realistically, the test should be treated as an informal measure.

Another strategy available to professionals is development of informal measures in the language of the student. As with norm-referenced tests, these should not be direct translations of English-language measures. The design of informal inventories, criterion-referenced tests, and other informal instruments requires proficiency in the child's language. If this is not available among the professional staff of the school or district, translators become necessary for the development of the assessments, and interpreters are needed for their administration. Again, this is not a perfect solution to the problem, but it is sometimes a workable alternative for students who speak uncommon languages.

It is interesting that even though the number of English-language learners is increasing, educators often do not get the information they need to support their students (Samson & Collins, 2012). This could have devastating effects. For example, Ballantyne, Sanderman, and Levy (2008) noted that students who are English-language learners have a higher dropout rate than students who are not

English-language learners. Samson and Collins (2012) reported that pedagogical coursework in teaching English-language learners is lacking in the training of teacher candidates. These researchers recommended applying guiding principles of oral language, cultural aspects, and academic language to high-impact areas, such as accrediting bodies and state regulations. Telléz and Waxman (2005) reported that not only is appropriate training not given to teachers, but students who are English language learners are more likely to have teachers first starting their profession or uncertified teachers Supporting English-language learners is essential as national data indicate significant differences in the performance of ELLs as compared to non-ELLs in reading and mathematics (U.S. Department of Education, 2007a, 2007b).

Bailey and Heritage (2014) discussed the concept of "learning progressions" in the assessment of students who were English-language learners. Learning progressions are supported by formative assessment and could be measured in smaller units than standards. Recently, the focus on standards has significantly affected ELLs in the areas of assessment and instruction (Kibler, Valdes, & Walqui, 2014). Teachers in authentic contexts of instruction and assessment support language learning through "language progressions."

 Breakpoint Practice 12.1
Click here to check your understanding of the assessment of English language learners.

WITHIN THE CONTEXT OF THE CLASSROOM

The classroom-learning environment is an important concern in the assessment of oral language skills, both for special students with educational needs in the area of oral language and for those who speak non-Standard English dialects or languages other than English. So far, discussion has focused on assessment strategies for gathering information about the student's performance. The emphasis now shifts to procedures and techniques for studying the classroom-learning environment and its influence on the student's oral language

skills. It is important to note that English-language fluency is not necessary to assess whether a student who is ELL has a disability (Hamayan, Marler, Sanchez-Lopex, & Damino, 2007).

The Instructional Environment

Oral language is not usually taught as a separate subject in general education classrooms, except in the early elementary grades. However, oral language demands pervade the entire curriculum. Students are expected to listen to and understand the teacher and others in the classroom. They are also expected to be fluent in the language of the classroom and to be capable oral communicators.

One aspect of the learning environment is the communication skill of the teacher. This is important both in the early elementary grades, where most of the instructional content is delivered orally, and in the secondary grades, where teachers rely heavily on the lecture as a method for presenting new information. Factors to consider are as follows:

- When oral directions are given, does the teacher prepare the students for what is to come?
- Does the teacher make sure that the purposes for listening are clear to each student?
- Is the teacher usually talking, or does the teacher listen to students as speakers? (Russell & Russell, 1959)

Other dimensions of teacher behavior that may influence students' ability to listen effectively are described by Alley and Deshler (1979):

1. *Nonlinguistic communication.* Does the teacher make effective use of gestures, eye contact, and pauses?
2. *Preorganizers.* Does the teacher present an overview that stresses the major points of the material to be covered?
3. *Organization.* Does the teacher present information in a logical, organized fashion?
4. *Pace.* Does the teacher present the information at varied paces—slowing down for important points and repeating them for emphasis?
5. *Examples.* Does the teacher use examples to illustrate points and give concrete examples of abstract information? (p. 289)

Another area of interest is the number and types of oral responses required of students in the classroom-learning environment. In the early years of elementary school, speaking is a primary way that students respond to classroom activities. They read aloud, answer questions orally, and participate in group discussions. In middle and high school, teachers continue to expect students to communicate orally. In a study by Knowlton and Schlick, reported in Schumaker and Deshler (1984), secondary teachers considered communication skills important and identified specific skills such as clear speech, explanations, spoken reports, and class discussions. Comprehension and decoding are also areas of interest (Geva & Massey-Garrison, 2013).

The teacher's instructional response to students with language differences or disorders should also be considered in assessment. In correcting student errors, does the teacher stress language form (i.e., articulation and grammar) or meaning and usage? What changes, if any, have been made in the standard instructional program to accommodate the needs of learners such as the student under assessment? Are listening tasks restructured for students with difficulty in receptive language? Are speaking tasks modified in any way for students with problems in language production?

Polloway and Smith (1982) provide specific suggestions for the instruction of students with special language needs, particularly those who speak dialectical English or languages other than English. These include the following:

- Avoid negative statements about the child's language, exercising particular caution in front of large groups. Rather than saying, "I don't understand you" or "You are not saying that right" several times, the teacher should use a statement such as, "Could you say that in a different way to help me understand?"
- Reinforce oral and written language production. A first goal in working with language-different students is to maintain and subsequently increase the language output. Reinforcing desired production will insure that this goal is reached.
- Set aside at least a short period during the day to stress language development.

- Involve persons from the linguistically different community in the total school program as much as possible so that these persons, as well as "native" speakers, can share language experiences.
- As the teacher, you should model Standard English usage. For example, when a student says, "Dese car look good," you could say, "Yes, these cars do look good." (pp. 83–84)

Waxman and Tellez (2002) suggested instructional methods to support high achievement in English-language learners. Examples included collaborative techniques, the use of technology, connected speech sequences, previous knowledge, and multiple representations.

The Interpersonal Environment

The interpersonal environment of the classroom is an important area of concern in the study of oral language performance because communication is a social event. At least two persons must participate: a speaker who transmits information and a listener who acts as the recipient.

In assessing the interpersonal dimension, it is necessary to determine whether students have opportunities to practice oral language skills as part of classroom activities. Some of the questions that can be asked are:

- Is the teacher the primary speaker in the classroom? That is, are students expected to act as listeners rather than speakers? How many opportunities per day, on the average, do students have to respond orally in class? What types of responses are most typical—yes and no answers, short responses of a few words, several sentences?
- Are there opportunities for students and the teacher to communicate in large group settings?
- Do students speak with the teacher individually or in small-group settings?
- Are students allowed or encouraged to communicate with each other?
- Are there opportunities for students to communicate in structured situations such as small group discussions, cooperative learning groups, role-playing activities, class meetings, debates, and panel discussions?

It is also important to evaluate the instructional interactions when classroom activities require oral communication. For example, when students make errors in speaking, how does the teacher respond? Is the error identified? Does the teacher correct it?

The Physical Environment

The way the physical environment of the classroom is arranged influences students' opportunities for interaction and the practice of oral communication skills. Cohen and Plaskon (1980) describe two classroom seating arrangements—one that inhibits student interaction and another that encourages communication among students. In the traditional classroom environment, students are seated at desks arranged in rows, so each student is isolated from all but a few peers. As Figure 12–2 shows, the modified classroom environment represents a more ideal arrangement because children have many chances to participate

in expressive language tasks. In addition, the teacher is able to interact with individual students as needed without calling attention to any particular student.

The physical environment can also affect listening skills. Soundproofing or carpeting decreases the overall noise level of the room. The areas of the classroom used for listening and independent study should be separated from the areas where less quiet activities take place. Some classrooms have listening centers where one or several students can listen to tapes or records through earphones. These centers can be used to provide instruction in listening skills and for free-time activities such as listening to music or stories.

Breakpoint Practice 12.2
Click here to check your understanding of classroom context.

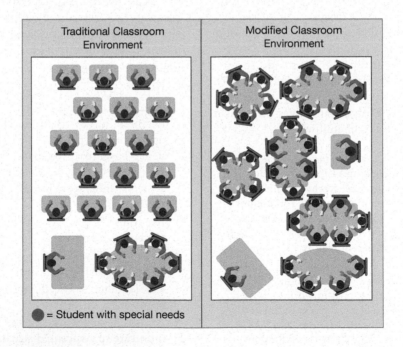

FIGURE 12–2
Classroom Seating Arrangements

Note: James A. McLoughlin; Rena B. Lewis; Effie P. Kritikos, *Assessing Students with Special Needs*, 8e., © 2018. Pearson Education, Inc., New York, NY.

ANSWERING THE ASSESSMENT QUESTIONS

Dynamic Assessment

Dynamic assessment has been discussed by researchers as an effective element in the assessment-to-instruction link (Robinson-Zanartu, 1996). Lidz and Pena (1996) note that intervention is the most essential aspect of this type of assessment. They add that dynamic assessment allows the assessor to look at how the student learns, how changeable the student is, and what types of instruction are most useful for the student. Dynamic assessment focuses on the use of this tool with students who are culturally and/or linguistically diverse.

For example, Ukrainetz, Harpell, Walsh, and Coyle (2000) investigated the relationship between dynamic assessment and language learning ability in Native American (Arapahoe/Shosone) children who were in kindergarten. Children's learning strategies (i.e., attending, planning, self-regulating, and responses) were related to more effective language learning. Pinpointing these skills can help professionals better discriminate the strength of language learning. Results supported the utilization of dynamic assessment in evaluating language learning skills in this population.

In addition, Gutierrez-Clellen and Pena (2001) compared dynamic assessment methods with assessment applications for students who are culturally and/or linguistically diverse. Three methods they examined included testing the limits (feedback and/or questioning during testing), graduated prompting (hierarchical), and test-teach-retest. The researchers noted that the test-teach-retest methods matched better with the concept of differentiation of disorders and differences (language and/or cultural). They discussed modifiability (changeability) based on Pena and Quinn's research (1997). The authors offered the protocol for assessing the student's responsiveness and the child's modifiability, and examining aspects that help with alteration in language areas.

Multicultural Considerations

Penegra (2000) noted that when individuals apply different meanings to words based on schemas and definitions, miscommunications and misperceptions may take place. This information has ramifications for communication exchanges in almost all areas of language as well as implications for the validity of assessment practices.

Language loss is another factor to consider when examining language and bilingual student populations. Paucity in both languages does not automatically indicate a language disorder. As individuals increase proficiency in a second language, a loss of proficiency may occur in the first language. This is considered a normal occurrence (Schiff-Myers, 1992). Even though an individual speaks English more proficiently than another spoken language, she or he may still have less exposure to English than a typical participant in the standardization sample. Consequently, he or she may not be familiar with the tasks necessary to do well on a test (Mattes & Omark, 1991).

Task Familiarity

In an example of exposure to tasks, Pena and Quinn (1997) investigated task familiarity and test results in Puerto Rican and African American children. They compared performances on description (familiar) and one-word labeling (unfamiliar) items. Results revealed that the participants did better on familiar test items. This type of test was more insightful in distinguishing typical language and atypical language when compared to unfamiliar test tasks (Pena & Quinn, 1997).

In addition, Campbell, Dollaghan, Needleman, and Janosky (1997) examined the effects of prior knowledge and experience on language assessment performance. They compared language measures dependent on knowledge and test measures dependent on processing in children. These participants came from the majority group (Caucasian) and from minority groups (African American, Asian, and Native American). Results revealed that the majority group participants scored higher than the minority group participants on measures that were dependent on knowledge. However, the groups did not perform differently on tasks that were processing measures.

Type of Task

The type of task may be a barrier to revealing valid assessment results. Rodekohr and Haynes (2001) performed a follow-up study comparing African American children (speaking African American English) with typical language, African American children with a language disorder (speaking African American English), Caucasian children (speaking Southern English) with typical language, and Caucasian children (speaking Southern English) with a language disorder in measures of knowledge-based and processing-based language tasks. Results revealed that the children who were African American did not do as well as the Caucasian children on knowledge-based tasks but performed the same as Caucasian children on processing-based tasks. A critical finding was that the processing-dependent measures distinguished typical and atypical language in both the African American and Caucasian children. Using processing measures that appear to be bias-free has strong implications for assessment of culturally and linguistically diverse individuals.

Research has been conducted in the area of comprehension tasks in the assessment of African American children from urban middle-income households (Craig, Washington, & Thompson-Porter, 1998). Researchers investigated relationships in responses to WH questions, performance on active/passive sentence task constructions, and chronological age/grade level. They found that the two tasks were appropriate to use in assessing the comprehension skills of young African American children.

In a follow-up study, Craig and Washington (2000) compared the language performance of African American children identified with language impairment who received school-based language therapy and two groups of typically developing peers (all speaking African American English) on five types of language measures. Those tasks included mean length of utterance (MLU), frequencies of syntax, numbers of different words (based on a language sample from play activity), comprehension of WH questions, and understanding of active/passive sentence forms. Students in the group with language impairments performed lower on all five measures. The authors supported the use of these informal tasks in the assessment of young African American children.

Gutierrez-Clellen, Restrepo, Bedore, Pena, and Anderson (2000) discussed code switching (moving from one language to another) and dialect as factors regarding the use of the Development Assessment of Spanish Grammar, mean length of response in words, mean length of terminable unit (no dependent clauses left over), and mean length of utterance in morphemes in Spanish-speaking children. Use of clinical methods for assessing individuals with limited English was suggested, including information regarding (1) Spanish morphosyntactic categories, (2) comparison of data from individuals of similar sociolinguistic backgrounds, (3) analysis of errors per simple or complex sentence (T-unit), (4) use of parent and teacher reports to validate observations, (5) clarification of issues of language loss, (6) investigation of second-language errors that may be associated with second-language acquisition, and (7) comparison of unexpected performance to children of similar sociolinguistic backgrounds.

Seymour, Bland-Stewart, and Green (1998), in their study of the shared features of African American English and Standard American English, used syntax analysis from language samples of children with and without language disorders. The features that the two dialects had in common (noncontrastive—features not unique to a dialect) were compared to features the two dialects did not share (contrastive—features unique to a dialect). The noncontrastive features were found to be different and the contrastive features not different (except in the past tense/ed/) in the two groups. Therefore, using these concepts in assessment may lead to better differentiation of language disorders in students speaking African American English.

McGregor, Williams, Hearst, and Johnson (1997) explored contrastive analysis in the process of differentiating a language difference from a language disorder. Specifically, they targeted the scenario of a speech-language pathologist coming from a different speech community than the client. They defined this method as taking apart speech-language patterns from the individual's first language or dialect compared to true errors.

They offered four procedures in this process: (1) being familiar with the dialect of the client, (2) collecting expressive language information from the assessment process, (3) comparing data to the dialect pattern to find "true errors," and (4) examining all of the pieces of the assessment process (i.e., case history).

Specific Quantitative Tests

Researchers have provided valuable information regarding specific tests and individuals who are culturally and/or linguistically diverse. Saenz and Huer (2003) looked at results from four standard and modified subtests of the Clinical Evaluation of Language Fundamentals—Third Edition (CELF-3) in bilingual Latino children. They found that scores improved with modification and repeated testing. The students had performed better on the second administration of the CELF-3, perhaps due to experience in the test taking.

In researching the area of articulation, Cole and Taylor (1990) examined the performance of African American children who spoke Black English Vernacular on three tests of articulation. Specifically, they investigated test–client correspondence (context appropriateness) on the Templin-Darley Tests of Articulation—Second Edition, Arizona Articulation Proficiency Scale—Revised (AAPS-R), and the Photo Articulation Test. The researchers not only examined test items of concern but also determined which tests might lead to misdiagnoses if dialect was not considered. They found that of the 10 participants, the following misdiagnoses would occur if dialect was not accounted for: AAPS-R, 7; Templin-Darley, 6; and Photo Articulation Test, 2. Dialect-sensitive scores were as follows: AAPS-R, 0; Templin-Darley, 2; and Photo Articulation Test, 1. Results reveal that if dialect variation is not considered during the assessment process, the outcome could be devastating.

Roberts, Medley, Swartzfager, and Neebe (1997) examined the use of the Communication and Symbolic Behavior Scales and found that the tool was appropriate in the area of internal consistency for African American 1-year-olds (Roberts et al., 1997).

Professionals' Judgment

Culture determines behavior as well as how behavior is judged (Kayser, 1995). Bebout and Arthur (1992) found differences in individuals' beliefs about the emotional health and potential for change in the speech of persons with speech disorders based on culture (i.e., North American-born and foreign-born). Participants included individuals born in the United States, Japan, Latin America, Southeast Asia, China, and Hong Kong. More specifically, in a question involving efforts to improve speech, participants from Southeast Asia, China, and Hong Kong more often reported that individuals with speech disorders could speak better if they tried harder. Chinese participants reported more frequently that a person with a speech disorder (such as cleft palate or hearing disorders) would have an emotional disturbance.

Speech-language pathologists are often asked to judge whether English-language learners have language disorders associated with learning difficulties. Many of these professionals are not well equipped to perform this task (Roseberry-McKibbin & Eicholtz, 1994). Roseberry-McKibbin (1994) presents interference, fossilization, interlanguage code switching, silent period, language loss, reduced exposure to both languages, and proficiency in both languages as learning processes involved in second-language acquisition. She adds that the ethnographic interview and case history are key components of the assessment. In analyzing the literature, Roseberry-McKibbin (1994) indicates support for the following informal assessment procedures: evaluating the student's language over time, focusing on the functional components of language, utilizing observations in authentic contexts, using questionnaires for various important individuals who interact with the student, using narratives, and employing spontaneous language samples. For a discussion of language sampling and multicultural issues please refer to Chapter 6.

In looking specifically at phonology, Yavas and Goldstein (1998) investigated phonological patterns in languages, sound pattern influence across languages, and guidelines for assessment practice. They indicated that case history, oral-peripheral examination (visual inspection of mouth and oral cavity), hearing screening, language, voice fluency, and phonological patterns should be in the battery of tests involved in this process. The authors considered sociocultural factors, assessing phonological skills in all languages, choosing an appropriate assessment tool, and using assessment alternatives (i.e., informal samples, dynamic assessment, and contextual sampling). In addition, the authors included describing common and uncommon phonological patterns in both languages, identifying bilingual phonological patterns, outlining interference patterns, and accounting for dialect features.

The information gleaned from this multitude of studies indicates that formal test results should be viewed with extreme caution. Useful information can be extracted to improve the assessment process. Language sampling and dynamic assessment appear to be fruitful in the assessment-to-instruction process.

ENHANCEDetext
Video Example 12.3
Watch this video to find out more about multicultural considerations.

Assessment in Action
Joseph

Joseph is a new student in your fourth-grade class who recently moved into the school district. He is bilingual in Spanish and English. Joseph's former teacher referred him for an evaluation. He had concerns regarding Joseph's language performance because Joseph was having a hard time keeping up with classroom discussions.

Joseph's parents reported that Joseph's birth and delivery were unremarkable. Developmental milestones, with the exception of communication, occurred within normal limits. Parents reported motor skills development of sitting unsupported at 6 months, crawling at 6 months, and walking independently at 12 months. Joseph's health history was marked by occasional colds, which were treated with decongestants. It was noted that an earache occasionally followed a cold.

Joseph lives at home with his mother, father, 10-year-old sister, 2-year-old brother, and paternal grandmother. Spanish and English are spoken within the home. Joseph's parents work outside the home.

What questions should be asked of Joseph, his family members, and his teachers?

Should formal and informal assessment measures be conducted?

If so, what informal assessment measures should be taken?

What formal tests should be administered?

What are some possible complicating factors?

When looking at the chapter-opening case study about Joseph, the earache information in his medical history raises questions regarding a possible hearing loss. A hearing screening would be the first checkpoint in the discussion of his possible language issues. Discussion or an interview with the parents with regard to their assessment of Joseph's language in the home and community setting would be the next checkpoint. Have they noticed any language issues in Spanish or English? How does his language use compare to that of his siblings? Observations of Joseph in multiple settings (i.e., with teachers, classmates, and family members) would be a window to his language functioning in Spanish and English. What percentage of the time does he use Spanish? English? With whom? In what contexts?

If the previous information points to difficulties with language, the assessment process can include language samples and classroom artifacts. Formal assessment practices could take place after a proper evaluation protocol has been completed. Possibilities for formal testing include the Peabody Picture Vocabulary Test, Expressive One-Word Picture

Vocabulary Test, Goldman-Fristoe Articulation Test, Test of Language Development—Intermediate, and the Test de Vocabulario en Imagenes Peabody. In the informal testing

domain, it would be appropriate to include interviews, observations, classroom artifacts, attendance data, language samples, and dynamic assessment.

SUMMARY

- Engquist (1974) describes the most common phono-logical variations in Black English:

  1. Softening of the *r* sound (e.g., sister/sistah, poor/po', Carter/Cahtuh).
  2. Lessening of the *l* sound (e.g., help/hep, all/awe, tool/too).
  3. Weakening of final consonants in clusters (e.g., past/pass, hold/hol, bent/ben).
  4. Specific sound substitutions (e.g., *f* for *th,* as in mouth/mouf; *d* for *th,* as in this/dis; *i* for *e,* as in pen/pin; *ah* for *i,* as in I/ah). (as cited in Polloway & Smith, 1982, pp. 72–73)

- Assessment of students who speak languages other than English has two purposes. The first is determination of the student's language proficiency, both in the first or home language (L1) and in English, the language of the school. With most students, English is the second language (L2), although English can be the child's third or even fourth language. Assessment of language proficiency provides professionals with information about the student's relative competence

in each language, so that the language or languages of assessment can be determined. Once this decision is made, assessment continues to explore the need for educational intervention.

- The dimensions of teacher behavior that may influence students' ability to listen effectively are described by Alley and Deshler (1979). Two examples include:

  1. *Nonlinguistic communication.* Does the teacher make effective use of gestures, eye contact, pauses?
  2. *Preorganizers.* Does the teacher present an overview that stresses the major points of the material to be covered? (p. 289)

- In addressing the assessment questions, language loss is another factor to consider when examining language and bilingual student populations. Paucity in both languages does not automatically indicate a language disorder. As individuals increase proficiency in a second language, a loss of proficiency may occur in the first language. Consequently, he or she may not be familiar with the tasks necessary to do well on a test (Mattes & Omark, 1991).

13

WavebreakMediaMicro/Fotolia

Reading

LEARNING OUTCOMES

After reading this chapter, you will be able to:

- Identify and describe three examples of considerations in assessment of reading.

- Name and discuss two examples of subtests in the *Woodcock Reading Mastery Tests—Third Edition*.

- Describe the purpose of the *Gray Oral Reading Tests—Fifth Edition*.

- Name and explain two Examples of Subtests in the *Test of Reading Comprehension—Fourth Edition*.

- Compare and contrast three measures of phonemic awareness and phonological processing.

- Describe an example of a curriculum-based reading fluency measure.

- Compare and contrast two informal reading inventories.

- Identify and explain two examples of other informal strategies.

- Name and discuss two major factors that relate to reading within the context of the classroom.

- Define and explain two examples of how reading assessment tools could vary in answering the assessment questions.

KEY TERMS

balanced literacy

phonemic awareness

phonological processing

decoding

sight vocabulary

phonics

fluency

comprehension skills

informal reading inventory

miscue analysis

cloze procedure

readability

Teachers, parents, and the American citizenry place great value on literacy, and reading is considered to be the most important literacy skill. In the elementary grades, much of the curriculum focuses on skill acquisition in reading, and in the secondary grades, reading is a major vehicle for the presentation of information in content subjects. In our society, people are expected to be proficient readers; illiteracy is a definite barrier to success.

The value placed on reading in the United States is highlighted by the Reading First program created under the 2001 No Child Left Behind Act. According to this act's website, Reading First provides grants to states to promote research-based strategies for students in lower elementary grades (U.S. Department of Education, n.d.).

Reading is often an area of difficulty for students with disabilities. Young students may not learn the basic skills of reading at the expected rate; they may fall far behind their classmates in their ability to decode and understand the written word. Older students who are even further behind in reading may lack the skills needed to use reading as a tool for learning other skills and subjects.

Once students are found eligible for special education services, the focus in assessment shifts to instructional planning. The question that guides this phase of assessment is, *What are the student's educational needs?* Because reading is often an area of need for students with mild disabilities, the assessment team may ask, *What is the student's current level of reading achievement? What are the student's strengths and weaknesses in the various skill areas of reading?*

At this level of questioning, the team is concerned more about the student's ability to perform important reading tasks than about how performance compares with that of other students. Although norm-referenced information can be useful in determining which reading skills are areas of need, criterion-referenced information and other types of informal data provide specific descriptions of the student's current status in skill development.

CONSIDERATIONS IN ASSESSMENT OF READING

Of all academic skills, reading is most often the subject of special education assessment. For many educators, reading is one of the most critical of all school subjects, particularly in the elementary curriculum that focuses on the acquisition of basic skills. In the secondary grades, students are expected to use their reading skills to gain information in subject areas such as English, history, and the sciences. Because many special students do not meet these expectations, reading is a major concern in special education assessment.

Purposes

Students' reading skills are assessed for several reasons. In determining eligibility for special education programs, overall school performance is investigated, and reading is an important component of school achievement. In addition, general education teachers monitor their students' progress in reading. Reading proficiency is one of the minimum competencies assessed by many schools and districts for grade advancement and high school graduation, and reading is always included on the state-mandated tests of school achievement that assess students' progress toward state performance standards.

In special education, reading skills are assessed not only for determining program eligibility, but also for planning instruction, and that is the focus of this chapter. Information from general achievement tests such as the *PIAT–R/NU,* the *WIAT–III,* or the *Woodcock-Johnson IV* is insufficient. It is necessary to gather additional data about the student's specific strengths and weaknesses to describe current levels of reading performance. It then becomes possible to develop appropriate annual goals for the student.

Reading assessment does not stop when the student's individualized educational program has been planned. Special educators begin to monitor the student's progress in acquiring targeted skills, and in ongoing assessment, data are gathered on a weekly or even a daily basis. Reading assessment continues throughout the student's special education program if reading is a focus of specialized instruction. At least once a year, the educational plan is reviewed, and evaluation data are gathered to determine the student's current levels of reading achievement.

Skill Areas

Reading is a complex process involving many skills. There is continuing debate over the nature of the reading process, but most experts acknowledge that reading involves the recognition and decoding of printed text and the comprehension of that text as meaningful information. According to Schreiner (1983), individuals interpret essential printed components and then give meaning to those components.

Three divergent models of proficient reading have been proposed (Chall & Stahl, 1982). These models differ in the amount of importance they attach to text and meaning, two aspects of the reading process. In the *bottom-up model,* it is hypothesized that proficient readers proceed from text to meaning; first, individual letters and words are perceived and decoded, and then comprehension of the text's meaning takes place. Reading is considered a text-driven or stimulus-driven activity; it depends on the reader's skill in lower-level processes such as word recognition. In contrast, the *top-down model* emphasizes what are considered the higher-level processes of comprehension. The skilled reader relies on prior knowledge and previous experience, questioning and hypothesis testing, and comprehension of the meaning of textual material rather than decoding of individual text elements. The third model is the *interactive model,* which emphasizes both text and meaning. In this model, reading is accomplished by applying previous knowledge to text so that the student can build a reply or answer (Walker, 1992).

The debate over the relative importance of text versus meaning or decoding versus comprehension carries over into the classroom and the strategies selected for reading instruction. More traditional approaches to reading instruction tend to be skills-based (i.e., bottom-up). Beginning instruction focuses on the development of decoding skills; comprehension skills are not emphasized until learners have some facility with decoding. Examples are traditional basal reader programs, phonics-based approaches, linguistic methods, and programmed instruction.

A newer approach, whole-language instruction, is based on the top-down and interactive models of reading. Reading is not broken down into subskills such as decoding. In fact, reading is integrated with the other language arts (speaking, listening, and writing). Whole language is often described as a philosophy rather than an instructional approach (Westby, 1992); in this philosophy, language is innate and has real-life application through literacy (Lapp & Flood, 1992). In the whole-language classroom, language learning takes place in a social context in which students use language for real (i.e., authentic) purposes. Students read whole texts, not fragments, and those texts tend to be children's literature rather than stories constructed solely for inclusion in textbooks. Throughout, meaning and motivation are emphasized; the development of isolated skills is deemphasized. Despite the popularity of whole language, research results do not point to the superiority of this approach over basal reader programs (e.g., Stahl & Miller, 1989). In addition, authors such as Lerner, Cousin, and Richeck (1992) and Mather (1992) warn that students with mild disabilities will require supplementary skills instruction if they are to succeed in a whole-language classroom.

In recent years, experts have come to recommend a combined approach to reading instruction, one that emphasizes the development of abilities not only in the decoding of print but also in the comprehension of textual meaning. A report of the National Research Council's Committee on the Prevention of Reading Difficulties in Young Children (Snow, Burns, & Griffin, 1998) describes the reading process in this way. They note that both form and context are essential cognitive conditions of reading.

One popular example is the **balanced literacy** approach. This approach includes both reading and writing and focuses on the acquisition of both decoding and comprehension skills. Cunningham (2003) describes the balanced literacy model called the Four Blocks framework. In this model, each day students engage in four types of literacy activities: working with words (i.e., word study), guided reading, self-selected reading, and writing (Cunningham & Allington, 1999; Cunningham, Hall, & Defee, 1991).

The federal education law, No Child Left Behind (NCLB), and its counterpart in special education, IDEA 2004, place great emphasis on the use of scientifically based instructional methods to promote student achievement. The *Report of the National Reading Panel: Teaching Children to Read* (National Institute of Child Health and Human Development, 2000) identified several components of evidence-based instruction in the area of reading:

- Phonemic awareness instruction
- Phonics instruction
- Fluency and guided oral reading
- Vocabulary instruction
- Text comprehension instruction

Walsh, Glaser, and Wilcox (2006) reported that the National Reading Panel's recommendations include foci on organized and overt instruction of phonics, oral reading, vocabulary construction and reading comprehension.

Phonemic awareness is an important readiness skill for the acquisition of beginning reading skills. Lerner (2000) defines this skill as identifying sound segments within words. Those individual sounds are called *phonemes,* thus the term *phonemic awareness.* Another term, **phonological processing**, is used to describe more complex operations with phonemes such as discrimination among phonemes, rhyming, sequencing, and recall. Because failure to develop phonological processing abilities can impede the acquisition of beginning reading skills, it is believed that young children with potential problems in this area should be identified so that they can receive appropriate training (Torgesen & Barker, 1995; Wagner & Torgesen, 1987). To this end, several measures of phonological processing skills have been developed in recent years.

In the assessment of reading itself (rather than reading readiness skills), traditional measures tend to be skills-based. They focus on the student's ability to decode text and respond to questions about the meaning of the text he or she has read. As Garner (1983) observed, these measures are product-oriented, and they are based on a bottom-up view of the reading act. Reading tests and inventories do not stress the interaction between the reader and the text. Thus, informal assessment strategies are needed to gather information about the student's background knowledge, language facility, knowledge of text structure, and the metacognitive strategies he or she chooses to use when interacting with text (Samuels, 1983).

Formal reading tests and inventories typically include measures of students' decoding and comprehension skills. **Decoding** skills are word recognition skills; decoding occurs when a student looks at a word, or the letters that make up the word, and then pronounces the word. Decoding can be accomplished in several ways. Words that are familiar to the student may be recognized by sight; such words are called sight words or **sight vocabulary.** When words are unfamiliar, the student may attempt to use phonic analysis, often called simply **phonics.** The student looks at each letter, or grapheme; recalls the sound, or phoneme, associated with the letter; and blends the sequence of sounds into a word. Another method of decoding unfamiliar words is structural analysis. In this method, words are broken into syllables to analyze prefixes, suffixes, root words, and endings. In yet another approach to decoding, the context of the sentence or paragraph in which the unfamiliar word appears is the subject of analysis. The student uses the meaning of the passage and the grammatical structure of the text as aids in word recognition. Phonic, structural, and contextual analyses are not necessarily independent strategies; students can use one, two, or all three of these methods to decode an unfamiliar word.

Decoding skills are assessed in several ways by reading tests and inventories. One typical method is to present students with a list of words to read aloud. The task may be untimed to allow students the opportunity to use phonic and structural analysis skills. However, tasks are timed if the purpose is to assess sight vocabulary or if the speed of decoding is a concern. Lists of phonetically regular words or nonsense words may be used to evaluate the student's ability to apply phonic analysis skills. Nonsense words force students to analyze each word rather than rely on sight recognition. Another common method of assessing decoding involves the reading of connected text rather than isolated words. Students are presented with sentences or paragraphs to read aloud. Passage reading provides students with the opportunity to use contextual analysis skills as well as other methods of decoding. Also, it becomes possible to observe the student's oral reading fluency and phrasing and his or her rate of reading connected text.

Fluency is the ability to perform a skill with both speed and accuracy. In the area of reading,

the term *fluency* typically refers to the ability to read text out loud quickly and with no or few errors. Fluency in oral reading is often measured using curriculum-based measurement techniques such as one-minute time samples.

On traditional reading tests and inventories, asking students questions about **comprehension skills** assesses material they have just read. Students may read the text silently or orally, depending on whether decoding skills are also under study. The text may be a sentence, a paragraph, or a series of paragraphs making up a story or essay. Comprehension questions may be multiple-choice or completion items, but most typically, the student provides oral responses to open-ended questions. Comprehension questions may probe the student's understanding of the literal meaning of the passage or require inferential thinking and critical analysis (Bartel, 1986b). For example, students may be asked to recall the details of the passage, remember a sequence of events, state the main ideas, explain the meaning of vocabulary words, make judgments, draw conclusions, or evaluate ideas or actions.

The ability to use reading skills in everyday situations is an area rarely included on measures of reading performance; informal techniques are needed to evaluate students' ability to apply their skills in decoding and comprehension to real reading tasks. Reading is a useful skill only when the student is able to read quickly and accurately enough to use it as a tool to gain new information. For example, in everyday life, readers apply their skills when they read signs, posters, letters, magazines and newspapers, television schedules, and the like. These important applications of reading should not be neglected in assessment.

Current Practices

In schools today, the assessment of reading achievement is common practice in both general and special education. Because of the high interest in reading and the complexity of this skill area, a great number and variety of measures and techniques are available to assess reading performance.

Academic achievement tests typically include one or more subtests designed to evaluate students' mastery of reading skills. This is true both for the group-administered achievement measures used in general education and for the individual tests preferred in special education. The school performance measures described in Chapter 11 each contain at least one reading achievement measure.

Norm-referenced reading tests are more directly related to instructional planning. Sometimes called diagnostic reading tests, these measures survey several subskills within the broad area of reading to identify specific strengths and weaknesses. Because these tests are norm-referenced, the information they provide is comparative.

A number of of reading tests are available, and these vary somewhat in the range of skills they assess. Some tests are designed for comprehensive assessment of the reading process and include measures of several of the important reading skills. One example is the *Woodcock Reading Mastery Tests—Third Edition.* Other measures concentrate on a particular component of reading. There are tests that assess only comprehension skills, others that assess only word recognition skills, and still others that evaluate reading fluency. On some measures, oral reading is the concern, whereas on others it is silent reading. The majority of reading tests are administered individually to allow testers the opportunity to observe students' performance.

Another type of measure often used in reading assessment is the **informal reading inventory.** Reading inventories are made up of graded word lists and graded reading selections. For instance, an inventory might contain a series of word lists and passages ranging from a primer reading level up to grade 8 reading level. Students begin by reading material at the lower grade levels; they continue reading until the material becomes too difficult to decode and/or to comprehend. These measures are grade-referenced, not norm-referenced. The standard of comparison is the grade level of the material the student is reading, not the performance of other students. Several informal reading inventories are available.

Inventories are only one type of informal strategy used in reading assessment. There are a great many informal assessment tools for reading, and these represent all of the standard types of measures and techniques. Among the most

commonly used are criterion-referenced tests of specific reading objectives, error analysis of students' oral reading performance, teacher checklists, diagnostic teaching, and clinical reading interviews. Informal techniques are also used to investigate the classroom learning environment and its relationship to students' reading performance.

Table 13–1 provides a listing of several of the reading measures used in special education. Each is categorized by type—formal test, informal reading inventory, criterion-referenced test, or curriculum-based measure—and information is included about the grades or ages for which each measure is intended and whether administration is group or individual. In addition, the table notes if the measure is designed to focus on the assessment of decoding skills, comprehension skills, or both.

This chapter describes each of the major strategies used in schools today for the assessment of reading. Formal reading tests are discussed first, and the next sections introduce three of these. Included are a comprehensive measure of reading, the *Woodcock Reading Mastery Tests—Third Edition* and two measures that concentrate on one major reading skill, the *Gray Oral Reading Tests—Fifth Edition* and the *Test of Reading Comprehension—Fourth Edition.* The following sections describe formal measures of phonological processing, followed by informal reading inventories and other informal assessment strategies.

 Breakpoint Practice 13.1
Click here to check your understanding of considerations regarding the assessment of reading.

WOODCOCK READING MASTERY TESTS—THIRD EDITION

The *Woodcock Reading Mastery Tests—Third Edition (WRMT™–3)* is a norm-referenced measure that is used to pinpoint students' strengths and weaknesses in reading. The original version of this test was published in 1973 and revised in 1987; another version with updated norms was published in 1998. According to its manual, the

TABLE 13–1
Measures of Reading

NAME (AUTHOR)	AGES OR GRADES	TYPE OF MEASURE*	GROUP OR INDIVIDUAL	SKILL AREA(S) ASSESSED	
				DECODING	COMPREHENSION
Analytical Reading Inventory (10th ed.) (Woods & Moe, 2015)	Primer to grade 9 functioning level	IRI	Individual	X	X
BRIGANCE® Assessment of Basic Skills—Revised, Spanish Edition (Brigance, 2007)	K to grade 8	CRT	Individual	X	X
BRIGANCE® Comprehensive Inventory of Basic Skills—II (Brigance, 2010b)	Pre-K to Grade 9	CRT	Individual	X	X
Classroom Assessment of Reading Processes (Swearingen & Allen, 2000)	Grades 1–9 functioning level	IRI	Individual	X	X
Classroom Reading Inventory—Twelfth Edition (Wheelock & Campbell, 2013)	Preprimer to grade 8 functioning level	IRI	Individual	X	X
Diagnostic Reading Scales (Spache, 1981)	Grades 1–8 functioning level	NRT	Individual	X	X
Durrell Analysis of Reading Difficulty—Third Edition (Durrell & Catterson, 1980)	Grades 1–6	NRT	Individual	X	X
Dynamic Indicators of Basic Early Literacy Skills (Good & Kaminski, 1996)	Grades K–6	CBM	Individual	X	X
Ekwall/Shanker Reading Inventory—Sixth Edition (Shanker & Ekwall, 2013)	Preprimer to grade 9 functioning level	IRI	Individual	X	X
English-Español Reading Inventory for the Classroom (Flynt & Cooter, 1999)	Preprimer to grade 9 functioning level	IRI	Individual	X	X
Flynt-Cooter Reading Inventory for the Classroom—Fifth Edition (Flynt & Cooter, 2004)	Preprimer to grade 12 functioning level	IRI	Individual	X	X
Formal Reading Inventory (Wiederholt, 1986)	Ages 7–18	NRT	Individual	X	X
Gates-McKillop-Horowitz Reading Diagnostic Test (Gates, McKillop, & Horowitz, 1981)	Grades 1–6	NRT	Individual	X	X
Gilmore Oral Reading Test (Gilmore & Gilmore, 1968)	Grades 1–8	NRT	Individual	X	X
Gray Diagnostic Reading Tests—Second Edition (Bryant, Wiederholt, & Bryant, 2004)	Ages 6–13	NRT	Individual	X	X

TABLE 13–1   *continued*

NAME (AUTHOR)	AGES OR GRADES	TYPE OF MEASURE*	GROUP OR INDIVIDUAL	SKILL AREA(S) ASSESSED	
				DECODING	COMPREHENSION
Gray Oral Reading Tests—Fifth Edition (Wiederholt & Bryant, 2012)	Ages 6–23	NRT	Individual	X	X
Gray Silent Reading Tests (Wiederholt & Blalock, 2000)	Ages 7–26	NRT	Individual or group		X
Hudson Education Skills Inventory (Hudson, Colson, Welch, Banikowski, & Mehring, 1989)	Grades K–12	CRT	Individual	X	X
Informal Reading Inventory—Eighth Edition (Roe & Burns, 2010)	Preprimer to grade 12 functioning level	IRI	Individual	X	X
Monitoring Basic Skills Progress: Basic Reading—Second Edition (Fuchs, Hamlett, & Fuchs, 1997)	Grades 1–7	CBM	Individual	X	X
Reading Miscue Inventory—Second Edition (Goodman, Watson, & Burke, 2005)	Grades 1–8+ functioning level	IRI	Individual	X	X
Slosson Oral Reading Test—Third Edition (Slosson & Nicholson, 2002)	Preschool to adult	NRT	Individual	X	
Standardized Reading Inventory—Second Edition (2nd ed.) (Newcomer, 1999)	Ages 6–14	NRT	Individual	X	X
Stanford Diagnostic Reading Test—Fourth Edition (Karlsen & Gardner, 1995)	Grades 1.5–13	NRT	Group	X	X
Stieglitz Informal Reading Inventory—Third Edition (Stieglitz, 2002)	Preprimer to grade 9 functioning level	IRI	Individual	X	X
Test of Early Reading Ability—Third Edition (Reid, Hresko, & Hammill, 2001)	Ages 3–8	NRT	Individual	X	X
Test of Reading Comprehension—Fourth Edition (Brown, Wiederholt, & Hammill, 2008)	Ages 7–18	NRT	Individual, small group		X
Test of Word Reading Efficiency (Torgesen, Wagner, & Rashotte, 2012)	Grades 1 to 12+, ages 6–25	NRT	Individual	X	
Woodcock-Johnson III Diagnostic Reading Battery (Woodcock, Mather, & Schrank, 2004)	Grades K–16.9, ages 4 to 90+	NRT	Individual	X	X
Woodcock Reading Mastery Tests—Third Edition (Woodcock, 2011)	Grades K–12, ages 5 to 79–11	NRT	Individual	X	X

*NRT = norm-referenced test, IRI = informal inventory, CRT = criterion-referenced test, and CBM = curriculum-based measure.

WOODCOCK READING MASTERY TESTS–REVISED/ NORMATIVE UPDATE (WRMT–R/NU)

R. W. Woodcock (2011)

Type: Norm-referenced test

Major Content Areas: Reading readiness, basic reading skills (word identification and word attack), word and passage comprehension

Type of Administration: Individual

Administration Time: 10 to 30 minutes

Age/Grade Levels: Grades K–12, ages 4–6 through 79–11

Types of Scores: Grade and age equivalents, percentile ranks, standard scores, and Relative Performance Index scores for subtests and clusters

Technology Aids: Q Global

Typical Uses: A broad-based reading test for the identification of strengths and weaknesses in reading skill development

Cautions: Reliability coefficients for several reliability types should be looked at with caution when coefficient numbers fall below the comfortable level.

Publisher: Pearson (*pearsonclinical.com*)

$WRMT^{TM}$–3 could be used for clinical assessment and diagnosis, individual program planning, selection and placement, and research.

Two parallel forms of the *WRMT–* are available: Form A and Form B.

- *Phonological Awareness.* Test taker hears sound, syllable, or word and identifies or names one of four illustrations or words, depending on the section. Thirty-three items across five sections include *First Sound Matching, Last Sound Matching, Rhyme Production, Blending* and *Deletion.* A score of 0 or 1 is achieved.

  - *Listening Comprehension. Test taker listens to passages that are either read by the examiner or played from an audio CD. They then respond to items regarding the passages. A 0 or 1 is earned for each of the 27 items.*
  - *Letter Identification.* Individual letters are arranged in rows, and the student must say the name (or sound) of each. Letters appear in upper- and lowercase, in manuscript and cursive, and in a variety of type styles. Test taker receives a score of 0 or 1 on 17 items.

- *Word Identification.* Students are shown rows of individual words (e.g., *is, listen*), and they must pronounce each of the 46 items within about 5 seconds. A score of 0 or 1 is achieved.
- *Rapid Automatic Naming. Test taker names 36 items as rapidly as possible. The time taken to name items, as well as number of errors are considered in this subtest.*
- *Oral Reading Fluency. Test taker reads passage/ passages and is timed by examiner who also records errors. Words read correctly in 10 seconds is measured in the score.*

- *Word Attack.* Nonsense words and syllables (e.g., *ift, lundy*) are presented instead of real words. The student reads each of the 26 items aloud for a score of 0 or 1 per item.
- *Word Comprehension.* This subtest includes three parts. On Antonyms, the student reads a word aloud and supplies its opposite. On Synonyms, the student reads a word and supplies a word that means the same. On Analogies, the student reads a row of three words representing an incomplete analogy

(e.g., *mother–big, baby–_____*) and supplies the missing word. Each response to the 86 items is scored as a 0 or 1.

- *Passage Comprehension.* This subtest uses a cloze procedure to assess comprehension skills. The student is presented with a brief passage with one word omitted. The student reads the passage silently and then attempts to supply the missing word. Easier passages are accompanied by drawings. Each of the responses to 38 items receives a score of 0 or 1.

The $WRMT^{TM}$–3 is designed for students from kindergarten through high school, but young children and nonreaders may experience success only on the readiness subtests. English-language skills are particularly important for the Word Comprehension and Passage Comprehension subtests, in which students must supply missing words. Students respond orally on all $WRMT^{TM}$–3 subtests; no writing is required.

Technical Quality

Norming was carried out with a sample of 3,360 individuals ages 4–6 to 79–11 across 45 states. Of those participants, 2,600 were students in kindergarten through grade 12. Approximately half of the students were males and half were females. The sample was selected to resemble the U.S. population as reflected in 2010 U.S. Census data. The sample appears to resemble the nation as a whole in terms of geographic region, parental education level (an indicator of socio economic status), and race or ethnic group. Also, the sample included K–12 students who receive services in special and gifted education. Students with learning disabilities in reading and intellectual disabilities were included.

In evaluating technical quality, it is also important to consider the reliability and validity of a test. Internal consistency reveals average means across age and grade groups in the .90s. Alternate forms reliability was performed between 9.3 and 19.5 days. Reliability coefficients were .84 to .94 for cluster scores and .62 to .93 for test scores. Test-retest scores for cluster scores ranged from .83 to .97, but test scores ranged from .51 to .95. Interscorer reliability was very high at .99

(Flowers, 2011). Concurrent validity of the $WRMT^{TM}$–3 was studied by examining its relationship to the reading tests including the *WJ-III, WRMT-R-NU, KTEA-II, RFI, CTOPP,* and *WIAT-III.*

Administration Considerations

Qualification B is required for the administration of this test (i.e., specialized degree). Examiners should study the test manual, administer at least two practice tests, and be observed and evaluated by an experienced examiner. Practice activities for administration, scoring, and interpretation are provided in the $WRMT^{TM}$–3 manual. The $WRMT^{TM}$–3 is a relatively easy test to administer, although scoring is somewhat complicated.

Each test indicates a starting point. The basal rule for most tests is three correct items, and not necessarily consecutive. The ceiling rule is four consecutive incorrect items. If a basal is not achieved, the examiner is instructed to go back to the previous starting point. It is not necessary to administer all subtests of the $WRMT^{TM}$–3; the tester can select any portion of the battery that is of interest. Subtests may be administered in any order.

Results and Interpretation

The $WRMT^{TM}$–3 offers a variety of scores. For each subtest, it is possible to obtain standard scores, grade equivalent, age equivalent, percentile rank, Relative Performance Index (RPI), and Growth Scale Value (GSV). The RPI score is a ratio; for example, an RPI of 85/90 indicates that the student is expected to perform tasks at 85 percent mastery that average students of his or her age or grade would perform at 90 percent mastery. Several other types of scores are available, including *T*-scores, stanines, normal curve equivalents, and standard scores with a mean of 100 and a standard deviation of 15. It is also possible to construct confidence intervals around scores so that RPI, percentile rank, and standard scores are expressed as ranges.

Subtest scores can be combined into cluster scores. The Readiness Cluster is made up of the three readiness subtests; the Basic Skills Cluster consists of the Word Identification and Word Attack subtests; and the Reading Comprehension Cluster, of the two comprehension subtests. The

Total Reading Cluster is a global score for the five reading achievement tests. The same types of scores that are available for subtests can be computed for clusters.

Error analysis is expanded in this new version of the WRMT™-3. Item-level error analysis is available for *Passage Comprehension*, *Listening Comprehension* and *Phonological Awareness*. Intraitem error analysis is available for *Word Attack* and *Word Identification*. It is also possible to compare performance in different reading skill areas.

Further information about strengths and weaknesses can be gathered by analyzing students' responses to specific test items. Results of the *WRMT™*–3 help the professional to determine the student's current levels of achievement in reading readiness, basic reading skills, and comprehension. These results are most useful for identifying areas of strengths and educational needs. They also provide valuable direction for further assessment. Informal strategies are used to further investigate weaknesses suggested by *WRMT™*–3 results and to probe skills not assessed.

GRAY ORAL READING TESTS (5TH ED.)

The *Gray Oral Reading Tests—Fifth Edition (GORT–5)* assess students' ability to read passages aloud quickly and accurately with adequate comprehension. The current version of this test is the fourth update of a popular measure developed by William S. Gray (1967). According to the manual, the *GORT–5* is designed to identify students with problems in reading, determine students' strengths and weaknesses, and document progress in reading.

Two alternate forms of the *GORT–5* are available: Forms A and B. Each contains 16 reading passages that increase in difficulty, and each passage is followed by five comprehension questions. The task remains the same throughout the test. The student reads the passage aloud as the tester records errors and times the student. Then the tester reads open-ended comprehension questions. Several types of questions are asked, including those that assess literal, inferential, critical, and affective comprehension.

ENHANCEDetext
Video Example 13.1
Watch this video to see administrator and teachers in action in a team meeting. Teachers discuss student achievement across class levels regarding reading.

The *GORT–5* is designed for students ages 6–0 to 23–11, and English-language skills are a necessity. Writing is not required; all student responses are oral.

Technical Quality

The *GORT–5* was standardized with 2,556 students from 33 states. The sample appears to approximate the national population in terms of geographic region, gender, urban–rural residence, race, ethnicity, and family income. Students with disabilities were also included in the normative group.

Internal consistency reliability is adequate for all scores on the *GORT–5,* as is the alternate form reliability. Test-retest reliability average coefficients are also between .82 and .90. Interrater reliability average coefficients ranged from .7 to .88 (Hall & Tannebaum, 2012). Concurrent validity was studied by examining the relationship between results from various editions of the *GORT* and those from five other measures of reading. In general, moderate correlations were found.

Administration Considerations

Because there is only one type of task on the *GORT–5,* administration is straightforward. Suggested starting points are provided by grade level

GRAY ORAL READING TESTS (5TH ED.) (GORT–5)

J. L. Wiederholt & B. R. Bryant (2012)

Type: Norm-referenced test

Major Content Areas: Oral reading rate, accuracy, fluency, and comprehension

Type of Administration: Individual

Administration Time: 15 to 45 minutes

Age/Grade Levels: Ages 6–0 to 23–11

Types of Scores: Percentile ranks, standard scores, Oral Reading Index

Technology Aids: N/A

Typical Uses: Identification of strengths and weaknesses in oral reading skills

Cautions: The *GORT–5* is a measure of oral reading skills; some students show better comprehension when reading silently. Further information is needed about the relationship of this test to other measures of reading commonly used in special education.

Publisher: PRO-ED (*www.proedinc.com*)

in a table on the examiner booklet. The Comprehension Score basal and ceiling are based on the student's performance on the comprehension questions following each passage. In contrast, the Fluency Score basal and ceiling are determined by considering the rate at which the student reads the passage (9 or 10 on two consecutive passages) and the number of oral reading errors he or she makes (0, 1, or 2 on two consecutive passages).

For each passage administered, the tester reads a sentence or two about the story as motivation and then tells the student to begin reading orally from the appropriate page in the Student Book. When the student has completed the passage, the tester asks open-ended comprehension questions and reads these aloud as the student looks on. The examiner scores either a 0 or 1 for the response to question. When the student is reading orally, the tester must do two things: (1) record any errors the student makes, and (2) time how many seconds it takes the student to read each passage.

In terms of recording errors, a slash mark (/) is used to denote deviations from the printed page.

A slash is made on each word that is not read correctly and in the space between words when errors such as additions, repetitions, or self-corrections occur. Each word and space can account for only one error. The student's response is written above the written word. Special notations are also identified for substitutions, additions, omissions, repetitions, reversals and self-corrections. If the student hesitates, the word is supplied by the tester and counted as an error. Students are allowed 10 seconds to sound out a word but only 5 seconds if there is no audible attempt to read the word.

Results and Interpretation

Each passage on the *GORT–5* produces four raw scores. The Comprehension raw score is simply the number of comprehension questions answered correctly. The Rate raw score is based on the time the student needed to read the passage; the Accuracy raw score reflects the number of times the student deviated from the text. Both Rate and Accuracy raw scores range from 1 to 5; they are determined from tables that accompany the passages. The Fluency raw score is simply the sum of the Rate and Accuracy scores.

Total Test Rate, Accuracy, Fluency Score, and Comprehension Score results are then converted to percentile ranks and standard scores. Standard scores are distributed with a mean of 10 and a standard deviation of 3. The Oral Reading Index (ORI) is a combined score of Fluency and Comprehension scaled scores. Other standardized scores include age equivalents, grade equivalents, and scaled scores (Mullis, 2012).

An important feature of the *GORT–5* is the procedure it provides for analysis of student errors or miscues. A portion of the protocol is used to record each substitution error and categorize the way in which it was similar to the text word. This system is based on the work of the Goodmans (Goodman, 1969, 1976; Goodman & Burke, 1972; Goodman, Watson, & Burke, 2005). Types of miscues include errors similar in meaning to the text word, errors similar in grammatical function, and errors with graphic/phonemic similarity. Errors due to multiple sources and self-corrections are also noted. The number and percentage of each type of miscue are then determined. For example, out of 10 miscues on a particular passage, 5 (or 50 percent) may have involved words with similar meanings, and 7 (or 70 percent) words with similar grammatical functions. The *GORT–5* protocol provides space for recording information about other types of miscues (omissions, additions, dialectical variations, and reversals) as well as observations of other reading behaviors.

The *GORT–5* is a useful measure for analyzing students' skills in oral reading. The *GORT–5* may underestimate the comprehension skills of those students for whom silent reading improves understanding. Results of the *GORT–5* provide information about the strengths and weaknesses related to oral reading, and they are best used to identify areas needing further assessment.

Another Gray measure is available if silent reading skills are of interest. The *Gray Silent Reading Tests* (Wiederholt & Blalock, 2000) for ages 7–0 to 25–11 are similar in format to the oral reading test: students read paragraphs silently, then answer comprehension questions. Also of note is the *Gray Diagnostic Reading Tests—Second Edition* (Bryant,

Wiederholt, & Bryant, 2004). This set of measures assesses both oral and silent reading and also includes several subtests that evaluate students' decoding skills. Subtests of *GDRT–2* are Letter/ Word Recognition, Phonetic Analysis, Reading Vocabulary, Meaningful Reading, and three supplemental subtests (Listening Vocabulary, Rapid Naming, and Phonological Awareness).

 Breakpoint Practice 13.2
Click here to check your understanding of individual reading assessment.

TEST OF READING COMPREHENSION (3RD ED.)

The *Test of Reading Comprehension—Fourth Edition (TORC–4)* does not attempt to measure all aspects of the reading process. Instead, it emphasizes comprehension skills, silent reading, and knowledge of word meanings.

The *TORC–4* contains five subtests. Instructions for each subtest are read to the student, and most subtests include one or two demonstration items. The student reads the test questions silently and then records responses on a separate answer sheet. The five subtests are used to determine the Reading Index, an index of general reading comprehension ability.

- *Relational Vocabulary.* The student is presented with three stimulus words that are related in some way. He or she then considers four possible responses and chooses two that relate to the stimulus words.

- *Sentence Completion.* Students silently read single sentences with two missing words. From a list of word pairs they select the appropriate response to complete the sentences.

- *Paragraph Construction.* Sentences that make up a paragraph are listed in random order. The student's task is to determine the sequence in which the sentences should appear.

- *Text Comprehension.* Students read paragraph selections and answer five multiple-choice questions about each. The questions require

TEST OF READING COMPREHENSION—FOURTH EDITION (TORC–4)

V. L. Brown, J. L. Wiederholt, & D. D. Hammill (2008)

Type: Norm-referenced test

Major Content Areas: Silent reading comprehension

Type of Administration: Individual or small group

Administration Time: 45 minutes or less

Age/Grade Levels: Ages 7–0 to 17–11

Types of Scores: Percentile ranks, standard scores, Reading Comprehension Index (RCI); age and grade equivalents

Computer Aids: N/A

Typical Uses: Identification of strengths and weaknesses in the development of comprehension skills and knowledge of word meanings

Cautions: The *TORC–4* is a measure of silent reading comprehension. To participate in *TORC–4*, administration and students must be able to work independently.

Publisher: PRO-ED (*www.proedinc.com*)

students to select the best title for the passage, recall details, and make inferences and negative inferences.

- *Contextual Fluency.* Students are allowed three minutes to identify single words in a series of passages. Passages are presented without punctuation or spaces in uppercase letters.

The *TORC–4* is designed for students ages 7–0 to 17–11. The manual points out that, because the *TORC–4* requires only silent reading, it is appropriate for students who speak a dialect, for those with articulation problems, and for deaf students. Students must be able to work independently. They answer all questions by writing. Proficiency in taking tests is expected because students write their answers on a separate answer sheet.

Technical Quality

The standardization sample for the fourth edition of the *TORC* consisted of 1,942 students from 14 states. The sample appears to approximate the national school-age population in terms of sex,

urban–rural residence, geographic region, race, and ethnicity. Students with disabilities who were enrolled in general education classes were included; for example, students with learning disabilities make up 6 percent of the norm group.

Coefficient alpha is .9 or higher for all subtests except the timed subtest, which does not receive a coefficient. Test-retest reliabilities were .8 for combined scores. Interrater reliability from two scorers was above .9. The *TORC–4* was compared to four other reading tests. Results indicate a moderate relationship between *TORC* results and those of other measures of reading.

Administration Considerations

Administration of the *TORC–4* requires no special training. However, in learning to administer this test, the manual recommends that professionals should administer the test to at least three different individuals and be observed by someone who is experienced in test administration, scoring, and interpretation.

The *TORC–4* is quite easy to administer. The tester reads the instructions for the subtest to the student, administers available demonstration items, and then allows the student to work independently. Students begin each subtest with item 1 and continue until a ceiling is reached. For Sentence Completion and Relational Vocabulary, the ceiling is three errors out of any five consecutive items. There is no ceiling on the Contextual Fluency subtest; students have 3 minutes. Testers should consult the manual for specific ceiling rules for the Text Comprehension and Paragraph Construction subtests.

Scoring the *TORC–4* is somewhat more difficult. For example, on the Relational Vocabulary subtest, students are to mark two responses; credit is given only if both responses are correct. Raw scores should be calculated carefully, particularly on Paragraph Construction. On this subtest, students can earn 0, 2, 3, 4, or 5 points for each question, depending on the order in which they arrange the sentences to form a paragraph.

Results and Interpretation

The *TORC–4* provides standard scores and percentile ranks for each subtest. Subtest standard scores have a mean of 10 and a standard deviation of 3. The Reading Comprehension Index (RCI) is a global score indicating the student's overall skill level in reading comprehension. This score is based on the results of the five subtests. The RCI is a standard score distributed with a mean of 100 and a standard deviation of 15. The RCI and subtest scores are plotted on the *TORC–4* profile.

More important than classifying students' scores in *TORC–4* interpretation is the identification of strengths and weaknesses in reading comprehension. The general comprehension subtests provide information about the student's ability to comprehend silently read material. The diagnostic subtests assess performance of classroom-related comprehension tasks. Of particular interest with younger elementary students is skill in reading and following written directions. With older elementary students and those in middle and high school, content areas become important, particularly when students are included in general education classes for these subjects.

TORC–4 results are helpful in determining the student's current levels of performance in several different comprehension skills. Informal techniques are then used to gather information about the specific skills that may require educational intervention. However, comprehension is related to the student's ability to recognize and pronounce words, and the *TORC–4* does not assess decoding skills or oral reading speed, as does the *GORT–5*. Also, it is not as complete a measure as the *WRMT*™–3. However, it addresses other important aspects of the reading process. Among the *TORC–4*'s features are the use of a standard classroom task to assess silent reading comprehension, the inclusion of a reading directions task for younger students, and the provision of standard score results for content area vocabulary subtests.

ENHANCEDetext
Video Example 13.2
Watch this video to see student working with small groups in a reading activity.

MEASURES OF PHONEMIC AWARENESS AND PHONOLOGICAL PROCESSING

In the past decade, several measures of phonological processing have been developed to assess students' phonemic awareness and phonological processing skills—that is, their awareness of the sounds that make up spoken words and their ability to recognize similarities and differences among sounds. Some measures, such as the *Test of Phonological Awareness—Second Edition: PLUS*

(Torgesen & Bryant, 2004) and the *Test of Phonological Awareness Skills* (Newcomer & Barenbaum, 2003), are designed for younger children in the elementary grades. Others, such as the *Comprehensive Test of Phonological Processing-2* (Wagner, Torgesen, Rashotte, & Pearson, 2013), are appropriate for both young children and older students in the elementary, middle, and high school grades.

The *Test of Phonological Awareness—Second Edition: PLUS (TOPA–2+)* contains two levels, one for kindergarten children (ages 5–0 through 6–11) and the other for early elementary grade students (ages 6–0 through 8–11). The *TOPA—2+* can be administered individually or to groups, and it requires 15 to 45 minutes depending on the level. On both levels, the examiner reads directions as children follow along in a student booklet. On most subtests, directions require that children attend to a row of four drawings as the examiner says the name of the first drawing (the stimulus figure) and the names of three possible response drawings. Students must then mark the one drawing that is similar to or different from the stimulus figure in some way.

The tasks on the kindergarten level of the *TOPA–2+* require students to locate drawings that begin with the same sound as the stimulus figure or that begin with a different sound. For example, in the first demonstration item, the stimulus is a drawing of a bat and the three possible responses are drawings of a horn, bed, and cup; students are asked to mark the drawing that starts with the same sound as *bat*. On the Early Elementary level, students must identify drawings that end with the same sound as the stimulus figure or that end with a different sound. The current edition of *TOPA* adds a letter–sound correspondence subtest to each level. On the kindergarten version of the test, students must find the letter that represents the sound made by the tester; on the version for older students, students are asked to write nonsense words pronounced by the tester. *TOPA–2+* results include percentile rank scores and standard scores (called ability scores and distributed with a mean of 100 and a standard deviation of 15).

The *Test of Phonological Awareness Skills (TOPAS)* is appropriate for elementary grade students ages 5–0 to 10–11. The *TOPAS* contains four subtests, although only the first two are administered to students below the age of 6. Administration requires 20 to 30 minutes, and the tester presents each item orally to the student.

According to the *TOPAS* manual, this measure assesses three important phonological constructs: sound comparison (subtest 1), phoneme blending (subtest 2), and phoneme segmentation (subtests 3 and 4). The four subtests are:

- *Subtest 1: Rhyming.* The tester reads an incomplete sentence emphasizing one word in the sentence; the student must supply the missing word that rhymes. The manual provides this example: "'I hurt my *knee* falling out of a . [tree]" (p. 6).
- *Subtest 2: Incomplete Words.* The tester says a word with one or more sounds missing; the student must say the whole word.
- *Subtest 3: Sound Sequencing.* This task requires the student to learn associations between individual speech sounds and colors. As the manual explains, "the child must listen to the sound sequences and arrange colored blocks in a corresponding sequence according to the sound each block represents" (p. 7). The manual notes that this subtest is based on the task used in the *Lindamood-Bell Auditory Conceptualization Test* (Lindamood & Lindamood, 2004).
- *Subtest 4: Phoneme Deletion.* The tester says a word and asks the student to repeat the word deleting a specific sound.

Age and grade equivalents, scaled scores, and percentile ranks are available for each *TOPAS* subtest. An overall test score, the Phonological Awareness Composite, can also be obtained. Subtest scaled scores are distributed with a mean of 10 and a standard deviation of 3; the overall Composite is a standard score with a mean of 100 and a standard deviation of 15.

The *Comprehensive Test of Phonological Processing-2 (CTOPP-2)* is designed for students ages 4–0 through 24–11. Two levels are available, one for ages 4 to 6 and the other for ages 7 and above. Both are based on a model of phonological processing that contains the following abilities: phonological awareness, phonological memory (i.e., the temporary storage of phonological information), and rapid naming (i.e., the retrieval of phonological information from long-term memory).

The *CTOPP-2* contains seven Core subtests and two Supplemental subtests for ages 7 to 24. Each phonological processing ability is assessed by two Core subtests; the Supplemental subtests provide additional information on phonological awareness, if desired. The Core subtests are as follows:

Phonological Awareness

- *Elision.* Students repeat a word and then must say what remains when one or more sounds are deleted from the word.
- *Blending Words.* When students hear two or more sounds that make up a word, they must say the word.
- *Phoneme Isolation.* Students isolate sounds within words.

Phonological Memory

- *Memory for Digits.* Students repeat numbers from memory; the digits are presented at the rate of two per second.
- *Nonword Repetition.* Students listen to nonsense words from 3 to 15 sounds long and then repeat them.

Rapid Symbolic Naming

- *Rapid Digit Naming.* Students must say the name of random numbers on a page.
- *Rapid Letter Naming.* Students must say the name of random letters on a page.

Similar measures are included on the *CTOPP-2* for younger students. They include nine core tests (*Elision, Blending Words, Sound Matching, Memory for Digits, Nonword Repetition, Rapid Digit Naming, Rapid Letter Naming, Rapid Color Naming, Rapid Object Naming*) and one supplemental test (*Blending Nonwords*).

Subtest raw scores can be converted to age and grade equivalents, percentile ranks, and standard scores (distributed with a mean of 10 and a standard deviation of 3). Composite scores are determined by combining subtest results. The following Composites are available on both

levels: Phonological Awareness, Phonological Memory, Rapid Symbolic Naming, and Rapid Nonsymbolic Naming Composites. On the level for older students, it is also possible to calculate the Alternate Phonological Awareness Composite, if appropriate supplemental subtests (*Blending Nonwords, Segmenting Words*) were administered.

Measures such as the *TOPA–2+, TOPAS,* and *CTOPP-2* assess reading readiness skills, not reading itself. Although information about students' phonological processing abilities may be useful when considering various instructional approaches, it does not shed light on current reading performance. Measures such as the formal tests described in the last section and the fluency measures and informal reading inventories, to be discussed next, provide that type of information.

READING FLUENCY MEASURES

Reading fluency, or the ability to read with both speed and accuracy, can be assessed formally with published measures or informally in classrooms with measures that teachers create. One example of a published assessment tool that includes a measure of fluency is the *Gray Oral Readings Tests—Fifth Edition*, described earlier in this chapter. The *GORT–5* offers Total Test Rate and Accuracy scores that are combined into Total Test Fluency score. These scores are converted into percentile ranks and standard scores, thus allowing norm-referenced comparisons.

Other norm-referenced measures of reading fluency are also available. Among these are the *Test of Silent Word Reading Fluency-2* (Mather, Hammill, Allen, & Roberts, 2004) and the *Test of Silent Contextual Reading Fluency-2* (Hammill, Wiederholt, & Allen, 2006). These tests used similar formats. On each, students are shown a block of text in uppercase letters with no spaces between words (for example, HERE IS AN EXAMPLE). The task is to draw a vertical line between words. The *Contextual Reading Fluency* measure presents words in sentences, whereas on the *Word Reading* measure the words are unrelated. Fluency is assessed by determining the number of lines correctly drawn within a

3-minute period. Norms are available for students in grades 1–12.

In the classroom, teachers can use curriculum-based measurement (CBM) techniques such as those described in Chapter 6 to evaluate how quickly students can accurately decode words in oral reading tasks. This type of assessment is considered curriculum-based because the reading materials are randomly selected from those to be taught during the school year. Tindal and Marston (1990) provide specific instructions for conducting a curriculum-based reading assessment. Two copies of a reading passage or word list are prepared; the teacher's copy should have numbers at the side of the text indicating the cumulative word count. The student reads aloud for 1 minute, and the teacher records errors. To begin, the teacher gives these directions:

> When I say "start," begin reading at the top of this page. If you wait on a word too long, I'll tell you the word. If you come to a word you cannot read, just say "pass" and go on to the next word. Do not attempt to read as fast as you can. This is not a speed reading test. Read at a comfortable rate. At the end of one minute, I'll say "stop." (Tindal & Marston, 1990, p. 148)

Substitutions, omissions, and reversals are counted as errors; words are pronounced by the teacher (and counted as errors) when the student hesitates for 3 seconds. Additions and self-corrections are not counted as errors; more than one mispronunciation of the same proper noun is considered only one error.

The teacher scores the CBM by determining the number of words read correctly during the 1-minute time period. Results are typically graphed so that the student's progress can be monitored over time. On the graph, the aim line represents the instructional goal for the student; the trend line is a record of actual progress.

It is possible to develop local norms for curriculum-based measures such as the reading fluency task just described (Howell, Fox, & Morehead, 1993; Tindal & Marston, 1990). By transforming an informal procedure into a norm-referenced one, it becomes possible to compare one student's rate to that of typical students in the same classroom or grade level in order to determine if a school performance problem exists. Shinn (1988) describes procedures for norms development.

One example of a commercially available curriculum-based reading measure is the *Reading Fluency Progress Monitor* (Ihnot, 2006), a component of the *Read Naturally* (Ihnot, 2000, 2001, 2003) instructional program mentioned in Chapter 6. This measure is designed to assess students' ability to read connected text quickly and accurately. Students are asked to read a passage aloud for 1 minute while the teacher marks errors. A booklet containing sets of passages is available for each grade from 1 through 8. The teacher determines the number of words read correctly in the 1-minute period. Three timed samples are administered, and the average number of words read correctly is calculated. That value can then be compared to the national norms for grades 1–8 based on the work of Hasbrouck and Tindal (2005). For example, at the grade 4 level, students at the 50th percentile rank read 94 words correctly per minute in the fall, 112 words correctly per minute in the winter, and 123 words correctly per minute in the spring.

Breakpoint Practice 13.3
Click here to check your understanding of individual reading testing.

INFORMAL READING INVENTORIES

Standardized tests are but one of the many types of assessment tools available for the study of students' reading skills. Another popular measure, particularly for classroom use, is the informal reading inventory (IRI). IRIs assess both decoding and comprehension skills. They are made up of graded word lists and reading selections that the student reads orally. The tester notes any decoding errors and records the student's answers to the comprehension questions accompanying each reading selection.

IRIs are grade-referenced measures; the word lists and passages are arranged in order of difficulty according to school grade levels. They are informal measures, and their purpose is to provide information about the student's reading skills in relation to the grade-level system of the general school curriculum.

The results obtained from IRIs are grade-level scores. Typically, informal inventories provide three reading levels: the Independent Level, the Instructional Level, and the Frustration Level. A student's Independent Level is the level of graded reading materials that can be read easily with a high degree of comprehension and few errors in decoding. At this level, the student reads independently, without instruction or assistance from the teacher. Reading materials at the student's Instructional Level are somewhat more difficult; this is the level appropriate for reading instruction. Materials at the Frustration Level are too difficult for the student; decoding errors are too frequent and comprehension too poor for instruction to occur. According to Kirk, Kliebhan, and Lerner (1978), the usual criteria for determining these three reading levels are:

- 98 to 100 percent word recognition accuracy and 90 to 100 percent accuracy in comprehension for the Independent Level;
- 95 percent word recognition accuracy and 75 percent accuracy in comprehension for the Instructional Level; and
- 90 percent or less word recognition accuracy and 50 percent or less accuracy in comprehension for the Frustration Level.

In the *Informal Reading Inventory—Eighth Edition* by Roe and Burns (2010), the tester introduces the task by reading a sentence that provides a purpose for reading. The student reads the selection orally and then responds to eight comprehension questions read by the tester. The number and percentage of word recognition and comprehension errors made by the student are recorded to determine whether the selection falls at the student's Independent, Instructional, or Frustration reading level.

Several published informal reading inventories are available for classroom use, or professionals can construct their own IRIs by selecting reading passages of various difficulty levels from a series of reading textbooks (Gillespie-Silver, 1979; Goodman et al., 2005; Johnson, Kress, & Pikulski, 1987). Designing an IRI requires time

and effort, but the advantage is that locally prepared inventories can reflect the reading series used in a particular school or district.

Selecting an Informal Reading Inventory

All informal reading inventories share several general characteristics. Their major emphasis is oral reading; they use lists of words and reading passages to assess reading skill; and they take both decoding and comprehension into account when determining the student's Instructional Reading Level. However, there are some differences that should be evaluated when selecting an IRI for use in assessment. Among the factors to consider are the number of forms provided, whether measures of listening skill and silent reading are included; the number and grade levels of word lists and passages; the types of comprehension questions asked; and the availability of optional tests and other features.

The *Analytical Reading Inventory (ARI)—Tenth Edition* by Woods and Moe (2015) is worthy of note for several reasons. First, it is one of the few inventories that provide a complete description of the procedures used in development and validation. Readability results are presented for each of the passages on the *ARI,* along with vocabulary diversity scores and information about average passage lengths.

Second, the *ARI* contains both narrative and expository passages carefully prepared to be inspirational. In addition, the content of the graded selections is consistent across the three forms of the *ARI.* At the grade 6 level, for example, all passages describe African American inventors or scientists. Because the content of a passage affects its appeal to readers, consistency helps to ensure the equivalence of alternate forms.

Third, the *ARI* provides several types of comprehension questions ranging from those that require literal thinking about the passage to those in which the reader must make interpretations about the text. The four question types (in order, from most to least literal) are retells of fact, put information together, connect author and reader, and evaluate and substantiate. At least one of each type of question accompanies each reading passage.

Fourth feature, the *ARI* encourages both quantitative and qualitative analysis of decoding errors. Drawing from the work of the Goodmans and others (Goodman, 1973a; Goodman & Burke, 1972), the authors of the *ARI* use the term *miscue* instead of *error*. Miscues are defined as deviations from the printed text. All readers make miscues, and miscues are not necessarily evidence of a problem in reading. For example, miscues such as the substitution of *the* for *a* do not change the meaning of the text and thus do not affect comprehension.

On the *ARI*, miscues can be analyzed both quantitatively and qualitatively. Quantitative analysis involves following the traditional procedure of counting the different types of errors made by the student (e.g., omissions, insertions, substitutions). In qualitative analysis, the examiner notes each miscue, and then determines how similar the miscue is to the original text. One important consideration is semantic similarity—that is, whether or not the miscue changes the meaning of the text. Figure 13–1 shows a sample passage from the *ARI* with miscues analyzed both quantitatively and qualitatively.

Most informal reading inventories are designed for elementary and middle school students. One exception is the *Informal Reading Inventory—Eighth Edition* (Roe & Burns, 2010), which contains passages from preprimer to grade 12 level. Another noteworthy measure is the *English-Español Reading Inventory for the Classroom* (Flynt & Cooter, 1999). It provides narrative and expository passages from preprimer to grade 9 levels both in English and in Spanish.Some IRIs include supplementary measures. For example, the *Ekwall/Shanker Reading Inventory—Sixth Edition* (Shanker & Ekwall, 2014) provides several strategies for the evaluation of Graded Reading Passages.

Two other measures attempt to make reading inventories less informal. The *Standardized Reading Inventory—Second Edition (SRI-2)* (Newcomer, 1999) has set procedures for administration and scoring, information is available about its reliability and validity, and it contains norms for students ages 6 to 14. Students read passages orally as the examiner records word recognition errors. Students then read the passage silently before answering comprehension questions. Scores are available for Passage Comprehension, Word Recognition Accuracy, and total test (Reading Quotient). An optional Vocabulary in Context subtest is also available. The *Formal Reading Inventory (FRI)* (Wiederholt, 1986) is a similar norm-referenced measure. The *FRI* is composed of a series of passages that students read silently and orally; standard score results are available for silent reading, and oral reading miscues can be analyzed informally.

OTHER INFORMAL STRATEGIES

Assessment for instructional planning in reading relies on informal strategies, including the informal reading inventories described in the previous section. Here the focus is on other types of informal techniques: teacher checklists, error analysis, cloze and maze procedures, diagnostic teaching and clinical reading interviews, criterion-referenced tests, curriculum-based measurement, questionnaires and interviews, and portfolio assessment.

Teacher Checklists

Checklists are a quick and efficient means of gathering information from teachers and other professionals about their observations and perceptions of students' reading skills. The reading behaviors described on checklists can be of any kind: decoding, comprehension, oral reading, silent reading, or a combination. Most typically, checklists are designed to identify difficulties in reading or are curriculum checklists used to record and monitor reading skills development. An example of a reading difficulty checklist appears in Figure 13–2.

Error and Miscue Analysis

One of the most frequently used techniques in the informal assessment of reading is error analysis. This traditional technique dates back to the 1930s when Marion Monroe (1932) described common types of oral reading errors. Error analysis is a study of the mistakes that students make. Unlike the more general procedure—response analysis—it does not take into consideration both

FORM C, LEVEL 2	Reader's Passages page 35

Prior Knowledge/Prediction

☐ Read the title and predict what the story is about. *About a road, its got a lot of cars*

Q: *What do you know about a busy road?*
SR: *We live near a road that has a lot of cars.*

☐ Read the first two sentences and add more to your prediction.
The boy yells at his dog because he's going to get hit.
Q: *What do you know about a dog getting hit on a road?*
SR: *I had a dog that got hit when she ran across the road.*

Prior Knowledge

☑ a lot
☐ some
☐ none

The Busy Road (Buzzy SC)	O	I	S	A	Rp	Rv
1 "Look out, you'll get hit!" I yelled as my dog ran across the						
2 busy road. *Thad SC* Thud was the *no SC / nose* noise I heard, and then I saw my pup						
3 lying in the street. "Oh, no!" I shouted. I felt scared *scar SC* inside. "Rex is						
4 my best friend!" I wanted to cry out. I knew that he was hurt, but						
5 he'd be all right *ready* if I could get help fast. I knew I had to be brave.			/			
6 "Mom! Dad!" I yelled as I ran *str SC* straight home. *hold* I tried to fight			/			
7 back the tears. They *The / street* started rolling down my face (anyway) as I	/		//			
8 blasted through the door. *to* "Rex has been hit, and he needs help			/			
9 now!" I cried out. "Please hurry so we can save him!"						
TOTALS						
Number of miscues __6__ Number of self-corrections __4__			1	5		

Fluency: Does the Reader . . .

☐ read smoothly, accurately, (in meaningful phrases?)
☐ read word-by-word, choppy, plodding?
☑ use pitch, stress, and intonation to convey meaning of the text?
☐ repeat words and phrases because s/he is monitoring the meaning (self-correcting)?
☑ repeat words and phrases because s/he is trying to sound out words?   *noise, straight*
☐ use punctuation to divide the text into units of meaning? *most times* ☐ ignore the punctuation?

Rating Scale: Circle One
4 = fluent reading / good pace   2 = choppy, plodding reading / slow pace
③ = fairly fluent / reasonable pace   1 = clearly labored, disfluent reading / very slow pace

Cueing Systems

LINE #	Miscue	Grapho-phonically Similar I M F (word level)	Syntactically Acceptable Unacceptable (sentence level)	Semantic Change in Meaning (CM) No Change in Meaning (NCM) (sentence level)
5	ready	I	A	CM
6	hold		A	NCM
7	The	IM	U	CM
7	street	I	U	CM
8	to	I	A	CM

Summary

☑ Most, ☐ few, ☐ no   miscues were graphophonically similar to the word in the passage.

☑ Most, ☐ few, ☐ no   miscues were syntactically matched.

☐ Most, ☑ few, ☐ no   miscues maintained the author's meaning.

☑ The self-corrections demonstrate that the reader monitors the meaning.

Form C, Level 2

FIGURE 13–1

Sample Analysis of Miscues from the *Analytical Reading Inventory*

Source: Woods, Mary Lynn; Moe, Alden J., Analytical Reading Inventory: Comprehensive Standards-Based Assessment for All Students Including Gifted and Remedial, 10Th Ed., © 2015. Reprinted and Electronically Reproduced by Permission of Pearson Education, Inc., New York, NY.

#	1st Check	2nd Check	3rd Check	Item	Category
1				Phonemic Awareness	Emergent Literacy Skills
2				Alphabet Knowledge	Emergent Literacy Skills
3				Basic Sight Words Not Known	Decoding Skills
4				General Sight Vocabulary Not Up to Grade Level	Decoding Skills
5				Phonics Difficulties: Consonants	Decoding Skills
6				Phonics Difficulties: Vowels	Decoding Skills
7				Phonics Difficulties: Blends, Digraphs, or Diphthongs	Decoding Skills
8				Structural Analysis Difficulties	Decoding Skills
9				Contractions Not Known	Decoding Skills
10				Inadequate Ability to Use Context Clues	Decoding Skills
11				Poor Pronunciation	Specific Oral Reading Difficulties
12				Omissions	Specific Oral Reading Difficulties
13				Repetitions	Specific Oral Reading Difficulties
14				Inversions or Reversals	Specific Oral Reading Difficulties
15				Insertions	Specific Oral Reading Difficulties
16				Substitutions	Specific Oral Reading Difficulties
17				Guesses at Words	Specific Oral Reading Difficulties
18				Word-by-Word Reading	Specific Oral Reading Difficulties
19				Incorrect Phrasing	Specific Oral Reading Difficulties
20				Voicing, Lip Movements, Finger Pointing, and Head Movements	Specific Oral Reading Difficulties
21				Word Meaning / Vocabulary Knowledge Inadequate	Comprehension Skills
22				Comprehension Inadequate	Comprehension Skills
23				Low Rate of Speed	Study Skills and Other Abilities
24				Inability to Adjust Reading Rate	Study Skills and Other Abilities
25				High Rate of Reading at the Expense of Accuracy	Study Skills and Other Abilities
26				Inability to Skim or Scan	Study Skills and Other Abilities
27				Inability to Locate Information	Study Skills and Other Abilities
28				Underdeveloped Dictionary Skills	Study Skills and Other Abilities
29				Written Recall Limited by Spelling Skill	Study Skills and Other Abilities

NAME _____   GRADE _____   TEACHER _____   SCHOOL _____

The items listed here represent the most common difficulties encountered by students in the reading program. Following each numbered item are spaces for notation of that specific difficulty. This may be done at intervals of several months. One might use a check to indicate difficulty recognized or the following letters to represent an even more accurate appraisal:

D—Difficulty recognized
P—Student progressing
N—No longer has difficulty

FIGURE 13–2
Reading Difficulty Checklist
Source: Locating and Correcting Reading Difficulties (8th ed.) by Shanker/Ekwall, © 2003. Reprinted by permission of Pearson Education Inc., Upper Saddle River, NJ.

correct and incorrect responses. In reading assessment, incorrect responses provide information about how the student is processing the text and suggest directions for instructional interventions.

Error analysis is generally used to investigate decoding mistakes in oral reading. The first step in conducting an error analysis is to select material for the student to read. That material may be a word list or some sort of connected text. If the teacher is interested in the student's ability to read common words—words that appear with high frequency in reading books and other text materials—the teacher could select a list like that shown in Table 13–2. This high-frequency word list is Johnson's (1971) updated version of the *Dolch Basic Sight Word List* (Dolch, 1953). It includes 220 words commonly found in reading texts for the primary grades.

Lists of "survival" reading words are also available. These contain words believed to be necessary for minimal literacy in today's society. Included are words found on warning signs and notices (e.g., "Danger," "Keep Out," "Poison") and words used to provide information (e.g., "Rest Rooms," "This Way Out," "Restaurant") (Kaluger & Kolson, 1978).

If connected text is the concern, the teacher can choose from the passages provided on informal inventories and some standardized tests, a series of graded textbooks for reading instruction, or other materials such as content area textbooks or library books on topics of interest. A basal reading series is a good source of reading selections, particularly if the teacher is also interested in determining the student's instructional reading level. The teacher should gather several levels of graded readers so that the student can begin reading at a level at which he or she can experience success.

The next step is to decide what types of responses will be considered errors and how these errors will be classified. In the reading of word lists, mispronunciations and nonpronunciations are typically viewed as errors. Mispronunciations occur when the student decodes a word incorrectly; for example, he or she may read *who* when the text says *how.* Mispronunciation errors are often classified by the types of letter sounds in which the mistakes occur: consonant sounds, vowel sounds, blends (e.g., the first two letters in *tree* and *glass*),

digraphs (e.g., the first two letters in *ship* and *chalk*), and diphthongs (e.g., the last two letters in *cow* and *toy*). Nonpronunciation occurs when the student fails to say a word. If word recognition speed is a major concern, the teacher can set a time limit for responding. For example, if 2 seconds are established as the time limit, correct responses produced after the 2-second time period would be scored as nonpronunciations.

Several types of errors can occur when students read connected text. Most systems of error analysis include at least four classes of errors:

- *Additions.* The reader adds words or parts of words to the printed text. For example, if the text is "the brown dog," the reader says, "the *big* brown dog."
- *Substitutions.* The reader mispronounces a word or parts of words; this type of error is also called a mispronunciation. For example, if the text is "the small house," the reader says, "the small *horse.*"
- *Omissions.* The reader fails to pronounce words or parts of words. This error occurs when readers skip words, when they hesitate in responding, or when they say they do not know a word and the teacher supplies it. For example, if the text is "the gnarled old tree," the reader might omit the word "gnarled" and read, "the old tree."
- *Reversals.* The reader changes the order of the words in a phrase or sentence or the order of sounds within a word. For example, if the text is "There were many seagulls," the reader says, "*Were there* many seagulls."

Repetitions are another type of reading behavior considered an error by some professionals. A repetition occurs when the reader repeats a word or a series of words. For example, if the text is "The man walked to the levee," the reader says, "The man walked to the *walked to the* levee." Other behaviors sometimes viewed as errors are disregard of punctuation and poor phrasing in oral reading. However, most educators agree that if a student makes and then corrects an error, the error is not counted.

When collecting a reading sample for error analysis, two copies of the reading material are needed: one for the student to read and another

TABLE 13–2
High-Frequency Word List

PREPRIMER	PRIMER	FIRST	SECOND	THIRD
1. The	45. when	89. many	133. know	177. don't
2. Of	46. who	90. before	134. while	178. does
3. And	47. will	91. must	135. last	179. got
4. To	48. more	92. through	136. might	180. united
5. A	49. no	93. back	137. us	181. left
6. In	50. if	94. years	138. great	182. number
7. That	51. out	95. where	139. old	183. course
8. Is	52. so	96. much	140. year	184. war
9. Was	53. said	97. your	141. off	185. until
10. He	54. what	98. may	142. come	186. always
11. For	55. up	99. well	143. since	187. away
12. It	56. its	100. down	144. against	188. something
13. With	57. about	101. should	145. go	189. fact
14. As	58. into	102. because	146. came	190. through
15. His	59. than	103. each	147. right	191. water
16. On	60. them	104. just	148. used	192. less
17. Be	61. can	105. those	149. take	193. public
18. At	62. only	106. people	150. three	194. put
19. By	63. other	107. Mr.	151. states	195. thing
20. I	64. new	108. how	152. himself	196. almost
21. This	65. some	109. too	153. few	197. hand
22. Had	66. could	110. little	154. house	198. enough
23. Not	67. time	111. state	155. use	199. far
24. Are	68. these	112. good	156. during	200. took
25. But	69. two	113. very	157. without	201. head
26. From	70. may	114. make	158. again	202. yet
27. Or	71. then	115. would	159. place	203. government
28. Have	72. do	116. still	160. American	204. system
29. An	73. first	117. own	161. around	205. better
30. They	74. any	118. see	162. however	206. set
31. Which	75. my	119. men	163. home	207. told
32. One	76. now	120. work	164. small	208. nothing
33. You	77. such	121. long	165. found	209. night
34. Were	78. like	122. get	166. Mrs.	210. end
35. Her	79. our	123. here	167. thought	211. why
36. All	80. over	124. between	168. went	212. called
37. She	81. man	125. both	169. say	213. didn't
38. There	82. me	126. life	170. part	214. eyes
39. Would	83. even	127. being	171. once	215. find
40. Their	84. most	128. under	172. general	216. going
41. We	85. made	129. never	173. high	217. look
42. Him	86. after	130. day	174. upon	218. asked
43. Been	87. also	131. same	175. school	219. later
44. Has	88. did	132. another	176. every	220. knew

Source: From "The Dolch List Reexamined" by D. D. Johnson, 1971, *The Reading Teacher, 24,* pp. 455–456. Copyright 1971 by the International Reading Association. Reprinted with permission of Dale D. Johnson and the International Reading Association.

for the teacher to record the student's responses. A standard set of symbols is used for noting errors:

- The symbol ∧ indicates an *addition;* the ∧ is placed in the text where the word or word part has been added, and the addition is written above the text. For example,

  big
  "The ∧ brown dog."

- A *substitution* is marked by crossing out the mispronounced word and writing the substituted word above it. For example,

  horse
  "The small house."

- *Omissions* are shown by drawing a circle around the word, word part, or series of words the student left out. For example,

  "The gnarled old tree."

- The symbol ⌐⌐ indicates a *reversal* of words or parts of a word. For example,

  "Were there many seagulls."

- *Repetitions* are marked by drawing an arrow under the word or words repeated. For example,

  "The man walked to the levee."

The next step is analysis of the student's errors. In the traditional approach to analysis, the professional simply counts the number of errors that occurred in each category. However, it is also necessary to decide which errors are instructionally important for the student under study. Most educators would agree that substitutions and omissions have instructional relevance, but other types of errors may be of less concern. Errors such as the addition of an *–s* ending or an occasional repetition usually do not alter the sense of the passage.

An alternate method of error analysis takes into account the quality of the errors that readers make. In this qualitative analysis system, errors are called miscues (Goodman, 1973a, 1973b; Goodman & Burke, 1972; Goodman, Watson, & Burke, 2005). According to Burke (1973), adults also make miscues often. As noted earlier, miscues are not necessarily cause for alarm. Efficient readers are still able to comprehend the meaning of text because the types of errors they make tend to preserve meaning. Inefficient readers, in contrast, make errors that change the meaning of the text (Goodman, 1973b).

Figure 13–2 provides an example of qualitative **miscue analysis.** Miscues are analyzed to determine whether they represent a change in meaning from the original text. For example, the substitution of *hold* for *fight* in *"fight back the tears"* is semantically correct and does not alter meaning. However, the substitution of *ready* for *right* in *"he'll be all right"* does change the sense of the passage.

The miscues that produce changes in meaning can be further analyzed. Burke (1973) suggests that the student's miscue and the original text should be compared in three ways:

1. Graphic Similarity: How much do the two words *look* alike?
2. Sound Similarity: How much do the two words *sound* alike?
3. Grammatical Function: Is the grammatical function of the reader's word the same as the grammatical function of the text word? (p. 23)

These questions are drawn from the short form of the *Reading Miscue Inventory* (Goodman & Burke, 1972). The most acceptable miscue is semantically correct. Less acceptable are errors that are grammatically correct but semantically incorrect and errors that fit the graphic or phonic characteristics of the text but are semantically and grammatically incorrect.

Error analysis techniques can be used to study comprehension as well as decoding skills. One way to do this is to ask students comprehension questions after they have finished reading a passage. Or students can be asked to retell the story they have read or summarize the major points of an expository passage. In selecting reading materials for the assessment of comprehension, the type of material is an important consideration. Expository, narrative, and other types of texts such as poetry and plays are organized differently, and the reader's experience with the type of text may affect comprehension. According to Lapp and Flood (1992), comprehension is influenced by previous contextual knowledge.

Several kinds of questions can be used to assess students' understanding of the meaning of a passage. To evaluate literal comprehension, the student can be asked to state the main idea of the passage, propose a title for the selection, recall details from the passage, remember a series of events or ideas, and explain the meaning of vocabulary words introduced in the reading selection. Inferential thinking is assessed by asking questions that force students to go beyond the information provided in the passage; students can be asked to draw conclusions, make predictions, evaluate ideas or actions, suggest alternative endings for a narrative, and so forth. In preparing comprehension questions to accompany a reading selection, professionals should ensure that the questions are text-dependent. Questions should be answerable only by students who have read the text.

Analysis of comprehension errors is conducted in the same way as analysis of decoding errors. A sample of the student's responses is gathered, and errors are noted and classified. Most typically, the classification system is based on the various types of comprehension questions: main idea, fact, sequence, vocabulary, inference, conclusion, and so forth. The number of errors in each category is totaled to help the professional identify the comprehension skills in which the student requires additional instruction. The book *Locating and Correcting Reading Difficulties—Tenth Edition* (Cockrum & Shanker, 2013) provides suggestions for analyzing errors not only in comprehension skills but also in the areas of emergent literacy, decoding, and study skills.

ENHANCEDetext
Video Example 13.3
Watch this video to see a teacher applying research-based strategies in assessing organizational skills. Organizing main ideas and outlining are discussed.

The Cloze Procedure

The **cloze procedure** (Bormuth, 1968; Jongsma, 1971) is an informal technique for determining whether a particular textbook or other reading material is within a student's instructional reading level. To use the cloze procedure, the teacher selects a passage of approximately 250 words. The first and last sentences of the passage are left intact. In the rest of the passage, every fifth word is deleted and replaced with a blank. For example, the sentence "The little dog sat down beside the boy" would become "The little dog sat _____ beside the boy." The student reads the passage and attempts to fill in each of the blanks. If the student correctly supplies between 44 and 57 percent of the missing words, the passage is considered to be at the student's instructional level (Bormuth, 1968; Burron & Claybaugh, 1977).

This technique is also useful for assessing comprehension skills. By omitting every fifth (or seventh or *n*th word), the teacher forces the student to rely on the context clues within the passage to derive meaning. Figure 13–3 provides an example.

Two variations of the cloze procedure are the maze and the limited cloze (Baumann, 1988). The maze is essentially the same as the standard cloze except that students are presented with choices for each omitted word; this changes the task from completion to multiple choice. In the limited cloze, the student may refer to a list of the omitted words arranged in random order. Baumann warns that evaluators should be aware that there is an inadequate literature base connecting cloze procedures to comprehension.

Diagnostic Teaching and Clinical Reading Interviews

In reading assessment, diagnostic teaching procedures are often based on the results of a clinical reading interview. Clinical reading interviews combine the techniques of observation, interviewing, and diagnostic probes. The professional observes the student who is engaged in some type of reading task, but assessment does not stop with observation. Students are questioned about their reading strategies, comprehension of the material,

Teacher reads these directions: "Here is a story with some words left out. Each time a word is left out, it has been replaced with a line. When you come to a line, try to figure out what word should be in that blank. Ready—begin."

Jan has a cat.

The cat's name is Tab.

Tab does not like dogs.

One day a dog ran after Tab.

Tab ran up a tree.

The dog could not go up the tree.

Then the dog went away.

Grade one reading level

Jan has a cat.

The cat's _____ is Tab.

Tab does not _____ dogs.

One day _____ dog ran after Tab.

_____ ran up a tree.

The dog could not go _____ the tree.

Then _____ dog went away.

FIGURE 13–3
The Cloze Procedure as a Measure of Comprehension Skills

Source: Cockrum, Ward; Shanker, James L., *Locating and Correcting Reading Difficulties*, 10Th Ed., © 2013. Reprinted with Electronically Reproduces by Permission of Pearson Education, Inc., New York, NY.

and background knowledge about passage content. In addition, the teacher can alter the nature of the reading task to determine how instructional adaptations will affect the student's reading performance. Clinical reading interviews are dynamic procedures. The professional observes, questions, changes the reading task, and then observes and questions again. The goal of the process is to provide information about promising strategies for reading instruction.

Clinical interviews focus on the interaction between the reader and the text; they allow the professional to go beyond the product of the reading act to evaluate the process. There are many important factors to consider when exploring the reading process, including the student's background knowledge, familiarity with the structure of the text (e.g., narrative or expository), understanding of anaphoric terms, facility with language, and use of metacognitive strategies (Samuels, 1983).

For example, students may or may not have background knowledge about the content and structure of the passage. These factors are critical for comprehension; if the student is totally unfamiliar with the content being presented, comprehension will suffer despite adequate decoding skills.

Anaphoric terms are words that are used as substitutes for words or phrases that have already appeared in a text. In the text "The dog and cat ate their supper. They liked it." there are three anaphoric terms: *their* and *they,* referring to the dog and cat, and *it,* referring to the supper. Students who are unable to identify the referents of anaphoric terms will lose the meaning of the passage.

Metacognitive strategies are the methods that readers use to think about their interactions with the text. Effective readers think about both the content of the material and the reading process. According to Samuels (1983), the active reader asks such questions as:

- Why am I reading this?
- Do I want to read this for superficial overview or for detail?
- Do I know when there is a breakdown in comprehension?
- When there is a breakdown in understanding, what can I do to get back on the track again?
- What are the major and minor points of this text?
- Can I summarize or synthesize the major points made in this text? (pp. 6–7)

The professional can adapt these questions and use them to investigate the way the student interacts with text during a clinical reading interview.

In addition to asking questions, the professional can introduce diagnostic probes. For example, if decoding skills are a concern, the teacher can change the task by reading aloud with the student, pronouncing the difficult words for the student, or providing clues for the difficult words. Sometimes the teacher may wish to have the student read the entire passage alone, without assistance, and then intervene. If the teacher discovers that the student has difficulty with a particular set of decoding skills such as medial vowel sounds or word endings, those skills can be taught, and then the student can attempt the passage again, with the teacher providing help as needed. Having the student do repeated readings of a passage is an excellent technique for evaluating his or her ability to learn and apply new skills.

What is learned about the student's skill levels and responsiveness to various types of instruction during the clinical reading interview is then used to design a diagnostic teaching sequence. Diagnostic teaching is a more structured process. Data are collected to describe the student's entry-level skills; then an instructional intervention is begun and consistently continued over several days. The student's performance is monitored daily to determine whether the intervention is effective and should be included as part of the instructional program.

Criterion-Referenced Tests

Criterion-referenced tests assess the student's mastery of specific skills within the reading curriculum. They are based on instructional objectives and, as Chapter 6 described, are quite easy to construct. For example, if mastery of high-frequency reading words is a goal of the instructional program, the teacher could use the word list presented in Table 13–2 as the basis of a criterion-referenced test. The objective for this test might be: *The student will read the high-frequency list aloud and pronounce at least 200 of the 220 words correctly.* The teacher would present each of the words to the student, keep track of errors, and then evaluate the student's performance to determine whether the objective had been achieved.

Several criterion-referenced tests of reading are commercially available, and professionals may select from these rather than constructing measures themselves. It is less time consuming to use a criterion-referenced test that has already been prepared, but the time saved is wasted unless the measure adequately reflects the classroom curriculum. In evaluating criterion-referenced tests, professionals should carefully study the objectives on which these measures are based to ensure that the skills included are important ones. Results of criterion-referenced tests should be relevant to the student's curriculum and immediately applicable to instruction.

The series of criterion-referenced tests by Brigance is one of the more popular sets of measures. This series includes the *BRIGANCE® Inventory of Early Development–III* (2013) for children from birth through age 7, the *BRIGANCE® Comprehensive Inventory of Basic Skills–II (CIBS–II)* (2010) for pre-kindergarten through grade 9, and the *BRIGANCE® Transition Skills Inventory* (2010) for older children and adults with "varying ability levels". Each of these measures contains several tests of reading; even the inventory for preschool children offers tests of readiness and basic reading skills.

The *CIBS–II* for elementary and middle school students assesses several types of reading skills: word recognition, grade placement, oral reading, reading comprehension, word analysis, and functional word recognition. In addition, some of the tests on the *CIBS–II* have been normed, and results can be expressed as standard scores, percentile ranks, and grade equivalents. In the area of reading, reading/English Language Arts (ELA) skills are assessed. Examples include readiness, word recognition, and word analysis. A technology program, the *CIBS–II Standardized Scoring Tool,* is available to assist in the scoring process.

The Transition Skills measure is intended for older elementary and secondary grade students. It contains the same types of tests as those found in the *CIBS–II,* but skills are assessed at post-secondary levels. For example, employment application/forms and job interview skills are assessed. Other features of both of these measures are the tests that assess functional skills such as reading direction words, warning and safety signs, and informational signs.

Many other criterion-referenced tests attempt to provide comprehensive coverage of the reading skill area. For example, the *Hudson Education Skills Inventory* (Hudson, Colson, Welch, Banikowski, & Mehring, 1989) provides criterion-referenced measures of reading readiness, sight vocabulary, phonic analysis, structural analysis, and comprehension skills for kindergarten through grade 12. In using a criterion-referenced instrument such as this, the professional selects and administers only those tests that address the skills of interest for the particular student.

Curriculum-Based Measurement

In the area of reading, curriculum-based measurement (CBM) techniques are most often used to evaluate oral reading fluency, that is, the rate at which students are able to accurately decode words in oral reading tasks. This type of assessment is considered curriculum-based because the reading materials are typically selected from those taught as part of the classroom curriculum. An earlier section of this chapter, Reading Fluency Measures, described this approach as well as other strategies for the assessment of skill in reading fluency.

CBM techniques can also be used to evaluate student progress in other areas of reading performance. For example, *Monitoring Basic Skills Progress (MBSP)—Second Edition* (Fuchs, Hamlett, & Fuchs, 1997) is a commercially available measure that is administered by computer. One of its four parts is Basic Reading, a test of comprehension. The student is presented with a 400-word reading passage, with every seventh word omitted. Students read silently, and when they come to a missing word, they click on the blank to see three possible responses. Students continue reading until the passage is completed or 2.5 minutes elapse, whichever comes first. Passages are available for grades 1–7, and each is a complete story.

As soon as a student has completed a passage, the program automatically computes and displays the student's current score as well as his or her progress over time. The score is the number of correct words. In addition, the program stores student data, so the teacher can access those data later.

The Dynamic Indicators of Basic Early Literacy Skills (DIBELS) is a measure commonly used in many schools. Included in this assessment are the necessary skills for learning to read and for improving specific aspects of reading. Educators use this tool to monitor student progress multiple times each year or on a daily or weekly basis. Each task takes one minute to complete and should not be seen as an in-depth assessment. Subtests include *Initial Sounds Fluency, Letter Naming Fluency, Phoneme Segmentation Fluency, Nonsense Word Fluency, DIBELS Oral Reading Fluency,* and *Word Use Fluency.*

Questionnaires and Interviews

Questionnaires and interviews are used in reading assessment to gather information about students' views and opinions: their attitudes toward reading, perceptions of the reading process, opinions of their own reading abilities, likes and dislikes in reading materials, and so on.

Interviews are preferred for younger students and those with poor reading skills; print question-naires are reserved for more mature students who are able to read with comprehension and answer in writing.

Students can be interviewed to find out their attitudes toward reading and preferences in read-ing materials. The teacher could ask questions such as:

- Is reading one of your better subjects in school?
- What types of reading activities are the easiest for you? Which are the hardest?
- If you could read a story about anything in the world, what would the story be about?
- What magazines do you read or look at?
- Do you ever read the newspaper? If so, what parts of the paper do you read?
- Would you rather read true stories or stories that the author makes up?
- What are your hobbies? Have you ever read a book, a story, or a magazine article about one of your favorite activities?
- What was the last thing you read for fun? When did you read it? What did you enjoy about it?

The purpose of this measure is to elicit infor-mation from students about their attitudes toward reading, their study skills and work habits, and their reading interests. In addition, students could be asked to describe the strategies they use when reading and to evaluate their own reading performance.

Portfolio Assessment

Reading is usually one of the areas represented in language arts portfolios. Separate portfolios for reading are not common. First of all, the act of reading typically does not result in a permanent product. Second, teachers using the whole-language approach tend to integrate the language arts so that reading and writing activities overlap. For example, students might keep written logs or journals to record their reactions to the books and stories they read.

Lapp and Flood (1992) suggest several types of information that can be placed in students'

portfolios to document progress in reading. Possibilities include (1) results of standardized tests and informal assessments, (2) student self-assessments, (3) samples of the types of materials read throughout the year as part of classroom instruction, and (4) information about participa-tion in a voluntary leisure reading program (e.g., number of books read each month). Cohen and Weener (2003) contribute these ideas for possible contents of reading portfolios:

- Measures that reflect and analyze students' decoding and vocabulary skills;
- Measures that reflect and analyze students' comprehension skills;
- Measures that require students to write as a reaction to reading across content areas with different forms of text and for different purposes;
- Measures of students' reading interests and attitudes;
- Lists and logs of students' actual reading experiences;
- Projects or products that are the outcomes of reading assignments;
- Teachers' progress notes, conference notes, or observational notes about the student when the student is engaged in reading activities; and
- Appraisal of the students' reading skills outside the school environment. (p. 72)

 Breakpoint Practice 13.4
Click here to check your understanding of individual reading testing.

WITHIN THE CONTEXT OF THE CLASSROOM

The assessment procedures described so far have been student-centered measures designed to eval-uate the student's current levels of performance in important reading skills. In this section, the emphasis shifts to assessment tools and tech-niques for studying the classroom-learning envi-ronment and its influence on the student's reading abilities.

The Instructional Environment

In the elementary grades, assessment of the instructional environment must take into account the reading curriculum and the instructional methods and materials used to implement that curriculum. The most common elementary reading program centers on either a basal reading series, children's literature, or a combination of the two. Some of the newer basals reflect this approach by including selections from children's literature. A basal series is a set of graded reading textbooks that span a number of grade levels, usually from the beginning reading levels (preprimer and primer) through the end of grade 6 or grade 8. Assessment of the instructional factors that influence younger students begins with a study of the classroom reading program:

1. What is the major component of the classroom reading program? A basal reading textbook? Children's literature? Another approach?

2. Does the classroom reading program stress text, meaning, or the interaction between text and meaning?

3. Do the reading materials build on the students' language and background experiences, or do they present unfamiliar content?

4. Is there a range of books or other reading materials to accommodate the range of student skills? Or if a third-grade classroom is under study, are only grade 3 reading books available?

5. What types of materials are used to supplement instruction? Workbooks? Worksheets? Computer-based instructional programs? Reading games? Leisure reading books?

6. What types of reading skills are stressed in classroom instruction? Decoding? Fluency? Comprehension? Oral reading? Silent reading?

7. Are decoding skills taught? If so, which are emphasized? Sight vocabulary? Phonic analysis? Structural analysis? Contextual analysis? A combination?

8. Is the reading curriculum organized so that the sequence of instruction is logical and the instructional steps are of appropriate size?

9. Is reading instruction based on ongoing assessment? How often are performance data collected for monitoring students' progress? What strategies are used to determine the starting points for students entering the program?

10. How are students grouped for reading instruction? Does the entire class receive instruction at one time? Is the class divided into large groups of 10 to 15 students each? Smaller groups of 5 to 8 students? How much individualization takes place in each group?

11. What instructional techniques does the teacher use to present new skills and information? Lecture? Discussion? Demonstration and modeling?

12. In what types of learning activities do students participate? Oral reading? Silent reading? Completing worksheets? Writing book reports?

13. How is supervised practice incorporated into the reading program? On the average, how many minutes per day do students spend practicing their reading skills?

14. What changes, if any, have been made in the standard reading program to accommodate the needs of special learners such as the student under assessment?

The nature of the materials that students are required to read is an important factor both for beginning readers and for secondary students who are expected to use reading as a tool for learning in other subject areas. Among the critical characteristics of reading materials are the topic of the text, the style in which the text is written, format, and readability (Samuels, 1983).

The topic of the text has a direct effect on the reader's ability to read with comprehension; more familiar topics are more easily understood. The clarity of the author's writing style also affects text comprehensibility. Passages that contain too many anaphoric terms, those with poor transitions from event to event or idea to idea, and those containing long sentences with too much information are difficult to comprehend. In addition, if there is a mismatch between the information presented in the text and the background knowledge of the reader, the author may fail to communicate with the intended audience. Format also plays a role in text comprehensibility. Reading materials should be printed clearly, and the text should be organized to facilitate reading and review. In evaluating the format of textbooks, professionals should check to see if chapters are structured with design features such as headings, subheadings, abstracts, summaries, and review questions.

The **readability** of a passage is influenced by its content, vocabulary, and organization, and by the structure of its sentences. However, most of the readability formulas available for measuring reading levels take only one or perhaps two of these factors into account. For example, Fry's (1968) readability graph, presented in Figure 13–4, uses sentence length and the number of syllables per word to estimate readability. The professional selects three 100-word passages from a book or article, counts the number of sentences and syllables in each passage, and then uses the graph to determine readability; readability estimates are stated in terms of grade level.

Readability formulas and graphs can help the professional evaluate reading materials and match the difficulty levels of materials to students' skill levels. This is particularly important with content area textbooks. Science, social studies, and other content subject texts are graded, but their grade levels refer to the difficulty of the subject matter, not to reading difficulty. Thus, a grade 9 science book is likely to contain grade 9 science material, but it may or may not be written at a grade 9 reading level. Readability graphs and formulas can also be used to determine the approximate reading levels of other types of materials, such as library books, short stories, passages in reference books, and magazine or newspaper articles. The Fry (1968) graph is a relatively quick and easy method for estimating readability. It can be used for materials that range from grade 1 to college level; extensions are available for pre-primer and primer materials (Maginnis, 1969) and for materials at college and graduate school levels (Fry, 1977).

The Interpersonal Environment

The major factors that relate to reading within the interpersonal environment of the classroom are the interactions between students and teachers and the social relationships among students. The most effective way of assessing these interpersonal dimensions is through observation. Classroom observations that are scheduled when students are engaged in reading activities can provide answers to the following questions:

- What occurs when a student makes an error in oral reading? Does the teacher correct the student? Ignore the error? Ask another student to assist?
- How does the student react to the teacher's corrections?
- What do other students do when a peer makes oral reading errors? Do they laugh, tease, or ridicule the student?
- Are poor readers accepted by others in the classroom? Do they participate with their peers in social and free-time activities?
- What happens when a student reads correctly? Does the teacher confirm the correct responses? Praise the student? Provide a tangible reward or token?
- Are students able to work independently on silent reading assignments and on workbook and other writing activities? Or do certain students require frequent assistance from the teacher?

Another factor to take into account when evaluating student–teacher interactions is the amount of time teachers spend teaching reading and students spend practicing reading skills. Early studies of programs for students with mild disabilities found that students were actively engaged in reading for only a few minutes each day (Leinhardt, Zigmond, & Cooley, 1981; Thurlow, Graden, Greener, & Ysseldyke, 1983; Zigmond, Vallecorsa, & Leinhardt, 1980). Engagement time must be a concern in assessment because the amount of time that students and teachers spend in instructional interactions is likely to have a direct effect on the amount of progress that students make in their attempts to develop reading skills.

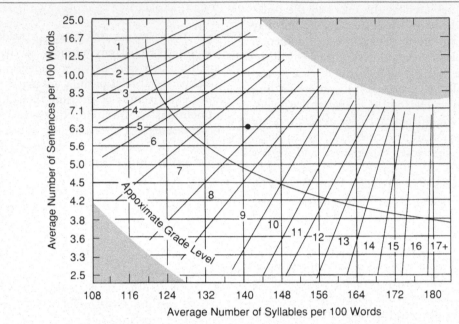

Directions: Randomly select 3 one hundred word passages from a book or an article. Plot average number of syllables and average number of sentences per 100 words on graph to determine the grade level of the material. Choose more passages per book if great variability is observed, and conclude that the book has uneven readability. Few books will fall in gray area but when they do, grade level scores are invalid.

Example:	Syllables	Sentences
1st hundred words	124	6.6
2nd hundred words	141	5.5
3rd hundred words	158	6.8
Average	141	6.3

Readability 7th grade (see dot plotted on graph)

FIGURE 13–4
Fry Readability Graph
Source: From *A Readability Formula That Saves Time* by E. Fry, McGraw-Hill Education.

The Physical Environment

The physical environment of the classroom can also affect students' reading performance. Environmental factors such as lighting, temperature, and ventilation influence the students' and the teacher's comfort levels and can either facilitate or hinder the teaching–learning process. In addition, the physical arrangement of the classroom is an important consideration, particularly in relation to seating configurations and allocation of classroom space.

Some of the questions that can be asked about the classroom's physical environment and its impact on reading instruction are as follows:

1. What seating arrangements are used for reading instruction? Are students seated so that they can easily see and hear the teacher?
2. Is the lighting in the classroom adequate for reading?
3. Is classroom space structured so that areas for noisier activities are separated from the areas for quieter activities like reading?
4. How are students' seats arranged for independent work? Are students' desks or tables positioned so that students do not distract one another?
5. Are there any quiet work areas or "offices" within the classroom where students can go to escape from distractions?
6. Is there a variety of reading materials in the classroom for student use? Do the materials cover a wide range of topics, interest levels, and reading levels? Are the materials accessible to students?
7. Is a computer available in the classroom for students to practice reading skills? Do students have access to a variety of educationally sound software programs in reading?
8. What types of reading materials are available in the school library or media center? Are these materials accessible to students?

ANSWERING THE ASSESSMENT QUESTIONS

The major purpose of reading assessment is to describe students' current levels of educational performance. There are many assessment tools designed for this purpose. They represent numerous types of techniques: diagnostic reading tests, fluency measures, informal reading inventories, error and miscue analysis procedures, clinical reading interviews, diagnostic teaching, cloze and maze procedures, criterion-referenced tests, curriculum-based measures, teacher checklists, interviews, observation, portfolios, and other informal strategies. Because of

the great number and diversity of assessment tools for reading, it is particularly important that the assessment process be carefully planned. Assessment begins with comprehensive measures that sample several reading skills. When potential problem areas are identified, these areas are assessed further, usually with informal measures and techniques.

Nature of the Assessment Tools

Tools for reading assessment vary in the range of reading skills they assess. Comprehensive measures such as the *Woodcock Reading Mastery Tests*—attempt to evaluate a wide range of reading skills, whereas an instrument such as the *Test of Reading Comprehension—Fourth Edition* focuses on a narrower set of skills. However, most measures today are comprehensive, and they assess both decoding and comprehension skills. Table 13–1 illustrated this point. Of the reading measures described, only a handful assess either decoding or comprehension, but not both.

Assessment tools can also vary in depth of skill coverage. Standardized tests typically sample several skills and levels but provide only a few representative test items in each area. For example, a subtest on phonic analysis may devote only two or three test items to the skill of decoding consonant-vowel-consonant words. Informal measures, particularly criterion-referenced tests, allow study of specific skills in much greater depth.

Measures of reading may also differ by the types of reading tasks that students are required to perform. Table 13–3 describes several of the more common measures of decoding and comprehension and the ways these measures go about assessment. Measures differ on the number of words on each list, the actual words included, and whether time limits are imposed.

In the area of comprehension, assessment tasks are much more varied. The *GORT–5* and the *Analytical Reading Inventory—Tenth Edition* use the standard tasks of reading graded passages and answering comprehension questions based on the content of the passages. However, questions are open-ended on the *ARI* but

TABLE 13–3
Assessment Tasks Used to Evaluate Reading Skills

READING SKILL	MEASURE	SUBTEST	PRESENTATION MODE	RESPONSE MODE
Decoding	*Gray Oral Reading Tests—Fifth Edition*	(entire test)	Look at a series of graded passages.	Read each passage aloud as quickly and accurately as possible.
	Analytical Reading Inventory—Tenth Edition	Word Lists	Look at lists of isolated words.	Read each word aloud.
	Woodcock Reading Master Tests—Third Edition	Word Attack	Look at lists of nonsense words and syllables.	Read each word or syllable aloud.
	Woodcock Reading Master Tests—Third Edition	Word Identification	Look at lists of isolated words.	Read each word aloud within 5 seconds.
Comprehension	*Gray Oral Reading Tests—Fifth Edition*	(entire test)	Look at a series of graded passages; listen to multiple-choice comprehension questions read aloud by the tester.	Read the passages orally; answer the comprehension questions by saying the letter of the correct answer.
	Analytical Reading Inventory—Tenth Edition	Graded Passages	Look at a series of graded passages; listen to questions read aloud by the tester.	Make predictions about each passage; read each passage orally; retell each passage and, if necessary, answer comprehension questions.
	Test of Reading Comprehension— Fourth Edition	Text Comprehension	Look at short passage, then read multiple-choice comprehension questions.	Silently read each paragraph and the comprehension questions that accompany it; mark answers on the separate answer sheet.
	Woodcock Reading Mastery Tests—Third Edition	Passage Comprehension	Look at a passage with one word missing.	Read the passage silently and say the missing word.

multiple choice on the *GORT–5*. The task on the *TORC–4* is somewhat different; students read standard types of passages and then read the multiple-choice comprehension questions themselves, rather than listening to the tester read them. The *WRMT*™–3 uses a cloze procedure to assess comprehension; no questions are asked. The student reads passages silently and then attempts to supply the words missing in each passage.

Oral reading is required on the comprehension tasks on the *GORT–5* and the *ARI;* the *WRMT*™–3 and the *TORC–4* employ silent reading tasks. Students respond orally on each measure except the *TORC–4*. The *TORC–4* and the *GORT–5* use multiple-choice comprehension questions; the *WRMT*™–3 a completion task; and the *ARI,* open-ended questions.

Clearly, measures of reading differ importantly in the ways they assess decoding and comprehension skills. These differences must be considered in selecting the tools for reading assessment and in interpreting the results of the assessment.

The Relationship of Reading to Other Areas of Performance

When the assessment team begins to evaluate and interpret its results, one of the major tasks is the study of the relationships among areas of performance. Academic skills such as reading may influence or be influenced by several other areas.

A student's general aptitude for learning can have an effect on the ease and speed with which reading skills are acquired. In general, students with lower than average general intelligence are expected to progress at a somewhat slower rate than students of average intellectual ability. Several attempts have been made to quantify the relationship between IQ and reading, and reading expectancy formulas have resulted (Bond & Tinker, 1967; Harris, 1970; Myklebust, 1968). These formulas use the student's current intellectual performance and sometimes other factors, such as age or years in school, to predict an expected reading level.

Expectancy formulas have several limitations; most notably their reliance on age and grade scores, and their use is not recommended. Instead, standard scores are preferred for comparing and contrasting IQ test results and results from measures of reading. Measures such as the *WRMT*™*–3*, the *Wechsler Individual Achievement Test–III,* and the *Woodcock-Johnson IV* provide procedures for the analysis of aptitude-achievement discrepancies.

Like general learning aptitude, specific learning abilities and strategies can influence the student's success in the acquisition and application of reading skills. Problems in attention, memory, or other areas such as phonological awareness can hinder skill development, particularly the acquisition of basic decoding skills. Inefficient learning strategies can interfere when students attempt to read with comprehension. In the secondary grades, poor learning strategies

may combine with poor reading skills to prevent students from successfully using reading as a study technique.

Classroom behavior may be related to reading performance. Inappropriate classroom conduct can impede classroom learning, including acquisition and application of reading skills. Poor achievement can also affect a student's behavior. Difficulty in reading can result in lowered self-concept and negative attitudes toward school and learning. Achievement problems can even influence peer relationships and the student's conduct in social and instructional situations.

Reading pervades the school curriculum. It has a direct impact on several other areas of school performance, particularly language arts subjects. Writing skills such as spelling and composition are directly affected by delayed development in reading. In written language, the expressive skill of writing is built on the receptive skill of reading. Similarly, the development of beginning reading skills is influenced by the student's oral language proficiency.

Reading can also affect the student's ability to perform successfully in mathematics and other subjects. Although arithmetic computation usually does not require reading skills, other mathematics tasks do. Students are often asked to read explanations in mathematics textbooks, to read the directions for mathematics worksheets or workbook pages, and to read word problems.

Reading is almost a necessity for content area subjects such as science, history, English, and social studies. Even in the elementary grades, students may be expected to use reading to acquire content area information. At the secondary level, reading assignments are routine. Students are expected to learn by reading textbooks and other materials. Students can bypass their poor reading skills by using aids such as taped versions of textbooks, but students with disabilities who are included in general education classrooms will still be expected to achieve at least a minimal level of reading proficiency.

In addition, there are very real reading demands in the adult world. Reading is a necessity for most occupations, and the average adult is constantly faced with text to read: street and traffic signs, signs on buildings and restroom doors, commercial ads, want ads, newspapers, magazines, television schedules, job application forms, postcards and letters, grocery labels, labels on cosmetics and medications, menus, and the like. The ability to read and comprehend everyday reading materials such as these is an important concern for all students, particularly older students with special instructional needs.

Documentation of Reading Performance

The general question that guides the assessment team in its study of reading skills is, *What are the student's educational needs?* The purpose of this phase of assessment is to describe precisely the student's current skill levels; these data then serve as the basis for planning the student's educational program. The first question that the team attempts to answer is, *What is the student's current level of reading achievement?* Then additional information is gathered about areas in which the student appears to be experiencing difficulty. The result is a description of the student's current performance in reading that is specific enough to answer the question, *What are the student's strengths and weaknesses in the various skill areas of reading?*

Data are gathered from many sources using many types of assessment tools. The team usually begins by reviewing school records, results of individual achievement tests, interviews with parents and teachers, and classroom observations to plan the reading assessment. Next, a diagnostic reading test may be administered to survey the student's skills in several areas of reading. Test results are used to identify potential problem areas, and these skills and subskills are further assessed with informal measures and techniques.

There are many alternatives for reading assessment—tests, inventories, error analysis procedures, and clinical leading interviews, among others—and the assessment team must choose its tools carefully to avoid duplication and ensure that assessment is as efficient as possible. As a general rule, the more specific measures and techniques such as criterion-referenced tests and clinical reading interviews are reserved for in-depth analysis of potential weaknesses.

ENHANCEDetext
Video Example 13.4
Watch this video to see a teacher working with a student on an individual reading assessment task in the context of probes and aim line (Curriculum Based Measurement).

Assessment in Action
Tyler

Tyler's problem in reading is one of the reasons Mr. Adams, his fourth-grade teacher, referred him for special education assessment. Tyler is unable to read any of the fourth-grade texts in his classroom, and he is now working in a beginning third-grade reading book. Results of individual achievement tests such as the *PIAT–III* confirmed that Tyler's reading performance is below that expected for his age and grade. Tyler considers reading one of his least favorites school subjects; he states that he is "dumb" in reading.

The assessment team believes that instruction in reading will be an important part of Tyler's individual education program. Evaluation of Tyler's current reading skills will begin with administration of the *Woodcock Reading Mastery Tests–3*, a norm-referenced measure that evaluates several components of the reading process, including sight word vocabulary, word attack skills, and passage comprehension. In addition, an informal reading inventory will be administered to gather information about Tyler's oral reading skills and his ability to derive meaning from the material he reads. Mr. Adams, Tyler's classroom teacher, will assist by gathering samples of Tyler's oral reading to assess reading fluency skills.

Then informal assessment strategies will be selected to further explore the particular reading skills that appear to be areas of weakness for Tyler. For example, if sight word vocabulary seems to be a need, the team could devise a criterion-referenced test to assess Tyler's mastery of standard lists of sight words for first-, second-, and third-grade students. Or, if comprehension skills are a concern, the team could analyze the types of errors Tyler makes in his attempts to answer comprehension questions.

The results obtained from these assessments will be used to develop part of the individualized special education program for Tyler.

Tyler is unable to read any of the grade 4 textbooks in his classroom. He is now working in a beginning third-grade, reading book with some success. Previous assessment with the *PIAT–R/NU* and interviews with Mr. Adams, Tyler's teacher, confirm that Tyler's current reading performance is below that expected for his age and grade.

The assessment team begins its study of Tyler's reading skills by administering the *Woodcock Reading Mastery Tests-3.* Tyler earns these scores:

Subtest	Standard Score Range
Word Identification	72–75
Word Attack	79–86
Word Comprehension	83–90
Passage Comprehension	79–85
Cluster	
Basic Skills	74–77
Reading Comprehension	81–82
Total Reading	77–80

Tyler's overall performance on the *WRMT*™–3 falls within the low-average range. His comprehension skills appear stronger than his decoding skills. Tyler shows low-average performance on the Word Identification subtest, a measure of sight vocabulary, and low-average to average performance on the Word Attack subtest, a measure of skill in phonic analysis of unknown words.

Next, the *Analytical Reading Inventory* is administered to gain more information about Tyler's oral reading abilities. According to this inventory, Tyler's Independent Reading Level is grade 1, his Instructional Level is grade 2, and his Frustration Level is grade 3. On the reading passages, Tyler makes very few comprehension errors until he reaches frustration level.

Tyler's oral reading responses on the *WRMT*™ 3 and the *ARI* are analyzed to identify patterns of errors. Tyler can recognize only a few words by sight. When he does not recognize a word, he attempts to decode it by sounding it out and by using available context clues. However, Tyler shows weak phonic analysis skills, and the majority of his decoding errors are substitutions that involve mispronunciation of vowel sounds. In reading connected text, Tyler appears to look at the initial consonant of the word and then guess from context. Most of his substitutions make sense in context and begin with the correct initial consonant sound.

A series of criterion-referenced tests are used for further analysis of Tyler's decoding skills. On the *BRIGANCE® Comprehensive Inventory of Basic SkillsRevised,* Tyler shows strengths in knowledge of consonant sounds, short vowel sounds, and consonant blends. However, results indicate that Tyler has not yet mastered long-vowel sounds, consonant digraphs, and diphthongs. The updated version of the Dolch high-frequency word list (Table 13–2) is used to assess Tyler's sight word vocabulary. Of the 220 words, Tyler is able to recognize 97; most of his errors occur in the second- and third-grade lists.

After careful analysis of these results, the assessment team is ready to describe Tyler's current levels of reading performance. Their conclusions are as follows:

- Tyler's current instructional reading level is grade 2, as measured by the *Analytical Reading Inventory.* At this level, Tyler comprehends well but requires assistance in decoding.
- In general, Tyler's comprehension skills are more advanced than his decoding skills. He uses context to help him decode unknown words.
- Tyler can recognize most preprimer and primer sight words. He has not yet mastered grades 1, 2, and 3 sight words.
- Tyler knows the sounds of consonants and consonant blends and the short sounds of vowels. He has not yet mastered long-vowel sounds, consonant digraphs, and diphthongs.

SUMMARY

- Students' reading skills are assessed for several reasons. In determining eligibility for special education programs, overall school performance is investigated, and reading is an important component of school achievement. In addition, general education teachers monitor their students' progress in reading. Reading proficiency is one of the minimum competencies assessed by many schools and districts for grade advancement and high school graduation, and reading is always included on the state-mandated tests of school achievement that assess students' progress toward state performance standards. In special education, reading skills are assessed not only for determining program eligibility, but also for planning instruction.

- Two examples of subtests from the *Woodcock Reading Mastery Tests–Third Edition* are the Rapid Automatic Naming Subtest and the Oral Reading Fluency Subtest. In the Rapid Automatic Naming Subtest, the test taker names 36 items as rapidly as possible. The time taken to name items, as well as the number of errors, are considered in this subtest. In the Oral Reading Fluency Subtest, the test taker reads passage/passages and is timed by examiner who also records errors. Words read correctly in 10 seconds are measured in the score.

- The *Gray Oral Reading Tests—Fifth Edition (GORT–5)* assess students' ability to read passages aloud quickly and accurately with adequate comprehension. The current version of this test is the fourth update of a popular measure developed by William S. Gray (1967). According to the manual, the *GORT–5* s designed to identify students with problems in reading, determine students' strengths and weaknesses, and document progress in reading.

- Two examples of subtests in the *TORC-4* are the *Sentence Completion and Paragraph Construction* subtests. In the *Sentence Completion* subtest, students silently read single sentences with two missing words. From a list of word pairs, they select the appropriate response to complete the sentences. In the *Paragraph Construction*, sentences that make up a paragraph are listed in random order. The student's task is to determine the sequence in which the sentences should appear.

- Some measures of phonemic awareness and phonological processing, such as the *Test of Phonological Awareness—Second Edition: PLUS* (Torgesen & Bryant, 2004) and the *Test of Phonological Awareness Skills* (Newcomer & Barenbaum, 2003), are designed for younger children in the elementary grades. Others, such as the *Comprehensive Test of Phonological Processing-2* (Wagner et al., 2013), are appropriate for both young children and older students in the elementary, middle, and high school grades.

- One example of a commercially available curriculum-based reading measure is the *Reading Fluency Progress Monitor* (Ihnot, 2006), a component of the *Read Naturally* (Ihnot, 2000, 2001, 2003) instructional program mentioned in Chapter 6. This measure is designed to assess students' ability to read connected text quickly and accurately. Students are asked to read a passage aloud for 1 minute while the teacher marks errors.

- Most informal reading inventories are designed for elementary and middle school students. One exception is the *Informal Reading Inventory—Eighth Edition* (Roe & Burns, 2010), which contains passages from preprimer to grade 12 level. Another noteworthy measure is the *English-Español Reading Inventory for the Classroom* (Flynt & Cooter, 1999). It provides narrative and expository passages from preprimer to grade 9 levels both in English and in Spanish.

- Checklists are a quick and efficient means of gathering information from teachers and other professionals about their observations and perceptions of students' reading skills. The reading behaviors described on checklists can be of any kind: decoding, comprehension, oral reading, silent reading, or a combination. Error analysis is a study of the mistakes that students make. Unlike the more general procedure—response analysis—it does not take into consideration both correct and incorrect responses. In reading assessment, incorrect responses provide information about how the student is processing the text and suggest directions for instructional interventions.

- In the elementary grades, assessment of the instructional environment must take into account the reading curriculum and the instructional methods and materials used to implement that curriculum. Another factor to consider when evaluating student–teacher interactions is the amount of time teachers spend teaching reading and students spend practicing reading skills.

- Tools for reading assessment vary in the range of reading skills they assess. Comprehensive measures such as the *Woodcock Reading Mastery Tests*– attempt to evaluate a wide range of reading skills, whereas an instrument such as the *Test of Reading Comprehension—Fourth Edition* focuses on a narrower set of skills. Assessment tools can also vary in depth of skill coverage. Standardized tests typically sample several skills and levels but provide only a few representative test items in each area. Informal measures, particularly criterion-referenced tests, allow study of specific skills in much greater depth.

14

Phil Boorman/Cultura/Getty Images

Mathematics

LEARNING OUTCOMES

After reading this chapter, you will be able to:

- Explain the purpose of mathematics assessment in the special education context in considerations in assessment of mathematics.

- Identify and describe two subtests of the *KeyMath 3*.

- Name and discuss two examples of other formal measures.

- Describe curriculum-based measures: *Monitoring Basic Skills Progress*.

- Compare and contrast two examples of other informal assessment procedures.

- Identify and discuss two examples within the context of the classroom.

- Discuss two ways mathematics measures vary when answering the assessment questions.

KEY TERMS

algorithms
problem solving
fluency

Mathematics, like reading, is one of the basic school subjects. Young students are expected to acquire the vocabulary of mathematics; learn to count, recognize, and write numerals and mathematical symbols; understand quantitative terminology; and begin to solve quantitative problems. Arithmetic operations are also a part of the elementary school curriculum; students learn to manipulate quantities with the computational processes of addition, subtraction, multiplication, and division. Mathematics learning continues in the secondary grades, where students are required to apply their knowledge of mathematics in solving quantitative problems. Some secondary students also expand their repertoire of skills by studying algebra, geometry, trigonometry, and perhaps even calculus.

Many students with special needs encounter difficulty in their attempts to learn the basic skills of mathematics and to apply these skills in mathematical problem solving. Although mathematics does not pervade the school curriculum in the same way that reading does, quantitative thinking is a necessity in the adult world. Mathematics-based tasks such as handling money, telling time, and measuring are a common part of daily life, as are problem-solving situations such as comparative shopping. Poor skill development in mathematics is a cause for concern, particularly when planning the educational program for students with special needs.

Math skills are assessed to gather information for instructional planning. The general question that the assessment team seeks to answer is, *What are the student's educational needs?* Two specific questions are asked: *What is the student's current level of mathematics achievement? What are the student's strengths and weaknesses in the various skill areas of mathematics?*

The major concern is description of the student's current levels of performance. Informal measures and techniques are preferred because they provide specific information about the student's status in skill development. Results of norm-referenced tests may help professionals differentiate educational needs from skills in which the student shows adequate progress.

Assessment for program planning is a selective process that concentrates on the skills and subskills that have been identified as possible problems. If a student's progress in an academic subject such as reading or mathematics is satisfactory, that subject will not be part of the student's special educational program and, thus, in-depth assessment is not necessary. However, if a student's progress is not at the level educators would expect, further assessment is often necessary.

CONSIDERATIONS IN ASSESSMENT OF MATHEMATICS

Students' mathematics and arithmetic skills are often the subject of special education assessment. One of the primary aims of the elementary school curriculum is the development of proficiency in mathematical thinking and computation, and elementary mathematics skills become the foundation for secondary grade mathematics. When students fail to meet the expectations of the general education curriculum in the acquisition and application of mathematics skills, mathematics becomes a major assessment concern.

Purposes

In general education, teachers routinely monitor their students' progress in mathematics, and it is one of the school skills evaluated by the group achievement tests administered at regular intervals throughout the grades. In addition, mathematics proficiency is a competency area that many schools and districts assess for grade advancement and high school graduation.

In special education, mathematics skills are investigated at the start of assessment to determine the student's eligibility for special education services. When mathematics is identified as an area of need for a particular student, assessment continues in order to gather the detailed information necessary for program planning. Precise information about the student's current status in mathematics is the basis for establishing the instructional goals of the individualized education program (IEP).

Assessment continues throughout the student's special education program. The cycle of gathering data about current skills, planning instructional interventions, and monitoring the success of those interventions is repeated for as long as the student needs specially designed mathematics instruction.

Skill Areas

Mathematical thinking begins in the preschool years when children acquire the rudiments of a quantitative vocabulary and start to learn counting and other fundamental skills. The written language of mathematics, made up of numerals and symbols, is built on this conceptual framework. Young students learn to read and write numerals and mathematical symbols and to manipulate quantities through computation. Mathematical problem solving is also introduced to young students as they are developing facility with computational operations.

The developmental nature of mathematics is apparent in the school curriculum. Skills are built one upon the other, and there is a set order for the acquisition of new learning. For example, the general mathematics skills taught in the elementary grades are prerequisite to the higher mathematics of the secondary grades and college.

It is important to distinguish between *mathematics,* the general field of study, and one of its components, *arithmetic.* Reid and Hresko (1981)

report mathematics as learning and use of concepts and associations of measurement concepts (e.g., mass, volume). Arithmetic is a computational skill (Reid & Hresko, 1981). It is concerned with the operations of addition, subtraction, multiplication, and division, and the algorithms involved in these operations. **Algorithms** are step-by-step procedures for solving computational problems (Ashlock, 2006).

Mathematics is much broader in scope than arithmetic. Although it includes computation, it also encompasses mathematical readiness, number systems and numeration, quantitative problem solving, geometry, measurement, the applications of time and money, and higher mathematics such as algebra and calculus. Skill in computation should not be equated with mathematics proficiency.

In the 1960s, the "new math" curriculum dominated mathematics instruction with its emphasis on exploration, discovery, and conceptual understanding. The back-to-basics movement of the 1970s changed the instructional focus to the development of basic skills. In the next decade, groups such as the National Council of Teachers of Mathematics (1980) called for educators to give problem-solving skills the highest priority in mathematics instruction.

In its landmark book, *Curriculum and Evaluation Standards for School Mathematics,* the National Council of Teachers of Mathematics (NCTM; 1989) called for a reform in mathematics instruction similar in scope to the whole-language movement in reading, writing, and other language arts. The NCTM proposed five general mathematics goals for all students:

1. that they learn to value mathematics,
2. that they become confident in their ability to do mathematics,
3. that they become mathematical problem solvers,
4. that they learn to communicate mathematically, and
5. that they learn to reason mathematically. (p. 5)

Accompanying these goals were recommendations for changes in the ways mathematics is taught. Students should be actively involved in authentic problem-solving activities, even at the earliest grade levels. For example, these controversial (Ma, 2013) *Standards* indicate that in kindergarten through grade 4, teachers should decrease reliance on memorization and worksheets and emphasize problem-solving approaches. Students should use manipulatives, calculators, and computers; they should engage in cooperative learning and write and talk about mathematics. The National Council of Teachers of Mathematics updated and amplified its recommendations in 2000 in the book *Principles and Standards for School Mathematics.*

Discussion within the discipline has taken place regarding whether or not elementary students should use calculators, as well as whether or not they should memorize multiplication and division tables (Kilpatrick, 2001). Recently, districts have made the shift from memorization to "guestimation." This change was made to focus on problem solving and higher-level thinking. However, negative consequences have occurred as test scores have dropped. On page xix of the 2008 U.S. National Mathematics Advisory report (National Mathematics Advisory Panel, 2008), recommendations shifted back to learning math facts. In addition, on page xxiv of that report use of calculators was not supported in lower grades before math facts are learned.

Despite these reforms, the measures traditionally used in special education assessment tend to focus on computational skills, problem solving, and the more common applications such as geometry and measurement. Computational skills are typically evaluated with paper-and-pencil tasks. The student is presented with written problems that require addition, subtraction, multiplication, or division of whole numbers, fractions, or decimals:

$$
\begin{array}{ccc}
5 & 26 & 639 \\
+4 & -19 & \times 748
\end{array}
$$

$$
4.2\overline{)509.3} \qquad \frac{3}{16} + \frac{5}{32} =
$$

The student then attempts to solve the problems, often within a specified time limit.

On most tests, students are allowed to use pencil and paper for calculation; however, some measures require mental computation. To solve computational problems, the student must read and understand numerals and symbols. Math facts must be recalled from memory or calculated. Then the student must select and correctly apply the appropriate algorithm when solving the problem.

Mathematical **problem solving** is often assessed by means of story problems that present a quantitative problem in a prose format. Within the story is the problem situation, the numerical data the student must manipulate, and information about the type of manipulation necessary. For example, the problem might state:

George had five apples. He gave two apples to Susan. How many apples did George have left?

The student must read or listen to the story, identify the problem and the pertinent data for its solution, select the appropriate operation and algorithm, and perform the computation correctly. On some tests, students are required to read the story problems themselves; this is not the best method of assessment for students with poor reading skills. As with computational tests, some measures of problem solving allow the use of paper and pencil, whereas others require mental computation.

In some ways, the distinction between computation and problem solving in mathematics is analogous to that between decoding and comprehension in reading. Just as comprehension relies on decoding, mathematical problem solving relies on arithmetic computation. And, as in reading, **fluency** is considered an important skill area in mathematics. Students are expected to perform computations and to solve problems quickly and with no errors.

As in reading, traditional measures of mathematics performance are product-oriented, not process-oriented. To investigate the interactions between the student and the mathematical "text," it is necessary to use informal strategies. Error analysis procedures provide some information about the student's strategies; clinical math interviews are useful when investigating the student's methods of interacting with story problems.

Mathematics measures often attempt to assess application skills as well as computation and problem solving. Most typically, the applications involve the everyday uses of geometry, time, money, and measurement. Application skills are based on mathematics fundamentals, but because they incorporate new subject matter, they extend beyond simple calculation. For example, to apply mathematics skills to money, the student must learn new symbols such as $ and ¢, new terms such as *penny* and *nickel,* and new facts and equivalencies such as *1 nickel = 5 pennies.* Application skills are an important part of mathematics competency because they represent the most typical ways that the average adult uses mathematics in daily life and the world of work.

Current Practices

Assessment of mathematics achievement is common practice today in both general and special education. Next to reading, mathematics is probably the most frequently assessed school skill. Mathematics assessment is a standard part of the elementary school curriculum, and both group and individual tests of academic achievement include measures of mathematics proficiency.

The assessment tools listed in Table 14–1 are more directly related to instructional planning in special education. Included are standardized tests of mathematics performance, informal inventories, and criterion-referenced tests. Fewer measures are available for the assessment of mathematics than for assessment of reading.

Most standardized tests of mathematics are survey instruments. They assess a wide range of skills within the broad area of mathematics in an attempt to identify the student's strengths and weaknesses. An example is the *KeyMath 3* The original version of this measure, the *KeyMath Diagnostic Arithmetic Test* (Connolly, Nachtman, & Pritchett, 1971, 1976), was consistently identified as one of the most often used tests in special education assessment (Mardell-Czudnowski,

1980; Thurlow & Ysseldyke, 1979), perhaps because there were few alternatives for the assessment of mathematics skills. At present, however, several standardized instruments are available, including the *Stanford Diagnostic Mathematics Test—Fourth Edition* and the *Test of Mathematical Abilities—Third Edition.*

In addition, there is a rich array of informal assessment strategies for the study of mathematics performance. These include all of the standard types of informal techniques, but among the most common are informal inventories, criterion-referenced tests of specific skills, error analysis procedures, curriculum-based measures, and clinical math interviews. As Table 14–1 shows, many of the criterion-referenced tests described as informal measures of reading assess mathematics skills as well.

This chapter describes each of the major strategies used in schools today for mathematics assessment. The *KeyMath 3* is discussed first. Then other formal measures of mathematics performance are described. Later sections of the chapter present information about informal measures and techniques.

▶ **ENHANCEDetext**
Video Example 14.1
Watch this video to find out more about teacher collaboration around mathematics assessment. A chapter test is discussed regarding fractions, equations, word problems and graphing.

TABLE 14–1
Measures of Mathematics Performance

NAME (AUTHOR)	AGES OR GRADES	TYPE OF MEASURE*	GROUP OR INDIVIDUAL
BRIGANCE® Assessment of Basic Skills—Revised, Spanish Edition (Brigance, 2007)	Grades K–8	CRT	Individual
BRIGANCE® Comprehensive Inventory of Basic Skills–II (Brigance, 2010)	Pre-K to grade 9	CRT	Individual
BRIGANCE Transition Skills Inventory	Middle and high school	CRT	Individual
Comprehensive Mathematical Abilities Test (Hresko, Schlieve, Herron, Swain, & Sherbenou, 2003)	Grades 3–12; ages 7–0 to 18–11	NRT	Individual
Diagnostic Test of Arithmetic Strategies (Ginsburg & Matthews, 1984)	Grades 1–6	II	Individual
Hudson Education Skills Inventory (Hudson, Colson, Welch, Banikowski, & Mehring, 1989)	Grades K–12	CRT	Individual
KeyMath–3 (Connolly, 2007)	Grades K–12; ages 4–6 to 22–11	NRT & CRT	Individual
Monitoring Basic Skills Progress: Basic Math Computation—Second Edition (Fuchs, Hamlett, & Fuchs, 1998)	Grades 1–6	CBM	Individual
Monitoring Basic Skills Progress: Basic Math Concepts and Applications (Fuchs, Hamlett, & Fuchs, 1999)	Grades 2–6	CBM	Individual
Stanford Diagnostic Mathematics Test—Fourth Edition (1995)	Grades 1.5–12.9	NRT	Group
Test of Early Mathematics Ability—Third Edition (Ginsburg & Baroody, 2003)	Ages 3–9	NRT	Individual
Test of Mathematical Abilities—Third Edition (Brown, Cronin, & Bryant, 2012)	Ages 8–0 to 18–11	NRT	Group or Individual

*NRT = norm-referenced test, II = informal inventory, CRT = criterion-referenced test, and CBM = curriculum-based measure.

KEYMATH-3 DIAGNOSTIC ASSESSMENT

The *KeyMath 3* is an individually administered test designed to assess mathematical skills and understandings. It is a norm-referenced test that also offers some of the features of criterion-referenced assessment. Test items are linked to skill domains and instructional objectives.

There are two forms of the *KeyMath–3*. Each contains 10 subtests that are organized into three major areas of mathematics: Basic Concepts, Operations, and Applications.

Basic Concepts Subtests

- *Numeration.* Items on this subtest are designed to evaluate the student's understanding of the number system. Among the skills assessed are counting, reading numbers, sequencing numbers, place value, and rounding.

- *Algebra.* Items include prealgebraic and algebraic concepts. In some tasks, the student sorts, classifies, describes patterns, solves equations, and determines proportions.

- *Geometry.* Included here are questions about spatial relations, likenesses and differences, pattern development, two- and three-dimensional shapes, and coordinate geometry.
- *Measurement.* In this subtest, the student answers questions relating to common units of measurement (both standard and metric) and the use of measurement tools such as rulers and thermometers.
- *Data Analysis and Probability.* This subtest assesses the student's ability to read and interpret graphs, charts, and tables. Simple problems involving probability and statistics are also included.

Operations Subtests

- *Mental Computation and Estimation.* Paper and pencil are not allowed on this subtest. The tester reads a computation problem or a series of problems, and the student must respond orally. On other questions, the student looks at a problem as the tester reads it aloud. Here, the student solves problems by estimating the answer. Included are problems involving whole numbers, fractions, and units of measurement.
- *Addition and Subtraction.* The student is given a page of problems and asked to write the answers. Included are problems requiring addition of multidigit numbers (with and without regrouping), fractions, decimals, and mixed numbers. Also, computations involve subtraction of multidigit numbers (with and without regrouping), fractions, decimals, and mixed numbers.
- *Multiplication and Division.* Algorithmic problems require multiplication and division of whole numbers, fractions, decimals, and mixed numbers.

Applications Subtests

- Foundations of *Problem Solving.* The student determines the components and operations necessary to solve mathematics problems.

- Applied Problem Solving. The student interprets problems and applies solutions in context.

KEYMATH 3 (KEYMATH–3)

A. J. Connolly (2007)

Type: Norm-referenced and domain-referenced test

Major Content Areas: Basic concepts, operations, and applications in mathematics

Type of Administration: Individual

Administration Time: 30 to 90 minutes

Age/Grade Levels: Grades K–12, ages 4–6 through 22–11

Types of Scores: Standard score and percentile ranks for subtests, area scores, Growth Scale Value (GSV) and total test; optional age and grade equivalents for area scores and total test

Aids: *ASSIST software*

Typical Uses: A broad-based mathematics test for the identification of strengths and weaknesses in mathematics skill development

Cautions: Reliability of the *KeyMath–* is best for total test and area scores. In administration, the Numeration Basal Item determines starting points for later subtests. Hand scoring is straightforward, but it can be time consuming if all types of results are desired.

Publisher: Pearson Assessments (*pearsonassessments.com*)

The *KeyMath–3* is designed for students from kindergarten through grade 12 and ages 4–6 through 22–11. Reading skills are not needed because the tester reads all questions and problems to the student. However, English-language skills are a necessity, particularly for subtests such as Problem Solving. On most *KeyMath–* subtests, students respond orally, but writing is required on two of the Operations subtests. Subtests are untimed and can be administered in more than one session.

Technical Quality

The *KeyMath–3* was normed with a sample of 3,630 individuals ages 4–6 to 22–11 based on the 2005 U.S. Census. Gender, race/ethnicity, geographic region, parent education, special populations (specific learning disability, speech-language impairment, intellectual disability, emotional/behavioral disturbance, developmental delay and other impairment-including sensory impairments, autism, and traumatic brain injury) were specified and included in the sample.

Split-half reliability revealed reliability scores of .85 to .97 for both forms A and B across all three areas (Basic Concepts, Operations, and Applications). Alternate form reliability coefficients for grade-based scores for adjusted *r* were .94 for Basic Concepts, .93 for Operations, .88 for Applications, and .96 for Total Test. Test-Retest reliability coefficients for grade-based scores for adjusted *r* were .95 for Basic Concepts, .93 for Operations, .93 for Applications, and .97 for Total Test.

Concurrent validity of the *KeyMath–3* was studied by examining its relationship to the *KeyMath–R, Normative Update* and to mathematics subtests on the Kaufman Test of Educational Achievement-II and the *Iowa Tests of Basic Skills*. In addition, Measures of Academic Progress and Group Mathematics Assessment and Diagnostic Evaluation were also used to compare the *Key-Math–3*. Total test scores of the two versions of the *KeyMath* are strongly related (.82 to .93); total mathematics subtest results from the group achievement tests show moderate correlations (.68 to .87) with *KeyMath–3* results (Pearson, 2007; Maccow, 2011).

Administration Considerations

The *KeyMath–3* should be administered and interpreted by qualified individuals. Those qualifications include coursework in measurement and interpretations, as well as "formal training" in mathematics.

There are consistent basal and ceiling rules for all *KeyMath–3* subtests. Basals are established by three consecutive correct responses, and ceilings by four consecutive errors. *KeyMath–* subtests must be administered in order. The test record provides a starting point for the subtest, Numeration. Starting points for the rest of the test are determined by the student's performance on Numeration. The basal is established and the "Numeration Basal Item" is identified; this is the *first* item in the string of three consecutive responses needed for the basal. For example, if the basal were established with successes on items 12, 13, and 14, the Numeration Basal Item would be item 12. This number is then used to locate the appropriate starting item for later subtests.

Test books are in easel format. On the examiner's side are the directions and questions to be read to the student, the correct answers, and any special scoring instructions. On some items, the tester must point to information on the student's side of the easel. On *KeyMath–* subtests, there are no time limits, and testers can repeat items for students as needed. Written computation is required on the two basic operation subtests; the test record form contains the problems, with ample space for computation.

On the *KeyMath–3* test items are scored as they are administered. Correct responses are circled "1" and incorrect responses "0." The tester records the student's performance (0 or 1) in the space provided for each item so that domain scores can be obtained. A line is drawn above the easiest item passed and below the most difficult item administered. Raw scores for domains are determined by counting the number of successes and the items assumed correct below the basal. The subtest's ceiling item is noted, and the total raw score for the subtest is computed by adding the scores.

Results and Interpretation

The *KeyMath–3* offers a variety of scores. Norms are available by age and grade; grade norms are provided for fall and spring testing dates. Subtest results are expressed as percentile ranks and scaled scores (standard scores with a mean of 10 and a standard deviation of 3). Additional scores are available for the three areas (Basic Concepts, Operations, and Applications) and for the Total Test: percentile ranks, standard scores with a mean of 100 and a standard deviation of 15, confidence intervals, age and grade equivalents, Growth Scale Values, normal curve equivalents, and stanines.

Results can be plotted on a Score Profile. The tester chooses a confidence level (68 or 90 percent) and consults a table to determine the values needed to construct intervals around observed scores. Standard scores are plotted for Total Test and area results and scaled scores for subtests. It is also possible to compare the student's performance on the three areas assessed by the *KeyMath–3*. The tester computes the observed difference between area standard scores and consults a table to determine whether these differences are significant at the .01 level, significant at the .05 level, or not significant.

The *KeyMath–3* provides procedures for analysis of students' performance by domain and by individual test item. *KeyMath–3* results help evaluators to determine the student's current achievement in basic mathematics concepts, computational operations, and applications such as problem solving, estimation, time, money, and measurement. Results can be linked to specific skills and subskills, thereby proving helpful in the selection or design of appropriate informal tools for in-depth assessment.

> **Breakpoint Practice 14.1**
> *Click here to check your understanding of KeyMath–3 diagnostic assessment.*

OTHER FORMAL MEASURES

There are several other formal measures of mathematics skills in addition to the *KeyMath–3* and four of these are described in the next sections.

Included are the *Stanford Diagnostic Mathematics Test–Fourth Edition*, a set of group-administered survey tests designed for grade 1 through high school; the *Test of Mathematical Abilities—Third Edition*, an instrument that assesses mathematical aptitudes and students' attitudes toward math; the *Comprehensive Mathematical Abilities Test*, a newer measure that assesses not only calculation and problem-solving skills but also more advanced subjects such as algebra as well as practical applications; and the *Diagnostic Test of Arithmetic Strategies*, a formal measure of the strategies that students use to solve computation problems.

Stanford Diagnostic Mathematics Test— Fourth Edition (SDMT)

The *SDMT* is a norm-referenced test of several types of mathematics skills designed for group use. Its major purpose is to identify areas of educational need.

Six levels of the *SDMT* are available to meet the needs of students in grades 1 through high school, and there is some overlap between levels to accommodate students with problems in mathematics. For example, both the Green and Purple Levels provide norms for fourth graders, but the Green Level is more appropriate for low achievers because its content is based on the skills taught in the early elementary grades. To facilitate retesting, parallel forms are available for the upper three levels.

Each level contains two separate tests: a multiple-choice test and a free-response test. The free-response format is available so that teachers can analyze how students go about solving mathematical problems. Each multiple-choice and free-response test is divided into two subtests: Concepts and Applications, and Computation. Several concept and skill domains are assessed by each of these subtests, although content varies somewhat from level to level:

Concepts and Applications

- Numeration
- Patterns and Functions
- Probability and Statistics
- Graphs and Tables
- Problem Solving
- Geometry and Measurement

STANFORD DIAGNOSTIC MATHEMATICS TEST—FOURTH EDITION
(SDMT) (1995)

Type: Norm-referenced test

Major Content Areas: Concepts and applications, computation

Type of Administration: Group

Administration Time: Approximately 1.5 hours

Age/Grade Levels: Red Level, Grades 1.5 to 2.5; Orange Level, Grades 2.5 to 3.5; Green Level, Grades 3.5 to 4.5; Purple Level, Grades 4.5 to 6.5; Brown Level, Grades 6.5 to 8.9; Blue Level, Grades 9.0 to 12.9

Types of Scores: Percentile ranks, stanines, scaled scores, grade equivalents, Progress Indicators

Technology Aids: Scoring services available from publisher

Typical Uses: A broad-based test for the identification of strengths and weaknesses in mathematics skill development

Cautions: The *SDMT* is designed for group administration. Some questions are multiple choice, some portions of the test are timed, and older students record their responses on a separate answer sheet. If students experience difficulty with group administration, the *SDMT* can be administered individually as long as the tester adheres to standard administration practices.

Publisher: Harcourt Assessment (*harcourtassessment.com*) retired

---

Computation

- Addition of Whole Numbers
- Subtraction of Whole Numbers
- Multiplication of Whole Numbers
- Division of Whole Numbers
- Operations with Fractions and Mixed Numbers
- Operations with Decimals and Percents
- Equations

It is possible to administer one or both subtests of the multiple-choice and free-response measures. To avoid tiring the students, it is suggested that only one subtest be given per day.

The *SDMT* is designed for group administration, and it is quite easy to administer. There are no basals or ceilings, and all responses are recorded by the student. The tester simply reads the specified directions to the student and times some of the tests. The *SDMT* can be hand-scored by the tester or sent to a commercial service for scoring.

To participate, students must be able to listen and attend to test directions and work independently. On the upper levels, students mark their responses on separate answer sheets. Several of the tests are timed. On the lower levels, reading skills are not required because the tester reads the word problems aloud. On the upper levels, students may request assistance in reading the questions.

Several types of scores are available for each *SDMT* subtest, including percentile ranks, scaled scores, stanines, and grade equivalents. Progress Indicator scores are also available. These scores provide information about how well the student is progressing in each of the concept and skill domains assessed by the *SDMT*. The student's raw score on each domain is compared to a cut-off score that indicates mastery of skills in that domain. If the student's score equals or exceeds the criterion, the Progress Indicator (PI) is 1, meaning adequate progress. If the student's score falls below the criterion, the PI is 2. The *SDMT* calls the PI a criterion-referenced score because its reference point is the test's content, not test norms.

Although the *SDMT* is a group test, it can be administered individually as long as standard testing procedures are followed. Its advantages include norms that extend through grade 12, so it can be used with older high school students. In addition, it offers precise descriptions of the skills it assesses and provides information about skill mastery through the Progress Indicators. Like other diagnostic tests, however, the *SDMT* is best used as a broad-based survey of several areas of mathematics proficiency.

Test of Mathematical Abilities— Third Edition (TOMA–3)

The *TOMA–3* is an interesting test because it attempts to extend mathematics assessment beyond the traditional skills of computation and problem solving. According to the *TOMA–3* manual, attitudinal, linguistic, and previous knowledge of mathematics are also essential components of mathematical abilities.

The *TOMA–3* contains five subtests:

- *Mathematical Symbols and Concepts.* Students are presented with multiple-choice items. They answer questions about signs, symbols, words, or phrases.
- *Computation.* Computational problems appear on a page in the test booklet. These problems sample the basic operations as well as manipulation of fractions, decimals, money, percentages, and other types of mathematical expressions. Students write their responses directly in the test booklet.
- *Mathematics in Everyday Life.* The student answers multiple-choice questions that they would use in a real-life situation.
- *Word Problems.* The student reads word problems, which start out simple and progressively become more difficult.
- *Attitude Toward Math (Supplemental).* The student answers questions regarding his or her perceived abilities in mathematics. Students listen and then check one of these responses: Yes, definitely; Closer to Yes; Closer to No; No, definitely. This subtest is an adaptation of the mathematics portion of the *Estes Attitude Scales* (Estes, Estes, Richards, & Roettger, 1981), which is described in Chapter 10.

Both reading and writing are required on the *TOMA–3,* and students with skill problems in these areas may have difficulty with some subtests. However, test tasks are not timed. Students must read sentences on the Word Problems subtest.

TEST OF MATHEMATICAL ABILITIES—THIRD EDITION (TOMA–3)

V. L. Brown, M. E. Cronin, & D. P. Bryant (2012)

Type: Norm-referenced test

Major Content Areas: Vocabulary, computation, general information, story problems, and attitude toward math

Type of Administration: Individual or group

Administration Time: 1 to 1½ hours

Age/Grade Levels: Ages 8–0 through 18–11

Types of Scores: Scaled scores, percentile ranks, Math Ability Index

Technology Aids: N/A

Typical Uses: Evaluation of attitudes toward mathematics and identification of strengths and weaknesses in mathematics skill development

Cautions: Students need both reading and writing skills to complete test tasks on the *TOMA–3.* Further information is needed about concurrent validity in relation to other measures of mathematics performance.

Publisher: PRO-ED (*www.proedinc.com*)

On the Vocabulary subtest, students must read terms and write definitions, although spelling, punctuation, and capitalization errors are not penalized. Clearly, English-language facility is a prerequisite for participation in the *TOMA–3*. If group administration procedures are used, then students must also be able to attend to test directions and work independently in a group.

The *TOMA–3* was standardized on approximately 1,456 students ages 8–0 to 18–11 from 21 states. The sample appears to resemble the national population in terms of gender, race, ethnicity, geographic region, and disability status. Internal consistency and test-retest reliability of the *TOMA–3* appear adequate, although one test-retest coefficient was below .8. Interscorer reliability revealed coefficients above .9. The concurrent validity of the original *TOMA* was studied in relation to the *Comprehensive Mathematical Abilities Test* and the *Iowa Algebra Aptitude Test-5*. Subtest score coefficients ranged from .5 to .74, while Index and composite scores ranged from .83 to .92. Further study is needed of the *TOMA–3*'s relationship to current versions of the individual tests of mathematics performance that are typically used in special education.

Formal training in assessment is recommended for testers who wish to administer the *TOMA–3*. The subtests should be presented in order. Students begin with item 1 on all subtests. On the Attitude toward Math subtest, students answer all items. On the other subtests, the ceiling is defined as three consecutive incorrect responses. When subtests are administered to groups, students are directed to complete as many items as they can; the tester then applies the ceiling rules when scoring the test.

Scaled scores and percentile ranks are available for each *TOMA–3* subtest. The scaled scores are distributed with a mean of 10 and a standard deviation of 3. A total test score, the Math Index, is derived by combining results of the four required subtests; it is distributed with a mean of 100 and a standard deviation of 15. Results of the *TOMA–3* are plotted on a profile in all areas.

The *TOMA–3* is a norm-referenced mathematics test that surveys several areas of performance. It assesses traditional mathematics skills and also offers measures of attitudes toward mathematics, mathematics vocabulary, and general mathematics information. As with other survey tests, the results of the *TOMA–3* are used to direct further assessment.

Comprehensive Mathematical Abilities Test (CMAT)

The *CMAT* is a newer measure that provides information about a broad range of mathematics skills. The core subtests address traditional computational and problem-solving skills. In addition, supplemental subtests provide information about higher mathematics skills and about the use of mathematics in daily life.

The *CMAT* is composed of 12 subtests. The first six make up the core subtests. Subtests 1 through 4 assess basic computational skills, whereas subtests 5 and 6 assess mathematical reasoning.

Core Subtests

- Subtest 1, Addition
- Subtest 2, Subtraction
- Subtest 3, Multiplication
- Subtest 4, Division
- Subtest 5, Problem Solving
- Subtest 6, Charts, Tables, and Graphs

The last six subtests are considered supplemental. Subtests 7, 8, and 9 measure more advanced math skills; in contrast, subtests 10, 11, and 12 are designed to assess the use of mathematics in daily life.

Supplemental Subtests

- Subtest 7, Algebra
- Subtest 8, Geometry
- Subtest 9, Rational Numbers
- Subtest 10, Time
- Subtest 11, Money
- Subtest 12, Measurement

One of the interesting features of the *CMAT* is that students are allowed to use calculators except on the computation subtests (tests 1 through 4). This reduces the effects of poor computation skills on the student's ability to respond to other types of mathematics questions. Subtests are not timed, and the tester can read items to

COMPREHENSIVE MATHEMATICAL ABILITIES TEST (CMAT)

W. P. Hresko, P. L. Schlieve, S. R. Herron, C. Swain, & R. J. Sherbenou (2003)

Type: Norm-referenced test

Major Content Areas: Basic calculations, mathematics reasoning, advanced calculations, and practical applications

Type of Administration: Individual

Administration Time: 45 to 60 minutes (core subtests)

Age/Grade Levels: Ages 7–0 through 18–11, grades 3 to 12

Types of Scores: Subtest standard scores, composite quotients, and percentile ranks

Technology Aids: Scoring program available from publisher

Typical Uses: A broad-based test for identification of strengths and weaknesses in various types of mathematics skills

Cautions: Calculators may be used except on the subtests that assess computation skills (subtests 1 through 4). Further information is needed about concurrent validity in relation to other individual measures of mathematics performance.

Publisher: PRO-ED (*www.proedinc.com*)

students and record their answers, if necessary. The manual states, "The **CMAT** is a test of mathematical ability *only.* Students should not be penalized for poor reading or poor handwriting" (p. 12).

The *CMAT* was standardized with 1,625 public and private school students from 17 states. The sample appears to resemble the national population in terms of gender, race, ethnicity, geographic area, urban–rural residence, and disability status. The reliability of the *CMAT* (internal consistency, test-retest, and interscorer) is adequate. Concurrent validity was studied in relation to the *Diagnostic Achievement Test for Adolescents—Second Edition, Woodcock-Johnson III,* and two group achievement tests. The General Mathematics composite of the *CMAT* showed a higher correlation with the Broad Mathematics score from the *WJ III* ($r = 83$) than with the *DATA-2's* Math Composite ($r = 60$). Equivalent correlations with results of group measures ranged from .65 to .95. The *CMAT* appears to differentiate between students with learning disabilities and others in the standardization sample. In addition, confirmatory

factor analyses support the model of mathematics underlying the *CMAT.* However, further study is needed regarding the relationship of the *CMAT* to the *KeyMath* series and other individual tests of mathematics performance typically used in special education.

The manual for this test recommends that formal training be a requirement for administration and interpretation of the CMAT. Subtests are to be administered in order, but it is not necessary to give the entire test. In fact, the Algebra and Geometry subtests should not be administered to students younger than 10–0 or those in grades 4 and below. Students younger than 10–0 begin with item 1 on each subtest; starting points are suggested for older students. Administration is straightforward with a basal of three correct responses for all subtests and a ceiling of three incorrect responses.

Subtest standard scores are distributed with a mean of 10 and a standard deviation of 3. Six composite scores are available: Basic Calculations (subtests 1–4), Mathematical Reasoning (subtests 5 and 6), General Mathematics (subtests 1–6),

DIAGNOSTIC TEST OF ARITHMETIC STRATEGIES (DTAS)

H. P. Ginsburg & S. C. Mathews (1984)

Type: Diagnostic inventory with standard administration and scoring procedures

Major Content Areas: Setting up problems, number facts, written calculation, and informal skills

Type of Administration: Individual

Administration Time: 20 minutes per subtest

Age/Grade Levels: Students in the elementary grades

Types of Scores: Norm-referenced scores are not available; results are the number and types of errors made by the student

Technology Aids: N/A

Typical Uses: Identification of successful and unsuccessful strategies for addition, subtraction, multiplication, and division

Cautions: The *DTAS* provides descriptive results rather than norm-referenced scores.

Publisher: PRO-ED (*www.proedinc.com*)

Advanced Calculations (subtests 7–9), Practical Applications (subtests 10–12), and Global Mathematics Ability make up of the results from all 12 subtests. The composite scores include Quotients (distributed with a mean of 100 and a standard deviation of 15) and percentile ranks.

The *CMAT* is a norm-referenced mathematics test that surveys a range of performance areas. It assesses traditional computation and problem-solving skills, and it also offers measures of more advanced subjects such as algebra and geometry. In addition, it is a measure of three important practical applications: time, money, and measurement. As with other survey tests, the results of the *CMAT* are best used to direct further assessment.

Diagnostic Test of Arithmetic Strategies (DTAS)

The *DTAS* is an older measure but one that is unique because it assesses the strategies students use in solving arithmetic computation problems. Although not norm-referenced, it is a formal assessment device with standard procedures for administration and scoring. Its scope is quite limited in comparison to tests like the *KeyMath*, *SDMT, CMAT,* and *TOMA–3.* Its purpose is the in-depth assessment of one important component of mathematical ability—arithmetic computation. See Figure 14–1.

The *DTAS* contains four subtests: Addition, Subtraction, Multiplication, and Division. Their focus is not the answers that students give to computation problems. Instead, they are designed to elicit information about the ways students go about solving computation problems. To accomplish this, each subtest is divided into four sections.

1. *Setting Up the Problem.* The tester reads problems to the student, who writes down each problem; the student is not required to solve the problems. For example, the tester might say, "Write down twenty-four plus eighteen." The student's responses are checked for several types of errors. Errors in writing numerals occur when the student writes 7. Errors in writing numbers occur when numbers are written as they sound (e.g., 204 for twenty-four) or when numbers are reversed. In addition, subtraction, and

SECTION IIB: WRITTEN CALCULATION

	Problems											
	5	6	7	8	9	10	11	12	13	14	15	16
1. Answer												
Correct (circle)	⟨39⟩	⟨27⟩	⟨46⟩	⟨72⟩	126	135	42	64	643	730	36	36
Incorrect (write in)	—	—	—	—	136	145	312	514	533	620	30	38
2. Standard school method	✓	✓	✓	✓	✓	✓	—	—	—	—	—	—
3. Informal method	—	—	—	—	—	—	—	—	—	—	—	—
4. Number fact error	—	—	—	—	✓	✓	—	—	—	—	—	—
5. Bugs												
A. Addition like multiplication	—	—										
B. Zero makes zero			—	—								
C. Add from left to right					—	—						
D. No carry: All digits on bottom							✓	✓	—	—		
E. No carry: Vanishing digit							—	—	✓	✓		
F. Carries wrong digit							—	—				
G. Wrong operation	—	—	—	—	—	—	—	—	—	—		
H. Add individual digits	—	—	—	—	—	—	—	—	—	—		
I. Other	—	—	—	—	—	—	—	—	—	—		
6. Slips												
A. Skips numbers	—	—	—	—	—	—	—	—	—	—	✓	—
B. Adds twice	—	—	—	—	—	—	—	—	—	—	—	✓
C. Other	—	—	—	—	—	—	—	—	—	—		

Notes: Debbie started out by doing the standard school method on problems 5-8 which do not involve carrying. When carrying was introduced, she obviously did not know how to deal with it and either put all digits on the bottom or ignored the numbers to be carried. On the last two problems, she was sloppy, making two slips.

FIGURE 14–1

Sample Results of the *Diagnostic Test of Arithmetic Strategies*

Source: From *Diagnostic Test of Arithmetic Strategies* (p. 34) by H. P. Ginsburg and S. C. Mathews, 1984, Austin, TX: PRO-ED. Copyright 1984 by PRO-ED. Reprinted by permission.

multiplication, alignment is incorrect if the student aligns numbers to the left rather than to the right. Sloppy alignment is also considered an error.

2. *Number Facts.* Students are shown a simple facts problem and are told to say the answer that comes into their head. The tester records how long it takes the student to respond and whether or not the response is correct. The skill under assessment is the student's ability to recall number facts quickly, accurately, and automatically. The tester observes the student and notes whether the student attempts to solve the problems by counting fingers, using whispered counting, or counting aloud.

3. *Written Calculation.* The student is presented with 12 computation problems of increasing difficulty. He or she is directed to read each problem out loud, show all work on the

answer sheet, and is told, "Tell me out loud what you are doing."

The tester then analyzes several aspects of the student's work. First, the professional determines whether the student's answer is correct or incorrect. Then the student's method of solving the problem is considered to see if the student used the standard school method or an informal one. The standard school method for addition involves beginning with the "ones" column and carrying when necessary. Informal methods are nonstandard procedures. For example, the student may begin with the larger number and count upwards; or a problem such as $42 + 54$ might be simplified into two problems, $40 + 50$ and $2 + 4$. Second, the tester looks for any number fact errors that may have occurred. "Bugs" are another concern. Also called defective algorithms (Ashlock, 2006), bugs are systematic but inappropriate procedures for problem solving. The *DTAS* scoring sheet lists several possible types of bugs. For instance, the student might approach an addition problem as if it were a multiplication problem. Or the student might follow the rule that "0 makes 0." With this bug, the sum of $15 + 20$ would be calculated as 30 because 0 plus any number is 0. "Slips" are another error category in Written Calculation. According to the *DTAS* manual, slips are are "relatively minor execution errors, and do not seem to result from basic faults in understanding or serious defects in the calculational procedure" (p. 4). Examples of slips in addition are skipping numbers and adding the same number twice.

4. *Informal Skills.* Here the tester reads computation problems, and the student must solve them mentally. For example, the tester might ask, "How much is 27 and 14?" The purpose of this activity is to require the student to go beyond the standard school methods of problem solving. The student is presented with nontraditional problems (nontraditional because they require mental computation), and informal problem-solving procedures are observed. The tester then records which strategy the student employs.

For example, on the Addition subtest, the tester notes whether the student used counting, simplification, imaginary column addition, or some other informal strategy. If the student fails to use an informal procedure, the tester prompts the student by suggesting a strategy.

According to the manual, the *DTAS* is appropriate for students "who are experiencing difficulty with addition, subtraction, multiplication, or division (roughly in grades 1–6)" (p. 9). Students must possess sufficient English-language skills to understand test directions and respond to questions. No reading skills are required, and students do not need to write letters or words. However, they are expected to write computation problems and solutions. None of the subtests are timed, but students are urged to work quickly on the Number Facts task. At first, students may be somewhat reluctant to explain how they are solving the problems on Written Calculation, but most will cooperate when encouraged by the tester.

Special training is not needed to administer the *DTAS*, but professionals should study the manual carefully and administer several practice tests. Subtests can be administered in any order, and it is not necessary to administer all subtests to any one student. The manual advises that a student be given only one of the four subtests during any one testing session. There are no basals and ceilings because students are encouraged to attempt all of the test items.

Scoring the *DTAS* requires more expertise than that required for many measures. The tester must evaluate the accuracy of the student's responses and also describe the methods the student used to arrive at these responses. The manual provides guidelines for scoring each subtest, standards for scoring, and examples. Testers should take advantage of these resources.

The *DTAS* does not produce norm-referenced results. Instead, the results are descriptive. For each basic operation, it is possible to identify the strategies the student uses and the types of errors that occur consistently. When faced with addition problems that require carrying (or regrouping), the student relies upon two types of bugs. She fails to carry and writes all digits:

$$\begin{array}{r} 15 \\ +29 \\ \hline 314 \end{array}$$

or she fails to carry but writes only the ones digit:

$$\begin{array}{r} 345 \\ +296 \\ \hline 531 \end{array}$$

Descriptive results have direct implications for instruction, if the skill in question is an area of educational need for the student. Because the *DTAS* is not normed, it is impossible to compare the student's performance with age or grade peers. For example, the student may be progressing satisfactorily but simply not have reached the point in the mathematics curriculum where regrouping skills are taught. However, if the skill deficiency is perceived as a problem, *DTAS* results may be used to plan a course of instructional action. The manual provides suggestions for remedial activities.

 Breakpoint Practice 14.2
Click here to check your understanding of formal mathematics assessment.

CURRICULUM-BASED MEASURES: MONITORING BASIC SKILLS PROGRESS

Monitoring Basic Skills Progress (MBSP) is a collection of commercially available curriculum-based measures that include computer components. Two of its four parts assess mathematics skills: Basic Math Computation (2nd ed.) (Fuchs, Hamlett, & Fuchs, 1998) and Basic Math Concepts and Applications (Fuchs, Hamlett, & Fuchs, 1999). The Computation portion of *MBSP* is designed for students in grades 1–6 and the Concepts and Applications portion for those in grades 2–6.

Unlike the Basic Reading measure of *MBSP,* the math portions are not administered by computer. Instead, students take timed, paper-and-pencil math tests and then enter their answers into a computer program. The program scores the test and provides students and teachers with detailed feedback on performance.

Each of the *MBSP* math measures includes a student disk, teacher disk, and a book of tests designed to be copied by the teacher. There are 30 tests at each grade level, and all tests at one grade level contain the same types of items. There are 25 items on the Computation tests and 18 to 25 items on the Concepts and Applications tests. The *MBSP* manuals recommend that tests be given once a week to general education students and twice a week to students in special education. The teacher must time tests. Time limits for the Computation measures range from 2 to 6 minutes, depending on grade level. Those for the Concepts and Applications measures range from 6 to 8 minutes.

The skills assessed by Basic Math Computation are the basic operations: addition, subtraction, multiplication, and division of whole numbers, fractions, and decimals. The Concepts and Applications measures, in contrast, assess a number of different skills, appropriate to the curricular changes from grades 2–6. Examples are counting, number concepts, numeration, measurement, charts and graphs, money, fractions, decimals, percentages, applied computation, word problems, geometry, ratios and probability, and variables. One important feature of both of these measures is the Skill Profile, a visual depiction of the skills the student has and has not mastered.

OTHER INFORMAL ASSESSMENT PROCEDURES

Assessment for instructional planning relies on several informal measures and techniques in addition to curriculum-based measurement. Among the most common are teacher checklists, informal inventories, error analysis, diagnostic teaching and clinical math interviews, criterion-referenced tests, questionnaires and interviews, and portfolio assessment.

Teacher Checklists

Checklists are a quick and efficient method for gathering information from teachers and other professionals about their observations of students' performance in mathematics. Some checklists are designed so that they are general in nature, surveying a wide range of mathematics content. Others are quite specific, focusing on a particular set of skills.

One major use of checklists is to document and monitor students' acquisition of mathematics skills. Curriculum checklists serve this purpose. Checklists could address application skills such as telling time, using a calendar, reading a thermometer, and applying consumer economics. This checklist could be completed during assessment and then updated as the student learns new skills.

Informal Inventories

Informal inventories survey a variety of skills to determine where the student's strengths and weaknesses lie. Inventories contain problems that require the basic operations of addition, subtraction, multiplication, and division. However, the inventory provides only one or two items, at most, to evaluate a particular skill such as addition of two-digit numbers with regrouping. If results point to a possible skill deficiency, it is necessary to collect further data with more precise measures such as criterion-referenced tests.

Inventories are quite easy to construct, and professionals can design their own to assess whatever skill areas are of interest. For instance, if the teacher is curious about a student's understanding of place value concepts, he or she could devise a set of questions to probe this area of mathematics. The teacher might include activities such as the following:

The number 48 is the same as 4 tens and 8 ones. Tell how many tens and ones make up these numbers.

$$15 = \underline{\hspace{1cm}} \text{ tens} + \underline{\hspace{1cm}} \text{ ones}$$

$$36 = \underline{\hspace{1cm}} \text{ tens} + \underline{\hspace{1cm}} \text{ ones}$$

$$72 = \underline{\hspace{1cm}} \text{ tens} + \underline{\hspace{1cm}} \text{ ones}$$

Or if the teacher is interested in the student's ability to tell time, the teacher could prepare a set of drawings of clock faces, each showing a different time. One set might assess telling time to the hour (e.g., 4:00), another telling time to the half hour (e.g., 7:30), and so forth. The teacher should also consider including clocks with digital displays (e.g., 8:42 or 4:23:15).

Mathematics skills are usually assessed with paper-and-pencil tasks, but there are many other alternatives. If the teacher wants to learn more about the student's knowledge of basic math facts, problems could be presented orally, on paper, on the chalkboard, with flashcards, in horizontal notation (2 + 3 =) or vertical notation, and so forth. Students could respond orally instead of writing their answers, and, if speed is a concern, the inventory can be timed.

Error Analysis

Mathematics is one of the school subjects best suited for error analysis because students respond in writing on most tasks, thereby producing a permanent record of their work. Also, there is usually only one correct answer to mathematical problems and questions, and scoring is unambiguous. Error analysis is a traditional technique in mathematics assessment; it dates back to the 1920s when professionals began to study the types of errors that characterize written computation (Brueckner, 1930; Buswell & John, 1925; Osborn, 1925).

Today, the most common use of error analysis in mathematics is assessment of computation skills. Cox (1975) differentiates between systematic computation errors and errors that are random or careless mistakes. With systematic errors, students are consistent in their use of an incorrect number fact, operation, or algorithm. Roberts (1968) studied the written computation of elementary grade students and identified four error types:

1. *Incorrect operation.* The student selects the incorrect operation. For example, if the problem requires subtraction, the student adds.
2. *Incorrect number fact.* The number fact recalled by the student is inaccurate. For example, the student recalls the product of 6×9 as 52.

3. *Incorrect algorithm.* The procedures used by the student to solve the problem are inappropriate. The student may skip a step, apply the correct steps in the wrong sequence, or use an inaccurate method. For example, in the subtraction problem 24–18, the student may begin by subtracting 4 from 8, using the algorithm "subtract the smaller number from the larger."

4. *Random error.* The student's response is incorrect and apparently random. For example, the student writes 100 as the answer to 42 × 6.

According to Roberts, the most frequent type of error among students with achievement problems is the random error. For other students, incorrect algorithms are most common.

The first step in conducting an error analysis is to gather a sample of the student's work. The professional could administer an informal mathematics inventory or a computation subtest from a formal test. Or samples of recent classroom work could be obtained from the student's teacher; these might be homework assignments, worksheets, workbook pages, or classroom tests or quizzes.

The math sample is then graded to identify the errors that the student has made. In most cases, scoring is a straightforward process. However, difficulties may arise when a student's handwriting is hard to read. If an answer is illegible, the professional should ask the student for help in deciphering it. By using this procedure, the teacher can evaluate the student's math skills separately from his or her writing skills.

Next, the student's errors are categorized by type. Random errors, incorrect operations, inaccurate number facts, and defective algorithms are the usual categories. The professional may also want to consider two other types of errors assessed by the *Diagnostic Test of Arithmetic Strategies:* slips (careless, nonsystematic errors) and mistakes in setting up the problem.

Sometimes the answer to a computational problem is wrong for more than one reason. For instance, the student may recall a number fact inaccurately *and* employ an inappropriate operation or algorithm. In the following problem, the student used addition rather than subtraction and also recalled one addition fact incorrectly:

$$
\begin{array}{r}
1 \\
36 \\
-18 \\
\hline
55
\end{array}
$$

Another concern is whether errors are systematic. If the student correctly adds 8 + 4 in four problems but not in the fifth, the error is probably a slip rather than a number facts problem. A response analysis of the student's work, in which both correct and incorrect answers are analyzed, can provide this kind of information. One error on one problem does not constitute an error pattern. The errors most relevant to instructional planning occur consistently over several problems and frequently over time.

Error analysis can also be used with mathematical problem-solving tasks such as story problems. Goodstein (1981) suggests that students' word problem errors be analyzed by following these steps:

1. Check to determine the magnitude of the discrepancy between the incorrect and correct response. Small discrepancies for large numbers will often indicate carelessness in the computational aspect of the task.
2. Check to determine if the magnitude of the response indicates selection of the proper operation....
3. Check to determine if the response could have been the combination of other numerical data in the problem. (Obviously, this step is only used when extraneous information is present) (pp. 42–43).

Clinical Math Interviews and Diagnostic Probes

Whereas error analysis techniques focus on students' written products, clinical interviews elicit information about the procedures that students use to arrive at those products. Clinical interviews are the most appropriate technique for process analysis.

In conducting a clinical interview, the professional combines several informal techniques. The student is observed going about the mathematics task, and the professional takes note of any behaviors of interest. For example, on a computation task, the student may attempt to solve problems by counting fingers or by making hatch marks on the paper. The student is interviewed to find out about the cognitive strategies he or she used to accomplish the task. Diagnostic probes are introduced to determine whether alternative strategies will improve the student's performance.

According to Cawley (1978), clinical math interviews are conducted *after* students have completed some mathematics task. The student's paper is scored, and then "[t]he student is asked to verbalize the procedure that he or she used to do both the correct and incorrect problems"(p. 224). However, Bartel (1986a) recommends that the interview take place *while* students are engaged in the mathematics activity. Bartel suggests these guidelines for math interviews:

1. One problem area should be considered at a time.
2. The easiest problem should be presented first.
3. A written record or tape should be made of the interview.
4. The student should simultaneously solve the problem in written form and "explain" what he or she is doing orally.
5. The student must be left free to solve the problem in his or her own way without a hint that he or she is doing something wrong.
6. The student should not be hurried. (p. 200)

Neither approach is the perfect solution (Ashlock, 2006). When interviews are conducted during the activity, the process of thinking out loud may influence the way the student approaches the problem. When interviews take place after the work has been completed, the student may be unable to recall all of the steps that were followed or the reasoning that prompted those steps. To compensate for the shortcomings of these methods, Ashlock advises using both. Thus, the professional could interview the student after he or she has completed one set of tasks and then conduct a second interview as the student attempts another set of tasks.

One use of clinical interviews is the study of computational processes. In the classroom, teachers can present the student with arithmetic problems and then listen to the student's explanation of the strategies selected for problem solving. Mercer and Mercer (1998) provide an example:

> The teacher gave Mary three multiplication problems and said, "Please do these problems and tell me how you figure out the answer." Mary solved the problems in this way:
>
> $$\begin{array}{ccc} 2 & 4 & 3 \\ 27 & 36 & 44 \\ \times 4 & \times 7 & \times 8 \\ \hline 168 & 492 & 562 \end{array}$$
>
> For the first problem, Mary explained,"7 times 4 equals 28. So I put my 8 here and carry the 2. 2 plus 2 equals 4, and 4 times 4 equals 16. So I put 16 here." Her explanations for the other two problems followed the same logic.
>
> By listening to Mary and watching her solve the problems, the teacher quickly determined Mary's error pattern: She adds the number associated with the crutch (the number carried to the tens column) *before* multiplying the tens digit (pp. 460–461).

Clinical interviews can also provide information about how students solve story problems. The solution involves several steps, and interviews are the best means for studying the student's skill in selecting and carrying out the appropriate procedures. According to Goodstein (1981), students must follow a four-step process in solving story problems:

1. Identification of the required arithmetic operation
2. Identification of the relevant set(s) of information
3. Appropriate and accurate display of the computation (this step is often unnecessary for simple computations and would be replaced by "accurate entry of the computational factors" if a calculator were to be used)
4. Accurate performance of the indicated computation (this step would automatically follow successful completion of steps 1–3, if a calculator were used). (p. 34)

To accomplish these steps, students must first read and comprehend the story problem. For many students with special needs, poor reading skills interfere with their ability to take this important first step. Next, the student must be familiar with the meanings of the quantitative terms that appear in the problem and the relationship between these terms and arithmetic operations. For example, when the problem asks, "How many are there *altogether?*" the addition operation is usually implied. When the student has identified the appropriate operation, the problem must be studied carefully to locate the values to add, subtract, multiply, or divide. To do this, relevant information must be recognized and irrelevant data discarded. For instance, if the problem says, "John has 3 kittens, Mary has 2 cats, and Marisol has 5 puppies," Marisol's pets are irrelevant if the student must determine "How many cats and kittens are there altogether?"

The professional can learn a great deal about the student's problem-solving skills by incorporating diagnostic probes into the clinical math interview. To do this, the student is given several story problems to solve and is instructed to "think out loud" throughout the entire process. When a problem area becomes apparent, the professional intervenes and provides a cue or an alternate strategy for accomplishing the task. Table 14–2 presents several diagnostic probes for use with story problems. For example, if the teacher suspects that poor reading skills are affecting the

TABLE 14–2
Diagnostic Probes for the Study of Problem-Solving Skills

SUSPECTED AREA OF DIFFICULTY	SUGGESTED INTERVENTION
Decoding the words in the story problem	Read the story problem aloud to the student, and see if he or she can then solve the problem correctly.
Understanding the meaning of the situation described in the story problem	Ask the student to draw a picture that illustrates the problem.
	Provide the student with a picture illustrating the problem.
Selecting the appropriate operation (addition, subtraction, multiplication, or division)	Ask the student to explain the meaning of key quantitative terms that appear in the problem (e.g., "How many apples are there *altogether?*" or "How many children were *left?*").
	Tell the student which operation to use and see if he or she can then solve the problem correctly.
Identifying the relevant and irrelevant information in the problem	If the problem requires knowledge of conceptual categories (e.g., dogs and cats are animals, but a doll is a toy), assess the student's understanding of the categories.
	Tell the student that the problem contains extra information, and ask him or her to try and find it.
Writing down the computational problem	Have the student dictate the problem while the professional writes it down.
Remembering number facts	Provide the student with manipulatives such as sticks or beans to use in figuring out the number facts that are needed.
	Provide the student with a calculator, and see if he or she can then solve the problem correctly.
Selecting the appropriate computational algorithm	If the student's algorithm is inaccurate, teach the student the appropriate procedure.
	Provide the student with a calculator, and see if he or she can then solve the problem correctly.

student's performance, the teacher can read the problem aloud to the student. If the student is then able to solve the problem successfully, reading becomes the instructional concern rather than mathematical problem-solving skills.

Criterion-Referenced Tests

Criterion-referenced tests are used to assess mastery of specific mathematics skills. For example, if the results of an informal math inventory or standardized test point to possible weaknesses in a particular set of skills, the professional can select or design a criterion-referenced test to evaluate the student's ability to perform those skills.

Professionals can prepare their own criterion-referenced measures based on the goals and objectives of the local curriculum, or they can select from commercially available tests. For example, mathematics skills are assessed by both the *BRIGANCE® Comprehensive Inventory of Basic Skills–II (CIBS–II)* (2010) for pre-kindergarten through grade 9 and the *BRIGANCE® Transition Skills* (2010) for middle and high school education. A Spanish edition of the *Basic Skills* inventory (Brigance, 2007) is also available.

The *CIBS–* includes several math readiness measures for younger students (e.g., counting, recognition of numerals, number comprehension). Measures for older students include *Number and Operations, Algebra, Geometry, Measurement,* and *Data Analysis and Probability.*

The *Transition Skills* Inventory stresses vocational as well as school skills and offers several tests of vocationally related mathematics abilities. For instance, there are 10 tests of Independent Living: Money and Finance, each of which is directed toward a real-world application of mathematics such as reading price signs and making change.

Questionnaires and Interviews

In mathematics assessment, questionnaires and interviews are used to gather information about students' viewpoints: their attitudes toward mathematics, perceptions of computation and the problem-solving process, opinions of their own abilities in the skill area of mathematics, and so

forth. Interviews are preferred for younger students and those with poor reading skills. Questionnaires are used only with students who can cope with reading and writing requirements.

Mercer and Mercer (1998) recommend sentence completion tasks for assessing students' attitudes toward arithmetic. In this procedure, the teacher reads an incomplete sentence to the student, who fills in the missing part. Examples of possible sentences are:

1. Math is very …
2. My best subject is …
3. During math I feel … (p. 461)

Interviews can also be used to find out about students' attitudes toward mathematics and perceptions of its usefulness in everyday life. For example, young students could be asked these open-ended questions:

- Is math one of your better subjects in school?
- What types of math activities are the easiest for you? Which are the hardest?
- Do you like to work addition problems? Subtraction problems? Multiplication? Division? Why or why not?
- Do you like to try to solve story problems? Why or why not?
- Most people use math skills every day. Can you name three things that people do with numbers?
- When was the last time you went to the store to buy something? How did you find out how much it cost? Did you pay for it? If you did, how did you figure out whether the salesperson gave you back the right change?
- Can you tell time? How do you do it?
- Suppose you wanted to find out how much you weigh. How would you do it? How could you find out how tall you are?
- Have you ever used a calculator to add or subtract numbers, or to multiply and divide? Is using a calculator easier than doing it in your head? Why or why not?

Several of these questions could be adapted into a questionnaire for older students by changing some of the terminology and substituting age-appropriate examples of everyday math activities.

Portfolio Assessment

In mathematics, as in language arts, students select several examples of their best work for inclusion in a portfolio. Those work samples might be classroom quizzes or assignments, group or individual projects, written math reports or math logs, or artwork related to mathematics. In the Vermont Portfolio Project, students must include five to seven "best pieces" of their mathematical work, other work samples, and a letter to the person who will evaluate their portfolio (Abruscato, 1993). Among the best pieces should be at least one investigation, one application, one puzzle, and no more than two group projects.

Mathematics portfolios can also contain results of standardized tests and informal assessments, student self-assessments, and student interest surveys and questionnaires. For instance, teachers might include checklists of student progress, graphs of results from curriculum-based math measures, and records of clinical math interviews.

ENHANCEDetext

Video Example 14.2

Watch this video to find out more about application of mathematics informal assessment in the classroom. See a teacher work with student in a small group activity where student self-assesses mathematics and organizational skills.

WITHIN THE CONTEXT OF THE CLASSROOM

Up to this point, discussion has focused on assessment tools for gathering information about the student's performance. Here the emphasis shifts to procedures and techniques for studying the classroom learning environment and its influence on the student's mathematics abilities.

The Instructional Environment

Assessment of the instructional environment must take into account the mathematics curriculum and the instructional methods and materials used to implement that curriculum. In the elementary grades, basal textbook series are often the foundation of the mathematics program. Basal series vary in their approach to the teaching of mathematics, but most emphasize both computation and problem-solving skills.

The questions that follow provide a framework for studying the classroom mathematics program:

1. Which mathematics series is used in the classroom?
2. Is more than one level of the mathematics series in use in the classroom?
3. What instructional materials supplement the mathematics textbooks? Are manipulatives provided as computational aids? Are calculators available? Computer programs?
4. What types of mathematics skills are stressed in classroom instruction? Computation? Problem solving? Fluency? Mathematics applications such as time, money, and measurement?
5. Is the mathematics curriculum organized so that development of new skills is based on the mastery of prerequisite skills? Are the instructional steps of appropriate size?
6. Is instruction based on ongoing assessment? How often are performance data collected for monitoring students' progress? What procedures are used to determine the starting points for students entering the mathematics program?
7. How are students grouped for mathematics instruction? How much individualization takes place in each group?
8. What instructional techniques does the teacher use to present new skills and information? Lecture? Demonstration? Discussion? Exploration? Cooperative learning?
9. In what types of learning activities do students participate? Do all mathematics

activities involve paper-and-pencil tasks, or do students sometimes have the opportunity to respond orally?

10. How is supervised practice incorporated into the mathematics program? On the average, how many minutes per day do students spend practicing their mathematics skills?

11. What changes, if any, have been made in the standard mathematics program to accommodate the needs of special learners such as the student under assessment?

Wiederholt, Hammill, and Brown (1978) suggest that it is also important to consider the teacher's attitudes, capabilities, and expectations in relation to mathematics instruction.

One major concern is the focus of the mathematics curriculum. The basic skills movement is still a powerful force in shaping instructional programs in mathematics, despite the recent emphasis on the teaching of problem solving. Basic skills programs tend to emphasize drill and practice as a means of achieving computational proficiency and fluency.

Also of importance are the academic skill demands placed on the student in mathematics activities. Reading is a part of many mathematics tasks, particularly in the upper elementary and secondary grades. Poor reading skills can interfere with the student's ability to read mathematics textbooks, the directions on math worksheets, story problems, and so forth. If reading is a concern, the reading level of the mathematics textbook or other material should be determined using the procedures described in Chapter 13. If the material is too difficult for the student's current skills, the text could be rewritten at an easier reading level or a more suitable text substituted.

Many mathematics activities also require writing skills. Students are expected to write the answers to computational problems, and students must sometimes copy questions or problems onto their papers from the chalkboard or from their textbooks. Such tasks may interfere with the mathematics performance of students with handwriting difficulties. Students who write slowly may be unable to finish their work. If the student's writing is difficult to read, both the student and the teacher may be unable to decipher it.

It is also useful to look at other characteristics of mathematics tasks: the number of questions or problems students are expected to complete, the requirements for speed, and the expectations for accuracy. Sometimes students have the necessary skills to succeed with mathematics assignments, but they fail because they cannot meet performance criteria. They may work the first few problems correctly and then become discouraged by the number of problems left to complete. Or they may work too slowly to finish within the required time period. It may be that classroom standards are unduly stringent and some adjustment can be made. For example, the teacher might be willing to allow more time for each assignment or reduce the number of problems that students are expected to complete.

The Interpersonal Environment

Social relationships among students are an important component of the classroom's interpersonal environment. Students with achievement problems are often not well accepted by their peers, but difficulties in mathematics seem to be better tolerated than difficulties in reading. Perhaps this is because, in mathematics, students make most of their responses privately, and peers are less aware of other students' performances. Another possible explanation relates to students' experiences with mathematics. All students make computational errors at one time or another, and this experience with failure may make achieving students more tolerant of those with persistent problems with mathematics. It is also possible that students value reading more highly than mathematics or that they perceive mathematics as the more difficult subject. Whatever the reason, mathematics skill deficiencies appear to be less socially debilitating than reading problems.

Interactions between students and teachers are also part of the interpersonal environment. In mathematics instruction, one of the primary ways the teacher communicates with students is by grading their math papers. There are several methods of grading, and some are more likely than others to encourage students in their efforts to learn mathematics skills. For example, for students with achievement problems, it is probably better to mark the correct responses rather than the errors. Such a paper is much less threatening than one covered with red checkmarks and a message such as "F—Try harder."

These questions should be considered when evaluating student–teacher interactions:

- In grading students' math papers, how does the teacher respond to errors? Does the teacher identify an incorrect response as an error? Correct it? Ignore the error?
- If the situation is a public one (e.g., students are solving problems at the board), what occurs when a student makes an error? Does the teacher use the same correction procedures as he or she uses in private interactions?
- How does the student react to the teacher's corrections? Is there a difference when the student is corrected in front of peers?
- What do other students do when a peer makes an error?
- What occurs when the student makes a correct response? Does the teacher confirm the response? Praise the student? Provide a tangible reward or token?
- Are students able to work independently on mathematics activities? Do certain students require frequent assistance from the teacher?

The Physical Environment

The physical environment of the classroom can also affect students' mathematics performance. The environment should be physically comfortable, with lighting, temperature, and ventilation at appropriate levels, and classroom space should be arranged to facilitate mathematics instruction. In assessing the classroom's physical characteristics, some of the questions that can be asked are the following:

1. Are all students seated so that they can easily see and hear the teacher? Can they see the chalkboard, if necessary?
2. Is the lighting in the classroom adequate?
3. Is the classroom space structured so that areas for noisier activities are separated from areas for quieter activities?
4. How are the students' seats arranged for independent work? Are students' desks or tables positioned so that students do not distract each other?

5. Are there any quiet work areas or "offices" within the classroom where students can go to escape from distractions?
6. Does the classroom offer a variety of mathematics learning materials, or are textbooks the only resource? If other materials are available, do they cover a wide range of skill levels? Are they accessible to students?
7. In elementary classrooms, is there a learning center for mathematics? If so, what materials and activities does it contain? Are manipulative materials such as computational aids available for student use?
8. Are calculators available to students? Are they accessible at all times, or are they reserved for special activities?
9. Is a computer available in the classroom for students to practice mathematics skills? Do students have access to a variety of educationally sound software programs in the area of mathematics?

 Breakpoint Practice 14.3
Click here to check your understanding of mathematics assessment within the context of the classroom.

ANSWERING THE ASSESSMENT QUESTIONS

Mathematics skills are assessed in order to describe the student's current levels of educational performance. A wide variety of assessment tools are available for this purpose, including both formal and informal measures and techniques.

Nature of the Assessment Tools

Measures of mathematics performance vary in the range of skills they assess. Some are quite comprehensive, whereas others are more limited. Four of the formal tests described in this chapter—the *KeyMath–3*, the *Stanford Diagnostic Mathematics Test—Fourth Edition*, the *Test of Mathematical Abilities—Third Edition* and the *Comprehensive Mathematical Abilities Test*—are considered wide-range measures because they assess a variety of skills. However, each covers a somewhat different set of skill areas. For example, the *KeyMath–3* the

SDMT, and the *CMAT* include computation, problem-solving, and mathematics applications. The *TOMA–3* does not assess mathematics applications but does evaluate areas that the *KeyMath–3* and the *SDMT* do not.

The criterion-referenced tests by Brigance are somewhat more restricted in range because they assess only application and computational skills. The *Diagnostic Test of Arithmetic Strategies* a measure that assesses only computational skills, is even narrower in scope. However, the *DTAS* also provides error analysis procedures for studying students' mistakes in computation.

Another area of difference is the thoroughness with which skills are assessed. Comprehensive tests such as the *KeyMath–* and the *SDMT* sample several skills and skill levels but provide only a few representative test items in each area. For example, on the *KeyMath–3,* several test items are used to evaluate the student's skill in addition of fractions. Informal measures evaluate skills in much greater depth. On the *BRIGANCE® CIBSII* for example, an entire subtest is devoted to addition of fractions and mixed numbers.

Measures can also differ in the types of assessment tasks used to evaluate skill development. For instance, there are many differences between the *KeyMath–3* and the *SDMT,* even though they both assess the same general skill areas. The *SDMT* requires written responses, whereas students usually answer orally on the *KeyMath–3.* Many *SDMT* questions are multiple choice, and several subtests are timed. The *KeyMath–3* imposes time limits on only one subtest, and most test questions are open-ended.

Mathematics measures are most similar in the assessment tasks they use to evaluate students' computational skills. Typically, paper-and-pencil tasks are used; students read the problem and then write the answer. There are fewer similarities in the ways that problem-solving skills are assessed, as Table 14–3 illustrates. Although story problems are the basic tasks for evaluating problem solving on the *KeyMath–3,* the *SDMT,* the *TOMA–3,* and the *CMAT,* task characteristics differ from measure to measure. Such differences can affect the student's ability to respond to test tasks. Task characteristics are important considerations in selecting the tools for assessment and in interpreting assessment results.

The Relationship of Mathematics to Other Areas of Performance

When assessment is complete, the special education team begins to interpret the results and study the relationships between areas of performance. Academic skills such as mathematics may influence or be influenced by several other areas.

General learning aptitude is a consideration in the acquisition of any skill, and the student's progress in mathematics should be evaluated in relation to estimated intellectual potential. In general, students with lower than average general intelligence are expected to progress at a somewhat slower rate than students of average intellectual ability. However, IQ may be a better predictor of mathematical problem-solving ability than of rote computational skills. As with reading, expectancy formulas are not the best means of estimating the student's expected level of achievement. Standard score procedures are preferred. For example, if the student's current scores on a measure of intellectual performance fall within the average range, that student would be expected to show average achievement in mathematics.

Specific learning abilities and strategies also play a role in the student's ability to acquire and apply mathematics skills. Difficulties in attention, memory, or other areas such as visual and auditory perception can hinder skill development, particularly the acquisition of mathematics readiness skills and computational proficiency and fluency. Inefficient learning strategies may interfere with the student's practice of mathematics skills, resulting in further underachievement. In the secondary grades, poor learning strategies may combine with poor mathematics skills to prevent students from applying mathematics in other subject areas.

Classroom behavior may be related to mathematics performance. Inappropriate conduct in the classroom can impede academic learning. Likewise, poor achievement can affect a student's behavior. For example, a student who is unable to cope with a classroom mathematics assignment may react by causing a disturbance. Poor achievement can also influence the student's self-concept, his or her relationships with peers, and the attitudes the student holds toward both school and mathematics.

TABLE 14–3
Assessment Tasks Used to Evaluate Mathematical Problem Solving

MEASURE	SUBTEST	PRESENTATION MODE	RESPONSE MODE
Key Math 3	Problem Solving	Listen to word problems read aloud by the tester; look at a test page with drawings and/or statements related to the problem.	Compute mentally and say the answer.
		Listen to word problems read aloud by the tester; look at a test page with drawings and/or statements related to the problem.	Tell how to solve the problem.
Stanford Diagnostic Mathematics Test—Fourth Edition	Concepts and Applications	Read brief story problem and a series of possible responses.	Write computations on scratch paper, as needed; select a response; mark the letter of the response on the appropriate space on the separate answer sheet; or, on the first three levels, mark the response in the test booklet.
Test of Mathematical Abilities—Third Edition	Story Problems	Read brief story problems.	Write computations in the workspace on the test page; write and circle the answer on the test page.
Comprehensive Mathematical Abilities Test	Problem Solving	Read brief word problems or listen to them read aloud by the tester.	Use a calculator or write computations on scratch paper; write answer in student response booklet.

The student's skills in mathematics may have an impact on other areas of school performance. Basic mathematics competencies are needed in any classroom. To locate page 42 in a spelling book, the student must be able to count and read numerals. Teachers' directions often include quantitative terminology such as *first, last, next,* and *greater than.* In art class, the student may need to measure the dimensions of a canvas; in physical education, students may be asked to "count off by 2s."

In the secondary grades, students are expected to use mathematics in several school subjects. Proficiency in mathematics is often a requirement in the sciences. Even in social studies, students must be able to read and interpret graphs and tables. Mathematics is necessary in almost all vocational subjects, and measurement skills are particularly important. Measurement is needed for cooking, sewing, carpentry, mechanics, agriculture, and many other vocational areas. Skills in handling money and telling time are also important, not only in vocational preparation classes, but also in daily life. Students who have not learned to tell time or deal with simple money exchanges will face real barriers in their attempts to deal with the demands of adult life.

Achievement problems in other curriculum areas can interfere with the acquisition of mathematics skills. Oral language is the foundation for all school learning, and students with language problems may have difficulty acquiring and using the quantitative vocabulary of mathematics. Reading is needed for many mathematics tasks and is a critical component of the process of solving story problems. Difficulties with handwriting can be a real liability. In beginning math instruction, students must learn how to read and write numerals and mathematical symbols, and writing continues to be a necessary part of math activities throughout the school years.

Documentation of Mathematics Performance

The general assessment question that guides the special education team in its investigation of mathematics is, *What are the student's educational needs?* In this phase of assessment, the goal is to obtain sufficient data to describe the student's current levels of educational performance. The team begins by asking, *What is the student's current level of mathematics achievement?* A wide range of mathematics skills is surveyed, and then additional information is gathered about the areas in which the student appears to experience difficulty. This results in a specific description of the student's current skills, and the assessment team is able to answer the question, *What are the student's strengths and weaknesses in the various skill areas of mathematics?*

In mathematics assessment, data are gathered from many sources using many types of assessment tools. Usually, the team begins by reviewing school records, the results of individual achievement tests, and the data collected in interviews with parents and teachers and in classroom observations. Next, a test that evaluates a range of mathematics skills is administered to identify possible problem areas. Informal measures and techniques are then used to learn more about potential weaknesses. For example, the team may administer a series of criterion-referenced tests to assess specific computational skills. Or a clinical math interview may be conducted to learn more about the student's problem-solving strategies.

Many types of tools are available for mathematics assessment. The assessment team should select its tools with care so that duplication is avoided and the assessment process is as efficient as possible. In general, the more specific procedures such as clinical interviews and criterion-referenced tests should be reserved for in-depth assessment of potential problem areas.

By answering the assessment questions about mathematics, the team moves closer to planning the student's IEP. Current levels of educational performance in mathematics are documented, and

the areas of educational need in mathematics are identified. For instance, David was referred for assessment because of his difficulties with mathematics.

ENHANCEDetext
Video Example 14.3
Watch this video to see a teacher present to students in a test review class session. The teacher models involving individual students in this review process.

Assessment in Action

David

His eighth-grade math teacher, Ms. Coolidge, has referred David for special education assessment. David's math grades were poor in seventh grade, and this year he is failing. In the classroom, he is not able to cope with eighth-grade math tasks and instead is reviewing basic number facts and operations. The results of individual achievement tests such as the *WRAT4* and the *Woodcock-Johnson IV* confirm that David's math performance is below that expected for his age and grade.

The assessment team has determined that David is eligible for special education services, and it is anticipated that specialized instruction in mathematics will be an important part of David's individualized program. To begin the study of David's math performance, the *KeyMath–3* will be administered. This measure assesses a wide variety of skills, and results will help the team determine the directions for further assessment.

As appropriate, informal measures and techniques will be used to explore the particular skills that appear to be areas of weakness for David. For example, if problem solving seems to need strengthening, the team may conduct a clinical math interview, observing and talking with David as he verbalizes his steps in solving a quantitative problem. Or if David's knowledge of number facts is a concern, the team may devise or select an informal inventory, criterion-referenced test, or curriculum-based measure to evaluate his command of specific addition, subtraction, multiplication, or division facts. David's individualized program in mathematics will be based on the results of these assessments.

To gather more information about David's skills across several areas of mathematics, Mr. Block, the special education resource teacher, administers the *KeyMath–3*. David's total test performance is within the standard score range of 75 to 81, which indicates overall below-average performance. His Operations and Applications skills are significantly lower than his Basic Concepts skills. David shows relative strengths in Numeration, Geometry, and Measurement. The areas in which David earns his lowest scores are Problem Solving and Multiplication and Division. Based on these results, the team decides to concentrate its efforts on assessing David's problem-solving and computation skills.

Next, portions of the *BRIGANCE® Comprehensive Inventory of Basic Skills–II* are administered to pinpoint David's computational difficulties. David shows mastery of addition and subtraction number facts but is less successful with multiplication and division facts; the majority of David's errors occur on problems involving multiples of 6, 7, 8, and 9. In basic operations with whole numbers, David consistently has difficulty with problems that require regrouping. In addition and multiplication, he often fails to carry and instead writes the entire number as part of the answer. When multiplying two multi-digit numbers, David uses the same strategy, and he does not cross-multiply; for example.

$$
\begin{array}{r}
25 \\
\times 34 \\
\hline
620
\end{array}
$$

In this problem, David multiplies 4×5 and writes the answer as 20. He then moves to the tens column and multiplies 3×2. In subtraction, he sometimes subtracts the smaller number from the larger, disregarding which is the minuend and which is the subtrahend. In division, he refuses to attempt problems that require regrouping, saying, "I can't do ones like this."

To assess David's skills in solving story problems, the team asks Ms. Coolidge, David's math teacher, to provide several samples of David's work. All of the papers provided to the assessment team had been graded *F*. However, most of David's errors were due to his failure to attempt all problems. On one assignment, for example, David solved the first two problems correctly and made a minor computational error on the third; he did not attempt the remaining seven problems, so his score on this paper was 20 percent.

The team uses clinical interviewing techniques to explore David's problem-solving skills. He is given 10 story problems and instructed to "think out loud" when solving them. He reads the problems accurately and is able to explain what operations are required. With simpler problems, David can identify the numbers to be used in computation and write the computational problem correctly. However, David's strategy is to include all of the numbers that the problem provides. With more difficult problems that contain extraneous information, this strategy is not successful. David also has difficulty carrying out the calculations. He works slowly, sometimes making hatch marks on his paper to help him figure out number facts, and 7 of his 10 solutions are incorrect. David says that he likes "the thinking part of these problems, but not the math part."

After a careful analysis of these results, the assessment team is ready to describe David's current levels of mathematics performance. Their conclusions are as follows:

- At present, David's overall level of achievement in mathematics is within the below-average range of performance, as measured by the *KeyMath–3*. His greatest areas of weakness are mathematics operations and applications.
- David shows adequate knowledge of addition and subtraction facts. He has not yet mastered multiplication and division facts and has particular difficulty with multiples of 6, 7, 8, and 9. David has some knowledge of regrouping procedures but fails to use them consistently. In addition and multiplication, David does not always carry, and in subtraction, he sometimes subtracts the smaller number from the larger. David does not appear to know how to solve division problems that require regrouping or how to cross-multiply in multidigit multiplication.

- David receives failing grades on story problem assignments because he completes only a few problems.

- David is able to determine how to solve simple story problems, but many of his answers are incorrect because of computational errors.

SUMMARY

- In special education, mathematics skills are investigated at the start of assessment to determine the student's eligibility for special education services. When mathematics is identified as an area of need for a particular student, assessment continues in order to gather the detailed information necessary for program planning. Precise information about the student's current status in mathematics is the basis for establishing the instructional goals of the IEP. Assessment continues throughout the student's special education program.

- *Geometry* and *Measurement* are two subtests of *KeyMath–3*. The *Geometry* subtest includes questions about spatial relations, likenesses and differences, pattern development, two- and three-dimensional shapes, and coordinate geometry. In the *Measurement* subtest, the student answers questions relating to common units of measurement (both standard and metric) and the use of measurement tools such as rulers and thermometers.

- The TOMA-3 and the CMAT are two other formal measures of mathematics assessment. The *TOMA–3* is an interesting test because it attempts to extend mathematics assessment beyond the traditional skills of computation and problem solving. According to the *TOMA–3* manual, attitudinal, linguistic and previous knowledge of mathematics are also essential components of mathematical abilities. The *CMAT* is a newer measure that provides information about a broad range of mathematics skills. The core subtests address traditional computational and problem-solving skills. In addition, supplemental subtests provide information about higher mathematics skills and about the use of mathematics in daily life.

- *Monitoring Basic Skills Progress (MBSP)* is a collection of commercially available curriculum-based measures that include computer components. Two of its four parts assess mathematics skills: Basic

Math Computation (2nd ed.) (Fuchs, Hamlett, & Fuchs, 1998) and Basic Math Concepts and Applications (Fuchs, Hamlett, & Fuchs, 1999). The Computation portion of *MBSP* is designed for students in grades 1–6 and the Concepts and Applications portion for those in grades 2–6.

- Error analysis and clinical interviews are two examples of other informal assessments. The first step in conducting an error analysis is to gather a sample of the student's work. The math sample is then graded to identify the errors that the student has made. Whereas error analysis techniques focus on students' written products, clinical interviews elicit information about the procedures that students use to arrive at those products. Clinical interviews are the most appropriate technique for process analysis.

- Two examples of considerations within the context of the classroom are instructional environment and physical environment in the classroom. Assessment of the instructional environment must take into account the mathematics curriculum and the instructional methods and materials used to implement that curriculum. In the elementary grades, basal textbook series are often the foundation of the mathematics program. The physical environment of the classroom can also affect students' mathematics performance. The environment should be physically comfortable with lighting, temperature, and ventilation at appropriate levels, and classroom space should be arranged to facilitate mathematics instruction.

- Measures of mathematics performance vary in the range of skills they assess. Some are quite comprehensive, whereas others are more limited. Another area of difference is the thoroughness with which skills are assessed. Comprehensive tests such as the *KeyMath–* and the *SDMT* sample several skills and skills levels but provide only a few representative test items in each area.

Tyler Olson/Fotolia

15

Written and Oral Language

LEARNING OUTCOMES

After reading this chapter, you will be able to:

- Identify and discuss the purpose regarding considerations in assessment of written language.

- Name and describe a common standardized test in the discussion of strategies for assessing spelling.

- Identify and describe two strategies for assessing handwriting.

- Name and discuss two strategies for assessing composition.

- Discuss interpersonal environment within the context of the classroom.

- Identify and describe a Brigance Assessment in answering the assessment questions.

- Describe the purpose in the context of special education regarding considerations in assessment of oral language.

- Name and describe an example of a comprehensive measure of oral language.

- Describe standardized testing as a strategy for assessing articulation.

- Identify and discuss an example of a formal strategy for assessing morphology and syntax.

- Name and describe a formal strategy for assessing semantics and pragmatics.
- Discuss the purpose of special education oral language assessment in answering the assessment questions.

KEY TERMS

written language
language
expressive language
receptive language
composition
oral language
phonology

articulation
morphology
syntax
semantics
pragmatics
language samples

Written language is a basic method of communication in today's society. Adults are expected to be literate, and literacy includes not only the ability to read but also the ability to write. As part of the routine of daily life, adults write shopping lists, business letters, e-mail and texts, and notes to friends. They complete job applications, fill out tax forms, and write checks. Writing skills are a requirement for most occupations, and some jobs demand a high degree of proficiency in written language.

Writing is also an important skill during the school years, and its acquisition is stressed in the elementary grades. In the upper elementary grades and in middle and high school, students are expected to be able to express their thoughts in writing. This poses grave difficulties for individuals with poor written expression skills, and many students with special needs fall within this group.

In special education assessment, students' written language skills are studied to gather information for instructional planning. The broad question that guides this portion of the assessment process is, *What are the student's educational needs?* When written language is the concern, this general question is refined into two specific questions: *What is the student's current level of achievement in written language? What are the student's strengths and weaknesses in the various skill areas of written language?*

CONSIDERATIONS IN ASSESSMENT OF WRITTEN LANGUAGE

Written language skills are critical for successful school performance. Students with poor written language are at a decided disadvantage in attempting to meet the academic demands of the general education curriculum. Because many students with mild disabilities experience difficulty in this area, written language is often one of the areas of focus in special education assessment.

Purposes

Written language skills are assessed for many different reasons. Writing is considered an important part of the general education curriculum; teachers routinely monitor their students' progress in the acquisition of spelling, handwriting, and composition skills. Spelling and some aspects of composition are often included among the skills assessed by group achievement tests, and proficiency in written language is frequently one of the competency areas evaluated for grade advancement and high school graduation.

In special education, written language skills may be investigated at the start of assessment to determine the student's eligibility for special education services. In many cases, however, assessment is limited to only one aspect of written language—spelling—because that is the language skill emphasized on the traditional individual tests of achievement used in special education. Further investigation is needed if there is reason to believe that other aspects of written language may be areas of educational need.

Several measures of written language are currently available to assist the assessment team in identifying academic skill deficiencies. Norm-referenced tests help to pinpoint specific areas of difficulty, and informal techniques and procedures are then used to gather the detailed information needed for planning the educational program. The student's current levels of performance are described, and specific strengths and weaknesses are noted in preparation for establishing the instructional goals and objectives of the individualized program plan.

Assessment continues when special education services begin, but it changes somewhat in character. The purpose becomes continuous monitoring of the student's educational progress. On an ongoing basis, special educators monitor the student's acquisition of targeted skills, and at least once each year, the educational plan is reviewed and modified as necessary.

Skill Areas

When considering the complex of skills and processes that contribute to proficiency in written language, it is important to understand the relationship between writing and other dimensions of language. **Language** is a communication system characterized by the use of symbols for the transmission of information. Language can be either spoken or written, and in both oral and written language there is an expressive and a receptive mode. In the **expressive** mode, the speaker or writer attempts to communicate ideas; in the **receptive** mode, the listener or reader attempts to comprehend the ideas expressed by the speaker or writer.

In the developmental sequence, oral language generally precedes written language. Most children begin to understand and use speech for communication within the first 3 years of life. Reading and writing skills come later, usually after children have completed some formal schooling. It also appears that receptive language skills emerge first: Young children learn to listen, then to speak; school-aged children learn to read, then to write.

In this developmental perspective, writing is the last skill to be acquired, and to some extent, it is dependent on the other language skills that underlie it. Poor oral language can inhibit the development of written language, just as lack of proficiency in reading can interfere with the acquisition of writing skills. However, students need not wait until they are proficient readers to begin writing; these skills can be developed simultaneously (Wells, 1981). As Westby (1992) points out, in the whole-language approach to instruction, the language arts are viewed as interdependent rather than separate skills that develop sequentially.

Writing is quite different from speech. Speech is essentially a social act (Litowitz, 1981). Both the sender and the receiver of the communication are present and are able to interact if a breakdown in communication occurs. Writing is a solitary act, and the writer is unable to exchange messages with the reader. In oral communication, information is transmitted in many ways, not only through spoken words. The facial expressions, gestures, posture, and body language of the participants all contribute to communication, as do the speaker's tone of voice and the loudness and speed with which the message is delivered. These methods of transmitting information are not available to the writer; the written symbols must stand alone.

In writing, the sender of the message must first conceptualize its content and then record the message so that it is available and comprehensible to the receiver. To do this, the writer must have some skill in handwriting (or typing or keyboarding) and in spelling. In recording the message, the writer uses a pencil or pen (or a keyboard) to form the smallest elements of written language, the individual letters, or graphemes. Letters are then combined into words, and the conventions of spelling determine how these letters are sequenced. As words are arranged into sentences, other conventions must be observed, including the rules for sentence formation, written syntax, and English usage. In addition, the writer must attend to the mechanical aspects of writing, factors that are not concerns in oral language: capitalization, punctuation, paragraphing, page format, and so forth.

In Smith's (1982) view, the act of writing imposes two distinct roles on the writer: author and secretary. The author's task is to generate ideas and compose the content of the writing. The secretary transcribes what the author composes. The secretary is concerned with the form of the writing and so attends to spelling, handwriting, capitalization, punctuation, and the like. Smith's analogy of the thinker and the scribe is a useful way of conceptualizing the writing process. It points out the range of skills required in writing (Nodine, 1983) and provides a framework for thinking about those skills.

Writing is a process that involves (or should involve) several steps (Graves, 1985), and each step places different demands on the writer. Polloway and Payne (1993) identify three stages of writing: prewriting, writing, and postwriting. In the prewriting stage, the author is the dominant participant. Influenced by past input, motivation, and the purpose for writing, the author plans the content. The writing stage requires both author and secretary. As the author composes, the secretary performs the physical act of writing, with attention to legibility, spelling accuracy, and other print conventions. The postwriting stage is the evaluation stage. While the secretary checks the accuracy of the mechanical aspects of the product, the author reviews the content: organization and sequence, logic and clarity, and the style in which it is written.

Mercer and Pullen (2005) divide the writing process into five stages. In the first, Prewriting, the student selects a topic, considers the purpose for writing and the audience, selects a format (e.g., story, essay, poem), and gathers and organizes ideas for writing. The second stage, Drafting, involves writing a first draft; here, the student pays most attention to content, not the mechanical aspects of writing. In stage three, Revising, the student reviews what he or she has written, asks other students for feedback, and revises the content of the composition. The fourth stage, Editing, involves correction of errors in spelling, capitalization, punctuation, and other mechanics. As needed, the student may confer with the teacher during the editing stage. In the last stage, Publishing, the student reads his or her work to an audience or publishes it as a classroom book or newspaper or magazine article.

Teaching students how to write clearly and cogently is a major goal of American education. Together with reading and mathematics, writing is considered one of the basic school skills. Despite this importance, past classroom practices often assigned writing only a minor role in the curriculum (Graves, 1978; Isaacson, 1988). Another concern was that when writing instruction did occur, it was directed more toward improving the performance of the writer-as-secretary than that of the writer-as-author. Writing instruction tended to emphasize mechanical aspects such as handwriting, spelling, and usage (Alexander, 1983).

In the past few years, important changes have occurred in how the teaching of writing is conceptualized (Moran, 1988; Nodine, 1983). One new direction is increased emphasis on writing as a thinking process and the stages that make up that process. Another is the whole-language approach to integrated language arts instruction, where writing is an essential component (Lerner, Cousin, & Richeck, 1992) In addition, writing is currently viewed as an appropriate means of expression in all areas of curriculum, including mathematics.

Concerns about the status of writing instruction in the United States have not abated. In 2003, the National Commission on Writing released its report titled *The Neglected "R": The Need for a Writing Revolution*. Among the recommendations of this report are increasing the emphasis placed on writing in the curriculum and increasing the amount of time students spend writing. In assessment, students should be required to write, not merely respond to multiple-choice test questions on the more mechanical aspects of written language.

Traditional measures of writing skills tend to focus on the skills of spelling, handwriting, and composition. Spelling is usually assessed with a paper-and-pencil task. The tester reads a word to the student, the word is read again in the context of a phrase or sentence, and the student responds by writing the word. Students can also be asked to spell orally, or spelling tasks can be designed in multiple-choice format. Multiple-choice tests usually present the student with several words, and the student selects the one that is correctly or incorrectly spelled.

Handwriting is generally assessed informally by comparing a sample of the student's writing with a set of performance criteria. An existing sample of the student's handwriting can be evaluated, or a new sample can be elicited. Depending on the age and skill level of the student, the sample may be written in manuscript (printing) or cursive handwriting.

Composition can be defined as the process by which a writer creates a written product. On measures of composition skills, students are typically presented with a writing task; the sample that the student produces is then subjected to analysis. Several aspects of the sample can be evaluated: content, vocabulary, organization, logic, writing style, productivity, creativity, and the more mechanical dimensions such as handwriting and spelling.

Traditional measures of composition are concerned with the product of writing, not the process. Their purpose is the evaluation of the student's responses, not the interaction between the student and the task throughout the series of stages involved in writing. To gather information about the process of writing and how the student approaches and completes the task of composition, informal assessment strategies are a necessity.

Another area that traditional measures often neglect is the ability to apply composition skills in daily life tasks. Writing is a common part of daily living. Students should be competent in performing tasks such as writing e-mails, notes and letters, memoranda, and shopping lists; completing job applications and tax forms; and the like.

Current Practices

Writing assessment receives less attention than either reading or mathematics assessment. There are fewer measures of writing skills available, and those that exist tend to emphasize the more mechanical aspects of the process. Although most survey tests of academic achievement contain some measure of written language, the skills most often assessed are spelling, usage, and grammar.

More directly related to instructional planning for students with disabilities are the assessment tools listed in Table 15–1. These include not only standardized tests but also criterion-referenced tests and other types of informal measures. The number of written language measures has increased dramatically in the past few years.

Some of the measures that are currently available are survey instruments. They are designed to assess a range of skills in order to identify the student's strengths and weaknesses. For instance, the *Test of Written Language–4* (Hammill & Larsen, 2009) assesses not only spelling and grammar, but also composition. Other measures concentrate on one specific skill area. The *Test of Written Spelling–5* (Larsen, Hammill, & Moats, 2013), for example, is limited to the investigation of spelling ability.

Informal strategies are a necessity in the assessment of writing skills because of the limited number of formal tools and the narrowness of their scope. Among the informal techniques most often used in writing assessment are observation, informal inventories, criterion-referenced tests, clinical interviews, work sample analysis procedures, and portfolio assessment. Informal strategies provide information not only about the student, but also about the characteristics of the classroom-learning environment.

This chapter is organized around three major skill areas in written language assessment: spelling,

TABLE 15–1
Measures of Written Language

Name (Author)	Ages or Grades	Type of Measure*	Group or Individual	SKILL AREA(S) ASSESSED		
				Spelling	Handwriting	Composition
BRIGANCE® Comprehensive Inventory of Basic Skills–II (Brigance, 2010)	Pre-K to grade 9	CRT	Varies	X	X	X
BRIGANCE® Inventory of Early Development–III (Brigance, 2013)	Birth to age 7	CRT	Individual		X	
BRIGANCE® Transition Skills Inventory (Brigance, 2010)	Middle and high school	CRT	Varies	X	X	X
Checklist of Written Expression (Poteet, 1980)	All	C	Individual	X	X	X
Denver Handwriting Analysis (Anderson, 1983)	Grades 3–8	II	Group or Individual		X	
Diagnostic Achievement Test in Spelling (Wittenberg, 1980)	Grades 2–10	NRT	Group		X	
Diagnostic Evaluation of Writing Skills (Weiner, 1980)	All	E	Individual	X	X	X
Diagnostic Spelling Test (Kottmeyer, 1970)	Grades 2–6	II	Group	X		
Hudson Education Skills Inventory (Hudson, Colson, Welch, Banikowski, & Mehring, 1989)	Grades K–12	CRT	Individual	X	X	X
Mather-Woodcock Group Writing Tests (Mather & Woodcock, 1997)	Grades 2–16	NRT	Group		X	X
Oral and Written Language Scales–II (Carrow-Woolfolk, 2011b)	Ages 3 to 21–11	NRT	Small Group or Individual	X		X
Picture Story Language Test (Myklebust, 1965)	Ages 7 to 17	NRT	Group or Individual		X	X
Spellmaster Assessment and Teaching System (Greenbaum, 1987)	Kindergarten to grade 10	II	Group	X		

continued

TABLE 15–1 *continued*
Measures of Written Language

Name (Author)	Ages or Grades	Type of Measure*	Group or Individual	SKILL AREA(S) ASSESSED		
				Spelling	Handwriting	Composition
Test of Adolescent and Adult Language–4 (Hammill, Brown, Larsen, & Wiederholt, 2007)	Ages 12–0 to 24–11	NRT	Group	X		X
Test of Early Written Language–3 (Hresko, Herron, Peak, & Hicks, 2012)	Ages 4–0 to 11–11	NRT	Individual	X	X	X
Test of Handwriting Skills–R (Milone, 2007)	Ages 5–0 to 18	NRT	Group or Individual		X	
Test of Legible Handwriting (Larsen & Hammill, 1989)	Ages 7–0 to 18–6; grades 2 to 12	NRT	Group or Individual		X	
Test of Written Expression (McGhee, Bryant, Larsen, & Rivera, 1995)	Ages 6–6 to 14–11	NRT	Group or Individual	X	X	
Test of Written Language–4 (Hammill & Larsen, 2009)	Ages 7–0 to 17–11	NRT	Group or Individual	X		X
Test of Written Spelling–5 (Larsen, Hammill, & Moats, 2013)	Ages 6–0 to 18–11	NRT	Group or Individual	X		
Woodcock Language Proficiency Battery–Revised (Woodcock, 1991)	Ages 3 to 80+	NRT	Individual	X		X
Word Identification and Spelling Test (Wilson & Felton, 2004)	Ages 7–0 to 18–11	NRT	Group or Individual	X		
Zaner-Bloser Evaluation Scales (n.d.)	Grades 1 to 6	R	Group		X	

*NRT = norm-referenced test, II = informal inventory, CRT = criterion-referenced test, C = checklist, E = error analysis procedure, and R = rating scale.

424

handwriting, and composition. Spelling is the first topic of discussion, and the section that follows describes the major formal and informal assessment strategies available for the study of special students' spelling skills. Techniques for assessing handwriting are described next, followed by procedures for evaluating proficiency in composition.

 Breakpoint Practice 15.1
Click here to check your understanding of norm-referenced, informal inventory, criterion-referenced, checklist, error analysis procedure, and rating scale measures of written language.

STRATEGIES FOR ASSESSING SPELLING

Spelling is an academic skill that is usually included on the individual achievement tests used in special education assessment to establish the presence of a school performance problem. However, it is important to recognize that broad-range achievement tests assess spelling skills in different ways. Many, like the *Wide Range Achievement Test–4* (Wilkinson & Robertson, 2006), use recall tasks in which the student is required to remember and then write the correct spelling of words. Others, like the *Peabody Individual Achievement Test—Revised/Normative Update* (Markwardt, 1998), employ recognition tasks in which the student must identify the correctly spelled word. Recognition tasks are essentially proofreading and are related to the editing stage of the writing process; recall tasks are related more to the writing stage. The *Woodcock-Johnson IV* (Schrank et al., 2014a) offers measures of both types of spelling skills in its Spelling and Editing subtests.

Broad-range achievement tests do not provide sufficient information for planning instructional programs in spelling. Thus, when a problem in spelling is indicated, further assessment must take place. The assessment team can select a norm-referenced test of spelling such as the *Test of Written Spelling–5*. In addition, a variety of informal techniques and procedures can be used to learn more about students' current spelling skills.

Test of Written Spelling–5

The *Test of Written Spelling–5 (TWS–5)* is a norm-referenced measure designed for students ages 6–0 to 18–11. Two forms of the *TWS–5* are available, Form A and Form B. Both are standard dictation tests. The tester reads a word to the student, reads the word in a sentence, and then reads the word again. The student responds by writing the word on the test answer sheet; no time limits are imposed. Each form contains 50 words (a compilation of words from the Predictable and Unpredictable subtests of earlier editions), and the manual provides suggested starting points by grade level. Guidelines for group administration of the *TWS–5* are also available in the manual.

The normative group included 1,634 students from 23 states. According to the *TWS–5* manual, the sample accounts for the U.S. school-age population in gender, urban–rural residence, race, geographic region, and ethnicity. No information is provided about the inclusion of students with disabilities in the norm groups. The reliability of the *TWS–5* is satisfactory (McCrimmon & Climie, 2011). Coefficients for internal consistency, alternative form, test-retest, and interrater reliability exceed .90. The manual presents evidence of adequate relationships between the *TWS–5* and results of group achievement tests and between the *TWS–5* and teachers' ratings of students' spelling skills. However, more information is needed about the relationship of the *TWS–5* to the individual measures of achievement typically used in special education.

Informal Techniques

Among the informal strategies that can provide information about spelling are work sample analysis, informal inventories, criterion-referenced tests, observation, and clinical interviews.

Work Sample Analysis

Spelling, like all written language skills, is well suited to work sample analysis because a permanent product is produced. Within every classroom, many types of spelling samples are available for analysis: students' essays, book reports, test

TEST OF WRITTEN SPELLING–5 (TWS–5)

S. C. Larsen, D. D. Hammill, & L. C. Moats (2013)

Type: Norm-referenced test

Major Content Areas: Spelling

Type of Administration: Individual or group

Administration Time: 20 minutes

Age/Grade Levels: Ages 6–0 to 18–11

Types of Scores: Standard score, percentile rank, age and grade equivalents

Technology: N/A

Typical Uses: Evaluation of students' spelling skills

Cautions: It is not known whether students with disabilities were included in the norm group. More information is needed about the relationship of the *TWS–5* to other individual tests of achievement used in special education assessment.

Publisher: PRO-ED (*www.proedinc.com*)

papers (including spelling tests), daily homework assignments, workbooks, and so forth. Error analysis procedures can be used to evaluate the spelling samples of older students who have achieved some proficiency. However, with younger students and others who are only beginning to acquire spelling skills, response analysis is the preferred technique.

Poplin (1983) points out that learning to spell is a developmental process, and young children go through a number of stages as they begin to acquire written language skills. Writing begins in the preschool years as young children observe and begin to imitate the act of writing. They practice with paper and pencil by drawing and scribbling, and they ask adults to write words for them so they can attempt to copy them. Soon children begin to write words and phrases on their own, using invented spellings. According to Poplin, spelling skills emerge in the following sequence:

(a) Only one to two consonants represent words or phrases.

(b) Most consonant sounds in words or phrases are represented, few or no vowels.

(c) Tense (long) vowels emerge without their silent counterparts; lax (short) vowels are missing.

(d) Lax vowels are represented by phonologically nearest tense vowel.

(e) Most consonants are present and correct—except possibly double consonants, consonant blends, consonant digraphs, final consonant blends, those associated with morphological endings (e.g., *ing, ed, er, tion,* and *sion*).

(f) Rules are overapplied to regular words (e.g., *goed*).

(g) Correct forms appear in a majority of instances. (p. 71)

These stages provide a framework for the work sample analysis of the spelling of beginning writers.

When students' skills mature to the extent that many of their written words are spelled correctly, error analysis becomes an appropriate procedure. Several systems for categorizing spelling errors have been devised. Edgington (1968), for example, includes additions, omissions, reversals, and phonetic spelling of nonphonetic words as errors.

The *Spellmaster Assessment and Teaching System* (Greenbaum, 1987) contains a series of inventories to assess students' skill in spelling regular words, irregular words, and homophones. There are eight levels of the Regular Word Test, corresponding roughly to grades kindergarten to 10, and the score sheet for each level is designed for analysis of the student's responses. Across the top are the spelling skills that are assessed on this level: beginning consonants, beginning blends, short vowels, and so on. The first spelling word, *lap*, is divided into three parts, and each letter appears under the appropriate heading. The tester circles the letter or letters where substitution errors occur; additions and omissions can also be noted on the score sheet. When all of the student's responses have been analyzed, a count is made of the number of errors in each category.

Others have suggested a simpler way to conceptualize errors in spelling: phonetic and nonphonetic misspellings (Howell & Kaplan, 1980; Mann, Suiter, & McClung, 1979). Phonetic misspellings take place when the student attempts, unsuccessfully, to use the rules of phonics to spell a word. Either the student applies the rules incorrectly, or the word does not adhere to those rules. For instance, a student might write *kat* instead of *cat.*

Nonphonetic spellings, in contrast, do not appear to be based on the application of phonics rules. Some nonphonetic spellings are close approximations of the correct sequence of letters. For example, the student may recall most of the appropriate letters correctly but forget one or two, add an extraneous letter, or jumble the sequence somewhat (e.g., *lenht* for *length*). In some cases, nonphonetic spellings bear little or no resemblance to the word in question (e.g., *ob* for *house*). Such attempts are usually considered random spellings.

Informal Inventories

Teachers may find it useful to design an informal inventory to learn more about students' current levels of performance. One strategy involves selecting representative words from the basal spelling series used in the school or classroom. A short list of words from the first-grade spelling textbook is assembled, a list from the second-grade text, and so on, depending on the student's skill level. Then the teacher dictates the lists to the student and asks him or her to write each word. Results provide a rough estimate of the student's status in relation to the skill demands of the classroom-spelling program.

Another strategy is to design an inventory around specific spelling skills. Mercer and Mercer (1998) provide an example designed to assess grades 2 and 3 spelling skills; it appears in Table 15–2. This is a diagnostic test because each item is intended to measure one particular aspect of spelling. Thus, skill in writing the letters that correspond to the short vowel sounds is assessed by the first five items. By evaluating the student's performance in terms of the specific spelling skills assessed, the teacher can determine which areas may be in need of further assessment with criterion-referenced tests and other procedures.

Criterion-Referenced Tests

These measures can help professionals identify which spelling skills have been mastered and which remain in need of instruction. Teachers can prepare their own criterion-referenced tests to measure progress toward curriculum objectives. For example, if spelling common words is an educational goal, the teacher could use the word list that appears in Figure 15–1 to construct a CRT. This list contains 250 words arranged in order of difficulty; each of the words included on the list is commonly found in children's writings. Criterion-referenced tests could also be designed to assess students' mastery of words that are often misspelled (spelling demons) or to evaluate progress in the classroom-spelling program.

There are also several published CRTs that offer tests of spelling. One example is the collection of tests by Brigance. The test for elementary students, the *BRIGANCE® Comprehensive Inventory of Basic Skills*–II (Brigance, 2010), features a Spelling Grade-Placement Test and measures of skill in spelling initial consonants, initial blends and digraphs, suffixes, and prefixes. These measures are also available on the secondary-level test, the *BRIGANCE® Transition Skills Inventory* (Brigance, 2010), testing functional writing skills.

Observation

Observations can help determine how the student approaches the task of spelling. The observation

TABLE 15–2
Diagnostic Spelling Test

SPELLING WORDS	SPELLING OBJECTIVES	SPELLING WORDS USED IN SENTENCES
1. man 2. Pit 3. dug 4. web 5. dot	short vowels and selected consonants	The *man* is big. The *pit* in the fruit was hard. We *dug* a hole. She saw the spider's *web*. Don't forget to *dot* the i.
6. mask 7. drum	words beginning and/or ending with consonant blends	On Halloween the child wore a *mask*. He beat the *drum* in the parade.
8. line 9. cake	consonant-vowel-consonant-silent *e*	Get in *line* for lunch. We had a birthday *cake*.
10. coat 11. rain	two vowels together	Put on your winter *coat*. Take an umbrella in the *rain*.
12. Ice 13. large	variant consonant sounds for *c* and *g*	*Ice* is frozen water. This is a *large* room.
14. mouth 15. town 16. boy	words containing vowel diphthongs	Open your *mouth* to brush your teeth. We went to *town* to shop. The *boy* and girl went to school.
17. bikes 18. glasses	Plurals	The children got new *bikes* for their birthdays. Get some *glasses* for the drinks.
19. happy 20. monkey	short *i* sounds of *y*	John is very *happy* now. We saw a *monkey* at the zoo.
21. war 22. dirt	words with *r*-controlled vowels	Bombs were used in the *war*. The pigs were in the *dirt*.
23. foot 24. moon	two sounds of *oo*	Put the shoe on your *foot*. Three men walked on the *moon*.
25. light 26. knife	words with silent letters	Turn on the *light* so we can see. Get a fork and *knife*.
27. pill	final consonant doubled	The doctor gave me a *pill*.
28. Bat 29. batter	consonant-vowel-consonant pattern in which final consonant is doubled before adding ending	The baseball player got a new *bat*. The *batter* hit a home run.
30. didn't 31. isn't	Contractions	They *didn't* want to come. It *isn't* raining today.
32. take 33. taking	final *e* is dropped before adding suffix	Please *take* off your coat. He is *taking* me to the show.
34. any 35. could	nonphonetic spellings	I did not have *any* lunch. Maybe you *could* go on a trip.
36. ate 37. eight 38. blue 39. blew	Homonyms	Mary *ate* breakfast at home. There are *eight* children in the family. The sky is *blue*. The wind *blew* away the hat.
40. baseball	compound words	They played *baseball* outside.

Note: From *Teaching Students with Learning Problems*, 5th ed., by Mercer/Mercer, © 1998. Reprinted by permission of Prentice Hall, Inc., Upper Saddle River, NJ.

Fry Words – The First Hundred

List 1	List 2	List 3	List 4
the	or	will	number
of	one	up	no
and	had	other	way
a	by	about	could
to	words	out	people
in	but	many	my
is	not	then	than
you	what	them	first
that	all	these	water
it	were	so	been
he	we	some	called
was	when	her	who
for	your	would	am
on	can	make	its
are	said	like	now
as	there	him	find
with	use	into	long
his	an	time	down
they	each	has	day
I	which	look	did
at	she	two	get
be	do	more	come
this	how	write	made
have	their	go	may
from	if	see	part

FIGURE 15–1
Fry's First 100 Words
Source: Fry, E. (2000). *1000 instant words.* Westminster, CA: Teacher Created Resources. Worksheet Design Copyright © 2013 K12reader.com. All Rights Reserved.

should be scheduled during a time when the student will be writing an essay or engaging in any other type of activity that requires spelling. The observer must be quite near the student to see exactly how the student proceeds. Of special interest are any strategies the student employs when he or she is unsure of the spelling of a word.

In the elementary grades where spelling is taught directly, students can also be observed as they attempt to learn new spelling words. The observer should watch for the ways that the student attacks or fails to attack the memorization task. Does the student open the spelling book and simply stare at the words? Or is there some indication that the student is actively rehearsing the new words? For example, does he or she write the words? Say the letters of each word aloud or subvocally? Look at a word, cover it, and then attempt to write it?

Clinical Interviews

Clinical interviews can take place while students are writing, but they may interrupt the students' thought processes and distract them from the task at hand. Because of this danger, it is probably best to simply observe until students have finished writing. Then they can be questioned about the ways they coped with the spelling demands of the writing task. Some of the questions that can be asked are as follows:

- When you're writing a sentence or a paragraph and you write down a word, how do you tell if you've spelled the word correctly?
- When you're not sure how to spell a word, what do you do?
  Do you guess at the spelling?
  Try to sound the word out?
  Write two or three possible spellings and then pick the one you think is right?
  Ask the teacher or a friend how to spell the word?
  Look the word up in a dictionary?
- Choose another word, one that you can spell?
- After you've finished writing, do you read and check what you've written?
- In checking your writing, what do you do if you find a word that you think may be spelled incorrectly?

Students can then be asked to look over the writing they have just completed and mark any words that they think might be incorrectly spelled. This provides some information about proofreading skills and the student's ability to spot errors in spelling.

ENHANCEDetext
Video Example 15.1
Watch this video to find out more about an example of writing assessment in a third-grade classroom.

STRATEGIES FOR ASSESSING HANDWRITING

Informal strategies such as rating scales, observation, error analysis, inventories, and criterion-referenced tests are used to assess the student's current proficiency in handwriting. Norm-referenced measures such as the *Test of Legible Handwriting* (Larsen & Hammill, 1989) are also available. With younger children, manuscript handwriting (i.e., printing) is the concern. With older students, cursive handwriting is analyzed.

Rating Scales

Rating scales provide a method for judging whether a student's handwriting is poor enough to be considered an area of educational need. However, rating scales rely on the judgment of the professional who evaluates the student's handwriting sample and, thus, their results can be somewhat subjective. Ratings can be made more objective if professionals are furnished with standards for judging students' handwriting, such as those described in the *Zaner-Bloser*.

Evaluation Scales

The *Zaner-Bloser Evaluation Scales* (n.d.) provide teachers with a standard method of collecting and

Example 3—**Average for Grade Three**

This is my best cursive handwriting. Can you read it?

CHECKPOINT

	Satisfactory	Needs Improvement
Shape	✓	
Slant	✓	
Spacing		✓
Size	✓	
Smoothness		✓

FIGURE 15–2

Writing Sample from the *Zaner-Bloser Evaluation Scales,* Grade 3

Note: From *Zaner-Bloser Evaluation Scales* © Zaner-Bloser, Inc. Used with permission from Zaner-Bloser, Inc. All rights reserved.

rating handwriting samples. A separate scale is available for grades 1–6; manuscript writing is evaluated on the scales for grades 1 and 2, and cursive writing on the scales for grades 3–6. A cursive scale for grade 2 is also available. Each scale contains a handwriting selection for the students to copy.

Five factors are considered in judging handwriting skill: shape, slant, spacing, size, and smoothness. To help the teacher evaluate these factors, the *Zaner-Bloser* provides examples of Excellent, Good, Average, Fair, and Poor handwriting at each of the grade levels. Figure 15–2 shows two examples from the Grade 3 Scale—Average and Poor.

The teacher rates the student's handwriting in relation to the five factors listed in the figure. Each is judged as either Satisfactory or Needs Improvement. If all of the five factors are judged satisfactory, the student's handwriting is considered Excellent. If four of the five factors are judged satisfactory, the sample is considered Good. Three satisfactory areas result in a rating of Average, two satisfactory areas in a rating of Fair, and one satisfactory area in a rating of Poor.

The *Zaner-Bloser Evaluation Scales* are most useful for providing an estimate of the overall quality of the student's handwriting. However, in interpreting results, it is necessary to remember that these scales are not designed to assess a typical sample of the student's handwriting. Instead, the student copies a selection, first practicing it and then attempting to write it in his or her best handwriting. Having the opportunity to practice may result in an improvement from the student's usual performance. On the other hand, fatigue may interfere with the second attempt. It is also important to note that the *Zaner-Bloser* is untimed. The quality of the student's handwriting may change dramatically when speed becomes a necessity.

Observation and Error Analysis

Both observations and error analyses can provide information about how students approach handwriting. A student can be observed during an activity that requires writing, and then error analysis procedures can be applied to the writing sample that the student produces. In implementing these informal assessment techniques, it is important to consider not only the legibility of the student's writing, but also speed. A student must be able to write quickly if handwriting is to become a useful tool for communication.

Speed can be studied in several ways. For example, the teacher can ask the student to copy a passage of 100 words (or some other known length) and time how long it takes the student to complete this task. Or the teacher can time the student during a writing activity and then count the number of letters or words the student produced. These data can then be transformed into a rate measure, such as the average number of letters the student writes per minute.

In classroom observations of handwriting performance, the professional should take note of several student behaviors:

- How is the student seated? Are the desk and chair of appropriate size? Is the student sitting upright with both feet on the floor under the desk?
- In what position is the student's paper? Is he or she holding it so it will not slip?

- How does the student hold the writing implement? Does the student grip the pen or pencil too tightly?
- Is the student writing with a pen or a pencil? Is it an appropriate size?
- On what type of paper is the student writing? What size is it? Is it lined? Are there guidelines between the lines? Are there margins?
- Does the student write with the right or left hand?
- When the student writes, does he or she move the entire hand smoothly across the page or move just the fingers in an attempt to draw each letter?
- Does the student press down when writing? Does he or she exert a great deal of pressure on the paper? If writing with a pencil, does the student break pencil points frequently?
- How often does the student erase or cross out mistakes?

When students are copying from the board or from a text or worksheet on the desk, they may make errors because they are unable to see the model clearly. If this occurs, it is important to determine if vision problems are a factor.

Any writing sample produced by the student can be used for error analysis, and daily classroom assignments are likely to provide the most typical sample of a student's handwriting. However, if written assignments require spelling and other language skills, poor handwriting may be the result of an attempt to compensate for poor skills in other areas. For instance, if a student is unsure whether to write *receive* or *recieve,* he or she may write the letters indistinctly, placing the dot for the *i* in the center between the two letters. Because such tactics interfere with the evaluation of handwriting, the teacher may wish to consider obtaining at least one writing sample in which the student copies the material.

Several systems of categorizing handwriting errors have been proposed. For example, Wiederholt, Hammill, and Brown (1978) suggest that the teacher examine the following features of students' manuscript writing:

1. Position of hand, arm, body, and/or paper
2. Size of letters: too small, large, etc.
3. Proportion of one letter or word to another

4. Quality of the pencil line: too heavy, light, variable, etc.
5. Slant: too much or irregular
6. Letter formation: poor circles or straight lines, lines disconnected, etc.
7. Letter alignment: off the line, etc.
8. Spacing: letters or words crowded or too scattered
9. Speed: too fast or too slow (p. 183)

Howell and Kaplan (1980) add that in analyzing cursive handwriting, teachers should take note of alignment, letter size, spacing, letter-form, and spatial orientation.

Inventories and Criterion-Referenced Tests

Teachers can design informal inventories to gain general information about students' handwriting abilities. An inventory assessing both manuscript and cursive writing skills appeared in Chapter 6 on classroom assessment. That chapter also presented a task analysis of the lowercase manuscript alphabet (Affleck, Lowenbraun, & Archer, 1980) in which letters were divided into several clusters based on difficulty (e.g., straight line letters, straight line and slant letters, and so forth). That analysis and one of cursive letters by Graham and Miller (1980) provide a framework for developing informal inventories of basic handwriting skills. According to Graham and Miller, the cursive alphabet can be divided into the following clusters based on how the letters are formed:

Lowercase Letters	*Uppercase Letters*
i, u, w, t, r, s	C, A, E
n, m, v, x	N, M, P, R, B, D, U, V, W,
e, 1, b, h, k, f	K, H, X
c, a, g, d, q	T, F, Q, Z, L
o, p, j	S, G
y, z	O, I, J, Y

The *Denver Handwriting Analysis* (Anderson, 1983) is a published inventory that assesses several cursive writing skills. It is designed for students in grades 3–8, but it can be used with other ages if cursive handwriting is a concern.

The skills sampled include near-point and far-point copying, writing the cursive alphabet from memory, and writing the cursive equivalent of manuscript letters.

Criterion-referenced tests can also provide information about students' current handwriting skills. For example, the measures by Brigance (1981, 1999, 2004, 2010, 2013) offer several tests of handwriting. Manuscript writing is assessed on the *BRIGANCE*® *Inventory of Early Development–III* and the *BRIGANCE*® *Comprehensive Inventory of Basic Skills–II*, and cursive writing is assessed on the basic skills measure as well as the *BRIGANCE*® *Transition Skills Inventory*. In addition, the essential skills battery includes measures of daily life handwriting tasks such as Addresses Envelope, Letter Writing, and Simple Application for Employment.

Test of Legible Handwriting

The *Test of Legible Handwriting (TOLH)* is a norm-referenced measure for students ages 7–0 to 18–6. It is an interesting test because the evaluation criteria it provides can be used to judge several types of handwriting samples. Possibilities include classroom work samples already produced by students and the story students write as part of the *Test of Written Language*. The *TOLH* also provides prompts for eliciting handwriting samples: picture prompts for story writing and verbal prompts for writing a biographical sketch and a letter. The picture prompts are the same as those used in the *Test of Written Language*. After the tester reads directions for the writing task, students are allowed 15 minutes to produce a sample.

Handwriting is scored holistically on the *TOLH*. The major criterion is legibility, and the tester makes a judgment by comparing the student's handwriting to models in the manual's scoring guides. Three scoring guides are available—one for manuscript writing, one for right slant or perpendicular cursive writing, and one for left slant cursive handwriting.

The raw score for each handwriting sample is converted to a standard score and percentile rank. Standard scores are distributed with a mean of 10 and a standard deviation of 3. When standard

---

TEST OF LEGIBLE HANDWRITING (TOLH)

S. C. Larsen & D. D. Hammill (1989)

Type: Norm-referenced test

Major Content Areas: Manuscript or cursive handwriting

Type of Administration: Individual or group

Administration Time: 20 minutes

Age/Grade Levels: Ages 7–0 to 18–6, grades 2–12

Types of Scores: Standard scores and percentiles for each writing sample; overall Legibility Quotient

Computer Aids: N/A

Typical Uses: Evaluation of students' ability to write legibly

Cautions: More information is needed about interrater reliability.

Publisher: PRO-ED (*www.proedinc.com*)

---

scores are available for at least two handwriting samples, a Legibility Quotient can be determined. The LQ is a standard score with a mean of 100 and a standard deviation of 15. In addition to rating each sample holistically, testers can also complete the Analysis of Handwriting Errors checklist on the back of the *TOLH* Profile/Record Form. Two checklists are available, one for cursive and one for manuscript, and each addresses letter formation (capital and lowercase), spatial relationships, and handwriting rate.

The *TOLH* was standardized in 1987 as part of the norming study for the second edition of the *Test of Written Language*. The *TOLH* standardization sample of 1,723 students from 19 states appears to approximate the national population in sex, urban–rural residence, race, and geographic region. Internal consistency, interscorer reliability, and test-retest reliability are all adequate. Interscorer reliability is particularly important with the *TOLH* because of its use of holistic scoring. A coefficient of .95 was reported in the manual for this type of reliability; however, the study included only two raters. The validity of the *TOLH* is supported by a strong correlation between *TOLH* results and teachers' independent ratings of handwriting samples ($r = .92$).

The *TOLH* is "the first nationally standardized measure of handwriting readability" (Bailet, 1991,

p. 178). As such, it is an important addition to the collection of measures available to professionals who are interested in the assessment of handwriting. Although more evidence supporting its interrater reliability is needed, the preliminary data reported in the *TOLH* manual are encouraging.

> **Breakpoint Practice 15.2**
> *Click here to check your understanding of measures of handwriting skills.*

STRATEGIES FOR ASSESSING COMPOSITION

A student's ability to plan, write, and revise a piece of original writing can be assessed formally with the aid of standardized tests or informally with techniques such as rating scales, work sample analysis, criterion-referenced tests, observation, clinical interviews, and portfolios. Most of these assessment strategies focus on the written product the student creates. Only the informal procedures of observation and clinical interviewing allow the professional to assess the process the student engages in to produce a sample of writing.

The primary concern in the assessment of composition skills is the content of the student's writing, not its form. Areas of interest include the

---

TEST OF WRITTEN LANGUAGE–4 (TOWL–4)

D. D. Hammill & S. C. Larsen (2009)

Type: Norm-referenced test

Major Content Areas: Conventional, linguistic, and conceptual components of written language

Type of Administration: Individual or group

Administration Time: 60 to 90 minutes

Age/Grade Levels: Ages 9–0 to 17–11

Types of Scores: Subtest standard scores, percentile ranks, and age and grade equivalents; composite standard scores called quotients for Contrived Writing, Spontaneous Writing, and Overall Writing

Technology Aids: *PRO-SCORE System*

Typical Uses: Identification of strengths and weaknesses in several of the written language skills involved in composition

Cautions: The tester must be thoroughly familiar with the scoring standards for evaluating both the writing sample and subtest responses. The test is lengthy. More information is needed about the relationship of the *TOWL–4* to other academic achievement measures.

Publisher: PRO-ED (*www.proedinc.com*)

---

organization of the writing, the vocabulary used to express ideas, the style in which the composition is written, and the originality of the ideas expressed. However, the mechanical aspects of writing also play a role, albeit a secondary one, because a composition's intelligibility can be impaired by mechanical errors. Thus, some measures of composition take into account areas such as syntax, usage, capitalization, punctuation, and even spelling and handwriting.

The sections that follow introduce a wide range of strategies for the assessment of composition skills. First to be discussed is the *Test of Written Language–4*, a formal measure that evaluates several of the important skills in writing. Next, other formal tests are introduced, and finally, a variety of informal techniques are described. Because few formal tests are available, informal strategies play a major role in the assessment of composition skills.

Test of Written Language–4

According to its manual, the *Test of Written Language–4 (TOWL–4)* is a test of comprehensive written expression. The fourth edition of this test

offers two forms. Each form is composed of seven subtests. Writing is elicited through both contrived (subtests 1–5) and spontaneous formats (subtests 6–7). Spontaneous writing is assessed by means of a writing sample that the student produces. The student is shown a picture and directed to write an original story about it. Contrived formats are artificial ways of eliciting written language responses, and they typically focus on one discrete element of language such as written grammar or spelling. Contrived methods include such devices as dictation spelling tests, proofreading tasks, and multiple-choice items.

There are seven subtests on the *TOWL–4*. Subtests 1 through 5 are contrived, and subtests 6 and 7 are spontaneous.

Contrived Format Subtests

- *Vocabulary.* A list of words appears in the Student Response Booklet. The student reads each word, and then writes a meaningful sentence that includes the word.
- *Spelling.* The tester dictates sentences, and the student writes them with attention to spelling (and to capitalization and punctuation).

- *Logical Sentences.* The student reads sentences that contain errors in logic (e.g., "Sally is as sweet as salt") and must rewrite each sentence so that it makes sense.
- *Sentence Combining.* The student reads two sentences and must write one new sentence that combines the original sentences.

Spontaneous Format Subtests

- *Contextual Conventions.* The student's writing sample is evaluated, and points are assigned for demonstration of specific capitalization and punctuation rules and for correct spelling.
- *Story Construction.* The content of the student's writing sample is evaluated in terms of its plot, sequence, characters, theme, and so on.

The *TOWL–4* was standardized in 2005 with 2,505 students from 17 states. The final sample approximates the national population in gender, urban–rural residence, race, geographic region, ethnicity, family income, and educational attainment of parents. Students with disabilities were included if they attended general education classes.

The reliability of *TOWL–4* global scores is well established. Internal consistency, alternate form, test-retest, and interscorer reliability coefficients all approximate or exceed .80 for the three composite scores. Subtest reliabilities are somewhat lower, as would be expected, although they are satisfactory. The concurrent validity of the *TOWL–4* was studied by examining its relationship to the WISC-4 and CTONI. Correlations were high to average in strength. The TOWL–4 was also compared to the WLOS, ROS, and TORC–4. A range or correlations was noted.

According to the manual, formal training in assessment is needed to administer and interpret results of the *TOWL–4*. For the first five subtests there is no basal, and testing continues until a ceiling of three consecutive errors is reached. The manual also provides guidelines for group administration of *TOWL–4* subtests.

TOWL–4 results include four types of scores for each subtest: percentile ranks, standard scores (mean = 10, standard deviation = 3), age equivalents, and grade equivalents. Three composite scores are also available: the Contrived Writing Quotient, the Spontaneous Writing Quotient, and the Overall Writing Quotient. Quotients are standard scores with a mean of 100 and a standard deviation of 15.

Results can be plotted on a profile form. The *TOWL–4* is a useful test because it includes methods for evaluation of several important components of written language. To do this, the *TOWL–4* departs from the typical format of standardized tests. While remaining within a norm-referenced framework, it incorporates one of the most valuable informal strategies for studying composition—the writing sample. Results are best used to identify strengths and weaknesses and to provide direction for further assessment.

Other Formal Measures

The *Test of Written Language–4* is only one of the formal measures that address comprehension skills. The *Picture Story Language Test* (Myklebust, 1965) is one of the earliest measures and is rarely used today. More recent measures include broad-based tests that assess a range of oral and written language skills and tests that focus only on written language. Broad-based tests include the *Test of Adolescent and Adult Language–4* (Hammill et al., 2007), the *Oral and Written Language Scale–II* (Carrow-Woolfolk, 2011b), and the *Woodcock Language Proficiency Battery–Revised* (Woodcock, 1991). Examples of measures that assess only writing skills are the *Mather-Woodcock Group Writing Tests* (Mather & Woodcock, 1997) and the *Test of Written Expression* (McGhee, Bryant, Larsen, & Rivera, 1995).

Test of Adolescent and Adult Language–4

The *Test of Adolescent and Adult Language (TOAL)–4)* is a norm-referenced measure developed for use with students ages 12–0 to 24–11. It assesses both spoken and written language, and professionals can also obtain an overall general language score.

Three of the six *TOAL–4* subtests assess written language:

- *Word Similarities.* The student reads a word and then must write a synonym for that word.
- *Sentence Combining.* Two sentences are presented. The student must write a new sentence that combines the meanings of the original sentences.

- *Orthographic Usage.* The student is shown sentences with capitalization, punctuation, and spelling errors and must find and correct each error.

Subtest results are expressed as percentile ranks and scaled scores. The student's performance on the three writing subtests is summarized by the Written Language Composite Index, a standard score with a mean of 100 and a standard deviation of 15. The *TOAL–4* manual provides guidelines for determining whether composite scores are significantly different. There must be at least an 8-point discrepancy between Index scores for statistical significance and at least 26 points for clinical usefulness.

The *TOAL–4* is one of the few tests of language designed specifically for older students. It is comprehensive in that it makes use of both types of receptive language, listening and reading, to assess both types of expressive language, speaking and writing. However, in the area of written language, students write only sentences, not passages of connected text. Results of the *TOAL–4* are most useful for identification of broad areas of educational need. As with most norm-referenced measures, further assessment is necessary before instructional planning can begin.

Oral and Written Language Scales

This measure is composed of four scales: two that assess oral language (Listening Comprehension and Oral Expression), one that assesses written language (Written Expression) and one that assesses reading (Reading Comprehension). The Written Expression Scale is designed for students ages 5 through 21–11. Items related to three skill areas are included: Conventions (e.g., letter formation, spelling, punctuation, and capitalization), Linguistics (e.g., verb forms, sentences), and Content (e.g., coherence, supporting ideas). On all items, the tester reads directions and the student answers by writing in the Response Booklet. Items for young students require writing first and last names, writing letters, and copying words and sentences; questions for older students require the composition of sentences and short paragraphs. This measure can be administered individually or to small groups of students.

Although this scale assesses several different written language skills, only total scale scores are available. The Written Expression Scale raw score can be converted to an age- or grade-based standard score (distributed with a mean of 100 and a standard deviation of 15), percentile rank, age equivalent, and grade equivalent. Results on the Written Expression Scale can be compared with those on the other scales and with composites. Like other broad-based measures, the Written Expression Scale helps to identify areas of need. However, the information it provides is not specific enough for planning the instructional program.

Mather-Woodcock Group Writing Tests

The *Group Writing Tests (GWT)* are an adaptation of the *Woodcock-Johnson Psycho-Educational Battery—Revised* (Woodcock & Johnson, 1989). According to the *GWT* manual, "although the *Group Writing Tests* are similar in format to the tests in the *WJ–R,* all items for the *GWT* are new" (p. 1). Unlike the *Woodcock-Johnson–R,* the *GWT* is designed for group administration. Three levels are available: Basic (grades 2–3), Intermediate (grades 4–7), and Advanced (grades 8–16 and adults). Each level contains four subtests: Dictation Spelling, Editing, Writing Samples, and Writing Fluency. The Editing subtest is equivalent to the Proofing subtest in the Language Proficiency Battery; Dictation Spelling is similar to Dictation, except that only spelling skills are assessed. The other two subtests, Writing Samples and Writing Fluency, are identical in format to their counterparts on the Language Proficiency Battery. The *GWT* also includes a rating scale, the Writing Evaluation Scale, which can be used to evaluate samples of the student's writing such as classroom assignments, stories, or essays.

When the *GWT* is hand-scored, it is possible only to determine age and grade equivalents for each of the subtests. To obtain other subtest scores and composite scores, it is necessary to purchase the computer program from the publisher—the *Scoring and Reporting Program for the Group Writing Tests.* That program produces standard scores, percentile ranks, and grade or age equivalents for each of the four subtests and three composite scores. The composites are Basic Writing Skills (composed of the spelling and editing subtests), Expressive Writing Ability (composed of the writing fluency and writing samples subtests), and Total Writing.

Test of Written Expression

The *Test of Written Expression (TOWE)* is a two-part test for ages 6–6 to 14–11. The two parts are considered contrived and spontaneous evaluations of writing. According to the manual, the first part, Items, is a contrived evaluation with short-answer questions that assess "a broad array of writing skills (i.e., ideation, vocabulary, grammar, capitalization, punctuation, and spelling)" (p. 5). The second part, Essay, is a spontaneous evaluation similar to the writing sample portion of the *TOWL–3*. However, on the *TOWE*, the student writes a story after the tester reads a story starter; there is no visual stimulus.

TOWE results include standard scores, percentile ranks, and grade equivalents for the two parts, Items and Essay. A total test score is not available. The *TOWE* Record Form contains an optional error analysis grid if the tester is interested in looking for patterns of errors among the different types of skills assessed by the Items portion of the test. Like most norm-referenced measures of writing skills, the *TOWE* helps to identify areas of need. Further assessment with informal techniques is necessary for planning the instructional program.

Informal Techniques

Writing skills are often evaluated with informal techniques rather than formal, norm-referenced tests. Results of informal measures and techniques are used to describe current skill levels, particularly in areas for which no test results are available. They are invaluable for providing direction for instructional planning.

Rating Scales and Checklists

There are several ways to analyze students' writing samples, and one common approach is the use of a rating scale or checklist. The teacher selects one or, preferably, several samples of the student's writing and then analyzes content, vocabulary, sentences, paragraphs, mechanics, handwriting, and spelling. To direct the teacher's examination of these skill areas, the scale provides specific questions such as, "Do the sentences in the paragraph relate to one topic?"

Poteet's (1980) *Checklist of Written Expression* covers four major concerns in writing: penmanship, spelling, grammar, and ideation. Composition skills are included in the section on ideation. When using the checklist, the teacher considers several aspects of the student's writing sample: type of writing, level of abstraction (or substance), productivity, comprehensibility, and relationship to the reality of the writing task. The last section in the checklist, Style, is divided into three subsections: sentence sense, tone, and word choice.

Checklists and rating scales typically assess skill development by breaking the broad skill of composition down into more specific subskill areas. Holistic evaluation is another approach to the assessment of writing. This method, as its name implies, considers the writing sample as a whole, not in relation to individual elements (Moran, 1988). Errors or particular features of the writing are not counted. Instead, holistic scoring emphasizes the content of writing (Bailet, 1991; Graham, 1982). Dagenais and Beadle (1984) suggest that training is needed before professionals can conduct holistic evaluations.

Writing Sample Analysis

In addition to checklists and rating scales, work sample analysis techniques can be used to study students' writing samples. Error analysis is most valuable for identifying possible areas of need in the mechanics of writing: spelling, handwriting, punctuation, capitalization, and so on. Response analysis, which takes into account both errors and correct responses, is the more useful technique for the evaluation of composition skills.

The *Diagnostic Evaluation of Writing Skills (DEWS)* (Weiner, 1980) is an error analysis procedure that focuses on six aspects of written language:

- Graphic (visual features)
- Orthographic (spelling)
- Phonologic (sound components)

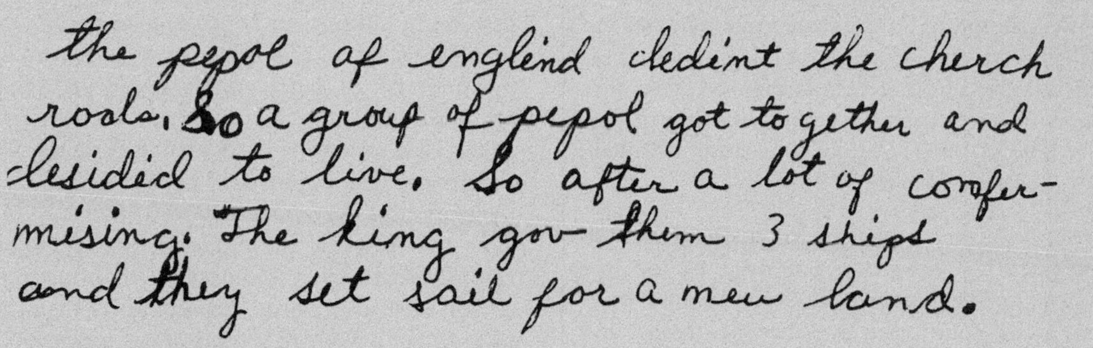

the pepol af englénd cledént the cherch roals. So a group of pepol got to gether and lesided to live. So after a lot of confer-mising. The king gov them 3 ships and they set sail for a mew land.

TRANSCRIPTION OF THE ENTIRE ESSAY

the pepol of englind didint the cherch roals. So a group of pepol got to gether and desidid to live. So after a lot of comfermising. The king gov them 3 ships and they set sail for a mew land. they sailed a long ways for a to long tine. then they saw it land it was North amareca. they landid on plymouth rock. ther they started to beld the ferst coliny. the firs winter wase the hardes a lot of pepol dide from being sick. After the winter was over the ingin's becom frinds with them and to them how to hunt and grow food.

ENTIRE ESSAY AS READ BY THE STUDENT

The people of England didn't like the church rules. So a group of people got together and decided to leave. So after a lot of compromising the King gave them three ships and they set sail for a new land. They sailed a long ways for a long time. Then they saw it. Land! It was North America. They landed on Plymouth Rock. Then they started to build the first colony. The first winter was the hardest and a lot of people died from being sick. After the winter was over the Indians became friendly with them and taught them how to hunt and grow food.

FIGURE 15–3
Student Writing Sample

- Syntactic (grammatical)
- Semantic (meaning)
- Self-Monitoring Skills

In the use of this procedure, students are asked to write an autobiography; approximately 30 minutes are allowed for writing and 15 minutes for revision. The writing sample is then studied to identify errors that may indicate a need for instruction. In the meaningful language category, the professional looks for errors in flexible vocabulary, coherence, logical sequencing, transitions, distinction between major and minor points, inferential thinking, and idiomatic and figurative language.

Content, organization, and vocabulary are among the critical factors that should be taken into account in the evaluation of composition skills (Wallace, Larsen, & Elksnin, 1992). As an example, consider the writing sample that appears in Figure 15–3. This essay was written by a 17-year-old student in grade 11 in response to an assignment in history class to describe the Pilgrims' journey to the New World. The first few sentences of the essay are presented in the student's own handwriting, followed by a verbatim transcription of the entire essay. Last is a record of the essay as read aloud by the student; note that, in reading the essay, the student filled in missing words and corrected many punctuation errors. An error analysis of this writing sample would document the extent of the student's difficulties with handwriting, spelling, capitalization, punctuation, and usage. However, a response analysis would reveal that the essay is meaningful, its content is expressed in an organized manner, and the student's word choice is accurate, if immature.

A number of other factors may be taken into account when analyzing students' writing (Polloway & Smith, 1982; Polloway, Patton, & Cohen, 1983). These include the following:

- *Productivity,* sometimes called fluency, refers to the quantity of writing produced by the student. The simplest way to evaluate productivity is to count the number of words and sentences in the writing sample and then determine the number of words per sentence. In general, longer sentences indicate a more mature writing style.
- *Sentences* can be analyzed according to their structure (simple, compound, complex, run-on, or fragment) and their type (declarative, interrogative, imperative, and exclamatory) (Polloway & Smith, 1982). Complete sentences are preferred to run-on sentences or sentence fragments, and compound and complex sentences are considered more advanced forms of expression than are simple sentences. In relation to sentence type, diversity is desirable when appropriate to content.
- *Vocabulary,* or the words selected by the student for inclusion in the writing sample, is another important consideration. The type–token ratio is a measure of the diversity of the vocabulary used by the writer. This ratio is determined by dividing the number of unique words in the writing sample by the total number of words in the sample. According to Polloway and Smith (1982), "a ratio of 1.0 would therefore indicate no redundancy while a ratio of .5 would suggest frequent repetition"(p. 344). In general, diversity of vocabulary is viewed as an indicator of mature writing.

Criterion-Referenced Tests

Criterion-referenced tests (CRTs) are a flexible type of assessment tool that can be used to measure a variety of different composition skills. For example, the teacher could develop CRTs to assess a student's ability to write complete sentences, an organized paragraph containing both a topic sentence and

several supporting sentences, or a brief story describing interactions between characters.

Published criterion-referenced tests such as the measures by Brigance (1981, 1999, 2010, 2013) also offer assistance in the study of composition skills. For example, a Sentence-Writing Grade Placement test is provided by the *BRIGANCE®* *Comprehensive Inventory of Basic Skills–II* (2010). This test assesses the student's ability to write complete and correct sentences that incorporate several stimulus words. For example, the student might be asked to compose a sentence that includes these possible words: *circus, escaped, after,* and *elephant.*

Criterion-referenced tests of practical writing skills appear on some of the Brigance measures. For example, the *BRIGANCE® Transition Skills Inventory* (2010) provides measures of daily life writing skills. Included are tests that assess skill in completing several common types of applications—employment, Social Security number, credit card, and driver's permit—as well as common forms such as income tax returns and forms for unemployment compensation. Another criterion-referenced measure, the *Hudson Education Skills Inventory* (Hudson et al., 1989), contains an array of composition measures that may be useful in classroom planning. Among the skills assessed are capitalization, punctuation, grammar, vocabulary, sentences, and paragraphs.

Observation and Clinical Interviews

Even though writing is essentially a private act, aspects of the writing process can be studied by observation. With classroom writing tasks, for example, it is possible to observe some of the actions the student takes in the three major steps of writing: preparing to write, writing, and reviewing and revising what has been written.

When a writing task is assigned, some students appear to engage in a planning process, whereas others begin to write immediately. Such observable behaviors are open to the scrutiny of the professional. For instance, the teacher could observe how much time is spent in the prewriting and postwriting stages as well as in the actual act of writing.

Table 15–3 lists the three major stages of writing and the typical behaviors expected of

TABLE 15–3
The Stages of Writing for Skilled and Unskilled Writers

STAGE	UNSKILLED WRITER	SKILLED WRITER
Planning	Does not participate in prewriting discussions.	Explores and discusses topic.
	Spends little time thinking about topic before beginning composition.	Spends time considering what will be written and how it will be expressed.
	Makes no plans or notes.	Jots notes; draws diagrams or pictures.
Transcribing	Writes informally in imitation of speech.	Writes in style learned from models of composition.
	Is preoccupied with technical matters of spelling and punctuation.	Keeps audience in mind while writing.
	Stops only briefly and infrequently.	Stops frequently to reread. Takes long thought pauses.
Revising	Does not review or rewrite.	Reviews frequently.
	Looks only for surface errors (spelling, punctuation).	Makes content revisions, as well as spelling and punctuation corrections.
	Rewrites only to make a neat copy in ink.	Keeps audience in mind while rewriting.

Note: From "Effective Instruction in Written language" (p. 291) by S. L. Isaacson, 1988, in *Effective Instructional Strategies for Exceptional Children* by E. L. Meyen, G. A. Vergason, and R. J. Whelan (Eds.), Denver: Love. Copyright 1988 by Love Publishing Company. Reprinted by permission.

skilled and unskilled writers at each stage. For example, in the planning stage, skilled writers may discuss the assigned topic, spend time thinking about what to write, and make notes or draw diagrams. The descriptions in this table could be converted into an observation checklist or a set of questions for a student interview.

It is important, however, to recognize that the writing process is not always made up of separate and distinct stages. As Graham (1982) observes, people approach writing in different ways. One person might write down thoughts as fast as they occur and then revise them later. Another might write and rewrite the first sentence until it is satisfactory and then proceed to the second sentence. Still another might carefully outline the story or essay and then write and edit it. A writer can also combine these strategies or switch from one to another during the act of writing.

Clinical interviews provide a method for gathering information about the nonobservable aspects of writing and the ways that the student interacts with the writing task. Interviews can be conducted before the student begins to write or after writing is completed (or both). However, while the student is writing, the professional should simply observe and not interrupt the student's thoughts with questions.

Among the dimensions of writing that can be explored in clinical interviews are the student's perceptions of the purposes for writing and the audience for which the writing is intended. Martin (1983) summarizes these dimensions with the questions, "What is the writing for?" and "Who is it for?" According to Martin, the function (or purpose) of expressive writing can be viewed as a continuum, with transactional writing at one end and poetic writing at the other. Phelps-Gunn and Phelps-Terasaki (1982) suggest that these purposes are related to the different modes of discourse—narration, description, exposition, and argument—that writers select to communicate their ideas to readers.

In school writing tasks, there are several different audiences: peers; the teacher, viewed as a trusted adult; the teacher, in the role of critic and dispenser of grades; the student himself or herself (as in writing a journal, class notes, and memoranda); or the general public (Martin, 1983). How students perceive the audience and the function of writing can influence how they approach the writing task. To find out about these and other dimensions of writing, the professional can ask these questions before the student begins to write:

- You're going to be writing something in a few minutes. Tell me about the assignment. What are you expected to do?
- Who will you be writing to? With whom will you try to communicate? Your teacher? A friend? Yourself? If you'll be writing to your teacher, do you expect the teacher to give you a grade—or to read what you have written and then help you make it better?
- What purpose will you try to accomplish in writing? Will you try to tell an exciting story? Give the reader information? Present an argument?
- What will you do before you begin writing? Will you think about what you're going to write? Make notes? Prepare an outline?

The interview can be continued after the student has completed the writing task:

- You've finished your essay (or paragraph, story, book report, etc.). Tell me about what you've written.
- When you finished, did you read over what you had written? Did you make any changes? What did you change?
- While you were writing, what did you think about? Did you consider...
  - The ideas you were writing about?
  - What should come first, second, and so on?
  - Choosing the exact words to express your meaning?
  - Spelling the words correctly, using correct punctuation, and following all the other rules for correct English?
- Do you think that you've accomplished your purpose in writing? Why or why not? If not, what do you need to change?
- You said that you would be writing to your teacher (or friend, self, etc.). Is your writing appropriate for that person? For example, is the vocabulary suitable? The tone? If not, what do you need to change?

Portfolio Assessment

Writing samples are the most common type of student work found in language arts portfolios. The "best pieces" that students select for their portfolios often represent a range of literary accomplishments: stories, poems, essays, reports, journals, plays, autobiographies, newspaper articles, movie and book reviews, student-authored books, and so on. In some cases, all drafts of a composition are included to document the process by which the final product was created. Self-evaluations and peer evaluations may also accompany some of the writing samples.

Teachers can contribute their evaluations of student work as well as results of formal and informal assessments. For example, with the *Language Arts Assessment Portfolio (LAAP)* (Karlsen, 1992), teachers rate the student's process of writing as well as the final product. Among the process concerns are the student's ability to engage in each of the stages of writing, his or her awareness of audience, and his or her independent editing skills. The teacher can also complete a spelling error analysis and rating scales on the mechanics of punctuation and capitalization. Students use the *LAAP* Self-Evaluation Booklets to describe what they have written and to rate themselves on writing process and product.

ENHANCEDetext
Video Example 15.2
Watch this video to find out more about an example of describing writing assessment results to parents.

WITHIN THE CONTEXT OF THE CLASSROOM

Students and their written products have been the focus of discussion up to this point in the chapter. Now the emphasis shifts to study of the classroom learning environment and its influence on students' spelling, handwriting, and composition skills.

The Instructional Environment

Assessment of the influence of the instructional environment on students' written language must take into account the classroom curriculum and the instructional methods and materials used to implement that curriculum. However, investigating the written language program may be a bit more difficult than studying classroom practices in reading and mathematics. In the elementary grades, written language can be divided into several subjects, each of which is taught directly but separately from the others: spelling, handwriting, and English (or language). There may be separate textbooks for each of these subjects, with composition subsumed under the subject of language or English. In contrast, teachers who use the whole-language approach may integrate writing into several areas of the curriculum, rather than teach it as one or more separate subjects. In the secondary grades, writing skills become part of the English curriculum, although students are expected to communicate in writing in all classes.

The amount of time devoted to instruction and the types of skills emphasized are two fundamental concerns in the evaluation of any instructional environment. These concerns are particularly important in written language instruction. Teachers who were studied in the 1980s did not allocate a great deal of instructional time to teaching writing skills (e.g., Alexander, 1983; Freedman, 1982; Leinhardt, Zigmond, & Cooley, 1981) and, when classroom time was spent on written language, the more mechanical aspects of writing such as spelling and handwriting were emphasized rather than composition. These problems should be less of a concern today because of the curricular changes brought about by whole-language, integrated language arts, and the process approach to teaching writing. However, not all classrooms have implemented these changes. Thus, one of the first steps in assessing the learning environment should be a study of the classroom schedule and how that schedule is implemented.

The following questions provide a framework for evaluating the classroom program for teaching written language skills:

1. Are spelling skills included within the written language curriculum? If so, what does the curriculum stress—regular words, irregular words, spelling rules, or a combination?
2. Are handwriting skills included? If so, is manuscript or cursive writing taught? Does the curriculum emphasize accuracy in letter formation? Speed? Legibility?
3. Are composition skills included? Are they taught as part of the language arts or English program? Or is there a separate program for teaching composition? If so, what are its major components?
4. Where do skills such as capitalization and punctuation fit? Are they taught in conjunction with composition or as a separate skill area?
5. What textbook series are used in the classroom to teach written language skills? Is there a text for spelling? Handwriting? Language? English?
6. Are multiple levels of each of the written language textbooks in use in the classroom?
7. What instructional materials supplement the textbooks in the basal series? Are computers used for writing?
8. What types of writing skills are stressed in classroom instruction? Writing mechanics? Composition and the use of writing as a means of communication?
9. Is any attempt made to integrate the teaching of composition with instruction in spelling, handwriting, and usage? If so, how is this accomplished?
10. Is the written language curriculum organized so that the sequence of instruction is logical?
11. Is instruction based on ongoing assessment?
12. How are students grouped for instruction? How much individualization takes place in each group?

13. What instructional techniques does the teacher use to present new skills and information? Lecture? Demonstration? Discussion? Exploration and discovery? Cooperative learning?

14. In what types of learning activities do students participate? In spelling and handwriting, do they complete workbook pages or worksheets? Do they copy each spelling word several times as a strategy for learning? In handwriting, do students practice writing letters, words, and symbols by copying from a model? What types of composition activities are available? Do students keep a journal? Write paragraphs? Stories? Letters? Poems? Book reports? Is expository or creative writing emphasized?

15. How is supervised practice incorporated into the written language program? On the average, how many minutes per day do students spend practicing their spelling skills? Handwriting skills? Composition skills?

16. What changes, if any, have been made in the standard program to accommodate the needs of special students such as the one under assessment?

Graham (1982) and Graham and Miller (1979, 1980) have summarized the research on effective methods for the teaching of spelling, handwriting, and composition in order to offer specific recommendations for classroom practice. These recommendations could serve as a set of standards for the evaluation of classroom practices.

According to Graham and Miller (1979), self-correction of spelling is essential. Some of the other research-based practices these authors advocate include setting aside an hour per week for spelling education, receiving spelling words in lists, and assessing learning of misspelled words. They also support writing words multiple times to increase memory of spelling. The researchers (Graham & Miller, 1980) also offer suggestions for handwriting instruction. Those include direct instruction, learning which is regular in short time increments, and handwriting used in authentic tasks. In relation to the teaching of composition skills, Graham (1982) suggests comprehensive and focused writing assignments, a

focus on positive writing accomplishments, and instruction based on assessment data.

It is also important to consider the performance demands imposed on students in writing tasks. These include expectations for quantity (i.e., the number of words, sentences, or paragraphs expected), the requirements for speed, and the expectations for accuracy. Performance demands become a concern whenever writing activities are a part of instruction: writing a composition in English class, copying mathematics problems from the board, writing answers to questions on a history test, writing entries in a science lab notebook, and so on.

Classroom standards should be considered in relation to the student under assessment. Standards may be unrealistically high for this student, and some adjustment can be made to better the student's chances for success. For example, the teacher may be willing to allow the student more time for composition activities or reduce the amount of writing required. If handwriting is an area of difficulty, the teacher may permit the student to type, tape record, or dictate assignments to a peer.

The Interpersonal Environment

The major factors within the interpersonal environment that are of concern in assessment are social relationships among students and student–teacher interactions. Often, students with achievement problems are not well accepted by their peers. This can occur when students experience difficulty with written language, particularly when their attempts to communicate in writing are open to view by their peers. In most classrooms, students have many opportunities to see and read what other students write. For instance, it is routine practice to ask students to write on the board and to collect their themes, stories, essays, and the like, placing them on public display on classroom bulletin boards.

In written language instruction, most teacher–student interactions center on the student's written product. The student writes in an attempt to communicate, and the teacher reads and then grades the communication. There are several methods of grading, and some are more likely than others to encourage students in their efforts to learn writing skills. Covering a student's paper with red ink by marking every error may only discourage the student from further attempts. For students with an achievement problem in some aspect of written expression, it is better to emphasize what they have done correctly by drawing attention to their correct responses rather than errors (Graham, 1982). It is also possible to assign more than one grade to a paper. For example, the teacher might give one grade for spelling and handwriting and another for the content.

The following questions are of interest when evaluating interactions between students and teachers in written language instruction:

- In private student–teacher interactions (e.g., when the teacher communicates with students by grading their papers), how does the teacher respond to an error? Does the teacher identify the response as an error? Correct it? Ignore the error?
- If the writing situation is a public one (e.g., students are writing on the board), what occurs when a student makes an error? Does the teacher use the same correction procedures in public and private interactions?
- How does the student react to the teacher's corrections? Is there a difference when the student is corrected in front of peers?
- What do other students do when a peer makes errors in writing?
- What happens when a student makes a correct writing response? Does the teacher confirm the response? Praise the student? Provide a tangible reward or token?
- Are students able to work independently on writing activities? Do certain students require frequent assistance from the teacher?

The Physical Environment

The physical environment of the classroom is an important consideration in written language instruction. General environmental factors such as lighting, temperature, and ventilation can affect the physical comfort of teachers and students, thereby influencing the teaching–learning process.

In addition, the seating arrangements for students and the writing tools provided can have an impact on their ability to perform, particularly in relation to handwriting. In assessing the classroom's physical environment, some of the major questions to consider are as follows:

1. Are appropriate chairs provided for students? Can each student sit comfortably with hips touching the back of the chair and both feet resting on the floor (Graham & Miller, 1980)?
2. Are student desks (or other types of writing surfaces such as tables) at an appropriate height for writing?
3. What types of writing implements are available in the classroom? Is there a selection of different types?
4. Are writing implements selected to meet the needs of individual students? For example, some students find primary-sized pencils easier to grip.
5. What types of paper are available in the classroom? Is there a selection of different types? For example, for younger students and those with severe handwriting problems, is there a supply of primary paper with guidelines between each pair of widely spaced lines?
6. Is the lighting in the classroom adequate for writing?
7. What seating arrangements are used for instruction in written language?
8. How are students seated for independent work?
9. Is the classroom space organized so that areas for noisier activities are separated from areas for quieter activities such as writing?
10. Are there any quiet areas within the classroom where students can escape from distractions?
11. Does the classroom offer a variety of learning materials, or are textbooks the only resource? For example, are computers and printers available in the classroom?

 Breakpoint Practice 15.3
Click here to check your understanding of assessment of writing within the context of the classroom.

ANSWERING THE ASSESSMENT QUESTIONS

The major purpose of assessing written language is to describe the student's current levels of educational performance in this important school skill. A number of different types of assessment tools are available for this purpose.

Nature of the Assessment Tools

The tools available for the study of written language vary in several ways. One important dimension is the range of skills they are designed to assess. Some measures are comprehensive and evaluate a number of the major skill areas of written language. Others are more limited in scope. For example, handwriting is the sole concern of the *Test of Legible Handwriting*, and the *Test of Written Spelling–5* concentrates on spelling.

Of the assessment tools listed in Table 15–1, six could be considered comprehensive measures. Of these, all are informal measures, except the *Test of Early Written Language–3*. If norm-referenced information is needed for decisions about the severity of students' skill deficits, relatively few formal tests are available. The most comprehensive are measures such as the *Test of Written Language–4* and *Mather-Woodcock Group Writing Tests,* although they do not assess handwriting performance.

Assessment tools can also vary in the depth with which skills are assessed. In general, informal measures are likely to provide the most thorough coverage of individual skills. For example, the *BRIGANCE® Comprehensive Inventory of Basic Skills–II* offers several tests of spelling, and each considers a specific skill in depth: spelling initial consonants, suffixes, prefixes, and so forth.

Assessment tools may also differ in the types of tasks used to evaluate skill development. For example, as Table 15–4 shows, there are three basic strategies for the study of spelling: dictation tests, analysis of students' writing samples, and error detection tasks. Error detection, the least frequently used assessment strategy, is essentially a proofreading task. It is important to remember that detecting spelling errors is not the same skill as recalling correct spellings from memory. If both skills are of interest, both should be assessed.

A variety of assessment tasks are used to evaluate handwriting skills. The major strategies are based on analysis of a sample of the student's handwriting, but they differ in the way the writing sample is obtained. On copying tests, students are provided with a model and are directed to copy that model in their best handwriting. In contrast, classroom-writing samples tend to represent the student's typical handwriting. Samples elicited on a test likely fall somewhere in between students' best and typical handwriting. A comparison of the handwriting samples that the student produces under divergent conditions can provide useful assessment information.

Composition skills are assessed in many ways, and writing samples are one common assessment task. However, the samples vary considerably in length, ranging from one sentence to a complete composition. On tests, students are directed to write a story about a standard stimulus such as one picture or a series of pictures. This technique is somewhat different from the collection of classroom writing samples. Because the task is standard for all students, norms can be developed for evaluating various aspects of written language performance. On the *Test of Written Language–4,* for example, the content of the writing sample is evaluated, vocabulary and sentence structure are assessed, and adherence to capitalization and punctuation rules is noted.

The Relationship of Written Language to Other Areas of Performance

A student's general aptitude for learning can affect the ease and speed with which academic skills are acquired. Hence, the student's current status in written language should be evaluated in relation to estimated intellectual performance. In general, students with lower than average general intelligence are expected to progress at a somewhat slower rate than students of average intellectual ability. The Verbal Comprehension Index is likely the best measure for estimating a student's potential for learning spelling and composition skills. In contrast, the Performance Index may provide a better estimate of handwriting ability because of the motor components of this skill.

TABLE 15–4

Assessment Tasks Used to Evaluate Written Language Skills

WRITTEN LANGUAGE SKILL	ASSESSMENT TASK	PRESENTATION MODE	RESPONSE MODE	EXAMPLES OF MEASURES USING THIS TYPE OF TASK
Spelling	Dictation test	Listen to a word (or a word and a sentence containing the word) read by the tester	Write the word	*Test of Written Spelling–5*, Kottmeyer's *Diagnostic Spelling Test*
		Listen to a sentence read by the tester	Write the sentence	Spelling subtest of the *Test of Written Language–4*
	Analysis of a classroom writing sample	Analyze an existing sample of the student's writing	–	*Checklist of Written Expression, Diagnostic Evaluation of Writing Skills*
	Error detection	Read a sentence that contains an error	Identify the error and correct it	Orthographic Usage subtest of the *Test of Adolescent and Adult Language–5*
Handwriting	Copying test	Look at a sentence or paragraph written in legible handwriting	Copy the model	*Zaner-Bloser Evaluation Scales, Denver Handwriting Analysis Checklist of Written Expression, Diagnostic Evaluation of Writing Skills, Test of Legible Handwriting*
	Analysis of a classroom writing sample	Analyze an existing sample of the student's writing	–	*Test of Legible Handwriting*
	Elicitation of a writing sample	Look at a picture	Write a story about the picture	*Test of Legible Handwriting*
		Listen to a prompt	Write an autobiography or a letter in response to the prompt	
Composition	Elicitation of a writing sample	Look at a picture	Write a story about the picture	*Test of Written Language–3, Picture Story Language Test*
		Listen to a prompt	Write a letter in response to the prompt	Written Expression subtest of *Wechsler Individual Achievement Test*, Essay portion of *Test of Written Expression*
	Sentence writing	Read a word	Write a sentence containing the word	Vocabulary subtest of *Test of Written Language–3*, Word Similarities subtest of *Test of Adolescent and Adult Language–4*
		Read a sentence that contains an error of logic	Rewrite the sentence and correct the error	Logical Sentences subtest of *Test of Written Language–4*, Writing Samples subtest of the *Woodcock Language Proficiency Battery–Revised* and of the *Mather-Woodcock Group Writing Tests*
		Read a prompt	Write a sentence in response to the prompt	
		Look at a picture; read three words	Write a sentence that describes the picture including the three words	Writing Fluency subtest of the *Woodcock Language Proficiency Battery–Revised* and of the *Mather-Woodcock Group Writing Tests*
	Sentence combining	Read two sentences	Write a new sentence that combines the meanings of the original sentences	Sentence Combining subtest of *Test of Written Language–4*, Sentence Combining subtest of *Test of Adolescent and Adult Language–4*

Specific learning abilities and strategies can influence the student's success in the acquisition and use of written language skills. Difficulties in attention, memory, or other areas such as visual perception and auditory discrimination can impede skill development, particularly the acquisition of basic spelling and handwriting skills. Fine-motor skills and eye–hand coordination are important considerations in relation to handwriting, the motor component of written language. Also, inefficient learning strategies can interfere with the student's attempts to learn new skills and apply already learned skills to the process of planning, writing, and revising a written product.

Classroom behavior may be related to written language performance. Inappropriate classroom conduct can impede any type of learning, including the acquisition of spelling, handwriting, and composition skills. Likewise, poor achievement can affect a student's behavior. Classroom writing activities often require that students work independently, and when written language is an area of difficulty, students may be unable to comply. The result may be disruptive behavior, frequent bids for the teacher's attention, and/or withdrawal from the academic situation.

In addition, achievement problems in other school skill areas can interfere with the acquisition of written language skills. In this regard, oral language and reading skills are the major concerns. Difficulties in the comprehension or expression of oral language can have a major impact on the student's ability to express thoughts in writing. Likewise, a lack of reading proficiency may inhibit the development of writing skills. Generally, students first learn to read words, and then learn to write and spell them. Also, reading exposes students to the formal conventions of written language—sentences, paragraphs, capitalization, punctuation, and the like—and to the structural, syntactical, and vocabulary differences between written and oral language.

Just as other school skills can affect written language, writing skills influence the student's chances for success in other academic areas. Beginning in the early elementary grades, writing is a primary way that students demonstrate what they have learned. As the student proceeds through the various levels of education—from the primary grades to the intermediate grades to middle school and so on—an increasing proportion of school tasks require writing.

Writing, like reading, is a skill that pervades the entire curriculum. Students with poor spelling, handwriting, and composition skills will have difficulty not only when these skills are taught directly, but also when writing proficiency is a requirement in other curriculum areas. Almost all school subjects involve some degree of writing. Students who write very slowly will have difficulty completing their assignments on time. Those who write illegibly may fail an exam or assignment even though their responses are correct. Poor spelling and syntax may lower students' grades, even in subjects like history or biology.

Writing skills are also necessary for adult life. Adults use writing as a memory aid when they make note of a telephone number, write down an address, or make out a shopping list. People also write to communicate with others; they write e-mail and instant messages to friends, fill out forms, and write notes and letters. Job applications are another feature of adult life, as are the forms that must be completed for a Social Security number, a driver's license, income taxes, and so on. In addition, some degree of writing proficiency is required in most occupations. In the assessment of written language, it is important to consider the student's ability to cope with adult writing tasks, as well as the degree of success in meeting classroom writing requirements.

Documentation of Written Language Performance

What are the student's educational needs? is the general assessment question that guides the special education team in its study of written language. The goal in this phase of assessment is to gather sufficient information for a precise description of the student's current levels of educational performance. The first question the team attempts to respond to is, *What is the student's current level of achievement in written language?* Additional data are then gathered about the writing skills that are possible areas of educational need. The result, a description of the student's current status in relation to written language, allows the team to answer this question: *What are the student's strengths and weaknesses in the various skill areas of written language?*

Oral Language

Oral language is a different form of language than written language and is the most basic communication skill. A person talks, another listens, and information is transmitted. This communication process begins in infancy when babies first learn to attend to the sound of their parents' voices. By the time most children enter school, they are experienced oral communicators, able to understand the messages spoken by others and to express their own thoughts in speech. Oral language is the foundation for school learning. In the first few years of school, most new information is presented orally; students learn by listening and demonstrate what they have learned by speaking. As students progress through the grades, reading and writing skills take on increased importance, but oral language remains a basic means of communication between teacher and student. It is also the fundamental communication process for daily life. In most communication situations at home, at work, and at play, people exchange information by talking.

For many students with special needs, oral language is an area of concern. Students with disabilities may have difficulty understanding the language of others, expressing themselves in speech, or in both comprehension and production of oral language. Oral language is a concern not only of students with disabilities, but also of students who are English learners or of those who speak a nonstandard version of English. If Standard English is the only language of communication in the classroom, linguistically diverse students may face real barriers in their attempts to understand and participate in instructional activities.

The purpose of oral language assessment is to gather information for instructional planning. The general question that guides this phase of assessment is, *What are the student's educational needs?* When oral language is the skill area under

study, two specific questions are asked: *What is the student's current level of development in oral language?* and *What are the student's strengths and weaknesses in the various skill areas of oral language?* These questions apply to both linguistically diverse students and those whose only language is Standard English. The goal in this phase of the assessment process is to describe the student's current levels of educational performance.

Assessment for instructional planning is a selective process. If the student is making satisfactory progress in oral language or another skill area, the student's special education program will probably not address this skill and, thus, extensive assessment is unnecessary. However, the assessment team often has little information about a student's current status in oral language. Before this or any other skill can be ruled out as an area of educational need, it is necessary to gather data to document the student's current performance.

ENHANCEDetext
Video Example 15.3
Watch this video to find out more about an example of an individualized education program (IEP) discussion regarding language skills.

CONSIDERATIONS IN ASSESSMENT OF ORAL LANGUAGE

Students' oral language skills are the subject of study in general, special, and bilingual education. This skill area, more than many others, illustrates the multidisciplinary nature of the assessment process. General, special, and bilingual education teachers are interested in promoting the language development of their students. They gather assessment data to measure students' progress. Speech-language pathologists serve students with severe oral communication disorders; their role in assessment is the administration of specialized measures to identify and describe disorders of speech and language.

Purposes

In general education, teachers monitor oral language skills to determine pupil progress and evaluate the effectiveness of the instructional program. However, after the early elementary grades, oral language is not usually taught as a separate school subject. Also, oral communication is not assessed by the group achievement tests that are used to measure students' school performance (although listening skills may be). This lack of attention to oral language reflects the assumption that students learn to listen and speak during the preschool years. Once in school, students are expected to be oral communicators, so the curriculum focuses on the acquisition of higher-level academic skills such as reading, writing, and mathematics.

In special education assessment, oral language may be a concern of the assessment team as it begins to gather data for planning the student's IEP. Many students with mild disabilities have special instructional needs in oral language. In particular, students with intellectual disabilities may show an overall delay in the acquisition of listening and speaking skills, and students with learning disabilities in written language may have equivalent needs in oral language. In addition, there is a large group of students for whom oral language is the primary disability area. This disability is called a communication disorder.

When oral language is identified as an area of educational need for a particular student, assessment is continued to gather the detailed information necessary for program planning. This occurs for all students with language needs, whatever the disability of the student or the language the student speaks. The goal at this point in assessment is to describe the student's current performance so that an appropriate educational program can be

designed. Once that program is implemented, the cycle of gathering data about current skills, planning instructional interventions, and evaluating the success of those interventions is repeated for as long as the student remains in need of specially designed instruction.

Skill Areas

Language is a symbol system used for communication, and speech is one medium used to express language. Like written language, oral language can be receptive or expressive, depending on the person's role in the communication process. In oral language, speech is the expressive component, and listening is the receptive component. Polloway and Smith (1982) suggest that just as language is a vehicle for communication, it is also a vehicle for thought. In this view, thinking is conceptualized as a type of communication process in which inner language plays a major role.

Language can be described in many ways, and the reception-expression dimension is only one approach. Another useful system is that proposed by Bloom and Lahey (1978), who suggest that language is composed of three interacting dimensions: form, content, and use. Language competence is the integration of these three dimensions of language.

Wiig and Semel's (1984) model of language includes similar components, as Figure 15–4 illustrates. In this model, four dimensions of language are described: language as sound sequences, language as a structured rule system (form), language as a meaning system (content), and language in communicative context (use).

The form of language is determined by the rules used to combine speech sounds into meaning units and meaning units into communications. Three aspects of language are involved: phonology, morphology, and syntax. **Phonology** is concerned with the smallest units of oral language, the speech sounds (phonemes). Expressive phonology is called **articulation**. Receptive phonology, the ability to recognize and comprehend phonemes, is auditory discrimination. The next level of language is **morphology**. A morpheme is the smallest meaningful unit of language. A morpheme may be a word such as *flower* or a

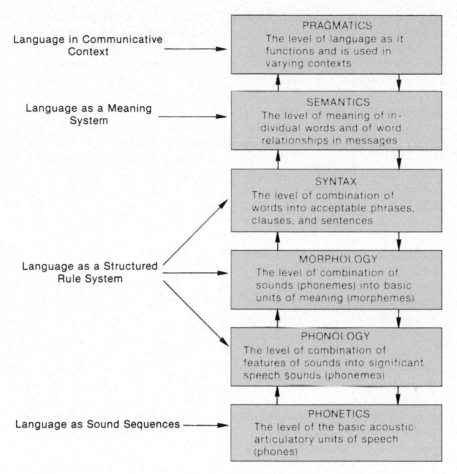

Language in Communicative Context →

Language as a Meaning System →

Language as a Structured Rule System →

Language as Sound Sequences →

PRAGMATICS
The level of language as it functions and is used in varying contexts

SEMANTICS
The level of meaning of individual words and of word relationships in messages

SYNTAX
The level of combination of words into acceptable phrases, clauses, and sentences

MORPHOLOGY
The level of combination of sounds (phonemes) into basic units of meaning (morphemes)

PHONOLOGY
The level of combination of features of sounds into significant speech sounds (phonemes)

PHONETICS
The level of the basic acoustic-articulatory units of speech (phones)

FIGURE 15–4

Dimensions of Oral Language

Note: From E.H. Whg; E. Semel-Mintz, E., *Language Assessment and Intervention for the Learning Disabled*, 1st Ed., © 1990. Reprint and Electronically reproduced by permission of Pearson Education, Inc., Upper Saddle River, New Jersey.

meaningful part of a word such as the *-ing* in *growing*. **Syntax** refers to the grammatical rules for combining morphemes into comprehensible utterances. Like phonology, morphology and syntax have receptive and expressive components. For example, expressive syntax refers to the ability to produce grammatically acceptable speech.

For communication to occur, language must have meaning as well as form, and language meaning is called semantics. **Semantics** is concerned with the meaning of individual words and with the meaning that is produced by combinations of words. Receptive semantics is language comprehension, and expressive semantics is the production of meaningful discourse.

Pragmatics, or language use, is concerned with the speaker's purposes for communication and the ways that language is used to carry out those intents. Adults are able to analyze the social contexts in which communications occur and alter their language accordingly. They are influenced by the setting of the communication, the characteristics of the participants, the topic of conversation, and the goals and objectives of each participant (Wiig & Semel, 1984). For example, if the communicative intent is to announce that dinner is ready, the language used to convey that message to one's family is likely to be different from that used with dinner guests.

Thus, oral language involves both reception and expression of communications, and those communications can be analyzed according to the dimensions of phonology, morphology, syntax, semantics, and pragmatics. In addition, oral communication is influenced by other aspects of the speech act (e.g., intonation, pitch, loudness, and stress) and by the nonverbal communications that accompany speech (e.g., facial expressions, body language, gestures). Children and adolescents can experience difficulty with any one or several of these dimensions.

In assessment, measures of oral language focus on the comprehension and production of language form and content. Pragmatics is a relatively new area of study and, thus, fewer measures have been developed for its assessment. In addition, traditional language measures are designed to evaluate students' products, not the process by which those products are created. When information is needed about a student's ability to use language in a variety of communicative contexts or about the cognitive processes that interact with language comprehension and production, informal measures are often the major type of assessment strategy available.

Many measures of oral language are designed for young children (preschoolers and children in the first few grades of school) because of the rapid rate at which language skills develop during this age period. Most measures are administered individually; this becomes a necessity when oral responses are required. Because language competence is such a complex skill area, many types of assessment tasks are used to evaluate students' oral language abilities.

Expressive phonology—the articulation of speech sounds—is assessed by eliciting samples of the student's speech. Auditory discrimination (receptive phonology) is measured by listening tasks. Tests of auditory discrimination were discussed in Chapter 8, the chapter on specific learning abilities and strategies, and thus will not be covered here.

Like articulation, expressive morphology and syntax are assessed by eliciting samples of the student's speech. With these skills, however, the concern is the structural adequacy of the utterance, not its phonological characteristics. Receptive skills are measured in a variety of ways, but one common technique involves having the student select a picture that illustrates a sentence read by the tester. For example, if the sentence is "The girl is talking to her mother," one picture might show a girl talking to her mother, another the mother talking while her daughter listens, and so forth.

The meaning component of language is the subject of assessment not only on measures of oral language but also on many tests of intellectual performance. Most often, expressive skills are the concern, and a typical test task is word definition. Recognition tasks are used to assess receptive skills. With this type of task, the student listens to a word and selects from several drawings or photos the one that best represents the word's meaning.

Current Practices

Assessment of oral language skills is not as common a practice as assessment of academic skills such as reading and mathematics. The group achievement and competency tests that are used in general education focus on written, not oral, language, and even individual tests of academic achievement rarely include listening and speaking skills. Two notable exceptions are the *Wechsler Individual Achievement Test—Third Edition* (2009) and the *Diagnostic Achievement Battery—Fourth Edition* (Newcomer, 2014).

Although oral language is not typically assessed by tests of academic achievement, it is often included on other types of measures. Tests of intellectual performance (unless they are designed as nonverbal measures) usually assess language skills in some way. For example, several of the subtests on the *Wechsler Intelligence Scale for Children—Fifth Edition* (Wechsler, 2014) are considered verbal comprehension measures, and half of the subtests on the *Stanford-Binet Intelligence Scale—Fifth Edition* (Roid, 2003) are verbal measures. In addition, oral language skills are frequently one of the performance domains assessed by measures of adaptive behavior. Some of the instruments used to assess specific learning abilities also evaluate oral language.

Measures designed specifically for the study of oral language skills are more directly related to instructional planning. Several of these assessment tools are listed in Table 15–5. These measures are divided into five categories according to

TABLE 15–5
Measures of Oral Language

Name (Author)	Ages or Grades	Group or Individual	SKILL AREA(S) ASSESSED	
			Reception	Expression
Survey Measures				
Bankson Language Test—Second Edition (Bankson, 1990)	Ages 3–0 to 6–11	Individual		X
BRIGANCE® Comprehensive Inventory of Basic Skills–II (Brigance, 2010)	Pre-K to grade 6	Individual	X	X
BRIGANCE® Diagnostic Inventory of Early Development—III (Brigance, 2013)	Birth to age 5	Individual	X	X
Clinical Evaluation of Language Fundamentals—Fifth Edition (Wiig, Semel, & Secord, 2013)	Ages 5 through 21–11	Individual	X	X
Illinois Test of Psycholinguistic Abilities–Third Edition (Hammill, Mather, & Roberts, 2001)	Ages 5–0 through 12–11	Individual	X	X
Oral and Written Language Scales–Ii (Carrow-Woolfolk, 2011a)	Ages 3 to 21	Individual	X	X
Test of Adolescent and Adult Language–4 (Hammill, Brown, Larsen, & Wiederholt, 2007)	Ages 12–0 to 24–11	Individual		X
Test of Early Language Development—Third Edition (Hresko, Reid, & Hammill, 1999)	Ages 2–0 through 7–11	Individual	X	X
Test of Language Development–4, Intermediate (Hammill & Newcomer, 2008)	Ages 8–0 to 12–11	Individual	X	X
Test of Language Development–4, Primary (Newcomer & Hammill, 2008)	Ages 4–0 to 8–11	Individual	X	X
Utah Test of Language Development—Fourth Edition (Mecham, 2003)	Ages 3–0 to 9–11	Individual	X	X
Woodcock Language Proficiency Battery—Revised (Woodcock, 1991)	Ages 3 to 80+	Individual	X	X
Phonology				
Arizona Articulation Proficiency Scale—Third Edition (Fudala, 2001)	Ages 1–6 to 18	Individual		X
Auditory Discrimination Test—Second Edition (Reynolds, 1987; Wepman, 1975)	Ages 4 to 8–11	Individual	X	
Goldman-Fristoe Test of Articulation—Third Edition (Goldman & Fristoe, 2015)	Ages 2 to 21–11	Individual	X	
Goldman-Fristoe-Woodcock Test of Auditory Discrimination (Goldman, Fristoe, & Woodcock, 1970)	Ages 4 to 70+	Individual	X	

continued

TABLE 15–5 *continued*
Measures of Oral Language

Name (Author)	Ages or Grades	Group or Individual	SKILL AREA(S) ASSESSED	
			Reception	Expression
Photo Articulation Test—Third Edition (Lippke, Dickey, Selmar, & Soder, 1997)	Ages 3–0 to 8–11	Individual	X	
Morphology and Syntax				
Carrow Elicited Language Inventory (Carrow-Woolfolk, 1974)	Ages 3–0 to 7–11	Individual	X	
Developmental Sentence Analysis (Lee, 1974)	Ages 2–0 to 7–11	Individual	X	
Language Sampling, Analysis, and Training—Third Edition (Tyack & Venable, 1999)	Young children	Individual	X	
Northwestern Syntax Screening Test (Lee, 1971)	Ages 3–11 to 7–1	Individual	X	X
Test for Auditory Comprehension of Language—Fourth Edition (Carrow-Woolfolk, 2014)	Ages 3–0 to 12–11	Individual	X	
Semantics				
Assessment of Children's Language Comprehension (Foster, Giddan, & Stark, 1983)	Ages 3 to 7	Individual	X	
Boehm-3-Preschool (Boehm, 2001)	Ages 3–0 to 5–11	Individual	X	
Boehm Test of Basic Concepts—Third Edition (Boehm, 2000)	Ages 5–0 to 7–11 Grades K–2	Group	X	
Comprehensive Receptive and Expressive Vocabulary Test—Third Edition (Wallace & Hammill, 2013)	Ages 5–0 to 89–11	Individual	X	X
Expressive One-Word Picture Vocabulary Test—Fourth Edition (Martin & Brownell, 2011)	Ages 2–80+	Individual	X	
Expressive Vocabulary Test—Second Edition (Williams, 2007)	Ages 2–6 to 90+	Individual		X
Peabody Picture Vocabulary Test—Fourth Edition (Dunn & Dunn, 2007)	Ages 2–6 to 90+	Individual	X	
Receptive One-Word Picture Vocabulary Test—Fourth Edition (Brownell, 2010)	Ages 2–70+	Individual	X	
Pragmatics				
Let's Talk Inventory for Children (Bray & Wiig, 1987)	Ages 4–8	Individual	X	X
Pragmatic Language Skills Inventory (Gilliam & Miller, 2006)	Ages 6–18–11	Individual rating scale	X	X
Test of Pragmatic Language-2 (Phelps-Terasaki & Phelps-Gunn, 2007)	Ages 5–0 to 13–11	Individual	X	
Test of Pragmatic Skills—Revised Edition (Shulman, 1986)	Ages 3–0 to 8–11	Individual	X	

the skills they assess. First are survey measures (instruments that assess more than one aspect of oral language), which are followed by measures of phonology, morphology and syntax, semantics, and pragmatics.

As Table 15–5 illustrates, many tools are available for the assessment of oral language, and these tools vary in the skill areas they address. Some measures are comprehensive, whereas others are limited to one domain. With the exception of pragmatics, each dimension of language is represented by a number of measures. For the most part, oral language assessments are designed for children in the elementary grades. However, some currently available measures extend oral language assessment into the secondary grades and even adulthood.

Informal techniques also play a role in oral language assessment. All of the standard types of informal devices and procedures are available, but the most common are criterion-referenced testing, informal inventories, language sample analysis, and checklists and rating scales.

 Breakpoint Practice 15.4
Click here to check your understanding of measures of oral language.

COMPREHENSIVE MEASURES OF ORAL LANGUAGE

Of the oral language measures available today, several are designed to assess a wide range of language skills. Two versions of the *Test of Language Development–4* are described here: the primary level for young children and the intermediate level for students in the later elementary grades. Also discussed is the *Oral and Written Language Scales-II* (Carrow-Woolfolk, 2011a), the *Test of Adolescent and Adult Language–4* (Hammill et al., 2007), and the *Illinois Test of Psycholinguistic Abilities—Third Edition* (Hammill, Mather, & Roberts, 2001).

Test of Language Development–4, Primary

The *TOLD–4 Primary* is an individual test of oral language for preschool and early elementary grade children. There are six core and three supplementary subtests on the *TOLD–4 Primary*. The *TOLD–4 Primary* assesses listening, organizing, and speaking skills in relation to phonology, syntax, and semantics. However, core subtests address only syntax and semantics.

The *TOLD–4* Primary subtests are:

Core Subtests

- *Picture Vocabulary* (Receptive Semantics). The tester reads a word, and the child points to the picture that best represents the word. The child chooses from four pictures.
- *Relational Vocabulary* (Organizational Semantics). The tester reads two words and the child must tell how they are alike.
- *Oral Vocabulary* (Expressive Semantics). The tester reads a word and asks the child to define it orally.
- *Syntactic Understanding* (Receptive Syntax). The tester reads a sentence, and the child must choose the picture that best illustrates the meaning of the sentence. The three pictures presented to the child represent syntactically similar sentences.
- *Sentence Imitation* (Organizational Syntax). On this subtest, the tester reads a sentence, and the child must repeat it verbatim.
- *Morphological Completion*. The tester reads an unfinished sentence, and the child must supply the missing word.

Supplemental Subtests

- *Word Discrimination* (Receptive Phonology). The tester reads two words, and the child must say whether the words are the same or different. Different word pairs differ in only one phoneme.

- *Word Analysis* (Organizational Phonology). The tester reads a word, then asks the child to repeat the word with one syllable deleted.

- *Word Articulation* (Expressive Phonology). Here the tester shows the child a picture and reads a sentence that describes it. The child is asked to name the picture.

According to the *TOLD–4 Primary* manual, the phonology subtests are most useful for children under the age of 7. However, norms are available for older children.

TEST OF LANGUAGE DEVELOPMENT–4 (TOLD–4), PRIMARY AND INTERMEDIATE

P. L. Newcomer and D. D. Hammill (1997); D. D. Hammill and P. L. Newcomer (2008)

Type: Norm-referenced test

Major Content Areas: Primary: receptive, organizational, and expressive skills in phonology, syntax, and semantics; Intermediate: receptive and expressive syntax and semantics

Type of Administration: Individual

Administration Time: Primary: 60 minutes; Intermediate: 30–60 minutes

Age/Grade Levels: Primary: ages 4–0 to 8–11; Intermediate: ages 8–0 to 17–11

Types of Scores: Percentile ranks, standard scores, and age equivalents for subtests; composite standard scores (quotients)

Technology Aids: *TOLD-P:4 Scoring Software and Reporting System, TOLD-I:4 Scoring Software and Reporting System*

Typical Uses: A broad-based test for the identification of strengths and weaknesses in oral language development

Cautions: The phonology subtests on the *TOLD–4, Primary* are most useful for children under age 7

Publisher: PRO-ED (*www.proedinc.com*)

To participate in *TOLD–4 Primary* administration, children must understand and speak English and be able to respond to oral questions. The subtests are not timed, and reading and writing skills are not required. This test is quite easy to administer and score. All subtests begin with item 1, and the ceiling for all of the core subtests is five consecutive incorrect responses. There are no ceilings on the supplemental subtests; all items are administered. It is not necessary to administer all subtests. For example, the tester can select only those subtests that assess a specific language ability such as syntax or semantics. However, if all subtests are administered, the three supplementary subtests should be given at a different time from the six core subtests to reduce student fatigue.

The *TOLD–4 Primary* was standardized in 2005 with 1,108 children from 16 states. This sample appears to approximate the national population in geographic region, gender, race, urban–rural residence, ethnicity, family income, and educational attainment of parents. Students with disabilities were included of the sample; most

common were those with speech-language disorders and learning disabilities.

The internal consistency (.97), test-retest (.80), and interrater (.90) reliabilities of the *TOLD–4 Primary* are adequate. The manual reports several investigations that support the concurrent validity of the previous edition of *TOLD Primary* with other tests of oral language and with vocabulary measures from tests of intellectual performance. Moderate to high correlations were found between the current edition of the *TOLD Primary* and language tests.

Percentile rank, standard scores, composite scores, and age equivalents are available for each subtest. Subtest standard scores are distributed with a mean of 10 and a standard deviation of 3. Quotients are standard scores (mean = 100, standard deviation = 15). *TOLD–4 Primary* results are plotted on a profile. The profile on the left shows the child's quotient scores, and subtest scores are plotted on the other profile. In this example, the child's performance falls within the low-average range in overall spoken language, listening skills, speaking skills, and semantics.

The *TOLD–4 Primary* is a useful measure for investigating the oral language skills of young children because it assesses several dimensions of language ability. It is best used at the start of language assessment to identify areas in which the child is proficient and areas that require further evaluation.

Test of Language Development–4, Intermediate

The intermediate level of the *TOLD–4* is designed for older elementary grade students. Like the primary version, it offers measures of receptive and expressive syntax and semantics. However, organizing skills are not assessed, and measures of phonology are not included.

Six subtests make up the *TOLD–4* Intermediate:

- *Sentence Combining* (Expressive Syntax). The tester reads two or more simple sentences, and the student must combine these into one new sentence.
- *Picture Vocabulary* (Receptive Semantics). The tester reads a two-word phrase and shows the student a Picture Card with six photos. The student must point to the photo that the phrase describes best.
- *Word Ordering* (Expressive Syntax). The tester reads several (three to seven) words in random order, and the student must put the words in order to form a sentence.
- *Relational Vocabulary* (Expressive Semantics). The tester reads three words, and the student must tell how the words are alike.
- *Morphological Comprehension* (Receptive Grammar). The student listens to the tester read sentences, some of which contain grammar errors. The student tells whether the sentence is correct or incorrect, but he or she is not required to provide corrections for errors.
- *Multiple Meanings* (Expressive Semantics). In this subtest, the tester reads a word and the student must say as many meanings possible.

The *TOLD–4 Intermediate* is somewhat more difficult to administer than the primary version of the test. Subtests must be administered in order. For Multiple Meanings, give all items. On Sentence Combining, Word Ordering and Relational Vocabulary ceiling is three consecutive incorrect items. Morphological Comprehension ceiling is 3 out of 5 incorrect (after #10). On Picture Vocabulary, ceiling is two consecutive incorrect items.

The *TOLD–4 Intermediate* was standardized in 2005 with 1,097 students from 14 states. The final sample appears to approximate the national population in geographic region, gender, race, urban–rural residence, family income, and educational attainment of parents. Students with disabilities were included in the study, with those with learning disabilities and speech-language disorders most common.

The internal consistency, test-retest, and interrater reliabilities of the *TOLD–4 Intermediate* are adequate. The *TOLD–4* manual reports two studies of validity showing relationships between this test and other measures. Moderate correlations were found between the *TOLD–4 Intermediate* and tests of academic achievement and language. Subtest scores on the *TOLD–4 Intermediate* are age equivalents, percentile ranks, composite quotients, and standard scores. The *TOLD–4 Intermediate* is a useful measure of oral language for older elementary grade students. Like the primary *TOLD–4*, it is best used at the start of assessment to identify the student's strengths and weaknesses in listening and speaking skills. Its results are not sufficiently specific to direct instructional planning.

Other Comprehensive Measures

In addition to the *TOLD–4*, several other comprehensive language measures are worthy of note. Those discussed in the next paragraphs attempt to broaden the scope of assessment by including not only oral, but also written, language skills.

Oral and Written Language Scales-II (OWLS-2)

The *OWLS-2* (Carrow-Woolfolk, 2011a) is composed of written language, reading, listening, and oral language scales. The Written Expression Scale was described earlier in this chapter. Of interest here are the two scales, Listening Comprehension and Oral Expression, which are designed for ages 3 through 21. On the Listening

Comprehension Scale, the tester reads an item, and the student responds by selecting one of four drawings. For example, the student may need to find the drawing of the doll or that of the smallest ball. On Oral Expression, the tester reads an item as the student looks at a drawing or drawings; the student must respond orally.

The oral language scales of the *OWLS* measure the student's ability to understand and use individual words, grammatical forms, and meaningful language. According to Carrow-Woolfolk (2011a), these scales assess the lexical, syntactic, pragmatic, and supralinguistic categories of oral language. The supralinguistic category refers to language tasks such as understanding humor.

Five Composite Scales are possible: Oral Language, Written Language, Receptive Language, Expressive Language, and Overall Language. Raw scores for Scales can be converted to a standard score (distributed with a mean of 100 and standard deviation of 15), percentile rank, and test-age equivalent. The oral language scales of the *OWLS-2*, like other broad-based measures, help to identify areas of need in oral language. However, further assessment is required in order to plan the instructional program.

Test of Adolescent and Adult Language–4 (TOAL–4)

The *TOAL–4* (Hammill et al., 2007) is a norm-referenced measure designed for students ages 12–0 to 24–11. It assesses both spoken and written language, and professionals can also obtain an overall general language score. The *TOAL–4* is of interest because it is one of the few tests of language designed specifically for older students.

Three of the six *TOAL–4* subtests assess oral language, and all must be administered individually:

- *Word Opposites.* The tester says a word, and the student must say a word that means the opposite.
- *Word Derivations.* The tester says a word and then reads two sentences. A form of the word must be used to complete the second sentence. The manual provides this example:

  The examiner says the key word *laugh* and then the sentences, "The play was very funny. The people broke out _____." The examinee should say, "laughing." (Hammill et al., 2007, p. 5).

- *Spoken Analogies.* The tester reads an analogy with a missing word. The manual gives this example, "Birds are to sing as dogs are to _____." (p. 5)

Subtest results are expressed as percentile ranks and scaled scores. The student's performance on the three oral language subtests is summarized by the Spoken Language Composite Index, a standard score with a mean of 100 and a standard deviation of 15. The *TOAL–4* manual provides guidelines for determining whether composite scores are significantly different (e.g., the Spoken Language Index versus the Written Language Index). There must be at least an 8-point discrepancy between Index scores for statistical significance and at least 26 points for clinical usefulness.

Illinois Test of Psycholinguistic Abilities— Third Edition

The *ITPA–3* is a thoroughly revised and up-dated version of the classic *Illinois Test of Psycholinguistic Abilities—Revised Edition* published in 1968 by Kirk, McCarthy, and Kirk. Unlike its predecessors, the *ITPA–3* contains measures of both oral and written language. The six oral language subtests are:

- *Spoken Analogies.* The student completes an analogy read aloud by the tester.
- *Spoken Vocabulary.* The student must produce an appropriate word when supplied a clue by the tester. The manual gives this example: "The examiner may say, 'I am thinking of something with a roof,' to which the child might respond, 'house'" (p. 7).
- *Morphological Closure.* The student fills in the blank when the tester presents prompts such as "small, smaller, _____."
- *Syntactic Sentences.* The student repeats a nonsense sentence read by the tester. Although nonsense, the sentence is syntactically correct.
- *Sound Deletion.* The student repeats words with parts deleted (e.g., a syllable or phoneme).
- *Rhyming Sequences.* The student repeats sequences of rhyming words read aloud by the tester.

The *ITPA–3* is designed for students ages 5–0 through 12–11. Standard scores and percentile ranks are available for all subtests and for several composites. Those pertaining to oral language are the Spoken Language Composite, Semantics Composite, Grammar Composite, and Phonology Composite. A total test score, the General Language Composite, is available if the six written language subtests are also administered.

ENHANCEDetext
Video Example 15.4
Watch this video to find out more about language assessment of a child of early childhood age.

STRATEGIES FOR ASSESSING ARTICULATION

Articulation refers to the production of speech sounds or phonemes. There are 44 speech sounds in the English language (Polloway & Smith, 1982). Twenty-five are consonantal sounds such as the initial phonemes in *mother* and *baby*. Consonantal sounds are produced by movements of the articulators (tongue, lips, teeth, palate, and so forth). There are also 19 vocalic sounds (e.g., the initial phonemes in *at* and *open*); when these are produced, the air passes through the mouth without obstruction. Table 15–6 presents the phonemes in the English language and examples of words containing these sounds. Some experts separate vocalic sounds into two categories: vowels and diphthongs. Diphthongs are made up of a combination of two vowel sounds. Examples are the medial phonemes in each of these words: *paid, time, couch,* and *boil* (Culatta & Culatta, 1985).

In the assessment of articulation, a sample of the child's speech is gathered, and the speech sounds that are produced are evaluated in terms of accuracy and intelligibility. One way to gather a speech sample is simply to record the spontaneous utterances of the child. However, this is not efficient because it may take the child some time to produce all of the speech sounds. Standardized measures of articulation use other strategies, and one of the most common is to present pictures or other stimuli to elicit the production of specific phonemes. For example, the *Photo Articulation Test—Third Edition* (Lippke, Dickey, Selmar, & Soder, 1997) contains 72 color photographs of objects. In naming these objects, the child produces all of the consonant, vowel, and diphthong sounds.

The *Goldman-Fristoe Test of Articulation— Third Edition* (Goldman & Fristoe, 2015) employs three strategies for eliciting speech sounds. The Sounds-in-Words subtest is a picture-naming task; the student is shown pictures of familiar objects and is asked to name or answer questions about them. The Sounds-in-Sentences subtest is more unusual. It contains stories that are accompanied by action pictures. The stories include words that have the speech sounds with which children most often have difficulty. The tester reads a story and then asks the student to retell it. The third subtest, Stimulability, is administered last. On this measure, the tester attempts to stimulate the student to produce phonemes that were misarticulated earlier in the test. The student is directed to watch and listen as the tester pronounces the target sound in a syllable, within a word, and in the context of a sentence.

Specially trained professionals such as speech-language pathologists usually administer norm-referenced tests of articulation. However, other professionals can collect preliminary data on students' articulation skills with informal procedures. The most common method is observation and analysis of the student's spontaneous speech. Also, any of the strategies used by formal measures can be adapted for informal assessment. For example, the student can be asked to name pictures or objects selected to represent the speech sounds.

TABLE 15–6
Phonemes of the English Language

I. CONSONANTAL (25)		II. VOCALIC (19)	
/b/	Ball	/ă/	cat
/ch/	Chip	/ā/	cake
/d/	Dog	/â/	air
/f/	Farm	/ä/	art
/g/	Goat	/ĕ/	leg
/h/	Home	/ē/	meal
/j/	Jump	/ĭ/	pin
/k/	Kite	/ī/	ice
/l/	Lamp	/ŏ/	log
/m/	Moon	/ō/	road
/n/	Nut	/ô/	stork, ball
/ng/	Song	/oi/	boy
/p/	Pig	/oo/	book
/r/	Rug	/ōō/	moon
/s/	Sun	/ou/	cow
/sh/	Ship	/ū/	cube
/t/	Top	/ŭ/	duck
/th/	Thumb	/û/	fur, fern
/th/	That	/ə/	sofa, circus
/v/	Vine		
/w/	Witch		
/wh/	White		
/y/	yo-yo		
/z/	Zipper		
/zh/	pleasure		

Note: From *Teaching Language Arts to Exceptional Learners* by E. A. Polloway and J. E. Smith, 1982, Denver: Love. Copyright 1982 by Love Publishing Company. Reprinted by permission.

STRATEGIES FOR ASSESSING MORPHOLOGY AND SYNTAX

Morphology and syntax, like phonology, are dimensions of language that relate to form. Morphology is concerned with the smallest meaningful units of language—morphemes—and how these are combined into words. Syntax is the relationship of words in phrases and sentences. Several formal measures of morphology and syntax are available for young children; in normal development, most of the formal features of language are learned during the preschool and early school years. The paragraphs that follow discuss formal measures of morphology and syntax as well as techniques for the analysis of language samples.

Formal Measures

Northwestern Syntax Screening Test (NSST)

The *NSST* (Lee, 1971) is designed to identify problems in either receptive or expressive syntax. Syntax, as defined by this test, includes morphology. It is an individual test that is appropriate for young children ages 3–0 to 7–4. Two subtests are included—Receptive and Expressive. On the Receptive subtest, the student is shown a page containing four line drawings. The tester reads a sentence, and the student must select the drawing that represents its meaning. Two sentences are read for each page of four drawings, and the sentences vary in only one grammatical element. For example, the first sentence might be "The dog is *in front of* the couch" and the second "The dog is *on top of* the couch." On the Expressive subtest, the student looks at two drawings, while the tester reads a sentence describing each. Then, for each drawing, the tester asks, "Now, what's this picture?" The student is expected to recall the sentences read by the tester. Again, the sentence pairs differ in only one grammatical element (verb tense, preposition, singular or plural verb, etc.).

Percentile rank scores are available for each subtest. According to the manual, scores at the second to third percentile are considered below average, and children earning such scores "are almost certain to be in need of interventional language teaching"(p. 9).

The *NSST* is a screening test; thus, its purpose is to identify children in need of further assessment. However, it is best used as an informal measure because of lack of information about technical quality. The manual does not discuss reliability and validity. In addition, the sample used to standardize this measure is inadequate. Only 344 children were included, half of whom were between the ages of 5–0 and 5–11. The children represented only seven schools from middle to upper-middle-income backgrounds.

Test for Auditory Comprehension of Language—Fourth Edition (TACL–4)

The purpose of the *TACL–4* (Carrow-Woolfolk, 1999) is assessment of receptive vocabulary, grammar, and syntax. It is an individual test for ages 3–0 through 12–11, and three subtests are included: Vocabulary, Grammatical Morphemes, and Elaborated Phrases and Sentences. The test format is similar to other measures of receptive language. A page with three full-color drawings is shown to the student, and the student must select the drawing that best represents the meaning of the word or sentence read by the tester.

The *TACL–4* was standardized with a national sample of 1,142 students selected to represent the U.S. population in terms of gender, race, ethnicity, geographic region, and disability. Several types of scores are available, including standard scores, percentile ranks, and age equivalents.

Carrow Elicited Language Inventory (CELI)

The *CELI*, also by Carrow-Woolfolk (1974), is a measure of expressive morphology and syntax for children ages 3–0 to 7–11. It is an individual test with one type of task: the tester reads and the child repeats a sentence. The imitation task was selected because research findings indicate a relationship between the form of children's spontaneous speech and the form of sentences they can imitate.

The 52 sentences on the *CELI* were constructed to assess several different grammatical categories and features: articles, adjectives, nouns, noun plurals, pronouns, verbs, negatives, contractions, adverbs, prepositions, demonstratives, and conjunctions. Percentile ranks are provided for the total test score as well as for each grammatical class. In addition, the student's errors are analyzed by type (substitution, omission, addition, transposition, reversal), and a percentile rank score is determined for each type. A Verb Protocol is available for in-depth analysis of the child's mastery of verb forms. Scoring the *CELI* is time consuming.

A small, restricted sample from only one city was used to standardize the *CELI*. Standardization took place in 1973 in Houston, Texas, and the sample contained 475 white children "from middle socioeconomic level homes" (p. 8). Reliability and validity were investigated, but the study samples included only 20 to 25 children. For these reasons, the *CELI* is best used as an informal measure of expressive syntax and morphology.

Analysis of Language Samples

Language samples are another method for the assessment of expressive syntax and morphology. A sample of the child's language is elicited, tape recorded, and transcribed. The transcription is then analyzed using one of the methods described in the following paragraphs.

Mean Length of Utterance

The simplest way of analyzing a child's language sample is to compute the mean length of utterance (MLU). A sample of 50 consecutive utterances, at minimum, is needed for this procedure. The professional counts the number of morphemes that the child produced and divides this total by the number of utterances. MLU, according to Wiig and Semel (1984), has been correlated with similar measures and has received adequate correlations.

Brown (1973) developed a set of procedures for calculating MLU that has been adopted by most language development researchers (Bartel, Bryen, & Keehn, 1973. In Brown's system, analysis begins with the second page of the transcription of the child's language sample. The first 100 utterances are counted, although 50 are sufficient for a preliminary estimate. Inflections such as the possessive *s* and the regular past tense *d* are counted as separate morphemes. Repetitions are not counted; nor are fillers such as "um" and "oh." Compound words are counted as one morpheme, as are diminutives (e.g., *kitty*) and catenatives (e.g., *gonna, wanna*).

According to Brown, these procedures are reasonable only for language samples with mean lengths of utterance up to approximately 4.0. Thus, this technique is most useful for young children and children with serious language disorders.

Developmental Sentence Analysis

Developmental Sentence Analysis (Lee, 1974) is another technique. This is a norm-referenced procedure designed for children ages 2–0 to 6–11. In an interview situation, a clinician elicits a sample of the child's language using stimulus materials such as toys or pictures. The sample is transcribed and analyzed to determine what proportion of the child's utterances are complete sentences. In this system, a complete sentence is defined as a noun and verb in subject–predicate relationship. Thus, "doggie bark" is considered a complete sentence.

Fifty complete, consecutive sentences are needed to use the Developmental Sentence Scoring system. First, each word is categorized by its grammatical type. Lee (1974) states that the categories of grammatical forms included are those "showing the most significant developmental progression in children's language" (p. 136). These are:

1. Indefinite pronoun or noun modifier
2. Personal pronoun
3. Main verb
4. Secondary verb
5. Negative
6. Conjunction
7. Interrogative reversal in questions
8. *WH*-question

A chart is then consulted to assign a point value to each word. Words representing higher developmental status receive higher point values. For example, among personal pronouns, first- and second-person pronouns such as *I* and *you* receive 1 point, third-person pronouns such as *he* and *she* receive 2 points, and plurals such as *we* receive 3 points. Point values range from 1 to 8.

The total number of points assigned to words in the sample of sentences is determined and then divided by the number of sentences (50) to produce the Developmental Sentence Score (DSS). This score can be expressed as a percentile rank. A chart is provided for determining where the score falls in relation to the 10th, 25th, 50th, 75th, and 90th percentiles for each 6-month age group between ages 2–0 and 6–6. The norms for this procedure were derived using a sample of

200 children. Thus, there were only 20 boys and 20 girls at each age level. The children were from middle-class, monolingual homes in four states. Split-half reliability was reported as .73 over all ages, but coefficients fell in the .50s for children aged 2, 3, and 4. No information is provided about concurrent validity.

Because norms are based on a limited sample, reliability is low for very young children, and validity is not established, this technique is best viewed as an informal assessment strategy.

Language Sampling, Analysis, and Training— Third edition (LSAT–3)

The *LSAT–3* (Tyack & Venable, 1999) is a similar approach to the analysis of children's expressive oral language. A sample of at least 100 sentences is elicited from the child and then transcribed. The number of words and the number of morphemes are counted for each sentence in order to determine the word–morpheme index. Then the child's utterances are analyzed according to several types of syntactical constructions: noun phrases, verb phrases, simple sentences, complex sentences, and questions and negatives. The results provide detailed information about the child's oral language needs in relation to expressive morphology and syntax.

 Breakpoint Practice 15.5
Click here to check your understanding of assessment of articulation, syntax and morphology.

STRATEGIES FOR ASSESSING SEMANTICS AND PRAGMATICS

Semantics is concerned with the meaning of language. A variety of tests and other procedures are available to assess students' comprehension of language content and production of meaningful discourse. In contrast, pragmatics is concerned with language use or, in the words of Wiig and Semel (1984), language in a communicative context. Meaning is one aspect of pragmatics, but the major focus is the speaker's intent and the way that language is used to fulfill that intent.

Assessment of Language Meaning

Formal measures are available to assess both receptive and expressive semantics skills. The most typical test format for receptive measures is a picture-identification task. The tester reads a word or a sentence, and the student selects from several pictures the one that best illustrates the meaning of the word or sentence. The best-known measure of receptive semantics is the *Peabody Picture Vocabulary Test—Fourth Edition* (Dunn & Dunn, 2007), which is described in the next sections along with the *Expressive Vocabulary Test—Second Edition* (Williams, 2007) and the *Comprehensive Receptive and Expressive Vocabulary Test—Third Edition* (Wallace & Hammill, 2013). Strategies for informal assessment are also discussed.

Peabody Picture Vocabulary Test— Fourth Edition (PPVT–4).

The *PPVT–4* is an individual test of receptive vocabulary designed for ages 2–6 through 90+. Two forms of the test are available, and administration typically requires 10 to 15 minutes. The test task remains the same throughout the *PPVT–4.* The student is shown a page containing four line drawings. The tester reads a word, and the student points to or says the number of the drawing that represents that word.

The *PPVT–4* includes four training items. In presenting an item, the tester shows the student a page with four different drawings and says, "Put your finger on _____," filling the blank with the label for one of the drawings. Once the tester is sure that the student understands the test task, these directions can be varied; for example, the manual recommends substitutions such as "Show me _____" or "What number is _____?" The *PPVT–4* contains 228 test items arranged in 19 sets of 12 each. The tester consults the protocol for a suggested starting point and then begins administration with the first item in the suggested set. The entire set is administered. A basal set is achieved when the student makes no more than one error in the 12-item set. The ceiling set is reached when there are eight or more errors in the 12-item set.

Until this edition of the *PPVT,* only age norms were available. The *PPVT–4* provides both age norms and grade norms (K–12). Only one result is obtained on this measure: an index of total test performance. Several types of scores are used to report that result, including standard scores (distributed with a mean of 100 and standard deviation of 15), percentile ranks, stanines, and age and grade equivalents. The student's score can be plotted on a profile and a confidence interval constructed around the score. The test form also provides a grid for error analysis of the parts of speech with which students might experience difficulty: nouns, verbs, and "attributes" (i.e., adjectives and adverbs).

The 2007 edition of the *PPVT* was standardized with a sample of 3,540 individuals ages 2–6 to 81+. The grade norm sample was a subset of the age norm sample. The age sample appears to resemble the U.S. population in terms of race/ethnicity, geographical region, and education level, an indicator of socialeconomic status. Representative numbers of students with disabilities were included in the norm group. However, English learners were not; English proficiency was one of the criteria for inclusion in the sample. Reliability of the *PPVT–4* appears adequate. In relation to validity, the manual provides evidence that results of the *PPVT–4* are related to those of oral language and reading measures. In addition, the *PPVT–4* appears to differentiate among students with identified disabilities, typical students in the norm group, and students identified as gifted.

The *PPVT–4* is a quick, easy-to-administer measure of receptive vocabulary. It is "*not,* however, a comprehensive test of general intelligence" (Dunn & Dunn, 1981, p. 2), as noted by the authors of the second edition of the *PPVT.* The misuse of the *PPVT* as an index of general intellectual ability continues today. In the current manual, for example, the fourth edition authors say that "for individuals whose primary language is English, vocabulary correlates highly with general verbal ability" (p. 1). Despite the merit of that assertion, the *PPVT–4* is best used as a screening tool to measure one of the many dimensions of oral language development, receptive vocabulary.

Expressive Vocabulary Test— Second Edition (EVT–2)

The *EVT–2* is an individual test of expressive vocabulary for ages 2–6 through 90+. Like the *PPVT–4* with which it was co-normed, it measures only one aspect of oral language. However, the *EVT–2* is composed of two types of test tasks, rather than one: labeling and synonyms. In the labeling items, students look at a picture and tell what they see; only one-word responses are acceptable. In the synonym items, the tester reads a word, and the student says a word that means the same.

As on the *PPVT–4,* one overall result is obtained. *EVT–2* total test performance can be expressed as a standard score, percentile rank, stanine, age equivalent, and grade equivalent. Results can also be plotted on a profile and compared with those of the *PPVT–4,* if there is interest in contrasting the student's receptive and expressive language skills. The co-norming of the two measures facilitates this type of comparison.

Comprehensive Receptive and Expressive Vocabulary Test—Second Edition (CREVT–3)

The *CREVT–3* is an interesting measure because it is one of the few tests that assesses both receptive and expressive semantics. The *CREVT–3* is designed for students ages 5–0 to 89. It contains two subtests: Receptive Vocabulary and Expressive Vocabulary. On Receptive Vocabulary, the student looks at a set of six color photographs and points to the one that best depicts the word spoken by the examiner. On Expressive Vocabulary, the examiner says a word and the student must tell what it means.

Results are available on the *CREVT–2* for Receptive Vocabulary, Expressive Vocabulary, and General Vocabulary (a total test score). These results include standard scores, percentile ranks, and age equivalents.

Informal Assessment Strategies

It is also possible to use informal procedures to evaluate a student's ability to comprehend and produce meaningful language. Any of the tasks used on formal tests could be adapted for this purpose. For example, if receptive vocabulary is the area of interest, the teacher can present a set of pictures or objects, name one, and direct the child to point to it. Or the child can be asked to demonstrate the meaning of action words ("Show me *jump*") or prepositions ("Put the apple in *front* of the book"). If expressive semantics is the concern, the student can be asked to label pictures or objects, define words, use words in sentences, provide synonyms or antonyms, describe objects or events, or tell a story.

A teacher can create a checklist for recording information about vocabulary development. It could list all kinds of vocabulary words to describe clothing, classroom objects, etc. The teacher could generate lists of words for each vocabulary type. These lists would vary from child to child due to differences in age, gender, interests, and environments. Once this checklist is expanded, it could form the basis for a series of observations of the student's language behavior. It could also provide the professional with a structure for designing a set of informal inventories to learn more about the student's receptive and expressive vocabulary.

Assessment of Language Use

Pragmatics refers to the way that language is used for communication in different situations. As language skills develop, children learn to modify their choice of words and grammatical structures according to the message they intend to convey and the situation in which the communication takes place. The context of the speech act is an important variable that is determined by several factors:

1. The social setting and occasion of the interaction
2. The location of the interaction
3. The characteristics of the participants (gender, race, ethnicity, etc.) in the interaction
4. The topic and purpose of the interaction
5. The spatial deployment of the participants (face-to-face, at a distance, nonvisible) in the interaction
6. The role or intent of the speaker. (Wiig & Semel, 1984, p. 57)

The speaker's intent influences the content and form of language and the way the message is delivered. One system for categorizing the several different purposes of communication has been proposed by Wells (1973). According to Wiig and Semel (1984), this system has five distinct language uses:

- *Ritualizing.* The ritualized use of language in social situations, as in greetings, farewells, introductions, turn taking, responses to requests, and so forth.
- *Informing.* The use of language to give or request information.
- *Controlling.* The use of language to control or influence the actions of the listener.
- *Feeling.* The use of language to express feelings or to respond to feelings or attitudes expressed by others.
- *Imagining.* The use of language to create an imaginary situation, as in storytelling, role playing, speculation, or the creation of fantasies.

By the end of the elementary grades, students are expected to comprehend the different functions of language and use language appropriately to accomplish each of these purposes (Wiig & Semel, 1984). As with other dimensions of language, competence in pragmatics develops over time. Findings from research by Wiig (1982b) and others suggest that children around the age of 6 communicate from a self-oriented perspective. However, by age 12, students adapt to the listener's needs. They are able to alter expectations, negotiate, state reasons and justifications, and communicate bad news so that its impact is softened.

Let's Talk Inventory for Children

The *Let's Talk Inventory for Children* (Bray & Wiig, 1987) is one of the few formal tools available for the assessment of pragmatic competence. It is an individual measure for ages 4 to 8. The assessment task is interesting. The student is shown a picture that illustrates a communication situation. Some pictures show peer interactions, others show interactions between a child and an adult. A short narrative is read to the student describing the situation and the intent of the speaker. The student's task is to formulate a speech act that is appropriate to the context, the audience, and the stated communicative intent.

Items are available to assess four of the major functions of language: ritualizing, informing, controlling, and feeling. The imagining function is not assessed, but the format of the test is role playing, a communication strategy that requires use of the imagining function. Items are also provided to assess receptive pragmatics, if the student experiences difficulty with the expressive tasks.

Test of Pragmatic Skills—Revised Edition

Shulman's (1986) *Test of Pragmatic Skills—Revised Edition* is designed for students ages 3 to 8. The test tasks are four guided play interactions in which the tester follows a script to elicit responses from the child. For example, in the first interaction, the student and tester use puppets to converse about favorite television shows. The test probes 10 types of communicative intents: requesting information, requesting action, rejection/denial, naming/labeling, answering/responding, informing, reasoning, summoning/calling, greeting, and closing conversation.

Test of Pragmatic Language— Second Edition (TOPL-2)

This measure by Phelps-Terasaki and Phelps-Gunn (2007) provides norms for students ages 6–0 to 18–11. It is designed to assess several aspects of pragmatic language, including the effects of context variables (setting, event, and audience) and message variables (topic and purpose). The communication purposes included in the model underlying the *TOPL-2* are requesting, informing, regulating, expressing, ritualizing, and organizing.

The test tasks are designed to elicit language from the student; expressive skills are emphasized. On most items, the tester shows the student a picture and then asks a question about the communication situation it depicts. Although the *TOPL-2* samples several types of pragmatic language skills, the only results it provides are an overall standard score and percentile rank.

Pragmatic Language Skills Inventory

This measure by Gilliam and Miller (2006) is a norm-referenced rating scale designed to be completed by teachers. Appropriate for students ages 5 to 12, the *Inventory* is made up of three subscales, each assessing a somewhat different aspect of pragmatic language: Classroom Interaction Skills, Social Interaction Skills, and Personal Interaction Skills. Teachers read descriptions of behaviors, then rate students on a nine-point scale from below average (ratings 1, 2, 3) to average (4, 5, 6) to above average (7, 8, 9). Standard scores and percentile ranks are available for each of the three subscales; a total test Pragmatic Language Index can also be calculated.

Informal Assessment Strategies

Informal strategies can also be used to investigate pragmatic performance. Mercer and Mercer (1998) suggest that a spontaneous sample of the student's speech can be analyzed to determine the types of language functions the student uses. Videotaping is the best way to record the language sample, because it allows the professional to study the situation in which the communication occurred. If this is not possible, the student can be audiotaped while an observer records the events that occur before and after each speech act. The professional evaluates each utterance in relation to the events that preceded and followed it and then assigns the utterance to a function category.

There are several other strategies for informal assessment of pragmatic competence. Students can be observed as they engage in conversational interactions with peers and adults, or the teacher can set up a role-playing situation to evaluate specific types of communications. For example, if observations reveal that a student rarely uses language for the ritualizing function, the student could be asked to participate in role plays such as meeting a friend on the way to school and leaving a party. Receptive skills can be probed with videotapes or pictures that present conversational interactions. For example, if the controlling function of language is of interest, the teacher could show a picture of two children, one of whom is playing with a toy

truck. The student would then be asked to select the more appropriate request: "Give me that truck!" or "May I please play with the truck a little while?"

ENHANCEDetext
Video Example 15.5
Watch this video to find out more about an example of a language sample at the middle school level.

ANSWERING THE ASSESSMENT QUESTIONS

The purpose of the study of oral language is to describe the student's current levels of performance in this important area of functioning. Many assessment strategies are available for this purpose. Many are norm-referenced tests, whereas others are informal measures such as language samples and informal inventories. These tools aid the assessment team in gathering information about the student's current status in oral language development.

Nature of the Assessment Tools

Measures of oral language vary along several dimensions, one of the most obvious being the language they assess. The most common language is, of course, English. However, several tests evaluate students' skills in Spanish, and some assess both English- and Spanish-language proficiency. Formal tests of proficiency in other languages are less common, although informal measures may be available.

Language measures also vary in the range of skills they assess. Some measures attempt to be comprehensive, whereas others concentrate on one or perhaps two of the major dimensions of language. Several current test batteries include measures of phonology, morphology, syntax, and semantics. However, measures are not truly comprehensive unless they include the newest area of language study—pragmatics.

Oral language is a complex skill made up of many subskills. Consequently, some measures attend to only one specific area of functioning. Examples include measures of articulation, those that assess morphology and syntax, and vocabulary tests. Some tests are so specific that they address an area as restricted as expressive syntax or receptive semantics.

Measures also differ in depth of skill coverage. Thus, norm-referenced tests tend to sample several skills and/or several skill levels, but only a few representative test items are provided in each area. Most informal measures are designed to evaluate skills in much greater depth. An example is language sample analysis in which every utterance is recorded, transcribed, and analyzed. A wealth of information concerning the student's productivity, the semantic aspects of the communication, and the specific morphological and syntactical characteristics of the student's language is the result.

Measures use different assessment tasks to evaluate similar oral language skills. For example, the student's command of morphology and syntax is assessed by tasks such as sentence repetition, sentence combination, and identification of pictures that best represent the meaning of sentences. Clearly, differences among test tasks must be considered when selecting the tools for assessment and interpreting results.

The Relationship of Oral Language to Other Areas of Performance

When assessment is complete, the special education team begins to interpret the results and study the relationships between and among areas of performance. General learning aptitude is one area of interest. Because general aptitude can influence the rate and success with which skills are acquired, the student's progress in oral language should be evaluated in relation to the estimated level of intellectual functioning. Verbal Index scores are most appropriate for this purpose. However, the relationship between language and intelligence is reciprocal. Just as intelligence can affect language development, students' language skills can affect performance on measures of intellectual performance. This is a particular concern with students whose language is dissimilar from the formal Standard English used on intelligence tests.

Specific learning abilities also play a role in the student's ability to acquire and use oral language skills. Difficulties in attention and memory can hinder language development, as can poor auditory discrimination. Again, the relationship is reciprocal. Language is an integral part of learning strategies such as verbal rehearsal, and students use language to regulate their own learning behavior and focus attention.

Classroom behavior may be influenced by language development. Students with poor receptive language skills may appear inattentive, fail to follow directions, or seem to ignore the teacher. Students with poor expressive skills may be reluctant to speak in class, especially in situations in which peers can take notice of their errors or the differences between their language and Standard English. Such students may refuse to answer questions and participate in class discussions; they may engage in disruptive behavior to draw attention away from their difficulties with language. Also, self-concept and attitude toward school are likely to be affected.

Oral language skills have an impact on other areas of school performance. All school subjects require at least some listening and speaking skills. In classrooms at all grade levels, from preschool through college, students are expected to learn by listening. The demands for speaking skills are almost as great. No matter what subject or what grade level, the teacher will ask questions and expect students to respond orally. Students who enter school with delays in receptive or expressive language development are likely to experience difficulty in the acquisition of reading, mathematics, and written language skills as well as content area subjects.

Oral language also pervades daily life. At home and at work, people communicate with each other through speech. They talk face to face and on the telephone to family members, friends, neighbors, and acquaintances; they talk to facilitate vocational pursuits and to accomplish routine tasks such as shopping. Students with severe language disorders may require training to succeed at the oral communication tasks that make up much of the fabric of daily life.

Documentation of Oral Language Performance

The general question that guides the assessment team in its study of student performance is, *What are the student's educational needs?* Two specific questions are asked in relation to the student's oral communication skills: *What is the student's current level of development in oral language? What are the student's strengths and weaknesses in the various skill areas of oral language?*

Many types of data are gathered to answer these questions. The team may begin by reviewing school records and the information collected in classroom observations and interviews with teachers and parents. Formal tests may then be administered to evaluate the student's oral language performance in relation to that of age or grade peers. Informal assessment strategies such as language sampling, informal inventories, and criterion-referenced tests may also play a role by describing the specific skill areas in which the student shows educational needs.

As with other areas of assessment, the team should select its tools with care so that duplication is avoided and the assessment process is as efficient as possible. This is an important concern in the study of oral language skills because of the great number of available formal measures. In addition, the more specific procedures such as language sampling should be reserved for in-depth assessment of potential problem areas. By answering the assessment questions about oral language, the team moves closer to planning the student's individualized education program.

Assessment in Actions
Sal

The team is now gathering data to assist in planning Sal's Individualized Education Program. From the reports of Sal's fourth grade teacher and from the results of individual achievement tests, the team is quite certain that Sal could benefit from specially designed instruction in at least two areas of written language: spelling and handwriting.

In spelling, Sal showed below-average performance on both the *PIAT–R/NU* and the *WIAT–II,* and he is working in a grade 2 spelling book in her fourth-grade classroom. To learn more about Sal's spelling skills, the team will administer the *Test of Written Spelling–5,* a measure that assesses the student's ability to spell phonetically regular and irregular words. Then informal techniques will be used to explore the particular spelling skills that appear to be areas of weakness for Sal. For example, if regular words appear to be a problem, the team may administer an informal inventory or criterion-referenced test that probes the student's ability to write the letters that correspond to various letter sounds.

Handwriting may also be an area of need for Sal. In the school that he attended last year, cursive writing was not introduced in the third grade, so Sal entered fourth grade at a disadvantage. Mr. Harvey, his fourth-grade teacher, has begun to teach Sal cursive writing, but Sal continues to print the majority of his assignments. Despite 3 years of instruction, Sal's printing is not good. To gather more information about handwriting, the assessment team will observe Sal as he writes and will collect several samples of his printing and cursive writing. The observational data and writing samples will be carefully analyzed to detect any pattern of errors.

As yet, the assessment team has no information about Sal's composition skills. Sal's ability to write sentences, themes, essays, stories, and the like was not mentioned by Mr. Harvey when he referred Sal for assessment, so the team will begin by interviewing Mr. Harvey. Then a broad-range measure such as the *Test of Written Language–4* will be administered to help the team pinpoint Sal's strengths and weaknesses in various composition skills. As necessary, informal procedures will be used to gather further information about specific areas of educational need. Sal's individualized program in written language will be based on the results of these assessments.

At this point in assessment, the team has some information about Sal's current skills in spelling and handwriting. In both areas, Sal's performance appears to be below average, and in his fourth-grade classroom, he is working in a second-grade spelling book and just beginning to learn cursive writing. However, little information is available about Sal's composition skills. Mr. Harvey, Sal's teacher, did not discuss composition when he made the referral, so the team decides to begin its in-depth study of written language by talking with him. In this interview, Mr. Harvey reports that Sal writes quite slowly, his handwriting is difficult to read, and his spelling is poor. Despite this negative assessment, Sal seems to have good ideas. Although his compositions are short and hard to read because of his difficulties with handwriting and spelling, he is able to express his thoughts in writing.

The team administers the *Test of Written Language–4* to learn more about Sal's composition skills, and the following results are obtained:

Subtests	Standard Scores
Vocabulary	7
Spelling	6
Punctuation	5
Logical Sentences	7
Sentence Combining	7
Story Construction	8
Composites	
Contrived Writing	75
Spontaneous Writing	83
Overall Writing	77

Sal's overall performance on the *TOWL–4* indicates low-average achievement in written language skills. However, on the writing sample, he shows strengths in Story Construction. Spelling and Style are areas of weakness. On the contrived subtests, Sal asked for

assistance in reading several of the words and sentences.

To investigate Sal's difficulties with spelling, the *Test of Written Spelling–5* is given. Sal's performance on this measure is consistent with his scores on the spelling subtests of the *PIAT–R/NU* and the *WIAT–II.* He earns an overall standard score of 69, indicating below-average performance in spelling.

Ms. Gale, the special education resource teacher, administers an informal spelling inventory (see Table 15–2) to determine Sal's pattern of errors with regular words. On this measure, Sal is able to spell the short sounds of vowels and words that follow the consonant-vowel-consonant-e pattern (e.g., *line* and *cake*). In the 15 words that he attempts, he makes no errors with consonants. However, he is unable to spell words with two vowels together (e.g., *coat*), with *ow-ou* spellings of the *ou* sound, long and short *oo,* and final *y* as short *i.* Sal is then asked to write the spellings of a portion of words in a high-frequency word list. He spells the first two groups of 10 words correctly but then begins to experience difficulty. For example, he spells *any* as *ene* and *eat* as *et.*

Handwriting is the next area of study. Samples of Sal's manuscript and cursive writing are obtained from Mr. Harvey and analyzed for possible error patterns. In manuscript, Sal's letters are large, poorly spaced, and often difficult to read. As the following sample shows, he seems to have special difficulty writing circular letters like *a, o,* and *e:*

Sal has just begun to learn cursive writing. He is able to write all of the lowercase letters and has started to learn capitals. His cursive writing is also large, but the spacing between letters and words is adequate. Letter formation is satisfactory, but he has not yet learned how to join some letters together with others.

A classroom observation is conducted when Sal is participating in a writing activity. Sal writes in manuscript to copy a paragraph from the board. His chair and desk are of appropriate size, his posture is adequate, and he holds his paper and pencil correctly. However, he writes with a standard pencil on lined paper with narrow spaces and no guidelines. In forming letters, he makes one line, lifts his pencil from the paper, repositions the pencil, and then writes a second line. For example, in writing an uppercase *M,* he makes four separate lines, lifting his pencil each time. This strategy, along with his frequent erasures, affects his writing speed.

After a thorough analysis of these results, the assessment team is prepared to describe Sal's current levels of written language performance. They have reached these conclusions:

- At present, Sal is functioning within the low-average range in composition skills, as measured by the *Test of Written Language–4.*
- Sal's spelling skills are quite deficient. On the *Test of Written Spelling–5,* he showed below-average performance in overall spelling.
- Sal's knowledge of regular spellings is limited to consonant and short vowel sounds and

words that follow the consonant-vowel-consonant-*e* pattern. He is able to spell only a very few irregular words.
- On most classroom assignments, Sal writes in manuscript. His manuscript writing is large, poorly spaced, and difficult to read because of poor formation of some letters (e.g., *a, e,* and *o*). A larger pencil and paper with guidelines between widely spaced lines might help improve his legibility.
- Sal's manuscript writing is slow because he lifts his pencil after each stroke and erases frequently.
- In cursive, Sal's spacing and letter formation are adequate, and his writing is legible. He needs to learn the uppercase cursive alphabet and procedures for joining letters together.

SUMMARY

- In special education, written language skills may be investigated at the start of assessment to determine the student's eligibility for special education services. Further investigation is needed if there is reason to believe that aspects of written language may be areas of educational need.

- The *Test of Written Spelling–5 (TWS–5)* is a norm-referenced measure designed for students ages 6–0 to 18–11. Two forms of the *TWS–5* are available, Form A and Form B. Both are standard dictation tests.

- Both observations and error analyses can provide information about how students approach handwriting. A student can be observed during an activity that requires writing, and then error analysis procedures can be applied to the writing sample that the student produces.

- A student's ability to plan, write, and revise a piece of original writing can be assessed formally with the aid of standardized tests or informally with techniques such as rating scales, work sample analysis, criterion-referenced tests, observation, clinical interviews, and portfolios.

- The major factors within the interpersonal environment that are of concern in assessment are social relationships among students and student–teacher interactions. Often, students with achievement problems are not well accepted by their peers. This can occur when students experience difficulty with written language, particularly when their attempts to communicate in writing are open to view by their peers.

- Assessment tools can also vary in the depth with which skills are assessed. In general, informal measures are likely to provide the most thorough coverage of individual skills. For example, the *BRIGANCE® Comprehensive Inventory of Basic Skills–II* offers several tests of spelling, and each considers a specific skill in depth: spelling initial consonants, suffixes, prefixes, and so forth.

- In special education assessment, oral language may be a concern of the assessment team as it begins to gather data for planning the student's IEP. Many students with mild disabilities have special instructional needs in oral language.

- The *TOLD–4 Primary* is an individual test of oral language for preschool and early elementary grade children. There are six core and three supplementary subtests on the *TOLD–4 Primary.* The *TOLD–4 Primary* assesses listening, organizing, and speaking skills in relation to phonology, syntax, and semantics.

However, core subtests address only syntax and semantics.

- Standardized measures of articulation use other strategies, and one of the most common is to present pictures or other stimuli to elicit the production of specific phonemes. In naming these objects, the child produces all of the consonant, vowel, and diphthong sounds.

- The *Test for Auditory Comprehension of Language—Fourth Edition TACL–4* (Carrow-Woolfolk, 1999) assesses receptive vocabulary, grammar, and syntax. It is an individual test for ages 3–0 through 12–11, and three subtests are included: Vocabulary, Grammatical Morphemes, and Elaborated Phrases and Sentences.

- The *Peabody Picture Vocabulary Test—Fourth Edition (PPVT–4)* is an individual test of receptive vocabulary designed for ages 2–6 through 90+. The student is shown a page containing four line drawings. The tester reads a word, and the student points to or says the number of the drawing that represents that word.

- The purpose of the study of oral language is to describe the student's current levels of performance in this important area of functioning. Numerous assessment strategies are available for this purpose. Many are norm-referenced tests, whereas others are informal measures such as language samples and informal inventories.

16

Andrey Kuzmin/Fotolia

Early Childhood Assessment

By Laura J. Hall

LEARNING OUTCOMES

After reading this chapter, you will be able to:

- Describe the importance of the interrelationship between the child and his or her family in the context of considerations in assessment of young children.

- Identify and define an example of a screening tool.

- Discuss the infant–toddler and family instrument as an example in ecological assessment, family interviews and rating scales, observation, and play-based assessment.

- Identify and discuss an example of curriculum-based or criterion-referenced assessment.

- Compare and contrast norm-referenced and dynamic assessment.

- Compare and contrast the *Receptive One-Word Picture Vocabulary Test-4* and the *Expressive One-Word Picture Vocabulary Test* in school readiness.

- Describe the use of activity-based interventions in program plans, goals, and objectives.

KEY TERMS

Individualized family service plan (IFSP)   transdisciplinary team
natural environments   play-based assessments
ecological assessments   dynamic assessment

An understanding of early childhood assessment is a necessity for special educators working with young children. It is also important for all educators to have knowledge about the philosophy, methods, instruments, and focus of early childhood assessment. This information is important for special education teachers in elementary schools, giving them an awareness of the differences between approaches and assessment techniques used by early childhood assessors compared with those used once families enter the school system. Teachers who have this understanding can be extremely helpful to families as they make the transitions from early intervention services to preschool programs and from preschool to elementary school services. Parents who have had experiences with early childhood assessment teams may expect similar attitudes and services once their child is enrolled in the school system. If teachers are aware of this expectation, then they can serve as effective communicators and true liaisons with the family.

Knowledgeable special education teachers can also speak about the similarities and differences in assessment instruments used in early intervention compared with the school system to assist with keeping families informed. For example, they may be able to tell a parent that an assessment used in elementary school (such as the *Vineland Adaptive Behavior Scales series*) uses the same format as one used during early childhood (*Vineland Social-Emotional Early Childhood Scales*). A broad understanding of the issues in assessment across all the age ranges can only serve to make a teacher the most effective.

Parents, relatives, physicians, child care providers, teachers, and others may notice a lag or unusual quality about a young child's development in one or more areas such as language, motor, social, or play skills. When children are in preschool, readiness for traditional schooling also becomes an important issue. Parents and others may indicate their concerns about their children's development and school readiness by comments such as "Jai often wakes up at night, does not play with toys for as long as the other children his age, and his day-care provider claims that he does not complete tasks that require sustained attention" or "Carla was premature, remains small for her age, and cries easily, especially when requested to follow directions."

When children are younger than school age, the assessment question is not whether they have a learning disability, intellectual disability, or emotional disturbance. Diagnostic queries are frequently avoided for very young children. Instead, assessment questions for this age group are focused on any apparent developmental delays or "risk" for delays they present, allowing suitable supports and interventions to be arranged in consultation with the family.

CONSIDERATIONS IN ASSESSMENT OF YOUNG CHILDREN

The most important consideration in the assessment of the young child is the interrelationship between the child and his or her family. In fact, the current philosophy guiding best practice indicates that questions about individual children are addressed through a focus of working with the family. Child assessment and family concerns are not considered two distinct areas, but since child issues and family issues are intertwined, together they form the focus of all assessment efforts. This family-centered approach (Dunst, Trivette, & Deal, 1988) to assessment and early intervention is recommended by the parents, teachers, and higher education personnel that comprise the Division of Early Childhood (DEC) of the Council for Exceptional Children (Trivette & Dunst, 2005). A goal of collaborative practices provides supports and resources to families so they could maximize positive results.

The assessor needs to be aware that the relationship with the family begins with the initial interaction. Tone of voice, language used, and expectations implied reveal a great deal about how the assessment will proceed. Contrast the following two introductory comments made to Ruben's parent:

a. "Hi, Mrs. Brookes, I am Dr. Jones, and I am a special educator from Early Start and I am calling to arrange a time when I can conduct an assessment on Ruben. I understand that he has been having some difficulties with language and communication, so the speech therapist and I would like to administer a few well-established assessments to determine the degree of his problem."

b. "Hi, Mrs. Brookes, my name is Mary Jones, and I am a special educator working with Early Start. I understand that you called about Ruben because you and his day-care provider, Mrs. Jackson, had some concerns about Ruben's communication. Is this a good time to talk? I was wondering if I could assist by obtaining additional information about Ruben's language and communication, and I am interested to know what type of information would be most useful for you and Mrs. Jackson."

Once family priorities are established prior to assessment, the context for the assessment is an issue for consideration. Current legislation requires that any form of early childhood intervention, including assessment, be conducted in the least restrictive and most "natural" environments. This may mean that assessments are conducted with parents in a comfortable environment for them, such as in their home, regardless of the form of assessment used.

Neisworth and Bagnato (2005) describe eight critical qualities for making assessment choices.

1. Assessment must be useful for early intervention and education (*Utility*) or must guide practice that contributes to beneficial outcomes. For example, assessment results that assist Ruben's parents and day-care provider to know what to teach in order to improve Ruben's use of language would be useful. Labeling his language difficulty alone may not be useful.

2. Professionals and families alike must mutually agree on assessment methods, styles, and materials (*Acceptability*). Assessor "b" in the previous example, who asked Ruben's mother and day-care provider what they considered important information for them, is more likely to conduct an assessment that is acceptable and valuable to the family.

3. Assessment tools and measures should be used in familiar settings and implemented in a manner that facilitates observation of child strengths and a realistic appraisal of skills and delays (*Authenticity*).

4. Assessment methods and styles should promote teamwork among professionals and families (*Collaboration*). A team approach to assessment, in which family members are essential team members and collaborative decision making takes place, is highly recommended (Neisworth & Bagnato, 2005).

5. Assessment should be based on a wide foundation of information, including use of multiple assessments and information from diverse sources (*Convergence*). Ruben may use language differently in day care, at home, with peers, with his parents, when upset, when most relaxed, and so on. In order to obtain a good

or valid understanding of Ruben's communication and language usage, several people using various methods would need to contribute information.

6. Individual differences should be accommodated *(Equity)* so that a fair and equitable assessment process is obtained.

7. Assessment materials need to be selected so that even the smallest increment of change can be detected *(Sensitivity)*.

8. Materials need to be designed and validated with young children who are similar to those who will be assessed *(Congruence)* (Neisworth & Bagnato, 2005).

Legislation

Federal legislation has had an impact on who is assessed, by whom, and where assessments take place. In 1975, PL 94-142 mandated a free, appropriate education in the least restrictive environment for all school-aged children with disabilities. It also gave parents the right to full involvement in decisions that related to classification and educational placement for their children. One section of the legislation offered small incentive grants to encourage states to develop programs for children with disabilities ages 3 to 5. In 1985, 24 states had mandates for serving children with disabilities younger than age 5, with the majority aimed at children ages 3 to 5 (Rossetti, 1990).

In 1986, PL 99-457 (Education of the Handicapped Act Amendments) was passed and required all states to provide services for all 3- to 5-year-old children with disabilities by the 1990–1991 school year. A section of this legislation, Title 1: Handicapped Infants and Toddlers, established a new discretionary program designed for infants and toddlers and their families. In addition to providing infants and young children with services, the family's needs were to be addressed in an individualized family service plan.

The Individuals with Disabilities Education Act Amendments (IDEA) of 1997 and regulations of 1999 contributed to the mandates for the assessment of and services for young children with disabilities by requiring the development and provision of services for young children birth through age 2 with developmental delays or "at risk" of

experiencing a substantial developmental delay (Part C). This legislation emphasizes that parents play a critical role in protecting the rights of their children with delays and in any decisions made regarding their child. Parental consent is required prior to conducting any evaluation or reevaluation of their child. Part C of the 1997 amendments states that early intervention services for infants and toddlers birth through age 2 are to be delivered in "natural environments." Education in the least restrictive environment and involvement with typical peers are also strengthened in all individualized family service plan, with the added requirement that there is an explanation regarding the extent to which children will *not* be involved with peers without disabilities followed by a rationale for this practice. This legislation also emphasizes accountability systems and outcome measures or benchmarks and goals.

Legislation requires that an **individualized family service plan (IFSP)** is devised for all recipients of early intervention services (birth through age 2). The IFSP must include the following components to comply with the law:

- A statement of the infant or toddler's present levels of physical (including hearing, vision, and health status), cognitive, communication, social or emotional, and adaptive development, based on acceptable, objective criteria.

- A statement of the family's resources, priorities, and concerns relating to enhancing the family's capacity to meet the developmental needs of their infant or toddler with a disability.

- A statement of the major outcomes expected to be achieved for the infant or toddler and family, and the criteria, procedures, and timelines to be used to track progress and to determine whether modifications of revisions of the goals or services are necessary.

- A statement of specific early intervention services based on peer-reviewed research necessary to meet the needs of the infant or toddler and the family and of the necessary frequency, intensity, and method of delivering services.

- A statement of the natural environments in which early intervention services shall be appropriately provided.

- The projected dates for initiation of services and the anticipated duration of such services.
- The name of the service coordinator, who is a member of the profession most immediately relevant to the infant's, toddler's, or family's needs, or who is otherwise qualified to carry out all the applicable duties, and who will be responsible for the implementation of the plan and for coordination with other people and agencies.
- The steps to be taken to support transition of the toddler with a disability to services provided by public school districts.

The legal requirements for the individualized educational plan for preschool-aged children ages 3 through 5 are the same as those for older students. The stated requirements for Part B of the IDEA clearly includes children ages 3 through 21 with disabilities.

The Individuals with Disabilities Education Improvement Act signed into law on December 3, 2004, with an effective date of July 1, 2005, provided some changes relevant to early childhood assessment and services (Yell, 2006). For example, more flexibility in regard to the services received by families with young children is allowed. Parents can provide informed written consent to the state to choose to continue early intervention services under Part C from the child's third birthday until their child enters kindergarten. Along with this change in legislation, funds are to be allocated to support the provision of early intervention services to promote school readiness, preliteracy, language, and numeracy skills to those children in families electing to continue receiving services under Part C. Early childhood special education services must be grounded in scientifically based research, and educators must be highly qualified.

Purposes

The reasons for early childhood assessment overlap with those described in Chapter 1 and include screening, eligibility, planning goals, monitoring progress, and program evaluation. The importance of early screening for possible developmental delays is well accepted. An in-depth assessment is conducted as a follow-up to a screening in order to determine the nature of any difficulties and to identify the appropriate services and sources of support to address them (Sandall, 1997a). Skills in one domain, such as language or motor, do not develop in isolation, and difficulties in one area can affect the others. For example, a child with language or motor delays may not play or interact with peers in the same way as typically developing children because of their problems in keeping up with the movement of their peers or because of difficulties in communication. Screening for and addressing delays when a child is very young may prevent greater delays in multiple areas in the future.

Assessment to determine service eligibility is an issue for early childhood as well as for school-aged children. Children ages birth through 2 years of age are eligible for services (1) if they are experiencing developmental delays in one or more areas of cognitive, physical, communication, social or emotional, and adaptive development; (2) if they have a diagnosed physical or mental condition that has a high probability of resulting in developmental delay; or (3) if they are at risk for developmental delays (at the state's discretion). Definitions of risk and delay, and the recommended assessment methods and instruments to determine risk and delay vary across and within states of the United States (Widerstrom, 1997).

Children ages 3 through 5 are eligible for special education services if they have an identified disability such as intellectual disability, speech or language impairment, or learning disability, or, at the discretion of the state, are experiencing developmental delays as defined by the state. Eligibility for services specific to a particular domain (e.g., speech) or disability requiring a particular pattern of delays (e.g., in communication and play), such as those that identify autism, may require an assessment that confirms these delays or disabilities.

Assessment data are used for planning any intervention or objectives included as part of individualized family service plans (IFSPs) used in infant and toddler programs and individualized education programs (IEPs) written when the child is in preschool. In addition to a focus on the child's delays, the assessment for the IFSP addresses the resources and sources of support available to the family and in the community as well as the priorities for the family. The aim of the

IFSP process is to enhance the child's development and the family's capacity to meet the child's unique needs (Turnbull, Turnbull, Erwin, & Soodak, 2006).

As the young child nears age 3 (if parents choose to change services), and again at elementary school age, it is critical to guarantee the continuation of vital support services during these transition phases. Successful transitions between school milestone levels decrease stress for students, families, and educators, thereby optimizing learning (Rosenkoetter, Hains, & Fowler, 1994). Parents report that not knowing what will happen to their child once the child enters kindergarten is a disempowering experience (Macvean, Hall, & Charlton, 2003). Information from current assessments may facilitate the exchange of information between early childhood agencies and any educational systems.

The final two reasons for assessment monitoring and evaluation are also purposes for assessment in early childhood (Sandall, 1997a). Any goals agreed upon in the IFSP/IEP are evaluated and changed as needed. Early childhood services are increasingly required to demonstrate the benefits of their programs, and accountability of services is an integral aspect of any reputable early intervention service. Furthermore, obtaining comprehensive research evidence of the factors that result in beneficial outcomes of early intervention is recommended so that program personnel can use their resources to maximize gains (Bryant & Maxwell, 1997). The No Child Left Behind Act emphasizes the use of research-based practices and the need for accountability in educational services (U.S. Department of Education, 2002b).

Areas Assessed

Consistent with the philosophy of viewing child development within the context of the family system, a complete assessment would address family strengths and concerns in addition to child strengths and delays. An understanding of the family system that includes all family members is necessary to understanding the young child (Turnbull et al., 2006). Sensitive family assessments would include the following considerations: use of a multimethod approach; an understanding

that the assessment process is an intervention that can influence the parent/professional relationship; evaluation of the timing when the assessment is conducted relative to becoming acquainted with the family; assignment of responsibility for conducting the assessment; and consideration of professional and parent perceptions for priorities and evaluation of assessment methods and procedures for usefulness (Bailey, 2004a).

The assessment of young children also encompasses all the main areas of development. Physical factors (hearing, vision, neurological status, etc.) figure prominently in any assessment, and children typically obtain a medical examination from a physician to determine if any delays are a result of a primarily physical anomaly. Concept formation and other cognitive functions such as attention and problem solving also are usually evaluated.

Another broad area assessed is language and communication skills, including both receptive and expressive use of vocabulary and pragmatics. Because language plays the key role in thinking, comprehension, and the formation of social relationships, speech and language are a frequent focus of early childhood assessment. Gross- and fine-motor skill delays would affect exploration and play; therefore, motor skills are another key area of assessment. Social-emotional development is assessed in the context of both the home and the play group or school setting. Because of the increased identification of pervasive development disorders (PDD), this domain had received increased attention, with a corresponding increase in screening tools for differences and delays compared with typical development. Self-help and adaptive skills is an important area addressed by assessment teams. Assessment that is useful will focus on what the child can do given any identified delays in order to determine the effect of any problems. If the child can function well during daily activities, including self-help activities, then it would be concluded that the effects of an identified delay were minimal.

When the child reaches ages 4 and 5, school readiness becomes a focus of evaluation and may include early reading, mathematics, and writing skills. Oral language and motor development continue to be major elements in assessment. The importance of social behavior expands to include typical classroom demands and expectations of teachers. School attitude and work habits, including the child's ability to follow directions and attend to tasks, are also evaluated during this period.

ENHANCEDetext
Video Example 16.1
Watch this video to see more information regarding setting up a preschool classroom.

Issues

Current legislation is emphasizing provision of services in **natural environments** those services that are natural or normal for the child's age peers without disabilities or delays, such as within community agencies, organizations, or homes. In these environments, children with delays or disabilities have an opportunity to interact and play with their typically developing peers. Providing services in natural environments can result in families building relationships within their community that may result in increased sources of support. Identifying and creating service opportunities in natural environments promotes a focus on child and family strengths. Services not conducted in natural environments require justification. It is the challenge for early intervention service providers to assure quality service that addresses identified benchmarks and objectives in natural environments.

It is highly recommended that assessment be linked to practice (Neisworth & Bagnato, 2005) or to curriculum (Bagnato, Neisworth, &

Munson, 1997; Puckett & Black, 2000), Therefore, it is important for the assessor to be aware of and to influence the curriculum that will be used during early intervention services. A curriculum includes planned methods connected to learning objectives (Hanson & Lynch, 1989). Ideally, any initial assessment would be instrumental in designing the individualized curriculum. The objectives for any group of young children would be incorporated into or serve as the framework for the activities and experiences designed by early intervention personnel.

Monitoring progress with objectives is recommended on an ongoing basis, so that engagement in activities is confirmed; changes to intervention or program activities can be made if the team determines progress to be too slow (Bagnato et al., 1997; Wolery, 2004). Assessment should be planned as an integral component of service delivery rather than as an event that occurs prior to, or periodically during, an early intervention or preschool program. However, combining a focus on child-led and typical routine activities, as well as incorporating progress monitoring systems requires personnel who value ongoing assessment, administrative support for program design that includes progress monitoring systems, and team members skilled in monitoring progress, modifying interventions, and communicating program changes with all team members. To accomplish this is a challenge for many services involving young children.

Although conventional, norm-referenced measures are not recommended owing to their lack of articulation with the commonly used, functional curriculum (Bagnato et al., 1997; Puckett & Black, 2000), and the lack of norms for children who are culturally and linguistically diverse (Barona & Santos de Barona, 2000; McLean, 2002), these measures are still being used. Pressures on assessors of young children to support eligibility decisions based on comparisons with chronologically aged peers and to demonstrate child progress with reliable and valid instruments are two reasons such measures continue to be used. Proponents of alternative assessment measures argue that young children in this age range are highly individualistic in the progression through developmental stages because of a variety of factors including the home and community environment.

Thus, there is considerable demand for **ecological assessments**. The child's development must be considered in light of the family and cultural context as well as other environmental factors. Ecological assessments require observations within a setting such as the home, and preferably multiple settings, so that the environmental effects on participants can be determined (Pellegrini, 1996). McCormick and Noonan (2002) describe a process of ecological assessment and planning that includes formulating goals and objectives by (1) listing daily routines and activities, (2) comparing the present skills and abilities of the child with special needs to the general expectations for their behavior in activities, and (3) determining how functional goals and objectives for the child will be embedded in activities throughout the day. Identifying any adaptations and supports needed and a method for monitoring progress are aspects of ecological assessment. The design, arrangement, and implementation of ecological assessments require skill, experience, and time.

At the same time, there is concern that, if the choice of assessment measures is too individual, then children can become overidentified. These concerns regarding the classification of PDD has resulted in the development of a state-of-the-art assessment system for identifying autism spectrum disorders called the *Autism Diagnostic Observation Schedule* (Lord, Rutter, DiLavore, & Risi, 2001). Proper implementation of the assessment requires training for professionals and time for both families and assessment teams to complete the sessions. It is currently being used as an assessment tool by clinical and school psychologists, who report that it is helpful in identifying specific behaviors relevant to autism spectrum disorders (Akshoomoff, Corsell, & Schmidt, 2006).

Similarly, assessment by a **transdisciplinary team** is recommended (McWilliam, 2005). A transdisciplinary assessment has the advantages of an emphasis on functional skills, greater family involvement, and an integrated therapy approach where professionals educated in various disciplines along with family members work to combine their strengths and creativity in

determining the needs of the child (Linder, 2004). However, arranging for multiple professionals to meet with a family for a sufficient amount of time to obtain the required information is a challenge for many services. Choosing the team members, the times and places for assessment, and when and how to interact with all team members, especially the child's family, are some of the choices made by assessors working with young children and their families. Each of these choices requires consideration of the issues that make up the choices, and effective assessors must continually balance these issues. Some of the issues that require this balancing act for the assessment team are listed in Table 16–1.

Current Practices

The Division of Early Childhood (DEC) has identified recommended practices involved in conducting authentic, collaborative, and useful assessments (Sandall, Hemmeter, Smith, & McLean, 2005; DEC, 2007). Recommended practices were devised from the synthesis of information from reviews of the research literature and from focus groups of parents, practitioners, administrators, and scientists (Smith, McLean, Sandall, Snyder, & Ramsey, 2005).

Curriculum-based assessment procedures obtain data on child competencies by evaluating the child's skills as they are displayed while interacting with the materials and peers within the curriculum used in early childhood programs. This form of assessment is classified as an informal assessment approach due to the fact that the behaviors observed, the questions asked by the assessor, and the tasks that create the assessment may vary across children and are usually not standardized. Experts in the area of early childhood assessment argue that by using curriculum-based assessment techniques the assessor obtains an "authentic" picture of the child's competencies in comparison to inauthentic assessment techniques, which include contrived tasks with unfamiliar materials administered in an unfamiliar setting (Bagnato et al., 1997). The use of curriculum-based assessment techniques is one of the hallmarks of current practices in early childhood special education.

TABLE 16–1
The Balancing Act of an Early Childhood Assessor

BALANCING:	WITH:
Collecting sufficient information	Intrusion in the family
Using a team for multiple perspectives	Intrusion in the family
Selecting and using ecologically valid assessments	Time and cost
Seeking multiple and diverse opinions	Interpretation of assessment information that is integrated and coherent
Developing an early intervention program in a natural environment with developmentally appropriate activities	Development of program evaluation that is ongoing, authentic, and addresses issues of efficacy of early intervention
Embedding educational goals in enjoyable activities with peers	Collection of ongoing, relevant data on individual child progress with established goals
Providing information to others to maximize outcomes	Preservation of confidentiality

Familiar physical and social environments are the recommended settings for obtaining information from assessment procedures. Using the child's own toys, common household items, common toys within the preschool setting, and toys with adaptive qualities helps to create an assessment that captures the child's strengths (Bagnato et al., 1997). Complete reliance on formally administered tests or parent and teacher interviews may provide a partial or biased perspective of abilities or disabilities.

The formation of an assessment team that includes family members as equal contributors is required by the Individuals with Disabilities Education Act (IDEA) and recommended practice (Sandall et al., 2005; Turnbull et al., 2006). It is recognized that no single agency or professional discipline can meet the diverse, individual, and often complex needs of young children with delays or disabilities and their families (Sandall, 1997b). Although the multiple perspectives of team members can be obtained using several models, one in which there is high collaboration in the planning, collection, and evaluation of assessment information across team members is highly recommended. The transdisciplinary model meets this criterion with the benefit of team members who possess various expertise (e.g., speech therapist, early childhood educator,

parent), learning from each other as they share the skills and information from their discipline (Sandall, 1997a; McWilliam, 2005).

Along with a growing understanding of the ways in which culture influences our communication style and interpretation of interactions, priorities, and customs, early interventionists are required to be aware of their own culture (Lynch, 2004) as well as the cultures of the families with whom they work. Culture is a dynamic context where day-to-day influences shape behavior (Hanson, 2004). Although it is important to have a broad understanding of the typical beliefs, values, and practices of the families that comprise the communities where the early interventionist works, it is also important to remain sensitive to the uniqueness of each family. As should be noted, a variety of beliefs and behaviors exist within a cultural group (Lynch, 2004). Cultural understanding enhances the assessor's ability to choose the most appropriate assessment methods and tools and to interact with the family effectively.

 Breakpoint Practice 16.1
Click here to check your understanding of assessment considerations in the early childhood setting.

SCREENING

In the first stage of the assessment process, the assessment question asked is: *Is there an indication of possible developmental delay(s) that will warrant further assessment?* A screening is a brief assessment aimed at identifying those infants/children who may be at risk for health and developmental delays due to differences as compared with standard expectations for children of the same age range and cultural background (Losardo & Notari-Syverson, 2001). Now that it is understood that early intervention can prevent the occurrence of more severe delays and difficulties for the child and family, an effort is being made to find children with developmental delays or those at risk for delays. Strategies for finding and screening young children vary and may include the following: educating the public regarding the importance of early intervention in order to build community awareness; establishing a formal network of informed agencies that serves as a referral system; disseminating information about the screening system and the number of families served as a means of maintaining local publicity and contacts; and canvassing the community for children in the designated age range to identify children who need screening by means of local announcements of screening events or through a systematic survey (Peterson, 1987).

The *Ages and Stages Questionnaires–3* (Squires & Bricker, 2009) is an example of a screening instrument designed to be easily disseminated. This instrument is a set of developmental surveys that are completed by parents periodically when their child is between 1 and 66 months of age. Each questionnaire, available in English and Spanish, contains 30 developmental items divided into five areas: communication, gross motor, fine motor, problem solving, and personal-social. Scoring can take as little as 10 minutes and can be completed by paraprofessional or clerical staff under the guidance of a professional (Squires & Bricker, 2009). The validity of the questionnaires has been obtained using standardized assessments with an overall agreement of .86; test-retest reliability for 145 parents is reported to exceed .92. The accompanying guide includes a section on cultural and language adaptations. This instrument assists parents in monitoring their own child's development and ensures that they have a critical role in any assessment of their child. Centers and agencies can purchase a program to manage data and generate reports entitled the ASQ (Ages and Stages Questionnaire) Manager.

Screening instruments used by professionals trained to implement them are typically divided into domains or areas that are evaluated. The *American Guidance Service Early Screening Profiles* (Harrison, 1990) is designed to assess delays or gifts and talents in the areas of cognitive/language, motor, and self-help/social for children ages 2 through 6. Additional information obtained from four surveys focused on articulation, behavior, health history, and the home environment completes the screening. The authors recommend a team approach to this screening process.

The *Developmental Observation Checklist System (DOCS)* is a screening tool consisting of three interrelated components: child development, child behavior, and the family's coping ability and stress (Hresko, Miquel, Sherbenou, & Burton, 1994). This multidimensional approach can be used with families that have children between the ages of birth and 6 years whose dominant language is English. The developmental checklist focuses on language, social, motor, and cognitive skills using functional activities. Parents rate their child's behavior as well as their own stress and support. The three components of the DOCS take approximately 30 minutes to complete (Hresko et al., 1994).

Another multiple-area screening tool available in English and Spanish is the *Developmental Indicators for the Assessment of Learning–4* (Mardell & Goldenberg, 2011) that includes language, concepts, motor skills, self-help, and social development domains. This screening tool is administered to children ages 2–6 through 5–11 and takes approximately 30 to 45 minutes to complete. The inclusion of a Parent Questionnaire facilitates obtaining the family perspective on the child's development. A brief version called the *Speed Dial–4* can be completed in 15 minutes and includes items from the language, motor, and concepts domains.

The *Denver Developmental Screening Test (Denver II)* (Frankenburg et al., 1990) was designed to screen developmental delays in children from birth through age 6 in the areas of personal, social, fine motor-adaptive, language, and gross motor. Typically, it is individually administered, resulting in a comparatively lengthy assessment time (Taylor, 2003). The comparison group used was from the Denver area that includes children with typically Anglo, African American, and Spanish surnames.

Screening tools consisting of items from more extensive instruments have been designed as a first step in identifying delays. The *Bayley Infant Neurodevelopmental Screener (BINS)* (Aylward, 1995) contains 11 to 13 items for screening infants ages 3 through 24 months for risk of neurological impairment or developmental delays. Brigance Screens include criterion-referenced skills that are typically performed by young children The *Infant & Toddler Screen* begins at birth through 23 months (Brigance & Glascoe, 2002), the *Early Preschool Screen III* (Brigance, 2013a) covers ages birth to 35 months, the *Preschool Screen* (Brigance, 2013b) is for children ages 3 to 5 years, and the *K–1 Screen* (Brigance, 2013c) is for children in kindergarten and first grade. Each of these screening tools includes developmentally relevant skills grouped by domains, such as visual/fine and graphomotor, gross motor, receptive and expressive vocabulary, articulation/verbal fluency, and syntax and, for older children, quantitative concepts, personal information, and prereading skills.

The *Infant-Toddler Developmental Assessment* is designed to be a family-centered, transdisciplinary process for families with children ages birth through 3 that bridges a screening tool and more in-depth assessment (Provence, Erikson, Vater, & Palmeri, 1995). It is conducted in six phases: (1) referral and pre-interview data gathering, (2) initial parent interview, (3) health review, (4) developmental observation and assessment, (5) integration and synthesis, and (6) sharing of findings, completion, and report. The developmental observation assessment form is divided across eight domains, with

items listed developmentally by age. Items are scored as present or observed, not observed, reported as present or absent, emerging, and refused. Items are summarized as "competent" or "of concern."

Screening instruments are also used if developmental delays appear to indicate a specific disability. For example, the *Autism Screening Instrument for Educational Planning–3* (Krug, Arick, & Almond, 2008) uses multiple measures to determine if the child has a pattern of skills and behaviors similar to individuals diagnosed with autism. The complete package includes an autism behavior checklist; an educational assessment that addresses the five areas of staying seated, receptive language, expressive language, body concept, and speech imitation; an interactive assessment that measures social responses and responses to requests; prognosis of learning rate; and an analysis of a sample of vocal behavior from the child. The *Checklist for Autism in Toddlers (CHAT)* (Baron-Cohen, Cox, Baird, Sweettenham, & Nightingale, 1996) is a nine-item screening tool for autism used with toddlers ages 18 through 36 months.

Screening procedures also may identify preschool-age children who are considered gifted and talented. The field of gifted education has emphasized the benefits of early intervention (Stile, 1996). Enriched preschool programs provide opportunities for these young children to demonstrate their strengths and an environment where their high potential can be nurtured (Kitano, 1990). The same recommendations of multiple measures and multiple approaches over multiple periods of time with more in-depth assessment following screening are relevant for young children, including those with disabilities, who are gifted and talented (Feldhusen & Jarwan, 2000; Stile, 1996).

Regardless of the screening procedures selected, it is important for assessors to ensure that those who administer screening instruments are well trained and experienced in performing screening tasks; that multiple sources of information are included; that family members are an integral part of the screening process; that all instruments are reliable, valid, and culturally sensitive; that familiar tasks and settings are used to obtain the most valid results; that screening tools are used for those purposes only; and that more in-depth assessments and, most importantly, follow-up services are available (McLean, 2004).

Screening and Assessment of Social-Emotional Development and Temperament

The understanding that delays and atypical behavior in the social-emotional development of young children can indicate a need for early intervention services has resulted in the design of assessment tools focused on this domain. Squires, Bricker, and Twombly (2015) have created a screening tool, the *Ages and Stages Questionnaires: Social Emotional–2,* in the same format as their screening tool for multiple domains. Eight surveys, to be completed by caregivers, have been designed covering ages birth to 6 years. The surveys include the areas of self-regulation, compliance, communication, adaptive behaviors, autonomy, affect, and interactions with others.

The *Vineland Social-Emotional Early Childhood Scales (SEEC)* (Sparrow, Balla, & Cicchetti, 1998) was designed to be completed in a semistructured interview format with an adult familiar with the child's social-emotional behavior. Responses to items are compared to a standardized sample of young children ages-birth through 5 years 11 months taken from the national sample obtained for the *Vineland Adaptive Behavior Scales* (Sparrow, Balla, & Cicchetti, 1984). Items are grouped in the following clusters: interpersonal relationships, play and leisure time, and coping skills with an overall social-emotional composite score also obtained (see Figure 16–1 for items). Administration of the SEEC scales takes approximately 15 to 25 minutes (Sparrow et al., 1998).

The *Temperament and Atypical Behavior Scale (TABS)* (Neisworth, Bagnato, Salvia, & Hunt, 1999) was designed to measure atypical behavior in young children ages 11 to 71 months. The *TABS Assessment Scale* (Bagnato, Neisworth, Salvia, & Hunt, 1999a) includes 55 items scored by a primary caregiver. The items are grouped in the categories of detached, hypersensitive/active,

underractive, and dysregulated. There is also a 15-item *TABS Screener* (Bagnato, Neisworth, Salvia, & Hunt, 1999b), with select items from the *Assessment Scale.* The results yield a temperament and regulatory index that is compared to a normed group to determine if the child is at risk for atypical development and in need of further assessment.

Social-emotional behaviors that may be indicators of autism spectrum disorders are a main component of both the *Childhood Autism Rating Scale (CARS)* (Schopler, Reichler, & Renner, 1988) and the *Gilliam Autism Rating Scale (GARS)* (Gilliam, 1995b). Both of these scales can be used with children as young as age 3, and both also include a focus on delays in communication and language skills. A parent report measure specifically designed to address behavioral issues that may indicate attention-deficit disorder is the *Home Situations Questionnaire (HSQ)* (Barkley, 1997). Parents rate the occurrence and severity of their child's behavior across 16 different home and public situations such as " chores" or "visiting someone's home." The *School Situations Questionnaire (SSQ)* uses the same rating scale for assessing attention-deficit/hyperactivity disorder (ADHD) symptoms as observed by teachers (Barkley & Murphy, 1998).

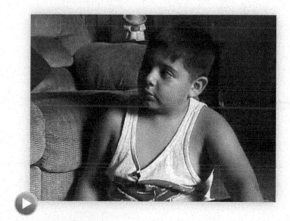

ENHANCEDetext
Video Example 16.2
Watch this video to see an educator assessing a young child through an individual interview format.

VINELAND SEEC SCALES ITEM CLUSTERS BY CONTENT CATEGORIES		
Scale	Content Category	Item Clusters
Interpersonal Relationships Scale	Responding to Others	A. Beginning responsiveness C. Responding to familiar people
	Expressing and Recognizing Emotions	B. Expressing emotions E. Recognizing emotions
	Imitating	D. Imitating phrases and movements
	Social Communication	F. Identifying others G. Responding to social communication J. Initiating social communication K. Cooperative interactions
	Friendship	H. Friendship
	Thoughtfulness	I. Giving gifts
	Belonging to Groups	L. Belonging to groups
Play and Leisure Time Scale	Playing	A. Playing with toys B. Interest in environment C. Playing with others D. Make-believe activities H. Playing games
	Sharing and Cooperating	E. Sharing and cooperating G. Following game rules
	Television and Radio	F. Watching television L. Using television and radio for entertainment and information
	Hobbies	J. Hobbies K. Extracurricular and nonschool activities
	Going Places with Friends	I. Beginning group activities M. Going places with friends independently
Coping Skills Scale	Manners	B. Beginning politeness C. Using manners in conversation G. Using table manners
	Following Rules	A. Following rules D. Being responsible for time
	Apologizing	I. Apologizing
	Keeping Secrets	F. Keeping secrets or confidences
	Controlling Impulses	E. Being sensitive to others H. Controlling Impulses
	Responsibility	J. Borrowing and returning

FIGURE 16–1

Clusters on the *Vineland Social-Emotional Early Childhood Scales*

Note: From *Vineland Social-Emotional Early Childhood Scales* (p. 31) by S. S. Sparrow, D. A. Balla, & D. V. Cicchetti. Circle Pines, MN: American Guidance Service. Copyright 1998 by American Guidance Service. Reprinted with permission.

ECOLOGICAL ASSESSMENT, FAMILY INTERVIEWS AND RATING SCALES, OBSERVATION, AND PLAY-BASED ASSESSMENT

Other important assessment questions are the following: *Given a particular context (home, an activity, an adult), which skills does the child display? Which skills are important to the family, community, and culture?* Keen observational skills are critical for the assessor working guided by current legislation and philosophy that emphasizes conducting assessments in natural environments using familiar contexts and materials. To comply with best practice recommendations, the assessor must obtain information about the child's developmental skills by observing the child interacting with and within the context of familiar settings. The format and focus of the observation will vary depending on the priorities and questions from the family and other assessment team members. The better the assessment team is at selecting methods that will result in the desired information, the more valid will be the assessment. If the assessors can draw upon a variety of skills in interview, observational, and play-based methods, the more likely the assessment will be conducted in an effective and valid manner.

Ecological Assessment

An ecological approach to assessment helps the team to understand the range of responses that a child and family may exhibit under a variety of conditions (McCormick & Noonan, 2002). The assessment team that uses the ecological approach focuses on understanding the interrelationship between the child and family, and the family and their environment (Bronfenbrenner, 1979; Turnbull et al., 2006) and uses this information to determine intervention and support strategies. The goal of the observer using the ecological approach is to identify patterns and sequences of behaviors given a specific context. The techniques selected and used should take into account the culture, socioeconomic status, and value system of the child and family (Hanson & Lynch, 2004; Lynch & Hanson, 2004b).

The family perspective is best obtained through culturally sensitive communication with family members (Turnbull et al., 2006). Kalyanpur and Harry (1999) support communication in a way that acknowledges cultural assumptions about priorities and interventions and demonstrates respect for diverse perspectives that they describe as the posture of cultural reciprocity. Assessment instruments and interview guides have been developed with the aim of obtaining an understanding of the family factors that influence the developmental outcomes for the child with disabilities or delays, or at risk for delays. It is important to note that when the term *family* is used, the broad definition of parents and family as described in Chapter 3, and the cultural considerations in determining family membership should be applied.

Family Interviews and Rating Scales

Although family assessment utilizes many methods, the family interview is particularly useful for gathering data about family characteristics, family strengths and priorities, and family perceptions of situations, events, goals, and services (Bailey, 2004a). A semistructured interview is better than paper-and-pencil tests because the interviewer can monitor whether he or she is being intrusive; language and questions can be changed to meet a family's values and culture; a family can more easily screen its responses; and there is more flexibility (Hanson & Lynch, 2004). The communication skills described in Chapter 3 would be necessary to conduct a sensitive and informative interview. Good listening skills are very important, as is the ability to maintain neutrality and listen and respond in a nonjudgmental manner. Parents and other family members must be regarded as equals; that is, their perceptions must be regarded as having equal value to those of other assessment team members. Finally, competence, openness, and a genuine desire to help the family are essential.

The *Infant-Toddler and Family Instrument (ITFI)* (Provence & Apfel, 2001) is a survey designed to guide a home visitor through completion of a thorough and sensitive interview and includes questions regarding the young child's characteristics, household and daily routines, caregiver–child interactions, family and friend support, health, growth and development, and family issues and concerns (see Figure 16–2 for sample questions from the Caregiver Interview). Information about development in the domains of motor, social-emotional, language, and coping and self-help skills is also recorded. The instrument contains a Checklist for Evaluating Concern to assist the interviewer in organizing family priorities. Owing to the amount of information obtained, the authors suggest that two 45- to 60-minute sessions be used to complete the interview (Apfel & Provence, 2001).

Family interview forms with suggested questions also have been developed to ensure that the family perspective and priorities are obtained as a component of the assessment. For example, *Family-Centered Interview* forms (Parks, 1994) are available as part of the HELP program (Parks et al., 1994). The interview comprises questions about the general health and history of the child, family preferences for the definition of family and the best method for receiving information, and family concerns, priorities, resources, and strategies for daily activities of the young child. Included as part of the Infant-Toddler Developmental Assessment is a *Parent Report* form to be used to gather input regarding the birth history and general temperament of the child and a *Health Recording Guide* to record a health history (Provence et al., 1995).

In addition to the general topics addressed in a family interview, information about a specific area of child development or parent–child interaction may be obtained using a parent report survey, questionnaire, or behavior scale. The *Vineland Adaptive Behavior Scales—Second Edition* is used to obtain a parent's opinion on the skills of his or her child in the domains of communication, daily living skills, socialization, and motor skills (Sparrow, Cicchetti, & Balla, 2005b). This scale can be used to discuss children from birth through adulthood and provides information about the developmental skills and adaptive behavior that is viewed by family members.

Family Strengths and Concerns

It is important to consider critical events in the lives of families because families of infants and children with disabilities and delays may experience added stress from both normal life events and stressful events. The diagnosis of a child's disability, the lack of developmental milestones, efforts in obtaining services, transitions such as preschool to elementary school programs, and medical crises can pose particular challenges for these families (Hanson & Lynch, 2004; Turnbull et al., 2006). It is important that any assessors are aware of whether such events are occurring for the families with whom they are working.

Support from family, friends (informal), and agency personnel (formal) is often needed to address stress and enhance coping. Inventories and surveys have been designed to assist early interventionists to assess the needs of families for resources including sources of support. An example is the *Family Strengths Profile* (Trivette, Dunst, & Deal, 1988) that records the family's current resources and strengths (e.g., commitment, sense of purpose, problem solving, positivism, flexibility).

The family's preferences for how concerns are addressed should be determined. Instruments that may facilitate this discussion include the *Family Needs Scale* (Dunst, Cooper, Weeldreyer, Snyder, & Chase, 1988), the *Family Needs Survey* (Bailey & Simeonsson, 1990), and the *Parent Needs Survey* (Seligman & Darling, 1989). Regardless of which surveys and inventories are used, it is the early childhood assessment team, including the family, that works to devise an individualized plan to address priorities, resources, and concerns.

Direct Observation

One means of determining patterns of behavior is through direct or systematic observation. For example, the assessment team might want to observe Ruben's use of communication during meal times at home. The question from the team would be formulated as follows: Given a familiar and comfortable environment (at home during meals with family), what vocalizations, words, and gestures does Ruben use? This question can be addressed through a variety of observational methods from which the team would need to choose.

Observers could use a developmental checklist with predetermined and defined communication and language skills where the item is checked when it is observed during the meal. A narrative recording could be used when observers attempt to write down the language as it is occurring within the context (Pellegrini, 1996). If the team has a well-defined question such as Ruben's use of vocalization and words or use of gestures, then the systematic observation of these behaviors could be obtained using event recording or a time-sampling method. These observational methods would enable the assessor to either count the number of times the behavior has occurred (event recording) or estimate the occurrence of the behavior (time-sampling) given the context (see Chapter 5 of this book for a more complete description of these observational techniques). The team could also use the same method across several settings and compare Ruben's communication between different contexts. In addition, the team could identify the factors in the environment that facilitated Ruben's best performance or helped Ruben to use his best language skills. This information would be very helpful for determining any educational strategies.

Many observation instruments have been designed to be used during play interactions. Examples include the *Social Interaction Assessment/ Intervention* (McCollum & Stayton, 1985) which scores turn-taking, imitation, and the like from videotaped play interactions, and the *ECO* (MacDonald & Gillette, 1989) which addresses turn-taking, communication, and conversational pragmatics through the use of a rating scale and interview. Early childhood assessors could consider how any of these observational instruments could be used in conjunction with a play-based assessment.

Play-Based Assessment

When observational methods are used in the context of play, they are referred to as **play-based assessments**. The behaviors that the assessment team may be interested in could be play behaviors and skills. For example, if the assessment team was concerned about the characteristics of autism, then observing the child at play and evaluating play skills would be very important since the lack of or unusual play skills is one of the defining characteristics of this disability. Pam Wolfberg (2003) has designed a *Play Questionnaire* to be implemented prior to participation in an Integrated Play Group. This assessment gathers information about the child's play experience (opportunities, settings, interactions with adults), play preferences (for people, activities, and characteristics), social play style (friendships, play patterns, mode of communication), and developmental play patterns. (Figure 16–2 provides the information from this part of the questionnaire.)

Play also can be used as the context for assessing one or more domains in addition to play skills. Play is one of the main contexts for young children and an activity frequently engaged in at home and in toddler programs and preschools. Therefore, it is an ideal "natural" environment in which to conduct an assessment. Using play as a means of assessing cognitive development can be considered an alternative approach to standardized or norm-referenced assessments (Linder, 2004). The assessor can observe the child organize materials, interact with playmates, and interact with toys in both structured and unstructured play situations as a means of determining strengths and weaknesses in the area of cognitive development.

If screening determines that further assessment is necessary to provide information about the quality and degree of Ruben's delays, and Ruben's family agrees to further assessment, then arranging a play environment would be an appropriate context for such an evaluation. Since Ruben likes cars it would be good to include tracks and tunnels for Ruben to use and to see if Ruben will pretend the car is on the track. It would be helpful to have peers playing nearby to see if Ruben will engage in parallel play with the cars and if he notices the other children nearby.

The *Transdisciplinary Play-Based Assessment–2 (TFBA-2)* approach assesses all major domains through structured and free-play situations (Linder, 2008). A transdisciplinary team designs, observes, and evaluates the skills of a young child who is interacting with the team, family, and materials in the context of play. Linder (1999) writes that, play opportunities

INTEGRATED PLAY GROUPS–PLAY QUESTIONNAIRE (PAGE 4 OF 4)

PART IV – DEVELOPMENTAL PLAY PATTERNS

Which best describes child's social play patterns?
(choose one category)

Isolate	Wanders without looking at peers	
	Briefly occupies self with anything of interest apart from adults	
	Plays alone apart from peers	
Orientation-Onlooker	Watches peers play	
	Orients body in direction of peers or their play activities	
	Imitates peer actions while watching them from distance	
Parallel-Proximity	Plays independently beside peers in same play space	
	Plays with similar play materials as peers	
	Imitates peers' actions while playing beside them	
Common Focus	Engages in reciprocal play with one or more peers	
	Takes turns in activities/shares materials with peers	
	Imitates/shares emotions (smiles, laughs) with peers	
Common Goal	Engages in cooperative play with one or more peers	
	Explicitly plans and carries out a common agenda with peers	
	Negotiates and compromises around divergent interests	

Which best describes child's representational play patterns?
(choose one category)

Manipulation-Sensory	Explores single objects (e.g., mouths, bangs, shakes)	
	Explores combined objects (e.g., lines up, fills and dumps)	
	Performs difficult feats with objects (e.g., balances, spins, lasso)	
Functional	Uses objects as intended (e.g., rolls car on floor, stacks blocks)	
	Associates related objects (e.g., puts teacup on saucer)	
	Simple scripts with realistic props (e.g., holds telephone to ear)	
Symbolic-Pretend	Uses one object to represent another (e.g., banana as telephone)	
	Attributes absent or false properties (e.g., wipes table as if wet)	
	Invents imaginary objects (e.g., motions with hand as if stirring pot)	
	Role plays characters/scripts with dolls and peers (e.g., tea party)	
Other	Does not display dominance in any one play level	
	Shows dominance in two or more play levels	

Please feel free to comment:

Do you have anything else to share or questions you'd like to ask about this child's play and peer relations?

THANK YOU FOR TAKING THE TIME TO FILL OUT THIS QUESTIONNAIRE!

FIGURE 16–2

Excerpt from the *Play Questionnaire* by Wolfberg (2003)

Note: This chart is an example of a sequence for one child. The sequence will vary depending on the child's needs. Structured and unstructured interactions are integrated throughout the play session.

Source: From *Peer Play and the Autism Spectrum* (p. 147) by P. J. Wolfberg. Copyright 2003 by Autism Asperger Publishing Company, Shawnee Mission, KS. Reprinted with permission.

and experiences influence cognitive understanding, emotional development, social skills, language usage, and physical and motor development and therefore are an important context for the evaluation of all of these skills. This ecological approach can be individualized to address the questions of the assessment team. The general structure and approximate time needed for each phase of a TPBA play session is outlined in Table 16–2. The challenges for assessors who use this approach are organizing the team, finding time to plan the individualized activities that elicit the priority behaviors, conducting the assessment over multiple periods of time and contexts, and developing a coherent plan as a consequence of the assessment (see Table 16–2).

 Breakpoint Practice 16.2
Click here to check your understanding of ecological assessment, family interviews and rating scales, observations and play-based assessment.

CURRICULUM-BASED AND CRITERION-REFERENCED ASSESSMENT

Another important assessment question in the early childhood years is the following: *Are young children able to perform the developmental skills needed in order to communicate, play and adapt to their daily routine successfully?* This question is addressed using curriculum-based assessment (CBA) by evaluating the young child's performance of the goals and objectives that are part of, or embedded in, the home routine, early intervention, or preschool program. The foundation of CBA is the developmental or hierarchical sequence of competencies that enable teams of parents and professionals to establish current functional levels (Neisworth & Bagnato, 2005). CBAs can be conducted in natural settings and during structured and unstructured activities (Neisworth & Bagnato).

Bagnato et al. have published a description, or "snapshot," and review of curriculum-based assessment instruments in their book *Linking*

TABLE 16–2
Transdisciplinary Play-Based Assessment Session

		TIME ALLOTTED
Phase I	Unstructured facilitation	20–25 minutes
Phase II	Structured facilitation	10–15 minutes
Phase III	Child–child interaction	5–10 minutes
Phase IV	Parent–child interaction	
	A. Unstructured	5 minutes
	B. Separation	
	C. Structured	5 minutes
Phase V	Motor play	
	A. Unstructured	5–10 minutes
	B. Structured	5–10 minutes
Phase VI	Snack	5–10 minutes
	Total Time	60–90 minutes

Note: From Linder, T. W. (1993). *Transdisciplinary Play-Based Assessment: A Functional Approach to Working with Young Children* (Rev. ed.), (p. 43). Baltimore: Brookes Publishing Co. Reprinted by permission.

Assessment and Early Intervention (1997). This book serves as an excellent guide for the selection of assessment measures. Each of the assessment instruments reviewed was rated on a scale of 1.0 (negligible) to 3.0 (exemplary) on six dimensions of quality. Several of the measures receiving high ratings in all six dimensions are described next.

The *Hawaii Early Learning Profile (HELP)* for ages birth to 3 (Parks et al., 1994) and preschoolers (ages 3–6) (Vort Corporation, 1995a) is an assessment designed to be completed by observing the child's activity under ongoing or arranged circumstances as well as through parent interviews (Bagnato et al., 1997). An assessor can record information on a checklist that organizes skills by age or by assessment strands (Parks, 1992; Vort Corporation, 1995b) that identify a range of skills within a dimension of competence (such as cognitive and regulatory/sensory organization). A full description of the following appear under each item: a complete definition of the item, the assessment materials needed, assessment procedures in easily replicable detail, adaptations that could be made to elicit the skill, instructional materials, and instructional activities that can be used to teach the item.

The *Assessment, Evaluation, and Programming System (AEPS)* is another set of assessment and curriculum materials for use with young children ages birth through 6 years. The administration guide, sample observational recording sheets, and sample IFSP/IEP goals and objectives are found in Volume 1 (Bricker, Pretti-Frontczak, Johnson, & Straka, 2002). Volume 2 contains the assessment items listed by domain and separated into two sections for birth through 3 years and 3 to 6 years (Bricker, Capt, & Pretti-Frontczak, 2002). The curriculum for teaching skills found to be delayed is outlined in Volume 3 for birth through 3 years (Bricker & Waddell, 2002a) and Volume 4 for 3 to 6 years (Bricker & Waddell, 2002b).

Six key domains organize assessment and curriculum items: social, social-communication, fine motor, gross motor, adaptive, and cognitive. The assessment tool is flexible enough to be used with children with motor and sensory impairments (Bagnato et al., 1997). In addition to the clear interface between measurement and curriculum

and the detailed descriptions of the directions and materials needed for each item, this curriculum-based system has a number of other noteworthy features. There is a goal and objective written for each item, and the objective contains a criterion for success. Suggestions for environmental arrangements to maximize skills are included, and the importance of the skill for each item in the curriculum is also described. Figure 16–3 is an example of the item "groups objects, people, or events on the basis of specified criteria" found in the cognitive domain in Volume 4. Bagnato and colleagues support the use of the AEPS (1997).

Another highly rated (Bagnato et al., 1997) and widely used set of curriculum-based measures is the *Carolina Curriculum for Infants and Toddlers with Special Needs* (Johnson-Martin, Attermeier, & Hacker, 2004) and the *Carolina Curriculum for Preschoolers with Special Needs* (Johnson-Martin, Hacker, & Attermeier, 2004). Organized into six domains of child development, child behaviors are listed following a suggestion for a situation for eliciting activities or a description of a position or activity where the skills are likely to be observed. The criterion skill or behavior is described for each item. A recording sheet, including a column for the date to record when the skill is mastered, is presented alongside each item. The curriculum includes daily routines and functional activities that would facilitate the development and learning of skills, including suggestions for group activities (Johnson-Martin et al., 2004).

The *Creative Curriculum* designed for infants and toddlers (Dombro, Colker, & Dodge, 2003) and for preschoolers (Dodge, Colker, & Heroman, 2006), provides suggestions for arranging the educational environment so that goals and objectives can be embedded into everyday routines and activities for infants and toddlers (Dombro et al., 2003) and within a daily schedule for preschool-age children (Dodge et al., 2006). Found in the appendix of the curriculum guide for infants and toddlers is a self-assessment to guide the identification of goals and objectives for teachers and caregivers. Also found is a form for individualizing goals and objects for young children organized by skill areas presented in a family-friendly manner, such as "to learn about others" and "to learn

Categorizing

STRAND B

Objective 1.1 Groups objects, people, or events on the basis of category
Objective 1.2 Groups objects on the basis of function
Objective 1.3 Groups objects on the basis of physical attribute

CONCURRENT GOALS

Adap A:1 Eats and drinks a variety of foods using appropriate utensils with little or no spilling
Cog A Concepts (all goals)
SC A:1 Uses words, phrases, or sentences to inform, direct, ask questions, and express anticipation, imagination, affect, and emotions
SC B:5 Uses descriptive words
Soc D:1 Communicates personal likes and dislikes

DAILY ROUTINES

Routine events that provide opportunities for children to group objects, people, or events on the basis of devised criteria include the following:
• Cleanup time
• Mealtime or snack time
• Transition time
• Unstructured playtime
    Example: During cleanup time, the interventionist asks Joey to put all of the toy animals in one basket and Latifa to put all of the toy people in another. (Cog B:1.1)

ENVIRONMENTAL ARRANGEMENTS

• Present materials during free play and routine events that are interesting and appealing to the children, and provide opportunities to group objects, people, or events on the basis of specified criteria; for example, present toys and materials that can be sorted according to the following:
    • Different functions (e.g., art materials, tools, toys that go in the water, things to eat, things to wear)
    • Different categories (e.g., food from different food groups)
    • Physical attributes (e.g., blocks of different sizes, foods with different textures such as crunchy or sweet, crayons of different colors)
    Example: While playing in the house play area, Manuel cleans house, putting away the food in the refrigerator and clothing in the dresser. (Cog B:1.2)
• Includes pictures, posters, books, and magazines in the environment that give children opportunities to group objects, people, or events on the basis of certain criteria; for example, posters of children playing could be categorized on the basis of sex, age, hair color, or any other criterion selected by the children or interventionist.

INTERVENTION ACTIVITIES

Two examples of how to embed this goal and the associated objectives within activities are presented next. For a list of intervention activities that address goals/objectives across areas, see Appendix A.

What Am I Thinking Of?

One child thinks of an animal and other children try to guess what it is. The interventionist provides miniature objects that represent different categories (e.g., animals that fly, animals that live in water, animals of different colors, farm or zoo animals). Other children each ask a question to narrow the possibilities. A child might ask, "Does it live in the water?" and, if the answer is yes, then all animals that do not live in water are removed. If each child has made a guess about the animal and no one has guessed correctly, then the first child gives another clue. The interventionist should provide the least level of assistance necessary for children to think up questions and subsequently categorize the objects.

FIGURE 16–3
Sample Item from the *Assessment, Evaluation, and Programming System for Infants and Children*
Note: From Bricker, D., and Waddell, M. (2002). *AEPS: Assessment, Evaluation, and Programming System for Infants and Children*. Baltimore: Paul H. Brookes Publishing Co., Inc., Reprinted by permission.

about moving and doing" (Dombro et al.). Age ranges that incorporate skills in 8- to 18-month periods present separate goals and objectives forms.

Criterion-Referenced Measures

Criterion-referenced tests (CRTs) measure a child's performance compared with a specified criterion of performance or mastery of a skill or sequence of skills (Bailey, 2004b). The focus on mastery or achievement of the criterion-referenced assessments used in early childhood is on developmental sequences and milestones. Since early childhood services and programs include activities designed to promote skills based on young children's typical developmental patterns, the criteria included in CRTs are often consistent with, or "compatible" with, the curriculum in these early childhood programs. Bagnato et al. (1997) describe criterion-referenced assessment instruments as those that are not part of a specific curriculum but are useful for instructional planning and ongoing assessment. Because criterion-referenced assessments include items that are listed in hierarchies or sequences, it is easy to develop objectives to address the domains assessed as the basis for the curriculum.

The *Brigance Inventory of Early Development III* (Brigance, 2013) is an example of a frequently used criterion-referenced measure. The instrument focuses on developmental skills divided into 11 domains and can be used for infants and children with a developmental age up to 7 years. The tool can be used to determine developmental age and to compare with normative data. Record books provide a means of scoring several assessment sessions on the same form as a way of assessing current performance and progress over time. The measure is appropriate for children with mild to moderate delays or disabilities. A compact disc with goals and objectives and a web-based management and scoring system also is available with this version of this assessment tool. Assessors could use the *Inventory of Early Development III (IED–III)*, along with other forms of assessment as part of the multiple measures recommended for best practice.

The *Pediatric Evaluation of Disability Inventory (PEDI)* is an example of an instrument designed for children with various sensory, motor, and neurological delays (Haley, Coster, Ludlow, Haltiwanger, & Andrellos, 1992). This instrument contains three measurement scales—caregiver assistance, functional skills, and modifications—for use with children ages 6 months to 7 years. Content domains include categories such as self-protection, getting in and out of the car, eating, and floor locomotion.

NORM-REFERENCED AND DYNAMIC ASSESSMENT

Sometimes the assessment team is interested in this question: *How do the child's skills compare with those of other children his or her age?* Norm-referenced tests use standardized procedures and materials to present selected tasks to elicit specific skills (Bailey, 2004b). Performance is evaluated to a set criteria, which is compared to a reference or normative group. The primary purpose of norm-referenced assessments is to measure a child's performance level in relation to that of other children. Norm-referenced tests can provide information about delays in development compared with typically developing peers, which is why they are used for eligibility purposes. If states define delay by a comparison with typical development using standard deviation or percentages (such as 25 percent delay) or months of delay, then comparisons with norms from reference groups from standardized assessment instruments are supported. When selecting and implementing norm-referenced assessments, several aspects should be considered: the year the sample testing was done to ensure the norms do represent current information; the characteristics of the normative sample (e.g., cultural and geographic representation); and whether or not children with disabilities were included in the sample (Bailey, 2004b).

Psychologists who receive specific training in the design, administration, and scoring of these instruments commonly administer norm-referenced tests. For example, the *Bayley Scales of Infant Development–III* (Bayley, 2006) is a three-part evaluation of a child from ages 1 year through 42 months, consisting of a Cognitive Scale (memory, learning, sensory-perception), a Language Scale (receptive and expressive) a Motor Scale (fine and gross motor), a Behavior Rating Scale (attention, interests, emotions, etc.), and an Adaptive Behavior Scale. Infants are observed while doing tasks, and parents report about performance or assist the child to complete the task successfully. The *Battelle Developmental Inventory—Second Edition (BDI–2)* (Newborg, 2004) can be used with infants and young children from birth through 7–11 years. Five domains of personal-social, adaptive, motor, communication, and cognitive contain 341 developmental skills, with suggestions for adaptations for specific sensorimotor disabilities. A screening tool, full assessment instrument, software for scoring, and an edition in Spanish (Newborg, 2005) are available. Additional norm-referenced tests that are used to measure intellectual performance that can be used with preschool-aged children (such as the *Stanford-Binet, WIPPSI, Woodcock-Johnson,* and *McCarthy Scales*) are described in Chapter 7.

The *Mullen Scales of Early Learning* (Mullen, 1995) is a standardized and norm-referenced assessment for young children ages birth through 68 months. Five scales that include the domains of expressive language, receptive language, visual reception, gross motor, and fine motor are evaluated using materials provided in a kit. Administration time varies depending on the age of the child, with up to 40–60 minutes for children age 5. Computer software is available to calculate and convert raw scores. Suggestions for developmentally appropriate tasks also are provided.

Dynamic assessment is a method that is considered an extension of existing, normed, static tests. The purposes of a dynamic assessment are to test, teach, and retest (Burton & Watkins, 2002). The aim is to determine which strategies, if any, assist the learner to be successful with test items. A dynamic assessment measure designed for use with preschool children, the *Preschool Learning Assessment Device (PLAD),* was created as an extension of the norm-referenced *Kaufman Assessment Battery for Children (K–ABC)* (Kaufman & Kaufman, 1983). In the *PLAD,* two subtests of the *K–ABC,* triangles and matrices, are administered first in the standardized fashion and then with pre-identified mediation strategies (Lidz & Thomas, 1987). For example, strategies used if

errors are made when the child is asked to draw a picture of a child include: modeling, using puzzles to describe body parts, helping the child to verbalize what the task is, asking the child how she or he plans to proceed, and encouraging additions and alternatives. Following the mediated activities, the item is repeated or the child is asked once again to draw a picture. Dynamic assessment methods help with the identification of child strengths, including gifts and talents (Kanevsky, 2000) and provide information on the processes the child uses to respond to test items. The original dynamic assessment, the *Learning Potential Assessment Device (LPAD),* is discussed in Chapter 7.

SCHOOL READINESS

In readiness assessment, the question of interest is the following: *Does the child have the pre-academic and behavioral skills that would facilitate learning in elementary school classrooms?* Screening instruments that include pre-academic and school readiness skills such as the *Brigance K–1 Screen–Revised* (Brigance, 2013) and the *Developmental Indicators for the Assessment of Learning–4* (Mardell & Goldenberg, 1998) have been described under the screening section in this chapter. The *Bracken Basic Concepts Scale–3* (Bracken, 2006) is a norm- and criterion-referenced assessment tool with 308 items that includes basic pre-academic concepts for children ages 3 years through 6 years, 11 months. This instrument can be used to identify and target areas to be addressed for school readiness. The *Bracken School Readiness Assessment–3* (Bracken, 2007) is a nonverbal screening tool for children the same ages that includes Colors, Letters, Numbers/Counting, Size/Comparison and Shapes. This tool takes approximately 10 to 15 minutes to complete.

Assessments have been designed for preschool-aged children that address specific pre-academic skills. The areas covered in these instruments include reading, math, language, and general kindergarten readiness skills. The *Test of Early Reading Ability (TERA–3)* (Reid, Hresko & Hammill, 2001) and the *Test of Early Mathematics Ability (TEMA–3)* (Ginsburg & Baroody, 2003) are two screening instruments that can be administered to preschoolers. The *TERA–3* requires children to listen, express themselves orally, and point to responses of print, pictures, and numerals in answer to three subtests: alphabet, conventions, and meaning. The *TEMA–3* contains 40 informal problems (counting and calculation) and 32 formal problems (numeral literacy, number facts, and concepts) to which children must respond verbally and nonverbally by writing numerical answers. Both of these norm-referenced instruments are reported to identify children who are significantly different from their preschool-aged peers in the early development of these skills.

Assessments that focus on expressive and receptive language skills have been designed to be used with young children. The *Expressive One-Word Picture Vocabulary Test*-4 (Brownell, 2010a) can be used with children as young as age 2 and through 70+. This norm-referenced tool contains test plates depicting actions or concepts, and the examinee is asked to name each full-color illustration. The assessment takes only 15 to 25 minutes to complete. Prompting to assist with identification of relevant aspects of the illustration is allowed. The *Hodson Assessment of Phonological Patterns (HAPP–3)* includes a Preschool Screening Form and a Comprehensive Evaluation Form (Hodson, 2004). Designed for children ages 3 to 12, this tool identifies atypical patterns of articulation and pronunciation. The screening tool contains 12 items for the child to state. If the child has difficulty in two or more areas identified in summary questions (e.g., consonant omissions, liquid phonemes), then the Comprehensive Evaluation is recommended. This evaluation has 50 words that can be transcribed to determine phonological patterns.

The *Receptive One-Word Picture Vocabulary Test*-4 (Brownell, 2010b) can be administered to individuals ages 2 through 70+. Test plates with items that were screened for bias are shown, and the examiner asks the examinee to identify the correct item. It takes 15 to 25 minutes to administer. There is also a Spanish-bilingual version of this receptive test (Brownell, 2012) that can be used with individuals ages 2 through 70+. It is intended for use with individuals who speak English and Spanish with varying levels of proficiency.

Norms were created from bilingual students in the United States, and the test takes into account the fact that scores may be lower in one language due to the acquisition of two languages rather than indicating a language delay—a result that may be concluded from a monolingual assessment tool (Brownell, 2012). This test takes 10 to 15 minutes to administer.

The *Peabody Picture Vocabulary Test—Fourth Edition (PPVT–4)* (Dunn & Dunn, 2007) can be used with children from age 21 months to determine receptive vocabulary abilities. The child responds to questions from the administrator by pointing to one of an array of four possible pictorial selections. The *Test of Early Language Development—Third Edition* (Hresko, Reid, & Hammill, 1999) assesses receptive and expressive grammatical forms and content of language for children from age 3. The *Test of Early Written Language* (Hresko, Herron & Peak, 1996) is designed to be used with children ages 3 through 10 to evaluate basic and contextual writing skills including the identification of writing materials and letters and the child's ability to draw and understand signs and words.

Skills that facilitate the transition to kindergarten (Chandler, 1993) and helpful entry-level skills for kindergarten (Rous & Hallam, 2002) have been identified. Skills recommended as important include: communicates wants and needs, follows simple directions, maintains peer interaction, shares toys and materials, takes turns, and is able to conduct self-care routines such as caring for toileting needs, eating independently, and taking outer clothing on and off. In addition, refraining from disturbing the activities of others, stopping activities when requested, working independently, completing tasks when given developmentally appropriate material, and waiting until directions are completed before beginning activities are all helpful skills to have at entry to kindergarten (Rous & Hallam). These authors recommend that preschool assessment include these skills (Chandler, Rous, & Hallam).

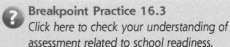
Breakpoint Practice 16.3
Click here to check your understanding of assessment related to school readiness.

PROGRAM PLANS, GOALS, AND OBJECTIVES

The important next step in assessment is development of the intervention plan. The team focuses on this question: *How will early intervention personnel assist young children and their families to maximize strengths and develop new skills?*

Individualized Family Service Plans

Families with a child, aged birth through age 2, who receive services must have an individualized family service plan (IFSP). Family-centered IFSP development is critical in achieving a useful working document for the child and family (Sandall, 1997c). Discussing family strengths during an initial interview sets a positive tone and facilitates family participation (Trivette & Dunst, 2005). A contributing factor to a family's strength is the resources available. Resources and sources of support can be described in four categories (Trivette, Dunst, & Deal, 1997): (1) personal and social network members that include those individuals to whom a family can turn to seek advice, assistance, and nurturance such as partners, friends, and neighbors; (2) associational groups such as church and outdoor groups, fitness clubs, and charities; (3) community programs and professionals including agencies that provide services and schools, and (4) specialized professional services such as special education and early intervention programs.

Given the resources available to the family, the assessment team identifies target outcomes. Outcomes specify what is to occur and what is expected as a result of these actions (Sandall, 1997c). Outcomes should be written in easily understood terms so that everyone on the assessment team will be able to know if the outcome has been reached. The criteria and timelines for meeting the goal or outcome should be identified, with particular attention to how family members define success in meeting the specific goals. A sample page from an IFSP that includes objectives fabricated for Timmy and his family is found in Figure 16–4. Note that the goals are written to strengthen family and child performance, with services delivered at home and in center-based and community-based programs.

When the child reaches age 3, the family may begin to receive services from the Department of Education that requires an individualized educational program, rather than the IFSP. This plan also includes goals and objectives as a means of evaluating progress with identified outcomes.

Program Monitoring and Ongoing Assessment

Although benchmarks, goals, and outcomes are required to be reviewed at least every 6 (IFSP) or 12 (IEP) months, an accountable early intervention service would plan to evaluate whether or not services were addressing goals on a much more frequent basis. Several challenges to ongoing assessment must be addressed. Curriculum-based assessments are recommended (Neisworth & Bagnato, 2005) because the transition from establishing areas of delay to defining the curriculum for addressing the delay with an accompanying measure of change is comparatively smooth. If measures are used that do not have an accompanying curriculum, such as norm-referenced instruments, then service providers must develop the curriculum based on results of these measures along with creating a monitoring system.

Service delivery in natural environments creates opportunity for group activities of children with and without disabilities or delays. Early childhood interventionists need to ensure that goals are being addressed in these heterogeneous groups as well as monitoring progress with the goals. Carrying pencil and paper to these activities may be cumbersome. Recalling observations made at the end of the day may be inaccurate, and using videotape to record activities, which is reviewed later, is time consuming and costly. With consideration of these challenges, a method for monitoring progress with identified outcomes is extremely important. Most young children with disabilities and delays and their families cannot wait 6 months to find out that an activity or method of service delivery was ineffective. Serial or ongoing assessment must be incorporated into the design of the service. The frequency of monitoring would depend on the importance of the goal, the degree to which progress is being made, and the demands on the caregivers (Wolery, 2004).

Name Timmy Brookes OPD.0 Family's Name Brookes IFSP# 1 FIPP Staff Member Jan Lee

Date / # — NEED/PROJECT OUTCOME STATEMENT	SOURCE OF SUPPORT/ RESOURCE	COURSE OF ACTION	FAMILY'S EVALUATION Date	FAMILY'S EVALUATION Rating
3-14 / 1 — Family has requested a workable transportation plan to meet all preferred appointments.	Jan will provide support and information. Grandparents, neighbors, and colleagues have volunteered some rides to specific appointments.	Jan will provide information on transportation funded by Early Start and on public transportation. Parents will talk with grandparents and colleagues about car pooling possibilities.	3-14-2008 5-22-2008	3 7
3-14 / 2 — The Brookes family would like "to see Timmy talk more," and the team will focus on getting Timmy to state, "I want" consistently to request desired items, objects, or events.	Sam (Early Start speech therapist) will work with Timmy weekly on this goal. Parents will communicate with Sam and provide consistent approach at home.	Sam will visit Timmy at the day care center once a week for speech and language service.	3-14-2008 5-22-2008	3 5
3-14 / 3 — Timmy will increase his vocabulary words to 25 words.	Parents, grandparents, neighbors, sister, Early Start staff and Mrs. Jackson (day-care provider) will all focus on teaching Timmy the identified vocabulary words.	Sam will establish a list of target words with parents and notify other Early Start staff and Mrs. Jackson.	3-14-2008 5-22-2008	3 3
3-14 / 4 — Mrs. Brookes would like Timmy and his sister to share toys during parallel play activities at least once a day.	Early Start Service Coordinator will suggest strategies. Mrs. Jackson will arrange activities during day-care.	Service coordinator will meet with parents and Mrs. Jackson to share strategies to promote play between Timmy and his sister. Preferred activities for both children will be identified.	3-14-2008 5-22-2008	4 6

Family's Evaluations

1...Situation changed, no longer a need
2...Situation unchanged, still a need, goal, or project
3...Implementation begun, still a need, goal, or project
4...Outcome partially attained or accomplished

5...Outcome accomplished or attained, but not to the family's satisfaction
6...Outcome mostly accomplished or attained to the family's satisfaction
7...Outcome completely accomplished or attained to the family's satisfaction

FIGURE 16–4
Portion of the IFSP for Timmy

The use of activity-based interventions where clearly defined goals are embedded in enjoyable activities (Pretti-Frontczak & Bricker, 2004) facilitates ongoing assessment. Incorporating goals into the family routine or in fun activities is an important component of service delivery. Observing the effect of these events on outcomes and recording these observations facilitates communication with other service delivery and assessment team members, and provides important information for future reference.

Program Evaluation

Outcome evaluations for individual programs and for the early intervention field have become increasingly in demand. Funding sources as well as participating families want to know if programs have been able to minimize or prevent developmental problems from occurring for children at risk (Guralnick, 1997). Two meta-analyses support the effectiveness of early intervention programs (Casto & Mastropieri, 1986; Shonkoff & Hauser-Cram, 1987). However, Guralnick (1997) writes that a major task for future research is to identify those specific program features (curriculum, intensity of service, role of parent involvement) that are associated with optimal outcomes for children and families. Regardless of the positive outcomes for the field in general, the evaluation of the effectiveness for specific programs also remains a key challenge.

In order to facilitate the incorporation of recommended practices, the Division of Early Childhood (DEC) has designed program assessment tools with the items comprised of their recommendations (Hemmeter, Joseph, Smith, & Sandall, 2001). Guidelines for evaluation programs are included. The DEC has also published a Parent Checklist for evaluating programs (Hemmeter & Salcedo, 2005) and a program evaluation to be used by administrators entitled Administrator's Essentials: Creating Policies and Procedures that Support Recommended Practices in Early Intervention/Early Childhood Special Education (EI/ECSE) (Smith, 2005).

When designing program evaluation methods, the constraints of resources, time, and political context need to be considered. The ethical and constitutional rights of participants in program evaluation need to be taken into account in evaluation design as well as the use of technical methods that are valid, reliable, accurate, fair, and replicable. Program evaluators for this early age frame need to participate in authentic context in order to collect valid information (Snyder & Sheehan, 1996). Accepting this challenge of continuing to improve the quality of services to best meet the priorities and needs of families who have young children with delays and disabilities through ongoing assessment is the responsibility of all early childhood special educators.

ENHANCEDetext
Video Example 16.3
Watch this video to see a language evaluation of a young child.

Assessment in Action
Timmy, a Child with Possible Delays

Timmy is an attractive 2-year-old who enjoys watching videos and playing outside on the slide, swings, and jungle gym. He has a lovely laugh that is particularly strong when his dad picks him up and holds him high in the air. Timmy's mother and his day-care provider, Mrs. Jackson, both have some concerns about Timmy's development, especially in the area of communication and language.

Although Timmy can say a couple of words, he typically communicates what he wants by grabbing objects or displaying a tantrum. Perhaps due to his lack of communication skills, he avoids playing near other children, including his 4-year-old sister. He will play with his toy cars for hours, but if his sister tries to join him he will turn away from her. Timmy's mother really wants her two children to learn to play well together.

The opportunity for Timmy to practice his language and communication skills and his ability to interact and play with his sister are the priorities for the Brookes family. Through multiple assessments (family interview, observation, play-based and curriculum-based), it was determined that Timmy has a developmental delay in the areas of communication and social-emotional development. He is also delayed in his play skills compared with other children his age. Timmy is eligible for early intervention services, and during the IFSP process it was agreed that the the team's efforts would focus on language and communication. His communication, language, and play skills would receive ongoing monitoring so that a change in emphasis could be arranged at any time. All team members are hoping that with a focus on speech and language now, and when Timmy is in preschool, he may be ready for kindergarten with his peers.

SUMMARY

- The most important consideration in the assessment of young children is the interrelationship between the child and his or her family. The current philosophy guiding best practice indicates that questions about individual children are addressed through working with the family. Child assessment and family concerns are not considered two distinct areas, but since child issues and family issues are intertwined, together they form the focus of all assessment efforts.

- The *AGS Early Screening Profiles* (Harrison, 1990) is designed to assess delays or gifts and talents in the areas of cognitive/language, motor, and self-help/ social for children ages 2 through 6. Additional information obtained from four surveys focused on articulation, behavior, health history, and the home environment completes the screening. The authors recommend a team approach to this screening process.

- The *Infant-Toddler and Family Instrument (ITFI)* (Provence & Apfel, 2001) is a survey designed to guide a home visitor through completion of a thorough and sensitive interview. It includes questions regarding the young child's characteristics, household and daily routines, caregiver-child interactions, family and friend support, health, growth and development, and family issues and concerns. Information about development in the domains of motor, social-emotional, language, coping, and self-help skills is also recorded.

- The *Hawaii Early Learning Profile (HELP)* for ages birth to 3 (Parks et al., 1994) and preschoolers (ages 3–6) (Vort Corporation, 1995a) is a curriculum-based assessment designed to be completed by observing the child's activity under ongoing or arranged circumstances as well as through parent interviews (Bagnato et al., 1997). An assessor can record information on a checklist that organizes skills by age or by assessment strands (Parks, 1992; Vort Corporation, 1995b) that identify a range of skills within a dimension of competence (such as cognitive and regulatory/sensory organization).

- Norm-referenced tests use standardized procedures and materials to present selected tasks to elicit specific skills (Bailey, 2004b). Performance is evaluated to set criteria, which are compared to a reference or normative group. The primary purpose of norm-referenced assessments is to measure a child's performance level in relation to other children. Dynamic assessment is a method that is considered an extension of existing, normed, static tests. The purposes of a dynamic assessment are to test, teach, and retest

(Burton & Watkins, 2002). The aim is to determine which strategies, if any, assist the learner to be successful with test items.

- The *Receptive One-Word Picture Vocabulary Test–4* (Brownell, 2010b) can be administered to individuals ages 2 through 70+. Test plates with items that were screened for bias are shown, and the examiner asks the examinee to identify (receptive) the correct item. The *Expressive One-Word Picture Vocabulary Test-4* (Brownell, 2010a) can be used with individuals ages 2 through 70+. This norm-referenced tool contains test plates depicting actions or concepts,

and the examinee is asked to name (expressive) each full-color illustration.

- The use of activity-based interventions where clearly defined goals are embedded in enjoyable activities (Pretti-Frontczak & Bricker, 2004) facilitates ongoing assessment. Incorporating goals into the family routine or in fun activities is an important component of service delivery. Observing the effect of these events on outcomes and recording these observations facilitate communication with other service delivery and assessment team members, and provide important information for future reference.

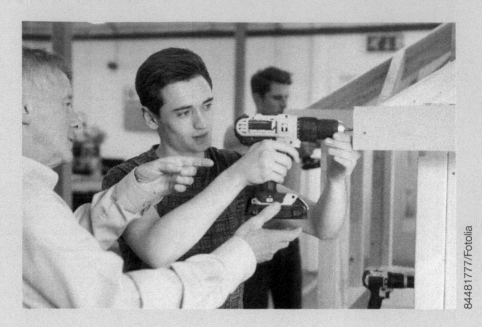

17

Assessment for Transition Education and Planning

By Bonnie R. Kraemer

LEARNING OUTCOMES

After reading this chapter, you will be able to:

- Describe conceptual framework for secondary education transition as it relates to the assessment of adolescents and young adults.
- Name and discuss strategies and approaches for transition assessment.
- Identify and describe assessment tools to assist in planning for future employment and adult life.
- Discuss person-centered planning when providing transition services.
- Discuss student responsibility related to support services in college and other postsecondary education settings.
- Identify and describe recommendations for improving transition practices.

KEY TERMS

transition
Summary of Performance (SOP)
job analysis

person-centered planning
self-determination
advocacy

W hen assessing adolescents and young adults with disabilities, it is critical to consider the individual's future adult roles and needed transition services. To address these issues, the assessment team must examine the transition process and the types of services and supports students will require to successfully move from the K–12 educational system to the adult world. Transition assessment is an individualized, ongoing process that helps students identify their interests, preferences, strengths, and abilities in relationship to preparation for adult roles, including employment, postsecondary education, independent living, community involvement, and social/personal relationships (Sitlington, Neubert, Begun, Lombard, & Leconte, 1996). Student assessment for transition should begin early and be an ongoing process. Early transition assessment leads to the identification of transition service needs and supports that are crucial in facilitating successful movement from high school to adult living. In addressing the needs of adolescents and young adults with disabilities, the general assessment question guiding data collection is: *What are the student's transition-related interests, preferences, strengths, and abilities?*

CONSIDERATIONS IN THE ASSESSMENT OF ADOLESCENTS AND YOUNG ADULTS

The **transition** from school to adult life has emerged as a primary focus for the secondary education of youth with disabilities. It has been argued that the secondary education of youth with disabilities is essentially the education of students for transition into adult life (Kohler, 1996). This emphasis emerged over the last 20 years following reports that youth with disabilities were not faring well upon leaving school (e.g., Hasazi, Gordon, & Roe, 1985). Compared to young people without disabilities, young people with disabilities are more likely to be unemployed, live with their parents, and be socially isolated (National Council on Disability, 2000). As an example, findings from the National Longitudinal Transition Study–2 indicate that 3 to 5 years after high school only about 50 percent of young people with disabilities are employed, compared to 69 percent of their peers (Wagner, Newman, Cameto, & Levine, 2005). The National Council on Disability (2000) reported that, significant needs existed in the post-school lives of our country's youth. Clearly, there is need to continue to improve the transition outcomes of students with disabilities.

This chapter presents the legal basis for transition planning and education followed by a conceptual framework that informs and guides transition assessment, planning, and education. Transition strategies and assessment tools for use in secondary settings are described, as well as emergent issues that impact the development and implementation of transition services. Strategies for college and postsecondary settings are included, in addition to recommendations for assuring that assessment practices result in effective transition programming.

Legal Framework for Transition Assessment

Since the mid-1970s, federal laws have established specific requirements for the education of children and youth with disabilities and for their access to postsecondary education and meaningful employment. The National Council on Disability (2000) listed examples, including the 1975 Education of All Handicapped Children Act, the

1990 Americans with Disabilities Act, the 1994 School-to-Work Opportunities Act, and the 1998 Higher Education Act.

Chief among these acts is the Individuals with Disabilities Education Act as amended in 1997 (IDEA, PL 105-17) and reauthorized in 2004 as the Individuals with Disabilities Education Improvement Act (IDEA, PL 108-446). This law clearly establishes school district responsibilities for planning the transition of youth with disabilities. The most significant responsibilities mandated by IDEA are:

1. provide a *coordinated set of activities* for a child with a disability that "is designed to be within a *results-oriented* process, that is focused on improving the academic and functional achievement of the child with a disability to facilitate the child's *movement from school to post-school* activities, including postsecondary education, vocational education, integrated employment (including supported employment), continuing and adult education, adult services, independent living, or community participation;"
2. develop a transition plan "based upon the individual *child's needs*, taking into account the *child's strengths, preferences and interests;*" and
3. offer transition education services that include "instruction; related services; community experiences; the development of employment and other post-school adult living objectives; and, when appropriate, acquisition of daily living skills and a functional vocational evaluation" (IDEA, 2004). [emphasis added]

School districts are also required to include statements describing the services that will be provided "beginning not later than the first individualized education program (IEP) to be in effect when the child is *16,* and updated annually thereafter" (emphasis added). Transition services (including courses of study) should help the child to achieve his or her appropriate, measurable postsecondary goals that are "based upon age appropriate transition assessments related to training, education, employment, and where appropriate, independent living skills" (IDEA, 2004).

This most recent reauthorization of IDEA added another provision for all students with disabilities who exit the school system. These students are required to have a **Summary of Performance (SOP)** upon exiting. This includes those who graduate from secondary school with a regular diploma or those who have exceeded the age eligibility for a free appropriate public education (FAPE) under state law. As stated in IDEA (2004), "a local education agency shall provide the child with a summary of the child's academic achievement and functional performance, which shall include recommendations on how to assist the child in meeting the child's postsecondary goals." An SOP that provides documentation of a student's disability, a summary of his or her educational performance, and recommendations on how to help the student achieve his or her postsecondary goals can help facilitate the transition from school to adult life and "bridge the gap" for students exiting from high school (Kochhar-Bryant, 2007).

Although not specifically written with students with disabilities in mind, the No Child Left Behind Act of 2002 (NCLB) also affects the transition of students with disabilities from high school to postsecondary settings. With its emphasis on meeting standards, NCLB requires students to be assessed in the areas of language arts, mathematics, and, by 2007–2008, science, at least once during grades 10–12. Indeed, to ensure that students have met federal and state standards before they graduate, as many as 26 states have or plan to adopt a High School Exit Exam (Center on Education Policy, 2006). Although the NCLB provides for "reasonable adaptations and accommodations for students with disabilities," in many states students with disabilities are required to pass a standardized assessment in order to receive their diplomas.

Federal laws mandate the responsibilities of schools for the transition planning of youth with disabilities and also provide a framework for implementation of transition assessment practices. Understanding this framework and the linkage between post-school outcomes and secondary transition education and planning is essential to understanding the function of transition assessment.

Post-school outcomes and goals for adulthood are *central* to the transition planning and education process. It is critical to establish a strong linkage between the student's instructional program (including the curriculum employed) and his or her post-school outcomes and goals. Curriculum and instruction must help the student acquire the knowledge, skills, and behaviors required to successfully achieve desired goals when he or she leaves school.

When a student reaches the age of 16, and every year thereafter for the duration of the student's schooling, the IEP must include a statement of needed transition services. This statement establishes the linkage between the types of services and supports that the student may need to achieve his or her post-school goals and outcomes. The IEP must include goals based on transition assessments and identify transition services needed for the student to meet these goals. These services and supports are planned and provided by the school district, state agencies (e.g., Department of Vocational Rehabilitation), and other community services providers. In 2011, the Office of Special Education Programs (OSEP) expanded language, more specifically measurable postsecondary goals in the areas of vocational training, employment, and independent living (OSEP, 2011).

Thus, post-school goals and outcomes are clearly the centerpiece for transition assessment. Therefore, it is essential to consider the possibilities for a student's future and to begin setting post-school goals and outcomes early. This will facilitate effective instructional planning and link the student and his or her family to the supports needed to achieve those goals.

Conceptual Framework for Transition Assessment

Given that secondary education is fundamentally preparation for adult life, it follows that *all* secondary education is fundamentally transition education and planning (Halpern, 1994; Kohler, 1996; Wehman, 2001). In addition, given the legal mandate of federal law, transition assessment must be considered an ongoing process in which *all* educational assessment conducted for students enrolled in secondary schools is fundamentally transition

assessment. This conceptualization significantly increases the scope of transition assessment.

One way in which transition assessment may be practically framed is by addressing a set of guiding questions:

1. What are the student's and his or her family's needs, preferences, interests, priorities, and expectations?
2. What are the student's and his or her family's goals upon graduating/completing school based on their preferences, interests, priorities, and expectations?
3. What are the most critical factors of each postsecondary goal that establish what must be in place for each goal to be achieved?
4. What is the student's current level of performance and his or her needs?
5. What performance criteria or standards may be established as measures or benchmarks for the student's successful achievement of his or her post-school goals and outcomes?
6. What curricular and instructional opportunities, activities, and strategies must be employed to ensure successful achievement of post-school goals and outcomes?
7. What adaptations, services, supports, and resources are or may be needed by the student (e.g., assistive technology, environmental modifications) to achieve post-school goals?

In this framework, transition assessment is driven by a futuristic perspective established by the student and his or her family in close collaboration with a multidisciplinary team composed of school and related service personnel, including representatives from community service providers, and, when appropriate, other local and state agencies. Transition planning is not a static process. It requires regular and continuous updating and improvement as the student and family's preferences, interests, expectations, and priorities change over time and become more clearly understood and established by the family, student, and school personnel.

The guiding questions lead to a series of outputs that enable the team to make important educational decisions. Table 17–1 presents the conceptual framework with respect to the guiding questions that must be addressed and the final outputs that must result. Any number of assessment strategies or

TABLE 17–1

Assessment for Transition Education and Planning: A Conceptual Framework

GUIDING QUESTIONS	INFORMATION OUTPUTS
1. What are the student's and his or her family's needs, preferences, interests, priorities, and expectations in the areas of: • High School Completion/Graduation • Regular Academics • Functional Academics • Career Development/Vocational Education and Training/Employment • Postsecondary Education • Living Arrangements • Leisure/Recreation • Personal Management • Personal/Social/Family Relationships • Health/Safety/Sexuality • Medical Services/Resources • Financial/Income • Transportation • Self-Determination/Advocacy/Legal • Community Access and Use	Statement of the preferences, interests, expectations, and priorities of the student and family
2. What are the student's and his/her family's goals upon graduating/completing school based on their preferences, interests, priorities, and expectations?	Post-school outcome and goal statements
3. What are the most critical factors of each postsecondary goal that establish what must be in place for each goal and outcome to be achieved with respect to: • Adult settings (places—where) • Adult roles (people—identity) • Adult activities (what is done in the setting—how) • Adult responsibilities (expectations, demands, and behaviors that must be met or demonstrated in each setting to successfully complete required activities) • Knowledge and skill requirements of the setting/activity (performance criteria for the completion of specific tasks) • Adaptations, services, supports, and resources that might be required by the student (e.g., assistive technology, environmental modifications)	Curricular and instructional components and elements of post-school goals and outcomes

TABLE 17–1   *continued*

GUIDING QUESTIONS	INFORMATION OUTPUTS
4. What is the student's current level of performance, and what are his or her needs with respect to prior and current knowledge and performance of and related to the post-school goals? • Opportunities to access and perform in adult settings related to post-school goals; • Knowledge and understanding of the roles and activities performed by adults in settings related to post-school goals; • Current level of performance with respect to adaptive behavior, social competence, social interaction, independence, self-determination, and other behaviors necessary for meeting the adult responsibilities, expectations, demands, and behaviors required by the settings and activities related to each post-school goal; • Current level of performance with respect to the knowledge and skills required to, independently or with support, perform typical and expected tasks and behaviors in the settings related to post-school goals; and, • Adaptations, services, supports, and resources needed by the student (e.g., assistive technology, environmental modifications) to achieve postschool goals.	Reliable measures and information about the student's current level of performance with respect to the curricular and instructional components of post-school goals and outcomes
5. What performance criteria or standards may be established as measures or benchmarks for the student's successful achievement of his or her post-school goals and outcomes?	Benchmarks or indicators of the successful achievement of post-school goals and outcomes
6. What curricular and instructional opportunities, activities, and strategies must be employed to ensure successful achievement of post-school goals outcomes?	Systematic and planned selection and development of curricular and instructional opportunities, activities, and strategies
7. What adaptations, services, supports, and resources are or may be needed by the student (e.g., assistive technology, environmental modifications) to achieve post-school goals?	Identification of adaptations, supports, services, and technologies needed

instruments may be employed to gather the information necessary to effectively address each question and develop a comprehensive student- and family-focused transition plan.

 Breakpoint Practice 17.1
Click here to check your understanding of the assessment of adolescents and young adults.

STRATEGIES AND APPROACHES FOR TRANSITION ASSESSMENT

The importance of assessment for transition education and planning has been well established in the literature (e.g., Clark, 2007; Cohen, Spenciner, & Twitchell, 2003; Hughes & Carter, 2000; Repetto, 2001; Sax & Thoma, 2002; Sitlington, 1996; Taylor, 2003; Wehman, 2001). The Division on Career Development and Transition (DCDT) of the Council for Exceptional Children defines transition assessment as:

> the ongoing process of collecting data on the individual's needs, preferences, and interests as they relate to the demands of current and future working, educational, living, and personal and social environments. Assessment data serves as the common thread in the transition process and forms the basis for defining goals and services to be included in the Individualized Education Program (IEP). (Sitlington, Neubert, & LeConte, 1997, pp. 70–71)

Sitlington et al. (1997) argued that transition assessment should be ongoing and emphasize the preferences, interests, and needs of the student with respect to current and future environments. They proposed a broad transition assessment process that involves three components:

1. *Student assessment* to identify strengths, interests, preferences, and needs through the use of various evaluation and assessment techniques
2. *Environmental analysis* to identify potential living, work, and educational settings and determine environmental demands and needed supports and accommodations
3. *Determining the match* between the student's strengths, interests, preferences, and needs with potential living, work, and educational demands, supports, and accommodations.

The assessment techniques employed are therefore often multidimensional. A variety of assessment techniques are available, some applicable for gathering many kinds of data and others only useful in specific cases (Clark, 1998a, 1998b; Sitlington et al., 1996). Several of these information-gathering techniques are briefly discussed next.

Cumulative Data Review

One vital aspect of transition assessment is examination of attendance records, grades, test scores, and available special education assessments of intellectual, academic, and behavioral areas. This information provides a context for understanding transition needs and choosing appropriate services.

Student, Parent, and Teacher Interviews

Students should be asked about interests and leisure-time activities, the type of work they have done at home, and the part-time and summer jobs they have held. Also, their knowledge about, and aspirations for, jobs and community life can be assessed informally through conversations or other informal methods. It is equally important to establish parents' aspirations for their children's future employment, schooling, and community life because these shape students' perceptions. Parents also can provide their view of their children's strengths and weaknesses and describe their perceptions of appropriate vocations and professions for their children. Teachers have a good deal of information about the cognitive and affective skills of students. Their experience with the work-related behaviors of students, such as attention and task completion, is also a valuable resource. They have knowledge about how students like to approach and complete tasks, as well as an awareness of instructional approaches that are successful for particular students. See Clark, Patton, and Moulton (2000) for a variety of helpful informal assessment tools that can be used during interviews with students, parents, and teachers.

Interest Inventories

Through the use of interest inventories, students are asked about occupational and other preferences. This can be done either formally or informally. Some students can clearly state their likes and dislikes in terms of future work and other adult outcomes, whereas other students will need additional supports and experiences to be able to identify their preferences and interests. In inventories and surveys, students choose among different types of activities and indicate the ones they like the most.

Vocational Aptitude/Ability Testing

General aptitude and ability tests are available to assess broad and multiple competencies for certain types of work. Also, there are specific aptitude tests for particular job skills such as fine- and gross-motor dexterity, use of tools, and speed and accuracy of motor and perceptual-motor performance. Although the results of these types of tests may suggest some aptitude or readiness for certain types of training or work, actual success or failure may be affected by many other factors (Wimmer, 1982). These tests may also present the opportunity to observe students' communication skills, physical endurance, work habits and attitudes, ability to follow directions, and tolerance for stress.

Job Readiness

This assessment concerns job-seeking skills such as interviewing skills. Job-keeping skills such as punctuality and response to supervision are also important to assess. This analysis can be conducted through a variety of means, including observation, testing, and interviews with teachers and parents.

Job Analysis

This procedure is a task analysis of the specific skills required by a job and is often a prerequisite for other assessments. Observations and interviews should be used to gather information to complete the following five basic steps of conducting a job analysis (McDonnell, Wilcox, & Hardman, 1991):

1. Identify the basic observable and measurable tasks necessary to complete a job.
2. Identify the environmental cues that prompt the completion of the job.
3. Identify the average time per task that makes up the job or number of products required to complete the job.
4. Identify the quality control for each job task.
5. Identify the exceptions to the normal routine.

Postsecondary Education Environment Analysis

This analysis concerns the identification of the courses, programs, and/or total postsecondary educational environment. Information gathered might include course load, course requirements, available academic and financial supports, supports for students with disabilities, and so forth.

Work Samples and Simulations

To reflect job placements in a particular location, work samples can be developed. They are simulated representations of work tasks or activities that represent an actual job or part of a job (Clark & Kolstoe, 1995). Such procedures not only reveal student competence on specific work tasks, but also provide information about work habits, stamina, and social skills. Students have the opportunity for hands-on exposure to job requirements before actually entering the market. Work samples may be a full-scale replica of a local job or a representation of one common job component in a variety of local jobs (e.g., using a cash register).

Ecological Analysis

This approach permits a systematic and functional analysis of the students' actual job performance. It involves specifying the work behavior being observed, describing the environmental work conditions, establishing the student's initial level of performance, initiating the job training program or actual job, and continuing observations during the program to establish improved skill competence.

Curriculum-Based Assessment

This assessment is related to the student's needs in the school curriculum. Beyond the academic evaluation mentioned in previous chapters, this assessment concerns determining the student's level of transition and community adjustment.

Situational Assessment

Students are also observed regularly by supervisory staff in performing training or actual work activities. This on-site assessment is quantified, or at least structured, on rating forms that cover areas of supervisor interest. Unforeseen strengths and weaknesses that go unnoticed in more artificial training activities often become apparent in such situations.

A multitude of assessment instruments can be used in the areas discussed previously to facilitate transition planning and implementation. These instruments have been described and reviewed by a number of authors (Cohen et al., 2003;

Everson, 1996; Flexer & Luft, 2001; Repetto, 2001; Rojewski & Black, 2002). However, Clark (1998a, 1998b, 2007) has provided the most complete review of transition assessment practices, instruments, and resources to date. Although Clark proposed that information be gathered to address the interests and concerns of the student, family, and school, he concluded that students and their families should be the two major sources for deciding what areas in transition planning are most important. He identified the following areas that may be addressed for the purpose of transition assessment:

- Interests
- Preferences
- Physical health and fitness
- Motor skills
- Speech and language
- Cognitive development and performance
- Adaptive behavior
- Socialization skills
- Emotional development and mental health
- Independent and interdependent living skills
- Leisure skills
- Preemployability, employability, and vocational skills
- Adaptive behavior
- Socialization skills
- Emotional development and mental health
- Independent and interdependent living skills
- Leisure skills
- Choice-making and self-determination skills
- Community participation
- Needed family or other supports
- Needed linkages with support services

Clark (1998a) also provided a comprehensive discussion and review of various assessment practices and instruments for transition planning, including standardized assessments, person-centered planning, computerized assessment systems, environmental assessments, curriculum-based assessments, and medical appraisals. Table 17–2 provides a listing of selected assessment instruments for transition planning.

Careful selection of appropriate instruments is essential to acquiring valid and reliable information that may be useful for transition education and planning. As with all assessment tools, caution is warranted to ensure that the design, construction, and properties of the instruments selected for use are appropriate for the student who may be assessed. Instruments should be selected on the basis of two primary criteria. First, the specific properties of the instrument will generate the information needed and are appropriate for the student under consideration. Second, instruments should be selected on the basis of the intended use of the information gathered. Information is only as useful as its ability to (1) guide the development of post-school outcomes and/or transition goals and objectives; (2) establish a clear indicator of a student's current level of performance, knowledge, or awareness; and (3) identify teaching and learning activities that promote the achievement of post-school outcomes.

ENHANCEDetext
Video Example 17.1
Watch this video to see an example of a transition plan.

ASSESSMENT TOOLS TO ASSIST IN PLANNING FOR FUTURE EMPLOYMENT AND ADULT LIFE

Awareness of Career Options

An important aspect of transition assessment is establishing the level of awareness and knowledge that students have about careers and jobs. Among

TABLE 17–2
Transition-Focused Assessment Tools

ASSESSMENT	AUTHOR/S	YEAR
SELF-DETERMINATION		
The ChoiceMaker Self-Determination Curriculum	Martin & Marshall	1995
Whose Future Is It Anyway?	Wehmeyer & Kelchner	1995
Next S.T.E.P.	Halpern et al.	1997
Self-Advocacy Strategy for Education and Transition Planning	Van Reusen et al.	1994
Goal Action Planning	Turnbull et al.	1996
COLLABORATION PLANNING		
Personal Futures Planning	Mount	1989
McGill Action Planning System	Pearpoint	1990
Circles of Support	Forest et al.	1993
Functional Skills Screening Inventory	Becker et al.	1986
COMPREHENSIVE TRANSITION ASSESSMENT		
Transition Planning Inventory	Clark & Patton	1997
Enderle-Severson Transition Rating Scale—Revised	Enderle & Severson	2003a
Enderle-Severson Transition Rating Scale III	Enderle & Severson	2003b
The Life Centered Career Education Knowledge Battery	Brolin	1992b
VOCATIONAL/ADJUSTMENT TOOLS		
Social and Prevocational Information Battery–Revised	Halpern & Irvin	1986
Transition Behavior Scale—Third Edition	McCarney & Arthaud	2012
Work Adjustment Inventory	Gilliam	1994
VOCATIONAL APTITUDE TOOLS		
Brigance Transition Skills Inventory	Brigance	2010
Wide Range Employability Sample Test	Jastak & Jastak	1980
Singer Vocational Evaluation System	Singer Company Career Systems	1982
Occupational Aptitude Inventory and Interest Schedule—Third Edition AS	Parker	2002
Apticom	VRI	1995
VOCATIONAL INTEREST TOOLS		
COIN Career Interest Survey and Occupational Index	Durgin, Ryan, & Ryan	1995
Reading-Free Vocational Interest Inventory	Becker	2000
The Self-Directed Search	Holland	1994
Wide Range Interest-Opinion Test	Glutting & Wilkinson	2003

the many procedures available is the *Social and Prevocational Information Battery—Revised (SPIB–R)* (Halpern & Irvin, 1986). The *SPIB–R* is a set of nine tests directly related to the long-range goals of work-study or work experience programs in secondary schools. The tests include job search skills, job-related behavior, banking, budgeting, purchasing, home management, physical health care, hygiene and grooming, and functional signs. The tests are administered orally; reading is not required. The *SPIB–R* was standardized on over 900 junior and senior high school students with intellectual disabilities in Oregon who were mostly Caucasian. Thus, the restrictiveness of this norm group may limit the *SPIB–R*'s usefulness for students who are culturally and linguistically diverse.

In addition, criterion-referenced tests such as the *Brigance Transition Skills* Inventory (Brigance, 2010) can be used to determine a student's level of awareness and knowledge about occupations, as well as to answer other assessment questions concerning reading and understanding employment vocabulary, abbreviations, and ads. The assessment team could select appropriate subtests to gather baseline information, and then readminister the same measures at a later date to determine if progress had been made. Brigance Transition Skills Activities (Brigance, 2012) could then be used to bridge instruction to assessment.

Job analysis is another form of assessment that can be adapted for transition assessment or programming. **Job analysis** is systematic observation of the performance of a job to determine what the worker does, how or why he or she does it, and the skills required. When opportunities are available for students to observe in the workplace, they can be encouraged to gather information about important aspects of jobs such as: (1) skills required for the job (academic skills, physical demands, etc.), (2) work conditions (noise, heating, lighting, etc.), (3) training requirements, (4) salary and hours, and (5) advantages and disadvantages of the job. This information can then be used in discussions with students about their career aspirations.

It is critical that the assessment team evaluate the results of examination of a student's awareness of vocational options in relation to that student's opportunities for experience, cultural and linguistic background, and other factors. Cognitive, academic, or behavioral disabilities may restrict an individual's ability to examine vocational options. Some students may be slower than their age peers in acquiring knowledge and interest in this area.

A student's work aptitudes can be measured in a variety of ways, including commercially available assessment tools. One measure that can be used in this area is the *Occupational Aptitude Survey and Interest Schedule—Third Edition (OASIS–3)* (Parker, 2002). The *OASIS–3* is composed of the *OASIS–3 Aptitude Survey* and the *OASIS–3 Interest Schedule*, each of which is norm-referenced for students in grades 8–12. The *OASIS–3 Aptitude Survey* assesses six broad areas of aptitude: general ability, verbal aptitude, numerical aptitude, spatial aptitude, perceptual aptitude, and manual dexterity. The *OASIS–3 Interest Schedule* is composed of 240 statements across 12 interest areas: artistic, scientific, nature, protective, mechanical, industrial, business detail, selling, accommodating, humanitarian, leading-influencing, and physical performing. Students mark whether they like, dislike, or are neutral about each interest item.

Figure 17–1 presents a sample *Aptitude Survey* profile for a ninth grader. Percentile ranks and stanines are available for each of the six aptitude factors. This student's scores all equal or exceed the 50th percentile or stanine 5. He has strengths in General Ability, Verbal Aptitude, Numerical Aptitude, and Spatial Aptitude. According to the *OASIS–3*, these scores suggest that he has the aptitude for many professions, including medical doctor, astronomer, and geologist.

The *COIN Basic Skills Test* (Durgin, Ryan, & Ryan, 1995) is another commercially available tool that can be used to determine a student's verbal and quantitative skills related to areas of employment. This tool helps students to determine if they can work successfully with the written materials and math requirements of specific jobs that interest them. Both the verbal and quantitative tests measure skills taught from elementary school through the 10th grade and, thus, are more appropriate for students with basic reading and math skills. The *COIN Basic Skills Test* is

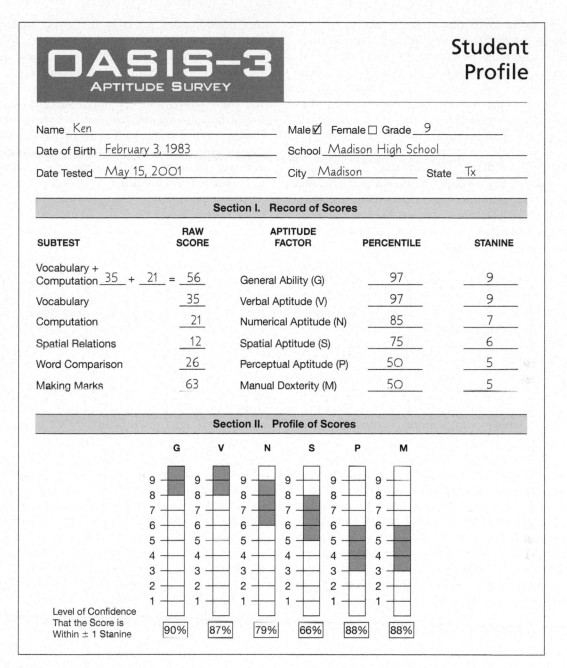

FIGURE 17–1

OASIS-3 Aptitude Survey

Note: From *OASIS-3 Aptitude Scale* by R. M. Parker, 2002, Austin, TX: PRO-ED. Copyright 2002 by PRO-ED. Reprinted with permission.

linked to the *COIN Career Interest Survey and Occupational Index*. When used in combination, these assessment tools provide skills scores linked to General Education Development levels (classification system used by the U.S. Department of Labor), provide interest assessment results that are linked to career clusters, and yield results that are linked to occupations.

Manual dexterity tests can be used to gather information about students' aptitude for the many occupations that require fine-motor dexterity and eye–hand coordination. Such tests generally require the placement and/or joining of small screws, bolts and nuts, and similar objects; tool usage may also be needed. These measures can assist determination of entry-level dexterity skills, help students identify realistic jobs, and provide motivation to acquire needed skills (Brolin, 1995). One example is the *Talent Assessment Program* (Talent Assessment, Inc., 1972, 1980, 1985, 1988). With this assessment, students perform 10 work samples requiring gross and fine finger and manual dexterity, visual and tactile discrimination, and retention of details. Based on the results of the 10 tasks, the *Talent Assessment Program* suggests potential occupations or occupational areas for the individual.

Dexterity measures can be quite frustrating for students with fine-motor coordination problems and a desire to enter occupations requiring such skills. When student frustration around fine-motor coordination tasks occurs, the assessment team can use results to guide instruction in areas of need and to explore alternative ways for students to perform such tasks (e.g., by using assistive technology). Professionals should avoid using performance on dexterity measures as a general predictor of vocational ability.

The *BRIGANCE Transition Skills Inventory* (Brigance, 2010) is an informal measure designed to assess the basic skills and employability skills needed to gain and maintain employment. This inventory helps to pinpoint skill levels in the areas of career awareness and understanding, job seeking and knowledge, reading skills, speaking and listening skills, preemployment writing, and math skills and concepts. Also, students can be rated in the areas of self-concept and attitudes, responsibility and self-discipline, motor coordination and job requirements, thinking skills/abilities and job requirements, job interview preparation, job interview skills, and work experience. The inventory is appropriate for use with secondary students with disabilities. Work and study habits are very important not only in school but also on the job and in postsecondary training settings. Methods of learning about students' current skills in these areas include observing students or interviewing them, their teachers, or members of their family.

Vocational Interests

Student interests and preferences form the foundation of a student's transition plan. However, not all interest inventories and assessment tools are appropriate for all students. It is critical that the tools that are used match the student's cognitive and communication skills. A variety of interest inventories are available for use with individuals with a range of disabilities. Some, such as the *COIN* and *OASIS–3 Interest Inventories* described previously, require higher levels of cognitive functioning and basic academic skills. The *Self-Directed Search* (Holland, 1994) is another interest inventory that can be used with students with milder disabilities. The *Self-Directed Search* is a career self-assessment tool, with a ninth-grade reading level, that, when completed, gives individuals a Holland Code that tells the relationship between job personalities, key characteristics, college majors, hobbies, abilities, and careers. The *Self-Directed Search* is linked to the Self-Directed Search Occupations Finder, which matches 1,309 occupations to Holland Codes. From the SDS Assessment, individuals search the Occupational Finder for occupations with matching or similar codes. They are the jobs that will be most satisfying to them.

For students with more severe disabilities, who have no or limited reading skills, the *Reading-Free Vocational Interest Inventory–2 (R-FVII–2)* (Becker, 2000) can be used. This inventory uses pictures, rather than text, to determine students' vocational interests. The *R-FVII–2* consists of 55 sets of three pictures; in each set, the student chooses the most appealing picture in terms of the work represented. The student must circle the picture of a person doing the job he or she would most like to do. There is no reading or writing involved. The tester reads the directions and also checks that students are marking the form correctly when working in a group. Results can be used for vocational planning and placement. Percentile ranks are derived for 11 interest areas, and areas of high and low interest are identified.

Vocational interest inventories have been created that utilize technology to simulate various occupations. For instance, both *Your Employment Selections (YES)* (Morgan, Ellerd, Gerity, & Tullis, 2000) and the *COIN Climb* series (COIN, 2003) use computer software to show students what various jobs entail. Having students watch actual video clips of individuals involved in various occupations gives them the opportunity to see different aspects of the job, where it is performed, how it is performed, what skills are needed to perform the job, and so forth. For instance, the *YES* program is a computer-based, vocational interest inventory that is geared for students with more severe disabilities. It does not require any reading skills but does specify that a student be able to make a choice of two options presented on the computer screen.

YES includes video of 120 jobs. Each video shows 2–4 minutes of critical tasks involved in each job. The *YES* program first guides students through a variety of screens showing different kinds of occupations to determine the type of work conditions that are most preferred (e.g., inside versus outside work, working with people versus working alone). Once the preferred work condition is determined, then students view 20 jobs that are performed in that type of setting. The jobs are presented in groups of two. For any pair of jobs, the student can select one of the two jobs, neither job, or both. Students select a job they like by clicking on the picture of the job. For each job in the program, the student can click on the "more info" link and access additional information, such as earnings and benefits, and training requirements.

In addition to surveying the student's vocational interests, the work community needs to be surveyed to establish current perceptions of students with disabilities, availability of jobs, and accommodations that need to be and can be made for students. For students who are interested in occupations requiring advanced training or with aspirations for higher education, technical schools and colleges need to be surveyed. These data should be combined with student interests to aid in realistic planning.

Unfortunately, students are often not asked about their career and vocational aspirations, impressions, and interests. Yet, it is paramount that the student's interests and preferences guide the transition planning process. Thus, it is highly recommended that students be interviewed about their career and vocational aspirations, impressions, and interests. Interviews are also useful vehicles for gathering information from students' families who influence their career and vocational aims. Parents and other family members shape a person's interests and aspirations by their own type of employment and experience, opinions about careers and work, and so forth. Such information may help to explain student entry behavior and alert educators to environmental factors that might influence student performance and motivation.

Specific Work Skills

Work samples are designed to assess students' ability to perform tasks that are similar to those they might encounter in actual work situations. Samples offer an opportunity to observe work habits and assess levels of interest. Although some commercially designed work samples are related to the specific jobs or job families described in the *Dictionary of Occupational Titles (DOT)* prepared by the U.S. Department of Labor, many of these assessment tools are not current. Examples of older measures are the *Wide Range Employability Sample Test (WREST)* (Jastak & Jastak, 1980) and the *Singer Vocational Evaluation System (VES)* (Singer Company Career Systems, 1982). Thus, when assessing specific work skills, it is often better to design your own work samples, use simulations, and employ other informal techniques. Simulations are a useful procedure to assess student aptitudes, skills, and interests in certain careers/jobs. As an example, some schools have set up student-run minibusinesses, such as stores to sell school supplies or snacks. Even having students perform a classroom project in an "industrial" fashion (e.g., using an assembly line) can prove useful by acquainting them with work basics and by providing a basis for discussion.

Community Adjustment

An essential aspect of addressing student needs is determining abilities and interests in a variety of domains that are specific to transition planning. These domains include not only employment, but also independent living skills, life skills, self-determination, postsecondary education, and personal-social skills (Brolin, 1995; Clark, 1998b). Among the available assessment tools that can be used in these areas are the *Transition Planning Inventory (TPI-2)* (Patton & Clark, 2014) and the *Life Centered Career Education (LCCE) Competency Assessment Knowledge Batteries* (Brolin, 1992b).

The *Transition Planning Inventory—Second Edition (TPI-2)* provides school personnel with a method to comply with federal transition mandates and assist students in their transition planning. The *TPI-2* is composed of (1) student forms, (2) a home form, (3) a school-based personnel form, and (4) a profile and further assessment recommendation form. The student, parents/guardians, and school professional complete these parts independently. New to this edition are two student interests and preference forms.

In the *TPI-2,* 57 transition planning statements are organized into the following areas: employment, further education/training, daily living, leisure activities, community participation, health, self-determination, communication, and interpersonal relationships. Each rater determines the student's level of functioning in these planning areas. In addition, the home form requests preferences and interests that are likely in post-school settings. Ratings and information are compiled on the Profile and Further Assessment Recommendation Form, which gives a visual display of data and is useful in developing the transition IEP. The *TPI-2* also contains a resource CD that can be helpful when completing the Profile and Further Assessment Forms.

The *Life Centered Career Education (LCCE) Competency Assessment Knowledge Batteries* is a curriculum-based assessment instrument. This tool assesses the career education knowledge and skills of students with disabilities in grades 7–12. The battery is a standardized, criterion-referenced set of 200 multiple-choice questions spread across the three domains of the LCCE model: awareness, exploration, and occupational guidance. This assessment is designed to be used with the *Life Centered Career Education (LCCE) Competency Assessment Performance Batteries* (Brolin, 1992c) as part of the LCCE curriculum program (Brolin, 1992a).

 Breakpoint Practice 17.2
Click here to check your understanding of assessment tools that assist in planning for future employment and adult life.

PROVIDING TRANSITION SERVICES

The conceptual framework presented earlier in this chapter suggests that the starting point for transition planning must be the development of post-school goals and outcomes. Unfortunately, Thompson, Fulk, and Piercy (2000) found little relationship between students' transition plans and the post-school outcomes and needs expressed by parents and students. Salembier and Furney (1997) reported that a significant portion of parents experienced limited participation and were not satisfied with the transition planning process. Parents also indicated that transition plans did not reflect individual interests or needs. In a statewide investigation of individualized transition plans, Everson, Zhang, and Guillory (2001) found that services specified in transition plans were unlikely to address outcome areas suggested by the state such as postsecondary education, employment, living arrangements, and financial and income needs. Indeed, these findings suggest that one of the most significant challenges to the transition planning process is establishing reasonable and achievable post-school goals and outcomes based on the preferences, needs, interests, expectations, and priorities of the student and their family and then ensuring that these goals and outcome areas are incorporated into an individual's transition plan.

The level of awareness and knowledge of adult roles, responsibilities, behaviors, tasks, and activities in multiple environments clearly restricts or expands the range of preferences, interests, expectations, priorities, and needs that may be identified by a student and his or her family. This, in turn, may result in a limited or expanded range of choices for post-school goals and outcomes. A limited range of choices has often been attributed to restricted exposure and learning opportunities. Repetto (2001) suggested that one of the most important aspects of career and vocational assessment is establishing the level of awareness and knowledge students may have about jobs. This may also apply to a student's awareness and knowledge of options in virtually all areas of adult living such as postsecondary education, independent living, income and financial support, and social relationships. Limited awareness and knowledge of adult roles and responsibilities in various settings and activities may be a function of a lack of opportunity, experience, and instruction.

DeFur, Todd-Allen, and Getzel (2001) found that the quality of the relationship between the family and service providers was the key factor affecting family involvement in transition planning. While IDEA mandates the inclusion of a statement of needed transition services beginning by age 16, it is essential that communication with and the involvement of families begin much earlier, preferably with the entrance of the student at elementary school age and intensifying in frequency and duration as the student progresses through middle school and high school. Students and families must be informed early of options and possibilities. This allows them to begin thinking about setting post-school goals and outcomes during the early years in order to effectively link educational programs and services to post-school goals.

Person-Centered Planning

Person-centered planning is an effective strategy for facilitating ongoing communication with and involvement of families and students leading to the development of post-school goals and outcomes based on the needs, preferences, and interests of the family and student. Person-centered planning is based on a philosophy that requires equal participation, positive and clear communication, and active involvement of the student and the student's family (Sax & Thoma, 2002). Though originally developed for including individuals with severe disabilities and their families in developing their own "futures" plan, this process has been adapted and expanded to address a much broader population.

A number of different strategies for person-centered planning have been developed. These include Making Action Plans (MAPS) (Vandercook & York, 1989), Planning Alternative Tomorrows with Hope (PATH) (Pearpoint, O'Brien, & Forest, 1995), and Circles of Support (Falvey, Forest, Pearpoint, & Rosenberg, 1994). Although these specific strategies differ slightly in their implementation, they have several elements in common. For instance, in person-centered planning, a number of group interviews are conducted with the student, his or her family, and others identified by the student and family as significant support partners. A standard format for person-centered planning involves gathering information about the student's history, places he or she goes, activities, preferred and nonpreferred choices, and expectations for the future (dreams). Additional information of importance to the student and family may also be gathered. Strong emphasis is placed on encouraging and facilitating the family to direct and control the discussion and planning process. This process involves identifying the strengths, preferences, interests, needs, expectations, and priorities of the student with his or her family and developing goals for the future that may be clearly established as post-school goals and outcomes.

An advantage of person-centered planning is that, through the process, transition-related activities, goals, objectives, and strategies can be identified that are then included in the IEP. Additionally, "person-centered planning has been found to increase the number of written IEP goals supported outside of school time; increase the number of non-paid individuals willing to provide support; and [result in] higher levels of satisfaction by both school personnel and families with the transition planning process" (Flannery et al., 2000, p. 135).

Finally, transition assessment instruments typically employed to determine vocational and career interests, aptitudes, work habits, and so forth become particularly important when the planning process arrives at the question of current level of performance in areas of interest to the student and his or her family. Thus, person-centered planning is certainly not intended to eliminate traditional assessment approaches, but rather to ensure the full participation of the student and family in planning their future. As seen in the case study of Phillip presented at the end of this chapter, person-centered planning can serve as a first step in the transition planning process. Through person-centered planning student and family priorities and post-school goals emerge, which can guide the transition assessment process.

Self-Determination

The importance of supporting and promoting the **self-determination** of adolescents from school to adult life has been well established (Agran, Snow, & Swaner, 1999; Field, Martin, Miller, Ward, & Wehmeyer, 1998; Hughes et al., 1997; Ward, 1988, 1991; Wehmeyer, 2001; Wehmeyer, Agran, & Hughes, 1998). Halloran (1993) argued that self-determination was education's ultimate goal, particularly for secondary level education. Wehmeyer and Schwartz (1997) found that, one year after graduation, students with learning disabilities or mental disabilities who were more self-determined were more likely to achieve positive post-school outcomes. Moreover, a study by Getzel and Thoma (2006) found that 34 individuals with disabilities (primarily learning disabilities and ADD) attending community and state colleges identified self-determination skills as important to their success in taking courses, finding the supports they needed, and advocating for their rights.

Wehmeyer (2001) listed 11 components of self-determined behavior that provide the basis for conducting transition assessment. These components are:

- Choice-making skills
- Decision-making skills
- Problem-solving skills
- Goal-setting and attainment skills
- Self-management skills
- Independence, risk-taking, and safety skills
- Self-advocacy and leadership skills
- Internal locus of control
- Positive attributions of efficacy and outcome expectancy
- Self-awareness
- Self-knowledge

Measures of self-determination are typically curriculum-based assessments integrated within a self-determination curriculum. For example, the *Arc's Self-Determination Scale* (Wehmeyer & Kelchner, 1995) is a self-report measure of self-determination that assesses a student's overall self-determination autonomy, self-regulation, psychological empowerment, and self-awareness. The Arc's self-determination curriculum *"Whose Future Is it Anyway?"* is organized for use with the *Self-Determination Scale*. It addresses self-awareness, self-confidence, choice and decision making, and goal attainment behavior for students with mild intellectual disabilities.

Another measure is the *Self-Determination Knowledge Scale (SDKS)* (Hoffman & Field, 2005). This curriculum-based measure is designed to be used as the pretest and posttest for *Steps to Self-Determination: A Curriculum to Help Adolescents Learn to Achieve Their Goals—Second Edition* (Hoffman & Field, 2005). The instrument assesses students' cognitive knowledge of self-determination in relationship to the skills taught in the curriculum. It has an approximately fifth-grade reading level.

Finally, the *ChoiceMaker Self-Determination Transition Curriculum and Program* (Martin & Marshall, 1995) is composed of three sections, including choosing goals, expressing goals, and taking action. The *ChoiceMaker Assessment* is a curriculum-referenced assessment that goes with the *ChoiceMaker Curriculum*. It contains 54 questions that assess student self-determination skills across the three areas just mentioned and opportunities at school for students to use those skills.

ENHANCEDetext

Video Example 17.2

Watch this video to find out more about transition to adult life with a kitchen example.

ASSESSMENT FOR COLLEGE AND OTHER POSTSECONDARY EDUCATION SETTINGS

More and more students with disabilities, particularly mild disabilities, will have goals to attend technical training schools and 2- and 4-year colleges. Students can earn a general high school education diploma while taking special education coursework/services (Walsh, 2012). According to Newman et al. (2011), just less than 20 percent of students with disabilities plan a four-year postsecondary education. The number of university freshmen claiming to have learning disabilities is increasing (Cowan, 2006; Harris & Robertson, 2001). Almost 11 percent (10.9) of all undergraduate college students were identified as having a disability in federal data from 2006 (National Center for Education Statistics, 2006). Data from 2011–2012 indicate a slight increase of that number, 11.1 percent (U.S. Department of Education, 2015).

In fact, an increasing number of students with learning disabilities are pursuing not only undergraduate, but also graduate and professional degrees (Henderson, 1995). Another indication of this increase is the 90 percent rise in the number of universities that are providing

support services to students with disabilities (Brinkerhoff, Shaw, & McGuire, 1993; Yost, Shaw, Cullen, McGuire, & Bigaj, 1994). According to the National Longitudinal Transition Study-2 (NLTS-2) (National Center on Secondary Education and Transition, 2002b), there has been a substantial increase in the number of students with learning disabilities attending all types of postsecondary education, particularly 2-year college programs.

The main legal imperatives requiring colleges to offer support services are Section 504 of the Rehabilitation Act of 1973, as it applies to postsecondary educational programs that receive federal monies (Vogel, 1982), and the Americans with Disabilities Act of 1990. Accurate identification and assessment procedures pose a particular challenge because the definitions of disabilities such as learning disabilities are vague and are not consistently used by colleges and universities. This is why IDEA's (2004) new requirement of a Summary of Performance (SOP) is critical for all students exiting the school system with a disability. In the case of students with milder disabilities transitioning to postsecondary education settings, the SOP, with appropriate accompanying documentation, provides information necessary under Section 504 of the Rehabilitation Act and the Americans with Disabilities Act to help establish a student's eligibility for reasonable accommodations and supports (Kochhar-Bryant, 2007).

Although many students are aware of their disabilities before leaving high school, others do not realize they have a learning disability until they are in college. Regardless of when the individual is diagnosed, it becomes the responsibility of postsecondary students to disclose their disability and the extent to which it may affect their academic success (Lynch & Gussel, 1996). These students become eligible for support services on the basis of appropriate documentation, and with the right accommodations they can experience success in college (Brackett & McPhearson, 1996; Larson & Aase, 1997).

Table 17–3 outlines possible admission requirements for students with mild disabilities who seek technical and advanced education (Patton &

TABLE 17–3
Postsecondary Education and Training Options

Option	Admission Requirements	Emphasis	DIMENSION	Outcome
			General Information	
Colleges, Universities	*Regular* High school diploma or GED SAT or ACT GPA and/or class rank *Special or Provisional* SAT/ACT may be waived or lower scores accepted Other factors (e.g., potential, goals) considered Remedial or study skills classes may be required *Cooperative (special program within college)* Joint decision between college and special program Must disclose disability Some require ACT/SAT Some require high school diploma/GED	4-year program Extensive selection of majors (>400) Sample a variety of courses during first 2 years Select major in last 2 years Some colleges specialize (music, design, technology)	Tuition varies greatly State-supported generally less costly Financial aid usually available Several sources of help available (counseling, peer tutoring, learning labs, math centers)	Bachelor of Science Degree, Bachelor of Arts Degree
Community and Junior Colleges, Public, 2-Year	Usually open admission 18 years or older Most require high school diploma or GED for credit courses	2-year program Liberal arts subjects Training in specific occupations (hotel management, auto mechanics, marketing, dental hygiene) Many also have remedial or developmental courses for upgrading basic academic skills Provides student with opportunity to try out college by taking one or two courses	Available in or near most cities Less expensive than 4-year programs Committed to serving educational and training needs of local communities Provides opportunity to build a better academic record that can be transferred to a 4-year program Provides opportunity to upgrade academic and job skills and work toward improved employment opportunities or a career change	Associates of Arts Degree, Certificate in Specific Occupations

TABLE 17–3 *continued*

		DIMENSION		
Option	Admission Requirements	Emphasis	General Information	Outcome
Junior Colleges, Private, 2-Year	High school diploma or GED Usually an entrance exam (SAT or ACT) Usually request GPA and/or class rank Experience and personal qualities usually considered	General course of study Prepares students to transfer to a 4-year liberal arts institution Opportunities to improve reading, writing, and math skills Opportunities to train for a new career	Most are small, residential schools Small class sizes Individualized attention	Associates of Arts Degree
Vocational Education Schools, Public and Private, 2 Years or Less	Usually open admission Some require high school diploma or GED Some require SAT, ACT, or admission tests	*Community Junior Colleges* Occupational training and liberal arts training can be combined *2-Year Technical Institutes/Colleges* Degree programs in skill areas needed to enter and advance in specific occupational fields Academic course usually related to occupational areas *Area Vocational Centers or Single-Specialty Public Vocational and Technical Schools* Available in a few areas Offer training in a single-specialty skill (e.g., aviation, truck driving, barbering) *Private* Trade, technical, or business schools Offers training in a variety of occupational skills Practical training in fields requiring 2 years or less	Great variability in patterns of service due to the state laws that govern (e.g., some states may offer vocational education through the community college system, whereas others might offer through technical institutes) Also great variability in state requirements for licenses to practice trades and courses of study to complete programs	Associates of Arts, Certificate

Adapted from *Unlocking Potential: College and Other Choices for Learning Disabled People. A Step-by-Step Guide* (pp. 46–47, 53–56, 81), by B. Scheiber & J. Talpers, 1987, Bethesda, MD: Adler & Adler.

Note: From *Transition from School to Young Adulthood* (pp. 41–43) by J. Patton and C. Dunn, 1998, Austin, TX: PRO-ED. Copyright 1998 by PRO-ED. Reprinted with permission.

Dunn, 1998; Scheiber & Talpers, 1987; Vogel, 1987). Some schools have open admissions, and students with special needs are automatically accepted. Other students meet the minimal entrance requirements just as typical students do; that is, they provide evidence of acceptable high school grades, performance on college admission tests like the SATs or American College Testing, and so forth. Still others request modifications of test administration procedures because of their learning disabilities, such as taking the tests untimed or having a reader or scribe. Other suggested modifications to evaluation procedures include providing essay exams instead of objective exams (or vice versa), allowing an exam to be taken in a separate room with a proctor, permitting alternate methods of demonstrating mastery of course objectives, allowing the use of computer exams and scoring sheets, and permitting the use of references and calculators (Gajar, Goodman, & McAfee, 1993; Vogel & Sattler, 1981).

There is no consistently used battery of tests for students to qualify as having a learning disability on college campuses and universities. However, the two most frequently utilized measures are the current versions of the *Wechsler Adult Intelligence Scale* and the *Woodcock-Johnson Psycho-Educational Battery*. These types of standardized assessments are important in providing documentation of a learning disability to a postsecondary institution. Most colleges require a comprehensive battery of assessments and a report of the results. This report should include a diagnosis of a learning disability and the results of assessments, including assessments of aptitude, academic achievement, and information processing. Additionally, a report needs to include the qualifications of the assessor, the date of the evaluation, and justification for the need for accommodations (Sitlington, 2003; Skinner & Lindstrom, 2003; Taymans & West, 2001).

Although formal, standardized assessment batteries are essential in documenting a learning disability for the purpose of receiving accommodations at colleges and universities, informal assessment techniques also figure prominently in postsecondary transition assessment, including observation and interviews. Vogel (1987) suggests:

- Ask students about the nature of their learning disability, things that were easy and hard to learn, their best and worst subjects, reasons for seeking more education and in what areas, their occupational plans.
- Ask institutions about the number of students with special needs on campus, the services available; preparation of advisors and instructors for accommodating students, the willingness of faculty to provide support.
- Ask faculty about their willingness to work with students with special needs, instructional style and individualization, and nature and flexibility of evaluation strategies.

Additional suggestions include:

- Use work samples, vocational interest and vocational aptitude assessments to help young adults identify skills and interests that will help them in transition decision making (Cummings, Maddux, & Casey, 2000).
- Assess assistive technology needs before the student transitions to college (Sitlington, 2003; Taymans & West, 2001).
- Help students contact disability services offices at the postsecondary institution and familiarize themselves with services offered and documentation required (Mandaus, 2005; Milsom & Hartley, 2005).

Areas that should frequently be the object for assessment are students' study habits (note taking, organization, time management, test taking); listening and comprehension skills for following class lectures and oral expression for participating in class activities; vocabulary, grammar, and production necessary for written expression; and the social, interpersonal, self-awareness and self-advocacy skills needed for interaction with teachers and peers (Cummings et al., 2000; Skinner & Lindstrom, 2003; Vogel, 1987).

Much can be accomplished with students like Joyce, whose learning disabilities were described in earlier chapters, long before they apply to or appear on a college campus. An appropriate transition assessment would establish Joyce's knowledge of and interest in possible fields of study. Many of the academic skills and learning strategies that are the subject of middle and high school assessment are applicable to the college setting and, when taught, provide an important foundation. Transitional plans for Joyce must prepare her for the college environment so that she can explain her needs well to instructors, seek out available services, use strategies independently to compensate for her disabilities, and cope with the increased demands for organizational, interpersonal, and other skills.

Of no less significance is a student's ability to engage in recreational and leisure-time activities. Researchers (Brolin, 1995; Clark & Kolstoe, 1995; White et al., 1983) indicate that students with learning disabilities, as well as others, need to be well prepared to use their free time and participate in the life of their communities. Also, the personal-social goals in the IEP should be extended to anticipate the transition to adult relationships, marriage, and child rearing. Full community adjustment is based on adequate preparation in all of these areas (Brolin, 1995; Clark & Kolstoe, 1995; Halpern, 1985). Students such as Phillip and Joyce require a transition plan conceptualized as part of their total preparation for and movement to the adult world.

 Breakpoint Practice 17.3
Click here to check your understanding of assessment for college and postsecondary education.

RECOMMENDATIONS FOR IMPROVING TRANSITION PRACTICES

Following are practical suggestions for educators and other professionals directly involved in coordinating and planning the transition process for students with disabilities:

1. Pay attention to and implement the research on validated practice (sometimes referred to as "best" practice) in transition. The success of your students depends upon your ability to employ the most effective intervention strategies. Among the most promising sources of information about validated practices are findings from the *National Longitudinal Transition Study* (Wagner, Blackorby, Cameto, Hebbeler, & Newman, 1993), the second iteration of this study (NLTS-2) (National Center on Secondary Education and Transition, 2002b; Wagner, Cameto, & Newman, 2003), and the *What Works Transition Research Synthesis Project* (National Center on Secondary Education and Transition, 2002a) recently funded by the Office of Special Education Programs. For example, Wagner et al. (1993) reported that students who are offered career and vocational education services, paid work experiences, community-based instruction, and access to and inclusion in regular education are more likely to be employed, earn higher wages, live independently, and be more involved in the community, and are less likely to drop out or be arrested.

2. Begin very early, on an ongoing and frequent basis, discussing with families and students their interests, preferences, needs, expectations, and goals for what the student will do when he or she graduates or exits school.

3. Select transition assessment instruments that were designed to be used with the students you are working with and for the purpose which you are intending to use them.

4. Understand that the best transition plan in the world is only as effective as the capacity for the plan to be fully and effectively implemented.

5. Document and record the student's successful home, school, work, and community experiences. Developing an individualized transition portfolio may help communicate the student's assets and strengths to others (Neubert & Moon, 2000).

6. Understand that the most important measures of the success of secondary education and the transition planning process are the outcomes achieved by students with disabilities after they leave school. To measure success, follow-up and follow-along surveys of

students who have graduated/exited school are essential.

7. Understand that students with disabilities who exit school continue to face the highest rates of drop-out, unemployment, poverty, and limited access to health care, housing, and community access. Therefore, **advocacy** is essential. Be an advocate and train your students to advocate for themselves, including their personal, social, educational, and political self-determination.

Assessment in Action
Phillip, a Ninth Grader

Phillip is a 16-year-old ninth grader who has been identified as a student with mild intellectual disabilities. At his last 3-year evaluation, Phillip performed in the below-average range on measures of general intelligence, adaptive behavior, and academic achievement. His primary instructional needs are in reading, mathematics, and written language; he also has poor fine-motor coordination. Phillip has difficulty with remembering, sequencing, and organizing his thoughts, as well as in making decisions. His parents and teachers agree that his program should stress functional skills for post-school community involvement, including vocational guidance and education.

As part of the assessment for this year's IEP review, several measures will be administered to gain more information about Phillip's transition needs. These measures will assess his interest, awareness, and knowledge of occupations; his aptitudes for certain jobs; and his strengths and needs in various areas of community life. As a means of gathering information, a person-centered planning process will be used with Phillip and his family to help identify post-school goals and outcomes. These goals and outcomes will then be used to help guide the transition assessment and planning process.

Following the person-centered planning meeting, the team will develop an individual assessment plan for Phillip. The plan will include several assessment questions related to planning his transition program. The questions will center around four areas: Phillip's knowledge of various careers; his interests in different occupations; his specific work-related skills; and his abilities and interests in other areas of community adjustment. To ascertain Phillip's interests and skills in various transition domain areas, members of the team will interview Phillip and administer interest inventories and work sample evaluations. In addition, Phillip, his parents, and his teacher will each complete portions of the *Transition Planning Inventory-2,* a set of measures designed to coordinate the planning process.

Planning Phillip's Program

The assessment team has finished gathering information to answer the assessment questions it posed about Phillip's educational program and needs in the area of transition. Among the team's conclusions are that Phillip would benefit from more information about the world of work and about realistic possibilities for future employment. Phillip's teachers and his mom and dad agree that Phillip needs help with developing better work habits, particularly in the areas of perseverance and asking for assistance when necessary. There is also agreement that Phillip needs to continue to mature socially and emotionally to be better prepared to work with others and to accept constructive criticism.

One aspect of the educational program for Phillip will focus on the development of academic skills useful for work and life in the community. For example, in language arts, Phillip will learn to read bus schedules, complete job applications, prepare a resume, and communicate on the telephone. In math, he will practice money use and management and learn how to use a calculator to help in computations. Phillip will also take a class called Career Exploration, which will assist him to begin making choices about potential career paths. In addition, for 3 hours a week, Phillip will participate in the community jobs program where he will be placed in an entry-level job in one of the stores or businesses in the neighborhood surrounding his high school.

SUMMARY

- Regarding conceptual framework in transition, given that secondary education is fundamentally preparation for adult life, it then follows that *all* secondary education is fundamentally transition education and planning (Halpern, 1994; Kohler, 1996; Wehman, 2001). In addition, given the legal mandate of federal law, transition assessment must be considered an ongoing process in which *all* educational assessment conducted for students enrolled in secondary schools is fundamentally transition assessment.

- *Cumulative Data Review:* One vital information-gathering technique of transition assessment is examination of attendance records, grades, test scores, and available special education assessments of intellectual, academic, and behavioral areas. This information provides a context in which transition needs can be understood and appropriate services chosen.

- An important aspect of transition assessment is establishing the student's level of awareness and knowledge about careers and jobs. Among the many procedures available is the *Social and Prevocational Information Battery—Revised (SPIB–R)* (Halpern & Irvin, 1986). The *SPIB–R* is a set of nine tests directly related to the long-range goals of work-study or work experience programs in secondary schools.

- Person-centered planning is an effective strategy for facilitating ongoing communication with and involvement of families and students leading to the development of post-school goals and outcomes based on the needs, preferences, and interests of the family and student. Though originally developed for including individuals with severe disabilities and their families in developing their own "futures" plan, this process has been adapted and expanded to address a much broader population.

- It is the responsibility of postsecondary students to disclose their disability and the extent to which it may affect their academic success (Lynch & Gussel, 1996). These students become eligible for support services on the basis of appropriate documentation, and with the right accommodations they can experience success in college (Brackett & McPhearson, 1996; Larson & Aase, 1997).

- One recommendation for improving transition practices is to begin very early, on an ongoing and frequent basis, discussing with families and students their interests, preferences, needs, expectations, and goals for what the student will do when he or she graduates or exits school.

GLOSSARY

Accommodations With tests, any changes in the ways in which a test is administered and/or scored.

Acuity The physiological ability to receive sensory information.

Adaptive behavior The ability to cope with the demands of the environment; includes self-help, communication, and social skills.

Advocacy Clear expression of support for the rights of persons with disabilities and their families.

Age score Also called *age equivalent;* a score that translates test performance into an estimated age; reported in years and months.

Algorithm A procedure used to perform a mathematical operation.

Alternate score A score resulting from the administration of standardized tests under altered conditions.

Anecdotal records Written notes kept by teachers on a daily basis about student performance and needed modifications of instructional programs.

Application skills The ability to use reading, mathematics, and other academic skills in real-life situations.

Articulation The production of the speech sounds or phonemes.

Assessment The systematic process of gathering educationally relevant information in order to make legal and instructional decisions about the provision of special services to students with disabilities.

Assistive technology Any technology, including computers, designed specifically to enhance the performance of individuals with disabilities.

Attention The selective narrowing or focusing on the relevant stimuli in a situation; a prerequisite for perception, memory, and all types of learning activities.

Attention deficit hyperactivity disorder (ADHD) A term used in psychiatric classification systems to describe individuals with poor attention, impulsivity, and sometimes hyperactivity.

Balanced literacy An approach to teaching reading in which both decoding and comprehension skills are stressed.

Basal In test administration, the point at which it can be assumed that the student would receive full credit for all easier test items.

Basic interpersonal communication skills (BICS) Fundamental spoken language skills; used in context-rich conversational settings.

Bilingual education The provision of special services to students whose primary language is not English; may include instruction in the primary language, training in English language skills, and development of multicultural awareness.

Ceiling In test administration, the point at which it can be assumed that the student would receive no credit for all more difficult test items.

Checklist An informal assessment device that allows an informant to quickly scan a list of descriptions and check those that apply to the student in question.

Chronological age The number of years and months since birth.

Classroom assessment Informal assessment that typically takes place in the classroom.

Classroom quiz An informal assessment tool, usually designed by teachers, to assess students' classroom learning.

Clinical approach An approach to teaching in which a new intervention is introduced and the student's progress monitored; similar to *diagnostic teaching*.

Clinical interview Asking a student questions about the strategies used to perform a task as it is performed or immediately afterwards.

Cloze procedure A technique for assessing reading skills in which words are omitted from a text and the student is asked to fill in the missing words.

Coaching In test administration, the practice of helping the student arrive at answers.

Code switching The ability to switch from one dialect to another depending upon the demands of the communication situation.

Cognitive-academic language proficiency (CALP) The set of language skills needed to function in academic school settings.

Composition Also called *written expression;* the subskill of written language in which writers produce connected text.

Comprehension skills In reading, the ability to understand what is read; may be assessed via oral or silent reading.

Computation skills In mathematics, the arithmetic operations of addition, subtraction, multiplication, and division as applied to whole numbers, fractions, and decimals.

Computer-assisted testing Assessment in which a computer administers a test and/or scores it.

Conferences Formal meetings at which professionals and parents of students with disabilities discuss assessment results, eligibility, placement, program design, and other matters.

Confidence interval A range of scores in which it is likely that the student's true score will fall; constructed by means of the standard error of measurement.

Continuous recording An observational technique in which all of the student's behaviors are studied.

Correlation A descriptive statistic that expresses the degree of relationship between two sets of scores.

Criterion-referenced test An informal assessment device that assesses skill mastery; compares the student's performance to curricular standards.

Curriculum-based assessment Any informal assessment technique or procedure that evaluates the student's performance in relation to the standard school curriculum.

Curriculum-based measurement A type of curriculum-based assessment characterized by frequent and direct measurement of critical school behaviors; often includes 1-minute timed samples of reading, math, and writing skills.

Decoding The process by which readers analyze a word in order to pronounce it; includes sight recognition, phonic analysis, structural analysis, and contextual analysis.

Demonstration In test administration, tasks similar to test items that are used to teach test procedures to the student.

Diagnosis The process of establishing the cause or causes of an illness or condition and prescribing appropriate treatment.

Diagnostic probe An informal technique in which a test task or instructional condition is altered in order to observe if a change in the student's performance results.

Diagnostic teaching An informal assessment strategy in which two or more instructional conditions are compared to determine which is most effective.

Dialect An alternate form of a language that differs in some way from the standard form.

Discrepancy analysis The procedure in which scores are compared to determine whether they are significantly different; most often used to compare expected and actual achievement in the identification of learning disabilities.

Due process Procedural safeguards established to ensure the rights of students with disabilities and their parents.

Duration recording An observational technique in which the length (or duration) of the target behavior is noted.

Dynamic assessment Also called *interactive assessment;* assessment using the test-teach-test format.

Ecological approach An approach to assessment that focuses on the student's interaction with the environment rather than on the deficits of the student.

English as a second language (ESL) Teaching English to speakers of other languages without regard to native languages.

English learner (EL) An individual who has not yet acquired proficiency in the English language.

Error analysis A type of work sample analysis in which the incorrect responses of the student are described and categorized.

Event recording An observational technique in which the frequency of the target behavior is noted.

Expressive language The production of language for communication; for example, speaking and writing.

Family-centered approach Approach to assessment and intervention in which child and family issues are considered most important.

Fine-motor skills In motor development, the use of the small muscles of the body, especially in eye-hand coordination tasks.

First language The language learned first by an individual; also called *home language, native language,* or *heritage language.*

Fluency The ability to perform a skill both quickly and accurately; used in relation to both reading and mathematics.

Formal assessment Assessment procedures that contain specific rules for administration, scoring, and interpretation; generally norm-referenced and/or standardized.

Functional assessment Also called *functional behavioral assessment;* a systematic procedure in which observational data are collected to determine the reasons for inappropriate behavior so that a behavior change program can be designed.

Grade score Also called *grade equivalent;* a score that translates test performance into an estimated grade; expressed in grades and tenths of grades.

Gross-motor skills In motor development, the use of the large muscles of the body.

Group test A test administered to more than one student at the same time.

Hyperactivity Excessive activity.

IDEA The Individuals with Disabilities Education Act and its amendments.

Inclusion Integration of students with disabilities physically, academically, and socially with age peers.

Individual test A test administered to one student at a time.

Individualized Assessment Plan (IAP) A plan in which the steps and procedures of the assessment are organized according to the reasons for the assessment.

Individualized Education Program (IEP) A written educational plan developed for each school-aged student eligible for special education.

Individualized Family Service Plan (IFSP) A written plan that describes the needs of infants and toddlers and their families and specifies the goals to be achieved and services they will receive to achieve those goals.

Individual transition plan Part of the IEP, this is a template for mapping out long-term adult outcomes from which annual goals and objectives are defined.

Informal assessment Assessment procedures without rigid administration, scoring, and interpretation rules; includes criterion-referenced tests, task analysis, inventories, and so forth.

Informal Reading Inventory (IRI) An informal assessment device that measures both word recognition and comprehension skills; scores include Instructional, Independent, and Frustration reading levels.

Intelligence The ability of an individual to understand and cope with the environment; generally assessed with intelligence or "IQ" tests that are measures of academic aptitude.

Interval The scale of measurement characterized by equal intervals (i.e., distances) between points in the scale.

Interview An informal assessment procedure in which the tester questions an informant.

Inventory An informal assessment device that samples the student's ability to perform selected skills within a curricular sequence.

IQ Intelligence quotient; a standard score yielded by measures of intellectual performance.

Job analysis A task analysis of the specific skills required by a job.

Language A communication system using symbols to transmit information.

Language proficiency The degree to which an individual is skilled in a language; when students speak languages other than English, proficiency is assessed to determine the primary language.

Language sample A sample of oral language used for analysis.

Latency In test administration, the amount of time between presentation of the test question and the student's response.

Learning aptitude The capacity for altering one's behavior when presented with new information; the ability to learn; generally measured by tests of intellectual performance and adaptive behavior.

Learning environment The instructional, interpersonal, and physical characteristics of the classroom that may influence student performance.

Learning strategies Methods used by individuals in their interactions with learning tasks.

Least restrictive environment (LRE) According to federal special education laws, the educational placement for students with disabilities that is as close to the general education classroom as feasible.

MA Mental age; a score yielded by some measures of intellectual performance.

Mainstream American English (MAE) The standard English dialect spoken in the United States.

Mean The arithmetic average; a measure of central tendency.

Median The middle score in a distribution of scores; a measure of central tendency.

Memory The ability to retrieve previously learned information.

Mild disabilities The disabilities of mild mental retardation, learning disabilities, and emotional disturbance (behavioral disorders); considered mild in relation to more severe disabilities.

Miscue A decoding error in reading.

Miscue analysis The error analysis procedure in reading in which errors that change the meaning of the text are considered most serious.

Mode The most common score; a measure of central tendency.

Morphology The study of morphemes, or the smallest meaningful units of language.

Motor skills Skills using the small and large muscles of the body; includes fine- and gross-motor skills.

Natural environment The environment expected to include individuals without disabilities who are peers of individuals with disabilities.

Nominal The scale of measurement in which data are sorted into categories.

Nondiscriminatory assessment Assessment that does not penalize students for their gender, native language, race, ethnicity, culture, or disability.

Normal curve equivalent (NCE) A normalized standard score with a mean of 50 and a standard deviation of 20.06; has the same range and midpoint as percentile rank scores but is an equal interval scale.

Norm-referenced test A test that compares a student's performance to that of the students in the norm group.

Observation An informal assessment technique that involves specifying, counting, and recording student behaviors.

Oral language The reception and expression of the pragmatic, semantic, syntactical, morphological, and phonological aspects of language; involves listening and speaking.

Ordinal The scale of measurement in which data are arranged in rank order.

Partnership A collaboration; often used to describe parent-professional relationships.

Percentile rank A score that translates student test performance into the percentage of the norm group that performed as well as or poorer than the student on the same test.

Perception The psychological ability to process or use information received through the sense organs.

Person-centered planning (PCP) A planning process that focuses on the needs of the student and his or her family; often used in transition planning.

Phonemic awareness The ability to recognize individual sounds within words.

Phonics The ability to decode unfamiliar words by identifying the speech sounds associated with letters.

Phonological processing Awareness of the sounds that make up words and the ability to recognize likenesses and differences among sounds.

Phonology Study of phonemes or speech sounds, the smallest units of oral language.

Play-based assessment A technique used in early childhood assessment in which young children are observed within the context of play.

Portfolio assessment The analysis of student work samples, self-evaluations, and other materials assembled in portfolios to document student progress over time.

Pragmatics Study of the use of language for communication.

Prereferral strategies Modifications of the general education program to promote student success and prevent referral to special education.

Primary language The language in which an individual is most proficient; also called *dominant language*.

Problem-solving skills In mathematics, the use of computational skills to solve a problem; usually assessed via word problems.

Profile A graph upon which scores are plotted.

Protocol The test form or student answer booklet.

Psychological processes Abilities for receiving and responding to incoming information; also called *information processes*.

Questionnaire An informal assessment device in which the informant reads questions and writes the answers.

Range A descriptive statistic that expresses the spread of a distribution.

Rapport The working relationship between student and tester.

Rating scale An informal assessment device in which the informant judges or rates the performance of the student.

Ratio The scale of measurement characterized by equal intervals between points in the scale and a true zero.

Raw score The first test score calculated; usually indicates the number of correct responses plus the number of items assumed correct.

Readability A measure of the ease with which a text can be read; usually expressed as a grade level.

Receptive language The processing of language, as in listening and reading.

Related services Special services that students with disabilities may need to benefit from special education; includes transportation, speech pathology and audiology, and counseling.

Reliability Refers to a test's consistency; types of reliability include test-retest, alternate form, split-half, and interrater.

Response analysis A type of work sample analysis in which both errors and correct responses are considered.

Response-to-intervention (RTI) The approach to the identification of learning disabilities in which the student's ability to profit from high quality instruction is studied.

Rubric A type of rating scale that describes various levels of student performance.

School performance The degree to which students succeed in academic pursuits; often equated with school grades.

Self-determination The ability of an individual to make choices and decisions for him- or herself.

Semantics The aspect of language that deals with meaning, concepts, and vocabulary.

Sequence analysis An observational technique in which the antecedents and consequences of the student's behaviors are studied.

Sight vocabulary The words the student can read automatically without the need to decode them.

Sociometric technique An assessment procedure used to determine how students perceive their peers.

Special education Specially designed instruction to meet the unique needs of students with disabilities.

Specific learning abilities Readiness skills such as attention, perception, and memory.

Standard deviation A descriptive statistic that expresses the amount of variability within a set of scores.

Standard error of measurement A statistic that estimates the amount of measurement error in a score.

Standard score A derived score with a set mean and standard deviation; examples are IQ scores, scaled scores, and T-scores.

Standardization sample The group used to establish scores on norm-referenced tests.

Standardized test A test in which the administration, scoring, and interpretation procedures are standard or set; usually norm-referenced.

Stanine A derived score equivalent to a range of standard scores; stanines divide the distribution into nine ranges.

Structural task analysis A type of task analysis in which the performance demands of the task (e.g., speed and accuracy requirements) are studied.

Summary of Performance (SOP) A description of capabilities that must accompany each student with disabilities who exits the school system as a young adult; required by IDEA 2004.

Supplementary aids and services Supports provided to students with disabilities to allow them to participate in the general education program.

Surrogate parent A person assigned by the state to represent a person with a disability if the parents cannot be identified, if the parents are unknown, or if the person is a ward of the state.

Syntax The grammatical structure of language.

Task analysis An informal assessment technique in which a task is broken into its essential components or subtasks.

Team approach An approach to assessment that requires the active involvement of professionals from many fields, parents, perhaps the person with a disability, and other interested parties.

Test A sample of student behavior collected under standard conditions.

Tester One who administers and scores tests.

Time-sample recording An observational technique in which it is noted whether the target behavior occurs at some time within a specified time interval; used with nondiscrete behaviors.

Transdisciplinary team A team of professionals representing several disciplines that is often used in assessment of infants, toddlers, and preschoolers with disabilities.

Transition The movement from one environment or service system to another; for example, the movement from school-based special education services to postsecondary education or vocational training options.

Validity The degree to which a test measures what it purports to measure; types of validity include content, criterion-referenced (predictive and concurrent), and construct.

Work sample A permanent product produced by the student (e.g., a homework assignment, test paper, or composition).

Work sample analysis An informal assessment technique in which samples of student work are studied.

Writing Expressive written language; includes spelling, handwriting, usage, and composition.

Writing sample A sample of the written language produced by the student that is used for analysis.

Written language Includes the receptive skill, reading, and the expressive skill, writing.

REFERENCES

CHAPTER 1

American Federation of Teachers. (1996). Making standards matter 1996. Washington, DC: Author.

American Federation of Teachers. (1996). Making standards matter 1996 [WWW document]. *http://www.aft.org// research/reports/standard/index.htm#Table*

American Occupational Therapy Association (2011). *About occupational therapy. http://www.aota.org/About-Occupational-Therapy.aspx.* Accessed June 30, 2015.

American Physical Therapy Association (2013). *About physical therapists. http://policy.apta.org/About/PTs/.* Accessed June 29, 2015.

Artiles, A. J., & Trent, S. C. (1994). Overrepresentation of minority students in special education: A continuing debate. *Journal of Special Education, 27,* 410–437.

Artiles, A.J., & Trent, S.C. (1994). Overrepresentation of minority students in special education: A continuing debate. The Journal of Special Education, 27, 410–437.

Barnett, D. W., Daly, E. J., III, Jones, K. M., & Lentz, F. E., Jr. (2004). Response to intervention: Empirically based special service decisions from single-case designs of increasing and decreasing intensity. *Journal of Special Education, 38*(2), 66–79.

Bell, F. (2010). Network theories for technology-enabled learning and social change. Connectivism and actor network theory. Paper presented at the Seventh International Conference Networked Learning. Aalborg, Denmark. Retrieved from *http://www.Lancsacuk/fss/ organisations/netlc/past/nlc2010/abstracts/Creanor.html* on June 12, 2015.

Benson, E. (2003). Intelligence across cultures. *Monitor on Psychology, 34*(2), 56–58.

Benson, E. (2003). Intelligent intelligence testing. *Monitor on Psychology, 34*(2), 1–48.

Birnbaum, B. W. (2006). *Foundations of special education leadership: Administration, assessment, placement and the law.* Lewiston, NY: Edwin Mellen Press.

Bransford, J. D., A. L. Brown, & Cocking, R.R., eds. (2000). How People Learn. Washington, D.C., National Academy Press.

Bransford, J. D., Brown, A. L., & Cocking, R. R. (Eds.) (2000). How people learn: Brain, mind, experience, and school (Expanded ed.). Washington, DC: National Academy Press.

Bush, G. W. (2001). *No Child Left Behind* [Online]. Washington, DC: U.S. Department of Education. Available: *http://www.ed.gov/inits/nclb/ index.html* [2001, June 1].

CASP Board of Directors. (2003). *Critical constructs and principles regarding the reauthorization of IDEA: Position paper of the California Association of School Psychologists.* Retrieved April 14, 2008, from *http://www.casponline.org/.*

Cegelka, P. T. (1995a). An overview of effective education for students with learning problems. In P. T. Cegelka & W. H. Berdine (Eds.), *Effective instruction for students with learning difficulties* (pp. 1–17). Boston: Allyn & Bacon.

Deno, S. L. (1985). Curriculum-based measurement: The emerging alternative. *Exceptional Children, 52,* 219–232.

Deno, S. L. (2003). Developments in curriculum-based measurement. *Journal of Special Education, 37*(3), 184–192.

Deno, S., & Mirkin, P. (1977). *Data-based program modification.* Minneapolis, MN: Leadership Training Institute for Special Education.

Dodd, J. M., Nelson, R., & Spint, W. (1995). Prereferral activities: One way to avoid biased testing procedures and possible inappropriate special education placement for American Indian students. *Journal of Educational Issues of Language Minority Students, 15,* 1–10.

Esparza Brown, J., & Sanford, A. (2011). RTI for English language learners: Appropriately using screening and progress monitoring tools to improve instructional outcomes. Washington, DC: U.S. Department of Education, Office of Special Education Programs, National Center on Response to Intervention. Retrieved from *http://www.rti4success.org/images/stories/pdfs/rtiforells.pdf.* Accessed June 13, 2015.

Fuchs, D. (2006a). Monitoring student progress in the classroom to enhance teaching and planning and student learning. *International Conference on Special Education 2006,* Hong Kong.

Fuchs, D. (2006b). On the changing definitions of learning disabilities and what it means for special education: A cautionary tale. *International Conference on Special Education 2006,* Hong Kong.

Fuchs, D., Fuchs, L. S., & Compton, D. L. (2004). Identifying reading disability by responsiveness-to-instruction: Specifying measures and criteria. *Learning Disability Quarterly, 27,* 216–227.

Fuchs, L. S., & Fuchs, D. (1986a). Curriculum-based assessment of reading progress toward long-term and short-term goals. *Journal of Special Education, 20,* 69–82.

Fuchs, L. S., & Fuchs, D. (1986b). Effects of systematic formative evaluation: A meta-analysis. *Exceptional Children, 53,* 199–208.

Fuchs, L. S., & Fuchs, D. (1997). Use of curriculum-based measurement in identifying students with disabilities. *Focus on Exceptional Children, 30,* 1–14.

Fuchs, L. S., & Fuchs, D. (1999). Monitoring student progress toward the development of reading competence: A review of three forms of classroom-based assessment. *School Psychology Review, 28,* 659–671.

Fuchs, L. S., & Fuchs, D. (2002). Curriculum-based measurement: Describing competence, enhancing outcomes, evaluating treatment effects, and identifying treatment non-responders. *Peabody Journal of Education, 77*(2), 64–84.

Gresham, F. M. (1991). Conceptualizing behavior disorders in terms of resistance to intervention. *School Psychology Review, 20,* 20–36.

Hosp, M. K., Hosp, J. L., & Howell, K. W. (2012). *The ABCs of CBM.* New York: Guilford Press.

Howell, K. W., & Nolet, V. (1999). *Curriculum-based evaluation: Teaching and decision making* (3rd ed.). Belmont, CA: Wadsworth.

IDEA 2004 Final Regulations. (2006, August 14). *Federal Register, 71*(156). Retrieved August 21, 2006, from *http://www.ed.gov/policy/speced/idea/idea2004.html*

Losen, D. J., & Orfield, G. (2002). Introduction. In D. J. Losen, & G. Orfield (Eds.), *Racial inequity in special education.* Cambridge, MA: Harvard Education Press.

Losen, D. J., & Orfield, G. (Eds.). (2002). *Racial inequity in special education.* Cambridge, MA: Harvard Education Press.

Massanari, C. (2004). Responsiveness to intervention LD identifier or schoolwide improvement. *MPRRC Today, 6*(3), 4–5.

Mellard, D. (2004). Understanding responsiveness to intervention in learning disabilities determination. *MPRRC Today, 6*(3), 6–8.

Murdick, N., Gartin, B., & Crabtree, T. (2002). *Special education law.* Upper Saddle River, NJ: Merrill/Pearson Education.

National Center for Educational Statistics (2015). *Fast facts. https://nces.ed.gov/fastfacts/display.asp?id=64.* Accessed June 30, 2015.

National Joint Committee on Learning Disabilities. (2010). Evaluation of students with disabilities report. LD Online. Accessed June 30, 2015.

Nelson, J. R., Smith, D. J., Taylor, L., Dodd, J. M., & Reavis, K. (1991). Prereferral intervention: A review of research. *Education and Treatment of Children, 14,* 243–253.

No Child Left Behind (NCLB) Act of 2001, Pub. L. No. 107–110, § 115, Stat. 1425 (2002).

Olson, K. (2006, Nov. 8). The wounds of schooling. *Education Week,* pp. 28–29.

Olson, M. L. (2006). A decade of effort. *Education Week, 25*(17), 8–16.

Patton, J. M. (1998). The disproportionate representation of African Americans in special education: Looking behind the curtain for understanding and solutions. *The Journal of Special Education, 32*(1), 25–31.

Patton, J., & Dunn, C. (1998). *Transition from school to young adulthood.* Austin, TX: PRO-ED.

Quenemoen, R., Thurlow, M., Moen, R., Thompson, S., & Morse, A. B. (2003). *Progress monitoring in an inclusive standards-based assessment and accountability system (Synthesis Report 53).* Minneapolis: University of Minnesota, National Center on Educational Outcomes. Retrieved June 29, 2006, from *http://education.umn.edu/NCEO/OnlinePubs/Synthesis53.html*

Salend, S. J., Garrick-Duhaney, L. M., & Montgomery, W. (2002). A comprehensive approach to identifying and addressing issues of disproportionate representation. *Remedial and Special Education, 23*(5), 1–15.

Sullivan, A. L. (2011). Disproportionality in special education identification and placement of English language learners. *Exceptional Children, 77,* 317–334.

Swain, K. D. (2005). CBM with goal setting: Impacting students' understanding of reading goals. *Journal of Instructional Psychology, 32*(3), 259–265.

Tindal, G. (2013). Curriculum-based measurement: A brief history of nearly everything from the 1970s to the present. *ISRN Education,* 1–29.

VanDerHeyden, A. M., & Jimerson, S. R. (2005). Using response-to-intervention to enhance outcomes for children. *The California School Psychologist, 10,* 21–32.

Vaughn, S., & Fuchs, L. S. (2003). Redefining learning disabilities as inadequate response to instruction: The promise and potential problems. *Learning Disabilities Research and Practice, 18,* 137–146.

Vellutino, F. R., Scanlon, D. M., & Lyon, G. R. (2000). Differentiating between difficult-to-remediate and readily remediated poor readers: More evidence against the IQ-achievement discrepancy definition of reading disability. *Journal of Learning Disabilities, 33,* 223–238.

Waitoller, F. R., & Artiles, A. J. (2013). A decade of professional development research for inclusive education: A critical review and notes for a research program. *Review of Educational Research, 83*(3), 319–356 DOI: 10.3102/0034654313483905 © 2013 AERA. *http://rer.aera.net.*

CHAPTER 2

Barnett, D. W., Daly, E. J., III, Jones, K. M., & Lentz, F. E., Jr. (2004). Response to intervention: Empirically based special service decisions from single-case designs of increasing and decreasing intensity. *Journal of Special Education, 38*(2), 66–79.

Bilingual Research Journal: The Journal of the National Association for Bilingual Education, 34(3), 316–333.

CASP Board of Directors. (2003). *Critical constructs and principles regarding the reauthorization of IDEA: Position paper of the California Association of School Psychologists.* Retrieved April 14, 2008, from *http://www.casponline.org/.*

DeMatthews, D. E., Edwards, D. B., & Nelson, T. E. (2014). Identification problems: US special education eligibility for English language learners. International Journal of Educational Research, 68, 27–34.

Deno, S. L. (1985). Curriculum-based measurement: The emerging alternative. *Exceptional Children, 52,* 219–232.

Deno, S. L. (2003). Developments in curriculum-based measurement. *Journal of Special Education, 37*(3), 184–192.

Deno, S., & Mirkin, P. (1977). *Data-based program modification.* Minneapolis, MN: Leadership Training Institute for Special Education.

Esparza Brown, J., & Sanford, A. (2011). RTI for English language learners: Appropriately using screening and progress monitoring tools to improve instructional outcomes. Washington, DC: U.S. Department of Education, Office of Special Education Programs, National Center on Response to Intervention. Retrieved from *http://www.rti4success.org/images/stories/pdfs/rtiforellspdf.* Accessed June 13, 2015.

Evans-Hampton, T., Skinner, C. H., Henington, C., Sims, S., and McDaniel , C. E. (2002). An investigation of situational bias: Conspicuous and covert timing during curriculum-based measurement of mathematics across African American and Caucasian students. School Psychology Review, 31, 529–539.

Fuchs, D. (2006a). Monitoring student progress in the classroom to enhance teaching and planning and student learning. *International Conference on Special Education 2006,* Hong Kong.

Fuchs, D. (2006b). On the changing definitions of learning disabilities and what it means for special education: A cautionary tale. *International Conference on Special Education 2006,* Hong Kong.

Fuchs, D., Fuchs, L. S., & Compton, D. L. (2004). Identifying reading disability by responsiveness-to-instruction: Specifying measures and criteria. *Learning Disability Quarterly,* 27, 216–227.

Fuchs, D., Fuchs, L. S., & Compton, D. L. (2012). Smart RTI: A next-generation approach to multilevel prevention. *Exceptional Children,* 78, 263–279. Retrieved from *http://www.cec.sped.org*

Fuchs, L. S., & Fuchs, D. (1986a). Curriculum-based assessment of reading progress toward long-term and short-term goals. *Journal of Special Education, 20,* 69–82.

Fuchs, L. S., & Fuchs, D. (1986b). Effects of systematic formative evaluation: A meta-analysis. *Exceptional Children, 53,* 199–208.

Fuchs, L. S., & Fuchs, D. (1997). Use of curriculum-based measurement in identifying students with disabilities. *Focus on Exceptional Children, 30,* 1–14.

Fuchs, L. S., & Fuchs, D. (1999). Monitoring student progress toward the development of reading competence: A review of three forms of classroom-based assessment. *School Psychology Review, 28,* 659–671.

Fuchs, L. S., & Fuchs, D. (2002). Curriculum-based measurement: Describing competence, enhancing outcomes, evaluating treatment effects, and identifying treatment non-responders. *Peabody Journal of Education, 77*(2), 64–84.

Gartin, B. C., & Murdick, N. L. (2005). IDEA 2004: The IEP. *Remedial and Special Education, 26,* 327–331.

Gresham, F. M. (1991). Conceptualizing behavior disorders in terms of resistance to intervention. *School Psychology Review, 20,* 20–36.

Hoover, J. J. (2010). Special education eligibility decision making in response to intervention models. *Theory into Practice, 49,* 289–296.

Hosp, M.K., Hosp, J. L., & Howell, K. W. (2012). The ABCs of CBM. New York: Guilford. Press.

Howell, K. W., & Nolet, V. (1999). *Curriculum-based evaluation: Teaching and decision making* (3rd ed.). Belmont, CA: Wadsworth.

Kranzler, J. H., Miller, M. D., & Jordon, L. (1999). An examination of racial/ethnic and gender bias on curriculum-based measurement of oral reading fluency. *School Psychology Quarterly, 14,* 327–342.

Kritikos, E.P. (2004). Special education assessment: Issues and strategies affecting today's classroom. Columbus, OH: Pearson.

MacMillan, P. (2000). Simultaneous measurement of reading growth, gender, and relative-age effects: Many-faceted Rasch applied to CBM reading scores. Journal of Applied Measurement, 1, 393–408.

Malecki, C. K., & Jewell, J. (2003). Developmental, gender, and practical considerations in scoring curriculum-based measurement writing probes. *Psychology in the Schools, 40*(4), 379–390.

Massanari, C. (2004). Responsiveness to intervention LD identifier or schoolwide improvement. *MPRRC Today, 6*(3), 4–5.

McCloskey, D., & Schicke Athanasiou, M. (2000). Assessment and intervention practices with second-language learners among school psychologists. *Psychology in the Schools, 37,* 209–225.

Mellard, D. (2004). Understanding responsiveness to intervention in learning disabilities determination. *MPRRC Today, 6*(3), 6–8.

-O'Halloran, P. (2008). Important factors for consideration when litigating special education due process hearings. Dissertation proceedings.

Ortiz, A. A., Robertson, P. M., Wilkinson, C. Y. , Liu, Y. J., McGhee, B. D., et al. (2011). The role of bilingual education teachers in preventing inappropriate referrals of ELLs to special education: Implications for response to intervention.

Quenemoen, R., Thurlow, M., Moen, R., Thompson, S., & Morse, A. B. (2003). *Progress monitoring in an inclusive standards-based assessment and accountability system (Synthesis Report 53)*. Minneapolis: University of Minnesota, National Center on Educational Outcomes. Retrieved June 29, 2006, from *https://www.osepideasthatwork.org/sites/default/files/ProgressMonitoring_InclusiveStandards.pdf*

Safer, N., & Fleischman, S. (2005). Research matters/how student progress monitoring improves instruction. *Educational Leadership, 62*(5), 81–83.

Salvia, J., Ysseldyke, J., & Bolt, S. (2006). Assessment in special and inclusive education (11th ed). Boston: Wadsworth.

Seaman, J., Guggisberg, K., Malyn, D., Payne, J., & Scheibe, R. (2001). Summary of results copying fluency sample. Communique, 30(2).

Sullivan, A. L. (2011). Disproportionality in special education identification and placement of English language learners. *Exceptional Children, 77*, 314–334.

Swain, K. D. (2005). CBM with goal setting: Impacting students' understanding of reading goals. *Journal of Instructional Psychology, 32*(3), 259–265.

Tindal, G. (2013). Curriculum-based measurement: A brief history of nearly everything from the 1970s to the present. *ISRN Education*, 1–29.

Turnbull, A. P., Strickland, B. B., & Brantley, J. C. (1982). *Developing and implementing individualized education programs* (2nd ed.). New York: Merrill/Macmillan.

VanDerHeyden, A. M., & Jimerson, S. R. (2005). Using response-to-intervention to enhance outcomes for children. *The California School Psychologist, 10*, 21–32.

VanDerHeyden, A., Witt, J., & Barnett, D. (2005). The emergence and possible futures of response to intervention. *Journal of Psychoeducational Assessment, 23*, 339–361.

Vaughn, S., & Fuchs, L. S. (2003). Redefining learning disabilities as inadequate response to instruction: The promise and potential problems. *Learning Disabilities Research and Practice, 18*, 137–146.

Vellutino, F., Scanlon, D., & Lyon, G. R. (2000). Differentiating between difficult-to-remediate and readily remediated poor readers: More evidence against the IQ-achievement discrepancy definition of reading disability. *Journal of Learning Disabilities, 33*, 223–238.

Wright, P. W. D (2006). *Summary of major changes*. Retrieved August 31, 2015, from *http://www.wrightslaw.com/idea/law/idea.regs.sumry.chngs.pdf*.

Zentall S. S., Beike S. (2012). Achievement and social goals of younger and older elementary students: Response to academic and social failure. *Learning Disability Quarterly, 35*, 39–53. doi:10.1177/0731948711429009

CHAPTER 3

Beckman, P. J., Frank, N., & Newcomb, S. (1996). Qualities and skills for communicating with families. In P. J. Beckman (Ed.), *Strategies for working with young children with disabilities* (pp. 31–46). Baltimore: Brookes.

Blue-Banning, M., Summers, J. A., Frankland, H.C., Nelson, L.L., & Beegle, G. (2004). Dimensions of family and professional partnerships: Constructive guidelines for collaboration. *Exceptional Children, 70*, 167–184.

Brandon, R., & Brown, M. (2009). African American families in the special education process: Increasing their level of involvement. *Intervention in School and Clinic, 45*(2), 85–90.

Chan, S., & Lee, E. (2004). Families with Asian roots. In E. W. Lynch & M. J. Hanson (Eds.), *Developing cross-cultural competence: A guide to working with children and their families* (3rd ed.) (pp. 21–298). Baltimore: Brookes.

Children's Defense Fund. (2014). Retrieved from *http://www.childrensdefense.org/library/state-of-americas-children* on August 29, 2015.

Cohen, L. G., Spenciner, L. J., & Twitchell, D. (2010). Youth in transition. In L. G. Cohen & L. J. Spenciner (Eds.), *Assessment of children and youth with special needs* (4th ed.) (pp. 459–479). Boston: Pearson Education.

Correa, V. I. (1991). Family-based applications. In C. V. Morsink, C. C. Thomas, & V. I. Correa, *Interactive teaming: Consultation and collaboration in special programs* (pp. 247–274). New York: Merrill/Macmillan.

Creighton, S., & Szymkowiak, A. (2014). The effects of cooperative and competitive games on classroom interaction frequencies. *Procedia-Social and Behavioral Sciences, 140*, 155–163. Retrieved from *http://www.sciencedirect.com/science/article/pii/S187704281403328X* on August 28, 2015.

Cummins, J. (1981). The role of primary language development in promoting educational success for language minority students. In California State Department of Education, *Schooling and language minority students: A theoretical framework* (pp. 3–49). Los Angeles: Evaluation, Dissemination & Assessment Center.

Cutler, B. C. (1995). *You, your child, and "special" education: A guide to making the system work*. Baltimore: Brookes.

Dardig, J. (2008). *Involving parents of students with special needs: 25 ready to use strategies*. Thousand Oaks, CA: Corwin Press.

Dunst, C. J., Trivette, C. M., & Deal, A. G. (1988). *Enabling and empowering families: Principles and guidelines for practice*. Cambridge, MA: Brookline.

Epstein, J. L. (1990). School and family connections: Theory, research, and implications for integrating sociologies of education and family. In D. G. Unger & M. B. Sussman (Eds.), *Families in community settings: Interdisciplinary perspectives* (pp. 99–124). New York: Haworth.

Ferrel, J. (2012). *Family engagement and children with disabilities: A resource guide for educators and parents.* Cambridge, MA: Harvard Family Research Project.

Garfinkel, L. (2010). Improving family involvement for juvenile offenders with emotional/behavioral disorders and related disabilities. *Behavioral Disorders, 36*(1), 52–60.

Hanson, M. J., & Lynch, E. W. (2004). *Understanding families: Approaches to diversity, disability, and risk.* Baltimore: Brookes.

Harry, B. (1992a). An ethnographic study of cross-cultural communication with Puerto Rican-American families in the special education system. *American Educational Research Journal, 29,* 471–494.

Harry, B. (1992b). Developing cultural self-awareness: The first step in values clarification for early interventionists. *Topics in Early Childhood Special Education, 12,* 333–350.

Hooper, S., & Umansky, W. (2009). *Young children with special needs* (5th ed.). Upper Saddle River, NJ: Merrill/Pearson Education.

Joe, J. R., & Malach, R. S. (2004). In E. W. Lynch & M. J. Hanson (Eds.), *Developing cross-cultural competence: A guide to working with children and their families* (3rd ed.) (pp. 109–139). Baltimore: Brookes.

Keogh, B. (1999). Revisiting families of children with learning disabilities. *Learning Disabilities, 9*(3), 81–85.

Kritikos, E., LeDosquet, P., & Melton, M. (2012). *Foundations of assessment in early childhood special education.* Columbus, OH: Pearson.

Kroth, R. L., & Edge, D. (1997). *Strategies for communicating with parents and families of exceptional children* (3rd ed.). Denver, CO: Love.

Langdon, H. W., Siegel, V., Halog, L., & Sánchez-Boyce, M. (1994). *The interpreter translator process in the educational setting.* Rohnert Park, CA: Resources in Special Education, Sonoma State University.

LeDosquet, P. (2010). *Early childhood.* In E. Kritikos, Special education assessment: Issues and strategies affecting today's classrooms. Columbus, OH: Pearson.

Lynch, E. W. (2004). Developing cross-cultural competence. In E. W. Lynch & M. J. Hanson (Eds.), *Developing cross-cultural competence: A guide for working with children and their families* (3rd ed.) (pp. 41–77) Baltimore: Brookes.

Lynch, E. W., & Hanson, M. J. (2004b). Family diversity, assessment, and cultural competence. In M. McLean, M. Wolery, & D. Bailey (Eds.), *Assessing infants and preschoolers with special needs* (3rd ed.) (pp. 77–122). Upper Saddle River, NJ: Merrill/Prentice Hall.

Lynch, E. W., & Hanson, M. J. (Eds.) (2004a). *Developing cross-cultural competence: A guide to working with children and their families* (3rd ed.). Baltimore: Brookes.

Lynch, E. W., & Stein, R. C. (1987). Parent participation by ethnicity: A comparison of Hispanic, Black, and Anglo families. *Exceptional Children, 54,* 105–111.

McCloskey, E. (2010). What do I know? Parental positioning in special education. *International Journal of Special Education, 25*(1), 162–170.

Mueller, T., Singer, G., & Draper, L. (2008). Reducing parental dissatisfaction with special education in two school districts: Implementing conflict prevention and alternative dispute resolution. *Journal of Educational and Psychological Consultation, 18*(3), 191–233.

Mulholland, R., & Blecker, N. (2008). Parents and special educators: Pre-service teachers' discussion points. *International Journal of Special Education, 23*(1), 49–53.

Nokali, N., Bachman, H., & Votruba-Drzal, E. (2010). Parent involvement in children's academic and social development in elementary school. *Child Development, 81*(3), 988–1005.

Olivos E. M., Gallagher R. J., Aguilar J. (2010). Fostering collaboration with culturally and linguistically diverse families of children with moderate to severe disabilities. *Journal of Educational and Psychological Consultation, 20,* 28–40. doi:10.1080/104744109035353/210.1080/10474410903535372

Santos, A., & Chan, S. (2004). Families with American Indian roots. In E. W. Lynch & M. J. Hanson (Eds.), *Developing cross-cultural competence: A guide to working with children and their families* (3rd ed., pp. 299–344). Baltimore: Brookes.

Staples, K., & Diliberto, J. (2010). Guidelines for successful parent involvement: Working with parents of students with disabilities. *Teaching Exceptional Children, 42*(6), 58–63.

Summers, J. A., Hoffman, L, Marquis, J., Turnbull, A., & Poston, D. (2005). Relationship between parent satisfaction regarding partnerships with professionals and age of child. *Topics in Early Childhood Special Education, 25,* 48–58.

Turnbull, A., & Turnbull, R. (2001). *Families, professionals, and exceptionality: Collaborating for empowerment* (4th ed.). Upper Saddle River, NJ: Merrill/Prentice Hall.

Wade, C., Mildon, R., & Matthews, J. (2006). Service delivery to parents with an intellectual disability: Family-centered or professionally centered? *Journal of Applied Research in Intellectual Disabilities, 20*(2), 87–98.

Wayman, K. I., Lynch, E. W., & Hanson, M. J. (1990). Home-based early intervention services: Cultural sensitivity in a family systems approach. *Topics in Early Childhood Special Education, 10,* 56–75.

Willis, W. O. (2004). Families with African American roots. In E. W. Lynch & M. J. Hanson (Eds.), *Developing cross-cultural competence: A guide to working with children and their families* (3rd ed.) (pp. 141–177). Baltimore: Brookes.

Zuñiga, M. E. (2004). Families with Latino roots. In E. W. Lynch & M. J. Hanson (Eds.), *Developing cross-cultural competence: A guide to working with children and their families* (3rd ed.) (pp. 179–217). Baltimore: Brookes.

CHAPTER 4

Abedi, J., Hofstetter, C. H., & Lord, C. (2004). Assessment accommodations for English language learners: Implications for policy-based empirical research. *Review of Educational Research, 74*, 1–28.

Alley, G., & Foster, C. (1978). Nondiscriminatory testing of minority and exceptional children. *Focus on Exceptional Children, 9,* 1–14.

American Educational Research Association, American Psychological Association, National Council on Measurement in Education, Joint Committee on Standards for Educational and Psychological Testing (U.S.) (1999). *Standards for Educational and Psychological Testing.* Washington, DC: American Educational Research Association.

Anastasi, A. (1988). *Psychological testing* (6th ed.). New York: Macmillan.

Anastasi, A., & Urbina, S. (1997). *Psychological testing* (7th ed.). Upper Saddle River, NJ: Prentice Hall.

Artiles, A.J., & Ortiz, A.A. (Eds.). (2002). Identification and instruction of English language learners with special education needs. Washington, D.C.: Center for Applied Linguistics & Delta Systems.

Ary, D., Jacobs, L. C., Sorensen, C., & Walker, D. (2013). *Introduction to research in education* (9th ed.). Belmont, CA: Wadsworth.

Best, J. W., & Kahn, J. V. (2005). *Research in education* (10th ed.). Boston: Allyn & Bacon.

Carlson, J. F., Geisinger, K.F., & Jonson, J. L. (Eds.). (2014). *The nineteenth mental measurements yearbook* (pp. 17–19). Lincoln, NE: Buros Center for Testing.

Cattell, R. B. (1950). *Culture fair intelligence test: Scale 1.* Champaign, IL: Institute for Personality and Ability Testing.

Cattell, R. B., & Cattell, A. K. S. (1960). *Culture fair intelligence test: Scale 2.* Champaign, IL: Institute for Personality and Ability Testing.

Cattell, R. B., & Cattell, A. K. S. (1963). *Culture fair intelligence test: Scale 3.* Champaign, IL: Institute for Personality and Ability Testing.

Cattell, R. B., & Cattell, A. K. S. (1977). *The culture fair intelligence tests (rev.).* Champaign, IL: Institute for Personality and Ability Testing.

Cheng, L. L., & Hammer, C. S. (1992). *The use of an interpreter/translator.* San Diego, CA: Los Amigos Research Associates.

Cohen, J., Cohen, P., West, S. G., & Aiken, L. S. (2003). *Applied multiple regression/correlation analysis for the behavioral sciences* (3rd ed.). Hillsdale, NJ: Lawrence Erlbaum Associates.

Cohen, L.G., & Spenciner, L.J. (2010). Assessment of children and youth: With special needs (4th ed.). New York: Longman.

Cooper, J. O., Heron, T. E., & Heward, W. L. (1987). *Applied behavior analysis.* New York: Merrill/Macmillan.

Council for Exceptional Children (2012). *CEC Initial Level Special Educator Preparation Standards.* Retrieved March 25, 2015, from *https://www.cec.sped.org/~/media/Files/Standards/Professional%20Preparation%20Standards/Initial%20Preparation%20Standards%20with%20Elaborations.pdf.*

Council for Exceptional Children (2012). Council for Exception Children Professional Standards. Retrieved March 25, 2015, from *http://www.cec.sped.org/Standards/Special-Educator-Professional-Preparation.*

Council for Exceptional Children. (2015). What Every Special Educator Must Know: Professional Ethics and Standards. Arlington, VA: CEC 4

Council for Exceptional Children. (2015). What Every Special Educator Must Know: Professional Ethics and Standards. Arlington, VA: CEC.

Diana v. State Board of Education. Civ. No. C-70 37 RFP (N.D. Cal. 1970, 1973).

Duffey, J. B., Salvia, J., Tucker, J., & Ysseldyke, J. (1982). Nonbiased assessment: A need for operationalism. *Exceptional Children, 47,* 427–434.

Dunn, L. M. (1968). Special education for the mildly retarded—Is much of it justifiable? *Exceptional Children, 35,* 5–22.

Feuerstein, R., in collaboration with Rand, Y., & Hoffman, M. D. (1979). *The dynamic assessment of retarded performers.* Baltimore: University Park Press.

Foegen, A., & Morrison, C. (2010). Putting algebra progress monitoring into practice: Insights from the field. *Intervention in School and Clinic, 46*(2), 95–103.

Frumkin, L. (2004). The joint committee on testing practices: Available publications on testing: In J. Wall & G. Walz (Eds.), Measuring up: assessment issues for teachers, counselors and administrators (pp. 745–755). Austin, TX: Pro Ed, Inc.

Fuchs, D. S., Fuchs, L. S., Benowitz, S., & Barringer, K. (1987). Norm-referenced tests: Are they valid for use with handicapped students? *Exceptional Children, 54,* 263–271.

Fuchs, L. S., Compton, D. L., Fuchs, D., Hollenbeck, K. N., Hamlett, C. L., & Seethaler, P. M. (2011). Two-Stage Screening for Math Problem-Solving Difficulty Using Dynamic Assessment of Algebraic Learning. *Journal of Learning Disabilities, 44*(4), 372–380. *http://doi.org/10.1177/0022219411407867*

Fuchs, L. S., Fuchs, D., & Zumeta, R. O. (2008). A curricular sampling approach to progress monitoring: Mathematics concepts and applications. *Assessment for Effective Intervention, 33,* 225–233.

Gagnon, J. C., & McLauglin, M. J. (2004). Curriculum, assessment, and accountability in day treatment and residential schools. *Exceptional Children, 70*(3), 263–283.

Gay, L. R. (1990). *Educational evaluation and measurement* (2nd ed.). Upper Saddle River, NJ: Merrill/Prentice Hall.

Gonzales, E. (1982). Issues in assessment of minorities. In H. L. Swanson & B. L. Watson (Eds.), *Educational and psychological assessment of exceptional children* (pp. 375–389). St. Louis, MO: Mosby.

Gravois, T. A., & Rosenfield, S. A. (2006). Impact of instructional consultation teams on the disproportionate referral and placement of minority students in special education. *Remedial and Special Education, 27*(1), 4–52.

Hallgren, K.A. (2012). Computing inter-rater reliability for observational data: An overview and tutorial. *Tutorials in Quantitative Methods for Psychology, 8,* 23–34.

Horn, C. (2003). High stakes testing and students: Stopping or perpetuating a cycle of failure? *Theory into Practice, 42*(1), 30–41.

Kritikos, E. P. (2010). *Special education assessment: Issues and strategies affecting today's classrooms.* Upper Saddle River, NJ: Pearson.

Lambert, N. M. (1981). Psychological evidence in *Larry P. v. Wilson Riles:* An evaluation by a witness for the defense. *American Psychologist, 36,* 937–952.

Laosa, L. M. (1977). Nonbiased assessment of children's abilities: Historical antecedents and current issues. In T. Oakland (Ed.), *Psychological and educational assessment of minority children* (pp. 1–20). New York: Brunner/Mazel.

Larry P. v. Riles. C-71–2270-RFP (N.D. Cal. 1972), 495 F. Supp. 96 (N.D. Cal. 1979) Aff'r (9th Cir. 1984), 1983–84 EHLR DEC. 555:304.

Luckner, J. L., Sebald, A. M., Cooney, J., Young, J., III, & Muir, S. G. (2006). An examination of the evidence-based literacy research in deaf education. *American Annals of the Deaf, 150*(5), 443–455.

Maddox, T. (Ed.). (2003). *Tests: A comprehensive reference for assessments in psychology, education, and business.* Austin, TX: PRO-ED.

Maloney, E. S., & Larrivee, L. S. (2007). Limitations of age-equivalent scores in reporting the results of norm-referenced tests. *Contemporary Issues in Communication Science and Disorders, 34,* 86–93.

Manly, J. J. (2005). Advantages and disadvantages of separate norms for African Americans. *The Clinical Neuropsychologist, 19,* 270–275.

Mercer, J. R. (1973). *Labeling the mentally retarded.* Berkeley, CA: University of California Press.

Miller, M. D., Linn, R. L., & Gronlund, N. E. (2009). *Measurement and assessment in teaching* (10th ed.). Upper Saddle River, NJ: Pearson.

Oakland, T. (1980). Nonbiased assessment of minority group children. *Exceptional Education Quarterly, 1*(3), 31–46.

Peña, E. (2001). Assessment of semantic knowledge: Use of feedback and clinical interviewing. *Seminars in Speech and Language, 22(1)* (Communicative Assessment of the Hispanic Child), pp. 51–63.

Popham, W. J. (2012). *Assessment bias: How to banish it.* Boston: Pearson.

Rhodes, R. L., Ochoa, S. H., & Ortiz, S. O. (2005). *Assessing culturally and linguistically diverse students: A practical guide.* New York: Guilford Press.

Roid, G. (2003). *Stanford-Binet intelligence scales, Fifth edition.* Itasca, IL: Riverside.

Roid, G. H., Miller, L. J., Pomplun, M., & Koch, C. (2013). *Leiter International Performance Scale-Third Edition.* Los Angeles: Western Psychological Services.

Rudner, L. M., & Schater, W. D. (2002). *What teachers need to know about assessment.* Washington, DC: National Education Association.

Salvia, J. S., Ysseldyke, J. E., & Bolt, S. (2010). *Assessment in special and inclusive education (11th Edition).* Boston: Wadsworth/Cengage Publications.

Salvia, J., & Ysseldyke, J. E. (2007). *Assessment in special and inclusive education* (10th ed.). Boston: Houghton Mifflin.

Samuda, R. (1975). *Psychological testing of American minorities.* New York: Dodd, Mead.

Schalock, R. L., Borthwick-Duffy, S. A., Bradley, V. J., Buntinx, W. H. E., Coulter, D. L., Craig, E. M., et al. (2010). *Intellectual disability: Definition, classification, and systems of supports.* Washington, DC: American Association on Intellectual and Developmental Disabilities.

Sotelo-Dynega, M., Ortiz, S. O., Flanagan, D. P., & Chaplin, W. (2013). The effect of English language proficiency on the Woodcock-Johnson tests of cognitive abilities-third edition. *Psychology in the Schools, 50,* 781–797.

Spinelli, C. G. (2011). *Classroom assessment for students with special needs in inclusive settings.* Upper Saddle River, NJ: Pearson.

Sternberg, R. J., & Grigorenko, E. L. (2002). *Dynamic testing.* Cambridge, England: Cambridge University Press.

Sulzer-Azaroff, B., & Mayer, G. R. (1977). *Applying behavior-analysis procedures with children and youth.* New York: Holt, Rinehart & Winston.

Tucker, W. H. (2009). *The Cattell controversy: Race, science, and ideology.* University of Illinois Press, pp. 50–52.

Valenzuela, J. S. de, & Cervantes, H. T. (1998). Procedures and techniques for assessing the bilingual exceptional children. In L. M. Baca & H. T. Cervantes (Eds.), *The bilingual special-education interface* (pp. 168–187). Upper Saddle River, NJ: Merrill/Prentice Hall.

Venn, J. (2014). *Assessing students with special needs* (4th ed.). Upper Saddle River, NJ: Pearson.

Williams, R. L. (1972). *The BITCH test (Black intelligence test of cultural homogeneity).* St. Louis, MO: Williams & Associates.

Williams, R. L. (1974). Black pride, academic relevance, and individual achievement. In R. W. Tyler & R. M. Wolf (Eds.), *Crucial issues in testing* (pp. 13–20). Berkeley, CA: McCutchan.

Winzer, M. A., & Mazurek, K. (1998). *Special education in multicultural contexts.* Upper Saddle River, NJ: Merrill/ Prentice Hall.

CHAPTER 5

Anastasi, A., & Urbina, S. (1997). *Psychological testing* (7th ed.). Upper Saddle River, NJ: Prentice Hall.

Code of Fair Testing Practices in Education. (2004) Washington, D.C.: Joint Committee on Testing Practices.

Kaplan, R.M., & Saccuzzo, D.P. (2012). *Psychological testing: Principles, applications, and issues* (6th ed.). Belmont, CA: Wadsworth.

Kessen, W. (1965). *The child.* New York: Wiley.

Klein, S. P., Le, V. and Hamilton, L. S. (2001). Does Matching Student and Teacher Racial/Ethnic Group Improve Math Scores? Santa Monica, CA: RAND Corporation. *http://www.rand.org/pubs/drafts/DRU2529.html*

Sattler, J. M. (1988). *Assessment of children* (3rd ed.). San Diego, CA: Author.

Terman, L. M., & Merrill, M. A. (1937). *Measuring intelligence.* Boston: Houghton Mifflin.

Wechsler, D. (2003a). *Wechsler intelligence scale for children– Fourth edition.* San Antonio, TX: Psychological Corp.

Wechsler, D. (2003b). *WISC-IV technical and interpretive manual.* San Antonio, TX: Psychological Corp.

CHAPTER 6

Abruscato, J. (1993). Early results and tentative implications from the Vermont Portfolio Project. *Phi Delta Kappan, 74,* 474–477.

Affleck, J. Q., Lowenbraun, S., & Archer, A. (1980). *Teaching the mildly handicapped in the regular classroom* (2nd ed.). New York: Merrill/Macmillan.

Airasian, P. W. (1996). *Assessment in the classroom.* New York: McGraw-Hill.

Airasian, P. W. (2005). *Classroom assessment* (5th ed.). Boston: McGraw-Hill.

Alberto, P. A., & Troutman, A. C. (1990). *Applied behavior analysis for teachers* (3rd ed.). Upper Saddle River, NJ: Merrill/Prentice Hall.

Bailey, D. B., & Harbin, G. L. (1980). Nondiscriminatory evaluation. *Exceptional Children, 46,* 590–596.

Barnett, D. W., Daly, E. J., III, Jones, K. M., & Lentz, F. E., Jr. (2004). Response to intervention: Empirically based special service decisions from single-case designs of increasing and decreasing intensity. *The Journal of Special Education, 38*(2), 66–79.

Barrett, E. (2005). Researching electronic portfolios and learner engagement. The REFLECT initiative. Retrieved on September 28, 2015, at *http://electronicportfolios.com/ portfolios/JAAL-REFLECT3.pdf*

Bennett, R. L. (1982). Cautions for the use of informal measures in the assessment of exceptional children. *Journal of Learning Disabilities, 15,* 337–339.

Berdine, W. H., & Cegelka, P. T. (1980). *Teaching the trainable retarded.* New York: Merrill/Macmillan.

Bradley, D. F., & Calvin, M. B. (1998). Grading modified assignments: Equity or compromise? *Teaching Exceptional Children, 31*(2), 24–29.

Browder, D., Trela, K., & Jimenez, B. (2007). Training teachers to follow a task analysis to engage middle school students with moderate and severe developmental disabilities in grade appropriate literature. *Focus on Autism and Other Developmental Disorders, 22*(4), 206–219.

Brown, F. G. (1981). *Measuring classroom achievement.* New York: Holt, Rinehart and Winston.

Bursuck, W.D., E.A. Polloway, L. Plante, M.H. Epstein, M. Jayanthi, and J. McConeghy. (1996). "Report Card Grading Adaptations: A National Survey of Classroom Practices." *Exceptional Children* 62, 4: 301–318.

Cawley, J., Hayden, S., Cade, E., & Baker-Kroczynski, S. (2002). Including students with disabilities into the general education science classroom. *Exceptional Children, 68* (4), 423–435.

Cegelka, P. T. (1995b). Identifying and measuring behavior. In P. T. Cegelka & W. H. Berdine (Eds.), *Effective instruction for students with learning difficulties* (pp. 47–79). Boston: Allyn & Bacon.

Christiansen, J., & Vogel, J. R. (1998). A decision model for grading students with disabilities. *Teaching Exceptional Children, 31*(2), 30–36.

Cohen, L.G., & Spenciner, L.J. (2007). *Assessment of children and youth: With special needs* (3rd ed.). New York: Longman.

Cooper, J. M., & TenBrink, T. (2003). *An educator's guide to classroom assessment.* Boston: Houghton Mifflin.

Cooper, J. O. (1981). *Measuring behavior* (2nd ed.). New York: Merrill/Macmillan.

Courtrade, G., Browder, D., Spooner, F., & DiBiase, W. (2010). Training teachers to use an inquiry-based task analysis to teach science to students with moderate and severe disabilities. *Education and Training in Autism and Developmental Disabilities, 45*(3), 378–399.

Davies, A, & Le Mahieu, P. (2003). Assessment for learning: reconsidering portfolios and research evidence. In M. Segers, F. Dochy, & E. Cascallar (Eds.), *Innovation and Change in Professional Education: Optimising New Modes of Assessment: In Search of Qualities and Standards* (p. 141–169). Dordrecht: Kluwer Academic Publishers.

Davies, A., & Le Mahieu, P. (2003). Assessment for learning: Reconsidering portfolios and research evidence. In M. Segers, F. Dochy, & E. Cascallar (Eds.), *Innovation and change in professional education: Optimising new modes of assessment: In search of qualities and standards* (pp. 141–169). Dordrecht: Kluwer Academic Publishers.

Deno, S. L. (1985). Curriculum-based measurement: The emerging alternative. *Exceptional Children, 52,* 219–232.

Deno, S. L., & Fuchs, L. S. (1988). Developing curriculum-based measurement systems for data-based special education problem solving. In E. L. Meyen, G. A. Vergason, & R. J. Whelan (Eds.), *Effective instructional strategies for exceptional children* (pp. 481–504). Denver, CO: Love.

Deno, S. L., Marston, D., & Mirkin, P. K. (1982). Valid measurement procedures for continuous evaluation of written expression. *Exceptional Children, 48,* 368–371.

Deno, S. L., Mirkin, P. K., & Chiang, B. (1982). Identifying valid measures of reading. *Exceptional Children, 49,* 36–45.

Deno, S.L., Mirkin, P. K., Lowry, L., Kuehnle, K. Relationships among simple measures of spelling and performance on standardized achievement tests (Research Report No. 21) January, 1980.

Duffey, J. B., Salvia, J., Tucker, J., & Ysseldyke, J. (1982). Nonbiased assessment: A need for operationalism. *Exceptional Children, 47,* 427–434.

Esparza Brown, J., & Sanford, A. (2011). *RTI for English language learners: Appropriately using screening and progress monitoring tools to improve instructional outcomes.* Washington, DC: U.S. Department of Education, Office of Special Education Programs, National Center on Response to Intervention. Retrieved June 13, 2015, from *http://www.rti4success.org/images/stories/pdfs/rtiforells.pdf.*

Feuer, M. J., & Fulton, K. (1993). The many faces of performance assessment. *Phi Delta Kappan, 74,* 478.

Friend, M. & Bursuck, W. (1996). *Including students with special needs: A practical guide for classroom teachers.* Boston: Allyn & Bacon.

Fuchs, L. S. (1986). Monitoring progress among mildly handicapped pupils: Review of current practice and research. *Remedial and Special Education, 7*(5), 5–12.

Fuchs, L. S., Deno, S. L., & Mirkin, P. K. (1984). The effects of frequent curriculum-based measurement and evaluation on pedagogy, student achievement, and student awareness of learning. *American Educational Research Journal, 21,* 449–460.

Gelfer, J. I., & Perkins, P. G. (1998). Portfolios: Focus on young children. *Teaching Exceptional Children, 31*(2), 44–47.

Gersten, R., Vaughn, S., & Brengelman, S. U. (1996). Grading and academic feedback for special education students and students with learning difficulties. In T. R. Guskey (Ed.), *Communicating student learning: 1996 yearbook of the ASCD* (pp. 47–57). Alexandria, VA: ASCD.

Goe, L., & Holdheide, L. (2011). Measuring teachers' contributions to student learning growth for nontested grades and subjects. Research and policy brief:

Vanderbilt. Retrieved September 26, 2015, from *http://www.gtlcenter.org/sites/default/files/docs/Measuring TeachersContributions.pdf.*

Grady, E. (1992). *The portfolio approach to assessment.* Bloomington, IN: Phi Delta Kappa Educational Foundation.

Groth, R. E. (2014). Using work samples from the National Assessment of Educational Progress (NAEP) to design tasks that assess statistical knowledge for teaching *Journal of Statistics Education, 22,* 3. Retrieved September 25, 2015, from *www.amstat.org/publications/jse/v22n3/groth.pdf.*

Guskey, T., & Jung, L. (2009). Grading and reporting in a standards-based environment: Implications for students with special needs. Paper presented at the annual meeting of the American Educational Research Association San Diego, CA. Retrieved on September 27, 2015, from *http://files.eric.ed.gov/fulltext/ED509343.pdf.*

Harris, L. P., & Wolf, S. R. (1979). Validity and reliability of criterion-referenced measures: Issues and procedures for special educators. *Learning Disability Quarterly, 2*(2), 84–88.

Hasbrouck, J. E., Woldbeck, T., Ihnot, C., & Parker, R. I. (1999). One teacher's use of curriculum-based measurement: A changed opinion. *Learning Disabilities Research & Practice, 14*(2), 118–126.

Howell, K. W., Kaplan, J. S., & O'Connell, C. Y. (1979). *Evaluating exceptional children.* New York: Merrill/Macmillan.

Ihnot, C. (2000, 2001, 2003). *Read naturally (fluency curriculum, levels. 8–8.0).* Saint Paul, MN: Read Naturally.

Ihnot, C. (2006). *Reading fluency progress monitor.* St. Paul, MN: Read Naturally.

Kritikos, E., LeDosquet, P., & Melton, M. (2011). *Foundations of education in early childhood special education assessment.* Columbus, OH: Pearson.

Lewis, R. B., & Doorlag, D. H. (2006). *Teaching special students in general education classrooms* (7th ed.). Upper Saddle River, NJ: Merrill/Prentice Hall.

Likert, R. (1932). A technique for the measurement of attitudes. *Archives of Psychology,* 140.

Mager, R. F. (1975). *Preparing instructional objectives* (2nd ed.). Belmont, CA: Fearon.

Martin, D. B. (1999). *The portfolio planner.* Upper Saddle River, NJ: Merrill/Prentice Hall.

McCormack, J. E., Jr. (1976). The assessment tool that meets your needs: The one you construct. *Teaching Exceptional Children, 8,* 106–109.

McLoughlin, J. A., & Kershman, S. (1978). Including the handicap. *Behavioral Disorders, 4,* 31–35.

Monroe, M. (1932). *Children who cannot read.* Chicago: University of Chicago Press.

Nilsson, N. L. (2008). A critical analysis of eight informal reading inventories. *The Reading Teacher, 61*(7), 526–536.

Oakland, T. (1980). Nonbiased assessment of minority group children. *Exceptional Education Quarterly, 1*(3), 31–46.

Oosterhof, A. (2003). *Developing and using classroom assessments* (3rd ed.). Upper Saddle River, NJ: Merrill/Prentice Hall.

Pierce, L. V., & O'Malley, J. M. (1992, Spring). *Performance and portfolio assessment for language minority students (NCBE Program Information Guide Series, No. 9).* Retrieved July 1, 1999, from *http://www.ncbe.gwu.edu/ncbepubs/pigs/pig9.htm*

Polloway, E., M.H. Epstein, W.D. Bursuck, T.W. Roderique, J.L. McConeghy, and M. Jayanthi. (1994). "Classroom Grading: A National Survey of Policies." *Remedial and Special Education* 15, 3: 162–170.

Salend, S. J. (1998). Using portfolios to assess student performance. *Teaching Exceptional Children, 31*(2), 36–43.

Scott, V. G., & Weishaar, M. K. (2003). Curriculum-based measurement for reading progress. *Intervention in School and Clinic, 38,* 153–159.

Silva, M., Munk, D. D., & Bursuck, W. D. (2005). Grading adaptations for students with disabilities. *Intervention in School and Clinic, 41,* 87–98.

Stiggins, R. J. (2001). *The unfulfilled promise of classroom assessment.* Portland, OR: Assessment Training Institute.

Strickland, B. B., & Turnbull, A. P. (1990). *Developing and implementing individualized education programs* (3rd ed.). New York: Merrill/Macmillan.

Wiggins, G. (1996). Practicing what we preach in designing authentic assessments. *Educational Leadership*, 18–25.

Wolf, K. P. (1991). Teaching portfolios: Focus for new clearinghouse and network. *Portfolio News, 3*(1), 7, 22.

CHAPTER 7

Anastasi, A., & Urbina, S. (1997). *Psychological testing* (7th ed.). Upper Saddle River, NJ: Prentice Hall.

Benson, E. (2003). Intelligence across cultures. *Monitor on Psychology, 34*(2), 56–58.

Bersoff, D. N. (1981). Testing and the law. *American Psychologist, 36,* 1047–1056.

Bickley, P. G., Keith, T. Z., & Wolfle, L. M. (1995). The three-stratum theory of cognitive abilities: Test of the structure of intelligence across the life span. *Intelligence, 20,* 309–328.

Binet, A., & Simon, T. (1905). Methodes nouvelles pour le diagnostic du niveau intellectual des anormaux. *L'Anee Psychologique, 11,* 191–244.

Binet, A., & Simon, Th. (1905). Méthodes nouvelles pour le diagnostic du niveau intellectuel des anormaux. *L'Année Psychologique, 11,* 191–255.

Bracken, B. A., & McCallum, R. S. (1998). *Universal nonverbal intelligence test.* Itasca, IL: Riverside.

Bracken, B. A., & McCallum, R. S. (2015). Universal Nonverbal Intelligence Test (UNIT). Rolling Meadows, IL: Riverside Publishing.

Brown, L. L., Sherbenou, R. J., & Johnsen, S. K. (1997). *Test of nonverbal intelligence* (3rd ed.). Austin, TX: PRO-ED.

Brown, L., Sherbenou, R. J., & Johnsen, L. K. (2010). The *Tests of Nonverbal Intelligence* (4th ed.) *(TONI–4).* Austin, TX: PRO-ED.

Budoff, M. (1987). Measures for assessing learning potential. In C. S. Lidz (Ed.), *Dynamic assessment: An interactional approach to evaluating learning potential* (pp. 173–195). New York: Guilford Press.

Burgemeister, B. B., Blum, L. H., & Lorge, I. (1972). *Columbia mental maturity scale* (3rd ed.). San Antonio, TX: Psychological Corp.

Carroll, J. B. (1993). *Human cognitive abilities: A survey of factor-analytic studies.* Cambridge, UK: Oxford University Press.

Carroll, J. B. (1997). The three-stratum theory of cognitive abilities. In D. P. Flanagan, J. L., Genshaft, & P. L. Harrison (Eds.), *Contemporary intellectual assessment: Theories, tests, and issues* (pp. 122–130). New York: Guilford Press.

Carroll, J. B., & Horn, J. L. (1981). On the scientific basis of ability testing. *American Psychologist, 36,* 1012–1020.

Carson, J. S., & Wiedl, K. H. (1992). Principles of dynamic testing: The application of a specific model. *Learning and Individual Differences, 4,* 153–166.

Cattell, R. B. (1950). *Culture fair intelligence test: Scale 1.* Champaign, IL: Institute for Personality and Ability Testing.

Cattell, R. B., & Cattell, A. K. S. (1960). *Culture fair intelligence test: Scale 2.* Champaign, IL: Institute for Personality and Ability Testing.

Cattell, R. B., & Cattell, A. K. S. (1963). *Culture fair intelligence test: Scale 3.* Champaign, IL: Institute for Personality and Ability Testing.

Cattell, R. B., & Cattell, A. K. S. (1977). *The culture fair intelligence tests (rev.).* Champaign, IL: Institute for Personality and Ability Testing.

Clarizio, H. F. (1979). In defense of the IQ test. *School Psychology Digest, 8,* 79–88.

Das, J. P., Naglieri, J. A., & Kirby, J. R. (1994). *Assessment of cognitive processes: The PASS theory of intelligence.* Boston: Allyn & Bacon.

Diana v. State Board of Education. Civ. No. C-70 37 RFP (N.D. Cal. 1970, 1973).

Diaz-Lefebvre, R. (2004). Multiple intelligences, learning for understanding, and creative assessment: Some pieces to the puzzle of learning. *Teachers College Record, 106*(1), 49–57.

Ebel, R. L. (1977). *The uses of standardized testing.* Bloomington, IN: Phi Delta Kappa Educational Foundation.

Esters, I., & Ittenbach, R. F. (1999). Contemporary theories and assessments of intelligence: A primer. *Professional School Counseling, 2*(5), 373–377.

Facon, B., & Facon-Bollengier, T. (1999). Chronological age and crystallized intelligence of people with intellectual disability. *Journal of Intellectual Disability Research, 43*(6), 489–496.

Feuerstein, R., in collaboration with Rand, Y., & Hoffman, M. D. (1979). *The dynamic assessment of retarded performers.* Baltimore: University Park Press.

Feuerstein, R., Miller, R., Hoffman, M. D., Rand, Y., Mintzker, Y., & Jensen, M. R. (1981). Cognitive modifiability in adolescence: Cognitive structure and the effects of intervention. *Journal of Special Education, 15,* 269–287.

Frisby, C. L., & Braden, J. P. (1992). Feuerstein's dynamic assessment approach: A semantic, logical, and empirical critique. *Journal of Special Education, 26,* 281–301.

Gardner, H. (1993). *Multiple intelligences: The theory in practice.* New York: Basic Books.

Geisinger, K. F. (Ed.). (1992). *Psychological testing of Hispanics.* Washington, DC: American Psychological Association.

Goodman, J. F. (1979). Is tissue the issue? A critique of SOMPA's models and tests. *School Psychology Digest, 8,* 47–62.

Guadalupe v. Tempe Elementary School District. Civ. Act. No. 71–435 (D. Ariz. 1972).

Hammill, D. D., Bryant, B., & Pearson, N. (1998). *Hammill multiability intelligence test.* Austin, TX: PRO-ED.

Hammill, D. D., Pearson, N. A., & Wiederholt, J.L. (1997). *Comprehensive test of nonverbal intelligence.* Austin, TX: PRO-ED.

Harth, R. (1982). The Feuerstein perspective on the modification of cognitive performance. *Focus on Exceptional Children, 15*(3), 1–12.

Helms, J. E. (1992). Why is there no study of cultural equivalence in standardized cognitive ability testing? *American Psychologist, 47,* 1083–1101.

Herrnstein, R. (1971). I.Q. *Atlantic Monthly, 228,* 43–64.

Holtzman, W. H., Jr., & Wilkinson, C. Y. (1991). Assessment of cognitive ability. In E. V. Hamayan & J. S. Damico (Eds.), *Limiting bias in the assessment of bilingual students* (pp. 247–280). Austin, TX: PRO-ED.

Horn, J. L., & Cattell, R. B. (1966). Refinement and test of the fluid and crystallized general intelligences. *Journal of Educational Psychology, 57,* 253–270.

Horn, J. L., & Hofer, S. M. (1992). Major abilities and development in the adult period. In R. J. Sternberg & C. A. Berg (Eds.), *Intellectual development* (pp. 44–99). Boston: Cambridge University Press.

Jones, R. L. (Ed.). (1988). *Psychoeducational assessment of minority group children, A casebook.* Berkeley, CA: Cobb & Henry.

Jones, R. L., & Wilderson, R. B. (1976). Mainstreaming and the minority child: An overview of issues and a perspective. In R. L. Jones (Ed.), *Mainstreaming and the minority child* (pp. 1–13). Reston, VA: Council for Exceptional Children.

Kanevsky, L. (2000). Dynamic assessment of gifted students. In K. A. Heller, F. J. Monks, R. J. Sternberg, & R. F. Subotnik (Eds.), *International handbook of giftedness and talent* (2nd ed.) (pp. 283–295). Oxford: Elsevier.

Kaufman, A. S., & Kaufman, N. C. (2004a). *Kaufman assessment battery for children, second edition.* Minneapolis, MN: Pearson Assessments.

Kaufman, A. S., & Kaufman, N. C. (2004b). *Kaufman test of educational achievement, second edition.* Minneapolis, MN: Pearson Assessments.

Kaufman, A. S., & Kaufman, N. L. (1993). *Kaufman adolescent & adult intelligence test.* Circle Pines, MN: American Guidance Service.

Kaufman, A. S., & Kaufman, N. L. (2004a). *Kaufman Assessment Battery for Children, second edition manual (KABC-II).* Circle Pines, MN: American Guidance Service.

Kaufman, A. S., Kaufman, J. C., Chen, T., & Kaufman, N. (1996). Differences on six Horn abilities for 14 age groups between 15–16 and 75–94 years. *Psychological Assessment, 8*(2), 161–171.

Kranzler, J. H., & Keith, T. Z. (1999). Independent confirmatory factor analysis of the Cognitive Assessment System (CAS): What does the CAS measure? *The School Psychology Review, 28*(1), 117–144.

Larry P. v. Riles. C-71–2270-RFP (N.D. Cal. 1972), 495 F. Supp. 96 (N.D. Cal. 1979) Aff'r (9th Cir. 1984), 1983–84 EHLR DEC. 555:304.

Li S., Lindenberger U., Hommel B., Aschersleben G., Prinz W., Baltes P. B. (2004). Transformations in the coupling among intellectual abilities and constituent cognitive processes across the life span. *Psychological Science, 15*(3), 155–163.

Lohman, D. F., & Hagen, E. P. (2001). *Cognitive abilities test, Form 6.* Itasca, IL: Riverside.

Losen, D. J., & Orfield, G. (Eds.). (2002). *Racial inequity in special education.* Cambridge, MA: Harvard Education Press.

McCarthy, D. (1972). *McCarthy scales of childrens abilities.* San Antonio, TX: Psychological Corp.

Mercer, J. R. (1973). *Labeling the mentally retarded.* Berkeley, CA: University of California Press.

Mercer, J. R., & Lewis, J. F. (1977a). *Adaptive behavior inventory for children.* San Antonio, TX: Psychological Corp.

Mercer, J. R., & Lewis, J. F. (1977b). *System of multicultural pluralistic assessment.* San Antonio, TX: Psychological Corp.

Naglieri, J. A. (2003). *Naglieri Nonverbal Ability Test.* San Antonio (2nd ed.), TX: Psychological Corporation.

Naglieri, J. A. (2003). *Naglieri nonverbal ability test.* San Antonio, TX: Psychological Corp.

Naglieri, J. A., & Das, J. P. (1997). *Das-Naglieri cognitive assessment system.* Itasca, IL: Riverside.

Nicholson, C. L., & Hibpshman, T. L. (1990). *Slosson intelligence test, SIT-R for children and adults* (1991 ed.). East Aurora; NY: Slosson.

Oakland, T. (1979). Research on the *Adaptive Behavior Inventory for Children* and the Estimated Learning Potential. *School Psychology Digest, 8*, 63–70.

Otis, A. S., & Lennon, R. T. (2002). *Otis-Lennon school ability test* (8th ed.). San Antonio, TX: Psychological Corp.

Parents in Action on Special Education v. Joseph P. Hannon. No. 74 C 3586 (N.D. III. 1980).

Patton, J. M. (1998). The disproportionate representation of African Americans in special education: Looking behind the curtain for understanding and solutions. *Journal of Special Education, 32*, 25–31.

Perrone, V. (1977). *The abuses of standardized testing.* Bloomington, IN: Phi Delta Kappa Educational Foundation.

Piaget, J. (1952). *The origins of intelligence in children.* New York: International Universities Press.

Raven, J. C. (1938). *Standard progressive matrices.* London: H. K. Lewis. [American distributor: Psychological Corporation]

Raven, J. C. (1947). *Coloured progressive matrices.* London: H. K. Lewis. [American distributor: Psychological Corporation]

Raven, J. C. (1962). *Advanced progressive matrices.* London: H. K. Lewis. [American distributor: Psychological Corporation]

Raven, J. C. (1998). *Raven's progressive matrices, comprehensive technical manual.* San Antonio, TX: Psychological Corp.

Raven, J.C. (2015). *Advanced Progressive Matrices.* NCS Pearson.

Reschly, D. J. (2005). Learning disabilities identification: Primary intervention, secondary intervention, and then what? *Journal of Learning Disabilities, 39*, 510–515.

Robinson, N. M., & Robinson, H. B. (1976). *The mentally retarded child* (2nd ed.). New York: McGraw-Hill.

Roid, G. (2003). *Stanford-Binet intelligence scales, Fifth edition.* Itasca, IL: Riverside.

Roid, G. H., & Miller, L. J. (1997). *Leiter International Performance Scale—Revised.* Wood Dale, IL: Stoelting.

Roid, G. H., Miller, L. J., Pomplun, M., & Koch, C. (2013). *Leiter International Performance Scale—Third Edition.* Los Angeles: Western Psychological Services.

Roid, G., & Miller, L. (1997). *Leiter international performance scale–revised.* Chicago: Stoelting.

Rosa's Law of 2010 (P.L. 111–256)

Sattler, J. M. (1988). *Assessment of children* (3rd ed.). San Diego, CA: Author.

Scarr, S. (1981). Testing *for* children: Assessment and the many determinants of intellectual competence. *American Psychologist, 36*, 1159–1166.

Schalock, R. L., Borthwick-Duffy, S. A., Bradley, V. J., Buntinx, W. H. E., Coulter, D. L., Craig, E. M., et al. (2010). *Intellectual disability: Definition, classification, and systems of supports.* Washington, DC: American Association on Intellectual and Developmental Disabilities.

Schalock, R. L., Borthwick-Duffy, S. A., Bradley, V. J., Buntinx, W. H. E., Coulter, D. L., Craig, E. M., et al. (2010). *Intellectual disability: Definition, classification, and systems of supports.* Washington, DC: American Association on Intellectual and Developmental Disabilities.

Schalock, R. L., Borthwick-Duffy, S. A., Bradley, V. J., Buntinx, W. H. E., Coulter, D. L., Craig, E. M., et al. (2010). *Intellectual disability: Definition, classification, and systems of supports.* Washington, DC: American Association on Intellectual and Developmental Disabilities.

Schrank, F. A., Mather, N., & McGrew, K. S. (2014). *Woodcock-Johnson IV Tests of Achievement.* Rolling Meadows, IL: Riverside.

Spearman, C. E. (1927). *The abilities of man.* New York: Macmillan.

Sternberg, R. J. (1988). *The triarchic mind: A new theory of intelligence.* New York: Viking.

Sternberg, R. J. (1999). The theory of successful intelligence. *Review of General Psychology, 3*, 292–316.

Sternberg, R. J., & Grigorenko, E. L. (2000). *Teaching for successful intelligence.* Arlington Heights, IL: Skylight.

Sternberg, R. J., & Grigorenko, E. L. (2002). *Dynamic testing.* Cambridge, England: Cambridge University Press.

Sternberg, R. J., & Grigorenko, E. L. (2004). Successful intelligence in the classroom. *Theory into Practice, 43*(3), 274–281.

Sternberg, R. J., Okagaki, L., & Jackson, A. (1990). Practical intelligence for success in school. *Educational Leadership, 48*, 35–39.

Sternberg, R. J., Okagaki, L., & Jackson, A. S. (1990). Practical intelligence for success in school. *Educational Leadership, 48*, 35–39.

Swanson, H. L. (1996). *Swanson-cognitive processing test.* Austin, TX: PRO-ED.

Thorndike, E. L. (1927). *The measurement of intelligence.* New York: Teachers' College Press.

Thorndike, R. L., Hagen, E., & Sattler, J. (1986). *Stanford-Binet intelligence scale: Fourth edition.* Chicago: Riverside.

Tyler, L. E. (Ed.). (1969). *Intelligence: Some recurring issues.* New York: Van Nostrand-Reinhold.

Valenzuela, J. S. de, & Cervantes, H. T. (1998). Procedures and techniques for assessing the bilingual exceptional children. In L. M. Baca & H. T. Cervantes (Eds.), *The bilingual special-education interface* (pp. 168–187). Upper Saddle River, NJ: Merrill/Prentice Hall.

Viadero, D. (1995). "Changes in attitude." *Education Week: 25.*

Vygotsky, L. S. (1978). *Mind in society.* Cambridge, MA: Harvard University Press.

Wechsler D. (2011). *Wechsler Abbreviated Scale of Intelligence–second edition (WASI-II).* San Antonio, TX: Psychological Corporation.

Wechsler, D. (2008). *Wechsler Adult Intelligence Scale* (4th ed.). San Antonio, TX: NCS Pearson.

Wechsler, D. (1974). *Wechsler intelligence scale for children– Revised.* San Antonio, TX: Psychological Corp.

Wechsler, D. (2003a). *Wechsler intelligence scale for children– Fourth edition.* San Antonio, TX: Psychological Corp.

Wechsler, D. (2005). *Wechsler intelligence scale for children– Fourth edition Spanish.* San Antonio, TX: Harcourt Assessment.

Wechsler, D. (2012). *Wechsler Preschool and Primary Scale of Intelligence, Fourth Edition: Canadian.* San Antonio, TX: NCS Pearson.

Wechsler, D. (2014a). *Wechsler intelligence scale for children* (5th ed.)*: Administration and scoring manual.* Bloomington, MN: Pearson.

Wechsler, D. (2014b). *Wechsler intelligence scale for children* (5th ed.)*: Administration and scoring manual supplement.* Bloomington, MN: Pearson.

Wechsler, D. (2014c). *Wechsler intelligence scale for children* (5th ed.)*: Technical and interpretive manual.* Bloomington, MN: Pearson.

Winzer, M. A., & Mazurek, K. (1998). *Special education in multicultural contexts.* Upper Saddle River, NJ: Merrill/ Prentice Hall.

Woodcock, R. W., & Mather, N. (1989). WJ-R tests of cognitive ability–Standard and supplemental batteries: Examiner's manual. In R. W. Woodcock & M. B. Johnson, *Woodcock-Johnson psycho-educational battery–Revised.* Chicago: Riverside.

Woodcock, R. W., Muñoz-Sandoval, A. F., McGrew, K. S., & Mather, N. (2005). *Batería III Woodcock-Muñoz.* Rolling Meadows, IL: Riverside.

CHAPTER 8

American Association on Intellectual and Developmental Disabilities. Retrieved November 22, 2015, from *http:// aaidd.org/intellectual-disability/definition#.VlZ514RG8dU.*

American Association on Mental Retardation. (1992). *Mental retardation: Definition, classification, and systems of supports* (9th ed.).Washington, DC: Author.

American Psychiatric Association. (2013). *Diagnostic and statistical manual of mental disorders* (5th ed.). Washington, DC: Author.

ARC. Retrieved November 22, 2015, from *http://www.thearc.org.*

Arias, B., Verdugo, M. A., Navas, P., & Gomez, L. E. (2013). Factor structure of the construct of adaptive behavior in children with and without intellectual disability. *International Journal of Clinical and Health Psychology, 13*(2), 155–166.

Beirne-Smith, M., Ittenbach, R.F., & Patton, J.R. (2006). Mental retardation (7th ed.). Upper Saddle River, NJ: Merrill/Prentice Hall.

Brown, L., & Leigh, J. (1986). *Adaptive behavior inventory.* Austin, TX: PRO-ED.

Bruininks, R. H., Warfield, G., & Stealey, D. (1982). The mentally retarded. In E. L. Meyen (Ed.), *Exceptional children and youth: An introduction.* Denver, CO: Love Publishing (Revised edition).

Bruininks, R. H., Woodcock, R. W., Weatherman, R. F., & Hill, B. K. (1996). *Scales of independent behavior–Revised.* Itasca, IL: Riverside.

Cheng, L. L. (1996). Enhancing communication: Toward optimal language learning for limited English proficient students. *Language, Speech, and Hearing Services in Schools, 27,* 347–352.

Damico, J. S., & Damico, S. K. (1993). Language and social skills from a diversity perspective: Considerations for the speech-language pathologist. *Language, Speech, and Hearing Services in Schools, 24,* 236–243.

Ditterline, J., Banner, D., Oakton, T., & Becton, D. (2008). Adaptive behavior profiles of students with disabilities. *Journal of Applied School Psychology, 24*(2), 191–208.

Doll, E. A. (1927). Borderline diagnosis. *Proceedings of the American Association for the Study of the Feebleminded, 32,* 45–59.

Doll, E. A. (1935). A genetic scale of social maturity. *American Journal of Orthopsychiatry, 5,* 180–188.

Doll, E. A. (1965). *Vineland social maturity scale* (rev. ed.). Circle Pines, MN: American Guidance Service.

Emerson, E., Hatton, C. R. S., & Thompson, T. (2004). *International handbook of applied research in intellectual disabilities.* DeKalb, IL: Wiley.

Greenspan, S. (1999). A contextualist perspective on adaptive behavior. In R. L. Schalock & D. L. Braddock (Eds.), *Adaptive behavior and its measurement* (pp. 61–80). Washington, DC: American Association on Intellectual and Developmental Disabilities.

Greenspan, S., & Switzky, H. N. (2006). Lessons learned from the Atkins decision in the next AAMR manual. In H. N. Switzky & S. Greenspan (Eds.), *What is mental retardation? Ideas for an evolving disability in the 21st century* (pp. 283–302). Washington, DC: American Association on Mental Retardation.

Grossman, H. J. (1983). *Classification in mental retardation.* Washington DC: American Association on Mental Deficiency.

Harrison, P. (2015). *Adaptive behavior assessment system—Third edition.* Minneapolis, MN: Pearson.

Harrison, P. L. (1987). Research with adaptive behavior scales. *Journal of Special Education, 21,* 37–68.

Heber, R. (1961). *A manual on terminology and classification in mental retardation* (Rev. ed.). Washington, DC: American Association on Mental Deficiency.

Hosp, J. L. (2003). Referral rates for intervention or assessment: A meta-analysis of racial differences. *Journal of Special Education, 37*(2), 67–80.

Iglesias, A. (1985). Communication in the home and classroom: Match or mismatch. *Topics in Language Disorders, 5,* 29–41.

Kamphaus, R. W. (1987). Conceptual and psychometric issues in the assessment of adaptive behavior. *Journal of Special Education, 27*(1), 27–35.

Kamphaus, R. W. (1987). Conceptual and psychometric issues in the assessment of adaptive behavior. *Journal of Special Education, 21,* 27–35.

Kramer, J. M., Coster, W. J., Kao, Y.-C., Snow, A., & Orsmond, G. I. (2012). A new approach to the measurement of adaptive behavior: Development of the PEDI-CAT for children and youth with autism spectrum disorders. *Physical and Occupational Therapy in Pediatrics, 32*(1), 34–47.

Kritikos, E. P. (2010). *Special education assessment: Issues and strategies affecting today's classrooms.* Columbus, OH: Pearson.

Kritikos, E. P., & Birnbaum, B. (2004). Parental perspectives of needs and services provided for families of children with mild disabilities. *Learning Disabilities: A Multidisciplinary Journal, 13*(2), 61–68. *Classification, and systems of supports.* 10th ed. Washington, DC: American Association on Mental Retardation.

Lambert, N., Nihira, K., & Leland, H. (1993). *AAMR adaptive behavior scale–School* (2nd ed.). Austin, TX: PRO-ED.

Luckasson, R., Borthwick-Duffy, S., Buntinx, W. H. E., Coulter, D. L., Craig, E. M., Reeve, A., et al. (2002). *Mental retardation: Definition, classification, and systems of supports* (10th ed.). Washington, DC: American Association on Mental Retardation.

Luckasson, R., Coulter, D. L., Polloway, E. A., Reiss, S., Schalock, R. L., Snell, M. E., Spitalnick, D. M., & Stark, J. A. (1992). *Mental retardation: Definition, classification, and systems of supports* (9th ed.). Washington, DC: American Association on Mental Retardation.

Marc J. Tassé, Ruth Luckasson, and Margaret Nygren (*2013*) AAIDD Proposed Recommendations for *ICD–11* and the Condition Previously Known as Mental Retardation. Intellectual and Developmental Disabilities: April 2013, Vol. 51, No. 2, pp. 127–131.

McCarney, S. B., & Arthaud, T. J. (2006a). *Adaptive behavior evaluation scale–Revised second edition: 4–12 years.* Columbus, MO: Hawthorne.

McCarney, S. B., & Arthaud, T. J. (2006b). *Adaptive behavior evaluation scale–Revised second edition: 13–18 years.* Columbus, MO: Hawthorne.

Mercer, J. R., & Lewis, J. F. (1977a). *Adaptive behavior inventory for children.* San Antonio, TX: Psychological Corp.

Morreau, L. E., & Bruininks, R. H. (1991). *Checklist of adaptive living skills.* Chicago: Riverside.

Nihira, K., Leland, H., & Lambert, N. (1993). *AAMR adaptive behavior scale–Residential and community* (2nd ed.). Austin, TX: PRO-ED.

O'Reilly, C., Northcraft, G. B., & Sabers, D. (1989). The confirmation bias in special eligibility decisions. *School Psychology Review, 18,* 126–135.

Panerai, S., Tasca, D., Ferri, R., Genitori D'Arrigo, V., & Elia, M. (2014). Executive functions and adaptive behavior in autism spectrum disorders with and without intellectual disability. *Psychiatry Journal,* Article ID 941809, 11 pp.

Pierangelo, R., & Guiliani, G.A. (2006). *Assessment in special education: A practical approach.* Boston, MA: Allyn & Bacon.

Pugliese, C. E., Anthony, L., Strang, J. F., Dudley, K., Wallace, G. L., & Kenworthy, L. (2014). Increasing adaptive behavior skill deficits from childhood to adolescence in autism spectrum disorder: Role of executive function. *Journal of Autism and Developmental Disorders, 45*(6), 1579–1587.

Reschly, D. J., Myers, T. J., & Hartel, C. R. (2002). *Mental retardation: Determining eligibility for social security benefits.* National Research Council (U.S.) Committee on Disability Determination for Mental Retardation. Washington, DC: National Academies Press.

Robinson, N. M., & Robinson, H. B. (1976). *The mentally retarded child* (2nd ed.). New York: McGraw-Hill.

Sattler, J. M., & Hoge, R. D. (2006). *Assessment of children: Behavioral, social and clinical foundations.* La Mesa, CA: Jerome Sattler.

Sattler, J.M. (2002). *Assessment of children: Behavioral and clinical applications* (4th ed.). San Diego, CA: Jerome M. Sattler.

Shapiro, J., Monzo, L. D., Rueda, R., Gomez, J. A., & Blesher, J. (2004). Alienated advocacy: Perspectives of Latina mothers of young adults with developmental disabilities on service systems. *Mental Retardation, 42*(1), 37–54.

Sparrow, S. S., Chicchetti, D. V., & Balla, D. A. (2005a). *Survey forms manual, Vineland adaptive behavior scales, Second edition.* Minneapolis, MN: Pearson Assessments.

Sparrow, S. S., Cicchetti, D. V., & Balla, D. A. (2005b). *Vineland adaptive behavior scales, Second edition.* Minneapolis, MN: Pearson Assessments.

Tasse, M. (2013). Adaptive behavior. *The Oxford Handbook of Positive Psychology and Disability* (Wehmeyer, M., Ed.). New York: Oxford University Press.

Tasse, M., & LeCavalier, L. (2000). Comparing parent and teacher ratings of social competence and problem behaviors. *American Journal on Mental Retardation, 105*(4), 252–259.

Tasse, M., Schalock, R. L., Balboni, G., Bersani, H., Borthwick-Duffy, S. A, Spreat, S., et al. (2012). The construct of adaptive behavior: Its conceptualization, measurement, and use in the field of intellectual disability. *American Journal on Intellectual and Developmental Disabilities, 117*(4), 291–303.

Thompson, J. R., Bryant, B. R., Campbell, E. M., Craig, E. M., Hughes, C., Rotholz, D. R., Silverman, W. P., Tasse, M. J., & Wehmeyer, M. L. (2004). *Supports intensity scale.* Washington, DC: American Association on Intellectual and Developmental Disabilities.

Ventola, P., Steinberg, E., Chawarska, & K, Klin, A. (2014). Early-emerging social adaptive skills in toddlers with autism spectrum disorders: an item analysis. *Journal–of Autism and Developmental Disorders, 44*(2), 283–293.

Voelker, S., Shore, D., Hakim-Larson, J., & Bruner, D. (1997). Discrepancies in parent and teacher ratings of adaptive behavior of children with multiple disabilities. *Mental Retardation, 35*(1), 10–17.

Weller, C., & Strawser, S. (1981). *Weller-Strawser scales of adaptive behavior for the learning disabled.* Novato, CA: Academic Therapy.

Westby, C. (1997). There's more to passing than knowing the answers. *Language, Speech, and Hearing in Schools, 28*, 274–287.

CHAPTER 9

Alley G.R., Deshler D.D., Clark F.L., Schumaker J.B., Warner M.M. (1983). Learning disabilities in adolescent and adult populations: Research implications (Part II). Focus on Exceptional Children, 15, 1–14.

Alley, G., & Deshler, D. (1979). *Teaching the learning disabled adolescent.* Denver, CO: Love.

Arter, J. A., & Jenkins, J. R. (1979). Differential diagnostic-prescriptive teaching: A critical appraisal. *Review of Educational Research, 49,* 517–555.

Baker, H. J., & Leland, B. (1967). *Detroit tests of learning aptitude* (rev. ed.). Indianapolis, IN: Bobbs-Merrill.

Beery, K. E., & Beery, N. A. (2004). *Developmental test of visual-motor integration* (5th ed.). Minneapolis, MN: NCS Pearson.

Beery, K. E., & Beery, N. A. (2006). *Addendum: Beery VMI adult norms.* Minneapolis, MN: NCS Pearson.

Beery, K. E., & Beery, N. A. (2010). *Administration, scoring, and teaching manual for the Beery-VMI* (6th ed.). San Antonio, TX: Pearson.

Bender, L. (1938). A visual motor gestalt test and its clinical use. *The American Orthopsychiatric Association Research Monographs, 3.*

Beverstock, C. (1991). *Your child's vision is important.* Newark, DE: International Reading Association.

Brown, V. L. (1978). Independent study behaviors: A framework for curriculum development. *Learning Disability Quarterly, 1*(2), 78–84.

Brown, W. F., & Holtzman, W. H. (1967a). *Survey of study habits and attitudes.* San Antonio, TX: Psychological Corp.

Brown, W. F., & Holtzman, W. H. (1967b). *Survey of study habits and attitudes, Spanish edition.* San Antonio, TX: Psychological Corp.

Bruininks RH, Bruininks BD. *Bruininks-Oseretsky Test of Motor Proficiency* (2nd ed.). Pearson, Minneapolis MN; 2005: 54–55.

Bruininks, R. H. & Bruininks, D. B. (2005) *Bruininks–Oseretsky Test of Motor Proficiency,* 2nd ed. Pearson Assessment, Minneapolis, MN, USA.

Bruininks, R. H. (1978). *Bruininks-Oseretsky test of motor proficiency.* Circle Pines, MN: American Guidance Service.

Bruininks, R. H., & Bruininks, B. D. (2005). *Bruininks-Oseretsky Test of Motor Proficiency, Second Edition.* Minneapolis, MN: Pearson Assessments.

California Association of School Psychologists. (2004). *CASP Board of Directors and RTI.* Accessed on February.

Carbo, M. (1982). *The reading style inventory.* Roslyn Heights, NY: Learning Research Associates.

Carbo, M. (1984). Research in learning style and reading: Implications for instruction. *Theory into Practice, 23*(1), 72–76.

Carbo, M., Dunn, R., & Dunn, K. (1986). *Teaching students to read through their individual learning styles.* Upper Saddle River, NJ: Prentice Hall.

Caton, H. R. (1985). Visual impairments. In W. H. Berdine & A. E. Blackhurst (Eds.), *An introduction to special education* (2nd ed.) (pp. 235–280). Boston: Little, Brown.

Cohen, S. B., & de Bettencourt, L. (1983). Teaching children to be independent learners: A step-by-step strategy. *Focus on Exceptional Children, 16*(3), 1–12.

Colarusso, R. P., & Hammill, D. D. (2003). *Motor-free visual perception test, third edition.* Novato, CA: Academic Therapy.

Colarusso, R., & Hammill, D. (2015). *Motor-Free Visual Perceptual Test,* (4th ed.). Novato: Academic Therapy Publications.

Coles, G. S. (1978). The learning disabilities test battery: Empirical and social issues. *Harvard Educational Review, 18,* 313–340.

Council for Learning Disabilities. (1986). *Inclusion of non-handicapped low achievers and under-achievers in learning disability programs.* A position paper of the Council for Learning Disabilities. Overland Park, KS: Author.

Demos, G. (1976). *The study skills counseling examination.* Los Angeles: Western Psychological Services.

Deshler, D. D., Alley, G. R., Warner, M. M., & Schumaker, J. B. (1981). Instructional practices for promoting skill acquisition and generalization in severely learning disabled adolescents. *Learning Disability Quarterly, 4,* 415–422.

Deshler, D. D., Schumaker, J. B., Alley, G. R., Warner, M. M., & Clark, F. L. (1982). Learning disabilities in adolescent and young adult populations: Research implications. *Focus on Exceptional Children, 15*(1), 1–12.

Dunn, R. (1984). Learning style: State of the science. *Theory into Practice, 23*(1), 10–18.

Dunn, R. (1988). Teaching students through their perceptual strengths or preferences. *Journal of Reading, 31,* 304–309.

Dunn, R., Dunn, K., & Price, G. E. (1979). *Learning style inventory.* Lawrence, KS: Price Systems.

Felton, R. H., & Wood, F. B. (1989). Cognitive deficits in reading disability and attention deficit disorder. *Journal of Learning Disabilities, 22,* 3–13.

Fiorello C. A., Hale J. B., Snyder L. E. (2006). Cognitive hypothesis testing and response to intervention for children with reading disabilities. *Psychology in the Schools, 43,* 835–854.

Fiorello C. A., Hale J. B., Snyder L. E., Forrest E., Teodori A. (2008). Validating individual differences through examination of converging psychometric and neuropsychological models of cognitive functioning. In Thurman S. K., Fiorello C. A. (Eds.), *Applied cognitive research in K-3 classrooms* (pp. 232–254). New York: Routledge.

Fiorello, C. A., & Primerano, D. (2005). Research into practice: Catell-Horn-Carroll cognitive assessment in practice: Eligibility and program development issues. *Psychology in the Schools, 42*(5), 525–537.

Fiorello, C. A., Hale, J. B., & Snyder, L. E. (2006). Cognitive hypothesis testing and response to intervention for children with reading problems. *Psychology in the Schools, 43*(8), 835–853.

Fiorello, C. A., Hale, J. B., Snyder, L. E., Forrest, E., & Teodori, A. (2008). Validating individual differences through examination of converging psychometric and neuropsychological models of cognitive functioning. *Applied Cognitive Research in K–3 Classrooms,* 232–254.

Frank, T. (1998). Hearing difficulties. In J. Salvia & J. E. Ysseldyke, *Assessment* (7th ed.) (pp. 409–430). Boston: Houghton Mifflin.

Frostig, M., & Horne, D. (1964). *The Frostig program for the development of visual perception.* Chicago: Follett.

Frostig, M., Lefever, W., & Whittlesey, J. R. B. (1966). *Developmental test of visual perception* (rev.). Palo Alto, CA: Consulting Psychologists Press.

Fuchs, D., Deshler, D., & Reschly, D. Learning Disabilities. Learning Disabilities Quarterly, 27(4), 189

Fuchs, D., Mock, M., Morgan, P. L., & Young, C. L. (2003). Responsiveness-to-instruction: Definitions, evidence, and implications for the learning disabilities construct. *Learning Disabilities Research & Practice, 18*(3), 157–171.

Fuchs, L. S. (2003). Assessing intervention responsiveness: Conceptual and technical issues. *Learning Disabilities Research & Practice, 18*(3), 172–186.

Goldman, R. M., Fristoe, M., & Woodcock, R. W. (1970). *Goldman-Fristoe-Woodcock test of auditory discrimination.* Circle Pines, MN: American Guidance Service.

Goldman, R. M., Fristoe, M., & Woodcock, R. W. (1976). *Goldman-Fristoe-Woodcock auditory skills test battery.* Circle Pines, MN: American Guidance Service.

Green, W. W. (1981). Hearing disorders. In A. E. Blackhurst & W. H. Berdine (Eds.), *Introduction to special education* (pp. 154–205). Boston: Little, Brown.

Hallahan, D. P. (Ed.). (1980). Teaching exceptional children to use cognitive strategies [Entire issue]. *Exceptional Education Quarterly, 1*(1).

Hallahan, D. P., & Cruickshank, W. M. (1973). *Psychoeducational foundations of learning disabilities.* Upper Saddle River, NJ: Prentice Hall.

Hallahan, D. P., & Reeve, R. E. (1980). Selective attention and distractibility. In B. K. Keogh (Ed.), *Advances in special education* (Vol. 1, pp. 141–181). Greenwich, CT: J.A.I.

Hammill, D. D. (1998). *Detroit tests of learning aptitude* (4th ed.). Austin, TX: PRO-ED.

Hammill, D. D., & Bryant, B. R. (1998). *Learning disabilities diagnostic inventory.* Austin, TX: PRO-ED.

Hammill, D. D., & Bryant, B. R. (2005). *Detroit tests of learning aptitude–Primary* (3rd ed.). Austin, TX: PRO-ED.

Hammill, D. D., & Larsen, S. C. (1974a). The effectiveness of psycholinguistic training. *Exceptional Children, 41,* 5–15.

Hammill, D. D., & Wiederholt, J. L. (1972). Review of the Frostig Visual Perception Test and the related training program. In L. Mann & D. Sabatino (Eds.), *The first review of special education, Volume I* (pp. 33–48). Philadelphia: Journal of Special Education Press.

Hammill, D. D., Bryant, B., & Pearson, N. (1998). *Hammill multiability intelligence test.* Austin, TX: PRO-ED.

Hammill, D. D., Goodman, L., & Wiederholt, J. L. (1974). Visual-motor processes: What successes have we had in training them? *The Reading Teacher, 27,* 469–478.

Hammill, D. D., Hresko, W. P., Ammer, J. J., Cronin, M. E., & Quinby, S. S. (1998). *Hammill multiability achievement test.* Austin, TX: PRO-ED.

Hammill, D. D., Mather, N., & Roberts, R. (2001). *Illinois test of psycholinguistic abilities* (3rd ed.). Austin, TX: PRO-ED.

Hammill, D. D., Pearson, N. A., & Voress, J. K. (1993). *Developmental test of visual perception* (2nd ed.). Austin, TX: PRO-ED.

Hammill, D. D., Pearson, N. A., & Voress, J. K. (1996). *Test of visual-motor integration.* Austin, TX: PRO-ED.

Hammill, D. D., Wiederholt, J. L., & Allen, E. A. (2006). *Test of silent contextual reading fluency.* Austin, TX: PRO-ED.

Hammill, D., Mather, N., & Roberts, R. (2001). *Illinois Test of Psycholinguistic Abilities—Third Edition.* Austin, TX: PRO-ED.

Hammill, D.D, Pearson, N.A., Voress, J.K. (2014). *Developmental Test of Visual Perception, 3rd ed.* Austin, TX: Pro-ed.

Heward, W. L. (2006). *Exceptional children* (8th ed.). Upper Saddle River, NJ: Merrill/Prentice Hall.

IDEA 2004 Final Regulations. (2006, August 14). *Federal Register, 71*(156). Retrieved August 21, 2006, from *http://www.ed.gov/policy/speced/ idea/idea2004.html*

Johnson, E., Humphrey, M., Mellard, D., Woods, K., & Swanson, H. L. (2010). Cognitive processing deficits and students with specific learning disabilities: A selective meta-analysis of the literature. *Learning Disability Quarterly, 33*(1), 3–18.

Kaufman, A.S., & Kaufman, N.L. (2014). *Kaufman Test of Educational Achievement,* (3rd ed.). Bloomington, MN: NCS Pearson.

Kaufman, A.S., & Kaufman, N.L. (2014). *Kaufman Test of Educational Achievement, 3rd ed.* Bloomington, MN: NCS Pearson.

Kavale, K. (1981). Functions of the Illinois Test of Psycholinguistic Abilities (ITPA): Are they trainable? *Exceptional Children, 47, 496–510.*

Kavale, K. A. (2005). Identifying specific learning disability: Is responsiveness to intervention the answer? *Journal of Learning Disabilities, 39,* 553–562.

Kirk, S. A., & Chalfant, J. C. (1984). *Academic and developmental learning disabilities.* Denver, CO: Love.

Kirk, S. A., & Kirk, W. D. (1971). *Psycholinguistic learning disabilities: Diagnosis and remediation.* Urbana: University of Illinois Press.

Kirk, S. A., McCarthy, J. J., & Kirk, W. D. (1968). *Illinois test of psycholinguistic abilities* (rev. ed.). Urbana, IL: University of Illinois Press.

Koppitz, E. M. (1963). *The Bender gestalt test for young children.* New York: Grune & Stratton.

Koppitz, E. M. (1975). *The Bender gestalt test for young children, Volume II: Research and application, 1963–1973.* New York: Grune & Stratton.

Larrivee, B. (1981). Modality preference as a model for differentiating beginning reading instruction: A review of the issues. *Learning Disability Quarterly, 4,* 180–188.

Larsen, S. C., & Hammill, D. D. (1975). Relationship of selected visual perceptual abilities to school learning. *Journal of Special Education, 9,* 282–291.

Larsen, S. C., Parker, R. R., & Hammill, D. D. (1982). Effectiveness of psycholinguistic training: A response to Kavale. *Exceptional Children, 49, 60–66.*

Larsen, S., Rogers, D., Sowell, V, The use of selected perceptual tests in differentiating between normal and learning disabled children. *Journal of Learning Disabilities, 1976, 9,* 85–90.

Learning Disabilities Association. (1990). *Eligibility for services for persons with specific learning disabilities.* A position paper of the Learning Disabilities Association. Pittsburgh, PA: Author.

Learning Disabilities Association. (2015). *Definition of learning disabilities.* Retrieved December 14, 2015, from *http://ldaamerica.org/sld-evaluation-linking-cognitive-assessment-data-to-learning-strategies.*

Lcnz, B. K., Ellis, E. S., & Scanlon, D. (1996). *Teaching learning strategies to adolescents and adults with learning disabilities.* Austin, TX: PRO-ED.

Lerner, J. (2000). *Learning disabilities* (8th ed.). Boston: Houghton Mifflin.

Lerner, J. (2006). *Learning disabilities and related disorder: characteristics and teaching strategies.* Boston: Houghton Mifflin.

Lerner, J., with Kline, F. (2006). *Learning disabilities and related disorders* (10th ed.). Boston: Houghton Mifflin.

Levine, M. D., Clarke, S., & Ferb, T. (1981). The child as a diagnostic participant: Helping students describe their learning disorders. *Journal of Learning Disabilities, 14,* 527–530.

Lewis, R. (1983). Learning disabilities and reading: Instructional recommendations from current research. *Exceptional Children, 50,* 230–240.

Lewis, R. B. (1988). Learning disabilities. In E. W. Lynch & R. B. Lewis (Eds.), *Exceptional children and adults* (pp. 352–406). Glenview, IL: Scott, Foresman.

Marston, D., Muyskens, P., Lau, M., & Canter, A. (2003). Problem-solving model for decision-making with high-incidence disabilities: The Minneapolis experience. *Learning Disabilities Research & Practice, 18*(3), 187–200.

Mascolo, J. T., Alfonso, V. C., & Flanagan, D. P. (2014) *Essentials of planning, selecting, and tailoring interventions for unique learners.* New York: John Wiley & Sons.

Mather, N., & Healey, W. C. (1989). Deposing aptitude-achievement discrepancy as the imperial criterion for learning disabilities. *Learning Disabilities, 1*(2), 40–48.

McCarney, S. B. (1996). *The learning disability evaluation scale–Renormed.* Columbia, MO: Hawthorne Educational Services.

McCarney, S. B., & Arthaud, T. J. (2007). *Learning Disability Evaluation Scale-Renormed—Second Edition.* Columbia, MO: Hawthorne Educational Services.

McCarney, S. B., & Bauer, A. M. (1991). *The parent's guide to learning disabilities.* Columbia, MO: Hawthorne Educational Services.

McCarney, S.B., & Bauer, A.M. (2006). *The Learning Disability Intervention Manual, Revised Ed.* Columbia, MO: Hawthorne Educational Services, Inc.

McCarney, S.B., Bauer, A.M., & House, S.N. (2006). *The Learning Disability Intervention Manual, Revised Ed.* Columbia, MO: Hawthorne Educational Services, Inc.

Meltzer, L. J. (1987). *Surveys of problem-solving & educational skills.* Cambridge, MA: Educators Publishing Service.

Michael, W. B., Michael, J. J., & Zimmerman, W. S. (1985). *Study attitudes and methods survey.* San Diego, CA: EdITS.

Minskoff, E. H. (1975). Research on psycholinguistic training: Critique and guidelines. *Exceptional Children, 42,* 136–144.

Moores, D. F., & Moores, J. M. (1988). Hearing disorders. In E. W. Lynch & R. B. Lewis (Eds.), *Exceptional children and adults* (pp. 276–317). Glenview, IL: Scott, Foresman.

Myers, I. B., & Myers, P. B. (1980). *Gifts Differing.* Palo Alto, CA: Consulting.

National Center for Response to Intervention. (2011). RTI State Database. Retrieved from *http://state.rti4success.org/index.php?option=com_chart&order=sld&asc=desc*

National Joint Committee on Learning Disabilities. (1994). *Collective perspectives on issues affecting learning disabilities.* Austin, TX: PRO-ED.

National Joint Committee on Learning Disabilities. (2005). *Responsiveness to intervention and learning disabilities.* PDF file *Njcld_rti2005.pdf* retrieved March 27, 2007, from *http://www.ncld. org/index.php?option=content&task=view&id=500*

National Joint Committee on Learning Disabilities. (2010). *Comprehensive assessment and evaluation of students with learning disabilities.* Retrieved from *www.ldonline.org/njcld*

National Joint Committee on Learning Disabilities. Learning Disabilities: Implications for Policy Regarding Research and Practice—A Report by the National Joint Committee on Learning Disabilities. (2011). *Learning Disability Quarterly, 34* (4), 237–241.

National Society to Prevent Blindness. (1977). *Signs of possible eye trouble in children* (Pub. G-112). New York: Author.

Newcomer, P. L., & Hammill, D. D. (1975). ITPA and academic achievement: A survey. *The Reading Teacher, 28,* 731–741.

Newcomer, P. L., & Hammill, D. D. (1976). *Psycholinguistics in the schools.* New York: Merrill/Macmillan.

O'Connor, R. E., Jenkins, J. R., Leicester, N., & Slocum, T. A. (1993). Teaching phonological awareness to young children with learning disabilities. *Exceptional Children, 59,* 532–546.

Office of Special Education Programs (OSEP), *56 IDELR* (2006).

President's Commission on Excellence in Special Education. (2002). *A new era: Revitalizing special education for children and their families.* Washington, DC: U.S. Department of Education Office of Special Education and Rehabilitative Services.

Pressley, M., Borkowski, J. G., Forrest-Pressley, D., Gaskins, I. W., & Wile, D. (1993). Closing thoughts on strategy instruction for individuals: The good information-processing perspective. In L. J. Meltzer (Ed.), *Strategy assessment and instruction for students with learning disabilities* (pp. 355–377). Austin, TX: PRO-ED. Psychologists Press.

Reschly, D. J. (2005). Learning disabilities identification: Primary intervention, secondary intervention, and then what? *Journal of Learning Disabilities, 39,* 510–515.

Reynolds, C. R., & Bigler, E. D. (1994). *Test of memory and learning.* Austin, TX: PRO-ED.

Reynolds, C. R., Pearson, N. A., & Voress, J. K. (2002). *Developmental test of visual perception-adolescent and adult.* Austin, TX: PRO-ED.

Reynolds, C., & Voress, J. (2007). *Test of memory and learning (TOMAL-2)* (2nd ed.). Austin, TX: PRO-ED.

Reynolds, W. M. (1987). *Wepman's auditory discrimination test manual* (2nd ed.). Los Angeles: Western Psychological Services.

Ringler, L. H., & Smith, I. (1973). Learning modality and word recognition of first grade children. *Journal of Learning Disabilities, 6,* 307–312.

Roach, E. G., & Kephart, N. D. (1966). *The Purdue perceptual-motor survey.* New York: Merrill/Macmillan.

Rose, M. D., Cundick, B. P., & Higbee, K. L. (1983). Verbal rehearsal and visual imagery: Mnemonic aids for learning disabled children. *Journal of Learning Disabilities, 16,* 352–354.

Salvia, J., & Ysseldyke, J. E. (1998). *Assessment* (7th ed.). Boston: Houghton Mifflin.

Schrank, F. A., Mather, N., & McGrew, K. S. (2014a). *Woodcock-Johnson IV Tests of Achievement.* Rolling Meadows, IL: Riverside.

Schrank, F. A., Mather, N., & McGrew, K. S. (2014b). *Woodcock-Johnson IV Tests of Oral Language.* Rolling Meadows, IL: Riverside.

Schrank, F. A., McGrew, K. S., & Mather N. (2015). *The WJ IV Gf-Gc Composite and its use in the identification of specific learning disabilities* (Woodcock-Johnson IV Assessment Service Bulletin No. 3). Rolling Meadows, IL: Riverside.

Schrank, F. A., McGrew, K. S., & Mather, N. (2014a). *Woodcock-Johnson IV.* Rolling Meadows, IL: Riverside.

Schrank, F. A., McGrew, K. S., & Mather, N. (2014b). *Woodcock-Johnson IV Tests of Cognitive Abilities.* Rolling Meadows, IL: Riverside.

Schumaker, J. B., Deshler, D. D., Alley, G. R., & Warner, M. M. (1983). Toward the development of an intervention model for learning disabled adolescents: The University of Kansas Institute. *Exceptional Education Quarterly, 4*(1), 45–74.

Sloan, W. (1954). *Lincoln-Oseretsky motor development scale.* Chicago: Stoelting.

Smolensky, J., Bonvechio, L. R., Whitlock, R. E., & Girard, M. A. (1968). *School health problems.* Palo Alto, CA: Fearon.

Snider, V. E. (1992). Learning styles and learning to read: A critique. *Remedial and Special Education, 54,* 228–239.

Snider, V. E. (1992). Learning styles and learning to read: A critique. *Remedial and Special Education, 13*(1), 6–18.

Snow, C. E., Burns, S., & Griffin, P. (Eds.). (1998). *Preventing reading difficulties in young children*. Washington, DC: National Academic Press.

Social Security Administration. (2002). *2.00 Special senses and speech*. Retrieved December, 14, 2015, from *https://www.ssa.gov/disability/professionals/bluebook/2.00-SpecialSensesandSpeech-Adult.htm*.

Sowell V., Parker R., Poplin M., & Larsen J. The effects of psycholinguistic training on improving psycholinguistic skills. *Learning Disability Quarterly*, 1979, 2(3), 69–77.

Sowell V., Parker R., Poplin M., Larsen S. (1979). The effects of psycholinguistic training on improving psycholinguistic skills. *Learning Disability Quarterly*, 2, 69–77.

Stahl, S. (1988). Is there evidence to support matching reading styles and initial reading methods? *Phi Delta Kappan, 70*, 317–322.

Stephens, T. M., Blackhurst, A., & Magliocca, L. (1982). *Teaching mainstreamed students*. New York: Wiley.

Sternberg, L., & Taylor, R. (2982). The insignificance of psycholinguistic training: A reply to Kavale. *Exceptional Children, 49*, 254–256.

Stroud, K. C., & Reynolds, C. R. (2006). School motivation and learning strategies inventory. Los Angeles: Western Psychological Services.

Swanson, H. L. (1989). Strategy instruction: Overview of principles and procedures for effective use. *Learning Disabilities Quarterly, 12*, 3–14.

Swanson, H. L. (1993). Principles and procedures in strategy use. In L. J. Meltzer (Ed.), *Strategy assessment and instruction for students with learning disabilities* (pp. 61–92). Austin, TX: PRO-ED.

Swanson, H. L. (1999). *Interventions for students with learning disabilities*. New York: Guilford.

Swanson, H. L., & Cooney, J. B. (1996). Learning disabilities and memory. In D. K. Reid, W. P. Hresko, & H. L. Swanson (Eds.), *Cognitive approaches to learning disabilities* (3rd ed.) (pp. 287–314). Austin, TX: PRO-ED.

Tarver, S. G., & Dawson, M. M. (1978). Modality preference and the teaching of reading: A review. *Journal of Learning Disabilities, 11*, 5–17.

Torgesen, J. K. (1977). The role of nonspecific factors in the task performance of learning disabled children: A theoretical assessment. *Journal of Learning Disabilities, 10*, 5–17.

Torgesen, J. K. (1980). Conceptual and educational implications of the use of efficient task strategies by learning disabled children. *Journal of Learning Disabilities, 13*, 364–371.

Torgesen, J. K., & Goldman, T. (1977). Rehearsal and short-term memory in reading disabled children. *Child Development, 48*, 56–61.

Torgesen, J.K. (1979). What shall we do with psychological processes? *Journal of Learning Disabilities, 12*, 514–522.

U.S. Department of Education, Office of Special Education Programs. (2006). *Topic Briefs: IDEA Regulations: Identification of Specific Learning Disabilities*. Retrieved December, 14, 2015, from *http://idea.ed.gov/explore/view/p/%2Croot%2Cdynamic%2CTopicalBrief%2C23%2C*.

Ulrich, D. A. (2000). *Test of gross motor development* (2nd ed.). Austin, TX: PRO-ED.

Vaughn, S., & Fuchs, L. S. (2003). Redefining learning disabilities as inadequate response to instruction: The promise and potential problems. *Learning Disabilities Research & Practice, 18*(3), 137–146.

Vaughn, S., & Fuchs, L. S. (2006). A response to "Competing views: A dialogue on response to intervention." *Assessment for Effective Intervention, 32*(1), 58–61.

Vaughn, S., Linan-Thompson, S., & Hickman, P. (2003). Response to instruction as a means of identifying students with reading/learning disabilities. *Exceptional Children, 69*, 391–409.

Vellutino, F., Scanlon, D., & Lyon, G. R. (2000). Differentiating between difficult-to-remediate and readily remediated poor readers: More evidence against the IQ-achievement discrepancy definition of reading disability. *Journal of Learning Disabilities, 33*, 223–238.

Wagner, R. K., & Torgesen, J. K. (1987). The nature of phonological processing and its causal role in the acquisition of reading skills. *Psychological Bulletin, 101*, 192–212.

Wagner, R. K., Torgesen, J. K., & Rashotte, C. (1993). *The efficacy of phonological awareness training for early reading achievement: A meta-analysis*. Unpublished manuscript, Florida State University.

Wallace, G., & McLoughlin, J. (1979). *Learning disabilities: Concepts and characteristics* (2nd ed.). New York: Merrill/Macmillan.

Waugh, R. P. (1973). Relationship between modality preference and performance. *Exceptional Children, 6*, 465–469.

Wechsler D. (2009). *Wechsler Memory Scale–Fourth Edition*. San Antonio, TX: Pearson.

Wechsler D. (2014a). *Wechsler Intelligence Scale for Children (5th ed.)*. Bloomington, MN: PsychCorp.

Wechsler, D. (1997b). *Wechsler memory scale–Third edition*. San Antonio, TX: Psychological Corp.

Wechsler, D. (2014b). *Technical and interpretive manual supplement: Special group validity studies with other measures and additional tables*. NCS Pearson.

Wepman J., Reynolds W. N. (1987). *Wepman's Auditory Discrimination Test* (2nd ed.). Los Angeles, CA: Western Psychological Services.

Wepman, J. M. (1975). *Auditory discrimination test* (rev. 1973). Palm Springs, CA: Research Associates.

Wiederholt, J. L., & Hammill, D. D. (1971). Use of the Frostig-Horne perception program in the urban school. *Psychology in the Schools, 8*, 268–274.

Wong, B. Y. L. (1980). Activating the inactive learner: Use of questions/prompts to enhance comprehension and retention of implied information in learning disabled children. *Learning Disability Quarterly, 3*(1), 29–37.

CHAPTER 10

Achenbach, T. M. (2001). *Child behavior checklist/6–18.* Burlington, VT: Research Center for Children, Youth, and Families.

Achenbach, T.M., & Reescorla, L.A. (2001). *Manual for the ASEBA school-ages forms and profiles.* Burlington: University of Vermont, Research Center for Children, Youth, & Families.

Affleck, J. Q., Lowenbraun, S., & Archer, A. (1980). *Teaching the mildly handicapped in the regular classroom* (2nd ed.). New York: Merrill/Macmillan.

Alberto, P. A., & Troutman, A. C. (1990). *Applied behavior analysis for teachers* (3rd ed.). Upper Saddle River, NJ: Merrill/Prentice Hall.

Algozzine, R., Ruhl, K., & Ramsey, R. (1991). *Behaviorally disordered? Assessment for identification and instruction.* Reston, VA: Council for Exceptional Children.

American Psychiatric Association. (1994). *Diagnostic and statistical manual of mental disorders, Fourth Edition.* Washington, DC: Author.

American Psychiatric Association. (2013). *Diagnostic and statistical manual of mental Disorders—Fifth edition.* Washington, DC: Author.

Artesani, A. J. (2001). *Understanding the purpose of challenging behavior.* Upper Saddle River, NJ: Merrill/Prentice Hall.

Asher, S. R., & Taylor, A. R. (1981). Social outcomes of mainstreaming: Sociometric assessment and beyond. *Exceptional Education Quarterly, 1,* 13–30.

Bagley, M. T., & Greene, J. F. (1981). *Peer attitudes toward the handicapped scale.* Austin, TX: PRO-ED.

Barnhill, G., Polloway, E. & Sumutka, B. (2011). A survey of personnel preparation practices in autism spectrum disorders. *Focus on Autism and other Developmental Disabilities 26* (2), 75–86.

Battle, J. (2002). *Culture-free self-esteem inventories* (3rd ed.). Austin, TX: PRO-ED.

Beyda Lorie, S. (2010). Behavior assessment. In E. P. Kritikos, *Special education assessment: Issues and strategies affecting today's classrooms.* Columbus, OH: Pearson.

Borich, G. D. (1999). *Observation skills for effective teaching* (3rd ed.). Upper Saddle River, NJ: Merrill/Prentice Hall.

Bracken, B. A. (1992). *Multidimensional self-concept scale.* Austin, TX: PRO-ED.

Brophy, J., & Good, T. (1969). *Teacher-child dyadic interaction: A manual for coding classroom behavior* (Report Series No. 127). Austin, TX: Research & Development Center for Teacher Education, University of Texas.

Brown, L. J., Black, D. D., & Downs, J. C. (1984). *School social skills rating scale.* East Aurora, NY: Slosson.

Brown, L. L., & Alexander, J. (1991). *Self-esteem index.* Austin, TX: PRO-ED.

Brown, L., & Hammill, D. D. (1990). *Behavior Rating Profile (2nd Ed.).* Austin, TX: Pro-Ed.

Brown, L., & Hammill, D. D. (1990). *Behavior rating profile.* (2nd ed.) Austin, TX: PRO-ED.

Bruininks, R. H., Rynders, J. E., & Gross, J. C. (1974). Social acceptance of mildly retarded pupils in resource rooms and regular classes. *American Journal of Mental Deficiency, 78,* 377–383.

Burks, H. F., & Gruber, C. P. (2006). *Burks behavior ratings scales* (2nd ed.). Los Angeles: Western Psychological Services.

Chandler, L. K., & Dahlquist, C. M. (2002). *Functional assessment.* Upper Saddle River, NJ: Merrill/Prentice Hall.

Chapman, R. N., Larsen, S. C., & Parker, R. M. (1979). Interactions for first-grade teachers with learning disordered children. *Journal of Learning Disabilities, 12,* 225–230.

Clarizio, H. F., & McCoy, G. F. (1983). *Behavior disorders in children* (3rd ed.). New York: Harper & Row.

Conners, C. K. (2008). *Conners rating scales* (3rd ed.). North Tonawanda, NY: Multi-Health Systems.

Cooper, J. O. (1981). *Measuring behavior* (2nd ed.). New York: Merrill/Macmillan.

Cooper, J. O., Heron, T. E., & Heward, W. L. (1987). *Applied behavior analysis.* New York: Merrill/Macmillan.

Coopersmith, S. (1981). *Coopersmith self-esteem inventories.* Palo Alto, CA: Consulting Psychologists Press.

Coopersmith, S., & Gilberts, R. (1981). *Behavioral academic self-esteem, A rating scale.* Palo Alto, CA: Consulting Psychologists Press.

Council for Exceptional Children. (1992). *Children with ADD: A shared responsibility.* Reston, VA: Author.

Eaves, R. C. (1982). A proposal for the diagnosis of emotional disturbance. *Journal of Special Education, 16,* 463–476.

Epstein, M. H., & Cullinan, D. (2010). *Scales for assessing emotional disturbance* (2nd ed.). Austin, TX: PRO-ED.

Epstein, M. H., & Sharma, J. (2004). *Behavioral and emotional rating scale* (2nd ed.). Boston. Houghton Mifflin-Harcourt.

Estes, T. H., Estes, J. J., Richards, H. C., & Roettger, D. (1981). *Estes attitude scales.* Austin, TX: PRO-ED.

Fahmie, T. A., & Iwata, B. A. (2011). Topographical and functional properties of precursors to severe problem behavior. *Journal of Applied Behavior Analysis, 44,* 993–997.

Federal Register, 2006, §300.8(c)(4).

Fitts, W. H., & Warren, W. L. (1996). *Tennessee self-concept scale* (2nd ed.). Los Angeles: Western Psychological Services.

Fitzsimmons, M. K. (1998). *Functional behavior assessment and behavior intervention plans (ERIC EC Digest #E571).* Reston, VA: ERIC Clearinghouse on Disabilities and Gifted Education. Retrieved July 4, 1999, from *http://www.ericec.org/digests/e571.htm*

Flanders, N. (1970). *Analyzing teacher behavior.* Menlo Park, CA: Addison-Wesley.

Gilliam, J. E. (2015). *Attention-deficit/hyperactivity disorder test* (2nd ed.). Austin, TX: PRO-ED.

Greenwood, C. R., Carta, J. J., Kamps, D., & Delquadri, J. (1997). *Ecobehavioral assessment systems software (EBASS), practitioner's manual* (version 3.0). Kansas City, KS: Juniper Gardens Children's Project, University of Kansas.

Gresham, F. M., & Elliott, S. N. (1990). *Social skills rating system.* Circle Pines, MN: American Guidance Service.

Gresham, F. M., Elliott, S. N., & Evans-Fernandez, S. (1992). *Student self-concept scale.* Circle Pines, MN: American Guidance Service.

Hallahan, D. P., & Kauffman, J. M. (1991). *Exceptional children* (5th ed.). Upper Saddle River, NJ: Prentice Hall.

Hanley, G. P. (2012). Functional assessment of problem behavior: Dispelling myths, overcoming implementation obstacles, and developing new lore. *Behavior Analysis in Practice, 5*(1), 54–72.

Hutton, J. B., & Roberts, T. G. (1986). *Social-emotional dimension scale.* Austin, TX: PRO-ED.

Hutton, J. B., & Roberts, T. J. (2004). *Social-emotional dimension scale* (2nd ed.). Austin, TX: PRO-ED.

Iwata, B. A., & Dozier C. L. (2008). Clinical application of functional analysis methodology. *Behavior Analysis in Practice, 1*, 3–9.

Kimball, S.T. (1974). *Culture and the Educative Process: An Anthropological Perspective.* New York: Teachers College Press.

Kroth, R. L. (1975). *Communicating with parents of exceptional children.* Denver, CO: Love.

Lambert, N., Hartsough, C., & Sandoval, J. (1990). *Children's attention and adjustment survey.* Circle Pines, MN: American Guidance Service.

Lerner, J. W., & Lerner, S. R. (1991). Attention deficit disorder: Issues and questions. *Focus on Exceptional Children, 24*, 1–17.

Lerner, J. W., & Lowenthal, B. (1993). Attention deficit disorders: New responsibilities for the special educator. *Learning Disabilities, 4*(1), 1–8.

Lerner, J. W., Lowenthal, B., & Lerner, S. R. (1995). *Attention deficit disorders.* Pacific Grove, CA: Brooks/Cole.

Lewis, R. B., & Doorlag, D. H. (2006). *Teaching special students in general education classrooms* (7th ed.). Upper Saddle River, NJ: Merrill/Prentice Hall.

Lewis, T. J., & Sugai, G. (1999). Effective behavior support: A systems approach to proactive schoolwide management. *Focus on Exceptional Children, 31*(6), 1–24.

LRE for LIFE Project. (1997). *Suggested guidelines for implementing positive behavior support strategies.* Knoxville, TN: Author. Retrieved July 4, 1999, from *http://web.ce.utk.edu/lre/full/sugguide.htm*

McArney, S. B., & Arthaud, T. J. (2014). *Behavior evaluation scale, fourth edition manual.* Columbia, MO: Hawthorne.

McCarney, S. B., & Arthaud, T. J. (2001). *Emotional and behavior problem scale–Second edition.* Columbia, MO: Hawthorne Educational Services.

McCarney, S. B., & Arthaud, T. J. (2013). *Attention deficit disorders evaluation scale* (4th ed.). Columbia, MO: Hawthorne Educational Services.

Michael, W. B., Smith, R. A., & Michael, J. J. (1984). *Dimensions of self-concept.* San Diego, CA: EdITS.

Miller, L. C. (1977). *School behavior checklist.* Los Angeles: Western Psychological Services.

Mooney, R. L., & Gordon, L. V. (1950). *The Mooney problem check lists* (rev. ed.). San Antonio, TX: Psychological Corp.

Naglieri, J. A., LeBuffe, P. A., & Pfeiffer, S. I. (1993). *Devereux behavior rating scales–School form.* San Antonio, TX: Psychological Corp.

Neeper, R., Lahey, B. B., & Frick, P. J. (1990). *Comprehensive behavior rating scale for children.* San Antonio, TX: Psychological Corp.

O'Neill, R.E., Horner, R.H., Albin, R.W., Sprague, J., Storey, K., & Newton, J.S. (1997). *Functional assessment and program development for problem behavior: A practical handbook.* Pacific Grove, CA: Brooks/Cole.

Oosterhof, A. (2003). *Developing and using classroom assessments* (3rd ed.). Upper Saddle River, NJ: Merrill/Prentice Hall.

Ortiz, A. A. (1991, November). Testimony before the CEC Task Force on children with Attention Deficit Disorders, New Orleans.

PACER Center. (1994). *What is functional assessment?* Minneapolis, MN: Author. Retrieved July 4, 1999, from *http://www.pacer.org.parent/function.htm*

Piers, E. V., & Herzberg, D. S. (2002). *Piers-Harris children's self-concept scale, Second edition.* Los Angeles: Western Psychological Services.

Popham, W. J., & Baker, E. L. (1970). *Systematic instruction.* Upper Saddle River, NJ: Prentice Hall.

Putnam, M. L., Deshler, D. D., & Schumaker, J. B. (1993). The investigation of setting demands: A missing link in learning strategy instruction. In L. J. Meltzer (Ed.), *Strategy assessment and instruction for students with learning disabilities* (pp. 325–353). Austin, TX: PRO-ED.

Quay, H. C., & Peterson, D. R. (1983, 1987). *Revised behavior problem checklist.* Coral Gables, FL: University of Miami.

Quay, H. C., & Peterson, D. R. (1996). *Revised behavior problem checklist-PAR edition.* Lutz, FL: PAR.

Quinn, M. M., Gable, R. A., Rutherford, R. B., Nelson, C. M., & Howell, K. (1998). *Addressing student problem behavior: An IEP team's introduction to functional behavioral assessment and behavior intervention plans* (2nd ed.). Washington, DC: Center for Effective Collaboration and Practice. Retrieved July 5, 1999, from *http://www.air-dc.org/cecp/ resources/ problembehavior/main.htm*

Reynolds, C. R., & Kamphaus, R. W. (2015). *BASC-3: Behavior assessment system for children, third edition manual.* Columbus, OH: Pearson.

Reynolds, C. R., & Kamphaus, R. W. (2016). *BASC Flex Monitor.* Columbus, OH: Pearson.

Reynolds, M. C., & Birch, J. W. (1977). *Teaching exceptional children in all America's schools.* Reston, VA: Council for Exceptional Children.

Shaywitz, S. E., & Shaywitz, B. A. (Eds.). (1992). *Attention deficit disorder comes of age.* Austin, TX: PRO-ED.

Shea, T. M. (1978). *Teaching children and youth with behavior disorders.* St. Louis: Mosby.

Shippen, M. E., Simpson, R. G., & Criters, S. A. (2003). A practical guide to functional behavioral analysis. *Teaching Exceptional Children, 35* (5), 36–44.

Silver, L. B. (1992). *Attention-deficit hyperactivity disorder.* Washington, DC: American Psychiatric Press.

Smith, R. M., Neisworth, J. T., & Greer, J. B. (1978). *Evaluating educational environments.* New York: Merrill/ Macmillan.

Sparrow, S. S., Balla, D. A., & Cicchetti, D. V. (1998). *Vineland social-emotional early childhood scales.* Circle Pines, MN: American Guidance Service.

Sulzer-Azaroff, B., & Mayer, G. R. (1977). *Applying behavior-analysis procedures with children and youth.* New York: Holt, Rinehart & Winston.

Swap, S. M. (1974). Disturbing classroom behaviors: A developmental and ecological view. *Exceptional Children, 41,* 163–172.

Thurman, S. K. (1977). Congruence of behavioral ecologies: A model for special education programming. *Journal of Special Education, 11,* 329–334.

Turnbull, A. P., & Schulz, J. B. (1979). *Mainstreaming handicapped students.* Boston: Allyn & Bacon.

Vannest, K.J. Reynolds, C. & Kamphaus, R. (2013) BASC-3 Manual. Pearson.

Walker, H. M. (1983). *Walker problem behavior identification checklist* (rev.). Los Angeles: Western Psychological Services.

Wallace, G., & Kauffman, J. M. (1986). *Teaching students with learning and behavior problems* (3rd ed.). New York: Merrill/Macmillan.

Witt, J. C., Daly, E. J., & Noell, G. H. (2000). *Functional assessments.* Longmont, CO: Sopris West.

Ysseldyke, J. E., & Christenson, S. (1993). *The instructional environment system-II.* Longmont, CO: Sopris West.

Ysseldyke, J. E., & Christenson, S. (2002). *Functional assessment of academic behavior.* Longmont, CO: Sopris West.

CHAPTER 11

Achievement. Rolling Meadows, IL: Riverside.

Blankenship, C. S. (1985). Using curriculum-based assessment data to make instructional decisions. *Exceptional Children, 52,* 233–238.

Bodner, J. R., Clark, G. M., & Mellard, D. F. (1987). *State graduation policies and program practices related to high school special education programs: A national study.* Lawrence, KS: University of Kansas.

Bolt, S. E., & Thurlow, M. L. (2004). Five of the most frequently allowed testing accommodations in state policy: Synthesis of research. *Remedial and Special Education, 25,* 141–152.

Brigance, A. H. (1999). *BRIGANCE® diagnostic comprehensive inventory of basic skills–Revised.* North Billerica, MA: Curriculum Associates.

Burns, T. G. (2010). Wechsler Individual Assessment Test-III: What is the "gold standard" for measuring academic achievement? *Applied Neuropsychology, 17*(3), 234–236.

Chiu, S. W. T., & Pearson, P. D. (1999). *Synthesizing the effects of test accommodations for special education and limited English proficient students.* Paper presented at the National Conference on Large Scale Assessment, Snowbird, UT. (ERIC Document Reproduction Service No. ED 433362)

Connolly, A. J., Nachtman, W., & Pritchett, E. M. (1971, 1976). *Key Math diagnostic arithmetic test.* Circle Pines, MN: American Guidance Service.

Copperman, P. (1979). The achievement decline of the 1970s. *Phi Delta Kappan, 60,* 736–739.

Cox, M. L., Herner, J. G., Demczyk, M. J., & Nieberding, J. J. (2006). Provision of testing accommodations for students with disabilities on statewide assessments: Statistical links with participation and discipline rates. *Remedial and Special Education, 27,* 346–354.

Cummins, J. (1984). *Bilingualism and special education: Issues in assessment and pedagogy.* Clevedon, England: Multilingual Matters.

Dee, T., & Jacob, B. A. (2010). The impact of No Child Left Behind on students, teachers, and schools. *Brookings Papers on Economic Activity* (pp. 149–207).

Deno, S. L. (1985). Curriculum-based measurement: The emerging alternative. *Exceptional Children, 52,* 219–232.

Deno, S. L., & Fuchs, L. S. (1988). Developing curriculum-based measurement systems fordata-based special education problem solving. In E. L. Meyen, G. A. Vergason, & R. J. Whelan (Eds.), *Effective instructional strategies for exceptional children* (pp. 481–504). Denver, CO: Love.

Dunn, L. M., & Dunn, L. M. (1981). *Peabody picture vocabulary test–Revised.* Circle Pines, MN: American Guidance Service.

Dunn, L. M., & Markwardt, F. C. (1970). *Peabody individual achievement test.* Circle Pines, MN: American Guidance Service.

Ebel, R. L. (1977). *The uses of standardized testing.* Bloomington, IN: Phi Delta Kappa Educational Foundation.

Elliott, S. N., Kratochwill, T. R., & Gilbertson, A. (1998). *The assessment accommodation checklist.* Monterey, CA: CTB/McGraw-Hill.

Elliott, S. N., Kratochwill, T. R., & Schulte, A. G. (1998). The assessment accommodation checklist. *Teaching Exceptional Children, 31*(2), 10–14.

Erickson, R., Ysseldyke, J., Thurlow, M., & Elliott, J. (1998). Inclusive assessments and accountability systems. *Teaching Exceptional Children, 31*(2), 4–9.

Fuchs, D. S., & Fuchs, L. S. (1988). Evaluation of the Adaptive Learning Environment Model. *Exceptional Children, 55,* 115–127.

Fuchs, D., & Fuchs, L.S.(1994). Inclusive schools movement and the radicalization of special education reform. *Exceptional Children, 60,* 294–309.

Fuchs, L. S., Fuchs, D., Eaton, S., & Hamlett, C. (2003). *Dynamic assessment of test accommodations.* San Antonio, TX: Psychological Corp.

Gallup, G. H. (1978). The 10th annual Gallup poll of the public's attitudes toward public schools. *Phi Delta Kappan, 60,* 33–45.

Glascoe, F. P. (1999). *CIBS-R standardization and validation manual.* North Billerica, MA: Curriculum Associates.

Hallahan, D. P., Keller, C. E., McKinney, J. D., Lloyd, J. W., & Bryan, T. (1988). Examining the research base of the Regular Education Initiative: Efficacy studies and the Adaptive Learning Environments model. *Journal of Learning Disabilities, 21,* 29–35, 55.

Hammill, D. D., Bryant, B., & Pearson, N. (1998). *Hammill multiability intelligence test.* Austin, TX: PRO-ED.

Hammill, D. D., Hresko, W. P., Ammer, J. J., Cronin, M. E., & Quinby, S. S. (1998). *Hammill multiability achievement test.* Austin, TX: PRO-ED.

Hammill, D. D., Leigh, J. E., Pearson, N. A., & Maddox, T. (1998). *Basic school skills inventory* (3rd ed.). Austin, TX: PRO-ED.

Heumann, J. E., & Warlick, K. R. (2000, August 24). *Questions and answers about provisions in the Individuals with Disabilities Education Act Amendments of 1997 related to students with disabilities and state and district-wide assessments.* Washington, DC: Office of Special Education and Rehabilitative Services.

Hoover, H. D., Dunbar, S. B., & Frisbie, D. A. (2001, 2003). *Iowa tests of basic skills.* Rolling Meadows, IL: Riverside.

Hoover, H.D., Dunbar, S.B., Frisbie, D.A. (2001). *Iowa Tests of Basic Skills (ITBS) Forms A, B, and C.* Rolling Meadows, IL: Riverside Publishing Company.

Jastak, J. F., & Jastak, S. R. (1978). *Wide range achievement test* (1978 rev. ed.). Wilmington, DE: Jastak.

Kaufman, A. S., & Kaufman, N. C. (2004b*). Kaufman test of educational achievement, second edition.* Minneapolis, MN: Pearson Assessments.

LaForte, E. M., McGrew, K. S., & Schrank, F. A. (2014). *WJ IV technical abstract* (Woodcock-Johnson IV Assessment Service Bulletin No. 2). Rolling Meadows, IL: Riverside.

Maccow, G. (2011). Administration, Scoring, and Interpretation of Wechsler Individual Achievement Test-III. Accessed from *http://images.pearsonassessments.com/ Images/PDF/Webinar/WIAT-III_Administration_and_ Scoring_Handout_September_2011.pdf* on 01/24/17.

Markwardt, F. C. (1989). *Peabody individual achievement test–Revised.* Circle Pines, MN: American Guidance Service.

Markwardt, F. C. (1998). *Peabody individual achievement test–Revised/normative update.* Circle Pines, MN: American Guidance Service.

Marston, D., & Magnusson, D. (1985). Implementing curriculum-based measurement in special and regular education settings. *Exceptional Children, 52,* 266–276.

Mather, N., & Wendling, B. J. (2014a). Examiner's Manual. *Woodcock-Johnson IV tests of achievement.* Rolling Meadows, IL: Riverside.

Munday, L. A. (1979). Changing test scores, especially since 1970. *Phi Delta Kappan, 60,* 496–499.

National Commission on Excellence in Education. (1983). *A nation at risk: The imperative for educational reform.* Washington, DC: U.S. Government Printing Office.

National Research Council. (1997). *Executive summary: Educating one & all, students with disabilities and standards-based reform.* Washington, DC: National Academy Press.

Newcomer, P. L. (2001). *Diagnostic achievement battery* (3rd ed.). Austin, TX: PRO-ED.

Newcomer, P.L. (2014). *Diagnostic Achievement Battery* (4th ed.). Columbia, MO: Hawthorne Educational Services.

Newcomer, P.L., & Bryant, B.R. (1993). *Diagnostic Achievement Test for Adolescents (2nd ed.).* Austin, TX: Pro-Ed.

Perrone, V. (1977). *The abuses of standardized testing.* Bloomington, IN: Phi Delta Kappa Educational Foundation.

Peterson, J., Heistad, D., Peterson, D., & Reynolds, M. (1985). Montevideo individualized prescriptive instructional management system. *Exceptional Children, 52,* 239–243.

Pipho, C. (1978). Minimum competency testing in 1978: A look at state standards. *Phi Delta Kappan, 59,* 585–588.

Popham, W. J. (1978). The case for criterion-referenced measurements. *Educational Researcher, 7,* 6–10.

Rogers, C. M., Lazarus, S. S., & Thurlow, M. L. (2014). *A summary of the research on the effects of test accommodations, 2011–2012* (Synthesis Report 94). Minneapolis, MN:

University of Minnesota, National Center on Educational Outcomes.

Roszmann-Millican, M., & Walker, S. (1998, November). *Accommodating students with learning disabilities in statewide performance assessments.* Paper presented at the annual meeting of Council for Learning Disabilities, Albuquerque, NM.

Rudman, H. C. (1977). The standardized test flap. *Phi Delta Kappan, 59,* 178–185.

Salend, S. J. (1998). Using portfolios to assess student performance. *Teaching Exceptional Children, 31*(2), 36–43.

Schrank, F. A., Mather, N., & McGrew, K. S. (2014a). *Woodcock-Johnson IV Tests of Achievement.* Rolling Meadows, IL: Riverside.

Schumaker, J. B., & Deshler, D. D. (1988). Implementing the Regular Education Initiative in secondary schools: A different ball game. *Journal of Learning Disabilities, 21,* 36–42.

Stainback, S., & Stainback, W. (1988). Educating students with severe disabilities. *Teaching Exceptional Children, 21*(1), 16–19.

Stainback, S., & Stainback, W. (1992). *Curriculum considerations in inclusive classrooms.* Baltimore: Brookes.

Stainback, S., & Stainback, W. (Eds.). (1985). *Integrating students with severe handicaps into regular schools.* Reston, VA: Council for Exceptional Children.

Stainback, S., Stainback, W., & Forest, M. (Eds.). (1989). *Educating all students in the mainstream of regular education.* Baltimore: Brookes.

State-wide Assessment Programs. (1998, Spring). *Research Connections in Special Education (No. 2).* Reston, VA: ERIC/OSEP Special Project, ERIC Clearinghouse on Disabilities and Gifted Education, Council for Exceptional Children.

Towles-Reeves, E., Kleinert, H., & Muhomba, M. (2009). Alternative assessment: Have we learned anything new? *Exceptional Children, 75*(2), 233–252.

Tucker, J. A. (1985). Curriculum-based assessment: An introduction. *Exceptional Children, 52,* 199–204.

U.S. Department of Education, National Center for Education Statistics. (1995). *1994 U.S. Census Data.* Washington, DC: U.S. Government Printing Office.

U.S. Department of Education, National Center for Education Statistics. (2006). *The Condition of Education 2006* (NCES 2006–071). Washington, DC: U.S. Government Printing Office.

U.S. Department of Education. (2002a). *Parents' guide to No Child Left Behind.* Washington, DC: Author.

U.S. Department of Education. (2002b). *The No Child Left Behind Act of 2001, Executive summary.* Retrieved July 7, 2003, from *http://www.ed.gov/offices/OESE/esea/esec-summ .html*

Valenzuela, J. S. de, & Cervantes, H. T. (1998). Procedures and techniques for assessing the bilingual exceptional children. In L. M. Baca & H. T. Cervantes (Eds.), *The bilingual special-education interface* (pp. 168–187). Upper Saddle River, NJ: Merrill/Prentice Hall.

Wang, M. C., & Walberg, H. J. (1988). Four fallacies of segregationism. *Exceptional Children, 55,* 128–137.

Wechsler, D. (2012). *Wechsler Preschool and Primary Scale of Intelligence* (4th ed.). San Antonio, TX: The Psychological Corporation.

Wendling, B. J., & Schrank, F. A. (2015). *Overview of the WJ IV interpretation and instructional interventions program* (Woodcock-Johnson IV Assessment Service Bulletin No. 5). Rolling Meadows, IL: Riverside.

Wilkinson, G. W., & Robertson, G. J. (2006). *Wide range achievement test: Fourth edition.* Lutz, FL: Psychological Assessment Resources.

Will, M. C. (1986). Educating children with learning problems: A shared responsibility. *Exceptional Children, 52,* 411–415.

Woodcock, R. W. (1973). *Woodcock reading mastery tests.* Circle Pines, MN: American Guidance Service.

Woodcock, R. W., & Johnson, M. B. (1977). *Woodcock-Johnson psycho-educational battery.* Chicago: Riverside.

Woodcock, R. W., Muñoz-Sandoval, A. F., McGrew, K. S., & Mather, N. (2005). *Batería III Woodcock-Muñoz.* Rolling Meadows, IL: Riverside.

Ysseldyke, J. E., & Olsen, K. (1999). Putting alternate assessments into practice: What to measure and possible sources of data. *Exceptional Children, 65,* 175–185.

Ysseldyke, J., Nelson, J. R., Christenson, S., Johnson, D. R., Dennison, A., Triezenberg, H., Sharpe, M., & Hawes, M. (2004). What we know and need to know about the consequences of high-stakes testing for students with disabilities. *Exceptional Children, 71,* 75–94.

Zhang, D., Wang, Q., Ding, Y., & Liu, J. J. (2014). Testing accommodation or modification? The effects of integrated object representation on enhancing geometry performance in children with and without geometry difficulties. *Journal of Learning Disabilities, 47*(6), 569–583.

CHAPTER 12

Achenbach, T. *Achenbach system of empirically based assessment (ASEBA).* (2010). Accessed January 31, 2016, from *http://www.aseba.org/index.html.*

Adler, S., & Birdsong, S. (1983). Reliability and validity of standardized testing tools used with poor children. *Topics in Language Disorders, 3*(3), 76–87.

Al-Hourani, A., & Afizah, T. N. (2013). Code switching in daily conversation. *International Journal of Social Science and Humanities Research, 1*(1), 40–43.

Alley, G., & Deshler, D. (1979). *Teaching the learning disabled adolescent.* Denver, CO: Love.

Aprenda: La prueba de logros en español, Tercera edición (2006). Hartcourt. Education.

Baca, L. (1998). Bilingualism and bilingual education. In L. M. Baca & H. T. Cervantes (Eds.), *The bilingual special education interface* (3rd ed.) (pp. 26–45). Upper Saddle River, NJ: Merrill/Prentice Hall.

Baca, L. M., & Almanza, E. (1991). *Language minority students with disabilities.* Reston, VA: Council for Exceptional Children.

Baca, L. M., & Cervantes, H. T. (1989). Assessment procedures for the exceptional child. In L. M. Baca & H. T. Cervantes (Eds.), *The bilingual special education interface* (2nd ed.) (pp. 153–181). Upper Saddle River, NJ: Merrill/Prentice Hall.

Bailey, A. L., & Heritage, M. (2014). The role of language learning professionals in improved instruction and assessment of English language learners. *TESOL Quarterly, 48*(3), 480–506.

Ballantyne, K. G., Sanderman, A. R., & Levy, J. (2008). *Educating English language learners: Building teacher capacity.* Washington, DC: National Clearinghouse for English Language Acquisition. Available at *http://www.ncela.gwu.edu/practice/mainstream_teachers.htm.*

Bartel, N. R., Grill, J. J., & Bryen, D. N. (1973). Language characteristics of black children: Implications for assessment. *Journal of School Psychology, 11,* 351–364.

Bebout, L., & Arthur, B. (1992). Cross-cultural attitudes toward speech disorders. *Journal of Speech and Hearing Research, 25,* 45–52.

Bebout, L., & Arthur, B. (1992). *Journal of Speech, Language, and Hearing Research,* Vol. 35, 45–52. doi:10.1044/jshr.3501.45.

Bergin, V. (1980). *Special education needs in bilingual programs.* Rosslyn, VA: National Clearinghouse for Bilingual Education.

Beringer, M. L. (1984). *Ber-Sil secondary Spanish test.* Rancho Palos Verdes, CA: Ber-Sil.

Beringer, M. L. (1987). *Ber-Sil elementary Spanish test.* Rancho Palos Verdes, CA: Ber-Sil.

Boehm, A. E. (2000). *Boehm test of basic concepts–Third edition.* San Antonio, TX: Psychological Corporation.

Brigance, A. H. (1999). *BRIGANCE® diagnostic comprehensive inventory of basic skills–Revised.* North Billerica, MA: Curriculum Associates.

Brigance, A. H. (2007). *BRIGANCE® assessment of basic skills-Revised, Spanish edition.* North Billerica, MA: Curriculum Associates.

Brown, L. L., & Hammill, D. D. (1982). *Perfil de evaluación del comportamiento.* Austin, TX: PRO-ED.

Brown, L. L., & Hammill, D. D. (1983). *Behavior rating profile.* Austin, TX: PRO-ED.

Brown, W. F., & Holtzman, W. H. (1967a). *Survey of study habits and attitudes.* San Antonio, TX: Psychological Corp.

Brown, W. F., & Holtzman, W. H. (1967b). *Survey of study habits and attitudes, Spanish edition.* San Antonio, TX: Psychological Corp.

Bruininks, R. H., Woodcock, R. W., Weatherman, R. F., & Hill, B. K. (1996). *Scales of independent behavior–Revised.* Itasca, IL: Riverside.

Burt, M. K., Dulay, H. C., & Hernández-Chávez, E. H. (1978). *Bilingual syntax measure I and II.* San Antonio, TX: Psychological Corp.

Camarota, S. A., & Zeigler, K. (2014). One in five U.S. residents speaks foreign language at home, record 61.8 million. Center for Immigration Studies. Available at *http://cis.org/sites/cis.org/files/camarota-language.pdf.*

Campbell, T., Dollaghan, C., Needleman, H., & Janosky, J. (1997). Reducing bias in language assessment: Processing-dependent measures. *Journal of Speech, Language, and Hearing Research, 40,* 519–525.

Cegelka, P. T. (1988). Multicultural considerations. In E. W. Lynch & R. B. Lewis (Eds.), *Exceptional children and adults* (pp. 545–587). Glenview, IL: Scott, Foresman.

Cheng, L. L. (1987). *Assessing Asian language performance: Guidelines for evaluating limited-English-proficient students.* Rockville, MD: Aspen.

Cohen, S. D., & Plaskon, S. P. (1980). *Language arts for the mildly handicapped.* New York: Merrill/Macmillan.

Cole, P. A., & Taylor, O. L. (1990). Performance on working class African-American children on three tests of articulation. *Language, Speech, and Hearing Services in Schools, 21,* 171–176.

Condon, E. C., Peters, J. Y., & Sueiro-Ross, C. (1979). *Special education and the Hispanic child: Cultural perspectives.* Philadelphia: Teacher Corps Mid-Atlantic Network, Temple University.

Craig, H. K., & Washington, J. A. (2000). An assessment battery for identifying language impairments in African American children. *Journal of Speech, Language, and Hearing Research, 43*(2), 366–380.

Craig, H. K., Washington, J. A., & Thompson-Porter, C. (1998). Performances of young African American children on two comprehension tasks. *Journal of Speech, Language, and Hearing Research, 41,* 445–457.

Critchlow, D. C. (1996). *Dos amigos verbal language scales, 1996 edition.* Novato, CA: Academic Therapy.

Cummins, J. (1981). The role of primary language development in promoting educational success for language minority students. In California State Department of Education, *Schooling and language minority students: A theoretical framework* (pp. 3–49). Los Angeles: Evaluation, Dissemination & Assessment Center.

Cummins, J. (1982, February). Tests, achievement, and bilingual students. *Focus* (National Clearinghouse for Bilingual Education), 9, 1–8.

Cummins, J. (1983). Bilingualism and special education: Program and pedagogical issues. *Learning Disability Quarterly, 6,* 373–386.

Diaz-Rico, L. T. (2008). *Strategies for teaching English language learners* (2nd ed.). New York: Pearson.

Duncan, S. E., & DeAvila, E. A. (1990). *Language assessment scales-oral.* Monterey, CA: CTB Macmillan/McGraw-Hill.

Dunn, L. M., & Dunn, L. M. (2007). *Peabody picture vocabulary test, fourth edition.* Minneapolis, MN: Pearson Assessments.

Dunn, L. M., Lugo, D. E., Padilla, E. R., & Dunn, L. M. (1986). *Test de vocabulario en imágenes Peabody.* Circle Pines, MN: American Guidance Service.

Echevarria, J., & Graves, A. (2007). *Sheltered content instruction* (3rd ed.). Boston: Pearson/Allyn & Bacon.

Engquist, G. (1974). *Black dialect: Deficient or different?* Unpublished manuscript, University of Virginia.

García, R. (2006). Language, culture, and education. In J. A. Banks (Ed.), *Cultural diversity and education* (5th ed.) (pp. 266–291). Boston: Pearson/Allyn & Bacon.

Geva, E., & Massey-Garrison, A. (2013). A comparison of the language skills of ELLs and monolinguals who are poor decoders, poor comprehenders, or normal readers. *Journal of Learning Disabilities, 46*(5), 387–340.

Gollnick, D. M., & Chinn, P. C. (1990). *Multicultural education in a pluralistic society (3rd ed.).* St. Louis: Mosby.

Gonzalez, V., Brusca-Vega, R., & Yawkey, T. (1997). *Assessment and instruction of culturally and linguistically diverse students with or at-risk of learning problems.* Boston: Allyn & Bacon.

Gutierrez-Clellen, V. F., & Pena, E. (2001). Dynamic assessment of diverse children: A tutorial. *Language, Speech, and Hearing Services in Schools, 32,* 212–224.

Gutierrez-Clellen, V. F., Restrepo, M. A., Bedore, L. M., Pena, E., & Anderson, R. (2000). Language sample analysis in Spanish-speaking children: Methodological considerations. *Language, Speech, and Hearing Services in Schools, 31*(1), 88–98.

Hamayan, E. V., Marler, B., Sanchez-Lopez, C., & Damino, J. S. (2007). *Reasons for the misidentification of special needs among ELLs.* Retrieved from LD Online: *http://www.ldonline.org/article/40715.*

Hammill, D. D., Larsen, S. C., Wiederholt, J. L., & Fountain-Chambers, J. (1982). *Prueba de lectura y lenguaje escrito.* Austin, TX: PRO-ED.

Hammill, D.D., Mather, N., & Roberts, R. (2001). *The Illinois Test of Psycholinguistic Abilities* (3rd ed.) (ITPA-3). Austin, TX: PRO-ED.

Hammill, D.D., Mather, N., Roberts, R. & Frias, M.G. (2009). *Prueba Illinois de habilidades psicolingüísticas (ITPA-3)* : manual del aplicador. México : Editorial El Manual Moderno.

Hammill, D.D., Mather, N., Roberts, R., & Frias, M. G. (2009). Prueba Illinois de habilidades psicolingüísticas (ITPA-3) : *manual del aplicador.* México: Editorial El Manual Moderno.

Heller, K. A., Holtzman, W. H., & Messick, S. (Eds.). (1982). *Placing children in special education: A strategy for equity.* Washington, DC: National Academy Press.

Herbert, C. H. (1996). *Basic inventory of natural language.* San Bernardino, CA: CHEC point Systems.

Hoover, H. D., Dunbar, S. B., & Frisbie, D. A. (2001, 2003). *Iowa tests of basic skills.* Rolling Meadows, IL: Riverside.

Hoover, H. D., Dunbar, S. B., & Frisbie, D. A. (2012). *Iowa tests of basic skills.* Rolling Meadows, IL: Riverside.

Hopstock, P. J., & Stephenson, T. G. (2003). *Descriptive study of services to LEP students and LEP students with disabilities. Special topic report #1: Native languages of LEP students.* Development Associates. Retrieved April 20, 2007, from *http://www.ncela.gwu.edu/resabout/research/descriptivestudyfiles/*

Hresko, W. P., Reid, D. K., & Hammill, D. D. (1982). *Prueba de desarrollo inicial de lenguaje.* Austin, TX: PRO-ED.

Hresko, W. P., Reid, D. K., & Hammill, D. D. (1999). *Test of early language development* (3rd ed.). Austin, TX: PRO-ED.

Juárez, M. (1983). Assessment and treatment of minority-language-handicapped children: The role of the monolingual speech-language pathologist. *Topics in Language Disorders, 3*(3), 57–66.

Kayser, H. (1995). *Bilingual speech-language pathology: An Hispanic focus.* San Diego, CA: Singular.

Kibler, A., Valdes, G., & Walqui, A. (2014). What does standards-based educational reform mean for English language learner populations in primary and secondary schools? *TESOL Quarterly, 48*(3), 433–453. Retrieved from *http://onlinelibrary.wiley.com/doi/10.1002.tesq.183/pdf.*

Lado, R. (1968). *Linguistics Across Cultures.* Ann Arbor, MI: University of Michigan Press.

Langdon, H. W. (1992). Speech and language assessment of LEP/bilingual Hispanic students. In H. W. Langdon & L. L. Cheng (Eds.), *Hispanic children and adults with communication disorders* (pp. 201–271). Gaithersburg, MD: Aspen.

Lee, L. L. (1971). *Northwestern syntax screening test.* Evanston, IL: Northwestern University Press.

Leonard, L. B., & Weiss, A. L. (1983). Application of non-standardized assessment procedures to diverse linguistic populations. *Topics in Language Disorders, 3*(3), 35–45.

Lidz, C., & Pena, E. D. (1996). Dynamic assessment: The model, its relevance as nonbiased approach, and its application to Latin American preschool children. *Language, Speech, and Hearing Services in Schools, 27,* 367–372.

Lynch, E. W., & Lewis, R. B. (1987). Multicultural considerations. In K. A. Kavale, S. R. Forness, & M. Bender (Eds.), *Handbook of learning disabilities, Volume I, Dimensions and diagnosis* (pp. 399–416). Boston: College Hill.

Mattes, L. J., & Omark, D. R. (1991). *Speech and language assessment for the bilingual handicapped* (2nd ed.). Oceanside, CA: Academic Communication Associates.

McGregor, K., Williams, D., Hearst, S., & Johnson, A. (1997). The use of contrastive analysis in distinguishing difference from disorder: A tutorial. *American Journal of Speech-Language Pathology, 6*(3), 45–56.

Mercer, J. R. (1983). Issues in the diagnosis of language disorders in students whose primary language is not English. *Topics in Language Disorders, 3*(3), 46–56.

Merino, B. J. (1992). Acquisition of syntactic and phonological features in Spanish. In H. W. Langdon & L. L. Cheng (Eds.), *Hispanic children and adults with communication disorders* (pp. 57–98). Gaithersburg, MD: Aspen.

Messick, S. (1984). Assessment in context: Appraising student performance in relation to instruction quality. *Educational Researcher, 13*(3), 3–8.

Muñoz-Sandoval, A. F., Cummins, J., Alvarado, C. G., & Ruef, M. L. (2005). *Bilingual verbal ability tests normative update.* Rolling Meadows, IL: Riverside.

Office for Civil Rights. (1975). Lau Remedies.

Office for Civil Rights. (1975). *Task force findings specifying remedies for eliminating past education practices ruled unlawful under Lau vs. Nichols.* Washington, DC: Author.

Ortiz, A. A., & Garcia, S. B. (1988). A prereferral process for preventing inappropriate referrals of Hispanic students to special education. In A. A. Ortiz & B. A. Ramirez (Eds.), *Schools and the culturally diverse exceptional student: Promising practices and future directions* (pp. 6–18). Reston, VA: Council for Exceptional Children.

Payan, R. M. (1989). Language assessment for the bilingual exceptional child. In L. M. Baca & H. T. Cervantes (Eds.), *The bilingual special education interface* (2nd ed.) (pp. 125–152). New York: Merrill/Macmillan.

Pena, E. D., & Quinn, R. (1997). Task familiarity: Effects on the test performance of Puerto Rican and African American Children. *Language, Speech, and Hearing in Schools, 28,* 323–332.

Penegra, L. M. (2000). *Your values, my values: Multicultural services in developmental disabilities.* Baltimore, MD: Brookes.

Plata, M. (1982). *Assessment, placement, and programming of bilingual exceptional pupils: A practical approach.* Reston, VA: ERIC Clearinghouse on Handicapped & Gifted Children, Council for Exceptional Children.

Reynolds, W. M. (1987). *Wepman's auditory discrimination test manual* (2nd ed.). Los Angeles: Western Psychological Services.

Roberts, J. E., Medley, L. P., Swartzfager, J. L., & Neebe, E. C. (1997). Assessing the communication of African American one-year-olds using the Communication and Symbolic Behavior Scales. *American Journal of Speech-Language Pathology, 6*(2), 59–65.

Robinson-Zanartu, C. (1996). Serving Native American children and families: Considering cultural variables. *Language, Speech, and Hearing in Schools, 27,* 373–384.

Rodekohr, R., & Haynes, W. (2001). Differentiating dialect from disorder: A comparison of two processing tasks and a standardized language test. *Journal of Communication Disorders, 34,* 1–18.

Roseberry-McKibbin, C. (1994). Assessment and intervention for children with limited English proficiency and language disorders. *American Journal of Speech Language Pathology, September.*

Roseberry-McKibbin, C. A., & Eicholtz, G. (1994). Serving children with limited English proficiency in the schools: A national survey. *Language, Speech, and Hearing Services in Schools, 25,* 156–164.

Roussel, N. (1991). Annotated bibliography of communicative ability tests. In E. V. Hamayan & J. S. Damico (Eds.), *Limiting bias in the assessment of bilingual students* (pp. 320–343). Austin, TX: PRO-ED.

Ruddell, R. B. (1974). *Reading language instruction: Innovative practices.* Upper Saddle River, NJ: Prentice Hall.

Russell, D. H., & Russell, E. F. (1959). *Listening aids through the grades.* New York: Bureau of Publications, Teachers College, Columbia University.

Saenz, T. I., & Huer, M. B. (2003). Testing strategies involving least biased language assessment of bilingual children. *Communication Disorders Quarterly, 24*(4), 184–194.

Samson, J. F., & Collins, B. A. (2012). *Preparing all teachers to meet the needs of English language learner. Applying research to policy and practice for teacher effectiveness.* Washington, DC: Center for American Progress. Retrieved from *http://files.eric.gov/fulltext/ED535608.pdf.*

Schiff-Myers, N. B. (1992). Considering arrested language development and language loss in the assessment of second language learners. *Language, Speech, and Hearing Services in Schools, 23,* 28–33.

Schrank, F. A., Wendling, B. J., Alvarado, C. G., & Woodcock, R. (2010). *The Woodcock-Muñoz language survey—Revised normative update.* Rolling Meadows, IL: Riverside Publishing.

Schumaker, J. B., Deshler, D. D., Alley, G. R., & Warner, M. M. (1983). Toward the development of an intervention model for learning disabled adolescents: The University of Kansas Institute. *Exceptional Education Quarterly, 4*(1), 45–74.

Sealey-Ruiz, Y. (2005). Spoken soul: The language of Black imagination and reality. *The Educational Forum, 70*(1), 37–46.

Seymour, H. N., Bland-Stewart, L., & Green, L. J. (1998). Difference versus deficit in child African American English. *Language, Speech, and Hearing Services in Schools, 29,* 96–108.

Sparrow, S. S., Cicchetti, D. V., & Balla, D. A. (2005b). *Vineland adaptive behavior scales, Second edition.* Minneapolis, MN: Pearson Assessments.

Taylor, O. L. (1990). Language and communication differences. In G. H. Shames & E. H. Wiig (Eds.), *Human communication disorders* (3rd ed.) (pp. 126–158). New York: Merrill/Macmillan.

Taylor, O. L., & Payne, K. T. (1983). Culturally valid testing: A proactive approach. *Topics in Language Disorders, 3*(3), 8–20.

Telléz, K., & Waxman, H. C. (2005). *Quality teachers for English language learners: A review of the research.* The Laboratory for Student Success, The Mid-Atlantic Regional Educational Laboratory at Temple University Center for Research in Human Development and Education. Retrieved January 25, 2016, from *http://www.temple.edu/Lss/pdf/ReviewOfThe ResearchTellezWaxman.pdf.*

Terrell, S. L., & Terrell, F. (1983). Distinguishing linguistic differences from disorders: The past, present, and future of nonbiased assessment. *Topics in Language Disorders, 3*(3), 1–7.

Toronto, A. S. (1973). *Screening test of Spanish grammar.* Evanston, IL: Northwestern University Press.

U.S. Census Bureau (2013). Detailed Languages Spoken at Home and Ability to Speak English for the Population 5 Years and Over: 2009–2013. Accessed on 01/24/17 from *http://www.census.gov/data/tables/2013/demo/2009-2013-lang-tables.html.*

U.S. Department of Education, Institute of Education Sciences, National Center for Education Statistics. (2007a). *National Assessment of Educational Progress (NAEP) 2007 Mathematics Assessment.* Washington DC: Author. Retrieved April 19, 2008, from *http://nces.ed.gov/nationsreportcard/nde.*

U.S. Department of Education, Institute of Education Sciences, National Center for Education Statistics (2007b). *National Assessment of Educational Progress (NAEP), 2007 Reading Assessment.* Washington DC: Author. Retrieved April 19, 2008, from *http://nces.ed.gov/nationsreportcard/nde.*

Ukrainetz, T. A., Harpell, S., Walsh, C., & Coyle, C. (2000). A preliminary investigation of dynamic assessment with Native American kindergarteners. *Language, Speech, and Hearing Services in Schools, 31*(2), 142–154.

Wald, B. (1982). On assessing the oral language ability of limited-English-proficient students: The linguistic bases of the noncomparability of different language proficiency assessment measures. In S. S. Seidner (Ed.), *Issues of language assessment* (pp. 117–124). Illinois State Board of Education.

Waxman, H., & Telléz, K. (2002). *Research synthesis on effective teaching practices for English language learners.* Philadelphia: Laboratory for Student Success, Temple University.

Wechsler, D. (2014). *Wechsler intelligence scale for children-fifth edition.* Bloomington, MN: Pearson.

Wepman, J. M. (1975). *Auditory discrimination test* (rev. 1973). Palm Springs, CA: Research Associates.

Wiig, E. H. (1982a). Communication disorders. In N. G. Haring (Ed.), *Exceptional children and youth* (3rd ed.) (pp. 81–109). New York: Merrill/Macmillan.

Wiig, E. H., & Semel, E. (1984). *Language assessment and intervention for the learning disabled* (2nd ed.). New York: Merrill/Macmillan.

Wilkinson, C. Y., Ortiz, A. A., Robertson, P. M., & Kushner, M. I. (2006). English language learners with reading-related LD: Linking data from multiple sources to make eligibility determinations. *Journal of Learning Disabilities, 39*(2), 129–141.

Willis, W. O. (2004). Families with African American roots. In E. W. Lynch & M. J. Hanson (Eds.), *Developing cross-cultural competence: A guide to working with children and their families* (3rd ed.) (pp. 141–177). Baltimore: Brookes.

Winzer, M. A., & Mazurek, K. (1998). *Special education in multicultural contexts.* Upper Saddle River, NJ: Merrill/Prentice Hall.

Woodcock, R. W., McGrew, K. S., & Mather, N. (2001a). *Woodcock-Johnson III tests of cognitive abilities.* Itasca, IL: Riverside.

Woodcock, R. W., McGrew, K. S., & Mather, N. (2001b). *Woodcock-Johnson III tests of achievement.* Itasca, IL: Riverside.

Woodcock, R. W., Muñoz-Sandoval, A. F., Ruef, M. L., & Alvarado, C. G. (2005). *Woodcock-Muñoz language survey–Revised.* Rolling Meadows, IL: Riverside.

Yates, J. R., & Ortiz, A. A. (1998). Developing Individualized Education Programs for exceptional language minority students. In L. M. Baca & H. T. Cervantes (Eds.), *The bilingual special education interface* (3rd ed.) (pp. 188–212). Upper Saddle River, NJ: Merrill/Prentice Hall.

Yavas, M., & Goldstein, B. (1998). Phonological assessment and treatment of bilingual speakers. *American Journal of Speech-Language Pathology, 7*, 49–60.

Yzquierdo, Z. A., Blalock, G., & Torres-Velásquez, D. (2004). Language-appropriate assessments for determining eligibility of English language learners for special education services. *Assessment for Effective Intervention, 29*(2), 17–30.

CHAPTER 13

Baumann, J. F. (1988). *Reading assessment.* New York: Merrill/Macmillan.

Bond, G. L., & Tinker, M. A. (1967). *Reading difficulties: Their diagnosis and correction* (2nd ed.). New York: Appleton-Century-Crofts.

Bormuth, J. R. (1968). The cloze readability procedure. *Elementary English, 45*, 429–436.

Brigance, A. H. (2007). *BRIGANCE® assessment of basic skills-Revised, Spanish edition.* North Billerica, MA: Curriculum Associates.

Brigance, A. H. (2010a). *Brigance comprehensive inventory of basic skills II math.* North Billerican, MA: Curriculum Associates.

Brigance, A. H. (2010b). *Brigance comprehensive inventory of basic skills II reading ELA.* North Billerican, MA: Curriculum Associates.

Brigance, A. H. (2010c). *Brigance transition skills inventory.* North Billerican, MA: Curriculum Associates.

Brigance, A. H. (2013). *Brigance inventory of early development III.* North Billerican, MA: Curriculum Associates.

Brown, V. L., Wiederholt, J. L., & Hammill, D. D. (2008). *Test of reading comprehension* (4th ed.). New York: Pearson.

Bryant, B. R., Wiederholt, J. L., & Bryant, D. P. (2004). *Gray diagnostic reading test–Second edition.* Austin, TX: PRO-ED.

Burke, C. (1973). Preparing elementary teachers to teach reading. In K. S. Goodman (Ed.), *Miscue analysis: Application to reading instruction* (pp. 15–29). Urbana, IL: ERIC Clearinghouse on Reading & Communication Skills.

Burron, A., & Claybaugh, A. L. (1977). *Basic concepts in reading instruction* (2nd ed.). New York: Merrill/Macmillan.

Chall, J. S., & Stahl, S. A. (1982). Reading. In H. E. Mitzel (Ed.), *Encyclopedia of educational research* (5th ed.) (pp. 1535–1559). New York: Free Press.

Cockrum, W., & Shanker, J.L. (2013) *Locating and Correcting Reading Difficulties-*(10th ed.). Boston: Allyn & Bacon.

Cunningham, P. (2003). *The four blocks literacy model.* Retrieved July 24, 2003, from *http://www.wfu.edu/%7Ecunningh/fourblocks/*

Cunningham, P. M., & Allington, R. L. (1999). *Classrooms that work* (2nd ed). New York: Longman.

Cunningham, P. M., Hall, D. P., & Defee, M. (1991). Non-ability grouped, multilevel instruction: A year in a first grade classroom. *Reading Teacher, 44,* 566–571.

Dolch, E. W. (1953). *The Dolch basic sight word list.* Champaign, IL: Garrard.

Durrell, D. D. & Catterson, J. J. (1980). *Durrell analysis of reading difficulty* (3rd ed.). San Antonio, TX: Psychological Corp.

Flowers, A. (2011). *WRMT-III.* Accessed on 01/24/17 at *http://cec.k12.ar.us/documents/wrmt-iii_af_trn_hnd.pdf*

Flynt, E. S., & Cooter, R. B. (1999). *English-español reading inventory for the classroom.* Upper Saddle River, NJ: Merrill/Prentice Hall.

Flynt, E. S., & Cooter, R. B. (2004). *Flynt-Cooter reading inventory for the classroom* (5th ed.). Upper Saddle River, NJ: Merrill/Prentice Hall.

Fry, E. (1968). A readability formula that saves time. *Journal of Reading, 11,* 513–516, 575–577.

Fry, E. (1977). Fry's readability graph: Clarifications, validity, and extension to level 17. *Journal of Reading, 21,* 242–252.

Fuchs, L. S., Hamlett, C. L., & Fuchs, D. (1997). *Monitoring basic skills progress: Basic reading* (2nd ed.). Austin, TX: PRO-ED.

Garner, R. (1983). Correct the imbalance: Diagnosis of strategic behaviors in reading. *Topics in Learning & Learning Disabilities, 2*(4), 12–19.

Gates, A. I., McKillop, A. S. & Horowitz, E. C. (1981). *Gates-McKillop. Horowitz reading diagnostic tests.* (2nd ed). New York: Teachers College Press.

Gillespie-Silver, P. (1979). *Teaching reading to children with special needs.* New York: Merrill/Macmillan.

Gilmore, J. V., & Gilmore, E. C. (1968). *Gilmore oral reading test.* San Antonio, TX: Psychological Corp.

Good, R. H., & Kaminski, R. A. (1996). Assessment for instructional decisions: Toward a proactive/prevention model of decision-making for early literacy skills. *School Psychology Quarterly, 11*(4), 326–336.

Goodman, K. S. (1969). Analysis of oral reading miscues: Applied psycholinguistics. *Reading Research Quarterly, 5,* 9–30.

Goodman, K. S. (1973b). Miscues: Windows on the reading process. In K. S. Goodman (Ed.), *Miscue analysis: Application to reading instruction* (pp. 1–14). Urbana, IL: ERIC Clearinghouse on Reading & Communication Skills.

Goodman, K. S. (Ed.). (1973a). *Miscue analysis: Application to reading instruction.* Urbana, IL: ERIC Clearinghouse on Reading and Communication Skills.

Goodman, Y. M., Watson, D. J., & Burke, C. L. (2005). *Reading miscue inventory* (2nd ed.). Katonah, NY: Richard C. Owen.

Goodman, Y., & Burke, C. (1972). *Reading miscue inventory.* New York: Macmillan.

Hall, A. H., & Tannebaum, R. P. (2012). Test review: J. L. Wiederholt & B. R. Bryant. (2012). *Gray oral reading tests* (5th ed.). Austin, TX: PRO-ED. *Journal of Psychoeducational Assessment, 31*(5), 516–520.

Hammill, D. D., Wiederholt, J. L., & Allen, E. A. (2006). *Test of silent contextual reading fluency.* Austin, TX: PRO-ED.

Harris, A. (1970). *How to increase reading ability* (5th ed.). New York: McKay.

Hasbrouck, J., & Tindal, G. (2005). *Oral reading fluency: 90 years of measurement* (Tech. Rep. No. 33). Eugene, OR: University of Oregon, College of Education, Behavioral Research and Teaching. Retrieved August 9, 2006, from *http://brt.uoregon.edu/tech_reports.htm*

Howell, K. W., Fox, S. L., & Morehead, M. K. (1993). *Curriculum-based evaluation* (2nd ed.). Pacific Grove, CA: Brooks/Cole.

Hudson, F. G., Colson, S. E., Welch, D. L. H., Banikowski, A. K., & Mehring, T. A. (1989). *Hudson education skills inventory.* Austin, TX: PRO-ED.

Ihnot, C. (2000, 2001, 2003). *Read naturally (fluency curriculum, levels.8–8.0).* Saint Paul, MN: Read Naturally.

Ihnot, C. (2006). *Reading fluency progress monitor.* St. Paul, MN: Read Naturally.

Johnson, M. S., Kress, R. A., & Pikulski, J. J. (1987). *Informal reading inventories* (2nd ed.). Newark, DE: International Reading Association.

Jongsma, E. (1971). *The cloze procedure as teaching technique.* Newark, DE: International Reading Association.

Kaluger, G., & Kolson, C. J. (1978). *Reading and learning disabilities* (2nd ed.). New York: Merrill/Macmillan.

Karlsen, B., & Gardner E. F. (1995). *Stanford diagnostic reading test, Fourth edition.* San Antonio, TX: Harcourt Brace Educational Measurement.

Kirk, S. A., Kliebhan, J. M., & Lerner, J. W. (1978). *Teaching reading to slow and disabled readers.* Boston: Houghton Mifflin.

Lapp, D., & Flood, J. (1992). *Teaching reading to every child* (3rd ed.). New York: Macmillan.

Leinhardt, G., Zigmond, N., & Cooley, W. (1981). Reading instruction and its effects. *American Educational Research Journal, 18,* 343–361.

Lerner, J. (2000). *Learning disabilities* (8th ed.). Boston: Houghton Mifflin.

Lerner, J. W., Cousin, P. T., & Richeck, M. (1992). Critical issues in learning disabilities: Whole language learning. *Learning Disabilities Research & Practice, 7,* 226–230.

Lindamood, C. H., & Lindamood, P. C. (2004). *Lindamood-Bell Auditory Conceptualization Test).* Austin, TX: PRO-ED.

Mather, N. (1992). Whole language reading instruction for students with learning disabilities: Caught in the crossfire. *Learning Disabilities Research & Practice, 7,* 87–95.

Mather, N., Hammill, D. D., Allen, E. A., & Roberts, R. (2004). *Test of silent word reading fluency.* Austin, TX: PRO-ED.

Monroe, M. (1932). *Children who cannot read.* Chicago: University of Chicago Press.

Mullis, R. (2012). *Test intro: Gray oral reading test* (5th ed.). Retrieved from *http://lcpsdiags.com/lcpsdiags/debsays/79-debs-tests/88-gray.*

Myklebust, H. R. (1968). Learning disabilities: Definition and overview. In H. R. Myklebust (Ed.), *Progress in learning disabilities* (Vol. I) (pp. 1–15). New York: Grune & Stratton.

National Institute of Child Health and Human Development. (2000). *Report of the National Reading Panel. Teaching children to read: an evidence-based assessment of the scientific research literature on reading and its implications for reading instruction.* Retrieved July 12, 2006, from *http://www.nichd.nih.gov/ publications/nrp/ smallbook.htm*

Newcomer, P. L. (1999). *Standardized reading inventory* (2nd ed.). Austin, TX: PRO-ED.

Newcomer, P. L., & Barenbaum, E. (2003). *Test of phonological awareness skills.* Austin, TX: PRO-ED.

Reid, D. K., Hresko, W. P., & Hammill, D. D. (2001). *Test of early reading ability* (3rd ed.). Austin, TX: PRO-ED.

Roe, B.D., & Burns, P.C. (2010). *Informal reading inventory* (8th ed.). Boston: Houghton Mifflin.

Samuels, S. J. (1983). Diagnosing reading problems. *Topics in Learning and Learning Disabilities, 2*(4), 1–11.

Schreiner, R. (1983). Principles of diagnosis of reading difficulties. *Topics in Learning and Learning Disabilities, 2*(4), 70–85.

Shanker, J. L., & Ekwall, E. E. (2013). *Ekwall/Shanker reading inventory* (6th ed.). Boston: Allyn & Bacon.

Shinn, M. R. (Ed.), (1988). *Curriculum-based measurement: Assessing special children.* New York: Guilford Press.

Slosson, R. L., & Nicholson, C. L. (2002). *Slosson oral reading test* (3rd ed.). East Aurora, NY: Slosson.

Snow, C. E., Burns, S., & Griffin, P. (Eds.). (1998). *Preventing reading difficulties in young children.* Washington, DC: National Academic Press.

Spache, G. D. (1981) *Diagnostic Reading Scales* (rev. ed.) Monterey, CA: CTB Macmillan/McGraw-Hill.

Stahl, S. A., & Miller, P. D. (1989). Whole language and language experience approaches for beginning reading: A quantitative research synthesis. *Review of Educational Research, 59,* 87–116.

Stieglitz, E. L. (2002). *Stieglitz informal reading inventory* (3rd ed.). Boston: Allyn & Bacon.

Swearingen, R., & Allen, D. (2000). *Classroom assessment of reading process* (2nd ed.). Boston: Houghton Mifflin.

Thurlow, M. L., Graden, J., Greener, J., & Ysseldyke, J. E. (1983). LD and non-LD students' opportunities to learn. *Learning Disability Quarterly, 6,* 172–183.

Tindal, G. A., & Marston, D. B. (1990). *Classroom-based assessment.* New York: Merrill/Macmillan.

Torgesen, J. K., & Barker, T. A. (1995). Computers as aids in the prevention and remediation of reading disabilities. *Learning Disability Quarterly, 18,* 76–87.

Torgesen, J. K., & Bryant, B. R. (2004). *Test of phonological awareness–Second edition: PLUS.* Austin, TX: PRO-ED.

Torgesen, J. K., Wagner, R. K., & Rashotte, C. A. (2012). *Test of word reading efficiency.* Austin, TX: PRO-ED.

Wagner, R. K., & Torgesen, J. K. (1987). The nature of phonological processing and its causal role in the acquisition of reading skills. *Psychological Bulletin, 101,* 192–212.

Wagner, R. K., Torgesen, J. K., Rashotte, C.A., & Pearson, N. A. (2013). *Comprehensive test of phonological processing* (2nd ed.). Austin, TX: PRO-ED.

Walker, B. J. (1992). *Diagnostic teaching of reading* (2nd ed.). New York: Merrill/Macmillan.

Walsh, K., Glaser, D., & Wilcox, D. D. (2006). *What education schools aren't teaching about reading and what elementary teachers aren't learning about reading.* Washington,

DC: National Council on Teaching Quality. Retrieved July 12, 2006, from *http://www.nctq.org/nctq/*

Westby, C. E. (1992). Whole language and learners with mild handicaps. *Focus on Exceptional Children, 24*(8), 1–16.

Wheelock, W. H., & Campbell, C. J. (2013). *Classroom reading inventory* (12th ed.). Boston: McGraw-Hill Higher Education.

Wiederholt, J. L. (1986). *Formal reading inventory.* Austin, TX: PRO-ED.

Wiederholt, J. L., & Blalock, G. (2000). *Gray silent reading tests.* Austin, TX: PRO-ED.

Wiederholt, J. L., & Bryant, B. R. (2012). *Gray oral reading test* (5th ed.). Austin, TX: PRO-ED.

Woodcock, R. W. (2011). *Woodcock reading mastery tests* (3rd ed.). New York: Pearson.

Woodcock, R., Mather, N., & Schrank, F. A. (2004). *Woodcock-Johnson III diagnostic reading battery.* Itasca, IL: Riverside.

Woods, M. L., & Moe, A. J. (2015). *Analytical Reading Inventory: Comprehensive standards-based assessment for all students, including gifted and remedial).* Boston: Pearson.

Zigmond, N., Vallecorsa, A., & Leinhardt, G. (1980). Reading instruction for students with learning disabilities. *Topics in Language Disorders, 1* (1), 89–98.

CHAPTER 14

Ashlock, R. B. (2006). *Error patterns in computation* (9th ed.). Upper Saddle River, NJ: Pearson.

Bartel, N. R. (1986a). Problems in mathematics achievement. In D. D. Hammill & N. R. Bartel (Eds.), *Teaching students with learning and behavior problems* (4th ed.) (pp. 178–223). Austin, TX: PRO-ED.

Brigance, A. H. (2007). *BRIGANCE® assessment of basic skills-Revised, Spanish edition.* North Billerica, MA: Curriculum Associates.

Brigance, A.H. (2010). *Comprehensive Inventory of Basic Skills-II.* North Billerica, MA: Curriculum Associates

Brown, V., Cronin, M. E., & Bryant, D. (2012). *Test of mathematical abilities-3.* Austin, TX: PRO-ED.

Brueckner, L. J. (1930). *Diagnostic and remedial teaching in arithmetic.* Philadelphia: Winston.

Buswell, G. T., & John, L. (1925). *Fundamental processes in arithmetic.* Indianapolis, IN: Bobbs-Merrill.

Cawley, J. F. (1978). An instructional design in mathematics. In L. Mann, L. Goodman, & L. L. Wiederholt (Eds.), *Teaching the learning-disabled adolescent* (pp. 201–234). Boston: Houghton Mifflin.

Connolly, A. J. (2007). *KeyMath-3 diagnostic assessment.* New York: Pearson.

Connolly, A. J., Nachtman, W., & Pritchett, E. M. (1971, 1976). *KeyMath diagnostic arithmetic test.* Circle Pines, MN: American Guidance Service.

Cox, L. S. (1975). Diagnosing and remediating systematic errors in addition and subtraction computations. *Arithmetic Teacher, 22,* 151–157.

Estes, T. H., Estes, J. J., Richards, H. C., & Roettger, D. (1981). *Estes attitude scales.* Austin, TX: PRO-ED.

Fuchs, L. S., Hamlett, C. L., & Fuchs, D. (1997). *Monitoring basic skills progress: Basic reading* (2nd ed.). Austin, TX: PRO-ED.

Fuchs, L. S., Hamlett, C. L., & Fuchs, D. (1998). *Monitoring basic skills progress: Basic math computation* (2nd ed.). Austin, TX: PRO-ED.

Fuchs, L. S., Hamlett, C. L., & Fuchs, D. (1999). *Monitoring basic skills progress: Basic math concepts and applications.* Austin, TX: PRO-ED.

Ginsburg, H. P., & Baroody, A. J. (2003). *Test of early mathematics ability* (3rd ed.). Austin, TX: PRO-ED.

Ginsburg, H. P., & Mathews, S. C. (1984). *Diagnostic test of arithmetic strategies.* Austin, TX: PRO-ED.

Goodstein, H. A. (1981). Are the errors we see true errors? Error analysis in verbal problem solving. *Topics in Learning and Learning Disabilities, 1*(3), 31–45.

Hresko, W. P., Schlieve, P. L., Herron, S. R., Swain, C., & Sherbenou, R. J. (2003). *Comprehensive mathematical abilities test.* Austin, TX: PRO-ED.

Hudson, F. G., Colson, S. E., Welch, D. L. H., Banikowski, A. K., & Mehring, T. A. (1989). *Hudson education skills inventory.* Austin, TX: PRO-ED.

Kilpatrick, J. (2001). Understanding mathematical literacy: The contribution of research. *Educational Studies in Mathematics, 47*(1), 101–116

Ma, L. (2013). A critique of the structure of U.S. elementary school mathematics. *Notices of the AMS, 60*(10). 1282–1296. Retrieved from *http://www.ams.org/notices/201310/rnoti-p1282.pdf.*

Maccow, G. (2011). *Overview of Key Math-3.* Accessed on 01/25/17 at *http://images.pearsonclinical.com/images/PDF/Keymath-3Handout.pdf.*

Mardell-Czudnowski, C. D. (1980). The four Ws of current testing practices: Who; what; why; and to whom—An exploratory survey. *Learning Disability Quarterly, 3*(1), 73–83.

Mercer, C. D., & Mercer, A. R. (1998). *Teaching students with learning problems* (5th ed.). Upper Saddle River, NJ: Merrill/Prentice Hall.

National Council of Teachers of Mathematics. (1980). *An agenda for action: Recommendations for school mathematics in the 1980's.* Reston, VA: Author.

National Council of Teachers of Mathematics. (1989). *Curriculum and evaluation standards for school mathematics.* Reston, VA: Author.

National Mathematics Advisory Panel. (2008). *Foundations for success: The final report of the National Mathematics Advisory Panel.* Washington, DC: U.S. Department of Education.

Osborn, W. J. (1925). Ten reasons why pupils fail in mathematics. *The Mathematics Teacher, 18,* 234–238.

Pearson. (2007). *Key Math 3 publication summary form.* Accessed on 01/25/17 at *http://images.pearsonclinical.com/images/pa/products/keymath3_da/km3-da-pub-summary.pdf*

Reid, D. K., & Hresko, W. P. (1981). *A cognitive approach to learning disabilities.* New York: McGraw-Hill.

Roberts, G. H. (1968). The failure strategies of third grade arithmetic pupils. *The Arithmetic Teacher, 15,* 442–446.

Thurlow, M. L., & Ysseldyke, J. E. (1979). Current assessment and decision-making practices in model programs for the learning disabled. *Learning Disability Quarterly, 2,* 15–24.

Wiederholt, J. L., Hammill, D. D., & Brown, V. (1978). *The resource teacher: A guide to effective practices.* Boston: Allyn & Bacon.

CHAPTER 15

Affleck, J. Q., Lowenbraun, S., & Archer, A. (1980). *Teaching the mildly handicapped in the regular classroom* (2nd ed.). New York: Merrill/Macmillan.

Alexander, N. (1983). A primer for developing a writing curriculum. *Topics in Learning & Learning Disabilities, 3*(3), 55–62.

Anderson, P. L. (1983). *Denver handwriting analysis.* Novato, CA: Academic Therapy.

Bailet, L. L. (1991). Written language test reviews. In A. M. Bain, L. L. Bailet, & L. C. Moats (Eds.), *Written language disorders* (pp. 165–187). Austin, TX: PRO-ED.

Bankson, N. W. (1990). *Bankson language test* (2nd ed.). Austin, TX: PRO-ED.

Bloom, L., & Lahey, M. (1978). *Language development and language disorders.* New York: Wiley.

Boehm, A. E. (2000). *Boehm test of basic concepts–Third edition.* San Antonio, TX: Psychological Corporation.

Boehm, A. E. (2001). *Boehm-3–Preschool edition.* San Antonio, TX: Psychological Corporation.

Bray, C. M., & Wiig, E. H. (1987). *Let's talk inventory for children.* San Antonio, TX: Psychological Corp.

Brigance, A.H. (2010). *Brigance Comprehensive Inventory of Basic Skills-II.* North Billerica, MA: Curriculum Associates

Brigance, A.H. (2013). *Brigance Inventory of Early Development.* North Billerica, MA: Curriculum Associates

Brigance, A.H. (2013). *Brigance Diagnostic Inventory of Early Development-III.* North Billerica, MA: Curriculum Associates.

Brown, R. (1973). *A first language: The early stages.* Cambridge, MA: Harvard University Press.

Brownell, R. (2010). *Receptive one word picture vocabulary test* (4th ed.). Novato, CA: Academic Therapy.

Carrow-Woolfolk, E. (1974). *Carrow elicited language inventory.* Chicago: Riverside.

Carrow-Woolfolk, E. (1999). *Test for auditory comprehension of language* (3rd ed.). Austin, TX: PRO-ED.

Carrow-Woolfolk, E. (2011a). *Oral and written language scale* (2nd ed.). *(OWLS-II)* listening comprehension/oral expression manual. Turrance, CA: Western Psychological Services.

Carrow-Woolfolk, E. (2011b). *Oral and Written Language Scale* (2nd ed.). *(OWLS-II)* reading comprehension/written expression manual. Turrance, CA: Western Psychological Services.

Carrow-Woolfolk, E. (2014). *Test for auditory comprehension of language* (4th ed.). Circle Pines, MN: AGS.

Culatta, R., & Culatta, B. K. (1985). Communication disorders. In W. H. Berdine & A. E. Blackhurst (Eds.), *An introduction to special education* (2nd ed.) (pp. 145–181). Boston: Little, Brown

Dagenais, D. J., & Beadle, K. R. (1984). Written language: When and where to begin. *Topics in Language Disorders, 4*(2), 59–85.

Dunn, L. M., & Dunn, L. M. (1981). *Peabody picture vocabulary test–Revised.* Circle Pines, MN: American Guidance Service.

Dunn, L. M., & Dunn, L. M. (2007). *Peabody picture vocabulary test, fourth edition.* Minneapolis, MN: Pearson Assessments.

Edgington, R. (1968). But he spelled it right this morning. In J. I. Arena (Ed.), *Building spelling skills in dyslexic children* (pp. 23–26). San Rafael, CA: Academic Therapy.

Foster, R., Giddan, J. J., & Stark, J. (1983). *Assessment of children's language comprehension.* Austin, TX: PRO-ED.

Fry, E. (2000). 1000 instant words. Westminster, CA: Teacher Created Resources. Worksheet Design Copyright © 2013 *K12reader.com.* All Rights Reserved

Fudala, J. B. (2001). *Arizona articulation scale* (3rd ed.). Los Angeles: Western Psychological Services.

Gilliam, J. E., & Miller, L. (2006). *Pragmatic language skills inventory.* Austin, TX: PRO-ED.

Goldman, R. M., Fristoe, M., & Woodcock, R. W. (1970). *Goldman-Fristoe-Woodcock test of auditory discrimination.* Circle Pines, MN: American Guidance Service.

Goldman, R., & Fristoe, M. (2015). *Goldman-Fristoe test of articulation* (3rd ed.). Bloomington, MN: Pearson Assessments.

Graham, S. (1982). Composition research and practice: A unified approach. *Focus on Exceptional Children, 14*(8), 1–16.

Graham, S., & Miller, L. (1979). Spelling research and practice: A unified approach. *Focus on Exceptional Children, 12*(2), 1–16.

Graham, S., & Miller, L. (1980). Handwriting research and practice: A unified approach. *Focus on Exceptional Children, 13*(2), 1–16.

Graves, D. (1978). *Balancing the basics: Let them write.* New York: Ford Foundation.

Graves, D. H. (1985). All children can write. *Learning Disabilities Focus, 1*(1), 36–43.

Greenbaum, C. R. (1987). *Spellmaster assessment and teaching system.* Austin, TX: PRO-ED.

Hammill, D. D., & Newcomer, P. L. (2008). *Test of language development—intermediate 4 (TOLD-I:4).* Austin, TX: PRO-ED.

Hammill, D. D., Brown, V. L., Larsen, S. C., & Wiederholt, J. L. (2007). *Test of adolescent and adult language* (4th ed.). Austin, TX: PRO-ED.

Hammill, D. D., Mather, N., & Roberts, R. (2001). *Illinois test of psycholinguistic abilities* (3rd ed.). Austin, TX: PRO-ED.

Hammill, H. H., & Larsen, S. C. (2009). *Test of written language* (4th ed.). Austin, TX: PRO-ED.

Howell, K. W., & Kaplan, J. S. (1980). *Diagnosing basic skills.* New York: Merrill/Macmillan.

Hresko, W. P., Reid, D. K., & Hammill, D. D. (1982). *Prueba de desarrollo inicial de lenguaje.* Austin, TX: PRO-ED.

Hresko, W., Herron, S., Peak, P., & Hicks, D. (2012). *Test of early written language* (3rd ed.). Austin, TX: PRO-ED.

Hudson, F. G., Colson, S. E., Welch, D. L. H., Banikowski, A. K., & Mehring, T. A. (1989). *Hudson education skills inventory.* Austin, TX: PRO-ED.

Isaacson, S. L. (1988). Effective instruction in written language. In E. L. Meyen, G. A. Vergason, & R. J. Whelan (Eds.), *Effective instructional strategies for exceptional children* (pp. 288–306). Denver, CO: Love.

Karlsen, B. (1992). *Language arts assessment profile.* Circle Pines, MN: American Guidance Service.

Kottmeyer, W. (1970). *Teacher's guide for remedial reading.* New York: McGraw-Hill.

Larsen, S. C., & Hammill, D. D. (1989). *Test of legible handwriting.* Austin, TX: PRO-ED.

Larsen, S., Hammill, D. D., & Moats, L. (2013). *Test of written spelling* (5th ed.). Austin, TX: PRO-ED.

Lee, L. L. (1971). *Northwestern syntax screening test.* Evanston, IL: Northwestern University Press.

Leinhardt, G., Zigmond, N., & Cooley, W. (1981). Reading instruction and its effects. *American Educational Research Journal, 18,* 343–361.

Leiter, R. G. (1948). *Leiter international performance scale.* Chicago: Stoelting.

Lerner, J. W., Cousin, P. T., & Richeck, M. (1992). Critical issues in learning disabilities: Whole language learning. *Learning Disabilities Research & Practice, 7,* 226–230.

Lippke, B. A., Dickey, S. E., Selmar, J. W., & Soder, A. L. (1997). *Photo articulation test* (3rd ed.). Austin, TX: PRO-ED.

Litowitz, B. E. (1981). Developmental issues in written language. *Topics in Language Disorders, 1*(2), 73–89.

Mann, P. H., Suiter, P. A., & McClung, R. M. (1979). *Handbook in diagnostic-prescriptive teaching* (2nd ed.). Boston: Allyn & Bacon.

Markwardt, F. C. (1998). *Peabody individual achievement test-Revised/normative update.* Circle Pines, MN: American Guidance Service.

Martin, N. (1983). Genuine communications. *Topics in Learning & Learning Disabilities, 3*(3), 1–11.

Martin, N., & Brownell, R. (2011). *Expressive one-word picture vocabulary test* (4th ed.). Novato, CA: Academic Therapy Publications.

Mather, N., & Woodcock, R. W. (1997). *Mather-Woodcock group writing tests.* Itasca, IL: Riverside.

McCrimmon, A. W., & Climie, E. A. (2011). Test review: D. D. Hammill & S. C. Larsen "Test of Written Language—Fourth Edition." Austin, TX: PRO-ED, 2009. *Journal of Psychoeducational Assessment, 29*(6), 592–596.

McGhee, R., Bryant, B. R., Larsen, S. C., & Rivera, D. M. (1995). *Test of written expression.* Austin, TX: PRO-ED.

Mecham, M. J. (2003). *Utah test of language development* (4th ed.). Austin, TX: PRO-ED.

Mercer, C. D., & Mercer, A. R. (1998). *Teaching students with learning problems* (5th ed.). Upper Saddle River, NJ: Merrill/Prentice Hall.

Mercer, C. D., & Pullen, P. C. (2005). *Students with learning disabilities* (6th ed.). Upper Saddle River, NJ: Merrill/Prentice Hall.

Milone, M. (2007). *Test of handwriting skills revised manual.* Novato, CA: Academic Therapy Publications.

Moran, M. R. (1988). Options for written language assessment. In E. L. Meyen, G. A. Vergason, & R. J. Whelan (Eds.), *Effective instructional strategies for exceptional children* (pp. 465–480). Denver, CO: Love.

Myklebust, H. R. (1965). *Development and disorders of written language. Volume one: Picture story language test.* New York: Grune & Stratton.

Newcomer, P. (2014). *Diagnostic Achievement Battery* (4th ed.) Austin, TX: Pro-Ed.

Newcomer, P. L., & Hammill, D. D. (1997). *Test of language development–3, Primary.* Austin, TX: PRO-ED.

Newcomer, P. L., & Hammill, D. D. (2008). *Test of language development—Primary 4 (TOLD-P:4).* Austin, TX: PRO-ED.

Nodine, B. F. (1983). Foreword: Process not product. *Topics in Learning & Learning Disabilities, 3*(3), ix–xii.

Phelps-Gunn, T., & Phelps-Terasaki, D. (1982). *Written language instruction.* Rockville, MD: Aspen.

Phelps-Terasaki, D., & Phelps-Gunn, T. (1992). *Test of Pragmatic Language.* Austin, TX: Pro-Ed.

Polloway, E. A., & Payne, J. S. (1993). *Strategies for teaching learners with special needs* (5th ed.). New York: Merrill/Macmillan.

Polloway, E. A., & Smith, J. E. (1982). *Teaching language skills to exceptional learners.* Denver, CO: Love.

Polloway, E. A., Patton, J. R., & Cohen, S. B. (1983). Written language for mildly handicapped children. In E. L. Meyen, G. A. Vergason, & R. L. Whelan (Eds.),

Promising practices for exceptional children: Curriculum implications (pp. 285–320). Denver, CO: Love.

Poplin, M. S. (1983). Assessing developmental writing abilities. *Topics in Learning and Learning Disabilities, 3*(3), 63–75.

Poteet, J. A. (1980). Informal assessment of written expression. *Learning Disability Quarterly, 3*(4), 88–98.

Reynolds, W. M. (1987). *Wepman's auditory discrimination test manual* (2nd ed.). Los Angeles: Western Psychological Services.

Roid, G. (2003). *Stanford-Binet intelligence scales, Fifth edition.* Itasca, IL: Riverside.

Sheehan, R. & Snyder, S. (1996). Recent trends and issues in program evaluation in early intervention. In M. Brambring, H. Rauh & A. Beemann (Eds), *Early childhood intervention* (pp. 281–304). Berlin: Walter de Gruyter.

Shulman, B. B. (1986). *Test of pragmatic skills* (rev. ed.). Tucson, AZ: Communication Skill Builders.

Smith, F. (1982). *Writing and the writer.* New York: Holt, Rinehart and Winston.

Tyack, D., & Venable, G. P. (1999). *Language sampling, analysis, and training* (3rd ed.). Austin, TX: PRO-ED.

Wallace, G., & Hammill, D. D. (2013). *Comprehensive receptive and expressive vocabulary test* (3rd ed.). Austin, TX: PRO-ED.

Wallace, G., Larsen, S. C., & Elksnin, L. K. (1992). *Educational assessment of learning problems* (2nd ed.), Boston: Allyn & Bacon.

Wechsler, D. (2014). *Wechsler intelligence scale for children-fifth edition.* Bloomington, MN: Pearson.

Weiner, E. S. (1980). Diagnostic evaluation of writing skills. *Journal of Learning Disabilities, 13,* 43–53.

Wells, C. G. (1981). *Learning through interactions: The study of language development.* Cambridge, England: Cambridge University Press.

Wells, G. (1973). *Coding manual of the description of child speech.* Bristol, England: University of Bristol School of Education.

Wepman, J. M. (1975). *Auditory discrimination test* (rev. 1973). Palm Springs, CA: Research Associates.

Westby, C. E. (1992). Whole language and learners with mild handicaps. *Focus on Exceptional Children, 24*(8), 1–16.

Wiederholt, J. L., Hammill, D. D., & Brown, V. (1978). *The resource teacher: A guide to effective practices.* Boston: Allyn & Bacon.

Wiig, E. H. (1982b). *Let's talk: Developing prosocial communication skill.* San Antonio, TX: Psychological Corp.

Wiig, E. H., & Semel, E. (1984). *Language assessment and intervention for the learning disabled* (2nd ed.). New York: Merrill/Macmillan.

Wiig, E. H., Semel, E., & Secord, W. A. (2013). *Clinical evaluation of test fundamentals* (5th ed.). Bloomington, MN: NCS Pearson.

Wilkinson, G. W., & Robertson, G. J. (2006). *Wide range achievement test: Fourth edition.* Lutz, FL: Psychological Assessment Resources.

Williams, K. T. (2007). *Expressive vocabulary test* (2nd ed.). Minneapolis, MN: Pearson Assessments.

Wilson, B. A., & Felton, R. H. (2004). *Word identification and spelling test.* Austin, TX: PRO-ED.

Wittenberg, W. (1980). *Diagnostic achievement test in spelling.* Baldwin, NY: Barnell Loft.

Woodcock, R. W. (1991). *Woodcock language proficiency battery–Revised.* Chicago: Riverside.

Woodcock, R. W., & Johnson, M. B. (1989). *Woodcock-Johnson psycho-educational battery–Revised.* Chicago: Riverside.

Zaner-Bloser evaluation scales. (n.d.). Columbus, OH: Zaner-Bloser.

CHAPTER 16

Akshoomoff, N., Corsell, C., & Schmidt, H. (2006). The role of Autism Diagnostic Observation Schedule in the assessment of autism spectrum disorders in school and community settings. *The California School Psychologist, 11,* 3–14.

Apfel, N. H., & Provence, S. (2001). *Manual for the infant-toddler and family instrument (ITFI).* Baltimore: Brookes.

Aylward, G. P. (1995). *Bayley infant neuro-developmental screener (BINS).* New York: Psychological Corporation.

Bagnato, S. J., Neisworth, J. T., & Munson, S. M. (1997). *Linking assessment and early intervention: An authentic curriculum-based approach.* Baltimore: Brookes.

Bagnato, S. J., Neisworth, J. T., Salvia, J., & Hunt, F. M. (1999a). *Temperament and atypical behavior scale: Assessment tool.* Baltimore: Brookes.

Bagnato, S. J., Neisworth, J. T., Salvia, J., & Hunt, F. M. (1999b). *Temperament and atypical behavior scale: Screener.* Baltimore: Brookes.

Bailey, D. B. (2004a). Assessing family resources, priorities and concerns. In M. McLean, M. Wolery, & D. B. Bailey (Eds.), *Assessing infants and pre-schoolers with special needs* (3rd ed.) (pp. 172–203). Upper Saddle River, NJ: Merrill/Prentice Hall.

Bailey, D. B. (2004b). Tests and test development. In M. McLean, M. Wolery, & D. B. Bailey (Eds.), *Assessing infants and preschoolers with special needs* (3rd ed.) (pp. 22–44). Upper Saddle River, NJ: Merrill/Prentice Hall.

Bailey, D. B., & Simeonsson, R. J. (1990). *Family needs survey.* Chapel Hill, NC: Frank Porter Graham Child Development Center, UNC.

Barkley, R. A. (1997). *ADHD and the nature of self-control.* New York: Guilford.

Barkley, R. A., & Murphy, K. R. (1998). *Attention-deficit hyperactivity disorder: A clinical workbook* (2nd ed.). New York: Guilford.

Baron-Cohen, S., Cox, S., Baird, G., Sweettenham, J., & Nightingale, N. (1996). Psychological markers in the detection of autism in infancy in a large population. *British Journal of Psychiatry, 168*(2), 158–163.

Barona, A., & Santos de Barona, M. (2000). Assessing multicultural preschool children. In B. A. Bracken (Ed.), *The psychoeducational assessment of preschool children* (3rd ed.) (pp. 282–297). Boston: Allyn & Bacon.

Bayley, N. (2006). *Bayley scales of infant and toddler development* (3rd ed.). San Antonio, TX: Harcourt Assessment.

Bracken, B. A. (2006). *Bracken basic concept scale—third edition: Receptive.* San Antonio, TX: Psychological Corporation.

Bracken, B.A. (2007). *Bracken School Readiness Assessment* (3rd ed.). San Antonio, TX: Harcourt Assessment.

Bricker, D., & Waddell, M. (2002a). *Assessment, evaluation, and programming system for infants and children: Vol. 3 AEPS curriculum for birth to three years.* Baltimore: Brookes.

Bricker, D., & Waddell, M. (2002b). *Assessment, evaluation, and programming system for infants and children: Vol. 4 AEPS curriculum for three to six years.* Baltimore: Brookes.

Bricker, D., Capt, B., & Pretti-Frontczak, K. (2002). *Assessment, evaluation, and programming system for infants and children: Vol. 2 test birth to three years and three to six years.* Baltimore: Brookes.

Bricker, D., Pretti-Frontczak, K., Johnson, J. J., & Straka, E. (2002). *Assessment, evaluation, and programming system for infants and children: Vol. 1 administration guide.* Baltimore: Brookes.

Brigance, A. H. (2013). *Brigance inventory of early development–III.* North Billerica, MA: Curriculum Associates.

Brigance, A. H., & Glascoe, F. P. (2002). *Infant & toddler screen.* North Billerica, MA: Curriculum Associates.

Brigance, A.H. (2013a). *Early Preschool Screen III.* North Billerica, MA: Curriculum Associates, Inc.

Brigance, A.H. (2013b). *Preschool Screen III.* North Billerica, MA: Curriculum Associates, Inc.

Brigance, A.H. (2013c). *K-1 Screen III.* North Billerica, MA: Curriculum Associates, Inc.

Bronfenbrenner, U. (1979). *The ecology of human development.* Cambridge, MA: Harvard University Press.

Brownell, R. (2010a). *Expressive One-Word Picture Vocabulary Test-4.* (2010). Novato, CA: Academic Therapy.

Brownell, R. (2010b). *Receptive One-Word Picture Vocabulary Test-4.* Novato, CA: Academic Therapy.

Brownell, R. (2012). *Receptive* and *Expressive One-Word Picture Vocabulary Test-4-Spanish Bilingual.* Novato, CA: Academic Therapy.

Brownell, R. (Ed.). (2000a). *Expressive one-word picture vocabulary test–2000 edition.* Novato, CA: Academic Therapy.

Brownell, R. (Ed.). (2000b). *Expressive one-word picture vocabulary test.* Novato, CA: Academic Therapy Publications.

Brownell, R. (Ed.). (2000b). *Receptive one-word picture vocabulary test–2000 edition.* Novato, CA: Academic Therapy.

Bryant, D., & Maxwell, K. (1997). The effectiveness in early intervention for disadvantaged children. In M. J. Guralnick (Ed.), *The effectiveness of early intervention.* (pp. 23–46). Baltimore: Brookes.

Burton, V. J., & Watkins, R. (2002). Dynamic assessment: Understanding children's development. In M. Ostrosky & E. Horn (Eds.), *Assessment: Gathering meaningful information. Monograph Series No. 4* (pp. 61–72). Longmont, CO: Sopris West.

Casto, G., & Mastropieri, M. A. (1986). The efficacy of early intervention programs: A meta-analysis. *Exceptional Children, 52,* 417–424.

Chandler, L. K. (1993). Steps in preparing for transition: Preschool to kindergarten. *Teaching Exceptional Children, 25*(4), 52–55.

Division of Early Childhood (DEC). (2007). *Promoting positive outcomes for children with disabilities: Recommendations for curriculum, assessment, and program evaluation.* Missoula, MT: Author.

Dodge, D. T., Colker, L. J., & Heroman, C. (2006). *The creative curriculum for preschool* (4th ed.). Washington, D.C.: Teaching Strategies.

Dombro, A. L., Colker, L. J., & Dodge, D. T. (2003). *The creative curriculum for infants & toddlers* (rev. ed.). Washington, D.C.: Teaching Strategies.

Dunn, L. M., & Dunn, L. M. (2007). *Peabody picture vocabulary test, fourth edition.* Minneapolis, MN: Pearson Assessments.

Dunst, C. J., Cooper, C. S., Weeldreyer, J. C., Snyder, K. D., & Chase, J. H. (1988). Family needs scale. In C. J. Dunst, C. M. Trivette, & A. G. Deal (Eds.), *Enabling and empowering families: Principles and guidelines for practice* (pp. 149–151). Cambridge, MA: Brookline.

Dunst, C. J., Trivette, C. M., & Deal, A. G. (1988). *Enabling and empowering families: Principles and guidelines for practice.* Cambridge, MA: Brookline.

Feldhusen, J. F., & Jarwan, F. A. (2000). Identification of gifted and talented youth for educational programs. In K. A. Heller, F. J. Monks, R. J. Sternberg, & R. F Subotnik (Eds.), *International handbook of giftedness and talent* (pp. 271–282). New York: Elsevier.

Frankenburg, W. K., Dodds, J., Archer, P., Bresnick, B., Mashka, P., Edelman, N., & Shapiro, H. (1990). *Denver developmental screening test (Denver II).* Denver, CO: Denver Developmental Materials.

Gilliam, J. E. (1995a). *Attention-deficit/hyperactivity disorder test.* Austin, TX: PRO-ED.

Gilliam, J. E. (1995b). *Gilliam autism rating scale.* Austin, TX: PRO-ED.

Ginsburg, H. P., & Baroody, A. J. (2003). *Test of early mathematics ability* (3rd ed.). Austin, TX: PRO-ED.

Guralnick, M. J. (1997). Second-generation research in the field of early intervention. In M. J. Guralnick (Ed.), *The effectiveness of early intervention* (pp. 3–20). Baltimore: Brookes.

Haley, S. M., Coster, W. J., Ludlow, L. H., Haltiwanger, J. T., & Andrellos, P. J. (1992). *Pediatric evaluation of disability inventory*. Boston: PEDI Research Group.

Hanson, M. J. (2004). Ethnic, cultural, and language diversity in service settings. In E. W. Lynch & M. J. Hanson (Eds.), *Developing cross-cultural competence: A guide for working with children and their families* (3rd ed.) (pp. 3–39). Baltimore: Brookes.

Hanson, M. J., & Lynch, E. W. (1989). *Early intervention: Implementing child and family services for infants and toddlers who are at-risk or disabled*. Austin, TX: PRO-ED.

Hanson, M. J., & Lynch, E. W. (2004). *Understanding families: Approaches to diversity, disability, and risk*. Baltimore: Brookes.

Harrison, P. (1990). *AGS early screening profile*. Circle Pines, MN: American Guidance Service.

Hemmeter, M.L., Joseph, G., Smith, B.J. & Sandall, S (EDs.) (2001) *DEC recommended practices program assessment: improving practices for young children with special needs and their families*. Missoula, MT: Division for Early Childhood.

Hemmeter, M. L., & Salcedo, P. S. (2005). Parent checklist. In S. Sandall, M. L. Hemmeter, B. J. Smith, & M. E. McLean (Eds.), *DEC recommended practices in early intervention/ early childhood special education: A comprehensive guide for practical application* (pp. 277–279). Longmont, CO: Sopris West.

Hodson, B. W. (2004). *Hodson assessment of phonological patterns* (3rd ed.). Novato, CA: Academic Therapy.

Hresko, W. P., Herron, W. P., & Peak, P. K. (1996). *Test of early written language* (2nd ed.). Austin, TX: PRO-ED.

Hresko, W. P., Miquel, S. A., Sherbenou, R. J., & Burton, S. D. (1994). *Developmental observation checklist system: Examiner's manual*. Austin, TX: PRO-ED.

Hresko, W. P., Reid, D. K., & Hammill, D. D. (1999). *Test of early language development* (3rd ed.). Austin, TX: PRO-ED.

Johnson-Martin, N. M., Attermeier, S. M., & Hacker, B. J. (2004). *The Carolina curriculum for infants and toddlers with special needs* (3rd ed.). Baltimore: Brookes.

Johnson-Martin, N. M., Hacker, B. J., & Attermeier, S. M. (2004). *The Carolina curriculum for preschoolers with special needs* (2nd ed.). Baltimore: Brookes.

Kalyanpur, M., & Harry, B. (1999). *Culture in special education: Building a posture of cultural reciprocity in parent-professional interactions*. Baltimore: Brookes.

Kanevsky, L. (2000). Dynamic assessment of gifted students. In K. A. Heller, F. J. Monks, R. J. Sternberg, & R. F. Subotnik (Eds.), *International handbook of giftedness and talent* (2nd ed.) (pp. 283–295). Oxford: Elsevier.

Kaufman, A. S., & Kaufman, N. L. (1983). *Kaufman assessment battery for children*. Circle Pines, MN: American Guidance Service.

Kitano, M.K. (1990). Intellectual abilities and psychological intensities in young children: Implications for the gifted. *Roeper Review, 13*, 5–10.

Krug, D., Arick, J., & Almond, P. J. (2008). *Autism screening instrument for educational planning* (3rd ed.). Austin, TX: PRO-ED.

Lidz, C. S., & Thomas, C. (1987). The preschool learning assessment device: Extension of a static approach. In C. S. Lidz (Ed.), *Dynamic assessment: An interactional approach to evaluating learning potential* (pp. 288–326). New York: Guilford.

Linder, T. W. (1999). *Transdisciplinary play-based assessment: A functional approach to working with young children* (rev. ed.). Baltimore: Brookes.

Linder, T. W. (2004). *Transdisciplinary play-based intervention: Guidelines for developing a meaningful curriculum for young children*. Baltimore: Brookes.

Linder, T. W. (2008). *Transdisciplinary play-based assessment* (2nd ed.). Baltimore: Paul H. Brooks Publishing Co.

Lord, C., Rutter, M., DiLavore, P. C., & Risi, S. (2001). *Autism diagnostic observation schedule*. Los Angeles, CA: Western Psychological Services.

Losardo, A., & Notari-Syverson, A. (2001). *Alternative approaches to assessing young children*. Baltimore: Brookes.

Lynch, E. W. (2004). Developing cross-cultural competence. In E. W. Lynch & M. J. Hanson (Eds.), *Developing cross-cultural competence: A guide for working with children and their families* (3rd ed.) (pp. 41–77) Baltimore: Brookes.

Lynch, E. W., & Hanson, M. J. (2004b). Family diversity, assessment, and cultural competence. In M. McLean, M. Wolery, & D. Bailey (Eds.), *Assessing infants and preschoolers with special needs* (3rd ed.) (pp. 77–122). Upper Saddle River, NJ: Merrill/Prentice Hall.

MacDonald, J., & Gillette, Y. (1989). *ECO: A partnership program*. Chicago: Riverside.

Mardell, C., & Goldenberg, D. (2011). *Developmental indicators for the assessment of learning–4*. Bloomington, MN: Pearson.

McCollum, J., & Stayton, V. (1985). Infant/parent interaction: Studies and intervention guidelines based on the SIAI model. *Journal of the Division of Early Childhood, 9(2)*, 125–135.

McCormick, L., & Noonan, M. J. (2002). Ecological assessment and planning. In M. Ostrosky & E. Horn (Eds.), *Assessment: Gathering meaningful information. Monograph Series No. 4* (pp. 47–60). Longmont, CO: Sopris West.

McLean, M. (2002). Assessing young children for whom English is a second language. In M. Ostrosky & E. Horn (Eds.), *Assessment: Gathering meaningful information. Monograph Series No. 4* (pp. 73–82). Longmont, CO: Sopris West.

McLean, M. (2004). Identification and referral. In M. McLean, M. Wolery, & D. B. Bailey (Eds.), *Assessing infants and preschoolers with special needs* (3rd ed.) (pp. 100–122). Columbus, OH: Merrill/Prentice Hall.

McWilliam, R. A. (2005). DEC recommended practices: Interdisciplinary models. In S. Sandall, M. L. Hemmeter, B. J. Smith, & M. E. McLean & (Eds.), *DEC recommended practices in early intervention/early childhood special education: A comprehensive guide for practical application* (pp. 127–146). Longmont, CO: Sopris West.

Mullen, E. M. (1995). *Mullen scales of early learning.* Circle Pines, MN: American Guidance Service.

Neisworth, J. T., & Bagnato, S. J. (2005). DEC recommended practices: Assessment. In S. Sandall, M. L. Hemmeter, B. J. Smith, & M. E. McLean & (Eds.) *DEC recommended practices in early intervention/early childhood special education: A comprehensive guide for practical application* (pp. 45–69). Longmont, CO: Sopris West.

Neisworth, J.T., Bagnato, S.J., Silvia, J., Hunt F. (1999). Temperament and Atypical behavior Scale (TABS); Early Childhood Indicators of Developmental Dysfunction: TABS Assessment and Intervention Manual. Baltimore, MD: Brookes.

Newborg, J. (2004). *Battelle developmental inventory* (2nd ed.) *(BDI-2).* Chicago: Riverside.

Newborg, J. (2005). *Battelle developmental inventory* (2nd ed., Spanish). Chicago: Riverside.

Parks, S. (1992). *HELP strands (birth–3).* Palo Alto, CA: Vort.

Parks, S. (1994). *HELP family-centered interview.* Palo Alto, CA: Vort.

Parks, S., Furono, S., O'Reilly, K., Inatsuka, T., Hoska, C. M., & Zeisloft-Falbey, B. (1994). *HELP at home (birth to 3).* Palo Alto, CA: Vort.

Pellegrini, A. D. (1996). *Observing children in their natural worlds: A methodological primer.* Mahwah, NJ: Erlbaum.

Peterson, N. (1987). *Early intervention for handicapped and at-risk children: An introduction to early childhood special education.* Denver, CO: Love.

Pretti-Frontczak, K., & Bricker, D. (2004). *An activity-based approach to early intervention* (3rd ed.). Baltimore: Brookes.

Provence, S., & Apfel, N. H. (2001). *Infant-toddler and family instrument (ITFI).* Baltimore: Brookes.

Provence, S., Erikson, J. Vater, S. & Palmeri, S. (1995). *Infant-toddler developmental assessment (IDA).* Itasca, IL: Riverside.

Puckett, M. B., & Black, J. K. (2000). *Authentic assessment of the young child.* Columbus, OH: Merrill.

Reid, D. K., Hresko, W. P., & Hammill, D. D. (2001). *Test of early reading ability* (3rd ed.). Austin, TX: PRO-ED.

Rosenkoetter, S. E., Hains, A. H., & Fowler, S. A. (1994). *Bridging early services for children with special needs and their families: A practical guide for transition planning.* Baltimore: Brookes.

Rossetti, L. M. (1990). *Infant-toddler assessment: An interdisciplinary approach.* Boston: College Hill.

Rous, B., & Hallam, R. A. (2002). Easing the transition to kindergarten: Assessing the social, behavioral, and functional skills of young children with disabilities. In M. Ostrosky & E. Horn (Eds.), *Assessment: Gathering meaningful information. Monograph Series No. 4* (pp. 97–110). Longmont, CO: Sopris West.

Rous, B., & Hallam, R. (Eds.) (2006). Tools for transition in early childhood: A step-by-step guide for agencies, teachers, and families. Baltimore: Brookes.

Sandall, S. R. (1997a). Developmental assessment in early intervention. In A. H. Widerstrom, B. A. Mowder, & S. R. Sandall (Eds.), *Infant development and risk: An introduction* (pp. 211–235). Baltimore: Brookes.

Sandall, S. R. (1997b). The family service team. In A. H. Widerstrom, B. A. Mowder, & S. R. Sandall (Eds.), *Infant development and risk: An introduction* (pp. 155–173). Baltimore: Brookes.

Sandall, S. R. (1997c). The individual family service plan. In A. H. Widerstrom, B. A. Mowder, & S. R. Sandall (Eds.), *Infant development and risk: An introduction* (pp. 237–257). Baltimore: Brookes.

Sandall, S. R., Hemmeter, M. L., Smith, B. J., & McLean, M. E. (2005). *DEC recommended practices in early intervention/early childhood special education: A comprehensive guide for practical application.* Longmont, CO: Sopris West.

Schopler, E., Reichler, R., & Renner, B. R. (1988). *The childhood autism rating scale (CARS).* Austin, TX: PRO-ED.

Seligman, M., & Darling, R. B. (1989). *Ordinary families, special children: A systems approach to childhood disability.* NY: Guilford.

Shonkoff, J. P., & Hauser-Cram, P. (1987). Early intervention for disabled infants and their families: A quantitative analysis. *Pediatrics, 80,* 650–658.

Smith, B. J. (2005). Administrator's essentials: Creating policies and procedures that support recommended practices in early intervention/early childhood special education. In S. Sandall, M. L. Hemmeter, B. J. Smith, & M. E. McLean (Eds.), *DEC recommended practices in early intervention/early childhood special education: A comprehensive guide for practical application* (pp. 267–275). Longmont, CO: Sopris West.

Sparrow, S. S., Balla, D. A., & Cicchetti, D. V. (1984). *Vineland adaptive behavior scales.* Circle Pines, MN: American Guidance Service.

Sparrow, S. S., Balla, D. A., & Cicchetti, D. V. (1998). *Vineland social-emotional early childhood scales.* Circle Pines, MN: American Guidance Service.

Squires, J., & Bricker, D. (2009). *Ages and stages questionnaires* (3rd ed.). Baltimore, MD: Brookes Publishing.

Squires, J., Bricker, D., & Twombly, E. (2015). *The ASQ: SE User's Guide for the Ages & Stages Questionnaires®: Social-Emotional: A parent-completed, child-monitoring system for social-emotional behaviors.* Baltimore, MD: Paul H. Brookes Publishing Co., Inc.

Stile, S. W. (1996). Early childhood education of children who are gifted. In S. L. Odom & M. E. McLean (Eds.), *Early intervention/early childhood special education: Recommended practices* (pp. 309–328). Austin, TX: PRO-ED.

Taylor, R. L. (2003). *Assessment of exceptional students* (6th ed.). New York: Allyn & Bacon.

Trivette, C. M., & Dunst, C. J. (2005). DEC recommended practices: Family-based practices. In S. Sandall, M. L. Hemmeter, B. J. Smith, & M. E. McLean (Eds.), *DEC recommended practices in early intervention/early childhood special education: A comprehensive guide for practical application* (pp. 107–126). Longmont, CO: Sopris West.

Trivette, C. M., Dunst, C. J., & Deal, A. G. (1988). Family strengths profile. In C. J. Dunst, C. M. Trivette, & A. G. Deal (Eds.), *Enabling and empowering families: Principles and guidelines for practice*. Cambridge, MA: Brookline.

Turnbull, A. P., Turnbull, H. R., Erwin, E., & Soodak, L. (2006). *Families, professionals, and exceptionality: Positive outcomes through partnerships and trust*. Upper Saddle River, NJ: Pearson Merrill Prentice Hall.

U.S. Department of Education. (2002b). *The No Child Left Behind Act of 2001, Executive summary*. Retrieved July 7, 2003, from *http://www.ed.gov/offices/OESE/esea/esec-summ.html*

Vort Corporation. (1995a). *HELP for preschooler*. Palo Alto, CA: Vort.

Vort Corporation. (1995b). *HELP for preschooler strands*. Palo Alto, CA: Vort.

Widerstrom, A. H. (1997). Newborns and infants at risk for or with disabilities. In A. H. Widerstrom, B. A. Mowder, & S. R. Sandall (Eds.), *Infant development and risk: An introduction* (pp. 3–19). Baltimore: Brookes.

Wolery, M. (2004). Monitoring children's progress and intervention implementation. In M. McLean, M. Wolery, & D. B. Bailey (Eds.), *Assessing infants and preschoolers with special needs* (3rd ed.) (pp. 545–584). Columbus, OH: Merrill Prentice Hall.

Wolfberg, P. (2003). *Peer play and the autism spectrum: The art of guiding children's socialization and imagination*. Shawnee Mission, KS: Autism Asperger.

Yell, M. (2006). *The law and special education* (2nd ed.). Columbus, OH: Pearson Merrill Prentice Hall.

CHAPTER 17

Agran, M., Snow, K., & Swaner, J. (1999). Teacher perceptions of self-determination: Benefits, characteristics, strategies. *Education and Training in Mental Retardation and Developmental Disabilities, 34,* 293–301.

Becker, H., Schur, S., & Hammer, E. (1986). *The Functional Skills Screening Inventory User's Guide*. Austin, TX: Functional Resources.

Becker, H., Schur, S., & Hammer, E. (1986). *The Functional Skills Screening Inventory User's Guide*. Austin, TX: Functional Resources.

Becker, R. L. (2000). *Reading-free vocational interest inventory* (2nd ed.). Columbus, OH: Elbern.

Brackett, J., & McPhearson, A. (1996). Learning disabilities diagnosis in postsecondary students: A comparison of discrepancy-based diagnosis models. In N. Gregg, C. How, & A. Gay (Eds.), *Adults with learning disabilities: Theoretical and practical perspectives* (pp. 68–84). New York: Guilford.

Brigance, A. H. (2010). *Brigance Transition Skills Inventory*. North Billerica, MA: Curriculum Associates, Inc.

Brigance, A. H. (2012). *Brigance Early Development III*. North Billerica, MA: Curriculum Associates, Inc.

Brinkerhoff, L. C., Shaw, S. E., & McGuire, J. M. (1993). *Promoting postsecondary education for students with learning disabilities: A handbook for practitioners*. Austin, TX: PRO-ED.

Brolin, D. (1992a). *Life centered career education (LCCE) curriculum program*. Reston, VA: Council for Exceptional Children.

Brolin, D. (1992b). *Life centered career education (LCCE) competency assessment knowledge batteries*. Reston, VA: Council for Exceptional Children.

Brolin, D. (1992c). *Life centered career education (LCCE) competency assessment performance batteries*. Reston, VA: Council for Exceptional Children.

Brolin, D. E. (1995). *Career education: A functional life skills approach* (3rd ed.). Upper Saddle River, NJ: Merrill/Prentice Hall.

Center on Education Policy (2006). *High school exit exams: Standards differ from the No Child Left Behind Act*. Exit Exam Policy Brief 4.

Clark, G. M. (1998a). Transition planning assessment for secondary-level students with learning disabilities. *Journal of Learning Disabilities, 29*(1), 79–62.

Clark, G. M. (1998b). *Assessment for transition planning: Transition series*. Austin, TX: PRO-ED.

Clark, G. M. (2007). *Assessment for transition planning* (2nd ed.). Austin, TX: Pro-Ed.

Clark, G. M., & Kolstoe, O. P. (1995). *Career development and transition education for adolescents with disabilities*. Boston: Allyn & Bacon.

Clark, G. M., & Patton, J. R. (1997). *Transition planning inventory*. Austin, TX: PRO-ED.

Cohen, L. G., Spenciner, L. J., & Twitchell, D. (2003). Youth in transition. In L. G. Cohen & L. J. Spenciner (Eds.), *Assessment of children and youth with special needs* (2nd ed.) (pp. 459–479). Boston: Pearson Education.

COIN Educational Products (2003). *COIN climb I*. Toledo, OH: COIN[3] Educational Products.

Cowan, R. J. (2006). Preparing high school students with learning disabilities for success in college: Implications for students, parents, and educators. *Learning Disabilities: A Multidisciplinary Journal, 14,* 5–13.

Cummings, R., Maddux, C. D., & Casey, J. (2000). Individualized transition planning for students with learning disabilities. *Career Development Quarterly, 49,* 60–73.

deFur, S. H., Todd-Allen, M., & Getzel, E. E. (2001). Parent participation in the transition planning process. *Career Development for Exceptional Individuals, 24*(1), 19–36.

Durgin, R. W., Ryan, J. M., & Ryan, R. M. (1995). *COIN basic skills and career interest survey.* Toledo, OH: COIN³ Educational Products.

Enderle J., Severson S. J. (2003). Enderle-Severson Transition Rating Scales. Moorhead, MN: ESTR Publications.

Enderle J., Severson S. J. (2003). Enderle-Severson Transition Rating Scale-J (Revised). Moorhead, MN: ESTR Publications.

Enderle, J., & Severson, S. (2003). *Enderle-Severson Transition Rating Scales III (ESTR-III).* Moorhead, MN: ESTR Publications.

Enderle, J., & Severson, S. (2003). *Enderle-Severson Transition Rating Scale-Revised (ESTR-J-R).* Moorhead, MN: ESTR Publications.

Everson, J. M. (1996). *Assessing the transition needs of young adults with dual sensory and multiple impairments. Assessment guidelines.* Volume 3. Columbus, OH: Great Lakes Area Regional Center for Deaf-Blind Education. (ERIC Document Reproduction Service No. ED438659)

Everson, J. M., Zhang, D., & Guillory, J. D. (2001). A statewide investigation of individualized transition plans in Louisiana. *Career Development for Exceptional Individuals, 24*(1), 37–49.

Falvey, M. A., Forest, M., Pearpoint, J., & Rosenberg, R. L. (1994). *All my life's a circle. Using the tools: Circles, MAPS, and PATH.* Toronto, Canada: Inclusion Press.

Field, S., Martin, J. E., Miller, R., Ward, M. J., & Wehmeyer, M. L. (1998). *A practical guide to teaching self-determination.* Reston, VA: Council for Exceptional Children.

Flannery, B., Newton, S., Horner, R., Slovic, R., Blumberg, R., & Ard, W. K. (2000). The impact of person centered planning on the content and organization of individual supports. *Career Development for Exceptional Individuals, 23,* 123–137.

Flexer, R. W., & Luft, P. (2001). Transition assessment and postschool outcomes. In R. W. Flexer, T. J. Simmons, P. Luft, & R. M. Baer (Eds.), *Transition planning for secondary students with disabilities* (pp. 197–226). Upper Saddle River, NJ: Prentice Hall.

Forest, M., Pearpoint, J., & Snow (Eds.), *The inclusion papers: Strategies to make inclusion work* (pp. 116–132). Toronto: Inclusion Press.

Gajar, A., Goodman, L., & McAfee J. (1993). *Secondary schools and beyond: Transition of individuals with mild disabilities.* New York: Merrill.

Getzel, E. E., & Thoma, C. A. (2006). Voice of experience: What college students with learning disabilities and attention deficit/hyperactivity disorders tell us are important self-determination skills for success. *Learning Disabilities, 14,* 33–39.

Gilliam, J. (1994). *Work Adjustment Inventory (WAI).* Austin, TX: PRO-ED.

Gilliam, J. (1994). *Work Adjustment Inventory (WAI).* Austin, TX: PRO-ED.

Glutting, J.J., & Wilkinson, G.S. (2003). *Wide Range Interest and occupation Test, Second edition (WRIOT-2).* Lutz, FL: Psychological Assessment Resources, Inc.

Glutting, J.J., & Wilkinson, G.S. (2003). *Wide Range Interest and Occupation Test, Second edition (WRIOT-2).* Lutz, FL: Psychological Assessment Resources, Inc.

Halloran, W. D. (1993). Transition services requirement: Issues, implications, challenge. In R. C. Eaves & P. J. McLaughlin (Eds.), *Recent advances in special education and rehabilitation* (pp. 210–224). Boston: Andover Medical.

Halpern, A. S. (1985). Transition: A look at the foundations. *Exceptional Children, 51,* 479–486.

Halpern, A. S. (1994). The transition of youth with disabilities to adult life: A position statement of the Division on Career Development and Transition, the Council for Exceptional Children. *Career Development for Exceptional Individuals, 17,* 115–124.

Halpern, A. S., & Irvin, L. K. (1986). *Social and prevocational information battery–Revised.* Monterey, CA: CTB Macmillan/McGraw-Hill.

Halpern, A.S., Herr, C.M., Wolf, N.K., Lawson, J.D., Doren, B., & Johnson, M.D. (1997). *Next S.T.E.P.: Student transition and educational planning.* Teacher manual. Eugene: University of Oregon.

Harris, R., & Robertson, J. (2001). Successful strategies for college-bound students with learning disabilities. *Preventing School Failure, 45,* 125–131.

Hasazi, S. B., Gordon, L., & Roe, C. A. (1985). Factors associated with the employment status of handicapped youth exiting high school from 1979 to 1983. *Exceptional Children, 51*(6), 455–469.

Henderson, C. (1995). The American freshman: National norms. *College freshmen with disabilities: A statistical profile.* Washington, DC: Health Resource Center, American Council on Education, U.S.

Hoffman, A., & Field, S. (2005). *Self-determination knowledge scale (SDKS) (2nd ed.).* Austin, TX: PRO-ED.

Hoffman, A., & Field, S. (2005). *Steps to self-determination: A curriculum to help adolescents learn to achieve their goals (2nd ed.).* Austin, TX: PRO-ED.

Holland, J. L. (1994). *The self-directed search: A guide to educational and vocational planning.* Odessa, FL: Psychological Assessment Resources.

Hughes, C., & Carter, E. W. (2000). *The transition handbook: Strategies high school teachers use that work!* Baltimore: Brookes.

Hughes, C., Hwang, B., Kim, J., Killian, J. J., Harmer, M. L., & Alcantara, P. R. (1997). A preliminary validation on strategies that support the transition from school to adult life. *Career Development for Exceptional Individuals, 20*(1), 1–14.

IDEA 2004 Final Regulations. (2006, August 14). *Federal Register, 71*(156). Retrieved August 21, 2006, from *http://www.ed.gov/policy/speced/ idea/idea2004.html*

Jastak, J. F., & Jastak, S. R. (1980). *Wide range employability sample test.* Wilmington, DE: Jastak.

Kochhar-Bryant, C. A. (2007). *What every teacher should know about transition and IDEA 2004.* Boston: Allyn & Bacon.

Kohler, P. D. (1996). *Taxonomy for transition programming: Linking research to practice.* Champaign, IL: Transition Research Institute, University of Illinois at Urbana-Champaign. Available online at *http://vms.cc.wmich.edu/~kohlerp/toc.html*

Larson, N., & Aase, S. (1997). *From screening to accommodation: Providing services to adults with learning disabilities.* Columbus, OH: AHEAD.

Lynch, R. T., & Gussel, L. (1996, March/April). Disclosure and self-advocacy regarding disability-related needs: Strategies to maximize integration in postsecondary education. *Journal of Counseling and Development, 74,* 352–357.

Mandaus, J. W. (2005). Navigating the college transition maze: A guide for students with learning disabilities. *Teaching Exceptional Children, 37*(3), 32–34.

Martin, J. E., & Marshall, L. H. (1995). Choice Maker: Infusing self-determination instruction into the IEP and transition process. In D. J. Sands & M. L. Wehmeyer (Eds.), *Self-determination across the life span: Independence and choice for people with disabilities* (pp. 215–236). Baltimore: Brookes.

McCarney, S., & Arthaud, T. (2012). *Transition behavior scale* (3rd ed.). Columbia, MO: Hawthorne Education.

McDonnell, J., Wilcox, B., & Hardman, M. (1991). *Secondary programs for students with developmental disabilities.* Boston: Allyn & Bacon.

Milsom, A., & Hartley, M. T. (2005). Assisting students with learning disabilities transitioning to college: What school counselors should know. *Professional School Counseling, 8,* 436–441.

Morgan, R. L., Ellerd, D. A., Gerity, B. P., & Tullis, M. D. (2000). *Your employment selections.* Logan, UT: TRI-SPED, Utah State University.

Mount, B. (1989). *Making futures happen: A manual for facilitators of personal futures planning.* St. Paul, MN: Governor's Council on Developmental Disabilities.

National Center for Education Statistics (2006).*Profile of undergraduates in U.S. postsecondary education institutions: 2003–2004.* (NCES2006–184). Available from *http://nces.ed.gov/pubsearch/pubsinfo.asp?pubid=52006184*

National Center on Secondary Education and Transition (NCSET). (2002a). *What works data brief. What works transition research synthesis project.* Minneapolis, MN: NCSET, Institute on Community Integration, University of Minnesota. *http://www.ncset.org/publications/whatworks/NCSET WhatWorks_1.1.pdf*

National Center on Secondary Education and Transition (NCSET). (2002b). *NLTS2 data brief. Introducing the NLTS2.* Minneapolis, MN: NCSET, Institute on Community Integration, University of Minnesota. *http://www.ncset.org/publications/nlts2/2002_01.pdf*

National Council on Disability (NCD). (2000). *Transition and post-school outcomes for youth with disabilities: Closing the gaps to post-secondary education and employment.* Washington, DC: Author. Available online at *http://www.ncd.gov/newsroom/publications/transition_11–1–00.html*

Neubert, D. A., & Moon, S. M. (2000). How a transition profile helps students prepare for life in the community. *Teaching Exceptional Children, 33*(2), 20–25.

Newman, L., Wagner, M., Knokey, A., Marder, C., Nagle, K., & Shaver, D. (2011). The post-high school outcomes of young adults with disabilities up to 8 years after high school: A report from the national longitudinal transition study-2 (NLTS2). *National Center for Special Education,* Retrieved from *http://www.eric.ed.gov/PDFS/ED524044.pdf.*

Nuehring, M.L. & Sitlington, P.L. (2003). Transition as a vehicle: Moving from high school to an adult vocational service provider. *Journal of Disability Policy Studies, 14* (1), 23–35.

OSEP. (2011). *Office of Special Education Program Part B of IDEA.* Retrieved from *http://idea.ed.gov/explore/view/p/, root, dynamic, QaCorner, 10.*

Parker, R. M. (2002). *Occupational aptitude survey and interest schedule* (3rd ed.). Austin, TX: PRO-ED.

Patton, J. M. (1998). The disproportionate representation of African Americans in special education: Looking behind the curtain for understanding and solutions. *Journal of Special Education, 32,* 25–31.

Patton, J. R., & Clark, G. M. (2014). *Transition planning inventory.* (2nd ed.). Dallas, TX: PRO-ED.

Pearpoint, J. (1990). *From behind the piano: The building of Judith Snow's unique circle of friends.* Toronto, ON: Inclusion Press.

Pearpoint, J., O'Brien, J., & Forest, M. (1995). *PATH: A workbook for planning positive possible futures.* Toronto, Canada: Inclusion Press.

Repetto, J. B. (2001). Assessment for transition planning. In J. A. McLoughlin & R. Lewis (Eds.), *Assessing students with special needs* (5th ed.) (pp. 550–582). Upper Saddle River, NJ: Merrill/Prentice Hall.

Rojewski, J. W., & Black, R. S. (2002). *Assessments that support the transition from school to work for adolescents with disabilities.* Reston, VA: Council for Exceptional Children.

Salembier, G., & Furney, K. S. (1997). Facilitating participation: Parents' perceptions of their involvement in the IEP/Transition planning process. *Career Development for Exceptional Individuals, 20*(1), 29–42.

Sax, C. L., & Thoma, C. A. (2002). *Transition assessment: Wise practices for quality lives.* Baltimore: Brookes.

Scheiber, B., & Talpers, J. (1987). *Unlocking potential: College and other choices for learning disabled people. A step-by-step guide.* Bethesda, MD: Adler & Adler.

Singer Company Career Systems. (1982). *Singer vocational evaluation system.* Rochester, NY: Singer.

Sitlington, P. L. (1996). Transition assessment—Where have we been and where should we be going? *Career Development for Exceptional Individuals, 19*(2), 159–168.

Sitlington, P. L., Neubert, D. A., & LeConte, P. J. (1997). Transition assessment: The position of the Division on Career Development and Transition. *Career Development for Exceptional Individuals, 20*(1), 69–79.

Sitlington, P. L., Neubert, D. A., Begun, W., Lombard, R. C., & Leconte, P. J. (1996). *Assess for success.* Reston, VA: Council for Exceptional Children.

Skinner, M. E., & Lindstrom, B. D. (2003). Bridging the gap between high school and college: Strategies for the successful transition of students with learning disabilities. *Preventing School Failure, 47,* 132–137.

Talent Assessment Inc. (1972, 1980, 1985, 1988). *Talent assessment program.* Jacksonville, FL: Author.

Taylor, R. L. (2003). *Assessment of exceptional students* (6th ed.). New York: Allyn & Bacon.

Taymans, J. M. & West, L. (2001). *Selecting a college for students with learning disabilities or attention deficit hyperactivity disorder (ADHD).* Arlington, VA: ERIC Clearinghouse on Disabilities and Gifted Education. (ERIC Document Reproduction Service No. ED461957)

Thompson, J. R., Fulk, B. M., & Piercy, S. W. (2000). Do individualized transition plans match the postschool projections of students with learning disabilities and their parents? *Career Development for Exceptional Individuals, 23*(1), 3–25.

Turnbull, A.P., Blue-Banning, M.J., Anderson, E.L., Turbull, H.R., Seaton, K.A., & Dinas, P.A. (1996). Enhancing self-determination through group action planning: A holistic emphasis. In D. J. Sands & M.L. Wehmeyer (Eds.), *Self-determination across the life span: Independence and choice for people with disabilities* (pp. 237–256). Baltimore: Paul H. Brookes.

U.S. Department of Education, National Center for Educational Statistics. (2015). *Chapter 3: Postsecondary education.*

Van Ruesen, A.K., Bos, C.S., Schumaker, J.B., & Deshler, D.D. (1994). *The Self-Advocacy Strategy for Education and Transition Planning.* Lawrence, KS: Edge Enterprises.

Vandercook, T., & York, J. (1989). The McGill Action Planning System (MAPS): A strategy for building the vision. *Journal of the Association for Persons with Severe Handicaps, 24*(3), 205–215.

Vogel, S. A. (1982). On developing LD college programs. *Journal of Learning Disabilities, 15,* 518–528.

Vogel, S. A. (1987). Issues and concerns in LD college programming. In D. Johnson & J. Blalock (Eds.), *Adults with learning disabilities* (pp. 239–276). Orlando, FL: Grune & Stratton.

Vogel, S. A., & Sattler, J. (1981). *The college student with learning disability: A handbook for university admissions officers, faculty, and administration.* Illinois Council for Learning Disabilities.

VRI Career Planning Solutions. (1995). *Career Score.* Retrieved on October 21, 2006, from *http://vri.org/careerscope/index.html.*

VRI Career Planning Solutions. (1995). *Career Score.* Retrieved on October 21, 2006, from *http://vri.org/careerscope/index.html.*

Wagner, M., Blackorby, J., Cameto, R., Hebbeler, K., & Newman, L. (1993). *The transition experiences of young people with disabilities: A summary of findings from the National Longitudinal Study of Special Education Students.* Menlo Park, CA: SRI. (ERIC Document Reproduction Services No. EC 302 815).

Wagner, M., Cameto, R., & Newman, L. (2003). *Youth with disabilities: A changing population.* A report of findings from the National Longitudinal Transition Study (NLTS) and National Longitudinal Transition Study-2 (NLTS2). Menlo Park, CA: SRI International. Available online from *http://www.nlts2.org/reports/changepop_execsum.html*

Wagner, M., Newman, L., Cameto, R., & Levine, P. (2005). *National longitudinal transition study 2: Changes over time in the early post-school outcomes of youth with disabilities.* Menlo Park, CA: SRI International.

Walsh, F. (2012). *Normal family processes* (4th ed.). New York: Guilford Press.

Ward, M. J. (1988). The many facets of self-determination. *Transition summary.* Washington, DC: National Information Center for Children and Youth with Handicaps.

Wehman, P. (2001). *Life beyond the classroom: Transition strategies for young people with disabilities* (3rd ed.). Baltimore: Brookes.

Wehmeyer, M. L. (2001). Self-determination and transition. In P. Wehman (Ed.), *Life beyond the classroom: Transition strategies for young people with disabilities* (3rd ed.) (pp. 35–60). Baltimore: Brookes.

Wehmeyer, M. L., & Kelchner, K. (1995). *Whose future is it anyway? A student-directed transition planning program.* Arlington, TX: Arc of the United States.

Wehmeyer, M. L., & Schwartz, M. (1997). Self-determination focus of transition goals for students with mental retardation. *Career Development for Exceptional Individuals, 21,* 75–86.

Wehmeyer, M. L., Agran, M., & Hughes, C. (1998). *Teaching self-determination to students with disabilities: Basic skills for successful transition.* Baltimore: Brookes.

White, W. J., Deshler, D. D., Schumaker, J. B., Warner, M. M., Alley, G. R., & Clark, F. C. (1983). The effects of learning disabilities on post-school adjustment. *Journal of Rehabilitation, 49,* 46–50.

Wimmer, D. (1982). Career education. In E. Meyen (Ed.), *Exceptional children in today's schools* (pp. 151–184). Denver, CO: Love.

Yost, D. S., Shaw, S. E., Cullen, J., McGuire, J. M., & Bigaj, S. (1994). Practices and attitudes of postsecondary LD services providers in North America. *Journal of Learning Disabilities, 27*(10), 631–640.

NAME INDEX

SUBJECT INDEX